Editorial Policy Committee

The Labor Law Group

Laura J. Cooper
University of Minnesota Law School

Dianne Avery
University at Buffalo Law School,
The State University of New York

Marion G. Crain
West Virginia University College of Law

Lance Compa
Cornell University, School of Industrial and Labor Relations

Kenneth G. Dau-Schmidt
Indiana University-Bloomington, School of Law

Deborah C. Malamud
New York University School of Law

Martin H. Malin
Chicago-Kent School of Law, Illinois Institute of Technology

Dennis R. Nolan
University of South Carolina School of Law

ADR
in the Workplace

Second Edition

by

Laura J. Cooper

*J. Stewart and Mario Thomas McClendon Professor in
Law and Alternative Dispute Resolution
University of Minnesota Law School*

Dennis R. Nolan

*Webster Professor of Labor Law
University of South Carolina School of Law*

and

Richard A. Bales

*Professor
Northern Kentucky University, Salmon P. Chase College of Law*

for

THE LABOR LAW GROUP

AMERICAN CASEBOOK SERIES®

THOMSON
™
WEST

Mat # 40161052

American Casebook Series and West Group are trademarks registered in the U.S. Patent and Trademark Office.

© 2005 By THE LABOR LAW GROUP
        610 Opperman Drive
        P.O. Box 64526
        St. Paul, MN 55164–0526
        1–800–328–9352

ISBN 0–314–14765–9

 TEXT IS PRINTED ON 10% POST CONSUMER RECYCLED PAPER

*For J. Stewart and Mario Thomas McClendon for their
Commitment to Education in Alternative Dispute Resolution
L.J.C.*

*For Connor Nolan McCloskey
D.R.N.*

and

*For Dennis and Emma
R.A.B.*

*

Foreword

The Labor Law Group is an association of law teachers, most of whom serve on faculties in the United States; others teach in Belgium, Canada, England, and Israel.

At the December 1946 meeting of the Labor Law Roundtable of the Association of American Law Schools, Professor W. Willard Wirtz (who became Secretary of Labor in 1962) delivered a compelling paper criticizing the labor law course books then available. His remarks so impressed those present that the Roundtable Council organized a general conference on the teaching of the subject. At the conference, held in Ann Arbor in 1947, some conferees agreed to exchange proposals for sections of a hoped-for new course book. The late Professor Robert E. Mathews served as coordinator. Beginning in 1948, a preliminary mimeographed version was used in seventeen schools; each user supplied comments and suggestions for change. In 1953, a hard-cover version was published under the title *Labor Relations and the Law*. The thirty-one "cooperating editors" were so convinced of the value of multi-campus collaboration that they gave up any individual claims to royalties. Instead, those royalties were paid to a trust fund to be used to develop and "provide the best possible materials" for training students in labor law and labor relations. The Declaration of Trust memorializing this agreement was executed November 4, 1953, and remains the Group's charter.

Cooperative ventures among legal scholars are often centered around ideological orthodoxies or common experiences or identities. In contrast, the Labor Law Group has tried to expand the scope of perceptions and experiences represented within its membership. Consistent with this goal, it has attained significant diversification in the racial, gender, national, and ideological composition of its participants and, additionally, has drawn its membership and leadership from institutions that are varied in size, styles, status, and geography.

The founding committee's hope that the initial collaboration would bear fruit has been fulfilled. Under Professor Mathews' continuing chairmanship, the Group's members produced *Readings on Labor Law* in 1955 and *The Employment Relation and the Law* in 1957, edited by Robert Mathews and Benjamin Aaron. A second edition of *Labor Relations and the Law* appeared in 1960, with Benjamin Aaron and Donald H. Wollett as co-chairmen, and a third edition was published in 1965, with Jerre Williams at the helm.

In June of 1969, the Group, now chaired by William P. Murphy, sponsored a conference to reexamine the labor law curriculum. The meeting, held at the University of Colorado, was attended by practitioners and by full-time teachers including nonmembers as well as members of the Group. The conference papers and discussion summaries were distributed to law school libraries and to participants. In meetings that followed the conference, the Group decided to reshape its work substantially. It restructured itself into ten task forces, each assigned a unit of no more than two hundred pages on a discrete topic such as employment discrimination or union-member relations. An individual teacher could then choose two or three of these units as the material around which to build a particular course. This multi-unit approach dominated the Group's work throughout much of the 1970s under Professor Murphy and his successor as chairman, Herbert L. Sherman, Jr. As the decade progressed and teachers refined their views about what topics to include and how to address them, some units were dropped from the series while others increased in scope and length. Under Professor Sherman's chairmanship, the Group planned a new series of six enlarged books to cover the full range of topics taught by labor and employment law teachers.

Professor James E. Jones, Jr., was elected chairman in 1978 and shepherded to completion the promised set of six full-size, independent casebooks. In addition, during this period supplements were published for some books. The Group continued to reevaluate its work and eventually decided that it was time to convene another conference of law teachers.

In 1984, the Group, now chaired by Robert Covington, sponsored another general conference to discuss developments in the substance and teaching of labor and employment law, this time at Park City, Utah. (The conference papers were distributed to law school libraries as well as participants.) Those discussions and a subsequent working session led to the conclusion that the Group should devote principal attention to three new conventional length course books, one devoted to employment discrimination, one to union-management relations, and one to the individual employment relationship. In addition, work was planned on more abbreviated course books to serve as successors to the Group's earlier works covering public employment bargaining and labor arbitration.

In 1989, with Alvin Goldman as Chair, the Group met in Breckenridge, Colorado, to assess its most recent effort and develop plans for the future. In addition to outlining new course book projects, the Group discussed ways to assist teachers of labor and employment law in their efforts to expand conceptual horizons and perspectives. In pursuit of the latter goals it co-sponsored, in 1992, a conference held at the University of Toronto Faculty of Law at which legal and nonlegal specialists examined alternative models of corporate governance and their impact on workers.

When Robert J. Rabin became Chair in 1996, the Group and a number of invited guests met in Tucson, Arizona, to celebrate the imminent fiftieth anniversary of the Group. The topics of discussion included the impact of the global economy and of changing forms of representation on the teaching of labor and employment law, and the impact of new technologies of electronic publishing on the preparation of teaching materials. The Group honored three of its members who had been present at the creation of the Group, Willard Wirtz, Ben Aaron, and Clyde Summers.

The Group next met in Scottsdale, Arizona in December, 1999, to discuss the production of materials that would more effectively bring emerging issues of labor and employment law into the classroom. Among the issues discussed were integration of international and comparative materials into the labor and employment curriculum and the pedagogical uses of the world wide web.

Laura J. Cooper became Chair of the Group in July, 2001. In June, 2003, the Group met in Alton, Ontario, Canada. The focus there was on labor law on the edge—looking at doctrinal synergies between workplace law and other legal and social-science disciplines, and workers on the edge—exploring the legal issues of highly-compensated technology workers, vulnerable immigrant employees, and unionized manufacturing employees threatened by foreign competition. The Group also heard a report from its study of the status of the teaching of labor and employment law in the nation's law schools and discussed the implications of the study for the Group's future projects.

In addition to this book on workplace dispute resolution, we presently have four other books in print all published by West Group.: *Employment Discrimination Law: Cases and Materials on Equality in the Workplace* by Robert Belton, Dianne Avery, Maria L. Ontiveros and Roberto L. Corrado (Seventh Edition); *Labor and Employment Law: Problems, Cases and Materials in the Law of Work* (Third Edition), by Robert J. Rabin, Eileen Silverstein, George Schatzki and Kenneth G. Dau-Schmidt; *Legal Protection for the Individual Employee* (Third Edition), by Matthew W. Finkin, Alvin L. Goldman, Clyde W. Summers and Kenneth Dau-Schmidt and *Public Sector Employment*, by Joseph R. Grodin, June M. Weisberger and Martin H. Malin. The Group is also currently at work on two additional projects. In 2005 Foundation Press will publish *Labor Law Stories*, a collection of historical essays about the most significant labor law decisions, edited by Laura J. Cooper and Catherine L. Fisk. We are also at work on an entirely new text on labor issues in the global economy.

At any one time, roughly twenty-five to thirty persons are actively engaged in the Group's work; this has proved a practical size, given problems of communication and logistics. Coordination and editorial review of the projects are the responsibility of the executive committee, whose members are the successor trustees of the Group. Governance is by consensus; votes are taken only to elect trustees and to determine whom to invite to join the Group. Since 1953, more than seventy persons have worked on Group projects; in keeping with the original agreement, none has ever received anything more than reimbursement of expenses.

The authors of this Second Edition of *ADR in the Workplace* here update their 2000 First Edition and its predecessor, the 1994 book, *Labor Arbitration: A Coursebook*, by Laura J. Cooper and Dennis R. Nolan. Laura J. Cooper and Dennis R. Nolan are memebers of the National Academy of Arbitrators and combine full-time academic careers with part-time practices in workplace mediation and arbitration. Professor Cooper is the J. Stewart and Mario Thomas McClendon Professor in Law and Alternative Dispute Resolution at the University of Minnesota. Professor Nolan is the Webster Professor of Labor Law at the University of South Carolina. Both have contributed to the scholarly literature of workplace dispute resolution, with a focus on labor arbitration. Among other publications, Professor Nolan is the author of *Labor and Employment Arbitration in a Nutshell* and the co-author of the textbook, *Labor Law: Collective Bargaining in a Free Society* (Fifth Edition), both published by West Group. Richard A. Bales was an employment litigator before joining the faculty of Northern Kentucky University, Chase College of Law. His significant body of scholarship focuses on employment litigation and alternative dispute resolution in the non-union workplace. He is the author of *Compulsory Arbitration: The Grand Experiment in Employment* (Cornell University ILR Press, 1998).

THE EXECUTIVE COMMITTEE
DIANNE AVERY
MARION G. CRAIN
LANCE COMPA
LAURA J. COOPER, *CHAIR*
KENNETH G. DAU-SCHMIDT
DEBORAH MALAMUD
MARTIN H. MALIN
DENNIS R. NOLAN

January, 2005

Preface

The final decades of the twentieth century brought an expansion of the substantive rights of employees. Although the number of employment claims in the courts, and particularly the federal courts, has been growing at a rapid rate, so too has grown the level of frustration with the limitations of litigation as a means to effectuate those rights. Employees represented by unions have long had the strongest workplace protections of all employees and enjoyed the most efficient and effective mechanism for the enforcement of those rights—labor arbitration. Arbitration of disputes arising under collective bargaining agreements has come to be the model for resolving many statutory and common law disputes outside the union context, although many of the characteristics that permitted success in the organized setting are absent in the nonunion workplace. In addition to borrowing arbitration from the union setting, employers and employees in nonunion workplaces are increasingly using other means of alternative dispute resolution, including mediation.

These mechanisms of dispute resolution fundamentally alter the role of the advocate and even the definition of employees' legal rights. The education of labor and employment advocates therefore requires study, not only of substantive rights, but also study of the alternative means of their enforcement. Cooper and Nolan, *Labor Arbitration: A Coursebook*, comprehensively covered labor arbitration. Its successor, *ADR in the Workplace*, updated the coverage of labor arbitration and added new material on alternative dispute resolution of statutory and common law employment rights of nonunion employees. This second edition of *ADR in the Workplace* again updates the coverage of labor arbitration, but also reflects the enormous recent growth of ADR in the nonunion sector. The second edition expands significantly the coverage of empirical and normative analysis as well as the ethical dilemmas that often arise for both attorneys and arbitrators in non-union ADR.

Courses in ADR in employment are useful for law schools, business schools, and schools of industrial relations. The scope of such courses varies considerably. Some courses may be limited to labor arbitration. Some may presume that students have already studied labor or employment law. Some provide a student's first look at these subjects. Others may see such a course primarily as a means to develop practical skills. Some courses may be limited to ADR in the nonunion setting. Some may be designed to focus on a comparison of union and nonunion dispute resolution mechanisms.

This book provides a comprehensive look at the world of employment ADR—its history, procedures, law, ethics and practice—that makes it suitable for use in any of these settings. It addresses ADR topics through a wide diversity of materials including judicial decisions, arbitration awards, essays, and questions and problems for class discussion. Sections on judicial determinations of arbitrability, judicial review, injunctions, deferral, and the duty of fair representation offer thorough coverage of legal issues for those teachers seeking to emphasize the legal context for labor arbitration. Extensive treatment of the substance and practice of labor arbitration provides teaching material for courses focusing on labor arbitration practice rather than law. Materials on dispute resolution in the nonunion setting address a broad range of issues including law, theory, practice and policy.

The chapters of the book are largely independent, allowing a teacher to design a course with as broad or as narrow a focus as the teacher desires. Those who want to look at labor arbitration as just one means of workplace dispute resolution will find here the materials to both understand other ADR mechanisms and to reflect upon them in this broader context. For teachers seeking to include advocacy skills training, the appendix includes a research guide and an essay on arbitration brief writing, and we have also made available materials for conducting classroom simulations of arbitration and mediation both in the union and nonunion setting. That book, Laura J. Cooper and Carolyn Chalmers, Workplace ADR: Simulations and Teacher's Guide (2d ed. 2005), is available for professors who have adopted the casebook.

We have attempted to edit the material unobtrusively. We did not indicate when we deleted internal footnotes and citations to authority, but we inserted asterisks when we deleted anything else. We retained ellipses whenever they were present in the original source. We sometimes revised citations in cases without indication, particularly to standardize the citation format. We usually retained parallel citations. Remaining footnotes have their original numbers.

LAURA J. COOPER
DENNIS R. NOLAN
RICHARD A. BALES

January, 2005

The Labor Law Group

Currently Participating Members

Steven D. Anderman
University of Essex School of Law

Harry W. Arthurs
Osgoode Hall Law School, York University

James Atleson
University at Buffalo Law School, The State University of New York

Dianne Avery
University at Buffalo Law School, The State University of New York

Richard A. Bales
Northern Kentucky University, Salmon P. Chase College of Law

Robert Belton
Vanderbilt University Law School

Roger Blanpain
Instituut voor Arbeidsrecht

Christopher David Ruiz Cameron
Southwestern University School of Law

Laura J. Cooper
University of Minnesota Law School

Lance Compa
Cornell University, School of Industrial and Labor Relations

Roberto L. Corrada
University of Denver College of Law

Robert N. Covington
Vanderbilt University Law School

Marion G. Grain
West Virginia University College of Law

Kenneth G. Dau-Schmidt
Indiana University-Bloomington, School of Law

Matthew W. Finkin
University of Illinois College of Law

Lucinda M. Finley
University at Buffalo Law School, The State University of New York

Catherine L. Fisk
Duke University School of Law

Joel W. Friedman
Tulane University School of Law

Julius G. Getman
The University of Texas School of Law

Alvin L. Goldman
University of Kentucky College of Law

Joseph R. Grodin
University of California, Hastings College of Law

Alan Hyde
Rutgers, The State University of New Jersey, S. I. Newhouse Center for Law and Justice

James E. Jones, Jr.
University of Wisconsin Law School (Emeritus)

Thomas C. Kohler
Boston College Law School

Brian A. Langille
University of Toronto, Faculty of Law

Deborah C. Malamud
New York University School of Law

Martin H. Malin
Chicago-Kent School of Law, Illinois Institute of Technology

Mordehai Mironi
University of Haifa Faculty of Law

Robert B. Moberly
Leflar Law Center, University of Arkansas, Fayetteville

Dennis R. Nolan
University of South Carolina School of Law

Maria L. Ontiveros
University of San Francisco School of Law

Robert J. Rabin
Syracuse University College of Law

George Schatzki
Arizona State University College of Law

Calvin W. Sharpe
Case Western Reserve University Law School

Eileen Silverstein
University of Connecticut School of Law

Clyde W. Summers
University of Pennsylvania Law School

Katherine Van Wezel Stone
University of California at Los Angeles School of Law

Lea Vander Velde
University of Iowa College of Law

June M. Weisberger
University of Wisconsin Law School (Emerita)

Marley Weiss
University of Maryland School of Law

Other Members

Benjamin Aaron
University of California at Los Angeles School of Law (Emeritus)

Alfred W. Blumrosen
Rutgers, The State University of New Jersey, S. I. Newhouse Center for Law and Justice

Acknowledgements and Permissions

The authors gratefully acknowledge the following permissions to reprint copyrighted materials:

Arbitration cases reproduced with permission from Labor Relations Reporter-Labor Arbitration Reports. Copyright by The Bureau of National Affairs, Inc., (800-372-1033), <http://www.bna.com>.

Arbitration cases from *Labor Arbitration Awards* (CCH) reproduced with permission from *Labor Arbitration Awards*, published and copyrighted by Commerce Clearing House, Inc., 2700 Lake Cook Road, Riverwoods, IL 60015. Copyright © 1969 & 1980, CCH Incorporated, All Rights Reserved.

National Academy of Arbitrators—Proceedings from Annual Meetings reprinted with permission. Excerpted from Proceedings of the 14th, 20th, 21st, 23rd, 30th, and 44th National Academy of Arbitrators Annual Meetings. Copyright © 1961, 1967, 1968, 1970, 1978, 1992 by The Bureau of National Affairs, Inc., Washington D.C. 20037. For copies of BNA Books publications call toll free 1-800-960-1220.

Chapter I

Dennis R. Nolan and Roger I. Abrams, *American Labor Arbitral ion: The Early Years*, 35 University of Florida Law Review 373 (1983) and Dennis R. Nolan and Roger I. Abrams, *American Labor Arbitration: The Maturing Years*, 35 University of Florida Law Review 557 (1983). Copyrights© 1983 by Dennis R. Nolan and Roger I. Abrams. All rights reserved. Reprinted by permission.

Chapter VI

Arnold M. Zack and Richard I. Bloch, *Problems of Proof—Evidence in Arbitration*, Labor Agreement in Negotiation & Arbitration, chapter 3, page 47 (2d ed. 1995). Copyright ©1995 by The Bureau of National Affairs, Inc., Washington DC 20037. Published by The Bureau of National Affairs, Inc. For copies of BNA Books publications call toll free 1-800-960-1220.

Elkouri & Elkouri, *Evidential Rules*, How Arbitration Works (Alan Miles Ruben, Editor-in-Chief, Sixth Edition, 2003), chapter 8, page 341. Copyright © 2003 by The Bureau of National Affairs, Inc., Washington DC 20037. Published by The Bureau of National Affairs, Inc. For copies of BNA Books publications call toll free 1-800-960-1220.

Chapter VII

Roger I. Abrams and Dennis R. Nolan, *Toward A Theory of "Just Cause" in Employee Discipline Cases*, 85 Duke Law Journal 594 (1985). Reprinted with permission from the authors and Duke Law Journal.

Marvin J. Hill, Jr. and Anthony V. Sincropi, *The Concept of Management Rights: An Overview*, in Management Rights: A Legal & Arbitral Analysis, page 3. Copyright © 1986 by The Bureau of National Affairs, Inc., Washington DC 20037. Published by The Bureau of National Affairs, Inc. For copies of BNA Books publications call toll free 1-800-960-1220.

Richard Mittenthal, *Past Practice and the Administration of Collective Bargaining Agreeements*, from Arbitration and Public Policy, chapter 2, page 30 (Proceedings of the Fourteenth Annual Meeting, National Academy of Arbitrators). Copyright © 1961 by The Bureau of National Affairs, Inc., Washington DC 20037. Published by The Bureau of National Affairs, Inc. For copies of BNA Books publications call toll free 1-800-960-1220.

Chapter VIII

Joseph R. Grodin and Joyce M. Najita, *Judicial Response to Public-Sector Arbitration*, in Public-Sector Bargaining, 229 (Benjamin Aaron, et al. eds.) (2nd ed.1988). Copyright © 1988 Industrial Relations Research Association. Reprinted by permission.

Alvin L. Goldman, *Settlement of Disputes over Interests in Comparative Labour Law and Industrial Relations in Industrialised Market Economies*, 541 (Roger Blanpain and Chris Engels eds.) (6th ed. Kluwer, 1999) Reprinted with permission from the publisher, Kluwer Law International.

Chapter IX

Creeping Legalism in Labor Arbitration: An Editorial, 13 Arbitration Journal 129 (1958). Reprinted with permission from the Arbitration Journal (now called the Dispute Resolution Journal), vol. 13 no. 3 (1958). Copyright © 1958 American Arbitration Association, publisher of the Dispute Resolution Journal, 335 Madison Avenue, New York, NY 10017-4506, www.adr.org.

Anthony F. Bartlett, *Labor Arbitration: The Problem of Legalism*, 62 Oregon Law Review 195 (1983). Copyright © 1983 Regents of the University of Oregon. All rights reserved. Reprinted by permission.

Paul Hays, *Labor Arbitration: A Dissenting View* (1966). Copyright © 1966 by Yale University Press. Reprinted with permission from the publisher, Yale University Press.

Saul Wallen, *Arbitrators and Judges—Dispelling the Hays Haze*, 9 California Management Review 17 (1967). Copyright © 1967 by the Regents of the University of California. Reprinted from the California Management Review, Vol. 9, No. 3. By permission of The Regents.

Katherine Van Wezel Stone, *The Structure of Post-War Labor Relations*, 11 New York University Review of Law and Social Change 125 (1982–83). Reprinted with permission from the New York University Review of Law and Social Change. Copyright © 1982 New York University Press. All rights reserved. Reprinted by permission.

John R. Phillips, *Their Own Brand of Industrial Justice: Arbitrators' Excesses in Discharge Cases*, 10 Employee Relations Law Journal 48 (1984). Reprinted with permission of Aspen Publishers.

Robert Coulson, *The Arbitrator's Role in Discharge Cases: Another Viewpoint*, 10 Employee Relations Law Journal 61 (1984). Reprinted with permission of Aspen Publishers.

James A. Gross and Patricia A. Greenfield, *Arbitral Value Judgments in Health and Safety Disputes: Management Rights over Workers' Rights*, 34 Buffalo Law Review 645 (1985). Copyright © 1985 by Buffalo Law Review. Reprinted with permission from the Buffalo Law Review.

Chapter XII

Samuel Estreicher, *Saturns for Rickshaws: The Stakes in the Debate Over Predispute Employment Arbitration Agreements*, 16 Ohio State Journal on Dispute Resolution 559 (2001). Reprinted with permission from the author and the Ohio State Journal on Dispute Resolution.

Lewis L. Maltby, *Employment Arbitration and Workplace Justice*, 38 University of San Francisco Law Review 105 (2003). Reprinted with permission from the University of San Francisco Law Review, copyright © 2003.

Martin H. Malin, *Ethical Concerns in Drafting Employment Arbitration Agreements After* Circuit City *and* Green Tree, 41 Brandeis Law Journal 779 (2003). Reprinted with permission from the author and the Ohio State Journal on Dispute Resolution.

Chapter XIII

Marc Galanter, *The Vanishing Trial: An Examination of Trials and Related Matters in Federal and State Courts*, to be published at 1 Journal of Empirical Legal Studies (Nov. 2004). Reprinted with permission from the author and the Journal of Empirical Legal Studies.

Jonathan R. Harkavy, *Privatizing Workplace Justice: The Advent of Mediation in Resolving Sexual Harassment Disputes*, 34 Wake Forest Law Review, 135 (1999). Reprinted with permission from the author and the Wake Forest Law Review.

E. Patrick McDermott and Ruth Obar, *What's Going On in Mediation: An Empirical Analysis of the Influence of a Mediator's Style on Party Satisfaction and Monetary Benefit*, 9 Harvard Negotiation Law Review 75 (2004). Reprinted with permission from the authors and the Wake Forest Law Review.

Joseph B. Stulberg, *The Theory and Practice of Mediation: A Reply to Professor Susskind*, 6 Vermont Law Review 85 (1981). Reprinted with permission from the author and the Wake Forest Law Review.

Laura Cooper and Carolyn Chalmers, *Alternative Dispute Resolution: An Introduction* (1997). Reprinted with permission from the authors.

Christopher W. Moore, The Mediation Process: Practical Strategies for Resolving Conflict (2003). Copyright © 2003 John Wiley & Sons, Inc. and Christopher W. Moore. Reprinted with permission from John Wiley & Sons, Inc. and Christopher W. Moore.

Uniform Mediation Act, copyright © 2003. Reprinted with permission from the National Conference of Commissioners on Uniform State Laws.

Norman Brand, *A Note on Mediator and Arbitrator Ethics*, in How ADR Works (Norman Brand, ed., 2002). Reprinted with permission from How ADR Works, editor-in-chief Norman Brand. Copyright © 2002 by The American Bar Association. Published by The Bureau of National Affairs, Inc., Washington D.C. 20037. For copies of BNA Books publications call toll free 1-800-960-1220.

Robert P. Burns, *Some Ethical Issues Surrounding Mediation*, 70 Fordham Law Review 691 (2001). Reprinted with permission from the author and the Fordham Law Review.

Richard N. Block, John Beck, and A. Robin Olson, *Low Profile/High Potential: A Look at Grievance Mediation*, 51 Dispute Resolution Journal 55(1996). Copyright © 1996 by American Arbitration Association. Reprinted with permission from the American Arbitration Association.

Chapter XIV

James N. Adler, *Drafting ADR Programs: Management-Integrated Conflict Management Systems*, in How ADR Works (Norman Brand, ed., 2002). Reprinted with permission from How ADR Works, editor-in-chief Norman Brand. Copyright © 2002 by The American Bar Association. Published by The Bureau of National Affairs, Inc., Washington D.C. 20037. For copies of BNA Books publications call toll free 1-800-960-1220.

Appendix A

Suzanne Thorpe and Laura J. Cooper, *Researching Labor Arbitration and Alternative Dispute Resolution in Employment*, original version published at 91 Law Library Journal 367 (1999). Reprinted with permission from the authors.

Appendix B

Uniform Arbitration Act, copyright © 2000. Reprinted with permission from the National Conference of Commissioners on Uniform State Laws.

Appendix C

American Arbitration Association, Labor Arbitration Rules, copyright © 2004 by the American Arbitration Association.

American Arbitration Association National Rules for the Resolution of Employment Disputes, copyright © 2004 by the American Arbitration Association.

Appendix D

Code of Professional Responsibility for Arbitrators of Labor-Management Disputes, as amended and in effect June 2003. Permission is granted by the National Academy of Arbitrators, for its part, to use this publication of the National Academy of Arbitrators, American Arbitration Association, and Federal Mediation and Conciliation Service.

Appendix F

Douglas E. Ray, *On Writing the Post-Hearing Brief*, Arbitration Journal 58-60 (Volume 47, Number 4, Dec. 1992). Copyright © 1992 by Arbitration Journal. Reprinted with permission from the Dispute Resolution Journal.

Special thanks to Holly Newell and Chester Edwards of the University of South Carolina Law School class of 2004, and to Rachel LeJeune and Wendy Bauer of Chase College of Law.

*

Summary of Contents

*

Table of Contents

---

*

Table of Cases

The principal cases are in bold type. Cases cited or discussed in the text are in roman type. References are to pages. Cases cited in principal cases and within other quoted materials are not included.

ADR
in the Workplace

*

Part 1

LABOR ARBITRATION

Chapter I

HISTORY AND BACKGROUND[1]

In contrast to most other countries, America's labor relations system has for a century or more rested on contract. As embodied in the National Labor Relations Act of 1935, the American model assumes that a defined group of employees, organized as a "bargaining unit," will select a union to serve as its "exclusive bargaining representative." That representative will then negotiate with the employer over the terms and conditions of employment applicable to all employees in the bargaining unit. If they can agree, they will sign a "collective bargaining agreement" spelling out their bargain.

The contractualist base of the labor relations system requires some enforcement mechanism. If one party thinks the other has breached the agreement, or if they cannot agree on the meaning or application of a contract term, the parties need some method of resolving the dispute. Two possible mechanisms, lawsuits and resort to economic pressure such as a strike or lockout, are slow or disproportionately costly. As a result, most unions and employers have chosen instead to use a private dispute-resolution mechanism, labor arbitration. Part I of this book explores the law and practice of American labor arbitration. Chapter I provides a description of the background to our modern system of arbitration.

A. EARLY JUDICIAL HOSTILITY

"Arbitration" refers to a method of resolving disputes by submitting them to the judgment of one or more impartial persons, usually outside the normal judicial process. Arbitration is probably as old as human society. References to its use appear in Greek mythology (Venus, Juno,

---

1. Bibliographic Suggestions: Robben W. Fleming, The Labor Arbitration Process 1–30 (1965); Gladys Gruenberg, Joyce Najita, and Dennis R. Nolan, The National Academy of Arbitrators: Fifty Years in the World of Work (1998); Dennis R. Nolan and Roger I. Abrams, *American Labor Arbitration: The Early Years*, 35 University of Florida Law Review 373 (1983) and *American Labor Arbitration: The Maturing Years*, 35 University of Florida Law Review 557 (1983); and Edwin Witte, Historical Survey of Labor Arbitration (1952).

and Pallas Athene agreed to let Paris decide which was the most beautiful), in the New Testament (in I Corinthians 6:1–7, Paul exhorts the early Christians to submit their disputes to arbitration rather than to the courts), in early Jewish and Roman law, and in Norse sagas.

Despite its lengthy history and popular acceptance, the common law courts did not welcome arbitration. The earliest judicial hostility reflected a concern for defense of judges' turf (and perhaps of the fees that came with the turf). Later judges adopted that hostility without examination.

> It has never been denied that the hostility of English-speaking courts to arbitration contracts probably originated (as Lord Campbell said in Scott v. Avery, 4 H.L. Cas. 811)—
>
> "in the contest of the courts of ancient times for extension of jurisdiction—all of them being opposed to anything that would altogether deprive every one of them of jurisdiction."
>
> A more unworthy genesis cannot be imagined. Since (at the latest) the time of Lord Kenyon, it has been customary to stand rather upon the antiquity of the rule than upon its excellence or reason:
>
> > "It is not necessary now to say how this point ought to have been determined if it were res integra—it having been decided again and again," etc. Per Kenyon, J., in Thompson v. Charnock, 8 T.R. 139.

United States Asphalt Refining Co. v. Trinidad Lake Petroleum Co. Ltd., 222 F. 1006, 1007–08 (S.D.N.Y.1915). Even so great a judge as Justice Joseph Story viewed arbitration with undisguised distaste, as the following case shows.

TOBEY v. COUNTY OF BRISTOL, ET AL.
Circuit Court, District of Massachusetts.
3 Story 800, 23 Fed. Cas. 1313 (1845) (Story, Circuit Justice).

[Tobey sued to compel county commissioners to submit his claim to arbitration pursuant to a bill of the Massachusetts legislature.]

No one can be found, as I believe, and at all events, no case has been cited by counsel, or has fallen within the scope of my researches, in which an agreement to refer a claim to arbitration, has ever been specifically enforced in equity. So far as the authorities go, they are altogether the other way. The cases are divided into two classes. One, where an agreement to refer to arbitration has been set up as a defence to a suit at law, as well as in equity; the other, where the party as plaintiff has sought to enforce such an agreement in a court of equity. Both classes have shared the same fate. The courts have refused to allow the former as a bar or defence against the suit; and have declined to enforce the latter as ill-founded in point of jurisdiction. * * *

* * * One of the established principles of courts of equity is, not to entertain a bill for the specific performance of any agreement, where it is

doubtful whether it may not thereby become the instrument of injustice, or to deprive parties of rights which they are otherwise fairly entitled to have protected. The specific performance of an agreement is, by no means, a matter of right which a party has authority to demand from a court of equity. So far from this, it is a matter of sound discretion in the court, to be granted or withheld, according to its own view of the merits and circumstances of the particular case, and never amounts to a peremptory duty. Now we all know, that arbitrators, at the common law, possess no authority whatsoever, even to administer an oath, or to compel the attendance of witnesses. They cannot compel the production of documents, and papers and books of account, or insist upon a discovery of facts from the parties under oath. They are not ordinarily well enough acquainted with the principles of law or equity, to administer either effectually, in complicated cases; and hence it has often been said, that the judgment of arbitrators is but rusticum judicium. Ought then a court of equity to compel a resort to such a tribunal, by which, however honest and intelligent, it can in no case be clear that the real legal or equitable rights of the parties can be fully ascertained or perfectly protected? * * *

At all events, it cannot be correctly said, that public policy, in our age, generally favors or encourages arbitrations, which are to be final and conclusive, to an extent beyond that which belongs to the ordinary operations of the common law. It is certainly the policy of the common law, not to compel men to submit their rights and interests to arbitration, or to enforce agreements for such a purpose. Nay, the common law goes farther, and even if a submission has been made to arbitrators, who are named, by deed or otherwise, with an express stipulation, that the submission shall be irrevocable, it still is revocable and countermandable, by either party, before the award is actually made, although not afterwards. This was decided as long ago as in Vynior's Case, 8 Coke, 8lb. The reason there given, is, that a man cannot, by his act, make such authority, power, or warrant not countermandable, which is by law, and of its own nature, countermandable; as if a man should, by express words, declare his testament to be irrevocable, yet he may revoke it, for his acts or words cannot alter the judgment of law, to make that irrevocable, which is of its own nature revocable. * * *

But where an award has been made before the revocation, it will be held obligatory, and the parties will not be allowed to revoke it, and the courts of law as well as equity will enforce it. In this view of the matter, courts of equity do but follow out the dictates and analogies of the law. When the law has declared, that any agreement for an arbitration is, in its very nature, revocable, and cannot be made irrevocable by any agreement of the parties, courts of equity are bound to respect this interposition, and are not at liberty to decree that to be positive and absolute in its obligation, which the law declares to be conditional and countermandable.

And this leads me to remark in the second place, that it is an established principle of courts of equity never to enforce the specific performance of any agreement, where it would be a vain and imperfect act, or where a specific performance is from the very nature and character of the agreement, impracticable or inequitable, to be enforced. * * *

In all these cases the reason is the same, the utter inadequacy of the means of the court to enforce the due performance of such a contract. The same principle would apply to the case of a specific contract by a master to paint an historical picture, or a contract by a sculptor to carve a statue or a group, historical or otherwise. From their very nature, all such contracts must depend for their due execution, upon the skill, and will, and honor of the contracting party. Now this very reasoning applies with equal force to the case at bar. How can a court of equity compel the respective parties to name arbitrators; and a fortiori, how can it compel the parties mutually to select arbitrators, since each must, in such a case, agree to all the arbitrators? * * *

So that we abundantly see, that the very impracticability of compelling the parties to name arbitrators, or upon their default, for the court to appoint them, constitutes, and must forever constitute, a complete bar to any attempt on the part of a court of equity to compel the specific performance of any agreement to refer to arbitration. It is essentially, in its very nature and character, an agreement which must rest in the good faith and honor of the parties, and like an agreement to paint a picture, or to carve a statue, or to write a book, or to invent patterns for prints, must be left to the conscience of the parties, or to such remedy in damages for the breach thereof, as the law has provided. * * *

Without going more at large into the subject, it appears to me, that the present is not a case in which this court can afford any relief whatsoever to the plaintiff, however strong his claims may be upon the justice of the county and its public functionaries. I shall, therefore, order the bill to be discharged, but without costs to the defendants.

Despite the courts' suspicion of arbitration—*rusticum judicium*, or rustic justice, as Justice Story termed it—many parties used it regularly. In addition to the special case of international adjudications, merchants of many types preferred arbitration to common law suits. Commercial arbitration, in fact, dates back at least to the middle ages, when merchants' needs for speedy, informal, inexpensive, and expert decision-making made regular litigation virtually worthless. Their choices demonstrated that arbitration offered substantial benefits the common law processes did not. In addition to the obvious procedural advantages, arbitration offered them a way to create and enforce a set of norms the common law courts might not recognize. (What might those norms be? Why would the courts not enforce them?) However popular arbitration might be in a given trade, it depended on mutual assent. A party to an arbitration agreement who was willing to risk ostracism from others in the trade could usually, as *Tobey* demonstrated, ignore the agreement with impunity.

Not until legislatures enacted laws expressly directing the courts to enforce arbitration agreements did judicial hostility ebb. Chief among these laws were the United States Arbitration Act (USAA) (now known as the Federal Arbitration Act or FAA), 9 U.S.C.A. §§ 1–14 (1999) and the Uniform Arbitration Act (UAA), both of which are reprinted in Appendix B. Enacted in 1925, the FAA applies to arbitration agreements in contracts "involving commerce" but not to those in "contracts of employment" of workers engaged in foreign or interstate commerce. In *dicta*, the Supreme Court has suggested that this excludes collective bargaining agreements, but even in those cases the courts frequently look to the FAA for guidance. United Paperworkers International Union v. Misco, Inc., 484 U.S. 29, 40 n. 9, 108 S.Ct. 364, 372 n. 9, 98 L.Ed.2d 286 (1987).

The Uniform Arbitration Act, which was designed to permit the expeditious enforcement of arbitration agreements in state courts, dates from 1956. Most states have now adopted it, although some of the statutes exclude labor agreements. Only after Congress enacted the Taft–Hartley Act in 1947, 29 U.S.C.A. §§ 141–97 (1998), did labor arbitration gain solid support from the judiciary, and most of that support did not develop until the Supreme Court interpreted the pertinent parts of Taft–Hartley in 1960. The key provision is § 301, which authorized federal courts to enforce collective bargaining agreements.

B. THE DEVELOPMENT AND ACCEPTANCE OF LABOR ARBITRATION

1. BEFORE THE SECOND WORLD WAR

Labor arbitration is of two types. In the first, termed "interest arbitration," the arbitrator determines the wages, hours, or conditions of employment—in short, the arbitrator writes the agreement for the parties (or at least fills in the gaps in the one they wrote for themselves). In the second, termed "grievance arbitration" (or sometimes "rights arbitration"), the arbitrator only interprets or applies the terms of an agreement already negotiated by the parties.

Collective bargaining agreements as we know them today are a relatively recent phenomenon, hence early arbitration was almost exclusively of the "interest" variety. A bitter dispute would arise, typically over wage rates, and a strike or lockout would ensue. If neither side could prevail simply by economic force, both might agree to let some neutral person or board decide the issue. Among the earliest examples were tripartite arbitrations (that is, arbitrations conducted with three arbitrators, one chosen by each party and one neutral) over terms of employment for freed slaves during Reconstruction. Planters would select one representative, the Freedmen's Bureau, an agency of the Federal government, would select another, and the freedmen would select the third. (Both planters and Freedmen's Bureau officials were initially surprised when the freedmen would chose one of their own to represent them, rather than selecting a sympathetic white man to do so.)

Well into the twentieth century, commentators used "arbitration" indiscriminately to refer to interest arbitration, to grievance arbitration, or even to what we now term conciliation (the use of a neutral to help the parties negotiate their own agreement). With the growth of individual employment arbitration in the 1990s, the term now applies to those sorts of disputes as well.

Labor arbitration faced a special barrier in courts until recently. In England and other common-law jurisdictions, courts did not regard collective bargaining agreements as contracts. Some courts thought them too vague to be enforceable. Others believed that parties to collective agreements did not intend them to be enforced in court. They were (and in the United Kingdom, still are) simply "gentlemen's agreements" that depended on honor and economic power for their force.

There are a few recorded instances of grievance arbitration as early as the Nineteenth Century, but scholars usually regard the settlement of the 1902 strike in the anthracite coal fields as the first major step in America toward modern labor arbitration. A commission appointed by President Theodore Roosevelt produced a lengthy and detailed award in 1903 and established a permanent Anthracite Board of Conciliation to interpret and apply the award. If the Board could not resolve a particular dispute, it referred the matter to a neutral arbitrator known as an umpire.

The next major advance occurred in parts of the clothing industry. Louis D. Brandeis, later an associate justice of the United States Supreme Court, helped to negotiate a "Protocol of Peace" that ended a strike against New York's cloak and suit manufacturers in 1910. The Protocol provided for a Board of Arbitration (which Brandeis chaired for four years) to resolve grievances. Because the Board's jurisdiction was open-ended, it engaged in interest arbitration as well as grievance arbitration. The following year a strike at Hart, Schaffner & Marx in Chicago ended with a similar and even more successful arrangement. The two negotiators in that dispute—one of whom was Clarence Darrow—named themselves the agreement's arbitrators.

Labor arbitration spread quite slowly before the First World War, although the concept itself was well publicized. Chief among its publicists was the National Civic Federation, a melange of business tycoons, labor leaders, and social reformers. During that War, the Federal Government created several agencies to resolve labor disputes, the most important of which was the National War Labor Board (NWLB), a tripartite body with labor, management, and public members. The NWLB's decisions were of dubious legal status, so parties often ignored them. Although the NWLB and its sister agencies were not especially successful, they did create a valuable precedent for post-war arbitration.

Fear of strikes during and after the War prompted several states, notably Colorado and Kansas, to prohibit strikes in essential industries and to compel parties to arbitrate unresolved grievance or interest disputes. Labor unions (and sometimes management as well) bitterly resisted these laws. The Supreme Court crimped the states' powers to impose compulsory arbitration when it declared the Kansas law unconstitutional in Charles Wolff Packing Co. v. Court of Industrial Relations, 267 U.S. 552, 45 S.Ct. 441, 69 L.Ed. 785 (1925). Despite that setback for compulsory arbitration, voluntary arbitration became increasingly popular, encouraged by passage of the United States Arbitration Act in 1925 and similar state laws, and by the United States Conciliation Service, a branch of the Department of Labor. When the Depression and New Deal legislation combined to spread labor unions to the mass production industries, labor arbitration was familiar enough to be quickly adopted.

AMERICAN LABOR ARBITRATION: THE EARLY YEARS

Dennis R. Nolan and Roger I. Abrams.
35 University of Florida Law Review 373 (1983).

Although governmental encouragement was a significant factor in labor arbitration's growth before World War II, nongovernmental events, such as the negotiation of arbitration clauses with major manufacturers, were equally important. In the 1930s, union organizing campaigns reached mass production industries such as automobiles, steel, rubber, electrical products and petroleum refining. These new industrial unions developed contract administration systems which differed significantly from those in the older craft unions. Multistep grievance procedures became commonplace and the newer contracts often limited the scope of the arbitrator's authority. These developments encouraged manufacturers and unions alike to move from grudging acceptance of ad hoc arbitration to voluntary establishment of permanent arbitration machinery.

A prime example of this trend is the relationship between the United Automobile Workers (UAW) and General Motors. In 1937, General Motors and the UAW agreed to establish a multistep grievance procedure culminating in arbitration before a mutually chosen arbitrator. The initial system pleased neither side, and they began to consider a permanent umpire system. Walter Reuther, then head of the UAW's General Motors Department, argued in 1940:

> You cannot strike General Motors plants on individual grievances. One plant going down will affect the 60 other plants. You have to work out something to handle individual grievances. * * * I don't want to tie up 90,000 workers because one worker was laid off for two months. That is a case for the umpire.

A new General Motors–UAW agreement accordingly established in 1940 the "Office of the Umpire" which remains substantially the same today.

This 1940 agreement expressly restricted the umpire to handling grievance disputes, rather than interest issues. Employers bitterly opposed unionization in the mass production industries and in the early years there was none of the spirit of accord that inspired earlier arbitration agreements such as the Hart, Schaffner & Marx agreement in Chicago. The continued tension and mutual suspicion were reflected in contract clauses which limited arbitrators to interpreting the written agreement.

The General Motors–UAW arbitration model both arose from and contributed to the popular support enjoyed by collective bargaining in the late 1930s. Similar multistep grievance procedures culminating in arbitration were negotiated at about the same time in most other mass production industries. From that point on, grievance arbitration was all but universal in the unionized sector of the American economy.

2. THE SECOND WORLD WAR

Like the First World War, the Second necessitated an alternative to strikes and lockouts. After some preliminary experiments with mediation, President Franklin Roosevelt in 1942 created the War Labor Board (WLB), a tripartite body modeled on the NWLB. The WLB's jurisdiction extended to any labor dispute that might interrupt war work, which, of course, meant almost every labor dispute. It could "finally determine" disputes by mediation, arbitration, or otherwise, but showed a distinct preference for third-party involvement. Swamped by its caseload, the WLB first encouraged and then required parties to include grievance arbitration provisions in their agreements. More importantly, it routinely accepted arbitration awards as binding, thus presaging the deference the National Labor Relations Board and the courts pay to arbitration today.

AMERICAN LABOR ARBITRATION: THE MATURING YEARS
Dennis R. Nolan and Roger I. Abrams.
35 University of Florida Law Review 557 (1983).

The reputation of the War Labor Board in the area of arbitration has changed in recent years. Earlier writers asserted, as did Foster Rhea Dulles, that the "full record of the National War Labor Board, for all its difficulties and for all the criticism it aroused, constituted a very real success for this unprecedented experiment in tripartite labor arbitration." Today a practitioner of the WLB period can claim that the Board actually delayed the development of labor relations. Another contemporary writer has criticized the Board for forcing labor organizations into weak "contract unionism" and excluding an alternate view of union activity based on the principles of industrial democracy. Most tellingly, one major study concluded that "the outlines of modern grievance arbitration were clear long before the war" and that the wartime no-strike pledge, rather than the WLB, forced labor and management to rely more heavily on arbitration.

The traditional and revisionist views of the relationship between the WLB and labor arbitration do not conflict as clearly as may first appear. After reviewing the history of labor arbitration, no one could deny that arbitration was solidly established before the Second World War and would have continued to develop even without the WLB. Nor would even the sharpest critics of the War Labor Board deny its boost to the popularity and use of labor arbitration. The contributions of the Board to labor arbitration were chiefly of three types: increases in the number and percentage of labor agreements containing arbitration clauses; refinement of certain arbitration concepts and rules; and creation of a large pool of experienced arbitrators.

The exact percentage of contracts with arbitration clauses is difficult to determine because the agreements are not recorded in a central file. By one set of figures, the percentage rose from 62 percent before World War II to 73 percent in 1944. By another set, the percentage grew from 76 percent in the pre-War period to 85 percent in the immediate postwar era. There is agreement on the upward trend, and on the WLB's partial responsibility for it. To the extent the increase can be attributed to the WLB, its impact was notable if not overwhelming.

Some of the Board's refinements of arbitration concepts and rules have already been discussed, such as the limitation of the arbitrator's contractual authority and the presumption of an award's validity on review. As the first major arbitration board of general jurisdiction, the WLB inevitably faced a myriad of issues endemic to every arbitration system. Its resolutions of those issues were often the first recorded decisions on point. Moreover, because WLB decisions were published and widely distributed, they were destined to be influential. Later arbitrators could hardly ignore War Labor Board principles, even though legally they might be free to depart from them.

The Board prescribed methods for an individual to settle grievances apart from a union as well as the proper use of time limits in a grievance procedure. The Board explored the relative merits of permanent versus ad hoc arbitrators and the possible methods for selecting an arbitrator. To increase voluntary arbitration and decrease management fears of impingement on managerial prerogatives, the WLB carefully defined the arbitrator's jurisdiction and strictly enforced jurisdictional limitations. It also specifically defined grievance arbitration as an adjudicatory process, "limited in jurisdiction and limited to an award based solely on the evidence presented at a hearing." Thus the Board not only encouraged arbitration generally, it established a particular model of arbitration. This was the judicial model rather than a mediatorial one. The Board's establishment of the judicial model during the War was a major factor in that model's postwar domination. Both as to substance and procedure, then, the Board's role as a leader in labor arbitration was unique.

Perhaps the Board's most important contribution to modern labor arbitration was the development of a body of experienced arbitrators, many of whom remained active after the War. There were few skilled labor arbitrators before the War and few of those viewed arbitration as a profession. Hundreds of new people served as arbitrators during World War II, either on the Board's staff, on its disputes panels, or as a result of selection by parties sent to arbitration by the WLB. In addition, the Board created a continuing long-term demand for the arbitration services of these people. Management and labor needed their expertise to operate the labor relations system bequeathed by the WLB. Seven years after the War, Edwin Witte accurately stated that the "great majority of the labor arbitrators of the present day gained their first direct experience in service on the staff of the War Labor Board or on its disputes panels." That remained true for many years thereafter.

Of greater importance than the percentage of WLB alumni among current arbitrators is their quality. The mere listing of WLB staff members who continued in arbitration after the War should impress anyone familiar with arbitration. Truly these men constituted "the hard core of the arbitration profession" up to the present day. Without the experience and expertise of these men, grievance arbitration may not have been so readily accepted.

Any evaluation of the WLB must consider all these effects. Together their impact on labor arbitration was immense. The War Labor Board, it is fair to conclude, was the most important single influence on the maturation of labor arbitration in America.

3. POST–WAR JUDICIAL AND LEGISLATIVE ACCEPTANCE

Judicial acceptance of labor arbitration began with Congressional endorsements of arbitration. In 1947, Congress passed the Taft–Hartley Act over President Truman's veto. In addition to several highly controversial provisions, the Act contained several statements of congressional policy about which there was little disagreement.

Section 201(b), which dealt with interest disputes, declared it the nation's policy to advance collective bargaining by providing government assistance for "conciliation, mediation, and voluntary arbitration." Section 203(c) ordered the Director of the Federal Mediation and Conciliation Service (FMCS) to encourage dispute resolution alternatives (presumably including arbitration) when the FMCS was unable to resolve a dispute by conciliation. Section 203(d) dealt with grievance disputes. It stated that "[f]inal adjustment by a method agreed upon by the parties" (again presumably including arbitration) is "the desirable method for settlement of grievance disputes arising over the application or interpretation of an existing collective-bargaining agreement."

By far the most important part of the Act for labor arbitration was § 301, which authorized the federal courts to enforce collective bargaining agreements. Section 301 wiped out the bases of the courts' reluctance to require parties to comply with arbitration agreements. That section presented many interpretive issues, but its essential message was clear: the federal courts were to carry out congressional labor policy by treating collective bargaining agreements as contracts and by enforcing

them as they would other contracts. Detailed treatment of the courts'
reactions to the Taft–Hartley Act's arbitration provisions will be deferred until Chapter III, but a brief synopsis of the major Supreme Court
decisions is appropriate at this point.

The first of the Supreme Court's major § 301 cases was Textile
Workers Union v. Lincoln Mills, 353 U.S. 448, 77 S.Ct. 912, 1 L.Ed.2d
972 (1957), an action to force a reluctant employer to abide by a promise
to arbitrate certain grievances. The primary question in the case was
whether § 301 was simply *jurisdictional* (that is, whether it gave federal
courts jurisdiction over the parties but left applicable state substantive
law intact), or whether it was *substantive* as well (that is, whether the
federal courts were to apply federal law when exercising their jurisdiction over collective bargaining agreements). If the section was substantive, a further question arose: what was the federal law the courts were
to apply? Writing for the Court, Justice Douglas termed the arbitration
agreement "the *quid pro quo* for an agreement not to strike." Viewed in
this light, he wrote, the legislation states a policy of enforcing arbitration
agreements to prevent strikes. The courts were to apply a new federal
substantive law of the collective bargaining agreement fashioned "from
the policy of our national labor laws" and supplemented by relevant
state law "absorbed as federal law."

The fullest statement of the Supreme Court's interpretation of
§ 301 came in the *Steelworkers Trilogy* written for the Court by Justice
Douglas in 1960.[2] The first two cases of the Trilogy, United Steelworkers
of America v. American Manufacturing Co., 363 U.S. 564, 80 S.Ct. 1343,
4 L.Ed.2d 1403 (1960), and United Steelworkers of America v. Warrior
and Gulf Navigation Co., 363 U.S. 574, 80 S.Ct. 1347, 4 L.Ed.2d 1409
(1960), like *Lincoln Mills*, involved suits to enforce agreements to
arbitrate. In *American Manufacturing*, the Court of Appeals for the
Sixth Circuit had upheld the district court's grant of summary judgment
against the union's attempt to force the employer to arbitrate. The court
termed the union's grievance "a frivolous, patently baseless one, not
subject to arbitration under the collective bargaining agreement." The
Supreme Court reversed, holding that the agreement (which contained a
standard arbitration provision providing arbitration for all disputes "as
to the meaning, interpretation and application of the provisions of this
agreement") was to submit *all* grievances to arbitration, "not merely
those that a court may deem to be meritorious." The function of a court
in such cases is very limited, according to Justice Douglas:

> It is confined to ascertaining whether the party seeking arbitration
> is making a claim which on its face is governed by the contract.
> Whether the moving party is right or wrong is a question of contract
> interpretation for the arbitrator.

2. For the inside story on the *Trilogy* litigation, see David E. Feller, *How the Trilogy Was Made*, 47 Proceedings of the Na- tional Academy of Arbitrators 329, 338–44 (1995).

363 U.S. at 568, 80 S.Ct. at 1346. This is so, said the Court, both because of the national labor policy favoring arbitration and because "[t]he processing of even frivolous claims may have therapeutic values of which those who are not a part of the plant environment may be quite unaware."

Warrior and Gulf's arbitration provision was similarly broad but contained an important exclusion: "matters which are strictly a function of management shall not be subject to arbitration." The union sought a court order forcing arbitration of its claim that the employer violated the agreement by contracting out certain work. The lower federal courts dismissed the complaint, agreeing with the employer that contracting out was "strictly a function of management."

Again the Supreme Court reversed. There is no room under federal labor policy for the hostility toward arbitration the courts have shown in commercial cases, said the Court. To the contrary, because arbitration in these cases is a substitute for labor strife rather than for litigation, the courts should read arbitration provisions in the manner most favorable to arbitration:

> An order to arbitrate the particular grievance should not be denied unless it may be said with positive assurance that the arbitration clause is not susceptible of an interpretation that covers the asserted dispute. Doubts should be resolved in favor of coverage.

363 U.S. at 582, 80 S.Ct. at 1353. Why should such matters of interpretation be left to arbitrators rather than the courts? Because the parties want them to be, answered Justice Douglas. The collective bargaining agreement is part of an attempt to establish a system of industrial self-government, the gaps in which "may be left to be filled in by reference to the practices of the particular industry and of the various shops covered by the agreement." Labor and management select an arbitrator for his or her knowledge of "the common law of the shop" and ability to bring to bear considerations which "may indeed be foreign to the competence of courts. * * * The ablest judge cannot be expected to bring the same experience and competence to bear upon the determination of a grievance, because he cannot be similarly informed." *Id*. at 581–82, 80 S.Ct. at 1352–53.

Moreover, Justice Douglas went on, because a no-strike clause is the usual trade-off for an arbitration agreement, an absolute no-strike clause (as was present in this case) "in a very real sense" subjects everything management does to the arbitration agreement. Any exceptions must be explicit, and the phrase "strictly a function of management" does not explicitly cover contracting out.

The third of the *Trilogy* cases, United Steelworkers of America v. Enterprise Wheel & Car Corp., 363 U.S. 593, 80 S.Ct. 1358, 4 L.Ed.2d 1424 (1960), asked whether and when the courts should enforce arbitration awards. In other words, are the courts any freer to interpret the meaning of the contract after the arbitrator has spoken than before? The dispute involved an arbitration award requiring reinstatement of discharged employees with back pay even for a period following the contract's expiration. The circuit court of appeals refused to enforce the portion of the award granting reinstatement and back pay beyond the expiration date.

Once again the Supreme Court reversed, holding that the policy of judicial deference to arbitration was proper after issuance of the award as well as before. This is not to say that arbitrators can do anything they wish; the arbitrator "does not sit to dispense his own brand of industrial justice." Rather, the award is legitimate "only so long as it draws its essence from the collective bargaining agreement." Because the arbitrator may seek guidance from many sources and need not provide reasons for the award, the court should not overturn the award merely because of an ambiguity in the opinion "which permits the inference that the arbitrator may have exceeded his authority." Where it is clear that the arbitrator's words "manifest an infidelity to this obligation," however, the court must refuse to enforce the award. In this case, though, there was no such infidelity. The lower court was therefore wrong to substitute its judgment on the merits for that of the arbitrator. "The refusal of the courts to review the merits of an arbitration award is the proper approach to arbitration under collective bargaining agreements. The federal policy of settling labor disputes would be undermined if the courts had the final say on the merits of the awards." 363 U.S. at 596, 80 S.Ct. at 1360.

Later cases affirmed the Supreme Court's whole-hearted endorsement of arbitration. In 1962, for example, the Court interpreted arbitration clauses as containing implied promises not to strike or sue over arbitrable matters. Teamsters Local 174 v. Lucas Flour Co., 369 U.S. 95, 82 S.Ct. 571, 7 L.Ed.2d 593 (1962); Drake Bakeries, Inc. v. Local 50, American Bakery and Confectionery Workers International, 370 U.S. 254, 82 S.Ct. 1346, 8 L.Ed.2d 474 (1962). In Boys Markets, Inc. v. Retail Clerks Union, Local 770, 398 U.S. 235, 90 S.Ct. 1583, 26 L.Ed.2d 199 (1970) and Buffalo Forge Co. v. United Steelworkers of America, 428 U.S. 397, 96 S.Ct. 3141, 49 L.Ed.2d 1022 (1976), the Court decided that the federal courts could enforce promises not to strike over arbitrable issues. Thereafter, federal courts could enjoin contract-breaking strikes, notwithstanding a federal statute severely limiting federal court injunctions in labor disputes. See the Anti–Injunction or Norris–LaGuardia Act of 1932, 29 U.S.C.A. §§ 101–15 (1998), discussed in Section III.D.

Three other cases, John Wiley & Sons, Inc. v. Livingston, 376 U.S. 543, 84 S.Ct. 909, 11 L.Ed.2d 898 (1964), Nolde Brothers, Inc. v. Local No. 358, Bakery & Confectionery Workers Union, 430 U.S. 243, 97 S.Ct. 1067, 51 L.Ed.2d 300 (1977), and Litton Financial Printing Division v. National Labor Relations Board, 501 U.S. 190, 111 S.Ct. 2215, 115 L.Ed.2d 177 (1991), held that the arbitration provision could survive the termination of the agreement in which it appeared. A post-expiration grievance is arbitrable, the Court said in *Litton*, when it involves matters that arose before expiration, or a right that vested under the agreement. Without some evidence of a contrary intention, however, the arbitration provision does not cover grievances over terms that continue in force only because the parties have not yet fulfilled their statutory duty to bargain to impasse.

In sum, labor arbitration has, since World War II, passed from an awkward step-child of the courts to their favorite off-spring. With the Supreme Court in the lead, the federal courts lent their considerable support to arbitration agreements, to the arbitration process, and to the enforcement of resulting arbitration awards. The success of labor arbitration was so great, in fact, that it encouraged the use of arbitration in other settings. Rightly or wrongly, much of the modern support for alternative dispute resolution stems from the example set by labor and management.

Chapter II

INTRODUCTION TO GRIEVANCE RESOLUTION

A. GRIEVANCE PROCEDURES

Part I of this book explores the use of arbitration to resolve grievances arising under collective bargaining agreements.[1] To understand this process of grievance arbitration, it is important first to distinguish between arbitration and mediation, and to then distinguish between grievance and interest arbitration.

Arbitration and mediation are often referred to as alternative dispute resolution methods. Both arbitration and mediation employ neutrals to resolve disputes. However, the function of the neutral in each method is quite different. In mediation, the neutral attempts to facilitate a voluntary agreement between the parties. The mediator may improve communication, encourage parties to make counterproposals, and offer suggestions for compromise. In mediation, if the parties cannot reach an agreement, the dispute remains unresolved. In arbitration, on the other hand, the parties have empowered the neutral to make a binding decision.

Two types of disputes may be resolved by labor arbitration—"interest" disputes and grievances. The interest arbitrator is asked by the parties to resolve their dispute about the provisions the collective bargaining agreement should contain. Interest arbitration is used after the parties' negotiations, often with a mediator, have been unsuccessful. The parties may then select an interest arbitrator to determine the contractual language of provisions on which they were unable to agree. Interest arbitration is most commonly used in the public sector where a union's right to strike may be limited or precluded by law.[2] Grievance arbitration, sometimes also called "rights arbitration," occurs after the parties

1. For discussion of arbitration of rights arising under common law or statute, see Part 2 *infra*, Individual Employment Arbitration. For discussion of mediation, including mediation of disputes arising under collective bargaining agreements, see Chapter XIV *infra*.

2. See Chapter VIII.A., *infra*.

16

have a collective bargaining agreement. Grievance arbitration is used to resolve disputes about interpretation or application of the agreement.

The desires of labor and management representatives, not the command of the law, make arbitration the pervasive mechanism for resolving grievances in the unionized workplace. Ninety-nine percent of collective bargaining agreements provide for arbitration of at least some types of grievances.[3] Collective bargaining agreements vary both in the nature of the arbitration procedures established and in their place in the grievance resolution process. Typically, arbitration is the final step in a multistep grievance procedure. Only those grievances that are not resolved by the parties in the earlier stages of the grievance process make their way to arbitration.

There may be from one to six steps in the grievance procedure, although three-step procedures are the most common. A grievance procedure normally begins when a union steward or an aggrieved employee presents the grievance to the employee's immediate supervisor. Most contracts require grievances to be submitted within a few days of the time the problem arose. Many contracts require this submission to be in writing. Most contracts also oblige management to respond within a few days. Unresolved grievances may proceed to later steps in the grievance process. In these later steps, union representatives of increasing rank (steward, officer, business agent) meet with management representatives of increasing rank (mid-level supervisor, industrial relations director, plant manager).

Most cases are either resolved or abandoned at one of these first steps. Unresolved cases may be submitted for arbitration, usually at the request of the union. Statistics collected by the Federal Mediation and Conciliation Service (FMCS) for fiscal 2004 reported that on average 159 days elapsed from the filing of a grievance to the request for a list of arbitrators.[4] Between request for a list and the hearing date, discussions between the parties continue. Most remaining grievances are settled or abandoned during this period. In fiscal 2004, for example, the FMCS reported seven times as many requests for lists of arbitrators as arbitration awards issued.[5] One study concluded that approximately 30 percent of panel requests result in an arbitration award.[6]

3.   Basic Patterns in Union Contracts 37 (14th ed. 1995). The Bureau of National Affairs (BNA) collected 4,000 current collective bargaining agreements from which it drew a sample of 400 contracts. The sample included a cross-section of industries, unions, number of employees covered and geographic areas. The statistical information about contract provisions presented here is taken from that sample.

4.   Federal Mediation and Conciliation Service. The FMCS annually reports a variety of statistics about arbitrations conducted by arbitrators selected through the agency's procedures. The types of statistics reported vary from year to year. Annual reports for fiscal years commencing with 2000 are available at the agency's web site: <www.fmcs.gov>.

5.   This statistic may overstate the number of cases settled prior to hearing because some arbitrators may neglect to report to the FMCS that the award was issued.

6.   Nels E. Nelson and Walter J. Gershenfeld, *The Appointment of Grievance Arbitrators by State and Local Agencies*, 52 Labor Law Journal 258, 262 (2001).

Contracts also typically provide for bypassing one or more steps of the pre-arbitration grievance procedure to expedite special kinds of grievances, such as discharge cases or safety matters. See Chapter II.H.3, *infra*. In a very small, but increasing, number of contracts, mediation is an intermediate step between the parties' grievance meetings and arbitration.

B.   VARIOUS ARBITRATION SYSTEMS

Collective bargaining agreements also differ in the nature of the arbitration tribunal established. While most contracts provide for a single arbitrator, 11% use a panel of three arbitrators and 4% use a panel of five. The contract may specify that the panel is to be composed entirely of neutrals; more commonly, the contract requires a tripartite panel including a neutral and one or two representatives of each party. Party-appointed arbitrators on a tripartite panel serve as advocates and not as neutrals. Their role is to provide technical assistance to the neutral so that the arbitrator does not misapprehend aspects of the dispute or the operation of the workplace that would be evident to one with greater familiarity with the matter. The parties' representatives on the panel gain an additional opportunity for advocacy because they may communicate with the neutral after the neutral has drafted a decision.

Even when the contract specifies a tripartite panel, the neutral often presides alone at the hearing by agreement of the parties. Because the use of a tripartite panel complicates scheduling, increases the costs of arbitration, and delays issuance of an award, parties often waive the panel and authorize the neutral to act alone.

C.   ARBITRATOR SELECTION[7]

Nearly all contracts specify the method that the parties will use to select an arbitrator. Under most collective bargaining agreements, the parties do not select an arbitrator until each grievance reaches the arbitration stage. Such *"ad hoc"* selection methods allow the parties to choose an arbitrator suited for the particular grievance. For example, in a case involving complex employment discrimination law, the parties may prefer as an arbitrator an attorney with expertise in employment discrimination. Or, a union might be perfectly willing to use a particular arbitrator in a discharge case but not in a promotion case because that

7.   Bibliographic Suggestions: Mai Liang Bickner, *Arbitrator Acceptability: Arbitrators' and Advocates' Perspectives*, 56 Proceedings of the National Academy of Arbitrators 247 (2004); W. Daniel Boone, *How Union Advocates Select Arbitrators*, 56 Proceedings of the National Academy of Arbitrators 266 (2004); Eric W. Lawson, Jr., *Arbitrator Acceptability: Factors Affecting Selection*, 36 Arbitration Journal 24 (December 1981); Walter J. Primeaux, Jr. and Dalton E. Brannen, *Why Few Arbitrators Are Deemed Acceptable*, 98 Monthly Labor Review 28 (September 1975); Julius Rezler and Donald Peterson, *Strategies of Arbitrator Selection*, 70 Labor Arbitration Reports 1307 (1978); John B. West, *Reflections on Selecting an Arbitrator*, 56 Proceedings of the National Academy of Arbitrators 272 (2004).

arbitrator has previously deferred to management decisionmaking in promotion cases.

The disadvantages of *ad hoc* selection systems are the delay caused by the selection process and the possibility of having to teach the arbitrator about the nature of the industry and workplace. With respect to delays, statistics collected by the Federal Mediation and Conciliation Service indicated that in fiscal 2004 an average of 106 days elapsed from the time parties were sent a list of possible arbitrators to the time that they selected the arbitrator to handle the grievance.

In order to avoid these disadvantages, 4% of collective bargaining agreements appoint a permanent arbitrator, sometimes called an umpire, for the life of the contract. In a very few companies or industries with a substantial arbitration caseload, umpires work on a full-time basis. More commonly, parties use the designated arbitrator as needed. Permanent arbitrators are relatively common in the automobile, aircraft, meat-packing, steel, rubber, apparel, and transportation equipment industries.[8]

Six percent of agreements employ an arbitration panel, a list of arbitrators who serve on a rotating basis as grievances arise. It may be difficult for the parties to agree upon a list of individuals acceptable for all types of grievances. Also, the parties' continued satisfaction with the arbitration system may be threatened if a party finds itself obligated to continue to use an arbitrator who has issued an unsatisfactory decision early in the life of the contract. For that reason, some contracts include provisions permitting removal of an arbitrator from the panel during the term of the agreement.

Contracts calling for *ad hoc* arbitrators usually specify the method of selection. Sometimes the contract may simply state that the arbitrator will be chosen by mutual agreement. Fifty-two percent of contracts, however, provide that the parties will select arbitrators through the facilities of an impartial agency, usually the Federal Mediation and Conciliation Service (FMCS), the American Arbitration Association (AAA), or one of twenty-six state and local mediation agencies that provide arbitration services. An individual arbitrator's name usually appears on the roster of several different agencies. A study of 1998 arbitration awards estimated that arbitrators selected under procedures of the AAA account for forty-seven percent of all awards issued, FMCS for twenty-eight percent, and state and local agencies for twenty-five percent.[9] In some regions of the country, the AAA is the most commonly used source for arbitrators while in other areas it is only rarely used.

In a common selection method, the parties receive from the agency a list of seven names. Following the toss of a coin or other method to determine which party proceeds first, the parties alternately strike

---

8. Elkouri & Elkouri, How Arbitration Works, 144–169 (Alan Miles Ruben, ed., 6th ed. 2003). See Chapter 4 of the Elkouri treatise for an excellent description of the various forms of arbitration tribunals and a comparison of their merits.

9. Nels E. Nelson and Walter J. Gershenfeld, note 6 *supra*, at 262.

names from the list. The name remaining after each party has removed three names is the person who will serve as the arbitrator. In another method, the agency supplies a list of names and each party strikes unacceptable arbitrators, ranks the rest of the arbitrators and returns the ranked list to the agency. The agency then names the most highly ranked arbitrator to hear the case.

Parties sometimes select arbitrators by a method other than that specified in their agreement. For example, the parties may in mid-contract decide to get arbitrators from a different agency than the one indicated in the contract because they have been dissatisfied with the lists they had received from the contractually-designated agency. Or, the parties simply may be able to agree on an arbitrator without having to request a list from the specified agency.

Appointing agencies try to meet the parties' desires for arbitrators with certain qualifications. Parties may request arbitrators with specific skills or experience, or arbitrators from a specific geographic area, or may get a list selected by the agency, which may or may not be random.

Sixty percent of contracts that specify an agency for arbitrator selection name the FMCS, an agency whose primary function is providing staff mediators for collective bargaining negotiations. A union or an employer, or often both jointly, may submit a request to the FMCS's Office of Arbitration Services in Washington, D.C. For a fee, the FMCS will provide names and brief biographies of seven arbitrators.[10] Alternatively, the parties may request the names and biographical information of all arbitrators in a particular geographic region, allowing the parties independently to employ their own selection method. In 2004 there were more than 1250 active arbitrators on the roster of the FMCS. The agency's requirements for listing arbitrators include demonstrated acceptability, usually shown by submitting five prior arbitration awards. The FMCS will, at a party's request, contact an arbitrator about a late award and will preclude an arbitrator with two late awards from obtaining additional cases. State mediation agencies have similar appointment procedures, although they vary considerably in the extent to which they are involved in the administration of cases. State agencies may be willing to open their rosters to less experienced arbitrators.

Thirty percent of collective bargaining agreements designating an agency for arbitrator selection specify the American Arbitration Association (AAA). In 2004, the AAA charged each party $175 per case for its services. For that fee, the AAA not only assists in the selection of the arbitrator, but also provides additional services. For example, the AAA can handle communications between the parties and the arbitrator to schedule the hearing and reserve a hearing room. Having the agency handle all pre-hearing communications regarding scheduling helps to avoid *ex parte* communications between the parties and the arbitrator.

---

10. In 2004, the FMCS charged $30 for panel requests submitted through its web   site and $50 for non-electronic requests.

The AAA will also contact the arbitrator following the hearing in an effort to assure that the arbitrator's award is rendered within thirty days. The AAA also helps resolve any subsequent questions about the arbitrator's bill. In 2003 there were 1025 labor arbitrators on the AAA's roster.

D.   THE ARBITRATION PROFESSION

Arbitrators are independent professionals selected and paid by the parties to hear an individual grievance. They are neither licensed nor directly regulated by government agencies. Ninety-one percent of collective bargaining agreements require parties to split the arbitrator's fee and expenses. When a tripartite panel is used, each party usually pays its own representative and the parties share the costs of the neutral. In 5% of the contracts with provisions governing arbitration expenses, the losing party pays the entire bill.

Normally, arbitrators charge the parties on a per diem basis. In 2004, the FMCS reported that arbitrators charged an average per diem of $838. Per diems ranged from $350 to $2400.[11] On average, cases require one day for the hearing and two days for "study time"—time for the arbitrator to review the evidence, undertake research and draft the award. Arbitrators also charge for time spent in travel. (Arbitrators typically also will charge a cancellation fee if a scheduled hearing is cancelled close to the hearing date.) In fiscal 2004, the average FMCS case consumed 3.91 days of arbitrator time and the average bill submitted by arbitrators was $3,541.62, including expenses.

The most comprehensive demographic study of arbitrators, conducted in 1986, concluded that "arbitration has been and remains a profession of elderly white men."[12] The study surveyed a representative sample of an estimated 3500 arbitrators nationally. The average age was fifty-seven; more than half had law degrees and about one quarter had doctorates. Ninety-seven percent of arbitrators were white, and only 9% were women.[13] A survey a decade later suggested that the profession had become only modestly more diverse in the intervening years. The 1998 study, surveying only members of the National Academy of Arbitrators, found that ninety-four percent were white and twelve percent were women.[14]

11. Per diems of AAA arbitrators in 2003 ranged from $250 to $2500. Twenty-three percent of AAA arbitrators charged $1000 or more per day in 2003, while 22% charged less than $700. Average per diems vary by region, with the highest amounts charged in New York, Washington, D.C., and San Francisco.

12. Mario F. Bognanno and Charles C. Coleman, Labor Arbitration in America: The Profession and Practice 148 (1992).

13. *Id*. at 24–27. See also Mario F. Bognanno and Clifford E. Smith, *The Demo-*

graphic and Professional Characteristics of Arbitrators in North America, 41 Proceedings of the National Academy of Arbitrators 266 (1989).

14. The average age of those surveyed was sixty-three; about ten percent were under age fifty and nearly seven percent were over age eighty. Sixty-one percent had law degrees and twenty-two percent had doctoral degrees. Michel G. Picher, Ronald L. Seeber, and David B. Lipsky, *The Arbitration Profession in Transition: Preliminary Results from a Survey of the National Acade-*

In 1986, the profession was largely a supplemental occupation with only 16.4% working full-time as arbitrators. Part-time arbitrators heard an average of 13.61 grievance cases in 1986 while full-time arbitrators heard an average of 63.77 cases. Approximately 17% of the profession were members of the National Academy of Arbitrators (NAA) whose members decided an average of 55.7 grievance cases in 1986. Nonmembers of the NAA, making up 73% of the profession, decided an average of only 16 cases that year. More than half of part-time arbitrators are teachers (usually of law, industrial relations or business). Other part-time arbitrators are commonly lawyers or are retired from other jobs.

Thirty percent of arbitrators served on at least one permanent panel and 10% had a permanent umpireship. In 1986, arbitrators reported an average of 43.5% of their cases in the public sector and 56.5% of their cases in the private sector. More recently, there has been a trend toward more full-time arbitrators and more labor arbitrators also serving as neutrals in non-union employment cases.

The National Academy of Arbitrators is a professional association of practicing arbitrators. The Academy was established in 1947 by a small group of arbitrators, mostly alumni of the War Labor Board, who wanted to professionalize the field. According to the NAA's first statement of purpose, its goals were:

> To establish and foster high standards and competence among those engaged in the arbitration of industrial disputes on a professional basis; to adopt canons of ethics to govern the conduct of arbitrators; to promote the study and understanding of the arbitration of industrial disputes.[15]

Unlike the FMCS and the AAA, the Academy is not a referral service. The Academy grants membership primarily on the basis of a record showing a large and diverse caseload over an extended period of years. Academy membership is viewed as a stamp of recognition in the field. In 1974, the Academy, along with the FMCS and AAA, jointly promulgated a "Code of Professional Responsibility for Arbitrators of Labor–Management Disputes." The Academy has formal procedures for enforcing the Code with respect to Academy members. Today, there are about 635 members of the NAA. The Academy also offers continuing education programs for its members.

Annual meetings of the Academy provide a forum for informed discussion on important issues facing labor arbitrators and the Academy. In the past, annual meetings have been the springboard for debate on

my of Arbitrators, 52 Proceedings of the National Academy of Arbitrators 241 (2000). Since only experienced arbitrators are eligible for membership in the National Academy of Arbitrators, the profession as a whole is likely somewhat younger and more diverse than these figures.

15.   Clare B. McDermott, *Some Developments in the History of the National Academy of Arbitrators*, 25 Proceedings of the National Academy of Arbitrators 27, 29 (1972). For a comprehensive history of the NAA, see Gladys W. Gruenberg, Joyce M. Najita and Dennis R. Nolan, The National Academy of Arbitrators: Fifty Years in the World of Work (1998). The book includes an fifty-year index of the proceedings of the annual meetings of the NAA.

concepts that are now well-settled principles of arbitration. For example, earlier meetings focused attention on the need for the publication of awards, the burden of proof in discharge cases, whether an employee must obey a management demand that violates the collective bargaining agreement, and the role of expedited arbitration procedures. Each year, the Annual Meeting's proceedings are published and serve as a rich source of information to arbitrators and others interested in labor arbitration.[16] Recently, the NAA has been reflecting on whether the Academy should seek to play a role in the development of employment arbitration, beyond its historic role in labor arbitration.

E. ADVOCATES IN ARBITRATION

The parties to the collective bargaining agreement select their own representatives to present their case at the arbitration hearing. On the union side, the advocate might be a union official who is a member of the bargaining unit or an attorney, but is most commonly a full-time union business agent. A typical union business agent began work as a member of the bargaining unit, participated actively in the union as an officer, steward, or bargaining committee member, and then became an employee of the union. On the management side, the representative might be an employee of the company's human resources department, a management consultant, or an attorney.

Estimates of the proportion of attorneys among arbitration advocates vary considerably, but all agree that employers use attorneys much more often than unions. A national survey of advocates requesting lists of arbitrators from the FMCS found that 25.6% of the union representatives and 34.4% of the management representatives were attorneys.[17] A Michigan survey found attorneys representing management in about 70% of cases but union attorneys appearing in substantially less than half.[18] In general, management's representatives have studied labor relations or law, while the union's representatives learned their skills on the job. The survey of those requesting FMCS lists found that union representatives were on average older than management representatives

---

16. See also William P. Murphy, *The Presidential Address: The Academy at Forty*, 40 Proceedings of the National Academy of Arbitrators 1 (1987).

17. Arthur Eliot Berkeley, *Arbitrators and Advocates: The Consumers' Report*, 41 Proceedings of the National Academy of Arbitrators 290, 298 (1989). This study may understate the proportion of attorneys representing parties in hearings because it is not uncommon for a party to participate in arbitrator selection before an attorney is retained to represent the party at the hearing. In AAA cases for 1990–1992, employers had attorneys 82% of the time and unions slightly more than half. Harry Graham and David Dinardo, *Grievance Arbitration Results in a Large Public Employer*, 24 Journal of Collective Negotiations 147, 149 (1995).

18. Jack Steiber, Richard N. Block and Leslie Corbett, *How Representative are Published Decisions?*, 37 Proceedings of the National Academy of Arbitrators 172, 179 (1985). A study of ten years of reported decisions in which employees were disciplined for drugs or alcohol found management attorneys in about 66% of cases and union attorneys in about 42% of cases. Stephen W. Crow and James W. Logan, *Arbitrators' Characteristics and Decision–Making Record, Gender of Arbitrators and Grievants, and the Presence of Legal Counsel as Predictors of Arbitral Outcomes*, 7 Employee Rights and Responsibilities Journal 169, 176 (1994).

(44.8 years vs. 42.0 years), twice as likely to be female (23.8% vs. 12.9%) and more than twice as likely to be Asian, Hispanic, or African–American (27.5% vs. 10.8%).

F.   THE ARBITRATION HEARING[19]

The arbitrator's first task is to schedule the hearing. Because of the difficulties in coordinating the schedules of the arbitrator, the parties' advocates, and the witnesses, there is frequently a considerable delay between the arbitrator's appointment and the hearing date. The FMCS reported that in fiscal 2004 there was, on average, six and one-half months between the arbitrator's selection and the hearing.

Most collective bargaining agreements contain no provisions regarding the conduct of the arbitration hearing, although some incorporate by reference the Labor Arbitration Rules of the American Arbitration Association or make brief reference to such matters as the nature of admissible evidence or the use of transcripts. Although an arbitrator thus has wide discretion in conducting the arbitration hearing, arbitrators tend to follow common procedural practices, modified by the desires and traditions of particular parties. Some parties prefer an arbitration hearing that looks very much like a judicial proceeding, complete with formal presentation of evidence, adherence to courtroom evidentiary standards, sworn witnesses, transcripts, and briefs. At the other extreme, some parties want a much less formal structure with few if any of those features. The degree of formality of most arbitration hearings falls somewhere between these extremes. Arbitration hearings are conducted in a variety of settings such as a union or company conference room, a hotel meeting room, or the conference room of a public building. In fiscal 2004, the average FMCS case took 1.09 days of hearing time. On average, transcripts are used in about 35% of the cases, although transcript practices vary significantly by region; in some regions transcripts are routine, in others extremely rare. In cases where transcripts are not made, the arbitrator may make a tape recording of the hearing or merely take notes by hand or on a laptop computer.

The arbitrator usually arrives at the hearing room with little or no information about the nature of the grievance. The arbitrator typically begins by making sure that there are no objections to the arbitrability of the grievance and by identifying the issue. Few collective bargaining agreements require the parties to submit written statements of the issue to the arbitrator. More often, the parties will attempt to state the issue at the start of the hearing.

The party bearing the burden of proof, generally the employer in disciplinary matters and the union in other cases, will offer a brief opening statement. The other side will either respond with an opening

---

19. Bibliographic Suggestion: Norman Brand (ed.), How ADR Works (2002) (Chapters 34–37); Dana Eischen, *The Arbitration Hearing: Administration, Conduct and Pro-* *cedures*, Labor and Employment Arbitration (Tim Bornstein, Ann Gosline and Marc Greenbaum, eds. 2003).

statement or reserve that opportunity until the conclusion of the opponent's case. The parties often agree to the admission of a group of joint exhibits, including the collective bargaining agreement, the grievance, and management's formal responses to the grievance. The party with the burden of proof presents evidence through witnesses and exhibits. Depending on the preferences of the parties and the authority of the arbitrator, witnesses may be sworn. Following the testimony of each witness, the other side has an opportunity for cross-examination. The arbitrator may ask occasional questions of witnesses, usually to clarify testimony rather than to engage in independent inquiries.

Following the opponent's presentation of evidence and any rebuttal evidence, the arbitrator will usually ask the parties if they would like to make closing arguments or if they would rather submit briefs. In fiscal 2004, briefs were submitted in 83% of FMCS cases. The parties and the arbitrator generally agree on a deadline of about a month after the hearing (or receipt of the transcript) for submission of briefs. The arbitrator's award is usually issued between a month and two months after the conclusion of the hearing.

A typical arbitrator's award will be from ten to twenty typed double-spaced pages. The award will state the issue, quote the relevant contract language, summarize the facts and the contentions of the parties, explain the arbitrator's conclusions, and, if the grievance is sustained, include a remedial order.

Notes and Questions

1.   Why aren't the terms of an ordinary collective bargaining agreement adequate to resolve the issues between the parties? Why do parties feel the need to include within their contracts a dispute resolution mechanism?

2.   In the absence of a system of grievance arbitration, how would the parties resolve contractual disputes? Why do 99% choose arbitration over these alternatives?

3.   When negotiating a grievance arbitration procedure, the parties must decide whether to receive lists of arbitrators from the Federal Mediation and Conciliation Service, the American Arbitration Association, or a state mediation agency. What factors should the employer and union consider when deciding which agency to use?

4.   What is likely to be the effect on the parties' resort to arbitration of a contractual provision that the losing party pays the entire arbitrator's fee? Why do so few contracts (5%) have such a provision?

5.   The employer discharges Bill after investigating a sexual harassment complaint filed against him by Sally, another member of the bargaining unit. The union takes to arbitration a grievance challenging Bill's discharge. What information should the union and the employer have before deciding which arbitrators to strike from the list? How can they get such information? (See the section, Information About Dispute Resolution Professionals, in Appendix A, Researching Labor Arbitration and Alternative Dispute Resolution in Employment.) What factors should the union and the

employer take into account in deciding which arbitrators to strike? Why should the union and the employer choose one arbitrator rather than another? Are the factors emphasized by the union and the employer likely to point toward the same arbitrator?

6.   The proportions of white women and men and women of color within the arbitration profession are substantially lower than within the unionized workforce. Is that a serious problem? Why or why not? If so, should action be taken to correct it? What and by whom?

7.   State and federal governments provide mediators at no cost to the parties to facilitate agreement on the terms of collective bargaining agreements. Should government also pay for or provide a paid staff of arbitrators for the resolution of grievances? (Until 1947, the United States Department of Labor did provide arbitrators free of charge and today the government pays neutrals resolving grievances in the railroad industry.) Is the fact that arbitration is today, except in the railroad industry, a private rather than a governmental function advantageous to labor and management? To society as a whole?

8.   Because arbitrators are hired by the parties, rather than the government, they must be acceptable to both unions and employers in order to obtain cases. Is this need to maintain acceptability likely to promote or undermine fair decisionmaking?

9.   If you wanted to become a labor arbitrator how would you go about it? See, Christopher A. Barreca, Anne Harmon Miller, and Max Zimny, eds., Labor Arbitrator Development: A Handbook (1983).

G.   THE RESOLUTION OF LABOR GRIEVANCES IN OTHER COUNTRIES[20]

The North American system of grievance arbitration under collective bargaining agreements generally is distinctive in three respects: (1) the rigid division in dispute resolution between rights and interests; (2) the absence of government from the adjudication of disputes; and (3) the absence of third-party conciliation efforts prior to adjudication.

In the North American system, usually the grievance process only recognizes rights previously created by contract; it has no power to

20. Bibliographic Suggestions: Alan Gladstone, *Settlement of Disputes over Rights*, Comparative Labour Law and Industrial Relations in Industrialized Market Economies (Roger Blanpain, ed., 8th ed., 2004) (the most comprehensive of the comparative essays); Alvin L. Goldman, Chair, *The Role of Neutrals in the Resolution of Shop Floor Disputes*, 9 Comparative Labor Law Journal 1 (1987) (including reports from twelve countries); J. Joseph Loewenberg, *International Comparison of the Role of Neutrals in Resolving Shop Floor Dis-*putes: Lessons for Arbitrators, 41 Proceedings of the National Academy of Arbitrators 247 (1989); J. Joseph Loewenberg, *The Neutral and Public Interests in Resolving Disputes: An Eight Nation Study by the Committee on International Studies of the National Academy of Arbitrators*, 13 Comparative Labor Law Journal 371 (1992); and Arnold M. Zack, *Managing International Work Place Disputes: Are United States Techniques Exportable?*, 27 Willamette Law Review 645 (1991).

create new contractual interests. In other countries, a single mechanism may define both "rights" and "interests." In Japan, for example, it is difficult to distinguish between rights and interests because of the abstract and vague nature of collective agreements. Even those disputes that in the United States would clearly be considered matters of rights, such as an employee discharge, are subject to mandatory collective bargaining. In Australia, on the other hand, a single agency has some responsibilities for both the creation and enforcement of labor agreements. The vesting of dual responsibilities in one agency blurs the distinction in Australia between rights and interests. The recognition of a clear distinction between rights and interests in North America is not, however, unique. It is also a characteristic of most European systems.

North American labor arbitration is most distinctive in the extent to which the parties themselves create both their substantive rights and enforcement procedures. In most other industrialized countries, public law establishes the rules governing the workplace, including those against unfair dismissal. Laws also establish the procedural mechanisms for enforcing employee rights. Such legally established tribunals include works councils with employee representatives in western Europe, administrative agencies in Australia, and labor courts in the United Kingdom and many continental European countries. The labor courts in most democratic countries are tripartite, with lay judges representing labor and management sitting with a professional judge. Unlike labor and management representatives who serve as partisans in tripartite arbitration in North America, labor and management representatives on these labor courts are expected to assess the cases in an objective manner and a high percentage of decisions are unanimous.

As in the United States, grievance resolution elsewhere commonly begins with efforts between management and labor to resolve the matter consensually, but in other countries there is more likely to be an effort at third-party conciliation, sometimes offered by a government agency, prior to the initiation of more formal procedures.

H.   ALTERNATIVE MECHANISMS FOR GRIEVANCE RESOLUTION

The arbitration process outlined in this chapter is, by a large margin, the most common device used in North American collective bargaining agreements to resolve grievances. Contracts, however, sometimes provide another mechanism for the resolution of grievances. Parties seek such alternatives to increase speed of resolution, reduce costs, or afford the parties greater control over the outcome. Some of these alternatives are designed to enhance the arbitration process and others are used to supplant it.

1.   JOINT FACT–FINDING

A joint fact-finding process begins as soon as a grievance is submitted. The union and the employer each appoint a fact-finder and the two investigate the grievance together, interviewing all witnesses and reviewing relevant documents. The fact-finders then prepare a report listing all facts that can be stipulated and those still in dispute. The report is submitted to company and union representatives who meet in an effort to settle the grievance. Many grievances are settled at this point. Unsettled grievances proceed to arbitration where no new evidence may be introduced.

Contracts providing for fact-finding may use a permanent arbitrator who reserves a day each month to hear all pending cases. The reports of stipulated facts expedite the hearings to such an extent that several cases can be presented in a single day. In one report, eleven cases (three discharges, four suspensions, and four contract interpretation disputes) were presented in a single session. During a three-year experience with joint fact-finding in the retail grocery industry, the parties found their arbitration costs to be only one-fifth of those under their prior traditional system.[21]

2. GRIEVANCE MEDIATION

Grievance mediation uses a neutral to facilitate settlement of a grievance before arbitration. Grievance mediation may be used on an *ad hoc* basis or may be an explicit step in the contractual grievance procedure. The parties may, by their contract, restrict the types of disputes subject to mediation. One contract may, for example, exclude discipline cases from mediation (coal industry), while another may send only discipline cases to mediation (telecommunications). Studies of grievance mediation systems have reported high settlement rates, significantly reduced costs, expeditious resolution of disputes, and high levels of participant satisfaction.[22]

3. EXPEDITED ARBITRATION

The parties may use an expedited arbitration process for particular categories of grievances specified in the collective bargaining agreement, such as employee discipline or safety issues, or they may refer grievances on an *ad hoc* basis to a previously agreed-upon expedited arbitration procedure.

---

21. See John Kagel, Kathy Kelly, and Patrick J. Szymanski, *Labor Arbitration: Cutting Cost and Time Without Cutting Quality*, 39 Arbitration Journal 34–41 (September 1984).

22. See Peter Feuille, *Grievance Mediation*, Employment Dispute Resolution and Worker Rights in the Changing Workplace (Adrienne E. Eaton and Jeffrey H. Keefe, eds. 1999); Deborah M. Kolb, *How Existing Procedures Shape Alternatives: The Case of Grievance Mediation*, 1989 Journal of Dispute Resolution 59; John Kagel, *Mediating Grievances,* 46 Proceedings of the National

Academy of Arbitrators 76 (1994); Matthew T. Roberts, Jeanne M. Brett and Stephen B. Goldberg, *Grievance Mediation in the Coal Industry*, 37 Industrial and Labor Relations Review 49–69 (1983); Deborah A. Schmedemann, *Reconciling Differences: The Theory and Law of Mediating Labor Grievances*, 9 Industrial Relations Law Journal 523–595 (1987); Roger S. Wolters, William H. Holley, Jr. and Hubert S. Feild, *Grievance Mediation: A Management Perspective*, 45 Arbitration Journal 15–23 (September 1990). For further discussion of mediation of grievances, see Chapter XIV. G. 3 *infra*.

An expedited arbitration procedure is characterized by brief time limits of no more than a couple of weeks for referral of cases to arbitration and requirements that arbitrators render their awards promptly, within time limits as short as forty-eight hours. Hearings are informal, without briefs and transcripts. Several cases may be heard in a single day. Arbitrators render short written awards which have no precedential weight. An expedited arbitration process will often use a pre-selected panel of arbitrators who have agreed to accept reduced fees. Expedited arbitration originated in the steel industry and is widely used in the bituminous coal industry and by the United States Postal Service.[23]

4. TEAMSTER JOINT COMMITTEES

The institution of joint committees for the resolution of grievances arising under Teamsters Union contracts dates back to 1938. In the 1960s, national Teamsters leaders encouraged locals to replace arbitration provisions in Teamsters contracts with provisions establishing joint grievance committees. Union and management representatives are made the primary decisionmakers in the hope that their industry experience and specific contract expertise will produce consistent outcomes that are practical to implement. Procedures are designed to resolve disputes to the extent possible at an institutional level closest to where the grievance arose and to use neutrals only when bipartite panels deadlock. Parties to Teamster agreements have promulgated procedural rules that expedite hearings by such features as prohibiting the use of attorneys in the presentation of cases, requiring parties to submit written statements of fact and restricting cross-examination to questions posed by panel members. Unlike most other collective bargaining agreements, some Teamster agreements protect the right to strike over certain disputes, such as the failure of an employer to make health and pension fund payments or to comply with the decision of a grievance panel or arbitrator.[24]

Today, contracts create a variety of structures for joint committees. Common characteristics include final and binding decisions by majority vote of a committee that consists of an equal number of employer and union representatives, none of whom can be from the union local or the company involved in the grievance. The contract may provide for committees to operate in tiers including local, area, and national levels. If a committee deadlocks at a lower level, the grievance is referred to a committee whose membership is drawn from a broader geographic area.

23. See American Arbitration Association, Streamlined Labor Arbitration Rules (2004); William Burrus, *Expedited Arbitration: U.S. Postal Service—A Union Perspective,* 36 Proceedings of the National Academy of Arbitrators 256–260 (1983); Cornelius J. Peck, *Report on a Survey of Academy Members on Expedited Arbitration,* 38 Proceedings of the National Academy of Arbitrators 265–274 (1986); John C. Sigler, *Mediation of Grievances: An Alternative to Arbitration?* 13 Employee Relations Law Journal 270–271 (1987).

24. See, for example, National Master Freight Agreement and Central Region Local Cartage and Over-the-Road, Motor Freight and Supplemental Agreement, Article 8, Section 3 (1998–2003).

Depending on the contract, when a deadlock is reached and there is no higher committee available, the grievance may simply end without resolution, proceed to arbitration before a neutral, or be subject to resolution by strike or lockout.

Some of the Teamsters contracts with the United Parcel Service employ an innovative procedure for resolution of deadlocks in cases involving employee discharges and suspensions. In these cases, a neutral arbitrator is present when the case is heard before a joint panel. In most cases, the arbitrator remains silent and the case is resolved by the panel. If the panel deadlocks, however, the arbitrator, already having heard the presentation to the joint panel, renders an immediate oral decision.[25]

At a regional level, a joint committee meeting can involve an enormous flurry of activity. Several panels meet simultaneously and several hundred persons are in attendance for a two-or three-day period to seek resolution of several hundred grievances. Typically hearings are held on about a third to a half of the cases on the docket while the remainder are settled or postponed. A single panel, with two to five representatives of labor and management, may hear fifteen to thirty cases in a day, spending about fifteen minutes hearing each case and five minutes discussing and deciding it. The committees render brief decisions that provide no explanations and have no precedential value.[26]

Some critics have argued that the brief hearings afforded are inadequate to obtain facts, that decisions are often based on *ex parte* communications, that the large number of matters considered simultaneously results in trading of grievances, that committees are subject to political pressures, and that the committees' composition of union and employer representatives personally subject to the same or similar contract provisions creates a significant potential for bias.[27] Such criticisms have additional significance because the National Labor Relations Board and the courts generally afford the decisions of Teamsters joint committees the same deference that they give to the awards of neutral arbitrators.[28]

5. SYSTEM BOARDS UNDER THE RAILWAY LABOR ACT

The Railway Labor Act governs labor relations in the railroad and airline industries.[29] As in collective bargaining relationships governed by

---

25. National Master United Parcel Service Agreement and Atlantic Area Supplemental Agreement, Article 49, Section 4(c) (2002–2008).

26. Clyde W. Summers, *Teamster Joint Grievance Committees: Grievance Disposal Without Adjudication*, 37 Proceedings of the National Academy of Arbitrators 130, 133–134 (1985). See also Gerry M. Miller, *Teamster Joint Committees: The Legal Equivalent of Arbitration*, 37 Proceedings of the National Academy of Arbitrators 118 (1985).

27. Clyde W. Summers, note 26 *supra*, at 136–149.

28. David E. Feller, *Arbitration Without Neutrals: Joint Committees and Boards, I. The Legal Background*, 37 Proceedings of the National Academy of Arbitrators 106 (1985); Gregory E. Zimmerman, *The Teamster Joint Grievance Committee and NLRB Deferral Policy: A Failure to Protect the Individual Employee's Statutory Rights*, 133 University of Pennsylvania Law Review 1453 (1985).

29. For a comprehensive discussion of the Railway Labor Act, see Douglas L. Leslie, ed., The Railway Labor Act (1995) and Supplement (2001). Chapter 5 addresses en-the National Labor Relations Act, parties under the Railway Labor Act are expected to make informal efforts to resolve grievances before resorting to formal procedures. For the railroad industry, the Act establishes a National Railroad Adjustment Board (NRAB) composed of members appointed by rail carriers and unions with jurisdiction to hear grievances, known as "minor disputes." In fiscal year 2003, NRAB closed 1313 cases.[30] It was earlier estimated that only twelve percent of railroad grievances are resolved by the NRAB.[31] Although authorized by statute, no similar government agency was ever created to hear grievances in the airline industry.

The Act also permits railroads,[32] and requires airlines,[33] to establish system boards of adjustment for the resolution of grievances. Air and rail carriers and their labor organizations determine the structure of their system boards by contract. System boards in the railroad industry are commonly tripartite. Airline contracts usually call for a bipartite board initially, but cases may be heard by a tripartite board if the bipartite board deadlocks or if the parties waive bipartite consideration. Much more rarely, usually in the case of a small airline, the system board is composed solely of one or more neutrals.[34] Contracts may specifically provide that the parties' representatives on bipartite and tripartite boards are to act in an independent manner rather than as partisans. System boards hold hearings at which evidence is presented and cases are decided by interpreting the requirements of the contract rather than by negotiating a settlement.

Bipartite boards, with an equal number of union and employer representatives, have the potential to resolve many grievances efficiently and inexpensively if the parties have a good working relationship. In one report from the mid–1980s concerning nine years of bipartite decision-making by United Air Lines and the Air Line Pilots Association, the system board heard 99 cases and resolved 68 without deadlock.[35] As a practical matter, though, the bipartite model has largely failed to achieve its objectives. In the railroad industry there is little incentive to resolve the case with a bipartite panel because the federal government will pay the costs of the neutral if the matter goes to a tripartite board. In the airline industry in recent years the contentious labor relations climate has made bipartite resolution highly unlikely. Today, airlines and their unions typically either treat the contractual bipartite step as *pro forma* or waive it entirely and go directly to a tripartite board with a neutral member whose vote effectively controls the outcome.

forcement of collective bargaining agreements.

30. National Mediation Board, Annual Performance Report, FY 2003, at 57.

31. Joshua M. Javits, Airline and Railroad Employment Law, Grievance Procedures: The Carrier's Perspective, American Law Institute–American Bar Association Continuing Legal Education (October 2000), on Westlaw at SF15 ALI–ABA 459.

32. 45 U.S.C. § 153. Second (2000).

33. 45 U.S.C. § 184 (2000).

34. Joshua M. Javits, note 31 *supra*.

35. Stuart Bernstein, *Bipartite Airline System Boards*, 37 Proceedings of the National Academy of Arbitrators 153, 157 (1985).

When bipartite systems boards are used, the labor contract will specify a procedure employing a neutral, typically as part of a tripartite board, to resolve deadlocks. Consideration by a tripartite board following a bipartite hearing is usually *de novo* in the airline industry and based on the record created at the bipartite hearing in the railroad industry.

In recent years, several airlines and their unions have made significant use of grievance mediation for cases that would otherwise be heard by system boards. These parties typically use an experienced arbitrator as a mediator so that if the parties fail initially to reach a mediated resolution, the mediator may offer an oral advisory opinion as a further inducement to settlement. If no agreement is reached, the grievance may proceed to a system board hearing. Parties using grievance mediation report improved labor relations and reduced costs.[36]

36.   Joshua M. Javits, note 31 *supra*.

Chapter III

FEDERAL COMMON LAW

A. CREATION OF THE FEDERAL COMMON LAW[1]

1. INTRODUCTION

Traditionally, courts were hostile to arbitration, viewing it as an institution that would deprive them of their jurisdiction.[2] Until the Second World War, such hostility left labor-management arbitration systems to operate quite independently of the law.

> [O]nce parties decided, voluntarily or under some compulsion, to use arbitration they had great freedom to structure the scope, form and jurisdiction of their arbitration system. Most industries voluntarily decided whether to use arbitration * * *. Moreover, the law generally left them alone once the agreement was made: it seldom enforced and only rarely interfered with such agreements.[3]

The legal system in the early 1940s was a hostile environment for labor arbitration. Under the common law, executory agreements to arbitrate were not judicially enforceable. Unions, as unincorporated associations, were not legal entities that could sue or be sued or be subject to money judgments. Collective bargaining agreements might not

1. Bibliographic Suggestions: Robert A. Gorman and Matthew W. Finkin, Basic Text on Labor Law: Unionization and Collective Bargaining § 23.4 (2004). Benjamin Aaron, *Arbitration in the Federal Courts: Aftermath of the Trilogy*, 9 UCLA Law Review 360 (1962); Alexander M. Bickel and Harry H. Wellington, *Legislative Purpose and the Judicial Process: The* Lincoln Mills *Case*, 71 Harvard Law Review 1 (1957); Archibald Cox, *Reflections Upon Labor Arbitration in Light of the* Lincoln Mills *Case*, 9 Proceedings of the National Academy of Arbitrators 24 (1959); David E. Feller, *How the Trilogy Was Made*, 47 Proceedings of the National Academy of Arbitrators 329 (1994); Stephen L. Hayford, *Unification of*

the Law of Labor Arbitration and Commercial Arbitration: An Idea Whose Time Has Come, 52 Baylor Law Review 781 (2000); Paul R. Hays, *Labor Arbitration: A Dissenting View* (1966); Bernard D. Meltzer, *The Supreme Court, Arbitrability and Collective Bargaining*, 28 University of Chicago Law Review 464 (1961); James E. Pfander, *Judicial Purpose and the Scholarly Process: The* Lincoln Mills *Case*, 69 Washington University Law Quarterly 243 (1991).

2. See, Chapter I.A., *supra*.

3. Dennis R. Nolan and Roger I. Abrams, *American Labor Arbitration: The Early Years*, 35 University of Florida Law Review 373, 420 (1983).

even be treated as contracts. Such issues were raised and responded to disparately in state courts because federal courts were unavailable in the absence of complete diversity of citizenship between the union's members and the employer.

Some within the labor arbitration system were satisfied with this independence and thought that law had no role to play, that law could not enhance and could only interfere with the parties' continuing relationship.[4] Others sought legal sanctions to assure that the enforceability of agreements did not depend wholly on economic power.[5]

In the end, it was not such academic debates, but the course of events that persuaded Congress that the law had a role to play in the enforcement of collective bargaining agreements. The end of World War II released unions from their wartime no-strike pledges, and workers' economic demands that had been constrained by the war fueled the greatest wave of strikes in the nation's history. Congress concluded that providing for the legal enforcement of collective bargaining agreements in the federal courts would promote industrial peace.

Congress thus included in the 1947 Labor Management Relations Act two paragraphs that granted jurisdiction to the federal courts and removed some of the technical, procedural obstacles to litigation over collective bargaining agreements. Section 301, now 29 U.S.C. § 185, provided:

(a) Suits for violation of contracts between an employer and a labor organization representing employees in an industry affecting commerce as defined in this Act, or between any such labor organizations, may be brought in any district court of the United States having jurisdiction of the parties, without regard to the amount in controversy or without regard to the citizenship of the parties.

(b) Any labor organization which represents employees in an industry affecting commerce as defined in this Act and any employer whose activities affect commerce as defined in this Act shall be bound by the acts of its agents. Any such labor organization may sue or be sued as an entity and in behalf of the employees whom it represents in the courts of the United States. Any money judgment against a labor organization in a district court of the United States shall be enforceable only against the organization as an entity and against its assets, and shall not be enforceable against any individual member or his assets.

Despite their seemingly modest objectives, these two paragraphs, interpreted by the United States Supreme Court over the next decade, revolutionized the labor arbitration process. The statute changed labor arbitration from a system independent of law into one entwined in a complex legal web.

4. Harry Shulman, *Reason, Contract, and Law in Labor Relations*, 68 Harvard Law Review 999, 1024 (1955).

5. Archibald Cox, *Grievance Arbitration in the Federal Courts*, 67 Harvard Law Review 591, 605–606 (1954).

This chapter addresses the creation of a federal common law to determine when the law will compel arbitration and when the law will enforce an arbitration award.

2. DECISIONS OF THE SUPREME COURT

TEXTILE WORKERS UNION v. LINCOLN MILLS
Supreme Court of the United States, 1957.
353 U.S. 448, 77 S.Ct. 912, 1 L.Ed.2d 972.

MR. JUSTICE DOUGLAS delivered the opinion of the Court.

Petitioner-union entered into a collective bargaining agreement in 1953 with respondent-employer, the agreement to run one year and from year to year thereafter, unless terminated on specified notices. The agreement provided that there would be no strikes or work stoppages and that grievances would be handled pursuant to a specified procedure. The last step in the grievance procedure—a step that could be taken by either party—was arbitration.

This controversy involves several grievances that concern work loads and work assignments. The grievances were processed through the various steps in the grievance procedure and were finally denied by the employer. The union requested arbitration, and the employer refused. Thereupon the union brought this suit in the District Court to compel arbitration.

The District Court concluded that it had jurisdiction and ordered the employer to comply with the grievance arbitration provisions of the collective bargaining agreement. The Court of Appeals reversed by a divided vote. 230 F.2d 81. It held that, although the District Court had jurisdiction to entertain the suit, the court had no authority founded either in federal or state law to grant the relief. * * *

There has been considerable litigation involving § 301 and courts have construed it differently. There is one view that § 301(a) merely gives federal district courts jurisdiction in controversies that involve labor organizations in industries affecting commerce, without regard to diversity of citizenship or the amount in controversy. Under that view § 301(a) would not be the source of substantive law; it would neither supply federal law to resolve these controversies nor turn the federal judges to state law for answers to the questions. Other courts—the overwhelming number of them—hold that § 301(a) is more than jurisdictional—that it authorizes federal courts to fashion a body of federal law for the enforcement of these collective bargaining agreements and includes within that federal law specific performance of promises to arbitrate grievances under collective bargaining agreements. Perhaps the leading decision representing that point of view is the one rendered by Judge Wyzanski in Textile Workers Union of America (C.I.O) v. American Thread Co., D.C., 113 F.Supp. 137. That is our construction of § 301(a), which means that the agreement to arbitrate grievance disputes, contained in this collective bargaining agreement, should be specifically enforced.

From the face of the Act it is apparent that § 301(a) and § 301(b) supplement one another. Section 301(b) makes it possible for a labor organization, representing employees in an industry affecting commerce, to sue and be sued as an entity in the federal courts. Section 301(b) in other words provides the procedural remedy lacking at common law. Section 301(a) certainly does something more than that. Plainly, it supplies the basis upon which the federal district courts may take jurisdiction and apply the procedural rule of § 301(b). The question is whether § 301(a) is more than jurisdictional.

The legislative history of § 301 is somewhat cloudy and confusing. But there are a few shafts of light that illuminate our problem.

The bills, as they passed the House and the Senate, contained provisions which would have made the failure to abide by an agreement to arbitrate an unfair labor practice. S.Rep. No. 105, 80th Cong., 1st Sess., pp. 20–21, 23; H.R.Rep. No. 245, 80th Cong., 1st Sess., p. 21. This feature of the law was dropped in Conference. As the Conference Report stated, "Once parties have made a collective bargaining contract, the enforcement of that contract should be left to the usual processes of the law and not to the National Labor Relations Board." H.R.Conf.Rep. No. 510, 80th Cong., 1st Sess., p. 42.

Both the Senate and the House took pains to provide for "the usual processes of the law" by provisions which were the substantial equivalent of § 301(a) in its present form. Both the Senate Report and the House Report indicate a primary concern that unions as well as employees should be bound to collective bargaining contracts. But there was also a broader concern—a concern with a procedure for making such agreements enforceable in the courts by either party. At one point the Senate Report, *supra*, p. 15, states, "We feel that the aggrieved party should also have a right of action in the Federal courts. Such a policy is completely in accord with the purpose of the Wagner Act which the Supreme Court declared was 'to compel employers to bargain collectively with their employees to the end that an employment contract, binding on both parties, should be made * * *.' "

Congress was also interested in promoting collective bargaining that ended with agreements not to strike.

The Senate Report, *supra*, p. 16 states:

> If unions can break agreements with relative impunity, then such agreements do not tend to stabilize industrial relations. The execution of an agreement does not by itself promote industrial peace. The chief advantage which an employer can reasonably expect from a collective labor agreement is assurance of uninterrupted operation during the term of the agreement. Without some effective method of assuring freedom from economic warfare for the term of

the agreement, there is little reason why an employer would desire to sign such a contract.

Consequently, to encourage the making of agreements and to promote industrial peace through faithful performance by the parties, collective agreements affecting interstate commerce should be enforceable in the Federal courts. Our amendment would provide for suits by unions as legal entities and against unions as legal entities in the Federal courts in disputes affecting commerce.

Thus collective bargaining contracts were made "equally binding and enforceable on both parties." *Id.*, p. 15. As stated in the House Report, *supra*, p. 6, the new provision "makes labor organizations equally responsible with employers for contract violations and provides for suit by either against the other in the United States district courts." * * *

Plainly the agreement to arbitrate grievance disputes is the *quid pro quo* for an agreement not to strike. Viewed in this light, the legislation does more than confer jurisdiction in the federal courts over labor organizations. It expresses a federal policy that federal courts should enforce these agreements on behalf of or against labor organizations and that industrial peace can be best obtained only in that way. * * *

It seems, therefore, clear to us that Congress adopted a policy which placed sanctions behind agreements to arbitrate grievance disputes, by implication rejecting the common-law rule, discussed in Red Cross Line v. Atlantic Fruit Co., 264 U.S. 109, 44 S.Ct. 274, 68 L.Ed. 582, against enforcement of executory agreements to arbitrate. We would undercut the Act and defeat its policy if we read § 301 narrowly as only conferring jurisdiction over labor organizations.

The question then is, what is the substantive law to be applied in suits under § 301(a)? We conclude that the substantive law to apply in suits under § 301(a) is federal law, which the courts must fashion from the policy of our national labor laws. See Mendelsohn, Enforceability of Arbitration Agreements Under Taft–Hartley Section 301, 66 Yale L.J. 167. The Labor Management Relations Act expressly furnishes some substantive law. It points out what the parties may or may not do in certain situations. Other problems will lie in the penumbra of express statutory mandates. Some will lack express statutory sanction but will be solved by looking at the policy of the legislation and fashioning a remedy that will effectuate that policy. The range of judicial inventiveness will be determined by the nature of the problem. See Board of Commissioners of Jackson County v. United States, 308 U.S. 343, 351, 60 S.Ct. 285, 288, 84 L.Ed. 313. Federal interpretation of the federal law will govern, not state law. Cf. Jerome v. United States, 318 U.S. 101, 104, 63 S.Ct. 483, 485, 87 L.Ed. 640. But state law, if compatible with the purpose of § 301, may be resorted to in order to find the rule that will best effectuate the federal policy. See Board of Commissioners of Jackson County v. United States, *supra*, 308 U.S. at pages 351–352, 60 S.Ct. at pages 288–289. Any state law applied, however, will be absorbed as federal law and will not be an independent source of private rights.

It is not uncommon for federal courts to fashion federal law where federal rights are concerned. See Clearfield Trust Co. v. United States, 318 U.S. 363, 366–367, 63 S.Ct. 573, 574–575, 87 L.Ed. 838; National Metropolitan Bank v. United States, 323 U.S. 454, 65 S.Ct. 354, 89 L.Ed. 383. Congress has indicated by § 301(a) the purpose to follow that course here. There is no constitutional difficulty. Article III, § 2, extends the judicial power to cases "arising under * * * the Laws of the United States * * *." The power of Congress to regulate these labor-management controversies under the Commerce Clause is plain. Houston East & West Texas R. Co. v. United States, 234 U.S. 342, 34 S.Ct. 833, 58 L.Ed. 1341; National Labor Relations Board v. Jones & Laughlin Corp., 301 U.S. 1, 57 S.Ct. 615, 81 L.Ed. 893. A case or controversy arising under § 301(a) is, therefore, one within the purview of judicial power as defined in Article III.

The question remains whether jurisdiction to compel arbitration of grievance disputes is withdrawn by the Norris–LaGuardia Act, 47 Stat. 70, 29 U.S.C. § 101 at seq., 29 U.S.C.A. § 101 et seq. Section 7 of that Act prescribes stiff procedural requirements for issuing an injunction in a labor dispute. The kinds of acts which had given rise to abuse of the power to enjoin are listed in § 4. The failure to arbitrate was not a part and parcel of the abuses against which the Act was aimed. Section 8 of the Norris–LaGuardia Act does, indeed, indicate a congressional policy toward settlement of labor disputes by arbitration, for it denies injunctive relief to any person who has failed to make "every reasonable effort" to settle the dispute by negotiation, mediation, or "voluntary arbitration." Though a literal reading might bring the dispute within the terms of the Act (see Cox, Grievance Arbitration in the Federal Courts, 67 Harv.L.Rev. 591, 602–604), we see no justification in policy for restricting § 301(a) to damage suits, leaving specific performance of a contract to arbitrate grievance disputes to the inapposite procedural requirements of that Act. * * *

The judgment of the Court of Appeals is reversed and the cause is remanded to that court for proceedings in conformity with this opinion.

Reversed.

MR. JUSTICE BLACK took no part in the consideration or decision of this case.

MR. JUSTICE BURTON, whom MR. JUSTICE HARLAN joins, concurring in the result.

This suit was brought in a United States District Court under § 301 of the Labor Management Relations Act of 1947, 61 Stat. 156, 29 U.S.C. § 185, 29 U.S.C.A. § 185, seeking specific enforcement of the arbitration provisions of a collective-bargaining contract. The District Court had jurisdiction over the action since it involved an obligation running to a union—a union controversy—and not uniquely personal rights of employees sought to be enforced by a union. Cf. Association of Westinghouse Salaried Employees v. Westinghouse Elec. Corp., 348 U.S. 437, 75 S.Ct. 489, 99 L.Ed. 510. Having jurisdiction over the suit, the court was not powerless to fashion an appropriate federal remedy. The power to decree specific performance of a collectively bargained agreement to arbitrate finds its source in § 301 itself, and in a Federal District Court's inherent equitable powers, nurtured by a congressional policy to encourage and enforce labor arbitration in industries affecting commerce.

I do not subscribe to the conclusion of the Court that the substantive law to be applied in a suit under § 301 is federal law. At the same time, I agree with Judge Magruder in International Brotherhood v. W.L. Mead, Inc., 1 Cir., 230 F.2d 576, that some federal rights may necessarily be involved in a § 301 case, and hence that the constitutionality of § 301 can be upheld as a congressional grant to Federal District Courts of what has been called "protective jurisdiction."

[Mr. Justice Frankfurter wrote a lengthy dissent. He reviewed the legislative history of § 301 and concluded that the provision was exclusively procedural and not intended to authorize federal courts to create substantive federal law. He stated that Congress did not intend to make arbitration clauses in collective bargaining agreements specifically enforceable. Moreover, he concluded that § 301 was unconstitutional.]

Notes and Questions

1. Review the text of § 301 and its legislative history, discussed in *Lincoln Mills*. Do you agree with Justice Douglas that Congress in § 301 authorized courts to create federal law to govern collective bargaining contracts? What would have been the effect of a contrary decision? Does the Constitution permit Congress to grant the federal courts jurisdiction over cases that are neither governed by federal law nor involve opposing parties from different states?

2. When Congress enacted the Norris–LaGuardia Act in 1932 it was, in part, seeking to limit the ability of the federal courts to define national labor policy. Is there evidence that by 1947 Congress had so changed its view of the federal courts that it intended, in enacting § 301, to authorize the federal courts to define substantive labor law?

3. Why didn't the Norris–LaGuardia Act preclude the federal court from issuing an injunction to compel arbitration in *Lincoln Mills*? If Congress had intended to exempt actions under § 301 from the requirements of the Norris–LaGuardia Act, wouldn't it have said so explicitly, as it did with the National Labor Relations Act? See National Labor Relations Act, § 10(h), 29 U.S.C. § 160(h) (2000).

4. Why did the Court conclude that a damage remedy alone would be insufficient for violations of collective bargaining agreements? *Would* a damage remedy alone be sufficient? Why or why not?

5. The majority opinion in *Lincoln Mills* did not expressly address the possible effect of the Federal Arbitration Act which authorizes federal courts to enforce arbitration agreements, but excludes from its coverage "contracts of employment of ... workers engaged in ... interstate commerce." 9 U.S.C. § 1 (2000). Justice Frankfurter, writing in dissent, thought that the majority's "silent treatment" of the FAA was an implicit holding that the FAA did not afford authority for the federal courts to enforce arbitration provisions in

collective bargaining agreements. 353 U.S. at 466. It was not until more than forty years later that the Supreme Court directly faced the question and held that the only employment contracts exempted by § 1 were those of transportation workers. Circuit City Stores, Inc. v. Adams, 532 U.S. 105, 121 S.Ct. 1302, 149 L.Ed.2d 234 (2001), Chapter X, *infra*. Had the majority in *Lincoln Mills* addressed the FAA issue and interpreted the statute as the Court later did in *Circuit City*, there likely never would have been a common law of labor arbitration. The Court has not, so far, suggested that *Circuit City* requires abandonment of decades of holdings defining the federal common law of labor arbitration. See, Major League Baseball Players Association v. Garvey, 532 U.S. 504, 532 U.S. 1015, 121 S.Ct. 1724, 149 L.Ed.2d 740 (2001), Chapter III.C.2., *infra*, (decided after *Circuit City*, applying traditional common law precedents without reference to the FAA). While the Supreme Court has not relied upon FAA precedents in deciding labor arbitration questions, it sometimes uses labor arbitration precedents interchangeably with FAA precedents in deciding commercial arbitration questions. See, for example, Howsam v. Dean Witter Reynolds, Inc., 537 U.S. 79, 123 S.Ct. 588, 154 L.Ed.2d 491 (2002). See also, Hayford, note 1 *supra* (advocating unification of the law of labor arbitration and the law of commercial arbitration developed under the FAA).

LOCAL 174, TEAMSTERS, CHAUFFEURS, WAREHOUSEMEN HELPERS v. LUCAS FLOUR CO.

Supreme Court of the United States, 1962.
369 U.S. 95, 82 S.Ct. 571, 7 L.Ed.2d 593.

Mr. Justice Stewart delivered the opinion of the Court.

The petitioner and the respondent (which we shall call the union and the employer) were parties to a collective bargaining contract within the purview of the National Labor Relations Act, 29 U.S.C.A. § 151 et seq. The contract contained the following provisions, among others:

Article II

The Employer reserves the right to discharge any man in his employ if his work is not satisfactory. * * *

Article XIV

Should any difference as to the true interpretation of this agreement arise, same shall be submitted to a Board of Arbitration of two members, one representing the firm, and one representing the Union. If said members cannot agree, a third member, who must be a disinterested party shall be selected, and the decision of the said Board of Arbitration shall be binding. It is further agreed by both parties hereto that during such arbitration, there shall be no suspension of work.

Should any difference arise between the employer and the employee, same shall be submitted to arbitration by both parties. Failing to agree, they shall mutually appoint a third person whose decision shall be final and binding.

In May of 1958 an employee named Welsch was discharged by the employer after he had damaged a new fork-lift truck by running it off a loading platform and onto some railroad tracks. When a business agent of the union protested, he was told by a representative of the employer that Welsch had been discharged because of unsatisfactory work. The union thereupon called a strike to force the employer to rehire Welsch. The strike lasted eight days. After the strike was over, the issue of Welsch's discharge was submitted to arbitration. Some five months later the Board of Arbitration rendered a decision, ruling that Welsch's work had been unsatisfactory, that his unsatisfactory work had been the reason for his discharge, and that he was not entitled to reinstatement as an employee.

In the meantime, the employer had brought this suit against the union in the Superior Court of King County, Washington, asking damages for business losses caused by the strike. After a trial that court entered a judgment in favor of the employer in the amount of $6,501.60. On appeal the judgment was affirmed by Department One of the Supreme Court of Washington. 57 Wash.2d 95, 356 P.2d 1. The reviewing court held that the pre-emption doctrine of *San Diego Building Trades Council v. Garmon*, 359 U.S. 236, 79 S.Ct. 773, 3 L.Ed.2d 775, did not deprive it of jurisdiction over the controversy. The court further held that § 301 of the Labor Management Relations Act of 1947, 29 U.S.C. § 185, 29 U.S.C.A. § 185, could not "reasonably be interpreted as pre-empting state jurisdiction, or as affecting it by limiting the substantive law to be applied." 57 Wash.2d, at 102, 356 P.2d, at 5. Expressly applying principles of state law, the court reasoned that the strike was a violation of the collective bargaining contract, because it was an attempt to coerce the employer to forego his contractual right to discharge an employee for unsatisfactory work. * * *

This case is thus properly before us, and we turn to the issues which it presents.

One of those issues—whether § 301(a) of the Labor Management Relations Act of 1947 deprives state courts of jurisdiction over litigation such as this—we have decided this Term in *Charles Dowd Box Co. v. Courtney*, 368 U.S. 502, 82 S.Ct. 519, 7 L.Ed.2d 483. For the reasons stated in our opinion in that case, we hold that the Washington Supreme Court was correct in ruling that it had jurisdiction over this controversy. There remain for consideration two other issues, one of them implicated but not specifically decided in *Dowd Box*. Was the Washington court free, as it thought, to decide this controversy within the limited horizon of its local law? If not, does applicable federal law require a result in this case different from that reached by the state court?

[The Court stated that Congress did not intend to permit state courts to apply state law in the interpretation of collective bargaining agreements. The Court expressed concern that conflicting substantive interpretations in state and federal courts would tend to prolong contract disputes and discourage parties from adopting arbitration provisions. It concluded that Congress required uniform federal law be applied to promote industrial peace.]

Whether, as a matter of federal law, the strike which the union called was a violation of the collective bargaining contract is thus the ultimate issue which this case presents. It is argued that there could be no violation in the absence of a no-strike clause in the contract explicitly covering the subject of the dispute over which the strike was called. We disagree.

The collective bargaining contract expressly imposed upon both parties the duty of submitting the dispute in question to final and binding arbitration. In a consistent course of decisions the Courts of Appeals of at least five Federal Circuits have held that a strike to settle a dispute which a collective bargaining agreement provides shall be settled exclusively and finally by compulsory arbitration constitutes a violation of the agreement. The National Labor Relations Board has reached the same conclusion. *W.L. Mead, Inc.*, 113 N.L.R.B. 1040. We approve that doctrine. To hold otherwise would obviously do violence to accepted principles of traditional contract law. Even more in point, a contrary view would be completely at odds with the basic policy of national labor legislation to promote the arbitral process as a substitute for economic warfare. See *United Steelworkers v. Warrior & Gulf Nav. Co.*, 363 U.S. 574, 80 S.Ct. 1347, 4 L.Ed.2d 1409.

What has been said is not to suggest that a no-strike agreement is to be implied beyond the area which it has been agreed will be exclusively covered by compulsory terminal arbitration. Nor is it to suggest that there may not arise problems in specific cases as to whether compulsory and binding arbitration has been agreed upon, and, if so, as to what disputes have been made arbitrable. But no such problems are present in this case. The grievance over which the union struck was, as it concedes, one which it had expressly agreed to settle by submission to final and binding arbitration proceedings. The strike which it called was a violation of that contractual obligation.

Affirmed.

Mr. Justice Black, dissenting.

* * * [I]t seems to me plain that the parties to this contract, knowing how to write a provision binding a union not to strike, deliberately included a no-strike clause with regard to disputes over broad questions of contractual interpretation and deliberately excluded such a clause with regard to the essentially factual disputes arising out of the application of the contract in particular instances. And there is not a word anywhere else in this agreement which indicates that this perfectly sensible contractual framework for handling these two different kinds of disputes was not intended to operate in the precise manner dictated by the express language of the two arbitration provisions. * * *

In any case, I have been unable to find any accepted principle of contract law—traditional or otherwise—that permits courts to change completely the nature of a contract by adding new promises that the parties themselves refused to make in order that the new court-made contract might better fit into whatever social, economic, or legal policies the courts believe to be so important that they should have been taken out of the realm of voluntary contract by the legislative body and furthered by compulsory legislation. * * *

The issue here involves, not the nature of the arbitration proceeding, but the question of whether the union, by agreeing to arbitrate, has given up all other separate and distinct methods of getting its way. Surely, no one would suggest that a provision for final and binding arbitration would preclude a union from attempting to persuade an employer to forego action the union was against, even where that action was fully within the employer's rights under the contract. The same principle supports the right of the union to strike in such a situation for historically, and as was recognized in both the Wagner and Taft–Hartley Acts, the strike has been the unions' most important weapon of persuasion. * * *

The additional burden placed upon the union by the Court's writing into the agreement here a promise not to strike is certainly not a matter of minor interest to this employer or to the union. The history of industrial relations in this country emphasizes the great importance to unions of the right to strike as well as an understandable desire on the part of employers to avoid such work stoppages. Both parties to collective bargaining discussions have much at stake as to whether there will be a no-strike clause in any resulting agreement. It is difficult to believe that the desire of employers to get such a promise and the desire of the union to avoid giving it are matters which are not constantly in the minds of those who negotiate these contracts. In such a setting, to hold—on the basis of no evidence whatever—that a union, without knowing it, impliedly surrendered the right to strike by virtue of "traditional contract law" or anything else is to me just fiction. It took more than 50 years for unions to have written into federal legislation the principle that they have a right to strike. I cannot understand how anyone familiar with that history can allow that legislatively recognized right to be undercut on the basis of the attenuated implications the Court uses here. * * *

I agree that the Taft–Hartley Act shows a congressional purpose to treat collective bargaining contracts and agreements for arbitration in them as one important way of insuring stability in industrial production and labor relations. But the fact that we may agree, as I do, that these settlements by arbitration are desirable is no excuse whatever for imposing such "contracts," either to compel arbitration or to forbid striking, upon unwilling parties. That approach is certainly contrary to the industrial and labor philosophy of the Taft–Hartley Act. Whatever else may be said about that Act, it seems plain that it was enacted on the view that the best way to bring about industrial peace was through voluntary, not compelled, labor agreements. Section 301 is torn from its roots when it is held to require the sort of compulsory arbitration imposed by this decision. I would reverse this case and relegate this controversy to the forum in which it belongs—the collective bargaining table.

Notes and Questions

1. Review Article XIV of the collective bargaining agreement quoted by the Supreme Court in *Lucas Flour*. Notice that it has two different paragraphs describing the nature of disputes subject to arbitration, only the first of which explicitly says that there shall be no suspension of work during arbitration.

(a) The Court holds that even if the dispute over Welsch's discharge fell within the second paragraph, without an explicit no-strike clause, a strike was precluded as a matter of federal common law. The Court says a contrary conclusion would "do violence to accepted principles of traditional contract law." Wouldn't traditional contract law instead allow the contracting parties to distinguish between types of disputes that include a no-strike obligation and those in which a suspension of work is permissible? How would a contrary conclusion "be completely at odds with the basic policy of national labor legislation"?

(b) Does Justice Stewart assume in *Lucas Flour* that the parties fully intended to bar strikes over non-interpretation disputes, but that their poor drafting of contract language failed to make that clear? If so, is the assumption valid?

2. If *Lucas Flour* is based, not on traditional contract law, but instead on the special federal common law governing collective bargaining agreements, what are its sources? The Court said in *Lincoln Mills* that that federal common law should be found in federal labor statutes and their policies. Doesn't the National Labor Relations Act protect rather than undermine freedom of contract? For example, the Supreme Court said of the NLRA in NLRB v. Insurance Agents' International Union, 361 U.S. 477, 488, 80 S.Ct. 419, 426, 4 L.Ed.2d 454 (1960), "Congress intended that the parties should have wide latitude in their negotiations, unrestricted by any governmental power to regulate the substantive solution of their differences." If *Lucas Flour* is not based on this strand of congressional labor policy, what source of labor policy mandates a contrary conclusion?

3. By establishing as a matter of law that an arbitration provision implies a no-strike obligation, the Supreme Court makes it unnecessary for employers to expend economic power at the bargaining table to obtain an explicit no-strike agreement and requires a union to expend economic power if it wants to retain a right to strike. Is this result consistent with the Supreme Court's prior statements in NLRB v. Insurance Agents' International Union, 361 U.S. 477, 80 S.Ct. 419, 4 L.Ed.2d 454 (1960), that (a) "The presence of economic weapons in reserve, and their actual exercise on occasion by the parties, is part and parcel of the system that the Wagner and Taft–Hartley Acts have recognized." (361 U.S. at 489, 80 S.Ct. at 427); and (b) that national labor policy does not authorize the government "to act at large in equalizing disparities of bargaining power between employer and union"? (361 U.S. at 490, 80 S.Ct. at 428).

4. The Court in *Lucas Flour* concludes that a strike should not be allowed to disrupt the entire workplace when a dispute over the discharge of a single employee could easily be resolved in arbitration. Should the Supreme Court's conclusion in *Lucas Flour*, that the arbitration provision defines the scope of the no-strike obligation, apply regardless of the nature of the dispute? What if the Union, objecting to the employer's reinstatement of foremen who have previously disregarded mine safety rules, has ignored the available grievance procedure and called a strike? See, Gateway Coal Co. v. United Mine Workers, 414 U.S. 368, 94 S.Ct. 629, 38 L.Ed.2d 583 (1974), also discussed in the concluding Note in Chapter III.D., *infra*.

5. The Supreme Court suggested that the NLRB had held in W.L. Mead, Inc., 113 NLRB 1040 (1955), that a provision for final and binding arbitration necessarily implies a no-strike obligation. *Mead*, however, was not based on the Board's view of statutory labor policy, but on the language of the collective bargaining agreement in that case, explicitly stating that arbitration was to be the "exclusive means" of resolving disputes. Did the collective bargaining agreement in *Lucas Flour* make arbitration the "exclusive means" of resolving the dispute over Welsch's discharge?

B. JUDICIAL DETERMINATION OF ARBITRABILITY[1]

1. INTRODUCTION

In *Lincoln Mills* (see Section III.A., *supra*), the courts assumed the responsibility to enforce collective bargaining agreements. Parties could seek judicial assistance in getting a reluctant collective bargaining partner to arbitrate. Courts now had to identify those disputes for which arbitration would be mandated. It was unclear at the outset whether courts would even be willing to decide whether a dispute was arbitrable or whether they might instead refer that issue to the arbitrator. And, if courts were willing to resolve disputes about arbitrability, it was uncertain what standard they would use to determine arbitrability.

Subsection 2 focuses upon two Supreme Court decisions that established the basic standard for assessing arbitrability. These two cases,

---

1. Bibliographic Suggestions: Robert A. Gorman and Matthew W. Finkin, Basic Text on Labor Law: Unionization and Collective Bargaining §§ 23.6–23.9 (2004). Mark M. Grossman, The Question of Arbitrability (1983); Benjamin Aaron, *Arbitration in the Federal Courts: Aftermath of the Trilogy*, 9 UCLA Law Review 360 (1962); Richard A. Bales, *The Arbitrability of Side and Settlement Agreements in the Collective Bargaining Context*, 105 West Virginia Law Review 575 (2003); Edgar A. Jones, Jr., *The Name of the Game Is Decision—Some Reflections on "Arbitrability" and "Authority" in Labor Law*, 46 Texas Law Review 865 (1968); Richard J. Medalie, *The New Appeals Amendment: A Step Forward for Arbitration*, 44 Arbitration Journal 22 (June 1989); Bernard D. Meltzer, *The Supreme Court, Arbitrability and Collective Bargaining*, 28 University of Chicago Law Review 464 (1961); Russell A. Smith and Dallas L. Jones, *The Impact of the Emerging Federal Law of Grievance Arbitration on Judges, Arbitrators, and Parties*, 52 Virginia Law Review 831 (1966); Clyde W. Summers, *The Trilogy and Its Offspring Revisited: It's a Contract Stupid*, 71 Washington University Law Quarterly 1021 (1993); Symposium, *50th Anniversary of the National Labor Relations Act and the 25th Anniversary of the Steelworkers Trilogy*, 7 Industrial Relations Law Journal 287 (1985); Harry H. Wellington, *Judicial Review of the Promise to Arbitrate*, 37 New York University Law Review 471 (1962).

United Steelworkers v. Warrior & Gulf Navigation Co. and United Steelworkers v. American Manufacturing Co., are part of the famous "Steelworkers Trilogy." (The final member of the Trilogy, United Steelworkers v. Enterprise Wheel, Chapter III.C.1., *infra*, articulated the standard for judicial review of arbitration awards.)

Subsection 3 addresses some of the more complex questions of arbitrability. Under what circumstances does an obligation to arbitrate survive the expiration of a collective bargaining agreement? What happens to a duty to arbitrate when the employer experiences a fundamental change of identity, such as by sale or merger? Are some questions of arbitrability to be left for an arbitrator to resolve? If so, under what circumstances?

This Section looks at judicial determinations of arbitrability. The related question of how arbitrators decide issues of arbitrability is addressed in Chapter VII. A., *infra*.

2. ESTABLISHING THE BASIC STANDARDS OF ARBITRABILITY

UNITED STEELWORKERS v. WARRIOR & GULF NAVIGATION CO.

Supreme Court of the United States, 1960.
363 U.S. 574, 80 S.Ct. 1347, 4 L.Ed.2d 1409.

Mr. Justice Douglas delivered the opinion of the Court.

Respondent transports steel and steel products by barge and maintains a terminal at Chickasaw, Alabama, where it performs maintenance and repair work on its barges. The employees at that terminal constitute a bargaining unit covered by a collective bargaining agreement negotiated by petitioner union. Respondent between 1956 and 1958 laid off some employees, reducing the bargaining unit from 42 to 23 men. This reduction was due in part to respondent contracting maintenance work, previously done by its employees, to other companies. The latter used respondent's supervisors to lay out the work and hired some of the laid-off employees of respondent (at reduced wages). Some were in fact assigned to work on respondent's barges. A number of employees signed a grievance which petitioner presented to respondent, the grievance reading:

> We are hereby protesting the Company's actions, of arbitrarily and unreasonably contracting out work to other concerns, that could and previously has been performed by Company employees.

> This practice becomes unreasonable, unjust and discriminatory in lieu [*sic*] of the fact that at present there are a number of employees that have been laid off for about 1 and 1/2 years or more for allegedly lack of work.

> Confronted with these facts we charge that the Company is in violation of the contract by inducing a partial lock-out, of a number

of the employees who would otherwise be working were it not for this unfair practice.

The collective agreement had both a "no strike" and a "no lockout" provision. It also had a grievance procedure which provided in relevant part as follows:

> Issues which conflict with any Federal statute in its application as established by Court procedure or matters which are strictly a function of management shall not be subject to arbitration under this section.

> Should differences arise between the Company and the Union or its members employed by the Company as to the meaning and application of the provisions of this Agreement, or should any local trouble of any kind arise, there shall be no suspension of work on account of such differences but an earnest effort shall be made to settle such differences immediately [through a five-step procedure ending with arbitration.]

Settlement of this grievance was not had and respondent refused arbitration. This suit was then commenced by the union to compel it.

The District Court granted respondent's motion to dismiss the complaint [and the Court of Appeals affirmed.]

We held in *Textile Workers v. Lincoln Mills*, 353 U.S. 448, that a grievance arbitration provision in a collective agreement could be enforced by reason of § 301(a) of the Labor Management Relations Act and that the policy to be applied in enforcing this type of arbitration was that reflected in our national labor laws. *Id.*, 353 U.S. at pages 456–457. The present federal policy is to promote industrial stabilization through the collective bargaining agreement. *Id.*, 353 U.S. at pages 453–454. A major factor in achieving industrial peace is the inclusion of a provision for arbitration of grievances in the collective bargaining agreement.[4]

Thus the run of arbitration cases, illustrated by *Wilko v. Swan*, 346 U.S. 427, becomes irrelevant to our problem. There the choice is between the adjudication of cases or controversies in courts with established procedures or even special statutory safeguards on the one hand and the settlement of them in the more informal arbitration tribunal on the other. In the commercial case, arbitration is the substitute for litigation. Here arbitration is the substitute for industrial strife. Since arbitration of labor disputes has quite different functions from arbitration under an ordinary commercial agreement, the hostility evinced by courts toward arbitration of commercial agreements has no place here. For arbitration of labor disputes under collective bargaining agreements is part and parcel of the collective bargaining process itself.

---

4. Complete effectuation of the federal policy is achieved when the agreement contains both an arbitration provision for all unresolved grievances and an absolute prohibition of strikes, the arbitration agreement being the *"quid pro quo"* for the agreement not to strike. *Textile Workers v. Lincoln Mills*, 353 U.S. 448, 455.

The collective bargaining agreement states the rights and duties of the parties. It is more than a contract; it is a generalized code to govern a myriad of cases which the draftsmen cannot wholly anticipate. See Shulman, Reason, Contract, and Law in Labor Relations, 68 Harv.L.Rev. 999, 1004–1005. The collective agreement covers the whole employment relationship. It calls into being a new common law—the common law of a particular industry or of a particular plant. As one observer has put it:[6]

> * * * [It] is not unqualifiedly true that a collective-bargaining agreement is simply a document by which the union and employees have imposed upon management limited, express restrictions of its otherwise absolute right to manage the enterprise, so that an employee's claim must fail unless he can point to a specific contract provision upon which the claim is founded. There are too many people, too many problems, too many unforeseeable contingencies to make the words of the contract the exclusive source of rights and duties. One cannot reduce all the rules governing a community like an industrial plant to fifteen or even fifty pages. Within the sphere of collective bargaining, the institutional characteristics and the governmental nature of the collective-bargaining process demand a common law of the shop which implements and furnishes the context of the agreement. We must assume that intelligent negotiators acknowledged so plain a need unless they stated a contrary rule in plain words.

A collective bargaining agreement is an effort to erect a system of industrial self-government. When most parties enter into contractual relationship they do so voluntarily, in the sense that there is no real compulsion to deal with one another, as opposed to dealing with other parties. This is not true of the labor agreement. The choice is generally not between entering or refusing to enter into a relationship, for that in all probability pre-exists the negotiations. Rather it is between having that relationship governed by an agreed-upon rule of law or leaving each and every matter subject to a temporary resolution dependent solely upon the relative strength, at any given moment, of the contending forces. The mature labor agreement may attempt to regulate all aspects of the complicated relationship, from the most crucial to the most minute over an extended period of time. Because of the compulsion to reach agreement and the breadth of the matters covered, as well as the need for a fairly concise and readable instrument, the product of negotiations (the written document) is, in the words of the late Dean Shulman, "a compilation of diverse provisions: some provide objective criteria almost automatically applicable; some provide more or less specific standards which require reason and judgment in their application; and some do little more than leave problems to future consideration with an expression of hope and good faith." Shulman, *supra*, at 1005. Gaps may be left to be filled in by reference to the practices of the particular

6. Cox, Reflections Upon Labor Arbitration, 72 Harv.L.Rev. 1482, 1498–1499 (1959).

industry and of the various shops covered by the agreement. Many of the specific practices which underlie the agreement may be unknown, except in hazy form, even to the negotiators. Courts and arbitration in the context of most commercial contracts are resorted to because there has been a breakdown in the working relationship of the parties; such resort is the unwanted exception. But the grievance machinery under a collective bargaining agreement is at the very heart of the system of industrial self-government. Arbitration is the means of solving the unforeseeable by molding a system of private law for all the problems which may arise and to provide for their solution in a way which will generally accord with the variant needs and desires of the parties. The processing of disputes through the grievance machinery is actually a vehicle by which meaning and content are given to the collective bargaining agreement.

Apart from matters that the parties specifically exclude, all of the questions on which the parties disagree must therefore come within the scope of the grievance and arbitration provisions of the collective agreement. The grievance procedure is, in other words, a part of the continuous collective bargaining process. It, rather than a strike, is the terminal point of a disagreement.

The labor arbitrator performs functions which are not normal to the courts; the considerations which help him fashion judgments may indeed be foreign to the competence of courts.

> A proper conception of the arbitrator's function is basic. He is not a public tribunal imposed upon the parties by superior authority which the parties are obliged to accept. He has no general charter to administer justice for a community which transcends the parties. He is rather part of a system of self-government created by and confined to the parties. * * * Shulman, *supra*, at 1016.

The labor arbitrator's source of law is not confined to the express provisions of the contract, as the industrial common law—the practices of the industry and the shop—is equally a part of the collective bargaining agreement although not expressed in it. The labor arbitrator is usually chosen because of the parties' confidence in his knowledge of the common law of the shop and their trust in his personal judgment to bring to bear considerations which are not expressed in the contract as criteria for judgment. The parties expect that his judgment of a particular grievance will reflect not only what the contract says but, insofar as the collective bargaining agreement permits, such factors as the effect upon productivity of a particular result, its consequence to the morale of the shop, his judgment whether tensions will be heightened or diminished. For the parties' objective in using the arbitration process is primarily to further their common goal of uninterrupted production under the agreement, to make the agreement serve their specialized needs. The ablest judge cannot be expected to bring the same experience and competence to bear upon the determination of a grievance, because he cannot be similarly informed.

The Congress, however, has by § 301 of the Labor Management Relations Act, assigned the courts the duty of determining whether the reluctant party has breached his promise to arbitrate. For arbitration is a matter of contract and a party cannot be required to submit to arbitration any dispute which he has not agreed so to submit. Yet, to be consistent with congressional policy in favor of settlement of disputes by the parties through the machinery of arbitration, the judicial inquiry under § 301 must be strictly confined to the question whether the reluctant party did agree to arbitrate the grievance or did agree to give the arbitrator power to make the award he made. An order to arbitrate the particular grievance should not be denied unless it may be said with positive assurance that the arbitration clause is not susceptible of an interpretation that covers the asserted dispute. Doubts should be resolved in favor of coverage.[7]

We do not agree with the lower courts that contracting-out grievances were necessarily excepted from the grievance procedure of this agreement. To be sure, the agreement provides that "matters which are strictly a function of management shall not be subject to arbitration." But it goes on to say that if "differences" arise or if "any local trouble of any kind" arises, the grievance procedure shall be applicable.

Collective bargaining agreements regulate or restrict the exercise of management functions; they do not oust management from the performance of them. Management hires and fires, pays and promotes, supervises and plans. All these are part of its function, and absent a collective bargaining agreement, it may be exercised freely except as limited by public law and by the willingness of employees to work under the particular, unilaterally imposed conditions. A collective bargaining agreement may treat only with certain specific practices, leaving the rest to management but subject to the possibility of work stoppages. When, however, an absolute no-strike clause is included in the agreement, then in a very real sense everything that management does is subject to the agreement, for either management is prohibited or limited in the action it takes, or if not, it is protected from interference by strikes. This comprehensive reach of the collective bargaining agreement does not mean, however, that the language, "strictly a function of management," has no meaning.

"Strictly a function of management" might be thought to refer to any practice of management in which, under particular circumstances prescribed by the agreement, it is permitted to indulge. But if courts, in order to determine arbitrability, were allowed to determine what is permitted and what is not, the arbitration clause would be swallowed up

---

7. It is clear that under both the agreement in this case and that involved in *American Manufacturing Co.*, *ante*, p. 564, the question of arbitrability is for the courts to decide. Cf. Cox, Reflections Upon Labor Arbitration, 72 Harv.L.Rev. 1482, 1508–1509. Where the assertion by the claimant is that the parties excluded from court determination not merely the decision of the merits of the grievance but also the question of its arbitrability, vesting power to make both decisions in the arbitrator, the claimant must bear the burden of a clear demonstration of that purpose.

by the exception. Every grievance in a sense involves a claim that management has violated some provision of the agreement.

Accordingly, "strictly a function of management" must be interpreted as referring only to that over which the contract gives management complete control and unfettered discretion. Respondent claims that the contracting out of work falls within this category. Contracting out work is the basis of many grievances; and that type of claim is grist in the mills of the arbitrators. A specific collective bargaining agreement may exclude contracting out from the grievance procedure. Or a written collateral agreement may make clear that contracting out was not a matter for arbitration. In such a case a grievance based solely on contracting out would not be arbitrable. Here, however, there is no such provision. Nor is there any showing that the parties designed the phrase "strictly a function of management" to encompass any and all forms of contracting out. In the absence of any express provision excluding a particular grievance from arbitration, we think only the most forceful evidence of a purpose to exclude the claim from arbitration can prevail, particularly where, as here, the exclusion clause is vague and the arbitration clause quite broad. Since any attempt by a court to infer such a purpose necessarily comprehends the merits, the court should view with suspicion an attempt to persuade it to become entangled in the construction of the substantive provisions of a labor agreement, even through the back door of interpreting the arbitration clause, when the alternative is to utilize the services of an arbitrator.

The grievance alleged that the contracting out was a violation of the collective bargaining agreement. There was, therefore, a dispute "as to the meaning and application of the provisions of this Agreement" which the parties had agreed would be determined by arbitration.

The judiciary sits in these cases to bring into operation an arbitral process which substitutes a regime of peaceful settlement for the older regime of industrial conflict. Whether contracting out in the present case violated the agreement is the question. It is a question for the arbiter, not for the courts.

Reversed.

MR. JUSTICE BLACK took no part in the consideration or decision of this case.

[The concurring opinion of JUSTICE BRENNAN, joined by JUSTICES FRANKFURTER and HARLAN, and the dissenting opinion of JUSTICE WHITTAKER have been omitted.]

UNITED STEELWORKERS v. AMERICAN MANUFACTURING CO.
Supreme Court of the United States, 1960.
363 U.S. 564, 80 S.Ct. 1343, 4 L.Ed.2d 1403.

MR. JUSTICE DOUGLAS delivered the opinion of the Court.

[The Union brought an action in the federal district court to compel arbitration of a grievance involving an employee who was denied employment two weeks after a determination that he was permanently partially disabled as the result of a workplace injury. The district court held that the employee was estopped to claim any employment rights by his acceptance of the worker's compensation settlement. The court of appeals affirmed on different grounds, holding that the grievance was "a frivolous, patently baseless one, not subject to arbitration under the collective bargaining agreement." *United Steelworkers v. American Manufacturing Co.*, 264 F.2d 624, 628 (6th Cir. 1959).]

Section 203(d) of the Labor Management Relations Act, 1947, 61 Stat. 154, 29 U.S.C. § 173(d), 29 U.S.C.A. § 173(d), states, "Final adjustment by a method agreed upon by the parties is hereby declared to be the desirable method for settlement of grievance disputes arising over the application or interpretation of an existing collective-bargaining agreement. * * * "That policy can be effectuated only if the means chosen by the parties for settlement of their differences under a collective bargaining agreement is given full play.

A state decision that held to the contrary announced a principle that could only have a crippling effect on grievance arbitration. The case was *International Assn. of Machinists v. Cutler–Hammer, Inc.*, 271 App.Div. 917, 67 N.Y.S.2d 317, aff'd 297 N.Y. 519, 74 N.E.2d 464. It held that "If the meaning of the provision of the contract sought to be arbitrated is beyond dispute, there cannot be anything to arbitrate and the contract cannot be said to provide for arbitration." 271 App. Div., at 918, 67 N.Y.S.2d, at page 318. The lower courts in the instant case had a like preoccupation with ordinary contract law. The collective agreement requires arbitration of claims that courts might be unwilling to entertain. In the context of the plant or industry the grievance may assume proportions of which judges are ignorant. Yet, the agreement is to submit all grievances to arbitration, not merely those that a court may deem to be meritorious. There is no exception in the "no strike" clause and none therefore should be read into the grievance clause, since one is the *quid pro quo* for the other. The question is not whether in the mind of the court there is equity in the claim. Arbitration is a stabilizing influence only as it serves as a vehicle for handling any and all disputes that arise under the agreement.

The collective agreement calls for the submission of grievances in the categories which it describes, irrespective of whether a court may deem them to be meritorious. In our role of developing a meaningful body of law to govern the interpretation and enforcement of collective bargaining agreements, we think special heed should be given to the context in which collective bargaining agreements are negotiated and the purpose which they are intended to serve. See *Lewis v. Benedict Coal Corp.*, 361 U.S. 459. The function of the court is very limited when the parties have agreed to submit all questions of contract interpretation to the arbitrator. It is confined to ascertaining whether the party seeking arbitration is making a claim which on its face is governed by the contract. Whether the moving party is right or wrong is a question of contract interpretation for the arbitrator. In these circumstances the moving party should not be deprived of the arbitrator's judgment, when it was his judgment and all that it connotes that was bargained for.

The courts, therefore, have no business weighing the merits of the grievance, considering whether there is equity in a particular claim, or determining whether there is particular language in the written instrument which will support the claim. The agreement is to submit all grievances to arbitration, not merely those which the court will deem meritorious. The processing of even frivolous claims may have therapeutic values of which those who are not a part of the plant environment may be quite unaware.[6]

The union claimed in this case that the company had violated a specific provision of the contract. The company took the position that it had not violated that clause. There was, therefore, a dispute between the parties as to "the meaning, interpretation and application" of the collective bargaining agreement. Arbitration should have been ordered. When the judiciary undertakes to determine the merits of a grievance under the guise of interpreting the grievance procedure of collective bargaining agreements, it usurps a function which under that regime is entrusted to the arbitration tribunal.

Reversed.

[JUSTICES FRANKFURTER and WHITTAKER concurred in the result. JUSTICE BLACK did not participate.]

Notes and Questions

1.   In *Wilko v. Swan*, 346 U.S. 427, 74 S.Ct. 182, 98 L.Ed. 168 (1953), a case involving a claim brought under the Securities Act of 1933, the Supreme Court refused to enforce an arbitration agreement because, the Court said, arbitration was an inadequate forum for resolving such claims. The *Warrior & Gulf* Court distinguishes *Wilko*. On what basis? Are you persuaded?

2.   The Supreme Court says in *Warrior & Gulf*, "A collective bargaining agreement is an effort to erect a system of industrial self-government." What does the Court mean? What, according to the Court, are the components of this self-government? What is the "law," and how is it created? What is the role of the federal and state governments? What is the role of the arbitrator?

---

6. Cox, Current Problems in the Law of Grievance Arbitration, 30 Rocky Mt.L.Rev. 247, 261 (1958), writes:

The typical arbitration clause is written in words which cover, without limitation, all disputes concerning the interpretation or application of a collective bargaining agreement. Its words do not restrict its scope to meritorious disputes or two-sided disputes, still less are they limited to disputes which a judge will consider two-sided. Frivolous cases are often taken, and are expected to be taken, to arbitration. What one man considers frivolous another may find meritorious, and it is common knowledge in industrial relations circles that grievance arbitration often serves as a safety valve for troublesome complaints. Under these circumstances it seems proper to read the typical arbitration clause as a promise to arbitrate every claim, meritorious or frivolous, which the complainant bases upon the contract. The objection that equity will not order a party to do a useless act is outweighed by the cathartic value of arbitrating even a frivolous grievance and by the dangers of excessive judicial intervention.

Are there any drawbacks to this paradigm for how labor relations should be ordered?

3. Assume that, following the Court's decision in *Warrior & Gulf*, the grievance concerning the contracting out comes before an arbitrator. Would it be appropriate for the arbitrator to consider whether the grievance is arbitrable?

(a) The Supreme Court has not decided the extent of the arbitrator's authority to determine arbitrability following a judicial finding of arbitrability. Nolde Brothers, Inc. v. Local No. 358, Bakery & Confectionery Workers Union, 430 U.S. 243, 255, n. 8, 97 S.Ct. 1067, 1074, n. 8, 51 L.Ed.2d 300 (1977). When Justice Douglas says in footnote 7 of *Warrior*, *supra*, that "the question of arbitrability is for the courts to decide," does he mean to preclude an arbitrator's subsequent consideration of the issue? Some arbitrators, notably the arbitrator in *Warrior* itself, have claimed the authority to determine arbitrability after a court order to arbitrate. Warrior & Gulf Navigation Co., 36 LA 695 (J. Fred Holly, 1961). See also Zoological Society of San Diego, 50 LA 1 (Edgar A. Jones, 1967) and Sun Life Insurance Co., 87 LA 598 (James M. Harkless, 1986).

(b) Under *Warrior & Gulf*, courts are not to decide whether the parties actually made a particular dispute arbitrable, but only if the dispute is arguably arbitrable. If, following a court's determination of arbitrability, an arbitrator is precluded from assessing the parties' actual intent then at no point in the process does anyone actually pay attention to the parties' contractual agreement. Does that make any sense?

4. In AT & T Technologies, Inc. v. Communications Workers of America, 475 U.S. 643, 106 S.Ct. 1415, 89 L.Ed.2d 648 (1986), the Supreme Court reaffirmed the statement in footnote 7 of *Warrior & Gulf* that a court presented with an issue of arbitrability may not simply refer the issue for decision by the arbitrator. In *AT & T*, the Court of Appeals had attempted to create an exception to *Warrior & Gulf* that would allow a court to avoid determining arbitrability where there was a standard arbitration provision, no clear exclusion of the issue, and where deciding arbitrability would entangle the court in interpretation of the substantive provisions of the agreement. The Supreme Court held that even in such cases the issue of arbitrability is to be decided by the court and not the arbitrator.

More recently, the Supreme Court explained that the principal rationale of *Warrior & Gulf*'s presumption of arbitrability is that "arbitrators are in a better position than courts to interpret the terms of a [collective bargaining agreement]." Wright v. Universal Maritime Service Corp., 525 U.S. 70, 78, 119 S.Ct. 391, 395, 142 L.Ed.2d 361 (1998). If this is true, why should courts rather than arbitrators decide questions of substantive arbitrability?

5. The Union submits a grievance alleging that the Citizens Manufacturing Company has violated the collective bargaining agreement by laying off 100 employees. The employees were laid off as a result of the Company's decision to have assembly work that had previously been done by these employees accomplished at another location not covered by the agreement. The Union alleges that the layoff violates the contract's recognition clause, Article I, which provides:

The Company recognizes the Union as the exclusive representative for purposes of collective bargaining with respect to hours of work, rates of pay, and other conditions of employment covered by this Agreement.

Article II of the contract provides:

Grievances may be submitted to arbitration involving the interpretation or application of a provision of this agreement. The arbitrator shall have no authority to rule upon management prerogatives.

Article III provides:

Included within the meaning of "management prerogatives," the Company has the right to subcontract and designate the work to be performed by the Company and the places where it is to be performed, which right shall not be subject to arbitration.

The Union requested arbitration, but the Company refused. Should a court order the Citizens Manufacturing Company to arbitrate the Union's grievance regarding the layoff of employees? See Boeing Co. v. UAW, Local 1069, 234 F.Supp. 404 (E.D.Pa.1964) (not arbitrable); Rochester Independent Workers, Local No. 1 v. General Dynamics Electronics Div., 54 Misc.2d 470, 282 N.Y.S.2d 804 (1967) (not arbitrable).

6. Following a strike, Gallo Winery and the Winery Workers Union signed a collective bargaining agreement that included the following three provisions:

Article A: Grievances, which are defined as disputes about the interpretation or application of this Agreement, may be taken to arbitration.

Article B: The Employer shall not discharge any employee without just cause.

Article C: There shall be no amnesty for strikers who engage in acts of violence or destruction of property. This matter is extracontractual (employees may assert their rights only under the National Labor Relations Act).

Gallo discharged nine employees on the ground that they had engaged in violent strike misconduct. The Union denied that the employees had engaged in violence. Gallo refused to arbitrate grievances regarding the discharges and the Winery Workers Union brought an action in federal district court seeking to compel arbitration.

(a) What should the union argue in support of its action? How should the company respond? Should the court compel arbitration?

(b) In deciding arbitrability, may a court receive evidence of bargaining history or must the court consider only the explicit language of the collective bargaining agreement? Are there reasons of policy to exclude evidence of bargaining history? What answer, if any, does the Court in *Warrior & Gulf* give to this question?

(c) Assume that Gallo seeks to introduce evidence that during the negotiations leading up to the adoption of Article B, the parties agreed that there would be just cause to discharge employees who engaged in any kind of strike misconduct regardless of whether it was violent. Should the court consider such evidence?

(d) Assume that Gallo seeks to introduce evidence that, during the negotiations leading up to adoption of Article C, the parties understood "violence" to encompass any kind of strike misconduct. Should the court consider such evidence?

Compare, Winery, Distillery & Allied Workers Union, Local 186 v. E & J Gallo Winery, Inc., 857 F.2d 1353 (9th Cir.1988), with Local No. 725, International Union of Operating Engineers v. Standard Oil Co. of Indiana, 186 F.Supp. 895 (D.N.D.1960). See also International Ass'n of Machinists & Aerospace Workers, Lodge No. 1777 v. Fansteel, Inc., 900 F.2d 1005 (7th Cir.), cert. denied, 498 U.S. 851, 111 S.Ct. 143, 112 L.Ed.2d 109 (1990); International Brotherhood of Electrical Workers, Local No. 4 v. KTVI–TV, Inc., 985 F.2d 415 (8th Cir. 1993); and Browning Ferris Industries v. Union De Tronquistas, Local 901, 29 F.3d 1 (1st Cir. 1994).

7.   The collective bargaining agreement between WXYZ–TV and the Electrical Workers Union provides that "all complaints, disputes or questions as to the interpretation, application or performance of this agreement which are not adjusted between the Employer and the Union" may be brought to arbitration. For many years, WXYZ–TV has provided a technician's lounge that employees have used while taking breaks and having meals. Some discussions between union members regarding collective bargaining and grievance handling have also taken place in the lounge. WXYZ–TV, without prior discussion with the Union, eliminated the technician's lounge. The Union sought arbitration of a grievance alleging that the elimination of the lounge violated the collective bargaining agreement. The Union, without pointing to any language in the agreement, claimed that the change violated "past practice." (See Section VII. D., *infra*.)

(a) Should a court order WXYZ–TV to arbitrate the grievance?

(b) Should a court order WXYZ–TV to arbitrate the grievance if the arbitration agreement defines arbitrable grievances as those involving a dispute about "the interpretation, application or performance of the *terms* of this agreement"?

(c) Should a court order WXYZ–TV to arbitrate the grievance if the arbitration agreement defines arbitrable grievances as those involving a dispute about "the interpretation, application, or performance of the *explicit written terms* of this agreement"? Would your answer be different if the Union also claimed that, in addition to past practice, loss of the lounge violated the recognition clause of the contract by interfering with the union's ability to bargain collectively and process grievances?

Compare International Brotherhood of Electrical Workers, Local 1228 v. WNEV–TV, 778 F.2d 46 (1st Cir.1985), cert. denied, 476 U.S. 1182, 106 S.Ct. 2916, 91 L.Ed.2d 545 (1986) (employer must arbitrate grievance concerning elimination of lounge), with Bridgestone/Firestone, Inc. v. Local Union No. 998, United Rubber Workers, 4 F.3d 918 (10th Cir.1993) (employer need not arbitrate grievance concerning elimination of employee suggestion plan).

8.   Professional hockey players in the East Coast Hockey League are represented by a union that has a collective bargaining agreement with the League. Section 5 of that Agreement states: "The President of the League may impose a penalty upon any player of a team, if the player has been

guilty of conduct prejudicial or detrimental to the League, as the President determines in his sole discretion." Section 10 of the Agreement, defining the scope of matters subject to arbitration, includes "any dispute, controversy, claim or disagreements . . . arising out of or relating to any term or condition of a player's employment." The President of the League imposed a lifetime suspension from the League on Brandon, a hockey player, for throwing a hockey stick at a patron. The President asserted that, under Section 5, the Union's grievance challenging Brandon's suspension was not arbitrable. Should a court order the League to arbitrate the grievance? If a court orders the League to arbitrate Brandon's grievance, can you draft language that the President might propose for the next Agreement that would preclude arbitration of such disciplinary actions in the future? East Coast Hockey League, Inc. v. Professional Hockey Players Ass'n, 322 F.3d 311 (4th Cir. 2003). See also Local 5–857 PACE v. Conoco, Inc., 320 F.3d 1123 (10th Cir. 2003) and Local 75, Teamsters v. Schreiber Foods, Inc., 213 F.3d 376 (7th Cir. 2000).

9.   The collective bargaining agreement between the Union and the Company permits the arbitration of grievances claiming that an employee was discharged without just cause. In February, employees Alexander and Baker were discharged after testing positive for illegal drug use. In March, the Union, the employees and the Company entered into an agreement, labeled a "Last Chance Agreement," under which the Employer agreed to reinstate Alexander and Baker under certain conditions. The agreement provided that they were to be subject to random drug testing and that if they used illegal drugs they would be discharged. The agreement further provided:

> Upon a positive test result, these employees will be afforded an opportunity to plead their cases before the Disciplinary Committee. The disposition of the Disciplinary Committee shall be final. Neither the employees nor the Union shall have recourse through the grievance and arbitration procedure to protest the disposition of the Disciplinary Committee.

In July, urine tests of both Alexander and Baker indicated the presence of illegal drugs; both were discharged. Alexander appeared before the Disciplinary Committee and maintained that the drug test was a false positive resulting from her vegetarian diet. Baker told the Committee that he had not used illegal drugs himself but had been at a party at which others were smoking marijuana. The Disciplinary Committee affirmed the discharges of Alexander and Baker. The Union filed grievances alleging that the discharges of Alexander and Baker violated the collective bargaining agreement, but the Company refused to arbitrate on the ground that the "Last Chance Agreement" relieved it of any duty to arbitrate these grievances. The Union brings an action in federal district court seeking an order compelling arbitration. How should a court rule? See the majority and dissenting opinions in United Steelworkers v. Lukens Steel Co., 969 F.2d 1468 (3d Cir.1992). See also Pace International Union v. Vacumet Paper Metalizing Corp., 91 Fed.Appx. 380, (6th Cir. 2004).

10.   The Supreme Court holds in *American Manufacturing* that federal common law requires arbitration even of grievances that a judge considers "frivolous." Why? Would an employer or a union ever want to pursue a frivolous grievance? Why? What are the "therapeutic values of which those

who are not a part of the plant environment may be quite unaware'"? See also Roger I. Abrams, Frances E. Abrams and Dennis R. Nolan, *Arbitral Therapy,* 46 Proceedings of the National Academy of Arbitrators 269 (1994).

3. SUCCESSORSHIP, PROCEDURAL ARBITRABILITY, AND POST–EXPIRATION ARBITRABILITY

John Wiley & Sons: The Successor's Duty to Arbitrate and Procedural Arbitrability

Successorship

The next arbitrability case before the Supreme Court posed two new issues. John Wiley & Sons, Inc. v. Livingston, 376 U.S. 543, 84 S.Ct. 909, 11 L.Ed.2d 898 (1964), articulated the federal common law governing arbitrability after a corporate merger and carved out matters of procedure from the scope of arbitrability questions appropriate for judicial resolution.

The Union represented 40 of 80 employees of Interscience, a publishing firm. During the term of the collective bargaining agreement, Interscience merged with John Wiley, a larger company with 300 employees, none of whom were represented by a union. The Union claimed that Wiley was obligated to recognize certain rights under the contract between Interscience and the Union, including seniority, severance and vacation pay, and to make pension fund payments. Wiley contended that the merger terminated the collective bargaining agreement for all purposes and it refused to recognize the Union as a bargaining agent. One week before the expiration of the Interscience bargaining agreement, the Union commenced an action in federal district court to compel arbitration of its grievance seeking to have Wiley abide by provisions of the Interscience agreement that the Union claimed had "vested."

The Supreme Court held that the issue of whether Wiley was obligated to arbitrate was a question for judicial determination. The Court compared the case to cases such as *Warrior & Gulf* where the issue was whether an employer, concededly bound by a contract, had agreed to arbitrate disputes of a particular kind. The Court stated, "just as an employer has no obligation to arbitrate issues which it has not agreed to arbitrate, so *a fortiori*, it cannot be compelled to arbitrate if an arbitration clause does not bind it at all." Looking to federal common law, the Court held

> that the disappearance by merger of a corporate employer which has entered into a collective bargaining agreement with a union does not automatically terminate all rights of the employees covered by the agreement, and that, in appropriate circumstances * * * the successor employer may be required to arbitrate with the union under the agreement.

The circumstances in *Wiley* warranting a duty to arbitrate included a "substantial continuity of identity in the business enterprise before and after a change," the Union's continuing assertion of its right to arbitrate, and a provision of state corporation law that precluded a merger from extinguishing corporate obligations.

The duty to arbitrate was consistent with federal labor policy, the Court said, because it would afford employees some protection from drastic changes in their employment without unduly interfering with the prerogative of owners to reorganize their businesses. While the Court acknowledged that ordinary contract law would not bind a nonconsenting successor to a contract it did not sign, it asserted that the labor policy derived from the National Labor Relations Act favoring arbitration overcame such traditional concepts.

It held that the duty to arbitrate was not affected by the fact of the merger or the expiration of the contract. The parties might well have agreed to the "accrual of rights during the term of an agreement and their realization after the agreement had expired."

The Court, however, made clear the limited scope of its holding:

> We do not hold that in every case in which the ownership or corporate structure of an enterprise is changed the duty to arbitrate survives. [T]here may be cases in which the lack of any substantial continuity of identity in the business enterprise before and after a change would make a duty to arbitrate something imposed from without, not reasonably to be found in the particular bargaining agreement and the acts of the parties involved. So too, we do not rule out the possibility that a union might abandon its right to arbitration by failing to make its claims known. Neither of these situations is before the Court. Although Wiley was substantially larger than Interscience, relevant similarity and continuity of operation across the change in ownership is adequately evidenced by the wholesale transfer of Interscience employees to the Wiley plant, apparently without difficulty. The Union made its position known well before the merger and never departed from it.

Procedural Arbitrability

Finally, Wiley contended that it had no obligation to arbitrate because the Union had failed to comply with two preconditions to arbitration. Under the contract, a duty to arbitrate only arose if grievances were filed within four weeks and if two preliminary steps in the grievance procedure, requiring conferences between the parties, had been completed. The Union argued that it would have been futile to pursue the preliminary steps of the grievance procedure because of Wiley's refusal to recognize the Union. Wiley argued that these issues of "procedural arbitrability" should also be decided by a court. The Supreme Court disagreed:

> Once it is decided * * * that the parties are obligated to submit the subject matter of a dispute to arbitration, "procedural" questions which grow out of the dispute and bear on its final disposition should be left to the arbitrator.

The Court reasoned that procedural questions often must be assessed in the context of the substantive issue raised so that requiring courts to decide procedural questions would involve them in assessing the merits and cause a duplication of effort. The Court also expressed concern that having courts decide procedural issues would impede the inexpensive and expeditious resolution of labor disputes.[2]

Subsequent Successorship Cases

Subsequent Supreme Court decisions have made clear the narrow scope of the Court's holding in *Wiley* with respect to the duties of a successor employer. In NLRB v. Burns International Security Services, Inc., 406 U.S. 272, 92 S.Ct. 1571, 32 L.Ed.2d 61 (1972), a case arising under § 8(a)(5) of the National Labor Relations Act, the Court held that a successor employer is not bound by operation of law to the predecessor's labor contract. Statutory bargaining duties arise, however, when a majority of the successor's workforce is comprised of the predecessor's employees, when the bargaining unit remains an appropriate one, and when there is substantial continuity in the enterprise. In rare situations, the bargaining duty may arise so early as to preclude the successor from making unilateral changes in the predecessor's employment terms. This could occur, for example, if the successor employer committed itself to hire all of its predecessor's employees without indicating that there would be new terms of employment. *Burns* was reaffirmed in Fall River Dyeing & Finishing Corp. v. NLRB, 482 U.S. 27, 107 S.Ct. 2225, 96 L.Ed.2d 22 (1987).

In Howard Johnson Co. v. Detroit Local Joint Executive Board, Hotel & Restaurant Employees, 417 U.S. 249, 94 S.Ct. 2236, 41 L.Ed.2d 46 (1974), a § 301 action, the Court held that the successor was not bound to arbitrate the extent of its obligations under the predecessor's labor contract. The successor purchased a motel and restaurant, leased the realty, and continued the operation with 45 employees, only nine of whom came from the predecessor's workforce of 53 employees. The Court noted that the case involved purchase of assets and rental of property, rather than merger, and that the predecessor continued to exist. The Court stressed that there was no continuity of identity in the business enterprise because the successor hired a new workforce with only a small minority coming from the predecessor. The key, said the Court, is whether the successor employer hires a majority of the predecessor's employees.[3]

2. The Supreme Court has recently applied to commercial arbitration cases *John Wiley*'s directive to leave procedural arbitrability questions to arbitrators. Howsam v. Dean Witter Reynolds, Inc., 537 U.S. 79, 123 S.Ct. 588, 154 L.Ed.2d 491 (2002).

3. See Robert A. Gorman and Matthew W. Finkin, Basic Text on Labor Law: Unionization and Collective Bargaining §§ 24.1–24.7 (2004). Marion Crain–Mountney, *The Unenforceable Successorship*

Clause: A Departure from National Labor Policy, 30 UCLA Law Review 1249 (1983); Jules I. Crystal, *Successor and Assigns Clauses: Do They Actually Require That a Purchaser Adopt the Seller's Contract?*, 33 Labor Law Journal 581 (1982); Sarah E. Siskind, *Employer Instability and Union Decline: Problems in the Law of Successorship*, 39 New York University Annual National Conference on Labor 8–1 (1986); Comment, *Bargaining Obligations After*

Post-Expiration Arbitrability[4]

The Supreme Court later also had occasion to expand upon its discussion in *Wiley* of the extent to which obligations to arbitrate continue to exist after expiration of the contract. Although the Supreme Court's decision in Nolde Brothers, Inc. v. Local No. 358, Bakery & Confectionery Workers Union, 430 U.S. 243, 97 S.Ct. 1067, 51 L.Ed.2d 300 (1977), addressed the issue of post-contract arbitrability, the ambiguity of its answer continued to create interpretive problems for more than a decade for the lower federal courts and the National Labor Relations Board.

In *Nolde*, the collective bargaining agreement made "any grievance" between the parties subject to arbitration. The contract contained a provision for severance pay on termination of employment, determined by an employee's wage and length of service. The contract terminated on August 27, 1973. On August 31, Nolde informed the Union of its decision to close the bakery permanently and operations ceased that day. Nolde refused to provide severance pay or to arbitrate the Union's severance pay grievance, contending that its contractual obligation to arbitrate terminated with the collective bargaining agreement.

The Supreme Court characterized the dispute as turning on interpretation of the severance pay provision of the contract. Did the parties intend, as Nolde argued, that any claim to severance pay must be made during the contract term? Or did the parties agree that rights accrued during the contract could be realized after its expiration, as the Union argued? The Court said that the dispute "although arising *after* the expiration of the collective-bargaining contract, clearly arises *under* that contract."

The Court acknowledged the validity of Nolde's argument that a "party cannot be compelled to arbitrate any matter in the absence of a contractual obligation to do so," but concluded that the argument did not require automatically extinguishing the duty to arbitrate upon contract termination. The Court noted that the duty to arbitrate surely extends beyond termination to allow post-termination entry of award in a case arbitrated during the life of the contract or to allow, as in *Wiley*, the completion of the arbitration process commenced during the contract term. The Court thought it irrelevant that the grievance in *Nolde*, unlike *Wiley*, was submitted after the contract's termination. The Court thought there was no reason to believe that the parties' desire to resolve their disputes promptly, inexpensively, and by an expert tribunal ended with the termination of the contract. The Court applied the presumption of arbitrability it had announced in *Warrior & Gulf* and held the dispute arbitrable because the parties had failed to exclude from arbitrability contract disputes arising after termination. The Court concluded,

Corporate Transformation, 54 New York University Law Review 624 (1979).

4. See Robert A. Gorman and Matthew W. Finkin, Basic Text on Labor Law: Unionization and Collective Bargaining § 23.9 (2004).

"where the dispute is over a provision of the expired agreement, the presumptions favoring arbitrability must be negated expressly or by clear implication."

In the wake of *Nolde*, some courts and the NLRB required that a right be vested or an event occur before expiration to be arbitrable after expiration, some courts applied the presumption of arbitrability regardless of whether the event occurred after expiration or whether the right could be considered to have vested, and other courts restricted *Nolde* to a limited time after expiration.

In Litton Financial Printing Division v. NLRB, 501 U.S. 190, 111 S.Ct. 2215, 115 L.Ed.2d 177 (1991), the Supreme Court, by a 5–4 vote, resolved the dispute by adopting the narrow interpretation of *Nolde*. In *Litton*, following expiration of an agreement that contained a provision that layoffs would follow seniority if aptitude and ability were equal, the employer laid off without regard to seniority. The NLRB held that it would not insist that employers fully abide by arbitration provisions following expiration, as it might if it followed the doctrine of NLRB v. Katz, 369 U.S. 736, 82 S.Ct. 1107, 8 L.Ed.2d 230 (1962), that an employer may not unilaterally change terms and conditions of employment. The Board stated that any duty to arbitrate should be imposed as a matter of contract and not of law. The Board held that, under *Nolde*, these layoff grievances did not "arise under" the expired contract and there was therefore no duty to arbitrate and thus no unfair labor practice. The Ninth Circuit reversed, rejecting the Board's requirement of accrual or vesting and instead relying upon the broad presumption of arbitrability. The Supreme Court, however, reversed and adopted the NLRB's interpretation of *Nolde*. The Court majority, in an opinion by Justice Kennedy, stated:

> A postexpiration grievance can be said to arise under the contract only where it involves facts and occurrences that arose before expiration, where an action taken after expiration infringes a right that accrued or vested under the agreement, or where, under normal principles of contract interpretation, the disputed contractual right survives expiration of the remainder of the agreement.

Applying this test to the layoff grievance, the Supreme Court held that the rights in question here were not vested or accrued because they involved an assessment of "aptitude and ability" which might well have changed after expiration of the agreement.

Four members of the Court dissented. Justice Stevens, joined by Justices Blackmun and Scalia, objected to the majority's holding that determination of whether the particular grievance "arose under" the expired contract was an issue for the court, rather than for the arbitrator. He said that the question of whether a particular right has accrued is a question of contract interpretation which should be referred to the arbitrator. Justice Marshall, also joined by Justices Blackmun and Scalia, agreed with Justice Stevens, but wrote separately to contend that the majority decision was unfaithful to *Nolde*'s broad presumption of arbitrability and inconsistent with sound labor policy. Justice Marshall expressed concern about the delay, high cost, and loss of expertise that would result from requiring a judicial interpretation of collective bargaining contract provisions.

The Third Circuit has suggested an additional basis for post-expiration arbitrability derived from the common law of contracts. In Luden's, Inc. v. Local Union No. 6 of the Bakery, Confectionery & Tobacco Workers' International Union, 28 F.3d 347 (3d Cir.1994), the court held that if, following expiration, the parties continue to act in accordance with the terms of the expired agreement, a presumption arises that the parties have entered into an implied-in-fact contract comprised of the terms of the expired agreement, including its arbitration provisions. Other courts have rejected implied-in-fact contract analysis on the basis that application of the theory is inappropriate in the labor context in which the National Labor Relations Act requires the employer to maintain terms and conditions of employment following contract expiration. Teamsters Local Union 1199 v. Pepsi–Cola General Bottlers, Inc., 958 F.2d 1331 (6th Cir.1992); Teamsters Local Union No. 122 v. August Busch & Co., 932 F.Supp. 374 (D.Mass.1996).

Notes and Questions on Successorship

1. Following the Supreme Court's decision in *Wiley*, the case reached the arbitrator. The arbitrator held that joint negotiations between Wiley and the Union effectively waived the pre-arbitral procedural requirements of the contract. The arbitrator stated that the same continuity of the identity of the business enterprise that required arbitration also required persistence of the contract until that identity changed. When, following the merger, Interscience employees were moved to the Wiley facility, the viability of the separate enterprise ended and the provisions of the contract ceased being enforceable. The arbitrator held that seniority guarantees ended upon expiration and that other clauses ended once Interscience employees were commingled with Wiley employees. The arbitrator ordered Wiley to pay vacation benefits accrued to former Interscience employees up to the date of their move to the Wiley facility. Interscience Encyclopedia, Inc., 55 LA 210 (Benjamin C. Roberts, 1970).

2. Articulate the present state of the law on the following issues:

    (a) A successor's duty to bargain.

    (b) A successor's duty to abide by a pre-existing contract.

    (c) A successor's duty to arbitrate.

Are there circumstances under which there would be a duty to arbitrate and no duty to bargain? When and why? Are there circumstances under which there would be a duty to bargain and no duty to arbitrate? When and Why? Are there any reasons why a successor's duty to arbitrate should be any broader than its duty to abide by other provisions of a pre-existing contract?

3. Employer A has 100 employees who are represented by a Union. Employer B buys Employer A's business assets and hires, as its entire workforce, 48 employees who had worked for Employer A. The Union seeks

to arbitrate with Employer B rights that it claims accrued under the collective bargaining agreement with Employer A.

(a) Would the decisions of the Supreme Court compel Employer B to arbitrate? As a matter of policy, should there be a duty to arbitrate in such a case? Would your answer be different if Employer A and Employer B had merged?

(b) What if the Union at Employer A's facility had won representational rights by a vote of 51 to 49 and the 48 former-A employees hired by Employer B join B's existing workforce of 47 employees? Should the question be whether the former-A employees each personally favored union representation, or whether they had the legal status of employees represented by a union by virtue of a union contract or the statutory doctrine of exclusive representation? Justice Rehnquist, dissenting in part in *Burns*, unlike the majority, thought the personal views of individual employees ought to be the only foundation for representation. 406 U.S. at 297, 92 S.Ct. at 1587.

(c) What if Employer B simply added the 48 former employees of Employer A to its existing workforce of 49 employees?

4. Should Wiley still have an obligation to arbitrate the grievances arising under the Interscience agreement if the employees at Wiley are already represented by another union? See, Arizona Portland Cement Co., 302 NLRB 36 (1991).

Notes and Questions on Procedural Arbitrability

1. The Supreme Court in *Wiley* held that questions of substantive arbitrability are for the courts to decide and questions of procedural arbitrability are for the arbitrator. The Supreme Court's explanation for the distinction, however, seems unpersuasive. Judicial determination of substantive arbitrability will even more likely involve consideration of the merits, and such consideration also causes delay and duplication of effort. The Court, nevertheless, is surely correct in suggesting that courts should decide such questions as whether a successor is bound to arbitrate or whether a specific provision in the agreement precludes arbitration of the grievance, and an arbitrator should decide such questions as whether a grievance was timely filed or whether pre-arbitral grievance steps have been followed. Can you provide a better test for the substance/procedure distinction than the Supreme Court offered in *Wiley*? What factors are relevant in deciding whether an arbitrability issue is appropriate for resolution by a court or by an arbitrator?

2. Although one would expect that forty years after *Wiley* employers would no longer be contesting the line between substantive and procedural arbitrability, appellate litigation over that issue continues. See, for example, Shaw's Supermarkets, Inc. v. UFCW, Local 791, AFL–CIO, 321 F.3d 251 (1st Cir. 2003) (whether grievances arising under multiple contracts between union and employer may be consolidated is an issue of procedural arbitrability for the arbitrator to decide); and International Ass'n of Bridge, Structural, Ornamental & Reinforcing Ironworkers, Shopman's Local 493 v. EFCO Corp., 359 F.3d 954 (8th Cir. 2004) (whether union's oral demand for arbitration was sufficient and timely was a question of procedural arbitrability).

3.   There are consequences for incorrectly labeling an issue as substantive rather than procedural. A court may order an attorney to pay its opponent's attorneys fees as a sanction for resisting arbitration on a matter the court considers to be procedural. Local 285, Service Employees International Union v. Nonotuck Resource Associates, Inc., 64 F.3d 735 (1st Cir. 1995); Washington Hospital Center v. Service Employees International Union Local 722, 746 F.2d 1503 (D.C.Cir.1984); IBEW Local Union No. 2022 v. Teletype Corp., 551 F.Supp. 676 (E.D.Ark. 1982).

4.   Kroger Grocery had a collective bargaining agreement with the Truckers Union covering its warehouse facilities in the Columbus area and a separate collective bargaining agreement with the Food Workers Union covering its meat processing facilities in the Columbus area. Each contract had its own provisions for grievance arbitration, covering such matters as arbitrator selection and procedures. As Kroger's meat processing activities at the North Columbus plant became more limited, employees represented by the Food Workers Union started doing warehousing work in the unused refrigerator space at North Columbus. The Truckers Union filed a grievance with Kroger, arguing that the assignment of warehouse work to the Food Workers at the North Columbus plant violated Kroger's collective bargaining agreement with the Truckers. When Kroger and the Truckers were unable to reach an agreement, the Truckers Union sought arbitration. Kroger said it would not arbitrate if the Food Workers Union would not participate in the arbitration and the Food Workers declined. The Trucker's Union has now brought an action in district court seeking to compel Kroger to arbitrate.

(a) Is the issue of whether Kroger should arbitrate this grievance a question for the court or the arbitrator?

(b) If it is a question for the arbitrator, does the arbitrator appointed under the Kroger–Truckers Union contract have the authority to order the Food Workers Union to participate in the arbitration? See, Stardust Hotel, 50 LA 1186 (Edgar A. Jones, Jr., 1968). See also Merton Bernstein, *Nudging and Shoving All Parties to a Jurisdictional Dispute into Arbitration: The Dubious Procedure of* National Steel, 78 Harvard Law Review 784 (1965), and Edgar A. Jones, Jr., *On Nudging and Shoving the* National Steel *Arbitration into a Dubious Procedure*, 79 Harvard Law Review 327 (1965).

(c) If it is a question for the court, what should the court decide? Can the court order Kroger to arbitrate in the absence of the Food Workers? See Carey v. Westinghouse Elec. Corp., 375 U.S. 261, 84 S.Ct. 401, 11 L.Ed.2d 320 (1964). Can the court order the Food Workers to participate in the arbitration even though it is not a party to the Truckers Union–Kroger contract? United Industrial Workers v. Kroger Co., 900 F.2d 944 (6th Cir.1990). Cf. Retail, Wholesale & Dept. Store Union, Local 390 v. Kroger Co., 927 F.2d 275 (6th Cir.1991). See also Emery Air Freight Corp. v. Teamsters Local 295, 23 F.Supp.2d 313 (S.D.N.Y.1998) (surveying the variety of judicial responses to the tripartite arbitration problem), aff'd, 185 F.3d 85 (2d Cir.1999); Miron Construction Co. v. International Union of Operating Engineers, Local 139, 44 F.3d 558 (7th Cir.), cert. denied, 514 U.S. 1096, 115 S.Ct. 1824, 131 L.Ed.2d 746 (1995); and Local 1351 Intern. Longshoremens Ass'n v. Sea–Land Service, Inc., Carriers' Container Council, 214 F.3d

566 (5th Cir. 2000) (inappropriate to order tripartite arbitration after another court had confirmed award from bipartite arbitration), cert. denied, 531 U.S. 1076, 121 S.Ct. 771, 148 L.Ed.2d 670 (2001).

Notes and Questions on Post–Expiration Arbitrability

1. The collective bargaining agreement between the Textile Manufacturing Company and the United Textile Workers (UTW) that expired on December 31 provided that there would be compulsory and binding arbitration over "all complaints, disputes, controversies and grievances of any kind." It further provided, "There shall be no strike, slowdown or work stoppage during the life of this agreement and any employee who violates this clause shall be subject to discipline up to and including discharge." Two days after expiration of the contract, on January 2, the employer discharged twelve employees. The UTW believed that the employees had been discharged because of their aggressive position in the ongoing collective bargaining negotiations. The UTW, on January 3, called a strike, in which 50 employees participated, to protest the discharge of the twelve employees. After the strike continued for a week, all of the strikers made unconditional offers to return to work. The employer responded that all of the strikers were fired for having violated their contractual no-strike obligations. The twelve employees who were fired on January 2 filed an unfair labor practice charge with the NLRB, but the NLRB dismissed the charge. The UTW filed with the NLRB a charge, alleging that the discharge of the 50 strikers violated §§ 8(a)(1) and 8(a)(3) of the National Labor Relations Act. What are the issues raised by this fact situation? How should the Board decide the case?

2. Did the majority or the dissenters have the better of the argument in *Litton*? Should the courts or the arbitrator decide questions of post-expiration arbitrability?

C. JUDICIAL REVIEW OF LABOR ARBITRATION AWARDS[1]

Supreme Court decisions on arbitrability, reviewed in Section B of this Chapter, established a strong presumption of arbitrability. That presumption exists to encourage the expeditious and inexpensive resolu-

---

1. Bibliographic Suggestions: Elkouri & Elkouri, How Arbitration Works, 64–78 (Alan Miles Ruben, ed., 6th ed. 2003); Fairweather's Practice and Procedure in Labor Arbitration 541 (Ray J. Schoonhoven, ed., 4th Ed. 1999); Robert A. Gorman and Matthew W. Finkin, Basic Text on Labor Law: Unionization and Collective Bargaining §§ 25–1–25.11 (2004). Benjamin Aaron, *Judicial Intervention in Labor Arbitration*, 20 Stanford Law Review 41 (1967); Charles J. Coleman and Gerald C. Coleman, *Toward a New Paradigm of Labor Arbitration in the Federal Courts*, 13 Hofstra Labor Law Journal 1 (1995); William B. Gould IV, *Judicial Review of Labor Arbitration Awards: Thirty* *Years of the* Steelworkers Trilogy: *The Aftermath of* AT & T *and* Misco, 64 Notre Dame Law Review 464 (1989); Edgar A. Jones, Jr., *His Own Brand of Industrial Justice: The Stalking Horse of Judicial Review of Labor Arbitration*, 30 UCLA Law Review 881 (1983); Lewis B. Kaden, *Judges and Arbitrators: Observations on the Scope of Judicial Review*, 80 Columbia Law Review 267 (1980); Clyde W. Summers, *Judicial Review of Labor Arbitration*, 2 Buffalo Law Review 1 (1952); Theodore J. St. Antoine, *Judicial Review of Labor Arbitration Awards: A Second Look at* Enterprise Wheel *and its Progeny*, 75 Michigan Law Review 1137 (1977).

tion of disputes by arbitrators who understand the workplace environment and are skilled at interpreting collective bargaining agreements. Achievement of these objectives also requires judicial reluctance to overturn arbitration awards. The Supreme Court has defined circumstances in which a court may vacate or refuse to enforce an award because it exceeds the arbitrator's authority, is procedurally flawed, or contrary to public policy. The Court has repeatedly emphasized the narrowness of these grounds for nonenforcement. Some lower federal courts, however, have found it extremely difficult to exercise the degree of restraint the Supreme Court's decisions seem to command.

1. ARTICULATING THE BASIC STANDARD FOR JUDICIAL REVIEW[2]

UNITED STEELWORKERS v. ENTERPRISE WHEEL & CAR CORP.

Supreme Court of the United States, 1960.
363 U.S. 593, 80 S.Ct. 1358, 4 L.Ed.2d 1424.

Opinion of the Court by MR. JUSTICE DOUGLAS.

Petitioner union and respondent during the period relevant here had a collective bargaining agreement which provided that any differences "as to the meaning and application" of the agreement should be submitted to arbitration and that the arbitrator's decision "shall be final and binding on the parties." Special provisions were included concerning the suspension and discharge of employees. The agreement stated:

> Should it be determined by the Company or by an arbitrator in accordance with the grievance procedure that the employee has been suspended unjustly or discharged in violation of the provisions of this Agreement, the Company shall reinstate the employee and pay full compensation at the employee's regular rate of pay for the time lost.

The agreement also provided:

> * * * It is understood and agreed that neither party will institute *civil suits or legal proceedings* against the other for alleged violation of any of the provisions of this labor contract; instead all disputes will be settled in the manner outlined in this Article III—Adjustment of Grievances.

2. Bibliographic Suggestions: Joseph H. Bornong, *Judicial Review By Sense of Smell: Practical Application of the* Steelworkers *Essence Test in Labor Arbitration Appeals*, 65 University of Detroit Law Review 643 (1988); David E. Feller, *Taft and Hartley Vindicated: The Curious History of Review of Labor Arbitration Awards*, 19 Berkeley Journal of Employment and Labor Law 296 (1998); Peter Feuille and Michael Le Roy, *Grievance Arbitration Appeals in the Federal Courts: Facts and Figures*, 45 Arbitration Journal 35 (March 1990); Walter Fogel, *Court Review of Discharge Arbitration Awards*, 37 Arbitration Journal 22 (June 1982); Timothy J. Heinsz, *Judicial Review of Labor Arbitration Awards: The* Enterprise Wheel *Goes Around and Around*, 52 Missouri Law Review 243 (1987).

A group of employees left their jobs in protest against the discharge of one employee. A union official advised them at once to return to work. An official of respondent at their request gave them permission and then rescinded it. The next day they were told they did not have a job any more "until this thing was settled one way or the other."

A grievance was filed; and when respondent finally refused to arbitrate, this suit was brought for specific enforcement of the arbitration provisions of the agreement. The District Court ordered arbitration. The arbitrator found that the discharge of the men was not justified, though their conduct, he said, was improper. In his view the facts warranted at most a suspension of the men for 10 days each. After their discharge and before the arbitration award the collective bargaining agreement had expired. The union, however, continued to represent the workers at the plant. The arbitrator rejected the contention that expiration of the agreement barred reinstatement of the employees. He held that the provision of the agreement above quoted imposed an unconditional obligation on the employer. He awarded reinstatement with back pay, minus pay for a 10-day suspension and such sums as these employees received from other employment.

Respondent refused to comply with the award. Petitioner moved the District Court for enforcement. The District Court directed respondent to comply. 168 F.Supp. 308. The Court of Appeals, while agreeing that the District Court had jurisdiction to enforce an arbitration award under a collective bargaining agreement, held that the failure of the award to specify the amounts to be deducted from the back pay rendered the award unenforceable. That defect, it agreed, could be remedied by requiring the parties to complete the arbitration. It went on to hold, however, that an award for back pay subsequent to the date of termination of the collective bargaining agreement could not be enforced. It also held that the requirement for reinstatement of the discharged employees was likewise unenforceable because the collective bargaining agreement had expired. 269 F.2d 327. We granted certiorari. 361 U.S. 929.

The refusal of courts to review the merits of an arbitration award is the proper approach to arbitration under collective bargaining agreements. The federal policy of settling labor disputes by arbitration would be undermined if courts had the final say on the merits of the awards. As we stated in United Steelworkers of America v. Warrior & Gulf Navigation Co., *ante*, p. 574, decided this day, the arbitrators under these collective agreements are indispensable agencies in a continuous collective bargaining process. They sit to settle disputes at the plant level— disputes that require for their solution knowledge of the custom and practices of a particular factory or of a particular industry as reflected in particular agreements.

When an arbitrator is commissioned to interpret and apply the collective bargaining agreement, he is to bring his informed judgment to bear in order to reach a fair solution of a problem. This is especially true when it comes to formulating remedies. There the need is for flexibility in meeting a wide variety of situations. The draftsmen may never have thought of what specific remedy should be awarded to meet a particular contingency. Nevertheless, an arbitrator is confined to interpretation and application of the collective bargaining agreement; he does not sit to dispense his own brand of industrial justice. He may of course look for guidance from many sources, yet his award is legitimate only so long as it draws its essence from the collective bargaining agreement. When the arbitrator's words manifest an infidelity to this obligation, courts have no choice but to refuse enforcement of the award.

The opinion of the arbitrator in this case, as it bears upon the award of back pay beyond the date of the agreement's expiration and reinstatement, is ambiguous. It may be read as based solely upon the arbitrator's view of the requirements of enacted legislation, which would mean that he exceeded the scope of the submission. Or it may be read as embodying a construction of the agreement itself, perhaps with the arbitrator looking to "the law" for help in determining the sense of the agreement. A mere ambiguity in the opinion accompanying an award, which permits the inference that the arbitrator may have exceeded his authority, is not a reason for refusing to enforce the award. Arbitrators have no obligation to the court to give their reasons for an award. To require opinions free of ambiguity may lead arbitrators to play it safe by writing no supporting opinions. This would be undesirable for a well-reasoned opinion tends to engender confidence in the integrity of the process and aids in clarifying the underlying agreement. Moreover, we see no reason to assume that this arbitrator has abused the trust the parties confided in him and has not stayed within the areas marked out for his consideration. It is not apparent that he went beyond the submission. The Court of Appeals' opinion refusing to enforce the reinstatement and partial back pay portions of the award was not based upon any finding that the arbitrator did not premise his award on his construction of the contract. It merely disagreed with the arbitrator's construction of it.

The collective bargaining agreement could have provided that if any of the employees were wrongfully discharged, the remedy would be reinstatement and back pay up to the date they were returned to work. Respondent's major argument seems to be that by applying correct principles of law to the interpretation of the collective bargaining agreement it can be determined that the agreement did not so provide, and that therefore the arbitrator's decision was not based upon the contract. The acceptance of this view would require courts, even under the standard arbitration clause, to review the merits of every construction of the contract. This plenary review by a court of the merits would make meaningless the provisions that the arbitrator's decision is final, for in reality it would almost never be final.

* * * [T]he question of interpretation of the collective bargaining agreement is a question for the arbitrator. It is the arbitrator's construction which was bargained for; and so far as the arbitrator's decision concerns construction of the contract, the courts have no business

overruling him because their interpretation of the contract is different from his.

We agree with the Court of Appeals that the judgment of the District Court should be modified so that the amounts due the employees may be definitely determined by arbitration. In all other respects we think the judgment of the District Court should be affirmed. Accordingly, we reverse the judgment of the Court of Appeals, except for that modification, and remand the case to the District Court for proceedings in conformity with this opinion.

It is so ordered.

[JUSTICE BLACK did not participate. JUSTICE BRENNAN filed a concurring opinion, in which JUSTICES FRANKFURTER and HARLAN joined. JUSTICE WHITTAKER dissented, contending that the arbitrator had no authority to order reinstatement or back pay for the period after expiration of the contract.]

Notes and Questions

1. How does the *Enterprise Wheel* standard for judicial review of arbitration awards differ from the standard appellate courts use in reviewing decisions of the NLRB and of lower courts? What accounts for the difference?

2. *Warrior & Gulf*, Chapter III.B.2, *supra*, sends grievances to arbitration if they are arguably arbitrable. *Enterprise Wheel* precludes courts from reviewing the merits of an arbitration award, once granted, so long as it "draws its essence from the collective bargaining agreement."

(a) Does the combination of the holdings of these two cases give too much power to arbitrators? Why or why not?

(b) If you believe the Court has given arbitrators too much power, do you think employers and unions would agree? If so, why, in the wake of *Warrior & Gulf* and *Enterprise Wheel*, do they continue to include arbitration agreements in 99% of their contracts?

(c) If employers and unions want to vest such powers in arbitrators, should the courts prevent them from doing so? Does anyone have a stake in the issue besides unions and employers? Professor Theodore J. St. Antoine suggests that the parties have jointly selected the arbitrator as their "contract reader" to fill in any gaps in their written text. He says that the arbitrator cannot "misinterpret" the parties' contract because the arbitrator's award *"is their contract."* Theodore J. St. Antoine, *supra* footnote 1 at 1140. St. Antoine therefore concludes that courts should only review awards for procedural error or harm to third parties. *Id.* at 1160–1161. See the Supreme Court's reliance on Professor St. Antoine's formulation in Part II of its opinion in *Eastern Associated Coal Corp.*, *infra* this Chapter.

3. Sheila Dixon asked her supervisor for a one-hour leave in the middle of the work day. When the supervisor asked why she needed the time, Sheila replied that she needed to take her truck to her daughter who had a doctor's appointment. When co-workers told the supervisor that Sheila had actually gone to pay an electric bill to avoid a utility shut-off, the employer fired

Sheila for "obtaining a leave of absence under false pretenses." The collective bargaining agreement under which Sheila is employed includes no "just cause" language, but it does provide:

   (1) An employee will be discharged immediately without prior warning for the following or similar reasons:....

      (c) Stealing, immoral conduct, or any act on the Company premises intended to destroy property or inflict bodily injury.

   (2) An employee will be subject to progressive discipline for the following or similar reasons:

      (a) Absenteeism.

      (b) Tardiness.

      (c) Inefficiency or poor work performance.

      (d) Abuse of rest periods and lunch periods.

      (e) Neglecting duty or failing to maintain work standards.

In cases where progressive discipline was applicable the employer was to impose discipline in the following order: verbal warning, written warning, three-day suspension, discharge.

The arbitrator held that the nature of the conduct reasonably called for progressive discipline rather than discharge, and the arbitrator overturned the discharge and ordered the employer to reinstate Sheila with a ten-day suspension.

The employer brought an action to vacate the arbitrator's award. How should the court rule? Would your answer be different if Paragraph (1) had listed "dishonesty" among the offenses for which immediate discharge was warranted? See, Bruce Hardwood Floors v. UBC, Southern Council of Industrial Workers, Local Union No. 2713, 103 F.3d 449 (5th Cir.) (2–1 decision vacating the award), cert. denied, 522 U.S. 928, 118 S.Ct. 329, 139 L.Ed.2d 255 (1997). What should be the result if, in addition to Paragraphs (1) and (2) above, the collective bargaining agreement also included the following provision, "The employer may discipline or discharge an employee only for just cause."? See, Coca–Cola Bottling Co. of New York, Inc. v. Local Union 1035, Teamsters, 973 F.Supp. 270 (D.Conn.1997) (distinguishing *Bruce Hardwood* on the ground that the contract there apparently did not include a "just cause" provision), aff'd, 175 F.3d 1007 (2d Cir.1999) (Table). See also, Arch of Illinois v. District 12, United Mine Workers of America, 85 F.3d 1289 (7th Cir.1996) (upholding arbitrator's award reducing discipline for sleeping on the job from discharge to one-month suspension where contract included "just cause" provision and listed "sleeping on the job" as an offense for which immediate discipline or discharge could be imposed).

   4. The collective bargaining agreement between the Union and the Employer was scheduled to expire on December 1. Section 15 of the contract stated:

     This agreement shall continue in full force from year to year thereafter, unless either party desiring to amend or terminate this Agreement shall serve upon the other party written notice at least sixty days prior to the date it desires to amend or terminate the agreement.

On September 15, the Employer sent the Union written notice of its intent to terminate the contract and it declined thereafter to negotiate with the Union about terms of a new contract. The Union filed a grievance alleging that the contract had "rolled over" and been extended for another year as a result of the Company's failure to offer to negotiate with the Union after giving notice of termination.

The arbitrator issued an award finding that the contract had rolled over and been extended for another year because the Company's failure to negotiate violated § 8(d) of the National Labor Relations Act, 29 U.S.C. § 158(d) (2000). That provision makes it an unfair labor practice for any party to a collective bargaining agreement to terminate a contract without offering to negotiate a new contract.

Should a court enforce the arbitrator's award? Why or why not? If not, could the arbitrator have written a different award reaching the same result that a court would have been obligated to enforce? Roadmaster Corp. v. Production and Maintenance Employees' Local 504, 851 F.2d 886 (7th Cir.1988). Compare Butler Mfg. Co. v. United Steelworkers of America, 336 F.3d 629 (7th Cir. 2003) (enforcing arbitration award relying on the Family and Medical Leave Act when the contract stated, "Butler Manufacturing Company offers equal opportunity for employment * * * in accordance with the provisions of law.")

5. For over twenty years the Company has paid its maintenance employees for their one-half-hour lunch breaks because they have been expected to work during lunch as the need arose. This assured employees one-half hour of overtime on most days because they had an additional eight hours of scheduled work. Recently, the Company announced that maintenance employees would not have to work during their half-hour lunch breaks and were free to leave the plant during that time. Employees stopped earning one half-hour of overtime every day. The Union submitted a grievance and challenged the new policy before the arbitrator as a violation of contractually-binding past practice. The Employer defended its actions, arguing that the practice was not binding and that its action was consistent with the contract's management rights provision.

The arbitrator ruled in favor of the Union, but didn't rely on the Union's past practice argument. Rather, the award rested on language in the Agreement that had not been addressed by either side. The contract had said that employees were entitled to overtime "for all time worked in excess of forty hours in any one week," and "for all time in excess of eight hours in any one day." The arbitrator said that because the word "worked" appeared in the former but not in the latter clause, the parties must have intended that the employees would receive overtime for any day they were required to be at the employer's premises in excess of eight hours, regardless of the time they were required to work on that day.

A court vacated the arbitrator's award. The court held that when an arbitrator construes an ambiguous provision of an agreement without seeking the parties' guidance as to its intent and evidence of their relevant past practices, the arbitrator's award does not draw its essence from the collective bargaining agreement. Was the court correct? Review the articulation of the "essence" standard in *Enterprise Wheel* and its restatement in Part II. A. of the Court's *Misco* decision in Chapter III.C.2., *infra*. International Wood-workers of America v. Weyerhaeuser Company, 7 F.3d 133 (8th Cir.1993), cert. denied, 511 U.S. 1128, 114 S.Ct. 2135, 128 L.Ed.2d 865 (1994).

6. An empirical study of federal court litigation between 1960 and 2001 to enforce or vacate arbitration awards found that both district courts and circuit courts of appeals enforced awards at a relatively consistent rate of approximately 70%. Authors of the study suggest that such a confirmation rate is consistent with the standards of *Enterprise Wheel*, reflecting "judicial deference without abandonment of reviewing responsibilities." Michael H. LeRoy and Peter Feuille, *Private Justice in the Shadow of Public Courts: The Autonomy of Workplace Arbitration Systems*, 17 Ohio State Journal on Dispute Resolution 19, 49, 59 (2001). They assert: "[M]ost critics of the judicial review of labor arbitration awards fail to give federal courts due credit for their continuing adherence to the *Trilogy*." *Id*. at 84. The study, however, "empirically validates the claim that some courts fail to adhere to the deferential standards of the *Trilogy*." *Id*. at 85. The study pinpointed abnormally low rates of confirmation of arbitration awards in federal courts wholly or partially in the South. Federal courts in such Southern circuits confirmed 56% of awards while those in the other circuits enforced 85% of awards. *Id*. at 85–86.

7. Judge Heaney of the Eighth Circuit has suggested that some courts are striking down arbitration awards simply because they disagree with the outcome and then disingenuously claiming that the awards fail to draw their essence from the contract. Trailways Lines, Inc. v. Trailways, Inc. Joint Council, 817 F.2d 1333 (8th Cir.1987) (Heaney, J., dissenting from order denying petition for rehearing en banc).

(a) If Judge Heaney is right, why would judges be so unwilling to follow the Supreme Court's directives?

(b) If some lower court judges are, in fact, refusing to follow *Enterprise Wheel*, does that suggest that the standard goes too far in insulating arbitration awards from judicial review?

(c) If the *Enterprise Wheel* "essence" test does not ensure that the lower courts exercise sufficient restraint, can you articulate a better formulation that would?

8. Although *Warrior & Gulf* and *Enterprise Wheel* try to discourage litigation of arbitrable disputes, a party determined to litigate both the arbitrability of a dispute and the validity of an award can make the process a costly one. As Judge Easterbrook of the Seventh Circuit has observed:

> Arbitration will not work if legal contests are its bookends: a suit to compel or prevent arbitration, the arbitration itself, and a suit to enforce or set aside the award. Arbitration then becomes more costly than litigation, for if the parties had elected to litigate their disputes they would have had to visit court only once.

Production and Maintenance Employees' Local 504 v. Roadmaster Corp., 916 F.2d 1161, 1163 (7th Cir.1990). Judge Easterbrook recommends that courts discourage such litigation by ordering parties to pay their opponent's legal fees if they "feebly" resist arbitration or an award.

Judge Easterbrook's Seventh Circuit has regularly imposed sanctions on parties that unsuccessfully seek vacation of an arbitration award. Jasper Cabinet Co. v. Steelworkers, 77 F.3d 1025 (7th Cir.1996) (in light of the broad deference afforded labor arbitrators, employer's claim that the arbitrator ignored the plain meaning of the contract language was without merit, justifying award of attorney's fees and costs to the union); Teamsters Local No. 579 v. B & M Transit, Inc., 882 F.2d 274 (7th Cir.1989) (company assessed $7,025 for union's attorney's fees); Hill v. Norfolk and Western Railway Co., 814 F.2d 1192 (7th Cir.1987) (attorney's fees for pursuit of frivolous appeal assessed personally against plaintiff's attorney). Will fear of sanctions be an equal disincentive to unions and management? Is judicial readiness to impose sanctions in arbitration litigation consistent with federal labor policy? See, Mark Berger, *Judicial Review of Labor Arbitration Awards: Practices, Policies and Sanctions*, 10 Hofstra Labor Law Journal 245, 282–295 (1992).

2. REFINING THE STANDARD FOR JUDICIAL REVIEW[3]

The Supreme Court's decision in *Enterprise Wheel* articulated the fundamental standard for judicial review of labor arbitration awards, but left many questions unanswered. One fundamental question was whether an award that might be consistent with the parties' agreement should nevertheless be vacated by a court if it violated public policy. The Court announced in *W.R. Grace & Co. v. Local Union 759, Rubber Workers*, 461 U.S. 757, 103 S.Ct. 2177, 76 L.Ed.2d 298 (1983), consistent with the common law of contracts, that courts may refuse to enforce awards that violate law or public policy. The following cases and notes demonstrate that even after more than two decades of judicial application of the

3. Bibliographic Suggestions: Paula A. Barran and Todd A. Hanchett, *Public Policy Challenges to Labor Arbitration Awards: Still a Safe Harbor for Silly Fact Finding?*, 38 Willamette Law Review 233 (2002); John E. Dunsford, *The Judicial Doctrine of Public Policy: Misco Reviewed*, 4 Labor Lawyer 669 (1988); Frank H. Easterbrook, *Arbitration, Contract, and Public Policy*, 44 Proceedings of the National Academy of Arbitrators 65 (1992); Harry T. Edwards, *Judicial Review of Labor Arbitration Awards: The Clash Between the Public Policy Exception and the Duty to Bargain*, 64 Chicago Kent Law Review 3 (1988); Ann C. Hodges, *Judicial Review of Arbitration Awards on Public Policy Grounds: Lessons from the Case Law*, 16 Ohio State Journal on Dispute Resolution 91 (2000); Michael H. LeRoy and Peter Feuille, *Final and Binding, but Appealable to Courts: Judicial Review of Labor and Employment Arbitration Awards*, 54 Proceedings of the National Academy of Arbitrators 49 (2002); Michael H. LeRoy and Peter Feuille, *Private Justice in the Shadow of Public Courts: The Autonomy of Workplace Arbitration Systems*, 17 Ohio State Journal on Dispute Resolution 19 (2001); Bernard D. Meltzer, *After the Labor Arbitration Award: The Public Policy Defense*, 10 Industrial Relations Law Journal 241 (1988); Deanna J. Mouser, *Analysis of the Public Policy Exception After Paperworkers v. Misco: A Proposal to Limit the Public Policy Exception and to Allow the Parties to Submit the Public Policy Question to the Arbitrator*, 12 Industrial Relations Law Journal 89 (1990); Judith Stilz Ogden, *Do Public Policy Grounds Still Exist for Vacating Arbitration Awards?* 20 Hofstra Labor and Employment Law Journal 87 (2002); Joan Parker, *Judicial Review of Labor Arbitration Awards: Misco and Its Impact on the Public Policy Exception*, 4 Labor Lawyer 683 (1988); Calvin William Sharpe, *Judicial Review of Labor Arbitration Awards: A View from the Bench*, 52 Proceedings of the National Academy of Arbitrators 126 (2000) (including a panel discussion by judges of the United States Court of Appeals for the Fifth Circuit); Todd M. Siegel, *Is Arbitration Final & Binding? Public Policy Says, "Not Necessarily!"*, 1995 Journal of Dispute Resolution 351; Comment, *Judicial Review of Labor Arbitration Awards: Reinstating Dangerous Employees*, 1990 University of Chicago Legal Forum 625.

public policy doctrine some of its contours remain disputed and unde-fined. The cases in this section also address other issues left uncertain after *Enterprise Wheel*. To what extent should courts overturn awards for procedural errors or misconduct by arbitrators? To what extent are courts free to second-guess an arbitral fact finding?

UNITED PAPERWORKERS INTERNATIONAL UNION v. MISCO, INC.

Supreme Court of the United States, 1987.
484 U.S. 29, 108 S.Ct. 364, 98 L.Ed.2d 286.

JUSTICE WHITE delivered the opinion of the Court.

The issue for decision involves several aspects of when a federal court may refuse to enforce an arbitration award rendered under a collective-bargaining agreement.

I

Misco, Inc., (Misco, or the Company) operates a paper converting plant in Monroe, Louisiana. The Company is a party to a collective-bargaining agreement with the United Paperworkers International Union, AFL–CIO, and its union local (the Union); the agreement covers the production and maintenance employees at the plant. Under the agree-ment, the Company or the Union may submit to arbitration any griev-ance that arises from the interpretation or application of its terms, and the arbitrator's decision is final and binding upon the parties. The arbitrator's authority is limited to interpretation and application of the terms contained in the agreement itself. The agreement reserves to management the right to establish, amend, and enforce "rules and regulations regulating the discipline or discharge of employees" and the procedures for imposing discipline. Such rules were to be posted and were to be in effect "until ruled on by grievance and arbitration procedures as to fairness and necessity." For about a decade, the Company's rules had listed as causes for discharge the bringing of intoxicants, narcotics, or controlled substances on to plant property or consuming any of them there, as well as reporting for work under the influence of such substances. At the time of the events involved in this case, the Company was very concerned about the use of drugs at the plant, especially among employees on the night shift.

Isiah Cooper, who worked on the night shift for Misco, was one of the employees covered by the collective-bargaining agreement. He oper-ated a slitter-rewinder machine, which uses sharp blades to cut rolling coils of paper. The arbitrator found that this machine is hazardous and had caused numerous injuries in recent years. Cooper had been repri-manded twice in a few months for deficient performance. On January 21, 1983, one day after the second reprimand, the police searched Cooper's house pursuant to a warrant, and a substantial amount of marijuana was found. Contemporaneously, a police officer was detailed to keep Cooper's car under observation at the Company's parking lot. At about 6:30 p.m.,

Cooper was seen walking in the parking lot during work hours with two other men. The three men entered Cooper's car momentarily, then walked to another car, a white Cutlass, and entered it. After the other two men later returned to the plant, Cooper was apprehended by police in the backseat of this car with marijuana smoke in the air and a lighted marijuana cigarette in the frontseat ashtray. The police also searched Cooper's car and found a plastic scales case and marijuana gleanings. Cooper was arrested and charged with marijuana possession.[3]

On January 24, Cooper told the Company that he had been arrested for possession of marijuana at his home; the Company did not learn of the marijuana cigarette in the white Cutlass until January 27. It then investigated and on February 7 discharged Cooper, asserting that in the circumstances, his presence in the Cutlass violated the rule against having drugs on the plant premises.[4] Cooper filed a grievance protesting his discharge the same day, and the matter proceeded to arbitration. The Company was not aware until September 21, five days before the hearing before the arbitrator was scheduled, that marijuana had been found in Cooper's car. That fact did not become known to the Union until the hearing began. At the hearing it was stipulated that the issue was whether the Company had "just cause to discharge the Grievant under Rule II.1" and, "[i]f not, what if any should be the remedy." App. to Pet. for Cert. 26a.

The arbitrator upheld the grievance and ordered the Company to reinstate Cooper with backpay and full seniority. The arbitrator based his finding that there was not just cause for the discharge on his consideration of seven criteria.[5] In particular, the arbitrator found that the Company failed to prove that the employee had possessed or used marijuana on company property: finding Cooper in the backseat of a car and a burning cigarette in the frontseat ashtray was insufficient proof that Cooper was using or possessed marijuana on company property. *Id.*, at 49a–50a. The arbitrator refused to accept into evidence the fact that marijuana had been found in Cooper's car on company premises because the Company did not know of this fact when Cooper was discharged and therefore did not rely on it as a basis for the discharge.[6]

---

3. Cooper later pleaded guilty to that charge, which was not related to his being in a car with a lighted marijuana cigarette in it. The authorities chose not to prosecute for the latter incident.

4. The Company asserted that being in a car with a lit marijuana cigarette was a direct violation of the company rule against having an illegal substance on company property. App. 23.

5. These considerations were the reasonableness of the employer's position, the notice given to the employee, the timing of the investigation undertaken, the fairness of the investigation, the evidence against the employee, the possibility of discrimination, and the relation of the degree of discipline to the nature of the offense and the employee's past record.

6. The arbitrator stated: "One of the rules in arbitration is that the Company must have its proof in hand before it takes disciplinary action against an employee. The Company does not take the disciplinary action and then spend eight months digging up supporting evidence to justify its actions. In addition, the use of the gleanings evidence prevented the Grievant from knowing the full extent of the charge against him. Who knows what action the Grievant or the Union would have taken if the gleanings evidence had been made known from the outset of the Company's investigation." App. to Pet. for Cert. 47a.

[The Company brought an action in federal district court to vacate the award on the ground that ordering reinstatement of an employee who had possessed marijuana on plant premises violated public policy. The district court vacated the award and the court of appeals affirmed.]

II

The Union asserts that an arbitral award may not be set aside on public policy grounds unless the award orders conduct that violates the positive law, which is not the case here. But in the alternative, it submits that even if it is wrong in this regard, the Court of Appeals otherwise exceeded the limited authority that it had to review an arbitrator's award entered pursuant to a collective-bargaining agreement. Respondent, on the other hand, defends the public policy decision of the Court of Appeals but alternatively argues that the judgment below should be affirmed because of erroneous findings by the arbitrator. We deal first with the opposing alternative arguments.

A

[The Court reviewed some of its prior decisions on judicial review of arbitration awards.]

* * * Because the parties have contracted to have disputes settled by an arbitrator chosen by them rather than by a judge, it is the arbitrator's view of the facts and of the meaning of the contract that they have agreed to accept. Courts thus do not sit to hear claims of factual or legal error by an arbitrator as an appellate court does in reviewing decisions of lower courts. To resolve disputes about the application of a collective-bargaining agreement, an arbitrator must find facts and a court may not reject those findings simply because it disagrees with them. The same is true of the arbitrator's interpretation of the contract. The arbitrator may not ignore the plain language of the contract; but the parties having authorized the arbitrator to give meaning to the language of the agreement, a court should not reject an award on the ground that the arbitrator misread the contract. *Enterprise Wheel, supra*, at 599. So, too, where it is contemplated that the arbitrator will determine remedies for contract violations that he finds, courts have no authority to disagree with his honest judgment in that respect. If the courts were free to intervene on these grounds, the speedy resolution of grievances by private mechanisms would be greatly undermined. Furthermore, it must be remembered that grievance and arbitration procedures are part and parcel of the ongoing process of collective bargaining. It is through these processes that the supplementary rules of the plant are established. As the Court has said, the arbitrator's award settling a dispute with respect to the interpretation or application of a labor agreement must draw its essence from the contract and cannot simply reflect the arbitrator's own notions of industrial justice. But as long as the arbitrator is even arguably construing or applying the contract and acting within the scope of his authority, that a court is convinced he committed serious error does not suffice to overturn his

decision. Of course, decisions procured by the parties through fraud or through the arbitrator's dishonesty need not be enforced. But there is nothing of that sort involved in this case.

B

The Company's position, simply put, is that the arbitrator committed grievous error in finding that the evidence was insufficient to prove that Cooper had possessed or used marijuana on company property. But the Court of Appeals, although it took a distinctly jaundiced view of the arbitrator's decision in this regard, was not free to refuse enforcement because it considered Cooper's presence in the white Cutlass, in the circumstances, to be ample proof that Rule II.1 was violated. No dishonesty is alleged; only improvident, even silly, factfinding is claimed. This is hardly a sufficient basis for disregarding what the agent appointed by the parties determined to be the historical facts.

Nor was it open to the Court of Appeals to refuse to enforce the award because the arbitrator, in deciding whether there was just cause to discharge, refused to consider evidence unknown to the Company at the time Cooper was fired. The parties bargained for arbitration to settle disputes and were free to set the procedural rules for arbitrators to follow if they chose. Article VI of the agreement, entitled "Arbitration Procedure," did set some ground rules for the arbitration process. It forbade the arbitrator to consider hearsay evidence, for example, but evidentiary matters were otherwise left to the arbitrator. App. 19. Here the arbitrator ruled that in determining whether Cooper had violated Rule II.1, he should not consider evidence not relied on by the employer in ordering the discharge, particularly in a case like this where there was no notice to the employee or the Union prior to the hearing that the Company would attempt to rely on after-discovered evidence. This, in effect, was a construction of what the contract required when deciding discharge cases: an arbitrator was to look only at the evidence before the employer at the time of discharge. As the arbitrator noted, this approach was consistent with the practice followed by other arbitrators. And it was consistent with our observation in *John Wiley & Sons, Inc. v. Livingston*, 376 U.S. 543, 557 (1964), that when the subject matter of a dispute is arbitrable, "procedural" questions which grow out of the dispute and bear on its final disposition are to be left to the arbitrator.

Under the Arbitration Act, the federal courts are empowered to set aside arbitration awards on such grounds only when "the arbitrators were guilty of misconduct * * * in refusing to hear evidence pertinent and material to the controversy." 9 U.S.C. § 10(c). See *Commonwealth Coatings Corp. v. Continental Casualty Co.*, 393 U.S. 145 (1968).[9] If we

---

9. The Arbitration Act does not apply to "contracts of employment of * * * workers engaged in foreign or interstate commerce," 9 U.S.C. § 1, but the federal courts have often looked to the Act for guidance in labor arbitration cases, especially in the wake of the holding that § 301 of the Labor Management Relations Act of 1947, 61 Stat. 156, 29 U.S.C. § 185, empowers the federal courts to fashion rules of federal common law to govern "[s]uits for violation of contracts between an employer and a labor

apply that same standard here and assume that the arbitrator erred in refusing to consider the disputed evidence, his error was not in bad faith or so gross as to amount to affirmative misconduct.[10] Finally, it is worth noting that putting aside the evidence about the marijuana found in Cooper's car during this arbitration did not forever foreclose the Company from using that evidence as the basis for a discharge.

Even if it were open to the Court of Appeals to have found a violation of Rule II.1 because of the marijuana found in Cooper's car, the question remains whether the court could properly set aside the award because in its view discharge was the correct remedy. Normally, an arbitrator is authorized to disagree with the sanction imposed for employee misconduct. In *Enterprise Wheel*, for example, the arbitrator reduced the discipline from discharge to a 10–day suspension. The Court of Appeals refused to enforce the award, but we reversed, explaining that though the arbitrator's decision must draw its essence from the agreement, he "is to bring his informed judgment to bear in order to reach a fair solution of a problem. *This is especially true when it comes to formulating remedies.*" 363 U.S., at 597 (emphasis added). The parties, of course, may limit the discretion of the arbitrator in this respect; and it may be, as the Company argues, that under the contract involved here, it was within the unreviewable discretion of management to discharge an employee once a violation of Rule II.1 was found. But the parties stipulated that the issue before the arbitrator was whether there was "just" cause for the discharge, and the arbitrator, in the course of his opinion, cryptically observed that Rule II.1 merely listed causes for discharge and did not expressly provide for immediate discharge. Before disposing of the case on the ground that Rule II.1 had been violated and discharge was therefore proper, the proper course would have been remand to the arbitrator for a definitive construction of the contract in this respect.

C

The Court of Appeals did not purport to take this course in any event. Rather, it held that the evidence of marijuana in Cooper's car

organization" under the federal labor laws. *Textile Workers v. Lincoln Mills*, 353 U.S. 448 (1957) (construing 29 U.S.C. § 185). See, *e.g., Ludwig Honold Mfg. Co. v. Fletcher*, 405 F.2d 1123 (3d Cir.1969); *Pietro Scalzitti Co. v. International Union of Operating Engineers, Local No. 150*, 351 F.2d 576 (7th Cir.1965).

10. Even in the very rare instances when an arbitrator's procedural aberrations rise to the level of affirmative misconduct, as a rule the court must not foreclose further proceedings by settling the merits according to its own judgment of the appropriate result, since this step would improperly substitute a judicial determination for the arbitrator's decision that the parties bargained for in the collective-bargaining agreement. Instead, the court should simply vacate the award, thus leaving open the possibility of further proceedings if they are permitted under the terms of the agreement. The court also has the authority to remand for further proceedings when this step seems appropriate. See, *e.g., Amalgamated Food & Allied Workers Union, Local 56 v. Great A & P Tea Co.*, 415 F.2d 185 (3d Cir.1969) (vacating and remanding to the arbitrators for decision after finding that the arbitrators declined to arbitrate the issues submitted). See also 9 U.S.C. § 10(e) ("Where an award is vacated and the time within which the agreement required the award to be made has not expired the court may, in its discretion, direct a rehearing by the arbitrators").

required that the award be set aside because to reinstate a person who had brought drugs onto the property was contrary to the public policy "against the operation of dangerous machinery by persons under the influence of drugs or alcohol." 768 F.2d, at 743. We cannot affirm that judgment.

A court's refusal to enforce an arbitrator's award under a collective-bargaining agreement because it is contrary to public policy is a specific application of the more general doctrine, rooted in the common law, that a court may refuse to enforce contracts that violate law or public policy. *W.R. Grace & Co. v. Rubber Workers*, 461 U.S. 757, 766 (1983) * * * That doctrine derives from the basic notion that no court will lend its aid to one who founds a cause of action upon an immoral or illegal act, and is further justified by the observation that the public's interests in confining the scope of private agreements to which it is not a party will go unrepresented unless the judiciary takes account of those interests when it considers whether to enforce such agreements. * * * In the common law of contracts, this doctrine has served as the foundation for occasional exercises of judicial power to abrogate private agreements.

In *W.R. Grace*, we recognized that "a court may not enforce a collective-bargaining agreement that is contrary to public policy," and stated that "the question of public policy is ultimately one for resolution by the courts." 461 U.S., at 766. We cautioned, however, that a court's refusal to enforce an arbitrator's *interpretation* of such contracts is limited to situations where the contract as interpreted would violate "some explicit public policy" that is "well defined and dominant, and is to be ascertained 'by reference to the laws and legal precedents and not from general considerations of supposed public interests.' "*Ibid.* (quoting *Muschany v. United States*, 324 U.S. 49, 66 (1945)). * * *

As we see it, the formulation of public policy set out by the Court of Appeals did not comply with the statement that such a policy must be "ascertained 'by reference to the laws and legal precedents and not from general considerations of supposed public interests.' " *Ibid.* (quoting *Muschany v. United States*, 324 U.S., at 66, 65 S.Ct., at 451). The Court of Appeals made no attempt to review existing laws and legal precedents in order to demonstrate that they establish a "well-defined and dominant" policy against the operation of dangerous machinery while under the influence of drugs. Although certainly such a judgment is firmly rooted in common sense, we explicitly held in *W.R. Grace* that a formulation of public policy based only on "general considerations of supposed public interests" is not the sort that permits a court to set aside an arbitration award that was entered in accordance with a valid collective-bargaining agreement.

Even if the Court of Appeals' formulation of public policy is to be accepted, no violation of that policy was clearly shown in this case. In pursuing its public policy inquiry, the Court of Appeals quite properly considered the established fact that traces of marijuana had been found in Cooper's car. Yet the assumed connection between the marijuana gleanings found in Cooper's car and Cooper's actual use of drugs in the work-place is tenuous at best and provides an insufficient basis for holding that his reinstatement would actually violate the public policy identified by the Court of Appeals "against the operation of dangerous machinery by persons under the influence of drugs or alcohol." 768 F.2d, at 743. A refusal to enforce an award must rest on more than speculation or assumption.

In any event, it was inappropriate for the Court of Appeals itself to draw the necessary inference. To conclude from the fact that marijuana had been found in Cooper's car that Cooper had ever been or would be under the influence of marijuana while he was on the job and operating dangerous machinery is an exercise in factfinding about Cooper's use of drugs and his amenability to discipline, a task that exceeds the authority of a court asked to overturn an arbitration award. The parties did not bargain for the facts to be found by a court, but by an arbitrator chosen by them who had more opportunity to observe Cooper and to be familiar with the plant and its problems. Nor does the fact that it is inquiring into a possible violation of public policy excuse a court for doing the arbitrator's task. If additional facts were to be found, the arbitrator should find them in the course of any further effort the Company might have made to discharge Cooper for having had marijuana in his car on company premises. Had the arbitrator found that Cooper had possessed drugs on the property, yet imposed discipline short of discharge because he found as a factual matter that Cooper could be trusted not to use them on the job, the Court of Appeals could not upset the award because of its own view that public policy about plant safety was threatened. In this connection it should also be noted that the award ordered Cooper to be reinstated in his old job or in an equivalent one for which he was qualified. It is by no means clear from the record that Cooper would pose a serious threat to the asserted public policy in every job for which he was qualified.[12]

[JUSTICE BLACKMUN wrote a concurring opinion in which JUSTICE BRENNAN joined.]

Notes and Questions

1. Review the Supreme Court's discussion of the arbitrator's decision not to consider the evidence the employer discovered after it discharged the employee, beginning in the second paragraph of Part II.B of its opinion in *Misco.*

(a) Does the decision of the arbitrator to exclude the evidence draw its essence from the collective bargaining agreement? Is that the proper test of this determination by the arbitrator?

(b) Is the *John Wiley* case, cited in the second paragraph in Part B, proper authority on the issue of the scope of judicial review of an arbitrator's

---

12. We need not address the Union's position that a court may refuse to enforce an award on public policy grounds only when the award itself violates a statute, regulation, or other manifestation of positive law, or compels conduct by the employer that would violate such a law.

procedural determinations? Was *John Wiley*, in saying that procedural questions were for the arbitrator, even addressing the issue of judicial review?

(c) After *Misco*, what standard should courts use in reviewing procedural decisions of arbitrators? Teamsters Local Union No. 61 v. United Parcel Service, Inc., 272 F.3d 600 (D.C.Cir. 2001) (arbitrator's decision on procedural matters entitled to "special" deference, broader than under *Garvey, infra* this Chapter); International Chemical Workers Union v. Columbian Chemicals Co., 331 F.3d 491 (5th Cir. 2003) (arbitrator's refusal to issue subpoena did not warrant vacation of award since conduct did not rise to the level of the misconduct described in section 10 of the FAA nor did it "yield a fundamentally unfair hearing"); Teamsters Local 688 v. SuperValu Inc., 2003 WL 145587, 171 LRRM 3270 (E.D. Mo. 2003) ("An arbitrator's procedural error must amount to bad faith or affirmative misconduct to warrant judicial intervention." "The courts have provided little or no guidance as to the standard to apply in assessing whether an arbitrator's rulings are simply erroneous or whether they rise to the level of affirmative misconduct and must be vacated."); and Finley Lines Joint Protective Bd. Unit 200 v. Norfolk Southern Ry. Co., 312 F.3d 943 (8th Cir. 2002) ("Arbitrators have broad procedural discretion.").

(d) After *Misco*, what sort of procedural action of an arbitrator might warrant vacation of an award? See Dover Elevator Systems, Inc. v. United Steel Workers, Local No. 3857, 1998 WL 527290, 160 LRRM 2720 (N.D.Miss. 1998) (award vacated where arbitrator relied on exhibit submitted *ex parte* by union with its brief when arbitrator had instructed parties not to submit new evidence with their briefs); Kuhlman Electric Corp. v. UAW, 1998 WL 863250, 159 LRRM 3022 (E.D.Ky.1998) (award of $1.6 million in back pay vacated on ground that arbitrator failed to provide employer with an opportunity to submit evidence on back pay issue); Kaplan v. Alfred Dunhill of London, Inc., 1996 WL 640901, 156 LRRM 2080 (S.D.N.Y.1996) (award vacated when arbitrator refused to allow employer to present any evidence despite notice to arbitrator immediately after hearing that employer had not received notice that hearing had been scheduled); United Food & Commercial Workers International Union v. SIPCO, Inc., 1992 WL 455167, 142 LRRM 2256 (S.D.Iowa 1992), aff'd, 8 F.3d 10 (8th Cir.1993) (award vacated where arbitrator had *ex parte* communications with nonparty and relied upon information not in evidence); and Flexsys America, L.P. v. Local Union No. 12610, 88 F.Supp.2d 600 (S.D.W.Va. 2000) (award vacated where arbitrator made *ex parte* telephone call to employer's counsel to determine the sexual orientation of a supervisor witness, saying that the case would be decided against the employer if the supervisor was gay, although sexual orientation was entirely irrelevant to the grievance). Compare M & A Electric Power Cooperative v. Local Union No. 702, IBEW, 977 F.2d 1235 (8th Cir.1992) (court refused to vacate award despite arbitrator's *ex parte* inquiry because information gained merely corroborated arbitrator's prior knowledge and evidence at the hearing); and Cemetery Workers and Greens Attendants Union, Local 365 v. Woodlawn Cemetery, 1995 WL 326541, 152 LRRM 2360 (S.D.N.Y.1995) (court refused to vacate award where arbitrator allowed employer to keep secret names of witnesses prior to their testimony). See also Perry A. Zirkel and Peter D. Winebrake, *Legal Boundaries for*

Partiality and Misconduct of Labor Arbitrators, 1992 Detroit College of Law Review 679.

(e) In *Misco*, the Supreme court borrowed its standard for review of procedural decisions of labor arbitrators from the Federal Arbitration Act, while at the same time suggesting, in footnote 9 of the opinion, that the FAA does not, by its terms, govern labor arbitration. Subsequently, the Supreme Court held that the FAA does govern employment arbitration agreements. Circuit City Stores, Inc. v. Adams, 532 U.S. 105, 121 S.Ct. 1302, 149 L.Ed.2d 234 (2001), Chapter X, *infra*. See Note 5 following the *Lincoln Mills* case in Chapter III.A., *supra*, for discussion of whether the Court might, following *Circuit City*, now hold that the FAA does in fact directly govern judicial review of labor arbitration awards.

2. Subsequent to its *Misco* decision, the Supreme Court addressed the question of the appropriate treatment of after-acquired evidence in deciding discrimination claims under the Age Discrimination in Employment Act. In McKennon v. Nashville Banner Publishing Co., 513 U.S. 352, 115 S.Ct. 879, 130 L.Ed.2d 852 (1995), the employer had discovered, in the course of defending a discrimination claim, that the employee had copied confidential company documents without authorization. The Supreme Court held that this after-acquired evidence, which might have established an independent basis for termination, could not be used to bar the discrimination claim because to do so would undermine the deterrent effect of the law. The Court held, however, that the after-acquired evidence could be considered in determining the appropriate remedy if a finding of discrimination were made, and that such evidence would be likely, in most cases, to preclude reinstatement and front pay. Does *McKennon* have any bearing on an arbitrator's use of information about an employee obtained after the employee's discharge?

3. To what extent does *Misco* refine the scope of the public policy exception recognized in *W.R. Grace*? Does *Misco* provide any additional information about the sources or scope of "public policy"?

EASTERN ASSOCIATED COAL CORP. v. UNITED MINE WORKERS OF AMERICA, DIST. 17

Supreme Court of the United States, 2000.
531 U.S. 57, 121 S.Ct. 462, 148 L.Ed.2d 354.

JUSTICE BREYER delivered the opinion of the Court.

A labor arbitrator ordered an employer to reinstate an employee truck driver who had twice tested positive for marijuana. The question before us is whether considerations of public policy require courts to refuse to enforce that arbitration award. We conclude that they do not. The courts may enforce the award. And the employer must reinstate, rather than discharge, the employee.

I

Petitioner, Eastern Associated Coal Corp., and respondent, United Mine Workers of America, are parties to a collective-bargaining agreement with arbitration provisions. The agreement specifies that, in arbitration, in order to discharge an employee, Eastern must prove it has "just cause." Otherwise the arbitrator will order the employee reinstated. The arbitrator's decision is final. App. 28–31.

James Smith worked for Eastern as a member of a road crew, a job that required him to drive heavy trucklike vehicles on public highways. As a truck driver, Smith was subject to Department of Transportation (DOT) regulations requiring random drug testing of workers engaged in "safety-sensitive" tasks. 49 CFR §§ 382.301, 382.305 (1999).

In March 1996, Smith tested positive for marijuana. Eastern sought to discharge Smith. The union went to arbitration, and the arbitrator concluded that Smith's positive drug test did not amount to "just cause" for discharge. Instead the arbitrator ordered Smith's reinstatement, provided that Smith (1) accept a suspension of 30 days without pay, (2) participate in a substance-abuse program, and (3) undergo drug tests at the discretion of Eastern (or an approved substance-abuse professional) for the next five years.

Between April 1996 and January 1997, Smith passed four random drug tests. But in July 1997 he again tested positive for marijuana. Eastern again sought to discharge Smith. The union again went to arbitration, and the arbitrator again concluded that Smith's use of marijuana did not amount to "just cause" for discharge, in light of two mitigating circumstances. First, Smith had been a good employee for 17 years. App. to Pet. for Cert. 26a–27a. And, second, Smith had made a credible and "very personal appeal under oath ... concerning a personal/family problem which caused this one time lapse in drug usage." *Id.*, at 28a.

The arbitrator ordered Smith's reinstatement provided that Smith (1) accept a new suspension without pay, this time for slightly more than three months; (2) reimburse Eastern and the union for the costs of both arbitration proceedings; (3) continue to participate in a substance abuse program; (4) continue to undergo random drug testing; and (5) provide Eastern with a signed, undated letter of resignation, to take effect if Smith again tested positive within the next five years. *Id.*, at 29a.

Eastern brought suit in federal court seeking to have the arbitrator's award vacated, arguing that the award contravened a public policy against the operation of dangerous machinery by workers who test positive for drugs. 66 F.Supp.2d 796 (S.D.W.V.1998). The District Court, while recognizing a strong regulation-based public policy against drug use by workers who perform safety-sensitive functions, held that Smith's conditional reinstatement did not violate that policy. *Id.*, at 804–805. And it ordered the award's enforcement., *Id.* at 805.

The Court of Appeals for the Fourth Circuit affirmed on the reasoning of the District Court. 188 F.3d 501, 1999 WL 635632 (1999) (unpublished). We granted certiorari in light of disagreement among the Circuits. Compare *id.*, at *1 (holding that public policy does not prohibit "reinstatement of employees who have used illegal drugs in the past"), with, *e.g.*, *Exxon Corp. v. Esso Workers' Union, Inc.*, 118 F.3d 841, 852 (1st Cir.1997) (holding that public policy prohibits enforcement of a similar arbitration award). We now affirm the Fourth Circuit's determination.

II

Eastern claims that considerations of public policy make the arbitration award unenforceable. In considering this claim, we must assume that the collective-bargaining agreement itself calls for Smith's reinstatement. That is because both employer and union have granted to the arbitrator the authority to interpret the meaning of their contract's language, including such words as "just cause." See *Steelworkers v. Enterprise Wheel & Car Corp.*, 363 U.S. 593, 599, 80 S.Ct. 1358, 4 L.Ed.2d 1424 (1960). They have "bargained for" the "arbitrator's construction" of their agreement. *Ibid.* And courts will set aside the arbitrator's interpretation of what their agreement means only in rare instances. *Id.*, at 596, 80 S.Ct. 1358. Of course, an arbitrator's award "must draw its essence from the contract and cannot simply reflect the arbitrator's own notions of industrial justice." *Paperworkers v. Misco, Inc.*, 484 U.S. 29, 38, 108 S.Ct. 364, 98 L.Ed.2d 286 (1987). "But as long as [an honest] arbitrator is even arguably construing or applying the contract and acting within the scope of his authority," the fact that "a court is convinced he committed serious error does not suffice to overturn his decision." *Ibid.*; see also *Enterprise Wheel, supra*, at 596, 80 S.Ct. 1358 (the "proper" judicial approach to a labor arbitration award is to "refus[e] ... to review the merits"). Eastern does not claim here that the arbitrator acted outside the scope of his contractually delegated authority. Hence we must treat the arbitrator's award as if it represented an agreement between Eastern and the union as to the proper meaning of the contract's words "just cause." See St. Antoine, Judicial Review of Labor Arbitration Awards: A Second Look at *Enterprise Wheel* and Its Progeny, 75 Mich. L.Rev. 1137, 1155 (1977). For present purposes, the award is not distinguishable from the contractual agreement.

We must then decide whether a contractual reinstatement requirement would fall within the legal exception that makes unenforceable "a collective bargaining agreement that is contrary to public policy." *W.R. Grace & Co. v. Rubber Workers*, 461 U.S. 757, 766, 103 S.Ct. 2177, 76 L.Ed.2d 298 (1983). The Court has made clear that any such public policy must be "explicit," "well defined," and "dominant." *Ibid.* It must be "ascertained 'by reference to the laws and legal precedents and not from general considerations of supposed public interests.'" *Ibid.* (quoting *Muschany v. United States*, 324 U.S. 49, 66, 65 S.Ct. 442, 89 L.Ed. 744 (1945)); accord, *Misco, supra*, at 43, 108 S.Ct. 364. And, of course, the question to be answered is not whether Smith's drug use itself violates public policy, but whether the agreement to reinstate him does so. To put the question more specifically, does a contractual agreement to reinstate Smith with specified conditions, see App. to Pet. for Cert. 29a, run contrary to an explicit, well-defined, and dominant public policy, as ascertained by reference to positive law and not from general considerations of supposed public interests? See *Misco, supra,* at 43, 108 S.Ct. 364.

III

Eastern initially argues that the District Court erred by asking, not whether the award is "contrary to" public policy "as ascertained by reference" to positive law, but whether the award "violates" positive law, a standard Eastern says is too narrow. We believe, however, that the District Court correctly articulated the standard set out in *W.R. Grace* and *Misco,* see 66 F.Supp.2d, at 803 (quoting *Misco, supra,* at 43, 108 S.Ct. 364), and applied that standard to reach the right result.

We agree, in principle, that courts' authority to invoke the public policy exception is not limited solely to instances where the arbitration award itself violates positive law. Nevertheless, the public policy exception is narrow and must satisfy the principles set forth in *W.R. Grace* and *Misco.* Moreover, in a case like the one before us, where two political branches have created a detailed regulatory regime in a specific field, courts should approach with particular caution pleas to divine further public policy in that area.

Eastern asserts that a public policy against reinstatement of workers who use drugs can be discerned from an examination of that regulatory regime, which consists of the Omnibus Transportation Employee Testing Act of 1991 and DOT's implementing regulations. The Testing Act embodies a congressional finding that "the greatest efforts must be expended to eliminate the . . . use of illegal drugs, whether on or off duty, by those individuals who are involved in [certain safety-sensitive positions, including] the operation of . . . trucks." Pub.L. 102–143, § 2(3), 105 Stat. 953. The Act adds that "increased testing" is the "most effective deterrent" to "use of illegal drugs." § 2(5). It requires the Secretary of Transportation to promulgate regulations requiring "testing of operators of commercial motor vehicles for the use of a controlled substance." 49 U.S.C. § 31306(b)(1)(A) (1994 ed., Supp. III). It mandates suspension of those operators who have driven a commercial motor vehicle while under the influence of drugs. 49 U.S.C. § 31310(b)(1)(A) (requiring suspension of at least one year for a first offense); § 31310(c)(2) (requiring suspension of at least 10 years for a second offense). And DOT's implementing regulations set forth sanctions applicable to those who test positive for illegal drugs. 49 CFR § 382.605 (1999).

In Eastern's view, these provisions embody a strong public policy against drug use by transportation workers in safety-sensitive positions and in favor of random drug testing in order to detect that use. Eastern argues that reinstatement of a driver who has twice failed random drug tests would undermine that policy—to the point where a judge must set aside an employer-union agreement requiring reinstatement.

Eastern's argument, however, loses much of its force when one considers further provisions of the Act that make clear that the Act's remedial aims are complex. The Act says that "rehabilitation is a critical component of any testing program," § 2(7), 105 Stat. 953, that rehabilitation "should be made available to individuals, as appropriate," *ibid.*, and that DOT must promulgate regulations for "rehabilitation programs," 49 U.S.C. § 31306(e). The DOT regulations specifically state that a driver who has tested positive for drugs cannot return to a safety-sensitive position until (1) the driver has been evaluated by a "substance abuse professional" to determine if treatment is needed, 49 CFR § 382.605(b) (1999); (2) the substance-abuse professional has certified that the driver has followed any rehabilitation program prescribed, § 382.605(c)(2)(i); and (3) the driver has passed a return-to-duty drug test, § 382.605(c)(1). In addition, (4) the driver must be subject to at least six random drug tests during the first year after returning to the job. § 382.605(c)(2)(ii). Neither the Act nor the regulations forbid an employer to reinstate in a safety-sensitive position an employee who fails a random drug test once or twice. The congressional and regulatory directives require only that the above-stated prerequisites to reinstatement be met.

Moreover, when promulgating these regulations, DOT decided not to require employers either to provide rehabilitation or to "hold a job open for a driver" who has tested positive, on the basis that such decisions "should be left to management/driver negotiation." 59 Fed.Reg. 7502 (1994). That determination reflects basic background labor law principles, which caution against interference with labor-management agreements about appropriate employee discipline. See, *e.g., California Brewers Assn. v. Bryant*, 444 U.S. 598, 608, 100 S.Ct. 814, 63 L.Ed.2d 55 (1980) (noting that it is "this Nation's longstanding labor policy" to give "employers and employees the freedom through collective bargaining to establish conditions of employment").

We believe that these expressions of positive law embody several relevant policies. As Eastern points out, these policies include Testing Act policies against drug use by employees in safety-sensitive transportation positions and in favor of drug testing. They also include a Testing Act policy favoring rehabilitation of employees who use drugs. And the relevant statutory and regulatory provisions must be read in light of background labor law policy that favors determination of disciplinary questions through arbitration when chosen as a result of labor-management negotiation.

The award before us is not contrary to these several policies, taken together. The award does not condone Smith's conduct or ignore the risk to public safety that drug use by truck drivers may pose. Rather, the award punishes Smith by suspending him for three months, thereby depriving him of nearly $9,000 in lost wages, Record Doc. 29, App. A, p. 2; it requires him to pay the arbitration costs of both sides; it insists upon further substance-abuse treatment and testing; and it makes clear (by requiring Smith to provide a signed letter of resignation) that one more failed test means discharge. The award violates no specific provision of any law or regulation. It is consistent with DOT rules requiring completion of substance-abuse treatment before returning to work, see 49 CFR § 382.605(c)(2)(i) (1999), for it does not preclude Eastern from assigning Smith to a non-safety-sensitive position until Smith completes the prescribed treatment program. It is consistent with the Testing Act's 1-year and 10-year driving license suspension requirements, for those requirements apply only to drivers who, unlike Smith, actually operated vehicles under the influence of drugs. See 49 U.S.C. §§ 31310(b), (c). The award is also consistent with the Act's rehabilitative concerns, for it requires substance-abuse treatment and testing before Smith can return to work.

The fact that Smith is a recidivist—that he has failed drug tests twice—is not sufficient to tip the balance in Eastern's favor. The award punishes Smith more severely for his second lapse. And that more severe punishment, which included a 90-day suspension, would have satisfied even a "recidivist" rule that DOT once proposed but did not adopt—a rule that would have punished two failed drug tests, not with discharge, but with a driving suspension of 60 days. 57 Fed.Reg. 59585 (1992). Eastern argues that DOT's withdrawal of its proposed rule leaves open the possibility that discharge is the appropriate penalty for repeat offenders. That argument fails, however, because DOT based its withdrawal, not upon a determination that a more severe penalty was needed, but upon a determination to leave in place, as the "only driving prohibition period for a controlled substances violation," the "completion of rehabilitation requirements and a return-to-duty test with a negative result." 59 Fed.Reg. 7493 (1994).

Regarding drug use by persons in safety-sensitive positions, then, Congress has enacted a detailed statute. And Congress has delegated to the Secretary of Transportation authority to issue further detailed regulations on that subject. Upon careful consideration, including public notice and comment, the Secretary has done so. Neither Congress nor the Secretary has seen fit to mandate the discharge of a worker who twice tests positive for drugs. We hesitate to infer a public policy in this area that goes beyond the careful and detailed scheme Congress and the Secretary have created.

We recognize that reasonable people can differ as to whether reinstatement or discharge is the more appropriate remedy here. But both employer and union have agreed to entrust this remedial decision to an arbitrator. We cannot find in the Act, the regulations, or any other law or legal precedent an "explicit," "well defined," "dominant" public policy to which the arbitrator's decision "runs contrary." *Misco*, 484 U.S., at 43, 108 S.Ct. 364; *W.R. Grace*, 461 U.S., at 766, 103 S.Ct. 2177. We conclude that the lower courts correctly rejected Eastern's public policy claim. The judgment of the Court of Appeals is

Affirmed.

JUSTICE SCALIA, with whom JUSTICE THOMAS joins, concurring in the judgment.

I concur in the Court's judgment, because I agree that no public policy prevents the reinstatement of James Smith to his position as a truck driver, so long as he complies with the arbitrator's decision, and with those requirements set out in the Department of Transportation's regulations. I do not endorse, however, the Court's statement that "[w]e agree, in principle, that courts' authority to invoke the public policy exception is not limited solely to instances where the arbitration award itself violates positive law." *Ante*, at 63. No case is cited to support that proposition, and none could be. There is not a single decision, since this Court washed its hands of general common-lawmaking authority, see *Erie R. Co. v. Tompkins*, 304 U.S. 64, 58 S.Ct. 817, 82 L.Ed. 1188 (1938), in which we have refused to enforce on "public policy" grounds an agreement that did not violate, or provide for the violation of, some positive law. See, *e.g.*, *Hurd v. Hodge*, 334 U.S. 24, 68 S.Ct. 847, 92 L.Ed. 1187 (1948) (refusing to enforce under the public policy doctrine a restrictive covenant that violated Rev.Stat. § 1978, at 42 U.S.C. § 1982).

After its dictum opening the door to flaccid public policy arguments of the sort presented by petitioner here, the Court immediately posts a giant "Do Not Enter" sign. "[T]he public policy exception," it says, "is narrow and must satisfy the principles set forth in *W.R. Grace*," *ante*, at 63, which require that the applicable public policy be "explicit," "well defined," "dominant," and "ascertained 'by reference to the laws and legal precedents and not from general considerations of supposed public interests.'" *W.R. Grace & Co. v. Rubber Workers*, 461 U.S. 757, 766, 103 S.Ct. 2177, 76 L.Ed.2d 298 (1983) (quoting *Muschany v. United States*, 324 U.S. 49, 66, 65 S.Ct. 442, 89 L.Ed. 744 (1945)). It is hard to imagine how an arbitration award could violate a public policy, identified in this fashion, without actually conflicting with positive law. If such an award could ever exist, it would surely be so rare that the benefit of preserving the courts' ability to deal with it is far outweighed by the confusion and uncertainty, and hence the obstructive litigation, that the Court's Delphic "agree[ment] in principle" will engender.

The problem with judicial intuition of a public policy that goes beyond the actual prohibitions of the law is that there is no way of knowing whether the apparent gaps in the law are intentional or inadvertent. The final form of a statute or regulation, especially in the regulated fields where the public policy doctrine is likely to rear its head, is often the result of compromise among various interest groups, resulting in a decision to go so far and no farther. One can, of course, summon up a parade of horribles, such as an arbitration award ordering an airline to reinstate an alcoholic pilot who somehow escapes being grounded by force of law. But it seems to me we set our face against judicial correction of the omissions of the political branches when we declined the power to define common-law offenses. See *United States v. Hudson*, 7 Cranch 32, 3 L.Ed. 259 (1812). Surely the power to invalidate a contract providing for actions that are not contrary to law (but "ought" to be) is less important to the public welfare than the power to prohibit harmful acts that are not contrary to law (but "ought" to be). And it is also less efficacious, since it depends upon the willingness of one of the parties to the contract to *assert* the public policy interest. (If the airline is not terribly concerned about reinstating an alcoholic pilot, the courts will have no opportunity to prevent the reinstatement.) The horribles that can be imagined—if they are really so horrible and ever come to pass—can readily be corrected by Congress or the agency, with no problem of retroactivity. Supervening law is always grounds for the dissolution of a contractual obligation. See Restatement (Second) of Contracts § 264 (1979).

In sum, it seems to me that the game set in play by the Court's dictum endorsing "in principle" the power of federal courts to enunciate public policy is not worth the candle. Agreeing with the reasoning of the Court except insofar as this principle is concerned, I concur only in the judgment.

Notes and Questions

1. Empirical research suggests, that although some lower courts have had difficulty in accepting the Supreme Court's limitations on overturning arbitration awards on public policy grounds, in the last decade arbitration awards challenged on public policy grounds have been confirmed at approximately the same rate as awards challenged on other grounds. Michael H. LeRoy and Peter Feuille, *Private Justice in the Shadow of Public Courts: The Autonomy of Workplace Arbitration Systems*, 17 Ohio State Journal on Dispute Resolution 19, 85 (2001). The confirmation rate of labor arbitration awards challenged on public policy grounds was 54.7% in 1960–1981, 55.3% in 1982–1987 and 72% in 1991–2001. *Id*. While lower courts have, in general, increasingly conformed to the public policy standards articulated by the Supreme Court, the authors of the study conclude that there is a seemingly irreducible systemic conflict in cases involving public safety where arbitral culture, valuing rehabilitation of errant employees, collides with judicial culture, valuing protection of the public. *Id*. at 73.

2. In the penultimate paragraph of Justice Scalia's concurrence in *Eastern Associated Coal*, he suggests as among the "parade of horribles" testing the limits of the public policy exception the hypothetical of an arbitrator reinstating an alcoholic pilot. Justice Scalia's scenario is not merely hypothetical. In 2002, seventeen commercial pilots tested positive for alcohol after being turned in by airline or airport workers, four tested positive after being turned in by security workers, and five others tested positive in random tests conducted by the FAA. Newsday, 2003 WL 56091283 (June 15, 2003). Assume that a commercial airline discharged a pilot for flying while intoxicated. Regulations of the Federal Aviation Administration prohibit consumption of alcohol within eight hours of flight. By the time of the arbitration hearing on the discharge, one year later, the pilot had completed chemical dependency treatment and had been recertified by the FAA as medically fit to fly. The arbitrator ordered the pilot reinstated without back pay. The airline brought an action in federal district court seeking to have the arbitration award vacated on the ground that it was

inconsistent with public policy. From the concurrence in *Eastern Associated Coal* we have a pretty good idea about how two justices would resolve the case. What about the Court majority? Would your answer be different if the arbitration award was based in part on the fact that twice previously the airline had permitted drunk pilots to obtain rehabilitation rather than be discharged? Compare Northwest Airlines, Inc. v. Air Line Pilots Association, 808 F.2d 76 (D.C.Cir.1987), cert. denied, 486 U.S. 1014, 108 S.Ct. 1751, 100 L.Ed.2d 213 (1988), with Delta Air Lines, Inc. v. Air Line Pilots Association, 861 F.2d 665 (11th Cir.1988), cert. denied, 493 U.S. 871, 110 S.Ct. 201, 107 L.Ed.2d 154 (1989) (both decided before *Eastern Associated Coal*). In January 2003, the FAA tightened its requirements for reinstatement of pilots who have flown while intoxicated. In addition to obtaining certification as medically fit to fly, such pilots now must wait a year and then retake all the written and flight tests for pilots. AP Online, 2003 WL 57309355 (June 17, 2003).

3.   The majority of the Court in *Eastern Associated Coal* agrees that a court's power to overturn arbitration awards on grounds of public policy is not limited to cases in which an award violates positive law. Assume that a nurse refuses to work overtime, claiming that under the collective bargaining agreement the hospital has no authority to require her to remain at the end of her shift. The hospital discharges the nurse, interpreting the contract differently and asserting credibly that her departure created a threat to patient safety. Would an arbitration award reinstating the nurse violate public policy according to the Court majority in *Eastern Associated Coal*? Compare Boston Medical Center v. Service Employees Intern. Union, Local 285, 260 F.3d 16 (1st Cir. 2001), cert. denied, 534 U.S. 1083, 122 S.Ct. 816, 151 L.Ed.2d 700 (2002) (no violation of public policy to reinstate nurse who made clinical misjudgment resulting in death of infant), with Illinois Nurses Ass'n v. Board of Trustees of University of Illinois, 318 Ill.App.3d 519, 251 Ill.Dec. 836, 741 N.E.2d 1014 (2001) (vacating on public policy grounds arbitration award reinstating nurse whose conduct endangered patients' lives)

4.   The employer determined that an employee, Mark, had engaged in conduct toward a female co-worker over a period of months that constituted sexual harassment (including one offensive phone call, repeated offensive remarks, and long periods of staring, despite repeated objections) and fired Mark. In its investigation Mark admitted most of the behavior, but denied that he had intended any harm. Mark's union challenged his discharge under the "just cause" provision of the collective bargaining agreement. The arbitrator found that Mark had engaged in sexual harassment, but found fault with the employer's failure to tell him to desist and its failure to permit him to enter its Employee Assistance Program. The arbitrator reduced the discharge to a nine-month suspension without pay.

Sexual harassment is unlawful employment discrimination under Title VII of the Civil Rights Act. A regulation of the federal Equal Employment Opportunity Commission makes an employer liable for the sexual harassment of its employees if it "knows or should have known of the conduct, unless it can show that it took immediate and appropriate corrective action." 29 C.F.R. § 1604.11(d) (2003). The Supreme Court has held, in the context of misconduct by a supervisor, that an employer must exercise "reasonable

care to prevent and correct promptly any sexually harassing behavior."
Faragher v. City of Boca Raton, 524 U.S. 775, 807, 118 S.Ct. 2275, 2293, 141
L.Ed.2d 662 (1998).

(a) Assume that the employer refused to comply with the award of the
arbitrator to reinstate Mark and instead filed an action in the federal district
court to vacate the arbitration award. What would be the best arguments
that the employer could make in support of its action to vacate?

(b) What would be the union's best arguments in opposition to the
employer's action to vacate?

(c) How should the federal court decide the matter?

Compare Westvaco Corp. v. United Paperworkers International Union, 171
F.3d 971 (4th Cir.1999) (no violation of public policy), Communication
Workers v. Southeastern Elec. Co-op., 882 F.2d 467 (10th Cir.1989) (no
violation of public policy), and Chrysler Motors Corp. v. International Union,
Allied Industrial Workers, 959 F.2d 685 (7th Cir.) (no violation of public
policy), cert. denied, 506 U.S. 908, 113 S.Ct. 304, 121 L.Ed.2d 227 (1992),
with Newsday, Inc. v. Long Island Typographical Union, 915 F.2d 840 (2d
Cir.1990) (violation of public policy), cert. denied, 499 U.S. 922, 111 S.Ct.
1314, 113 L.Ed.2d 247 (1991). See also Weber Aircraft Inc. v. General
Warehousemen and Helpers Union Local 767, 253 F.3d 821 (5th Cir. 2001)
(there is no public policy precluding the reinstatement, following a suspension, of a sexual harasser); E.E.O.C. v. Indiana Bell Telephone Co., 256 F.3d
516 (7th Cir. 2001) (it is not a defense to a Title VII action for sexual
harassment that the employer's discipline of an employee for alleged sexual
harassment would be subject to "just cause" protection under a collective
bargaining agreement); and City of Brooklyn Center v. Law Enforcement
Labor Services, Inc., 635 N.W.2d 236 (Minn. App. 2001) (vacating on public
policy grounds arbitration award reinstating police officer who had engaged
in sexual harassment). See Carrie G. Donald and John D. Ralston. *Arbitral
Views of Sexual Harassment: An Analysis of Arbitration Cases, 1990–2000*,
20 Hofstra Labor and Employment Law Journal 229 (2003).

(d) Would the employer have a stronger or weaker case for vacation of
the award on public policy grounds if the arbitrator did not reach the
question of whether sexual harassment had occurred but nevertheless reinstated the employee on the ground that the employer's investigation of the
matter did not satisfy standards of procedural fairness? See Stroehmann
Bakeries v. Local 776, Teamsters, 969 F.2d 1436 (3d Cir.), cert. denied, 506
U.S. 1022, 113 S.Ct. 660, 121 L.Ed.2d 585 (1992). (The arbitrator's award is
reproduced in Chapter VII.B.3, *infra*). In *Stroehmann*, the court said, "Under the circumstances present here, an award which fully reinstates an
employee accused of sexual harassment without a determination that the
harassment did not occur violates public policy." 969 F.2d 1436, 1442. Does
that suggest that if the arbitrator finds that the employee *did* engage in
sexual harassment but should nevertheless be reinstated because of a
procedural violation by the employer, the award does *not* violate public
policy? Compare Jamaica Buses, Inc. v. Transport Workers' Union, Local
100, 2003 WL 1621026 (E.D.N.Y. 2003) (no violation of public policy despite
failure of arbitrator to determine whether alleged sexual harassment occurred).

MAJOR LEAGUE BASEBALL PLAYERS ASSOCIATION v. GARVEY

Supreme Court of the United States, 2001.
532 U.S. 504, 121 S.Ct. 1724, 149 L.Ed.2d 740, 532 U.S. 1015.

PER CURIAM.

[Following grievances submitted by the Major League Baseball Players Association alleging that baseball clubs had colluded in the market for free-agent players, arbitration awards established a fund to compensate injured players. Under an agreed Framework, a player was eligible for compensation if he could prove that a club made a specific offer of a contract extension, prior to collusion, and then withdrew it once the collusion scheme was initiated. Retired San Diego Padres' first baseman Steve Garvey submitted a grievance that alleged that Padres' President Ballard Smith had offered to extend Garvey's contract for the 1988 and 1989 seasons, but then refused to negotiate further regarding an extension once collusion commenced. In support of his claim, Garvey presented a June 1996 letter from Padres' President Smith stating that, before the end of the 1985 season, Smith offered to extend Garvey's contract through the 1989 season, but that the Padres refused to negotiate with Garvey thereafter due to collusion. The arbitrator noted that Smith's letter was contradicted by Smith's testimony in the 1986 arbitration proceedings regarding collusion in which Smith denied there had been any collusion and asserted that the Padres had independently determined that a contract extension was unwarranted. The arbitrator also noted Garvey's failure to provide evidence of a specific offer of extension. The arbitrator decided to discredit both the 1996 letter and further statements Smith made in 1996 consistent with the 1996 letter. The arbitrator concluded:]

> " '[t]he shadow cast over the credibility of the [1996] Smith testimony coupled with the absence of any other corroboration of the claim submitted by Garvey compels a finding that the Padres declined to extend his contract not because of the constraints of the collusion effort of the clubs but rather as a baseball judgment founded upon [Garvey's] age and recent injury history.' " *Ibid.*

Garvey moved in Federal District Court to vacate the arbitrator's award, alleging that the arbitrator violated the Framework by denying his claim. The District Court denied the motion. The Court of Appeals for the Ninth Circuit reversed by a divided vote. The court acknowledged that judicial review of an arbitrator's decision in a labor dispute is extremely limited. But it held that review of the merits of the arbitrator's award was warranted in this case, because the arbitrator " 'dispensed his own brand of industrial justice.' " [*Garvey v. Roberts*, 203 F.3d 580, 589 (9th Cir. 2000).] The court recognized that Smith's prior testimony with respect to collusion conflicted with the statements in his 1996 letter. But in the court's view, the arbitrator's refusal to credit Smith's letter was "inexplicable" and "border[ed] on the irrational," because a panel of arbitrators, chaired by the arbitrator involved here, had previously concluded that the owners' prior testimony was false. *Id.*, at 590. The court rejected the arbitrator's reliance on the absence of other corroborating evidence, attributing that fact to Smith and Garvey's direct negotiations. The court also found that the record provided "strong support" for the truthfulness of Smith's 1996 letter. *Id.*, at 591–592. The Court of Appeals reversed and remanded with directions to vacate the award.

The District Court then remanded the case to the arbitration panel for further hearings, and Garvey appealed. The Court of Appeals, again by a divided vote, explained that *Garvey I* established that "the conclusion that Smith made Garvey an offer and subsequently withdrew it because of the collusion scheme was the only conclusion that the arbitrator could draw from the record in the proceedings." No. 00–56080, 2000 WL 1801383, at *1 (9th Cir., Dec. 7, 2000), (unpublished), judgt. order reported at 243 F.3d 547. (*Garvey II*). Noting that its prior instructions might have been unclear, the Court clarified that *Garvey I* "left only one possible result—the result our holding contemplated—an award in Garvey's favor." 2000 WL 1801383, at *1. The Court of Appeals reversed the District Court and directed that it remand the case to the arbitration panel with instructions to enter an award for Garvey in the amount he claimed.

[Although Garvey's claim arose under the Framework, the Court characterized it as essentially a claim under a collective bargaining agreement.]

Judicial review of a labor-arbitration decision pursuant to such an agreement is very limited. Courts are not authorized to review the arbitrator's decision on the merits despite allegations that the decision rests on factual errors or misinterprets the parties' agreement. *Paperworkers v. Misco, Inc.*, 484 U.S. 29, 36, 108 S.Ct. 364, 98 L.Ed.2d 286 (1987). We recently reiterated that if an " 'arbitrator is even arguably construing or applying the contract and acting within the scope of his authority,' the fact that 'a court is convinced he committed serious error does not suffice to overturn his decision.' " *Eastern Associated Coal Corp. v. Mine Workers*, 531 U.S. 57, 62, 121 S.Ct. 462, 148 L.Ed.2d 354 (2000) (quoting *Misco, supra*, at 38, 108 S.Ct. 364). It is only when the arbitrator strays from interpretation and application of the agreement and effectively "dispense[s] his own brand of industrial justice" that his decision may be unenforceable. *Steelworkers v. Enterprise Wheel & Car Corp.*, 363 U.S. 593, 597, 80 S.Ct. 1358, 4 L.Ed.2d 1424 (1960). When an arbitrator resolves disputes regarding the application of a contract, and no dishonesty is alleged, the arbitrator's "improvident, even silly, fact-finding" does not provide a basis for a reviewing court to refuse to enforce the award. *Misco*, 484 U.S., at 39, 108 S.Ct. 364.

In discussing the courts' limited role in reviewing the merits of arbitration awards, we have stated that " 'courts ... have no business weighing the merits of the grievance [or] considering whether there is equity in a particular claim.' " *Id.*, at 37, 108 S.Ct. 364 (quoting *Steelworkers v. American Mfg. Co.*, 363 U.S. 564, 568, 80 S.Ct. 1343, 4 L.Ed.2d 1403 (1960)). When the judiciary does so, "it usurps a function which ... is entrusted to the arbitration tribunal." Id., at 569, 80 S.Ct. 1343; see also *Enterprise Wheel & Car Corp.*, *supra*, at 599, 80 S.Ct. 1358 ("It is the arbitrator's construction [of the agreement] which was bargained for ..."). Consistent with this limited role, we said in *Misco* that "[e]ven in the very rare instances when an arbitrator's procedural aberrations rise to the level of affirmative misconduct, as a rule the court must not foreclose further proceedings by settling the merits according to its own judgment of the appropriate result." 484 U.S. at 40–41, n. 10, 108 S.Ct. 364. That step, we explained, "would improperly substitute a judicial determination for the arbitrator's decision that the parties bargained for" in their agreement. *Ibid.* Instead, the court should "simply vacate the award, thus leaving open the possibility of further proceedings if they are permitted under the terms of the agreement." *Ibid.*

To be sure, the Court of Appeals here recited these principles, but its application of them is nothing short of baffling. The substance of the Court's discussion reveals that it overturned the arbitrator's decision because it disagreed with the arbitrator's factual findings, particularly those with respect to credibility. The Court of Appeals, it appears, would have credited Smith's 1996 letter, and found the arbitrator's refusal to do so at worst "irrational" and at best "bizarre." *Garvey I*, 203 F.3d, at 590–591. But even "serious error" on the arbitrator's part does not justify overturning his decision, where, as here, he is construing a contract and acting within the scope of his authority. *Misco, supra*, at 38, 108 S.Ct. 364.

In *Garvey II*, the court clarified that *Garvey I* both rejected the arbitrator's findings and went further, resolving the merits of the parties' dispute based on the court's assessment of the record before the arbitrator. For that reason, the court found further arbitration proceedings inappropriate. But again, established law ordinarily precludes a court from resolving the merits of the parties' dispute on the basis of its own factual determinations, no matter how erroneous the arbitrator's decision. *Misco, supra*, at 40, n. 10, 108 S.Ct. 364; see also *American Mfg. Co.*, 363 U.S. at 568, 80 S.Ct. 1343. Even when the arbitrator's award may properly be vacated, the appropriate remedy is to remand the case for further arbitration proceedings. *Misco, supra*, at 40, n. 10, 108 S.Ct. 364. The dissent suggests that the remedy described in *Misco* is limited to cases where the arbitrator's errors are procedural. *Post*, at 512 (opinion of STEVENS, J.). *Misco* did involve procedural issues, but our discussion regarding the appropriate remedy was not so limited. If a remand is appropriate even when the arbitrator's award has been set aside for "procedural aberrations" that constitute "affirmative misconduct," it follows that a remand ordinarily will be appropriate when the arbitrator simply made factual findings that the reviewing court perceives as "irrational." The Court of Appeals usurped the arbitrator's role by resolving the dispute and barring further proceedings, a result at odds with this governing law.[2]

For the foregoing reasons, the Court of Appeals erred in reversing the order of the District Court denying the motion to vacate the arbitrator's award, and it erred further in directing that judgment be entered in Garvey's favor. The judgment of the Court of Appeals is reversed, and the case is remanded for further proceedings consistent with this opinion.

It is so ordered.

JUSTICE GINSBURG, concurring in part and concurring in the judgment.

I agree with the Court that in *Garvey v. Roberts*, 203 F.3d 580 (9th Cir.2000) (*Garvey I*), the Ninth Circuit should not have disturbed the arbitrator's award. Correction of that error sets this case straight. I see no need to say more.

JUSTICE STEVENS, dissenting.

It is well settled that an arbitrator "does not sit to dispense his own brand of industrial justice." *Steelworkers v. Enterprise Wheel & Car Corp.*, 363 U.S. 593, 597, 80 S.Ct. 1358, 4 L.Ed.2d 1424 (1960). We have also said fairly definitively, albeit in dicta, that a court should remedy an arbitrator's "procedural aberrations" by vacating the award and remanding for further proceedings. *Paperworkers v. Misco, Inc.*, 484 U.S. 29, 40–41, n. 10, 108 S.Ct. 364, 98 L.Ed.2d 286 (1987). Our cases, however, do not provide significant guidance as to what standards a federal court should use in assessing whether an arbitrator's behavior is so untethered to either the agreement of the parties or the factual record so as to constitute an attempt to "dispense his own brand of industrial justice." Nor, more importantly, do they tell us how, having made such a finding, courts should deal with "the extraordinary circumstance in which the arbitrator's own rulings make clear that, more than being simply erroneous, his finding is completely inexplicable and borders on the irrational." *Garvey v. Roberts*, 203 F.3d 580, 590 (9th Cir.2000) (case below). Because our caselaw is not sufficiently clear to allow me to conclude that the case below was wrongly decided—let alone to conclude that the decision was so wrong as to require the extraordinary remedy of a summary reversal—I dissent from the Court's disposition of this petition.

---

2. In any event, no serious error on the arbitrator's part is apparent in this case. The fact that an earlier panel of arbitrators rejected the owners' testimony as a whole does not compel the conclusion that the panel found Smith's specific statements with respect to Garvey to be false. The arbitrator's explanation for his decision indicates that he simply found Smith an unreliable witness and that, in the absence of corroborating evidence, he could only conclude that Garvey failed to show that the Padres had offered to extend his contract. The arbitrator's analysis may have been unpersuasive to the Court of Appeals, but his decision hardly qualifies as serious error, let alone irrational or inexplicable error. And, as we have said, any such error would not justify the actions taken by the court.

Without the benefit of briefing or argument, today the Court resolves two difficult questions. First, it decides that even if the Court of Appeals' appraisal of the merits is correct—that is to say, even if the arbitrator did dispense his own brand of justice untethered to the agreement of the parties, and even if the correct disposition of the matter is perfectly clear—the only course open to a reviewing court is to remand the matter for another arbitration. That conclusion is not compelled by any of our cases, nor by any analysis offered by the Court. As the issue is subject to serious arguments on both sides, the Court should have set this case for argument if it wanted to answer this remedial question.

Second, without reviewing the record or soliciting briefing, the Court concludes that, in any event, "no serious error on the arbitrator's part is apparent in this case." *Ante*, at 511, n. 2. At this stage in the proceedings, I simply cannot endorse that conclusion. After examining the record, obtaining briefing, and hearing oral argument, the Court of Appeals offered a reasoned explanation of its conclusion. See 203 F.3d, at 589–592; see also *id.*, at 593–594 (Hawkins, J., concurring). Whether or not I would ultimately agree with the Ninth Circuit's analysis, I find the Court's willingness to reverse a factbound determination of the Court of Appeals without engaging that court's reasoning a troubling departure from our normal practice.[1]

Accordingly, I respectfully dissent.

Notes and Questions

1. In petitioning for certiorari, lawyers for the Players Association said that the Ninth Circuit's decision in *Garvey* was so clearly erroneous that it warranted a summary reversal. 2001 WL 34091962. Counsel for Garvey contended that the Ninth Circuit's decision was consistent with Supreme Court precedent and, in any case, so dependent upon its unique facts that Supreme Court review was unwarranted. 2001 WL 34090262. An amicus brief by Professor David Feller, on behalf of the National Academy of Arbitrators, told the Court that, although the case did have its unique facts, it was an example of an egregious pattern in the lower federal courts:

> Many of the lower federal courts have adopted a simple formula when faced with a decision with which they disagree: First set out the correct rule that a court has no business vacating an arbitration award simply because it believes it to be wrong. Cite *Enterprise* and *Misco*. Then, go ahead and find some reason why the particular award involved nevertheless has to be set aside because it is wrong.

2001 WL 34091989. Professor Feller agreed with the Players Association that oral argument was unnecessary, but, unlike the Association, he suggest-

---

1. The Court's opinion is somewhat ambiguous as to its reasons for overturning the portion of the Court of Appeals' decision setting aside the arbitration. It is unclear whether the majority is saying that a court may never set aside an arbitration because of a factual error, no matter how perverse, or whether the Court merely holds that the error in this case was not sufficiently severe to allow a court to take that step. If it is the latter, the Court offers no explanation of what standards it is using or of its reasons for reaching that conclusion.

ed that the lower courts needed stronger chastisement than a summary reversal would provide. He encouraged the Supreme Court to remind the lower courts at least every decade of the degree of deference required by *Misco*. He therefore urged the Court to do what it ended up doing in *Garvey*, that is, dispensing with further briefing and oral argument and issuing an explanatory per curiam opinion. (Professor Feller's brief also asked the Court to order briefing and oral argument on the question of whether the Federal Arbitration Act was applicable to judicial review of collective bargaining agreements, a request the Court did not grant.)

While *Garvey* seems to have produced its intended effect of increasing judicial deference, some courts continue to reassess arbitral fact-finding, engage in independent contract interpretation, and make judicial determinations of remedy. See, for example, American Eagle Airlines, Inc. v. Air Line Pilots Ass'n, International, 343 F.3d 401 (5th Cir. 2003), cert. denied, ___ U.S. ___, 124 S.Ct. 1655, 158 L.Ed.2d 355 (2004) and Citgo Asphalt Refining Co. v. Paper, Allied–Industrial, Chemical & Energy Workers Int'l Union, 385 F.3d 809 (3d Cir. 2004). The Ninth Circuit described *Garvey* with this sardonic statement: "The Supreme Court recently reminded us that it's not enough to recite the correct legal standard; we must actually apply it." Abovian v. I.N.S., 257 F.3d 971, 971 n.1 (9th Cir. 2001).

2. In *Misco*, the Court said that courts should not disregard an arbitrator's factual findings even if they are improvident or silly (Part II.B. of the Opinion). The *Misco* Court also said that a court was not to reject an arbitrator's factual findings merely because the Court disagreed with them (Part II.A. of the Opinion). Did the majority opinion in *Garvey* narrow, reaffirm or broaden the standard for judicial review of arbitral fact finding articulated in *Misco*? Does *Garvey* make *Misco*'s standard for judicial review of fact finding more or less clear than it was before *Garvey*? See Footnote 1 in Justice Stevens opinion. Do you agree with his assessment there of the majority opinion?

3. The Court of Appeals in *Garvey* thought that the arbitrator's fact finding was irrational; the Supreme Court thought not. Does it matter? After *Garvey*, may a court overturn an arbitrator's irrational finding of fact?

4. If an arbitrator concludes that an employee discharged for misconduct is unlikely to engage again in misconduct if reinstated, is such a conclusion a finding of fact wholly insulated from judicial review? If so, will an award escape vacation on the grounds of public policy anytime an arbitrator makes such a finding?

5. The *Garvey* Court reaffirms the language in *Enterprise Wheel* that a court may overturn an award in which the arbitrator is dispensing the arbitrator's "own brand of industrial justice." After *Garvey*, can an arbitrator's erroneous fact finding be the basis of a conclusion that an arbitrator was dispensing a personal sense of justice rather than interpreting and applying an agreement? What's left of the "own brand of industrial justice" standard after *Garvey*?

6. The Supreme Court majority noted that while the Ninth Circuit had correctly articulated the standards for judicial review, its application of them was "baffling." Is the problem that the Ninth Circuit didn't understand the Supreme Court's directives or that it its sense of justice precluded it from

exercising the degree of restraint the Supreme Court decisions commanded? See Note 7 following *Enterprise Wheel*.

7. The Supreme Court's *Garvey* majority states that when an arbitrator's award properly may be vacated, "the appropriate remedy is to remand the case for further arbitration proceedings," not to decide it on the merits as the Court of Appeals did in *Garvey II*.

(a) Compare the remedy in *Garvey* with the remedy used by the Supreme Court for cases in which an arbitrator is thought to have reached an erroneous result because of a union's breach of the duty of fair representation in its representation of an employee. In *Vaca v. Sipes*, 386 U.S. 171, 87 S.Ct. 903, 17 L.Ed.2d 842 (1967), *infra* Chapter V.A., the Court held that if a court, in deciding a DFR case, substantially determined the underlying contract claim, the court would be free to decide the contract claim and award damages or to remand the case to an arbitrator. Is there any reason why a court should have less remedial discretion in a § 301 case than in a DFR case?

(b) Justice Stevens in part objects to the majority's remedial limitation on the ground that the majority resolved the issue without oral argument that might have highlighted the arguments on each side. What are the arguments on each side? Which are more persuasive?

D. INJUNCTIONS[1]

The 1932 Norris–LaGuardia Act, 29 U.S.C. § 101, Appendix B., *infra*, was one of the earliest pieces of federal labor legislation. Unlike later federal legislation, such as the National Labor Relations Act, which defined substantive rights of labor and management, the operative language of the Norris–LaGuardia Act only restricted federal courts' issuance of injunctions in labor cases. Congress focused upon the injunction because Congress was persuaded that federal judges, narrowly defining the rights of labor in the course of issuing injunctions, had effectively precluded union organization and collective action.[2]

The Norris–LaGuardia Act denied federal courts jurisdiction to issue injunctions in "labor disputes" absent a showing that unlawful acts or property damage were threatened and would occur. The statute included

1. Bibliographic Suggestions: Robert A. Gorman and Matthew W. Finkin, Basic Text on Labor Law: Unionization and Collective Bargaining §§ 26.1–26.7 (2004). James B. Atleson, *The Circle of* Boys Market: *A Comment on Judicial Inventiveness*, 7 Industrial Relations Law Journal 88 (1985); Jonathan G. Axelrod, *The Application of the* Boys Markets *Decision in the Federal Courts*, 16 Boston College Industrial and Commerce Law Review 893 (1975); Norman L. Cantor, Buffalo Forge *and Injunctions Against Employer Breaches of Collective Bargaining Agreements*, 1980 Wisconsin Law Review 247; William B.

Gould, *On Labor Injunctions, Unions and the Judges: The* Boys Markets *Case*, 1970 Supreme Court Review 215; William B. Gould, *On Labor Injunctions Pending Arbitration: Recasting* Buffalo Forge, 30 Stanford Law Review 533 (1978); Eileen Silverstein, *Collective Action, Property Rights and Law Reform: The Story of the Labor Injunction*, 11 Hofstra Labor Law Journal 97 (1993); Stephen C. Vladeck, Boys Markets *and National Labor Policy*, 24 Vanderbilt Law Review 93 (1970).

2. See, Felix Frankfurter and Nathan Greene, The Labor Injunction (1930).

a very broad definition of "labor dispute." Even in cases of violence, the Act prohibited enjoining conduct that the Act defined as lawful labor activity such as joining labor organizations and participating in peaceful strikes. The Act also imposed strict procedural limitations on labor injunctions, including provisions to ensure fair notice and hearing and narrowly drafted injunctive orders.

In 1935, when Congress enacted the National Labor Relations Act, it included specific language to make clear that federal courts acting under the NLRA would not be governed by the anti-injunction provisions of Norris–LaGuardia. NLRA § 10(h), 29 U.S.C. § 160(h). In 1947, however, when Congress enacted the Labor Management Relations Act, including § 301, creating jurisdiction in the federal courts to enforce collective bargaining agreements, it made no reference to Norris–LaGuardia. To what extent would federal courts, acting in this new role, be free to issue injunctions?

The Supreme Court initially confronted the interrelationship between the Norris–LaGuardia Act and § 301 in Textile Workers Union v. Lincoln Mills, 353 U.S. 448, 77 S.Ct. 912, 1 L.Ed.2d 972 (1957), see Chapter III. A.2, *supra*. The issue there was whether the anti-injunction statute precluded a federal court from ordering an employer specifically to perform its agreement to arbitrate grievances. In *Lincoln Mills*, the Court acknowledged that the language of the statute was broad enough to encompass such a dispute. It said, however, that "[t]he failure to arbitrate was not a part and parcel of the abuses against which the Act was aimed." It concluded that congressional policy favoring peaceful resolution of labor disputes precluded reading the statute to bar effective judicial enforcement of arbitration provisions.

In *Lincoln Mills*, it was relatively simple to say that a statute written to prevent employers from obtaining injunctions against peaceful union strike activity did not apply to injunctions obtained by unions to compel employers to arbitrate. A much more difficult question was whether the Norris–LaGuardia Act would preclude federal courts from issuing injunctions against peaceful union strikes over arbitrable grievances.

In 1962, in Sinclair Refining Co. v. Atkinson, 370 U.S. 195, 82 S.Ct. 1328, 8 L.Ed.2d 440, the Supreme Court held that the Norris–LaGuardia Act denied a federal court jurisdiction to enjoin a union's strike over an arbitrable grievance. Eight years later, in *Boys Markets*, the Court overturned *Sinclair*.

BOYS MARKETS, INC. v. RETAIL CLERKS UNION, LOCAL 770
Supreme Court of the United States, 1970.
398 U.S. 235, 90 S.Ct. 1583, 26 L.Ed.2d 199.

MR. JUSTICE BRENNAN delivered the opinion of the Court.

[The contract between the Union and Boys Markets had broad arbitration and no-strike provisions. The Union objected to the employer permitting nonmembers of the bargaining unit to rearrange frozen food in a grocery case. The Union struck when the employer refused to have the food case stripped and restocked by Union personnel. The Market obtained a temporary restraining order against the strike in state court, but shortly thereafter the Union removed the case to federal district court. The federal trial court enjoined the strike and ordered the parties to arbitrate the dispute. The court of appeals reversed, relying upon *Sinclair*.]

[The Supreme Court majority, in an opinion by Justice Brennan, thought it appropriate to reconsider *Sinclair*, despite the recency of the decision, for several reasons. The Court saw *Sinclair* interfering with promotion of peaceful settlement of disputes through arbitration. It thought an intervening decision permitting removal of labor cases to federal court effectively would deprive state courts of jurisdiction of labor cases. It rejected the idea that congressional silence in the wake of *Sinclair* should be construed as concurrence in the decision.]

[The Supreme Court reviewed its decisions since *Lincoln Mills* articulating the federal common law governing labor arbitration, including Charles Dowd Box Co. v. Courtney, 368 U.S. 502, 82 S.Ct. 519 (1962), holding that Congress intended state courts to have concurrent jurisdiction of § 301 cases enforcing collective bargaining agreements, and Avco Corp. v. Aero Lodge No. 735, 390 U.S. 557, 88 S.Ct. 1235 (1968), holding that § 301 actions filed in state courts could be removed to federal courts.]

The decision in *Avco*, viewed in the context of *Lincoln Mills* and its progeny, has produced an anomalous situation which, in our view, makes urgent the reconsideration of *Sinclair*. The principal practical effect of *Avco* and *Sinclair* taken together is nothing less than to oust state courts of jurisdiction in § 301(a) suits where injunctive relief is sought for breach of a no-strike obligation. Union defendants can, as a matter of course, obtain removal to a federal court, and there is obviously a compelling incentive for them to do so in order to gain the advantage of the strictures upon injunctive relief which *Sinclair* imposes on federal courts. The sanctioning of this practice, however, is wholly inconsistent with our conclusion in *Dowd Box* that the congressional purpose embodied in § 301(a) was to *supplement*, and not to encroach upon, the pre-existing jurisdiction of the state courts. It is ironic indeed that the very provision that Congress clearly intended to provide additional remedies for breach of collective-bargaining agreements has been employed to displace previously existing state remedies. We are not at liberty thus to depart from the clearly expressed congressional policy to the contrary.

On the other hand, to the extent that widely disparate remedies theoretically remain available in state, as opposed to federal, courts, the federal policy of labor law uniformity elaborated in *Lucas Flour Co.*, is seriously offended. This policy, of course, could hardly require, as a practical matter, that labor law be administered identically in all courts, for undoubtedly a certain diversity exists among the state and federal systems in matters of procedural and remedial detail, a fact that Congress evidently took into account in deciding not to disturb the traditional jurisdiction of the States. The injunction, however, is so important a remedial device, particularly in the arbitration context, that its availability or nonavailability in various courts will not only produce rampant forum shopping and maneuvering from one court to another but will also greatly frustrate any relative uniformity in the enforcement of arbitration agreements.

Furthermore, the existing scheme, with the injunction remedy technically available in the state courts but rendered inefficacious by the removal device, assigns to removal proceedings a totally unintended function. While the underlying purposes of Congress in providing for federal question removal jurisdiction remain somewhat obscure, there has never been a serious contention that Congress intended that the removal mechanism be utilized to foreclose completely remedies otherwise available in the state courts. Although federal question removal jurisdiction may well have been intended to provide a forum for the protection of federal rights where such protection was deemed necessary or to encourage the development of expertise by the federal courts in the interpretation of federal law, there is no indication that Congress intended by the removal mechanism to effect a wholesale dislocation in the allocation of judicial business between the state and federal courts. Cf. City of Greenwood v. Peacock, 384 U.S. 808, 86 S.Ct. 1800, 16 L.Ed.2d 944 (1966).

It is undoubtedly true that each of the foregoing objections to *Sinclair–Avco* could be remedied either by overruling *Sinclair* or by extending that decision to the States. While some commentators have suggested that the solution to the present unsatisfactory situation does lie in the extension of the *Sinclair* prohibition to state court proceedings, we agree with Chief Justice Traynor of the California Supreme Court that "whether or not Congress could deprive state courts of the power to give such [injunctive] remedies when enforcing collective bargaining agreements, it has not attempted to do so either in the Norris–LaGuardia Act or section 301." McCarroll v. Los Angeles County Dist. Council of Carpenters, 49 Cal.2d 45, 63, 315 P.2d 322, 332 (1957), cert. denied, 355 U.S. 932, 78 S.Ct. 413, 2 L.Ed.2d 415 (1958). * * *

An additional reason for not resolving the existing dilemma by extending *Sinclair* to the States is the devastating implications for the enforceability of arbitration agreements and their accompanying no-strike obligations if equitable remedies were not available.[15] As we have previously indicated, a no-strike obligation, express or implied, is the *quid pro quo* for an undertaking by the employer to submit grievance

15. It is true that about one-half of the States have enacted so-called "little Norris–LaGuardia Acts" that place various restrictions upon the granting of injunctions by state courts in labor disputes. However, because many States do not bar injunctive relief for violations of collective-bargaining agreements, in only about 14 jurisdictions is there a significant Norris–LaGuardia–type prohibition against equitable remedies for breach of no-strike obligations.

disputes to the process of arbitration. See Textile Workers Union v. Lincoln Mills, *supra*, 353 U.S., at 455, 77 S.Ct. at 917. Any incentive for employers to enter into such an arrangement is necessarily dissipated if the principal and most expeditious method by which the no-strike obligation can be enforced is eliminated. While it is of course true, as respondent contends, that other avenues of redress, such as an action for damages, would remain open to an aggrieved employer, an award of damages after a dispute has been settled is no substitute for an immediate halt to an illegal strike. Furthermore, an action for damages prosecuted during or after a labor dispute would only tend to aggravate industrial strife and delay an early resolution of the difficulties between employer and union.

Even if management is not encouraged by the unavailability of the injunction remedy to resist arbitration agreements, the fact remains that the effectiveness of such agreements would be greatly reduced if injunctive relief were withheld. Indeed, the very purpose of arbitration procedures is to provide a mechanism for the expeditious settlement of industrial disputes without resort to strikes, lockouts, or other self-help measures. This basic purpose is obviously largely undercut if there is no immediate, effective remedy for those very tactics that arbitration is designed to obviate. Thus, because *Sinclair*, in the aftermath of *Avco*, casts serious doubt upon the effective enforcement of a vital element of stable labor-management relations—arbitration agreements with their attendant no-strike obligations—we conclude that *Sinclair* does not make a viable contribution to federal labor policy.

IV

We have also determined that the dissenting opinion in *Sinclair* states the correct principles concerning the accommodation necessary between the seemingly absolute terms of the Norris–LaGuardia Act and the policy considerations underlying § 301(a). * * *

The literal terms of § 4 of the Norris–LaGuardia Act must be accommodated to the subsequently enacted provisions of § 301(a) of the Labor Management Relations Act and the purposes of arbitration. Statutory interpretation requires more than concentration upon isolated words; rather, consideration must be given to the total corpus of pertinent law and the policies that inspired ostensibly inconsistent provisions. * * *

The Norris–LaGuardia Act was responsive to a situation totally different from that which exists today. In the early part of this century, the federal courts generally were regarded as allies of management in its attempt to prevent the organization and strengthening of labor unions; and in this industrial struggle the injunction became a potent weapon that was wielded against the activities of labor groups. The result was a large number of sweeping decrees, often issued *ex parte*, drawn on an *ad hoc* basis without regard to any systematic elaboration of national labor policy. * * *

In 1932 Congress attempted to bring some order out of the industrial chaos that had developed and to correct the abuses that had resulted from the interjection of the federal judiciary into union-management disputes on the behalf of management. See declaration of public policy, Norris–LaGuardia Act, § 2, 47 Stat. 70. Congress, therefore, determined initially to limit severely the power of the federal courts to issue injunctions "in any case involving or growing out of any labor dispute * * *." § 4, 47 Stat. 70. Even as initially enacted, however, the prohibition against federal injunctions was by no means absolute. See Norris–LaGuardia Act, §§ 7, 8, 9, 47 Stat. 71, 72. Shortly thereafter Congress passed the Wagner Act, designed to curb various management activities that tended to discourage employee participation in collective action.

As labor organizations grew in strength and developed toward maturity, congressional emphasis shifted from protection of the nascent labor movement to the encouragement of collective bargaining and to administrative techniques for the peaceful resolution of industrial disputes. This shift in emphasis was accomplished, however, without extensive revision of many of the older enactments, including the anti-injunction section of the Norris–LaGuardia Act. Thus it became the task of the courts to accommodate, to reconcile the older statutes with the more recent ones. * * *

The *Sinclair* decision, however, seriously undermined the effectiveness of the arbitration technique as a method peacefully to resolve industrial disputes without resort to strikes, lockouts, and similar devices. Clearly employers will be wary of assuming obligations to arbitrate specifically enforceable against them when no similarly efficacious remedy is available to enforce the concomitant undertaking of the union to refrain from striking. On the other hand, the central purpose of the Norris–LaGuardia Act to foster the growth and viability of labor organizations is hardly retarded—if anything, this goal is advanced—by a remedial device that merely enforces the obligation that the union freely undertook under a specifically enforceable agreement to submit disputes to arbitration. We conclude, therefore, that the unavailability of equitable relief in the arbitration context presents a serious impediment to the congressional policy favoring the voluntary establishment of a mechanism for the peaceful resolution of labor disputes, that the core purpose of the-LaGuardia Act is not sacrificed by the limited use of equitable remedies to further this important policy, and consequently that the Norris–LaGuardia Act does not bar the granting of injunctive relief in the circumstances of the instant case.

V

Our holding in the present case is a narrow one. We do not undermine the vitality of the Norris–LaGuardia Act. We deal only with the situation in which a collective-bargaining contract contains a mandatory grievance adjustment or arbitration procedure. Nor does it follow from what we have said that injunctive relief is appropriate as a matter of course in every case of a strike over an arbitrable grievance. The dissenting opinion in *Sinclair* suggested the following principles for the guidance of the district courts in determining whether to grant injunctive relief—principles that we now adopt:

> A District Court entertaining an action under § 301 may not grant injunctive relief against concerted activity unless and until it decides that the case is one in which an injunction would be appropriate despite the Norris–LaGuardia Act. When a strike is sought to be enjoined because it is over a grievance which both parties are contractually bound to arbitrate, the District Court may issue no injunctive order until it first holds that the contract *does* have that effect; and the employer should be ordered to arbitrate, as a condition of his obtaining an injunction against the strike. Beyond this, the District Court must, of course, consider whether issuance of an injunction would be warranted under ordinary principles of equity—whether breaches are occurring and will continue, or have been threatened and will be committed; whether they have caused or will cause irreparable injury to the employer; and whether the employer will suffer more from the denial of an injunction than will the union from its issuance. 370 U.S., at 228, 82 S.Ct., at 1346. (Emphasis in original.)

In the present case there is no dispute that the grievance in question was subject to adjustment and arbitration under the collective-bargaining agreement and that the petitioner was ready to proceed with arbitration at the time an injunction against the strike was sought and obtained. The District Court also concluded that, by reason of respondent's violations of its no-strike obligation, petitioner "has suffered irreparable injury and will continue to suffer irreparable injury." Since we now overrule *Sinclair*, the holding of the Court of Appeals in reliance on *Sinclair* must be reversed. Accordingly, we reverse the judgment of the Court of Appeals and remand the case with directions to enter a judgment affirming the order of the District Court.

It is so ordered.

[Justice Marshall took no part in the decision of the case. Justice Stewart concurred, agreeing with the majority opinion despite having earlier joined in the majority opinion in *Sinclair*. Justice Black dissented, maintaining that by altering its interpretation of the Norris–LaGuardia Act, the Court was usurping a legislative function. He noted that Congress had not enacted introduced bills to overturn *Sinclair*. He stated that correct interpretation of labor laws was less important than the proper division of functions between branches of government. Justice White dissented, relying upon the expression of his views in the majority opinion in *Sinclair*.]

Notes and Questions

1. Was the Court correct, in *Boys Markets*, in overruling *Sinclair*? Are the factors to be taken into account in overruling an interpretation of a

statute different from those considered in overruling an interpretation of the Constitution? How?

2.   To what extent will traditional equitable doctrines limit the granting of injunctions under *Boys Markets*?

3.   To what extent, if any, are other limits of the Norris–LaGuardia Act applicable to the granting of *Boys Markets* injunctions? For example, must a *Boys Markets* injunction comply with § 7 of Norris–LaGuardia (prohibiting *ex parte* hearings), § 8 (requiring reasonable efforts of settlement) or § 9 (requiring fact findings and narrowly written injunctive orders)? The text of the Act is included in Appendix B, *infra*.

4.   One of the reasons the Supreme Court offered in *Boys Markets* for overruling *Sinclair* was that if injunctions were unavailable, employers would "be wary of assuming obligations to arbitrate specifically enforceable against them." 398 U.S. at 252, 905 S.Ct. at 1593. Professor Atleson contends that the Supreme Court's assumption of employer behavior was demonstrably incorrect. He reports that two years after *Sinclair* there were arbitration provisions in 94% of collective bargaining agreements and that the number of arbitration provisions continued to grow after the decision. James B. Atleson, footnote 1, *supra* at 102.

A NOTE ON *BUFFALO FORGE*

Six years after *Boys Markets*, the Court, in a 5–4 decision, declined to expand the implied exception to the injunction restrictions of the Norris–LaGuardia Act to permit a federal court to enjoin a sympathy strike. In Buffalo Forge Co. v. United Steelworkers of America, 428 U.S. 397, 96 S.Ct. 3141, 49 L.Ed.2d 1022 (1976), the Steelworkers Union represented employees in two separate units, one with production and maintenance employees (P & M) and one with office clerical-technical personnel (O & T). The contract covering the P & M employees had a broad no-strike provision. The Union had recently organized the O & T employees and was bargaining for their initial collective bargaining agreement. When the O & T employees struck in support of their contract demands, P & M employees honored the picket lines. The employer brought an action in federal district court against the Union under § 301, seeking to enjoin the strike by the P & M employees.

The parties disagreed about whether the no-strike provision in the P & M contract prohibited the sympathy strike. The Court said that issue was for an arbitrator to decide, but that the issue before the Court was whether the strike could be enjoined pending that arbitration. The Court majority, in an opinion by Justice White, construed the holding of *Boys Markets* as a "narrow one," dealing only with the situation in which the strike is over a dispute subject to arbitration. Norris–LaGuardia's anti-injunction policy should be accommodated to § 301 only to the extent necessary to prevent strikes over arbitrable grievances where the strike would interfere with the arbitration process. The Court said this strike was not over an arbitrable grievance. The arbitrator would have no authority to decide the merits of the dispute over the terms of the contract covering O & T employees. The strike had neither the purpose nor effect of evading arbitration. Nor was an injunction available because of the allegation that the strike violated the contract. If federal courts were empowered to enjoin contract violations, contract disputes would be resolved in the courts, rather than in the arbitral forum chosen by the parties.

Justice Stevens, joined by three other members of the Court, including liberal justices Brennan and Marshall, dissented. The dissenters thought Norris–LaGuardia no barrier to specific enforcement of a contractual no-strike obligation. If the contract clearly prohibits the strike, there is no reason to await the arbitrator's decision. The dissenters thought that federal labor law afforded the employer enforcement of its contractual promise of uninterrupted production.

Notes and Questions

1. Is *Warrior & Gulf*'s test of "arguably arbitrable" the proper one to determine arbitrability for the purpose of determining the availability of injunctions under *Boys Markets* and *Buffalo Forge*? Chicago Dist. Council of Carpenters Pension Fund v. K & I Construction, Inc., 270 F.3d 1060 (7th Cir. 2001) (yes); Allied Systems Ltd. v. Teamsters, 179 F.3d 982 (6th Cir.), cert. denied, 528 U.S. 965, 120 S.Ct. 401, 145 L.Ed.2d 313 (1999) (no) (no injunction can issue against a strike where the union presents a colorable argument that a provision of the agreement precludes arbitration of the underlying claim); Standard Food Prods. Corp. v. Brandenburg, 436 F.2d 964 (2d Cir.1970) (same).

2. Assume a contract has a broad arbitration provision, but *no* no-strike provision. The union calls a strike over an *arbitrable* grievance. May a federal court enjoin the strike? See Gateway Coal Co. v. United Mine Workers, 414 U.S. 368, 94 S.Ct. 629, 38 L.Ed.2d 583 (1974). May the employees participating in the strike be discharged? May the employer obtain damages from the union?

3. Assume a contract has a broad no-strike clause. The union calls a strike over a *non-arbitrable* issue. May the strike be enjoined in federal court? May the employees participating in the strike be discharged? May the employer obtain damages from the union?

4. If, in question 2 or 3 above, the employer has a right to damages from the union, may the employer pursue its damage remedy in litigation, or is it obligated to arbitrate its damage claim? Some courts have ordered employers to arbitrate on the basis of the general presumption of arbitrability, Domino Sugar Corp. v. Sugar Workers Local 392, 10 F.3d 1064 (4th Cir.1993), while others have inferred from the typical language of arbitration clauses speaking only of grievances submitted by unions, that employers are not required to arbitrate damage claims, Rental Services Corp. v. Operating Engineers, Local 150, 1999 WL 1144904 (N.D.Ill. 1999); United Parcel Service, Inc. v. Teamsters Local 705, 1998 WL 699670, 159 LRRM 2968 (N.D.Ill.1998).

5. Suppose Buffalo Forge filed a grievance alleging that the union's sympathy strike violated the collective bargaining agreement. Following

expedited arbitration, the arbitrator concluded that the strike violated the agreement, but the strike continued. May a court now enjoin the strike?

6.   The contract between the Union and the Employer contains broad arbitration and no-strike provisions. The Union calls a strike over an arbitrable issue. If the Employer brings an action in state court to enjoin the strike, may the state court issue the injunction? What would have been the surest way for the Employer to avoid the possibility of denial of an injunction?

7.   The contract between the Union and the Employer contains broad arbitration and no-strike provisions. The Union calls a strike over a non-arbitrable issue. The Employer brings an action in state court to enjoin the strike and the state court issues the injunction. Should the state court injunction be overturned on appeal? Could the Union, even more easily, end the injunction by removing the case to federal court? Does the Union's ability to remove the case to federal court undermine the Supreme Court's reliance in *Boys Markets* on *Avco* as a basis for overturning *Sinclair*?

8.   Judge Michael Boudin of the First Circuit has said:

> If this [curtailment of equitable relief] seems an eccentric limitation on a useful remedy now customarily available to litigants, the short answer is that the Norris–LaGuardia Act reflects a unique historical experience. See Frankfurter & Greene, The Labor Injunction (1930). Perceived judicial abuses gave rise to severe restrictions on federal court authority; and the restrictions, being statutory, persist even though the climate that led to abuses has altered. Courts have assumed a lot of authority in recent years, but the authority to repeal statutes still belongs to Congress.

Tejidos de Coamo, Inc. v. International Ladies' Garment Workers' Union, 22 F.3d 8, 15 (1st Cir. 1994). Is Judge Boudin right that the Norris–LaGuardia Act is an anachronism? If so, why hasn't it been repealed by Congress?

9.   *Reverse Boys Market Injunctions.* The contract between the Union and the Manufacturing Company contains an arbitration provision covering "all grievances and disputes" between the parties. The Company has always scheduled each employee to one of three shifts: the day, evening or night shift. The Manufacturing Company has announced that next month all employees will be assigned to work teams that will rotate every two weeks among the day, evening and night shifts. The Union has filed a grievance with the Employer alleging that the schedule change violates the collective bargaining agreement. Employees are complaining about the significant disruption to their lives that will result from the rotating shifts including difficulties with child care, the necessity of quitting second jobs, and health problems. The Union brings an action in federal district court to enjoin the change in schedules pending arbitration of its grievance.

Does the Norris–LaGuardia Act prevent the court from issuing the injunction? Was the Norris–LaGuardia Act designed to protect employers from injunctions? Does the employer have an implied duty to maintain the status quo pending arbitration, just as the union has an implied duty not to strike pending arbitration? Would your answer be different if the grievance arose from the employer's announcement that it was closing the plant and moving all the machinery to another facility? If the Norris–LaGuardia Act does permit a federal court to enjoin employer action pending arbitration, must the union prove a likelihood of success on the merits in order to obtain an injunction? Independent Oil & Chemical Workers v. Procter & Gamble, 864 F.2d 927 (1st Cir.1988). See also Communications Workers of America v. Verizon Communications, Inc., 255 F.Supp.2d 479 (E.D.Pa. 2003); IUE–CWA, Local 628 v. Flowserve Corp., 239 F.Supp.2d 527 (M.D.Pa.2003); Local Union 15, IBEW v. Exelon Corp., 191 F.Supp.2d 987 (N.D.Ill.2001); Teamsters Local Union 299 v. U.S. Truck Co. Holdings, Inc., 87 F.Supp.2d 726 (E.D.Mich.2000); Norman L. Cantor, footnote 1 *supra*; and William P. Kratzke, *Enjoining Employers Pending Arbitration: Some Misconceptions and Clarifications*, 24 St. Louis University Law Journal 92 (1979).

10. An employer's successful effort to exclude a matter from a contract's arbitration clause can have unintended consequences for the employer with regard to its protection from injunctions. In Aeronautical Industrial District Lodge 91 v. United Technologies Corp., 230 F.3d 569 (2d Cir. 2000), the employer agreed to a contract provision obligating itself to "make every effort to preserve the work" of bargaining unit employees but insisted that the provision not be subject to arbitration. Later, when the employer proposed to transfer bargaining unit work the union was able to enjoin the employer's action because violations of that provision were not arbitrable. The court held that an injunction under such circumstances did not violate the intent of either the Norris–LaGuardia Act or § 301.

A FURTHER NOTE ON INJUNCTIONS AND NO–STRIKE OBLIGATIONS

While the focus of this Section is on injunctions related to the arbitration process, decisionmaking by a union contemplating a strike and an employer facing a strike needs to take into account other legal rules apart from the availability of injunctions. Decisions by the United States Supreme Court have further defined the scope of *Boys Markets* and *Buffalo Forge* and the rights and responsibilities of unions and employers when strikes occur.

In Jacksonville Bulk Terminals, Inc. v. International Longshoremen's Association, 457 U.S. 702, 102 S.Ct. 2672, 73 L.Ed.2d 327 (1982), the Supreme Court held that the anti-injunction provisions of the Norris–LaGuardia Act apply to politically motivated work stoppages (union refusal to handle Russian cargo to protest Russian intervention in Afghanistan), and that such stoppages could not be enjoined under § 301 pending an arbitrator's decision on whether the strike violated the labor contract. Neither the language nor the legislative history of Norris–LaGuardia indicates a political motivation exception. Further, held the Court, the *Buffalo Forge* rationale precludes an injunction based on the no-strike clause because the underlying dispute is not arbitrable.

Section 502 of the NLRA, 29 U.S.C. § 143, provides, "nor shall the quitting of labor by an employee or employees in good faith because of abnormally dangerous conditions for work at the place of employment of such employee or employees be deemed a strike under this Act." Section 502 thus creates a limited exception to an express or implied no-strike obligation. Even when employees are covered by a comprehensive no-strike clause in their labor contract, a work stoppage called solely to protect employees against immediate danger is authorized by § 502 and cannot form the basis for either a damage award or injunction. Subjective good faith and honest belief in the existence of abnormally dangerous work conditions does not invoke the protection of § 502. Rather, there must be ascertainable, objective evidence supporting the conclusion that an abnormally dangerous working condition exists. See Gateway Coal Co. v. United Mine Workers, 414 U.S. 368, 94 S.Ct. 629, 38 L.Ed.2d 583 (1974). See also Marshall v. Whirlpool Corp., 593 F.2d 715, 731 (6th Cir.1979), aff'd on other grounds, 445 U.S. 1, 100 S.Ct. 883, 63 L.Ed.2d 154 (1980).

In *Gateway Coal*, the Supreme Court held that § 502 did not protect an employee work stoppage based upon the employees' belief that the foremen's failure to record a reduced air flow in the mines created an abnormally dangerous working condition, where the district court had conditioned injunctive relief on the suspension of the foremen pending arbitration and thereby, in the Court's view, eliminated any safety issue.[3]

In Carbon Fuel Co. v. United Mine Workers of America, 444 U.S. 212, 100 S.Ct. 410, 62 L.Ed.2d 394 (1979), the Supreme Court held that absent a showing of common-law agency responsibility, neither the international union nor its district union were liable in damages for "wildcat" strikes engaged in by the local unions, notwithstanding the failure of the international and district unions to make reasonable efforts to end the strikes. The Court held that liability may only be imposed on an international or district union (1) if the local acted as its agent under a "fundamental agreement of association" or (2) if the international or district "instigated, supported, ratified, or encouraged" the strike.[4]

---

3. Compare Whirlpool Corp. v. Marshall, 445 U.S. 1, 100 S.Ct. 883, 63 L.Ed.2d 154 (1980) (upholding OSHA regulation permitting an employee to refuse a job assignment because of a reasonable apprehension of death or serious injury coupled with a reasonable belief that no less drastic alternative is available). See also Note, *Refusals of Hazardous Work Assignments: A Proposal for a Uniform Standard*, 81 Columbia Law Review 544 (1981). For a recent example, see Airborne Freight Corp. v. Teamsters Local 705, 216 F.Supp.2d 712 (N.D.Ill. 2002) (union's strike over denial of access to water during heat wave was subject to injunction because temperatures had cooled prior to work stoppage).

4. See also Atkinson v. Sinclair Refining Co., 370 U.S. 238, 82 S.Ct. 1318, 8 L.Ed.2d 462 (1962) (individual union officers and members not liable for damages for union breach of no-strike clause); Complete Auto Transit, Inc. v. Reis, 451 U.S. 401, 101 S.Ct. 1836, 68 L.Ed.2d 248 (1981) (individual employees not liable for damages for wildcat strike breaches of no-strike clause); and Jerald R. Cureton and Victor J. Kisch, *Union Liability for Illegal Strikes: The Mass Action Theory Redefined*, 87 West Virginia Law Review 57 (1984–85). When employers have satisfied the legal standards for union responsibility for unlawful strike activity, unions have been ordered to pay hundreds of thousands of dollars in damages. See, for example, R.L. Coolsaet Const. Co. v. Local 150, Operating Engineers, 177 F.3d 648 (7th Cir.), cert. denied, 528 U.S. 1004, 120 S.Ct. 498, 145 L.Ed.2d 384 (1999); Security Farms v. Teamsters, 124 F.3d 999 (9th Cir. 1997); Quick Air Freight, Inc. v. Teamsters Local No. 413, 62 Ohio App.3d 446, 575 N.E.2d 1204 (1989).

In Metropolitan Edison Co. v. NLRB, 460 U.S. 693, 103 S.Ct. 1467, 75 L.Ed.2d 387 (1983), the Supreme Court held that an employer may not discipline union officials more severely than other union employees for participating in an unlawful work stoppage. The Court agreed with the NLRB that such conduct is inherently destructive of protected individual rights in violation of §§ 8(a)(1) and (3) of the NLRA because it discriminates solely based upon union status. It found that an employer's contractual right to be free from an unauthorized strike does not counterbalance the discriminatory effects of particularly harsh treatment. The Court said that imposing greater discipline on union officials may have only an indirect effect on the rank and file's decision to strike but may well deter qualified employees from seeking union office.[5]

Strikes in breach of the no-strike provisions of a collective bargaining contract are generally deemed unprotected under §§ 7 and 8(d) of the NLRA, leaving employees subject to discharge. See NLRB v. Sands Mfg. Co., 306 U.S. 332, 59 S.Ct. 508, 83 L.Ed. 682 (1939). A no-strike clause does not effect a waiver of the right to strike against "serious" unfair labor practices, but will render strikes against "non-serious" practices unprotected.[6]

5. See Note, *Selective Discipline of Union Officials After* Metropolitan Edison v. NLRB, 63 Boston University Law Review 473 (1983).

6. See Mastro Plastics Corp. v. NLRB, 350 U.S. 270, 76 S.Ct. 349, 100 L.Ed. 309 (1956); Arlan's Dep't Store, 133 NLRB 802 (1961); Dow Chem. Co., 244 NLRB 1060 (1979), enf. denied, 636 F.2d 1352 (3d Cir. 1980), cert. denied, 454 U.S. 818, 102 S.Ct. 97, 70 L.Ed.2d 87 (1981).

Chapter IV

DEFERRAL AND PREEMPTION

A. DEFERRAL TO ARBITRATION[1]

1. INTRODUCTION

Most arbitrable workplace grievances only allege violations of the collective bargaining agreement. Sometimes, however, the facts of the grievance also raise issues under state and federal laws, such as those addressing labor relations, health and safety, wages and hours, employment discrimination, and workers' compensation.

What should a government agency do if a dispute that it would otherwise address could be (or has been) sent to an arbitrator? Should an employee be able to pursue the same claim before both the agency and an arbitrator? If not, may the employee choose between the two? Or will the agency insist that one procedural avenue be taken to the exclusion of others? What if an arbitration award has already been rendered? Will the

---

1. Bibliographic Suggestions: The Developing Labor Law, 1365–1449 (Patrick Hardin and John E. Higgins, Jr., eds., 4th ed., 2001) and 326–334 (Howard Z. Rosen, Peter A. Janus and Barry J. Kearney, eds., Supp. 2003); Elkouri & Elkouri, How Arbitration Works, 530–536 (Alan Miles Ruben, ed., 6th ed. 2003); Robert A. Gorman and Matthew W. Finkin, Basic Text on Labor Law: Unionization and Collective Bargaining §§ 31.1–31.11 (2004). Gerald E. Berendt and David A. Youngerman, *The Continuing Controversy over Labor Board Deferral to Arbitration—An Alternative Approach*, 24 Stetson Law Review 175 (1994); Harry T. Edwards, *Deferral to Arbitration and Waiver of the Duty to Bargain: A Possible Way Out of Everlasting Confusion at the NLRB*, 49 Ohio State Law Journal 23 (1985); John H. Fanning and John J. Pendergast, III, *NLRB Deferral Policies*, Labor and Employment Arbitration, (Tim Bornstein, Ann Gosline and Marc D. Greenbaum, eds., 2d ed. 2003); William B. Gould IV, *The NLRB's Deferral to Arbitration Policy*, 10 The Labor Lawyer 719 (1994); Charles J. Morris, *NLRB Deferral to the Arbitration Process: The Arbitrator's Awesome Responsibility*, 7 Industrial Relations Law Journal 290 (1985); Cornelius J. Peck, *A Proposal to End NLRB Deferral to the Arbitration Process*, 60 Washington Law Review 355 (1985); Douglas E. Ray, *Independent Rights and NLRB Deferral to the Arbitration Process: A Proposal*, 28 Boston College Law Review 1 (1986); Calvin William Sharpe, *NLRB Deferral to Grievance–Arbitration: A General Theory*, 48 Ohio State Law Journal 595 (1987); John C. Truesdale, *NLRB Deferral to Arbitration: Still Alive and Kicking*, 53 Proceedings of the National Academy of Arbitrators 55 (2001); Benjamin W. Wolkinson, *The Impact of the* Collyer *Policy of Deferral: An Empirical Study*, 38 Industrial and Labor Relations Review 377 (1985).

agency consider the dispute *de novo*, consider it only if arbitration failed to meet certain minimum standards, or refuse to consider it at all?

This Section addresses the issue of deferral to arbitration, the manner in which institutions coordinate their enforcement of workplace laws with the process of labor arbitration. Subsection 2 focuses upon the National Labor Relations Board's interaction with the arbitration process. Subsection 3 looks at the interaction between labor arbitration and other workplace laws.

2. THE NATIONAL LABOR RELATIONS BOARD

The National Labor Relations Board has two principal statutory functions. Section 8 of the National Labor Relations Act empowers the Board to prevent the commission of unfair labor practices. 29 U.S.C. § 158. Section 9 directs the Board to oversee procedures for designation of exclusive bargaining representatives. 29 U.S.C. § 159.

Some arbitrable workplace disputes also raise issues under Section 8 or 9. A union steward's discharge for use of obscene language while handling an employee grievance, an arguable violation of the "just cause" contract provision, might also be considered discrimination for union activities violating §§ 8(a)(1) and 8(a)(3) of the NLRA. An employer's change in wage rates or subcontracting practices might be challenged as a contract violation or a violation of § 8(a)(5), as unilateral action inconsistent with the employer's duty to bargain in good faith. An employer's refusal to apply a contract's provisions to a new facility could be regarded as a violation of the contract's recognition clause or as a bargaining unit dispute subject to NLRB resolution under § 9.

Sometimes the statutory issue can be resolved independently of the contract language. The NLRB could determine the legality of the discharge of the union steward, for example, exclusively by interpreting the NLRA without having to consider the meaning of the "just cause" contract provision. In other cases, resolution of the statutory issue may depend completely on interpretation of the agreement. For example, deciding whether employer subcontracting is an unlawful unilateral change may turn on whether the employer's action was permitted by the contract's subcontracting provision.

Regardless of whether resolution of the statutory dispute requires interpretation of the collective bargaining agreement, Congress authorized the NLRB to resolve those disputes. Section 10(a) of the NLRA states that the Board's power to prevent unfair labor practices "shall not be affected by any other means of adjustment or prevention that has been or may be established by agreement, law, or otherwise." Although contract interpretation is normally a task for an arbitrator, the Supreme Court has held that it is entirely appropriate for the NLRB to interpret a contract when necessary to resolve an unfair labor practice claim. NLRB v. C & C Plywood Corp., 385 U.S. 421, 87 S.Ct. 559, 17 L.Ed.2d 486 (1967).

To say that the NLRB *may* address a dispute that could be or has been decided by an arbitrator is not, of course, to say that it *should*, let alone that it *must*. The NLRB may have the legal authority to consider an arbitrable dispute, but choose not to do so for policy reasons. NLRB policy development has focused upon two different points at which the deferral issue may arise. The Board's postarbitration deferral policy determines whether, and under what circumstances, the Board will consider disputes already arbitrated. The Board's prearbitration deferral policy defines when the Board will abate its consideration of a case because there is an opportunity to arbitrate. The materials in this Section outline the Board's current policies of arbitral deferral and offer an opportunity to consider both their legality and wisdom.

(a) Postarbitration Deferral

In Spielberg Manufacturing Co., 112 NLRB 1080 (1955), the Board first stated that it would, in appropriate cases, recognize the decision of an arbitrator and decline to decide the merits of an unfair labor practice charge. The NLRB's brief decision in *Spielberg* is still cited today as the origin of the principal requirements of deferral, but the factual context that gives meaning to the holding is often forgotten.

In *Spielberg*, a manufacturer of ladies' handbags had agreed, following a strike, to reinstate all but four employees. The employer claimed that during the strike the four women had used profane language toward company officials and other workers. The employer and the union agreed that the cases of the four employees would be submitted to a "special board of arbitration." The arbitration panel included the company's attorney and a representative of another union that had assisted the union in negotiations during the strike. These two selected as a third member of the arbitration board an accountant who had known the company attorney for twenty years and who had no prior experience in such matters. The company attorney and the accountant had represented mutual clients. The company attorney told the accountant that the proceedings "wouldn't last long" and "would be more or less of a formality." Following a two-hour meeting at which the company president read a statement and the employees were asked some questions, the company attorney and the accountant wrote a decision that merely stated that the company was justified in not reinstating the women. The union representative dissented. At a meeting a few weeks later, the discharged women met with officials of their union and the union that had assisted in the negotiations. An official of the latter union told them, "Well, in a case like this some people have to sacrifice their job to get a union contract in, that is what happened here." He said that they should look upon the loss of their jobs as a "sacrifice for the overall good of the rest of the workers."

The four women filed charges with the NLRB alleging violations of §§ 8(a)(1) and 8(a)(3) of the NLRA. The Trial Examiner who heard the evidence concluded that much of the testimony by company witnesses was not credible and that other employees who had been reinstated had used similarly vile language. The Trial Examiner found that the nature of the language used was, under Board precedent, within the bounds of permissible and predictable picket line conduct. The Trial Examiner recommended that the four employees be reinstated with back pay.

The Board, however, disagreed and announced a new policy of deferral toward arbitration awards. The Board stated it would defer when the proceedings were fair and regular, the parties had agreed to be bound, and the arbitration award was not clearly repugnant to the purposes and policies of the Act. Without mention of the unusual nature of the "special board," the questionable neutrality of the accountant board member, the conflict of interest between the union and the discharged employees, and Board precedent accepting profanity as commonplace on picket lines, the Board found that under this standard deferral was appropriate. The Board therefore dismissed the unfair labor practice complaint.

Board decisions since *Spielberg* have modified the deferral standard. In 1963, the Board added the requirement that the arbitrator actually have considered the unfair labor practice issue. Raytheon Co., 140 NLRB 883 (1963). In Suburban Motor Freight, 247 NLRB 146 (1980), the Board placed upon the party seeking deferral the burden of proving that the requirements for deferral had been met.

In Olin Corp., 268 NLRB 573 (1984), however, the Board fundamentally altered the standards for postarbitration deferral by reversing Suburban Motor Freight and substantially redefining the requirements of *Spielberg* and *Raytheon*. This is the Board's statement of its holding in *Olin*:

> We would find that an arbitrator has adequately considered the unfair labor practice if (1) the contractual issue is factually parallel to the unfair labor practice issue, and (2) the arbitrator was presented generally with the facts relevant to resolving the unfair labor practice. In this respect, differences, if any, between the contractual and statutory standards of review should be weighed by the Board as part of its determination under the *Spielberg* standards of whether an award is "clearly repugnant" to the Act. And, with regard to the inquiry into the "clearly repugnant" standard, we would not require an arbitrator's award to be totally consistent with Board precedent. Unless the award is "palpably wrong," i.e., unless the arbitrator's decision is not susceptible to an interpretation consistent with the Act, we will defer.

> Finally, we would require that the party seeking to have the Board reject deferral and consider the merits of a given case show that the above standards for deferral have not been met. Thus, the party seeking to have the Board ignore the determination of an arbitrator has the burden of affirmatively demonstrating the defects in the arbitral process or award.

Notes and Questions

1.   When the NLRB adopted its postarbitration deferral policy in *Spielberg* the only explanation it offered was that deferral would "encourag[e] the voluntary settlement of labor disputes." As a matter of national labor policy, are there other advantages gained when the NLRB refuses to consider the statutory issues raised by a dispute that has already been arbitrated? Are there disadvantages that result when the NLRB defers? See Sharpe, *supra* footnote 1.

2.   In what ways do the NLRB and arbitral forums differ? Consider such factors as the nature of the parties, which party bears the burden of proof, costs, procedures, nature of the decisionmaker, access to professional representation, and the availability of administrative and judicial review.

3.   Different types of cases demand different kinds of factfinding and analytical skills, skills that are not present in equal measure in the arbitral and NLRB forums. Compare, for example a "just cause" dismissal case in which there is an allegation of anti-union discrimination with an employer unilateral action case. In the latter, a union claims that the employer, without contractual authority, has changed an employment condition, without having bargained with the union. NLRB deferral policy after *Olin* does not take into account the nature of the issue in determining the propriety of deferral. Should it?

4.   Even within the category of cases that could be examined as violations of a "just cause" provision as well as violations of NLRA §§ 8(a)(1) and (3), there may be significant differences in the relevance of NLRA expertise to the resolution of the issue. This category includes largely factual disputes such as whether the employer's motivation for discharge was employee productivity or union activity. However, it may also encompass questions of law and legal policy such as whether an employee's disclosure of information in violation of an employer confidentiality rule is nevertheless legally protected activity because of the significance of the information to union activities. Does NLRB deferral doctrine take into account these subtle differences in the nature of issues in determining the propriety of deferral? Should it? Could it?

5.   Would unions and management have any general reasons to prefer the Board or the arbitrator? If so, why? Despite expansion of the Board's deferral policy, 99% of contracts still include arbitration provisions.

6.   How significant is *Olin*'s shift in the burden of proof? How easy will it be for the General Counsel to prove what evidence was presented to the arbitrator?

7.   The Supreme Court has stated that courts will not enforce arbitration awards "based solely upon the arbitrator's view of the requirements of enacted legislation." United Steelworkers of America v. Enterprise Wheel & Car Corp., 363 U.S. 593, 80 S.Ct. 1358, 4 L.Ed.2d 1424 (1960). See also *supra* Chapter III.C. As an arbitrator aware of this standard of enforcement, how likely are you to rest your award on statutory grounds? Is the NLRB expecting parties to receive analysis of their statutory rights from arbitrators who have been cautioned by the Supreme Court not to assume that task?

See question 6 *infra* in the Notes and Questions of Subsection 2(b) of this Section.

8. Before *Olin*, the Board would defer in cases in which the arbitrator actually considered and decided the unfair labor practice issue. After *Olin*, the Board will defer simply because the statutory and contract issues are factually parallel. Does the rationale for deferral suggest that deferral is equally appropriate in both of these circumstances? A more recent case creates some doubt about the Board's continuing acceptance of mere factual parallelism. In Phoenix Transit System, 337 NLRB 510 (2002), enforced, 63 Fed.Appx. 524 (D.C.Cir. 2003), the employee was discharged for publishing in a union newsletter criticism of the employer's handling of sexual harassment complaints despite an employer directive to keep the harassment investigation confidential. Although the arbitrator heard evidence about the publication and the employer's confidentiality directive, the Board adopted the Administrative Law Judge's decision not to defer because the "arbitrator's award fails to consider or decide whether or not workers have a right protected by the Act to complain to their employer concerning perceived sexual harassment, or whether or not discussions between employees concerning such complaints, and their redress, are protected by the Act."

9. An empirical study in two NLRB regional offices found that the NLRB refused to defer in 18.9% of cases before *Olin* and 3.8% of cases after *Olin*. Patricia A. Greenfield, *The NLRB's Deferral to Arbitration Before and After* Olin: *An Empirical Analysis*, 42 Industrial and Labor Relations Review 34 (1988).

10. You submit an unfair labor practice charge concerning a dispute that is also arbitrable. The NLRB regional office stays its investigation pending arbitration and then, after the award is issued, the Board defers under *Olin*. The arbitrator did not actually consider the unfair labor practice issue. What procedural steps could you take to obtain judicial review of the *Olin* deferral standard? See Leedom v. Kyne, 358 U.S. 184, 79 S.Ct. 180, 3 L.Ed.2d 210 (1958); Cornelius J. Peck, *A Proposal to End NLRB Deferral to the Arbitration Process*, 60 Washington Law Review 355, 374–77 (1985).

11. Does the National Labor Relations Act preclude the NLRB from deferring to an arbitration award in which the arbitrator did not actually consider or decide the unfair labor practice issue? See Taylor v. NLRB, 786 F.2d 1516 (11th Cir.1986); Darr v. NLRB, 801 F.2d 1404 (D.C.Cir.1986). What about a case in which the parties settled the grievance prior to arbitration? Plumbers and Pipefitters Local Union No. 520 v. NLRB, 955 F.2d 744 (D.C.Cir.1992) (Board's policy of granting deference to pre-arbitration settlement agreements is consistent with the NLRA). But see Titanium Metals Corp., 340 NLRB No. 88 (2003) (NLRB did not consider settlement fair or regular when it was reached without the grievant's participation or knowledge and it appeared to be an effort by the employer and union to disguise the real reason for the grievant's discharge).

12. One might have expected, in light of the criticism generated by the *Olin* decision, that it would have likely been overturned once nominees of a Democratic President gained majority status on the NLRB. The fact that *Olin* was not overturned by Board members appointed by President Clinton perhaps suggests a broad consensus in support of its strong postarbitration

deferral policy. Former NLRB Chairman William B. Gould IV, however, suggests another explanation. He believes that Board inaction on major policy issues during the Clinton administration was caused at least in part by Board members' fear that a retaliatory Republican Senate would otherwise doom their confirmations (both reappointments and confirmations following a presidential recess appointment). William B. Gould IV, *The Labor Board's Ever Deepening Somnolence: Some Reflections of a Former Chairman,* 32 Creighton Law Review 1505 (1999). One should however be alert to the possibility that, while the articulation of deferral standards may remain constant over time, case outcomes may not be consistent as Board members with different political perspectives apply elements of the standard with varying strictness. Compare, for example, the treatment of the issue of repugnancy in The Motor Convoy, Inc., immediately below, with U.S. Postal Service, 332 NLRB 340 (2000) (Board adopted decision of Administrative Law Judge finding that arbitrator's award was repugnant to the Act because it was inconsistent with Board doctrine, in the absence of any assessment of whether the award was susceptible to an interpretation consistent with the Act).

THE MOTOR CONVOY, INC.
National Labor Relations Board, 1991.
303 NLRB 135.

Opinion by Mary Miller Cracraft, Member, Dennis M. Devaney, Member, John N. Raudabaugh, Member:

* * * The judge refused to defer to a grievance panel arbitration award and found that the Respondent Company violated Section 8(a)(1) and (3) of the Act and the Respondent Union violated Section 8(b)(1)(A) and (2) of the Act by giving the Union steward, Donald Malone, superseniority for the purpose of job bidding. We disagree. For the reasons that follow, we find that the complaint should be dismissed by deferring to the arbitral award.

The Company has three types of driver positions: city drivers, short country drivers, and over-the-road drivers.* In 1981, pursuant to the collective-bargaining agreement's superseniority provision, Union Steward Malone obtained the one permanent city driver slot, which the judge found to be the most lucrative position. In 1987, three employees, including the Charging Party, filed a grievance over the superseniority issue. The arbitration panel upheld the superseniority practice.

The judge found this case is controlled by *Dairylea Cooperative,* 219 NLRB 656 (1975), enfd. sub nom. *NLRB v. Teamsters Local 338,* 531 F.2d 1162 (2d Cir.1976), which held that steward superseniority for

---

* [Editor's Note: The Administrative Law Judge noted that most employees are over-the-road drivers who transport cars from 150 to 250 miles and take from 2 to 4 days to complete a trip. Three short country drivers deliver up to 125 miles from the terminal, make one or two trips in a day, and can return to the terminal without spending a night on the road. The single city driver averages three trips a day. The city driver works fewer days, fewer hours per day, and makes approximately $17,000 more per year than the short country drivers.]

purposes other than layoff and recall is presumptively unlawful, but the presumption may be rebutted by a showing of legitimate and substantial business justification. After reviewing the facts concerning the steward's duties; the method of processing grievances; and the availability of a driver to serve as steward when holding the city driver as opposed to the country day driver position, the judge concluded that the Respondents did not show that Malone needed the city driver job in order to serve as steward and, therefore, did not rebut the *Dairylea* presumption. The judge found it inappropriate to defer to a grievance panel's arbitration award because, according to the judge, the panel's decision is inconsistent with his conclusion and, therefore, repugnant to the Act.

* * * Our dissenting colleagues assert that the issue in this case is not suitable for deferral. We disagree. The issue in this case is whether the Respondent Union justified the superseniority accorded to Steward Malone, i.e., whether Malone could have effectively performed his steward duties in a position other than that of city driver. We see no reason why an arbitrator cannot make this factfinding based on evidence presented by the parties. Indeed, the parties and the arbitrator are probably in a better position than the Board to make a determination of the needs of the shop.

In support of their position, the dissenters cite *Auto Workers Local 1161 (Pfaudler Co.)*, 271 NLRB 1411 (1984), enfd. sub nom. *NLRB v. Auto. Workers Local 1161*, 777 F.2d 1131, 1140–1141 (6th Cir.1985). The case is wholly inapposite. In the first place, the case involved prearbitration deferral under *Collyer Insulated Wire*,[1] not postarbitration deferral under *Olin*. Secondly, the case involved a clause that was unlawful on its face. * * *

Our dissenting colleagues also claim the arbitral proceedings were not fair and regular. It is true that the Board has found deferral to arbitration inappropriate when there is proof that an actual conflict of interest existed between individual employee grievants and the union representing them. *Tubari Ltd.*, 287 NLRB 1273 fn. 4 (1988). Under *Olin*, however, the General Counsel bears the burden of raising and proving the argument that an actual conflict of interest impaired the fairness of arbitration proceedings.

In this case, the General Counsel has not even raised the fairness issue. Further, the grievants' position in arbitration was supported by the Employer, and there is no showing that the Employer did anything less than vigorously oppose the grant of superseniority. In these circumstances, we cannot say that the General Counsel has shown that the arbitral proceedings were not fair and regular.[3]

1. 192 NLRB 837 (1971).

3. The fact that the Employer, as a co-Respondent with the Union in this case, may now have a somewhat different position with regard to the necessity of superseniority than it argued to the panel does not establish that the proceedings were not fair and regular. To the contrary, the fact that the Employer might be charged with an unfair labor practice if it granted superseniority, as of course it was, provided the Employer with a substantial reason to vig-

The only other argument made against deferral is the dissent's assertion that the arbitration panel's award is repugnant to the Act. In determining repugnancy, the Board will weigh the difference, if any, between the contractual standard used by an arbitrator and the statutory standard used by the Board. *Olin*, supra at 574. In the instant case, the statutory standard is whether there was a need for superseniority for job bidding purposes, i.e., whether Malone could have effectively performed his steward duties in a position other than that of city driver. *Electronic Workers IUE Local 663 (Gulton Electro Voice)*, 276 NLRB 1043 (1985). In the arbitration proceeding, the Union's position was that superseniority was necessary for Malone to perform his steward duties. The contract provided that superseniority may be granted if it "may be useful" in the performance of steward duties. The arbitral opinion states only that Malone "did not use the right to bid for monetary gain."

In light of the brevity of the arbitral conclusion, there is a possibility that the panel's award was based on a contractual standard requiring less showing of need for superseniority than the statutory *Dairylea* standard. The test under *Olin*, however, is whether the arbitral opinion is *susceptible to an interpretation* consistent with the Act. In the instant case, the General Counsel does not dispute that the arbitration concerned the steward's need for superseniority to perform his duties. Nor does the General Counsel claim that the arbitration panel was not presented generally with the facts relevant to resolving the unfair labor practice. Given the Union's position in arbitration that superseniority was necessary for the performance of steward duties, and given the arbitration panel's ultimate agreement with the Union, the arbitral opinion is at least "susceptible" to the interpretation that the panel found that superseniority was necessary to the performance of steward duties. In any event, the General Counsel has not met his burden of showing that the award is not susceptible to the above interpretation.

The dissent also relies on the language of the contract and the language of the award. Concededly, neither the contract nor the award read expressly in terms of the *Gulton* standard. However, *Olin* does not require that the contract or the award read expressly in terms of statutory standards. The question is whether the arbitral award is *susceptible to an interpretation consistent with the Act.* * * * [This] award is susceptible to an interpretation consistent with the Act even though it does not read in statutory terms. This is particularly so in light of the fact that the Union presented evidence that the grant of superseniority was necessary for the performance of Malone's duties as steward. * * *

In *Olin*, the Board said that it would not require that the arbitral award be totally consistent with Board precedent. In *Dennison National Co.*, 296 NLRB 169 (1989), an arbitrator found that, under the contract's

orously pursue the employees' claims and oppose the Union and the grant of superseniority.

management-rights clause, an employer was privileged to make a unilateral change. The General Counsel argued that the award was repugnant because the arbitrator failed to use the statutory standard of whether the management-rights clause clearly and unmistakably waived the right to bargain. In spite of the difference in standards, the Board deferred. The Board said that deferral is appropriate notwithstanding that the arbitral award may be inconsistent with Board precedent.[6] * * *

Accordingly, we shall defer to the grievance panel arbitration award and dismiss the complaint.

Dissent by James M. Stephens, Chairman, Clifford R. Oviatt, Jr., Member:

We dissent from our colleagues' decision to defer to the award of the bipartite arbitration panel. We agree with the judge that deferral is inappropriate because it is evident that the arbitration panel applied a standard that is repugnant to the Act. We would also decline to defer on two additional grounds. In our view, the statutory issue here was not appropriate for resolution by an arbitral panel; and the proceedings were not fair and regular because employees Helm and Driver, the alleged discriminatees in this case, were not adequately represented in the arbitral proceedings.

Addressing first the question whether the issue is even suitable for arbitration, we would find that deferral of the issue in this case is contrary to the Board's holding in *Auto Workers Local 1161 (Pfaudler Co.)*, 271 NLRB 1411 (1984), enfd. sub nom. *NLRB v. Auto. Workers Local 1161*, 777 F.2d 1131, 1140–1141 (6th Cir.1985). * * *

[The dissenters thought *Pfaudler* controlling despite the fact that it concerned prearbitral rather than postarbitral deferral and despite the fact that in *Pfaudler* the provision was challenged on its face rather than as applied. They contended that an issue inappropriate for prearbitral deferral would not become deferable merely because the arbitration had already occurred. They also maintained that once the Board permitted a contract provision to be construed inconsistently with the Act the provision would thereafter function just like a provision unlawful on its face.]

We note also that the employee right at issue under the *Dairylea* doctrine—the right not to suffer a relative loss of job benefits simply because one is not the union steward—is not a right that unions may waive on behalf of unit employees. Just as an employer and union may not lawfully agree on a clause that suppresses the workplace solicitation rights of union dissidents (*NLRB v. Magnavox*, 415 U.S. 322 (1974)), so

---

6. Compare *Ciba-Geigy Pharmaceuticals Division*, 264 NLRB 1013 (1982), enfd. 722 F.2d 1120, 1126 (3d Cir.1983). In that case, the arbitrator based his opinion on a noncontractual residual rights theory under which management could make unilateral changes unless the contract forbids them. The Board refused to defer to the arbitral opinion. Because waiver of the right to bargain is bottomed on party consent, the arbitral award based on something other than a contract clause or party conduct was repugnant to the Act. By contrast, both *Dennison* and the instant case involve contractual provisions.

they may not lawfully agree on a clause that confers benefits on union stewards or officers without adequate justification. * * *

Even assuming arguendo that the grant of superseniority here is a proper subject for deferral, we would find the award repugnant. The operative portion of the contract clause at issue in this case—granting *"such other employment preferences as may be useful* in the performance of his duties as Steward as requested by the Local Union in writing" (emphasis added)—is presumptively unlawful under *Dairylea.* * * *

The majority contends that the arbitration panel's award is susceptible to an interpretation that the panel found superseniority was necessary to the performance of steward duties. In our view nothing in the award supports such an interpretation. The award speaks only to the purported motive for the steward's receipt of superseniority—that it was not pursued for "monetary gain." Such a finding, even if true, is not connected to the statutory requirement that superseniority be necessary for the performance of the steward's duties, or even that it be "useful" to those duties. Indeed, the panel's finding has nothing at all to do with the "need" for superseniority, only with the steward's "good faith." Further, the award's repugnancy is seriously compounded by the fact that, as noted above, the award must be evaluated within the context that the grant of superseniority here is presumptively unlawful. Therefore, any such evaluation must contain some ground that would *overcome* this presumption under current Board law.

In these circumstances, this case is distinguishable from those cases cited by the majority in which the Board deferred even though the arbitrator's analysis perhaps did not "comport precisely" with Board precedent. *Postal Service,* 275 NLRB 430, 432 (1985). Here the majority defers to an award validating a presumptively unlawful grant of superseniority when the only ground available to it to do so is that the steward did not act for monetary gain. Because we find that such a reason bears no relationship to any meaningful statutory inquiry pertinent to the issue presented, we find that the award is repugnant to the Act.

As stated above, we would also find deferral inappropriate because the proceedings were not fair or regular. Given the adverse position that the Respondent Union took to the challenge to Malone's exercise of superseniority to claim the city driver position, the Union obviously could not adequately represent the employee grievants in the arbitral procedure—nor did it even attempt such representation. The grievants were "represented" instead by the Respondent Employer. We do not question the integrity of the Employer, but the fact remains that whatever the vigor of its challenge to the Union's interpretation of the provision before the bipartite panel, its interests were not fully congruent with those of the grievants (the alleged discriminatees); and, unlike the Union, the Employer owed them no duty of fair representation. * * *

Because we would not defer to the arbitral award, we would reach the merits of the case. For the reasons stated by the judge, we would find that the Respondent Union violated Section 8(b)(1)(A) and (2) of the Act and that the Respondent Employer violated Section 8(a)(3) and (1). * * *

Notes and Questions

1. The "arbitration award" in *Motor Convoy* to which the Board deferred was not the decision of a neutral third party, but rather the decision of a bipartite panel made up an equal number of employer and union representatives under a Teamster contract. See the description of Teamster Joint Committees in Chapter II.H.4, *supra*. Did the nature of the grievance panel in *Motor Convoy* affect the Board's decision? Should the Board be as willing to defer to decisions of bipartite panels as to decisions of neutrals? Is the reason for deferral to the decisions of arbitrators the extent to which their procedures parallel those of the Board or is it rather that arbitration is the process the parties selected? See Taylor v. NLRB, 786 F.2d 1516 (11th Cir.1986); Gregory E. Zimmerman, *The Teamster Joint Grievance Committee and NLRB Deferral: A Failure to Protect the Individual Employee's Statutory Rights*, 133 University of Pennsylvania Law Review 1453 (1985); and other articles cited *supra* Chapter II.H.4. If the Board defers to negotiated settlement agreements, is there any reason not to defer to decisions of bipartite boards?

2. Board precedent in *Dairylea Cooperative* presumes that steward superseniority for purposes other than layoff and recall is unlawful in the absence of legitimate and substantial business justification. Does that precedent protect the Motor Convoy employees senior to steward Malone who were unable to obtain the lucrative city driver slot? Does the Board requirement that waiver of statutory rights be accomplished by clear and unmistakable language accomplish its objective if the Board will defer to arbitrators' decisions that do not apply such a high standard? What protection do these legal standards provide to nearly all unionized employees who are employed in workplaces governed by contractual arbitration provisions? Is there some function served by having an agency make law that does not, in practice, apply to anyone? Or do these questions overstate the impact of the Board majority's "repugnancy" standard?

3. Two Board members who joined in the majority opinion in *Motor Convoy* were members of a Board panel that decided another repugnancy case just fifteen days earlier. In Bath Iron Works Corp., 302 NLRB 898 (1991), the employer had previously had plant rules that prohibited the use of alcohol and drugs on the premises, permitted the employer to test employees thought to be under the influence of drugs or alcohol, and specified appropriate discipline for violation of the rules. The contract also had a management rights clause that granted management the right to discipline and discharge for just cause and to require employees to observe its rules. Nine years after implementation of the rules, the employer announced new rules that included, as grounds for discharge, possession of drug paraphernalia and any employee's conviction for a drug-or alcohol-related crime. The arbitrator found the new rules valid under both the contract and the NLRA. The arbitrator said that the new rules were not a significant departure from the earlier drug and alcohol rules and there was

thus no obligation to bargain with the union. The arbitrator did not specifically rely upon the management rights language as authority for the new rules, but merely approved them as an extension of the prior policy.

The Board declined to defer to the arbitrator's decision. The Board stated that the arbitrator's assessment that the new provisions were insignificant extensions of the old policy was "palpably wrong" and repugnant to the Act because under the new rules employees could be discharged for conduct that would not have violated the earlier rules. The Board declined even to consider whether, had the arbitrator relied on the management rights language, the decision would have been repugnant to the Act. Is this case consistent with *Motor Convoy*? If not, what meaning of "repugnancy" ought be applied by (a) parties deciding whether to pursue an unfair labor practice charge after an arbitration award has been rendered; (b) NLRB Regional Directors deciding whether to issue a complaint; (c) Administrative Law Judges deciding unfair labor practice cases raising deferral issues? Recall the purposes of deferral. How likely are these to be achieved if those who must make decisions in light of the Board's deferral policy are uncertain about its content and application?

4. If one were to follow the dissent's view of repugnancy in *Motor Convoy*, would the Board ever defer when the result reached by the arbitrator was different than the result which would have been reached by the Board? If so, can you state generally the dissent's standard for repugnancy? If not, what's the point of having a deferral doctrine if it requires in each case a determination of what would have been the Board's answer in the absence of an arbitration decision?

5. Are there situations in which deferral, in the form of collateral estoppel (issue preclusion), might be appropriate with respect to arbitral fact finding but not with respect to the substantive implication of facts under the National Labor Relations Act?

6. In footnote 6 of the majority opinion in *Motor Convoy*, the Board distinguishes an award based on an interpretation of management rights language to which it would defer and an award based on "noncontractual residual rights theory under which management could make unilateral changes unless the contract forbids them" to which it would not. See also Columbian Chemicals Co., 307 NLRB 592 (1992),enforced, 993 F.2d 1536 (4th Cir.1993). Should this be a relevant distinction in deciding the propriety of deferral? Do you agree that an arbitrator's decision relying on residual management rights is "noncontractual"? Would such a decision fail to draw its essence from the contract and therefore be unenforceable under *Enterprise Wheel* (Chapter III.C.1., *supra*)?

7. The deferral requirement that a decision result from proceedings that are "fair and regular" has been a part of Board doctrine since *Spielberg*. From the perspective of the senior employees at Motor Convoy, was the proceeding fair if their Union opposed them in the grievance and the employer had no particular reason nor any legal obligation to represent their interests? What remains, in the view of the Board majority, of the prior doctrine that the Board will not defer when there is an actual conflict between individual employee grievants and their union?

(b) Prearbitration Deferral

In cases concerning postarbitration deferral, such as *Olin* and *Motor Convoy*, the parties have already completed arbitration and the NLRB must decide whether it should hear a case, aspects of which have already been decided in another forum. The prearbitration deferral issue, on the other hand, arises when a party that could arbitrate chooses instead to seek relief from the NLRB. Should the NLRB nevertheless defer and refuse to hear the case because the arbitral forum is available?

The Board announced its initial approach to prearbitration deferral in Collyer Insulated Wire, 192 NLRB 837 (1971). In *Collyer*, the employer unilaterally increased some incentive pay rates. The contract prohibited the employer from making any "change in the general scale of pay," but authorized "adjustments in individual rates" for proper purposes. Whether the employer's wage adjustment was an unlawful refusal to bargain in violation of § 8(a)(5) of the NLRA thus turned entirely upon interpretation of the contract language. The Board dismissed the complaint, but retained jurisdiction, if necessary, after arbitration to assure that the arbitration process had met the standards of *Spielberg, supra.* The Board said deferral was appropriate in *Collyer* because the parties had had a long and productive collective bargaining relationship, there was no claim of employer animosity to employees' statutory rights, the contract permitted arbitration of a broad range of disputes, the arbitration agreement clearly encompassed the dispute, and the employer was willing to arbitrate. The Board considered the dispute well suited to resolution by arbitration because contract interpretation was at its center. The Board introduced its prearbitral deferral policy to promote resolution of disputes by a mechanism selected by the parties and to permit expeditious and informal dispute resolution. Some scholars and Board members condemned *Collyer* and expressed fear that it would too easily be extended to cases of individual employees, as it indeed soon was.

In 1972, in National Radio Co., 198 NLRB 527 (1972), the Board applied its prearbitration deferral doctrine to include § 8(a)(1) and 8(a)(3) cases. In a typical § 8(a)(3) claim, a discharged employee asserts that the reason for discharge was union activities. The grievance generally turns on application of a "just cause" contract provision, while the unfair labor practice issue may depend on statutorily based doctrines. The Board nevertheless expanded deferral to such individual rights cases. It acknowledged, however, that here, unlike *Collyer*, resolution of the contract issue would not necessarily resolve the unfair labor practice issue.

Five years later, however, the Board reversed itself. In General American Transportation Corp., 228 NLRB 808 (1977), the Board stated that it would no longer defer in cases involving allegations of violations of §§ 8(a)(1), 8(a)(3), 8(b)(1)(A), and 8(b)(2) because it had concluded that arbitration was not suited to resolve statutory issues that did not depend on contract interpretation.

Seven years later the Board reversed itself again. In United Technologies Corp., 268 NLRB 557 (1984), a divided Board once again applied prearbitration deferral to cases alleging individual rights violations. *United Technologies* has remained Board precedent despite substantial changes in the political composition of the NLRB. In a speech in 2000, the Chairman of the NLRB said that the Board in recent years had been deferring to arbitration under *Collyer* in approximately 1300 cases per year. Truesdale, footnote 1 *supra*, at 61–62.

Notes and Questions

1.   In what respects is the deferral issue different when posed before rather than after arbitration?

2.   Reconsider the facts in *Collyer*. A union came to the NLRB seeking enforcement of its statutory right to bargain prior to an employer's change in a term and condition of employment. That right can be contractually waived by the union in its collective bargaining agreement. As a matter of labor policy, should the NLRB insist that the union instead arbitrate the claim? What is gained? What is lost? Who gains? Who loses?

3.   Consider the facts in a typical § 8(a)(1) or (3) case. An employee, active in concerted or union activities, is discharged and believes those activities were the reason for her discharge. She asks the NLRB to enforce her statutory right to be free of anti-union discrimination. The labor contract under which she works permits arbitration of discharge claims. Is there any rational basis for having a different deferral policy for individual rights cases? Was the Board's policy better in *General American Transportation* or in *United Technologies*?

4.   Does *United Technologies* violate the National Labor Relations Act? Consider § 10(a) of the NLRA and § 203(d) of the Labor Management Relations Act. Although the Supreme Court has never addressed the legality of NLRB deferral, it has assumed the existence of the deferral doctrine in addressing other legal issues. See, for example, NLRB v. City Disposal Systems Inc., 465 U.S. 822, 838–39, 104 S.Ct. 1505, 1515, 79 L.Ed.2d 839 (1984). For several different perspectives on the legality of NLRB deferral see the opinions of Judges Wald, Edwards, and Mikva in Hammontree v. NLRB, 925 F.2d 1486 (D.C.Cir.1991) (en banc). The majority opinion of Judge Wald found that the Board's deferral policy did not violate any of these statutory provisions. Judge Edwards, restating a theory he had earlier articulated in a law review article (see *supra* footnote 1), thought the deferral policy was lawful insofar as the employee claims subject to deferral involve statutory rights that a union is empowered to waive on behalf of those it represents. In a lengthy dissent, Chief Judge Mikva reviewed legislative history that he thought mandated a conclusion that Congress permitted deferral of claims involving interpretation or application of a collective bargaining agreement but not those involving individual employee rights.

5.   In addition to the reasons for nondeferral mentioned previously in this Subsection (including repugnancy, conflict of interest between union and employee, and employer unwillingness to arbitrate), the NLRB also will not defer in some other categories of cases:

(a) Union requests for access or information needed for processing grievances. See American National Can Co., 293 NLRB 901 (1989), enforced, 924 F.2d 518 (4th Cir.1991); General Dynamics Corp., 268 NLRB 1432 (1984). The Board's rationale is that nondeferral avoids the delays of a two-tiered arbitration process in which an arbitrator first considers the procedural issue and later the substantive issue. But the Board's nondeferral inevitably requires a two-tiered process (Board and arbitrator) which will take longer simply because Board procedures are much slower than those of arbitration. See Laura J. Cooper, *Discovery in Labor Arbitration,* 72 Minnesota Law Review 1281, 1320–24 (1988). Concerns about the Board's policy of nondeferral in information cases has also recently come from within the agency. In a speech in 2002, then-NLRB Chairman John C. Truesdale repeated Professor Cooper's observations about timeliness and said that the Board's procedures may cause more delay than the parties anticipate at the time an unfair labor practice charge is filed. Truesdale, footnote 1 *supra*, at 65. In 2002, the NLRB's General Counsel announced that his office would begin to advance in pending cases the argument that the Board should reconsider its deferral policy in refusal-to-furnish-information cases. General Counsel Arthur Rosenberg suggested that deferral would expedite the process, take advantage of the contract-interpretation skills of the arbitrator, and conserve Board resources. NLRB General Counsel, Report on Recent Case Developments, R–2464 (November 8, 2002). The Board subsequently, however, reaffirmed its intention to refuse to defer in information cases. Shaw's Supermarkets, Inc., 339 NLRB No. 108 (2003) (Chairman Battista, dissenting, would permit deferral of information disputes arising during efforts to enforce arbitration awards).

The Board's policy of nondeferral in information disputes may offer unions an escape from deferral in cases in which deferral would otherwise be ordered. The Board will not defer in cases in which deferrable and nonde-ferrable issues are intertwined. A union may therefore avoid deferral on an otherwise deferrable substantive claim if it can couple the substantive claim with a claim that the employer refused to provide information relevant to the substantive claim. United States Postal Service, 302 NLRB 918 (1991) (Board refused to defer a § 8(a)(5) charge involving a unilateral change in premium pay because it was "intimately connected" with an employer's refusal to provide information).

When the parties have already arbitrated an information dispute, however, the Board may defer to the decision of the arbitrator. American Broadcasting Co., 290 NLRB 86 (1988).

(b) Allegations of discrimination for filing NLRB charges or giving testimony under the NLRA. See Superior Forwarding Co., 282 NLRB 806 (1987). Section 8(a)(4) of the NLRA makes it an unfair labor practice for an employer to discriminate against an employee "because he has filed charges or given testimony under this Act." The Board has said that it would be inappropriate for it to delegate the responsibility for safeguarding the integrity of the Board's processes.

(c) Representation cases. The Board will not defer representation questions, such as accretion, definition or clarification of an appropriate bargaining unit. Port Chester Nursing Home, 269 NLRB 150 (1984); Williams

Transportation Co., 233 NLRB 837 (1977). Nondeferral seems clearly appropriate here because arbitration assumes the existence of a valid collective bargaining contract while representation issues raise the more fundamental question of whether a contract covers these employees at all. Representation cases also are inappropriate for arbitration because one of the critical parties to the representation dispute, a rival union or unrepresented employees, usually is not a party to the arbitration process. Statutory standards governing representation issues are often entirely unrelated to interpretation of the contract. Finally, in representation cases, unlike unfair labor practice cases, the Board process is often more expeditious than arbitration. Despite its general policy of nondeferral in representation cases, the Board sometimes selectively relies on portions of an arbitration award when appropriate in a representation case. Westinghouse Electric Corp., 162 NLRB 768, 771 (1967) (respecting some of the arbitrator's factual findings, but considering additional evidence not available to the arbitrator).

Representation issues should be distinguished from "jurisdictional disputes." A representational dispute addresses which union represents particular workers. A jurisdictional dispute concerns which workers are entitled to perform certain work. For example, both a masons union and a laborers union might claim the right to have workers it represents bring concrete blocks across a construction site to the masons' work location. Section 10(k) of the National Labor Relations Act mandates that the Board not consider unfair labor practice charges under § 8(b)(4)(D) in a jurisdictional dispute if the parties have, within ten days, notified the Board that they have agreed upon a method for voluntary settlement of the dispute. The agreement for voluntary settlement must include the employer and both unions. The Board has held, for example, that it will proceed to a hearing where the employer is bound by two different arbitration agreements that provide for conflicting methods of resolving jurisdictional disputes, Operating Engineers Local 318 (Foeste Masonry), 322 NLRB 709 (1996), or where one union declines to participate in an arbitration between the employer and a competing union, Carpenters Local 624 (T. Equipment Corp.), 322 NLRB 428 (1996).

6. An employee has filed a grievance under the collective bargaining agreement alleging he has been discharged without "just cause." He also files an unfair labor practice charge alleging violations of § 8(a)(1) and (3) of the NLRA. The NLRB regional office defers to arbitration. You are the arbitrator. The collective bargaining agreement states that the arbitrator's powers are limited to "determination of the facts and interpretation and application of this Agreement."

(a) The Union seeks to argue at the arbitration hearing that the discharge violated the NLRA. The Employer asks you to exclude the argument and confine your decision to the contract. Should you allow the Union to make its NLRA argument? Should you consider the NLRA argument in making your decision? Suppose you sustain the discharge, relying on the contract without mentioning the NLRA. If the employee returns to the Board, would the Board, relying on *Spielberg* and *Olin*, defer to your award? Why or why not?

(b) Would you be more likely to consider the Union's arguments if the contract contained a provision prohibiting the Employer from discriminating against an employee because of Union activities? What if the contract had a clause prohibiting the Employer from violating the NLRA?

(c) Assume the contract makes no reference to either anti-union discrimination or the NLRA, but the parties agree that they would like you to decide whether the discharge violated the NLRA. Should you decide that issue?

3. ARBITRATION DEFERRAL AND OTHER WORKPLACE LAWS

While the United States Supreme Court has never ruled on the legality of NLRB deferral policies,[2] the Court has held that an adverse arbitrator's award under a collective bargaining agreement does not preclude pursuit of rights under several other statutes.

In Alexander v. Gardner–Denver Co., 415 U.S. 36, 94 S.Ct. 1011, 39 L.Ed.2d 147 (1974), a black employee was told that he was discharged for producing too many defective parts. The contract under which the employee worked prohibited discrimination on the basis of race and precluded discharge in the absence of "just cause." The employee submitted a grievance under the collective bargaining agreement and filed with a state agency a charge of race discrimination under Title VII of the 1964 Civil Rights Act. The state agency referred the statutory claim to the federal Equal Employment Opportunity Commission and later the employee filed an action in federal district court.

At the arbitration hearing the union argued that others who had had similar problems with defective parts had been transferred rather than discharged. The arbitrator, however, found just cause for the employee's discharge. The federal district court dismissed the employee's complaint, saying he was bound by the adverse decision of the arbitrator.

The court of appeals affirmed the dismissal, but the Supreme Court reversed. It rejected the employer's alternative arguments that arbitration precluded pursuit of the statutory remedy and that courts should defer to arbitral decisions if the collective bargaining agreement prohibited discrimination. With respect to the preclusion issue, the Court found that Congress intended to accord "parallel or overlapping remedies against discrimination." The Court said, "The distinctly separate nature of these contractual and statutory rights is not vitiated merely because both were violated as a result of the same factual occurrence." The Court compared the Title VII issue to cases arising under the NLRA where an arbitration award does not prevent the NLRB from considering the claim.

The Supreme Court rejected the argument that the employee had waived his right to pursue the discrimination claim under Title VII:

> We are also unable to accept the proposition that petitioner waived his cause of action under Title VII. To begin, we think it

2. It has, however, assumed the existence of the deferral doctrine in addressing other legal issues. See, for example, NLRB v. City Disposal Systems Inc., 465 U.S. 822, 838–39, 104 S.Ct. 1505, 1515, 79 L.Ed.2d 839 (1984).

clear that there can be no prospective waiver of an employee's rights under Title VII. It is true, of course, that a union may waive certain statutory rights related to collective activity, such as the right to strike. *Mastro Plastics Corp. v. NLRB*, 350 U.S. 270 (1956); *Boys Markets v. Retail Clerks Union*, 398 U.S. 235 (1970). These rights are conferred on employees collectively to foster the processes of bargaining and properly may be exercised or relinquished by the union as collective-bargaining agent to obtain economic benefits for union members. Title VII, on the other hand, stands on plainly different ground; it concerns not majoritarian processes, but an individual's right to equal employment opportunities. Title VII's strictures are absolute and represent a congressional command that each employee be free from discriminatory practices. Of necessity, the rights conferred can form no part of the collective-bargaining process since waiver of these rights would defeat the paramount congressional purpose behind Title VII. In these circumstances, an employee's rights under Title VII are not susceptible of prospective waiver. * * *

The actual submission of petitioner's grievance to arbitration in the present case does not alter the situation. Although presumably an employee may waive his cause of action under Title VII as part of a voluntary settlement, mere resort to the arbitral forum to enforce contractual rights constitutes no such waiver. Since an employee's rights under Title VII may not be waived prospectively, existing contractual rights and remedies against discrimination must result from other concessions already made by the union as part of the economic bargain struck with the employer. It is settled law that no additional concession may be exacted from any employee as the price for enforcing those rights. *J. I. Case Co. v. NLRB*, 321 U.S. 332, 338–339 (1944).

The Court also considered the arbitral forum ill-suited to the task of resolving issues of public law:

As the proctor of the bargain, the arbitrator's task is to effectuate the intent of the parties. His source of authority is the collective-bargaining agreement, and he must interpret and apply that agreement in accordance with the "industrial common law of the shop" and the various needs and desires of the parties. The arbitrator, however, has no general authority to invoke public laws that conflict with the bargain between the parties:

An arbitrator is confined to interpretation and application of the collective bargaining agreement; he does not sit to dispense his own brand of industrial justice. He may of course look for guidance from many sources, yet his award is legitimate only so long as it draws its essence from the collective bargaining agreement. When the arbitrator's words manifest an infidelity to this obligation, courts have no choice but to refuse enforcement of the award. *United Steelworkers of America v. Enterprise Wheel & Car Corp.*, 363 U.S. 593, 597 (1960).

If an arbitral decision is based "solely upon the arbitrator's view of the requirements of enacted legislation," rather than on an interpretation of the collective-bargaining agreement, the arbitrator has "exceeded the scope of the submission," and the award will not be enforced. *Ibid.* Thus the arbitrator has authority to resolve only questions of contractual rights, and this authority remains regardless of whether certain contractual rights are similar to, or duplicative of, the substantive rights secured by Title VII.

Emphasizing the arbitrator's responsibility to the contract, the Court added, "Where the collective-bargaining agreement conflicts with Title VII, the arbitrator must follow the agreement."

The Court described the arbitral process as "comparatively inferior to judicial processes in the protection of Title VII rights." It noted that arbitrators may lack expertise in the law and that many are not lawyers. The Court identified procedural differences between the courts and the arbitration process:

> Moreover, the factfinding process in arbitration usually is not equivalent to judicial factfinding. The record of the arbitration proceedings is not as complete; the usual rules of evidence do not apply; and rights and procedures common to civil trials, such as discovery, compulsory process, cross-examination, and testimony under oath, are often severely limited or unavailable. * * * And as this Court has recognized, "arbitrators have no obligation to the court to give their reasons for an award." * * * Indeed, it is the informality of arbitral procedure that enables it to function as an efficient, inexpensive, and expeditious means for dispute resolution. This same characteristic, however, makes arbitration a less appropriate forum for final resolution of Title VII issues than the federal courts.

In a footnote, the Court suggested how the Union's involvement in the process of arbitration might further limit its ability satisfactorily to resolve discrimination claims:

> A further concern is the union's exclusive control over the manner and extent to which an individual grievance is presented. See *Vaca v. Sipes*, 386 U.S. 171 (1967) * * *. In arbitration, as in the collective-bargaining process, the interests of the individual employee may be subordinated to the collective interests of all employees in the bargaining unit. See *J. I. Case Co. v. NLRB*, 321 U.S. 332 (1944). Moreover, harmony of interest between the union and the individual employee cannot always be presumed, especially where a claim of racial discrimination is made. See, *e.g.*, *Steele v. Louisville & N.R. Co.*, 323 U.S. 192 (1944) * * *. And a breach of the union's duty of fair representation may prove difficult to establish. See *Vaca v. Sipes*, *supra* * * *. In this respect, it is noteworthy

that Congress thought it necessary to afford the protections of Title VII against unions as well as employers.

The Court rejected the suggestion that concerns about arbitration could be allayed by applying a more demanding deferral standard to arbitration awards on issues of discrimination:

> [A] standard that adequately insured effectuation of Title VII rights in the arbitral forum would tend to make arbitration a procedurally complex, expensive, and time-consuming process. And judicial enforcement of such a standard would almost require courts to make *de novo* determinations of the employees' claims. It is uncertain whether any minimal savings in judicial time and expense would justify the risk to vindication of Title VII rights.

Although the *Alexander* Court held that an arbitration award does not foreclose a Title VII claim, it nevertheless suggested, in footnote 21 of its opinion, that a court in a Title VII case could give some weight to an arbitration award:

> We adopt no standards as to the weight to be accorded an arbitral decision, since this must be determined in the court's discretion with regard to the facts and circumstances of each case. Relevant factors include the existence of provisions in the collective-bargaining agreement that conform substantially with Title VII, the degree of procedural fairness in the arbitral forum, adequacy of the record with respect to the issue of discrimination, and the special competence of particular arbitrators. Where an arbitral determination gives full consideration to an employee's Title VII rights, a court may properly accord it great weight. This is especially true where the issue is solely one of fact, specifically addressed by the parties and decided by the arbitrator on the basis of an adequate record. But courts should ever be mindful that Congress, in enacting Title VII, thought it necessary to provide a judicial forum for the ultimate resolution of discriminatory employment claims. It is the duty of courts to assure the full availability of this forum.

The Supreme Court subsequently relied on *Alexander* in rejecting a preclusive effect for arbitration in two other statutory schemes. In Barrentine v. Arkansas–Best Freight System, Inc., 450 U.S. 728, 101 S.Ct. 1437, 67 L.Ed.2d 641 (1981), the Court held that an adverse arbitration award did not preclude employees from pursuing a claim under the Fair Labor Standards Act for failure to comply with minimum wage requirements. In McDonald v. West Branch, 466 U.S. 284, 104 S.Ct. 1799, 80 L.Ed.2d 302 (1984), the Court held that a police officer could pursue a civil rights claim under 42 U.S.C. § 1983 against his municipal employer despite an arbitrator's determination that his discharge has been for "just cause."

Subsequently, the Supreme Court looked with greater favor on arbitration in the employment context, at least in the nonunion workplace. In Gilmer v. Interstate/Johnson Lane Corp., 500 U.S. 20, 111 S.Ct. 1647, 114 L.Ed.2d 26 (1991), the employee was required by his employer to register as a securities representative with the New York Stock Exchange.[3] His registration included an agreement to arbitrate all employment disputes. Subsequently the employee was terminated and brought an action claiming violation of the federal Age Discrimination in Employment Act (ADEA). The Supreme Court majority held that the employee was compelled to arbitrate the age discrimination claim.

The Court distinguished the issue in *Gilmer* from the issues in *Alexander*, *Barrentine*, and *McDonald*:

> There are several important distinctions between the *Gardner-Denver* line of cases and the case before us. First, those cases did not involve the issue of the enforceability of an agreement to arbitrate statutory claims. Rather, they involved the quite different issue whether arbitration of contract-based claims precluded subsequent judicial resolution of statutory claims. Since the employees there had not agreed to arbitrate their statutory claims, and the labor arbitrators were not authorized to resolve such claims, the arbitration in those cases understandably was held not to preclude subsequent statutory actions. Second, because the arbitration in those cases occurred in the context of a collective-bargaining agreement, the claimants there were represented by their unions in the arbitration proceedings. An important concern therefore was the tension between collective representation and individual statutory rights, a concern not applicable to the present case. Finally, those cases were not decided under the [Federal Arbitration Act], which * * * reflects a "liberal federal policy favoring arbitration agreements." * * * Therefore, those cases provide no basis for refusing to enforce Gilmer's agreement to arbitrate his ADEA claim.

The Court in *Gilmer* also specifically retracted its statements in *Alexander* that arbitration is procedurally inferior to the judicial process for the resolution of statutory claims. In a footnote, the Court suggested that its denigration of arbitration in *Alexander* had been the product of unreasonable judicial suspicion of the arbitration process.

Subsequently, the Supreme Court acknowledged that there was some tension between *Alexander,* that had held that statutory rights were not subject to prospective waiver, and *Gilmer*, that had permitted an arbitration agreement to waive a judicial forum for consideration of statutory rights. The question in Wright v. Universal Maritime Service Corp., 525 U.S. 70, 119 S.Ct. 391, 142 L.Ed.2d 361 (1998), was whether a collective bargaining agreement providing for arbitration of workplace disputes precluded judicial consideration of an employee's claim under the Americans with Disabilities Act. The Court declined to decide the validity of a union-negotiated waiver because it unanimously concluded that the provision in the contract before it, which established a grievance procedure including arbitration for "[m]atters under dispute which

3. The Supreme Court's decision in *Gil-*   X.B., *infra.*
mer is reproduced and discussed in Chapter

cannot be promptly settled" was not a "clear and unmistakable" waiver of the right to seek a judicial forum for statutory employment claims.

The Supreme Court's imposition of the unmistakable waiver standard has demonstrably constrained courts previously inclined to interpret contract language as constituting a waiver. Brown v. ABF Freight Systems, Inc., 183 F.3d 319 (4th Cir. 1999). The same circuit has also found that a collective bargaining agreement did waive an employee's right to a judicial forum for ADA and FMLA claims when the contract stated, "Any and all claims regarding equal employment opportunity . . . under any federal or state employment law shall be exclusively addressed by an individual employee or the Union under the grievance and arbitration provisions of this Agreement." Singletary v. Enersys, Inc., 57 Fed.Appx. 161 (4th Cir. 2003). For a survey of post-*Wright* judicial decisions assessing the language of collective bargaining agreements see Mary K. O'Melveny, *One Bite of the Apple and One of the Orange: Interpreting Claims that Collective Bargaining Agreements Should Waive the Individual Employee's Statutory Rights*, 19 Labor Lawyer 185 (2003).

Notes and Questions

1. Does the Court's holding in *Alexander* suggest that the NLRB's *Spielberg-Olin* postarbitral deferral policy is unlawful, or is *Alexander* distinguishable?

(a) Does it matter that Title VII rights are nonwaivable, but that some NLRA rights are subject to waiver? Would that suggest a relevant distinction between 8(a)(5) employer unilateral action cases and 8(a)(3) individual rights cases?

(b) Is workplace race discrimination a more important public policy concern than discrimination on the basis of union activities?

(c) Is there an assumption that arbitrators can be trusted fairly to consider claims alleging violation of the National Labor Relations Act but cannot be expected fairly to decide discrimination cases?

(d) Is it relevant that there is a right to a private cause of action under Title VII, the Fair Labor Standards Act, and § 1983, but there is no private right of action for unfair labor practices?

2. Does *Gilmer* strengthen or weaken the precedential use of *Alexander* in a legal challenge to the NLRB's deferral policy? Consider *Gilmer*'s appreciation of both the quality of arbitration's procedures and the difference between individual and collective contracts.

3. The Supreme Court said in *Alexander* that although an arbitration award could not preclude a discrimination claim, it could nevertheless be given "great weight" in resolving a factual question. 415 U.S. at 60 n. 21, 94 S.Ct. at 1025 n. 21. Some lower courts have relied upon that language in footnote 21 in deciding employment cases brought under Title VII as well as other workplace laws, but other courts have afforded varying levels of deference to the decisions of labor arbitrators. For example, in Collins v. New York City Transit Authority, 305 F.3d 113, 119 (2d Cir.2002), the Second Circuit in a Title VII case held that an arbitrator's award was

"highly probative of the absence of discriminatory intent." In Truax v. City of Portsmouth, 2001 WL 716120 (D.N.H. 2001), the district court declined to give an arbitration award any weight in determining sex discrimination because the issue of "just cause" was different than the question of Title VII discrimination and because the arbitrator's award did not address the question of whether the employee's discharge decision was tainted by discrimination. In Baker v. Union Pacific Railroad Co., 145 F.Supp.2d 837 (S.D.Tex.2001), the district court found the arbitration award "plainly relevant" but "not dispositive" of discrimination issues under Title VII and § 1981. A post-*Alexander* empirical study of 1761 arbitration awards involving Title VII issues found that employees also litigated the discrimination claims in 307 cases and obtained a result different than the arbitration award in only 21 cases. Michele Hoyman and Lamont Stallworth, *The Arbitration of Discrimination Grievances in the Aftermath of* Gardner–Denver, 39 Arbitration Journal 49 (September 1984)

4. As a union representative, would you be inclined to negotiate a provision in a collective bargaining agreement that constituted a "clear and unmistakable" waiver of the employees' right to take employment discrimination claims to court? If you did, would you have violated the union's duty of fair representation to the employees it represents?

When Congress in 1991 amended several federal anti-discrimination statutes, including Title VII, it provided:

Where appropriate and to the extent authorized by law, the use of alternative means of dispute resolution, including settlement negotiations, conciliation, facilitation, mediation, factfinding, minitrials, and arbitration, is encouraged to resolve disputes arising under the Acts or provisions of Federal law amended by this title.

Section 118, Civil Rights Act of 1991, Pub. L. No. 102–166, 105 Stat. 1071. If federal law encourages arbitration of employment discrimination claims, could a union's negotiation of a contract provision requiring arbitration of Title VII disputes violate the duty of fair representation? (For general discussion of the scope of the duty of fair representation, see Chapter V.A., *infra*.)

B. SECTION 301 PREEMPTION[1]

Employees governed by collective bargaining agreements sometimes seek to enforce legal rights against employers outside the grievance and

1. Bibliographic Suggestions: The Developing Labor Law 2221–2241 (Patrick Hardin and John E. Higgins, Jr., eds., 4th ed., 2001) and 467–472 (Howard Z. Rosen, Peter A. Janus and Barry J. Kearney, eds., Supp. 2003); Robert A. Gorman and Matthew W. Finkin, Basic Text on Labor Law: Unionization and Collective Bargaining §§ 32.9–32.11 (2004). Robert E. Williams and Thomas R. Bagby, Allis–Chalmers Corporation v. Lueck: The Impact of the Supreme Court's Decision on Wrongful Discharge Suits and Other State Court Employment Litigation (1986); Richard A. Bales, *The Discord Between Collective Bargaining and Individual Employment Rights: Theoretical Origins and a Proposed Solution*, 77 Boston University Law Review 687 (1997); Michael C. Harper, *Limited Section 301 Preemption: Three Cheers for the Trilogy, Only One for* Lingle *and* Lueck, 66 Chicago–Kent Law Review 685 (1990); Laura W. Stein, *Preserving Unionized Employees' Individual Employment Rights: An Argument Against Section*

arbitration procedures of the agreement. When contractual and noncontractual rights are parallel, a government agency responsible for enforcement of the noncontractual remedy may choose to defer to the contractual remedy and preclude or limit access to the noncontractual remedy. See Section A. of this Chapter. Sometimes, however, the federal statutory scheme governing enforcement of collective bargaining agreements will entirely preclude an employee's enforcement of state common law or statutory rights under the doctrine of preemption.

The Supreme Court has said that the Supremacy Clause of Article VI of the United States Constitution grants Congress power to preempt state law when it interferes with the implementation of federal labor legislation. One line of labor preemption cases—sometimes called "*Garmon* preemption" after San Diego Building Trades Council v. Garmon, 359 U.S. 236, 79 S.Ct. 773, 3 L.Ed.2d 775 (1959)—protects the regulatory and remedial scheme of the National Labor Relations Act by depriving state and federal courts of jurisdiction over subject matter that is clearly or arguably controlled by the National Labor Relations Board. A successful preemption challenge to a lawsuit under the *Garmon* doctrine results in the court dismissing the claim on jurisdictional grounds. This Section discusses another line of preemption doctrine, distinct from *Garmon* preemption, that arises not from the NLRA but rather from § 301 of the Labor Management Relations Act. Section 301 preemption was first described in Local 174, Teamsters v. Lucas Flour Co., 369 U.S. 95, 82 S.Ct. 571, 7 L.Ed.2d 593 (1962), Chapter III.A.2., *supra*.

Lucas Flour held that Congress intended that the federal common law developed to govern enforcement of collective bargaining agreements uniformly prevail over inconsistent state law. The Court was concerned that disparate interpretation of collective bargaining agreements would inhibit the negotiation of agreements, stimulate and prolong disputes about their meaning, and discourage parties from agreeing to arbitration provisions. Claims of violation of collective bargaining agreements had to be brought under § 301 and decided according to federal law. The need for uniformity would compel preemption not only of state law actions to enforce collective bargaining agreements but also of any type of cause of action that required a court to define the meaning of a term in a collective bargaining agreement.[2] Subsequent Supreme Court decisions have indicated that inclusion of a subject in a collective bargaining agreement enforceable under § 301 may bar employees from pursuing various state tort, contract, and statutory actions. But because Congress

301 Preemption, 17 Berkeley Journal of Employment and Labor Law 1 (1996); Katherine Van Wezel Stone, *The Legacy of Industrial Pluralism: The Tension Between Individual Employment Rights and the New Deal Collective Bargaining System*, 59 University of Chicago Law Review 575 (1992); Rebecca Hanner White, *Section 301's Preemption of State Law Claims: A Model for Analysis*, 41 Alabama Law Review 377 (1990).

2. This should be distinguished from a case in which state law merely provides a minimum standard for employment conditions, a case in which there is no preemption. Federal labor law does not foreclose state regulatory power over issues simply because they may be the subject of collective bargaining. See Fort Halifax Packing Co., Inc. v. Coyne, 482 U.S. 1, 107 S.Ct. 2211, 96 L.Ed.2d 1 (1987).

has never sought to occupy the entire field of labor and employment legislation, a court must determine, for each state law claim, whether Congress intended it to be precluded by federal law.

The Supreme Court applied § 301 preemption analysis in Allis–Chalmers Corp. v. Lueck, 471 U.S. 202, 105 S.Ct. 1904, 85 L.Ed.2d 206 (1985), to hold that a employee's tort action against an employer for bad faith handling of an insurance claim was preempted. Employee Lueck was covered by a collective bargaining agreement that included a disability plan funded by the employer and administered by a life insurance company. The agreement provided for resolution of insurance-related disputes by a procedure ending in arbitration. Lueck commenced receiving disability benefits for a nonoccupational back injury, but he alleged that he was harassed by interruptions of his payments and repeated requests for medical examinations. Without attempting to grieve his dispute, Lueck brought an action against both his employer and the insurance company alleging that they had handled his disability insurance in bad faith. The Wisconsin Supreme Court held that the action was not preempted because it did not arise under § 301 and because the tort claim was independent of the contractual relationship.

The United States Supreme Court reversed, rejecting the distinctions drawn by the state court:

> The interests in interpretive uniformity and predictability that require that labor-contract disputes be resolved by reference to federal law also require that the meaning given a contract phrase or term be subject to uniform federal interpretation. Thus, questions relating to what the parties to a labor agreement agreed, and what legal consequences were intended to flow from breaches of that agreement, must be resolved by reference to uniform federal law, whether such questions arise in the context of a suit for breach of contract or in a suit alleging liability in tort. Any other result would elevate form over substance and allow parties to evade the requirements of § 301 by relabeling their contract claims as claims for tortious breach of contract.

471 U.S. at 211, 105 S.Ct. at 1911. The Court said that the test for § 301 preemption was whether state law conferred rights independent of any contract right or instead whether evaluation of the state law claim was "inextricably intertwined with consideration of the terms of the labor contract." *Id.* at 213, 105 S.Ct. at 1912. The Court concluded that here a court would be unable to determine if the employer and insurance company had acted in bad faith without first determining what express and implied obligations for timely payment of disability benefits arose from the collective bargaining agreement. The Court cautioned that its holding did not require that "every state-law suit asserting a right that relates in some way to a provision in a collective-bargaining agreement, or more generally to the parties to such an agreement, necessarily is preempted by § 301." *Id.* at 220, 105 S.Ct. at 1915. Instead, the Court

said preemption determinations would have to be made on a case-by-case basis.

In Lingle v. Norge Div. of Magic Chef, Inc., 486 U.S. 399, 108 S.Ct. 1877, 100 L.Ed.2d 410 (1988), the Court made a further effort to define the scope of § 301 preemption. There, an employee covered by a collective bargaining agreement sued her employer under state law claiming that she had been discharged in retaliation for filing a workers' compensation claim. The federal district court and court of appeals held that the retaliatory discharge claim was preempted because it was "inextricably intertwined" with the collective bargaining agreement's "just cause" provision. The court of appeals considered the state law claim preempted because if the discharge violated the contractual "just cause" provision, a state court would be deciding the same issue as an arbitrator.

The Supreme Court rejected that approach, saying that factual parallelism was not the touchstone of preemption.[3] Rather, the test was whether resolution of the state law claim of retaliatory discharge required construing the collective bargaining agreement:

"[T]o show retaliatory discharge, the plaintiff must set forth sufficient facts from which it can be inferred that (1) he was discharged or threatened with discharge and (2) the employer's motive in discharging or threatening to discharge him was to deter him from exercising his rights under the Act or to interfere with his exercise of those rights." * * * Each of these purely factual questions pertains to the conduct of the employee and the conduct and motivation of the employer. Neither of the elements requires a court to interpret any term of a collective-bargaining agreement. To defend against a retaliatory discharge claim, an employer must show that it had a nonretaliatory reason for the discharge * * *; this purely factual inquiry likewise does not turn on the meaning of any provision of a collective-bargaining agreement. Thus, the state-law remedy in this case is "independent" of the collective-bargaining agreement in the sense of "independent" that matters for § 301 pre-emption purposes: resolution of the state-law claim does not require construing the collective-bargaining agreement.

486 U.S. at 407, 108 S.Ct. at 1882.

The Supreme Court in *Lingle* repeated its caveat in *Lueck* that not every dispute tangentially involving a provision of a collective bargaining agreement is preempted by § 301. The Court's effort at explaining this principle, however, seemed to raise more questions than it answered. The Court said:

A collective bargaining agreement may, of course, contain information such as rate of pay and other economic benefits that might be helpful in determining the damages to which a worker prevailing in

3. Compare the NLRB's doctrine of retrospective deferral in which factual parallelism between an claim heard by an arbitrator and a claim under the National Labor Relations Act will preclude the Board from hearing the statutory claim. See *supra* Chapter IV. A.

a state-law suit is entitled * * *. Although federal law would govern the interpretation of the agreement to determine the proper damages, the underlying state-law claim, not otherwise pre-empted, would stand. 486 U.S. at 413 n.12, 108 S.Ct. at 1885 n.12.

The Supreme Court had an opportunity to clarify its preemption doctrine in Livadas v. Bradshaw, 512 U.S. 107, 114 S.Ct. 2068, 129 L.Ed.2d 93 (1994). In *Livadas*, a state labor commissioner refused to enforce an employee's state statutory right to immediate payment of wages upon discharge on the ground that she was covered by a collective bargaining agreement. The commissioner contended that § 301 preemption prevented the agency from interpreting the collective bargaining agreement to determine the employee's contractual wage rate, the basis for calculation of the statutory penalty. The Supreme Court held there was no preemption. It said determining whether the employer had willfully failed to pay the wages upon termination was independent of the collective bargaining agreement. The Court said that it need not go beyond *Lingle* to be able to conclude that "when liability is governed by independent state law, the mere need to 'look to' the collective-bargaining agreement for damages computation is no reason to hold the state-law claim defeated by § 301." 512 U.S. at 125, 114 S. Ct. at 2079. The Court emphasized the narrowness of its holding by stating that in other circumstances, apparently if the contractual wage rate would have been less clear, a claim under the same state statute might be preempted. 512 U.S. at 125 n.19, 114 S. Ct. at 2079 n.19.

Although the Supreme Court in *Livadas* acknowledged that the lower courts had reached different interpretations of *Lingle* and *Lueck*, the Court declined to use *Livadas* as an opportunity to provide further clarification of its prior decisions. *Id.* at n.18. Moreover, in an intriguing footnote, the Court intimated that its resolution of the preemption problem might, in the future, take a quite different direction. The Court observed, in agreement with the suggestion of amicus AFL–CIO, that "[h]olding the plaintiff's cause of action substantively extinguished may not * * * always be the only means of vindicating the arbitrator's primacy as the bargained-for contract interpreter." *Id.*[4]

The Supreme Court's lack of guidance has left a degree of uncertainty about the law that encourages employers bound by collective agreements regularly to move to dismiss employee lawsuits on the ground of § 301 preemption. In recent years, employers have sought to preempt employee claims based on claims for breach of contract, breach of covenants of fair dealing, tortious interference with contract, fraud, misrepresentation, defamation, civil conspiracy, invasion of privacy, intentional infliction of emotional distress, tortious drug testing, negligence, retaliation under workers' compensation and other laws, violation

4. The Supreme Court illustrated a possible alternative means of addressing the preemption problem by citing Collyer Insulated Wire, 192 NLRB 837 (1971), *supra* Chapter IV.A., in which the NLRB prospectively deferred consideration of an unfair labor practice charge until an arbitrator had the opportunity to decide an underlying issue requiring interpretation of the collective bargaining agreement.

of state wage and hour laws and various employment discrimination statutes.[5] State courts[6] and lower federal courts have had difficulty providing consistent application of preemption standards to the myriad factual and legal claims of employees covered by collective bargaining agreements.[7]

Notes and Questions

1. Employee Gomez was injured on the job and received workers' compensation benefits. The Company concluded that Gomez was physically unable to work and dismissed him. Gomez filed an action claiming he had been discharged in retaliation for exercising his rights under the state workers' compensation law. The Company contends its action was authorized by a provision of the collective bargaining agreement permitting it to dismiss physically incapable employees. The Company moves to dismiss the action on the ground that it is preempted by § 301. Gomez responds that the collective bargaining agreement is irrelevant because the lawsuit turns on whether the Employer's motivation for discharge was the filing of the workers' compensation claim. Gomez contends that if the court finds that the Employer had another motive it need not determine its legitimacy.

(a) Should the court dismiss Gomez's lawsuit on the ground of preemption? Compare Sullivan v. Raytheon Co., 262 F.3d 41 (1st Cir. 2001), cert. denied, 534 U.S. 1118, 122 S.Ct. 931, 151 L.Ed.2d 893 (2002) (potential conflict with management rights clause requires preemption) with Trevino v. Ramos, 197 F.3d 777 (5th Cir. 1999), cert. denied, 531 U.S. 1036, 121 S.Ct. 625, 148 L.Ed.2d 534 (2000) (no preemption because issue is factual matter of employer motivation).

(b) Would your answer be different if the state statute, in addition to providing a cause of action for retaliation for filing a workers' compensation

5. The Developing Labor Law, 468–470 (Howard Z. Rosen, Peter A. Janus and Barry J. Kearney, eds., Supp. 2003).

6. As a matter of tactics, plaintiffs may prefer to bring actions for enforcement of state law claims in state rather than federal court out of belief that state courts may be less inclined to hold that their laws are preempted. If the preemptive effect of § 301 were similar to the preemptive effect of other federal statutes, the defendant employer would be unable to have the case removed to federal court to permit a federal court to decide the preemption issue, because there is no federal question jurisdiction if the complaint raises only state law issues and the federal issue is raised only as a defense. However, in Avco Corp. v. Aero Lodge No. 735, 390 U.S. 557, 88 S.Ct. 1235, 20 L.Ed.2d 126 (1968), the Supreme Court held that § 301 preemption was so expansive that claims based exclusively on state law not only were preempted, but also became from their inception federal question claims, and therefore could be removed to federal court. In Franchise Tax Board v. Construction Laborers Vacation Trust, 463 U.S. 1, 22, 103 S.Ct. 2841, 2853, 77 L.Ed.2d 420 (1983), the Court called this "complete preemption" doctrine "an independent corollary of the well-pleaded complaint rule." See also Caterpillar, Inc. v. Williams, 482 U.S. 386, 393, 107 S.Ct. 2425, 2430, 96 L.Ed.2d 318 (1987). Courts, however, have questioned whether the complete preemption doctrine also applies to employees in the railroad and airline industries governed by the Railway Labor Act. Geddes v. American Airlines, Inc., 321 F.3d 1349 (11th Cir.), cert. denied, 540 U.S. 946, 124 S.Ct. 386, 157 L.Ed.2d 276 (2003).

7. The Supreme Court noted in *Livadas* that the courts of appeals had "not been entirely uniform in their understanding and application of the principles set down in *Lingle* and *Lueck*." 512 U.S. at 125 n.18, 114 S. Ct. at 2079 n.18. See Bales, *supra* footnote 1, at 709–718 (collecting and categorizing preemption cases in the lower courts).

claim, also included the following provision, "In the event that any right set forth in this section is inconsistent with an applicable collective bargaining agreement, such agreement shall prevail."? See Martin v. Shaw's Supermarkets, Inc., 105 F.3d 40 (1st Cir.1997) (preempted) and Biagini v. Berkshire Concrete Corp., 190 F.Supp.2d 170 (D. Mass. 2002) (preempted).

(c) Gomez might also have a claim against his employer for discrimination under the federal Americans with Disabilities Act. Depending on the nature of the determinative issues, a disability claim based on state law may not be preempted. Zuckerman v. Volume Services America, Inc., 304 F.Supp.2d 365 (E.D.N.Y.2004) (state law claim of disability discrimination not preempted when it turns on factual issue of employer motivation).

2.   As a result of § 301 preemption, employees working under collective bargaining agreements may be denied the opportunity to bring legal actions, available to unrepresented employees, for violation of state statutory and common law rights.

(a) Is this result consistent with national labor policy? See Stone, *supra* footnote 1. See also, Bales, *supra* footnote 1 (suggesting that it would be better to change the law to facilitate labor arbitrators hearing employees' common law and statutory claims than to expand represented employees' access to the judicial forum).

(b) If you believe this result undermines national labor policy, should § 301 preemption be scrapped entirely, or merely differently defined? If the problem is one of definition, how should the scope of the doctrine be redefined?

(c) Would the concerns that gave rise to § 301 preemption doctrine be better satisfied if courts, rather than dismissing preempted claims, were to suspend consideration of a represented employee's statutory or common law claim until an arbitrator had an opportunity to interpret any provision of a collective bargaining agreement necessary to resolution of the legal claim?

(d) As an employer preparing campaign materials for a union representation campaign under the current preemption regime, would it be a good idea to explain to employees that they may lose state law employee protections if they unionize?

3.   The Agreement between the Union and the Employer provides for creation of a joint safety committee responsible for monitoring safety in the workplace. An employee working under the collective bargaining agreement is injured on the job.

(a) Is the injured worker's tort action against the Union, alleging that the Union failed properly to monitor safety conditions, preempted by § 301?

(b) Assume instead that the employee's tort action alleged that the employee was injured as a result of a union member of the joint safety committee having disengaged a safety device. Would the employee's action be preempted by § 301?

See United Steelworkers of America v. Rawson, 495 U.S. 362, 110 S.Ct. 1904, 109 L.Ed.2d 362 (1990); IBEW v. Hechler, 481 U.S. 851, 107 S.Ct. 2161, 95 L.Ed.2d 791 (1987); and Galvez v. Kuhn, 933 F.2d 773 (9th Cir.1991). See also Szarka v. Reynolds Metals Co., 17 F.Supp.2d 115

(N.D.N.Y.1998) (claim against union for negligent supervision of a steward preempted).

4.   The Company wrote a letter to employee Gates stating that Gates was being discharged for "dishonesty." Gates' work for the Company was governed by a collective bargaining agreement.

(a) Gates filed an action for defamation against the Company for having distributed copies of the discharge letter to eight supervisors at the Company. Is Gates' action for defamation preempted by § 301?

(b) Gates filed an action for defamation against the Company for having sent the Union a copy of the discharge letter. A provision in the collective bargaining agreement requires the Company to send copies of discharge letters to the Union. Is Gates' action preempted by § 301? Would your answer be the same if there were no explicit provision in the agreement requiring notice to the Union?

See Tellez v. Pacific Gas and Electric Co., 817 F.2d 536 (9th Cir.), cert. denied, 484 U.S. 908, 108 S.Ct. 251, 98 L.Ed.2d 209 (1987) (action for letter distributed to managers not preempted); Barbe v. Great Atlantic & Pacific Tea Co., 722 F.Supp. 1257 (D.Md.1989), aff'd, 940 F.2d 651 (4th Cir.1991), cert. denied, 502 U.S. 1059, 112 S.Ct. 939, 117 L.Ed.2d 109 (1992) (action for letter distributed to supervisors and to union preempted). See also Garley v. Sandia Corp., 236 F.3d 1200 (10th Cir. 2001) (defamation claim preempted when necessary to determine if employer's actions authorized by collective bargaining agreement); Carpenter v. C.W.A., 163 LRRM 3023 (N.D.Ga. 2000) (defamation claim not preempted when collective bargaining agreement may need to be consulted, but need not be interpreted, to determine scope of union privilege).

5.   A state Wage Payment Act requires that all vacation benefits owed to employees must be paid within two weeks after an employee's termination. At the time of her termination, employee Chan was working under a collective bargaining agreement providing for vacation time in accordance with years of service. Chan's employer maintains that it does not owe Chan any benefits. Is Chan's action under the state Wage Payment Act for the Company's failure to pay vacation benefits preempted by § 301? Does it matter whether the agreement's provision determining amounts of vacation time is clear as applied to Chan? If "clarity" is relevant to determination of preemption, how should clarity be determined? Consider the language from *Lingle* and *Livadas*, quoted above, regarding use of the contract as the measure of damages for a claim based on state law. See National Metal-crafters v. McNeil, 784 F.2d 817, 824–25 (7th Cir.1986) (preempted), distinguishing Whelan's, Inc. v. Kansas Dept. of Human Resources, 235 Kan. 425, 681 P.2d 621 (1984), on the basis that in *Whelan's* there was no dispute about the amount of benefits due; Norcon, Inc. v. Kotowski, 971 P.2d 158 (Alaska 1999) (preemption of wage claim only if contractual wage rate language is subject to "conflicting interpretations"). See also Barton v. Creasey Co., 718 F.Supp. 1284 (N.D.W.Va.1989), aff'd, 900 F.2d 249 (4th Cir.1990), cert. denied, 498 U.S. 849, 111 S.Ct. 137, 112 L.Ed.2d 104 (1990) (finding preemption without any concern about the clarity of the agreement); Hisle v. Todd Pacific Shipyards Corp., 113 Wash.App. 401, 54 P.3d 687 (2002) (claim for non-negotiable minimum wages not preempted al-

though collective bargaining agreement may have to be consulted); and Gregory v. SCIE, LLC, 317 F.3d 1050 (9th Cir. 2003) (majority and dissent disagree about whether state law overtime claim requires interpretation of collective bargaining agreement).

6.   A state statute provides that an employer must offer an employee who tests positive for drugs or alcohol an opportunity for rehabilitation before taking any adverse personnel action. Under a collective bargaining agreement, employees are entitled to a leave of absence for alcohol abuse rehabilitation only if they request it prior to commission of an act subject to disciplinary action. Watkins is discharged for drunk driving and is not permitted a leave of absence for rehabilitation. She brings an action alleging that she was discharged in violation of the state statute. Is her action preempted by § 301? Visnovec v. Yellow Freight System, Inc., 754 F.Supp. 142 (D.Minn.1990) (action under some provisions preempted, some not); Robinson v. Fred Meyers Stores, Inc., 252 F.Supp.2d 905 (D. Ariz. 2002) (claims based on state drug testing statute preempted); Karnes v. Boeing Co., 335 F.3d 1189 (10th Cir. 2003) (majority holds no preemption of claim for violation of state drug testing statute; dissent disagrees). Does it matter whether, as a matter of state law, employees are permitted prospectively to waive their statutory right to rehabilitation?

Chapter V

IMPACT OF LAW

A. THE DUTY OF FAIR REPRESENTATION[1]

1. INTRODUCTION

Although the labor arbitration process is created by private agreement between union and management, arbitration operates within an environment of public law that also defines the rights and duties of the participants. One element of this environment, the union's duty of fair representation, profoundly affects the manner in which unions represent workers in the grievance process and arbitration. The existence of the union's duty also affects, indirectly but very significantly, the arbitration process and its other participants.

The Supreme Court first recognized the duty of fair representation (DFR) as a limitation upon the union's discretion in the collective

---

1. Bibliographic Suggestions: Timothy J. Boyce and Ronald Turner, Fair Representation, The NLRB, and the Courts (rev. ed. 1984); The Developing Labor Law, 1857–1960 (Patrick Hardin and John E. Higgins, Jr., eds., 4th ed., 2001) and Cumulative Supplement 399–414 (2003); The Duty of Fair Representation (Jean T. McKelvey, ed. 1977); Robert A. Gorman and Matthew W. Finkin, Basic Text on Labor Law: Unionization and Collective Bargaining §§ 30.1–30.11 (2004). Fairweather's Practice and Procedure in Labor Arbitration 689 (Ray J. Schoonhoven, ed., 4th ed. 1999); David E. Feller, *A General Theory of the Collective Bargaining Agreement*, 61 California Law Review 663 (1973); Matthew W. Finkin, *The Limits of Majority Rule in Collective Bargaining*, 64 Minnesota Law Review 183 (1980); Michael J. Goldberg, *The Duty of Fair Representation: What the Courts Do in Fact*, 34 Buffalo Law Review 89 (1985); Michael C. Harper and Ira C. Lupu, *Fair Representation as Equal Protection*, 98 Harvard Law Review 1211 (1985); Karl E. Klare, *The Quest for Industrial Democracy and the Struggle Against Racism: Perspectives from Labor and Civil Rights Law*, 61 Oregon Law Review 157 (1982); William Levin, *Duty of Fair Representation: The Role of the Arbitrator*, 33 Proceedings of the National Academy of Arbitrators 309 (1982); Martin H. Malin, *The Supreme Court and the Duty of Fair Representation*, 27 Harvard Civil Rights–Civil Liberties Law Review 127 (1992); Russell G. Pearce, *The Union Lawyer's Obligations to Bargaining Unit Members: A Case Study of the Interdependence of Legal Ethics and Substantive Law*, 37 South Texas Law Review 1095 (1996); Clyde W. Summers, *The Individual Employee's Rights Under the Collective Agreement: What Constitutes Fair Representation?*, 126 University of Pennsylvania Law Review 251 (1977); Lea S. VanderVelde, *A Fair Process Model for the Union's Fair Representation Duty*, 67 Minnesota Law Review 1079 (1983); Lea S. VanderVelde, *Making Good on* Vaca's *Promise: Apportioning Back Pay to Achieve Remedial Goals*, 32 UCLA Law Review 302 (1984).

bargaining process. The duty was later imposed upon unions engaged in handling grievances, both before and during arbitration. Although the Supreme Court later narrowed the extent of the union duty in the bargaining setting, the scope of the union's duty in grievance handling continues to be sufficiently broad to give rise to a substantial amount of litigation.

This section explores the origins of the duty of fair representation, its expansion to grievance handling, problems of defining the scope of the duty in the grievance setting, and procedural and remedial issues.

2.   ORIGINS OF THE DUTY OF FAIR REPRESENTATION IN THE CONTEXT OF COLLECTIVE BARGAINING

To understand the nature and scope of the union's duty of fair representation in the context of arbitration, we need first to understand its creation and development within the context of collective bargaining. When, in 1944, the Supreme Court encountered an obvious racial injustice in collective bargaining in the absence of any explicit statutory text affording a remedy, it creatively announced the existence of a duty of fair representation to fill the gap.

In Steele v. Louisville & Nashville Railroad Co., 323 U.S. 192, 65 S.Ct. 226, 89 L.Ed. 173 (1944), the Brotherhood of Locomotive Firemen and Enginemen was the exclusive collective bargaining representative for all firemen employed by the railroad. The Brotherhood allowed only whites to be members of the union.[2] The union negotiated a series of supplemental agreements with the Railroad under which, initially, vacancies were assigned to white firemen. Later, African–American fireman were transferred to more arduous, longer, and less remunerative work. The African–American firemen were not given notice or an opportunity to be heard before these agreements were put into effect. A group of African–American firemen sued both the union and the railroad in Alabama state court. The plaintiffs sought, among other remedies, damages and an injunction against enforcement of the discriminatory agreements. The Supreme Court of Alabama held that the plaintiffs' complaint stated no cause of action. It found that the union had plenary authority to negotiate with the Railroad without any obligation to protect the rights of minorities from discrimination, however gross.

In an opinion by Chief Justice Stone, the Court said that problematic constitutional questions would arise if the Railway Labor Act were construed to vest a union with the exclusive right to negotiate with an employer but then not impose upon it a duty to act fairly on behalf of all those it represented. It said that a duty of fair representation could be inferred from the statutory grant of exclusivity because the statute deprived employees of the right to bargain individually with their employer and because, in the absence of such a duty, the Act would not achieve its objective of labor peace. The Court said, "The fair interpreta-

---

2. It was not until enactment of Title VII of the Civil Rights Act of 1964, two decades after *Steele*, that race discrimination in union membership became unlawful.

tion of the statutory language is that the organization chosen to represent a craft is to represent all its members, the majority as well as the minority, and it is to act for and not against those whom it represents." As the Court did not find any administrative mechanism clearly available for this cause of action, the duty of fair representation would be enforceable by actions in court for damages and injunctions. Courts could also invalidate agreements that were a product of violations of the duty.

While the Court in *Steele* prohibited a union from discriminating against a racial minority in negotiation of a collective agreement, it was willing to leave other racial discrimination fully intact. It said that the Railway Labor Act "does not deny to such a bargaining labor organization the right to determine eligibility to its membership." Justice Murphy, in a concurrence, was troubled by the failure of the Court to address the constitutionality of affording a union the power of exclusive representation while permitting it to exclude employees from membership on the basis of race. He said, "Racism is far too virulent today to permit the slightest refusal, in the light of a Constitution that abhors it, to expose and condemn it wherever it appears in the course of a statutory interpretation."

After declaring the existence of the duty the Court immediately realized the difficulty of defining its scope without unduly undermining the union's bargaining autonomy. It began the task analytically, suggesting an analogy with the obligations of a legislature elected by majority vote:

> We think that the Railway Labor Act imposes upon the statutory representative of a craft at least as exacting a duty to protect equally the interests of the members of the craft as the Constitution imposes upon a legislature to give equal protection to the interests of those for whom it legislates. Congress has seen fit to clothe the bargaining representative with powers comparable to those possessed by a legislative body both to create and restrict the rights of those whom it represents, * * * but it has also imposed on the representative a corresponding duty. We hold that the language of the Act * * * read in the light of the purposes of the Act, expresses the aim of Congress to impose on the bargaining representative of a craft or class of employees the duty to exercise fairly the power conferred upon it in behalf of all those for whom it acts, without hostile discrimination against them.

The Court knew from the start that it could not simply say that a union was prohibited from negotiating agreements that offered different benefits to different employees because such distinctions are fundamental to labor agreements.

> This does not mean that the statutory representative of a craft is barred from making contracts which may have unfavorable effects on some of the members of the craft represented. Variations in the terms of the contract based on differences relevant to the authorized

purposes of the contract in conditions to which they are to be applied, such as differences in seniority, the type of work performed, the competence and skill with which it is performed, are within the scope of the bargaining representation of a craft, all of whose members are not identical in their interest or merit.

Unions had the authority to make those kinds of distinctions, but they did not have the authority to treat employees differently in the absence of "relevant differences." While the Court acknowledged that it might not always be easy to know when differences in conditions would warrant differences in contractual benefits, it could at least resolve the case before it. Discriminations based on race alone, it said, "are obviously irrelevant and invidious." The only guidance it offered for defining the limits of permissible difference was that in bargaining and making contracts a union was required to act "without hostile discrimination, fairly, impartially, and in good faith."

The Court suggested that the duty of fair representation imposed procedural as well as substantive limits upon a union's conduct in collective bargaining. It said that whenever it was necessary, in order to treat minorities fairly, a "union is required to consider requests of nonunion members of the craft and expressions of their views with respect to collective bargaining with the employer and to give to them notice of and opportunity for hearing upon its proposed action."

The Supreme Court's decision in *Steele* had found a duty of fair representation implicit in the text of the Railway Labor Act. The Court, in Ford Motor Co. v. Huffman, 345 U.S. 330, 73 S.Ct. 681, 97 L.Ed. 1048 (1953), assumed the duty similarly arose from the text of the National Labor Relations Act and confronted the question of whether contractual distinctions between employees on grounds other than race also might violate the duty of fair representation.

Ford Motor arose from a contract provision between the United Auto Workers and Ford which, in the aftermath of World War II, granted employees workplace seniority for pre-employment military service. During postwar layoffs, some employees who started at Ford after military service retained their jobs while employees with more time at Ford were laid off. The Court distinguished *Steele* and held that the UAW had not violated the duty of fair representation. The Court explained:

> Inevitably differences arise in the manner and degree to which the terms of any negotiated agreement affect individual employees and classes of employees. The mere existence of such differences does not make them invalid. The complete satisfaction of all who are represented is hardly to be expected. A wide range of reasonableness must be allowed a statutory bargaining representative in serving the unit it represents, subject always to complete good faith and honesty of purpose in the exercise of its discretion.
>
> Compromises on a temporary basis, with a view to long-range advantages, are natural incidents of negotiation. Differences in

wages, hours and conditions of employment reflect countless variables. Seniority rules governing promotions, transfers, layoffs and similar matters may in the first instance, revolve around length of competent service. Variations acceptable in the discretion of bargaining representatives, however, may well include differences based upon such matters as the unit within which seniority is to be computed, the privileges to which it shall relate, the nature of the work, the time at which it is done, the fitness, ability or age of the employees, their family responsibilities, injuries received in course of service, and time or labor devoted to related public service, whether civil or military, voluntary or involuntary.

Subsequently, the Supreme Court emphasized the narrowness of the union's duty of fair representation in the collective bargaining context. In Air Line Pilots Association, International v. O'Neill, 499 U.S. 65, 111 S.Ct. 1127, 113 L.Ed.2d 51 (1991), the Court explained that a union's behavior exceeds the "wide range of reasonableness" afforded in *Ford Motor* only if its conduct is irrational. In the *Air Line Pilots* case, the Union's agreement with Continental Airlines provided for striking pilots to obtain a limited number of positions at the conclusion of a strike. The Fifth Circuit Court of Appeals thought that the union's agreement left the pilots worse off than a unilateral termination of the strike under which, it assumed, they would have been entitled to reemployment on the basis of seniority. The Supreme Court, however, found that legal uncertainties about the seniority rights of former strikers and the possibility of protracted litigation made the settlement reasonable. It said, "In labor disputes, as in other kinds of litigation, even a bad settlement may be more advantageous in the long run than a good lawsuit." The Supreme Court concluded that even if the pilots were in fact worse off as a result of the agreement, the contract was not irrational when viewed "in light of the factual and legal landscape at the time of the union's actions."

Later, the Supreme Court described the *Air Line Pilots* case as holding that a "union's conduct can be classified as arbitrary only when it is irrational, when it is without a rational basis or explanation." Marquez v. Screen Actors Guild, Inc., 525 U.S. 33, 119 S.Ct. 292, 142 L.Ed.2d 242 (1998). There the Supreme Court held that a union did not violate its duty of fair representation when it negotiated a union security clause that tracked the language of the National Labor Relations Act, even though that meant it did not fully detail all employee rights under such a clause. The Supreme Court also cautioned employees that casting claims of violation of the National Labor Relations Act as violations of the duty of fair representation could not be used to circumvent the primary jurisdiction of the National Labor Relations Board over unfair labor practices. "When a plaintiff's only claim is that the union violated the NLRA, the plaintiff cannot avoid the jurisdiction of the NLRB by characterizing this alleged statutory violation as a breach of the duty of fair representation." Federal courts have jurisdiction to hear a duty of fair representation claim only if the employee alleges facts suggesting that "the union's violation of the statute was arbitrary, discriminatory, or in bad faith."

3. DEFINING THE DUTY OF FAIR REPRESENTATION IN THE CONTEXT OF GRIEVANCE ARBITRATION

VACA v. SIPES
Supreme Court of the United States, 1967.
386 U.S. 171, 87 S.Ct. 903, 17 L.Ed.2d 842.

MR. JUSTICE WHITE delivered the opinion of the Court.

[Benjamin Owens was employed by the Swift meat packing company and represented by the Packinghouse Workers union. Owens had been under treatment for high blood pressure for a long time. Following a sick leave, he was certified by his family physician as ready to return to work, but Swift discharged him for poor health. The Union filed a grievance on Owens' behalf seeking his reinstatement and pursued it through the fourth step of the grievance procedure. When the Union received a new medical report that did not support Owens' position, the Union decided not to take the grievance to arbitration.]

[Owens then filed this action in state court in Missouri against his union alleging that he had been discharged from employment and that the union had "arbitrarily, capriciously and without just or reasonable reason or cause" refused to take his grievance to arbitration. Owens filed a separate suit for breach of contract against Swift which was still pending in the trial court at the time of the United States Supreme Court's consideration of his action against the union.]

[In the trial court, the union asserted that the state court lacked jurisdiction because the claim was properly posed as an unfair labor practice under the National Labor Relations Act.]

In his charge to the jury, the trial judge instructed that petitioners would be liable if Swift had wrongfully discharged Owens and if the Union had "arbitrarily * * * and without just cause or excuse * * * refused" to press Owens' grievance to arbitration. Punitive damages could also be awarded, the trial judge charged, if the Union's conduct was "willful, wanton and malicious." However, the jury must return a verdict for the defendants, the judge instructed, "if you find and believe from the evidence that the union and its representatives acted reasonably and in good faith in the handling and processing of the grievance of the plaintiff." R., at 161–162.

[A jury awarded Owens compensatory and punitive damages, but the trial judge set aside the verdict on the ground that the NLRB had exclusive jurisdiction. The Supreme Court of Missouri disagreed and directed reinstatement of the verdict.]

II.

Petitioners challenge the jurisdiction of the Missouri courts on the ground that the alleged conduct of the Union was arguably an unfair labor practice and within the exclusive jurisdiction of the NLRB. Petitioners rely on *Miranda Fuel Co.*, 140 N.L.R.B. 181 (1962), enforcement denied, 326 F.2d 172 (2d Cir.1963), where a sharply divided Board held for the first time that a union's breach of its statutory duty of fair representation violates N.L.R.A. § 8(b), as amended. With the NLRB's adoption of *Miranda Fuel*, petitioners argue, the broad pre-emption doctrine defined in *San Diego Building Trades Council v. Garmon*, 359 U.S. 236, becomes applicable. For the reasons which follow, we reject this argument.

[The Court noted that the duty of fair representation had been created by the courts before the NLRB had been given unfair labor practice jurisdiction over unions. The Court observed that the Board had adopted and applied the doctrine as it had developed in the federal courts. It questioned whether the Board had any special expertise in understanding collective bargaining negotiations and grievance machinery because those matters were not normally within the Board's jurisdiction. The Court expressed concern that if the NLRB remedy were the only one available, the injured employee might be foreclosed from bringing a meritorious claim because of the unreviewable discretion of the Board's General Counsel in deciding whether to issue an unfair labor practice complaint. The Court was also influenced by the fact that limiting the employee to an NLRB claim would preclude the employee from overcoming the employer's argument in a breach of contract claim that the employee had failed to exhaust contractual remedies.]

For these reasons, we think the wrongfully discharged employee may bring an action against his employer in the face of a defense based upon the failure to exhaust contractual remedies, provided the employee can prove that the union as bargaining agent breached its duty of fair representation in its handling of the employee's grievance. We may assume for present purposes that such a breach of duty by the union is an unfair labor practice, as the NLRB and the Fifth Circuit have held. The employee's suit against the employer, however, remains a § 301 suit, and the jurisdiction of the courts is no more destroyed by the fact that the employee, as part and parcel of his § 301 action, finds it necessary to prove an unfair labor practice by the union, than it is by the fact that the suit may involve an unfair labor practice by the employer himself. The court is free to determine whether the employee is barred by the actions of his union representative, and, if not, to proceed with the case. And if, to facilitate his case, the employee joins the union as a defendant, the situation is not substantially changed. The action is still a § 301 suit, and the jurisdiction of the courts is not pre-empted under the *Garmon* principle. This, at the very least, is the holding of *Humphrey v. Moore, supra*, with respect to pre-emption, as petitioners recognize in their brief. And, insofar as adjudication of the union's breach of duty is concerned, the result should be no different if the employee, as Owens did here, sues the employer and the union in separate actions. There would be very little to commend a rule which would permit the Missouri courts to adjudicate the Union's conduct in an action against Swift but not in an action against the Union itself.

For the above reasons, it is obvious that the courts will be compelled to pass upon whether there has been a breach of the duty of fair representation in the context of many § 301 breach-of-contract actions. If a breach of duty by the union and a breach of contract by the employer are proven, the court must fashion an appropriate remedy. Presumably, in at least some cases, the union's breach of duty will have enhanced or contributed to the employee's injury. What possible sense could there be in a rule which would permit a court that has litigated the fault of employer and union to fashion a remedy only with respect to the employer? Under such a rule, either the employer would be compelled by the court to pay for the union's wrong—slight deterrence, indeed, to future union misconduct—or the injured employee would be forced to go to two tribunals to repair a single injury. Moreover, the Board would be compelled in many cases either to remedy injuries arising out of a breach of contract, a task which Congress has not assigned to it, or to leave the individual employee without remedy for the union's wrong. Given the strong reasons for not pre-empting duty of fair representation suits in general, and the fact that the courts in many § 301 suits must adjudicate whether the union has breached its duty, we conclude that the courts may also fashion remedies for such a breach of duty.

It follows from the above that the Missouri courts had jurisdiction in this case. Of course, it is quite another problem to determine what remedies may be available against the Union if a breach of duty is proven. See Part IV, *infra*. But the unique role played by the duty of fair representation doctrine in the scheme of federal labor laws, and its important relationship to the judicial enforcement of collective bargaining agreements in the context presented here, render the *Garmon* pre-emption doctrine inapplicable.

III.

Petitioners contend, as they did in their motion for judgment notwithstanding the jury's verdict, that Owens failed to prove that the Union breached its duty of fair representation in its handling of Owens' grievance. Petitioners also argue that the Supreme Court of Missouri, in rejecting this contention, applied a standard that is inconsistent with governing principles of federal law with respect to the Union's duty to an individual employee in its processing of grievances under the collective bargaining agreement with Swift. We agree with both contentions. * * *

A.   * * * Quite obviously, the question which the Missouri Supreme Court thought dispositive of the issue of liability was whether the evidence supported Owens' assertion that he had been wrongfully discharged by Swift, regardless of the Union's good faith in reaching a contrary conclusion. This was also the major concern of the plaintiff at trial: the bulk of Owens' evidence was directed at whether he was medically fit at the time of discharge and whether he had performed heavy work after that discharge.

A breach of the statutory duty of fair representation occurs only when a union's conduct toward a member of the collective bargaining unit is arbitrary, discriminatory, or in bad faith. * * *

Though we accept the proposition that a union may not arbitrarily ignore a meritorious grievance or process it in perfunctory fashion, we do not agree that the individual employee has an absolute right to have his grievance taken to arbitration regardless of the provisions of the applicable collective bargaining agreement. In L.M.R.A. § 203(d), 61 Stat. 154, 29 U.S.C. § 173(d), Congress declared that "Final adjustment by a method agreed upon by the parties is * * * the desirable method for settlement of grievance disputes arising over the application or interpretation of an existing collective-bargaining agreement." In providing for a grievance and arbitration procedure which gives the union discretion to supervise the grievance machinery and to invoke arbitration, the employer and the union contemplate that each will endeavor in good faith to settle grievances short of arbitration. Through this settlement process, frivolous grievances are ended prior to the most costly and time-consuming step in the grievance procedures. Moreover, both sides are assured that similar complaints will be treated consistently, and major problem areas in the interpretation of the collective bargaining contract can be isolated and perhaps resolved. And finally, the settlement process furthers the interest of the union as statutory agent and as coauthor of the bargaining agreement in representing the employees in the enforcement of that agreement. See Cox, Rights Under a Labor Agreement, 69 Harv. L. Rev. 601 (1956).

If the individual employee could compel arbitration of his grievance regardless of its merit, the settlement machinery provided by the contract would be substantially undermined, thus destroying the employer's confidence in the union's authority and returning the individual grievant to the vagaries of independent and unsystematic negotiation. Moreover, under such a rule, a significantly greater number of grievances would proceed to arbitration.[15] This would greatly increase the cost of the grievance machinery and could so overburden the arbitration process as to prevent it from functioning successfully. See NLRB v. Acme Industrial Co., 385 U.S. 432, 438; Ross, Distressed Grievance Procedures and Their Rehabilitation, in Labor Arbitration and Industrial Change, Proceedings of the 16th Annual Meeting, National Academy of Arbitrators 104 (1963). It can well be doubted whether the parties to collective bargain-

15. Under current grievance practices, an attempt is usually made to keep the number of arbitrated grievances to a minimum. An officer of the National Union testified in this case that only one of 967 grievances filed at all of Swift's plants between September 1961 and October 1963 was taken to arbitration. And the AFL–CIO's amicus brief reveals similar performances at General Motors Corporation and United States Steel Corporation, two of the Nation's largest unionized employers: less than .05% of all written grievances filed during a recent period at General Motors required arbitration, while only 5.6% of the grievances processed beyond the first step at United States Steel were decided by an arbitrator.

ing agreements would long continue to provide for detailed grievance and arbitration procedures of the kind encouraged by L.M.R.A. § 203(d), *supra*, if their power to settle the majority of grievances short of the costlier and more time-consuming steps was limited by a rule permitting the grievant unilaterally to invoke arbitration. Nor do we see substantial danger to the interests of the individual employee if his statutory agent is given the contractual power honestly and in good faith to settle grievances short of arbitration. For these reasons, we conclude that a union does not breach its duty of fair representation, and thereby open up a suit by the employee for breach of contract, merely because it settled the grievance short of arbitration.

For these same reasons, the standard applied here by the Missouri Supreme Court cannot be sustained. For if a union's decision that a particular grievance lacks sufficient merit to justify arbitration would constitute a breach of the duty of fair representation because a judge or jury later found the grievance meritorious, the union's incentive to settle such grievances short of arbitration would be seriously reduced. The dampening effect on the entire grievance procedure of this reduction of the union's freedom to settle claims in good faith would surely be substantial. Since the union's statutory duty of fair representation protects the individual employee from arbitrary abuses of the settlement device by providing him with recourse against both employer (in a § 301 suit) and union, this severe limitation on the power to settle grievances is neither necessary nor desirable. Therefore, we conclude that the Supreme Court of Missouri erred in upholding the verdict in this case solely on the ground that the evidence supported Owens' claim that he had been wrongfully discharged.

B. Applying the proper standard of union liability to the facts of this case, we cannot uphold the jury's award, for we conclude that as a matter of federal law the evidence does not support a verdict that the Union breached its duty of fair representation. As we have stated, Owens could not have established a breach of that duty merely by convincing the jury that he was in fact fit for work in 1960; he must also have proved arbitrary or bad-faith conduct on the part of the Union in processing his grievance. The evidence revealed that the Union diligently supervised the grievance into the fourth step of the bargaining agreement's procedure, with the Union's business representative serving as Owens' advocate throughout these steps. When Swift refused to reinstate Owens on the basis of his medical reports indicating reduced blood pressure, the Union sent him to another doctor of his own choice, at Union expense, in an attempt to amass persuasive medical evidence of Owens' fitness for work. When this examination proved unfavorable, the Union concluded that it could not establish a wrongful discharge. It then encouraged Swift to find light work for Owens at the plant. When this effort failed, the Union determined that arbitration would be fruitless and suggested to Owens that he accept Swift's offer to send him to a heart association for rehabilitation. At this point, Owens' grievance was suspended in the fourth step in the hope that he might be rehabilitated.

In administering the grievance and arbitration machinery as statutory agent of the employees, a union must, in good faith and in a nonarbitrary manner, make decisions as to the merits of particular grievances. See *Humphrey v. Moore*, 375 U.S. 335, 349–350; *Ford Motor Co. v. Huffman*, 345 U.S. 330, 337–339. In a case such as this, when Owens supplied the Union with medical evidence supporting his position, the Union might well have breached its duty had it ignored Owens' complaint or had it processed the grievance in a perfunctory manner. See Cox, Rights under a Labor Agreement, 69 Harv. L. Rev., at 632–634. But here the Union processed the grievance into the fourth step, attempted to gather sufficient evidence to prove Owens' case, attempted to secure for Owens less vigorous work at the plant, and joined in the employer's efforts to have Owens rehabilitated. Only when these efforts all proved unsuccessful did the Union conclude both that arbitration would be fruitless and that the grievance should be dismissed. There was no evidence that any Union officer was personally hostile to Owens or that the Union acted at any time other than in good faith. Having concluded that the individual employee has no absolute right to have his grievance arbitrated under the collective bargaining agreement at issue, and that a breach of the duty of fair representation is not established merely by proof that the underlying grievance was meritorious, we must conclude that that duty was not breached here.

IV.

[The Supreme Court also found that the Missouri Supreme Court had erred in requiring the union to compensate the employee for damages resulting from the employer's alleged breach of contract. The Court said that the union's breach was no reason to exempt the employer from its obligation for contractual damages.]

Petitioners urge that an employee be restricted in such circumstances to a decree compelling the employer and the union to arbitrate the underlying grievance. It is true that the employee's action is based on the employer's alleged breach of contract plus the union's alleged wrongful failure to afford him his contractual remedy of arbitration. For this reason, an order compelling arbitration should be viewed as one of the available remedies when a breach of the union's duty is proved. But we see no reason inflexibly to require arbitration in all cases. In some cases, for example, at least part of the employee's damages may be attributable to the union's breach of duty, and an arbitrator may have no power under the bargaining agreement to award such damages against the union. In other cases, the arbitrable issues may be substantially resolved in the course of trying the fair representation controversy. In such situations, the court should be free to decide the contractual claim and to award the employee appropriate damages or equitable relief.

A more difficult question is, what portion of the employee's damages may be charged to the union: in particular, may an award against a union include, as it did here, damages attributable solely to the employer's breach of contract? We think not. Though the union has violated a statutory duty in failing to press the grievance, it is the employer's unrelated breach of contract which triggered the controversy and which caused this portion of the employee's damages. The employee should have no difficulty recovering these damages from the employer, who cannot, as we have explained, hide behind the union's wrongful failure to act; in fact, the employer may be (and probably should be) joined as a defendant in the fair representation suit, as in *Humphrey v. Moore, supra.* It could be a real hardship on the union to pay these damages, even if the union were given a right of indemnification against the employer. With the employee assured of direct recovery from the employer, we see no merit in requiring the union to pay the employer's share of the damages.[18] The governing principle, then, is to apportion liability between the employer and the union according to the damage caused by the fault of each. Thus, damages attributable solely to the employer's breach of contract should not be charged to the union, but increases if any in those damages caused by the union's refusal to process the grievance should not be charged to the employer. In this case, even if the Union had breached its duty, all or almost all of Owens' damages would still be attributable to his allegedly wrongful discharge by Swift. For these reasons, even if the Union here had properly been found liable for a breach of duty, it is clear that the damage award was improper.

Reversed.

MR. JUSTICE FORTAS, with whom THE CHIEF JUSTICE and MR. JUSTICE HARLAN join, concurring in the result. [The justices joining in the concurrence voted to reverse the state court decision on the ground of *Garmon* preemption, concluding that the state court lacked jurisdiction because an alleged violation of the duty of fair representation was within the exclusive jurisdiction of the National Labor Relations Board.]

MR. JUSTICE BLACK, dissenting.

The Court today opens slightly the courthouse door to an employee's incidental claim against his union for breach of its duty of fair representation, only to shut it in his face when he seeks direct judicial relief for his underlying and more valuable breach-of-contract claim against his employer. This result follows from the Court's announcement in this case, involving an employee's suit against his union, of a new rule to govern an employee's suit against his employer. The rule is that before an employee can sue his employer under § 301 of the L.M.R.A. for a

---

18. We are not dealing here with situations where a union has affirmatively caused the employer to commit the alleged breach of contract. In cases of that sort where the union's conduct is found to be an unfair labor practice, the NLRB has found an unfair labor practice by the employer, too, and has held the union and the employer jointly and severally liable for any back pay found owing to the particular employee who was the subject of their joint discrimination. *E.g., Imparato Stevedoring Corp.,* 113 N.L.R.B. 883 (1955); *Squirt Distrib. Co.,* 92 N.L.R.B. 1667 (1951); *H.M. Newman,* 85 N.L.R.B. 725 (1949). Even if this approach would be appropriate for analogous § 301 and breach-of-duty suits, it is not applicable here. Since the Union played no part in Swift's alleged breach of contract and since Swift took no part in the Union's alleged breach of duty, joint liability for either wrong would be unwarranted.

simple breach of his employment contract, the employee must prove not only that he attempted to exhaust his contractual remedies, but that his attempt to exhaust them was frustrated by "arbitrary, discriminatory, or * * * bad faith" conduct on the part of his union. With this new rule and its result I cannot agree. * * *

Owens, who now has obtained a judicial determination that he was wrongfully discharged, is left remediless, and Swift, having breached its contract, is allowed to hide behind, and is shielded by, the union's conduct. I simply fail to see how it should make one iota of difference, as far as the "unrelated breach of contract" by Swift is concerned, whether the union's conduct is wrongful or rightful. * * *

Today the Court holds that an employee with a meritorious claim has no absolute right to have it either litigated or arbitrated. * * * If the Court here were satisfied with merely holding that in this situation the employee could not recover damages from the union unless the union breached its duty of fair representation, then it would be one thing to say that the union did not do so in making a good-faith decision not to take the employee's grievance to arbitration. But if, as the Court goes on to hold, the employee cannot sue his employer for breach of contract unless his failure to exhaust contractual remedies is due to the union's breach of its duty of fair representation, then I am quite unwilling to say that the union's refusal to exhaust such remedies—however nonarbitrary—does not amount to a breach of its duty. Either the employee should be able to sue his employer for breach of contract after having attempted to exhaust his contractual remedies, or the union should have an absolute duty to exhaust contractual remedies on his behalf. The merits of an employee's grievance would thus be determined by either a jury or an arbitrator. Under today's decision it will never be determined by either. * * *

The Court suggests three reasons for giving the union this almost unlimited discretion to deprive injured employees of all remedies for breach of contract. The first is that "frivolous grievances" will be ended prior to time-consuming and costly arbitration. But here no one, not even the union, suggests that Benjamin Owens' grievance was frivolous. The union decided not to take it to arbitration simply because the union doubted the chance of success. Even if this was a good-faith doubt, I think the union had the duty to present this contested, but serious, claim to the arbitrator whose very function is to decide such claims on the basis of what he believes to be right. Second, the Court says that allowing the union to settle grievances prior to arbitration will assure consistent treatment of "major problem areas in the interpretation of the collective bargaining contract." But can it be argued that whether Owens was "fit to work" presents a major problem in the interpretation of the collective bargaining agreement? The problem here was one of interpreting medical reports, not a collective bargaining agreement, and of evaluating other evidence of Owens' physical condition. I doubt whether consistency is either possible or desirable in determining whether a particular employee is able to perform a particular job. Finally, the

Court suggests that its decision "furthers the interest of the union as statutory agent." I think this is the real reason for today's decision which entirely overlooks the interests of the injured employee, the only one who has anything to lose. Of course, anything which gives the union life and death power over those whom it is supposed to represent furthers its "interest." I simply fail to see how the union's legitimate role as statutory agent is undermined by requiring it to prosecute all serious grievances to a conclusion or by allowing the injured employee to sue his employer after he has given the union a chance to act on his behalf. * * *

Today's decision, requiring the individual employee to take on both the employer and the union in every suit against the employer and to prove not only that the employer breached its contract, but that the union acted arbitrarily, converts what would otherwise be a simple breach-of-contract action into a three-ring donnybrook. It puts an intolerable burden on employees with meritorious grievances and means they will frequently be left with no remedy. Today's decision, while giving the worker an ephemeral right to sue his union for breach of its duty of fair representation, creates insurmountable obstacles to block his far more valuable right to sue his employer for breach of the collective bargaining agreement.

Notes and Questions

1. (a) Justice Black's dissent assumes that the employer breached the contract. Note that the jury so found, but only in a case in which the employer did not participate. (Owens had a separate suit against the employer.) If the employee sues the union in a hybrid duty of fair representation/breach of contract suit, is the employer a necessary party? If not, what happens when separate judges or juries differ over the question of the alleged breach? If the employee sues the employer in a hybrid case, is the union a necessary party? Or can the union and employer be counted on to represent each other's interests?

(b) Justice Black asserts that the employee should be able to sue for breach of contract even if the union fairly concludes the case is not worth arbitrating. The typical collective bargaining agreement, however, makes the grievance and arbitration procedure the *exclusive* remedy, and gives the union *exclusive* control over that procedure. If the contract in *Vaca* contained those clauses, shouldn't Owens lose as a matter of contract law? Or is Black asserting a *statutory* right to sue regardless of the contract's terms? If so, what is the source of that statutory right? Read § 301 of the Labor Management Relations Act in Appendix B. Does this grant Owens a right to sue?

(c) If Justice Black's opinion were the law, how would you advise employer (or union) clients to react? Does your answer to this question suggest a reason why the majority did *not* agree with Justice Black?

2. Professor Clyde Summers has described *Vaca* as creating a "Rube Goldberg device" and "a confusion of roles which rivals the Marx brothers in *A Night at the Opera*" because the "guilty union defends by pleading the

virtue of the employer" and the "guilty employer defends by pleading the virtue of the union." Clyde W. Summers, *The Individual Employee's Rights Under the Collective Agreement: What Constitutes Fair Representation,* 27 Proceedings of the National Academy of Arbitrators, 14, 15–16 (1975). Is the litigation structure created by *Vaca* as convoluted and paradoxical as Professor Summers suggests?

3. The *Vaca* Court noted that the National Labor Relations Board considers a breach of the duty of fair representation to be an unfair labor practice. This gives a potential plaintiff a choice of forum. What factors would you consider in advising a client whether to sue or to file an unfair labor charge?

4. *Vaca* had suggested that an employee would have an action for breach of contract against an employer when a union's failure to pursue a grievance violated its duty of fair representation. The Supreme Court went further, in Hines v. Anchor Motor Freight, Inc., 424 U.S. 554, 96 S.Ct. 1048, 47 L.Ed.2d 231 (1976), when it held that even if a grievance had been fully considered under contractual grievance resolution procedures, the employer could still be sued for breach of contract if the grievance procedure was tainted by the union's violation of the duty of fair representation. The Supreme Court quoted its statement from *Vaca* that a union could violate the duty if it ignored an employee's complaint or processed it in a "perfunctory manner."

In *Hines*, truck drivers had been discharged for dishonesty for seeking reimbursement for motel expenses in excess of the actual charges. The company had receipts presented by the drivers showing charges in excess of those shown on the motel's registration cards. The employer also had a notarized statement of the motel clerk asserting the accuracy of the cards and an affidavit from the motel owner stating that the registration cards were accurate. The union pursued the employees' grievance to a hearing before a joint arbitration committee. At the hearing, the employees denied dishonesty but the union did not present any further evidence to contradict the documents presented by the employer. The joint committee sustained the discharges.

The discharged employees sued both their employer and the union. They claimed that the employer discharged them in breach of contract and that the union had violated its duty of fair representation by failing adequately to investigate the charges against them. In the course of discovery, the motel clerk revealed in a deposition that he had falsified the records and pocketed the difference between the amounts shown on the receipts and the registration cards. The Sixth Circuit Court of Appeals held that the facts precluded summary judgment in favor of the union but that the employer was entitled to summary judgment because of the provision of the collective bargaining agreement making decisions of the joint arbitration committee "final and binding." The employees sought review of the decision affirming the summary judgment granted on behalf of the employer. The Supreme Court, in an opinion by Justice White, reversed.

The Court held that a union's breach of the duty of fair representation relieves the employees of an express or implied requirement that grievances be settled through contractual grievance procedures. The Court said:

> [W]e cannot believe that Congress intended to foreclose the employee from his § 301 remedy otherwise available against the employer if the contractual processes have been seriously flawed by the union's breach of its duty to represent employees honestly and in good faith and without invidious discrimination or arbitrary conduct.

The Court emphasized that the employees would not prevail merely by showing that the charges against them were false and that they were fired without just cause. Nor would it be sufficient to show that the union made errors of judgment in representing them. Contractual finality provisions would be enforced unless the union had been dishonest or acted in bad faith or in a discriminatory fashion.

Justices Rehnquist and Burger dissented in *Hines*, maintaining that the employer should be protected from liability by the finality provisions of the collective bargaining agreement.

5. The Supreme Court in *Hines* did not address whether the contractual finality issue should be handled differently because the grievance was considered by a joint committee made up of employer and union representatives, rather than by a neutral arbitrator. For further discussion of the legal status of Teamster Joint Committees, see Chapter II.H.4 and the first note following the *Motor Convoy* case in Chapter IV.A.2.(a).

6. In a subsequent case addressing the duty of fair representation outside the grievance context, the Supreme Court articulated a narrow definition of the scope of the union's duty of fair representation in language that may apply as well to the grievance processing context. In United Steelworkers of America v. Rawson, 495 U.S. 362, 110 S.Ct. 1904, 109 L.Ed.2d 362 (1990), survivors of miners who had died in an underground mine fire brought an action against the union alleging that the deaths were the result of the union's negligence in conducting mine safety inspections with the mine owner pursuant to the collective bargaining agreement. The Court majority found that the plaintiffs had no claim for violation of the duty of fair representation because there was no showing that the union's conduct was "arbitrary, discriminatory, or in bad faith." The Court continued:

> The courts have in general assumed that mere negligence, even in the enforcement of a collective-bargaining agreement, would not state a claim for breach of the duty of fair representation, and we endorse that view today.

The National Labor Relations Board has also held that "mere negligence" does not breach the duty of fair representation. National Association of Letter Carriers, Local 3825, 333 NLRB 343, 348 (2001).

7. The Union submitted to the Employer a grievance alleging that the employee's discharge violated the collective bargaining agreement. The Employer denied the grievance. Under the collective bargaining agreement, the Union was required to submit a written request to arbitrate within three days of the Employer's denial of the grievance. The Union submitted the written request for arbitration one day late because the Union's business agent was on vacation. An arbitrator upheld the employee's discharge on the ground that the request for arbitration was untimely. The employee filed an

action against the Union for breach of the duty of fair representation. The Union moved for summary judgment.

(a) The employee argues to the court that summary judgment should be denied because, under Air Line Pilots Association, International v. O'Neill, 499 U.S. 65, 111 S.Ct. 1127, 113 L.Ed.2d 51 (1991), *supra*, the Union's conduct was "irrational," that is, lacking in reason. The Union, however, argues it is entitled to summary judgment because the Supreme Court stated in United Steelworkers of America v. Rawson, 495 U.S. 362, 110 S.Ct. 1904, 109 L.Ed.2d 362 (1990), *supra*, that "mere negligence, even in the enforcement of a collective-bargaining agreement, would not state a claim for breach of the duty of fair representation." How should the court rule on the Union's motion for summary judgment? See Vencl v. International Union of Operating Engineers, Local 18, 137 F.3d 420 (6th Cir.) (absent justification, a union's failure to take a basic and required step is arbitrary and perfunctory conduct violating the DFR), cert. denied, 525 U.S. 871, 119 S.Ct. 168, 142 L.Ed.2d 138 (1998); Beavers v. United Paperworkers International Union, Local 1741, 72 F.3d 97 (8th Cir.1995) (unexplained untimely submission of grievance may violate DFR); Neal v. Newspaper Holdings, Inc., 349 F.3d 363 (7th Cir. 2003) (negligent failure to file grievance on time does not breach DFR); Scott v. New York Health and Human Services Union, 172 LRRM 2231 (S.D.N.Y. 2003) (same).

(b) As a matter of policy, should unions be liable under the duty of fair representation for negligent failure to submit grievances in a timely fashion? Compare a situation in which an employee, not represented by a union, has an individual employment contract that precludes dismissal without just cause. The employee is dismissed in violation of the contract and hires an attorney to sue the employer. The attorney fails to sue prior to the running of the statute of limitations. What remedy does the former employee have against the lawyer? Against the former employer? If persons and institutions are normally liable for the harm caused by their negligent conduct, what basis can there be for holding in *Rawson* that unions are exempt from liability for negligence? Do reasons of policy justify different treatment of the unionized and nonunionized employer?

(c) Assume that under the facts given the Union's conduct would be considered a breach of the duty of fair representation. Would it still be a violation if the collective bargaining agreement permitted both the Union and employees to request arbitration? Assume that allowing employees to seek arbitration would relieve a union from any claim that the duty of fair representation had been violated by the union's failure to request arbitration. If that were the case, would you recommend that unions negotiate agreements that allow individual employees to bring grievances to arbitration? What might a union lose by negotiating such a provision?

(d) Assume that the Union failed to file the grievance in a timely manner because of the race of the dismissed employee. Can the employee recover lost wages in a claim for violation of the duty of fair representation even if the Union can demonstrate that the employee's discharge was for just cause? If the employee cannot recover lost wages, can the employee recover attorneys fees? Some courts have permitted such plaintiffs to recover attorneys fees on the theory that absent the union's breach of the duty of fair representation, the employee would not have had to obtain an attorney to pursue contract remedies against the employer. Ames v. Westinghouse Electric Corporation, 864 F.2d 289, 293–94 (3d Cir. 1988); Dutrisac v. Caterpillar Tractor Co., 749 F.2d 1270 (9th Cir. 1983); Del Casal v. Eastern Airlines, Inc., 634 F.2d 295 (5th Cir.), cert. denied, 454 U.S. 892, 102 S.Ct. 386, 70 L.Ed.2d 206 (1981); Stanton v. Delta Air Lines, Inc., 669 F.2d 833, 838 (1st Cir. 1982); Self v. Drivers, Chauffeurs, Warehousemen & Helpers, Local Union No. 61, 620 F.2d 439, 444 (4th Cir. 1980); Zeman v. Office & Professional Employees International Union Local 35, 91 F.Supp.2d 1247 (E.D.Wis.2000). A sole dissenting voice comes from the Sixth Circuit which says that it is not sound judicial policy to encourage the bringing of frivolous actions in which no underlying right can be vindicated. Wood v. International Brotherhood of Teamsters, Chauffeurs, Warehousemen and Helpers of America, Local 406, 807 F.2d 493, 503 (6th Cir.1986), cert. denied, 483 U.S. 1006, 107 S.Ct. 3232, 97 L.Ed.2d 738 (1987). See also Ooley v. Schwitzer Division, Household Manufacturing Inc., 961 F.2d 1293 (7th Cir.) (granting summary judgment in favor of the union upon a finding that the plaintiffs' underlying contract claim lacked merit, despite evidence suggesting bad faith reasons for failure to pursue the grievance), cert. denied, 506 U.S. 872, 113 S.Ct. 208, 121 L.Ed.2d 148 (1992) .

(e) How should the existence of the union's duty of fair representation affect the conduct of the employer? Assume that the union, through negligence, misses a grievance deadline. Should the employer allow the untimely grievance to be arbitrated anyway out of concern that, if the union's conduct violated its duty of fair representation, the employer could be forced to bear some financial liability? See *infra* Chapter V.A.4. for discussion of the remedial obligations of unions and employers in hybrid DFR/§ 301 cases.

8.   Jane, a member of the bargaining unit, complains to the Company that she is being sexually harassed by Bill, another member of the bargaining unit. Following investigation of Jane's complaint, the Company discharges Bill. Bill asks the Union to file a grievance challenging his discharge. Bill threatens to sue the Union for breach of the duty of fair representation if it fails to take his claim to arbitration. Jane tells the Union that she will sue the Union for breach of the duty of fair representation if it takes Bill's grievance to arbitration. You are an attorney representing the Union. What do you advise it to do? See Reginald Alleyne, *Arbitrating Sexual Harassment Grievances: A Representation Dilemma for Unions*, 2 University of Pennsylvania Journal of Labor and Employment Law 1 (1999); Mary K. O'Melveny, *Negotiating the Minefields: Selected Issues for Labor Unions Addressing Sexual Harassment Complaints by Represented Employees*, 15 Labor Lawyer 321 (2000).

9.   The Supreme Court said in *Vaca*, and repeated in *Hines*, that "a union may not arbitrarily ignore a meritorious grievance or process it in perfunctory fashion." What does "perfunctory" mean in this context? Dictionary definitions include "characterized by routine" and "lacking in interest or enthusiasm." Does inclusion of "perfunctory" in articulation of the standard suggest considerably less deference than a standard requiring "arbitrary" conduct? A number of courts have labeled union conduct as "perfunctory" in finding a breach of the duty. See Webb v. ABF Freight System, Inc., 155 F.3d 1230 (10th Cir.1998) (union's conduct was perfuncto-

ry by, among other things, failing to present claim of retaliation and in misleading both the grievant and the grievance panel about the significance of the grievant's absence from the hearing), cert. denied, 526 U.S. 1018, 119 S.Ct. 1253, 143 L.Ed.2d 350 (1999); Lampkin v. Automobile Workers, Local 1093, 154 F.3d 1136 (10th Cir.1998) (union failed to advise employer that reason for employee's absenteeism was his wife's serious injury in an automobile accident); and Beavers v. United Paperworkers International Union, Local 1741, 72 F.3d 97 (8th Cir.1995) (union's untimely handling of grievance was perfunctory because the "union acted without concern or solicitude, or gave a claim only cursory attention").

10. Did the union in *Hines* violate the duty of fair representation?

11. Although there are no recent empirical studies of duty of fair representation cases, an informal review of DFR cases from 2000–2004 indicates that employees continue to bring DFR cases in large numbers, but that their successes are few. That suggests that employees and their attorneys are reluctant to accept the notion that a union's misjudgment in handling a grievance, even if it costs the employee's job, does not ordinarily give rise to a cause of action. Courts, on the other hand, appear to have now widely accepted the degree of deference to union decisionmaking dictated by Supreme Court decisions.

4. REMEDIAL AND PROCEDURAL ISSUES IN ENFORCING THE DUTY OF FAIR REPRESENTATION

BOWEN v. UNITED STATES POSTAL SERVICE

Supreme Court of the United States, 1983.
459 U.S. 212, 103 S.Ct. 588, 74 L.Ed.2d 402.

JUSTICE POWELL delivered the opinion of the Court.

The issue is whether a union may be held primarily liable for that part of a wrongfully discharged employee's damages caused by his union's breach of its duty of fair representation.

I.

On February 21, 1976, following an altercation with another employee, petitioner Charles V. Bowen was suspended without pay from his position with the United States Postal Service. Bowen was a member of the American Postal Workers Union, AFL-CIO, the recognized collective-bargaining agent for Service employees. After Bowen was formally terminated on March 30, 1976, he filed a grievance with the Union as provided by the collective-bargaining agreement. When the Union declined to take his grievance to arbitration, he sued the Service and the Union in the United States District Court for the Western District of Virginia, seeking damages and injunctive relief.

Bowen's complaint charged that the Service had violated the collective-bargaining agreement by dismissing him without "just cause" and that the Union had breached its duty of fair representation. His evidence at trial indicated that the responsible Union officer, at each step of the grievance process, had recommended pursuing the grievance but that the national office, for no apparent reason, had refused to take the matter to arbitration.

Following the parties' presentation of evidence, the court gave the jury a series of questions to be answered as a special verdict.[1] If the jury found that the Service had discharged Bowen wrongfully and that the Union had breached its duty of fair representation, it was instructed to determine the amount of compensatory damages to be awarded and to apportion the liability for the damages between the Service and the Union. In explaining how liability might be apportioned, the court instructed the jury that the issue was left primarily to its discretion. The court indicated, however, that the jury equitably could base apportionment on the date of a hypothetical arbitration decision—the date at which the Service would have reinstated Bowen if the Union had fulfilled its duty. The court suggested that the Service could be liable for damages before that date and the Union for damages thereafter. Although the Union objected to the instruction allowing the jury to find it liable for any compensatory damages, it did not object to the manner in which the court instructed the jury to apportion the damages in the event apportionment was proper.

Upon return of a special verdict in favor of Bowen and against both defendants, the District Court entered judgment, holding that the Service had discharged Bowen without just cause and that the Union had handled his "apparently meritorious grievance * * * in an arbitrary and perfunctory manner * * * " 470 F.Supp. 1127, 1129 (1979). In so doing, both the Union and the Service acted "in reckless and callous disregard of [Bowen's] rights."[4] *Ibid.* The court found that Bowen could not have proceeded independently of the Union and that if the Union had arbitrated Bowen's grievance, he would have been reinstated. *Ibid.*

The court ordered that Bowen be reimbursed $52,954 for lost benefits and wages. Although noting that "there is authority suggesting that only the employer is liable for damages in the form of back pay," it observed that "this is a case in which both defendants, by their illegal acts, are liable to plaintiff * * *. The problem in this case is not one of liability but rather one of apportionment * * *." *Id.*, at 1130–1131. The jury had found that the Union was responsible for $30,000 of Bowen's

---

1. The jury sat only as an advisory panel on Bowen's claims against the Service. See 28 U.S.C. § 2402 ("Any action against the United States under section 1346 shall be tried by the court without a jury").

4. The District Court had instructed the jury that both the Union and the Service could be liable for punitive damages if either had acted "maliciously or recklessly or in callous disregard of the rights of the Plaintiff [Bowen]." 3 Record 597. The jury found that the Service and the Union were liable for punitive damages of $30,000 and

$10,000, respectively. App. to Pet. for Cert. A22. The District Court determined, however, that punitive damages could not be assessed against the Service because of sovereign immunity. 470 F.Supp., at 1131. Although the court found that the Union's actions supported the jury's award of punitive damages, it set the award aside. It concluded that it would be unfair to hold the Union liable when the Service was immune. *Ibid.* Bowen did not appeal the District Court's decision on this point.

damages. The court approved that apportionment, ordering the Service to pay the remaining $22,954.[6]

On appeal by the Service and the Union, the Court of Appeals for the Fourth Circuit overturned the damages award against the Union, 642 F.2d 79 (1981). It accepted the District Court's findings of fact, but held as a matter of law that, "[a]s Bowen's compensation was at all times payable only by the Service, reimbursement of his lost earnings continued to be the obligation of the Service exclusively. Hence, no portion of the deprivations * * * was chargeable to the Union. Cf. *Vaca v. Sipes*, 386 U.S. 171, 195 * * * (1967)." *Id.*, at 82 (footnote omitted). The court did not alter the District Court's judgment in any other respect, but "affirmed [it] throughout" except for the award of damages against the Union. *Id.*, at 83.

Thus, the Court of Appeals affirmed the District Court's apportionment of fault and its finding that both the Union and the Service had acted "in reckless and callous disregard of [Bowen's] rights."[7] Indeed, the court accepted the District Court's apportionment of fault so completely that it refused to increase the $22,954 award against the Service to cover the whole of Bowen's injury. Bowen was left with only a $22,954 award, whereas the jury and the District Court had awarded him lost earnings and benefits of $52,954—the undisputed amount of his damages.

II.

In *Vaca v. Sipes*, 386 U.S. 171 (1967), the Court held that an employee such as Bowen, who proves that his employer violated the labor agreement and his union breached its duty of fair representation, may be entitled to recover damages from both the union and the employer. The Court explained that the award must be apportioned according to fault:

> "The governing principle, then, is to apportion liability between the employer and the union according to the damage caused by the fault

---

6. The District Court found as a fact that if Bowen's grievance had been arbitrated he would have been reinstated by August 1977. Lost wages after that date were deemed the fault of the Union: "While the [Service] set this case in motion with its discharge, the [Union's] acts, upon which [Bowen] reasonably relied, delayed the reinstatement of [Bowen] and it is a proper apportionment to assign fault to the [Union] for approximately two-thirds of the period [Bowen] was unemployed up to the time of trial." 470 F.Supp., at 1131.

7. In a footnote added after the opinion was first filed, the court noted that it made "no revision in the judgment of $22,954.12 against the Postal Service. In this connection we note that no appeal was entered by [Bowen] from the judgment against the Ser-

vice in the amount of $22,954.12." 642 F.2d, at 82, n.6.

The court's view that the judgment against the Service could not be increased because of Bowen's failure to appeal is erroneous. Bowen won an unambiguous victory in the District Court. He established that he had been discharged by the employer without just cause and that the Union had breached its duty of fair representation. The amount of lost wages and benefits was not in dispute, and the jury and the District Court awarded him all of his damages, apportioning them between the Union and the Service. Bowen had no reason to be unhappy with the award and should not have been deprived of the full amount of his compensatory damages because of his failure to cross-appeal.

of each. Thus, damages attributable solely to the employer's breach of contract should not be charged to the union, but increases if any in those damages caused by the union's refusal to process the grievance should not be charged to the employer." *Id.*, at 197–198.

Although *Vaca*'s governing principle is well established, its application has caused some uncertainty. The Union argues that the Court of Appeals correctly determined that it cannot be charged with any damages resulting from a wrongful discharge. *Vaca*'s "governing principle," according to the Union, requires that the employer be solely liable for such damages. The Union views itself as liable only for Bowen's litigation expenses resulting from its breach of duty. It finds support for this view in *Vaca*'s recognition that a union's breach of its duty of fair representation does not absolve an employer of all the consequences of a breach of the collective-bargaining contract. See *id.*, at 196. The Union contends that its unrelated breach of the duty of fair representation does not make it liable for any part of the discharged employee's damages; its default merely lifts the bar to the employee's suit on the contract against his employer.

The difficulty with this argument is that it treats the relationship between the employer and employee, created by the collective-bargaining agreement, as if it were a simple contract of hire governed by traditional common-law principles. This reading of *Vaca* fails to recognize that a collective-bargaining agreement is much more than traditional common-law employment terminable at will. Rather, it is an agreement creating relationships and interests under the federal common law of labor policy.

A.

[The Court reviewed its decision in *Vaca v. Sipes, supra.*]

The interests thus identified in *Vaca* provide a measure of its principle for apportioning damages. Of paramount importance is the right of the employee, who has been injured by both the employer's and the union's breach, to be made whole. In determining the degree to which the employer or the union should bear the employee's damages, the Court held that the employer should not be shielded from the "natural consequences" of its breach by wrongful union conduct. *Id.*, at 186. The Court noted, however, that the employer may have done nothing to prevent exhaustion. Were it not for the union's failure to represent the employee fairly, the employer's breach "could [have been] remedied through the grievance process to the employee-plaintiff's benefit." The fault that justifies dropping the bar to the employee's suit for damages also requires the union to bear some responsibility for increases in the employee's damages resulting from its breach. To hold otherwise would make the employer alone liable for the consequences of the union's breach of duty.

Hines v. Anchor Motor Freight, Inc., 424 U.S. 554 (1976), presented an issue analogous to that in *Vaca*: whether proof of a breach of the duty of fair representation would remove the bar of finality from an arbitral decision. We held that it would, in part because a contrary rule would prevent the employee from recovering

> even in circumstances where it is shown that a union has manufactured the evidence and knows from the start that it is false; or even if, unbeknownst to the employer, the union has corrupted the arbitrator to the detriment of disfavored union members. 424 U.S., at 570.

It would indeed be unjust to prevent the employee from recovering in such a situation. It would be equally unjust to require the employer to bear the increase in the damages caused by the union's wrongful conduct.[11] It is true that the employer discharged the employee wrongfully and remains liable for the employee's backpay. See *Vaca*, 386 U.S., at 197. The union's breach of its duty of fair representation, however, caused the grievance procedure to malfunction resulting in an increase in the employee's damages. Even though both the employer and the union have caused the damage suffered by the employee, the union is responsible for the increase in damages and, as between the two wrongdoers, should bear its portion of the damages.[12]

Vaca's governing principle reflects this allocation of responsibility. As the Court stated, "damages attributable *solely* to the employer's breach of contract should not be charged to the union, but *increases* if any in those damages caused by the union's refusal to process the grievance should not be charged to the employer." *Id.*, at 197–198 (emphasis added). The Union's position here would require us to read out of the *Vaca* articulation of the relevant principle the words emphasized above. It would also ignore the interests of all the parties to the collective agreement—interests that *Vaca* recognized and *Hines* illustrates.

B.

* * * Although each party participates in the grievance procedure, the union plays a pivotal role in the process since it assumes the responsibility of determining whether to press an employee's claims. The employer, for its part, must rely on the union's decision not to pursue an employee's grievance. For the union acts as the employee's exclusive representative in the grievance procedure, as it does in virtually all matters involving the terms and conditions of employment. Just as a nonorganized employer may accept an employee's waiver of any challenge to his discharge as a final resolution of the matter, so should an organized employer be able to rely on a comparable waiver by the employee's exclusive representative.

11. We note that this is not a situation in which either the union or the employer has participated in the other's breach. See *Vaca*, 386 U.S. at 197, n.18.

12. Although the union remains primarily responsible for the portion of the damages resulting from its default, *Vaca* made clear that the union's breach does not absolve the employer of liability. Thus if the petitioner in this case does not collect the damages apportioned against the Union, the Service remains secondarily liable for the full loss of backpay.

There is no unfairness to the union in this approach. By seeking and acquiring the exclusive right and power to speak for a group of employees, the union assumes a corresponding duty to discharge that responsibility faithfully—a duty which it owes to the employees whom it represents and on which the employer with whom it bargains may rely. When the union, as the exclusive agent of the employee, waives arbitration or fails to seek review of an adverse decision, the employer should be in substantially the same position as if the employee had had the right to act on his own behalf and had done so. Indeed, if the employer could not rely on the union's decision, the grievance procedure would not provide the "uniform and exclusive method for [the] orderly settlement of employee grievances," which the Court has recognized is essential to the national labor policy. See *Clayton v. Automobile Workers*, 451 U.S. 679, 686–687 (1981).

The principle announced in *Vaca* reflects this allocation of responsibilities in the grievance procedure—a procedure that contemplates that both employer and union will perform their respective obligations. In the absence of damages apportionment where the default of both parties contributes to the employee's injury, incentives to comply with the grievance procedure will be diminished. Indeed, imposing total liability solely on the employer could well affect the willingness of employers to agree to arbitration clauses as they are customarily written.

Nor will requiring the union to pay damages impose a burden on the union inconsistent with national labor policy. It will provide an additional incentive for the union to process its members' claims where warranted. See *Vaca*, 386 U.S., at 187. This is wholly consistent with a union's interest. It is a duty owed to its members as well as consistent with the union's commitment to the employer under the arbitration clause. See *Republic Steel*, 379 U.S., at 653. * * *

IV.

In this case, the findings of the District Court, accepted by the Court of Appeals, establish that the damages sustained by petitioner were caused initially by the Service's unlawful discharge and increased by the Union's breach of its duty of fair representation. Accordingly, apportionment of the damages was required by *Vaca*.[19] We reverse the judgment of the Court of Appeals and remand for entry of judgment allocating damages against both the Service and the Union consistent with this opinion.

It is so ordered.

19. We need not decide whether the District Court's instructions on apportionment of damages were proper. The Union objected to the instructions only on the ground that no back wages at all could be assessed against it. It did not object to the manner of apportionment if such damages were to be assessed. Nor is it necessary in this case to consider whether there were degrees of fault, as both the Service and the Union were found to have acted in "reckless and callous disregard of [Bowen's] rights."

[Justice White, joined by Justices Marshall, Blackmun, and Rehnquist, dissented on the apportionment issue. Justice White said that the majority's position had "been rejected by every Court of Appeals that has squarely considered it, does not give due regard to our prior precedents, to equitable principles, or to the national labor policy." The dissenters thought that the employer should be primarily liable for all backpay. The union's liability should be measured by the extent that its misconduct adds to the difficulty and expense of collecting from the employer, as for example, paying attorneys fees and other litigation expenses. The chronological method of apportionment approved by the majority would make the union responsible for more than half of the back pay liability. Under that method, the extent of the union's liability would be unrelated to its comparative culpability and the union would have no way of limiting its constantly increasing liability. The dissenters feared that the majority's holding would impair labor policy by encouraging unions to take nonmeritorious grievances to arbitration. Those joining Justice White, with the exception of Justice Rehnquist, would have increased the judgment against the employer, making it responsible for the entire amount of Bowen's backpay. Justice Rehnquist, in a separate opinion, though it unnecessary to decide whether the employer's liability should have been increased.]

Notes and Questions

1. Assume that a DFR remedial scheme should satisfy the following objectives: (a) the plaintiff is fully compensated for his or her injuries; (b) neither the employer nor the union is required to pay more than its appropriate share of the damages; (c) the extent of damages imposed on unions provides a significant deterrent to breaches of the duty; (d) the extent of employer responsibility for damages is sufficient to encourage employers promptly to reconsider and reverse unwarranted disciplinary decisions; and (e) the union's responsibility is not so large as to undermine the collective interest of all employees and the public in the proper use of limited union funds.

(a) How well does the chronological method, approved in *Bowen,* satisfy these objectives? Consider the chronology of the *Vaca* case, set out in Justice White's opinion in *Bowen*:

> The employee in that case had been discharged in January 1960. Sometime after February 1961, the union refused to take the matter to arbitration, and, in February 1962, the employee filed suit, claiming that the union's refusal to go to arbitration violated his rights. The trial began in June 1964, and the matter was not finally adjudicated until this Court rendered its decision in February 1967.

Is this sort of chronology likely to occur in most duty of fair representation cases? If so, after *Bowen,* how are damages in duty of fair representation cases likely to be apportioned?

(b) Does the Supreme Court's decision in *Bowen* mandate that courts apportion damages according to its chronological method, or does *Bowen* merely indicate that chronological apportionment is simply one permissible approach? Subsequent to *Bowen*, many courts have apportioned damages according to its chronological method, but several courts have apportioned damages on the basis of fault. See Schoonover v. Consolidated Freightways Corp., 147 F.3d 492 (6th Cir.1998) (65% to the employer and 35% to the union), cert. denied, 525 U.S. 1139, 119 S.Ct. 1029, 143 L.Ed.2d 39 (1999); Webb v. ABF Freight System, Inc., 155 F.3d 1230 (10th Cir.1998) (80% to the employer and 20% to the union), cert. denied, 526 U.S. 1018, 119 S.Ct. 1253, 143 L.Ed.2d 350 (1999); and Cruz v. Local Union Number 3, IBEW, 34 F.3d 1148 (2d Cir.1994) (union ordered to pay 90% to one plaintiff and 100% to seven others).

(c) Can you design a remedial scheme that satisfies the listed objectives better than *Bowen* does?

2.   What are the likely affects of *Bowen?*

(a) How will *Bowen* affect the behavior of unions in processing grievances? Is it possible for a union, through the collective bargaining process, to limit the impact of *Bowen*?

(b) How will *Bowen* affect the behavior of employers litigating DFR suits? How much incentive will employers have to settle pending claims?

(c) Do you expect the union liability imposed in *Bowen* to have an effect upon the way in which the scope of the union's duty is defined?

A NOTE ON ADDITIONAL REMEDIAL AND PROCEDURAL ISSUES

Several United States Supreme Court cases define other remedial and procedural characteristics of the cause of action for breach of the duty of fair representation. These cases address statutes of limitations, punitive damages, exhaustion of remedies and the right to jury trial.

In DelCostello v. International Brotherhood of Teamsters, 462 U.S. 151, 103 S.Ct. 2281, 76 L.Ed.2d 476 (1983), the Court held that when an employee brings a hybrid claim, suing the union for breach of the duty of representation and the employer for breach of contract, the statute of limitations is six months. The Court acknowledged that absent an expressly applicable federal limitations period, courts usually borrow the most closely analogous state law limitations period. The Court rejected that solution here because such periods might be too short to permit the worker to investigate and obtain counsel or too long to permit rapid final resolution of labor disputes. Moreover, different limitations periods for claims against the employer and union would make the litigation unreasonably complex. The Court decided to borrow the six-month limitations period for unfair labor practices under the National Labor Relations Act as the limitations period for an action claiming both breach of the collective bargaining agreement and of the duty of fair representation.

In International Brotherhood of Electrical Workers v. Foust, 442 U.S. 42, 99 S.Ct. 2121, 60 L.Ed.2d 698 (1979), the Supreme Court held that DFR plaintiffs could not recover punitive damages. The Court rejected punitive damages, fearing such awards would "impair the financial stability of unions and unsettle the careful balance of individual and collective interests." The Court thought substantial, unpredictable windfall punitive damage awards could deny unions necessary resources to represent workers. The Court reasoned that the additional deterrent effect of punitive damages would impose too great a price for workers. The Supreme Court also was concerned that punitive damages could unduly limit union discretion in grievance handling. The Court thought unions must retain discretion to pursue grievances to promote settlements, avoid processing of frivolous grievances and strengthen employer confidence in the union. Four justices concurred in the holding that punitive damages were inappropriate in this case, but would not have precluded punitive damages where appropriate.

The Supreme Court in Clayton v. United Auto. Workers, 451 U.S. 679, 101 S.Ct. 2088, 68 L.Ed.2d 538 (1981), considered whether a DFR plaintiff must first exhaust available internal union appeals procedures. The Supreme Court held that exhaustion could be required if (1) the internal union procedure were fair and reasonable; (2) the internal union process offered the grievant either complete relief or the reopening of the grievance; and (3) the internal procedure would not unreasonably delay the employee's opportunity to obtain a judicial hearing on the merits. The Court held exhaustion unnecessary here because the UAW appeals procedures could not provide either reinstatement or the opportunity to reactivate the grievance.

In Chauffeurs, Teamsters, and Helpers, Local 391 v. Terry, 494 U.S. 558, 110 S.Ct. 1339, 108 L.Ed.2d 519 (1990), a DFR plaintiff sought a jury trial on the issue of back pay. A majority of the Court held that the Seventh Amendment affords a right to a jury trial on a back pay claim. In the wake of *Terry*, judges must decide how to handle cases in which some remedies are subject to jury trial and other remedies, such as reinstatement, vacation of the arbitration award, or back pay from the employer, may not be. The Eighth Circuit has suggested that because there is no constitutional right to a nonjury trial, juries should decide facts regarding both legal and equitable claims in a hybrid duty of fair representation/breach of contract case. Brownlee v. Yellow Freight System, Inc., 921 F.2d 745 (8th Cir.1990).

B. THE ROLE OF EXTERNAL
LAW IN ARBITRATION

1. INTRODUCTION

Few subjects have prompted more debate among arbitrators and scholars of arbitration than the role of external law in labor arbitration. In essence, the question is this: when, if ever, may an arbitrator apply external law? That general inquiry breaks down into several narrower questions. May an arbitrator look to statutes, regulations, or court decisions for guidance? If so, when? May the external authorities overrule the terms of the contract, or may they only supplement it with consistent terms? Or may the arbitrator only use external authorities to help resolve an ambiguity in the contract? The issue is a recurring one, which the reader will encounter in several later chapters.

The debate may be more limited than it first appears.

(a) No one doubts that the parties may authorize the arbitrator to decide external law questions, either by incorporating the law in the collective bargaining agreement or by posing the external law issue in the submission agreement. In Alcoa Building Products, 104 LA 364 (Jack P. Cerone, 1995), for example, the parties stipulated that the arbitrator could decide an Americans with Disabilities Act (ADA) issue.

(b) Nor does anyone doubt that an arbitrator may use external law as an interpretive aid; for example, if one resolution to a contractual ambiguity is legal and another illegal, an arbitrator might reasonably conclude that the parties intended the legal meaning. External authorities may also flesh out general concepts such as "just cause." In Thermo King Corp., 102 LA 612 (Jonathan Dworkin, 1993), the arbitrator used the ADA to help decide whether a discharge was "just and fair." In Schuller International, Inc., 103 LA 1127 (Richard F. Allen, 1994), the arbitrator used tax law to determine an employee's earnings for the purpose of calculating vacation benefits.

(c) Finally, the parties might implicitly authorize the use of external law. Adoption of contractual language paralleling a statute, for instance, strongly suggests that the parties intended their provision to incorporate the relevant law. In those instances, the arbitrator's consideration of external law is inevitable as well as appropriate. A good example is American Sterilizer Co., 104 LA 921 (Richard W. Dissen, 1995). The contract contained a severability clause stating that a provision found to conflict with federal law "will not abrogate any of the other provisions of this Agreement." Following an earlier arbitrator's lead, Arbitrator Dissen held that the clause (and a later internal management memorandum) were "sufficient to include [the ADA] within the agreement between the parties." A general provision obliging the parties to "comply with federal and state laws," however, does not incorporate all those laws into the agreement, Los Angeles Community College District, 87 LA 252 (Walter N. Kaufman, 1986).

The real dispute, then, is whether and when an arbitrator may use external law *instead of* the terms of the agreement. Whatever the limits, some arbitrators simply cannot resist the temptation to imitate a federal court judge. In Stone Container Corp., 101 LA 943 (Marvin J. Feldman, 1993), the arbitrator first concluded that he had no authority to apply the ADA. Rather than ending the topic at that point, he added this sentence: "However, a discussion of that law might be noteworthy herein." He then went on to decide that the grievant's evidence failed to prove a "mental disorder" under that statute.

The Supreme Court has provided relatively little guidance. In United Steelworkers of America v. Enterprise Wheel & Car Corp., 363 U.S. 593, 597, 80 S.Ct. 1358, 1361, 4 L.Ed.2d 1424 (1960), the Court said in *dicta* that an award "based solely upon the arbitrator's view of the requirements of enacted legislation * * * would mean that he exceeded the scope of the submission." In Alexander v. Gardner–Denver Co., 415 U.S. 36, 53, 94 S.Ct. 1011, 1022, 39 L.Ed.2d 147 (1974), again in *dicta*, the Court cited *Enterprise Wheel* for the proposition that an arbitrator "has no general authority to invoke public laws that conflict with the bargain between the parties." "Where the collective-bargaining agreement conflicts with" federal law, the Court added four pages later, "the arbitrator must follow the agreement." More recently, in W.R. Grace & Co. v. Local Union 759, International Union of the United Rubber, Cork, Linoleum & Plastic Workers of America, 461 U.S. 757, 103 S.Ct. 2177, 76 L.Ed.2d 298 (1983), the Court upheld an arbitration award that expressly declined to apply federal law. Thus the cases suggest, without actually deciding, that an arbitrator should not apply external law instead of the contractual terms.

The excerpts in Subsection 2 provide a range of opinions about the use of external law in labor arbitration. As you read these excerpts, ask yourself what each author's theory would mean in practice, and how each theory differs from the others. Subsection 3 shows how arbitrators have dealt with the issue in specific cases. The rise of individual employment arbitration (discussed at length in Part 3) has complicated matters by creating a branch of arbitration that exists in large part precisely to apply external law. Many if not most individual arbitration disputes involve claims of discrimination or other violations of statutory or common law. The process would have little utility if arbitrators ignored the legal bases of those claims.

2. THE DEBATE

RUMINATIONS ABOUT IDEOLOGY, LAW AND LABOR ARBITRATION
Bernard Meltzer.
20 Proceedings of the National Academy of Arbitrators 1, 14–17 (1967).

Arbitral fidelity to the agreement is also involved in the last question I shall discuss, i.e., the arbitrator's responsibility when an award warranted by the agreement would be repugnant to an applicable federal or state policy or rule of public policy.

The following situations suggested by recent cases illustrate the general questions involved: First, a grievant who volunteered to attend a training course paid for by the employer claims overtime for travel to and from school. Under the governing contract, read in the light of the past practice, it is clear that the grievant's claim should be denied, but the arbitrator reads the FLSA [Fair Labor Standards Act] as requiring payment for travel time. Second, a layoff is plainly consistent with the agreement but is attacked as involving discrimination repugnant to Title VII of the Civil Rights Act. * * *

In the first two situations I have described, what effect, if any, should the arbitrator give to the law, which, we will assume, would be contravened by an award based on that agreement?

Before exploring that question, it is appropriate to distinguish it from other questions that have a surface similarity but are fundamentally different. One such question is how the just-cause standard should be applied and the applicable burden of persuasion defined where a grievant's employment, as in the case of an airline pilot, involves substantial risks to the public and to fellow employees and where regulation imposes duties on employers that reflect the risks involved. In such situations there is no necessary incompatibility between the contractual standard and that drawn from regulation or public policy; for the contractual standard is formulated loosely, presumably for the purpose of permitting consideration of all relevant factors, including, of course, the relevant regulation or public policy. Similarly, where a contractual provision is susceptible to two interpretations, one compatible with, and the other repugnant to, an applicable statute, the statute is a relevant factor for interpretation. Arbitral interpretation of agreements, like judicial interpretation of statutes, should seek to avoid a construction that would be invalid under a higher law. In both of the situations just mentioned, the art of construction and the actual or imputed intention of the parties make it possible to avoid a direct conflict between the agreement and the law.

Where, however, there is an irrepressible conflict, the arbitrator, in my opinion, should respect the agreement and ignore the law. My position is based on several interrelated considerations: The first one is the mandate implicit in the following statement from *Enterprise Wheel*: "[The award] may be read as based solely upon the arbitrator's view of the requirements of enacted legislation which would mean that he exceeded the scope of his submission."

The basis of this approach is, of course, that the parties typically call on an arbitrator to construe and not to destroy their agreement.[37] There is, moreover, no reason to credit arbitrators with any competence, let alone any special expertise, with respect to the law, as distinguished from the agreement. A good many arbitrators lack any legal training at all,[38] and even lawyer-arbitrators do not necessarily hold themselves out

37. The parties may, of course, submit to an arbitrator either the issue of whether a given agreement is compatible with a pertinent statute or "problems" that result from the need to accommodate an agreement and the law. But such submissions, which may call for the reshaping of the agreement, are infrequent. In any event, there is not, in my opinion, any persuasive basis for giving any special deference to arbitral determinations as to the reach of the law. If, however, the parties have agreed to submit to the arbitrator issues as to the impact of regulation on the agreement and if his award calls for action that is compatible with both the submission agreement and the law, there is no reason for the courts to withhold enforcement of the award.

38. It is true that NLRB members are not necessarily lawyers. But those who rely on that point to support an argument for broad arbitral jurisdiction over legal issues often ignore important differences between arbitrators and Board members: (1) The latter have colleagues who are lawyers, as well as a staff of legal advisors. (2) Board hearings are conducted by trial examiners who, under recent Civil Service requirements, must be duly licensed lawyers. U.S. Civil Service Comm., Announcement No. 318, *Hearing Examiners* 5 (1965). (3) Board members deal continuously with a single statute whereas arbitrators, if required to deal with the law governing collective agreements, would from time to time be confronted with a considerably broader

as knowledgeable about the broad range of statutory and administrative materials that may be relevant in labor arbitrations. Indeed, my impression—and it is only that—is that nonlawyer arbitrators are more willing to rush in where lawyers fear to tread.... [A]n analogy to administrative tribunals is instructive. Such agencies consider themselves bound by the statutes entrusted to their administration and leave to the courts challenges to the constitutional validity of such statutes. Arbitrators should in general accord a similar respect to the agreement that is the source of their authority and should leave to the courts or other official tribunals the determination of whether the agreement contravenes a higher law. Otherwise, arbitrators would be deciding issues that go beyond not only the submission agreement but also arbitral competence. Arbitrators would, moreover, be doing so within a procedural framework different from that applicable to official tribunals. Finally, they would be impinging on an area in which courts or other official tribunals are granted plenary authority. Under such circumstances, the limited judicial review appropriate for arbitral interpretations of the agreement would be wholly inappropriate for arbitral interpretation of the law.

THE ARBITRATOR, THE NLRB, AND THE COURTS

Robert G. Howlett.
20 Proceedings of the National Academy of Arbitrators 67 (1967).

There are distinguished arbitrators who advance the thesis that an arbitrator is responsible solely for determination of contract issues, and that all questions involving statutory violation should be deferred to the NLRB. * * *

I submit that, subject to the caveat expressed below, arbitrators *should* render decisions on the issues before them *based on both contract language and law*. Indeed, a separation of contract interpretation and statutory and/or common law is impossible in many arbitrations. This impossibility of separation has been well stated:

> "In short, no regulation of unilateral action during the term of an agreement can escape the dilemma that, if the regulation be by the NLRB, it will involve that body in the administration of agreements, and that, if the regulation be by court or arbitrator, it will involve them in determining as a contractual question the discharge of what is also a statutory obligation. Adjudication by either overlaps the function of the other."[108]

Arbitrators, as well as judges, are subject to and bound by law, whether it be the Fourteenth Amendment to the Constitution of the United States or a city ordinance. All contracts are subject to statute and common law; and each contract includes all applicable law. The law is

range of national and unpreempted state regulation.

108. Dunau, *Contractual Prohibition of Unfair Labor Practices: Jurisdictional Prob-* *lems*, 57 Columbia Law Review 52, 79 (1957).

part of the "essence [of the] collective bargaining agreement" to which Mr. Justice Douglas has referred. * * *

An award that does not consider the law may result in error. Consider obvious examples. Should an arbitrator enforce a contract that provides for payment of wages lower than those established in the Fair Labor Standards Act or, if applicable, a state minimum wage law? Or is he performing his function if he overlooks limitations on hours for women and minors, or maximum loads that women may carry in industrial employment? I think not.

Indeed, an arbitrator who decides a dispute without consideration of legal issues disserves his management-union clients, and acts inconsistently with the decisions of both the NLRB and the courts that sanction arbitral decisions. * * *

That an arbitrator should consider the statute is consistent with the *Spielberg* [Spielberg Manufacturing Co., 112 NLRB 1080 (1955)] doctrine. *Unless an arbitrator has passed upon the statutory issue, his award will not be honored.* And the arbitrator should not confine statutory interpretation to those situations in which the collective bargaining contract, as is sometimes the case, parrots the statute. In keeping with the concept that arbitrators' awards will be honored if due process is recognized, as the *Spielberg* doctrine holds, and if the settlement of disputes through a private, rather than a public, agency is to be encouraged, arbitrators should not hesitate in their application of the applicable statute. * * *

Questions are raised as to whether an arbitrator should "probe" to determine whether a statutory issue is involved. If he is to be useful in reducing the NLRB caseload, he should, particularly in discharge cases, inquire as to the possibility of Section 8(a) and 8(b) violations, the latter if there is any suggestion of collusion between the parties. Unless he does so, neither the General Counsel nor the Board will "defer" to the arbitrator's decision; and, if the statute has run, the arbitrator's failure to act may result in an injustice to an employee. * * *

Suggestion was also made at the [NAA] regional meetings that not all arbitrators are lawyers; therefore, interpretation of legal provisions should not be within the role of arbitrators. There is nothing in the National Labor Relations Act which requires that members of the NLRB be lawyers. This has not prevented the NLRB's non-lawyer members from participating in the decision of legal questions.

THE ROLE OF LAW IN ARBITRATION
Richard Mittenthal.
21 Proceedings of the National Academy of Arbitrators 42 (1968).

Arbitrators tend to be passive, by profession if not by nature. Our job is to settle controversies, not start them. The purpose of this paper, however, is to continue and perhaps enlarge the controversy over the role of law in arbitration. At last year's Academy meeting, Bob Howlett called for a marriage of law and arbitration. He stated that "every agreement incorporates all applicable law" and that arbitrators "should render decisions * * * based on both contract language and law." At the same meeting, Professor Meltzer opposed such a marriage. He stated that arbitrators are "the proctor of the agreement and not of the statutes" and that we, therefore, "should respect the agreement and ignore the law" where the two conflict.

It seems to me that both of these positions are somewhat extreme. I choose to occupy the middle ground between them, a position more in keeping with the diversity of language in collective bargaining agreements and the diversity of disputes in which the role of law may become an issue. My concern here is with what arbitrators should do when asked to consider the law in resolving a grievance dispute. * * *

B. AREAS OF CONTROVERSY

Let me turn now to the areas of controversy. Howlett's view is based in part on the belief that "all applicable law" is, *by implication*, incorporated in "every agreement." Some courts and some arbitrators have drawn this implication. Indeed, the U.S. Supreme Court said in 1866 that "the laws which subsist at the time and place of the making of a contract, and where it is to be performed, enter into and form a part of [the contract], as if they were expressly referred to or incorporated in its terms" [Von Hoffman v. Quincy, 71 U.S. 535, 550]. Thus, it can be argued that Howlett's position is supported by the law of contracts.

I find no merit in such an argument. First, the implication is highly artificial. Where courts imply that the law is part of the contract, they must necessarily assume that (1) "everybody knows the law" and (2) "everybody makes his contract with reference to [the law] and adopts its provisions as terms of the agreement." These assumptions involve the piling of one fiction upon another and have nothing to do with people's real intentions.

Second, the implication is unnecessary. Courts can and do apply the law in a contract dispute without indulging in such multiple fictions. A judge has two functions to perform. He must interpret the contract; he must also determine the legal operation of the contract, that is, the legal remedies (if any) for its enforcement. He is, in other words, "concerned not only with the [contract] but also with the law that limits and governs it." It is only in connection with the legal operation of the contract that it is necessary for the judge to refer to any applicable constitution or statute. Realistically, what happens is that he interprets the contract and then imposes upon his interpretation the relevant rules of law. Given this view of judicial decision-making, there is no need to imply that the law is incorporated in the contract.

Third, for these reasons the implication is opposed by eminent authorities on the law of contracts. Williston believes the implication is "too broad to be accepted without qualification." Corbin believes an implication "in such general terms * * * can not be accepted as correct." Indeed, Corbin flatly asserts that "statutes and rules of law are certainly not incorporated into the contract."

This analysis suggests two conclusions. First, the broad implication is not sound and is not supported by the weight of authority. If this is true of contracts in general, there is no reason why it should not be true of collective bargaining contracts. Second, judges concern themselves with applicable law because they exercise the coercive power of the state and must determine the legal operation of the contract. Arbitrators, unlike judges, are not an arm of the state and do not determine the legal operation of the collective bargaining contract. We determine contract rights and questions of interpretation and application, nothing more. We are the servants of the parties, not the public. We derive our powers from the contract, not from the superior authority of the law. Hence, even if courts had a rational basis for implying that law is part of the contract, arbitrators would have no justification for doing the same.

If, as I have argued, Howlett's implication is not borne out by the law of contracts, is it supported by the contract itself? Arbitrators have the authority to establish implied conditions. The source of this authority is the parties' will, the parties' common understanding. We may find implications which can reasonably be inferred from some provision of the contract or even from the contract as a whole. The implication that all applicable law is incorporated in the contract would be warranted where there was a real or tacit understanding to that effect during negotiations. While such an understanding may exist in some relationships, it is more than doubtful that there is any general understanding among employers and unions as to the role of law during the term of the contract.

The typical contract does mention the law. It is not unusual for the parties to refer to statutory law regarding union security, checkoff, reemployment of veterans, and supplemental unemployment benefits. Those who draft such provisions are certainly aware of the impact of law upon employee rights. Their limited reference to the law suggests that they intend a limited role for the law. Their failure to state, in these circumstances, that all applicable law is part of the contract must have some significance. Thus, Howlett's implication seems inconsistent with the language found in most contracts.

Finally, even if the implication could somehow hurdle all of these objections, it would be confronted by the arbitration clause. Ordinarily, the arbitrator is confined to the interpretation and application of the agreement and forbidden to add to or modify the terms of the agreement. If he rules that the law is part of the contract, he must read into the parties' contract a new and indeterminate set of rights and duties. By doing so, however, he would be adding to the terms of the contract and thus ignoring the limitations on his authority. The purpose of a narrow arbitration clause is to limit us to questions of private rights which arise out of the contract. That purpose would certainly be defeated if we were to draw an implication which would transform arbitration into a forum for the vindication of not just private rights but public rights as well. In the absence of any evidence that the parties intend such a drastic departure from the normal arbitration system, the implication should be rejected.

For these reasons, I find nothing in the collective bargaining contract to support the implication that the law is incorporated in the contract.

C.   WHERE CONTRACT AND LAW CONFLICT

Let me turn now to more specific problems. What should an arbitrator do where the contract and the law conflict, where an award affirming a clear contract obligation would require either party to violate a statutory command?

Professor Cox gave us an excellent example of this problem at an earlier meeting. He noted that after World War II a conflict developed between the Selective Service Act and contract seniority. This statute was interpreted by the Supreme Court to require employers to give veterans preference over nonveterans in the event of layoffs during the first year after their discharge from the armed forces. The typical contract gave veterans only the seniority they would have had if they had not been drafted. A dispute arose when an employer, in reducing the work force, retained a veteran and laid off a nonveteran even though he had more contract seniority. The nonveteran grieved, relying upon the contract. The employer defended his action, relying upon the law. Who should prevail?

There are two possible points of view. Cox tells us to deny this grievance—that is, to respect the law and ignore the contract.

He argues that:

> * * * The parties to collective bargaining cannot avoid negotiating and carrying out their agreement within the existing legal framework. It is either futile or grossly unjust to make an award directing an employer to take action which the law forbids—futile because if the employer challenges the award the union cannot enforce it; unjust because if the employer complies he subjects himself to punishment by civil authority.

Furthermore, such an award demeans the arbitration process by inviting noncompliance, appeals to the courts, and reversal of the award.

Professor Meltzer, on the other hand, tells us to grant the grievance—that is, to respect the contract and ignore the law. His argument includes three main points, each of which deserves some comment.

First, Meltzer says:

> There is * * * no reason to credit arbitrators with any competence, let alone any special expertise, with respect to the law, as distinguished from the agreement. A good many arbitrators lack any legal training at all, and even lawyer-arbitrators do not necessarily hold

themselves out as knowledgeable about the broad range of statutory and administrative materials that may be relevant in labor arbitrations.

No one can quarrel with this description. Arbitrators are not omniscient. Most of us do not have the time, the energy, or the occasion to become truly knowledgeable about the law. But some of our members—Smith, Aaron, Cox, Meltzer himself, to name but a few—surely possess the necessary expertise. Such men are well equipped to decide grievance disputes which raise both contractual and legal questions. It is not unusual for the parties to fit the arbitrator to the dispute, to choose a man qualified by experience or learning for the particular task involved An example of this is the use of industrial engineers to arbitrate time-study or incentive issues. There is no reason why the parties, when confronted by a difficult legal question, cannot exercise this same selectivity in finding a man with experience in both the contract and the law.

Second, Meltzer says:

> * * * an analogy to administrative tribunals is instructive. Such agencies consider themselves bound by the statutes entrusted to their administration and leave to the courts challenges to the constitutional validity of such statutes. Arbitrators should in general accord a similar respect to the agreement that is the source of their authority and should leave to the courts or other official tribunals the determination of whether the agreement contravenes a higher law.

This analogy is appealing. But another analogy can be constructed to support a different conclusion. For example, an administrative agency would refuse to enforce the terms of its enabling statute in a given case if enforcement would require conduct that is unlawful under some other statute. An arbitrator should likewise refuse to enforce a particular contract provision if enforcement would require action forbidden by the law. My point is not that Meltzer's analogy is wrong but rather that his analogy, by itself, is not sufficient reason to adopt his point of view.

Third, Meltzer says that "the parties typically call on an arbitrator to construe and not to destroy their agreement." His position is that an arbitrator is not construing the contract if he defers to the law and ignores the terms of the contract. He would adhere strictly to the contract even where it means requiring one of the parties to act unlawfully.

This is really the crux of the problem. No one would disagree with Meltzer's view that the arbitrator is supposed to construe, rather than destroy, the contract. The question is what exactly is the arbitrator doing when he takes notice of the conflict between the law and the contract and refuses to order the commission of an act required by contract but forbidden by law? Is he destroying the contract by refusing to issue such an order? I do not think so. A strong case can be made for the proposition that the arbitrator, when exercising this kind of restraint, is ordinarily construing the contract.

Consider some of the language in the typical contract. First, it is not unusual to find a "separability" or "saving" clause. Such a clause says that if any contract provision "shall be or become invalid or unenforceable" by reason of the law, "such invalidity or unenforceability shall not affect" the rest of the contract. The parties thus intend to isolate any invalidity so as to preserve the overall integrity of the contract. But they also recognize the fact that a contract provision can be held "invalid" or "unenforceable" because of a state or federal statute. They do not wish to be bound by an invalid provision. The implication seems clear that the arbitrator should not enforce a provision which is clearly unenforceable under the law.

Second, it is not unusual to find an arbitration clause which says the arbitrator's awards will be "final and binding" upon the employer, the union, and the employees concerned. If the arbitrator ignores the law and orders the employer to commit an unlawful act, he invites noncompliance and judicial intervention. He knows that his award, under such circumstances, is not going to be "final and binding." Either the employer asks a court to reverse the award, or the employer refuses to comply and the union asks a court to affirm the award. In either event, the dispute continues beyond the grievance procedure. That could hardly be what the parties intended when they adopted arbitration as the final step in the grievance procedure as the means of terminating the dispute. The implication seems clear that the arbitrator must consider the law in this kind of situation if his award is to have the finality which the contract contemplates.

Thus, it may well be that contracts can be construed to justify resort to the law to avoid an award which would require unlawful conduct.

On balance, the relevant considerations support Cox's view. The arbitrator should "look to see whether sustaining the grievance would require conduct the law forbids or would enforce an illegal contract; if so, the arbitrator should not sustain the grievance." This principle, however, should be carefully limited. It does not suggest that "an arbitrator should pass upon all the parties' legal rights and obligations" or that "an arbitrator should refuse to give effect to a contract provision merely because the courts would not enforce it." Thus, although the arbitrator's award may permit conduct forbidden by law but sanctioned by contract, it should not require conduct forbidden by law even though sanctioned by contract.

WHEN SHOULD ARBITRATORS FOLLOW FEDERAL LAW?

Michael I. Sovern.
23 Proceedings of the National Academy of Arbitrators 29, 38–45 (1970).

I believe that an arbitrator may follow federal law rather than the contract when the following conditions are met:

1. The arbitrator is qualified.

2.   The question of law is implicated in a dispute over the application or interpretation of a contract that is also before him.

3.   The question of law is raised by a contention that, if the conduct complained of does violate the contract, the law nevertheless immunizes or even requires it.

4.   The courts lack primary jurisdiction to adjudicate the question of law. * * *

[Earlier Professor Sovern had described a recent case, National Dairy Products Corp. v. Milk Drivers and Dairy Employees Union, Local 680, 308 F.Supp. 982 (S.D.N.Y. 1970). The collective bargaining agreement prohibited the company from operating an ice cream plant outside the New York area for sales within New York. Instead, the company sold products from a Philadelphia plant to a third party who then distributed them in New York. At arbitration the company claimed that the union's interpretation would violate the antitrust laws. The arbitrator declined to decide the antitrust issue and found a violation of the contract. The district court upheld the award.]

Let me illustrate by referring back to the *National Dairy* case. Suppose the arbitrator was an initiate in the mysteries of antitrust law and hot-cargo clauses. My first condition would then have been met. * * * My second and third conditions were me because the arbitrator was asked to resolve a dispute over the meaning of the contract and the employer claimed that the antitrust laws required him to violate the agreement if the union's interpretation of it were upheld.

As to the antitrust question, however, my fourth condition was not met. Federal district courts have full authority to deal with antitrust questions. The antitrust defense could, therefore, be raised in a court action to enforce the award and the question resolved by the appropriate tribunal. Since the arbitrator's decision on a question of antitrust law would not be entitled to the finality attaching to his interpretation of the contract, little would be gained by having him decide it first. * * *

With respect to the first condition, who is to decide whether the arbitrator is qualified to tackle the issue of law? The answer is simple: The arbitrator himself must resolve that question. If he feels unqualified to resolve a statutory issue pressed on him by a party, his only duty is to avoid possible confusion by making it clear that he has limited his consideration to the contract question. An arbitrator whose training and areas of specialization have not equipped him to resolve a particular statutory question serves himself, the parties, and the system best by saying so. (If the statutory question is a part of the submission expressly agreed upon by the parties, the unqualified arbitrator should, of course, decline the case.)

Not all arbitrators are notable for their humility and some may assume they are qualified when they are not. The parties can often protect against this in their selection. And, of course the arbitrator's decision is not final on statutory matters. The risk of immodesty seems worth running.

My second condition—that the question of law be implicated in a contract-interpretation dispute that is also before the arbitrator—is necessary because unless it is met the parties belong in some other forum altogether. Consider again my seniority hypothetical in which an employer lays off black workers pursuant to a departmental seniority system and they grieve to arbitration. Their claim ... was not that the contract was misconstrued, but that the action violated Title VII of the Civil Rights Act of 1964. Congress has designated the Equal Employment Opportunity Commission and the federal courts to handle such cases. Unless all of the parties expressly agreed to submit the dispute to an arbitrator, there is no reason why he should assume jurisdiction over it. * * *

When my third condition is not met, the arbitrator should not decide the question of law. The reason, as we have just seen, is that the consequences of decision seem worse than those of abstention. Abstention has the virtue of clarity: The arbitrator decides the contract question and the Board decides the statutory question, and everyone concerned can know who is to do what. If the arbitrator decides, there is always the chance that his decision will conclude the matter, but if it does not, he may have succeeded only in dragging the courts into the case in addition to or in place of the NLRB.

To put the point another way, when an employer claims his conduct, if a breach of contract, is required by law, the case is tangled enough to warrant an arbitrator's gambling on improving matters. Deciding the statutory question might help greatly and can't hurt much. When that condition is lacking, the case though complex, is not so badly snarled and there is a serious risk that a decision by the arbitrator will make things much worse. * * *

For a case in which the first three conditions are met, let us return to an earlier hypothetical: An employer ignores a department seniority provision and lays off whites with greater department seniority than recently transferred blacks; the white employees grieve to arbitration; the employer defends on the ground that his decision was required by Title VII. Under my formula, the arbitrator should decide the Title VII issue only if the courts lack primary jurisdiction to adjudicate it.

As I read Title VII, that condition is not met. The preliminary recourse to the Equal Employment Opportunity Commission required by that statute is intended to permit conciliation, not to obtain an adjudication from a specialized tribunal. Indeed, the EEOC has no power to adjudicate. A complainant whose case is not voluntarily settled must come to federal court if he wishes to have the matter adjudicated.

Since the courts are entrusted with primary jurisdiction to decide Title VII questions, my fourth condition is not satisfied and the arbitrator should not decide the statutory question. In our hypothetical, he would presumably decide that the employer violated the agreement, that the white grievants are, insofar as the contract is concerned, entitled to the jobs. He should also make it absolutely clear that he is not deciding the Title VII issue. Then, in the ensuing action to enforce or set aside the award, the court can apply Title VII to the award and, if appropriate, invalidate it. * * *

JUDICIAL REVIEW OF LABOR ARBITRATION AWARDS: A SECOND LOOK AT *ENTERPRISE WHEEL* AND ITS PROGENY

Theodore J. St. Antoine.
30 Proceedings of the National Academy of Arbitrators 29 (1977).

One final, perhaps controversial, lesson flows from my theory of the arbitrator as contract-reader. It has previously been assumed, by others as well as by me, that insofar as an arbitrator's award construes a statute, it is advisory only, and the statutory question will be examined de novo if the award is challenged in the courts. I no longer think this is the necessary result. As between the parties themselves, I see no impediment to their agreeing to a final and binding arbitral declaration of their statutory rights and duties.[26] Obviously, if an arbitrator's interpretation of an OSHA requirement did not adequately protect the employees, or violated some other basic public policy, a court would not be bound by it. But if the arbitrator imposed more stringent requirements, I would say the award should be enforced. The parties agreed to that result, and their agreement should be accorded the same finality as any other arbitration contract.

Whatever damage may be done to the pristine purity of labor arbitration by this increased responsibility for statutory interpretation, I consider an expanded arbitral jurisdiction inevitable. Such recent statutes as Title VII of the Civil Rights Act, the Pension Reform Act (ERISA), and OSHA are so interwoven in the fabric of collective bargaining agreements that it is simply impracticable in many cases for arbitrators to deal with contractual provisions without taking into account statutory provisions. Since I believe that, as between the parties, the arbitrator's rulings on the law should have the same finality as his rulings on the contract, I conclude, in contrast to the forebodings of my friend Dave Feller, that we are actually entering a new "golden age" for the arbitration process. * * *

Notes and Questions

1. Which view on the consideration of external law impresses you the most? Why?

2. Recall that Howlett justified his activism by suggesting that an award that does *not* decide legal issues "may result in error" and would

26. Although the decisions are somewhat divided, there is clear authority that arbitrators may be made the final judges of law as well as fact, and that awards issued under misconception of the law will be upheld. See Annotation, 112 A.L.R. 873 (1938), and cases cited.

disserve the parties. Is that necessarily so? When Howlett applied his theory, he ran into trouble. In *Roadmaster Corporation*, he sustained a grievance over an employer's termination of the collective agreement on the ground that the employer had violated the National Labor Relations Act. As in the excerpt above, Arbitrator Howlett asserted that the collective agreement automatically included all applicable law. The employer challenged the award in federal district court. The court overturned the award, holding that the arbitrator exceeded the scope of the submission by basing his award on law rather than on the agreement. Roadmaster Corp. v. Production & Maintenance Employees' Local 504, Laborers' International Union of North America, 655 F.Supp. 1460 (S.D.Ill.1987), affirmed, 851 F.2d 886 (7th Cir.1988).

3.   Howlett also argued that the National Labor Relations Board would not defer to an award that failed to decide the NLRA issue. That may have been the law when Howlett wrote, but it is no longer true. For an explanation of the Board's changing deferral doctrine, see Chapter IV.A. and footnote 26 in the excerpt from Professor St. Antoine's article.

4.   Mittenthal concluded that although an award "may *permit* conduct forbidden by law but sanctioned by the contract, it should not *require* conduct forbidden by law even though sanctioned by contract" [emphasis added]. Do you understand that distinction? Are you persuaded by it? Here is Professor Meltzer's response, *The Role of Law in Arbitration: Rejoinders*, 21 Proceedings of the National Academy of Arbitrators 58, 59–61 (1968):

> The implications and desirability of that qualification may be clarified if we examine it in the context of two grievances. The first, suggested by Mr. Mittenthal, was filed by a *nonveteran* who, when laid off, requested reemployment and back pay on the ground that his layoff violated an agreement that granted veterans only their plant seniority plus the seniority they would have accumulated had they not been drafted. The employer supported his layoff of the nonveteran, even though the latter had more seniority than the retained veteran on the following ground: The Selective Service Act of 1940 required the layoff of nonveterans rather than veterans during the first year after the veteran's discharge from military service, even though the veteran's seniority, including credit for his military service, was less than the nonveteran's.

> Although Mr. Mittenthal's statement of his hypothetical case rests on what I believe to be a misreading of *Fishgold v. Sullivan Corp.* [328 U.S. 275, 66 S.Ct. 1105 (1946)], I will assume, for the purpose of this discussion, that his reading of *Fishgold* is correct. Mr. Mittenthal suggests that the arbitrator should follow the statute and deny the grievance because an award calling for the nonveteran's reinstatement and the veteran's displacement would require the employer to engage in conduct forbidden by the law.

> The second grievance involves the same basic situation, except for this variation: The employer laid off the *veteran*, who filed a grievance requesting reinstatement (and displacement of the nonveteran) and back pay. Mr. Mittenthal, if I follow his distinction, suggests that the arbitrator should deny the veteran's grievance even though the award

would be contrary to the law, for "the arbitrator's award may permit conduct forbidden by law but sanctioned by contract." Our hypothetical arbitrator is not requiring legally proscribed conduct; he is merely permitting it or refusing to grant a remedy for it.

Whatever one's view of the larger issue as to the role of law in arbitration, I cannot see an acceptable basis for Mr. Mittenthal's formula. It is not supported by the authority conferred on the arbitrator by the parties; or by the expertise imputed to arbitrators and courts; or by the twin desires for finality of arbitration awards and the limitation of judicial intervention. Under Mittenthal's approach, the role accorded to law would depend on how an employer resolved a controversy and not on its essential character or the functions properly delegated to different adjudicative agencies. In my opinion, such an approach transforms an accidental consideration into a decisive one. His formula, incidentally, also appears to run contrary to Cox's suggestion, on which he relies; for Cox admonished the arbitrator to "look to see whether sustaining the grievance would require conduct the law forbids or would enforce an illegal contract; if so, the arbitrator should not sustain the grievance." In my opinion, if the arbitrator is viewed as "enforcing" contracts, he "enforces" an illegal contract equally whether he causes an employer to engage in an act prohibited by statute or, by denying a remedy, condones the prohibited act already executed by the employer.

It is, however, worth noting, that, in a strict sense, the arbitrator does not "enforce" the contract. Enforcement is left to the courts, and, regardless of whether the arbitrator purports to apply the law or to ignore it, the courts stand ready to enforce the condition that his award is not repugnant to the law.

Are you *still* persuaded by Mittenthal?

5. (a) Meltzer and Howlett mark the debate's poles; the rest of the commentators fall somewhere between those poles. When faced with difficult choices, most people tend to look for intermediate positions. Are any of the intermediate positions here satisfactory? Or might this be the rare case in which one of the extremes is correct, and all the intermediate positions are faulty?

(b) If you favor a middle position, do Professor Sovern's four conditions provide a comfortable resting place? Why should an arbitrator follow federal law only if the question arises by a contention that the law immunizes or requires the challenged conduct (condition 3)? Does this differ from Mittenthal's approach?

6. Professor St. Antoine's excerpt alludes to his theory of the arbitrator as the parties' chosen "contract reader"—that is, a person designated to "read" their contract and tell them, authoritatively and finally, what they meant.

(a) In the quoted excerpt, he argues that the contract reader's construction of a statute should be binding *between the parties* even if it is incorrect, at least if it imposed more stringent requirements than a court would. Why? Wouldn't this approach necessarily favor one party in almost every case? Which one? Why?

(b) Professor St. Antoine would make the arbitrator's interpretation of the law binding as between the parties only if it imposed "more stringent requirements" than the law itself actually does. Like a ratchet, his device would work only in one direction. Why should that be so?

7. (a) Does a contract with no provision about the applicability of external law indicate that the parties wanted the arbitrator to avoid extra-contractual questions? Or only that the parties did not consider the problem? See Alexander v. Gardner–Denver Co., 415 U.S. 36, 53, 94 S.Ct. 1011, 1022, 39 L.Ed.2d 147 (1974) ("The arbitrator, however, has no general authority to invoke public laws that conflict with the bargain between the parties").

(b) Suppose you were negotiating a collective bargaining agreement. Would you raise the external-law problem? If so, how would you deal with it? Would it matter whether you represented the employer or the union?

(c) What should the arbitrator do if an attorney representing one party raises a statutory question and the other party does not use an attorney?

8. Where would an arbitrator gain the *authority* to resolve external law questions, if the parties do not expressly or impliedly confer it?

(a) The office of arbitrator is created by the agreement, and the typical arbitration clause forbids the arbitrator to "add to, subtract from, or otherwise modify" the underlying agreement. Could the arbitrator get authority to resolve the external law issue from some other part of the agreement? If so, which? Consider these possibilities: (I) a nondiscrimination provision; (ii) a "just cause for discharge" provision; (iii) a "savings" clause.

(b) Or could the authority come from the pertinent statute? If so, how?

(c) Or could the authority come from the Labor Management Relations Act or from federal labor policy? If so, how? Consider NLRA §§ 203(d) and 301 in Appendix B.

9. Even if arbitrators have *authority* to apply external law, do they have the necessary *competence*? Professor (now Judge) Harry Edwards surveyed members of the National Academy of Arbitrators in 1975 about arbitration of discrimination cases. His results were shocking. Only half the respondents said that they kept abreast of Title VII developments and only 14% believed they could accurately define basic employment-discrimination terms such as "bona fide occupational qualification." Despite their limited knowledge of the field, 72% of the surveyed arbitrators stated that they were professionally competent to decide legal issues in discrimination cases. Edwards, *Arbitration of Employment Discrimination Cases: An Empirical Study*, 28 Proceedings of the National Academy of Arbitrators 59 (1976). Is that expression of self-confidence really surprising? Might an arbitrator reasonably expect the advocates to present the information necessary to resolve legal questions? Only half the respondents in Professor Edwards's survey were lawyers. Are non-lawyers capable of resolving complex legal issues in arbitration, with or without help from the parties?

10. *Should* arbitrators decide legal issues, even if they possess both authority and competence? Professor David Feller passionately argued that resolution of legal issues would inevitably harm the arbitration process. By breaking down the walls that insulated collective bargaining's "autonomous, self-contained system of private law," he argued, arbitral interpretations of

external law would invite judicial second-guessing. *The Coming End of Arbitration's Golden Age, supra* note 1. For a more optimistic view of arbitration's ability to survive the introduction of external-law issues, see Harry Edwards, *Labor Arbitration at the Crossroads: The 'Common Law of the Shop' v. External Law*, 32 Arbitration Journal 65 (1977).

3.   APPLYING THE THEORIES[1]

EVANS PRODUCTS CO.

70 LA 526 (David Feller, 1978).*

[The contract forbade discrimination "on the basis of age." A federal regulation prohibited the employment of any person under the age of 18 "in the occupations of setting up, adjusting, repairing, oiling, or cleaning power-driven wood-working machines." Believing that the regulation applied to a particular job that required cleaning a mechanical saw, the employer refused to hire 17–year-old Adrian Landers for that position. The union believed the regulation did not apply to the job in question.]

The principal issue presented by this grievance—the extent of an arbitrator's authority to resolve a grievance on the basis of law external to the collective bargaining agreement—has been the subject of much controversy among arbitrators. See the articles and speeches cited in Feller, The Coming End of Arbitration's Golden Age, in ARBITRA-TION–1976, Proceedings, 29th annual Meeting, National Academy of Arbitrators (BNA, 1976) at p. 110. I have participated in that controversy and my views are reasonably well known. Indeed, subsequent to my appointment in this case but prior to the hearing, I provided to the parties citations to my published work on this question, and in the case of the employer, reprints of two recent articles: The Impact of External Law Upon Labor Arbitration, in THE FUTURE OF LABOR ARBITRA-TION IN AMERICA (American Arbitration Association, 1976) 83 and Arbitration: The Days of Its Glory Are Numbered, 2 Industrial Relations Law Journal 97 (1977). The views there expressed parallel recent decisions by both courts and arbitrators. Thus, the Court of Appeals for the Ninth Circuit wrote the following in March 1977:

> " * * * The function of an arbitration panel is to resolve disputes based upon the expressed commitment of the parties to the collective bargaining agreement and to the arbitration procedure incorporated therein. Consequently, the arbitrator's domain mainly covers question of contractual interpretation. Alexander v. Gardner–Denver Co., 415 U.S. 36 (1974). The Board, meanwhile, is concerned

---

1. For an enlightening survey of arbitral practices in this area, see Bonnie G. Bogue, *Melding External Law with the Collective Bargaining Agreement*, 50 Proceedings of the National Academy of Arbitrators 82 (1997). See also Perry A. Zirkel, *The Use of External Law in Labor Arbitration: An Analysis of Arbitral Awards*, 1985 Detroit College of Law Review 31.

with the prevention of unfair labor practices under the federal labor laws and is thus primarily concerned with the statutory and policy consideration." Stephenson v. NLRB, 550 F.2d 535, 539, 94 LRRM 3224.

See also Southbridge Plastics Division v. Local 759, 565 F.2d 913, 16 FEP Cases 507 (5th Cir.1978). Of even more relevance is the recent decision by the distinguished arbitrator Charles O. Gregory to the following effect:

> "After extensive reading and reflection I have concluded that the grievance herein is arbitrable and that I had best fulfill my responsibility as an arbitrator acting under the agreement, in accord with the terms of that agreement, leaving to the courts the interpretation and appropriateness of the various federal anti-discrimination laws, rulings and sanctions." USM Corp., 69 Lab. Arb. Rep. 1050 (1977).

Other arbitrators have a different view. The cases are summarized in The Impact of External Law on Arbitration. For a recent example of a contrary position see International Paper Co., 69 Lab. Arb. Rep. 857 (F. Jay Taylor, 1977).

Whatever one's views may be on this subject in general, however, decision in a particular case must depend upon the authority granted to the arbitrator by the particular agreement which sets forth his jurisdiction. In this case the agreement is particularly clear. It provides that the arbitrator has no "authority to modify or add to any of the terms and provisions of this Agreement, nor to make any decisions on matters not covered by specific provisions of this Agreement." Unless otherwise modified by some other provision of the agreement, this seems to limit me to consideration of whether the employer has violated any specific provision of the agreement, leaving to other tribunals the decision as to whether that violation is justified by a prohibition imposed by law external to the agreement.

The employer argues that the limitation on my authority contained in Section 18(f) is modified by the provisions of Section 9(I). Section 9(I) provides that if any provision of the agreement is found to be illegal, the parties intend that the remaining portions of the agreement shall remain in full force and effect. As I indicated at the hearing, the purpose of this provision seems to be to preserve the remainder of the agreement if some portion of it is found to be invalid rather than to vest the arbitrator with authority to find that a portion of the agreement or its application in a particular case is invalid under external law.

I therefore conclude that, whatever the general authority of arbitrators may be, the only authority I have under this agreement is to decide whether the employer's action in refusing to hire Mr. Adrian Landers on July 5, 1977, was a violation of the "specific provisions of this Agreement." Since I find that there is no specific provision which incorporates into the agreement the provisions of the Fair Labor Standards Act or any other federal statute, I am left with the question of whether the employer's action constituted a violation of the provision in Section 9(h) prohibiting discrimination against an applicant for employment on the basis of age.

The question is somewhat more difficult than might first appear and differs substantially from the case where an arbitrator is asked to ignore an admitted violation of the agreement because of the anti-discrimination provisions of external law (as in the decision by Arbitrator Gregory cited above). The question is what "discrimination" in this agreement means. It might be possible to argue that this provision, properly construed, refers only to such discrimination as is prohibited by the Age Discrimination in Employment Act and therefore does not reach a refusal to hire an applicant under the age of 40. The employer, at the hearing, however, although raising the question, specifically declined to rest upon any such interpretation of the agreement. The only defense tendered, counsel asserted, was the alleged restriction imposed by the Fair Labor Standards Act.

It might also be possible to argue that the only kind of discrimination intended to be prohibited is invidious or hostile discrimination and that a refusal to hire because of an arguable prohibition under the Fair Labor Standards Act does not constitute discrimination of the kind prohibited by Section 9(h). Alternatively, it might be possible to contend that it is not discrimination to refuse to hire an individual who because of his age is incapable of performing the job for which he has applied—as would be the case if the applicant were five years old—and that the regulations issued under the Fair Labor Standards Act place such restrictions upon the work which Mr. Landers could perform that he was thereby rendered unable to fill the requirements of the job. Neither of these latter two arguments, however, was presented to me. The employer rested on the contention that the refusal to hire Mr. Landers because of his age was justified by the Fair Labor Standards Act and that Section 9(I) gave me authority to determine the validity of that defense, and declined to proceed further when I indicated my preliminary view that I found no such authority in that section.

Concluding as I do that Section 9(I) is not such a grant of authority and that I am required, in the absence of agreement to the contrary, to limit myself to the "specific provisions of this Agreement," I am compelled to conclude that the conceded refusal of the employer to hire Mr. Landers solely because he was 17 years old was discrimination against an applicant for employment on the basis of his age in violation of the provisions of Section 9(h) of the agreement.

There remains the question of remedy. Any remedy which I might direct is obviously subject to nullification by a court having authority to determine the disputed question of federal law. I need not, therefore, concern myself with any unfairness in providing a remedy if the employer should prove to be correct in the contention with respect to the applicability of federal law to the present case. If, on the other hand, the union should prove to be successful in its view that the federal regulation did not prohibit the employment of Mr. Landers I must decide what, under this agreement, is the appropriate remedy.

There is no express provision in the agreement as to the remedy to be provided for an applicant who is refused employment in violation of the provisions of the agreement. The union argued, at the hearing, that the appropriate remedy to be implied into the agreement is a direction that Mr. Landers be currently employed by the employer with retroactive salary, benefits, and rights to the date of July 5, 1977, those rights to be equivalent to those enjoyed by the person or persons hired in lieu of Mr. Landers from that period to the date when Mr. Landers is actually employed by the employer. The employer declined to present argument as to the appropriate remedy.

The question of remedy in the case of a refusal to employ is apparently a novel one under this agreement and there has been no experience or practice. In the case of a discharge found to be without just case, the usual remedy is reinstatement to the position from which the employee was discharged with full back pay minus any compensation from employment earned by the grievant during the period of his discharge and minus any unemployment compensation which the employee might have received during the period of discharge which he is not required to repay. The remedy in case of a refusal to hire should it seems to me be similar, subject only to the uncertainty as to whether the job for which the applicant applied was a permanent job which would have paid full wages for the period in question. Since that cannot be determined on the record made by the parties, the award will simply set forth the principles to be applied in the determination or retroactive pay. Such an award is similar to the remedy provided by the National Labor Relations Board in cases of discriminatory refusal to hire in violation of that Act, see Phelps Dodge Corp. v. NLRB, 313 U.S. 177, 8 LRRM 439 (1941), and it seems appropriate to imply agreement upon such a remedy into this agreement.

Award

The employer, having violated Section 9(h) of the agreement between the parties by refusing to employ Adrian Landers on July 5, 1977, for non-production off-bearing tailoff work because of his age, shall offer employment to him in that position with retroactive salary, benefits and rights equivalent to those person or persons hired in lieu of Mr. Landers, from that date to the date actually employed.

INTERNATIONAL PAPER CO., SOUTHERN KRAFT DIVISION, BASTROP MILL
69 LA 857 (F. Jay Taylor, 1977).*

[The parties' collective bargaining agreement required the employer to allow the senior qualified employee to transfer to an apprenticeship. It also provided that the arbitrator "shall have no power to add to or subtract from or modify any of the terms of this agreement." In 1973, the company awarded an apprenticeship to a qualified but junior black employee instead of a qualified but senior white employee.]

[The company was subject to Executive Order 11,246, which obliged federal contractors to adopt an affirmative action plan and make good-faith efforts to correct the underutilization of minority employees. A group of black employees had recently sued International Paper for race discrimination in violation of Title VII of the Civil Rights Act of 1964. The settlement agreement in that suit contained a term stating that the collective bargaining agreement's seniority provisions "are not racially discriminatory in their terms or operation."]

[The company challenged the arbitrability of the white employee's grievance because ultimately the federal courts would have to determine the legality of the company's action. On the merits, it argued that its affirmative action plan required it to select the junior black applicant because of the low representation of blacks in apprenticeships in the Bastrop mill. It refused, however, to give the union a copy of its affirmative action plan. The arbitrator first found the dispute arbitrable because federal law did not prohibit the union from processing the grievance.]

On the merits, I find that I must consider the obligations of the equal employment policies of this nation, and the many laws and executive orders which spell out that policy. When there is a direct conflict between job discrimination laws and the collective bargaining agreement in a grievance, the choice becomes even more difficult.

I fully recognize that an Arbitrator is a creature of the Contract. His powers are created in the Contract and are limited by the Contract. And I have asked myself the questions—Does the Arbitrator have greater authority to fashion a remedy in discrimination cases other than what is set forth in the Collective Bargaining Agreement? Can the Arbitrator go outside the Collective Bargaining Agreement and apply the law if there is conflict? My answer must be: When a group of employees, as is clearly evident in this case, has been found to be the victims of past discrimination, and the Company through its Affirmative Action Program has fashioned a remedy to alleviate the problem, then I must conclude that this remedy is exempt from contractual obligations.

Not to so rule places the Company in an impossible position. The Company has no alternative but to comply with the directives of the Office of Contract Compliance. Failure to do so would be a violation of Executive Order 11246 and would jeopardize the economic well being, even survival, of the International Paper Company. One requirement of executive Order 11246 is to maintain an Affirmative Action Program which would afford relief for those persons suffering the effects of past discrimination. Such a program is a condition of the employer being found in compliance. Those not found in compliance would suffer potential loss of government contracts and sub-contracts as well as facing charges of violating applicable Federal law. Thus, the Company faced drastic consequences if it failed to follow the directions of Federal enforcement authority.

Was, then, the remedial action devised by the Company justified under the conditions that prevailed at its Bastrop Mill in May of 1973? I shall not attempt to establish conclusively with any kind of final certainty the state of present law on this complex issue. Nor could I do so if I were inclined. I can only make a reasonable, good-faith determination that affirmative action on the Company's part was not only justified but demanded. Consider the following unrefuted facts:

(a) There had never been a Black admitted to the apprentice program prior to May, 1973.

(b) Even today Blacks represent only 15% of the apprentices at that Mill.

(c) There is still not one Black among the 58 journeymen employed at the Mill.

(d) Without the Company's Affirmative Action Program only a token number of Blacks would have been assigned to apprenticeship positions during the past four years. Within the Company's ten mills, only four of 97 Blacks now apprenticed would have been selected and the program would currently consist of 343 Whites and four Blacks.

(e) It would be at least 10 years before Black bidders could accumulate enough seniority to compete proportionately with Whites for apprenticeship vacancies.

These facts make it quite apparent that since the apprenticeship program was the established route for promotion into the craft skills, the Company was particularly vulnerable to charges of discriminatory practices. To this Arbitrator this conclusion, which I deem to be valid, carries far more weight than the lengthy testimony produced at the Hearing and the dozens of court cases cited and analyzed by the advocates. Thus, I feel that the Company was justified in failing to observe the specific terms of the Agreement in fashioning a remedy which would meet the problems of its Black employees. Failure to take such action would likely result in a violation of Federal law and the consequences that could result from such violations (to say noting of moral principles) render the alternatives totally unacceptable.

This leads me to the conclusion that the remedial action program required of the Company by appropriate Federal authorities are [sic] paramount to the provisions of the Labor Agreement even though it does alter Section D(3). Under the circumstances noted above I simply cannot look at the Agreement alone, but it must be considered in the context of applicable law, particularly Title VII. And Executive Order 11246, upon which the Company's action is based, has the force of law. Not to adopt such a position would, in my opinion, result in the abdication of my function and responsibility as an arbitrator. * * *

I do fault the Company for not making known the specific provisions of its Affirmative Action Plan which it wishes to implement. This failure, however, in the light of the circumstances, is not sufficient grounds to estop the employer from raising Affirmative Action as a basis for its actions. Regardless of any written plan, however, the Company is still required to show a good-faith effort to correct underutilization of minorities in the apprenticeship program.

Finally, I would add that I am sympathetic to the frustrations which the Union must feel in an issue such as this. The Contract is clear and unequivocal. In matters related to transfers the Agreement states that "The Company will consider the applicant for transfer into any department on the basis of seniority consistent with ability." Certainly this provision of the Contract was not intended to discriminate against anyone. Nor is there the slightest shred of evidence that the Union wishes to perpetrate discrimination. The Union simply believed that it had, in good faith, negotiated an agreement on questions of transfers and seniority, and now it finds this agreement altered by a Federally mandated remedial action program. Nevertheless, such sympathy did not alter my conclusions. I shall sign an AWARD denying the grievance.

Award

Grievance denied.

Notes and Questions

1.   Collective bargaining agreements almost always forbid an arbitrator to modify the agreement. If you represented the employer in *Evans Products*, how would you have dealt with the union's likely argument that Section 9(h) barred consideration of the statutory question? What would you recommend as your client's next step?

2.   Arbitrator Feller notes that he provided parties with citations to his articles on the role of external law before the hearing. Why did he do that? Should an arbitrator do so? *Must* the arbitrator do so? Consider that in most cases the arbitrator knows nothing about the issue in a case until the hearing.

Feller also stated the he need not concern himself with the possible unfairness of ordering the employer to do something illegal because a court will nullify any legal error in the award. Is that a responsible attitude for an arbitrator? What else could he have done, short of deciding and applying the legal issue? In fact, the California courts did vacate his award, just as he expected: Evans Products Co. v. Millmen's Union No. 550, 205 Cal.Rptr. 731, 159 Cal.App.3d 815 (1984) (award was unenforceable on grounds of illegality because it would have compelled the employer to violate the child labor provisions of the FLSA).

3.   (a) In his *International Paper* decision Arbitrator Taylor recognizes that the arbitrator is a "creature of the contract" whose powers are "limited

by the contract." Why then does he conclude that he can apply the law rather than the contract? Is his answer persuasive? Why or why not?

(b) Arbitrator Taylor finds a "direct conflict between job discrimination laws and the collective bargaining agreement." Is that how you read the situation? What about the settlement agreement stating that the seniority provisions were *not* discriminatory? He also accepts the company's assertion that its affirmative action plan required it to select the junior black applicant, yet he never quotes the plan. Why not? Is there any evidence that he (unlike the union) even saw the plan?

(c) Title VII of the Civil Rights Act of 1964 expressly protects *bona fide* seniority agreements. Assuming that the contract in this case is *bona fide*, should the arbitrator nevertheless allow a company's unilaterally-adopted affirmative action plan to trump the seniority provision?

4. (a) Arbitrator Taylor is not a lawyer. Should that matter to his decision? Does it?

(b) David Feller was one of the towering figures of modern labor arbitration. After graduating from Harvard Law School, where he served on the Law Review, he worked as a Supreme Court clerk and later practiced labor law in Washington, D.C. Among other major activities, he successfully argued the *Steelworkers Trilogy* cases for the union and served as General Counsel for the Steelworkers. He left full-time practice to become a law professor at Berkeley, where he proceeded to write many important works on labor law, including articles on the role of external law in arbitration. On top of all that, he became a distinguished labor arbitrator. If any arbitrator in the country was qualified to resolve statutory questions, he was. Given that background, why did he hesitate? Does the task require a nonlawyer like Taylor?

(c) Or is there a more practical explanation? There were both factual and interpretive disputes at issue in *Evans Products*. The regulation prohibited the employment of any person under the age of 18 "in the occupations of setting up, adjusting, repairing, oiling, or cleaning power-driven woodworking machines." The employer argued that the job in question required cleaning the saw as well as taking material away from the saw (the "tailoff work"). The union argued that the job did not include cleaning the saw itself, and that even if it did, the cleaning was not the kind envisioned by the regulation. Rather than getting into the saw with soap and water, the union claimed, the employee simply used a high-powered hose. In light of the ambiguity of the regulation and the facts, perhaps Arbitrator Feller simply thought it wiser to let the Department of Labor apply its own regulations.

5. Enderby Manufacturing Company unilaterally changed from a five-day to a seven-day production schedule. For the first time in the Company's history, some employees were required to work regular weekend shifts. The union grieved, and the parties selected Professor Susan Fair to hear the case. The union charged that the unilateral change violated the NLRA as well as the agreement's recognition clause. The employer responded that the NLRA was irrelevant and that the agreement's management-rights clause authorized it to "determine the methods of production."

(a) Should Arbitrator Fair decide the NLRA question? Why or why not? Reread endnote 2 after the St. Antoine excerpt.

(b) Assume that Arbitrator Fair sustains the grievance on the basis of the NLRA issue. If the employer thinks her interpretation of the law incorrect, what recourse, if any, does it have?

(c) Assume, alternatively, that she does not decide the legal issue and denies the grievance on the merits. What recourse, if any, does the union have?

6.   The external-law debate has focused on statutory law. Contract law presents less of a problem, because it usually assists interpretation. Seldom would it conflict with an agreement. Some advocates cite common-law rules to bolster their interpretations, often to the arbitrator's discomfort. Here is the helpful advice of one distinguished contracts scholar:

> In short, nonlawyer arbitrators should refuse to be snowed by lawyers thundering out what they will insist are inviolable principles of contract law. Lawyer arbitrators should reevaluate those principles to which they were exposed in law school and have unquestioningly accepted since. I submit that the correct applicable principles in any given case are those that an intelligent arbitrator can and will arrive at—and arrive at more surely—by the thoughtful application of everyday standards of relevance, by consideration of the purpose and function of collective bargaining agreements, by careful attention to the total environment in which the dispute with which he is faced arose, and, forgive me, by the use of common sense.

Addison Mueller, *The Law of Contracts—A Changing Legal Environment*, 31 Proceedings of the National Academy of Arbitrators 204, 217 (1979).

7.   Whether or not the arbitrator may use external law to decide the merits of a question, may he or she use it to expand the remedies normally available in arbitration? Professor Carlton Snow has forcefully argued "that, as a general rule, parties to a collective bargaining agreement expect the law of the land to be used to inform remedies fashioned by an arbitrator." *Make-Whole and Statutory Remedies—I. Informing the Silent Remedial Gap*, 48 Proceedings of the National Academy of Arbitrators 150 (1996). He qualifies that broad statement, however, by stating that arbitrators should not award remedies that exceed the parties' expectations and should consider the potentially different goals of the statute and the agreement. Using those qualifications, he suggests that arbitrators normally should not award punitive damages or oblige the losing party to pay the other's attorney fees.

8.   Perhaps there is no satisfactory answer to the general question of external law. If not, then we need guidelines rather than purported rules. Leonard L. Scheinholtz and Philip A. Miscimarra, *The Arbitrator as Judge and Jury: Another Look at Statutory Law in Arbitration*, 40 Arbitration Journal, June 1985, at 55, argue that each case should be decided on its own, considering: (a) arbitral authority (does the contract authorize or prohibit arbitrators from applying external law?); (b) arbitral competence (does the arbitrator have the knowledge and training required for statutory interpretation?); (c) arbitration procedure (does the negotiated procedure contain elements that may be necessary for resolving statutory issues, *e.g.*, evidentia-

ry rules, subpoena power, and right to counsel?); and (d) finality or redundancy (would arbitral determination of the statutory question lead to or duplicate other proceedings?). Should an arbitrator be more willing to decide a statutory question if no other agency or court is likely to do so? How would these considerations apply in *Evans Products* and *International Paper*?

9.   Even if arbitrators do tackle statutory questions, there is no guarantee they will do so correctly or even consistently. A famous example of the problems arbitrators can cause is W. R. Grace and Co. v. Local Union No. 759, International Union of the United Rubber, Cork, Linoleum and Plastic Workers of America, 652 F.2d 1248 (5th Cir.1981), affirmed on other grounds, 461 U.S. 757, 103 S.Ct. 2177, 76 L.Ed.2d 298 (1983), discussed in Chapter VI.D., *infra*. The first arbitrator held that a conciliation agreement the employer signed with the Equal Employment Opportunity Commission overrode the collective bargaining agreement's seniority provisions and therefore denied a grievance. The second arbitrator held that the first arbitrator should not even have considered the conciliation agreement and therefore sustained an identical grievance. That left the employer with contradictory awards. (To learn how the dispute came out, read ahead in Chapter VI.D.)

10.   How important is the external law question? Recall the comments in the Introduction about the narrow scope of the debate. One study found that external law played a significant role in only 5% of a sample of 100 published arbitration awards. Perry A. Zirkel, *The Use of External Law in Labor Arbitration: An Analysis of Arbitral Awards*, 1985 Detroit College of Law Review 31, at 45–46. Here is the author's conclusion:

> In conclusion, the importance of the external-law controversy seems to be largely * * * in theory, not practice * * *. Examination of a cross section of reported arbitration decisions reveals that a solid third of the cases do not involve any trace of the law, even merely in terminology or technique. Most of the rest were decided without according the external law even a secondary role—relying instead on nontechnical evaluation of evidence, interpretation, or contractual provisions, and application of industrial equity * * *. Further, where the issue of the proper place of public law in the private law arena of labor arbitration has arisen as a possible stumbling block, it has typically been skipped over or sidestepped, with an irrepressible conflict scarcely ever being perceived as present. In sum, although the arbitral role of external law may be significant in terms of complexity, with regard to frequency the Decade of Debate—loosely paraphrasing Shakespeare—seems to be much ado about relatively little.

A NOTE ON CURRENT ISSUES OF EXTERNAL LAW

As the decisions by Arbitrators Feller and Taylor show, arbitrators have had to deal with questions of external law for many years. Several recent developments have exacerbated the challenges for arbitrators. Congress has passed more laws regulating employment, including the Age Discrimination in Employment Act (ADEA), the Employee Retirement and Income Security Act (ERISA), the Americans with Disabilities Act (ADA), and the Family and Medical Leave Act (FMLA). More parties have adopted contract provisions either explicitly or implicitly incorporating statutory rights. Individual contracts of employment commonly require employees to arbitrate any statutory claims against the employer. Finally, employees are more willing to assert statutory protections in arbitration, either to enforce them through the arbitration process rather than through administrative or court procedures, or to challenge employer actions that may violate statutes. The result has been a dramatic increase in the number, complexity, and variety of external law problems.

Consider just one of the these statutes, the FMLA. This law guarantees covered employees up to twelve weeks of unpaid leave each year for absences due to a "serious health condition" of the employee or of a member of the employee's immediate family. The FMLA has played a role in many recent arbitrations. The following examples are just a sampling from BNA's Labor Arbitration Reports. Note the many different ways in which the arbitrators used the statute.

• In System Sensor, 111 LA 1186 (Vicki Peterson Cohen, 1999), the FMLA provided background for the discharge of an employee for excessive absenteeism after she had exhausted her FMLA leave time.

• In Sibley County Sheriff's Department, 111 LA 795 (Mario Bognanno, 1998), the arbitrator used the FMLA in resolving an interest arbitration dispute. The employer wanted to eliminate a leave provision, saying the rights were already guaranteed by the FMLA and other statutes. The arbitrator denied the request, partly because he was not certain whether the statutory benefits were congruent with the contractual language.

• In IKO Production, 118 LA 887 (Louis V. Imundo, Jr., 2003), an employer argued that a claim was not arbitrable because it would require the arbitrator to interpret certain FMLA provisions. The arbitrator rejected the argument, holding that when interpretation of a statute is relevant to the disposition of a grievance, the arbitrator has a clear responsibility to interpret and apply the law.

• In Koppers Industries, 115 LA 152 (Carl F. Jenks, 2000), the employer fired an employee who worked another job while on FMLA because of an alleged total disability. The arbitrator denied the grievance because the employee falsified company documents to get his FMLA leave and because the employee's violation of the requirements for FMLA leave would have forfeited his right to that leave.

• In Cargill, Inc., 111 LA 571 (Sidney S. Moreland, IV, 1998), the employer unilaterally adopted a tougher absenteeism policy. The arbitrator found that policy unreasonable because it did not incorporate FMLA requirements.

• In BF Goodrich Aerospace Ice Protection Division, 111 LA 602 (Michael Paolucci, 1998), the arbitrator reduced a discharge to a suspension because the employee wrongly but in good faith believed she was entitled to FMLA leave to care for her son.

● In ATC/VANCOM, 111 LA 268 (Lionel Richman, 1998), the arbitrator sustained the discharge of an employee for excessive absenteeism despite the grievant's claim that he was entitled to FMLA leave. Applying the statute, the regulations adopted pursuant to it, and several court cases, the arbitrator concluded that the grievant's absences were not due to a "serious health condition."

Similarly, the ADA is increasingly coming into play when grievants raise it as a shield to an employer's discipline or other detrimental employment decision, *e.g.*, Shell Oil Co., 109 LA 965 (Barry J. Baroni, 1998) (discharge of an employee who could no longer perform his job); City of Tampa, 111 LA 65 (Robert B. Hoffman, 1998) (discharge for inability to perform job after a back injury); City of Akron, 111 LA 705 (Matthew M. Franckiewicz, 1998) (layoff for alleged inability to work) and Frito–Lay, Inc., 115 LA 1573 (Kathy L. Eisenmenger, 2001) (no violation of the ADA in paying a lower wage to partially-disabled employees reassigned to a lesser classification job because the ADA does not provide pay protection). Other grievants have used the ADA as a sword to gain accommodations in work assignments, as in the City of Tampa case (arbitrator denied a grievance demanding that the employer create a new position the grievant could perform); Mead Products, 114 LA 1753 (Harvey A. Nathan, 2000) (ADA does not give a disabled employee the right to bump into another employee's job because reasonable accommodation cannot be at the expense of non-disabled employees); and Bowater, Inc., 116 LA 382 (Joe M. Harris, 2001) (the ADA did not oblige the employer to eliminate part of a job that the grievant could no longer perform).

These developments raise several questions about the current role of external law in arbitration. Given the ubiquity of statutory claims, is it any longer possible for arbitrators to take the Meltzer position? If arbitrators must resolve statutory claims (as they do when the contract so provides or when both parties ask the arbitrator to do so), is the typical labor arbitration procedure adequate? Can nonlawyer advocates satisfactorily debate, or nonlawyer arbitrators satisfactorily decide, complicated issues of statutory interpretation? Are the parties really willing to pay for the amount of time it would take for an arbitrator to do the necessary legal research?

Chapter VI

EVIDENCE AND PROCEDURE

A. EVIDENCE[1]

1. INTRODUCTION

The United States Supreme Court has made clear that arbitrators have wide discretion in resolving evidentiary issues. In United Paperworkers International Union v. Misco, Inc., 484 U.S. 29, 108 S.Ct. 364, 98 L.Ed.2d 286 (1987), Chapter III.C.2., *supra*, it said that courts cannot overturn an arbitrator's evidentiary error unless it was made in "bad faith" or is "so gross as to amount to affirmative misconduct."[2] For those hearings administered by the American Arbitration Association, labor arbitrators explicitly are given broad evidentiary authority:

> The parties may offer such evidence as is relevant and material to the dispute, and shall produce such additional evidence as the arbitrator may deem necessary to an understanding and determina-

---

1. Bibliographic Suggestions: Elkouri & Elkouri, How Arbitration Works, 339–426 (Alan Miles Ruben, ed., 6th ed. 2003); Fairweather's Practice and Procedure in Labor Arbitration 326–372 (Ray Schoonhoven, ed., 4th ed. 1999); Marvin F. Hill, Jr. and Anthony V. Sinicropi, Evidence in Arbitration (2d ed. 1987); Arnold M. Zack and Richard I. Bloch, Labor Agreement in Negotiation and Arbitration 47–62 (2d ed. 1995); Marvin F. Hill, Jr. and Tammy M. Westhoff, *"I'll Take it for What it is Worth"—The Use of Hearsay Evidence by Labor Arbitrators: A Primer and Modest Proposal*, 1998 Journal of Dispute Resolution 1; John Kagel, *Practice and Procedure*, The Common Law of the Workplace: The Views of Arbitrators (Theodore J. St. Antoine, ed., 1998); Michael S. Winograd, *Rules of Evidence in Labor Arbitration*, 55 Dispute Resolution Journal 45 (May, 2000), Steven M. Wolf, *Evidence In Arbitration*, Labor and Employment Arbitration (Tim Bornstein, Ann Gos-

line and Marc Greenbaum, eds., 2d ed., 2003). Significant parts of two annual meetings of the National Academy of Arbitrators were devoted to issues of evidence. 19 Proceedings of the National Academy of Arbitrators 86–355 (1967) (Chapters IV–XII present and discuss the findings of four regional tripartite committees that addressed common evidentiary issues). 35 Proceedings of the National Academy of Arbitrators 107–137 (1983) (Chapter 5 contains discussion of six hypothetical evidentiary questions). See also, 51 Proceedings of the National Academy of Arbitrators 89–101 (1999) (A Debate: Should Arbitrators Receive Evidence for "What It's Worth"?).

2. The Court borrowed the standard of review from the Federal Arbitration Act, saying that while the Act is not directly applicable, its standards provide useful guidance. 484 U.S. at 40, 108 S.Ct. at 372, n.9.

tion of the dispute. * * * The arbitrator shall be the judge of the relevance and materiality of the evidence offered and conformity to legal rules of evidence shall not be necessary. * * *[3]

The Revised Uniform Arbitration Act states that arbitrators may "determine the admissibility, relevance, materiality and weight of any evidence."[4]

What have arbitrators done with this broad discretion? Although not required to, have they followed evidentiary rules used by courts? Have they accepted all evidence regardless of its nature or source? Or have arbitrators followed some middle ground, applying standards of evidence less rigid than judicial evidentiary rules? And if so, is there some established consensus among arbitrators about what those standards are, or must parties enter an arbitration process in which evidentiary standards are wholly *ad hoc* and unpredictable?

PROBLEMS OF PROOF—EVIDENCE IN ARBITRATION

Arnold M. Zack and Richard I. Bloch.
Labor Agreement in Negotiation and Arbitration 47 (Second Edition 1995).

Perhaps the only predictable element in an arbitration hearing is that there will be an argument over evidence. It is not clear whether this is due to too many lawyers or too few, whether, instead, it arises from the occasional mix of lawyers and nonlawyers. Some say the half-formal, half-informal nature of the proceedings is at the heart of the problem. Were it clearly a legal proceeding or clearly not, all would know the rules, it is argued. Perhaps, on the other hand, arguments exist simply because the process is adversarial.

For whatever reason, substantial blocks of valuable hearing time are spent arguing admissibility and weight of various pieces of evidence. * * *

One must immediately confess to a bias that may be self-evident. The very act of discussing rules of evidence suggests they have a place in an arbitration hearing. This means the arbitrator will be serving to filter, to a certain extent, materials proffered by the parties in support of their respective cases. It is here that one must part company with those who simply refuse to make evidentiary rulings—who routinely prefer, instead, to "let it in for what it's worth." One proceeds with recognition of Clare McDermott's Presidential Address to the National Academy of Arbitrators in 1980, where he warned that "litigation and its formalistic trappings are for dead and dying relationships, whereas arbitration is for living ones." He noted:

3. American Arbitration Association, Labor Arbitration Rules, Rule 28.

4. Revised Uniform Arbitration Act, § 15(a) (2000). The first Comment to Section 15 includes the following language: "[T]he rules of evidence are inapplicable in an arbitration proceeding except that an arbitrator's refusal to consider evidence material to the controversy that substantially prejudices the rights of a party is a ground for vacatur under Section 23(a)(3)."

It could be dangerous to arbitration's health if some practitioners were to succeed in transplanting techniques suitable to the law into arbitration, without very careful and critical analysis.

There is no reason to quarrel with the notion that arbitration dare not elevate the form of the presentation over its substance. To do so would, as McDermott observes, challenge its vitality. Nevertheless, no matter how informal the hearing process, there comes a time when it is unsatisfactory and potentially unfair to deny the parties guidance on the use to which the arbitrator intends to put certain proffered materials. To be sure, many disputed points may reasonably be glossed over by the neutral with the wholly defensible intent of progressing to hear the essence of the case. Many points will have no impact on the case: time spent in wrestling with niceties of admissibility is better spent moving on with the case. But there are also times when a particular piece of evidence becomes undeniably critical, when "letting it in for what it's worth" is unfair because the parties must reasonably be told, then and there, what indeed that evidence is worth. This is not to say that the arbitrator must disclose the weight a given portion of the evidence may have. Yet, the parties should not be surprised by learning, for the first time, in the opinion that evidence has or has not been admitted. A key document submitted in lieu of an absent witness may well require a definitive ruling. If the holding is that the contents would be accepted as the functional equivalent of testimony, then the offering party may forego the time and expense of securing the individual witness. At the same time, the other party should be well advised not to rely on the arbitrator's later discounting that material as, for example, hearsay: the immediate search for rebuttal materials may be essential.

* * * [A]rbitration continues to function as an important internal dispute settlement procedure precisely because of its ability to provide an informal and flexible forum for the airing of disputes. * * * [A]rbitrators and the parties must not sacrifice basic fairness in the name of informality. When a question arises concerning evidence, it should be answered. * * *

EVIDENCE

Elkouri & Elkouri, How Arbitration Works 341.
(Alan Miles Ruben, Editor-in-Chief, Sixth Edition, 2003).

Unless directed by the contract, strict observance of legal rules of evidence is not necessary in arbitration. While the parties may expressly require the arbitrator to observe legal rules of evidence, they seldom do so. In fact, they may sometimes specifically provide that strict observance of such rules shall not be required. * * *

As stated by one federal court:

In an arbitration the parties have submitted the matter to persons whose judgment they trust, and it is for the arbitrators to determine the weight and credibility of evidence presented to them without restrictions as to the rules of admissibility which would apply in a court of law.

Another federal court, in reviewing an arbitration award within the court's jurisdiction under § 301(a) of the Labor Management Relations Act (LMRA), wrote "[i]t is well established that rules of evidence as applied in court proceedings do not prevail in arbitration hearings." This has long been the rule under common law, and it is the rule under most of the state statutes which deal with the matter. Where a case is covered by a state arbitration statute which is either silent or not specific on a point, the common law would ordinarily apply.

In the absence of legislatively imposed limitations, courts have ruled not only that arbitrators are not bound by the "technical" exclusionary rules—in particular the rule against admission of hearsay evidence—but also that they may not exclude relevant evidence because of "technical" procedural reasons. * * *

The *Code of Professional Responsibility for Arbitrators of Labor–Management* * * * in Section 5.A.1. [states] that an arbitrator "must provide a fair and adequate hearing which assures that both parties have sufficient opportunity to present their respective evidence and argument." Seemingly, it acknowledges the parties' interests in having leeway to present what they deem important. * * *

Arbitrators recognize the need to achieve a satisfactory balance between procedural efficiency and other interests:

> At the hearing the arbitrator must provide for procedural efficiency, and at the same time assure himself that he is getting all that he needs to decide the case. To be successful at this he must bear in mind simultaneously a number of complex considerations. The attorneys must be allowed to present their cases fully as they see them. Witnesses should be allowed to say what they feel is important, sometimes even when it is technically irrelevant. It is sometimes necessary to be aware of political considerations within the union or among management people involved in the case, or between union and management in the plant or industry.

The net result of the flexible approach toward the admission of evidence is that, in a majority of cases, "any evidence, information, or testimony is acceptable which is pertinent to the case and which helps the arbitrator to understand and decide the problem before him."

In regard to the flexible application of legal rules of evidence in arbitration proceedings, one arbitrator concluded that:

> [Arbitrators] have established the pattern of ordered informality; performing major surgery on the legal rules of evidence and procedure but retaining the good sense of those rules; greatly simplifying but not eliminating the hearsay and parole evidence rules; taking the rules for the admissibility of evidence and remolding them into rules for weighing it; striking the fat but saving the heart of the

practices of cross-examination, presumptions, burden of proof, and the like. * * *

Arbitration, as originally conceived and practiced, supported the general rule of free admissibility of testimony and other evidence and rejected the judicial exclusionary rules of evidence in order that arbitration be as fully informed as possible about the dispute to be resolved.

First, the exclusionary rules were developed principally in the context of jury trials, to prevent lay jurors from being misled.... A second and broader consideration is how the exclusion of evidence may affect the perception of the employees and supervisors who are not familiar with legal technicalities. They want to tell the arbitration what *they* think is important. If they are denied the opportunity to do so and are on the losing side, they will feel they were denied a fair hearing....

A third consideration is that the arbitrator who is asked to exclude evidence as irrelevant or immaterial is not in a very good position to make an intelligent ruling. A trial judge has the benefits of pleadings, pretrial conferences, and frequently pretrial briefs. This familiarity enables the judge to make informed rulings....

The inapplicability of the legal rules restricting the admission of evidence results in the parties being given a free hand to present any type of evidence thought to strengthen and clarify their case. Indeed, it has been observed that "the more serious danger is not that the arbitrator will hear too much irrelevancy, but rather that he will not hear enough of the relevant."

In fact, the liberal reception of evidence is not as extreme a departure from traditional judicial practice as many persons might believe. Judges who are trying cases without a jury typically receive evidence very freely, on the basis that they can determine its weight and relevancy after the entire case has been presented. * * *

Perhaps the most extreme position—free and unrestricted reception of all evidence—was advanced as follows:

One of the fundamental purposes of an arbitration hearing is to let people get things off their chest, regardless of the decision. The arbitration proceeding is the opportunity for a third party, an outside party, to come in and act as a sort of father confessor to the parties, to let them get rid of their troubles, get them out in the open, and have a feeling of someone hearing their troubles. Because I believe so strongly that that is one of the fundamental purposes of arbitration, I don't think you ought to use any rules of evidence. You have to make up your own mind as to what is pertinent or not in the case. Lots of times I have let people talk for five minutes, when I knew all the time that they were talking it had absolutely nothing to do with the case—just completely foreign to it. But there was a fellow testifying, either as a worker or a company representative, who had something that was important for him to get rid of. It was a good time for him to get rid of it.

Even adherents of a more formal and structured approach to evidentiary issues frequently recognize that some excursions into extraneous matter may help the arbitrator get the background of the case or may help in understanding the viewpoints of the parties. Moreover, the relevance of evidence offered in arbitration, though it may appear at first glance not to be germane to the case, cannot always be determined accurately until the entire case has unfolded. Accordingly, from a procedural standpoint arbitrators often accept evidence while reserving their response thereto until the challenged evidence can be evaluated in the light of the whole record. The objection to the evidence, even if overruled, will serve to caution the arbitrator to examine the challenged evidence more closely before giving it weight.

Actually, the admission of proffered evidence is much less likely to render the proceedings vulnerable to court challenge than is exclusion of it. Indeed, under many statutes an arbitrator's refusal to hear evidence may provide a ground for a vacating the award.[39]

Notes and Questions

1. For discussion of the issues of burden of proof, quantum of proof, and assessment of credibility, see questions 1, 2 and 4 *infra* in the Notes and Questions following the *Stroehmann Bakeries* case in Chapter VII.B.3.

2. Rule 401 of the Federal Rules of Evidence defines relevancy as "evidence having any tendency to make the existence of any fact that is of consequence to the determination of the action more probable or less probable than it would be without the evidence." The Rules permit the admission of all relevant evidence (Rule 402), but permit exclusion of relevant evidence if "its probative value is substantially outweighed by the danger of unfair prejudice, confusion of the issues, or misleading the jury, or by considerations of undue delay, waste of time, or needless presentation of cumulative evidence." Rule 403. Is there any reason why the bounds of relevancy should be broader in a labor arbitration proceeding?

3. Rule 408 of the Federal Rules of Evidence makes offers of compromise or the willingness to accept an offer of compromise inadmissible to prove liability for or invalidity of the claim or its amount. Conduct or statements made in settlement negotiations are also inadmissible under the Rule.

(a) Assume that at an earlier step in the grievance procedure an employer offered to reinstate the employee without back pay, but the union refused to accept the offer. At the arbitration hearing on the employee's discharge, the union seeks to introduce evidence of the employer's settlement offer to show that the employee continues to be an acceptable worker. Is the evidence relevant? Should the arbitrator admit it? What is the rationale of Rule 408? Is it applicable in arbitration? What if the employer, seeking to persuade the arbitrator that, even if reinstatement is ordered,

---

39. The [Uniform Arbitration Act] so provides. * * *

back pay would be inappropriate, offers evidence that the union offered to settle the case for reinstatement without back pay? See Hill and Sinicropi, *supra* footnote 1, at 153–156.

(b) In accordance with Step 3 of the parties' grievance procedure, a meeting was held between the grievant, the union business agent and the employer's manager of human resources to discuss the grievant's discharge and to seek to settle the grievance. In the course of the meeting, the grievant explained what he had done. At the subsequent arbitration hearing on the grievance, the employer sought to question the manager of human resources about what the grievant had said at the Step 3 meeting. How should the arbitrator rule if the union objects to the question on the basis that statements made in the course of settlement negotiations are inadmissible?

4. A hospital discharges a psychologist for releasing patient information, allegedly in violation of the hospital's confidentiality policy. At an arbitration hearing to determine whether the psychologist's discharge was for "just cause," the Union argues that the confidentiality policy was unclear and that the hospital failed to provide adequate staff training on application of the policy. The Union seeks to introduce evidence that, following discharge of the psychologist, the hospital provided training programs for its staff in the application of the confidentiality policy. Is the evidence relevant? Under Rule 407 of the Federal Rules of Evidence, evidence regarding the subsequent training would likely be excluded. Rule 407, Subsequent Remedial Measures, states in relevant part:

> When, after an injury or harm allegedly caused by an event, measures are taken that, if taken previously, would have made the injury or harm less likely to occur, evidence of the subsequent measures is not admissible to prove negligence, culpable conduct, a defect in a product, a defect in a product's design, or a need for a warning or instruction.

Why does Rule 407 exclude evidence of subsequent remedial measures? Are those policies equally applicable in the arbitration setting? Should the arbitrator in the case of the discharged psychologist exclude the evidence of subsequent training?

5. State law provides for a wide variety of testimonial privileges, precluding admission in court of certain communications such as those between wife and husband, attorney and client, and physician and patient.

(a) Should an arbitrator respect such assertions of privilege under state law even though the privilege statutes and common law only seek to govern admission of evidence in court?

(b) Should an arbitrator who would respect a state law attorney-client privilege for communications between a company's manager and its in-house or outside counsel recognize a similar privilege for communications between a union steward and the union's business representative if the union is using its business representative rather than an attorney to present its case in arbitration? If the arbitrator were to exclude the testimony about the union communication, would the arbitrator's award be likely to be vacated by a court for the arbitrator's refusal to hear all relevant evidence? See American Airlines, Inc. v. Superior Court (DiMarco), 114 Cal.App.4th 881, 8 Cal. Rptr.3d 146 (2003) (declining, in a lawsuit for discrimination and wrongful termination, to recognize a privilege for communications between a union vice president and employees represented by the union).

6. In an arbitration concerning an employee's discharge, an employer makes the following contentions regarding a previous unemployment compensation hearing in which the administrative law judge concluded that the employee had been discharged for misconduct and was thus ineligible for unemployment compensation: (a) the transcript from the unemployment compensation hearing should be admitted "for what it's worth," (b) the administrative law judge's finding of the employee's misconduct precludes the arbitrator from concluding that the employee's discharge lacked just cause. How should the arbitrator rule on each of the employer's contentions? See Hill and Sinicropi, *supra* footnote 1, at 370–375, and *infra* Chapter VI.D.3. Some states provide by statute that the record of an unemployment compensation proceeding is inadmissible in any other forum. See Minnesota Statutes, Chapter 268.105, subd. 5(c) (2002). Is a labor arbitrator in a private sector case compelled to follow such a state statute? See *supra* Chapter IV. B., regarding the preemptive effect of § 301 of the Labor Management Relations Act.

Would your response be different if the prior proceeding was not an unemployment compensation hearing but rather a criminal case in which the employee (a) was found guilty, (b) pled guilty, (c) pled "nolo contendere" (Latin for "I do not wish to contest") , or (d) was acquitted of theft from the employer's premises? See Hill and Sinicropi, *supra* footnote 1, at 375–384; United States Postal Service, 89 LA 495 (Dennis R. Nolan, 1987) (arbitrator reinstated grievant who had been discharged for having pled "nolo contendere" to a charge of sexual assault of his daughter where the employer introduced no other evidence of misconduct); and Space Gateway Support, 118 LA 1633 (Roger I. Abrams, 2003) (employee's nolo plea does not prevent him contesting in arbitration the facts alleged in a police report). Compare Eaton Corp., 116 LA 1584 (William P. Daniel, 2001) (nolo plea was additional evidence of guilt of drug trafficking); and Interkal, Inc., 115 LA 553 (Glen M. Bendixsen, 2001) (because discharge occurred prior to nolo plea, employer may not rely on plea as proof employee engaged in violent conduct).

7. For discussion of the question of whether arbitrators should admit improperly obtained evidence, see *infra* Chapter VI.B.3 (b).

2. ADMISSIBILITY OF EVIDENCE

AMBASSADOR CONVALESCENT CENTER, INC.

83 LA 44 (Nathan Lipson, 1984).*

The jointly stipulated issue in this case is:

Was the suspension of August 19, 1983, and the subsequent termination of L on August 22, 1983, for just and sufficient cause? If not, what shall the remedy be?

FACTS OF THE CASE

[Grievant, who had been an orderly at a patient care facility for two years, was terminated for patient abuse for hitting a patient, D, on August 15, 1983.]

Patient D, who is now deceased, was approximately 70 years old and had had both legs amputated. On August 15, 1983, at approximately 10:30 a.m., G, the patient's sister, visited D in his room. G testified that D had been bathed, and she noticed that his left eye was red and watering.

G stated that her brother told her that a fellow had hit him that morning, and that it was "the nurse Jack Taylor". D explained that the employee got mad at him because he had had a bowel movement during the bath, and that a lady was there at the time. The patient went on to state that this was the first time he had hit him like this, and asked G to go to the desk and find out who had bathed him that morning.

It was G's continued testimony that she then spoke to the nurse and stated what D had reported. The nurse on duty told G that L had taken care of D that morning. At that point, the Grievant was brought into the patient's room, and D, in the presence of his relatives and several nurses, pointed to L and said, "He's the one who hit me—there was a lady in the bathroom". The testimony was that L denied hitting D, and said, "I'll refuse to wait on you if you say such things about me".

G stated that she was acquainted with the Grievant as a result of frequent visits to the facility. She also stated that a few weeks earlier during a visit she heard another patient yell as L was twisting his arm. She claimed that the Grievant explained that the patient had to be restrained because he had just hit him. On August 17, D was transferred out of the Convalescent Center at his own request.

Bolden Fisher, a friend of the patient who frequently visited him, testified that in June, 1983, he saw L in a scuffle with a slender white male patient in his late fifties. Fisher stated that he saw L twist the patient's arm and hit him, and that the patient yelled. L stated, "He just hit me in the eye".

Mr. Fisher claimed that D was mentally alert and fundamentally aware of occurrences or events. On August 15, 1983, Fisher visited D after lunch and noted that the patient's eye was red or watery. Fisher asked for an explanation, and D stated, "Jack Taylor hit me because I did something in the bathtub". D also stated that a lady nurse was there at the time.

It was Fisher's continued testimony that a head nurse came in and asked D to describe the person that hit him, and that the patient's response was, "He was light skinned and curly haired". Shortly thereafter, the Grievant was brought into the room, and D was asked, "Is this the guy who hit you?" The response was, "Yes, that's him".

Nursing Supervisors Margaret Boggerty and Queen Dowdell, who worked the same shift as the Grievant, also testified. The nurses heard about an incident involving patient D and went into his room prior to noon on August 15, 1983. Both witnesses confirmed that in the presence of friends and relatives, the patient stated that "Jack Taylor hit me".

The nurses testified that one of D's eyes was red, but no actual injury was observed. The Grievant was called into D's room, and Nurse Dowdell asked, "Was that the Orderly who hit you?" The testimony was that D answered, "That's the one", and pointing at L said, "You hit me". The patient also stated that L had put soap in his eyes.

The nurses pointed out that in addition to the Grievant, Orderlies Charles Foster and Jack Taylor cared for patient D. However, only L had contact with D on August 15, 1983. In contrast to the Grievant, who is light skinned, Taylor and Foster are of brown or dark complexion. The other Orderlies were not assigned to the second floor on the morning of August 15, 1983.

Grievant L, who was hired as an Orderly on August 14, 1981, testified that he bathed patient D on August 15, at approximately 9:30 a.m., with the help of Nursing Assistant Annie Long. During the bath, D said, "Please don't drown me". Otherwise, however, the bath proceeded normally, and D was placed in the day room at approximately 9:50 a.m. During the noon hour, the Grievant was asked to come to D's room.

The Grievant stated that Nurse Boggerty asked D, "Did he hit you?" L claimed that the patient said nothing, but nodded affirmatively. The Grievant did not notice anything wrong with the patient's eyes. L clearly and strongly denied striking the patient. L also pointed out that he had never been informed that an incident report had been filed by the Employer.

The Grievant's position was supported by Nursing Assistant Annie Long, who worked with him on the shift in question. Long pointed out that bathing D was a two-person job, and recalled assisting L. Annie Long stated that the patient did not have a bowel movement during the bath, and that nobody struck the patient.

The Employer pointed out that patient abuse is prohibited both by law and Convalescent Center policy, and that the staff has been so instructed. * * *

FINDINGS AND CONCLUSIONS

It is clear that the bulk of the Employer's case consists of hearsay evidence i.e., the patient, who was the actual victim of alleged abuse, did not testify, but his statements went into the record through the testimony of other witnesses. The situation requires an inquiry into the role of hearsay evidence in discharge cases in general, and the significance of the kind of hearsay that is in the present record.

It is well known that fundamentally speaking, hearsay evidence is not admitted in courts of law or other tribunals functioning under the Rules of Evidence to prove a fact that will determine the outcome in a case. Thus, it has been said:

It is a general rule, which is subject to many exceptions, that hearsay evidence is incompetent and inadmissible to establish a fact. 'Hearsay' has been defined as evidence which derives its value, not solely from the credit to be given to the witness upon the stand, but in part from the veracity and competency "of some other person."

Many of the reasons for the exclusion of hearsay are self-evident. For example, the declarant is not available for cross-examination, and the trier of fact is consequently hampered in determining the credibility and veracity of the person who was the source of the evidence. Nevertheless, hearsay is usually admitted in arbitration, because such proceedings are generally not governed by the Rules of Evidence. Accordingly, an arbitrator will frequently accept hearsay evidence "for what it is worth," or will regard the hearsay nature in determining the weight to be given the evidence.

There are good reasons for accepting hearsay evidence in a labor arbitration proceeding. Arbitration is generally informal and the participants are frequently nonlawyers, who can not be expected to handle cases on the basis of legal technicalities, including the Rules of Evidence. Facts are determined, not by a jury, but by an arbitrator, who is expected to have the experience and expertise to evaluate evidence and to accord the appropriate weight to hearsay. Frequently, hearsay is the only evidence available in the work place setting, and the automatic exclusion of same could result in an incomplete record and a failure to accomplish a just result. On the other hand, an arbitrator must carefully bear in mind the inherent weaknesses in hearsay evidence, particularly in the context of a discipline case where the employer has the burden of proving just cause.

As has been noted above, there are exceptions to the exclusion of hearsay evidence—two important exceptions are germane to the present case. Thus, the Federal Rules of Evidence includes the following:

Rule 803. Hearsay Exceptions; Availability of Declarant Immaterial

The following are not excluded by the hearsay rule, even though the declarant is available as a witness:

(1) Present sense impression.—A statement describing or explaining an event or condition made while the declarant was perceiving the event or condition, or immediately thereafter.

(2) Excited utterance.—A statement relating to a startling event or condition made while the declarant was under the stress of excitement caused by the event or condition.

The Federal Rules of Evidence also provides as follows:

Rule 804. Hearsay Exceptions: Declarant Unavailable

(a) Definition of unavailability.—"unavailability as a witness" includes situations in which the declarant—* * *

(4) is unable to be present or to testify at the hearing because of death * * *

(b) Hearsay exceptions.—The following are not excluded by the hearsay rule if the declarant is unavailable as a witness: * * *

(5) Other exceptions.—A statement not specifically covered by any of the foregoing exceptions but having equivalent circumstantial guarantees of trustworthiness, if the court determines that (A) the statement is offered as evidence of a material fact; (B) the statement is more probative on the point for which it is offered than any other evidence which the proponent can procure through reasonable efforts; and (C) the general purposes of these rules and the interests of justice will best be served by admission of the statement into evidence.

There can be no doubt that the above-identified exceptions to hearsay evidence exclusion are applicable to the present case. Certainly, D, the declarant or source of the evidence, was unavailable to testify due to his death, his evidence was "offered as evidence of material fact," and "the statement is more probative on the point than any other evidence which the proponent can procure through reasonable efforts." There can be no debate that "the interests of justice will best be served by admission of the statement into evidence," since otherwise there can be no inquiry into an accusation of patient abuse, a serious matter in the nursing home context.

It is also probable that D's statement was a "present sense impression," in that it was made shortly after his allegedly being struck by the Grievant. Moreover, the Arbitrator believes that D made an "excited utterance," in that he identified the Grievant under stress when confronted by L after the alleged incident. In sum, the Arbitrator concludes that even under the Rules of Evidence, the hearsay statement was properly received and should play a role in the outcome.

The overwhelming weight of the evidence establishes that on August 15, 1983, D stated that he had been struck by an employee named Jack Taylor. Shortly thereafter, when the Grievant came to D's room, the patient pointed out the Grievant and uttered words making it clear that it was L who had struck him. The Grievant, of course, denied any such act, and his contention was supported by co-worker Annie Long.

Accordingly, it is the Arbitrator's task to decide whether D's hearsay statement should prevail over the Grievant's denial, which was corroborated by Annie Long. It must be noted that D's declaration is supported by evidence and surrounding circumstances. Thus, the Arbitrator is convinced that the patient suffered an eye injury. It is clear that the Grievant, and no other male Orderly, bathed D on August 15. The two other Orderlies whose names appear in the record were not on duty and could not have been involved that morning. Moreover, the evidence is that Foster and Taylor do not resemble the Grievant, so that confusion as to appearance was unlikely.

The Union and Grievant, however, contend that the patient was confused and that his statements should not be accepted. As has been indicated above, there is and should be concern about accepting testimony which can not be cross-examined to establish a crucial fact. Nevertheless, the Arbitrator must be impressed by the clear and unequivocal testimony of relatives, friends, and uninterested professional staff that the patient was competent to identify a person who had struck him.

While great weight must be given to the sworn testimony of the Grievant and co-worker Long, in which misconduct was denied, it must be recognized that said testimony can not be deemed impartial. The Grievant certainly has an interest in a decision that would result in his reinstatement and back pay, and it is understandable that a friend or co-worker would tend to support his assertions. In contrast, there is nothing in the record to suggest that D had a motive to frame or unjustly accuse the Grievant. Thus, a careful consideration of the facts and circumstances lead to the conclusion that the Employer has made a clear and convincing case that L struck patient D on the morning of August 15, 1983.

From the above, it can only follow that the Employer has established that the Grievant was suspended and discharged for just and sufficient cause. It is obvious that patient abuse can not be tolerated in a health care facility. This is the case, not only because the law and humanitarian considerations make such behavior unacceptable, but because proper treatment of patients is the heart of the Employer's business. Accordingly, there is no doubt that the severest discipline is justified for a health care employee who abuses his patients.

Award

For all of the above reasons, it is determined that the suspension of August 19, 1983, and the subsequent termination of L on August 22, 1983, was for just and sufficient cause. This grievance is denied.

Notes and Questions

1. Rule 801(c), of the Federal Rules of Evidence, defines hearsay as "a statement, other than one made by the declarant while testifying at the trial or hearing, offered in evidence to prove the truth of the matter asserted."

2. The foundation of hearsay doctrine is the concern that statements within the definition pose four risks (misperception, faulty memory, misstatement, and distortion) that would be substantially reduced by the safeguards of the trial process (testimony under oath, opportunity to observe demeanor, and cross-examination). Were any of these risks present in the hearsay testimony admitted by the arbitrator in *Ambassador*? Note, for example, that the patient told two people that the person who hit him was "Jack Taylor," not the Grievant L.

3. The arbitrator acknowledges the inapplicability of the Rules of Evidence to arbitration hearings, but then goes on to consider their applicability to the facts of the case. That approach is not atypical. Why?

4. Does arbitrator Lipson correctly apply the exceptions to the hearsay rule that he finds permit the admission of the patient's statements?

(a) *Present Sense Impression.* The underlying justification for this exception is that statements of perception substantially contemporaneous with an event are highly trustworthy because simultaneity avoids problems of memory, precludes time for calculated misstatement, and results in the statement being made to one who also observed the event and who can check misstatements. In this case, the statements were not made to persons who also observed the alleged event. Apparently a couple of hours passed between the patient's morning bath and his identification of the Grievant. Was that sufficient time for problems of memory or calculated misstatement to arise? In a case with facts similar to those in *Ambassador*, a court refused to apply the exception where two hours had passed between the time a hospital patient received an injection and the time the patient, under questioning, identified the nurse who administered the injection. United States v. Narciso, 446 F.Supp. 252, 285–291 (E.D.Mich.1977) (also citing other cases).

(b) *Excited Utterance.* This exception requires that the declarant be "under the stress of excitement caused by the event." The arbitrator says that he believes the patient was under stress, but cites no evidence supporting that conclusion. The *Narciso* court refused to admit as an excited utterance the statement identifying a nurse. The court there said that there was no specific evidence to demonstrate that the patient who had suffered cardiac arrest was under stress at the time he made the statement and that the period of two hours between event and statement provided an opportunity to reflect that would negate the assumption of reliability under Rule 803(2). In another similar case, a labor arbitrator admitted hearsay evidence that the grievant had hit a patient, a mentally retarded adult, but rejected the employer's argument that the statement was credible because it was an excited utterance. The arbitrator concluded that the patient's statement, made only five or ten minutes after the alleged incident, was not made under the stress of the incident because, between the incident and the patient's report to the supervisor, the patient had had two routine conversations with the supervisor, asking about a newspaper and an opportunity to smoke. Wisconsin Department of Health & Social Services, 84 LA 219 (Sharon K. Imes, 1985). See also, Aviva Orenstein, *"MY GOD!": A Feminist Critique of the Excited Utterance Exception to the Hearsay Rule*, 85 California Law Review 159 (1997) (reviewing psychological research on the relationship between stress and accuracy and also suggesting that the exception is underinclusive and relies on gendered stereotypes that undermine women's credibility).

(c) *Declarant Unavailable.* The arbitrator perhaps correctly applies the requirements of elements (A), (B) and (C) of Rule 804(b)(5) (now Residual Exception, Rule 807, of the Federal Rules of Evidence), but what about the critical requirement that the arbitrator does not discuss, that the statement have "equivalent circumstantial guarantees of trustworthiness" to those specifically listed in the rule (prior testimony under oath, statement under belief of impending death, statement against interest, and statement of family history)? What circumstantial guarantees were there of the patient's identification of the Grievant as the one who had hit him when he had just before told two others that the person who had hit him was Jack Taylor?

5. Was there a better means to analyze the evidentiary issue in *Ambassador* than by resort to the Federal Rules of Evidence? How should the issue have been decided?

6. Should an arbitrator's willingness to rely on hearsay evidence vary depending on the nature of the conduct for which the grievant was discharged? An arbitrator has suggested that in those cases in which the grievant has been discharged for conduct constituting moral turpitude, such as patient abuse, an employer is required to prove its case by clear and convincing evidence and such a standard cannot be satisfied by hearsay evidence alone. Edgewater Systems, 117 LA 1677 (Dorothy Lupton Moran, 2002) (inadequate proof of patient abuse when employer's evidence consisted of written statements by delusional schizophrenic patients and their hearsay comments to a supervisor).

7. In the United States, a judge could not overturn the award in *Ambassador* merely because of a disagreement with the arbitrator's admission of the patient's statements. See, Chapter III. C., *supra*. In Canada, however, a similar arbitration award was overturned by a court on the ground that reliance on such hearsay violated "natural justice and procedural fairness." In Bond v. New Brunswick (Board of Management), 325 Atlantic Provinces Reports 149 (New Brunswick Court of Appeal 1992), a patient, diagnosed as psychotic and schizophrenic, accused a hospital employee of sexual assault. Upon the recommendation of her psychiatrist, the patient did not testify. Her statements to others regarding the alleged sexual assault were admitted by the arbitrator who sustained the employee's discharge. The court remanded the case for rehearing before a different arbitrator. Although the *Ambassador* and *Bond* cases are similar, in *Ambassador* the declarant was dead while in *Bond* the declarant was mentally ill. Is that a material difference?

8. Consider the following hypothetical:

> As the basis for its termination of an employee, the employer introduces three letters of complaint received from customers over a six-month period. The union objects to introduction, stating that letters cannot be cross-examined. The employer, a hotel, says the witnesses wrote from their homes in California, Texas and Canada and cannot be brought to the hearing; further, the letters are admissible as "normal business records" and must be credited since all witnesses "spontaneously" reported similar performance by the employee.

(a) Should the arbitrator admit the letters? Exclude the letters? Or admit them for some limited purpose?

(b) This hypothetical was posed in a survey to which over one thousand arbitrators responded. In the survey, only 7.9% of the arbitrators said they would exclude the letters as hearsay; 27.1% would admit them without limitation and 65% would admit the letters only to prove the reason for discharge. Jeffrey Small and J. Timothy Sprehe, *Report of American Arbitration Association Survey of Labor Arbitrators*, 234 Daily Labor Report E–1 (December 5, 1984). The arbitrators' response to the hypothetical is somewhat puzzling. The issue in the termination case is whether the employer *had* just cause for termination, not whether it *believed* it had a reason for discharge. Why would most arbitrators admit the letters only for their relationship to an issue that the arbitrator is not called upon to decide? On the other hand, is the source of the puzzle to be found in the methodology of the survey? Might some respondents have assumed that this was the only evidence against the grievant while others assumed that it could serve to corroborate testimony regarding similar misconduct? Might some have assumed instead that the union was challenging the employer's explanation as a pretext for a discriminatory dismissal?

(c) While use of telephonic testimony might remedy problems of distance, what if the employer still declines to call customers as witnesses for reasons of customer relations? Regardless of where the customer is located, should arbitrators generally be willing to admit hearsay evidence of customer complaints rather than requiring employers to subpoena their customers? Does it matter whether the complaints were unsolicited by the employer? SuperShuttle of Los Angeles, 118 LA 1552 (Lionel Richman, 2003) (accepting hearsay customer complaints as evidence but declining to rely on such complaints alone to sustain a discharge, especially when they were in some respects contradictory).

(d) If an employer's business reasons would warrant permitting an employer to rely on hearsay evidence of customers, would employer business reasons also permit accepting hearsay evidence rather than insisting on direct testimony of present, or former, co-workers? See Wackenhut Corrections Corp., 118 LA 63 (Donald T. O'Connor, 2003) (arbitrator overturned discharge for insubordination when employer's only evidence of grievant's conduct was the hearsay written statement of a former employee whom employer did not call to testify); General Mills, 118 LA 1292 (Richard W. Dissen, 2003) (arbitrator would not sustain discharge for threatening a co-worker on basis of hearsay statement of co-worker when employer did not call co-worker to testify). In another recent case, the arbitrator also found a lack of just cause for a discharge for threatening to poison the office buffet where the discharge was based on the oral and written statements of a subsequently discharged co-worker who was not called to testify. Lucas County Auditor's Dept., 119 LA 1063 (Saundria Bordone, 2003). Arbitrator Bordone explained that although arbitrators rely on hearsay when circumstances suggest it is trustworthy and reliable, in this case the hearsay statements of the co-worker were themselves inconsistent as well as inconsistent with the recollections of others who were present at the same time yet did not hear the alleged threat. Sometimes, by rule or custom, parties prohibit bargaining unit members from testifying against one another.

9. Arbitrator Lipson notes that arbitrators will frequently admit hearsay evidence "for what it is worth" without immediately advising the parties of whether the evidence will be given any weight at all. Arbitrators Arnold M. Zack and Richard I. Bloch, in their book excerpted earlier in this Section, say that such an approach can sometimes be unfair to the parties. Was it appropriate for arbitrator Lipson to make his decision about the hearsay statement's admissibility in his award rather than at the hearing? Are there reasons why evidentiary decisions should not be left to resolution in the writing of the award? Are there circumstances under which such a delay would be appropriate? In a rare case vacating an arbitration award on an evidentiary matter, the Fifth Circuit found arbitrator misconduct not because of the arbitrator's evidentiary decision, but rather because the arbitra-

tor had misled the employer's counsel by making his evidentiary decision in the course of writing the award rather than at the hearing, when the employer would have had an opportunity to respond. The arbitrator, in the hearing of that case, admitted a marijuana drug test as evidence and declined to allow the employer's counsel to establish that it was a business record. Later, however, in his award, the arbitrator refused to consider the drug test report on the ground that it was hearsay and not a business record. Gulf Coast Industrial Workers Union v. Exxon Co., 70 F.3d 847 (5th Cir.1995).

10. The arbitrator in *Ambassador* not only admitted the patient's hearsay statement, but ultimately found it more credible than that of the Grievant or of Annie Long, who had assisted in giving the patient his bath, both of whom testified under oath.

(a) Was the arbitrator correct in discounting the Grievant's testimony because of self-interest? Is the arbitrator suggesting that every credibility dispute between a grievant and a supervisor or other person should be resolved against the grievant?

(b) Was the arbitrator correct in discounting Annie Long's testimony because of her status as a co-worker? Should her status affect her credibility?

(c) What protection is afforded employees by imposing the burden of proof on employers in discipline cases if the testimony of grievants and co-workers is deemed inherently suspect simply because of their status?

11. Arbitrators generally recognize the difficulty of making credibility determinations. Only about a third of arbitrators in a survey responded that they agreed or strongly agreed with the statement, "I can tell if witnesses testifying before me are truthful." Members of the National Academy of Arbitrators, who are more experienced, were *less* likely than other arbitrators to agree with the statement. See *supra* Jeffrey Small and J. Timothy Sprehe, note 8(b). See Gerald R. Miller and Judee K. Burgoon, *Factors Affecting Assessments of Witness Credibility*, The Psychology of the Courtroom 169–194 (Norbert L. Kerr and Robert M. Bray, eds. 1982). In Paul Ekman, Maureen O'Sullivan and Mark G. Frank, *A Few Can Catch a Liar*, 10 Psychological Science 263 (1999), the authors review studies suggesting that most people cannot tell from demeanor whether others are lying. Federal law enforcement officers (Central Intelligence Agency and Secret Service agents) are the most successful at detecting deception, doing better than federal judges and clinical psychologists.

12. There are relatively few reported decisions regarding evidence in labor arbitration. Arbitrators resolve most evidentiary issues in the course of the hearing, rather than in their written awards. The limited opportunity for successful judicial review of an arbitrator's evidentiary rulings makes court decisions regarding evidence extremely rare. As a result, it is difficult to obtain an accurate picture of how arbitrators in fact handle evidentiary issues.

One view of that elusive world is provided by a survey of over one thousand arbitrators conducted in 1983. The study concluded that arbitrator's reactions to hypotheticals posing evidentiary questions were remarkably consistent regardless of arbitrators' demographic characteristics (such as age, caseload, lawyer status, and experience). See Jeffrey Small and J. Timothy Sprehe, *supra* note 8(b). For an attempt to articulate "generally accepted approaches" to the admission of evidence in labor arbitration cases, see John Kagel, *supra* footnote 1.

B.　DUE PROCESS OF ARBITRATION[1]

1.　INTRODUCTION

The title of this section comes from Willard Wirtz's pathbreaking 1958 paper to the National Academy of Arbitrators. Arguing that arbitrators had an obligation to exercise their authority "with a 'due' regard to the balancing of the two kinds of interests, individual and group interests, that are involved in every situation arising in a complex society," Wirtz set off a debate that continues today. The dispute centers on the nature and scope of the individual employee's rights *within the arbitration process*, as distinguished from the individual's rights to fair treatment *from the employer*.

Although the debate frequently uses the constitutional term, "due process," the Constitution itself usually does not apply. Except for governmental employers (and perhaps a few highly-regulated government contractors[2]), labor arbitration does not involve sufficient state action to bring the Constitution into play. Nevertheless, some commentators have urged arbitrators to incorporate constitutional protections in their procedural and substantive decisions.[3] In addition, a few arbitrators expressly apply constitutional norms in private-sector employment disputes. See, for example, King Company, 89 LA 681, 685 (Joseph L. Bard, 1987):

> Today, there can be little doubt that the Fifth Amendment of the Constitution creates a privilege against self-incrimination which is available outside of the criminal court proceedings and serves to

1. Bibliographic Suggestions: Benjamin Aaron, *The Role of the Arbitrator in Ensuring a Fair Hearing*, 35 Proceedings of the National Academy of Arbitrators 30 (1982); Norman J. Brand, *Due Process in Arbitration*, Chapter 15 of Labor and Employment Arbitration (Tim Bornstein, Ann Gosline, and Mark Greenbaum, 2d ed. 2001); R. W. Fleming, The Labor Arbitration Process 107–98 (1967) and *Some Problems of Due Process and Fair Procedure in Labor Arbitration*, 13 Stanford Law Review 235 (1961); James Gross & R. Daniel Bordoni, *Reflections on the Arbitrator's Responsibility to Provide a Full and Fair Hearing: How to Bite the Hands that Feed You*, 29 Syracuse Law Review 877 (1978); *Mitigation and Labor Arbitration*, 47 Proceedings of the National Academy of Arbitrators 22–41 (1994) (two papers on mitigation of discipline because of an employer's due-process violations); James Oldham, *Procedural Due*

Process, in The Common Law of the Workplace: The Views of Arbitrators 186 (Theodore J. St. Antoine, ed. 1998); Jeffrey Small and J. Timothy Sprehe, *Report of American Arbitration Association Survey of Labor Arbitrators*, 234 Daily Labor Report E–1 (December 5, 1984); Willard Wirtz, *Due Process of Arbitration*, 11 Proceedings of the National Academy of Arbitrators 1 (1958).

2. The leading example is Holodnak v. Avco Corp., 381 F.Supp. 191 (D.Conn.1974), affirmed in relevant part, 514 F.2d 285 (2d Cir.), cert. denied 423 U.S. 892, 96 S.Ct. 188, 46 L.Ed.2d 123 (1975).

3. See especially Julius G. Getman, *What Price Employment? Arbitration, the Constitution, and Personal Freedom*, 29 Proceedings of the National Academy of Arbitrators 61 (1976), and Gross & Bordoni, *supra* footnote 1.

protect persons in all settings in which their freedom of action is curtailed in any significant way from being compelled to incriminate themselves. See Miranda v. Arizona, 384 U.S. 436, 467 (1966).

There is probably nothing in a person's life, other than his family and his freedom of greater importance than his job. An employee who feels that he must confess or tell the truth to an employer at the risk of violating a company rule is under enormous psychological compulsion to do so * * *. There can be no doubt whatsoever that to use the threat of termination or suspension to seek a confession of criminal conduct clearly impinges upon the Fifth Amendment rights of the grievants.

Even without reference to the Constitution, providing a fundamentally fair proceeding—"due process of arbitration" or, more commonly, "contractual due process"—necessarily involves the arbitrator in familiar subjects such as asserted rights to notice, counsel, confrontation, and opportunity to present one's case. Even modest arbitral efforts to ensure more "fairness" than the agreement explicitly provides annoy many advocates. One distinguished union lawyer, for example, charged that arbitrators pursuing "due process" have "bastardized" arbitration practices; if unchecked, she argued, that arbitral view "will kill the process." Judith P. Vladeck, *Comment*, 35 Proceedings of the National Academy of Arbitrators 55, 57–58 (1983). Vladeck feared that by applying external standards of procedural justice, arbitrators were taking arbitration away from its creators.

"Due process of arbitration" covers a wide variety of problems. The rest of this section deals with a few of the main ones. Subsection 2 addresses employees' asserted rights to knowledge of and access to the arbitration procedure, the claims of grievants to separate representation, and third-party intervention. Subsection 3 deals with miscellaneous evidentiary problems, including questions of compelled testimony and missing or reluctant witnesses. Subsection 4 deals with contractual due process rights. Subsection 5 covers privacy issues. Finally, subsection 6 explores the ethical dilemmas posed by "agreed" or "informed" arbitration cases.

Notes and Questions

1. *Should* the Constitution govern private-sector arbitration proceedings? See Note, *Due Process Considerations in Grievance Arbitration Proceedings*, 2 Hastings Constitutional Law Quarterly 519 (1975) (arguing that federal regulation of labor relations and judicial review of arbitration awards constitute sufficient state action to bring the Constitution into play). Do you agree?

2. What about policy considerations? Who would win and who would lose if the Constitution applied to the grievance and arbitration process?

3. Professor John Dunsford argues that the *dissimilarities* between arbitration and the criminal law process make constitutional protections inappropriate in arbitration: *Comment*, 29 Proceedings of the National

Academy of Arbitrators 71, 77–85 (1976). For example, he argues that the Fifth Amendment privilege against self-incrimination stemmed from "concerns about abuse of governmental power going back to Star Chamber proceedings and the thumbscrew and the rack, elements that do not loom large in the modern American factory."

2. ACCESS TO ARBITRATION, SEPARATE REPRESENTATION, AND THIRD–PARTY INTERVENTION

(a) Access to Arbitration[4]

Does a dissatisfied employee have a right to grieve and arbitrate a dispute even over the union's objection? Most collective bargaining agreements specify that the aggrieved employee may present a complaint to the employee's immediate supervisor (frequently termed Step 1 of the grievance procedure). One could say that the employee "owns" the grievance at that stage. If the supervisor does not resolve the problem to the employee's satisfaction, some agreements authorize the employee to file a written grievance, while others provide only for union-filed written grievances. At some point in almost all grievance procedures, however, the union takes control of the grievance. Without the union's consent, in other words, and subject only to the duty of fair representation, the grievant may not proceed to the last steps of the grievance process or to arbitration. When the union takes control, it comes to "own" the grievance. The union can then press the grievance, compromise it, or drop it, all without the employee's approval.

The union's control of access to arbitration can leave the grievant without an effective remedy for an employer's contract breach. The union and the employee might differ about the merits of the complaint, for example, or about whether even a valid complaint is worth pursuing to arbitration. The union might consciously oppose the employee's position in the interest of some broader concern such as a desire to conserve resources for disputes affecting more employees. The union might trade off some grievances to win others or might simply believe that the modest possible gain from arbitrating a particular dispute would not be worth the cost of the process. Finally, the union's leaders might use their control of the grievance process to enhance their political position, processing only the grievances of their supporters or refusing to challenge discharges of their opponents. On the other hand, without union

---

4. See R. W. Fleming, *Due Process and Fair Procedure in Labor Arbitration*, 14 Proceedings of the National Academy of Arbitrators 69 (1961); Herbert L. Sherman, Jr., *The Role and Rights of the Individual in Labor Arbitration*, 15 William Mitchell Law Review 379 (1989); and Jerre S. Williams, *Intervention: Rights and Policies*, 16 Proceedings of the National Academy of Arbitrators 266 (1963).

The classic debate on whether the individual employee should have a right to arbitration against the wishes of the union was between Professors Clyde Summers and Archibald Cox. See, *e.g.*, Cox, *Rights Under a Labor Agreement*, 69 Harvard Law Review 601 (1956) and *Individual Enforcement of Collective Bargaining Agreements*, 8 Labor Law Journal 850 (1957); Summers, *Individual Rights in Collective Agreements—A Preliminary Analysis*, 12 N.Y.U. Annual Conference on Labor 63 (1959) and *Individual Rights in Collective Bargaining Agreements and Arbitration*, 37 N.Y.U. Law Review 361 (1962).

control of the grievance process, the union could not guarantee consistent interpretation of the agreement, could not prevent meritless disputes from burdening the process, could not speak with the single voice needed to balance the employer's authority in the workplace, and might lose in arbitration part of what it gained in negotiations.

These conflicting interests—the union's in controlling interpretation of the collective agreement and the individual employee's in redressing the employer's breaches—have troubled scholars and judges for decades. No answer resolves all of the problems; each answer imposes certain costs.

● One possibility is for the employee to sue the employer directly if the union refuses to arbitrate the complaint. If the employee's grievance alleges a breach of the agreement, however, how could the employee escape the agreement's provision making arbitration the exclusive remedy for alleged breaches? What would the arbitration provision be worth to the employer if it did not provide the exclusive remedy for grievances?

● Alternatively, the employee might seek to arbitrate the grievance even over the union's objection. For many years Professor Clyde Summers argued that employees should be able to insist on access to arbitration, whether or not the union agreed. Professor Archibald Cox and others responded that this would weaken the union and undermine the agreement itself. An individual right to arbitration would certainly destroy the union's ability to control interpretation of the agreement. In addition, an individual right to arbitration would require the decision-maker to ignore language giving the union exclusive right to invoke arbitration. Moreover, it would lessen the value of the arbitration agreement to the employer, because the provision would not bar even those grievances the union found worthless.

● Finally, the employee might have a remedy against the union for an unfair refusal to arbitrate. This would leave the union in control of the process but would subject that control to outside evaluation, primarily through duty of fair representation claims. See Section V.A.

When Congress amended the Wagner Act in 1947, it added a few words to § 9(a) that provided fuel for the debate. The new part of § 9(a) appears below in italics:

> Representatives designated or selected for the purposes of collective bargaining by the majority of the employees in a unit appropriate for such purposes, shall be the exclusive representatives of all the employees in such unit for the purposes of collective bargaining in respect to rates of pay, wages, hours of employment, or other conditions of employment: Provided, That any individual employee or a group of employees shall have the right at any time to present grievances to their employer *and to have such grievances adjusted, without the intervention of the bargaining representative, as long as the adjustment is not inconsistent with the terms of a collective-bargaining contract or agreement then in effect: Provided*

further, That the bargaining representative has been given opportunity to be present at such adjustment.

Individual-rights advocates interpreted the amendment as granting employees a statutory right to arbitrate their grievances. Their opponents interpreted it as simply allowing employers, if they wished, to deal directly with employees without fear of violating the legal obligation to bargain with the exclusive representative.

The Supreme Court finally settled the dispute in Vaca v. Sipes, 386 U.S. 171, 87 S.Ct. 903, 17 L.Ed.2d 842 (1967) (excerpted above in Section V.A.4.). The individual has no "absolute right to have his grievance taken to arbitration regardless of the provisions of the applicable collective bargaining agreement," said the Court. Rather, the individual has a right to be represented fairly by the union. Only if the employee first proved the union breached its duty of fair representation could he or she sue the employer for the alleged breach of the contract. Although *Vaca* dealt with § 301 (which authorizes suits to enforce collective bargaining agreements) rather than § 9(a), the Court's leaning was unmistakable. In Emporium Capwell Co. v. Western Addition Community Organization, 420 U.S. 50, 61 n. 12, 95 S.Ct. 977, 984 n. 12, 43 L.Ed.2d 12 (1975), the Court removed any remaining doubt by stating that § 9(a) permits but does not require an employer to deal with individual grievants. Professor Summers later advocated a statutory right for *all* employees, whether or not represented by unions, to arbitrate claims of unjust dismissal: *Individual Protection Against Unjust Dismissal: Time for a Statute*, 62 Virginia Law Review 481 (1976).

Notes and Questions

1. Does the grievant have a right to be present when the union arbitrates the grievance? Technically, the parties to any labor arbitration are the employer and the union—the signatories to the contract that includes the arbitration agreement—even though the grievance may involve only a single employee. Most parties routinely invite grievants to the arbitration hearing but a few do not. There is no express legal requirement that the grievant have notice and an opportunity to attend the hearing, but any union wishing to avoid duty of fair representation suits would be well advised to include the grievant in the hearing. One court did interpret § 9(a) to allow employees to attend meetings on their grievances, Local Union 1110, United Mine Workers of America v. Consolidation Coal Co., 531 F.Supp. 734 (N.D.W.Va.1982), but there the union wanted them present and only the employer resisted.

2. Apart from any possible legal requirements, some arbitrators will not proceed in a disciplinary case without the grievant (or at least without a good reason for the grievant's absence). Does it matter whether the case primarily concerns the grievant, as in a discharge arbitration, or primarily involves group interests, as in an overtime grievance where the amount of money claimed by any individual is trivial?

3. Suppose a grievant participates in an arbitration hearing but advances a position opposed by both the union and the employer. How is the

arbitrator likely to rule? Why? Would an arbitrator even allow the grievant to present a position in the hearing if the union objects?

(b) Separate Representation[5]

Even if the union does arbitrate the dispute, the grievant might doubt the union's ability, commitment, or fairness. A discharged union dissident, for instance, might well wonder how vigorously the union will fight to overturn the discharge. Occasionally a grievant will attend the arbitration hearing with independent counsel. Does the employee have the right to participate as a separate party, or does the union have the exclusive right to represent the grievant?

The law is clear. As one court concisely put it, the employer has the right to deal only with the union in an arbitration proceeding: "The parties to the proceeding are the Union and the employer. An employee is not a party to such an arbitration proceeding." Blake v. USM Corp., 94 LRRM 2509, 2509–10 (D.N.H.1977). Several other courts have reached the same result, *e.g.*, Castelli v. Douglas Aircraft Co., 752 F.2d 1480 (9th Cir.1985), and Valentin v. United States Postal Service, 787 F.2d 748 (1st Cir.1986). The arbitrators' code of professional responsibility recognizes the problem but remains strictly neutral.[6]

Despite the potential unfairness, arbitrators uniformly hold that only the parties to the agreement—the employer and the union—may participate. Almost as uniformly, however, they seek to work out an accommodation, such as allowing the grievant's counsel to assist the union's representative. Some arbitrators warn the union's representative about the risks of legal action if the union does not allow the grievant's attorney to participate. When the union refuses to budge, though, the employee's only recourse is a suit or unfair labor practice charge alleging that the union breached its duty of fair representation.

(c) Third–Party Intervention

Occasionally employees other than the grievant seek to intervene in an arbitration. That may happen, for example, during the arbitration of a grievance challenging an employer's promotion of a junior employee. At the hearing the union will almost always represent the interests of the senior employee because seniority is such a highly prized principle. Can the employer be counted on to represent the junior? Should the junior employee receive notice of the hearing and have a chance to attend? To participate? If the junior employee does not participate, will he or she be bound by an adverse award? Could the displaced junior

---

5. See Jesse Simons, *Grievants' Use of Private Counsel*, 36 N.Y.U. Conference on Labor § 8–1 (1983); James S. Youngdahl, *Uneasy Second Thoughts on the Independent Participation by Employees in Labor Arbitration Proceedings*, 33 Arkansas Law Review 151 (1979).

6. Code of Professional Responsibility for Arbitrators of Labor–Management Disputes § 2.C.1.a. (1974): "Occasionally, special circumstances may require that an arbitrator rule on such matters as attendance and degree of participation of counsel selected by a grievant."

employee file a separate grievance? Or sue the union for breach of its duty of fair representation?

In a widely-criticized opinion, Clark v. Hein–Werner Corp., 8 Wis.2d 264, 99 N.W.2d 132 (1959), cert. denied 362 U.S. 962, 80 S.Ct. 878, 4 L.Ed.2d 877 (1960), the Wisconsin Supreme Court held:

> where the interests of two groups of employees are diametrically opposed to each other and the union espouses the cause of one in the arbitration, it follows as a matter of law that there has been no fair representation of the other group. This is true even though, in choosing the cause of which group to espouse, the union acts completely objectively and with the best of motives. The old adage, that one cannot serve two masters, is particularly applicable to such a situation.

99 N.W.2d at 137. Because the union did not tell the plaintiffs, whose seniority interests were threatened by the union's position, about the hearing, the court held that the award did not bind them. Cf. Smith v. Hussmann Refrigerator Co., 619 F.2d 1229 (8th Cir.1980), cert. denied sub nom. Local 13889, United Steelworkers v. Smith, 449 U.S. 839, 101 S.Ct. 116, 66 L.Ed.2d 46 (1980) (union breached its duty of fair representation by not inviting affected employees to attend an arbitration hearing). Despite these cases, few arbitrators allow third-party intervention over the union's objection. Remember, according to the typical contract, the union owns the grievance.

Suppose that affected employees did show up and were allowed to participate. What could they add to the hearing? How much influence would they be likely to have?

For a strong argument in favor of third-party intervention, see the Williams article cited at footnote 4; for strong arguments to the contrary, see the comments following that article.

3. EVIDENTIARY CONCERNS BEARING ON DUE PROCESS[7]

Although neither the Constitution nor judicial rules of evidence apply in the typical private-sector labor arbitration, arbitrators often reach the same results that a judge would in evidentiary disputes. The most common due-process evidentiary issues involve employees' claims to protection from "self-incrimination"; the lack of opportunities for confrontation; search and seizure questions; and "surprise" evidence such as issues or arguments raised at the hearing or in the post-hearing briefs.

(a) Self–Incrimination

The Constitution usually does not apply to private-sector arbitration, so employees have no legal right to refuse to testify. Among other distinctions, arbitration does not decide whether the grievant committed

---

7. See Ann Gosline, *Witnesses in Labor Arbitration: Spotters, Informers, and the Code of Silence*, 43 Arbitration Journal 44 (March, 1988); Marvin Hill and Anthony Sinicropi, Evidence in Arbitration 131–53, 229–78, and 305–333 (2d ed. 1987).

a crime, even if the employee's alleged offenses are criminal in nature. As a practical matter, however, an arbitrator lacks the power to compel attendance or testimony. Although in most states an arbitrator can issue a subpoena, enforcement of the subpoena requires a court order. The most an arbitrator could do if a witness refused to testify would be to draw an adverse inference.

There may be a few small exceptions to the general statement that the Constitution does not apply to arbitration. Public-sector cases obviously present a different situation. If a public-sector employer compelled an employee's testimony at an arbitration by threat of discharge, its demand might pose sufficient "state action" to invoke the U.S. Constitution. Possibly even a private-sector arbitrator's issuance of a subpoena, expressly or impliedly invoking statutory authority, could be considered state action. There are no reported cases on point, however, and there is little chance of such a situation arising.

Even if the U.S. Constitution did apply to an arbitration hearing, the Fifth Amendment might not shield the employee. A question about possible criminal conduct could present a Fifth Amendment issue; a question about non-criminal misconduct would not.

Notes and Questions

1. *Should* the arbitrator draw an adverse inference from the grievant's silence? Compare these two excerpts:

> The Arbitrator disregards any adverse inferences which might be drawn from the Grievant's not being present at the hearing. While this is in no sense a criminal matter, there is an inescapable analogy between the absence from an arbitration hearing of the Grievant in a disciplinary case and the rule of law that a defendant in court may not be required to take the stand if he chooses not to do so, and it should not be held against him if he does not.

American International Aluminum Corp., 68–2 ARB ¶ 8591 (John F. Sembower, 1968).

In Quaker Oats Co., 110 LA 816 (Charles J. Crider, 1998), the employer suspended an employee indicted for shooting his wife. The local newspaper reported the attack, the grievant's subsequent arrest, and other information. The grievant declined to testify at the arbitration hearing because of the pending criminal charges. Arbitrator Crider wrote:

> S_ opted to remain silent at the arbitration about the Dallas Morning News article and would say nothing about both of the pending indictments. The grievant's silence leaves the arbitrator with only the media account and Dallas County criminal records to consider. While he has the right to remain mute on these matters to protect himself against self incrimination in governmental proceedings, S_ cannot reasonably expect reinstatement while offering no explanation at all about the charges against him. As arbitrator Turkus put it in United Parcel Service, 45 LA (BNA) 1050, 1052 (Turkus, 1965):

> As broad and comprehensive as it so properly is in protection of the innocent as well as the guilty when the privilege of self incrimination is invoked, the Constitution, however, neither guarantees to a grievant exercising the privilege, the right to his job or reinstatement to employment. * * *

Are the views of arbitrators Sembower and Crider incompatible? Why or why not? If they are, with which do you agree? Why?

2. When an arbitrator considers a grievant's failure to testify, does it matter whether the employer is a governmental or a private entity? Rejecting a public-sector grievant's claim of protection from compelled testimony, one arbitrator asserted that the nature of the employer was irrelevant. The proper focus, he wrote, was the general consideration of fair procedure:

> The privilege against self-incrimination is largely related to admissions or confessions in a criminal setting. It is meant to protect the individual against the power of the State, which is trying him for an alleged crime. This is different from the role of the State as an employer. Arbitration is not conducted under the rules of the criminal court, and it is expected to be an informal system of adjudication. Thus, the primary application of self-incrimination in arbitration, if any at all, relates to an interest in fair procedure. The Arbitrator in the subject case required the City to make a *prima facie* case re its charges before allowing it to call the grievant as a witness. Most arbitrators probably would engage in a similar procedure.

City of San Antonio, 90 LA 159, 162 (J. Earl Williams, 1987). Do you agree? Why or why not?

Arbitrator Williams is an economist, not a lawyer. Perhaps because of that, his decision does not consider court decisions protecting government employees from discharge for invoking the privilege against self-incrimination, *e.g.*, Gardner v. Broderick, 392 U.S. 273, 88 S.Ct. 1913, 20 L.Ed.2d 1082 (1968) and Uniformed Sanitation Men Association, Inc. v. Commissioner of Sanitation, 392 U.S. 280, 88 S.Ct. 1917, 20 L.Ed.2d 1089 (1968). Would that rule help private-sector employees?

3. Suppose an arbitrator decides to draw an adverse inference from an employee's refusal to testify. What does that amount to? Would the adverse inference alone be enough to prove the employee's guilt in a discipline case? If the arbitrator insists on corroborating evidence, is the employee any worse off because of the adverse inference? Would the answer depend on what other evidence the union had to refute the employer's evidence? See, for example, Southern Bell Telephone & Telegraph Co., 25 LA 270, 273 (Whitley McCoy, 1955):

> Inferences may be resorted to in aid of evidentiary facts; they cannot supply facts of which there is no evidence. Findings of fact must be based on credible evidence. The failure to deny or refute incredible evidence does not change the character of that evidence from incredible to credible. Testimony that is merely weak can gain strength from failure to deny; but testimony that is utterly incredible can never become credible in that way.

Perhaps the concern for the constitutional issue is overdrawn in self-incrimination cases. The biggest problem for the reluctant grievant may well be that without his or her testimony the employer's evidence will stand unrefuted. See, for example, Republic Airlines, Inc., 83 LA 127, 131 (Marshall J. Seidman, 1984) (failure of the grievant to testify in the face of the evidence against him leads the arbitrators to infer that he "had no adequate explanation of his conduct to offer, leading to the conclusion that he was guilty" of the charges against him). Should it matter whether the employee is still subject to criminal prosecution for the alleged misconduct? In *Republic Airlines*, for example, the employee had already been acquitted and could not have been tried again.

4.   The employment relationship complicates what might otherwise be a straightforward constitutional issue. A government may not normally require an individual to provide information, but a governmental employer, like any other employer, can demand that its employees cooperate with investigations into possible wrongdoing. If the employee and the suspected wrongdoer are one and the same, may the employer fire a non-cooperating employee? See City of Indianapolis, 117 LA 911 (Ellen J. Alexander, 2002) (animal-control officer's invocation of his constitutional right against self-incrimination did not bar his discharge because there is no constitutional right to refuse to cooperate with one's employer).

5.   A common defense to disciplinary action is the claim that supervisors have condoned the conduct on which the employer has based the discipline. For example, the union might claim that supervisors have consistently allowed employees to violate an attendance policy. The problem for the union is to find a way to prove its allegation. The most obvious method, by presenting testimony from employees who have violated the policy without penalty, raises the risk that the witnesses might be disciplined after admitting their own violations. Should such witnesses have immunity from discipline based on their testimony? In Paxar Systems Group, 102 LA 75 (Judith A. La Manna, 1994), the arbitrator looked to federal labor law for guidance on that question. Relying on Public Service Electric and Gas Co., 268 NLRB 361 (1983), which held that witnesses in NLRB proceedings had no such immunity, she denied the union's request for testimonial immunity. How else might the union prove its assertion?

6.   Even if self-incrimination is not an issue, may the employer call the grievant as its first witness? In most civil proceedings a party may call any relevant witness, but this simple question bedevils labor arbitrators. See, for example, the transcript of a discussion by several arbitrators and advocates in 35 Proceedings of the National Academy of Arbitrators 157–62 (1983). One poll found that more than a third of the responding arbitrators would not allow an employer to call the grievant as its first witness. Jeffrey Small and J. Timothy Sprehe, *supra* footnote 1. In some bargaining relationships it is even considered bad form to call *any* witness from the opposing side.

The problem arises because of the way in which arbitration reverses the burden of proof in discharge cases. In a civil action for wrongful discharge, the plaintiff would have the burden of proving the discharge was wrongful. Typically, the plaintiff would be an early witness for his or her side. The employer would thus be able to cross-examine the plaintiff before presenting its own case. In a "just cause" arbitration, however, the employer has the burden of proof. The employer may then want the discharged employee to testify as part of its case, perhaps because of fear the employee would otherwise tailor the testimony to address the employer's evidence. Union representatives often feel that the employer is interfering with the union's ability to present its own case.

It is not easy to pin down the reason why some arbitrators are uncomfortable with the civil procedure approach; usually the explanation begs the question by asserting that the employer should prove its case with its own witnesses. Here is one arbitrator's attempt to explain:

> It really is not a fair procedure. It amounts to moving cross-examination of the grievant up front. As a matter of orderly procedure, I would rather hear the company say what they saw, what they heard, and why they did what they did. Then in due course you can cross-examine the grievant. It is not as if there is something new to be disclosed. The parties know what has happened. They have been living with the case through the grievance hearings before it gets to arbitration. That is why the traditional argument in favor of such testimony, to avoid perjury or influence by other witnesses makes no sense.

Edgar A. Jones, Jr., *Selected Problems of Procedure and Evidence*, in Arbitration in Practice 48, 58–59 (Arnold M. Zack ed., 1984). Are you persuaded? What difference does it make *when* a grievant testifies? The grievant usually attends the whole hearing. Would not Arbitrator Jones's approach permit the very "tailoring" of the grievant's later testimony that employers fear? Why should a grievant or any other witness have that option? Arbitrator Jones assumes the union will call the grievant as a witness so that the company will have an opportunity for cross-examination. Is this a safe assumption? The ultimate choice of allowing or prohibiting the questioning is within the arbitrator's discretion. Local 560, International Brotherhood of Teamsters v. Eazor Express Inc., 95 N.J.Super. 219, 230 A.2d 521 (App.Div.1967).

(b) Search and Seizure

Many searches by employers are lawful in situations when searches by police would not be. For example, many employers routinely search employees' lockers (or rather, lockers the employer loans to employees) for contraband. Others search departing employees and their vehicles to deter theft. If the search was reasonable and the employee knew that it might occur, few arbitrators would exclude evidence found in the search. What if the search actually or arguably violates a state or federal constitutional provision? Should arbitrators apply an exclusionary rule?

COMMODITY WAREHOUSING CORP.
60 LA 1260 (Lawrence F. Doppelt, 1973).*

[Police arrested an employee named Lott after discovering meat stolen from the employer in the course of a search of his car. After his

* Reprinted with permission from *Labor Arbitration Reporter–Labor Arbitration Reports*, 60 LA 1260. Copyright 1973 by The Bureau of National Affairs, Inc. (800–372–1033) <http://www.bna.com>.

arrest, Lott told police and the employer that the grievant had helped him steal the meat. A court later ruled the search illegal and dismissed criminal charges against Lott and the Grievant. Lott testified at the arbitration hearing that he and the grievant stole meat on several occasions. The grievant denied any involvement in the thefts.]

At the outset, the union moves to quash all evidence seized as a result of the police search of L— on May 5, 1972, wherein the stolen meat which was allegedly traced to grievant was discovered, as well as all evidence resulting from such search. The union alleges such evidence was secured as the result of an illegal search and seizure and is thus tainted and inadmissible under the Fourth and Fourteenth Amendments to the United States Constitution. Presumably, it was on such basis that the criminal actions against Lott and grievant were dismissed, although there is no direct evidence showing the reasons for the latter dismissal.

The union's motion is herewith denied. There are several reasons therefor.

First, it is questionable whether the motion serves any real purpose. Even if the evidence of the discovered meat is quashed, there is still L—'s confession to the police to consider. And even if L—'s confession is quashed as resulting from an illegal search and seizure, there is still L—'s direct testimony *de novo* at the arbitration hearing implicating grievant in a theft and describing in detail the events of May 5. It is highly questionable whether the union's motion can properly include such latter testimony. Thus, detailed evidence relating to the incidents of May 5 is, in any event, part of the record, and the evidence which the union moves to quash is merely corroborative of other direct evidence properly before the Arbitrator.

Second, labor arbitrators should tread lightly when it comes to interpreting exclusionary rules of evidence based on criminal and constitutional law. The parties have chosen the arbitrator for his presumed expertise in matters pertaining to labor-management relations, not as an expert on rules of evidence in criminal cases. To point this out, the employer here says the Fourth and Fourteenth Amendments would not, in any event, protect grievant because grievant was not himself the victim of an illegal search and seizure, and such Amendments are designed to protect the victim of an illegal search and seizure, not implicated third parties. (Citing *Alderman v. U.S.*, 394 U.S. 165 (1969); *Jones v. United States*, 362 U.S. 257 (1960); and others.) Thus, says the employer, evidence secured through an illegal search and seizure of L— may be used against grievant even if it cannot be used against L—. The union, on the other hand, says the Fourth and Fourteenth Amendments protect grievant as well as L— from evidence garnered through an illegal search and seizure of L—. This dispute points up the traps confronting a labor arbitrator when he attempts to resolve issues involving the interpretation of intricate rules of evidence applicable to criminal and constitutional law matters.

Third, there is a serious question whether the exclusionary rules of evidence applicable in criminal proceedings should, in any event, be uniformly applied to labor arbitration. Aside from the difficulties inherent in having a labor arbitrator decide issues involving such, as above shown, different policies are involved in the two proceedings. Criminal law pertains to vindicating the rights of society against individuals who have broken society's laws. In vindicating such rights, the individual must be protected against certain possible governmental abuses, and exclusionary rules of evidence help afford that protection. Labor arbitration, on the other hand, adjudicates the rights and responsibilities of employers, unions, and employees under a labor contract. It involves private disputes without any spectre of governmental excesses. It is doubtful whether all the various evidentiary rules necessary to protect individuals against possible governmental abuses should automatically be applied in employer-employee relations matters which involve private disputes.

Indeed, the main issue in many arbitration matters is whether the employer acted in a reasonable manner. And this cannot be determined unless the arbitrator is aware of all the evidence based on which an employer acted. To exclude certain evidence which motivated an employer's actions, and then to ignore such evidence in labeling an employer's activities unreasonable, could well work an injustice on the employer.

This is not to say that an employee does not have certain basic procedural and substantive due process rights under a contract requiring that an employee not be discharged except for "cause". Of course, he does, and arbitration cases are replete with examples of such. Indeed, such contract language implies the imposition of certain rights and duties on employers and employees. However, the rights accorded an employee are not necessarily the same as those granted individuals under exclusionary rules of evidence in criminal matters.

Thus, in this case the Arbitrator cannot determine whether the employer had "cause" unless he knows all the facts based on which the employer acted. And the evidence and confession secured pursuant to the police search of May 5 were clearly what motivated the employer herein. To exclude such evidence would be to ignore the whole basis on which the employer acted.

Finally, the Arbitrator cannot say the employer acted unreasonably in securing the evidence in the manner it did in this case. Theft is a cancer which eats away at the employer. It affects the employer's very ability to stay in business and provide jobs for itself and its employees. The employer must have leeway to take all reasonable action to protect itself against theft. When a theft is reasonably suspected, as it was here, the employer must be allowed reasonable action to detect and smother such. Calling in the police to apprehend an employee reasonably suspected of theft, and relying on the police action, is not unreasonable under circumstances such as are here present.

Accordingly, for all the above reasons, the union's motion to quash is denied. This, it should be noted, is in accord with the general arbitration practice that exclusionary rules of evidence applicable in criminal proceedings are not automatically or uniformly to be applied in arbitration proceedings. See Elkouri & Elkouri, How Arbitration Works (BNA, Rev. Ed.) at p.174, wherein it is stated:

> Flexible arbitral application of formal rules of evidence is particularly justified in regard to those rules of proof which come from criminal law. The application of these principles of proof in the field of arbitration, which deals with intra-plant employer-employee relations, probably should not be accepted in all cases without some consideration of the appropriateness of their use * * *.

Thus, the issue herein is whether, based on all the evidence before it, the employer had cause to discharge grievant for theft. [The arbitrator concluded that, even with the challenged evidence, the employer had not met its burden of proof.]

Notes and Questions

1. Most arbitrators would agree with Arbitrator Doppelt's reluctance to apply criminal law evidentiary rules in labor arbitration. There are a few dissenters. In Aldens, Inc., 58 LA 1213 (John P. McGury, 1973), for example, hospital security guards saw suspicious conduct in the neighboring parking lot owned by a department store and approached the grievant's car. On their demand, the grievant, an Aldens employee, opened his trunk revealing shoes from Aldens. The grievant and a companion were charged with a crime but the court suppressed the evidence found by the guards. The union representing the grievant argued that the arbitrator should apply the exclusionary rule. Arbitrator McGury agreed because of "the seriousness of the consequences to the grievant." See also U.S. Government Printing Office, 82 LA 57 (William Feldesman, 1983) (excluding items seized without a warrant from the grievant's apartment by a government investigator because the government owed the grievant a duty not to invade his privacy).

Do you agree with the majority or the minority? Why? Or do you need more information before making up your mind? If so, what more would you need to know? Who wins and who loses when arbitrators apply exclusionary rules?

In a later *Aldens* case on the same point, 61 LA 663, 666 (David Dolnick, 1973), the arbitrator said that Arbitrator McGury's decision was the only one he could find supporting the union's position, then added:

> I have read and reread that decision carefully. I cannot agree with the concepts or with the reasons given for sustaining the motion to suppress. It appears to me that the conclusion is inconsistent with the legal and arbitral principles enunciated in the opinion. It will serve no useful purpose to detail my disagreements with each of the purported reasons in the findings. Suffice it to say that I do not accept the Award in that case as a binding precedent.

2.   Are arbitrators competent to decide the legal aspects of search and seizure questions? Roughly half are not lawyers. Many of the rest are full-time arbitrators who have not practiced law for many years and may never have practiced criminal law. Given the rapid changes in this area of constitutional law in the last few years, it might be difficult for most judges to say what the law is. Should arbitrators even try?

(c) Confrontation

In several typical disciplinary situations, employers either cannot or will not call certain witnesses against the employee. In service industries, customers may complain about an employee's behavior but refuse to participate in an arbitration. Alternatively, the employer may fear alienating customers by trying to get them to participate. In other cases, the employer may use undercover agents or "spotters" (persons acting as customers in order to observe employees at work) whose utility would disappear once their identity became known. In some bargaining relationships, employers will not call bargaining unit employees to testify against their colleagues, perhaps out of fear for their safety or their relationships with co-workers, or out of concern for social frictions that might impair productivity. In other cases, employees refuse to testify against one another, occasionally under threat of union discipline. The result is a "code of silence" that hampers the arbitrator's work. As Willard Wirtz said many years ago (*supra* footnote 1, at 18), "the tradition against the company's calling bargaining-unit witnesses does more than any other single element to prevent reliable fact determination in [arbitration] cases."

If the arbitrator insists on live testimony, the employer may not be able to prove its case, or may be able to do so only at a cost it finds unacceptable. If the arbitrator does not insist on testimony, though, and instead allows the employer to prove its case by hearsay, the grievant cannot cross-examine the accusers.

The problem is not merely one of hearsay, for arbitrators routinely accept many other types of hearsay. The greater difficulty is in the arbitrator's inability to determine the truth without hearing the witnesses. On their own, or at the instance of the arbitrator, some parties have worked out practical compromises, for example, allowing the arbitrator to contact complaining customers, or allowing undercover agents to testify behind a screen or over a telephone. See generally, Gosline, *supra* footnote 7.

But what if the parties cannot agree on a way to deal with the problem? Should the arbitrator insist that the employer provide the accusers? That is what Arbitrator James Duff did in York Wallcoverings, 110 LA 300 (1998). The employer issued the grievant a verbal warning for "harassment of co-workers and otherwise improperly interfering with the work of other employees" but flatly refused to identify the complaining workers. Although the employer had promised the workers confidentiality and legitimately feared that disclosing their names might lead to reprisals, Arbitrator Duff sustained the grievance:

The Company has every right to honor any commitments it made and to decline to identify or produce as witnesses whomever it chooses to so protect and its integrity in that regard is beyond reproach.

What the Company cannot accomplish however is to refuse to disclose the exact nature of the charges against the Grievant, as well as the names of witnesses it plans to use against him and times of the critical events, and yet succeed in having any discipline imposed upon him sustained. As the undersigned pointed out at the Arbitration Hearing, such strategic decisions are not insulated from harm where the Party making them has the burden of proof. Phenomena such as fear of reprisal are unfortunately part of the reality parties must always account for in planning their presentations. While special safeguards may be tailored to minimize the impact of such factors, fear of reprisal cannot alone shield failure to furnish information necessary to investigate and defend against disciplinary charges; if the rule were otherwise, unions would be forced to defend in the dark in a Star–Chamber like atmosphere.

With regard to co-workers, the parties' mutual adherence to the "code of silence" should at least permit wider use of hearsay and negate any adverse inference from the employer's failure to call a specific witness, but problems in obtaining or presenting testimony will not relieve the employer from its burden of proof.

In the case of undercover agents and spotters under the employer's control, the grievant's right to confront accusers requires their testimony, although the arbitrator should take necessary precautions to preserve the agents' utility. Those precautions, however, may prejudice the grievant's defense. It is virtually impossible to investigate a witness's credibility without knowing the witness's identity. In Indianapolis Plant of Carrier Corp., 103 LA 891 (Nathan Lipson, 1994), the arbitrator tried to balance the parties' interests. He accepted the evidence of an undercover agent who testified from behind a screen but held that

concealment of the identity of the informant limited the effectiveness of his cross-examination, and therefore must diminish the weight given to his testimony. Accordingly, this Arbitrator must agree with the words set forth above and the Union's admonition that this testimony *alone* cannot establish the Grievant's guilt.

Because the employer presented substantial supporting evidence, Arbitrator Lipson sustained the discharge.

Customers and other outsiders who are not under the employer's control present the most difficult issue. See generally, Jeffrey Small and J. Timothy Sprehe, *supra* footnote 1.

Tangentially related to the right of confrontation is the asserted right to interview possible witnesses before the arbitration. Labor arbitration does not have a formal discovery process during which a party could take a witness's deposition. Because most witnesses are employees, however, the employer can usually question them about their knowledge before the hearing. The union lacks that power. Some witnesses might be happy to speak with the union representative, of course, but many are not. In those situations, the union can only ask the employer to make the witnesses available. If the employer denies the union's request, does the employee have a serious due process claim? In Stone Container Corp., 114 LA 395 (Louis V. Immundo, Jr., 2000), the company discharged the grievant for sexual harassment but refused to allow the union business agent to interview the grievant's accuser and another witness. The arbitrator held that due process required such access so long as there was no reason to believe the union representative would seek to intimidate or influence the witnesses. Despite the due-process violation, he refused to overturn the discharge because the union knew the witnesses and the nature of their charges and because another union official had opportunities to speak to them.

(d) Surprise

There are several varieties of surprise. A party may raise an entirely new issue at an arbitration hearing, or may present evidence the other side has never seen. A party may raise a new argument only in its post-hearing brief, or may attempt to introduce new evidence in the brief. How should an arbitrator respond?

Most arbitrators try to determine the degree of surprise and the possibility of harm to the surprised party. In the case of an entirely new issue, for example, the party may be offering what is, in effect, a different grievance. If so, the arbitrator would almost certainly sustain an objection. On the other hand, the purported new issue might only be a rephrasing or elaboration of the one discussed in the grievance procedure; if so, no arbitrator would bar it. For a good discussion of the distinction, see Crittenton Hospital, 85 LA 177, 180–83 (George T. Roumell, Jr., 1985). The one case of surprise on which arbitrators are virtually unanimous is that in which the employer offers at the hearing a new reason for discharging the grievant. Normally discharges must stand or fall on the reason the employer used to make the decision. Hill and Sinicropi, *supra* footnote 7, at 308–10. Nevertheless, a newly-discovered reason such as a falsified job application might limit the appropriate remedy or provide a basis for a new discharge without affecting the legitimacy of the first discharge.

Arbitrators deal with new evidence as they do with new arguments and issues, by attempting to protect both the parties' opportunities to make their cases and the efficiency of the grievance and arbitration process. If the proffered evidence is merely cumulative or explanatory, the surprised party might be entitled to a recess to prepare a response but (absent a contractual prohibition) most arbitrators would still accept it. Even if the evidence is substantively different but newly-discovered, most arbitrators would accept it.

However, if one party deliberately withheld the evidence from the other, perhaps intending to spring it as a trap in arbitration, most arbitrators would sustain an objection. The case for rejecting the evidence is especially strong when the party offering it denied the other party's timely request for all pertinent evidence. Implicit in a negotiated grievance process is the obligation to try one's best to resolve differences. Hiding relevant evidence violates that obligation. Rather than proceed without the evidence, however, an arbitrator might refer the case back to the parties' grievance procedure for consideration in light of the new material.

A recent case offers a possible compromise approach. In Bill Kay Chevrolet, 107 LA 302 (Aaron S. Wolff, 1996), the employer had discharged the grievant for "theft of services" by falsely claiming to have repaired a customer's car. After the discharge but before the hearing, the employer learned of a similar incident involving the grievant. It did not disclose that evidence to the union until the day of the hearing. Arbitrator Wolff accepted and relied on the evidence of the second incident but penalized the employer for not disclosing the information before the hearing:

> Had the Union been aware prior to the arbitration that two cars were implicated rather than one, it might well have decided not to proceed to arbitration with its attendant costs.... Under these circumstances, it seems appropriate to require the Company to reimburse the Union for one-half of the Union's share of the costs of this arbitration.

The easiest issue in this category is that of the new argument or evidence offered in a post-hearing brief. Arbitrators routinely reject such belated offerings. In rare cases of newly-discovered and previously-unavailable material information, however, the arbitrator may reopen the hearing. Most arbitrators would also ignore new arguments because the other party would have no chance to deal with them. Deciding whether the offered evidence or argument is truly "new" can be tricky, given the lack of clarity in many parties' presentations. If a new theory occurs to the arbitrator after the close of the hearing, the safest course is to ask the parties for their comments on it, rather than basing a decision on a ground offered by neither side.

Problem

The employer fired the employee for violating the attendance policy. The critical issues were whether the grievant knew of the company's policy requiring employees to call in if they were going to miss work and whether he did in fact call in. The only evidence on those points was testimony from the grievant and his supervisors, so a credibility determination was essential and would likely be decisive. At the end of the hearing, the arbitrator announced that the record was closed except for the submission of briefs. Later, but before the due date for briefs, the employer moved to reopen the hearing to receive in evidence a newly-discovered certain letter written by the grievant that, the company claimed, would prove the grievant a liar. The company's representative helpfully enclosed a copy of the letter.

What should the arbitrator do? Accept and read the letter? Ignore it? Telephone the union's representative and ask if the union objects to the arbitrator's consideration of the letter? Write a letter to both parties announcing that the arbitrator will consider written arguments from the parties concerning whether the record should be reopened? If the arbitrator does consider reopening the record, what information would he or she need? If the arbitrator decides to reopen the record, should the union be able to respond to the employer's evidence by submitting its own evidence, by brief, or by a further hearing? See Westvaco, Virginia Folding Box Division, 91 LA 707 (Dennis R. Nolan, 1988) (the test for reopening is "good cause shown"; in applying that test, the arbitrator should consider the timing of the request, whether the information was or should have been available at the time of the hearing, whether the evidence is pertinent and likely to affect the outcome, and whether admission of the evidence would improperly prejudice the other party).

4. CONTRACTUAL DUE PROCESS RIGHTS

GENERAL DYNAMICS CONVAIR DIV.
95 LA 500 (Edgar A. Jones, Jr., 1990).*

[The Company's Security Officer heard "from a confidential source" that the grievant had drugs, possibly for distribution, on the Company's property. He went to her car and saw through a window what he thought were marijuana seeds on the floor. Company investigators then questioned the grievant in an interview room around 9:00 a.m., without a union representative. They asked if she had drugs in the car but did not mention the seeds. She denied having illegal drugs but refused their request to inspect her car. Two and a half hours later, they took her to her car where she met with a Union steward called by the Company. After speaking to the steward and hearing the Company's warning of discipline if she did not allow the inspection, she repeated her refusal. Neither then nor in later discussions inside the plant did the Company representatives mention the seeds to her or to the steward. Finally, around 2:30 p.m., the Company suspended the Grievant. It later fired her for insubordination.]

[A Memorandum of Understanding (MOU) between the Company and the Union prohibited possession of illegal drugs on Company property. Notices posted pursuant to Paragraph 4.A.(1) of this policy warned employees that entering the plant indicated consent to searches of their vehicles. Paragraph 4.B.(6) permits inspection of employee cars outside the "controlled perimeter" (as the grievant's car was) only when "there is a reasonable cause to believe that alcohol or illegal drugs" are in the vehicle." Paragraph 5.B.(1).a. defines "reasonable cause" as "those circumstances were the Company has information, based on facts, about the employee's conduct in the workplace that would cause a reasonable

* Reprinted with permission from *Labor Arbitration Reporter–Labor Arbitration Reports*, 75 LA 500. Copyright 1991 by The Bureau of National Affairs, Inc. (800–372–1033) <http://www.bna.com>.

person to believe that the employee * * * has used * * * illegal drugs on Company property." These other parts of Paragraph 4.B. also apply:

> (2) Special inspections (as defined in (1) above), shall usually be made by no fewer than two management officials, one of which is from the Human Resources or Security function. A Union representative shall be offered an opportunity to be present for the inspection if a representative is on the premises.

> (4) Employees who refuse to permit an inspection shall not be forcibly detained nor inspected. However, they are to be advised that [refusal to submit] to such inspections will result in immediate suspension without pay and subject them to disciplinary action or discharge.]

For "just cause" to exist in this case to discharge Grievant, it is contractually prerequisite that there be compliance by the Company with the express and implied due process components of just cause that are applicable to inspections of employee vehicles on suspicion of the presence of illegal drugs. See *Federated Dept. Stores v. UFCW Local 1442*, 901 F.2d 1494, 1497 (9th Cir.1990) ("[T]he arbitrator considered minimum procedural due process to be a component of good cause * * *. [B]ecause it is not unusual for an arbitrator to apply due process notions to just cause, the arbitrator derived his decision from the essence of the collective bargaining agreement.") Several of the due process procedural requisites of the MOU and the basic Agreement are applicable to Grievant's circumstances. First, employees must be put on notice by the posting of a sign on entrances to Company property that entering constitutes consent to the inspection of their vehicles. (Para. 4.A(1)) In this case, there was compliance with that requirement.

Second, where a vehicle is parked on Company property that is not "within the controlled perimeter"—which Grievant's car was not—an inspection is categorized as "special" and there must, therefore, exist a "reasonable cause" to inspect it. That phrase is only defined in the MOU relative to "for-cause" testing for alcohol and drugs. (Para. 5.B.(1).a) But it is reasonably inferable that the words are applicable by implication to the inspection of vehicles.

To constitute "reasonable cause" to inspect, therefore, there must be "circumstances where the Company has information, based on facts, about the employee's conduct in the workplace that would cause a reasonable person to believe that the employee * * * has * * * illegal drugs on company property."

In this case, the observation through Grievant's car window by the two security investigators, [led] there to survey the car by an informant's tip, was that they had visually identified marijuana seeds. That was sufficient to cause a reasonable person to believe that Grievant may have brought marijuana onto Company property. That perception constituted the requisite "reasonable cause" to proceed to institute an inspection of the interior of the vehicle.

Third, once the Company for whatever reason, becomes suspicious that an employee possesses an illegal drug on its property, it undertakes, as it did in Grievant's case what it called in Investigations Department Instruction No. 1 "a suspect interview." That departmental instruction to investigators requires that the suspected employee be advised that disciplinary action could result. It also directs postponement of the interview until a Union steward is available to be present, but only "[i]n the event the employee requests Union representation." To that extent, the instruction does not conform, as it must, to MOU Paragraph 4.B.(2) which requires that a Union steward be contacted "to be present for the inspection." It is irrelevant whether the suspected employee requests Union representation. It must in any event be provided.

From the moment—at about 8:15 a.m. that morning—that the security investigator became convinced that marijuana seeds were present in the car, it was clear that an inspection of the vehicle would ensue. Indeed that was when the "inspection" may be said to have commenced. The next step in the inspection process is to contact the suspected employee. Before any contact is made with that employee, however, the obligation arises to contact and assure the presence of a Union representative at that next step in the inspection.

In Grievant's case, that was not done. In a serious deviation from the prescribed procedure, instead of arranging for the presence of a steward—and postponing the commencement of the interview until one was available—the investigators started the interview process by going to Grievant's work station, unaccompanied by a steward. They took her into their custody, commencing the "suspect interview" as they removed her from her work station in their vehicle to Security.

Inexplicably—and, on this record, unexplained—for some reason the security investigators sequestered her for two and one-half hours at Security without making any effort whatsoever to contact a Union representative to be present throughout their effort to obtain her consent to an inspection of her vehicle. As each testified, she vacillated back and forth, expressing her uncertainty of what their and her rights might be in the circumstances, and what she should do, uncertain of what she should answer to their constant querying about whether she would give her consent to inspect her vehicle. That state of irresolution graphically exemplifies why it is essential that a Union representative be brought into the "suspect interviews" from the outset, even if it has to be postponed to achieve that presence.

Repetitive experience counsels that an employee in that isolated psychological situation cannot be expected to respond coolly and rationally to this livelihood-threatening situation. The common tendency is to equivocate, uncertain of what to do or say, which is how she acted. The presence of someone sympathetic to the employee's plight ameliorates that sense of isolation and better enables rational responses to it, which serves both the employer's interest and the employee's.

It was only shortly before 11:30 a.m. that Security and Human Resources contacted a Union steward. And even then, they did not disclose to the steward—nor, indeed, even to the suspected employee— that they believed that they had observed marijuana seeds in her car, which was why they were asking her consent to inspect it. Nor did they even take the steward over to the car to observe the seeds they were later to allege to be marijuana in their testimony. This assertion that there were marijuana seeds, or any seeds, was without the readily available but unsummoned confirmation—indeed, with the considerable and warranted skepticism—of the steward and the suspected employee. Common sense and the contract unite to demand complete and candid disclosure in these circumstances.

Instead of withholding the knowledge they thus far believed themselves to have uncovered, they should have been intent from 8:15 a.m. on to assure that they shared their preliminary findings of fact with Grievant and a Union representative duly summoned by them to the scene so that the inspection could proceed in the procedurally fair manner contemplated and required by the MOU procedures.

Fourth, MOU Paragraph 4.B(4) mandatorily declares that an employee who refuses to submit to an inspection "shall not be forcibly detained nor inspected."

Investigators must be made to understand that coercion need not be overt; it is inherent in the adversarial situation in which they have "requested" someone to accompany them to Security for a "suspect interview." The more so is this true in the absence of any sympathetic person—for example, a union steward—from whom to draw support and counsel. Intimidation is implicit in those circumstances.

A female employee who feels compelled, as did Grievant, to ask male investigators if she can go to the bathroom, or if she can use the telephone, and disclose to whom she wants to call, is someone who is being demeaningly detained, which is to say, "forcibly" within the prescriptive intent of the MOU. It is not necessary to threaten physical violence in order "forcibly" to detain a suspected employee. The term encompasses—and prohibits—non-violent constructive force as well as actual force. The fear of loss of livelihood may be a very real and irresistible force deterring a detained suspected employee from feeling free to leave. It is unquestionable in these circumstances that the security investigators exercised their will unremittingly and successfully—without any physical coercion—that she remain in the interview room for those two and one-half hours by herself, much of it spent in unwelcome silence, until she would make a decision to submit or not to submit to the inspection by signing the proffered waiver form.

Fifth, the Union contends that the Company rule declaring insubordination to be dischargeable conduct has been superseded by the 1988 MOU establishing the drug and alcohol program. It asserts that a direct order by a supervisor to grant access to the employee's vehicle is not authorized by the MOU. But Paragraph 4.B.(4) provides that "submission to such inspections is a condition of employment and failure to permit such an inspection will result in immediate suspension without pay and subject them to disciplinary action or discharge."

That creates the offense of insubordination in the case of an employee who, despite reasonable cause to conduct an inspection, refuses to submit. The Company's procedure in this case of having the employee's immediate supervisor issue a twice repeated direct order is not only allowable, it is a preferable way to proceed. It presents this important choice unambiguously to the employee from a recognized supervisor rather than from some stranger from Human Resources or Security.

Sixth, and finally, the deviations from the prescribed due process precautions were so pervasive and blatant in those circumstances that Grievant's discharge must be held to have been without just cause. Only her reinstatement with retroactive compensation will compel adherence to the MOU due process procedures and, thereby, assure the integrity of the parties' enforcement program. The importance of the due process procedures created by the parties in their Alcohol and Drugs MOU must be recognized. These are not mere technicalities to be sloughed off by security investigators unduly intent upon ferreting out wrongdoing, but at the unrecognized expense of the substantial dignitary values certified by the parties in the terms of their MOU to inhere in the person of each suspected employee, whether ultimately disclosed to be innocent or guilty of wrongful conduct.

Award

The Award is that W—shall be reinstated with straight-time compensation retroactive to the date of her discharge and without loss of seniority or other contractual benefits. She shall submit a sworn statement of all earnings, if any, received by her in lieu of her Company earnings during the period of her termination, which shall be deducted from the pay due her; provided, however, that any unemployment compensation payments received by her shall not be so deducted because of her legal obligation to reimburse the State of California personally from the proceeds of her back pay.

Jurisdiction is retained to resolve any disputes that may arise in the course of administering this Award.

Notes and Questions

1. Can you precisely and concisely state Arbitrator Jones's holding?

2. Arbitrator Jones writes: "A female employee who feels compelled, as did Grievant, to ask male investigators if she can go to the bathroom, or if she can use the telephone, and disclose to whom she wants to call, is someone who is being demeaningly detained, which is to say, 'forcibly' within the prescriptive intent of the MOU." Is that a condescendingly sexist remark? Or is it an accurate statement of the situation? Would it be equally true of a male employee interviewed by female investigators? By male investigators?

3.   Arbitrator Jones's opinion demonstrates the importance of contractual due-process terms. Do you agree with his result? Would you, if your safety depended on the grievant's clear-headedness? Do the employer's procedural violations affect the merits of the insubordination charge? If not, why does the arbitrator reinstate the grievant?

4.   Is sustaining the grievance the only (or the best) remedy for an employer's breach of due-process rights? In Stroehmann Bakeries, Inc., 98 LA 873 (John E. Sands, 1990) (reprinted in Section VII.B.3.), the arbitrator sustained a grievance challenging the discharge of an employee for sexually harassing a customer. Arbitrator Sands found that the employer's agents "never once asked [the grievant] himself what had happened. . . . Instead, withholding warning and opportunity to prepare, they cornered [him] alone and confronted him with scurrilous accusations of scurrilous behavior that [they] had already accepted as Gospel." He ordered the employer to reinstate the grievant with full back pay. Do you agree with the arbitrator that the employer's violation of the grievant's procedural rights invalidated the discharge? How would you have dealt with the case?

Stroehmann's challenged the award in court and prevailed at the court of appeals. The court held that reinstating an alleged harasser without determining the merits of the charge violated "a well-defined and dominant public policy concerning sexual harassment in the workplace." The court remanded the case for a de novo hearing before a different arbitrator. Stroehmann Bakeries, Inc. v. Local 776, International Brotherhood of Teamsters, 969 F.2d 1436 (3rd Cir.), cert. denied, 506 U.S. 1022, 113 S.Ct. 660, 121 L.Ed.2d 585 (1992). How should the court deal with a similar case today in light of Eastern Associated Coal Corp. v. United Mine Workers of America, Dist. 17, 531 U.S. 57, 121 S.Ct. 462, 148 L.Ed.2d 354 (2000), reprinted in Section III.C.? If the award does not violate public policy under the Supreme Court's latest iteration, would the tone of the award, illustrated by the quote above, justify vacatur?

5.   County of Cook, 105 LA 974 (Aaron S. Wolff, 1995) was another case in which the employer failed to provide union representation required by the contract to an employee disciplined for fighting. The arbitrator found that the grievant had committed the offense but stated that

> it does not follow that the 5–day suspension must stand. If it did, the Employer would escape all responsibility for its breach of the Contract and, in future cases, would reduce, if not eliminate, the need for the Employer to follow the Contract in an important procedural respect. Accordingly, the appropriate remedy here will be to reduce the suspension imposed from five days to one day.

Do you agree?

C.   DISCOVERY[1]

While pursuing rights under a contractual grievance procedure, a union or an employer may want information from the other side. The

---

1. Bibliographic Suggestions: Laura J. Cooper, *Discovery in Labor Arbitration*, 72   Minnesota Law Review 1281 (1988); Linda J. French, *Arbitral Discovery Guidelines for*

need for information may arise when a party decides whether a grievance should be filed or pursued to arbitration, when a party prepares its case for arbitration, or when a party seeks to implement an arbitrator's remedial order. Unlike the parties in litigation (who are often total strangers to one another), the parties to a collectively bargained grievance procedure already know much about one another. For example, the union has ready access to information known by employees within the company. In addition, union contracts often provide union representatives access to the employer's premises to investigate grievances. Moreover, in the early stages of a grievance procedure, which amount to a series of settlement conferences, the parties are likely to present information supporting their position in an effort to persuade the other side to settle. Although these informal procedures rarely yield the volume of information typically exchanged in litigation, usually parties in arbitration have significantly less need for formal discovery procedures.

Nevertheless, circumstances do arise in which one party desires information that the other side is reluctant to disclose. Should the labor arbitration process accommodate these desires? Or will discovery introduce unwanted delay, cost, and formality to the arbitration process?

The extent to which discovery is available in arbitration depends to some extent on the legal source from which the authority to discover is claimed. Labor and management may obtain discovery because of provisions in the collective bargaining agreement, rights afforded by the National Labor Relations Act, or orders of an arbitrator.

1. CONTRACTUAL PROVISIONS

Some collective bargaining agreements explicitly oblige the employer to provide information. For example, a contract between Sanyo Manufacturing Corp. and the Electronic Workers provides:

> In the course of a grievance discussion, the Union and the employee shall have reasonable access to Company records necessary to resolve the grievance. Such records shall be obtained through the Human Resources office.[2]

A contract between Group Health Association, Inc. and the Registered Nurses and Physical Therapists Association assured the union access to all "nonconfidential information as is relevant and appropriate to the negotiation, maintenance and enforcement of this agreement."[3] Where such provisions exist, an arbitrator may refuse to admit in evidence

---

Employers, 50 University of Missouri Kansas City Law Review 141 (1982); Alvin L. Goldman and Paula K. Goldman, *Discovery and the Duty to Disclose*, Labor and Employment Arbitration (Tim Bornstein, Ann Gosline and Marc Greenbaum, eds., 2d ed., 2003); Timothy J. Heinsz, *The Use of Arbitral Subpoenas*, Labor and Employment Arbitration (Tim Bornstein, Ann Gosline and Marc Greenbaum, eds., 2d ed., 2003); Edgar A. Jones, Jr., *The Accretion of Federal Pow-*

er in Labor Arbitration—*The Example of Arbitral Discovery*, 116 University of Pennsylvania Law Review 830 (1968); Harold C. White and Lynn M. Meyer, *Employer Obligation to Provide Information*, 35 Labor Law Journal 643 (1984).

2. Bureau of National Affairs, Collective Bargaining Negotiations and Contracts 140:1001 (1998).

3. *Id.*

information a noncomplying party failed to disclose, especially if prejudice results, or may require the noncomplying party to pay additional costs incurred if a continuance is required for the other side to respond to the new evidence. A noncomplying party would also be subject to ordinary means for enforcement of contract violations, including arbitration. Contracts, however, seldom have such explicit language. Where the contract is silent regarding arbitral discovery, the parties have two alternative avenues for relief, the National Labor Relations Board and the procedural authority of the arbitrator.

2. DISCOVERY UNDER THE NATIONAL LABOR RELATIONS ACT

Sections 8(a)(5) and 8(b)(3) of the National Labor Relations Act, 28 U.S.C. §§ 158(a)(5) and 158(b)(3), require the parties to bargain in good faith. The NLRB interprets that requirement to include a duty to provide information needed for the proper performance of duties arising from the collective bargaining relationship. NLRB v. Truitt Manufacturing Co., 351 U.S. 149, 76 S.Ct. 753, 100 L.Ed. 1027 (1956). The Supreme Court has endorsed the Board's finding that it is an unfair labor practice to refuse to provide information to assist a union in deciding whether to submit a grievance under the collective bargaining agreement, NLRB v. Acme Industrial Co., 385 U.S. 432, 87 S.Ct. 565, 17 L.Ed.2d 495 (1967), and in preparing a case for presentation at an arbitration hearing, Detroit Edison Co. v. NLRB, 440 U.S. 301, 99 S.Ct. 1123, 59 L.Ed.2d 333 (1979). In *Acme*, the union was able to get information about the employer's removal of equipment from the plant to assess whether the employer was violating contractual limitations on subcontracting. Other decisions of the NLRB had affirmed the right of unions to obtain information on such matters as wage rates, overtime hours and workplace conditions related to health and safety. Further expanding the duty, appellate courts have agreed with the NLRB that employers must sometimes permit union representatives access to the employer's facility when necessary for handling grievances. NLRB. v. Holyoke Water Power Co., 778 F.2d 49 (1st Cir.1985), cert. denied, 477 U.S. 905, 106 S.Ct. 3274, 91 L.Ed.2d 565 (1986). Circuit courts, however, have reached different conclusions about whether specific factual circumstances warrant imposition of the duty. See, for example, Brown Shoe Co. v. NLRB, 33 F.3d 1019 (8th Cir.1994).

In assessing claims for information, the NLRB requires the requesting party to demonstrate that the information sought is relevant and necessary. The NLRB defines relevance broadly and describes its standard as similar to the scope of discovery in civil litigation. Although the Board's articulated standard requires the requesting party to demonstrate "necessity," in practice, the Board requires disclosure even if the requesting party could obtain the information through an independent course of investigation. Illinois–American Water Co., 296 NLRB 715 (1989), enforced, 933 F.2d 1368 (7th Cir.1991). Once the requesting party has demonstrated relevance and necessity, the party from whom the information has been requested may present defenses to the disclosure of information such as burdensomeness, employee privacy concerns, or protection of trade secrets, which may limit or defeat the discovery request. If the defenses are legitimate, the requesting party's needs must be weighed against the defenses to determine whether, in the particular circumstances, the information must be provided and, if so, in what form. *Detroit Edison Co., supra*, at 314. The Board may require the parties, in the first instance, to seek through bargaining an accommodation of their competing concerns. Oil, Chemical & Atomic Workers Local Union No. 6-418, AFL-CIO v. N.L.R.B., 711 F.2d 348, 363 (D.C. Cir. 1983).

The statutory right to obtain information has two critical limitations. First, the statutory obligation to provide information is subject to waiver by "clear and unmistakable" language. New York Telephone Co., 299 NLRB 351 (1990), enforced, 930 F.2d 1009 (2d Cir.1991). Second, and most significant, the procedural delays endemic to NLRB proceedings mean that a party seeking a legally-enforceable order to disclose information may have to wait for years. A request for information, brought as an unfair labor practice charge, may be followed by an agency investigation, a hearing before an administrative law judge, and review by the NLRB and a federal court of appeals. Such delays make the NLRB process incompatible with arbitration's objective of speedy resolution of grievances. Under current policy, the Board will itself decide unfair labor practice allegations related to failure to provide information rather than defer such questions to arbitrators, but the Board's General Counsel has urged it to reconsider this position. See Note 5(a) in Chapter IV.A.2. (b), *supra*.[4]

3. THE AUTHORITY OF THE ARBITRATOR

The final alternative means of obtaining discovery for labor arbitration is resort to the procedural authority of the arbitrator. Using the arbitrator to facilitate discovery avoids the most critical limitation of the NLRB. The arbitrator is able to render a final decision much more quickly. The Supreme Court has held that where a collective bargaining agreement does not specify the applicable procedures, the arbitrator is free to resolve procedural questions. United Paperworkers International Union v. Misco, 484 U.S. 29, 108 S.Ct. 364, 98 L.Ed.2d 286 (1987), *supra* Chapter III.C.2.

In exercising that discretion, the arbitrator may look to the decisions of other arbitrators on discovery matters and to state law. Unfortunately, because of the infrequency of discovery requests and the informality with which they are usually resolved, there are few published arbitration awards addressing discovery. Arbitrators therefore may seek guidance from NLRB decisions regarding information disclosure in arbitration. The arbitrator may want to follow the NLRB's definition of the scope of

---

4. For a summary of NLRB caselaw on an employer's duty to disclose information, see Robert A. Gorman and Matthew W. Finkin, Basic Text on Labor Law: Unionization and Collective Bargaining §§ 20.4–.6 (2004).

discovery and appropriate defenses to disclosure. The arbitrator might also seek guidance from state law, which the Supreme Court has held may be incorporated as federal law where compatible with its purposes. Textile Workers Union v. Lincoln Mills, 353 U.S. 448, 77 S.Ct. 912, 1 L.Ed.2d 972 (1957), Chapter III.A.2, *supra*. Such state law may include the Uniform Arbitration Act which affords arbitrators subpoena authority, or the Revised Uniform Arbitration Act (2000), adopted as of 2004 in nine states, that explicitly grants the arbitrator authority to conduct discovery.[5]

Despite the availability of arbitral discovery, employers and unions rarely require such assistance. Because parties in arbitration begin with common general knowledge of the workplace and acquire specific information in the preliminary steps of the grievance process, they never employ all of the discovery devices commonly used in civil litigation. The desire for a quick and inexpensive process often results in relatively limited pre-hearing preparation by the parties. Time-consuming or expensive discovery devices such as depositions or interrogatories are rare, except in unusually important or complex cases or where loss of vital evidence is otherwise threatened.

Usually a party desiring an arbitrator's assistance in obtaining information only requires a subpoena to compel hearing testimony or a subpoena *duces tecum* for the production of documents. Authority to issue subpoenas may be derived from the collective bargaining agreement, state arbitration statutes (including the Uniform Arbitration Act), or federal common law under § 301 of the Labor Management Relations Act governing the labor arbitration process. See *supra* Chapter III. A.[6] Ordinarily parties will comply with arbitrators' subpoenas, but in some cases of noncompliance litigation to enforce subpoenas is undertaken, adding to cost and delay. Federal courts have jurisdiction over causes of action to enforce subpoenas issued by labor arbitrators. Teamsters National Automotive Transporters Industry Negotiating Committee v. Troha, 328 F.3d 325 (7th Cir.), cert. denied, 540 U.S. 826, 124 S.Ct. 180, 157 L.Ed.2d 48 (2003).

5. "An arbitrator may permit such discovery as the arbitrator decides is appropriate in the circumstances, taking into account the needs of the parties to the arbitration proceeding and other affected persons and the desirability of making the proceeding fair, expeditious, and cost effective." Revised Uniform Arbitration Act, § 17(c) (2000). In cases outside the jurisdiction of federal labor law, such as those involving a state or its municipalities, state law, such as the Uniform Arbitration Act, will directly control the arbitrator's authority to issue subpoenas and manage discovery.

6. For useful practical suggestions for parties requesting subpoenas and arbitrators issuing subpoenas, see Timothy Heinsz, *An Arbitrator's Authority to Subpoena: A Power in Need of Clarification*, 38 Proceedings of the National Academy of Arbitrators 219 (1986) and Timothy J. Heinsz, *supra* footnote 1, § 6.05.

RALSTON PURINA CO.

82 LA 983 (Erwin B. Ellman, 1984).*

A prehearing Motion for Production of Relevant Information, supported by an affidavit and memorandum, has been filed by the Union in this matter.

The grievance, dated April 25, 1983, recites:

On or about April 18, 1983, the Company transferred duties and responsibilities normally assigned to members of Local 66 to salaried personnel. These duties are, in general, associated with inventory control of items necessary to maintain repair of equipment in the plant, and the initial step or steps of the ordering of such items. We grieve that the Company cease and desist from this practice. Further, that any member of Local 66 adversely affected by this action be placed in such status as would have been attained had this practice not been instituted.

On February 7, 1984, the President of Local 66, Thomas J. Powers, who signed the grievance, requested that "a representative of Local 66, a non-member qualified in computer technology, be allowed the opportunity to observe the processes and procedures used in the inventory control of the 'Maintenance Stockroom'." It was anticipated this individual would be accompanied by management personnel and a Union representative.

On February 24th Plant Manager A. L. Murray responded that the request was "considered to be unnecessary and inappropriate at this time." The Company indicated its willingness to meet to explain "the procedures being used in the areas of your concern" but it saw no need to "expose ourselves to the outside world." It requested that the Union indicate the specific information it desired. From the Union's Memorandum it appears that the "outsider" for whom the Union seeks access is experienced in computer technology and is employed at a collegiate computer user service center.

The Union urges that the information it seeks is relevant to the grievance; that it does not have specialized expertise in computer technology; and that use of an outside expert is desirable. It seeks direct inspection by such expert rather than use of a nonexpert as an intermediary, as the Company suggests. The Union states that it is willing to assure discreet handling of any information obtained to meet the Company's apprehensions that its "security" will be compromised.

Though copies of the moving papers were apparently transmitted to the Company, no response was offered by it.

1.   At this stage I have no knowledge of the underlying collective bargaining agreement or any understanding between the parties which might shed light on the issue raised. I do not know whether this arbitration, submitted through the Federal Mediation and Conciliation

* Reprinted with permission from *Labor Arbitration Reporter–Labor Arbitration Reports*, 82 LA 983. Copyright 1984 by the Bureau of National Affairs, Inc. (800–372–1033) <http://www.bna.com>.

Service, is to be governed by the rules of the American Arbitration Association, the Federal Arbitration Act, or any other special rules or regulations. Since no controlling doctrine has specifically been called to my attention, I assume that I am governed by general "arbitral common law."

2. I read National Labor Relations Board v. Acme Industrial Co., 385 U.S. 432 (1967) cited by the Union, to impose an obligation on the employer to furnish information to the Union sufficient to enable it to perform its statutory duties, including the processing of grievances. But this obligation is normally to be enforced by the NLRB, as it was in that case. * * * Should the Union proceed before the Board and move to adjourn the arbitration hearing until resolution of those proceedings, I would give serious consideration to such a request. I do not think, however, that I have a roving commission as an arbitrator to do the work which Congress has committed to the NLRB.

3. Traditionally it has been assumed that "there is no discovery in labor arbitration" although this dogma has been somewhat abraded and qualified in recent years. * * * But it should not be replaced by equally dogmatic assimilation of the arbitration process to discovery procedures prevailing in federal court civil litigation. In the absence of any statutory or contractual guidance, I am reluctant to embrace the facile notion that because I have control over "procedural" matters, I should grant the Union's request. The limited insight I presently have concerning the background of the grievance does not permit a confident ruling as to the necessity of the steps the Union proposes to take, the substantiality of the claim that the Employer has security interests which must be accommodated, or the techniques which might be appropriate to meet the legitimate interests of both parties. I accordingly deny the motion at this time, without prejudice to its later renewal.

4. The parties should be aware, however, that at the hearing, upon request of either party or sua sponte, should I deem it appropriate, I will personally inspect any plant premises germane to the issue presented, and will permit a reasonable number of nominees of each side to accompany me. When necessary, I will not hesitate to question any witness if what I feel to be relevant information is not otherwise made available. Should it then appear that the information obtained requires evaluation justifying postponement of the hearing, I will consider such a request. This could elongate the hearing and aggravate burdens and expenses to all concerned. For this reason, the parties may find it desirable and expedient to reach some pre-hearing accommodation on the issue presented.

Notes and Questions

1. Did the arbitrator in *Ralston Purina* properly handle the union's request to allow its computer expert to observe the employer's inventory control operation?

(a) How might the union have presented to the arbitrator a more persuasive case for access than it did?

(b) How persuasive is the arbitrator's assertion that he was not given a "roving commission * * * to do the work which Congress has committed to the NLRB"?

(c) Was the arbitrator justified in being reluctant to make procedural decisions in the absence of statutory or contractual guidance?

(d) Is the arbitrator's resolution of the problem more sensible than simply allowing the union's computer expert access before the hearing?

2. The Company received and investigated complaints from Customer A and Customer B about the conduct of an employee. In the course of its investigation, the Company discussed with the employee the complaint from Customer A and asked the employee about the incident with Customer A. The Company has in its files a signed statement from Customer A and an investigative report summarizing Customer A's concerns and the employee's response. It also has in its files information about Customer B's complaints although no signed statement from Customer B. The Company has not disclosed Customer B's identity to the employee or the Union nor does the employer intend to call Customer B as a witness at the arbitration hearing. The Union submits a grievance challenging the employee's discharge for conduct involving Customer A. The Union requests that the Company produce three items: (i) the Company's investigative report; (ii) the statement of Customer A; and (iii) the identity of any other customers besides Customer A who complained about the employee's conduct. Which items, if any, should the arbitrator order the Employer to produce?

(a) In deciding this question, should the arbitrator use the NLRB's general analytical scheme, determining whether the information is "relevant and necessary" and, if so, whether the Employer has available any defenses sufficient to defeat the Union's access to the information? If the arbitrator follows this analysis, how would the arbitrator decide the union's request for production? If you don't think the arbitrator should follow the NLRB's general scheme, how should the arbitrator resolve the issue?

(b) The NLRB, in determining whether an employer has committed an unfair labor practice, looks to a detailed body of precedent that defines the scope of the employer's duty to produce information. See NLRB v. New Jersey Bell Telephone Co., 936 F.2d 144 (3d Cir.1991) (employer must disclose investigatory report in case in which identity of customer already known to employee); distinguishing, Anheuser–Busch, Inc., 237 N.L.R.B. 982 (1978) (employer need not disclose witness statements); and GTE California Inc., 324 N.L.R.B. 424 (1997) (employer need not disclose name and telephone number of complaining customer in case in which union permitted to interview anonymous customer by telephone).) Should the arbitrator in deciding the Union's request for production attempt to follow these precedents? Should the arbitrator insist, before deciding the case, that the parties submit briefs examining NLRB precedent and its application to the case?

(c) Issues of evidence related to testimony of customers is addressed in Question 8 following the case of *Ambassador Convalescent Center, Inc., supra* Chapter VI.A.

3. Prior to a hearing, the arbitrator issued a subpoena requiring the Company to produce certain documents. The Company has neither raised any objections to production nor produced the documents. How should the arbitrator rule at the hearing if the Union moves that the arbitrator, in response to the Company's failure to produce, should: (a) decide the case on the merits in favor of the Union? (b) grant the Union a continuance so that it might seek a court order enforcing the subpoena? (c) draw an adverse inference from the Company's failure to produce the documents? (d) preclude the Company from introducing the documents in evidence? Would some other sanction or response be appropriate? See Alvin L. Goldman and Paula K. Goldman, *supra* footnote 1, § 2.10.

4. Should parties to arbitration devote more time and resources to gathering information before arbitration hearings? Or do interests in inexpensive and expeditious dispute resolution outweigh the interest in having decisions based on complete and accurate information?

5. Does existing legal authority to engage in discovery in labor arbitration already go too far toward permitting the process to be encumbered by the costs and delay of information exchange?

6. Does one side more frequently benefit from the scarcity of discovery in arbitration?

7. The limited number of published arbitration decisions regarding discovery and the absence of current empirical studies on the subject make it difficult to ascertain whether arbitrators today generally would be more willing to permit discovery than Arbitrator Ellman.

8. For a discussion of the use of discovery in employment arbitration, see Chapter XI.E., *infra*.

D. THE ROLE OF PRECEDENT[1]

1. INTRODUCTION

Precedent plays several important roles in labor arbitration, just as it does in litigation. "Precedent" in this context means prior arbitration awards, court, and administrative decisions involving the same parties, and arbitration awards involving other parties. (Administrative and court decisions involving *other* parties form the "external law" whose impact on arbitration is discussed in Section V.B.) Some commentators welcome the development and use of arbitral precedent because it guides later arbitrators and provides parties with greater predictability. See, for example, Dallas L. Jones and Russell A. Smith, *Management and Labor Appraisals and Criticisms of the Arbitration Process: A Report with*

1. Bibliographic Suggestions: The most authoritative treatment of the role of precedent in labor arbitration is Carlton J. Snow, *An Arbitrator's Use of Precedent*, 94 Dickinson Law Review 665 (1990). See also Jay E. Grenig, *Contract Interpretation and Respect for Prior Proceedings*, Chapter 9 of Labor and Employment Arbitration (Tim Bornstein, Ann Gosline, and Mark Greenbaum, eds., 2d ed. 2001); Marvin Hill, Jr., and Anthony Sinicropi, Evidence in Arbitration 369–409 (2d Ed. 1987); Peter Seitz, *The Citation of Authority and Precedent in Arbitration (Its Use and Abuse)*, 38 Arbitration Journal 58 (Dec. 1983); Allan D. Vestal & Marvin Hill, Jr., *Preclusion in Labor Controversies*, 35 Oklahoma Law Review 281 (1982).

Comments, 62 Michigan Law Review 1115, 1151–52 (1964). Others, like Peter Seitz in the article cited in footnote 1, vehemently oppose the use of arbitral precedent in most cases, arguing that it mistakes the nature of arbitration and increases arbitration's time and cost.

For good or ill, however, parties and arbitrators alike frequently refer to previous decisions. Parties usually do so in the hope that previous awards will persuade the arbitrator of the merits of their positions, not because they regard the awards as binding. Arbitrators usually do so to justify their decisions.

To appreciate precedent's roles in arbitration, one must first understand three distinct but closely-related legal concepts.

- *Stare decisis*, a Latin term meaning "to stand decided," refers to the legal doctrine that makes certain previous court decisions binding in later court cases. Decisions are binding only if they are from the same court or from courts of superior rank in the same jurisdiction. (Courts owe only "due regard" to decisions by courts of equal rank.[2]) An intermediate appellate court in State A, for instance, is bound by the decisions of State A's highest court but not by those of its trial courts or other intermediate appellate courts, or even those of State B's highest court. The doctrine therefore presumes a hierarchy of tribunals whose decisions are published and thus available for reference. Moreover, prior decisions are binding only when the issue is the same and the facts are substantially similar—in a popular legal term, when the new case stands "on all fours" with the older one. The obvious goals of the doctrine are stability and predictability in the law.

Once thought to be quite rigid, *stare decisis* is really quite flexible. Skillful judges and litigants are often able to distinguish the issues or facts, and the highest court of any jurisdiction may overrule its own precedents.

- *Res judicata*, a Latin term meaning "a thing adjudged," is the principle that once a competent court has decided a dispute on the merits, the original parties or their successors may not reopen or challenge the result (except, of course, by appealing the judgment). It does not bar later challenges by other parties, differing in this respect from *stare decisis*. In short, *stare decisis* binds everyone, but *res judicata* binds only the parties. Like *stare decisis*, *res judicata* reflects a desire for stability and predictability in the law. In addition, however, *res judicata* seeks to end a particular dispute by preventing relitigation. The preferred modern term is "claim preclusion," suggesting that the earlier decision bars any attempt to revive the original claim, even by asserting new arguments which could have been, but were not, presented in the first case.

2. Robert Von Moschzisker, *Stare Decisis in Courts of Last Resort*, 37 Harvard   Law Review 409, 412 (1923–24).

- *Collateral estoppel* bars relitigation by the parties or their successors of previously determined *issues* (as opposed to the previously determined *claims* affected by *res judicata*). The preferred modern term is "issue preclusion," suggesting that the parties may not relitigate the decided issue even in a different claim.

Strictly speaking, none of the three legal concepts applies in arbitration, but *stare decisis* should have the least impact of all. Apart from arbitration's vaunted informality, which should discourage legal rigidities, arbitration lacks the necessary hierarchy of tribunals: each arbitration constitutes a new and equal forum. Each arbitrator therefore owes no more than "due regard" to the decisions of other arbitrators. Nor is there complete publication of awards. Those published form only a small, and not necessarily representative, portion of the whole. Many parties have no convenient access to the publishing services, and many parties forego the use of lawyers who could discover and argue the pertinent precedents.

Nevertheless, previous arbitration awards can be useful. On novel questions, they provide the parties and the arbitrator with other arbitrators' analyses. On common questions, they may reveal a consensus in the labor relations community of which parties should be aware and to which later arbitrators should defer. Precedent's force in arbitration is limited, however, because there is no superior authority to force adherence to previous awards. Even if there were, arbitration cases are less likely than court cases to be "on all fours." Contractual language, evidence of the drafters' intentions, and the parties' past practices differ widely. The same words may mean different things in different bargaining relationships. Factual contexts are usually unique. Seldom will accidents occur in exactly the same way; seldom will two seniority systems operate identically.

Accordingly, prior awards involving other agreements or other parties are at most persuasive, not authoritative. The better reasoned and better written the award, the greater will be its power of persuasion. Thus Arbitrator David Wolff gave some weight to another arbitrator's award even though it used different contract language and practices to resolve a dispute between different parties:

> On the other hand, points of similarity may not be disregarded. In addition, the Chairman has high regard for Dr. [Harry] Shulman's sincerity, clarity of thought, and reasoning processes. The Chairman does not propose to unthinkingly adopt Dr. Shulman's determination in another case as his own in the instant case. However, to the extent to which he believes it here applicable, he makes use of it with appreciation.

Chrysler Appeal Board Case No. 573 (1948), quoted in Elkouri and Elkouri, How Arbitration Works 620 (Marlin M. Volz and Edward P. Goggin, eds., 5th Ed. 1997).

Res judicata and collateral estoppel raise different concerns. The need to put a dispute to rest is equally strong in arbitration and litigation. Most parties obliquely refer to that need by providing in their agreements that an arbitrator's award is to be "final and binding." The parties know of their previous arbitrations, so access to that source of precedent presents no problem. Given the essential similarity of parties, language, and issues, these concepts logically should influence arbitrators. Thus, with only a few exceptions, arbitrators regard previous awards under the same contract as becoming *part of* that agreement until the parties amend it. This is particularly true if the parties have renegotiated the agreement without changing the interpreted language. Arbitrator Roger Abrams concisely discussed the principle in a recent decision:

> A decision by one arbitrator does not bind a subsequent arbitrator in the same way an appellate court decision becomes binding precedent within a jurisdiction. However, to maintain stability in a collective relationship it is best that contract interpretations not be disturbed, especially if the parties have had the opportunity, as they have here, to negotiate clarifications in contract language in the interim.

Kroger Co., 117 LA 737 (2002).

In effect, arbitrators follow a form of *stare decisis*, but one that is limited to decisions under the same contract.

2. THE EFFECT OF PRIOR ARBITRATION AWARDS

PAN AMERICAN REFINING CORP.
9 LA 731 (Whitley P. McCoy, 1948).*

These two grievances, though separately filed, one by two men and the other by five, involve precisely the same question and will be treated together. The issue submitted in each case reads: "Are the complaining employees entitled to the Painter's rate * * *?"

On November 4, 1947, J. E. Berry and J. C. Ferguson, classified as "helpers, Mechanical Department, Paint Division," applied the priming coat of paint to a number of stanchions. On the same day, C. F. Brown, E. E. Whitacre, L. C. Turner, E. P. White, and R. E. Davis, having the same classification, applied the priming coat to structural steel. They claim pay for the time thus spent at the painter's rate, under Article VB, reading as follows:

> If an employee formally assigned to one classification is required to perform work peculiar to another classification carrying a higher wage rate, he shall be paid at such higher rate for so long as he performs such work * * *

In the absence of any agreement between the parties, either by way of agreed upon job descriptions or long established practice, I should be much inclined, if the matter were one of first impression, to uphold this grievance. A line must be drawn somewhere between the work of the painter and the work of the painter's helper, and I can think of no more logical and certain line than that contended for by the Union. The Union's position is that when the helper picks up a paint brush and starts painting he becomes, for the time, a painter.

This essentially logical position is fortified by the practices and working rules of the Painters Union, A.F. of L. Under these rules, an apprentice cleans surfaces for painting (among other duties), a helper carries and sets up ladders and paint, raises and lowers the painters to scaffolding, etc., but does not paint, the painter mixes paint and paints. Of course, the working rules of the Painters Union, A.F. of L., would not in any event be binding upon this Union and this Company, and they are referred to only as supporting the logic of the Union's position.

However, the matter is not one of first impression: the precise question was presented by this Company and Union, under identical contract provisions and job descriptions, to another arbitrator and was decided adversely to the Union's contention. Matter of Pan American Refining Corporation and Oil Workers International Union, Local 449, 4 LA 773, decided September 2, 1946. That decision, based upon a finding that the parties had agreed upon a consolidation of the duties of helper and 3rd class painter, held that when a helper applies a priming coat he is not performing painter's work within the meaning of the contract clause in question, but is performing helper's work. It thus construed that contract clause as not covering facts in all respects identical with the facts before me. This raises the question as to how far one arbitrator's decision should be binding upon another.

Of course it should not be binding at all when another company and union are involved, but should be at most merely persuasive, entitled to as much weight as, but no more than, its inherent logic, common sense, and reasonableness dictate. Where the prior decision involves the same company and union, but is essentially a decision on facts rather than on the interpretation of a contract clause, it is entitled to no weight whatever under a different set of facts, though general statements of principle may or may not be persuasive. But where, as here, the prior decision involves the interpretation of the identical contract provision, between the same company and union, every principle of common sense, policy, and labor relations demands that it stand until the parties annul it by a newly worded contract provision.

Otherwise, in what position would the parties find themselves? If I should decide to the contrary of the prior decision, which decision would be binding for future cases? Obviously neither, for if Dr. Abernathy's decision is not binding neither is mine. When similar facts arose next week, the Company would refuse to pay, the case would go to arbitration, and a third arbitrator would be called upon to decide the same question because both Abernathy and I would have to refuse to serve if appointed, having already expressed an opinion. So every week or two the parties would find themselves arbitrating the same question, each time with a new arbitrator. Such a situation would be intolerable.

I find that the precise issue before me, having been already decided between these parties adversely to the Union's contention, is not open to a new determination in arbitration, but must be settled, if at all, by agreement of the parties. The questions submitted will therefore be answered in the negative.

AWARD

It is the award of the arbitrator that: * * * The questions submitted on Grievances No. 147 and 148, filed in behalf of certain helpers, Mechanical Department, Paint Division, are answered in the negative.

SPECIALIZED DISTRIBUTION MANAGEMENT, INC.

1997 WL 828804 (Carlton J. Snow, 1996).

[On April 18, 1995, Arbitrator Luella Nelson sustained a grievance brought by Teamsters Local 439 on behalf of drivers employed by Specialized Distribution Management, Inc. (SDMI). That grievance charged that SDMI violated the agreement by sending home and temporarily replacing drivers who refused to cross a United Food and Commercial Workers (UFCW) picket line at Pak–N–Sav, a subsidiary of Safeway Stores. Shortly before Arbitrator Nelson issued her award, the UFCW struck Safeway Stores in a separate dispute. SDMI again temporarily replaced drivers who refused to cross the UFCW picket line. Drivers who refused to cross the picket lines thus lost a day's pay. Local 439 filed a new grievance but also filed a motion requesting that the SDMI first show cause why it should be permitted to proceed to arbitration. Local 439 argued that the principle of res judicata controlled the new grievance and thus precluded relitigation of the issue. SDMI responded that the Nelson award was not binding because the facts of the second grievance differed from those of the first and that the earlier award was erroneous because Arbitrator Nelson considered extrinsic evidence even though the agreement was unambiguous.]

III.   RELEVANT CONTRACTUAL PROVISIONS

Article V—No Strike/Lockout

Picket Line. It shall not be a violation of this Agreement, nor shall it be cause for discharge of an employee or disciplinary action of any kind if an employee refuses to cross or work behind a lawful, primary picket line, approved by the Unions party to this Agreement and sanctioned by the appropriate Joint Council, including picket lines at the Employer's place of business. A seventy-two (72) hour written notice shall be required prior to observing a lawful, primary picket line directed at the Employer's facility from the time actual picketing commences. * * *

VI. ANALYSIS

A. The Principle of Res Judicata

As a threshold issue, the Union asserted that the principle of res judicata precludes the arbitrator from asserting jurisdiction in the case. Res judicata literally means "a thing decided," and it refers to a collection of concepts that limit opportunities to resolve in a second proceeding matters that were or could have been resolved in a prior hearing. With roots in Roman law, the principle of res judicata is a well-established concept in Anglo–American common law. * * *

The principle of res judicata in common law is used to describe rules covering both claim preclusion and issue preclusion. Rules covering claim preclusion prevent a party from pursuing in a later proceeding any matter that was a part of the same claim decided in an earlier proceeding. Claim preclusion prevents relitigating claims that could have been pursued earlier, even though such claims were not actually resolved in a prior proceeding. Rules covering issue preclusion, however, bar a party from pursuing issues actually determined in an earlier action from being relitigated in a later proceeding. * * *

Some scholars cover only rules of claim preclusion under the topic of res judicata. In such an organization of the principle of res judicata, the topic of issue preclusion is covered under the topic of collateral estoppel. Restatement (Second) of Judgments uses the term "res judicata" to cover both claim and issue preclusion. (See, p. 131 (1982)).

The concept of res judicata has taken root in arbitration, and arbitrators more often than not have used the term to refer to issue preclusions. (See, *e.g.*, Pan American Refining Corp., 9 LA 731 (1948); and Board of Education of Cook County, 73 LA 310 (1979)). As one arbitrator observed:

> Preclusive effect may be given to a prior award only where the issues are identical and the subsequent dispute cannot be distinguished from the one earlier ruled upon. Thus, the second arbitrator must first be satisfied that the issue he is required to decide is identical to that presented in the previous case. Next, assuming he has made that determination, the arbitrator must ascertain whether there have been any changes in the circumstances or conditions material to the original holding which make inappropriate continued adherence to the earlier ruling. (See, Burnham Corp., 88 LA 931, 935 (1987).)

For the Union to prevail on the matter of issue preclusion, it is necessary for the issue arbitrated in the first proceeding to be the same as the issue before this arbitrator. While common law courts traditionally have not required total congruency, several factors may be used to test whether the two issues are the same. For example, is there substantial congruency between evidence and arguments in the two proceedings? Second, is the same arbitral principle involved in both proceedings? Third, did preparation for the first proceeding embrace most matters to be covered in the second proceeding? The focus in issue preclusion is on what was actually arbitrated in the first case and not what might have been pursued by a party.

Evidence submitted to the arbitrator makes it reasonable to conclude that the grievance advanced by the Union in this case is not precluded by a prior decision rendered by Arbitrator Nelson. Although both cases are factually similar, the case before this arbitrator is easily distinguishable from the former dispute. It is noteworthy that the parties are not necessarily identical. Although Safeway Stores owns Pak–N–Sav, the effect of the Safeway strike on SDMI was different from the impact of the Pak–N–Sav strike.

The Pak–N–Sav strike affected only a small number of stores within a short delivery distance. The Safeway strike affected over 200 stores over a greater distance. Arbitrator Nelson specifically limited her award to facts of that case. For example, she held:

> It is irrelevant, for this case, that the Employer serves a large area overall. The stores affected by the Pak–N–Sav dispute were in the same or adjoining counties within relatively short driving distances. The question of the Employer's rights when faced with a distant delivery location is best left to a case directly raising that issue. * * *

The point is that Arbitrator Nelson did not fully address all issues that are relevant in the case before this arbitrator.

Since the date Arbitrator Nelson rendered her decision, the National Labor Relations Board has become involved in the dispute. In other words, not only are factual circumstances clearly distinguishable, but also the circumstances have changed. Although Arbitrator Nelson's decision is significant in the dispute before this arbitrator, it is not dispositive and does not preclude the arbitrator from addressing the merits of the case. * * *

B. Impact of the Agreement

Does the parties' agreement prohibit temporary replacement of workers who refuse to cross picket lines? Article V of the parties' agreement prevents management from discharging or disciplining employees who decide to honor a picket line. The parties promised each other that:

> Picket Line. It shall not be a violation of this Agreement, nor shall it be cause for discharge of an employee or disciplinary action of any kind if an employee refuses to cross or work behind a lawful, primary picket line, approved by the Joint Council, including picket lines at the Employer's place of business. * * *

[The union argued that by waiving its right to discipline employees who refused to cross a picket line, the employer also waived its right to replace reluctant drivers with others. Arbitrator Snow held that the impact of the no-discipline clause depended on the parties' intent.]

An influential factor in understanding the intent of the parties is the arbitration decision of Arbitrator Luella Nelson. She interpreted the exact language at issue in this case under similar circumstances. The Employer argued quite correctly that a strict doctrine of stare decisis is not applicable in arbitration. In fact, there is a long history of arbitrators using other decisions as a source of guidance without affording them precedential value. As a general rule, an arbitrator must be aware of prior decisions; and it is reasonable to expect an arbitrator to make a greater effort to explain an award if a great body of decisions on the same topic customarily come to a different conclusion from the one reached by the arbitrator.

A prior decision by an arbitrator involving similar circumstances and exactly the same language bears closer scrutiny, even though such an award is not binding on the arbitrator. Closer scrutiny is merited in the interest of continuity of interpretation. It is in the interest of the parties to know that arbitral determinations are based on reason and reflect more than random judgments. As the eminent Harry Shulman of Yale Law School observed many years ago:

> Even in the absence of arbitration, parties themselves seek to establish a form of stare decisis or precedent for their own guidance—by statements of policy, instructions, manuals of procedure, and the like. This is but a means of avoiding the pain of rethinking every recurring case from scratch, of securing uniformity of action among the many people of co-ordinate authority upon whom each of the parties must rely, of assuring adherence in their actions to the policies established by their superiors, and of reducing or containing the possibilities of arbitrary or personal discretion. (See, Shulman, "Reason, Contract, and Law in Labor Relations," 68 Harv. L. Rev. 999, 1020 (1955).)

While prior awards on the same issue might have considerable persuasive power, they merit no weight at all if logically flawed or analytically erroneous. One arbitrator has stated the general rule when he observed that "words have been reversed in a subsequent proceeding if found to be clearly erroneous." (See, Pacific Tel. & Tel. Co., 77 LA 1088, 1096 (1981)). Arbitrators disregard prior decisions that are clearly erroneous. (See, Coleman Co., Inc. 52 LA 357 (1969)).

The Employer argued that Arbitrator Nelson's decision deserved no weight because it clearly was erroneous and logically flawed. In evaluating a prior award, arbitrators should not merely substitute their judgment for that of the prior decision maker. The prior award should be disregarded if the earlier arbitrator was clearly mistaken in his or her statement of facts and in logically applying relevant principles to the facts. Yet, if a prior decision on essentially the same issue is to be considered by a subsequent arbitrator, the earlier decision should be used as an important source of guidance if its analysis is sound. Any other approach undermines the stability of arbitration, reduces the usefulness of prior decisions as a source of guidance for the parties, and unleashes the risk of arbitrariness on the part of the subsequent arbitrator.

The Employer asserted that Arbitrator Nelson made two significant mistakes in her analysis of the earlier case. First, she allegedly erred by considering extrinsic evidence when language of the parties' agreement was clear and unambiguous. It is the position of the Employer that extrinsic evidence may not be used to inform an arbitrator's judgment when contractual language is plain and unambiguous. This conclusion, however, does not accurately reflect modern principles of contract interpretation. [Arbitrator Snow concluded that, "while the 'plain meaning' rule is far from dead," modern contract law, as stated in the Restatement (Second) of Contracts and the Uniform Commercial Code, allows consideration of extrinsic evidence to interpret the contract even if the language seems unambiguous.]

The interpretation asserted by the Union in this case is not contrary to the language of the parties' agreement. While the verbiage standing alone may not appear to be ambiguous, the Union presented evidence in the previous arbitration hearing that demonstrated a latent ambiguity. * * * Extrinsic evidence may be used to demonstrate an ambiguity in the language. At the time the ambiguity became apparent, it was not erroneous for Arbitrator Nelson to rely on extrinsic evidence to determine the intention of the parties. Even under a "plain meaning" rule, it is appropriate for a decision maker to evaluate extrinsic evidence in order to determine whether there is an ambiguity in the language. As one court observed, "proof on the issue of ambiguity may encompass * * * the surrounding circumstances, common usage and custom * * * and subsequent conduct of the parties." (See, Eskimo Pie Corp. v. Whitelawn Dairies, 284 F.Supp. 987 (S.D.N.Y. 1968)). Nor was there any showing that undisputed documentary evidence disproved the allegation of ambiguity in the language.

The Employer also asserted that Arbitrator Nelson made a second mistake in her analysis of the case she decided. The Employer contended that Arbitrator Nelson erred in her determination that the union presented sufficient evidence regarding the parties' contractual intent. There allegedly was insufficient evidence to support a conclusion that the union's interpretation of the disputed language represented the mutual intent of the parties when they entered into an agreement. A transcript of the previous arbitration proceeding as well as Arbitrator Nelson's decision, however, both indicated that she received evidence and testimony regarding this issue and that it was from such documentary evidence and testimony that she drew her conclusions. Evidence submitted to the arbitrator failed to establish that Arbitrator Nelson was erroneous in the decision she rendered. A contrary decision by this arbitrator merely would be substituting one arbitrator's judgment for another's. There is no basis for rejecting her decision as logically flawed or analytically incorrect.

C.   The Persuasive Value of the Nelson Award

There are circumstances of the case before this arbitrator that are different from the previous case. The geographic area is larger, and a greater number of delivery sites were affected. But the language to be interpreted remains the same. This is the language for which the parties bargained. If a party has concluded that the language is ineffective, the solution is to be found in the bargaining process and not in the grievance procedure. The manner in which the Employer dispatched routes and its unwillingness to consider alternatives to subcontracting demonstrated the arbitrary nature of the Employer's action. If there had been no intent to discipline drivers, it is reasonable to conclude that management would have allowed workers to continue to bid for routes outside of their start time. The Employer's justification failed to provide a basis for violating the agreement of the parties. Courts continue to honor the old-fashioned notion that knowledgeable negotiators are free to contract imprudently as well as prudently. (See, Black Industries, Inc. v. Bush, 110 F.Supp. 801 (1953)).

As Restatement (Second) has instructed, "the objective of interpretation and the general law of contracts is to carry out the understanding of the parties rather than to impose obligations on them contrary to their understanding." (See, s 201, comment c, p. 84 (1981)). It is not for an arbitrator to make a new agreement for the parties. The long-term benefits of a contractual commitment depend on the good faith of both parties in adhering to their promises, whether or not the terms later prove to be prudent. The solution to unfavorable terms, once dickered into existence by the parties, can only be found at the bargaining table, absent proof of unconscionability or some other significant excusing condition. None has been proved in this case. Accordingly, the grievance must be sustained.

AWARD

Having carefully considered all evidence submitted by the parties concerning this matter, the arbitrator concludes that the Employer violated the parties' collective bargaining agreement by temporarily replacing grievants who refused to cross the UFCW–Safeway Stores picket lines in April of 1995. The grievants shall be made whole for any loss of pay and benefits resulting from their temporary replacement.
* * *

Notes and Questions

1. Arbitrator McCoy in *Pan American Refining* gave the previous award preclusive effect. Arbitrator Snow in *SDMI* did not. Why did their conclusions differ? Did their differences affect the outcomes? Arbitrator Snow is a law professor. (Or would you have already guessed that from his opinion in *Specialized Distribution*?) While most arbitrators would reach the same result he did, few would do so in such a scholarly way.

2. As both cases indicate, an earlier award will control the second decision only (if at all) when the parties, issues, facts, and contract language are substantially identical.

(a) *Parties.* The "parties" to a labor arbitration case are almost always the employer and the union, even though an individual employee may be the only reason for the grievance. Thus a decision involving the union should control a second case on the same issue even if there is a different grievant. In Arch of Illinois, Conant Mine, 105 LA 445 (Marvin J. Feldman, 1995), an earlier arbitrator had held that an individual's compensation for paid days off (sick days, vacation days, and holidays) includes the average amount of overtime the employee would have worked. The grievant in that case was a man named Ridgeway.

The grievance presented to Arbitrator Feldman involved the same union, the same employer, and the same contract language, but sought a similar remedy on behalf of all bargaining unit employees. Arbitrator Feldman sustained the grievance:

> * * * even though the prior case concerned only one grievant and the instant case involved the entire bargaining unit, the fact of the matter is, that the parties are still the same. The rule established for Ridgeway is being sought to be established for the entire unit and quite frankly the company argument attempting to disturb the Ridgeway rule on the basis that the parties are different must be held for naught. The award in that case governed the parties and the dispute between them. In that regard the Ridgeway dispute, when he was a member of local 15, is no different than the unit dispute of local 15 with the company * * * .
>
> From all of that, it can be determined that the company argument that the parties are different is simply not true. While it is true that the first grievance was held for the benefit of Ridgeway, local 15 has many faces. It has as many faces as there are bargaining unit members but an individual cannot bring a grievance. While an individual may sign off on a grievance the right to bring that grievance and to pursue it and to perpetuate it belongs to the union and in this particular case the union was a party to both events of arbitration, namely the case before Arbitrator Cohen and namely the instant matter.

Compare *Arch of Illinois* with Bayshore Concrete Products Co., 92 LA 311 (William S. Hart, 1989). The employer announced rules for punching in and out to ensure proper recording of work hours. It then suspended five employees from the Iron Workers bargaining unit and four from the Operating Engineers bargaining unit for violating the rules. The Operating Engineers filed the first grievance, but the two unions agreed that a settlement of that grievance would bind both of them. The parties could not resolve the first grievance, so both unions then took their grievances to arbitration.

In the first case, Arbitrator Harold Leeper found that the employer had just cause for suspending the Iron Workers employees. In the second case, before Arbitrator William Hart, the company asserted that the Operating Engineers were collaterally estopped by the other arbitration decision involving the same facts, issues, and contract language, especially after the unions had agreed to be jointly bound by any resolution. Arbitrator Hart refused to apply collateral estoppel because the first arbitration did not include the

Operating Engineers. The agreement between the unions was no bar, he ruled, because it concerned only settlements, not arbitration awards.

Suppose the Iron Workers in the previous case brought a second, identical grievance on behalf of different employees (same union, same company, different grievants). Would *res judicata* bar the second claim? If not, would collateral estoppel bar relitigation of the "just cause" issue? See the chapter by Professor Grenig cited at footnote 1. How would you explain your conclusions to the discharged grievants?

(b) *Issues.* Virgin Islands Water & Power Authority, 89 LA 809 (Thomas L. Watkins, 1987), shows how a difference in issues can be critical. The employer suspended an employee during an investigation of a possible theft. When she failed to respond or to return to work, it fired her for those reasons. An arbitrator reduced the discharge to a suspension. When she returned to work, the employer then fired her for the alleged misappropriation. The discharge grievance went before Arbitrator Watkins. He held that the first decision did not control the case before him because the grounds for discharge differed and thus the first arbitrator did not resolve same the issue. He found, however, that it was too late for the employer to revive the two-year-old charge of misappropriation. Nevertheless, clearly troubled by strong evidence of the grievant's guilt, he declined to order the usual remedy of reinstatement with back pay. Instead, he gave the employer the choice of reinstating her *without* back pay or of giving her back pay without reinstatement. Moreover, some issues like credibility determinations may require the arbitrator to observe the witnesses rather than to rely on an earlier arbitrator's decision. See Northern Indiana Public Service Co., 116 LA 426 (Gerard A. Fowler, 2001) ("I was not present for the hearing of the grievance presented by the clerical union and assumptions I might draw concerning the credibility of the witnesses or evidence in that matter would be nothing more than crass speculation").

(c) *Facts.* Cannelton Industries, Inc., 118 LA 1446 (Lawrence Roberts, 2003), shows how a modest difference in facts can be crucial. The dispute involved contracting out of bargaining unit work. The contract prohibited subcontracting of "repair and maintenance work" but permitted some subcontracting of "construction work." The line between the two categories, as one arbitrator put it, "is not a glaringly bright one." Several earlier awards had found disputed work ("laying down shot rock, filter paper, and crushed stones" in one case and "filling a slip" in another) to fall in the first category. The grievance before Arbitrator Roberts involved converting a general access road to use in coal hauling. Even though the work required "repair," the arbitrator concluded that it was closer to new construction and found that the earlier awards did not ban the subcontracting.

(d) *Contract language.* In Saint–Gobain Calmar, 118 LA 585 (Calvin William Sharpe, 2003), a 1989 award held that under Section 14(a) of the agreement management could remove "lead persons" from their positions without regard to their seniority. In 2002, the Company removed certain lead persons and reassigned them to a lower classification. Because the contract had changed in small but significant ways after the first case, Arbitrator Sharpe held that the earlier award did not require him to deny the new grievance.

3. Apart from these legal doctrines, a party can easily find itself in an awkward position if it adopts a different position in a new case. Regions Hospital, 118 LA 26 (Mario F. Bognanno, 2002), involved a dispute as to whether part-time pharmacists were inside or outside the bargaining unit. In 1994 the union successfully argued before Arbitrator Bognanno that only pharmacists who worked 32 or more hours per pay period were covered by the collective bargaining agreement. In this 2002 case, it argued that the unit included *all* pharmacists. Even though the hospital had become private after the first award, the arbitrator found that the earlier award still controlled, noting that "the Union took a position under the same contract language that it now seeks to avoid."

4. A multiplicity of prior arbitration awards may make it difficult to determine the "law," as in Boeing Satellite Systems, 119 LA 241 (Lionel Richman, 2003):

> The issue of the permissible area of subcontracting is one that has arisen time and again, for some 37 years, under the agreement between the Union and Hughes Aircraft Company, as well as its various successors. In this Arbitrator's award of January 5, 2001, he traced the history of many of the prior arbitration awards. In fact, since several arbitrators had heard more than one case, he began numbering them. (This will be Richman Award 5.) Not unexpectedly, each of the parties has cited the Arbitrator to a number of prior awards. The Union points to Richman Award 4, the Company points to Richman Award 2. It likewise cites Fellman Award 1, dismissing the grievance; and ignores Fellman Award 2, sustaining the grievance. The sole stranger in these proceedings is the award of Arbitrator Collins, dated October 1, 1994.

The Arbitrator has again reviewed the prior awards.

A NOTE ON ARBITRAL SECOND GUESSES AND THE COURTS

Even when the issues, facts, and parties are the same, arbitrators may decline to follow an earlier award in certain circumstances. Arbitrator Roy Ray listed these circumstances in General Portland Cement Co., 62–2 ARB ¶ 8611 (1962):

> (1) The previous award was clearly an instance of bad judgment; (2) the decision was made without benefit of some important and relevant facts; (3) the decision was based upon an obvious and substantial error of fact or law; (4) a full and fair hearing was not afforded in the prior case.

Other arbitrators use different descriptions for the same point: a second arbitrator is not bound by a decision that was procedurally flawed or substantively insupportable.

The best-known example of each arbitrator's authority to second-guess previous arbitrators is the case of W. R. Grace and Co. v. Local Union No. 759, International Union of the United Rubber, Cork, Linoleum and Plastic Workers of America, 652 F.2d 1248 (5th Cir.1981), affirmed on other grounds, 461 U.S. 757, 103 S.Ct. 2177, 76 L.Ed.2d 298 (1983). Under pressure from the Equal Employment Opportunity Commission (EEOC), the employer signed a conciliation agreement that conflicted with the collective bargaining agreement's seniority provisions. When the union tried to arbitrate a seniority grievance arising from the employer's actions under the conciliation agreement, the employer sought and received an injunction against the arbitration; the district court also issued a declaratory judgment that the conciliation agreement bound all parties. While the union's appeal of that decision was pending, the Supreme Court in another case approved seniority provisions like those the EEOC challenged. The Fifth Circuit therefore reversed the district court's decision, and several grievances went to arbitration.

The first grievance to be decided involved an employee laid off while the district court's order was in effect. The arbitrator agreed with the union that the employer had breached the agreement's seniority clause. Because the employer acted in good faith pursuant to the court order, however, the arbitrator felt "[i]t would be inequitable and manifestly unfair to penalize the Employer under these circumstances." Other grievances went to a second arbitrator who declined to follow the first award. He ruled that the first arbitrator had no jurisdiction to consider the "fairness" question because the Agreement limited the arbitrator to "the interpretation and application of the express provision or provisions of this Agreement." The second arbitrator therefore sustained the grievances. The employer then challenged the second award in court. The Fifth Circuit, in an opinion by Judge Jerre Williams, a former labor arbitrator, held that the first arbitrator exceeded his contractual jurisdiction; the second arbitrator was therefore free to ignore that award. The Court of Appeals ordered enforcement of the second award.

The Supreme Court affirmed, but only on the question of enforceability of the second award. It specifically rejected the Fifth Circuit's suggestion that the validity of the first award was the crucial question. In other words, whether or not the second arbitrator correctly decided that the first award did not bind him, the district court should have enforced the second award if it drew its essence from the collective agreement.

Suppose two arbitrators reach plausible but conflicting results on identical disputes under the same contract. If each losing party challenges its loss in court, what should the court do? Enforce both awards? Neither? The best one? The Supreme Court in *W. R. Grace* hinted that the courts should enforce both. *Compare* Connecticut Light & Power Co. v. Local 420, International Brotherhood of Electrical Workers, 718 F.2d 14, 21 (2d Cir.1983) (favoring the "better reasoned" and "more persuasive" award) *with* Trailways Lines, Inc. v. Trailways, Inc. Joint Council, 624 F.Supp. 880, 884–85 (E.D.Mo.1985), aff'd on other grounds, 807 F.2d 1416 (8th Cir.1986) (rather than selecting the better award, the court should "refuse to sustain a later contrary award which for no legal reason ignores the 'final and binding' provision of the contract as applied to a prior award which draws its essence from the contract") *with* Northern Indiana Public Service Company v. United Steelworkers of America, 243 F.3d 345 (7th Cir. 2001) ("While the awards are opposite in interpreting the same issue involving different bargaining units, we concur with the second arbitrator's statement that both awards draw their essence from the contract").

In a vigorous dissent to the Eighth Circuit's denial of a rehearing *en banc* in *Connecticut Light*, Judge Heaney argued that arbitrators are free to disregard earlier awards; the district court, he asserted, should therefore have enforced the second award. The Court of Appeals for the District of Columbia adopted Judge Heaney's approach in Hotel Association of Washington, D.C., Inc. v. Hotel and Restaurant Employees Union, Local 25, 963 F.2d 388 (D.C.Cir.1992) (absent a contract clause making an arbitration decision binding on later arbitrators, the extent to which the second arbitrator is bound is itself a matter of interpretation for that arbitrator), and a majority of the circuit courts of appeal now hold that position. A good recent example is International Union v. Dana Corp., 278 F.3d 548 (6th Cir. 2002). An employer sought to vacate an arbitration award because the decision differed from that of a previous arbitrator who interpreted the same provision. The Sixth Circuit concluded : "[w]e adopt the reasoning of the majority of other circuits to have examined this issue and hold that absent a contractual provision to the contrary, the preclusive effect of an earlier arbitration award is to be determined by the arbitrator." The court also held that a clause making the arbitrator's decision "final and binding" on both parties "only requires that an arbitrator not reopen an earlier arbitration decision."

Notes and Questions

1. Will an arbitration award preclude a claim or issue in the context of a new incident? That may depend on the wording of the award. If the award is specifically prospective, it controls subsequent cases with *material* factual similarity. In Oil, Chemical and Atomic Workers International Union, Local 4–16000 v. Ethyl Corp., 644 F.2d 1044 (5th Cir. Unit A, 1981), an arbitrator found that the employer violated a clause limiting the use of salaried employees to perform hourly-employees' jobs. He ordered the company to "desist from violations such as that involved here." When the union sued to prevent later alleged violations, the Court of Appeals ruled that it had the right to provide "the aid of the judicial strong arm in preventing" the Company from similar violations. It remanded the case, however, for a determination of whether the appropriate next step in the new case was an injunction action before the District Court or deferral to an arbitrator. On remand, the District Court declined to decide the underlying issue and sent the matter to arbitration. The Court of Appeals affirmed, 703 F.2d 933 (1983).

If the award restricts itself to one incident, however, subsequent arbitrators have to determine for themselves whether they are bound by the first award. The parties in Oil, Chemical and Atomic Workers Local 4–367 v. Rohm & Haas, Texas, Inc., 677 F.2d 492 (5th Cir.1982), asked an arbitrator to resolve a particular overtime pay dispute, and the arbitrator expressly declined to make a prospective ruling. When the union later sought to enforce the award to stop later alleged violations, the Court of Appeals held that the award's future effect "itself is a proper subject for arbitration."

What if the award is *neither* specifically prospective *nor* specifically retrospective? Can an award be "inherently prospective?" See Boston Shipping Association v. International Longshoremen's Association, 659 F.2d 1 (1st Cir.1981).

2.   In a case almost as complex as *W. R. Grace*, Arbitrator Howard Bard declined to follow a previous award that, he said, mischaracterized and refused to follow a still earlier award. McQuay–Perfex, Inc., 93 LA 1289 (1990). Could a fourth arbitrator find that Arbitrator Bard's award exceeded his jurisdiction, showed bad judgment, or committed an obvious error of fact or law, and follow the second award? Reread the last three paragraphs of *Pan American Refining Corp., supra.*

3.   What types of errors in the first award will justify a second arbitrator's refusal to give it preclusive effect? See, *e.g.*, General Shale Products Corp., 60 LA 387 (William H. Mills, 1973) (reasoning of earlier award was unsound); International Paper Co., 60 LA 447 (Roy R. Ray, 1973) ("clearly erroneous" standard); Henry Vogt Machine Co., 68–2 ARB ¶ 8650 (Vernon L. Stouffer, 1968) (declining to adopt reasons and findings "with which he could not in good conscience agree").

4.   Last year the Teamsters filed a grievance with United Parcel Service protesting the company's assignment of certain overtime work to junior employees. Just before the scheduled arbitration hearing, the union withdrew the grievance. A similar case has now arisen. Does the union's withdrawal of the first grievance bind the arbitrator in the second grievance? Suppose that instead the parties had settled the first grievance with a small payment to the by-passed senior employees. Would that settlement bind the arbitrator? See the Grenig chapter cited in footnote 1.

5.   Changed circumstances and even changed attitudes may deprive earlier decisions of preclusive force. Consider Superior Coffee & Foods, 103 LA 609 (Reginald Alleyne, 1994). In a grievance challenging the company's discharge of an employee for sexual harassment, the union relied on arbitration decisions (involving other parties) overturning discharges based on far more serious misconduct. Arbitrator Alleyne rejected those holdings:

> I find the cited cases on sexual harassment not in keeping with current arbitral thinking on the subject. They are 1986 and 1987 decisions, and both societal and judicial views on the seriousness of sexual harassment have undergone dramatic change between then and now. * * * I believe that [the cited decisions] are no longer valid precedents, assuming they ever were, and I will not follow them.

6.   The mere passage of time will not moot earlier decisions. In Arch of Illinois, Captain Mine, 104 LA 1102 (Gerald Cohen, 1995), the employer sought to discount several old decisions relied on by the union. The arbitrator rejected that argument:

> The Company has advanced a number of arguments that deserve consideration. The first is that the cases cited by the Union in support of its position are all quite old, many of the cases dated in the late 1970s. The Company is correct. However, the contract language that we are considering in this situation is identical today to the contract language in the late 1970s. There has been, literally, no change in the language. It is the same today as it was in, say, 1978. * * * In every one of the other cases that the Union has cited, eleven in number, the contract language has not varied.

7. This section dealt only with the impact of arbitration awards in subsequent arbitrations. For a thorough analysis of the impact arbitration awards have (and should have) in later court cases, see Hiroshi Motomura, *Arbitration and Collateral Estoppel: Using Preclusion to Shape Procedural Choices*, 63 Tulane Law Review 29 (1988).

3. THE EFFECT OF PRIOR ADMINISTRATIVE OR JUDICIAL DETERMINATIONS

Somewhat different considerations apply when a party asserts that an administrative or judicial determination precludes the other's claim or assertion of an issue in arbitration. See generally, Note, *Res Judicata/Collateral Estoppel Effect of a Court Determination in Subsequent Arbitration*, 45 Albany Law Review 1029, 1048–56 (1981). One serious problem is that in most such proceedings the parties will not be the same. Under the typical collective agreement, the only parties are the union and the employer. In unemployment compensation and workers' compensation disputes, on the other hand, the employer and the individual employee are the parties; the union has no formal standing. In criminal cases, the state and the employee are parties. In private suits, the union and the employer may or may not be the parties. In NLRB proceedings initiated by a union, the Board treats the union as a party even after the General Counsel issues a complaint against the employer. Although the charging party retains some rights to participate in subsequent proceedings, the General Counsel may settle the case without the charging party's approval. On the other hand, as an aggrieved "person" the union may seek judicial review of the Board's decision.

More importantly, the issues and standards are likely to differ. "Just cause" in a discharge arbitration, for example, does not mean the same thing as "misconduct attributable to the employee" in an unemployment compensation case. The award of unemployment compensation benefits thus does not resolve the issue of whether the employer breached the agreement by firing the employee. Moreover, the administrative process in unemployment hearings often lacks arbitration's ability to discover and develop evidence. So too with burden of proof problems. In a discipline case, for example, the employer bears the burden of proving just cause by a "preponderance of the evidence" or "clear and convincing evidence." In a criminal law case, the state must prove the defendant's guilt "beyond a reasonable doubt." A "not guilty" verdict thus does not prove that the employee was innocent, and an arbitrator may sustain a discharge for conduct for which the jury refused to convict. See, for example, Associated Grocers of Alabama, Inc., 83 LA 261 (James Odom, 1984). For further discussion of these issues in the context of disciplinary grievances, see Chapter VII, Section B.3.

For these reasons, arbitrators usually do not treat as conclusive the determinations of administrative agencies or courts. A good example is City of Oak Creek, 90 LA 710 (Rose Marie Baron, 1988). The arbitrator refused to accept as binding a court decision denying the employees the reinstatement they sought. The union was not involved in the suit, she noted, so there was no identity of parties. Moreover, the suit did not raise the breach of contract claim, so there was no identity of issues. Indeed, it was not even clear that the court would have considered the contractual issue had the employees raised it. Similarly, the arbitrator in Triborough Bridge and Tunnel Authority, 92 LA 684 (Steven J. Goldsmith, 1989), refused to give collateral estoppel effect to an administrative agency's determination. The agency found that the employer did not violate the state labor relations act by failing to negotiate a work rule. Negotiability and breach of contract are separate issues, said the arbitrator, and the agency did not construe the contract. See generally, Hill and Sinicropi, *supra* footnote 1, at 369–85.

In some situations, though, employees may have to choose which road to follow. In Central Pennsylvania Institute of Technology, 114 LA 513 (John Joseph D'Eletto, 2000), the school demoted two employees and eliminated the job of a third. The employees exercised their statutory right to take their cases to the school's Joint Operating Committee, which ruled against them. Arbitrator D'Eletto found that the Committee evaluated all the relevant issues and ruled that the grievants had "elected a remedy under the School Code and they are barred from raising the substantive issues previously litigated now."

Prior administrative or judicial determinations may be influential even when they are not determinative. In Hill Air Force Base, Utah, 114 LA 1670 (Paul D. Staudohar, 2000), the employer had fired an employee for off-duty misconduct, having consensual sex with a male minor in a public bathroom. The minor was 16 years and seven months old, just five months shy of the legal age of consent in Utah. In a plea bargain, he pled guilty to sexual assault on a minor. Instead of finding him guilty, however, the judge deferred adjudication and placed him on probation for seven years. If he did not commit a similar offense during that period, the conviction would never be entered. The lenient sentence impressed the arbitrator: "There is no doubt that the Grievant exercised dreadfully poor judgment in his actions. But he would not have gotten off with probation had the encounter been more serious from the standpoint of the criminal law." In light of the court's evaluation of the off-duty offense as relatively minor, the lack of any evidence showing a nexus with his employment, and other evidence showing the grievant to be a good employee, the arbitrator found that the discharge was not for just cause.

Notes and Questions

1. You can easily understand, can't you, why an *acquittal* of a criminal charge would not bind an arbitrator in a later grievance over the same conduct? Surely, then, dismissal of criminal charges because of technical defect should have no greater force. In Bruno's Food Fair, Inc., 104 LA 306 (William S. Hart, 1995), the employer discharged the grievant for theft. She was found guilty in the trial court but prevailed in an appeal because the warrant used to obtain certain evidence was faulty. The union argued that "Grievant was exonerated of the charges against her in the eyes of the

court." Arbitrator Hart rejected the union's argument because "charges brought in the courts are for the purpose of enforcing applicable laws whereas the disciplinary process applied by the employer is for the purpose of enforcing the terms of the Labor Agreement."

2. But what about a criminal *conviction*? Because the state had to meet a higher burden of proof, the conviction should resolve the issue in arbitration, shouldn't it? In *dicta*, several arbitrators have said that neither a conviction nor an acquittal would bind the arbitrator, *e.g.*, New York State Department of Correctional Services, 69 LA 344 (Daniel Kornblum, 1977), and Meyer's Bakery of Blytheville, Inc., 70–2 ARB ¶ 8582 (LeRoy Autrey, 1970). Do you agree? For the other side of the argument, see City of Lebanon v. District Council 89, American Federation of State, County and Municipal Employees, 36 Pa.Cmwlth. 442, 388 A.2d 1116 (1978), in which the court overturned an arbitration award because the arbitrator refused to accept a jury's finding that the grievants committed the acts for which they were discharged. Even in such a case, however, the jury's finding of facts would not settle the just cause question. At first glance, a guilty plea seems conclusive evidence, but is it really? Might someone plead guilty for a reason other than actual guilt?

3. After an internal investigation of suspected drug sales by employees on its premises, Teddy Bear Toy Company called in the police. The district attorney eventually prosecuted three employees for selling marijuana at work. John Smith pled guilty and received probation. Robin Jones pled not guilty but was convicted and sentenced to probation. Jane Adams pled *nolo contendere* and was placed in a pre-verdict diversionary program; if she successfully completes the program, her criminal record will be expunged. The employer fired all three. The union has taken all three subsequent grievances to you for a decision. The employer argues that the criminal proceedings bar relitigation of the employees' guilt. How would you rule? *Compare* Means Services, Inc., 81 LA 1213, 1216 (Llewellyn E. Slade, 1983); Carlisle Corp., 87 LA 99, 102 (Marvin J. Feldman, 1986); and United States Postal Service, 89 LA 495 (Dennis R. Nolan, 1987).

4. There are exceptions to the principle that previous administrative or court decisions have neither *res judicata* nor collateral estoppel effect. In Los Angeles County Public Social Services Department, 93 LA 164 (Anita Christine Knowlton, 1988), the arbitrator found that a county was estopped from challenging the arbitrability of a grievance after it had obtained a court finding of arbitrability in a similar case. If an employee argues one position in court and the opposite in arbitration, the arbitrator may well apply collateral estoppel, lest the employee "have his cake and eat it too," Loma Corp., 1975 ARB ¶ 8068 (Henry L. Sisk, 1975).

Chapter VII

THE SUBJECTS OF LABOR ARBITRATION

This Chapter surveys the most significant issues considered by labor arbitrators. The Chapter begins with decisions concerning arbitrability. In a minority of cases, before an arbitrator can address the substance of the grievance, the arbitrator must first consider whether the particular grievance is subject to arbitration under the terms of the collective bargaining agreement. The remainder of the Chapter deals with the most common substantive issues considered by arbitrators. Consideration of substantive issues begins with discipline and discharge, by far the largest single category of cases decided by arbitrators. The Chapter then looks at two pervasive themes that affect analysis of other contract interpretation issues—management rights (the claim that an employer's action does not violate the agreement because it is among those rights the contract reserved to the employer) and past practice (the claim that an employer's action violates the contract because it is inconsistent with the parties' past practices). Finally, the Chapter explores a series of discrete substantive issues—seniority, wages and hours, fringe benefits, subcontracting, and union security.

Data reported by the Federal Mediation and Conciliation Service for fiscal year 2004 suggest the distribution of some of these substantive issues within the arbitration caseload. Thirty-nine percent of cases involved discipline and discharge, 5% wages and hours, 5% seniority, 4% fringe benefits and 2% subcontracting.[1]

The topics included in the Chapter illustrate not only the rich diversity of issues resolved in arbitration but also wide variations in the extent to which the text of the agreement plays a significant role in the arbitrator's analysis. Questions of past practice, for example, sometimes

---

1. The Federal Mediation and Conciliation Service publishes statistics regarding its labor arbitration caseload at its web site <www.fmcs.gov>. The statistics are drawn from arbitrators' reports of closed cases and are therefore likely incomplete. Prior to 2003, statistics generally indicated that discipline and discharge cases represented approximately half or more of the FMCS arbitration caseload.

are arbitrated without any reference whatsoever to the contract's text. In discipline and discharge cases the arbitrator may obtain no more guidance from the contract than the directive that employees not be disciplined without "just cause." On the other hand, disputes about such issues as wages, hours, and fringe benefits often require detailed textual analysis of complex written provisions.

A. ARBITRABILITY[1]

1. INTRODUCTION

Arbitrability is the jurisdictional question of whether the parties' agreement grants the arbitrator authority to hear the particular dispute. Courts may consider arbitrability issues in an action to compel arbitration or an action seeking a declaratory judgment that a dispute is not subject to arbitration. The Supreme Court has said that if the issue presented is one of substantive arbitrability, the court is to decide the matter and not simply refer the issue of arbitrability to an arbitrator. The Court, however, said that issues of procedural arbitrability should be decided by arbitrators.[2] See *supra* Chapter III.B.

Generally, arbitrability issues comprise only a small part of arbitrators' work. In fiscal year 2004, only 4% of the cases reported to the Federal Mediation and Conciliation Service raised an issue of arbitrability. Of the arbitrability issues heard by arbitrators that year, 64% concerned procedural arbitrability; 19% substantive arbitrability and 16% both substantive and procedural arbitrability.

Why is it that arbitrators hear issues of substantive arbitrability despite the Supreme Court's directive that courts should not leave substantive arbitrability questions for arbitrators to decide? There are a variety of circumstances in which a substantive arbitrability issue could be presented to an arbitrator. A party may, for example, choose to raise its substantive arbitrability argument before an arbitrator rather than incur the costs and delay of litigating the matter or resisting arbitration. The parties may have agreed in their collective bargaining agreement to vest the power to decide arbitrability issues in the arbitrator rather than

---

1. Bibliographic Suggestions: Elkouri & Elkouri, How Arbitration Works, 277–290 (Alan Miles Ruben, ed., 6th ed. 2003); Fairweather's Practice and Procedure in Labor Arbitration 116 (Ray J. Schoonhoven, ed., 3d ed. 1999); Arnold M. Zack and Richard I. Bloch, Labor Agreement in Negotiation and Arbitration 160 (2d ed. 1995); Richard I. Bloch, *Arbitration: Time Limits and Continuing Violations*, 96 Michigan Law Review 2384 (1998); Harvey A. Nathan and Sara McLaurin Green, *Challenges to Arbitrability*, Labor and Employment Arbitration (Tim Bornstein, Ann Gosline and Marc Greenbaum, eds., 2003); Carlton J. Snow,

Contract Interpretation, The Common Law of the Workplace: The Views of Arbitrators §§ 2.22–2.23 (Theodore J. St. Antoine, ed. 1998).

2. Substantive arbitrability issues address whether the dispute is one of the types of disputes the parties have agreed to arbitrate. Procedural arbitrability issues concern whether the dispute is not arbitrable because a contractual precondition to arbitration, such as a time limitation, has not been satisfied. For a further exploration of the subtleties in this distinction, see *supra* Chapter III.B.3.

a court.[3] Or a party ordered to arbitrate by a court may still want to raise questions of substantive arbitrability before the arbitrator. Such a party may contend that the court has only determined that the dispute is arguably arbitrable and that an arbitrator may still find that the dispute is not in fact arbitrable. (See *supra* Question 3 in the Notes and Questions following *American Manufacturing* in Chapter III.B.2.)

If arbitrators hear substantive and procedural arbitrability issues, how will they decide them? The Supreme Court, perhaps never anticipating the volume of substantive arbitrability issues that would come before arbitrators, has provided no guidance to arbitrators about how to analyze substantive arbitrability. Do judicial standards for substantive arbitrability also govern arbitrators? Further, although the Supreme Court expected arbitrators to decide procedural arbitrability issues, there too it never articulated an analytical framework for their resolution. This section, therefore, addresses how arbitrators decide issues of procedural and substantive arbitrability.

2.   PROCEDURAL ARBITRABILITY

YOKOHAMA TIRE CORP.
117 LA 509 (Stanley H. Sergent, 2002).*

STATEMENT OF THE CASE

Yokohama Tire Corporation ("Company") and Local Union No. 1023 of the United Steelworkers of America ("Union") are parties to a collective bargaining agreement which became effective July 24, 1997. The Agreement governs the wages, hours, and other terms and conditions of employment of members of the bargaining unit employed at the Company's Salem, Virginia, plant. It also provides for a grievance procedure culminating in final and binding arbitration as the mechanism to be used to resolve any disputes concerning the interpretation or application of its terms.

[Following workplace injuries, the grievant was on a leave of absence and was receiving workers' compensation benefits. On July 30, 2001, the Company informed the grievant that he was being terminated from employment because it had no jobs that the grievant could perform in light of a physician's statement that the grievant could not work more than four hours a day nor lift more than ten pounds. On August 30, 2001, the Union submitted a grievance alleging that the discharge was not for just cause. The Union maintained that the grievant should have been placed instead on a leave of absence. It also contended that he regained his ability to work shortly after his termination.]

---

3. United Steelworkers v. Warrior and Gulf Navigation, 363 U.S. 574, 583 n. 7, 80 S.Ct. 1347, 1353 n. 7, 4 L.Ed.2d 1409 (1960), *supra* Chapter III.B.2.

* Reprinted with permission from *Labor Arbitration Reporter–Labor Arbitration Re-* ports, 117 LA 509. Copyright 2004 by The Bureau of National Affairs, Inc. (800–372–1033) <http://www.bna.com>.

Article V

Grievance Procedure

Section 1—Representation and Responsibility

The supervisor and employee will consult directly on any dissatisfaction relating to the application or interpretation of this Agreement. * * * The supervisor will follow through in such matter and attempt to adjust it, in the event a satisfactory adjustment is not made, then the employee or employees may submit his or their complaint in writing as a grievance, but this must be done within five (5) working days of the time when the employee reasonably should have had knowledge of the occurrence or event, otherwise, the grievance or complaint shall be considered dropped and not for further consideration. When filing a grievance, the grievant will give all facts known, and the Company will give in writing a detailed reply in all steps of the grievance procedure.

Article VI

Arbitration

The arbitrator ... shall have the power to make determinations of fact of the Agreement alleged to have been violated, so long as the grievance is submitted to him in accordance with the provisions, limitations and procedures specified in this Agreement. No arbitrator shall have the jurisdiction or authority to add to, take from, nullify, or modify any of the terms of this Agreement....

Article X

Seniority

Section 10—Leaves of Absence

(c) An employee with seniority who receives workers' compensation payments shall accumulate seniority during the period covered by compensation payments. If at the end of such period he is physically unable to return to work on [sic] his classification or in another classification to which he might be eligible to transfer, he shall be placed on a leave of absence without pay for an additional period not to exceed three (3) years during which he shall furnish satisfactory medical evidence of continuing disability.

DISCUSSION AND DECISION

A. *Procedural Issue*

Prior to considering the merits of this dispute a threshold issue of arbitrability which was raised by the Company must be addressed. It concerns the Company's argument that the grievance should be dismissed as procedurally non-arbitral because it was not filed within the five day time limit set out in Article V, Section 1 of the bargaining agreement. Consequently, the issue of arbitrability must be addressed in order to determine whether or not the arbitrator has the authority to consider the merits of the dispute.

As a beginning point in analyzing the timeliness issue it should be noted that it is axiomatic that adherence to the time limits contained in a collective bargaining agreement for the filing and processing of grievances is a condition precedent to arbitration. Arbitrators and the judiciary have repeatedly recognized that timeliness is a jurisdictional issue based on the fact that the parties have agreed to withhold from an arbitrator any jurisdiction or authority to consider grievances that are not timely filed. Therefore, where the contract specifies time limitations for the filing of grievances, a grievance submitted outside those time limits is not arbitrable, absent waiver, estoppel, or fraud. As explained by authors Elkouri and Elkouri in their authoritative treatise *How Arbitration Works*, 276 (BNA 5th Ed., (1997)):

> If the agreement does contain clear time limits for the filing and prosecuting grievances, failure to observe them will generally result in dismissal of the grievance if the failure is protested. Thus, the practical effect of late filing in many instances is that the merits of the dispute are never decided.

Similar reasoning has been expressed by other authorities:

> When a grievance has not been filed within the time limits set forth in the collective bargaining agreement the arbitrator generally will dismiss the claim as non-arbitrable unless the opposing party has waived this procedural defect. Since the parties have limited the cases which they agree to arbitrate according to the terms of their agreement, the arbitrator has no authority to hear a claim presented too late because it has not properly entered the procedure and hence has not reached the arbitration "step." Arbitrators have supported the dismissal ... on the ground that the arbitrator must receive authority to hear the grievant's claim from the agreement....

Fairweather, *Practice and [Procedure] in Labor Arbitration*, 101 (BNA 2nd Ed., 1982).

Notwithstanding the deference which must be accorded the time limits contained in a collective bargaining agreement, arbitrators are frequently reluctant to dismiss a grievance without reaching the merits of a dispute where the procedural shortcoming is not clearly proved, where it results from innocent inadvertence or excusable neglect, and where the opposing party is not injured thereby either in [its] ability to present its case or in the extent of damages that are suffered. While it is understood that arbitrators cannot exceed the authority vested in them by the Agreement by ignoring or overlooking clear procedural violations which deny them jurisdiction, they do often favor arbitration by interpreting ambiguous facts or contract language in a liberal manner that permits the merits to be addressed.

The timeliness issue is governed by several provisions of the collective bargaining agreement. First of all, Article V, Section 1 of the

Agreement states that grievances must be filed in writing "within five (5) working days" or else the grievance "shall be considered dropped and not for further consideration." * * *

Another contract provision that governs the timeliness issue is Letter #24, which became a part of the collective bargaining agreement in 1994. The letter memorialized the parties' commitment to abide strictly by the time limits of the grievance procedure. It states, in pertinent part, as follows:

> Effective upon the ratification of the new agreement the parties agree to strictly enforce the time limits of the grievance procedure unless the time limits are extended by mutual agreement and so noted on the grievance form.

This letter, of course, has the same force and effect as any other provision of the collective bargaining agreement.

Finally, Article VI confers jurisdiction on an arbitrator to decide the merits of a dispute concerning the interpretation or application of the Agreement only if "the grievance is submitted to him in accordance with the *provisions, limitations and procedures* specified in this Agreement." [Emphasis added.]

Based on the foregoing contract provisions, it is abundantly clear that the Agreement does specify a clear and unequivocal time limitation for the filing of a grievance and bars the processing of a grievance if the time limit has not been met. Moreover, the fact that the instant grievance was not filed within the requisite time limit is beyond legitimate dispute. The grievant was terminated on July 31, 2001, and his termination was the "occurrence or event" which gave rise to his right to file a grievance. Inexplicably, he did not file his grievance until August 30, 2001, well beyond the prescribed period, and there was no "mutual agreement . . . so noted on the grievance form" extending the time limits in this case, as required by Letter #24 in the collective bargaining agreement. To the contrary, at each step of the grievance procedure the Company reiterated that the grievance is untimely. * * *

The Union does not dispute the fact that the grievance was filed well beyond the date that the grievant was terminated. It argues, nonetheless, that the grievance is not untimely because the violation alleged in the grievance is a "continuing" one. This argument is without merit both as a matter of law and of common sense. A "continuing" violation is one that recurs on a regular basis, such as to provide a new cause of action or grievance for each occurrence, as opposed to a single, isolated and completed transaction. An employment action that is more discrete and final than discharge is hardly conceivable. Moreover, as the Company has aptly noted, to hold that a discharge is susceptible to the application of a "continuing violation" analysis would eviscerate the impact of every limitations period of every kind.

A "continuing" violation is one that is ongoing and repetitive in nature. A classic example of such a violation is one involving an Employer's regular and recurring failure to pay an employee the proper rate of pay for the work he is performing. In that type of situation, every day that the employee is not being properly compensated is a new violation under the contract and the grievance is therefore continuing in nature, although relief would ordinarily be limited to the time of filing. In contrast, because a discharge involves a single, isolated, and completed transaction, judicial decisions uniformly hold that they are not susceptible to a "continuing violation" theory.

The National Labor Relations Board has followed this same line of reasoning in denying the applicability of the "continuing violations" doctrine to discharge decisions in unfair labor practice cases. Likewise, arbitrators have found that discharges and layoffs are not continuing violations.

In summary, the grievant's employment with the Company came to an end on July 31, 2001, when he was terminated as a result of his physical inability to perform work at the plant. It was that event which gave rise to this grievance and any legal claims that he had against the Company matured at that time. Although the collective bargaining agreement provides for a five day time limit for filing a grievance, he did not file it until thirty days later. Consequently, as a result of the late filing this arbitrator has no jurisdiction or authority to consider the merits of the grievance. Accordingly, it must be dismissed as untimely and non-arbitrable.

AWARD

In accordance with the foregoing opinion and for the reasons set forth therein the grievance must be dismissed as untimely and non-arbitrable.

Notes and Questions

1. Consider the variety of interpretive problems that may arise even in a simple case of procedural arbitrability concerning the timeliness of a grievance. When a contract calls for submission of a grievance within a specified number of "days," does it mean calendar days or working days? From what point is the time measured? From the date of the employer's announcement of its policy or from the date that policy has a detrimental impact on an employee? Is the time measured from when the action occurred, when the union first learned of it, or when the union should have learned of it? Assuming that the parties do not offer evidence of other contract language or bargaining history suggesting the meaning of these contract terms, on what basis is an arbitrator to decide such questions?

2. What purposes are the parties trying to accomplish when they establish time limits for the submission of grievances? Why do parties to collective bargaining agreements set time limits for the submission of grievances that are so much shorter than typical statutes of limitation? While statutes of limitations usually are measured in numbers of years, even the limitations period for unfair labor practice charges submitted to the

National Labor Relations Board is six months. Why would the parties in *Yokohama Tire* have agreed to a five-day limit?

3.   In *Yokohama Tire*, Article X, Section 10(c) of the parties' agreement, quoted in the arbitrator's award, seems to protect from discharge an employee with a workplace injury if he is able to show that, within three years, he recovered from his injury. This grievant though fails to receive the protection of the contract language. Does this strike you as unfair? If so, is it the arbitrator's job to remedy the unfairness? If the grievant doesn't have a remedy in arbitration, does he have one elsewhere? See materials on the duty of fair representation in Chapter III.A. *supra*.

4.   Arbitrator Sergent notes that arbitrators generally interpret ambiguous time limits in collective bargaining agreements "in a liberal manner that permits the merits to be addressed." Why would this be so? Is there a reason why arbitrators should bring a presumption either way to this interpretive task? An arbitrator's discretion is obviously considerably more limited if the contract includes language, as in Letter #24 in *Yokohama Tire*, declaring that time limits will be strictly enforced or language that specifically says that untimely grievances are considered to have been waived.

5.   Arbitrator Sergent acknowledges the existence of the continuing violation theory but finds it inapplicable to a discharge grievance.

(a) Why should an employer action that has a continuing impact upon employees ever be subject to arbitration months or years later despite contractual time limits for filing grievances?

(b) If the continuing violation theory is ever appropriate, why is it appropriate in wage payment cases but not in discharge cases? See Richard I. Bloch, *supra* footnote 1.

(c) In wage payment cases, when arbitrators permit a claim to be heard under the continuing violation theory, they typically limit retroactive remedies only to wages paid within the contractual time limit for the filing of grievances. Does hearing the grievance but imposing such a remedial limitation fully vindicate the employer's reasons for having a short time limit for the submission of grievances?

6.   Should the continuing violation theory allow a union to challenge an employer's layoff as long as the employee remains on layoff? Centel Business Systems, 90 LA 172, 173 (Hy Fish, 1987). Should a union have to challenge a no-beard policy at the time it is adopted or may it wait until the policy has an adverse effect upon an employee? Gulf South Beverages, Inc., 87 LA 688, 689 (John F. Caraway, 1986).

7.   An arbitrator may find that the contract does not explicitly state any time limitation for the submission of grievances or that the time limitations are applicable only to other categories of grievances. In such cases, is an arbitrator to permit a grievance regardless of how long after the occurrence the grievance is submitted? If instead the arbitrator should impose a limitation of reasonableness, as might a court applying the doctrine of laches, how is the meaning of reasonableness determined? Compare Custom Cartage Services Division, 111 LA 353 (Aaron S. Wolff, 1998) (permitting a grievance to be submitted ten years after failure to make a pension contribution) and Saks Fifth Avenue, 118 LA 1398 (Robert Herzog, 2003) (permitting

arbitration of a change in commission rates seven months after the change), with Nashville Gas Co., 96 LA 897 (Dennis R. Nolan, 1991) (holding untimely a grievance submitted nine months after the employer's adoption of a policy on outside work) and Aerofin Corp., 98 LA 582 (Dennis R. Nolan, 1991) (grievance submitted four years after a change in job duties was untimely).

3. SUBSTANTIVE ARBITRABILITY

Problem

Andrew Dailey is employed as a maintenance worker at Sci–Fi Industries and is represented by the Maintenance Workers Union. The contract between Sci–Fi and the Union includes the following provisions:

Article I. Management Rights. The Company shall have, among others, the right to hire new employees, to direct the working force * * * to decide the methods, schedules and standards of production, including the means and processes of manufacture. All other rights of management that it has by law are also expressly reserved, even though not enumerated above, unless they are limited by the provisions of this Agreement.

Article II. Arbitration. The rights of management enumerated in Article I, and all other rights of management not limited by this Agreement, are not subject to the arbitration provisions of this Agreement.

Article III. Grievances. The Union may file a grievance on behalf of any employee who claims a violation of rights under this Agreement. [Following compliance with three steps of a grievance procedure] grievances may be submitted to arbitration.

Maintenance employees at Sci–Fi are required to supply their own hand tools. The Company provides a locker in which employees may leave their hand tools overnight and on weekends. Dailey left his tools in the locker overnight and returned in the morning to discover that someone had broken into the plant, opened the locker, and removed the lock from Dailey's tool box. All of Dailey's tools, valued at $850, were taken. Dailey's supervisor told him to purchase replacement tools and the Company would reimburse him. When Dailey presented his receipt for the replacement tools to the Plant Manager he was told that the Company had no policy for replacing employee tools and that it would not reimburse Dailey.

The Union filed a grievance on Dailey's behalf, alleging that the Company was responsible for replacing the tools. The Union alleged that, in the past, the Company had lent employees tools to replace those that were lost or broken. The Union's grievance did not cite any explicit written provision in the Agreement.

The grievance was processed through the first three steps of the grievance procedure and the parties selected an arbitrator.

Notes and Questions

1. At the arbitration hearing, the Company, for the first time in the grievance process, asserts that the grievance is not arbitrable under the Agreement.

(a) The Company announces at the hearing that it is unwilling to arbitrate the issue of substantive arbitrability. Should the arbitrator decide the issue of arbitrability despite the employer's objection? Denver Public Schools, 88 LA 507 (Thomas L. Watkins, 1986).

(b) Assume instead that the employer raises the arbitrability issue for the first time at the hearing and asks the arbitrator to find that the grievance is not arbitrable. Should the arbitrator hold that the Company waived its objections to arbitrability by not raising the issue earlier in the grievance process? Compare Akal Security, 115 LA 1121 (Colman R. Lalka, 2001) (waiver), with Keebler Co., 118 LA 326 (William H. Holley, Jr., 2003) (no waiver).

2. Assume that the arbitrator has decided to resolve the dispute about arbitrability.

(a) Should the arbitrator, at the same hearing, consider the merits of the Union's grievance? Or should the arbitrator instead issue a decision on arbitrability and then, if the grievance is arbitrable, schedule another hearing on the merits? Would different circumstances compel a different answer to this question? If so, what circumstances? See Elkouri & Elkouri, *supra* footnote 1, at 287–289. As an advocate for an employer or for a union, what circumstances would warrant your requesting a bifurcated, or nonbifurcated, hearing?

(b) If you were an employer claiming that the dispute was not substantively arbitrable, should you be concerned that the arbitrator has a personal financial interest in finding the dispute arbitrable? If the arbitrator finds that it is arbitrable, the arbitrator will be paid for the additional hearing and study time to consider the dispute on the merits. In light of this conflict of interest, should you request that the arbitrator consider only the arbitrability issue and leave to another arbitrator the possible consideration of the issue on the merits? Or, do the costs and inefficiencies of using a second arbitrator warrant subordinating any concerns about conflict of interest?

(c) Does *Warrior & Gulf* require the arbitrator to consider the grievance presumptively arbitrable? Is *Warrior & Gulf* based on a belief that arbitrators have better procedures and greater expertise for contract interpretation, or based on a belief that labor peace is best furthered by having as many disputes as possible resolved in the arbitration process? The Supreme Court identified the former as the "principal rationale" of *Warrior & Gulf*. Wright v. Universal Maritime Service Corp., 525 U.S. 70, 78, 119 S.Ct. 391, 395, 142 L.Ed.2d 361 (1998). There is a disagreement among arbitrators regarding applicability to arbitrators of the *Warrior & Gulf* presumption. See Elkouri & Elkouri, *supra* footnote 1, at 286; Carlton J. Snow, *supra* footnote 1, § 2.22; and Harvey A. Nathan and Sara McLaurin Green, *supra* footnote 1, § 8.01[3].

(d) What evidence or arguments should the parties present to the arbitrator on the issue of arbitrability?

(e) Is it possible for the arbitrator to decide the arbitrability issue without considering the merits of the grievance? See Reyco Industries, Inc., 85 LA 1034 (Melvin L. Newmark, 1985).

(f) Absent a presumption, how should the arbitrator decide the arbitrability question?

(g) Disputes about employer liability for stolen employee tools are apparently commonplace. While some arbitrators have found employers liable on theories of negligence, bailment, or implicit contract, other arbitrators have found the dispute nonarbitrable or denied the grievance on the merits. See Elkouri & Elkouri, *supra* footnote 1, at 1169–1174.

3. If the Company arbitrates the grievance without raising any objection to arbitrability, should a court later allow the Company to challenge the arbitrator's award on the ground that the dispute was not arbitrable?

4. If the Company, in the arbitration proceeding, contests arbitrability and loses, may it later obtain judicial review of the arbitrator's arbitrability decision? If the answer to that question were "no," how would that affect a party's willingness to arbitrate a case in which it disputes arbitrability? Compare Van Waters & Rogers, Inc. v. Teamsters Local Union 70, 913 F.2d 736 (9th Cir.1990) (a party who contests arbitrability before an arbitrator and fails expressly to reserve the issue for later judicial consideration has waived judicial review of the arbitrability issue), with Teamsters, Local 249 v. Western Pennsylvania Motor Carriers Association, 574 F.2d 783, 786 (3d Cir.) (making jurisdictional arguments before a dispute resolution panel did not waive judicial review of the jurisdictional issue), cert. denied, 439 U.S. 828, 99 S.Ct. 102, 58 L.Ed.2d 122 (1978). In the commercial arbitration context, the Supreme Court has held that contesting arbitrability before an arbitrator does not constitute a waiver of judicial consideration of the arbitrability issue. First Options of Chicago, Inc. v. Kaplan, 514 U.S. 938, 115 S.Ct. 1920, 131 L.Ed.2d 985 (1995). See the following note for discussion of the issue of whether the Supreme Court's holding in *First Options* establishes precedent for labor, in addition to commercial, arbitration.

5. If a court subsequently undertakes judicial review of the arbitrator's arbitrability decision, what is the appropriate standard of review? Should the court assess arbitrability *de novo* with a presumption of arbitrability, as it would have had the arbitrability issue been raised in a court prior to arbitration? Or should the arbitrator's arbitrability decision be overturned only if it fails to "draw its essence" from the collective bargaining agreement, the much more deferential standard courts use in reviewing awards on the merits under *Enterprise Wheel*, *supra* Chapter III.C.1? Or should the court decide the issue independently, without any presumption of arbitrability?

It is possible that the Supreme Court has answered this question in the context of deciding a commercial arbitration case. In First Options of Chicago, Inc. v. Kaplan, 514 U.S. 938, 115 S.Ct. 1920, 131 L.Ed.2d 985 (1995), the Supreme Court held that if the parties did not clearly agree that the arbitrator had the authority to decide the arbitrability issue, courts were empowered to decide the issue independently, without deference to the arbitrator's resolution of the arbitrability issue. If on the other hand, the parties had agreed that the arbitrator could decide the arbitrability issue, the arbitrator's arbitrability decision should be reviewed under the same deferential standard used for arbitrators' decisions on the merits. The Court said that, in assessing whether the parties had agreed to permit the arbitrator to resolve the arbitrability issue, the fact that they argued the issue to the arbitrator would not be determinative. The unanimous Court relied interchangeably on precedents from both labor and commercial arbitration.

This perhaps suggests that *First Options'* analysis would be applicable to labor arbitration. The Ninth Circuit, however, on remand of a case that had been vacated by the Supreme Court for reconsideration in light of *First Options*, held that the decision governed only commercial arbitration. Pacesetter Construction Co. v. Carpenters 46 Northern California Counties Conference Board, 116 F.3d 436 (9th Cir.) (party's contest of arbitrability before the arbitrator constituted consent to have the arbitrator decide arbitrability, thereby waiving judicial review), cert. denied, 522 U.S. 1014, 118 S.Ct. 599, 139 L.Ed.2d 488 (1997). The Ninth Circuit distinguished labor from commercial arbitration on the grounds that there was a stronger federal policy in favor of labor arbitration and that the parties to labor contracts expected arbitrators to engage in more "gap filling." Subsequently, the Ninth Circuit cited *First Options* in holding that an employer who had appeared before an arbitration board without objection, presented arguments on the merits, and failed to reserve any issue for initial determination by a court, could not judicially challenge arbitrability. District Council of Iron Workers v. Pitner & Zenor, 246 F.3d 673 (9th Cir.2000) (Table). See also Kennametal, Inc. v. United Steelworkers, 262 F.Supp.2d 663 (W.D.Va. 2003) (relying on *First Options* and holding that court should review arbitrability decision of arbitrator *de novo* since employer objected to arbitrability in arbitration), aff'd, 96 Fed.Appx. 851 (4th Cir.2004); Rock–Tenn Co. v. United Paperworkers, 184 F.3d 330 (4th Cir.1999) (relying on *First Options* to hold that company's voluntary submission to arbitration of the dispute, its vigorous participation on the merits in arbitration, its failure to challenge there the arbitrator's authority to determine the dispute or explicitly to preserve the issue for resolution by the court, manifested the employer's willingness to have arbitrability determined by the arbitrator); and U.S. Postal Service v. American Postal Workers Union, 204 F.3d 523 (4th Cir. 2000) (when parties have manifest agreement to submit arbitrability decision to the arbitrator, arbitrator's determination should be reviewed by court under "essence" standard).

B. DISCIPLINE AND DISCHARGE[1]

1. INTRODUCTION

Protection from unjust discipline and discharge may be the most significant benefit bestowed upon employees covered by collective bar-

---

1. Bibliographic Suggestions: Norman Brand, ed., Discipline and Discharge in Arbitration (1998) and Supplement (2001); Tim Bornstein, Ann Gosline and Marc Greenbaum, eds., Labor and Employment Arbitration, (Chapters 14, 16–21) (2004); Elkouri & Elkouri, How Arbitration Works, 923–1002 (Alan Miles Ruben, ed., 6th ed. 2003); Theodore J. St. Antoine, ed., The Common Law of the Workplace (Chapter 6) (1998); Adolph M. Koven and Susan L.

Smith, Just Cause: The Seven Tests (2d ed. 1992, Revised by Donald F. Farwell); Arnold M. Zack, Arbitrating Discipline and Discharge Cases (2000); *Arbitral Discretion: The Tests of Just Cause*, 42 Proceedings of the National Academy of Arbitrators 23–64 (Essays of John E. Dunsford, Donald W. Cohen, and Robert J. Mignin) (1990); *The Discipline and Discharge Case: Two Devil's Advocates on What Arbitrators Are Doing Wrong*, 32 Proceedings of the National

gaining agreements. Despite recent expansion of individual employment rights, an employee without union representation has little recourse against unjust discipline. Generally, the unrepresented worker can challenge an employer's decision only through litigation and can prevail only upon proof of specific discriminatory intent or of violation of some very limited common law right. Nearly every worker represented by a union has vastly broader protection. An employer's reprimand, demotion, suspension, or discharge of a union-represented employee may be overturned if an arbitrator concludes the action was undertaken without "just cause." And, such a protection is not merely theoretical. Arbitrators do, with regularity, order employers to reinstate employees, provide back pay, and rescind suspensions and reprimands.[2] Arbitrators consider protection from unjust dismissal so basic an element of the collective bargaining relationship that they commonly find it to exist even when the contract contains no "just cause" provision.[3] Protection from unjust discipline is not only the centerpiece of the unionized employee's benefits, it is also the centerpiece of the arbitration process itself. Arbitrators hear overwhelmingly more discipline and discharge grievances than any other kind of case.

Academy of Arbitrators 63–91 (Essays of William M. Saxton, Bruce A. Miller, and William J. Fallon) (1980); Walter J. Gershenfield and Gladys Gershenfield, *Current Issues in Discharge Arbitration,* 55 Dispute Resolution Journal 48 (May 2000); Marvin F. Hill, Jr. and Mark L. Kahn, *Discipline and Discharge for Off-Duty Misconduct: What Are the Arbitral Standards?*, 39 Proceedings of the National Academy of Arbitrators 121 (1987); *Just Cause and the Troubled Employee*, 41 Proceedings of the National Academy of Arbitrators 21–74 (Essays of Daniel G. Collins, Thomas R. Miller and Susan M. Oliver, and Linda Lampkin) (1989); Jean T. McKelvey, *Discipline and Discharge*, Arbitration in Practice 88 (Arnold M. Zack, ed., 1984).

2. One study of 435 discharge cases in Michigan found that arbitrators overturned the employer's discipline in 55.6% of the cases. Grievants received full back pay in 15.2% of the cases, partial back pay in 14.7% and no back pay in 25.7%. Jack Stieber, Richard N. Block, and Leslie Corbitt, *How Representative are Published Decisions?*, 37 Proceedings of the National Academy of Arbitrators 176 (Table 1) (1985). A review of 539 published discharge decisions between 1982 and 1986 found the discharge upheld in 51% of the cases, full back pay in 20%, partial back pay in 8%, and reinstatement without back pay in 21%. John C. Shearer, *Reinstatement Without Back Pay—An Appropriate Remedy?*, 42 Arbitration Journal 47 (December 1987).

More recent studies, examining arbitration decisions in both the public and private sectors, have found that unions prevailed in between 55% and 60% of discharge cases. David A. Dilts and Edwin C. Leonard, Jr., *Win-Loss Rates in Public Sector Grievance Arbitration Cases: Implications for the Selection of Arbitrators*, 18 Journal of Collective Negotiations 337 (1989); Lawrence J. Haber, Ahmad R. Karim and J. Douglas Johnson, *A Survey of Published, Private-Sector Arbitral Decisions*, 48 Labor Law Journal 431 (1997); Debra J. Mensch and Dan R. Dalton, *Arbitration in Practice: Win, Lose or Draw?* 4 The Human Resources Professional 37 (1992). (Generally, in such studies, an employer is considered to have "won" a case only if management's action was upheld in its entirety.)

3. State of Montana, Department of Transportation, 107 LA 1060 (Jack C. Calhoun, 1997); Superior Products, 116 LA 1623 (Earle William Hockenberry, 2002). *Contra*, Mercury Consolidated, Inc., 101 LA 309 (Robert C. Schubert, 1993); Westvaco, 92 LA 1289 (Dennis R. Nolan, 1989) (previous arbitrator had held no implicit just cause protection and parties had not subsequently amended contract); Kimberly–Clark Corp., 82 LA 1090 (Frank A. Keenan, 1984). In SFIC Properties, Inc. v. Machinists, District Lodge 94, 103 F.3d 923 (9th Cir.1996), the court refused to overturn an arbitrator's decision finding a just cause requirement implicit "in all modern day collective bargaining agreements."

Although discipline cases dominate the work of labor arbitrators, the text of collective bargaining agreements provides less guidance in resolving these disputes than perhaps any other issue except "past practice." (See *infra* Part D of this Chapter.) Ninety-two percent of collective bargaining agreements provide that employees may be disciplined or discharged only for "cause" or for "just cause."[4] Often that is all they say. Typically, parties to collective bargaining agreements do not detail the kinds of conduct warranting discipline, the nature of appropriate discipline, the circumstances mitigating discipline, or the remedies to be afforded if discipline is found inappropriate.

This section addresses the body of arbitral theory and decisionmaking that has developed to answer these fundamental questions of discharge and discipline. Subsection 2 examines two efforts to provide a general definition of just cause. Subsection 3 provides examples of arbitrators' just cause decisionmaking. The cases in subsection 3 are not a representative sample of discipline cases. For example, they underrepresent the proportion of cases in which arbitrators affirm the employer's discipline. The cases, instead, offer an opportunity to discuss some of the most common reasons for employee discipline (including absenteeism, misconduct, incompetence, and insubordination) and the application of commonly applied requirements for just cause (including procedural fairness, fair warning, use of progressive discipline, and equal treatment). Subsection 4 discusses the variety of remedial issues that arise in discipline cases.

2. ARTICULATING A THEORY OF JUST CAUSE

What do the parties to collective bargaining agreements expect arbitrators to do when their contracts preclude employee discipline without just cause, but fail to define the concept? Does such silence mean that the parties are willing to vest the arbitrator with unlimited discretion to second-guess employer personnel decisions on an *ad hoc* and personal basis? Or are the parties willing to use such unspecific contractual language because they expect the arbitrator to be constrained by some consistent body of previous arbitrators' decisions interpreting and applying the concept or by some commonly understood theory of just cause? Professor Clyde Summers has observed:

> Although arbitrators often cite no other decisions in their opinion and never consider other cases as binding precedents, they usually are quite aware of the pattern of decisions by other arbitrators and are reluctant to deviate far from that pattern. Results in a discipline case may well depend on the length of the arbitrator's foot, but that leads to relatively small differences, for there are few peg-legs or abominable snowmen among arbitrators, and no one follows in their footsteps.[5]

4. Basic Patterns in Union Contracts 7 (14th ed. 1995).

5. Clyde W. Summers, *Individual Protection Against Unjust Dismissal: Time for* *a Statute*, 62 Virginia Law Review 481, 501 (1976).

This subsection examines two efforts to articulate a general understanding of just cause: Carroll R. Daugherty's seven tests of just cause and Roger I. Abrams and Dennis R. Nolan's theory of just cause.

Arbitrator Carroll R. Daugherty has suggested that there is a consensus or "common law" of "just cause." In the appendix to a 1966 arbitration decision, Daugherty articulated the most frequently cited formulation of the concept in what has come to be called "The Seven Tests of Just Cause."[6] Daugherty's introduction explained, "A 'no' answer to any one or more of the following questions normally signifies that just and proper cause did not exist." He then listed his seven questions:

1. Did the company give to the employee forewarning or foreknowledge of the possible or probable disciplinary consequences of the employee's conduct?

2. Was the company's rule or managerial order reasonably related to (a) the orderly, efficient, and safe operation of the company's business and (b) the performance that the company might properly expect of the employee?

3. Did the company, before administering discipline to an employee, make an effort to discover whether the employee did in fact violate or disobey a rule or order of management?

4. Was the company's investigation conducted fairly and objectively?

5. At the investigation, did the "judge" obtain substantial evidence or proof that the employee was guilty as charged?

6. Has the company applied its rules, orders, and penalties evenhandedly and without discrimination to all employees?

7. Was the degree of discipline administered by the company in a particular case reasonably related to (a) the seriousness of the employee's proven offense and (b) the record of the employee in his service with the company?

Notes and Questions

1. Review Arbitrator Daugherty's seven questions.

(a) Which questions can be answered objectively? Which require the exercise of subjective judgment?

(b) Would reliance on the seven tests significantly limit the arbitrator's exercise of discretion? Should tests for "just cause" provide greater limitations on arbitrators' discretion?

6. Enterprise Wire Co., 46 LA 359 (Carroll R. Daugherty, 1966). The Daugherty appendix in *Enterprise Wire* includes, in addition to the questions listed in the text, a number of explanatory notes. Daugherty's first published version of the questions was in Grief Bros. Cooperage Corp., 42 LA 555 (Carroll R. Daugherty, 1964). An entire treatise on discipline and discharge is structured around Daugherty's seven tests. Adolph M. Koven and Susan L. Smith, Just Cause: The Seven Tests (2d ed. 1992, revised by Donald F. Farwell).

(c) Or do Daugherty's tests provide excessive limitations on the arbitrator's exercise of judgment? Arbitrator John Dunsford has written of such tests:

[T]he difficulty is that a process whose strength and uniqueness lies in the personal responsiveness of the decision maker to the daily problems of flesh and blood human beings in the shop may be transformed into an academic exercise, as tests and rules imported from extraneous sources begin to dominate the discretion and judgment of the arbitrator.

John E. Dunsford, *Arbitral Discretion: The Tests of Just Cause*, 42 Proceedings of the National Academy of Arbitrators 23, 37 (1990).

2. Is it appropriate for an arbitrator to determine answers to each of the seven questions or should the arbitrator merely focus upon the objections to the discipline specifically raised by the union?

3. Daugherty's first question requires that the Company give the employee forewarning of the "possible or probable disciplinary consequences of the employee's misconduct." Which degree of forewarning is required— "possible" consequences, "probable" consequences, or both? Is some conduct so obviously improper that it would be silly to make forewarning a condition for discipline?

4. Daugherty's questions 3, 4, and 5 focus upon the employer's decisionmaking process. Daugherty suggests that a "no" answer to any of these questions should result in overturning the discipline. Assume that the employer's investigation was incomplete and conducted by a supervisor biased against the employee. Should the discipline nevertheless be overturned if the other questions are answered in the affirmative? If the procedural error caused no harm, should it bar an otherwise proper discipline?

5. Some commentators have questioned whether Daugherty's insistence on these procedural matters accurately reflects arbitral practice. John E. Dunsford, *supra* Question 1(c), at p. 31:

Even a cursory survey of the literature and published cases reveals that arbitrators differ radically on the issue of whether a failure to accord a complete and fair investigation and hearing prior to the arbitration requires an invalidation of discipline under the just cause standard.

See also Christine D. Ver Ploeg, *Investigatory Due Process and Arbitration*, 45 Proceedings of the National Academy of Arbitrators 220 (1993) (after review of ten years of decisions on the issue, concluding that there is no consensus among arbitrators). A decade later, another arbitrator thought VerPloeg's assessment remained accurate. Jack Clarke, *To What Extent Do and Should the Seven Tests Guide Arbitrators or the Parties?*, 55 Proceedings of the National Academy of Arbitrators 51, 57 (2003). In another study, arbitrators were asked in a survey how likely they were to reduce discipline in a series of alternative scenarios varying the nature of the disciplinary offense and the nature of the employer procedural violation. The authors concluded:

[A]rbitrators do not believe in blindly applying the seven tests to procedural violations and finding lack of just cause for discharge if procedural error is established. Rather, arbitrators are more likely to mitigate some types of major offenses than others, and some procedural violations more than others.

James P. Begin and Michael A. Zigarelli, *An Academy Survey: Do You Mitigate?*, 47 Proceedings of the National Academy of Arbitrators 30, 40 (1994). Arbitrators were less likely to reduce the disciplinary sanction because of a procedural violation if the offense was either theft or use of alcohol or drugs on the premises. They were also less likely to reduce the discipline if the procedural violation occurred at the investigatory stage, unless the violation was denial of union representation.

6. Daugherty's questions, and particularly his three procedural inquiries, suggest that the arbitrator's appropriate role is to act more like an appellate court reviewing the employer's decision, than like a trial court assessing the discipline *de novo*. Which role is it likely the union envisioned for the arbitrator? Which role is it likely the employer envisioned for the arbitrator? See the comments of union and management representatives in *Arbitral Discretion: The Tests of Just Cause*, 42 Proceedings of the National Academy of Arbitrators 50–64 (1990). If the parties did not have a common understanding of the arbitrator's appropriate role when they chose to include "just cause" language in their contract, which role should the arbitrator assume?

7. John E. Dunsford's criticism of Daughterty's seven tests was not limited to concerns about the significance of procedural violations and the role of arbitral discretion. Dunsford called the seven tests "misleading in substance and distracting in application." He suggested that the tests arose out of Daughterty's particular experience as a referee on the National Railroad Adjustment Board and thus were not applicable more broadly. Dunsford noted that in the railroad industry the hearings did not involve the testimony of fact witnesses or grievants and there were special concerns about due process within the industry. See John E. Dunsford, *supra* Question 1(c).

8. The variety of inquiries included within Daugherty's seven tests imposes significant limits on employer discretion. How likely is it that an employer who signs a collective bargaining agreement without a "just cause" provision implicitly agreed to those limitations? Should an arbitrator ever infer the existence of a "just cause" provision? See cases cited in footnote 3, *supra*.

TOWARD A THEORY OF "JUST CAUSE" IN EMPLOYEE DISCIPLINE CASES
Roger I. Abrams and Dennis R. Nolan.
85 Duke Law Journal 594 (1985).

[While Daugherty's seven tests purport to provide a definition of "just cause" based on decisions of arbitrators, Professors Abrams and Nolan propose a theory of just cause derived from the fundamental understanding between all employees and employers, as modified by the collective bargaining agreement and the congruent interests of unions and employers. They begin by defining that fundamental understanding.]

THE FUNDAMENTAL UNDERSTANDING

A potential employer is willing to part with his money only in return for something he values more highly, the time and satisfactory work of the employee. The potential employee will part with his time and work only for something he values more, the money offered by the employer. * * *

This fundamental understanding of the employment relationship can be easily summarized: both parties realize that the employer must pay the agreed wages and benefits and that the employee must do "satisfactory" work. "Satisfactory" work, in this context, has four elements: (1) regular attendance, (2) obedience to reasonable work rules, (3) a reasonable quantity and quality of work, and (4) avoidance of any conduct that would interfere with the employer's ability to operate the business successfully. * * *

For the employees, the most important effect of the collective agreement is the correction of what they perceive to be the major flaw of the fundamental understanding—the insecurity of the relationship. * * * Thus, the main addition to the fundamental understanding that unions seek in collective agreements is job security. * * * [Most frequently,] the agreement protects job security by limiting the employer's power to discipline and discharge. * * * [T]he fundamental understanding, as amended in the collective bargaining agreement, can be stated as follows: employees will provide "satisfactory" work, in return for which the employer will pay the agreed wages and benefits, and will continue the employment relationship unless there is just cause to terminate it.

Just cause is obviously not a precise concept. It cannot be applied to a particular dispute by an employer or an arbitrator without analysis and the exercise of judgment. The concept is so vague, in fact, that it produces confusion and inconsistent arbitration awards. There will never be a simple definition of "just cause," nor even a consensus on its application to specific cases, but this does not mean the phrase is devoid of meaning. On the contrary, it is possible to make sense of the term and to give it substance. This can be done by viewing the just cause standard as an amended form of the fundamental understanding. Just cause, in other words, embodies the idea that the employee is entitled to continued employment, provided he attends work regularly, obeys work rules, performs at some reasonable level of quality and quantity, and refrains from interfering with his employer's business by his activities on or off the job. An employee's failure to meet these obligations will justify discipline. * * *

The nature and severity of the employee's offense, among other things, will determine what form of discipline is appropriate. A small departure from "satisfactory" work may result in a verbal or written warning. A more serious or repeated offense may produce a suspension without pay. In an extreme case, the employer may be justified in discharging an employee. The employee may protest the discipline through the contractual grievance procedure. If the parties fail to resolve the grievance, the union may take the case to an impartial arbitrator for final and binding resolution. The question for the arbitrator is whether the employee's conduct constituted a sufficiently serious breach of his obligation under the fundamental understanding to warrant the discipline imposed.

The fundamental understanding forms the very core of just cause. Management seeks efficient production from its workforce and engages individual employees to achieve that goal. When an employee fails to fulfill the employer's reasonable expectations, he breaches his obligations under the fundamental understanding. On the other hand, when an employer fires an employee for an illegitimate reason, it breaches its obligation under the amended version of the fundamental understanding. The employee's offense and the employer's decision to fire can both be tested against the just cause standard. * * *

[Abrams and Nolan suggest the appropriateness of employee discipline may be assessed in light of this fundamental understanding of the employment relationship, amended by the collective bargaining agreement, and further refined by an understanding of the congruence of management and union interests.]

MANAGEMENT'S INTERESTS

Why would management discipline an employee? Whim or prejudice explain some disciplinary decisions, but such cases are rare. The profit motive alone discourages arbitrary discipline. Wrongful or disproportionate discipline creates employee dissatisfaction, which in turn makes it more difficult to hire and retain qualified employees. In particular, wrongful discharge may impose significant costs on an employer, who must seek out, employ, and train a replacement for the terminated worker. The employer's common law authority to suspend or discharge workers at will is thus no indication of his actual willingness to use that authority in a capricious manner.

Most discipline is imposed for more rational purposes. There are at least three possible motivations for employee discipline: (1) rehabilitation, (2) deterrence, which may be either specific or general, and (3) protection of profitability. Rehabilitation is the most obvious objective. An employee who seems to be developing poor work habits, such as absenteeism or carelessness, may, as the result of disciplinary prodding, become fully satisfactory. Perhaps the employee's mistakes stemmed from some correctable personal problem or a lack of awareness as to their seriousness. By applying discipline in gradually increasing doses, the employer might impress upon the employee the need for change. The objective is to cure a specific problem and make the employee's work satisfactory.

Specific deterrence is closely related to rehabilitation. The employer's objective is to deter an employee from repeating a certain error by imposing one penalty and threatening to impose a more serious one in the future. Where the employee's conduct indicates that rehabilitation is impossible, specific deterrence will be ineffective. In such cases, the employer will discharge the employee, having determined that he is incorrigible. Both the rehabilitation and specific deterrence objectives reflect the employer's attempt to predict an employee's future performance on the basis of past performance. If the employee's past performance indicates that he could do satisfactory work in the future, some discipline short of discharge is appropriate. If, on the other hand, the employee's prior conduct indicates an inability to fulfill the essential elements of the job, termination may be the appropriate decision. * * *

The final purpose for which management may discipline an employee, protection of profitability, is something of a catch-all. Certain employee conduct, though not prohibited by a specific rule, may still interfere with the employer's operation of the enterprise. For instance, employees can mar a carefully nurtured public image and can harm relationships with customers or suppliers. Discipline up to and including dismissal might be appropriate even when it cannot be directly tied to motives of rehabilitation or deterrence. The largest category of employee conduct falling under this third objective involves off-duty activity.

The generally accepted rule is that an employer may not discipline an employee for off-duty conduct unless the conduct can be shown to harm the employer. * * *

The just cause standard precludes one common objective for discipline—retribution. Management may not discipline an employee merely to punish him for his transgressions. Indeed, it has no economic interest in doing so. Individual managers may desire retribution, but a business entity has no legitimate interest beyond productivity and profitability.

All of the legitimate management interests in discipline are consistent with the fundamental understanding. Rehabilitation and specific deterrence are aimed at improving the transgressing employee's work. General deterrence serves to reinforce the work rules which all employees must observe if the business is to prosper. Finally, protection of profitability justifies prohibition of conduct that harms the employer's business relations.

The Union's Interests

What does a union seek in a discharge or discipline case? A cynic might argue that the union's goal is unqualified job security. Like the extreme management ideal of unlimited discretion, such a union goal cannot be considered legitimate; nor does it reflect true union interests. A union cannot reasonably expect management to carry on its employment rolls someone who has breached the fundamental understanding. A union may certainly question the extent to which a particular instance of employee conduct may harm productivity, but it must acknowledge that an employee's failure to meet his obligations works to the detriment of other employees as well as the employer. In the short run, an unsatisfactory employee simply makes the jobs of co-workers more difficult. In the long run, continued tolerance of substandard performance will endanger the employer's competitive position, and that, in turn, will threaten the wages and even the jobs of the rest of the workforce. The economic welfare of workers and management is interdependent.

The union's real interest in disciplinary matters is fairness. A union pursues this interest in a variety of ways. First, it seeks fairness in disciplinary procedures. For example, employees must have actual or constructive notice as to their work obligations. Posted disciplinary rules are fairly common, but even in the absence of such rules, arbitrators reasonably presume that employees are aware of basic, though unwritten, behavioral standards. A union also seeks fairness in the administration of discipline. Disciplinary measures must be based on facts; management must ascertain what actually occurred before it imposes discipline. Management must also give the employee an opportunity to explain and must allow him union representation during the investigation, if he so requests. Finally, discipline should be imposed in gradually increasing degrees. These concerns for procedural fairness might be termed "industrial due process."

A union will also seek procedural fairness in the arbitration process, particularly in the allocation of the burden of proving just cause. A disciplinary grievance, like other grievances, alleges that the employer breached the collective bargaining agreement. Although the burden of proof usually rests with the party asserting the breach, the union will seek to shift the burden of proof to management when the case involves discipline. The fundamental understanding, as amended by the collective agreement, provides for continued employment unless there is just cause for discipline. Management, in the union's view, thus bears the burden of demonstrating just cause. It has singled out an individual employee for disciplinary action or termination, it knows why it took the action, and for that reason it should bear the burden of explaining why discipline is justified.

The second way in which a union seeks "fairness" in discipline is through consistent treatment of similar cases. For example, if one employee is not punished for certain conduct, co-workers who engage in the same conduct should be treated in the same manner. Like cases should be treated alike. In a disciplinary situation, a union seeks what might be termed "industrial equal protection."

Finally, a union seeks "fairness" for the disciplined individual by compelling management to consider mitigating factors. Perhaps the most important of these is the employee's work record. For any given offense, an employee with a long record of excellent work and no prior discipline should be treated more leniently than a junior employee with a history of unsatisfactory work and several prior offenses. Other mitigating factors may be tied to the particular offense. If two employees have been fighting, the aggressor deserves more severe discipline than the victim. In appropriate cases, an employee's attitude, demeanor, and other personal factors might warrant mitigation of the penalty. The union thus seeks fairness through individualized treatment.

This third goal initially may appear to conflict with the union's interest in equal protection. The two objectives, however, are compatible. Like cases should be treated alike, but different cases should be treated differently. The just cause standard requires reasonable discipline in each case; it does not require that each category of offense carry a single mandatory penalty. * * *

[Professors Abrams and Nolan next conclude that the effectuation of union interests in industrial due process, industrial equal protection and individualized treatment also ultimately serves management's interest in productive efficiency. The authors then summarize their theory of just cause and, in a section omitted here, apply that theory to the resolution of concrete cases.]

A THEORY OF JUST CAUSE

The legitimate interests of management and labor regarding discipline are consistent both with the fundamental understanding and with each other. From this congruence, a theory of just cause can be derived, a theory which accommodates the parties' needs and reflects their mutual understanding.

A. Just cause for discipline exists only when an employee has failed to meet his obligations under the fundamental understanding of the employment relationship. The employee's general obligation is to provide satisfactory work. Satisfactory work has four components:

1. Regular attendance.

2. Obedience to reasonable work rules.

3. A reasonable quality and quantity of work.

4. Avoidance of conduct, either at or away from work, which would interfere with the employer's ability to carry on the business effectively.

B. For there to be just cause, the discipline must further one or more of management's three legitimate interests:

1. Rehabilitation of a potentially satisfactory employee.

2. Deterrence of similar conduct, either by the disciplined employee or by other employees.

3. Protection of the employer's ability to operate the business successfully.

C. The concept of just cause includes certain employee protections that reflect the union's interest in guaranteeing "fairness" in disciplinary situations.

1. The employee is entitled to *industrial due process*. This includes:

a. actual or constructive notice of expected standards of conduct and penalties for wrongful conduct;

b.   a decision based on facts, determined after an investigation that provides the employee an opportunity to state his case, with union assistance if he desires it;

c.   the imposition of discipline in gradually increasing degrees, except in cases involving the most extreme breaches of the fundamental understanding. In particular, discharge may be imposed only when less severe penalties will not protect legitimate management interests, for one of the following reasons: (1) the employee's past record shows that the unsatisfactory conduct will continue, (2) the most stringent form of discipline is needed to protect the system of work rules, or (3) continued employment would inevitably interfere with the successful operation of the business; and

d.   proof by management that just cause exists.

2.   The employee is entitled to *industrial equal protection*, which requires like treatment of like cases.

3.   The employee is entitled to *individualized treatment*. Distinctive facts in the employee's record or regarding the reason for discipline must be given appropriate weight.

Notes and Questions

1.   Compare the Abrams and Nolan articulation of the "just cause" standard to Daugherty's seven tests:

(a) Do they differ in the extent to which they control the arbitrator's exercise of discretion?

(b) Does the Abrams and Nolan model view the role of the arbitrator as a *de novo* decisionmaker or as an appellate reviewer of the employer's decision?

(c) Do they differ in the extent to which the nature of the employer's investigation and decisionmaking process determine the outcome of the arbitration?

2.   Abrams and Nolan assert that discipline for whim and prejudice is likely to be rare. If they are wrong about this, the unionized employee's "just cause" protection is even more important. The authors of a textbook have challenged the Abrams and Nolan assertion:

Certainly, acting on the basis of whim and prejudice is not profitable. However, discipline is not imposed by the "rational profit-maximizing firm" but by individual supervisors whose interests are only loosely related to the economic self-interests of the firm. Internal controls may not deal effectively with such supervisors.

Charles A. Sullivan, Deborah A. Calloway, and Michael J. Zimmer, Cases and Materials on Employment Law 15 (1993). Arbitrators report anecdotally that it is not uncommon for senior management officials to be surprised by information they learn at the arbitration hearing about the conduct of their supervisors in discharge cases. One might expect an immediate offer of settlement by upper management in such cases, but often no such offer is made. Why not? Does upper management value maintaining supervisory morale or management solidarity above doing justice? Does it value an arbitral rejection of supervisory misconduct as a worthwhile educational experience for a wayward supervisor?

3. COMMON REASONS FOR DISCHARGE AND REQUIREMENTS FOR JUST CAUSE

STROEHMANN BAKERIES, INC.

98 LA 873 (John E. Sands, 1990).*

On March 29, 1990 the parties agreed to submit the following issue to arbitration by me:

Was there just cause for the discharge of grievant L on November 20, 1989? If not, what shall be the remedy?

This sexual misconduct case turns less on determinations of witnesses' credibility than on the adequacy of Stroehmann's investigation prior to its discharge decision. Indeed, the *relevant* facts are undisputed. Until November 20, 1989 L was a transport driver who had been with Stroehmann's for seventeen years. L drove a tractor-trailer, making night deliveries of large baked goods orders to supermarkets. One of his regular stops was Stauffer's Lititz store. For ten years L had been shop steward of Stroehmann's small Teamster unit. At the time of his discharge L was Stroehmann's sole remaining transport driver. (On L's nights off, a garage mechanic covered L's routes.)

Since mid-August 1989 W has been night custodian/receiving clerk at that facility. L was a friend of W's father, having helped him get his job with Stauffer's; and L was friendly with W too.

Three or four times each week L made deliveries to Stauffer's in Lititz while W was working. They frequently exchanged banter and conversation as they did their respective jobs.

L is a forty-year-old, married man with two children, aged fifteen and thirteen. He stands well over six feet tall and appears to weigh more than two hundred pounds. W is five feet four and weighs 224 pounds. She does not have an active social life. W accuses L of having sexually assaulted her on Sunday night, November 12, 1989.

This is how L's discharge came about and how the question of just cause has come to me. On Tuesday morning, November 14, 1989 Stroehmann's management received word of a serious incident that had occurred at Stauffer's Lititz supermarket on Sunday night, November 12th. Harrisport sales activator Steve Garrett and branch manager Joe Jacobs took this report from Stauffer's store manager Ken Zimmerman:

> The night person who lets our store door driver in the store, W, told her mother on Tuesday, 11/14/89, that when L was done

* Reprinted with permission from *Labor Arbitration Reporter–Labor Arbitration Reports*, 98 LA 873. Copyright 1992 by The Bureau of National Affairs, Inc. (800–372–1033) <http://www.bna.com>.

delivering product in the store, that L came up behind her and grabbed her breast and pushed himself against her and that L also had an erection. Right after this took place, L told W "Do not tell your father because we are real good friends." W's father works at this store. Ken Zimmerman does not want L to serve any of the four (4) Stauffer's stores anymore. Steve and I assured Ken that corrective action would be taken immediately.

W's mother told Ken Zimmerman that she is considering taking legal action against L.

At 5:20 that evening, Steve Garrett and Joe Jacobs reached W by telephone and prepared this statement of what she had said in their twenty-minute conversation:

Steve Garrett and Joe Jacobs called W on Tuesday 11/14/89, at 5:20 P.M. L stopped his truck out in front of the Stauffer store and then drove out to the back dock. He rang the buzzer and W opened the back door and let L in. L proceeded to tell W that he was just talking to two girls on his CB radio and they were going to have an orgy and that he was excited about this. He started to unload the bread order and continued to talk about this orgy. W asked him if he was married and L replied that he was married, but he still had sex with other women. L told W that he would not cheat on his wife anymore, however, would still like to feel other women, but was afraid of Aids [sic].

When he finished unloading the bread order, L went to the produce cooler and took an orange. He asked W if her breasts were as hard as that orange. He then attempted to pull up her shirt. She resisted and pulled her shirt back down. W then walked to the front of the store and L followed her. She checked to see if the instore baker had arrived. The other employee had not arrived yet. W then went to the back of the store and L was in front of her and he asked W why she was following him. L then said, I know why you are following me, you want to look at my ass. They then were at the back door and W said she had to follow him back to make sure the doors were locked. L then was behind W and reached around her and grabbed both her breasts. She again resisted and held the door open for L to leave. L said, "What is your hurry? Are you trying to get rid of me?" L told W to not say anything to her father because they were friends and he did not want anything to change. L then left and W locked the door.

Witnesses to this conversation with W were: Steve Garrett and Joe Jacobs, over a speaker phone with W's permission.

According to Jacobs, more than half-way through that conference call W became upset and began to sob. Garrett picked up the telephone handset and ended Jacobs' observation of W's statement. Garrett and Jacobs both confirmed that Garrett was very solicitous of W's feelings, "went easy" on her, and never questioned any of the apparent differences between her account and Zimmerman's version of her mother's report to him of what W had originally said to her mother.

On Wednesday, November 15th, Garrett and Jacobs had a negotiating session with the Teamsters which L attended as shop steward. They mentioned nothing to L or his union representative about W's accusations. Instead, Jacobs called L at home after the negotiations' 2:30 or 3:00 conclusion and told him to come in to discuss a "problem" that Jacobs declined to describe on the telephone. Jacobs mentioned nothing about potential discipline, and, to L's question whether he should bring a union representative, Jacobs replied, "It's up to you." Jacobs gave that answer even though he conceded that, prior to that meeting, he had already decided to suspend L "pending further investigation and discharge." (Indeed, Jacobs had *already* arranged for someone else to cover L's route that night!) Under these circumstances, Stroehmann's cannot seriously claim that L knowing [sic] waived his right to union representation in a disciplinary meeting with management.

L came right in to Jacobs' office without a union representative. There Garrett, Jacobs, and Paul Blair (L's supervisor) confronted L with the Zimmerman and W write-ups. Jacobs asked L for his reaction. Jacobs testified that L responded that he would not so jeopardize his marriage and job and wouldn't do this, that W was a "wacko," and that he denied everything she had said. L specifically stated that W had to have been lying about L's "orgy" statement because his CB radio was broken, and L invited Jacobs and the others to come out to his tractor and see for themselves. They declined.

Jacobs wrote this summary of L's response in the "Employee's Reaction or Comments" portion of the Employee Contact Report that Jacobs prepared and had L sign at the interview:

> L claims that none of this information is not [sic] true and that W is a waco [sic]. L [sic] told myself, P. Blair Steve Garritt [sic] that he loved his wife and would not consider jeapordizing [sic] his job and marrage [sic].

For "Nature of Report," Jacobs had already written, "Suspending pending dismissal" for violation of "Group III—Major Offense—Paragraph 10—Immoral conduct or indecency on company property or while on duty."

According to Stroehmann's "Disciplinary Program 'Sales Department,' " Group III infractions are subject to immediate dismissal. Note #1 to Company Exhibit 4 provides, however:

> *Dismissal*—When immediate action is necessary, supervisors should suspend violators with intention to dismiss. *This will allow higher management to investigate and collect the facts* before a final and official dismissal is declared. [Emphasis added.]

In fact, no further investigation, fact-gathering, or confirmation efforts occurred. All that happened was a "run-by" past Stroehmann's "higher-ups" of L's dismissal and a November 17th meeting at which

Zimmerman advised Jacobs that he believed W's story because she was "a very Christian girl" and "bashful." So much for Note #1's admonition to investigate and collect facts!

On Monday, November 20th, Jacobs called L to advise him of his dismissal. In that conversation Jacobs heard for the first time L's account of what had happened on November 12th, none of which would have been culpable under or inconsistent with Stroehmann's rules, acceptable standards of social intercourse, or what W and L's bantering business relationship had been. Certainly nothing L admitted fulfilled W's charges of sexual assault.

By this time, however, Jacobs' discharge decision was firm. Jacobs testified that he had believed W's accusations and rejected L's denials based on these three considerations:

(1) W had told her mother, so her story was credible.

(2) W had told Garrett and Jacobs in their telephone conference, and her crying lent additional weight to the inherent credibility of having told strangers such an embarrassing tale.

(3) In L's shoes Jacobs would have gone down to Stauffer's to try to "work it out" with Stauffer's and W, but L had made no such effort.

This grievance ensued, and the union has timely processed it to arbitration by me.

On these facts Stroehmann's argues (a) that Jacobs' judgment to believe W and disbelieve L was reasonable; (b) that W's testimony at the hearing before me was thoroughly credible and supported Jacobs' judgment that she had no reason to lie; and (c) that the union's claim of antiunion animus is an unsupported "red herring." The union, on the other hand, contends (a) that the company's failure to make a fair and objective investigation deprived grievant of his right to industrial due process; (b) that Stroehmann's failed to establish grievant's guilt beyond a reasonable doubt; and (c) that Stroehmann's decision to discharge a seventeen-year employee based on such flimsy evidence could only have been motivated by anti-union animus.

On the entire record before me, including my assessments of witnesses' credibility and the probative value of evidence, I must sustain L's grievance as meritorious and grant the remedy the union seeks for him. I reach that conclusion for the following reasons.

First, it is essential at the outset to eliminate what this decision does *not* involve. It does *not* involve any fine questions of quantum of proof, relative credibility of witnesses, seriousness of charged misconduct, or presence of anti-union animus. If Stroehmann's investigation had been at all consistent with the severity of W's accusations and of their consequences for L's life and if that investigation had provided an adequate basis to believe L had behaved as charged, Stroehmann's discharge decision would have been unassailable. And it would not have mattered whether Stroehmann harbored anti-union animus, whether

Rule III.10 applies by its terms to transport as well as sales department personnel, whether or not W is a "very Christian girl," or whether W's words or acts may have invited L's alleged misconduct. The simple truth is that, even if W had been the most celebrated slattern in seven states, sexual misconduct of the kind charged is absolutely inappropriate and should support immediate discharge.

Second, what *is* involved in this case is the absolute insufficiency of Stroehmann's response to the information its management received on November 14th from Zimmerman and W. Although both Jacobs and Garrett testified to the necessity for establishing facts before making any decision, their professed concern was mere lip service.

Neither Jacobs nor Garrett did anything more to determine what in fact had happened on November 12th than to accept uncritically W's telephone account of bizarre behavior on L's part. No one probed the apparent inconsistencies between W's statement and Zimmerman's double hearsay account to them (and triple hearsay in Company Exhibit 3–B) of what W's mother had told him W had told her. No one met W in person to evaluate her appearance and demeanor. (For example, at the hearing before me W stopped cold and then blushed furiously when a simple question about the location of an orange pointed out a hole in her story. It really does not matter where the orange in fact had been. What did matter was W's embarrassment that everyone saw at the hearing but no one in Stroehmann's management had an opportunity to see in their limited investigation.) No one even required W's timely signature on Jacobs' account of her telephone statement. (In fact, Jacobs sent that statement to Stauffer's for W's execution, a process that required more than two months and three or four telephone reminders.)

More important, Jacobs and Garrett never once asked L himself what had happened at Stauffer's Lititz store on November 12th. Instead, withholding warning and opportunity to prepare, they cornered L alone and confronted him with scurrilous accusations of scurrilous behavior that Jacobs and Garrett had already accepted as Gospel. (Indeed, before having sought the facts according to L, Jacobs had already arranged for L's suspension and replacement on November 15th.) And between that time and the November 20th discharge decision, Stroehmann's management did nothing more to investigate the facts than to confirm Zimmerman's impressions of W's bashfulness and of her status as a "very Christian girl." Not only am I mystified by the relevance of those issues to the charges against L, but I am equally stumped, assuming their relevance, by Stroehmann's failure to consider with equal weight L's Christianity or his status as a married father of two.

Third, as a result of the absolute insufficiency of Stroehmann's investigation, it could not possibly have made a supportable judgment concerning the charges against L. This is not to say that I believe W was lying and L was truthful. The point is that, even on the complete record before me, I have insufficient evidence to resolve the credibility conflict between W and L. And if that were the determinative question before me, Stroehmann's would have had to lose for having failed to bear its burden of proof.

Finally, Jacobs' stated reasons for having believed W's story defy logic. He believed W because she had told her mother, because she had told two strangers, and because L had made no effort to make peace with Stauffer's and W between November 15th and 20th.

Yet the unchallenged "facts" Jacobs accepted as true can also support the equally illogical conclusion that W, unattractive and frustrated, could have fabricated a disturbing incident to titillate herself and attract her mother's caring attention. And, her story having gained sufficient momentum, W was unable to disengage from it. Whether one casts either W or L as the victim, neither scenario can stand scrutiny based on Stroehmann's burlesque of an investigation.

Nor can I, on this record, find evidence that antiunion animus motivated Jacobs and Garrett. In truth, I believe that they were both shocked and embarrassed by W's story and, as well, hobbled in their response by puritan unwillingness to pursue a necessary inquiry into the tabu subject matter she raised. The result—an uncritical acceptance of W's charges—is as reprehensible as would have been a sexist assumption that W had been "asking for" whatever she got. In this scenario it was only coincidental that L's discharge also satisfied a large customer's demand that L stop servicing their stores.

The bottom line is that Stroehmann's discharge decision lacked just cause, and it must accordingly reinstate L to employment with full back pay and benefits less interim earnings.

By reason of the foregoing, I issue the following

AWARD

1. Stroehmann's Bakeries, Inc. lacked just cause to discharge grievant L from employment on November 20, 1989.

2. The company shall reinstate grievant to employment effective November 20, 1989 with full back pay and benefits less interim earnings.

Notes and Questions

1. Consistent with arbitration practice generally, Arbitrator Sands' analysis assumes that the employer bears the burden of proving that it had just cause for discharging the employee. Which party would bear the burden of proof if the union had alleged violation of some other provision of the contract, such as a requirement to pay overtime or to promote on the basis of seniority if the senior employee is qualified for the position? Which party would bear the burden of proof if L had challenged his discharge in a civil action for wrongful discharge or an action under Title VII alleging discrimination? Which party would bear the burden of proof if the NLRB had pursued a charge that L had been discharged for his union activities? In labor arbitration, why should an employer bear the burden of proving that it *didn't* violate the contract in discharging or disciplining an employee?

2. Assuming that the employer bears the burden of persuasion, what quantity of proof is required to satisfy that burden? The Union argued in *Stroehmann Bakeries* that the employer had to prove L's guilt "beyond a reasonable doubt." Is that the appropriate standard? Or should it be the "preponderance of the evidence" standard typically used in civil lawsuits and for other arbitration issues? Is there any reason why arbitrators should require a higher level of proof in discharge cases generally? Or in certain kinds of discharge cases?

In cases involving charges of moral turpitude or criminal conduct, some arbitrators use the criminal law standard of "beyond a reasonable doubt." Others use an intermediate standard such as "clear and convincing evidence." Still others reject these higher standards of proof, either because they would not be required if allegations of criminal conduct were made in civil litigation or because one should distinguish between the seriousness of criminal punishment and the less serious consequences of discharge from employment. Other arbitrators dismiss the debate entirely, as "just playing games with words," on the ground that such legal terminology is inappropriate in labor arbitration where what is at issue is the simpler question: Is the arbitrator persuaded that the employer had just cause for discharge? See Marvin F. Hill, Jr. and Anthony V. Sinicropi, Evidence in Arbitration 32–39 (2d ed. 1987) (discussing the variety of opinions within the arbitral community). See also Norman Brand, *supra* footnote 1, at 335 ("There is a divergence of opinion among arbitrators as to which standard of proof applies in disciplinary proceedings.") and Kenneth W. Thornicroft, *Arbitrators, Social Values, and the Burden of Proof in Substance Abuse Discharge Cases*, 40 Labor Law Journal 582 (1989) (empirical study of substance abuse discharge cases found arbitrators using all three burdens of proof—beyond a reasonable doubt, clear and convincing, and preponderance of the evidence— in substance abuse discharge cases).

3. Arbitrator Sands concludes that employee L must be reinstated because Stroehmann Bakeries conducted an inadequate investigation of the sexual harassment charge.

(a) What did the employer do to investigate the charge? In the view of Arbitrator Sands, what else should it have done to conduct an adequate investigation?

(b) Do you agree with Arbitrator Sands that the investigation was inadequate?

(c) The contract has no language establishing specific procedures for employer investigations. How was the employer to know in advance of L's discharge what kind of investigation an arbitrator would later have expected of it? Even if the employer could not have foreseen the specific investigatory standards that an arbitrator might retrospectively impose upon it, is it nevertheless reasonable for an arbitrator to impose such standards? (Take another look at the excerpts in subsection 2.)

(d) Assume that the arbitrator was convinced that an employee's conduct was sufficiently egregious to warrant discharge. Why should the arbitrator nevertheless reinstate the employee because of inadequacies in the employer's investigation? Was the reliability of evidence presented at the arbitration hearing reduced by the shortcomings of the employer's investigation?

4. If Arbitrator Sands had reached the merits of the discharge issue, he would have had to determine whether the employer's factual conclusions about the incident were correct. When an arbitrator hears witnesses, testifying under oath, tell conflicting stories, how is the arbitrator to determine which witness is credible? Which witness did you think was credible here? Why? Is your ability to assess credibility in this case hindered by the fact that you did not observe the witnesses testifying? (If so, what does that say about the company's decision to discharge L?) What factors other than witness observation are likely to affect the arbitrator's assessment of credibility? For a discussion of factors influencing arbitrator's determinations of credibility, see Norman Brand, *supra* footnote 1, at 355–357. Would an arbitrator's personal views about typical characteristics of men and women affect the arbitrator's determination of credibility in a sexual harassment case? (Arbitrator Sands permitted the union attorney to ask branch manager Jacobs: "Would you think an average man or yourself would make a pass at a woman that weighs 225 pounds?" Stroehmann Bakeries, Inc. v. Local 776, International Brotherhood of Teamsters, 969 F.2d 1436, 1446 (3d Cir.1992). Can either male or female arbitrators be "neutral" in assessing credibility in a sexual harassment case?

5. Assume that Arbitrator Sands reached the merits of the discharge issue and believed the testimony of W regarding L's conduct.

(a) Would that provide just cause for the discharge of L, a seventeen-year employee? If so, why? If not, is there some other disciplinary action, such as a suspension without pay, for which there would be just cause? If the arbitrator believes a suspension would be the appropriate discipline, how long should it be? Should it be for the period from discharge until the date of the arbitrator's award (reinstatement without back pay)? Six months? One month? Two weeks? On what basis is an arbitrator to make such a decision? Or do you need more information in order to decide? If so, what? See the discussion in subsection 4 of this section on duration of back pay awards.

(b) Although Arbitrator Sands did not mention it in his award, employee L testified at the hearing as follows:

> [T]hey always have oranges sitting on the outside which are mostly throwaways and which her dad always gave me. So I picked up an orange and we were carrying on, and I said I wish my wife's breasts were as hard as this. She said, "You're awful." (Transcript at p. 241.)

Assume that L's testimony quoted here was the only evidence the employer had of L's misconduct. Would his comment to W have provided just cause for discipline or discharge?

6. Arbitration awards are rarely challenged in the courts and even more rarely overturned, but Arbitrator Sands' award was subsequently vacated by a federal district court on the ground that it violated public policy. Stroehmann Bakeries v. Local 776, International Brotherhood of Teamsters, 762 F.Supp. 1187 (M.D.Pa.1991), affirmed, 969 F.2d 1436, 1442 (3d Cir.) ("[A]n award which fully reinstates an employee accused of sexual harassment without a determination that the harassment did not occur

violates public policy."), cert. denied, 506 U.S. 1022, 113 S.Ct. 660, 121 L.Ed.2d 585 (1992). Does it? What about the public policy favoring due process and the presumption of innocence? Or is sexual harassment such an evil that we can dispense with such niceties? The Third Circuit probably would have been less likely to have affirmed vacation of the arbitrator's award in *Stroehmann Bakeries* had the case arisen subsequent to the Supreme Court's decision in Eastern Associated Coal Corp. v. United Mine Workers of America, Dist. 17, 531 U.S. 57, 121 S.Ct. 462, 148 L.Ed.2d 354 (2000), in which the Court clarified and narrowed the public policy ground for overturning an arbitration award. See Chapter III.C.2. *supra*.

7. The court of appeals concluded that the district court correctly remanded *Stroehmann Bakeries* for hearing before a different arbitrator because the arbitrator's use of language in the award demonstrated he was biased in favor of L. Did you notice any use of language in the award that would substantiate a conclusion of bias? If the arbitrator's language suggests he was biased in favor of the grievant, could the employer have successfully challenged the award in court on the ground that the arbitrator was biased?

8. Would there be just cause to discharge a delivery driver, regardless of the merits of a sexual harassment charge, simply because one of the employer's major customers would no longer, as a result of the charge, permit the driver to deliver goods at its stores?

9. For general discussions of the treatment of sexual harassment in labor arbitration, see Stephen M. Crow and Clifford M. Koen, *Sexual Harassment: New Challenge for Labor Arbitrators?* 47 Arbitration Journal 6 (June 1992); Carrie G. Donald and John D. Ralston, *Arbitral Views of Sexual Harassment: An Analysis of Arbitration Cases, 1990–2000*, 20 Hofstra Labor and Employment Law Journal 229 (2003); Anita Christine Knowlton and Robert Simmelkjaer, *Sexual Harassment*, Labor and Employment Arbitration (Tim Bornstein, Ann Gosline and Marc Greenbaum, eds., 2004); William A. Nowlin, *Sexual Harassment in the Workplace: How Arbitrators Rule*, 43 Arbitration Journal 31 (December 1988). For a discussion of the role of the union in the arbitration of sexual harassment cases, see Reginald Alleyne, *Arbitrating Sexual Harassment Grievances: A Representation Dilemma for Unions*, 2 University of Pennsylvania Journal of Labor and Employment Law 1 (1999).

CHICAGO TRIBUNE COMPANY

119 LA 1007 (Harvey A. Nathan, 2003).*

I. THE ISSUES

The parties agreed that the issues in this case are as follows:

1. Did the Company violate the Collective Bargaining Agreement when it terminated the grievant, W?

2. If so, what is the appropriate remedy?

II.   APPLICABLE CONTRACT PROVISIONS

The applicable provisions of the Collective Bargaining Agreement between the parties are as follows:

[The contract's management rights clause authorized the Company "to establish and enforce reasonable rules and regulations" and to "discharge regular employees for just cause."]

CHICAGO TRIBUNE COMPANY STANDARDS OF CONDUCT ATTENDANCE POLICY

* * * ABSENCES CONSIDERED OCCURRENCES

The following will be considered occurrences under the Attendance Policy:

Sick days used in excess of five (5). Any absence of one or more consecutive days for a single illness or injury will be considered one occurrence.... Time spent off work by an employee for Family Medical Leave Act (FMLA) qualifying reasons will not be considered occurrences....

More than three (3) tardies in a calendar year. Employees are eligible for three (3) tardies in a calendar year after completion of the probationary period. Starting with the fourth tardy, each tardy will be counted as a single occurrence. Tardiness is defined as not being at the work station ready to work at the starting time and at the prescribed time after rest and meal breaks....

Failure to call in within the specified time period to report an absence. Employees are requested to call in on a daily basis as far in advance of the start of their shift, but no later than sixty (60) minutes prior to the start of their shift to report absences with the exception of employees on approved medical leaves of absence. *Failure to call in within the appropriate time frame will classify the absence as a no show/no call and will be considered as two occurrences....* (Emphasis in original.)

REPORTING ABSENCES

To report an absence, an employee is required to call his/her immediate supervisor in accordance with departmental procedures.... * * *

ATTENDANCE CORRECTIVE ACTION LEVELS

... When corrective action becomes necessary, the employee will progress through levels of the corrective action as stated below.

Level	Number of Occurrences	Corrective Action
1	1	Counseling
2	2	Verbal Warning
3	3	Written Warning
4	4	2nd Written Warning
5	5	3-day suspension
6	6	Termination of employment

ACCELERATION OF ATTENDANCE POLICY/ATTENDANCE PROBATION

Any employee who reaches the suspension level twice within a 24-month revolving period will be terminated. . . .

III. THE FACTS

W was hired by the Company in July, 1985. About two or three years later she became a press operator. W was discharged effective January 7, 2003 for violation of the Company's attendance policy. She had been tardy on seven occasions in 2002, and on December 19th she was charged with a no call/no show violation when she was tardy again and failed to call the plant in a timely manner. According to the Company, this gave her six chargeable "occurrences," which under the attendance policy, warranted discharge.[1] Although orally advised of the discharge on January 7th, W subsequently received a written notice of the action dated February 28, 2003. After reviewing her tardiness record, the notice stated as follows:

> On December 19, 2002 you failed to notify your supervisor one hour prior to the start of your shift that you were going to be late. This classifies your absence as a no call/no show and constitutes two occurrences. Based on your record, this brings you to the termination level for attendance. * * *

W missed a lot of time from work in 2001 due to medical complications related to childbirth. She was on a short disability leave and used all twelve weeks of FMLA leave that year. She was approved to return to work on December 13, 2001. In 2002, her attendance was good. Except for the above-recited tardies, two occasions of funeral leave and her earned vacation time, she was at work. In 2002, W's mother, Kathryn, was seriously ill and unable to take care of herself. She lived near W and

---

1. The first three tardies were not chargeable. The next four gave her four "occurrences," each of which gave rise to progressive discipline. The final incident, classified as a no call/no show because of when W called in, cost two occurrences. Six occurrences in a rolling twelve month period called for termination of employment.

W became the primary care giver for Kathryn. During the day and evening of December 18, 2002, W was taking care of Kathryn, first by taking her out and then at her home. That night Kathryn's blood pressure was out of control and W, in consultation with Kathryn's physician, was monitoring her medication. W stayed with her mother until about midnight that night. When she went home she found that her one year old child was having difficulty sleeping. W rocked the child in a rocking chair and they both fell asleep.

W was due at work at 6:00 a.m. the following morning. She awoke at 5:50 and called the plant to notify them of what had happened. She asked to speak with her supervisor but he was unavailable. She spoke with another supervisor and asked if she should come in. That supervisor said yes and W immediately left for work, arriving at about 6:20. However, when she arrived her supervisor met her at the door and told her she was suspended pending investigation.

[When W met with company representatives on December 23 to discuss what had occurred on December 18-19, W explained why she had to take care of her mother. Jennifer Klinger from Human Resources replied that] "there might be cause for FMLA, and we were doing everything possible to come up with a way to save W's job." W testified that [her department manager] Kunz told her that they were going to give her another chance, that she would be given some FMLA forms to be filled out by Kathryn's doctor.

W then went with Klinger to get some forms. Klinger told her that while her son's ailments were not qualified under FMLA, her mom's seemed to be. Klinger then filled out the front page of the FMLA forms and checked the boxes indicating that W was "eligible for leave under the FMLA, pending receipt of medical certification if requested." Klinger told W to return the forms no later than January 3rd. [W submitted to the employer a physician's statement saying that Kathryn was seriously ill, that she needed the care of her daughter and that Kathryn had had hypertension and forgetfulness through December 19, 2002.]

On January 6th W met with Kunz and Debbie Gleason, a Human Resources Manager. W discussed the facts with Gleason, who testified that W told her that on the days in question she had taken care of her mother and then her child, and then fell asleep and overslept. * * * On the following day, January 7th W got a telephone call from Murtaugh and Kunz advising her that she was being terminated effective that day. She was told that her application for FMLA leave had been denied because she had no eligible time left in 2002. According to W she did not get any other explanation. W asked for a statement of the reasons in writing. The letter she received dated February 28th, after a grievance meeting, said nothing about the FMLA.

Debbie Gleason testified that she is one of the Company representatives who reviews FMLA applications and she consults with Company lawyers and physicians where necessary. In this case, she testified, she did not have to make such a review because she realized that the tardiness was not related to Kathryn's illness but was caused by W's having overslept. According to Gleason, oversleeping was not an "FMLA event." Gleason did acknowledge that had W's tardiness been an FMLA event she would have been eligible because more than 12 months had passed since W had last returned from leave. * * *

Additionally, Gleason prepared and gave the Union a statement of position at a grievance meeting held on January 23, 2003. * * * [The statement said that because the grievant had taken a nearly four-month leave of absence after her pregnancy in 2001 she was ineligible for FMLA leave in 2002. It said she was terminated because she hadn't provided documentation for her absence, was ineligible for FMLA and was at the termination level of the attendance policy. No one from the Company suggested at this, or a later grievance meeting, that W had been discharged for giving oversleeping as the reason for her tardiness.]

IV.   Positions of the Parties

A.   *The Company*

The Company argues that the tight deadlines which keep the newspaper competitive require teamwork and the presence of every employee at work at his/her task every day. The Company's attendance policy makes clear that tardiness and unexcused absence will not be tolerated. Because W violated the policy in the face of repeated warnings, the Company argues, her termination was for just cause.

The Company argues that much of the testimony and arguments raised by the Union obfuscate the real issues in this case. * * * The rules are fair and applied evenhandedly. The grievant violated the rules, was repeatedly warned, and then accumulated enough occurrences of tardiness to justify the discharge. In this case, the Company argues, it bent over backwards to accommodate the grievant, even to the point of suggesting on its own that her last incident might qualify for FMLA leave.

According to the Company, at first it appeared that the grievant was ineligible because she had used up her available leave time within the preceding twelve months. Subsequently a closer look found that not to be the case but, rather, that the grievant did not qualify because the reason for tardiness was not a qualifying event. Her tardiness on December 19th was not caused by her need to take care of her mother at a time that she was due at work. Rather, her tardiness was caused by oversleeping which was the result of attending to her children when she got home late on the night of December 18th. The grievant did not qualify for FMLA leave. There was nothing unreasonable in this conclusion, the Company argues. Had she missed time from work because she had to take her mother to the hospital, or some other medical emergency, that would have been a different case. Here, however, the Company points out, the grievant was tardy because she fell asleep rocking her child. Under these circumstances and given that the grievant had been repeatedly warned about tardiness she had an obligation to arrange her personal obligations in a manner which enabled her to come to work on time. * * * [11]

B.   The Union

The Union makes a multitude of arguments in support of the grievance. It argues that the grievant was the primary care-giver for her mother who was disabled with serious hypertension. It argues that the grievant needed to stay with her mother until late on December 18th and that when she finally got home she was so exhausted that she fell asleep with her child in her arms and overslept. The Union argues that the oversleeping was the result of the grievant's exhaustion from taking care of her mother. This was an FMLA qualified event, as the Company initially recognized. FMLA was granted to the grievant on December 23rd, the Union argues, subject only to her submission of supporting medical documentation. According to the Union the grievant supplied exactly what she was told to do and in the time allotted.

According to the Union, the Company's rationales for denying FMLA leave were inconsistent, contradictory and transparent. The Company should have known that its own policy established a 12 month rolling eligibility period and that by December 19th the grievant was eligible. [The Union complained that the Company kept changing its rationale for the grievant's discharge, first saying it was because she was ineligible for FMLA leave, then that it was because of her no call/no show, and then, at the hearing, saying it was because her oversleeping was not an FMLA event.] The Union argues that the Company's shifting rationales demonstrate the lack of integrity and justness of its decision. Indeed, the Union argues, none of the rationales are valid. Thus, the Union points out, by its own terms the one hour call-in requirement does not apply to tardiness, and its application as an "oral rule" makes no sense because often employees do not know they are going to [be] late an hour before it occurs. Likewise, the Union maintains, the grievant was clearly eligible for FMLA . * * * The oversleeping was clearly the result of the grievant's exhausting efforts taking care of her mother all day and late into the night. That she had to rock her son to sleep when she got home is simply a coincidence and does not take away from the efforts W expended that day in the care of her mother.

V.   ANALYSIS AND CONCLUSIONS

The primary difficulty with the Company's attractive arguments in its well-crafted brief is that the facts do not support the conclusions. There is little doubt that had the facts been proven as the Company asserts, its cause would have been just and sufficient. It is not the arbitrator's function to second-guess an employer in a discipline case

---

11. The Company further points out that even if the arbitrator were to find that the grievant's actions on December 19th were not a no call/no show situation, she still would have been eligible for discharge because this was the second time in 24 months that she had reached the suspension stage of the attendance rules. Under the rules, discharge occurs when an employee reaches the suspension stage twice within a 24 month period.

provided its procedure is fair, it follows its own rules and it has sufficient facts to support its allegations. The burden is on the Company to prove its case. The grievant need not establish her innocence.

[The arbitrator was unimpressed with the Union's argument about the Company's varied explanations for the grievant's discharge. He thought the Company should not be bound by its initial error in calculating periods of FMLA eligibility.] The issue for the parties has always been whether the grievant, despite the tardiness, was excused because of the operation of the FMLA. While the process would have been a lot more palatable had the Company had its act together from the beginning, the precise words used in effectuating discipline should not be determinative. Here the grievant was told from the beginning that the issue was whether she qualified for FMLA coverage or not.

That being said, the case comes down to whether the grievant qualified for FMLA coverage because the Company's rules provide that time spent off work due to FMLA qualifying reasons will not be considered as occurrences. Thus, because the Company has incorporated the FMLA into its rules, and the rules are in play because they are sanctioned by the Management Rights clause which also contains a "just cause" provision for discharge, the arbitrator, in determining whether the Company followed its own rules, is put in the position of deciding whether the tardiness on December 19th was an FMLA qualifying event. Through the adoption of these rules and the grievance-arbitration procedure in the collective bargaining agreement, the arbitrator has derivative authority to determine FMLA applicability as part of the just cause examination.[15]

As the arbitrator understands the Family and Medical Leave Act, the employee is entitled to twelve weeks of unpaid leave in any twelve month period. Despite the initial confusion, the Company's witnesses agreed at the arbitration hearing that the grievant had the requisite amount of qualifying time to be eligible for FMLA coverage should an FMLA event occur. The issue comes down to whether the tardiness on December 19th was such an event and whether it was properly supported by medical documentation.

The tardiness was a qualifying event because the manner in which the grievant fell asleep is immaterial. She was clearly enervated from her day and evening experience with her mother. The time she missed from work was time she needed to recover from this experience. It was directly related to the care-giving function for her mother. Undoubtedly had the grievant known of the statutory coverage at the time she might have called the Company that night and taken time off to recover. Had she done so she would have been protected by the Act. Her ignorance of her statutory rights should not affect the validity of her position in a just

15. In this regard, even if the arbitrator misconstrues the law, the parties have bargained for his interpretation of the statute when that law was incorporated by reference in the collective bargaining agreement. In a sense, the arbitrator is not defining the law. He is interpreting the contract.

cause for discharge contractual setting. She was entitled to take time off under the Company's rules to engage in direct care for her mother in time of serious illness.

The time she spends in the pursuit of this protected function need not be continuous. Thus, had she taken a nap during the day and evening when she was with her mother she would not have lost her protection. If she was the certified necessary care-giver, as her medical statement indicated, she need not be in direct patient contact every minute of the day or night. It is sufficient that her mother was at high risk and needed supervision. Thus, oversleeping is a qualified event when it is directly tied to the grievant's status as a protected care-giver.

Nor is it material that she fell asleep holding her son. That intervening fact does not alter the gist of her exhaustion. It was not her son that caused her to oversleep. That is simply a detail of her day, and not a defining feature. FMLA coverage for family illness is for a state of being, a role being served, not the actual act of administering to the patient at all times. The grievant might have been a qualifying care-giver for her mother even if she were not with her mother a good part of the day or evening, provided her availability was necessary for the care and treatment of the patient. Thus, that she may have expended a few minutes with her son does not disqualify her as the primary care-giver for her mother.

[The arbitrator rejected the Company's argument that W's medical documentation was insufficiently specific, saying that such documents didn't need to be construed as "common law pleadings."] In the event the data was insufficient for the Company, it had an obligation to inquire, not to simply dismiss the entire application. Accordingly, the Company failed to follow its own attendance policy when it discharged W, and for this reason the discharge was not for just cause.

Award

1. The Company violated the Collective Bargaining Agreement when it terminated the grievant, W.

2. The Company shall reinstate the grievant to her former position in the Pressroom with full seniority and make her whole for all wages and benefits lost.

3. The arbitrator retains jurisdiction of this case for a period of thirty days from the receipt of this Award for the purposes of resolving any disputes regarding the remedy in this Award.

Notes and Questions

1. One study of arbitration cases found that excessive absenteeism was the most common reason for discharge. Howard A. Cole, *How Representative are Published Decisions?*, 37 Proceedings of the National Academy of Arbitrators 183 (1985). For general discussions of arbitration decisions concerning absenteeism, see Barbara Zausner Tener and Ann Gosline, *Absenteeism and Tardiness*, Tim Bornstein, Ann Gosline and Marc Greenbaum, eds.,

supra footnote 1, at Chapter 17; and, *Attendance*, Norman Brand, ed., *supra* footnote 1, at Chapter 3.

2. Absenteeism causes significant problems for employers:

The absentee must be replaced. That often means calling in a replacement or holding over someone from the previous shift. In either event, overtime costs are incurred. Or perhaps the vacancy can be filled by transferring an employee from some other job. But that solution often involves an inexperienced replacement who may affect the quantity or quality of the product. All of these arrangements impose administrative burdens on management, particularly when seniority rights or overtime distribution rules must be applied. Thus, absenteeism is bound to lessen productivity and increase costs.

Howard Block and Richard Mittenthal, *Arbitration and the Absent Employee*, 37 Proceedings of the National Academy of Arbitrators 78–79 (1985).

3. On the other hand, employees, for a variety of reasons, may be unable to come to work. Some of those reasons will be legitimate, others not. If an employer attempts to assess the legitimacy of each absence it finds itself intruding into employee privacy, taking on a cumbersome administrative task, and having to draw difficult lines between excused and unexcused absences. In order to avoid such problems, employers, such as the Chicago Tribune, promulgate "no-fault" attendance policies in which employees receive graduated discipline for specific numbers of absences without regard to the reason for the absence. Such policies typically permit employees periodically to clear their attendance records by some specified period of perfect or near-perfect attendance. When an employee is ultimately discharged under such a plan, however, the arbitrator may find it difficult to reconcile the dismissal of a "faultless" employee with the contractual requirement of "just cause." As one arbitrator has described the conflict:

> In labor relations law, no fault attendance plans are one of many battle-grounds for efficiency and equity, two factors which often are diametric. Equity here is used synonymously with reasonableness and, hence, just cause, and efficiency refers to productive efficiency. Enhancing one may correspondingly reduce the other. Employers often hope that their no fault attendance plans will raise productive efficiency by liberating their managerial staff from the tedium of evaluating the veracity and reasonableness of an everlasting procession of employees' excuses for their attendance problems. Employers also want their no fault attendance plans to reduce or eliminate the inequities, real or perceived, associated with attendance problems. Employees often allege disparate treatment when supervisors try to tailor their decisions to the specific facts of the absentee dispute in question. Workers invariably will perceive differences among supervisors' decisions and conclude that the supervisors treated similarly situated employees differently and, thereby, discriminated when applying rules of attendance. * * *

> When attempting to strike a reasonable balance between equity and efficiency, employers should avoid pure no fault attendance plans which ignore fault altogether. * * * Instead, equity requires that employers leave employees some basic opportunity to address questions of fault.

T & M Rubber Co., 100 LA 84, 89 (Robert Brookins, 1992). Arbitrators Block and Mittenthal, *supra* Question 2, at 103–104, reach the same conclusion. ("A rule calling for automatic enforcement of penalties is modified by a provision for equitable exception to the rule as a safeguard against perverse applications.") See also, M. David Vaughn, *Current Issues in Attendance*, 55 Proceedings of the National Academy of Arbitrators, 39, 44 (2003) ("[E]ven in no-fault programs it is almost impossible to remove from analysis the fact that some reasons for absence are simply more excusable—more forgiveable—than others.") For one arbitrator's assessment of the reasonableness of a no-fault attendance policy, see the case of Chanute Manufacturing Company, *infra* Part C of this Chapter.

4. The Chicago Tribune's Attendance Policy imposes a three-day suspension without pay as the "corrective action" for an employee's fifth "occurrence." Arbitrator W. David Vaughn has written, "The customary management response of punishing absent employees through the use of additional forced absences is illogical and mutually unproductive." Vaughn, Question 3 *supra* at 45. Do you agree?

5. Assume that Grievant W in the *Chicago Tribune* case actually had exhausted her available leave under the FMLA as the employer had initially erroneously believed. Would there then have been just cause to discharge her? Would there have been "just cause" to discharge an employee who was late to work because she overslept after taking care of her critically ill mother? What about an employee who had exhausted FMLA leave but who continued to have chronic absences because of a heart condition? The arbitrators quoted in Question 3, *supra*, conclude that arbitrators must still address the question of fault when an employee is dismissed under a no-fault attendance policy. Does that mean they would overturn a discharge in a case like this hypothetical variant of *Chicago Tribune* or the case of the employee with the chronic heart condition? Is the issue *ability to work* rather than *fault*? Does the expectation of regular attendance justify both dismissal for failure to work when well and dismissal for chronic inability to work regardless of the reason?

6. Notice that the Chicago Tribune Company initially made a mistake in calculating whether W had worked sufficient hours since her previous FMLA leave to be again eligible for FMLA leave. The Tribune's Human Resources Manager testified in that case that she sometimes needed to consult with lawyers and physicians to make decisions on FMLA coverage. The provisions of the Family and Medical Leave Act, 29 U.S.C. §§ 2601–54 (2000), and its regulations, 29 C.F.R. Part 825 (2003), are complex and many issues remain unclear. As in *Chicago Tribune*, employers may require outside assistance to comply with the law, but even those service providers can make mistakes that need to be disentangled in the arbitration process. See, for example, Verizon Wireless, 117 LA 589 (Gerald B. Chattman, 2002) (employer used an outside company to make FMLA determinations, its decisions took four to six weeks, followed by an appeal process, and, despite its purported expertise, its record-keeping and decisionmaking were seriously flawed). Many non-lawyers or even lawyer advocates may lack the technical FMLA expertise to avoid making arguments that misconstrue or misapply the FMLA, further complicating the arbitrator's task. See, for example, Electrolux Home Products, 117 LA 46 (Stephen F. Befort, 2002) (union

claimed FMLA coverage but arbitrator, relying on regulatory history, concluded that hours not worked because of illness or accident do not count toward the required number of hours worked necessary for an employee to receive FMLA coverage).

7. In order to comply with the FMLA an employer may need to determine such issues as whether the employer itself is a covered employer at particular locations, whether the employees' hours of work since the last FMLA leave make the employee eligible for current leave, whether the employee has already exhausted the allowable twelve weeks of leave, whether the employee or the family member for whom the employee is caring has a "serious health condition," and whether a caregiver's assistance was in fact necessary. There may also be disputes about the timeliness and adequacy of documentation. With so many possible questions, it is easy to see how an otherwise simple case of absenteeism can raise complex and uncertain legal questions.

(a) Notice that the Employer's attendance policy in *Chicago Tribune* specifically stated that FMLA leaves would not be considered "occurrences" subjecting the employee to possible discipline. Notice how Arbitrator Nathan equates the employer's policy with the text of the collective bargaining agreement by saying that the employer's rules were authorized by the agreement's management rights clause authorizing the employer to promulgate rules. Was Arbitrator Nathan right to say, as he did in footnote 15, that in interpreting the FMLA he was "not defining the law" but "interpreting the contract"?

(b) Regulations implementing the FMLA provide that employers are prohibited from counting a FMLA leave as an absence under a no-fault attendance program. 29 C.F.R. § 825.220(c)(2003). If the Chicago Tribune's policy or its collective bargaining agreement made no reference to the FMLA, would it still be appropriate for the arbitrator to decide the same FMLA issue that Arbitrator Nathan decided?

(c) Arbitrator Nathan does not cite to any legal authorities to support his conclusion that the FMLA entitles an employee to leave for oversleeping after caring for a seriously ill family member. Should he have? Does it matter whether Arbitrator Nathan's conclusion was right as a matter of law? Is he correct in saying in footnote 15 that the parties have bargained for him to construe (and to misconstrue) the law?

(d) Was Arbitrator Nathan actually construing the FMLA or was he just cloaking his assessment of fairness and fault in the mantle of law? Does it matter if he was?

(e) For an extended discussion of the role of external law in labor arbitration, see Chapter V. B. *supra*.

8. The FMLA is not the only law that may affect just-cause decision-making in cases of discharge for excessive absenteeism or tardiness. The Americans with Disabilities Act (ADA), 42 U.S.C. § 12101 et seq. (2000), requires employers to make "reasonable accommodations" for disabled workers. Does "reasonable accommodation" require an employer to afford a disabled employee more absences than other employees under a no-fault attendance policy? Does "reasonable accommodation" preclude an employer

from *ever* discharging a disabled employee for excessive absenteeism? Or is a regularly absent employee unable to perform the "essential functions" of the job so as not to be entitled to ADA protection? See Charles T. Joyce, *The Impact of the Americans with Disabilities Act on Attendance Issues: An Anachronism in the Making?*, 55 Proceedings of the National Academy of Arbitrators 30 (2003) (suggesting that the ADA is unlikely to afford protection to employees subject to discharge for excessive absenteeism). In addition to the FMLA and the ADA, some states and localities have laws that impose additional medical and parenting leave requirements on employers.

EG & G MOUND APPLIED TECHNOLOGIES
98 LA 923 (Langdon D. Bell, 1992).*

BACKGROUND

EG & G Mound Applied Technologies (hereafter the "employer") operates a facility in Miamisburg, Ohio, commonly referred to as the "Mound plant," under contract with the United States Department of Energy ("DOE"). The employer is here engaged in the research, development, testing, and production of radioactive and conventional components for nuclear weapons and heat sources used in the N.A.S.A. space program.

Given the nature of the operations being conducted at the Mound plant and the potential adverse impact upon national security interests, it is the subject of intense security efforts, both in terms of physical measures at the site and the size and training of its security force, all of which are subject to orders and audits of the D.O.E. * * *

[The Employer discharged a seven-year employee, a security inspector, for tampering with, and rendering inoperable a safety and security emergency notification system.]

DECISION

[T]he security requirements covering this 300 acre facility are extensive, and overseen by the United States Department of Energy via issuance of orders to the contractor/employee and detailed audits to assure compliance. Several communication systems exist at the facility which are used independently and in conjunction with one another. * * * The public address system is the only emergency notification vehicle by which details and information concerning an emergency can be communicated to the plant's total employee population.

In late 1990 the plant's manager of security began receiving complaints from safety and building personnel that the public address system in and for building 102 was being turned down during the weekends at its controls. * * * [An elaborate investigation identified the Grievant by use of a dusting powder that adhered to the Grievant's uniform. The Grievant then acknowledged that he had unplugged the unit and had turned down the volume on two or three other occasions. The Employer concluded that the Grievant's deliberate and repeated actions to alter the operability of the emergency/PA system were totally unacceptable and contrary to the assigned mission of security inspectors.]

[The Employer had promulgated "general orders" that required security inspectors to "abide by all plant safety rules and regulations" and to "[r]efrain from tampering with, or using, any equipment or office machines." There was conflicting evidence presented at the hearing about whether the Grievant had ever received any specific instruction not to tamper with the public address system. The Union presented evidence that the security system had been tampered with on some dates on which the Grievant had not worked or had not been assigned to that building, although there was evidence that the Grievant sometimes visited the building despite not being assigned there.]

[The Employer has in place a five-step progressive discipline policy which includes discussion between the employee and the employee's immediate supervisor, a written reprimand, discussion between the employee and a more senior supervisor and a second written reprimand, a suspension without pay, and termination. The policy states, "if an individual does not perform in an acceptable manner, appropriate action will be taken. In such instances, the emphasis will be on corrective, rather than punitive action." The Employer's policy also states that serious work rules violations may render progressive discipline inapplicable.]

The employer asserts on brief that the potential consequences flowing from the grievant's deliberate and repeated actions to alter the operability of the emergency/PA system provide "just cause" and warrant discharging the grievant. This is particularly so for a member of the security force who served as a communications center officer and possessed knowledge of the critical importance of the system for the protection and security of the property and population at the plant. It cites the progressive protective measures taken by management to protect the system from tampering, the formation announcements, and the published general orders as providing clear notice and warning to the grievant that tampering with the system was prohibited.

The criticality of the hazardous operations conducted at this facility heighten the seriousness of this breach. As its manager of security testified, this facility has a much higher level of responsibility to the community than a General Motors' "warehouse" because of the nuclear work done here. Every exercise conducted at this facility utilizes and relies upon the proper functioning of this system to communicate emergencies and operational need announcements. The criticality of this system's operational capability is underscored by the D.O.E.'s surveillance of this system. As recently as 1989–1990 the D.O.E. sent an assembled group of 70 experts to the plant for a five week period to review and assess the site's ability to respond to simulated nuclear material accidents with medical, fire, and security personnel. Such response is "orchestrated" through the use of this very system which the grievant disengaged, placing in potential jeopardy the health and safety of the building's sixty occupants.

The employer's position is that the admitted action of the grievant is absolutely so contrary to the mission of the protective force as to demand the imposition of the discharge penalty. It is, in the employer's view, akin to a security officer abandoning his post in a vital area, for which discharge penalties have been imposed in the past.

The evidence and argument presented at the hearing and on brief by the Union was directed to demonstrate that the employer failed to prove the grievant "repeatedly" disabled the building 102 PA system and that the level of the grievant's June 22, 1991 admitted misconduct does not rise to that level which justifies discharge of a seven year employee with no prior disciplinary record.

The Union stresses the evidence demonstrating that, for the period of time the system was disabled in this single building no one was permitted in the building other than security officers, fire fighters or individuals accompanied by security officers possessing radios which carry the identical announcements made over the building's PA system. As such, it contends that the effect of the PA system disablement was isolated to this vacant building for a limited period of time, which was of no consequence because of the redundancy attendant to the security officer's possession of hand radios. Moreover, it asserts the existence of operative bells and claxton alarms situated in the building and area enable communication of the need to evacuate or take other action in the event of high level alarms, thus lessening the criticality of an operable building PA system.

On this later point the Union asserts that its evidence demonstrates the employer is exaggerating the criticality of an operable PA system. It cites its unrefuted evidence that the PA system in the SM/PP cafeteria has not been working for more than a year; that the building PA systems have volume controls in several meeting rooms and reception areas, as well as the guard shacks, where occupants regularly adjust the volume so as to avoid potential distraction. While not disputing the same, the employer notes that such action does not disable the system within the building and, in any event, announcements through speakers in adjacent rooms can yet be heard by occupants in the room where the volume has been turned down.

Finally, the Union asserts that the grievant lacked any scienter, ill-motive, or malicious intent. Instead, the grievant simply was irritated by the "muzak" regularly coming over the PA system, which had a tendency to make him drowsy on his midnight shift; that his actions did not physically damage or harm the system; and that he reactivated the building's system at the end of his tour by plugging it back in * * * something that was not done on prior tampering occasions, when the grievant wasn't even in the area.

This arbitrator is persuaded by the evidence that the hazardousness of this facilities' operation renders critical the mission of the protective force. This mandates strict adherence by the protective force to its general orders. Yet, based upon the totality of the evidence presented and the arguments presented by counsel representing the employer and the grievant the arbitrator is compelled to conclude that the employer failed to prove, by the preponderance of the evidence, that it possessed "just cause" for the termination of grievant's employment under the circumstances of this case.

The arbitrator's determination that the employer has failed to carry its burden of proof of establishing just cause for discharge has not been reached lightly. To the contrary, this arbitrator will not substitute his sense of work place justice for that of management, absent compelling reason. Arbitrators do not have the day to day responsibility of effectively and efficiently managing the business giving rise to employment producing collective bargaining agreements. The same is patently true and reflected in the case at bar where, following the issuance of this award, this arbitrator's task has ended * * * yet management continues to shoulder the day in and day out responsibility of protecting the health and safety of several hundred employees and government property of immense value in an extremely critical and hazardous nuclear environment. It is this employer, not this arbitrator, that is and will remain accountable to the D.O.E. for its security requirements at this site.

The imposition of disciplinary penalties is driven by two fundamental objectives: retribution and deterrence. As clearly revealed by this employer's guide to correcting unacceptable performance and behavior, the focus of this employer's disciplinary objectives is the deterrence of unacceptable conduct by corrective action, not simply retribution. Section. 1.b of that guide expressly provides that:

> No employee will be discharged for *continuing* poor work performance or *continuing* unacceptable behavior without prior documented warning that his/her performance or behavior is unacceptable and his/her continued employment is in jeopardy. [emphasis in original]

In the case at bar the employer failed to comply with its own guidelines by dismissing this seven year employee with no prior disciplinary record without the required documented warning of unacceptable behavior and the jeopardization of his continued employment. The circumstances here extant are not such as to reasonably provide the grievant with notice that such conduct would place his continued employment in jeopardy. There is not the slightest hint in the record of this case that any penalty short of discharge is incompatible, inconsistent, or detractive of the employer's ability to effectively meet its objectives, or that the grievant is anything other than ready, willing, able, and desirous of correcting his unacceptable behavior.

Instead, it appears from the record evidence that other security inspectors were engaging in the same unacceptable conduct, evidenced by the tampering occurrences at times when the grievant was demonstrated not to be, or not likely to be, in the area on the dates in which the tampering occurred. The penalty here imposed was either an over-reaction, or alternatively used as a stringent example so as to deter others from such conduct. The Union argues on brief that the extensive evidence mitigating the seriousness of the grievant's conduct is inconsistent with any discipline that would cause him to lose back pay and that, at most, grievant should be issued a letter of warning. Accordingly the Union requests grievant's reinstatement with full back pay, lost over-time, ill [sic] fringe benefits and seniority.

The Union's request simply misses the mark in this case. While such a request might well warrant serious consideration were the grievant's unacceptable behavior to have occurred in a General Motors' warehouse, it warrants absolutely no consideration within the context of this case. The responsibilities borne by this employee to his employer, the D.O.E., and to the community in which its facility is situated requires that the employer possess all reasonable means to impress upon its employees the serious potential hazards that exist and that absolute adherence to its safety and operational orders is required. In this instance, reinstatement without back pay or fringe benefits would effectively reduce the disciplinary action imposed to an eight month suspension. Such a penalty for the unacceptable conduct here found to exist, while not normally used at this facility, is found to be reasonable and necessary for the employer to meet its responsibilities, and appropriate as a deterrent to such unacceptable conduct in the future.

AWARD

It is the arbitrator's finding and award that the employer failed to establish by a preponderance of the evidence that its discharge of the grievant was for just cause, and the grievant is ordered reinstated without back pay or other fringe benefits.

Notes and Questions

1. Imagine yourself as the advocate for the Employer at EG & G Mound. In a few sentences articulate your vision of this case as you might at the beginning of the Employer's opening statement at the arbitration hearing. Now do the same thing as the advocate for the union. The parties' radically different interpretations of the same essentially uncontested facts illustrate the reason why unions and employers sometimes find grievance disputes irreconcilable in the absence of a neutral arbitrator.

2. The arbitrator notes that the employer has the burden of proving just cause for discharge, but also states that he will not "substitute his sense of work place justice for that of management, absent compelling reason." Are these assertions inconsistent?

3. The arbitrator overturned the Grievant's discharge because of the Employer's failure to issue a warning that his behavior was unacceptable

and its repetition could warrant discharge. Does the Employer's policy, quoted in the arbitrator's award, from Section 1.b of the Employer's guide, preclude discharge without warning in all cases? Note that the Employer's policy also stated that serious work violations could render progressive discipline inapplicable. What if the Grievant had shot a supervisor at work? Would the Employer's policy preclude his discharge until after he had been warned that repetition could result in discharge? If some serious misconduct makes warning prior to discharge unnecessary, did the Grievant's conduct here fall into that category? Consider *supra* item C.1.c. from Professors Abrams and Nolan's outline of their theory of just cause.

4.   There were apparently other employees who had tampered with the emergency public address system whom management was unable to identify. Does the requirement of "industrial equal protection," that like cases be treated alike, preclude the Employer from disciplining the Grievant because it is unable to identify the others? Or, to the contrary, is particularly harsh discipline against the Grievant warranted because of the need to deter others remaining in the workforce who have tampered with the equipment in the past and might otherwise do it again?

5.   The arbitrator concludes that the discharge must be overturned because the Grievant was not warned, yet he imposes an eight-month suspension without pay. If there was not just cause for discharge without warning, why is there just cause for an eight-month loss of pay without warning? See *infra* the discussion of the duration of back pay awards in subsection 4 of this Section.

BRIGGS DIVISION, JPI PLUMBING PRODUCTS, INC.

97 LA 386 (Robert W. Kilroy, 1991).*

FACTS

The Company is engaged in the manufacture and distribution of ceramic toilet accessories at its Robinson, Illinois facilities. Grievant had been employed by the Company for more than twelve years. His last classification was Vacation Relief. In this classification, grievant was assigned to work vacant positions of employees on vacation. On the evening of January 7, 1991, grievant was assigned to the toilet tank line as a fitter. This is a three position line where the tank grader inspects ceramic tanks and places them on the line. The tank fitter installs the ballcock and flush assemblies, and the packer labels and crates the finished tanks.

Prior to beginning work on this date, grievant filed a grievance because he had been denied the opportunity as senior man to fill another vacancy on an easier production line.

On the morning of January 8, 1991, a routine quality control check revealed serious deficiencies in the production of the tank line by both

* Reprinted with permission from *Labor Arbitration Reporter–Labor Arbitration Reports*, 97 LA 386. Copyright 1992 by The Bureau of National Affairs, Inc. (800–372–1033) <http://www.bna.com>.

the fitter and packer. These included flush valves installed backwards, plastic screw-type fittings stripped, and ballcocks off location interfering with the lever assembly. The packer had failed to apply numerous labels to the product and the carton flaps were not properly folded. These deficiencies resulted in the entire shift production being audited and demonstrated a 30% defective rating on the fitter, 6.5% of mislabeling by the packer, and 100% failure of the packer to properly fold cartons.

In conference with management on the matter, grievant's only excuse was that he was rushed to fit 705 pieces on a shift.

After investigating the matter, the Company terminated grievant for gross negligence by letter dated January 11, 1991. The packer was also discharged. Subsequently, after grievances were filed protesting both discharges, the Company reduced the discharge of the packer to a disciplinary suspension upon the Union's request for leniency and the employee's [assurances] of better performance.

Grievant's discharge was allowed to stand. During his term of employment, grievant had never been disciplined for conduct, performance or absenteeism.

Applicable Contractual Provisions

[The contract contained a just cause provision.]

Position of the Company

The Company contends that there was just cause to discharge grievant upon the uncontradicted facts. The Company argues that grievant knew his job as a tank fitter but yet produced the largest quality disaster in management's memory. The company states that grievant purposely created the defects found and it was in retaliation for not being transferred to another job.

Position of the Union

The Union argues that grievant's discharge was not for just cause because of disparate treatment. The Union states that the grievant's alleged state of mind as stated by the Company superintendent was based on hearsay, and further the facts do not support the conclusion of management that grievant purposely put out defective work. In mitigation of poor work, the Union argues that grievant had not performed that job for almost two years and had twelve years of good service with the Company. * * *

Discussion

Based on the evidence, the arguments of the parties, and the collective bargaining agreement, the Arbitrator finds there was not proper cause to discharge grievant.

In evaluating proper cause or just cause for discipline, the Arbitrator must affirmatively find that a valid rule existed for the safe and efficient operation of the plant, the employee was aware of the rule, the employee violated the rule, that a fair and full investigation was made of the matter, that the discipline was proportionate to the offense, and that the grievant was treated as other individuals who violated like and similar rules. The burden of proof is upon the Company to affirmatively establish all of the above by a preponderance of the evidence.

No plant rules or regulations governing employee conduct and/or performance were introduced into evidence. Nor was any evidence introduced as to what by practice between the parties or by unilateral action established gross negligence as applied to other employees. * * *

In the absence of any specific rule * * * the Company has amply demonstrated negligence on the part of the employee and his failure to perform assigned tasks with care. Whether or not it is gross or intentional is less convincing in the absence of corroborating data as to performance on the tank line by others upon like and similar product in like and similar amounts of production. What makes the bare statistics offered by the Company less convincing is the lack of relationship with other objective factors when balanced against the employee's claim that the line was running too fast. While the Company investigation in terms of actual defects by grievant is convincing, and demonstrates poor work performance, standing alone it does not constitute gross negligence.

While grievant's excuse may be self serving, and may even be suspicious in view of his attempts to get off the worst job in the factory, it remains uncontradicted by Company evidence that others have done just as much with [nowhere] near the same amount of defects. Having established by complete investigation that grievant failed to perform to expectations, and his failure causing damage to the Company, it remains to evaluate grievant's treatment.

This Arbitrator is of the school of thought that management is charged with and responsible for determining what is a proper penalty. It is only when this determination is demonstrated to be arbitrary, capricious, invidious or mistaken that an Arbitrator can legitimately set aside the decision of management. In this case, the decision of the Company is capricious. Here, we have two individuals, grievant and the packer, on the same line failing to perform as expected. There is no evidence before the Arbitrator as to why the discharge of the packer was reduced to a disciplinary suspension while grievant remained on discharge. Certainly, mislabeling and carton folds are not the same as inverted flush valves or crooked ballcocks. Even more certain are the facts that on a percentage basis, the packer had been less and more of the same thing, failure to perform as required. In the absence of some rational and business related reason to be more lenient to the packer, the treatment of the grievant is capricious. It is excessive in terms of the number of years grievant has been employed without any problems whatsoever. In simple terms, it is not fair and equal treatment for like offenses.

For all the foregoing reasons, the Arbitrator makes the following Award.

AWARD

Grievance granted. Grievant is to be reinstated upon the same date the packer was returned to work. * * *

Notes and Questions

1. Did the arbitrator make a finding of fact regarding the Employer's claim that the Grievant had deliberately created the defects? If not, was that a significant omission by the arbitrator?

2. On the basis of the evidence described in the award, how should the arbitrator have decided the question of whether the Grievant intentionally caused the defects? Is this a case in which the rule that the employer bears the burden of proof in discharge cases would have a significant effect upon resolution of the question?

3. Assume that the Grievant's production of defects was *not* intentional and that the Grievant was simply incapable of satisfying production standards. Under what circumstances would there be just cause to discipline an employee for incompetence? Consider such factors as how an employer should establish production standards, what notice of expectations should be provided to employees, and whether just cause requires warnings and an opportunity to improve performance. Does just cause require that an employer offer an employee a transfer before initiating a discharge for incompetence? Assuming that there was no proof of intentional misconduct in *Briggs Division*, was there just cause to support the suspension actually imposed by the arbitrator? For a general discussion of arbitration decisions concerning discipline for poor work performance, see Norman Brand, *supra*, footnote 1 (Chapter 4, Job Performance Problems).

4. The arbitrator's finding of lack of just cause rests partly on the Employer's failure to treat equally the Grievant and the packer whose discharge was reduced, in a settlement between the Employer and the Union, to a suspension. The arbitrator's decision was premised on the requirement of industrial equal protection that like cases be treated alike. But what is a "like" case? Two cases will rarely be identical. What factors ought to be taken into account in determining whether two cases are sufficiently alike as to warrant equal treatment? Were the cases of the Grievant and the packer sufficiently similar so as to require equal treatment or were there significant distinguishing factors?

5. If you represented the company in this case, how would you have argued the case? What additional evidence would you have wanted to provide?

CHAMPION INTERNATIONAL
96 LA 325 (C. Gordon Statham, 1991).*

[The issue was whether the Grievant, A, was discharged for just cause. The contract contained an explicit "just cause" provision, as well

* Reprinted with permission from *Labor Arbitration Reporter–Labor Arbitration Reports*, 96 LA 325. Copyright 1991 by The Bureau of National Affairs, Inc. (800–372–1033) <http://www.bna.com>.

as an appendix that detailed Rules for Employee Conduct, including the
following:]

> Any employee who commits any of the following acts or other
> acts which are properly and customarily the subject of disciplinary
> action, may be disciplined, including discharge from employment,
> either after a warning or immediately without warning, depending
> on the seriousness, nature and circumstances of the violation(s).
> * * *

> 31. Being convicted of violating any civil or criminal law which
> is of such a nature that whether a period of confinement is ordered
> or not, conviction reflects unfavorably upon the Company, other
> employees, or upon the employee involved. * * *

[The Employer's Substance Abuse Policy expressed concern for drug
and alcohol use by employees that impaired safety or performance. It
emphasized rehabilitation. It stated that any employee found selling
drugs or alcohol on the Mill site would be subject to immediate termination.]

BACKGROUND

The Grievant, A, was terminated September 13, 1989 pursuant to
Rule 31 of the Appendix of the Company–Union Agreement and the
Company's substance abuse policy based upon his plea of guilty to the
State of Alabama felony charge of "Unlawful Distribution of Controlled
Substances" for which he was sentenced to five (5) years in the State
Penitentiary and fined $500.00 which sentence was commuted to four (4)
years probation effective November 16, 1989.

[The Grievant was a material handler who had worked for the
Employer for nearly sixteen years. He gave the following testimony at
the arbitration hearing regarding the circumstances that gave rise to his
guilty plea.]

> I was in Town Creek riding around. I was—a off day or—and riding
> down through town, and I saw this guy that I've known all my life, a
> friend of mine, and he stopped me and we were talking, and he had
> a girl with him, and asked me if I knew where he could get a half a
> gram of cocaine. And I told him possibly I—I probably did, and I told
> him the guy's name that he could get it from, and he said, "Well, I
> don't know him. Could you pick it up for me?" I said, "Yeah, I will."
> And he said, "Well, I'll meet you back down here in a little while."
> And I said, "All right. I'll be back through town in about 20 or 30
> minutes, something like that." I left and went to this other guy's
> house right outside of Town Creek, pick up a half a gram of cocaine
> from him, brought it back and gave it to this guy, this friend of
> mine, and charged him exactly for what I had to give for it. It was
> $50 for a half a gram of cocaine, and I gave it to him. He left, and
> I—I just drove off and didn't have any idea of what, you know, what
> had happened or who it was or anything.

[The Grievant also testified that sometime later the same friend asked him to buy some cocaine for him again and the Grievant refused.]

[The Company contended that the Grievant had clearly violated Rule 31 because drug dealing reflects unfavorably upon all those named in the rule. It maintained that the reasonableness of the rule could not be questioned because it was part of the agreement between the parties. The Company asserted that the existence of the rule makes it unnecessary for it to demonstrate a nexus between the conviction and the Grievant's employment, but that it could nevertheless demonstrate such a nexus because (1) the arrest and conviction occurred and were publicized locally; (2) local residents knew the Grievant was employed at the Company; and (3) the Company is active in community affairs and this incident damaged its reputation. It asserted that an officer on the Drug Task Force indicated that the Grievant may have been more involved in drugs than this conviction alone would suggest.]

[The Union contended that there was no nexus between the Grievant's off-duty misconduct and his work at the Mill. It stated that the nature of the Company's product precluded any loss of business as a result of the conviction. It stated that other employees had unanimously supported the arbitration, indicating that they had no reluctance to continue working with the Grievant. The Union presented a letter from the Grievant's probation officer stating that he had been a model probationer and that the officer was not aware of any other dealing or drug use by the Grievant prior to his conviction. The Union also claimed that the Company had not uniformly discharged employees convicted of crimes.]

Does Negotiated Rule No. 31 Grant to the Company Uncontestable Rights which Negate Reasonableness and Nexus?

The language of Rule No. 31 is extremely broad and would seem to grant to the Company unrestricted discretion to terminate an employee for violation of any civil or criminal law which reflected unfavorably upon the employee, other employees or the Company.

The key to this language is the word unfavorably. This must be construed in the context of arbitration law. Therefore, the Arbitrator is of the opinion that to reflect unfavorably there must be a nexus established and the Company must meet the test generally accepted in labor-management disputes. Further, in cases of termination, the Company must meet the standard of just cause as it relates to the basis for the termination.

Therefore, the Arbitrator rules that the Company, in applying Rule No. 31, must establish the reasonableness of the application of the rule and that a nexus existed as a basis for the termination.

[The arbitrator found that the Grievant's circumstances were distinguishable from those of an employee convicted of misdemeanor drug possession and an employee reinstated after serving time for murder.]

Nexus

The Grievant lived in Town Creek, population 1,200–1,400, located approximately six miles from the mill. [Another employee at the Company testified that the Grievant was well known in the community, known to work at Champion and, therefore, Champion's reputation was damaged.]

[The arbitrator noted that none of the newspaper articles mentioned that the Grievant was an employee of Champion. The arbitrator also observed that there was no effect on the Employer's customers, other employees did not oppose the Grievant's reinstatement and the Grievant's conviction did not directly preclude him working as a material handler.]

Severity of the Offense

[The arbitrator commented that criminal convictions can vary substantially in their seriousness and that it was important to take into account the particular circumstances of the Grievant's conviction. The arbitrator reviewed the facts of the conviction about which the Grievant had testified at the arbitration hearing.]

The friend who set up the Grievant did so in order to get a guns violation dismissed. The Grievant was advised by the Drug Task Force that if he would cooperate and make a buy of drugs at Champion the charges would be dismissed. The Grievant refused feeling that it would jeopardize the safety of his wife and children.

It is apparent from the facts that the Grievant was not a principal player in a high profile drug conspiracy. In fact, the Grievant was not the source, nor the broker, of the drug deal. There was no evidence that the Grievant had any other drug contacts other than his friend. According to the newspaper account, 47 persons had indictments returned as a result of a nine months investigation by the Northwest Alabama Drug Task Force. * * *

The evidence regarding the Grievant did not establish that he was involved in a drug conspiracy, therefore, the Arbitrator concludes that there is no relationship between the Grievant and the indictment of 47 persons for drug related charges.

[The arbitrator said that he was impressed by the fact that the Grievant did not profit from the sale of the cocaine and that he declined to make an additional purchase of drugs at the request of the undercover agent. He also noted the favorable letter from the probation officer.]

The Arbitrator can reasonably conclude that whatever the Grievant's involvement with drugs, the evidence would indicate that it was minimal.

The Arbitrator, to the contrary, would have absolutely no feelings of mitigation if the evidence had established that the Grievant was a source of controlled substances, planned the flow and distribution, controlled the money and brokered the deals. Such evidence would have established a major drug involvement dedicated to the drug culture. Any employer would have total justification to terminate such an employee.

CONCLUSION

Rule No. 31 does not constitute a basis for the Grievant's termination, even under Rule No. 31, the Company must establish the necessary nexus for the Grievant's off duty conduct and its adverse effect upon the Company, which the evidence failed to establish. Further, although the Grievant violated a criminal statute such violation per se is not a termination offense, especially if the evidence mitigates in the Grievant's behalf.

These type cases present a dilemma for employers.

The Company evaluated the circumstances and made a good faith judgment that Rule No. 31 constituted proper justification to terminate the Grievant. The Arbitrator notes, however, that the Grievant has been employed for 16 years and length of seniority is always a factor of consideration. The Grievant has been off the payroll for 17 months and this is sufficient discipline for the offense.

[The arbitrator ordered that the Grievant be reinstated without back pay.]

Notes and Questions

1. When there is a "just cause" provision in a collective bargaining agreement, one of the following circumstances will exist: (a) there are no specific rules on employee conduct; (b) the employer has unilaterally promulgated rules of employee conduct; or (c) the union and the employer collectively bargained for rules of employee conduct. *Champion International* is an example of the third category. How should the arbitrator's task differ in each of the three categories?

2. Rule 31 of the appendix to the parties' agreement in *Champion* stated that the Employer could discharge an employee for any conviction that "reflects unfavorably upon the Company, other employees, or upon the employee involved." The arbitrator acknowledged that this language, on its face, appeared to grant the employer "unrestricted discretion to terminate" any employee whose conviction caused an unfavorable reflection. The arbitrator nevertheless concluded that the term "unfavorably" should be construed "in the context of arbitration law" to require proof of a nexus between the conviction and the Grievant's work. Was the arbitrator correct in imposing a requirement of nexus when the contract language required only an unfavorable reflection? Why or why not? Don't parties have the authority to negotiate a just cause scheme in which an employer has greater discretion to discharge employees than would exist in the absence of such specific language? Did they do so here?

3. Arbitrator Statham did not provide any citation to support his assertion that "arbitration law" requires a nexus. He nevertheless accurately reports the consensus among arbitrators regarding the circumstances under which, in the absence of more specific contract language, off-duty

misconduct may establish just cause. In their comprehensive and widely-cited article, arbitrators Marvin Hill and Mark Kahn conclude:

> In general, arbitrators are reluctant to sustain discipline or discharge based on off-duty misconduct (i.e., conduct that occurs off the premises during nonworking time) absent some relationship or "nexus" to the job.

Marvin F. Hill, Jr. and Mark L. Kahn, *Discipline and Discharge for Off–Duty Misconduct: What are the Arbitral Standards?*, 39 Proceedings of the National Academy of Arbitrators 121, 124 (1987). The authors found that arbitrators find nexus satisfied in four categories:

> (a) damage to the employer's business or reputation or to both; (b) unavailability of the employee (incarceration); (c) impact of grievant's reinstatement on fellow employees (their refusal to work with the off-duty offender or their potential exposure to danger from the offender); and (d) unsuitability for continued employment in light of the misconduct.

Id. at 126. See also Marvin F. Hill, Jr. and James A. Wright, Employee Lifestyle and Off–Duty Conduct Regulation (1993) and Theodore J. St. Antoine, ed., *supra* footnote 1 at § 6.6. For examples of arbitrators' application of the nexus requirement, see S.B. Thomas, Inc., 106 LA 449 (Reginald Alleyne, 1995) (insufficient nexus between conviction for participation in scheme to defraud insurance company of $33,000 for false claim of stolen personal property and job as a bakery products delivery truck driver with no responsibility for handling employer money); and North Oakland Medical Centers, 106 LA 488 (William P. Daniel, 1996) (sufficient nexus between assault conviction for off-duty stabbing and work as a hospital food service worker because of history of angry confrontations with co-workers and access to sharp objects in the hospital kitchen). More recently, in U.S. Foodservice, 114 LA 1675 (Joseph Chandler, 2000), the arbitrator held that the employer did not have just cause indefinitely to suspend an employee who killed another parent in the course of a fight at a youth hockey practice session. In 2004, the employee's six to ten year prison sentence for involuntary manslaughter was pending on appeal. Boston Herald, May 5, 2004, 2004 WL 57720994.

4. Arbitrator Statham found that the Company had not demonstrated nexus. Do you agree? Does it matter that the Employer was apparently a manufacturer and wholesaler and had no customers in the community? Is it relevant that the newspaper reported the Grievant's conviction, that the newspaper did not mention where the Grievant was employed, but that residents of the small community may have known the Grievant to be an employee of Champion? In a larger community, would it be "just" for an employee's right to retain a job to turn on whether a newspaper happened to report the employee's place of employment? In a study of off-duty substance abuse arbitration awards, in every one of three cases in which an employer's name was mentioned in media publicity about the incident, the arbitrator denied the grievance. Helen Elkiss, *Employee Rights vs. Employer Concerns: Substance Abuse Off–Duty*, 49 Dispute Resolution Journal 79, 80 (March 1994).

5.   If the arbitrator had concluded that Rule 31 should be applied to the facts without regard to matters of nexus, should the arbitrator have concluded that the conviction here "reflect[ed] unfavorably upon the Company, other employees, or upon the employee involved"? If so, would that necessarily demonstrate just cause for discharge?

6.   Assume that a seventeen-year material handler at Champion was convicted of selling cocaine under circumstances indicating that the employee was dealing on a regular basis, but neither using drugs nor selling them at work. Assume that the employee's guilty plea also resulted in a sentence of probation. In such a case would there clearly be a nexus between the conviction and the employee's work warranting discharge? Why or why not? Compare Trane Co., 96 LA 435 (James L. Reynolds, 1991) (outside dealing involving other employees has a corrupting influence on the workplace), with Brockway Pressed Metals, Inc., 98 LA 1211 (Len Mayer, 1992) (the employer could not prove the employee's conduct had an adverse effect upon the employer's enterprise).

7.   *Reinstatement without backpay.*

(a) In *Champion*, the arbitrator, after saying that just cause requires a nexus, concludes that there was no nexus between the Grievant's conviction and any adverse effect upon the Company. The arbitrator nevertheless imposes upon the Grievant a seventeen-month suspension without pay. If there was no nexus, why was there just cause for a seventeen-month suspension?

(b) The arbitrator was troubled by what he perceived as a dilemma: The Employer had discharged the Grievant in good faith reliance upon its interpretation of Rule 31. When an arbitrator later disagrees with that interpretation, should the Employer be required to pay seventeen months of wages, for which no work was obtained, to a convicted drug dealer? Do you agree with the arbitrator that these circumstances create a dilemma? If so, how should it be resolved?

(c) Assume that the Grievant's conduct in *Champion* established just cause for a suspension of some duration. Why was it that the just length of the suspension was the period of seventeen months that elapsed from the date of discharge to the date of the arbitrator's award? If the arbitrator's award had been issued five months after discharge would there be just cause for a five-month suspension? See the discussion of the duration of back pay awards in subsection 4 of this Section, *infra*.

(d) In *Champion*, the judicial system had concluded that the Grievant's conviction warranted a sentence, as commuted, of probation without payment of a fine. As a result of the arbitrator's award, however, the Grievant lost tens of thousands of dollars of wages as a penalty for the conviction. Is it the appropriate role of the workplace to penalize employees for nonworkplace misconduct far beyond penalties imposed by the criminal justice system?

8.   For comprehensive discussions of drug and alcohol issues in arbitration, see Frank Elkouri and Edna Asper Elkouri, Resolving Drug Issues (1993); Norman M. Brand, ed., Discipline and Discharge in Arbitration (Chapter 6, Substance Abuse) (1998); M. David Vaughn, Linda K. Shore,

Beth A. Paulson and Andrée Y. McKissick, *Drug and Alcohol Issues*, Labor and Employment Arbitration (Tim Bornstein, Ann Gosline and Marc Greenbaum, eds., 2004). See also Tia Schneider Denenberg and R.V. Denenberg, Alcohol and Other Drugs: Issues in Arbitration (1991); Tia Schneider Denenberg, *The Arbitration of Employee Drug Abuse Cases, I. An Arbitrator's Perspective*, 36 Proceedings of the National Academy of Arbitrators 90 (1984); *Substance Abuse: The Problem That Won't Go Away*, 40 Proceedings of the National Academy of Arbitrators 67 (essays by William A. McHugh, Jr., Willis J. Goldsmith, and Leroy D. Clark) (1988).

4. REMEDIAL ISSUES IN DISCIPLINE CASES[7]

Reinstatement. If an arbitrator finds that an employer lacked just cause for discharging an employee, the arbitrator must determine the appropriate remedy. Although courts do not order specific performance of employment contracts, reinstatement is the most common remedy for wrongful termination in labor arbitration.[8] Courts have assumed that a compelled employment relationship is unlikely to be successful.[9] It may be, however, that the conditions within a union workplace make reinstatement more likely to be successful. Although the complexity of relevant factors makes it difficult to draw general conclusions about the success rate of reinstatements in the union setting,[10] several studies suggest that they are usually successful.[11] A thorough study of 19 cases found that most reinstated employees actually returned to work. Those who did so performed at least as well as they had before discharge.[12] An

7. See generally, Norman M. Brand, ed., Discipline and Discharge in Arbitration (Chapter 12, Remedies for Inappropriate Discipline) (1998); Marvin Hill, Jr. and Anthony V. Sinicropi, Remedies in Arbitration (Chapter 7, Reinstatement, and Chapter 8, Back Pay) (2d ed. 1991); Theodore J. St. Antoine, ed., The Common Law of the Workplace: The Views of Arbitrators (Chapter 10, Part II, Remedies in Discharge and Discipline Cases) (1998).

8. Dallas L. Jones explains this unusual presumption of the appropriateness of reinstatement in American arbitration as the result of the fact that employee terminations were very frequent at the time that unions first gathered strength in the 1930s and that job security was of central importance to American unions. Dallas L. Jones, *Ramifications of Back–Pay Awards in Discharge Cases*, 22 Proceedings of the National Academy of Arbitrators 163, 163–164 (1970). Professor Martha West suggests that reinstatement was assumed to be appropriate in grievance arbitration because grievance arbitration evolved from interest arbitration in which arbitrators had routinely reinstated groups of discharged striking employees. Martha West, *The Case Against Reinstatement in Wrongful Discharge*, 1988 University of Illinois Law Review 1, 22–23.

9. West, *supra* footnote 8, at 10–11.

10. See I. B. Helburn, *Seniority and Postreinstatement Performance*, 43 Proceedings of the National Academy of Arbitrators (1991) (reviewing several prior studies). See also David Lewin, *Theoretical and Empirical Research on the Grievance Procedure and Arbitration: A Critical Review*, Employment Dispute Resolution and Worker Rights in the Changing Workplace 137, 164 (Adrienne E. Eaton and Jeffrey H. Keefe, eds., 1999) (concluding a summary of the findings of studies of postreinstatement turnover rates by saying that most are flawed by the absence of control groups of nongrievants).

11. William E. Simkin, *Some Results of Reinstatement by Arbitration*, 41 Arbitration Journal 53 (September 1986). Arbitrator Simkin reports on his own reinstatements at one company over a period of more than twelve years. Of 120 employees reinstated, he found that forty-five were later discharged. It is difficult to compare this study with others because of the long time after reinstatement (as long as fourteen years in some cases) that employee status was assessed.

12. Jones, *supra* footnote 8, at 171.

earlier survey of 159 reinstated employees concluded that the "post-reinstatement employee becomes or continues to be a stable, reliable, and generally acceptable and satisfactory employee with whom there is no further serious work or disciplinary problem."[13] There is also evidence that the reinstatement of a discharged employee does not in most cases adversely affect the performance and behavior of other employees.[14]

Advocates should take note of an interesting study on the relationship between the passage of time from discharge to arbitration award and the likelihood of employee reinstatement. Researchers found that each one-month increase in the time from discharge to award reduced the grievant's odds of reinstatement by 8.6%.[15] That suggests that unions should seek prompt hearing dates and prefer arbitrators with a history of issuing prompt awards.

Conditional Reinstatement. While most arbitrators' reinstatement awards are unconditional, some make reinstatement dependent on conditions to be satisfied either before or after reinstatement.[16] For example, if the discharged employee's conduct resulted from a physical or mental problem, or from chemical dependency, an arbitrator may condition reinstatement on certification from a health care provider that the employee has completed treatment and may return to work. Or an arbitrator may order reinstatement conditioned on nonrepetition of the circumstances giving rise to the discharge. For example, in such a "last chance" order, an arbitrator might state that an employee would be subject to immediate discharge if future attendance did not meet a specified standard. Marvin Hill and Anthony Sinicropi have criticized such conditional reinstatement orders on the grounds that they are

---

13. Arthur Anthony Malinowski, *An Empirical Analysis of Discharge Cases and the Work History of Employees Reinstated by Labor Arbitrators*, 36 Arbitration Journal 31, 46 (March 1981). Despite the employees' success, Malinowski found that employers nevertheless consider the reinstatement "a personal affront and a challenge to their decision-making authority." *Id.* One researcher, after describing several surveys of employer opinion about the effectiveness of reinstatement concluded, "Taken as a whole, these studies also suggest that employers believe that incidence of postreinstatement disciplinary infractions by reinstated employees do not differ significantly from the incidence of infractions among other employees and that reinstatement does not have detrimental effects on employer authority, supervisory relations, or work group performance." Lewin, *supra* footnote 10, at 164.

14. Jones, *supra* footnote 8, at 172–173.

15. Nels E. Nelson and A.N.M. Meshquat Uddin, *The Impact of Delay on Arbitrators' Decisions in Discharge Cases*, 23 Labor Studies Journal 3 (1998). The au-

thors theorize that the "status quo tendency" in decisionmaking generally predisposes arbitrators to interpret evidence in such a way as to support the status quo of the employee's discontinued employment; the longer the employee remains unemployed, the stronger the tendency.

16. Arbitrators generally consider that the authority to determine "just cause" includes the discretion to modify the penalty. See Norman Brand, ed., *supra* footnote 1, at 389–391, 400. Courts have generally upheld arbitrators' awards reducing the extent of discipline imposed by the employer. Way Bakery v. Truck Drivers Local 164, 363 F.3d 590 (6th Cir. 2004). See also, United Paperworkers International Union v. Misco, Inc., 484 U.S. 29, 108 S.Ct. 364, 98 L.Ed.2d 286 (1987) ("Normally, an arbitrator is authorized to disagree with the sanction imposed for employee misconduct."), Chapter III.C.2, *supra*. But see, Poland Spring Corp. v. UFCW Local 1445, 314 F.3d 29 (1st Cir. 2002) (when agreement said that employees guilty of insubordination "shall" be subject to discharge, arbitrator lacked authority to reduce the penalty).

difficult to implement and are likely to give rise to subsequent disputes and continuing antagonisms between the parties.[17] Parties may disagree about whether the employee has satisfied the conditions. Also, last chance orders, which state or suggest that an employee who does not satisfy the arbitrator's conditions may be discharged without recourse to the grievance procedure, are likely to cause disputes about arbitrability of any subsequent discharge.

Duration of Back Pay Awards. The arbitrator must also decide whether the reinstated employee should receive back pay and if so, the appropriate period for back pay.[18] The arbitrator may have found that there was no just cause for any discipline. Or the arbitrator may have concluded that discharge was too severe a penalty, but that the employer had just cause to impose a suspension of some duration. Logically, one would think that an employee discharged without just cause should receive back pay for the entire period from discharge to reinstatement, except for any period determined by the arbitrator to be the appropriate length for a suspension. Surprisingly, many arbitrators do not take that approach. One study found that fewer than half the reinstated grievants received back pay. Nearly half of the reinstatements without back pay were in cases in which the arbitrators had *not* relied upon either an excessive penalty or the presence of mitigating circumstances. In these cases, arbitrators denied back pay despite findings that (1) the charge was not supported by the evidence; (2) the company failed to meet its burden of proof; (3) there was no clear company policy or lax enforcement; (4) discriminatory treatment was demonstrated; or (5) the grievant's action was justified.[19] Recall that the arbitrator in *Champion International*, in this chapter, ordered reinstatement without back pay despite findings about nexus suggesting any discipline would be inappropriate.

Even when arbitrators find just cause for discipline short of discharge, they often award reinstatement without any back pay rather than calculate what would be the appropriate length suspension. One study found that in 42% of cases in which arbitrators awarded reinstatement without back pay, the principal reason was that they considered discharge an excessive penalty.[20] When an employer imposes a suspension without pay as progressive discipline under a collective bargaining agreement, the duration is usually only one or two days, rarely two weeks and very rarely a full month. The result in arbitration is that an employee who might appropriately have received no more than brief suspension instead loses many months of pay. One study of over five hundred cases found that when arbitrators reinstated without back pay

17. Marvin Hill, Jr. and Anthony V. Sinicropi, *supra* footnote 7, at 169–171.

18. In rare circumstances, where reinstatement is precluded because an employee was discharged for just cause, some arbitrators nevertheless have awarded some back pay as a remedy for an employer's violation of the employee's due process rights, such as denial of union representation in a disciplinary interview. See, for example, Bi-State Development Agency, 105 LA 319 (Robert G. Bailey, 1995).

19. Malinowski, *supra* footnote 13, at 35.

20. Shearer, *supra* footnote 2, at 51.

the *average* duration of the resulting suspension was thirty-three weeks. In one case, the effective suspension was 111 weeks![21]

Why do so many arbitrators impose suspensions whose length turns on the time it takes to process the grievance rather than on the circumstances of the case? Commentators have offered four possible reasons that explain but do not justify the phenomenon.[22] First, some arbitrators may regard a substantial back pay award to a grievant guilty of some misconduct as an unwarranted "windfall." The grievant would receive a large sum of money for work never done. Yet, the employer in fact violated the contract, causing the employee that amount of harm. (Normally back pay awards provide for reduction if the employee has had interim earnings.)

Second, some arbitrators may find it difficult to calculate the appropriate length of the suspension when parties have declined to offer evidence on that issue. They may fear compromising their respective positions for denial or sustaining of the grievance. The arbitrator could solve that procedural problem, however, by imposing a suspension of the maximum length employers generally use (for example, one month). Alternatively, the arbitrator could remand the issue to the parties for negotiation,[23] perhaps retaining jurisdiction to choose between their final offers if negotiations are unsuccessful.[24]

Third, some arbitrators may impose suspensions of such extraordinary length as an act of clemency. That is, they may believe the employer's discharge was contractually proper but that the circumstances (for example, a serious offense by a long-term employee) warrant clemency. Would it be better for the arbitrator in such a case to sustain the discharge and merely recommend reinstatement? Or would that cause other problems?

Fourth, some arbitrators may view reinstatement without back pay as a means to provide partial satisfaction to both sides—to give the employee the job back and to save the employer from having to pay any money. Critics complain that arbitrators avoid all-or-nothing awards out of a fear that such decisions would alienate advocates who might otherwise select the arbitrator for future cases. These arbitrators may, however, be miscalculating the effect of such split awards on future arbitrator selection. Some parties may be disinclined to select arbitrators who are reluctant to make all-or-nothing awards when circumstances warrant.

Calculating the Amount of Back Pay. Even after the arbitrator determines the appropriate duration of back pay, calculating the amount due may involve complex questions. Resolution of these questions may

21. *Id.* at 48.

22. *Id.* at 49–52, and authorities cited therein.

23. Peter Seitz, *Substitution of Disciplinary Suspension for Discharge (A Proposed 'Guide for the Perplexed' in Arbitra-* *tion)*, 35 Arbitration Journal 27 (June 1980).

24. Dallas M. Young, *My Use of the Final–Offer Principle*, 38 Proceedings of the National Academy of Arbitrators 239, 242–246 (1986).

require a substantial amount of information beyond that presented on the just cause issue at the hearing. Should the arbitrator ask for substantial additional evidence that may be irrelevant if the discipline is upheld or the arbitrator orders reinstatement without back pay? Or should an arbitrator simply decide the period for which back pay should be awarded and let the parties try to settle the exact amount due? Would that be wise if the arbitrator knows that a failure of back pay negotiations will create yet another dispute requiring arbitration? One common method of resolving the dilemma is for the arbitrator to remand the calculation of back pay to the parties, but (with or without the express consent of the parties) to retain jurisdiction for a specified period of time to decide any remedial issues the parties are unable to resolve.[25]

The purpose of a back pay award is to make the employee whole for the losses suffered as a result of the employer's wrongful disciplinary action. This straightforward proposition, however, may give rise to a number of disputed issues in an attempt to reconstruct the wages and benefits the grievant would have received if not wrongfully discharged. Standards for calculating back pay can be found in the relatively few arbitration cases that actually calculate back pay amounts. These principles guide unions and employers in the large proportion of cases in which back pay amounts are determined by negotiation of the parties, rather than by the arbitrator.

Back pay calculations require a number of considerations. One needs to determine the grievant's wage rate and any changes or bonuses occurring while the grievant was unemployed. One must also determine the extent of overtime the grievant would likely have worked. Those calculations may depend on whether overtime is mandatory or voluntary, on the availability of overtime during the period of the grievant's absence, and on the grievant's history of working or declining overtime. Back pay awards should include amounts that would have been contributed to pension and health and welfare plans.

The arbitrator must also consider possible reductions in the amount due. The so-called "duty to mitigate" requires subtraction of the employee's interim earnings. If the grievant had no interim earnings, or the earnings appear meager, the arbitrator might have to evaluate the grievant's efforts to mitigate damages by finding new employment. The arbitrator may have to separate earnings from a second job the grievant held (or could have held) concurrently with the job sought in the grievance. The arbitrator normally will not deduct earnings from a second job unless they increased because of the grievant's increased availability for work because of the discharge. Evidence of post-discharge

25. Marvin Hill, Jr. and Anthony V. Sinicropi, *supra* footnote 7, at 186–190. For a discussion of legal and ethical issues related to retention of jurisdiction, see John E. Dunsford, *The Case for Retention of Remedial Jurisdiction*, 31 Georgia Law Review 201 (1996); John E. Dunsford, *Should Arbi-* *trators Retain Jurisdiction over Awards?* 51 Proceedings of the National Academy of Arbitrators 102 (1999); George Nicolau, *O Functus Officio: Is it Time to Go?*, 51 Proceedings of the National Academy of Arbitrators 115 (1999).

misconduct or employer post-discharge discovery of pre-discharge misconduct is sometimes also used to reduce an employer's backpay liability.[26]

Arbitrators, of course, must follow any directives regarding back pay remedies contained in the collective bargaining agreement. For federal employees, back pay calculations are governed by federal statutes and regulations that include provisions for payment of attorneys fees and interest on back pay awards. 5 U.S.C. § 5596 (2000); 5 C.F.R. § 550.801 et seq. (2004).

The issues of whether to award interest and to deduct unemployment compensation benefits in awarding back pay are among the issues discussed in the following case and its Notes and Questions.

RALPH'S GROCERY CO.
108 LA 718 (Donald S. Prayzich, 1997).*

At the outset of the hearing, the following issues were framed and agreed to by the Parties:

1. [The first issue concerned the nature of the documentation the grievant was obliged to provide to the employer to demonstrate the amount of earnings since his discharge. The arbitrator held that the grievant had provided appropriate documentation.]

2. What deductions, if any, should be made from Arbitrator Maxwell's Award to O, dated January 20, 1997?

3. What monies, if any, is the Company required to pay?

BACKGROUND

* * * The Grievant, O, is an employee of the [Ralphs Grocery] Company in the classification of Janitor–Foreman. At the time of his discharge, on or about November 16, 1995, the Grievant was employed at the Company's Chula Vista store. His discharge was grieved; the dispute over his termination could not be resolved and was submitted to Arbitrator Eugenia B. Maxwell. In an Award dated January 20, 1997, Arbitrator Maxwell found that O was not terminated for just cause and stated "Grievant should be reinstated with full back pay and benefits" * * *.

POSITIONS OF THE PARTIES

Union Position

The Union stresses that Grievant O is entitled to all lost back pay, (straight time and overtime hours) and benefits in accordance with Arbitrator Maxwell's January 20, 1997 Award. Further, that Award

---

26. Elkouri & Elkouri, *supra* footnote 1, at 977–980.

* Reprinted with permission from *Labor Relations Reporter–Labor Arbitration Re-* ports, 108 LA 718. Copyright 1997 by The Bureau of National Affairs, Inc. (800–372–1033 <http://www.bna.com>).

makes no reference to a reduction in the Employer's liability for back pay, either by earnings or unemployment compensation received by the Grievant during the period he was off the job. Accordingly, the Union's position is now modified, to a request for a ruling from this Arbitrator, for all lost pay and benefits with no reduction from the amount he would have earned, had he not been wrongfully terminated. Moreover, because of the Company's refusal to comply with the back pay and benefits award, the Union requests a ruling from this Arbitrator of an additional penalty payment of $1,000 as punitive damages and/or interest for the Grievant, and further, that the Company be required to pay this Arbitrator's fee in its entirety.

* * * So far as the Company's argument that the Grievant has "failed in his duty to mitigate the amount of his loss," the Union submits that the Company has not produced evidence to support this contention. * * * Accordingly, the Company has not established that O failed to make reasonable efforts to mitigate his losses. The Grievant's testimony, in contrast, establishes that he pursued other employment with "ordinary diligence". The Union also stresses that O's efforts to seek employment satisfied State of California requirements for unemployment compensation. The Union stresses that the Company is attempting to place a higher standard on the Grievant than that required by the State. In conclusion, the Union argues that the Grievant had no incentive to not seek interim employment, in that the outcome of his discharge arbitration was uncertain. Accordingly, the Union seeks a ruling awarding the Grievant all lost wages (regular and overtime hours he would have worked), and an additional payment of $1,000 plus full payment of this Arbitrator's fee.

Company Position

The Company submits, that no back pay, or at most, one month's pay, is due the Grievant. The main thrust of the Company's arguments [focuses] primarily on O's failure to take "reasonable steps to mitigate his losses". The Company rejects, out of hand, the Union's contentions, that there was no obligation to mitigate because mitigation was not expressed in Arbitrator Maxwell's award. Moreover, the information furnished to the Company, regarding the Grievant's pursuit of employment, amounted to only one contact per day and resulted in no job offers. The Company argues, that based upon the Grievant's testimony, his job hunting consumed only three hours per week. Further, the Grievant testified that he wrote down each company that he contacted on his calendar, but had nothing written down for the period May 12, 1996 through January 16, 1997. The Company submits that such activity cannot be construed as "reasonable diligence." Citing *Orlando Transit and Amalgamated Transit Union 1326*, 71 LA (BNA) 897, the Company parallels that case with the dispute at hand. In *Orlando*, Arbitrator Serot held that attending school six hours per day, narrowed the number of job opportunities, and therefore, the Grievant did not "make reasonable efforts to find other employment."

So far as penalties, fees and interest, the Company submits that all are inappropriate and had the Company's demand letter of February 13, 1997, been complied with, there would not have been the need for the instant arbitration proceeding. Referencing Arbitrator Howard S. Block's reasoning in *Permanente Medical Group and Hospital and Institutional Workers Local 250*, 52 LA (BNA) 217 (1968), the Company submits that the Grievant should have been able to find replacement employment within no more than one month of his termination. Additionally, citing *Elkouri & Elkouri in How Arbitration Works*, at P. 408, the Company argues that unemployment benefits should be subtracted from any back pay awarded the Grievant.

Opinion of the Arbitrator

* * * Back pay is intended not to penalize an employer, but to make a grievant whole, by placing him in the same position financially, that he would have been in, had the employer not acted wrongfully. This is accomplished by awarding an affected employee what he would have earned, (but for the employer's wrong), subject to appropriate deductions. Those [deductions] clearly include interim earnings from employment during the period of time the affected employee was off the job. While there is some split of opinion among Arbitrators regarding the deduction of unemployment compensation from back pay, the majority view is that such compensation is deductible. Additionally, Arbitrators generally believe that an employee who has been wronged has a duty to mitigate, within reason, the amount of back pay lost. Further, some Arbitrators go so far as to hold that an employee has a recognized duty to mitigate his losses even where the applicable Collective Bargaining Agreement expressly states that an employee who was unjustly discharged shall be "paid for all time lost." It is within the foregoing general guidelines that the facts as established by the evidentiary record, so far as the issues before this Arbitrator, will be reviewed.

* * * With respect to Issue No. 2: "What deductions, if any, should be made from Arbitrator Maxwell's Award to O, dated January 20, 1997[?]" A breakdown of the approximate 14 months in question, into the following time periods seems appropriate:

1.　November 16, 1995 (date of discharge), through May 13, 1996, (date initial period of unemployment compensation ceased).

2.　May 14, 1996 through December 16, 1996, (Grievant testified that he attended training and/or retraining during the period June 24, 1996 to December 16, 1996).

3.　December 17, 1996 through date of reinstatement in January 1997.

The Grievant was terminated on or about November 16, 1995. The Company stresses that Union Exhibit No. 1 (a list of places where the Grievant sought employment during November and December 1995), was not produced until April 28, 1997, the date of the instant arbitration and does not establish diligence. Nonetheless, Union Exhibit No. 1

stands unrebutted and the Arbitrator is persuaded that it must be considered as being provided in good faith, absent evidence to the contrary, and will be credited accordingly. As previously stated, a discharged employee has an obligation to mitigate his losses by using "reasonable diligence." This standard does not require a Grievant to search for work on a full-time basis, but the efforts made must be viewed overall as reasonable under the circumstances. For the first period of time (November 17, 1995 through May 13, 1996), the Arbitrator is satisfied that O used reasonable diligence in his job hunting efforts. While it seems unusual that he was unable to secure replacement employment, in light of the nature of his work and the experience and job skills he possesses, he nonetheless satisfied the Employment Development Department of the State of California, in that he was deemed eligible for unemployment compensation through May 13, 1996. Therefore, a determination is warranted that full back pay calculated on the basis of regular and overtime hours, that the Grievant would have worked for the period November 17, 1995 through May 13, 1996, is appropriate. The Grievant testified, that he stopped looking for work when his unemployment compensation ceased on or about May 13, 1996. Therefore, no back pay is warranted for the period May 14, 1996 through June 23, 1996. Unemployment compensation received during the period November 1995 to May 13, 1996, is to be deducted from the back pay due for this first time frame.

Addressing the period June 24, 1996 through December 16, 1996: The record establishes that the Grievant received an approximate six-month extension in unemployment compensation, which apparently was conditioned upon his acceptance of training or retraining in related fields commencing June 24, 1996. Specifically: The Grievant received Certificates of Completion in "Professional Growth," "Landscape Maintenance," and "Commercial Cleaning". The evidentiary record is somewhat unclear as to the total time spent by O in pursuit of these goals * * * , but there was testimony that the training took approximately 20 hours per week. With regard to the pursuit of replacement employment during training and this extended period of unemployment compensation, (June 24, 1996 through December 16, 1996), there is little evidence, (other than a representation by the Union, that the Grievant looked for work between classes and on Saturdays), for purposes of satisfying the required standard of using reasonable diligence to mitigate losses. It was obviously not a requirement of the Department of Employment during this period to actively pursue employment, as it was for the period November 17, 1995 to May 13, 1996. The fact that the Grievant failed to keep a calendar of contacts after May 13, 1996, confirms this conclusion. Accordingly, the weight of the evidence persuades this Arbitrator that the Grievant restricted himself time wise, by accepting the extended unemployment compensation and retraining, and that factor, coupled with the lack of documentation regarding job hunting efforts, mandates a conclusion that he cannot be deemed to have exercised reasonable diligence in attempting to mitigate his losses during the period June 24, 1996 to December 16, 1996.

So far as the time frame December 17, 1996 (date training ended), to the date of his reinstatement, the Grievant testified that he repeatedly attempted to find work. The Arbitrator will accept that representation without written documentation, and therefore concludes, that for the period December 17, 1996 to date of reinstatement in January 1997, the Grievant shall be made whole for all lost straight and overtime hours he would have worked.

Accordingly, the following determinations regarding back pay due the Grievant and deductions from that back pay are summarized below:

1. From November 17, 1995 through May 13, 1996—full back pay (all regular and overtime hours the Grievant would have worked), less unemployment compensation received during this same period.

2. For the period May 14, 1996 through December 16, 1996, no back pay is due for the reasons expressed above.

3. For the period December 17, 1996 to the date of Grievant's reinstatement, full back pay (all regular and overtime hours the Grievant would have worked); no unemployment compensation received during this period, therefore no deduction.

The actual calculation of monies and benefits due, in accordance with the foregoing is remanded to the Parties. [The Arbitrator will retain jurisdiction, for purposes of resolving any dispute which may arise with regard to implementation of this Award.] So far as the Union's request for $1,000, (punitive damages and/or interest), neither is provided for in the Collective Bargaining Agreement. Moreover, such penalties are generally appropriate only in situations where there is evidence of bad faith, intentional delays or other evidence that a penalty is appropriate. The record here, is sans such evidence. While there was a substantial delay in resolving this matter, this Arbitrator is persuaded that it was the result of good faith dealing and firm pursuit of respective positions as adversaries and nothing more. The request is therefore denied. So far as the Union's request for full payment of the Arbitrator's fee by the Company, that request is in direct conflict with the provisions of Article XIII E, which states in part: "The expenses of the arbitrator shall be borne equally by both the Employer and the Union." Moreover, the Union's request in this regard is also punitive in nature and clearly not warranted under the circumstances, for the reasons discussed above. Accordingly, this request is also denied. * * *

Notes and Questions

1. Arbitrator Maxwell's award ordering reinstatement with "full back pay" made no reference to any obligation on behalf of the grievant to mitigate wage loss following his discharge. Nor did the collective bargaining agreement apparently contain any explicit obligation to mitigate. Nevertheless, Arbitrator Prayzich imposes a duty to mitigate because other arbitrators generally impose such a duty. These arbitrators use an analysis of

mitigation issues that parallels common law contract doctrine, including such concepts as the existence of a duty to mitigate, a burden of proof on the party claiming a failure to mitigate, excusing an employee from quickly accepting a lesser position and deducting wages actually earned. Is it appropriate for labor arbitrators deciding discipline cases to adopt the mitigation requirement and its particulars developed in common law contract law? What is the rationale for requiring mitigation of contract damages? Is the doctrine equally applicable here?

2.   Arbitrator Prayzich's award does not make clear on which side he is imposing the burden of persuasion on the issue of reasonable mitigation. Most arbitrators impose the burden on the employer to prove than an employee failed reasonably to mitigate. Norman Brand, *supra* footnote 1, at 382. This amounts to a rebuttable presumption of reasonable mitigation.

(a) Why should we effectively assume that a discharged employee made reasonable efforts to mitigate?

(b) Why should the employer be required to offer proof of lack of mitigation when the employer is unlikely to have access to the necessary evidence?

(c) If you were the employer in this case, what evidence could you produce to demonstrate that a janitor who failed to find work for a period of fourteen months had not made a reasonable effort to mitigate his damages?

3.   The arbitrator in *Ralph's* found that during the period from November 16, 1995, through May 13, 1996, the employee O made one employment contact per day, spending approximately three hours per week seeking employment. Although the arbitrator finds it surprising that the grievant failed to find work as a janitor during that period, he nevertheless concludes that O's efforts were reasonable. Do you agree? Was the arbitrator correct that satisfaction of the state's job search requirements for establishing eligibility for unemployment compensation should necessarily satisfy the duty of mitigation in the context of arbitration?

4.   The arbitrator denies back pay for the period that the grievant was in training, in part because he offered no documentation or testimony that he engaged in job search efforts during this period. With regard to the period following training, however, the arbitrator accepts the grievant's testimony that he sought work, despite the absence of any documentation. Did the arbitrator properly deny back pay for the period of training? Did he properly award back pay for the period following training?

5.   Arbitrator Prayzich denies the union's request for interest on the grounds that the collective bargaining agreement did not call for interest on back pay amounts and that interest would only be appropriate as a penalty in cases of bad faith or intentional delay.

(a) Consider this counterargument:

I do not consider interest to be punitive. Interest is a natural and consequential result from a breach of contract. I consider it necessary to make an employee whole who has been denied the use of funds for a period of time and, similarly, denies to the employer the unjust enrichment it has derived by improperly maintaining those funds during the period of the suspension and discharge.

Champlain Cable Corp., 108 LA 449 (David F. Sweeney, 1997) (also saying that it was irrelevant that the collective bargaining agreement did not explicitly authorize interest and noting that the award of interest "remains a minority trend.") Do you agree with Arbitrator Prayzich or Arbitrator Sweeney?

(b) If arbitrators do not traditionally award interest on back pay awards, and the collective bargaining agreement does not mention interest as necessary to a back pay award, should an arbitrator nevertheless include interest in the remedial order if the arbitrator considers interest necessary to make the employee whole? Although historically arbitrators have generally only awarded interest when the employer's conduct was egregious or the employer was unusually dilatory in the arbitration process or in compliance with the award, there appears to be a very modest recent trend in favor of the awarding of interest in the absence of special circumstances. Stephen H. Jordan, *Interest Awards of Back–Pay: Strengthening Make–Whole Remedies*, 55 Proceedings of the National Academy of Arbitrators 17 (2003). See also, Homer Electric Association, 119 LA 525 (M. Zane Lumbley, 2003); Reno Police Department, 118 LA 926 (Howard G. D'Spain, 2003); USAIR Shuttle, 108 LA 496 (Earle William Hockenberry, 1997); Atlantic Southeast Airlines, 101 LA 515 (Dennis R. Nolan, 1993) ("Given the choice between fully compensating a wrongly discharged employee at extra cost to the breaching employer on the one hand, and inadequately compensating the employee to save money for the breaching employer on the other, justice demands the first remedy.").

(c) Although the National Labor Relations Act makes no mention of the payment of interest on back pay remedies in unfair labor practice cases, since 1962 the National Labor Relations Board has routinely added interest to its back pay orders. Isis Plumbing & Heating Co., 138 NLRB 716 (1962). The Board has described interest as necessary to "encourage timely compliance with Board orders, discourage the commission of unfair labor practices, and more fully compensate discriminatees for their economic losses." New Horizons for the Retarded, Inc., 283 NLRB 1173, (1987) (establishing the interest rate charged by the Internal Revenue Service for the underpayment of taxes as the interest rate on NLRB back pay awards). Is this NLRB practice relevant to arbitrators deciding whether to award interest on back pay?

6.   Arbitrator Prayzich reduces the employee's back pay award for the period from November 1995 to May 1996 by the amount the employee received in unemployment compensation benefits without explaining why such a deduction was appropriate. His decision was likely influenced by California law, under which, if an arbitration award does not make a deduction for unemployment compensation benefits, the employee is obliged to reimburse the state. Cal. Unemp. Ins. Code § 1375 (West Supp. 2004), § 1382 (West 1986). In the absence of state law requiring an employee reinstated with back pay to reimburse the state for unemployment benefits, many arbitrators do not reduce employees' back pay awards by the amount of unemployment compensation received. These arbitrators appear to be following the analysis of the United States Supreme Court upholding the practice of the NLRB not to deduct unemployment benefits from back pay awards remedying unfair labor practices:

Payments of unemployment compensation were not made to the employees by respondent [the employer] but by the state out of state funds derived from taxation. True, these taxes were paid by employers, and thus to some extent respondent helped to create the fund. However, the payments to the employees were not made to discharge any liability or obligation of respondent, but to carry out a policy of social betterment for the benefit of the entire state.

NLRB v. Gullett Gin Co., 340 U.S. 361, 364, 71 S.Ct. 337, 95 L.Ed. 337 (1951). See also Norman Brand, *supra* footnote 1, at 384 and David P. Andrews, *Monetary Issues in Labor Arbitration Awards: Management Perspective*, 55 Proceedings of the National Academy of Arbitrators 25, 25 (2003) ("Arbitrators are split on the issue of whether to deduct unemployment compensation from back pay awards."). Is there any more reason for arbitrators to follow the NLRB's treatment of unemployment compensation than to follow its inclusion of interest on back pay awards?

C. MANAGEMENT RIGHTS[1]

When an employer enters into a collective bargaining relationship, it is likely to fear that the union's assertion of rights may impair its ability to manage an efficient and profitable business. Employers, therefore, both in the process of collective bargaining and in arbitration, seek to define certain aspects of their business as management rights, areas of decisionmaking in which the union will not be allowed to participate.

Management may be able to secure from the union an explicit provision in the collective bargaining agreement regarding management rights. Eighty percent of collective bargaining agreements contain some statement of management rights. Such provisions typically list, in varying degrees of generality, functions reserved to the employer. For example, 76% of contracts with management rights provisions reserve to management the right to direct the work force and 74% the right to manage the business. Contracts may guarantee management the right to control production (39%), issue company rules (43%), or determine employee duties (28%). Forty-four percent of contracts with a management rights provision include a savings clause stating that the employer retains all rights not restricted by the contract or that listed manage-

---

1. Bibliographic Suggestions: Elkouri & Elkouri, How Arbitration Works, 631–833 (Alan Miles Ruben, ed., 6th ed. 2003); Marvin Hill, Jr. and Anthony V. Sinicropi, Management Rights: A Legal and Arbitral Analysis (1986); Gladys W. Gruenberg, *Management Rights: Common Issues*, Labor and Employment Arbitration (Tim Bornstein, Ann Gosline and Marc Greenbaum, eds., 2003); Gladys Gershenfeld and Walter J. Gershenfeld, *Management Rights: Overview and Case Review*, Labor and Employment Arbitration (Tim Bornstein, Ann Gosline and Marc Greenbaum, eds., 2003);

Arthur J. Goldberg, *Management's Reserved Rights: A Labor View*, 9 Proceedings of the National Academy of Arbitrators 118 (1956); Gladys W. Gruenberg, *Management and Union Rights: Overview*, The Common Law of the Workplace: The Views of Arbitrators (Theodore J. St. Antoine, ed. 1998); James C. Phelps, *Management's Reserved Rights: An Industry View*, 9 Proceedings of the National Academy of Arbitrators 102 (1956); Arnold M. Zack and Richard I. Bloch, *Management Rights*, Labor Agreement in Negotiation and Arbitration (2d ed. 1995).

ment rights are not exclusive.[2] The following is an illustrative management rights provision:

> The Management of the Company and the direction of the working force, including the right to plan, direct and control plant operations; to schedule and assign work to Employees, to determine the means, methods, processes and schedules of production, to determine the products to be manufactured, the location of its plants and the continuance of its operating departments; to establish and require Employees to observe Company rules and regulations; to hire, lay off or relieve Employees from duties; and to maintain order and to suspend, demote, discipline and discharge Employees for just cause, are the sole rights of the Company. * * * [3]

Arbitrators may be asked to interpret the language of such a provision or evaluate a claim of an inherent managerial right. Arbitrators considering the existence and extent of inherent rights have generally divided into two camps, following the theory of "reserved rights" or of "implied obligations." The reserved rights theory holds that management retains all rights it possessed before the commencement of collective bargaining except for those rights defined in the contract. The implied obligations theory asserts that the introduction of collective bargaining has fundamentally changed the relationship giving management an implicit obligation to maintain existing working conditions and other company policies until it has negotiated a change. While arbitrators following the reserved rights theory may still reject employer actions that they find arbitrary, capricious or discriminatory, arbitrators using the implied obligations theory may more broadly assess whether employer actions are reasonable and fair.[4]

Regardless of whether employers rely on specific contract language or on a theory of reserved rights, they are apparently highly successful in protecting management prerogatives in the arbitration process.[5] Arbitrators Gladys Gershenfeld and Walter Gershenfeld studied 284 reported awards in management rights cases, decided in four different decades. They found that employers prevailed in 72.2% of the cases.[6] The researchers made these additional observations:

2. Basic Patterns in Union Contracts 79 (14th ed. 1995). Data reported are from a data base created by the Bureau of National Affairs of 400 current contracts representing a cross-section of industries, unions, number of employees covered and geographic areas.

3. Collective Bargaining Agreement between Avery Dennison Corporation, Industrial Products Division, Cleveland Ohio and Graphic Communications Industrial Union Local 546M, reported in Avery Dennison Corp., 119 LA 1170 (Louis V. Imundo Jr., 2004). The contract also included an explicit reserved rights provision, saying that this enumeration of rights "shall not be deemed to exclude other rights of Management, not specifically set forth" and that the Company retained "all rights not otherwise specifically covered by the Agreement."

4. Gladys W. Gruenberg, *Management Rights: Common Issues*, Labor and Employment Arbitration § 11B.01[2]-[3] (Tim Bornstein, Ann Gosline and Marc Greenbaum, eds., 2003)

5. Gladys Gershenfeld and Walter J. Gershenfeld, *supra* footnote 1, at § 11A.05.

6. *Id.*, at § 11A.03[2].

Specific supportive contract language, in a management rights or other clause, is clearly helpful to a party's position. Management, whether or not contractually required to do so, benefits from prior consultation when a case goes to arbitration. Union positions are frequently enhanced when the viability of the bargaining unit is threatened or when job-loss procedures are being circumvented.[7]

When challenging an employer-promulgated rule, the study observed, unions could succeed if they could demonstrate that the rule violated some provision of the agreement, was procedurally flawed, or was unreasonable. Even in these cases, however, the authors commented: "A holding for a union may be pyrrhic in that the employer is often free subsequently to make necessary process or content changes to meet the arbitrator's spelled-out basis for disqualification."[8]

THE CONCEPT OF MANAGEMENT RIGHTS: AN OVERVIEW

Marvin J. Hill, Jr. and Anthony V. Sinicropi.
Management Rights: A Legal and Arbitral Analysis 3 (1986).

No area of labor-management relations evokes so much emotion and controversy as does "management rights," for it is the concept of management rights and its counterpart—the union's quest for job security and other substantive protections for its members—that are at the core of the conflict between labor and management. * * * To understand the root causes of this conflict, the goals and purposes of management and labor must be considered.

In the tradition of Adam Smith, management has been described as being dedicated to the goal of profit maximization. Indeed, many prominent economists view profit maximization as the only legitimate goal of managers who, if not owners themselves, are the guardians of the financial interests of stockholders. If this is an accepted predicate, it follows (in the eyes of many observers) that management must have control over all decision-making factors of the enterprise if it is to operate efficiently. Economic efficiency, in turn, requires maximum flexibility to make unencumbered decisions involving the commitment of resources and the direction of the work force.

[Professor Neil] Chamberlain * * * stress[es] the nature of authority or managerial decision making under collective bargaining and its effect on efficiency:

This aim of management [control] is based on efficiency concepts, in which the functioning parts of the business organism—including of course the personnel—have their assigned roles. In the business organism there can be only one mind and one nerve center if the various parts are to be coordinated into a harmonious whole.

7. *Id.*, at § 11A.05.   8. *Id.*, at § 11A.03[4].

The union, however, constitutes a second center of authority, which speaks in terms of welfare rather than efficiency.

Often management assesses its ability to be efficient and in control by determining how much flexibility it has with regard to decision making, particularly when directing the work force is at issue. Employers maintain that any union penetration into this area is an intrusion of management's inherent right to manage. Union advocates argue that the right to direct the work force, where it involves wages, hours, or working conditions is only a procedural right that does not imply some right over and above labor's right. On this point, former Supreme Court justice Arthur Goldberg argues as follows:

[The right to direct] is a recognition of the fact that somebody must be boss; somebody has to run the plant. People can't be wandering around at loose ends, each deciding what to do next. Management decides what the employee is to do. However, this right to direct or to initiate action does not imply a second-class role for the union. The union has the right to pursue its role of representing the interest of the employee with the same stature accorded it as is accorded management. To assure order, there is a clear procedural line drawn: the company directs and the union grieves when it objects. To make this desirable division of function workable, it is essential that arbitrators not give greater weight to the directing force than the objecting force.

At the same time employees, acting through their unions, often view management behavior as unpredictable and unfair. Cullen and Greenbaum, for example, point out that if efficiency and low costs are the only goals of our society, then perhaps society should outlaw unions and let management make all the decisions on wages, hours, and working conditions. This argument is posed by union leaders to those who accuse them of invading management's right to manage.

Thus the conflict is born. The dual union objective of predictability of managerial behavior and job-security protections for employees challenges management's dual goals of organizational flexibility and efficiency. Within this relationship management invariably attempts to negotiate an agreement in which its exclusive and explicit rights are incorporated in the labor contract.

In addition to explicit management rights that have their genesis in the language of the labor agreement, there are those "implied," "residual," or "reserved" rights that exist within the relationship between the parties but are not found within the four corners of the agreement. These inherent management rights arise and, under certain conditions, are sometimes lost, by the operation of custom or past practice of the parties, or what is frequently referred to as the "common law of the shop."

The "reserved rights theory"—the doctrine that holds that management's authority is supreme in all matters except those it has expressly agreed to share with or relinquished to the union—has been the topic of much debate. Such rights are often challenged on the basis of 1) the reasonableness of the specific management right, or 2) the equitable administration and application of that inherent right.

* * * [I]t is argued that management has an implied obligation in exercising its inherent rights, when challenged by the union, to demonstrate that these rights are reasonably related to the safe and efficient operation of the business, and that the application of such rights has been consistent and equitable. Prasow and Peters, who inquired into this area at some length, discuss the reserved management rights controversy as follows:

> * * * Stated in an unqualified simplistic form, the reserved-rights theory holds that management's authority is supreme in all matters except those it has expressly conceded in the collective agreement and in all areas except those where its authority is restricted by law. Put another way, management does not look to the collective agreement to ascertain its rights; it looks to the agreement to find out which and how many of its rights and powers it has conceded outright or agreed to share with the union. The reserved-rights theory is somewhat analogous to the Tenth Amendment of the United States Constitution.

Professor Dennis Nolan has argued that arbitrators, faced with questions of interpretation arising from issues that are not addressed in the contract, sometimes hold that management retains all rights not limited by the agreement.

> Usually termed the "reserved rights doctrine," this principle is based on the argument that because the employer possessed all rights to run the business before the union came on the scene it must still possess those the union did not succeed in limiting. If this were not so, it would mean either that all such rights passed *sub silentio* to the union or that they simply disappeared, and neither of these possibilities is very reasonable.

Prasow and Peters also submit that an important corollary to the reserved-rights theory is that of "implied obligations."

> * * * The implied-obligations doctrine acknowledges the employer's right to alter or abolish employee benefits when the contract is open for negotiations, but once a new contract has been signed, he is no longer free to withdraw existing benefits. He has an implied obligation to maintain them, including those benefits which were not revoked by him during negotiations and to which the contract makes no reference.

CHANUTE MANUFACTURING COMPANY
101 LA 765 (Mark Berger, 1993).*

* * * [T]he proper formulation of the issue is as follows:

Is the Company's revision of its Policy Concerning Absences, Tardiness and Early Departure from Work subject to arbitration under

* Reprinted with permission from *Labor Arbitration Reporter–Labor Arbitration Reports*, 101 LA 765. Copyright 1994 by The Bureau of National Affairs, Inc. (800–372–1033) <http://www.bna.com>.

the terms of the collective bargaining agreement between the parties? If so, does the Policy violate the terms of the collective bargaining agreement and, if so, what remedy is appropriate?

FACTS

[The Company's new General Manager, Michael McGuire, instituted a number of new systems of operation in an effort to enhance productivity and competitiveness. He also sought to address concerns about employee absenteeism.]

Using available statistics Mr. McGuire was able to identify a significant number of employees who stayed within the prior attendance policy but had absences from work not otherwise excused at levels as high as fifty-three days in a nine-month period. Foremen reported that employees would sometimes take off for such personal matters as fishing and going to the races. Sometimes they would simply leave early if they were annoyed with the foreman or did not wish to perform assigned tasks. This made the performance of assignments exceedingly difficult and, in Mr. McGuire's estimation, cost the Company over $100,000 per year.

These matters were discussed with the Union in the context of an effort to develop a new attendance control policy. Several drafts of the policy were framed until the final version emerged for implementation in early January, 1993.

As finally framed, the policy was formulated as a no-fault attendance program, as had been the case for the predecessor policy. However, whereas the predecessor policy led to termination after the accumulation of eighteen points, the new policy would result in termination after the accumulation of nine negative attendance points. This reduction in point accumulation for termination was mitigated, however, by the implementation of a personal day off (PDO) system. Employees were given four PDO's during the calendar year which they could use any way they saw fit. Thus, if an employee was absent and did not wish to be assigned a negative point, he could use his PDO for this purpose. The decision could even be made after the day of work was missed. On the other hand, if the employee was not in attendance difficulty, he could use the personal day off to handle personal business. The result of the PDO system, according to the Company, was to effectively increase the point total for termination to thirteen as opposed to nine negative points. It was also true, moreover, that employees could use their paid floating holiday to cover an absence if they so desired, thereby also alleviating the significance of the change in the point totals.

Employees may earn credit against the attendance control program for having no full-point negative attendance assessments against them during a calendar month.

The new policy also reduced the triggering point for the award of credit for working overtime under the attendance control program. Previously forty hours of overtime during a month was required before credit could be earned, but this was lowered to thirty hours. The program set a limit, however, in the amount of credit possible. Specifically, an employee's record could go to minus three under the program, but no more.

The philosophy behind the provisions allowing for the earning of credit under the attendance program was that good attendance should be rewarded. However, that is the only way that an employee can improve his status under the program's provisions. Previously the program involved a nine-month rolling total. Under this system negative credits earned would drop off the employee's record after nine months. Under the revised program, in contrast, all negative points stay on the record of the employee. However, he is able to earn credit to reduce the total through either satisfactory attendance for a calendar month in which there was no negative assessment of a full point during that period, as well as the working of sufficient overtime hours.

Another change from the prior program involved multi-day absences. Previously if an employee had multi-day absences as a result of illness, point assessments would be capped at two. Under the new program, an employee who brought in a doctor's note supporting the fact that the absence was medically related would have multi-day absences capped at one. The Company also noted that a leave of absence can be granted to deal with special problems.

Pursuant to the policy notice must be given to employees of their attendance program status after the sixth and eighth points. If there are continuing absences and no opportunity to deliver the notice, this requirement need not be satisfied.

The Company also introduced evidence concerning the implementation of the program and its impact upon attendance levels. For the first six months of 1993, attendance problems dropped dramatically. Even though there were two more employees during this period as opposed to the comparable period in 1992, hours lost as a result of absences were reduced by approximately twenty percent. Moreover, the number of employees with fifteen or more absences dropped from nineteen to seven. Statistics accumulated under the new program also revealed that seventy-eight percent of the employees had accumulated three points or less, with fifty-one percent accumulating zero points or less.

DISCUSSION

[The arbitrator concluded that the dispute was arbitrable under the Management Rights clause, Article X, that granted the Company the right to "make or change reasonable rules, regulations and practices."

Article X further stated that all other management rights are retained by the Company except as "abridged, delegated or modified by this Agreement."]

The standard governing rules and regulations formulated by the Company, as stated in the management rights clause, is that of reasonableness. To apply this standard to the Company's attendance policy requires that individual features of the policy, along with its overall impact, be separately analyzed. It would thus be possible to conclude that the policy is unreasonable on its face and therefore totally unenforceable. Equally permissible is the conclusion that the policy is generally reasonable, but specific features violate the management rights clause standard. Finally, the policy could be deemed reasonable both as to its individual components as well as its overall scope. As indicated below, it is my conclusion that the policy meets the general standard of reasonableness subject to only one area in which I conclude that the labor contract has been violated.

Even though the program is a no-fault attendance policy, it nevertheless satisfies the management rights clause reasonableness test. At this juncture no-fault attendance programs have achieved wide acceptability, and have been specifically approved in two prior rulings by this Arbitrator.

So too, all but one of the features of the program satisfy the reasonableness test and are themselves consistent with prevailing arbitration standards in this area.

The Union initially objects that the Company failed to provide any justification for its adoption of a new attendance program. However, the evidence revealed significant efforts by the Company to identify the scope and extent of employee absences, along with an attempt to calculate their financial impact upon Company profitability. Sufficient evidence was presented at the hearing to demonstrate that the Company faced an identifiable attendance problem, and that an effort to restructure its absence control program constituted a reasonable Company objective. While it may be conceivable that circumstances would make the very effort to revise a policy unreasonable, more than ample justification was produced for the policy revision in the instant case. The Company, in short, was reasonable in concluding that a policy revision was appropriate.

One of the major features of the policy was to change the number of negative points required for termination. On its face the reduction appears to be from an eighteen point level to a nine point level. But as the evidence at the hearing demonstrated, alternatives were available which effectively served to increase the employees' ability to avoid negative attendance program point assessments. This derived in part from both the floating holiday provisions of the contract along with the establishment of a personal day off system. The combination of these two procedures allows employees five additional days of non-attendance without being subject to point assessments under the attendance program. So understood, the reduction is actually from a level of eighteen negative points to a level of fourteen negative [points]. Allowing an employee to be discharged after experiencing attendance program violations to this degree cannot be deemed unreasonable.

It should be noted that point assessments under the program may be made at a level of 1.0 points or .5 points, depending on whether or not more than an hour absence from work is involved. The fourteen points can therefore actually represent as much as twenty-eight separate occurrences. But even if it is assumed that all occurrences were at the one-point level, it remains true that the total is reasonable and consistent with generally prevailing practices.

A further concern of the Union is that the new policy does not mandate a progressive disciplinary system. This is based primarily on the fact that the policy calls for written warning notices after the accumulation of six and eight points, but only "if possible." If the qualifying "if possible" language meant that the decision whether or not to notify the employee was purely up to the Company's discretion, the Union would have a valid complaint. Instead, the Company indicated at the hearing that the thrust of this phrase was to cover situations where employees do not come back to work, and therefore providing notice to them is not feasible. So understood, the policy does not give the Company unstructured discretion as to whether or not notice must be provided. And with the provision of notice, the policy directive that employees are "responsible" for knowing their status under the program is not unreasonable.

Another factor in support of the reasonableness of the policy is that it permits employees to earn credit which can reduce their negative attendance program points. This result can be achieved by reaching appropriate levels of overtime work during the month or by having a month of perfect attendance. The Union has raised no objection to the reasonableness of the credit system based upon overtime. However, it does argue that awarding credit against negative attendance points for perfect attendance during a calendar month is unreasonable. As the Union points out, an employee could have fifty-nine days of perfect attendance, but nevertheless would be denied any credit because of having missed the first day of work of the first month, and the last day of work of the second month.

In response to this concern the Company maintained that awarding credit for perfect attendance during any thirty-day period, whether or not it coincides with a calendar month, would be administratively impractical. To attempt to keep track of employee attendance other than by simply looking at the monthly attendance sheet would require substantial attendance tracking for all Company employees.

There is, of course, a measure of force to the Union's argument. The Company has agreed that employees can be rewarded for good attendance, but has structured the system in a way that good attendance over a significant period of time may not lead to credit because of the fact that it does not perfectly coincide with the calendar-month system the Company has chosen to rely upon. Nevertheless, based upon the Company's record keeping system and my belief that the administrative difficulties would be greater than the Union concedes, I cannot conclude that the choice to base the system on a calendar month of perfect attendance is unreasonable.

The Union also complains about the fact that the personal day off system requires that an entire day be taken in order for the employee to avoid negative attendance program point assessments. There is no provision in the policy to allow partial day absences where the employee would return to work on the very same day. From the Union's perspective, this prevents employees from taking short absences from work for such things as medical appointments.

After careful consideration, the decision to limit personal day off requests to entire day units is in my judgment within the permissible limits of the Company's discretion. It is not unreasonable to conclude that time off during the day, even if the employee is prepared to return to work the same day, is too disruptive to productivity for it to be part of the personal day off procedure. The Company may be legitimately concerned that it would face employees taking their days off in bits and pieces and substantially disrupting the work place. The reasonableness standard created by the management rights clause is not violated by such a conclusion.

Finally, there is one aspect of the Union's grievance which I find has merit. Employees under the program are limited in their ability to reduce their negative attendance program points. They may achieve this objective by working sufficient overtime, but this is a factor largely out of their control. Employees are not guaranteed overtime, and therefore cannot count on this opportunity. What they can depend upon, in contrast, is that they may earn credit through perfect attendance, albeit limited to a calendar month calculation. Otherwise, negative attendance points remain on the employee's record forever. This is a significant change from the prior policy pursuant to which negative attendance points more than nine months old were erased from the employee's record. After careful consideration, I find myself in agreement with the Union's complaint that this aspect of the policy violates the reasonableness standard of the management rights clause.

It is common in arbitration rulings on no-fault attendance programs to encounter policies which allow for the elimination of old or stale attendance points from an employee's record. Although the Company previously allowed this to occur after nine months, arbitration rulings appear to support a more typical twelve-month rolling period.[7]

The impact of not using a rolling period in the administration of the attendance program is to leave employees under a continuing cloud as a

---

7. E.g., Universal Frozen Foods, 100 LA (BNA) 24 (Lacy, 1992); T & M Rubber Co., 100 LA (BNA) 84 (Brookins, 1992); Cooper Industries, 94 LA (BNA) 831 (Yarowsky, 1990); Union Camp Corp., 91 LA (BNA) 749 (Clarke, 1988).

result of absence problems which are stale. That creates a situation which in my judgment represents an unreasonable exercise of management authority.

The response of the Company is that employees remain able to improve their record by demonstrating good attendance practices. But, as previously noted, even fifty-nine days of perfect attendance may not necessarily lead to an improvement in the employee's attendance record. Indeed, even thirty days of perfect attendance within a calendar month, but which also includes a very short lateness which might be the result of unavoidable circumstances, would leave the employee without any improvement in his attendance program record.

The Company responds that it may grant a leave of absence and thereby eliminate the risk that employees will face attendance program difficulties when they have legitimate reasons for their absences. However, the leave of absence program is entirely a matter of Company discretion. The employee does not appear to have a right to demand a leave of absence and so has no guarantee that planned absences will not lead to negative attendance program points. While the new Family and Medical Leave Act may provide some protection, I remain unconvinced that it is sufficient to meet the standards of the management rights clause. For this reason I find that the total elimination of the use of a rolling period of time in the administration of the attendance program violates the labor contract.

This conclusion, however, does not mean that the Company is obligated to reinstitute the nine-month period it used previously. I am convinced that the Company provided sufficient evidence to demonstrate that the nine-month period was too easily abused by a limited number of employees with serious attendance problems. For this reason, I would advise the parties that a twelve-month period would be an acceptable alternative. But the absence of any provision for wiping out old absences cannot be sustained.

AWARD

The Company had the right to formulate a revised attendance policy under the management rights clause. The reasonableness standard within that clause supports the adoption of a no-fault program. However, under all the facts and circumstances presented, that portion of the plan which totally eliminates the use of a rolling period of time in the calculation of attendance program points is unreasonable and unenforceable. The use of a twelve-month rolling period, however, would meet the reasonableness test [of] the management rights clause. Furthermore, in all other respects the program is consistent with labor contract standards.

Notes and Questions

1. For further discussion of the problem of employee absenteeism and arbitral review of no-fault attendance policies, see the Notes and Questions

following the case of *Chicago Tribune Company, supra* Chapter VII.B.3. See also Barbara Zausner Tener and Ann Gosline, *Absenteeism and Tardiness*, Labor and Employment Arbitration (Tim Bornstein, Ann Gosline and Marc Greenbaum, eds., 2003).

2.   The arbitrator in *Chanute* suggested that the Family and Medical Leave Act (FMLA) might provide some protection for employees who had legitimate reasons for absences, but that the granting of leaves of absence was a matter of management discretion. The FMLA, 29 U.S.C. § 2601 et seq. (2000), requires certain employers to grant leaves of absence up to twelve workweeks in any twelve-month period to employees seeking leave because of the birth, adoption, foster care placement of a child, the serious health condition of the employee, or the need of the employee to care for a family member with a serious health condition. Employers are prohibited from counting a FMLA leave as an absence under a no-fault attendance program. 29 C.F.R. § 825.220(c)(2003). Following enactment of the FMLA in 1992, covered employers had to amend their no-fault policies to preclude negative consequences for employees taking FMLA leave. For discussion of several cases in which arbitrators addressed issues under the FMLA in resolving disputes arising under collective bargaining agreements, see the section, Notes on Current Issues of External Law, in Chapter V.B.3., *supra*.

3.   The parties to a collective bargaining agreement might deal with the issue of a management right to promulgate rules in one of four ways: (1) the management rights clause, as in *Chanute,* could grant the employer specific authority to promulgate reasonable rules; (2) the management rights clause could grant the employer authority to make rules, but not mention any requirement of reasonableness; (3) the management rights clause could specifically state that the employer retained all rights protected by the reserved rights doctrine; or (4) the contract could make no mention of management rights or the right to promulgate work rules.

(a) Does an employer have the authority, in all of four these circumstances, to promulgate work rules?

(b) Is an employer free, in any of these four circumstances, to promulgate unreasonable rules?

(c) Does an employer, in a workplace without a union, have the right to promulgate unreasonable work rules? If so, if a collective bargaining agreement explicitly states that an employer retains all rights protected by the reserved rights doctrine, does that mean that the employer has the right to promulgate unreasonable rules?

In *Rock-Tenn Company*, 1996 WL 942630 (William H. Holley, Jr., 1996), the agreement included the following language: "All right and authority heretofore exercised by or inherent in the Company and not expressly contracted away by the terms of this agreement are hereby expressly reserved to the Company * * *." When the union challenged the employer's right to change attendance rules, the arbitrator concluded:

> [S]uch a fundamental right is retained by the Employer unfettered, even in the absence, as here, of an express contractual reservation of the right, unless the contract either expressly or impliedly restricts that Management right. It is "reserved" to the Company. The parties in the

instant case have entered into a collective bargaining agreement in which the customary rights of management are reserved. The Employer under the rubric of its management rights had the right to unilaterally revise its attendance policy* * *.

Do you agree? Does Arbitrator Holley mean that where the employer possesses authority as a "reserved right," its decisionmaking is not subject to challenge on the basis of reasonableness? Certainly, some arbitrators believe that is so. City of Albuquerque, 1997 WL 612398 (Robert F. Oberstein, 1997) ("The Reserved Rights or Management Rights Doctrine endows Management not only with the right to manage but also, absent any stated violations, with the opportunity and right to mismanage.") A broad review of arbitral practice, however, concluded that, regardless of whether the employer gets its authority to promulgate rules from an explicit provision or as a reserved right, arbitrators consistently permit the union to challenge the rule for reasonableness. Hill and Sinicropi, *supra* footnote 1, at 65. For an example, see South Charleston Stamping & Mfg., 115 LA 710 (Marvin J. Feldman, 2001) (although agreement gave employer explicit right to determine schedules of work, reasonableness was implicitly required). In Avery Dennison Corp., 119 LA 1170 (Louis V. Imundo Jr., 2004), although the contract included explicit reserved rights language, quoted in footnote 3 *supra*, the arbitrator held that it was unreasonable for the employer to count consecutive days of absence as independent "occurrences" in the employer's no-fault attendance program.

4.   In *Chanute*, the arbitrator assumed that the union had the right to challenge the attendance policy on its face. Do you agree? Or do you believe the union should have waited until the employer disciplined an employee? If the union could have proceeded either way, what factors should the union consider in deciding whether to challenge the policy on its face or as applied in a particular case?

5.   How does an arbitrator determine whether a management rule is reasonable? Does reasonableness require both a reasonable objective and a reasonable means? Was it appropriate for the arbitrator in *Chanute* to consider "wide acceptability" and "prevailing arbitration standards"? Are there other measures of reasonableness that the arbitrator should have, but did not, consider?

(a) On what basis did the arbitrator conclude that it was reasonable to reduce the number of points that would result in termination? Do you agree with his conclusion?

(b) Do you agree with the arbitrator's conclusion that the requirement of perfect attendance in a calendar month to eliminate a negative attendance point was reasonable? Why or why not?

(c) Do you agree with the arbitrator's conclusion that the failure to permit the passage of time to eliminate negative attendance points was unreasonable? Why or why not?

6.   The arbitrator appears to be careful not to impose on the employer a twelve-month rolling period, but rather to hold the absence of a passage-of-time provision to be unreasonable and simply to advise that a twelve-month rolling period would be reasonable. Why do you think the arbitrator re-

frained from ordering the employer to adopt a twelve-month rolling period? Was it appropriate for the arbitrator to refrain from such an order?

7. An employer violates § 8(a)(5) of the National Labor Relations Act when it alters a term or condition of employment without first bargaining with the union to impasse. NLRB v. Katz, 369 U.S. 736, 82 S.Ct. 1107, 8 L.Ed.2d 230 (1962). An attendance policy is a term or condition of employment. Roll and Hold Warehouse and Distribution Corp., 325 NLRB 41 (1997), enforced, 162 F.3d 513 (7th Cir.1998). Notice that the arbitrator in *Chanute* mentions that the employer discussed its proposed policy with the union, but there is no indication that the parties had bargained to impasse on the issue. Should the arbitrator have considered whether the National Labor Relations Act had been violated? Did the employer's promulgation of the attendance policy in *Chanute* violate § 8(a)(5)? Or did the management rights provision in the collective bargaining agreement waive the union's rights under § 8(a)(5)? See Reid Carron and Angela Broughton, *When Is "No" Really "No"?—The NLRB's Current Position on the Freedom of Contract, Management Rights, and Waiver*, 13 The Labor Lawyer 299 (1997); Kenneth L. Wagner, *"No" Means "No" When a Party "Really" Says So: The NLRB's Continued Adherence to the Clear and Unmistakable Waiver Doctrine in Unilateral Change Cases*, 13 The Labor Lawyer 325 (1997).

D. PAST PRACTICE[1]

The arbitrator's interpretive tools in resolving a grievance are not limited to the words of the collective bargaining agreement. Often the parties ask the arbitrator to find that their past conduct explains the meaning of ambiguous contract language, defines general language, or alters the meaning of seemingly unambiguous language. Most significantly, they may also claim that practice, unsupported by explicit contract language, creates a binding condition of employment.

It is not unusual in an ordinary commercial contract to look to the parties' conduct to interpret the language of their agreement,[2] but the broad scope of implicit rights recognized in labor arbitration distinguishes the collective bargaining agreement from other contracts. Labor arbitrators may recognize a past practice, not mentioned in the contract, as binding on the parties. Participants in labor arbitration, therefore, must be able to understand and distinguish the wide variety of functions

1. Bibliographic Suggestions: Elkouri & Elkouri, How Arbitration Works, 605–630 (Alan Miles Ruben, ed., 6th ed. 2003); Arthur Dobbelaere, Jr., William H. Leahy and Jack Reardon, *The Effect of Past Practice on the Arbitration of Labor Disputes*, 40 Arbitration Journal 27 (December 1985); Ira F. Jaffe, *Past Practice, Maintenance of Benefits, and Zipper Clauses*, Labor and Employment Arbitration (Tim Bornstein, Ann Gosline and Marc Greenbaum, eds. 2003); Richard P. McLaughlin, *Custom and Past Practice in Labor Arbitration*, 18 Arbitration Journal 205 (1963); Richard Mitten-

thal, *The Ever–Present Past*, 47 Proceedings of the National Academy of Arbitrators 184 (1994); Carlton J. Snow, *Contract Interpretation*, The Common Law of the Workplace: The Views of Arbitrators 62 (Theodore J. St. Antoine, ed. 1998); Saul Wallen, *The Silent Contract vs. Express Provisions: The Arbitration of Local Working Conditions*, 15 Proceedings of the National Academy of Arbitrators 117 (1962).

2. Restatement of the Law, Second, Contracts §§ 219–223 (1981).

that past practice plays in the interpretation of collective bargaining agreements. How do labor arbitrators use practice to interpret the language of collective bargaining agreements? Why should practices unreflected in contract language ever be binding? What sorts of practices can become binding? By what process can they become binding? If a practice is considered binding, under what circumstances can it be changed?

Although much has been written in arbitration awards and scholarly journals about the role of past practice, no writing better explains the concept than this paper by Arbitrator Richard Mittenthal.

PAST PRACTICE AND THE ADMINISTRATION OF COLLECTIVE BARGAINING AGREEMENTS
Richard Mittenthal.
14 Proceedings of the National Academy of Arbitrators 30 (1961).

Custom and practice profoundly influence every area of human activity. Protocol guides the relations between states; etiquette affects an individual's social behavior; habit governs most of our daily actions; and mores help to determine our laws. It is hardly surprising, therefore, to find that past practice in an industrial plant plays a significant role in the administration of the collective agreement. Justice Douglas of the United States Supreme Court recently stated that "the labor arbitrator's source of law is not confined to the express provisions of the contract, as the industrial common law—the past practices of the industry and the shop—is equally a part of the collective bargaining agreement although not expressed in it." [*United Steelworkers of America v. Warrior & Gulf Navigation Co.*, 363 U.S. 574, 581–582 (1960), Chapter III.B.1, *supra.*]

Past practice is one of the most useful and hence one of the most commonly used aids in resolving grievance disputes. It can help the arbitrator in a variety of ways in interpreting the agreement. It may be used to clarify what is ambiguous, to give substance to what is general, and perhaps even to modify or amend what is seemingly unambiguous. It may also, apart from any basis in the agreement, be used to establish a separate, enforceable condition of employment. I will explore each of these functions of past practice in some detail. And I will seek to describe the nature of a practice as well—that is, its principal characteristics, its duration, and so on.

THE NATURE OF A PRACTICE

The facts in a case may be readily ascertainable but the arbitrator then must determine what their significance is, whether they add up to a practice, and if so, what that practice is. These questions confront us whenever the parties base their argument on a claimed practice. They cannot be answered by generalization. For a practice is ordinarily the unique product of a particular plant's history and tradition, of a particular group of employees and supervisors, and of a particular set of circumstances which made it viable in the first place. Thus, in deciding the threshold question of whether a practice exists, we must look to the plant-setting rather than to theories of contract administration.

Although the conception of what constitutes a practice differs from one employer to another and from one union to another, there are certain characteristics which typify most practices. These characteristics have been noted in many arbitration decisions. For example, in the steel industry, Sylvester Garrett has lucidly defined a practice in these words:

> A custom or practice is not something which arises simply because a given course of conduct has been pursued by Management or the employees on one or more occasions. A custom or a practice is a usage evolved * * * as a normal reaction to a recurring type situation. It must be shown to be the *accepted* course of conduct characteristically repeated in response to the given set of underlying circumstances. This is not to say that the course of conduct must be *accepted* in the sense of both parties having agreed to it, but rather that it must be *accepted* in the sense of being regarded by [those] involved as the *normal* and *proper* response to the underlying circumstances presented.

In short, something qualifies as a practice if it is shown to be the understood and accepted way of doing things over an extended period of time.

What qualities must a course of conduct have before it can legitimately be regarded as a practice?

First, there should be *clarity* and *consistency*. A course of conduct which is vague and ambiguous or which has been contradicted as often as it has been followed can hardly qualify as a practice. But where those in the plant invariably respond in the same way to a particular set of conditions, their conduct may very well ripen into a practice.

Second, there should be *longevity* and *repetition*. A period of time has to elapse during which a consistent pattern of behavior emerges. Hence, one or two isolated instances of a certain conduct do not establish a practice. Just how frequently and over how long a period something must be done before it can be characterized as a practice is a matter of good judgment for which no formula can be devised.

Third, there should be *acceptability*. The employees and the supervisors alike must have knowledge of the particular conduct and must regard it as the correct and customary means of handling a situation. Such acceptability may frequently be implied from long acquiescence in a known course of conduct. Where this acquiescence does not exist, that is, where employees have constantly protested a particular course of action through complaints and grievances, it is doubtful that any practice has been created.

One must consider, too, the *underlying circumstances* which give a practice its true dimensions. A practice is no broader than the circumstances out of which it has arisen, although its scope can always be enlarged in the day-to-day administration of the agreement. No meaningful description of a practice can be made without mention of these circumstances. For instance, a work assignment practice which develops on the afternoon and midnight shifts and which is responsive to the peculiar needs of night work cannot be automatically extended to the day shift. The point is that every practice must be carefully related to its origin and purpose.

And, finally, the significance to be attributed to a practice may possibly be affected by whether or not it is supported by *mutuality*. Some practices are the product, either in their inception or in their application, of a joint understanding; others develop from choices made by the employer in the exercise of its managerial discretion without any intention of a future commitment.

Subject Matter

Practices usually relate to some phase of the contractual relationship between the employer and [the] employees. They may concern such subjects as scheduling, overtime, promotions, and the uses of seniority, all of which are covered to some extent in the typical collective agreement. But practices may also involve extra-contractual considerations— from the giving of Thanksgiving turkeys and Christmas bonuses to the availability of free parking.

Still other practices, although this characterization may be arguable, have more to do with managerial discretion in operating a plant than with the employment relationship. For example, the long-time use of inter-departmental hand trucks for moving material might be regarded as a practice, and the truckers who do this work certainly have an interest in preserving this method of operation. But could it be seriously argued that this practice would prohibit the employer from introducing a conveyor belt to replace the hand trucks? Most agreements provide, usually in a management-rights clause, that methods of manufacture are solely within the employer's discretion.

There may even be practices which have nothing whatever to do with the employment relationship. The long-time assignment of a certain number of foremen to a given department might be viewed by some as a practice, but it could hardly preclude the employer from using fewer foremen. What I am suggesting here is that the mere existence of a practice, without more, has no real significance. Only if the practice clarifies an imperfectly expressed contractual obligation or lends substance to an indefinitely expressed obligation or creates a completely independent obligation will it have some effect on the parties' relationship. * * *

FUNCTIONS OF PAST PRACTICE

Clarifying Ambiguous Language

The danger of ambiguity arises not only from the English language with its immense vocabulary, flexible grammar and loose syntax but also from the nature of the collective bargaining agreement. The agreement is a means of governing "complex, many-sided relations between large numbers of people in a going concern for very substantial periods of time." It is seldom written with the kind of precision and detail which characterize other legal instruments. Although it covers a great variety of subjects, many of which are quite complicated, it must be simply written so that its terms can be understood by the employees and their supervisors. It is sometimes composed by persons inexperienced in the art of written expression. Issues are often settled by a general formula because the negotiators recognize they could not possibly foresee or provide for the many contingencies which are bound to occur during the life of the agreement.

Indeed, any attempt to anticipate and dispose of problems before they arise would, I suspect, create new areas of disagreement and thus obstruct negotiations. Sooner or later the employer and the union must reach agreement if they wish to avoid the economic waste of a strike or lockout. Because of this pressure, the parties often defer the resolution of their differences—either by ignoring them or by writing a provision which is so vague and uncertain as to leave the underlying issue open.

These characteristics inevitably cause portions of the agreement to be expressed in ambiguous and general terms. With the passage of time, however, this language may be given a clear and practical construction, either through managerial action which is acquiesced in by the employees (or, conceivably, employee action which is acquiesced in by management) or through the resolution of disputes on a case-by-case basis. This accumulation of plant experience results in the development of practices and procedures of varying degrees of consistency and force. * * *

Implementing General Contract Language

Practice is also a means of implementing general contract language. In areas which cannot be made specific, the parties are often satisfied to state a general rule and to allow the precise meaning of the rule to develop through the day-to-day administration of the agreement.

For instance, the right to discipline and discharge is usually conditioned upon the existence of "just cause." Similarly, the right to deviate from a contract requirement may be conditioned upon the existence of "circumstances beyond the employer's control." General expressions of this kind are rarely defined. For no definition, however detailed, could anticipate all the possibilities which might take place during the term of the agreement.

But, in time, this kind of general language does tend to become more concrete. As the parties respond to the many different situations confronting them—approving certain principles and procedures, disputing others, and resolving their disputes in the grievance procedure—they find mutually acceptable ways of doing things which serve to guide them in future cases. Instead of rearguing every matter without regard to their earlier experiences, acceptable principles and procedures are applied again and again. * * *

Modifying or Amending Apparently Unambiguous Language

What an agreement says is one thing; how it is carried out may be quite another. A recent study at the University of Illinois revealed that differences between contract provisions and actual practice are not at all unusual. Thus, an arbitrator occasionally [is] confronted with a situation where an established practice conflicts with a seemingly clear and unambiguous contract provision. Which is to prevail? The answer in many cases has been to disregard the practice and affirm the plain meaning of the contract language.

* * * The real question, however, is whether as serious a matter as the modification of clear contract language can be based on practice alone. Some arbitrators have held, I think with good reason, that practice should prevail only if the proofs are sufficiently strong to warrant saying there was in effect *mutual agreement* to the modification. The parties must, to use the words in one decision, "have evinced a positive acceptance or endorsement" of the practice. Thus, I believe that the modification is justified not by practice but rather by the parties' agreement, the existence of which may possibly be inferred from a clear and consistent practice.

* * * But what of a situation where practice conflicts with the real meaning of a truly unambiguous provision? * * * I would find no violation on the ground that practice can be decisive only if there is some uncertainty, however slight, with respect to the parties' original intention * * * [I]f the "living document" notion is carried to its logical conclusion, a violation may exist on the ground that the practice, being a product of joint determination, amounts to an amendment of the contract and that thereafter the practice could only be changed by mutual agreement. * * *

As a Separate, Enforceable Condition of Employment

Past practice may serve to clarify, implement, and even amend contract language. But these are not its only functions. Sometimes an established practice is regarded as a distinct and binding condition of employment, one which cannot be changed without the mutual consent of the parties. Its binding quality may arise either from a contract provision which specifically requires the continuance of existing practices or, absent such a provision, from the theory that long-standing practices which have been accepted by the parties become an integral part of the agreement with just as much force as any of its written provisions. * * *

Most agreements * * * say nothing about management having to maintain existing conditions. They ordinarily do not even mention the subject of past practice. The question then is whether, apart from any basis in the agreement, an established practice can nevertheless be considered a binding condition of employment. The answer, I think, depends upon one's conception of the collective bargaining agreement. * * *

Employers tend to argue that the only restrictions placed upon management are those contained in the agreement and that in all other respects management is free to act in whatever way it sees fit. Or to put the argument in the more familiar "reserved rights" terminology, management continues to have the rights it customarily possessed and which it has not surrendered through collective bargaining. If an agreement does not require the continuance of existing conditions, a practice, being merely an extra-contractual consideration, would have no binding force regardless of how well-established it may be. It follows that management may change or eliminate the practice without the union's consent.

Unions take an entirely different view of the problem. They emphasize the unique qualities of the collective bargaining agreement and the background against which the agreement was negotiated, particularly those practices which have come to be accepted by employees and supervisors alike and have thus become an important part of the working environment. The agreement is executed in the light of this working environment and on the assumption that existing practices will remain in effect. Therefore, to the extent that these practices are unchallenged during negotiations, the parties must be held to have adopted them and made them a part of their agreement.

Many arbitrators have, at some time in their careers, been confronted by these arguments. Some have held that the agreement is the exclusive source of rights and privileges; others have held that the agreement may subsume continuation of existing conditions. The latter is the more prevalent view. Those who follow it have prohibited employers from unilaterally changing or eliminating practices with regard to efficiency bonus plans, paid lunch periods, wash-up periods on company time, maternity leaves of absence, free milk, and home electricity at nominal rates.

The reasoning behind these decisions begins with the proposition that the parties have not set down on paper the whole of their agreement. "One cannot reduce all the rules governing a community like an industrial plant to fifteen or even fifty pages."

Thus, the union-management contract includes not just the written provisions stated therein but also the understandings and mutually acceptable practices which have developed over the years. Because the contract is executed in the context of these understandings and practices, the negotiators must be presumed to be fully aware of them and to have relied upon them in striking their bargain. Hence, if a particular practice is not repudiated during negotiations, it may fairly be said that the contract was entered into upon the assumption that this practice would continue in force. By their silence, the parties have given assent to "existing modes of procedure." In this way, practices may *by implication* become an integral part of the contract.

* * *

Still another problem exists. Those of us who accept the principle that an agreement may require the continuance of existing practices recognize that this principle cannot be allowed to freeze *all* existing conditions. For instance, the long-standing use of hand-controlled grinding machines could hardly be regarded as a practice prohibiting the introduction of automatic grinding machines. Or the long-time use of pastel colors in painting plant interiors could not preclude management from changing to a different color scheme. Plainly, not all practices can be considered binding conditions of employment. * * *

A better test, I think, is suggested by what Shulman said in a decision[53] he made as umpire under the Ford–UAW agreement, an agreement which did not require the continuance of existing practices. He urged that the controlling question in this kind of case is whether or not the practice was supported by "mutual agreement." He explained his position in these words:

> A practice thus based on mutual agreement may be subject to change only by mutual agreement. Its binding quality is due, however, not to the fact that it is past practice but rather to the agreement in which it is based.

> But there are other practices which are not the result of joint determination at all. They may be mere happenstance, that is, methods that developed without design or deliberation. Or they may be choices by Management in the exercise of managerial discretion as to convenient methods at the time. In such cases there is no thought of obligation or commitment for the future. Such practices are merely present ways, not prescribed ways, of doing things. The relevant item of significance is not the nature of the particular method but the managerial freedom with respect to it. Being the product of managerial determination in its permitted discretion, such practices are, in the absence of contractual provisions to the contrary, subject to change in the same discretion. . . . But there is no requirement of mutual agreement as a condition precedent to a change of a practice of this character.

> A contrary holding would place past practice on a par with written agreement and create the anomaly that, while the parties expend great energy and time in negotiating the details of the Agreement, they unknowingly and unintentionally commit themselves to unstated and perhaps more important matters which in the future may be found to have been past practice.

Under this test, only a practice which is supported by the mutual agreement of the parties would be enforceable. Such a practice would be binding, regardless of how minor it may be and regardless of the extent to which it may affect a traditional function. Absent this mutuality, however, the practice would be subject to change in management's discretion. * * *

53.   [Ford Motor Co., 19 LA 237 (Harry Shulman, 1952).]

DURATION AND TERMINATION OF A PRACTICE

Once the parties become bound by a practice, they may wonder how long it will be binding and how it can be terminated.

Consider first a practice which is, apart from any basis in the agreement, an enforceable condition of employment on the theory that the agreement subsumes the continuance of existing conditions. Such a practice cannot be unilaterally changed during the life of the agreement. For, as I explained earlier in this paper, if a practice is not discussed during negotiations most of us are likely to infer that the agreement was executed on the assumption that the practice would remain in effect.

The inference is based largely on the parties' acquiescence in the practice. If either side should, during the negotiation of a later agreement, object to the continuance of this practice, it could not be inferred from the signing of a new agreement that the parties intended the practice to remain in force. Without their acquiescence, the practice would no longer be a binding condition of employment. In face of a timely repudiation of a practice by one party, the other must have the practice written into the agreement if it is to continue to be binding.

Consider next a well-established practice which serves to clarify some ambiguity in the agreement. Because the practice is essential to an understanding of the ambiguous provision, it becomes in effect a part of that provision. As such, it will be binding for the life of the agreement. And the mere repudiation of the practice by one side during the negotiation of a new agreement, unless accompanied by a revision of the ambiguous language, would not be significant. For the repudiation alone would not change the meaning of the ambiguous provision and hence would not detract from the effectiveness of the practice.

It is a well-settled principle that where past practice has established a meaning for language that is subsequently used in an agreement, the language will be presumed to have the meaning given it by practice. Thus, this kind of practice can only be terminated by mutual agreement, that is, by the parties rewriting the ambiguous provision to supersede the practice, by eliminating the provision entirely, etc.

Consider finally the effect of changing circumstances on the viability of a practice during the contract term. Where the conditions which gave rise to a practice no longer exist, the employer is not obliged to continue to apply the practice. * * *

Notes and Questions

1. Why should an arbitrator ever permit past practice to have the binding force of written contract language?

2. The Supreme Court has held that § 8(a)(5) of the National Labor Relations Act prohibits an employer from unilaterally changing a term or condition of employment without first bargaining about the matter with the union to an impasse. NLRB v. Katz, 369 U.S. 736, 82 S.Ct. 1107, 8 L.Ed.2d 230 (1962). Does that principle, established subsequent to Mittenthal's

essay, give statutory support to Mittenthal's analysis of the proper use of past practice? Or, might the statutory principle undercut Mittenthal's approach by precluding an employer from disestablishing a past practice through an accumulation of contrary actions?

3. Does permitting past practice to have the binding effect of written contract language have any negative effects upon the parties, their relationship, or the collective bargaining process? Any positive effects?

4. Many contracts include a provision stating that the arbitrator "has no authority to add to or subtract from or modify" any of the terms of the agreement. Does such language preclude an arbitrator from finding that a past practice has become contractually binding?

5. Some contracts expressly reject reliance on past practice. If the parties fail to include such a provision in their contract, is it reasonable for an arbitrator to conclude that they intend past practices to be contractually binding?

6. Three years ago, before any of its employees were represented by a Union, the College promulgated a policy regarding work of maintenance employees on days when the College was closed because of snow. On such "snow days," employees unable to get to work would nevertheless be compensated and employees who were able to work would receive the hours worked on the snow day as compensatory time off. This year the College's maintenance employees became represented by a Union. The first collective bargaining agreement between the Union and the College makes no mention of snow days but it does provide:

§ 2: Any and all prior agreements, resolutions, practices, policies, rules and regulations regarding terms and conditions of employment, to the extent inconsistent with the provisions of this Agreement, are hereby superseded.

§ 3: The parties mutually acknowledge that during the negotiations that resulted in this Agreement, each had the unlimited opportunity to make demands and proposals regarding terms and conditions of employment. All understandings and agreements arrived at by the parties are set forth in this Agreement.

Assume that in the absence of the quoted contract language, the arbitrator would find that the "snow day" policy is a binding past practice. What arguments should the College make to support the proposition that the quoted language precludes such a finding? What arguments should the Union make to support the proposition that the quoted language does not preclude a finding of a binding past practice? How should the arbitrator rule? Compare, Augsburg College, 91 LA 1166 (Thomas P. Gallagher, 1988) (past practice not binding), with Wallace Murray Corp., 72 LA 470 (Roger I. Abrams, 1979) (past practice binding). The type of language included in § 3 is often referred to as a "zipper clause." See Jaffe, *supra* footnote 1, at § 10.03[5].

7. The collective bargaining agreement between the School District and the Education Association that represents the classroom teachers contains the following provision:

> A teacher shall be allowed full pay for up to four days absence from school in any one school year, on account of serious illness or death of the teacher's spouse, child, sibling, parent or grandchild.

Grievant, a fourth grade teacher, has a fourteen-month-old child who was suffering from respiratory problems. The child had been hospitalized for her condition. The child's physician advised the parents that the child had to remain in a tent filled with a misted water vapor, and that the child could remain in the tent in the hospital or the environment could be provided at home with rented equipment. The teacher decided to care for her child at home and she was absent from school for three days as a result. The Superintendent of Schools denied the teacher wages for the three days on the ground that the contractual term "serious illness" was limited to those illnesses requiring hospital confinement. The Education Association pursued to arbitration the teacher's grievance challenging the Superintendent's decision.

At the arbitration hearing to consider the grievance, the Association maintained that the contract does not require hospitalization in order to constitute "serious illness," and that the teacher's child was suffering from a serious illness. At the hearing, the Superintendent testified that she had, for the past six years, denied paid family illness leave unless the leave requested coincided with hospital confinement. She said that this test for serious illness was much easier to administer than a subjective test of seriousness. The Superintendent also testified that many requests for paid leave had been determined according to the hospitalization standard. The Association representatives testified that they had never been notified by the Superintendent that the hospitalization standard was being applied.

Should the arbitrator rule that the contractual term "serious illness" has been defined by past practice to require hospital confinement of the family member? Why or why not? Independent School District No. 22, 83 LA 66 (Thomas P. Gallagher, 1984) Note that contract language is different than the critical phrase in the Family and Medical Leave Act ("serious health condition") and that the facts in the cited case arose prior to enactment of the FMLA. Should the result be different if the case arose *after* enactment of the FMLA? (No provision of the FMLA requires an employer to provide paid leave.)

8. The collective bargaining agreement between the parties states that the employer "agrees to pay" for employees' health insurance. Despite this language, for at least twenty years, the employer has deducted from each employee's wages the sum of $10 per pay period toward the cost of the health insurance premium. Without notice to the Union, the employer recently started deducting 10% of the premium cost, rather than the much lower sum of $10. The Union asserts that it was unaware of the twenty-year practice and that deducting any amount for health insurance from employee wages violates the unambiguous language of the agreement. The Employer asserts that the increased cost of health insurance permits it to increase the employees' existing co-payment to 10%. Is the Employer right? The Union? Neither? If there is a past practice allowing the employer to charge a $10 premium co-payment, would the significant increase in the cost of health care insurance be a sufficient change in circumstances to allow the employer

to increase the amount of the co-payment? See, American Sand & Gravel Co., 118 LA 535 (Gregory P. Szuter, 2003) (arbitrator considered explicit language amended by past practice to permit $10 employee payment but not to permit increase to 10%).

9.   For more than ten years, the production employees at the Company have had access to vending machines located adjacent to the shop floor from which they have purchased snacks at break and meal times. The collective bargaining agreement between the Company and the Union makes no reference to vending machines. The Production Manager of the Company received information from supervisors suggesting that some employees had been using the vending machines during working time and that litter from vending machine products had been left about the production areas and also been placed in bins of scrap material that the Company collects and sells. The Production Manager therefore had the vending machines moved to the Company Cafeteria which is on the floor above the production area. As a result, employees who want to obtain food from the vending machines during their breaks have found it nearly impossible to get food and get back to their work stations in the brief break periods. The Union submits a grievance to the Company, asserting that the Company's removal of the vending machines violates past practice.

(a) What arguments should the parties make? How should the arbitrator rule on the Union's grievance? Compare Tecumseh Products Co., 80 LA 568 (L. D. May, 1983) (past practice requires employer to return vending machines to shop floor) with Mechanical Products, Inc., 91 LA 977 (George T. Roumell, Jr., 1988) (past practice of allowing employees to use vending machines during working time did not preclude implementation of a new rule restricting their use to break and lunch periods).

(b) The Supreme Court held in Ford Motor Co. v. NLRB, 441 U.S. 488, 99 S.Ct. 1842, 60 L.Ed.2d 420 (1979), that an employer violated § 8(a)(5) of the National Labor Relations Act when it refused to bargain with the union over changes in vending machine prices. If the provision of in-plant food services is a mandatory subject of bargaining, did the employer here violate the National Labor Relations Act when it moved the vending machines from the shop floor to the cafeteria? Should the fact that the provision of in-plant food services is a mandatory subject of bargaining influence the arbitrator's decision of whether the employer violated the collective bargaining agreement by moving the vending machines?

(c) For cases in which arbitrators have held that changed circumstances permitted an employer to terminate an established past practice, see Goodyear Tire & Rubber, 107 LA 24 (Stanley H. Sergent, 1996) (employer no longer had to exempt employees with a religious objection from Sunday work where employer had changed from occasional use of Sunday overtime to regular Sunday operations, substantially increasing the employer's cost of allowing an exemption); and Packaging Corp., 102 LA 1099 (James J. Odom, Jr., 1994) (employer not required to maintain a forty-year practice of having a nurse on second and third shifts because of changed circumstances—now there are substantially fewer employees on those shifts, alternative emergency care is available in the community, and employees have been trained to provide emergency care).

10. For more than fifteen years the Employer has had a service award program. The program is not mentioned in the parties' collective bargaining agreement. Employees at five-year intervals of their employment with the company are invited to select an award from a list of awards for employees with at least that number of years of service. Awards include such things as jewelry, clocks and small appliances. A few times the Employer changed some of the specific items available for the various years of service. One employee approaching the thirtieth anniversary of employment was looking forward to getting a three-diamond gold ring that several of his co-workers had previously received for their twenty-fifth anniversary. When he received the current booklet for service awards, however, the ring now was only available to employees with forty years of service. The union filed a grievance on behalf of the employee alleging that the denial of the ring to the thirty-year employee violated past practice. Did the Employer violate the contract? Could the employer eliminate the service award program in its entirety? Commonwealth Industries, 117 LA 580 (Hyman Cohen, 2002) (employer could change the awards available from time to time without violating past practice).

11. Ten years ago, when County employees were not represented by any union, the County adopted a compensation plan providing that real estate appraisers would be given a greater number of vacation days than other employees, but appraisers would be allowed overtime compensation only at straight time rates. Five years ago, the Union became the collective bargaining representative for all County employees including the real estate appraisers. The agreement entered into between the Union and the County provided for fewer vacation days than the real estate appraisers had previously been receiving, but it allowed overtime compensation at the rate of time and one-half. The agreement stated, "All personnel policies provided by this contract, unless otherwise stated, shall be applied uniformly across the entire bargaining unit." Years later, after adoption of two additional collective bargaining agreements containing identical provisions, the County converted to a computerized personnel system. The County discovered that there were six real estate appraisers who had continued, throughout the life of the three collective bargaining agreements, to receive more vacation days than specified in the collective bargaining agreement. The appraisers had also continued to receive only straight time compensation for overtime. The six appraisers were notified that they would no longer receive the extra vacation days.

The appraisers submitted a grievance challenging the County's decision to deny them the additional vacation days and the Union pursued their grievance to arbitration.

(a) What are the County's best arguments for why it could discontinue the extra vacation days for appraisers?

(b) What are the Union's best arguments for why the County is bound by its past practice of providing appraisers with extra vacation days?

(c) How should the arbitrator decide the case? Why? See, Ramsey County v. American Federation of State, County and Municipal Employees, 309 N.W.2d 785 (Minn.1981) (court upheld arbitration award based on past practice contradicting express contract language). Cf., Judsen Rubber Works,

Inc. v. Manufacturing, Production & Service Workers Union, Local No. 24, 889 F.Supp. 1057 (N.D.Ill. 1995) (court refused to enforce arbitration award that had relied upon past practice rather than explicit contract language). See also Anheuser–Busch, Inc. v. Teamsters, 280 F.3d 1133 (7th Cir. 2002) (court refused to enforce arbitration award relying on past practice contradicting express contract language when contract contained a zipper clause precluding practices from superceding written provisions).

(d) Should past practice ever be permitted to outweigh explicit and unambiguous language in a collective bargaining agreement? See Rexroth Corp., 101 LA 94 (Mollie H. Bowers, 1993) (employer did not violate contract when it followed forty-year scheduling practice rather than explicit contract language); and Cook County, 117 LA 1025 (Aaron S. Wolff, 2002) (although contract explicitly required a bidding procedure for assignment of overtime, employer did not violate agreement when it followed a past practice using a rotation system to assign overtime). Notice that in both of these cases it was the *employer* rather than the union that sought to make a past practice binding. See also Elkouri & Elkouri, footnote 1 *supra*, at 628 (citing arbitration awards finding "that a party's failure to file grievances or to protest past violations of a clear contract rule does not bar that party, after notice to the violator, from insisting on compliance with the clear contract requirement in future cases").

12.   A successor employer assumes the collective bargaining agreement of its predecessor. Can the successor be bound by the past practices of the predecessor? Compare North Baking Co., 116 LA 1788 (Elliott H. Goldstein, 2002) (yes, but no binding practice under the facts of the case), with Supervalu Holdings, Inc., 116 LA 417 (John M. Felice, 2001) (no).

13.   How would you go about proving to an arbitrator that a past practice was or was not contractually binding?

14.   As a union representative, what might you do in the next collective bargaining negotiations to strengthen the binding effect of current practices? As an employer representative, what might you do in the next collective bargaining negotiations to provide the employer with maximum discretion in changing current practices? For examples of contract language see City of Woodward, 114 LA 289 (Ronald E. Bumpass, 2000) (precluding the modification of past practices except by explicit written agreement) and North Baking Co., 116 LA 1788 (Elliott H. Goldstein, 2002) (precluding past practices from becoming binding). Knowing that a past practice may sometimes benefit an employer and sometimes a union, is it wise for either side to seek contract language that determines, in advance, the effect of past practices?

15.   If a past practice has become binding, how can a party terminate its binding effect? Is it sufficient for a party simply to announce during the contract period that it no longer will be bound by the practice? If not, is it sufficient to announce prospective termination of the practice during negotiations for the next contract? Or is it necessary to obtain a written agreement between the parties for the binding effect to end? If a written agreement is not necessary, would you nevertheless recommend that parties seek in negotiations a written agreement to terminate a practice?

16.   What is the relationship between the management rights and past practice doctrines? Can an employer lose what would otherwise be a management right through its past practices? Compare, Wellman Friction Products, 117 LA 1101 (James Clair Duff, 2002) (employer violated binding past practice by eliminating a paid lunch break despite managements rights provision giving employer the right to "to establish and change working schedules"), with Shell Chemical Co., 116 LA 503 (Diane Dunham Massey, 2001) (basic management rights, such as vacation scheduling, cannot be modified by past practice).

17.   In 1994, Richard Mittenthal reflected back on the topic of his 1961 essay on past practice. He concluded that, although arbitrators' analysis of the past practice issue had not changed during that time, the labor relations climate had changed in two ways that had the effect of reducing the parties' opportunities to establish past practices. First, collective bargaining agreements had grown in length so that what had been general provisions subject to clarification by practice were now fully articulated sets of rules and subrules. Second, employers increasingly obtained provisions in agreements that expressly negated the application of the past practice doctrine. Richard Mittenthal, *The Ever–Present Past*, 47 Proceedings of the National Academy of Arbitrators 184 (1994).

E.   SENIORITY

1.   INTRODUCTION[1]

Unions prize seniority provisions above almost any other part of the collective bargaining agreement. As a result, 91% of the contracts surveyed by BNA in 1995 contain such provisions.[2]

In the employment context, "seniority" refers to length of service. Seniority comes in several varieties, among them seniority on a particular job, in a department, at a plant, with an employer, or in a given industry. It is not uncommon for employees to accrue several types of seniority to be used for different purposes. Job seniority might determine promotion in a line of progression, plant seniority might control the order of layoffs, company seniority the length of the employee's vacation, and industry seniority the size of the employee's pension. The possible permutations are almost infinite.

The distinctions between types of seniority can be critical. In Saint–Gobain Calmar, 118 LA 585 (Calvin William Sharpe, 2003), for example, the agreement provided that layoffs of employees who had passed their

---

1. Bibliographic suggestions: Benjamin Aaron, *Reflections on the Legal Nature and Enforceability of Seniority Rights*, 75 Harvard Law Review 1532 (1962); Roger I. Abrams and Dennis R. Nolan, *Seniority Rights Under the Collective Agreement*, 2 The Labor Lawyer 99 (1986); Mollie Bowers, *Layoffs, Bumping, and Recall*, Chapter 28 of Labor and Employment Arbitration (Tim Bornstein, Ann Gosline, and Mark Greenbaum, eds., 2d ed. 1997; Harry T. Edwards, *Seniority Systems in Collective Bargaining*, in Arbitration in Practice 119 (Arnold Zack ed. 1984); Thomas J. McDermott, *Types of Seniority Provisions and the Measurement of Ability*, 25 Arbitration Journal 105 (1970).

2. Bureau of National Affairs, Basic Patterns in Union Contracts 85 (14th ed. 1995).

"qualifying period" would be in reverse order of plant seniority but layoffs of those during the qualifying period would follow classification seniority. The company removed three employees from one classification and assigned them to a lower classification in what it alleged was a restructuring rather than a layoff. The transferred employees had less classification seniority but more plant seniority than others retained by the employer. After finding that the shift was actually a layoff and that the grievants had passed their qualifying period, the arbitrator held that their layoff was improper because the company should have used plant seniority. He ordered the company to restore them to their former positions with full compensation.

The two primary purposes of seniority are to choose between employees competing for a scarce benefit ("competitive status seniority") and to decide eligibility for, or to calculate the amount of, fringe benefits ("benefit seniority"). Examples of competitive status seniority are selections for promotions, transfers, layoffs, recalls, work assignments, shift preferences, and vacation periods. Examples of benefit seniority are eligibility for sick leave, vacation and holiday pay, and pensions. The distinction is imperfect because competitive status seniority might accrue as a right, just as benefit seniority does. If two firms merge and have to lay off some employees, the senior employees will surely argue for the preservation of their competitive seniority for bidding purposes. Benefit seniority produces few disputes. This section therefore discusses only competitive status seniority.

Seniority serves a third and less obvious function in unionized workplaces. It delineates some aspects of job control by limiting management's discretion. When seniority is of limited importance, management retains power; when seniority is of decisive importance, the union has seized some of that power. The clearest examples involve conflict between seniority and ability in promotions and work assignments. Without a contractual limitation, an employer could arbitrarily award a desirable job to any employee. Employers oppose strong seniority clauses, arguing that they frustrate newer but more able employees, reduce flexibility, and inhibit productivity. Unions, on the other hand, typically seek to make seniority the sole or at least a decisive criterion, arguing that such an objective measure is necessary to prevent managerial favoritism and encourage stability in the work force. A seniority provision could embody either of these views or some hybrid; for example, the contract might require promotion of the "senior qualified" employee even if the junior is *more* qualified, or it might favor the most senior employee only if the competitors' abilities are "relatively equal."

In the unionized workplace, seniority is purely a contractual concept, created and defined by the collective bargaining agreement. When the collective bargaining agreement ends, so—normally—does the competitive status seniority accrued pursuant to it. Local 1251, UAW v. Robertshaw Controls Co., 405 F.2d 29 (2d Cir.1968) (*en banc*); Interscience Encyclopedia, Inc., 55 LA 210, 221–22 (Benjamin C. Roberts, 1970). Whether benefit seniority continues is a frequent subject for litigation.

Without a seniority provision an employer could still choose to allocate benefits according to length of service, but nothing in the employment relationship or the law requires it to do so. Many nonunionized employers, however, use informal seniority systems.

Because seniority is purely contractual, the wording of the seniority provision can be decisive. In St. Croix Alumina, L.L.C., 116 LA 641 (D. L. Howell, 2001), the employer had acquired the plant in 1995 from a predecessor, VIALCO, and had hired the VIALCO employees. The collective bargaining agreement between St. Croix Alumina and the Steelworkers defined seniority as length of service "with the Company." It also provided severance pay that increased with length of service. When St. Croix Alumina decided in 2000 to shut down the plant, the parties could not agree whether the grievants should received receive severance pay based on their VIALCO service date or on their St. Croix Alumina service date. The arbitrator denied the grievance, holding that the contract used the phrase "the Company" to refer to the current employer, St. Croix Alumina, not its predecessor VIALCO.

All these factors—the almost-universal adoption of seniority provisions, the multiple purposes served by seniority, and the wide variety of contractual language on seniority—make seniority a fertile ground for grievances. Among the major problem areas arbitrators encounter are these:

Acquisition and Calculation of Seniority. Who may acquire seniority, and when? In which unit or units—department, plant, company, or industry—does one accumulate seniority?

Retention, Accumulation, and Loss of Seniority. What effect does a break in service have, for example, a leave, layoff, or assignment outside the bargaining unit? What happens if units with different seniority lists are combined after a sale or merger?

Use of Seniority. How much weight does seniority have against ability when an employer assigns a job? What do "ability" and "qualified" mean? Is a senior employee "qualified" if he or she would need training before safely performing a certain job, or if he or she would need some "break-in" time before becoming efficient? Does "ability" refer to objective standards or also to subjective evaluations? Is an employee's disciplinary record (absenteeism, for example) relevant to an evaluation of "ability?" Does long seniority count as a mitigating factor in discipline cases? If so, to what degree?

Superseniority. Many contracting units give some union officials "superseniority," placing them above all other employees for certain purposes. Many such agreements are of dubious legality because they discriminate against other employees. Who is entitled to superseniority? When does it begin and end? How does superseniority relate to requirements that an employee be "qualified" for a job assignment? Does a union violate its duty of fair representation when it negotiates superseniority provisions?

Seniority and Discrimination. Because of past discrimination or demographic factors, women and minorities may be concentrated at the bottom of a seniority list. If so, does use of seniority amount to discrimination? How do contractual seniority rights relate to consent decrees and affirmative action requirements? When drafting Title VII of the Civil Rights Act of 1964, Congress expressly provided [in § 703(h)] that applying different standards of compensation or other terms of employment "pursuant to a bona fide seniority or merit system" would not be an unlawful employment practice. Similarly, negotiated seniority rules may limit what an employer need do when trying to offer a "reasonable accommodation" to an employee with a disability covered by the Americans with Disabilities Act. Protection of seniority systems was essential to guarantee union support for antidiscrimination legislation. Congress and the courts may also believe seniority so essential to fairness or to settled expectations that it outweighs antidiscrimination objectives.

This section of Chapter VII deals with the first four topics. The last is beyond the scope of this book.

2. THE ACQUISITION AND CALCULATION OF SENIORITY

(a) Seniority Units

An employee obtains seniority in one or more seniority units—typically the department, plant, or employer—pursuant to a collective bargaining agreement. Outside that context, seniority has no binding effect. Working for ten years in the Shipping Department of XYZ Department Store may affect an employee's life at work in many ways; working for several employers at different times ever since graduating from high school will not. One of the first things an arbitrator dealing with a seniority dispute must do, therefore, is determine the unit or units in which the employee has acquired seniority.

Usually the collective bargaining agreement specifies whether seniority accrues in, for example, a department or the plant, or both, and which seniority date applies to which decision. In Heckett Company, 48 LA 184 (R.R. Williams, 1966), for instance, the agreement specified that for vacation and pension calculations, seniority was "the length of continuous service with the Company from the day when the employee was last hired for work at the Company's Gadsden, Alabama, plant"; the arbitrator therefore denied an employee's effort to add to his seniority years served at another plant. If the contract is silent and there is no binding past practice, arbitrators usually assume the parties intended plant-wide seniority. Great Lakes Homes, Inc., 44 LA 737 (Neil Gundermann, 1965).

(b) Seniority Dates

Employees usually do not begin to accumulate seniority until they complete a probation period. Once they do so, however, their seniority may date from the first day of employment. The probation period typically allows the employer to "do with probationary employees what they will," Hughes Tool Co., 22 LA 540, 543 (Jerre S. Williams, 1954)—even to discharge them without cause and without recourse.

Notes and Questions

1.   Each potential seniority unit has its advantages and disadvantages. Industrial unions (as opposed to craft unions) usually favor broader seniority units because they enhance the value of seniority rights. Employers traditionally favored narrower units that give more weight to experience in specific jobs. Can you explain the normal preference? Sometimes the positions are reversed. Recently, for example, employers have pushed for fewer but broader seniority units. When might a union favor a narrower unit and an employer a broader one?

2.   Occasionally two or more employees hired on the same day will bid on an assignment controlled by seniority. How should the employer (or the arbitrator) decide between them? Obviously some nondiscriminatory rule is desirable. In one grievance, the arbitrator ordered the employees to toss a coin to decide which should be laid off. McCall Corp., 49 LA 183, 186 (Robert G. McIntosh, 1967). Was that a fair decision? If not, what should the arbitrator have done?

3.   Employers normally post or distribute seniority lists so employees can check them for accuracy. Does an erroneous list, if unchallenged for some time, bind the parties? Suppose an employer lays off A, the junior employee on a seniority list that has been posted for several years, but later learns A was actually senior to B. Would A be entitled to reinstatement and back pay? What would B say? See Universal Printing Co., 67 LA 456, 460 (Robert H. Kubie, 1976). Would the situation be different in a case involving benefit seniority rather than competitive status seniority? For example, may (or must) an employer continue to make pension payments calculated on the basis of an erroneous seniority list even after it discovers the error? See General Plywood Corp., 36 LA 633 (Arthur R. Porter, Jr, 1961). If you would decide these cases differently, how would you distinguish between them?

3.   RETENTION, ACCUMULATION, AND LOSS OF SENIORITY

An employee's work history may affect seniority. In particular, breaks in service and work outside the bargaining unit raise knotty questions as to whether seniority accumulates, remains frozen, or disappears. A well-drafted seniority provision would answer these questions, but not all are well-drafted. Layoffs and leaves usually stop the accumulation of seniority but do not terminate it. See Klein Mfg. Co., 101 LA 18 (Duane Traynor, 1993) (an employer may adjust an employee's seniority date to reflect a period on layoff). Arbitrators disfavor forfeitures, so they will rarely treat a temporary interruption in service as ending all seniority. Very seldom will anything other than a lengthy or ostensibly permanent break in employment end an employee's seniority. Beyond some reasonable period, though, no employee can expect to retain reemployment rights. Resignation or discharge for cause, on the other hand, immediately terminates all seniority rights.

If the employee continues to work with the employer but moves out of the seniority unit (for example, to take a supervisory position), new problems arise. If there is a layoff, should the former supervisor be able to bump back into the bargaining unit? If so, with the same seniority he or she had when leaving the unit, with increased seniority, or with no seniority at all? Absent any hard evidence of the parties' intentions, most arbitrators presume they intended employees working outside the unit to retain but not accumulate seniority, *e.g.*, Folger Coffee Co., 60 LA 353, 355 (Stanford C. Madden, 1973). Is this a reasonable assumption? Why or why not?

Several business decisions can bring different seniority lists into conflict. An employer may consolidate two operations into one, acquire a new plant, merge with another employer, or establish a new operation using employees from two or more units. How should the new seniority list be crafted? If there are not enough jobs for all employees, which should stay and which should go? When you read the following case, try to determine the basis of the arbitrator's decision.

BURNSIDE–GRAHAM READY MIX, INC.
86 LA 972 (Harold G. Wren, 1986).*

[In 1984, two southern Indiana concrete firms, Burnside–Graham Ready Mix, Inc. and Hi Hill Ready Mix, Inc., both organized by Teamsters Local 135, formed a new operation known as the Joint Venture. Burnside–Graham then ceased most operations in the area, transferred assets to the Joint Venture, and laid off its employees. Hi Hill employees constituted the Joint Venture's work force. The Union grieved, contending that Burnside–Graham violated the agreement by not recognizing its employees' seniority. Burnside–Graham argues that the Joint Venture is a successor to Hi Hill and is therefore subject to the Hi Hill contract. The Union argues that the Joint Venture is successor to Burnside–Graham and is therefore subject to the Burnside–Graham contract. The Joint Venture does not have enough jobs for both sets of employees.]

[Article 23 of the Burnside–Graham agreement provided:

This Agreement shall be binding upon the parties hereto, their successors, administrators, executors and assigns. In the event an entire operation is sold, leased, transferred or taken over by sale, transfer, lease, assignment, receivership or bankruptcy proceeding, such operation shall continue to be subject to the terms and conditions of this Agreement for the life thereof. On the sale, transfer or lease of an individual run or runs, only the specific provisions of this contract, excluding supplements or other conditions, shall prevail. It is understood by this Section that the parties hereto shall not use any leasing device to a third (3rd) party to evade this contract * * *.

[The arbitrator concluded that Hi Hill and Burnside–Graham were *both* predecessors of the joint venture. He then cited John Wiley & Sons v. Livingston, 376 U.S. 543 (1964), as recognizing the flexibility an arbitrator has to determine the seniority rights of employees affected by business changes.]

From this, it is clear that we have the authority to fashion a remedy within the essence of the collective bargaining agreement before us. The Union has sought to have the Burnside–Graham Contract extended to the Joint Venture as of January 1, 1985. In the alternative, the Union requests that the Arbitrator award damages to the Burnside–Graham employees for the Company's failure to require that Hi Hill Ready Mix Company recognize the collective bargaining agreement between the Union and Burnside–Graham.

The Arbitrator has no basis for granting the Union either of these awards. The management of Burnside–Graham and Hi Hill have acted with consummate good faith from the outset. In the absence of any bad faith or capricious action, any monetary arbitral award would commence only from the time that the Company had deliberately refused to recognize the rights of the Burnside–Graham employees vis-a-vis the Hi Hill employees. To date, this time has yet to arrive. We find no basis for making an award for any past lost wages. Both the Company and the Union have adhered to the view that the employees of one of the joint venturers must be "endtailed" to the employees of the other. They differ only as to which group of employees should be endtailed. Both the Company and the Union base their arguments on the "surviving-group principle." See T. Kennedy, *Merging Seniority Lists*, Labor Arbitration and Industrial Change 1–34 (BNA, Inc., 1963). This principle is normally applied where employer A purchases employer B, and the acquiring company's employees receive seniority preference over the acquired company's employees. By the Union's theory Burnside–Graham is in the role of A, and Hi Hill, the role of B. The Company argues the opposite.

Neither the Company nor the Union is correct, since the transaction here is more nearly analogous to a merger or consolidation. A merger is formally distinguished from a consolidation in that the former involves only *two companies*. In a consolidation, two or more corporate entities combine to form a third corporate entity. Apart from the fact that the Joint Venture is, by definition, an unincorporated association, the present situation is analogous to this type of transaction. If we apply an *aggregate*, as distinct from an *entity*, theory to the Joint Venture, we would be compelled to say that both Burnside–Graham and Hi Hill succeeded to their respective portions of the ready mix concrete business. A more correct view is that the Joint Venture, as an *entity*, succeeded to the contract rights and obligations of both Burnside–Graham and Hi Hill.

In applying the consolidation analogue, there are at least four different bases for merging the seniority lists:

1.   The length-of-service principle;

2. The follow-the-work principle;

3. The absolute-rank principle;

4. The ratio-rank principle.

Each of the four principles has been used by arbitrators, singly or in combination, to dovetail seniority lists. Under the length-of-service principle, a combined seniority list of all truck drivers in the order of the length of service, regardless of whether they worked for Burnside–Graham or Hi Hill would be prepared, and become the seniority list for the Joint Venture.

Under the follow-the-work principle, the employees are given the opportunity to follow their work with the seniority rights to such work being protected by continuation of separate seniority lists. Since the work of the production employees of the two companies was the same, this principle is inapplicable to the facts of the case before us.

Under the absolute-rank principle, there would be a new merged seniority list prepared on the basis of the rank that employees held on their respective seniority lists. The two employees who were first on the two former lists would be assigned the first two places on the merged list, with the employee having the longer service getting the first place, and the other employee getting the second. The next two employees who were second on the two original lists, would then be given the third and fourth places on the merged list; and so on. The ratio-rank principle follows the absolute-rank principle, but makes allowance for differences in the size of the two employers. For example, if seniority list A has 200 employees and seniority list B has 100 employees, two of the first three places on the merged seniority list would be allocated to employer A, and one to employer B. In the absence of any evidence before us with respect to the rankings of the employees of Burnside–Graham and Hi Hill, we have no basis for applying either the absolute-rank or the ratio-rank principle. Accordingly, we conclude that the length-of-service principle should be applied.

The question remains whether this Arbitrator has the power to issue an award that would direct the parties to dovetail the Burnside–Graham seniority list into a combined seniority list for the Joint Venture on a length-of-service principle. We have no doubt that we have the power to fashion such a remedy. Our award is legitimate * * * "so long as it draws its essence from the collective bargaining agreement." United Steelworkers v. Enterprise Wheel & Car Corp., 363 U.S. 593, 597, 34 LA 569 (1960). We impose no additional contractual obligation on the parties, but apply the existing Contract, including the successor clause. As the Third Circuit has remarked:

> [The predecessor's] collective bargaining agreement as an embodiment of the law of the shop, remained the basic charter of labor relations at the * * * plant after the change of ownership. But, in the arbitration of any grievance thereunder, the arbitrator may properly give weight to any change of circumstances created by the

transfer of ownership which may make adherence to any term or terms of the agreement inequitable.

United Steelworkers v. Reliance Universal, Inc., 335 F.2d 891, 895, 56 LRRM 2721 (3d Cir.1964).

Since the Supreme Court has empowered arbitrators to use "flexible procedures" in situations such as that before us (see John Wiley & Sons v. Livingston, supra), it is appropriate to issue an award directing the Company to dovetail the production employees of Burnside–Graham into a combined seniority list for the Joint Venture, based on the length-of-service principle. Such an award satisfies the Union's duty under 29 U.S.C. § 185, to provide fair representation to the employees of Hi Hill, as well as the employees of Burnside–Graham. See Humphrey v. Moore, 375 U.S. 335, 55 LRRM 2031 (1964); Ferrara v. Pacific Intermountain Express Co., 301 F.Supp. 1240, 71 LRRM 2872 (D.Ill.1969). To insure the implementation of this award, we retain jurisdiction of this matter.

Award

Within thirty days from the receipt of this Award, the Company shall dovetail the seniority of those Burnside–Graham production employees who desire to work for the Joint Venture, based on the length-of-service principle outlined in the foregoing opinion. The dovetailing shall operate prospectively only; no employee shall be entitled to recover for lost wages for any period from January 1, 1985, until the completion of the combined seniority list. Either party may apply for an extension of time for the implementation of this Award for good cause shown.

Notes and Questions

1. The first steps in evaluating this decision are to identify the parties, determine the arbitrator's authority, and decide what the remedy will do.

(a) Apparently neither the Joint Venture nor Hi Hill nor their employees were parties to this arbitration. Nevertheless, the arbitrator's order directly (and in some cases drastically) affects their economic lives. The same union represented both bargaining units. Why would it favor the Burnside–Graham employees? Or would the union have objected on behalf of the Hi Hill employees if the Joint Venture had employed only the Burnside Graham employees?

(b) How could the arbitrator have such (or any) authority over nonparties? The award seems to assume that Burnside–Graham can unilaterally control the Joint Venture's hiring decisions. Is there any basis for that assumption? If not, how can the grievants enforce the award? What would happen if the Hi Hill employees sought arbitration under *their* contract?

(c) Assuming Arbitrator Wren correctly decided to dovetail seniority lists using the length-of-service principle, is his remedy fair to the former Burnside employees? Why does he rule that the dovetailing "shall operate prospectively only?" Does his remedy harm anyone? If so, were the harmed individuals fairly represented before the arbitrator?

2.   Did the arbitrator adequately explain his choice between the possible controlling principles? Some employees will lose their jobs because of his decision. Did he owe them a better explanation? Was he right to reject the ratio-rank method simply because the actual seniority lists were not in evidence?

3.   The senior former employees of Burnside–Graham seem to have lost two years' income because the Joint Venture hired only the former employees of Hi Hill, yet Arbitrator Wren declined to order the employer to compensate them. He states that a monetary award would be appropriate only when Burnside–Graham "deliberately refused" to recognize its employees' rights and that this has not yet happened. Hasn't it? Why does he insist on a "deliberate refusal" before ordering compensation? Aren't employees harmed even by a good faith breach of contract entitled to be "made whole?"

4.   At first glance, dovetailing by length of service seems the obvious and perhaps the only fair way to deal with post-consolidation seniority. When, then, would an arbitrator find "endtailing" (adding all employees of one unit at the end of the other unit's seniority list) appropriate? Are you persuaded by the following argument?

> Dovetailing has a superficial aura of fairness about it, but the equities are not so clear. Length of service is certainly an important part of seniority, and dovetailing reflects that importance. There is another important aspect, however. For many employees, relative ranking is of greater concern than absolute seniority, and employees may as reasonably wish to preserve their standing as their seniority date. Dovetailing gives no weight to that factor. The senior person in a department may, as a result, find himself dovetailed to the bottom half of a merged seniority list. Employees facing that prospect, particularly employees of the larger entity, can be expected to argue for endtailing, and not without some justification. Resolving disputes of this sort can be extraordinarily difficult for a union, especially since the losing group may charge the union with breach of the duty of fair representation.

Roger I. Abrams and Dennis R. Nolan, *Seniority Rights Under the Collective Agreement, supra* footnote 1, at 123 (footnotes omitted).

5.   How serious is the duty of fair representation (DFR) risk? Union officials often find themselves in difficult positions when companies merge. When large employer *A* merges with small employer *B*, the union representing *A*'s workforce is likely to represent the new workforce. The president of the local representing *A*'s employees has a strong incentive to promise constituents to protect their seniority rights by endtailing the former *B* employees—but that amounts to a promise to discriminate against the endtailed workers. Compare the two cases Abrams and Nolan cite at that point: Truck Drivers and Helpers, Local Union 568 v. NLRB, 379 F.2d 137 (D.C.Cir.1967) (union representing employees at the larger of two merged facilities violated the DFR by promising to discriminate against the employees of the other facility when merging seniority lists); O'Donnell v. Pabst Brewing Co., 12 Wis.2d 491, 107 N.W.2d 484 (1961) (union's decision to dovetail rather than endtail seniority lists of merged plants did not violate the DFR because it was neither arbitrary nor capricious.). Would negotiating

any alternative to dovetailing violate the union's duty of fair representation? If so, which and why?

6.   When would an arbitrator select one of the other dovetailing principles in preference to length of service?

(a) Consider Delta Air Lines, Inc., 72 LA 458 (Harry Platt, 1979). In 1972 Delta merged with Northeast Airlines. The Civil Aeronautics Board directed Delta to integrate the flight attendant seniority lists "in a fair and equitable manner." After much consideration, Delta integrated the lists by date of hire for flight attendants with more than twenty years or less than one year of service. For all others, it used the ratio-rank principle; one Northeast flight attendant was slotted after every four or five Delta employees (with a few other modifications). Delta would thus offer jobs in order to (i) very senior employees, by date of hire; (ii) mid-seniority employees, by ratio-rank; and (iii) very junior employees, by date of hire. Arbitrator Platt found the Delta plan "fair and equitable." Can you suggest some reasons why Delta selected this plan? Why might it have used ratio-rank for (only) mid-seniority employees? Are these reasons sufficient to make that method "fair and equitable?" See also Superior Products Co., 42 LA 517 (Russell A. Smith, 1964) (arbitrator used a combination of follow-the-work and ratio-rank).

(b) Amax Coal Co., 104 LA 790 (Carl F. Stoltenberg, 1995) is a good illustration of the absolute rank approach. After a reduction-in-force, the employer combined two seniority units that had worked in different parts of one mine and were represented by different locals of the same union, but it retained the separate facilities and functions. It decided to merge the units' seniority lists on a one-to-one rank basis rather than using straight seniority. (That is, the senior employee in each former unit got the first two jobs, the second senior employees got the next two, and so on.) The result was to give greater job security to the members of the smaller unit, because the jobs ran out before all the larger unit's members were employed. The employer's objective apparently was to ensure that enough employees of the smaller unit remained on the job to carry out the unit's operations.

Arbitrator Stoltenberg distinguished previous awards in cases involving merger of two or more mines rather than the simple merger of seniority lists involved in this case. The other cases involved closing or merging operations. The controlling clause of the agreement, he found, was the reduction-in-force clause that obliged the employer to retain "employees with the greatest seniority in the mine." Notwithstanding the employer's asserted business justification, he concluded that use of the absolute rank approach violated the contract. For some unexplained reason, the grievance did not seek compensation for the wrongly laid off employees. As a result, the arbitrator simply ordered the company to realign the surviving seniority list to rank employees by mine seniority regardless of their rank on the old seniority lists.

7.   Should the nature of the business change make any difference? If Company A purchases smaller Company B, do B's employees have less claim to dovetailing than if the two firms had merged or (as in *Burnside-Graham*) had established a joint venture? *Cf.* Associated Brewing Co., 40 LA 680

(Mark L. Kahn, 1963) (A merger required dovetailing but a plant shutdown would have required endtailing).

8. Because unions prize seniority above almost any other principle, they can usually be counted on to represent the senior employee over the junior in a layoff or promotion dispute, no matter what the issue. One extremely rare exception is St. Clare Hospital, 112 LA 602 (Michael E. Cavanaugh, 1998). The collective bargaining agreement provided that in the event of a layoff, "seniority shall be the determining factor providing that skill, competency, ability in a specific area, and prior job performance are considered equal in the opinion of the Employer." The employer laid off a junior ultrasound technologist, Frank Roberts, and retained the senior employee, Brenda Sloan, after it determined that their qualifications were equal. The Union argued that Roberts's qualifications were so superior to those of Sloan that the Employer's judgment about their relative abilities was "completely without merit."

The arbitrator held that because seniority "is one of the hallmarks of the unionized workplace," it "should take a back seat only when there is clear contractual language supporting it and a compelling difference in demonstrated skills and abilities favoring the junior employee." He found no "compelling reasons for bypassing seniority" in that case.

4. THE USES OF SENIORITY

CITY OF FOND Du LAC*

69–2 ARB ¶ 8520 (Robert Moberly, 1969).

The parties stipulated that the issue is as follows:

"Did the Municipal Employer give appropriate consideration to the grievant's qualifications, records of performance and seniority in denying a promotion to grievant from the classification of Truck Driver to Electrician's Helper?"

PERTINENT CONTRACT PROVISIONS

The parties also stipulated that the contract provisions involved are as follows: * * *

ARTICLE X

PROMOTION

"Vacancies in positions above the entrance level (i.e., Laborer I or equivalent classification) shall be filled by promotion whenever in the judgment of the Employer it is in the best interest of the City to do so. Appropriate consideration shall be given to the applicant's qualifications, record of performance and seniority. All employees must possess the qualifications necessary for the position to which they seek promotion. The division head and the department head shall be responsible for determining whether or not an employee possesses the necessary qualifications for promotion to a particular position. Appropriate tests may be given to aid in this determination. * * *

FACTS

In the spring of 1968 a vacancy for the classification of Electrician's Helper occurred in the Electrical Division of the Municipal Employer. The Electrical Division is comprised of a Supervisor, an Electrician, an Electrician's Apprentice, and an Electrician's Helper. The function of the Electrician's Helper in the division is to assist the Electricians in construction, repair and maintenance work, and to perform other related duties.

In accordance with the Working Conditions Agreement, the Municipal Employer posted the position, stating that certain knowledge and abilities were essential and certain training and experience was desirable. Included in the training and experience which was desirable was "previous work experience preferably in the repair and maintenance of electrical equipment." Seventeen employees made application for the position, including [P] and the grievant [B]. [P] was selected to fill the position, and the promotion became effective May 6, 1968. On April 13, 1968, [B] filed a grievance protesting the appointment of [P] and specifically alleged that in making such appointment the Municipal Employer violated Article X of the Agreement regarding consideration of his seniority. The Municipal Employer's response to the grievance stated that the position was filled in compliance with Article X of the Agreement, and that the selection was made on the recommendation of a division head and concurrence of the department head to the effect that the selected employee was best qualified to fill the position. The parties could not reach agreement through the grievance procedure, and the issue, along with certain other unrelated issues, was submitted to arbitration before Arbitrator Neil Gundermann, appointed by the Wisconsin Employment Relations Commission.

At the hearing in the arbitration proceeding before Mr. Gundermann on July 24, 1968, the Municipal Employer took the position that the issue of whether appropriate consideration was given to an employee was not arbitrable, and limited its argument and evidence to the question of arbitrability. The arbitrator therefore limited his award to the question of arbitrability and issued an award stating that "under the provisions of the working agreement the issue of whether an employee was given 'appropriate consideration' is arbitrable." In making this award, Arbitrator Gundermann made the following comment:

"It is the suggestion of the undersigned that the City provide the Union with a written statement explaining what consideration was given the applicants' qualifications, records of performance and seniority. Clearly the Union should not be compelled to accept merely the City's assertion that 'appropriate consideration' was given the applicants without any facts regarding what the city considered in making its judgment."

Following this award, the Municipal Employer issued a Memorandum to the President of the Union, purporting, in conformance with the suggestion of Arbitrator Gundermann, to "set forth reasons for the City's selection of [P] for the position of Electrician's Helper." The Memorandum continued as follows:

"In a small operation such as the City's Electrical Division, it is extremely essential to have a balanced and harmonious work force. The men must all be willing and able to learn and take direction in a co-operative spirit in the conduct of day-to-day operations. Further, the City must be concerned with the long range view of developing supervisory personnel for the future.

"With these thoughts in mind, the City evaluated each candidate and, after numerous discussions between appropriate division and departmental supervisors, it was decided that [P] was the most qualified individual for this position. Evaluation of work performance, desire and potential ability for future advancement in the City's operations indicated that [P's] selection for the position was in the best interest for the continuation of efficient operation of the Electrical Division of the Department of Public Works."

The dispute was not resolved between the parties, and the present arbitration proceeding was instituted for a determination of the merits.

A short description of the grievant [B] and of [P] is in order. The grievant, 35 years old, was employed over eight years at the time of the job posting. Although he is presently employed as a Truck Driver for the Municipal Employer, grievant successfully completed training courses as an electrician's helper and also attended diesel school while in the armed forces. He then spent the remaining portion of his two years in military service working as an electrician's helper. Grievant further testified that he had accumulated six years' additional electrical experience in the Signal Department of the Chicago and North Western Railway, where he performed such tasks as wiring electrical boxes, installing cross-way protections and signals, and working with relays. In a general intelligence test which was given to fourteen of the employees interested in this position, grievant along with two other employees ranked fifth. The Municipal Employer does not dispute the fact that grievant's past work performance has been satisfactory.

[P], the employee who was selected for the position, was 23 years old and had been on the job for approximately seven months at the time of the job posting. He was the least senior of the seventeen employees applying for the position. Up to the time of his promotion, he was employed as a Laborer I in the Construction–Maintenance Division, and he ranked second on the general intelligence test referred to above. There was no evidence to show that he had any previous related education, training or experience to qualify him for the position of Electrician's Helper.

POSITION OF THE PARTIES

The Municipal Employer argues that it complied with Article X in filling the position, and that [P] was the most qualified person for the position.

The Union argues that the Municipal Employer in its evaluations gave insufficient consideration to grievant's seniority. It points out that grievant had eight years' seniority as compared to seven months for [P], and that [P] had the least seniority of the employee applicants. It also argues that the unreasonableness in promoting [P] over grievant is further demonstrated by comparing grievant's extensive experience in electrical work, including course work, and [P's] total lack of education or experience in this area.

DISCUSSION

* * * The usual manner of accommodating the competing interests [of labor and management in seniority matters], of course, is through the collective bargaining process. Predictably, the promotional policies established thereby vary considerably from contract to contract. Some contracts make no provision governing promotions. Under such contracts, the employer has unilateral authority in the promotion of employees. However, most contracts, including the agreement in question here, contain clauses which call for some evaluation of both seniority and qualifications in determining which employee should receive a promotion, and are commonly referred to in labor relations as "modified seniority" clauses.

Among modified seniority clauses, a distinction is made between (1) "relative ability" clauses, which state that the senior employee will be given preference if he possesses qualifications equal to that of junior employees; (2) "sufficient ability" clauses, wherein preference is given to the senior employee provided he is qualified for the job; and (3) "hybrid" clauses, which require only that the employer give consideration to both seniority and qualifications, without indicating the relative weight to be accorded these factors.

Article X of the Working Conditions Agreement must be given an interpretation based on its particular language and on all the specific facts and circumstances of this case. Nonetheless, by providing that "appropriate" consideration shall be given to both seniority and qualifications (which the arbitrator interprets as including record of performance), Article X may fairly be placed in the general category of "hybrid" clauses in that it requires that some consideration be given to both seniority and qualifications but does not specify the weight to be accorded each. Thus the arbitrator may be guided in interpreting Article X by certain general criteria commonly applied in labor relations to "hybrid" clauses.

Under "hybrid" clauses, the consideration given by the Employer to both seniority and qualifications must be reasonable and not arbitrary or capricious. The determination must be made through a reasonable balancing of the two factors. As stated in the following work on the subject:

"It seems clear that under 'hybrid' clauses the relative claims of seniority and of ability must be determined by comparing and weighing against each other the relative difference in seniority of competing employees and the relative difference in their abilities. Thus, in comparing two or more qualified employees, both seniority and ability must be considered, and where the difference in length of service is relatively insignificant and there is a relatively significant difference in ability, then the ability factor should be given greater weight; but where there is a relatively substantial difference in seniority and relatively little difference in abilities, then length of service should be given greater weight." Elkouri & Elkouri, How Arbitration Works (BNA 1960).

In balancing the factors of seniority and qualifications, the Employer is entitled to make the initial determination, and its determination is presumed to be reasonable. The issue before the arbitrator is whether the decision of the Municipal Employer to promote [P] instead of grievant [B] to the position of Electrician's Helper was unreasonable under the facts, capricious or arbitrary.

After a thorough review of the testimony and exhibits presented at the hearing, it is apparent to the arbitrator that the Employer's determination to promote [P] to the position of Electrician's Helper over the grievant [B] was in fact unreasonable under the circumstances, and that the Employer therefore violated Article X of the Working Conditions Agreement by failing to give "appropriate" consideration to the grievant's "qualifications, record of performance and seniority." This conclusion follows of necessity from (1) the evidence (or lack of it) with regard to the actual consideration given by the Municipal Employer to the factor of seniority, and (2) the actual facts of the qualifications and seniority of the individuals involved.

A strong piece of evidence against the Municipal Employer's position was provided by the Municipal Employer itself in its response to Arbitrator Gundermann's suggestion that it provide the Union with a written statement explaining what consideration was given the applicants' qualifications, records of performance and seniority. The Municipal Employer listed several items which it claimed to have considered in making the determination, but no reference was made to the factor of seniority. Thus the Municipal Employer's own statement tends to verify the Union's contention that the Municipal Employer gave almost no consideration to the grievant's substantially greater seniority in making the selection.

The evidence presented at the hearing did nothing to encourage a contrary conclusion. A representative of the Municipal Employer stated that it gave consideration to the following factors in making the promotional determination:

1. Work records with the City.

2.   Results of aptitude tests.

3.   Examination of the personnel files.

4.   Seniority.

After the flat opening statement that the Municipal Employer "considered" these matters, the Municipal Employer introduced certain exhibits and then closed its case without presenting any testimony. There was no evidence with respect to work records of the applicants. There was no evidence with respect to the contents of the personnel files or how such contents were evaluated by the Municipal Employer in making the judgment to promote [P]. There was no evidence with respect to what weight, if any, was given to the seniority factor. The City did introduce the results of an aptitude test given the applicants, and the seniority of each was stipulated to. When the Union in the presentation of its case called the personnel officer and attempted to delve further into the considerations which the Municipal Employer allegedly took into account, the personnel officer mentioned that the Municipal Employer considered the work records, the results of the aptitude test and the examination of the personnel files, but he made no mention of seniority. Under such circumstances, it is impossible to make a finding that the Municipal Employer gave weight in its deliberations to the factor of seniority.

Further, the actual facts of the qualifications and seniority of the individuals involved can result in no other conclusion but that the promotion of [P] over grievant was unreasonable under the facts. The grievant had over eight years of employment with the Municipal Employer at the time of the job posting as compared to the approximately seven months [P] had been employed. Of the seventeen municipal employees who applied for the position, [P] was the least senior. Seniority, of course, is not the only factor to be considered and a municipal employer, in passing over sixteen more senior employees to select the least senior employee, might not be found to be in violation if it could show circumstances which could reasonably justify the complete disregard of seniority. Such circumstances might exist, for example, where it is shown that the person selected had sufficiently greater qualifications than the more senior employee. While the Municipal Employer argues that [P] was more qualified for the position than grievant, this claim is not substantiated by the record. In fact, the opposite appears to be true. [P] had no relevant (1) education or (2) prior work experience which would assist him in the position of Electrician's Helper, even though the job posting called for such qualities. By contrast, the grievant successfully completed training courses in the armed forces as an electrician's helper, and also gathered relevant working experience in that capacity while fulfilling his military obligation. He has further acquired six years of related work experience while employed by the Chicago & North Western Railway.

The Employer administered a general intelligence test of the type which, according to the description manual of the test, could be used "as an indication of an individual's general capacity to learn.'' [P] ranked second on the test, and grievant, along with two other employees, ranked fifth. The Municipal Employer does not contend that grievant's score is unsatisfactory for the Municipal Employer's purposes.

The use of a general intelligence test is a proper effort to obtain some objective measure of the qualifications of the applicants. However, such a test, being general in nature rather than relating to the specific requirements for the position in question, also has limits in the use an employer may make of it to justify the ignoring of seniority. Such limits are clearly exceeded when, as here, the test results are set forth as almost the only justification for promotion of a junior employee over a senior employee whose test results are not said to be unsatisfactory, and who has substantially greater seniority, substantially greater relevant education, and substantially greater prior related work experience.

Other than the test results, the City did not introduce any tangible, objective evidence to demonstrate that [P] would have a greater likelihood of successful performance in the position. It stated in its memorandum explaining its selection of [P] that it was extremely essential to have a balanced and harmonious work force, that the men must be willing and able to take direction in a cooperative spirit, and that the City must be concerned with developing supervisory personnel for the future. These factors, while all proper considerations, are all subjective rather than objective considerations. As such, they are more easily subject to abuse in their application. When a promotion is based primarily on such subjective factors rather than objective factors (i.e., prior job experience an work performance), the employer is obliged to demonstrate through such evidence as testimony by supervisors that the least senior employee was superior when viewed in light of these subjective considerations. Yet in the instant case the City made no attempt to compare the abilities of the two men involved with respect to the subjective characteristics it was seeking. It introduced no testimony showing that [P] was more "willing and able to take direction in a cooperative spirit" or that the promotion of [P] rather than grievant would result in a more "balanced and harmonious work force." While the City expressed concern with developing supervisory personnel for the future and implied that [P] had more potential for a supervisory position than grievant, there again was a lack of evidence from present supervisors or from any other person as to whether, why or how [P] had more potential than grievant for future promotion to a supervisory position. Thus there is a total lack of evidence which would demonstrate that [P] is superior to grievant even with respect to the subjective criteria cited by the City.

In summary, we have a situation where the Employer gave almost no consideration to the factor of seniority; and in addition, on the evidence presented there was no basis by which the Municipal Employer could reasonably conclude that [P's] qualifications and record of performance called for his promotion over the more senior employee. Under such circumstances, the arbitrator must find that the decision of the

Employer to promote [P] over grievant was unreasonable under the facts, and therefore was in violation of Article X of the Working Conditions Agreement requiring that "appropriate consideration" be given to an applicant's qualifications, record of performance and seniority. * * *

AWARD

The Municipal Employer, in selecting [P] rather than grievant for the position of Electrician's Helper, violated Article X of the Working Conditions Agreement, relating to promotions, by failing to give "appropriate consideration" to the applicants' qualifications, records of performance and seniority. The Municipal Employer shall remedy the violation by taking the following action: (1) immediately offer to the grievant, [B], the position of Electrician's Helper now occupied by [P], without prejudice to any rights and privileges of that position which would have accrued from May 6, 1968, the effective date of the promotion; and (2) make grievant whole for any loss of wages incurred as a result of the violation.

Notes and Questions

1. How *should* the employer have handled the promotion? Compare Nordson Corp., 104 LA 1206 (Matthew M. Franckiewicz, 1995). Like *City of Fond du Lac*, that case involved a "hybrid" clause requiring the employer to consider both seniority and ability. When a vacancy in the Machinist Leader category occurred, the employer promoted a junior employee with less experience. Unlike the earlier case, however, the employer first adopted several highly subjective criteria—"interpersonal skills, communication skills, initiative, and attitude," naturally finding the junior employee superior in those categories. The arbitrator held that the attributes sought by the employer were relevant and that he could not say that the company's ratings were erroneous. He therefore denied the grievance.

2. *City of Fond du Lac* involved a "hybrid" form of modified seniority provision. The other two forms, "relative ability" and "sufficient ability" clauses, pose different problems.

(a) **"Head and Shoulders" Doctrine.** Seldom can "ability" be measured solely by objective data, yet use of subjective evaluations (for example, a supervisor's opinion) permits an employer to negate the impact of a relative ability clause. Arbitrators have reacted to this risk by developing the "head-and-shoulders" doctrine—that is, an employer subject to a relative ability clause may promote the junior employee only if it can prove the junior clearly and significantly more able than the senior. This is one of the oldest arbitral doctrines, dating back at least to a 1941 opinion (Umpire Decision No. B–52) of George Taylor, during his term as Umpire for General Motors Corporation and the United Automobile Workers. Consider this statement of the doctrine:

> Competence, ability, etc., are difficult to evaluate and impossible to measure precisely. Therefore it would be impractical to insist that the senior employee's qualifications be exactly equal to those of the junior employee before length of service becomes the ruling consideration. Rough or approximate equality will suffice; conversely, if the junior

employee is preferred, he should be "head and shoulders" above the senior.

San Francisco News–Call Bulletin, 34 LA 271, 273 (Arthur M. Ross, 1960). In what ways does the head-and-shoulders doctrine strengthen the union's position?

The Kroger Company, 117 LA 737 (Roger I. Abrams, 2002), represents a simple application of the head-and-shoulders test under a relative-ability clause. The employer selected the junior applicant (Sheppard) for the position of head grocery clerk and defended its choice by pointing to his familiarity with the particular store, its computer system, and its personnel system. The grievant (Jennings) had been the head grocery clerk at another store in the chain for 25 years and had set up the same computer system at his store. Arbitrator Abrams noted that the managers who interviewed the applicants found both of them "acceptable" and ruled that " 'Acceptable' is all it takes" to give the senior applicant preference. Sheppard, he wrote, did the job well but that is not the test under the Agreement. Seniority rights cannot be so easily disregarded. Jennings might not have been a better pick than Sheppard, but he did have the right to the job under the Agreement as long as he was acceptable to the Company and had a measure of ability about as good as Sheppard.

(b) **Relative Ability Clauses.** Suppose an employer subject to a relative ability clause administers a test to employees applying for a certain promotion and then selects the highest scorer, who happens to be the junior bidder. Would the promotion violate the agreement? What further information would an arbitrator need to make a ruling? Why did the test results in *City of Fond du Lac* not satisfy Arbitrator Moberly?

Normally the union bears the burden of proof in non-disciplinary cases. In seniority cases involving questions of relative ability, however, arbitrators often demand that the employer prove that element of its case. Thus the employer must prove the junior to be head and shoulders above the senior; the union need not prove them of relatively equal ability. Why?

(c) **Sufficient Ability Clauses.** Is "sufficient ability" any clearer than "relative ability?" A typical sufficient-ability clause permits a laid-off employee to "bump" into a lower-rated job if the "bumper" possesses the "ability" to perform it. Does that mean the employee must be able to perform all parts of the job without any additional training? Or would it suffice if the employee had all the natural skills needed even though he or she would need several weeks of additional instruction to master the job? Compare these two positions:

> An employee possesses sufficient ability when he has the skills to perform the job after the customary break-in instruction that is involved in any new job. The senior employee should not be disqualified simply because he cannot step in and perform the work without any instruction.

Abrams and Nolan, *supra* footnote 1, at 127–28.

> [Under a clause permitting bumping if the employee has "the present necessary fitness and ability to satisfactorily do the required work"], that one is "good enough" to fill-in temporarily on occasion does not

equate to "present necessary ability." Even Union witnesses honestly testify that they do not believe G _____ was fully trained in January, 1983, to the point where she could operate on her own without advice and supervision, especially if something out of the ordinary were to occur on her machine * * *. Hence, it appears the Company was fully justified in not allowing G _____ to replace a completely qualified employee. * * *

Container Corporation of America, 84 LA 604, 608 (A. Dale Allen, Jr., 1985). Does the choice between these positions depend on the circumstances? For example, should an arbitrator require the employer to train a partially-qualified employee if the layoff is likely to be short?

Even when the seniority clause requires the senior employee to demonstrate only "sufficient ability," the employer has broad discretion to judge the applicants' qualifications against some standard of sufficiency. See International Association of Fire Fighters, 105 LA 560 (Marvin C. Wahl, 1995) (management's determination of ability must be upheld so long as it is not arbitrary, discriminatory, unreasonable, or in bad faith), and Sandusky International, Inc., 118 LA 916 (William C. Heekin, 2003) (no violation in retaining junior employee and laying off senior employees when the junior was the only person able to maintain critical machines). What the employer subject to a sufficient ability clause may *not* do is compare the applicants' general abilities with one another.

3. What sort of proof must the employer provide? Yale Law School Dean Harry Shulman, one of the most distinguished arbitrators of his era, made these comments, which most arbitrators would still regard as "good law":

> On the company's side, there is some tendency to overemphasize supervision's personal judgment of merit and ability and forget seniority. Some members of management or supervision seem to think that it is sufficient for them to form and assert strongly the belief that one employee is superior to another. That is clearly not enough. They must be able to support this belief with specific, concrete reasons. Sec. 53 expressly declares that disputes as to merit and ability are subject to the grievance procedure. The several agencies in the grievance procedure, including the umpire, are thereby given a positive task to perform. The provision is not an empty formalism; and the agencies of the grievance procedure, including the umpire, are not expected merely to rubber stamp the assertions of one side or the other or to make decisions merely on the basis of the strength or positiveness of the assertions. To perform their tasks, they must be given adequate basis for judgment. A supervisor's testimony that he honestly believes one employee to be superior to another with respect to the promotion is certainly a factor to be considered. It is not, however, either conclusive or sufficient. The supervisor must be prepared to state the basis for his belief and to support it, not by repeated assertion but by specific and understandable evidence—evidence which relates to capacity for the job in question, not merely to the employee's general character.

Ford Motor Co., 2 LA 374, 375–76 (1945).

4. The City of Fond du Lac asserted that it considered aptitude test results before deciding which employee to promote. That case did not turn on the permissibility, accuracy, or relevancy of those tests, but the issue has come up in other arbitrations. For example, some employers use personality tests, "honesty" tests, and other psychological tests as well as aptitude tests. Most experts in the field have serious doubts about the utility of these sorts of tests for job decisions. For a thorough discussion of the issues involved in psychological testing, see 49 Proceedings of the National Academy of Arbitrators 123–63 (1997).

5. Collective bargaining agreements often allow a laid off employee to displace a junior employee in comparable or lower-ranked job classification. This practice is known as "bumping down." The object is to lay off the most junior employees, even if the reduction starts with jobs held by senior employees. Parties naturally assume (and frequently require) that the bumping employee is qualified to perform the job into which he or she would like to bump. That works smoothly if the employee seeks to bump into a lower rated job in the same classification, but may a displaced employee bump into a *different* classification? Arbitrator John Felice, in Brentwood Medical Associates, 118 LA 1313 (2003), held that a provision requiring that layoffs be by seniority "in the classifications affected" could not "be interpreted to prohibit senior employees affected by a layoff from exercising their 'bargaining unit-wide' seniority rights and bump less senior employees outside of their classification, provided they are qualified."

If the contract is silent, may a laid off but qualified senior employee bump *up*—that is, displace a junior employee who holds a higher job classification? In Container Corporation of America, 84 LA 604, 607 (A. Dale Allen, Jr., 1985), Arbitrator Allen wrote:

> In short, in construing [the contract's] language as a whole, the strong implication is that normally employees transfer or demote downwardly in the event of a layoff and move up to a higher rated position only in the context of a promotion. Obviously, one could draw the conclusion, therefore, that a senior employee cannot "promote himself" during a layoff situation by demanding to be "bumped up" the promotional ladder. * * *

See also U.S. Rubber Company, 25 LA 417 (Hiram S. Hall, 1955) (upward bumping "would make a shambles out of the job classification system and would create a maze of inconsistencies with resultant grievances").

5. SUPERSENIORITY

"Superseniority" refers either to a special kind of seniority worth more than others or to an extra grant of seniority. Its purpose is to favor certain employees, particularly in layoffs, by placing them at the top of their unit's seniority list. Many years ago some newly-unionized companies insisted on granting superseniority to "key" employees. Unions responded by demanding superseniority for union officials. The former sort is now rare, but the latter is relatively common.

Although superseniority for union officials is generally lawful, Aeronautical Indus. Dist. Lodge 727 v. Campbell, 337 U.S. 521, 528, 69 S.Ct. 1287, 93 L.Ed. 1513 (1949), it can harm employees who do not hold union offices, *e.g.*, nonunion employees and employees who are not active members of the union. As a result, the National Labor Relations Board allows parties to use superseniority only to protect from layoff those union officers essential to contract administration. These usually include the local president and "stewards"—elected or appointed shop-floor representatives who file grievances and usually process them at the first step or two of the grievance procedure. Gulton Electro–Voice, Inc., 266 NLRB 406 (1983), *enforced*, 727 F.2d 1184 (D.C.Cir.1984). Presumably the same rationale would legitimize some other protections such as a prohibition on bumping union stewards off their shifts.

What should an arbitrator do when an employer challenges a superseniority provision as illegal under *Gulton*? Compare Heil–Quaker Corp., 79 LA 513, 518 (Carl Cabe, 1982) (ignoring the contract in favor of the law because "to rule otherwise would be a dereliction of duty") with Hunter Engineering Co., Inc., 82 LA 483, 485 (Reginald Alleyne, 1984) (applying the contract and "leaving pure questions of contractual legality to those authorized by law to resolve such questions"). See Chapter V.B of this book for further discussion of the role of external law in labor arbitration.

Superseniority attaches to the named union offices, not to individuals. Thus, an employee will possess superseniority as soon as, and as long as, he or she holds a specified office. Newly-elected but laid-off officers will be entitled to immediate recall even if they have to bump senior employees, Lydall Eastern, Inc., 85 LA 329 (George F. Larney, 1985); Keller Industries, Inc., 63 LA 1230, 1234 (A. Howard Bode, 1974). Similarly, an employee loses protection by leaving the specified office, Matlock Trailer Corp., 75 LA 263 (Donald Crane, 1980); American Safety Razor Co., 69 LA 157, 161 (Max B. Jones, 1977).

Superseniority clauses typically oblige the employer to retain protected officers in a layoff only if they can do the available work. This may require the employer to lay off a better employee to retain a supersenior employee who can do only part of the job:

> [I]t is a widely accepted premise of contract law that the fundamental purpose of superseniority provisions is to assure, to the fullest extent possible, union representation at the worksite by experienced representatives. Consequently arbitrators generally, and in this case in particular, liberally construe such provisions to safeguard the legitimate purpose for which they were negotiated.

Lamar & Wallace, Inc., 83 LA 625, 629 (Mollie H. Bowers, 1984). An employer need not retrain a union officer who lacks the current ability to do the job, however. Kennecott Corp., 80 LA 1142 (Mei L. Bickner, 1983).

F. WAGES AND HOURS[1]

1. INTRODUCTION

Wage issues are usually the most hotly-debated subjects in collective negotiations, although in certain economic circumstances job security or health care may temporarily take over that position. Until recently unions sought to "take wages out of competition," as the saying went, by setting "the rate for the job." Translated, that meant that unions strove for a common wage scale covering all persons in a classification, for whomever they worked. A strong union representing employees of all the employers in a given industry could, through multi-employer negotiations (simultaneously negotiating with several employers) or pattern bargaining (using the first negotiated agreement as a firm model for later negotiations), set a single rate for each job. Taking wages out of competition would protect negotiated wage rates by preventing one employer from under-pricing another by means of lower labor costs.

Unions never quite achieved that goal but they did come close in some industries (tires, autos, steel) in some periods (particularly the 1950s through 1970s). With the increase of foreign competition and the growth of nonunion sectors in most industries during the late twentieth century, the dream faded, leaving individual companies to negotiate wages reflecting their peculiar competitive situation. Many multi-employer bargaining units and much pattern bargaining simply disappeared. During the 1980s some parties even negotiated "two-tier" wage scales that paid new employees much less than present employees for the same work in the same plant. This allowed an employer to reduce wages over time with minimal effect on current employees. (Not incidentally, two-tier systems shifted the burden of wage adjustments from those who could vote on ratification of the agreement to those with no voice in the union at the time of ratification.)

At first glance, the wage question seems uncomplicated, however hotly debated: the Union demands X dollars per hour, the employer counters with Y dollars, and the parties eventually end up somewhere between. Were hourly rates the only aspect of wages, the matter might indeed be that simple. In practice, however, parties often choose far more diverse and complicated compensation systems.[2] Some do rely on

---

1. Bibliographic Suggestions: Roger I. Abrams and Dennis R. Nolan, *Buying Employees' Time: Guaranteed Pay Under Collective Agreements*, 35 Syracuse Law Review 867 (1984), and *Time at a Premium: The Arbitration of Overtime and Premium Pay Disputes*, 45 Ohio State Law Journal 837 (1984); Timothy J. Buckalew, *Work Schedules and Compensation for Work–Related Time*, Chapter 29 of Labor and Employment Arbitration (Tim Bornstein, Ann Gosline, and Marc Greenbaum, eds., 2d ed. 1997); Gladys Gershenfeld, *Overtime*, Chapter 33 of Labor and Employment Arbitra-

tion (Tim Bornstein, Ann Gosline, and Marc Greenbaum, eds., 2d ed. 1997); Steven Kropp, *Compensation Systems and Job Evaluation*, Chapter 34 of Labor and Employment Arbitration (Tim Bornstein, Ann Gosline, and Marc Greenbaum, eds., 2d ed. 1997); and Jack Stieber, *Job Classification, Overtime, and Holiday Pay*, in Arbitration in Practice 103 (Arnold M. Zack ed. 1984).

2. See Bureau of National Affairs, Basic Patterns in Union Contracts 111–21 (14th ed. 1995), for a thorough analysis of the prevalence of different wage provisions.

hourly, monthly, or annual rates, of course, but others use piece-rates or other quantity-based systems; some use productivity measures; others use any of several profit-sharing methods. Still others use a combination of methods. Moreover, most employers supplement current wages with forms of deferred wages such as pension plans and vacations.

Even when the parties do use an hourly rate, setting that rate may be complicated. They may set it by using economic leverage and negotiating ability or by referring to some external index (industry averages, for example, or inflation rates since the last contract). Many businesses still attempt to set the proper wage for each job by comparing it with other jobs in the company or industry or by separately evaluating each component of the job. The "job evaluation" systems necessary for the last option can become extraordinarily intricate, requiring lengthy evaluation books, time-study experts, and pounds of comparative materials, not to mention time spent negotiating or arbitrating.

As if that were not enough complexity, the agreed base rate may change depending on the employee's shift (unpopular shifts often receive a "shift differential") or the type of work ("dirty" or dangerous work may receive a premium) or with inflation ("cost-of-living" provisions). Some employees may have a "guaranteed" pay of so many hours per week or year, or may receive a certain minimum number of hours for being "called in" or for "reporting." Employees may also receive overtime pay. Typically the overtime agreement provides pay at time-and-one half the usual rate for hours over 40 hours in a week (the statutory requirement employees covered by the federal Fair Labor Standards Act of 1938, or FLSA), but a contract may reduce the number of hours before overtime pay kicks in or may provide it for work over a certain number of hours in a day. Other premium pay provisions may apply to work on weekends, holidays, or vacations. One recurring subject of arbitration is "pyramiding" premium rates: what rate applies to an employee called in for overtime third-shift work on Saturday when she was supposed to be on vacation? Time-and-half for the overtime, surely, but at what base rate? The usual third-shift rate? The weekend rate? The vacation-pay rate? All of the above?

The issue of working hours is just as complicated. For office workers on a nine-to-five schedule, there is not much to debate about hours. Other jobs may have frequent disputes over the number of hours to be worked (with some unions trying to decrease and others trying to increase the work week), the regularity of assignments (because some parties favor and others despise rotating shifts), the allocation of hours (eight a day for five days or ten a day for four, for example), and the flexibility of hours.

Scholars have written whole books just on incentive plans and on job evaluation schemes. This section seeks only to introduce you to the major problems and to suggest the range of potential issues that end up in arbitration.

2. WAGE DISPUTES

Overtime pay requirements produce more arbitrations than any other single aspect of wages. FLSA § 7 requires covered employers to pay covered employees at a rate of time-and-one-half for all hours worked over 40 in a single week. The primary objective of that New Deal law was to discourage employers from using overtime so that they would instead hire more workers. Today the primary rationale is to compensate employees for working longer than the statutorily-defined workweek. Many collective bargaining agreements have expanded the right to overtime pay, often requiring it after eight hours in a single day.

Contractual overtime disputes fall in four categories: arguments over the employer's power to require overtime, selection of the proper employee to perform the overtime, determination of the proper rate of pay, and the remedy for improper assignment of overtime. The first category is conceptually the easiest: absent some limiting contract clause, arbitrators generally hold that employers may require a "reasonable" amount of overtime. See, *e.g.*, Georgetown Steel, 73 LA 233 (Malcolm J. Hall, 1979). The following case illustrates the second and fourth categories.

LITHONIA HI TEK—VERMILLION
109 LA 775 (Matthew M. Franckiewicz, 1997).*

The contract provisions involved are:—* * *

ARTICLE 12 OVERTIME PROVISION

Overtime in the various classifications shall be equally distributed among the employees on their respective jobs insofar as possible.

> A.   The regular work week shall be Monday through Friday and shall consist of five (5), eight (8) hour days, excluding a thirty (30) minute lunch break; however, there shall be no daily or weekly guarantee of hours.
>
> B.   All time worked in excess of eight (8) hours in any single work day, Monday through Friday, inclusive, shall be paid at the overtime rate of one and one-half (1½) times the regular rate of pay.
>
> C.   All Saturday work will be paid at one and one-half (1½) times the regular rate of pay providing the employee's starting time occurs on Saturday (exclusive of third shift operations).
>
> D.   All Sunday work will be paid at two (2) times the regular rate of pay providing the employee's starting time occurs on Sunday (exclusive [of] third shift operations).
>
> E.   Employees in a probationary or temporary status will not be offered overtime until all full-time regular employees in the

* Reprinted with permission from *Labor Arbitration Reporter–Labor Arbitration Reports*, 129 LA 775. Copyright 1998 by The Bureau of National Affairs, Inc. (800–372–1033) <http://www.bna.com>.

classification have been asked. An employee shall be required to work daily overtime if notified prior to the end of his/her previous shift. Friday overtime shall be optional except for inventory if an employee is scheduled to work on Saturday. An employee shall be required to work on Saturday or Sunday if notified on Thursday. * * *

THE FACTS

The Company typically schedules overtime in increments of one to four hours, although Saturday overtime may be scheduled in eight hour increments. Overtime may be voluntary or mandatory, depending on the amount of advance notice given. The Company maintains records of the amount of overtime charged to each employee. Employees are charged for both overtime worked and overtime declined. Apparently these overtime logs are "reset" to zero hours charged each July, at the beginning of a new contract year. * * *

From these employer overtime records, the Union prepared summaries reflecting two types of disparities in overtime distribution.

First the Union compared the maximum overtime charged to an employee on one shift with the minimum charged to an employee on the other shift. The Union found 13 classifications, out of the 37 total classifications, in which this differential exceeded 16 hours, during the contract year from July 1995 through July 1996. The Union's summary suggests that in general, although not in all cases, greater overtime opportunities were afforded to first shift employees than to second shift employees. The Union refers to this type of differential as "cross shift" differential.

The Union also prepared a summary indicating that for two classifications in which there were no second shift employees, the difference between the highest and lowest overtime charged to first shift employees exceeded eight hours. The Union refers to this type of differential as "within shift" differential. In addition, by my calculation, the Union's cross shift summary also discloses 12 cases (seven on the first shift, five on the second shift) in which the difference between the highest and the lowest overtime charged to employees in the same classification on a given shift exceeded eight hours.

For the 15 classifications in which there was * * * a cross shift differential in excess of eight hours, the Union computed the average overtime by dividing the total overtime charged to all employees (regardless of shift) by the total number of employees (regardless of shift). The Union next identified all employees within the classification who were below this average, and calculated how far each of these employees trailed the average overtime charged. This difference ranged from as low as 0.44 hours to as high as 54.69 hours in the Assembly Packer Operator classification, and from as low as 0.48 hours to as high as 74.51 hours in the Material Handler Warehouse classification.

The Employer did not offer any evidence to explain the disparities. It did offer evidence regarding prior grievances concerning overtime equalization. The Union objected to this evidence, and I deferred ruling on the objection. My ruling and the rationale for it [are] set forth below in the Analysis and Conclusions section in this Award. * * * [The arbitrator held that evidence of prior grievance settlements was admissible.]

It appears that there has been no case in which employees were paid money in consequence of alleged failure to equalize overtime.

In negotiations, the parties discussed, but never agreed to, a standard for the permissible level of overtime disparity.

Issue

The issue, as agreed to by the parties, is whether the Employer violated the overtime equalization provision in Article 12 of the collective bargaining agreement during the year of the contract which ran from July 1995 through July 1996, and if a violation is found, what the appropriate remedy is. * * *

Position of the Union

[The union argued that its proposed benchmarks of 16 hours of cross shift differential and 8 hours within shift differential were reasonable, so disparities exceeding those benchmarks violated the agreement. Because the company did not rebut the union's evidence of larger overtime disparities, the union asserted that the only issue was the appropriate remedy. On that question, the union argued that precedent required a monetary remedy rather than an opportunity for employees to make up the missed overtime.]

Position of the Employer

[The employer rejected the union's proposed benchmarks and asserted that the union failed to offer concrete evidence of any contractual violation. Under Article 12, the employer need only equalize overtime "insofar as possible." That phrase requires a case by case analysis rather than a fixed formula. If there has been a violation, the employer need only offer the affected employees an opportunity to make up the missed overtime.]

Analysis and Conclusions

Although the facts in this case are undisputed and fairly straightforward, the questions raised by the parties' arguments are complex, and require fairly detailed discussion. * * *

II. The Standard of Proof

I am satisfied that the Union has sustained its burden of proof in this case. The Union's statistical approach demonstrates disparities in overtime among employees in the same classification. Its method addresses a number of considerations which are implicit in the overtime equalization provision.

First is that overtime need not be equalized on a daily or weekly basis. No contract violation occurs if the Company temporarily permits some employees to exceed others in overtime assignments, so long as the disadvantaged employees are later permitted to catch up. But if the Company fails to even out the overtime opportunity over a reasonable period of time, a contract violation has occurred. I conclude that a year is a reasonable time within which the Company should accomplish the equalization. This is especially appropriate given the parties' prior history, which suggests a mutual understanding that a contract year (from July to July) is the appropriate measuring period.

The second notion that is inherent in the overtime equalization provision, and taken into account in the Union's statistical method, is that exact mathematical precision is not to be expected in overtime distribution. Even if two employees had identical overtime accounts as the end of the contract year approached, the need to have a single employee work overtime on a Saturday for eight hours could create an eight hour imbalance. Factors such as special skills and availability could account for some degree of disparity. (In this regard, however, the large number of different classifications at the facility suggests that skill differentials may be more apparent across different classifications than within a given classification. Further, the practice of charging employees for declined overtime should minimize the importance of availability in accounting for overtime disparities.) Given that overtime is normally assigned in increments of one to four hours (with up to eight hours on Saturdays), I conclude that the Union, by demonstrating a variation of over eight hours among the employees in a classification on the same shift, has sustained its burden of proof, at least to the extent of shifting to the Employer the burden of coming forward with evidence to explain the disparity. Since the Employer is in the best position to present the evidence of why it assigned overtime to one employee over another, it is appropriate to shift the burden to it, once the Union has demonstrated that a disparity of over eight hours has occurred.

The third proposition inherent in the overtime equalization provision (or perhaps it is only a special case of the second) is that a greater degree of disparity between employees on different shifts may fairly be expected. Considerations which do not obtain in the within shift situation may affect the assignment of overtime to employees on one shift rather than another shift, for example the need to complete a "rush" assignment quickly, or limitations on equipment or work stations which may make it infeasible on some occasions to assign work to employees on one shift or the other. The Union's statistical method, utilizing a standard of in excess of 16 hours disparity in cross shift situations, addresses this issue. I conclude that by showing disparities of over 16 hours in cross shift situations, the Union has sustained its burden of proof, at least to the extent of shifting to the Company the burden of producing evidence to explain the disparity.

Since the Company has not offered evidence to explain the disparities in either the within shift or cross shift situations, I conclude that the Union has demonstrated violations of the agreement.

III. The Remedy

[After extended discussion of the appropriate remedy, the arbitrator awarded compensation to affected employees who had left the company or no longer held the same classification. He awarded make-up opportunities to all other employees. For further discussion of this issue, see note 2 below.]

AWARD

The grievance is sustained. The Company shall take remedial action as set forth above. Jurisdiction is retained for the limited purpose of resolving any disagreements which may arise in connection with this award.

Notes and Questions

1.   The *Lithonia* provision requiring equalization "insofar as possible" is fairly typical. Without an equalization clause, the most senior employees might receive all the overtime opportunities and the junior employees might receive none. Even worse, from the union's perspective, is the possibility that supervisors could award overtime opportunities disproportionately to their favorite employees. As in *Lithonia*, it is often difficult to determine just what is "possible." Most arbitrators interpret "possible" to mean "reasonably" possible. But how much equalization is "reasonable," and at what cost? Equalization within what group? All employees? All employees qualified to do certain work? All within a classification? Or only among those on a given shift? Equalization *when*? Every day? Week? Month? Year?

2.   *Remedies for Overtime Bypasses.*

(a) Arbitrator Franckiewicz dealt at length with the common remedial dispute as to whether the bypassed employees are entitled to pay for the overtime they would have worked (monetary relief) or to an extra opportunity to work overtime (make-up relief). Monetary relief is the most common remedy, as Arbitrator John Thornell stated in Georgia–Pacific Corp., 93 LA 4, 5 (1989):

> Where the remedy is not specified in the contract the weight of arbitral authority is to award monetary relief. This is especially so where the contract, as here, provides for overtime assignment on a seniority basis as opposed to an equalization basis. This is because when overtime is by seniority, giving Grievant make-up overtime will infringe upon rights other employees may have to that make-up overtime. If Grievant would otherwise be entitled to the overtime that is being given him as a remedy he is not being compensated because he would have received the overtime anyway.

> Where arbitrators have sanctioned make-up overtime in an equalization situation it is usually based on the rationale that when overtime is assigned to the wrong employee he is charged with it and will receive

that much less work in the long run among members of the overtime equalization unit. The overtime is not lost to the employee who should have received the assignment as he is only entitled to his approximately equal share of the overtime work available to employees in the equalization unit. So long as he receives his share over the period of time involved he has not lost any earnings.

The practice of paying for lost overtime, in the absence of express contract language, is consistent with fundamental contract law that one who has suffered monetary loss due to breach of contract will be compensated by payment of damages. Giving the Grievant the right to work for pay at some time in the future is not the payment of damages.

I conclude that apart from whether or not there is a practice of paying, the correct way to remedy this contract violation in assigning overtime work is to pay Grievant for the four hours of missed overtime.
* * *

Do you agree? Is the monetary remedy really "consistent with fundamental contract law," or at least any more consistent than make-up relief? Ask yourself what the grievants really lost when they were bypassed, then consider this excerpt from Abrams and Nolan, *Time at a Premium*, *supra* footnote 1, at 852:

Some arbitrators have held that the employee is entitled to overtime pay for the missed hours as damages. This position improperly describes the damages suffered by the employee who misses an overtime assignment. The actual loss is not the money the employee would have earned but the opportunity to earn that money. The difference between the two positions can be illustrated by an example of a simple problem of sales. If A breaches an agreement to sell a car worth $10,000 to B for $9,000, B's damages are measured not by the value of the car but by that value less what he would have paid for it—$1,000 rather than $10,000. Similarly, the grievant in the typical overtime case has lost not the amount of overtime pay but rather the chance to exchange labor for the promised amount. To give the employee the money without requiring him to work for it would be to give him more than he bargained for; it would, in other words, overcompensate him. Monetary relief is thus inappropriate in the normal overtime case because it overcompensates the grievant and imposes a penalty on the employer. In both respects, monetary relief departs from proper principles of contract remedies.

Which position is correct? Are they even in conflict? (Note Arbitrator Thornell's distinction between contract provisions awarding overtime opportunities according to seniority and provisions requiring equalization of overtime.)

Arbitrator Franckiewicz in *Lithonia* concluded that the arbitrator's role was to place all parties "where they would have been had there been no violation." When applied to an "equalization" overtime clause like that in *Lithonia*, his standard points toward make-up relief:

To simply award them money without requiring them to do the work which otherwise would have been the prerequisite to earning that money, would make them more than whole, since it would place them in a better position than they would have enjoyed had there been no violation. (In this regard I note that at least some overtime is voluntary. Some employees prefer not to work overtime. An employee who would have declined additional overtime if it had been offered lost nothing by virtue of the Company's failure to equalize overtime. For such an employee, a monetary remedy would be simply a windfall.) A make-up remedy only postpones, but does not deprive, the employees of the overtime (and earnings) which they should have received earlier.

(b) Even if make-up relief is the better remedy in general, there will be many cases in which it would not work, either because a grievant is no longer available to perform the make-up overtime or because the make-up remedy would penalize some other employee. If the employer's initial error was to assign work outside the appropriate overtime unit, for example, giving the grievant an extra opportunity will deprive some other employee within the unit of overtime that would otherwise have come his or her way. If some grievants have left the employer or moved to other overtime units, if new employees have joined the overtime unit, or if the period for equalizing overtime has passed, it may be impossible to award a make-up opportunity that would not come at someone else's expense. In such a situation, monetary relief may be the only fair option. Thus Arbitrator Franckiewicz awarded monetary compensation to grievants who had left the company or transferred to other classifications.

3. *Methods of Wage Payment.* Broadly speaking, there are two methods of payment, incentive and non-incentive. Non-incentive workers receive a salary or an hourly wage regardless of their productivity, the company's profits, or anything else. Incentive workers may receive a commission, payment for quantity of production, a premium for individual or group production over some stated norm, or a bonus calculated by a designated formula measuring quantity, productivity, profits, or some other factors.[3] In theory, incentive payment systems encourage employees to work harder or better. In practice, they often fall short of the goal. If the plan's incentives are small, if the plan is too complex to understand or to administer easily, or if employees perceive the plan as unfair or overly demanding, the incentive scheme may be useless or counter-productive. Incentives for group performance may cause tensions among employees. Harder-working employees may resent rewards given to those they regard as slackers, while those less concerned about income may resent pressures from their colleagues to work faster or harder.

Unions may resist or sabotage incentive programs because they believe the employer will simply raise the expected norms (institute a "speed-up") once it discovers how efficient the employees can be; doing so would leave the employees with more work for the same pay. Some studies have shown that employees occasionally defeat incentive schemes by adopting their own preferred norms and punishing "rate busters." (Compare the ostracized high school—or law school—"curve wrecker.") Not everyone runs faster to grab the dangling carrot. Some people prefer leisure to money.

3. More than a quarter of the collective bargaining agreements in one study discussed incentive pay, although 4% prohibited such arrangements without union consent. Incentive pay was much more common in manufacturing (42%) than in other contracts (7%). Basic Patterns, *supra* note 2, at 19–21.

4. Changed conditions usually prompt one party or the other to call for changed wages. For example, a new machine may require a new job classification, but at what wage rate? Or an employer may reduce a crew from five people to four, or buy a machine that lets an employee produce twice as many widgets per hour while exerting less energy. How should these changes affect wages? One arbitral principle is that a wage increase should accompany any material increase in workload. This works reasonably well on the upside for hourly employees, but what if the change *decreases* the workload? (Unions usually argue that any reduction in work is more than balanced by an increase in responsibility, mental exertion, or value to the employer.)

Incentive-rate employees present a trickier problem. Doubled productivity might mean doubled income under an incentive program, even if the only change is an expensive machine paid for by management. Would that be fair? Arbitrators try to apply principles such as "maintenance of prior earnings" or "maintenance of the ratio of earnings to effort." It is far easier to state these principles than to apply them. See generally, Elkouri and Elkouri, How Arbitration Works 672 (Alan Miles Rubin, Editor-in-Chief, 6th ed. 2003).

5. *Guaranteed Pay Provisions.* Imagine that you are an hourly-paid worker. You report to work one day after your usual half-hour commute, only to learn that a power failure has closed the plant for the day. Because you can't work, you don't get paid. Or imagine that your employer calls you in on Sunday for a special assignment, then quickly sends you home with fifteen minutes' pay. From the employer's perspective, in each case you have received just what the contract calls for—pay at the appropriate rate for the time you worked—but from your perspective, you've wasted a lot of time for nothing.

To prevent employers from taking their workers' time lightly, unions often negotiate "guaranteed pay" provisions. Typically these provisions guarantee employees a minimum of four hours' pay when they report for work ("reporting pay") or are called in for work at an unusual time ("call-in pay").[4] Employers thus have a strong incentive to notify employees of any work interruption and to schedule work to avoid interrupting the employees' free time.

Guaranteed pay provisions provide a small but steady flow of arbitration cases. One problem is the conflict between overtime and call-in. Suppose your foreman tells you to stay after your regular shift for a few hours. That may constitute overtime but not a new "call-in." Suppose, however, that she tells you to report two hours earlier than usual the next day. Is that a call-in? See McGraw–Edison Co., 41 LA 1136 (John Sembower, 1963) (scheduled or pre-arranged pre-shift work does not constitute a call-in).

Reporting pay provisions raise other problems. Suppose an employee covered by a reporting pay provision comes to work five minutes late. Should he lose the four hours' guaranteed pay? But what if another employee reports two hours late? Should she receive the four hours' pay? Or two hours' pay? Or none? An express provision, for example one requiring employees to report punctually, will of course control. See, for example,

---

4. Of the contracts in a 1995 study, 80% provided for reporting pay and 69% for call-in pay. A majority in each category set the minimum at four hours' pay. Basic Patterns, *supra* footnote 2, at 116–17, 121.

Canton Drop Forging & Mfg. Co., 63 LA 483 (Rankin Gibson, 1974) (denying reporting pay to an employee who arrived three minutes late). Absent such an express provision, the general requirement of reasonableness applies.

Reporting pay clauses often contain express or implied exceptions for emergencies and other conditions beyond the control of management. (Note that these exceptions shift the risk of unexpected occurrences from employer to employee.) Of course the exceptions should not apply if the employer was responsible for the problem, Federal Mogul Bower Bearings, 43 LA 12 (Arthur Ross, 1964), or unreasonably delayed a decision to close until it was too late to notify employees. For example, in Thiokol Corporation, 103 LA 1025 (Barnett M. Goodstein, 1994), the employer denied reporting pay to employees sent home early due to an ice storm. The arbitrator sustained the grievance even though the contract exempted closures because of "conditions beyond the control of the Company." Arbitrator Goodstein held that the company could easily have decided whether to shut the plant before the employees reported.

Usually reporting pay is not due if the employer used reasonable means to notify the employee not to report. What is "reasonable" depends on the circumstances. In many northern cities with frequent snow storms, an announcement over a previously designated radio station might be reasonable. The snowfall should alert employees to listen to the radio just as Minnesota school children do. If the problem is equipment failure, however, employees would have no reason to listen for the announcement, so that would not be a reasonable method of notification. An employer wishing to avoid liability in such a situation should try to call each employee.

The notice must also be timely. If the employer knows that employees are likely to leave for work an hour before the scheduled starting time, a radio announcement or even a telephone call later than that would not be timely. Gould Pumps, Inc., 71 LA 551 (Irwin Dean, Jr., 1978); Keystone Carbon Co., 103 LA 623 (John Felice, 1994).

6. *Incentive Pay Plans.* Many employers find that their employees are more productive when paid incentives for the quantity or quality of their work. As with most other wage disputes, the devil is in the details. An employer thinking of adopting an incentive pay arrangement must consider what sort of incentives to offer, what standards to apply, how much to pay for performance at various levels, how to evaluate performance, and, not least, how to keep employees from "gaming" the system—that is, finding ways to maximize incentive pay without actually being as productive as the system expects. The devilish details of incentive plans are usually too complicated and too tentative to be resolved in negotiations. As a result, collective bargaining agreements more often grant the employer authority to maintain a current plan or design a new one subject to consultation with the union. The simplest form of incentive is a commission on sales.

In The Seattle Times Co., 119 LA 1109 (William F. Reeves, 2004), an agreement negotiated in 2001 allowed the newspaper to establish and modify assignments, policies, and commission structures for advertising employees who worked on commission provided it notified the employees six months before implementation (Sections 2, 3, and 4). Section 5 reserved for management the right to establish or change "goals for each Commission Sales

Employee" but did not contain an express 6–month notice period. Over the next year the employer developed standards of performance (SOPs) for these employees and published them in October 2002. The SOPs contained disciplinary provisions (the stick) as well as incentive payments (the carrot). The union challenged the SOPs because they were unreasonable, the disciplinary scheme was arbitrary, and the employer did not provide six months' notice. The arbitrator carefully examined the details of the plan and found them generally reasonable even though several provisions troubled him: "In the absence of clear evidence that unrealistic or unreasonable standards or workloads have been adopted by an employer, even unusual or difficult rules should be upheld. * * * I find that while the requirements may be difficult there is no clear evidence that the SOPs are unreasonable." Although the notice requirement for "policies" in Section 3 applied to Section 5 Performance Plan Guidelines, the arbitrator found that the parties had a binding past practice of allowing monthly changes to "performance goals." Even though there was a notification violation involving some of the new rules, the arbitrator awarded no remedy because more than six months had passed, and that period belatedly satisfied the notice period.

A NOTE ON JOB–EVALUATION SYSTEMS

(a) Description

Employers often tie pay to the perceived demands of the job. A position that requires more education or more skills deserves a higher wage than another with lower requirements. A position that imposes more physical or mental demands or more responsibility is worth more than another without those demands. A position performed in irregular shifts or in dangerous or uncomfortable working conditions should provide greater rewards than a steady 9–to–5 job in an office. There are many ways to evaluate jobs, as the following excerpt explains.

Job Ranking.

This is commonly thought to be the simplest method. Each job is considered as a whole and then is given a ranking in relation to all other jobs. A ranking table is then drawn up and the ranked jobs grouped into grades. Pay levels can then be fixed for each grade.

Paired Comparisons.

This is a simple method. Each job is compared as a whole with each other job in turn and points (0, 1 or 2) are awarded according to whether its overall importance is judged to be less than, equal to or more than the other. Points awarded for each job are then totaled and ranking order produced.

Job Classification.

This is similar to ranking except that it starts from the opposite end; the grading structure is established first and individual jobs fitted into it.

A broad description of each grade is drawn up and individual jobs considered typical of each grade are selected as "benchmarks." The other jobs are then compared with these benchmarks and the general description [and] are placed in their appropriate grade.

Points Assessment.

This is the most common system in use. It is an analytical method, which, instead of comparing whole jobs, breaks down each job into a number of factors—for example, skills, responsibility, physical and mental requirements and working conditions. Each of these factors may be analysed further.

Points are awarded for each factor according to a pre-determined scale and the total points decide a job's place in the ranking order. Usually, the factors are weighted so that, for example, more or less weight may be given to hard physical conditions or to high degree of skill.

Factor Comparison.

This is also an analytical method, employing the same principles as points assessment but using only a limited number of factors, such as skill, responsibility and working conditions.

A number of "key" jobs are selected because their wage rates are generally agreed to be "fair." The proportion of the total wage attributable to each factor is then decided and a scale produced showing the rate for each factor of each key job. The other jobs are then compared with this scale, factor by factor, so that a rate is finally obtained for each factor of each job. The total pay for each job is reached by adding together the rates for its individual factors.

Eaton Ltd. v. Nuttall, 6 I.R.L.R. 71 (Employment Appeals Tribunal [England] 1977), *quoted in* Robert N. Covington, *Equal Pay Acts: A Survey of Experience Under the British and American Statutes*, 21 Vanderbilt Journal of Transnational Law 649, 663 (1988).

(b) Application

In practice, evaluation of jobs is far more complicated than this description suggests. Here is an example of a "points assessment" evaluation using a sophisticated job evaluation manual (76 printed pages) negotiated between a major paper company and the United Paperworkers International Union. The evaluation system rates each job in the plant on twelve factors: manual skill, mental skill, experience, physical effort, visual application, responsibility for material, responsibility for tools and equipment, responsibility for direction of others, responsibility for operations, responsibility for safety of others, hazards, and working conditions. Each factor has between four and seven ratings ("degrees"). Each degree carries an agreed number of points. The total number of points determines the job's pay grade.

Introduction of new paper-making machines in the 1980s required the parties to re-evaluate almost every job in a large mill. Jobs on which they could not agree were taken to arbitration. The arbitrators then had to judge management's preliminary rating of each disputed factor. In one tiny part of one job among many on one machine, the arbitrator had to decide the degree of manual skill required for the reconstituted entry-level job of "Utility Assistant." The company rated the job's manual-skill factor at "3b" (worth .9 points), defined in the job-evaluation manual as "manipulate multiple controls of machines or equipment at a rapid pace involving a high degree of coordination." The union rated it as "4b" (1.8 points), defined as "high degree of hand and eye coordination for sustained periods." (Note the vagueness of the definitions.)

The arbitrator heard substantial testimony about this job and comparison jobs, then rode around in the wood-hauling equipment while an employee demonstrated the work. He concluded that in the abstract the union's rating of 4b was accurate but that the Utility Assistant performed essentially the same tasks as a predecessor job the parties rated at 3b. He therefore sustained the employer's rating on that factor, then resolved similar disputes about six other factors on that job, then evaluated similar factors for the next four jobs in the job sequence. The entire arbitration award took 32 single-spaced pages. Total costs of the arbitration to the parties, considering the parties' time as well as the arbitrator's fee and expenses, must have exceeded $20,000—just to get the opinion of an outsider who surely knew less about the work than they. The parties had at least three other arbitrations to resolve similar job-evaluation disputes in other lines of progression.

Several questions must occur to any arbitrator in a complicated job-evaluation dispute. Is it really possible to analyze jobs as accurately as job-evaluation systems presume? Or are the job's factors too subtle and too numerous for such precision? Even if an accurate evaluation is theoretically possible, is the resulting wage rate likely to be any fairer (or the process any more cost-effective) than one set by the parties' economic power or by supply and demand? Arbitrator Jack Stieber, *supra* footnote 1, at 107, expressed his frustration about an evaluation of a new position of "tool room machinist":

> In this kind of case, both sides usually call expert witnesses. A toolmaker, who was in the bargaining unit, testified that, in his opinion, this job would duplicate the duties of a toolmaker to the extent of 90 percent. For the other side, management engineers testified that, in their judgment, duplication between the two jobs would not exceed 50 percent. The arbitrator, who may not have understood the difference between a toolmaker and a machinist, had to decide this dispute. In cases like this, the parties would be well advised not to rely on arbitration. They should realize that the arbitrator is less likely to reach an intelligent decision than they are if they work it out themselves. Yet, all too often, the parties cannot agree, and they prefer any decision to no decision.

Despite these problems, job evaluation systems are still common, perhaps because they add a veneer of scientific and mathematical accuracy to an inherently subjective process. In fact, job evaluation has made something of a comeback as public officials and others have grappled with concerns over "comparable worth." Anti-discrimination laws prohibit paying men more than women for the same work, but in many workplaces men and women do different work. To address what some regard as another form of discrimination—a predominantly male classification like truck driver paying more than a predominantly female classification like administrative assistant, for example—some state and local governments and a few private parties have used job-evaluation systems to determine the relative worth of different jobs. If a points assessment rates two jobs equally, then the pay ranges presumptively should be comparable.

Needless to say, it all depends on the evaluator's choice of relevant factors, relative weight, and application of the facts, which factors the evaluator considers, and how much weight he or she gives to each of them. Two experts, each applying the paper mill's factors to the truck drive/administrative assistant example could produce radically different results. One might conclude that truck drivers should earn more because of the job's required physical effort, hazards, and uncomfortable working conditions. The other might conclude the administrative assistants should earn more because of their job's required mental skill and responsibility for operations.

Does job evaluation serve the same function in wage-setting generally as it does in the implementation of comparable worth? Is it likely to work better in one than in the other? Why or why not?

Finally, what relationship should a job evaluation system (whether in a collective bargaining relationship or in a "comparable worth" plan) have to the market value of the respective jobs? Suppose a job-evaluation system rates the administrative assistant classification as "worth" more than the trucker classification, but the market disagrees. What would be the result?

3. HOURS DISPUTES

GOODYEAR TIRE AND RUBBER CO.*
80–2 ARB ¶ 8468 (Gordon F. Knight, 1980).

BACKGROUND: [The Union grieved the Company's failure to pay night shift premium to employees working a split shift. The Employer's third-step answer stated]

> * * * the contract clearly states that premium shift differential shall be paid to employees according to shift starting time as follows: Second shift, 3:00 pm to 11:00 pm—$.190 per hour: Third shift, 11:00 pm to 7:00 am—$.235 per hour. Since none of our employees worked shifts starting at 3:00 pm or 11:00 pm none are entitled to night shift pay.

Article V, Section 8 of the current contract states:

A premium shift differential shall be paid to employees according to shift starting time as follows: Second shift—$.190/hr.; Third shift—$.235/hr.

Elsewhere in Article V the first shift is specified as 7:00 am to 3:00 pm; Second shift—3:00 pm to 11:00 pm; and Third shift—11:00 pm to 7:00 am.

The premium shift differential was $.09/hr. for all work performed between the hours of 7:00 pm and 7:00 am in the first contract between the parties at this location in 1969 and remained unchanged in 1972 and 1976.

In October of 1976 certain adjustments were made as a result of the Reopening clause incorporated in the local contract signed earlier that year. The Reopener was for the purpose of reflecting the impact of the Master Contract negotiations in the local contract. The Reopener specified that all work performed on the second shift between 3:00 pm and 11:00 pm was to receive a shift differential or $.103/hr. in October, 1976 with increases in the following two years. A shift differential of $.148/hr. was to be paid for work performed on the third shift between 11:00 pm and 7:00 am with increases for the following two years.

The subsequent application of this article produced a grievance wherein the Union claimed shift differential for those employees on the first shift who worked overtime beyond 3:00 pm. In the negotiation of the current contract the Union agreed to the shift differential in terms of starting times and in return the Employer compensated employees with claims under the grievance previously mentioned.

The Employer's facility is a tire distribution center. In January of 1980 there were 15 employees on the first shift and 6 on the second. With the production slowdown in the automotive assembly plants and reduced retail sales, 5 employees were laid off on February 7, 1980 and the entire second shift was eliminated on February 11, 1980.

At the same time, in order to accommodate the problems of the loading of trucks occasioned by the elimination of the second shift, the Employer assigned 3 employees to a split shift working from 11:00 am to 7:00 pm. On February 20, 1980 the manpower was increased while retaining the split shift. The grievance was filed on February 27, 1980 and reflects these conditions. On March 3, 1980 the split shift was eliminated and the second shift restored.

On April 28, 1980 the hours of the first shift were changed from 7:00 am–3:00 pm to 8:00 am–4:00 pm. The second shift was eliminated and the split shift (11:00 am–7:00 pm) was reinstituted.

On June 16, 1980 the hours of the split shift were changed to 12:00 pm–8:00 pm.

Article V. Section 12 of the contract states:

The Employer may adjust the daily starting times for any portion of employees. Notice of such changes must be made at least five (5) days in advance to employees and appropriate Local Union Representative advising reasons for such change.

[POSITIONS OF THE PARTIES]

The Union's position is that this shift differential was negotiated in good faith as part of an over-all package settlement. This was negotiated at the Master Contract level and translated in the local contract in the manner described earlier. For the Employer to avoid the payment of this negotiated benefit by resorting to the alteration of shift starting times is unreasonable. The Employer's theory would permit it to avoid payment of shift differential for the second shift by changing the starting time from 3:00 pm to 3:15 pm. The Union further contends that for the arbitrator to rule in favor of the Employer would be in violation of his contractually specified power.

The Employer argues there is no contract violation. It eliminated the second shift entirely when it created the split shift. The payment of shift differential is linked by contract to shift starting times. The Employer's authority to adjust working hours is clear. No shift differential for those on the split shift are mandated by the contract.

DISCUSSION AND AWARD

It is easy to sympathize with the Union's concerns here. From its view, it negotiated a benefit, in this case the shift differential for work on the less desirable shifts—namely, the second and third shifts. The selection of this benefit presumably was in lieu of some other possible benefit. Now the Employer by altering the shift hours avoids the payment of this benefit. Further, this benefit had been in existence for several years and only recently altered.

However much the arbitrator may understand the Union's view in this and every grievance, the provisions of the contract must be looked to first.

It is clear the language in the current contract was chosen carefully to preclude the type of liability arising from the wording in the prior October, 1976 contract. The latter specified shift differentials be paid for work during certain hours. This required the payment of the differential if the first shift worked overtime into the hours of the second shift or, similarly, the second shift into the hours of the third shift.

The problems involved produced the language in the current contract which relates shift differentials to shift starting times.

It is clear that the Employer is authorized by the contract to alter starting times. It is likewise clear that in the current fact situations the starting times of the split shifts did not conform to those specified in the contract for which shift differentials would be mandated.

The Union's point cannot be ignored however. Can the Employer evade the payment of shift differentials by altering the shift starting times by an insignificant amount? Clearly this would be unreasonable.

In the original situation, however, the split shift started some 4 hours earlier—a significant time change. Moreover, the reason for the change was related to considerations of operating efficiency. This was unchallenged. Subsequent changes in shift starting times were presumably for reasons of efficient operations also.

In short, the Employer used its authority to alter the shift starting times by a significant amount for legitimate reasons. In doing so the contract does not require the payment of any shift differential inasmuch as the starting time of the split shift which was created does not conform to the shift starting times which would mandate the payment of such differential.

Setting the contract language aside for the moment, the reason for the payment of shift differentials merits examination. Such differentials are paid to compensate employees for the disruptions to family and social life associated with such working hours. Certainly the inconvenience and disruption to the lives of employees working the split shift (11:00 am to 7:00 pm or later, 12:00 pm to 8:00 pm) is not as great as the conventional second shift from 3:00 pm to 11:00 pm.

The fact that the Union feels it has been denied part of a package of benefits that it negotiated is unfortunate. Yet it should have been readily apparent that some benefits such as this one here are more vulnerable to legitimate actions of the Employer than are others.

It should be clear that the impact of language relating to shift differentials in prior contracts must be ignored in the face of the clear and unambiguous language governing this grievance.

In summary, the Union has failed to meet its burden of proof. The Employer, for sound business reasons, exercised its authority to alter the shift starting times—more accurately, created a new split shift. Because the starting time of the split shift was significantly different from the starting times specified for the payment of shift differential, the contract makes no requirement for the payment of any shift differentials to employees on the split shift.

The reasoning here applies equally to the circumstances of the grievance as well as those claims arising from subsequent shift changes referred to.

AWARD

Grievance denied.

Notes and Questions

1. Pretty sneaky of Goodyear, wasn't it? Suppose the employer changed the second shift's hours from 3:00–11:00 p.m. to 3:15–11:15 p.m., as the union feared it might. Would that eliminate the obligation to pay the

shift differential? Isn't that just an exaggerated form of what Goodyear did in this case?

2. Agreements commonly state a "normal" workday or workweek. Unions frequently rely on those definitions to challenge changes in hours. The cases differ on the question of whether such definitions constitute enforceable guarantees. Compare these two awards by distinguished arbitrators. In Anchor Hocking Corp., 81 LA 502 (Roger I. Abrams, 1983), the contract stated that "Eight (8) hours shall constitute a normal work day." To cut costs, the employer changed its methods of assignment with the result that many employees worked fewer hours each day. When the union protested, the company asserted that the definition of a normal work day was no guarantee and therefore did not bar the change. Arbitrator Abrams disagreed:

> Arbitrators have long recognized that the customary contractual definition of a "normal work day" does not constitute a "guarantee." See, Libby, McNeill & Libby, 11 LA 872 (Fleming, 1948). For example, when employees are sent home on any given day for lack of work during a shift, the "normal work day" language would not require payment for a full eight hours. That, however, is not the issue raised in this case. The Company is not sending home employees on an occasional day when during a shift it discovers that there is no work to perform. The Company's change contested here involves a fundamental restructuring of the scheduling procedure in the Select & Pack Department. * * *

> The parties wrote Article 13, Section 1 in their Agreement. They obviously intended that it mean *something* even if it would not create a "guarantee" or be used as a measure for overtime calculation. The Arbitrator's responsibility is to determine what the parties intended when they agreed that eight hours shall constitute a normal work day.

> A reasonable reading of the "normal work day" language would be that in the usual, ordinary, and regular situation, eight hours shall constitute an employee's daily work period. See, e.g., Caribe Circuit Breaker Co., 63 LA 261, 262 (Pollock, 1974). Of course, on occasion some employees would work more than eight hours because of overtime. On other occasions, employees might work less than eight hours. This latter possibility has been recognized by the parties in their reporting pay provision, Article 15. Thus in the unusual, nonordinary, irregular situation, less or more than eight hours might constitute the work day. But the parties agreed that eight hours shall constitute the normal work day. Under the Company's change of operations contested here, many employees were not working eight hours as a "normal work day." * * *

> Pursuant to its reserved managerial rights, the Company cannot deny employees their expectation expressly protected by the Contract to an eight hour normal work day. See, e.g. North American Systems, Inc., 82–2 ARB para. 8508 (Feldman, 1983). What the Company's change has done, in effect, is convert many full-time employees to irregular, part-time or casual status. It is uncontroverted that the Company had never employed selectors or any other hourly employees on that basis in the past.

81 LA at 507–08.

In Ampco–Pittsburgh Corp., 80 LA 472 (Steven Briggs, 1982), the Agreement defined the "regular work week of an employee" as "five (5) consecutive eight (8) hour days." After a major loss of business, the company laid off a large part of its work force, then decided to reduce the daily hours of its clerical workers from eight to seven. The union argued that the contract provision barred the reduction, but Arbitrator Briggs, citing other arbitration awards, disagreed:

> If the above language is construed as a guarantee that employees shall receive eight hours' work per day and forty per week, then it must be concluded that the Company did, in fact, violate the agreement. But that interpretation cannot be given to Paragraph 48. Such guarantees cannot be implied, they must be specifically stated. For example, consider the following language deemed by Arbitrator Thomas T. Roberts to be void of an hours of work guarantee:

>> The normal work week for all employees within the unit shall consist of forty (40) hours to be worked at the rate of eight (8) hours per day, from M–F inclusive (General Precision, Inc., 42 LA 589).

> Also consider the language that Arbitrator Walter Boles, Jr. decided did not contain a guarantee of any number of hours per day or week:

>> The normal workday shall be eight (8) hours per day, exclusive of lunch period. The normal work week shall consist of forty (40) hours per week, that is, five normal work days, Monday through Friday (Cook Machinery Company, 35 LA 845).

> This Arbitrator recognizes that exacting parallels cannot be drawn between the language of one labor agreement and that of another. Each exists in its own context and within its own unique background. About all that can be said about a comparison of the above quoted two clauses is that neither contains an express guarantee of hours for employees, nor does Article XIII, Paragraph 48 in the instant case. But language in that Paragraph is still far from pellucidly clear. The Arbitrator therefore looks to the record for evidence of the parties' mutual intent in negotiating that Paragraph. The Union claimed during the hearing that a work hour guarantee was intended, but there is nothing else in the record to substantiate that claim. Accordingly, the Arbitrator has concluded that Article XIII, Paragraph 48 does not guarantee employees eight hours' work per day or forty hours' work per week.

80 LA at 477–78. Which arbitrator, Abrams or Briggs, is right? Could *both* be right? How? If Arbitrator Briggs is right, what *is* the meaning of the quoted contract language about a "regular work week?"

3. Both cases in the previous note involved the use of "work sharing" (that is, reducing hours or days of work to spread the pain of a reduction in total hours) as a way of avoiding layoffs. Why would an employer prefer work sharing? Isn't work sharing much more egalitarian than layoffs? Why then would the union oppose it?

4. One problem unions face in these cases is the employer's ability to manipulate hours to maximize productivity at the expense of employee expectations and convenience. A good example is Air System Components, 104 LA 477 (Donald P. Goodman, 1995). The contract guaranteed a 15–

minute break "after lunch." Breaks often result in some loss of production beside the obvious 15 minutes, for example because employees might have to spend additional time shutting down and starting up complicated machinery. Perhaps for that reason, Air Systems Components rescheduled employees' breaks for the last 15 minutes of the work day. Even though the break provision did not expressly prohibit that rescheduling, the arbitrator sustained the grievance because an industrial relations dictionary defined a "rest period" as "A short interruption *during* the work period" (emphasis added).

Of course a negotiated management right may protect even more radical employer changes in hours. In University of Chicago Hospitals, 103 LA 558 (Irwin M. Lieberman, 1994), the employer unilaterally eliminated three 12–hour night shift positions, changed one position to 12 hours on the day shift, and posted two new eight-hour night shift vacancies. The arbitrator denied the grievance because the agreement reserved to management the right to "determine and change starting times, quitting times, and shifts" and to "determine staffing patterns."

5. Among the many other types of hours disputes are differences over the existence, length, timing, and changing of meal breaks, rest breaks, restroom breaks, and wash-up time. Space constraints prevent covering those topics here. See instead Buckalew, *supra* footnote 1, at § 29.06.

G. FRINGE BENEFITS

1. INTRODUCTION

"Fringe benefits" is a broad phrase that includes virtually anything an employer can grant an employee other than wages and hours, from something as valuable as health insurance to something as mundane as a Thanksgiving turkey. The historical tendency has been for some employers to grant a new benefit, then for unions to negotiate a contractual right to that benefit, and finally for employees to come to look on it almost as a natural right. Thus, paid vacations and holidays began as gratuities, then became subjects of negotiation. Today, few employers could imagine *not* offering them to full-time employees. In addition to health insurance, vacations, and holidays, the most important fringe benefits are pension and profit-sharing plans and leaves of absence (for sickness, funerals, union business, and personal business). This section provides a brief introduction to a few of these topics.

2. HOLIDAY PAY[1]

In contrast to most other industrialized countries, the U.S. has left holiday entitlements largely to the market and to collective bargaining.

---

1. Bibliographic Suggestions: Roger I. Abrams and Dennis R. Nolan, *Resolving Holiday Pay Disputes in Labor Arbitration*, 33 Case Western Reserve Law Review 380 (1983); Timothy J. Buckalew, *Holidays and Holiday Pay*, Chapter 32 of Labor and Employment Arbitration (Tim Bornstein, Ann Gosline, and Marc Greenbaum, eds., 2d ed. 1997); Shyam Das, *Fringe Benefits*, The Common Law of the Workplace: The Views of Arbitrators (Theodore J. St. Antoine, ed. 1998), 306, 311–20; Arnold M. Zack and Richard I. Bloch, Labor Agreement in Nego-

Almost all collective agreements provide for paid holidays. The median number of paid holidays in union contracts in the most recent large survey was 11, but about ten per cent of the contracts provided for fewer than eight holidays while only seven per cent provided 14 or more holidays. Until 1989 there was a steady increase in the number of paid holidays. There has been little change since then.[2] By European standards, these numbers are modest. Most European countries statutorily require 15 or more holidays.

OUTBOARD MARINE CORP.

54 LA 112 (Louis C. Kesselman, Chairman, 1969).[1]

STIPULATED ISSUE

Did the Company act within the spirit and letter of Article 11.5 of the contract, as well as past practice, in denying L.A. DeJaynes holiday pay for December 24 and 25, 1968, after he had received permission from his supervisor to take off one-half hour early to play Santa Claus and was absent the day after the holiday?

STATEMENT OF FACTS

The grievant had been a volunteer, non-paid, Santa Claus in Oquawka, Illinois, approximately 35 miles from the plant for about eight years. He customarily left the plant after his regular shift, if a work day was involved, and drove to Oquawka where he performed before various civic groups.

On or about December 18, 1968, the grievant informed Maintenance Supervisor McGrew that he would again be playing Santa for a city-sponsored Christmas party at Oquawka on December 23. On the latter date, the grievant told Acting Maintenance Supervisor Brown that he was scheduled to appear in Oquawka at 5:00 P.M. and asked permission to leave the plant at 4:00 P.M., one-half hour before the end of his shift. He also asked permission to work through his lunch period to make up the time, which was denied on the ground that it was contrary to plant policy. However, Brown gave him a pass to leave the plant one-half hour early, after reminding him not to miss the day after the holiday "if at all possible."

The grievant was ill on December 25 and 26 and did not report for work until December 27, 1968. When the Company denied him Christmas holiday pay on the ground that he had not worked his full regularly scheduled work days prior to and following the holiday, as required by Article 11.5 of the Agreement, he filed a grievance on January 29, 1969, charging that the company had violated Articles 3.1, 5.1, 11.4 and 11.5

tiation and Arbitration 272–83 (2d ed. 1995).

2. Bureau of National Affairs, Basic Patterns in Union Contracts 57–66 (14th Ed. 1995).

1. Reprinted with permission from *Labor Arbitration Reporter–Labor Arbitration Reports*, 54 LA 112. Copyright 1970 by The Bureau of National Affairs, Inc. (800–372–1033) <http://www.bna.com>.

by failing to pay him holiday pay for December 24 and 25, 1968 and asking that he be "reimbursed for all losses." * * *

DISCUSSION

Everybody loves Santa Claus and nobody wants to be a Scrooge and penalize those who spread his holiday cheer. However, the issue in this case is not whether an employee can be denied holiday pay for playing Santa but rather whether Article 11.5 entitles an employee to holiday compensation if he is excused to leave work early on the last work day before a holiday and fails to work on the day following the holiday because of illness.

It has become almost universal in American labor contracts to provide holiday pay benefits for holidays not worked to enable employees to enjoy holidays with their families without loss of earnings. It has also become common for labor contracts to specify qualifications for entitlement to holiday pay in the form of work requirements before and after the holiday. Paid holidays are a contractual rather than an absolute right and employees must meet all requirements agreed upon by the parties in collective bargaining.

Many contracts also specify exceptions to the qualifications which permit an employee to be absent on the required work days and still receive holiday pay. These exceptions commonly include illness and other excused absences. But, regardless of whether the exceptions are spelled out or not, holiday pay clauses have provided considerable employment for arbitrators as the number of published awards on the subject will attest. The general pattern of awards, as set out by Arbitrator Madden in American Beauty Macaroni Company (67–2 ARB 8524) after reviewing many awards is that arbitrators are strongly inclined to decide cases in favor of grievants even where their absences are caused by reasons other than those stated in the exceptions. The basis for most of these awards which favor the aggrieved employees is that arbitrators generally agree that "the purpose of eligibility provisions in holiday pay clauses is to discourage the tendency on the part of some employees to stretch the holiday into an absence from work for one or more days beyond the holiday itself" (Kaiser Steel Corporation, 31 LA 567, 574).

In his review of published awards, the Impartial Arbitrator has found that arbitrators have awarded holiday pay in many situations not covered by the Agreement where they have been satisfied that the purpose of the absence was not deliberately to prolong the holiday. For example:

Standard Beverage, Inc. (69–2 ARB 8806)—employee who reported for work on day before holiday and [was] then discharged was awarded holiday pay.

Fruehauf Trailer Company (69–2 ARB 8613)—employee who reported sixteen minutes late on first qualifying day was awarded holiday pay on ground that the purpose of provision was to prevent holiday stretching and not to penalize lateness. * * *

Harvey Probber, Inc. (68–2 ARB 8669)—one employee in court as a defendant and one as a witness awarded holiday pay because their absence was beyond their control and not to stretch their holiday. * * *

Greenfield Top & Die Corp. (15 LA 536)—Arbitrator upheld a holiday pay grievance where the employee did not work either day before or after a holiday because of illness on ground that his intent was not to stretch the holiday. * * *

Obviously, the above awards were made under contracts and circumstances different from those involved in the case before us and their citation is intended solely to indicate the general pattern of thinking of arbitrators when confronted with grievances involving denial of holiday pay for failure to meet contract attendance requirements for entitlement to pay. The Impartial Arbitrator admits that he shares the common view among arbitrators that work requirements before and after holidays are intended to prevent the stretching of holidays. Nevertheless, he recognizes that he must apply the spirit and letter of Article 11, Section 5 to the instant grievance rather than a general theory of holiday pay qualifications.

Article 11.5 provides:

> To qualify for holiday pay, employees must have worked their full regularly scheduled work day prior to and their full regularly scheduled work day following a holiday unless their absence on either of such days has been authorized by the Company * * *. Employees on sick or accident leaves or on a leave of absence shall not receive holiday pay unless such employees worked either the day prior to or the day following a holiday.

The language of Article 11.5 makes it clear that an employee, in order to be eligible for holiday pay, must work the "full regularly scheduled" work days surrounding a holiday. According to Article 5.2, a full regularly scheduled work day is eight hours.

However, Article 11.5 also permits exceptions. If ill etc. one need work only one of the two days to qualify for holiday pay. Furthermore, in the first line of this section an additional exception is stated: " * * * unless their absence on either of such days has been authorized by the Company."

No dispute exists over the grievant's absence on December 26, 1968, which resulted from illness and therefore automatically excused him from working the day after the holiday. The disagreement centers on whether his departure from work one-half hour early on December 23, 1968, was proper cause for the Company to deny him Christmas pay for 1968.

The Board of Arbitration has examined both Article 11.5 and the evidence with references to its past application and makes the following findings:

1. The phrase "authorized by the Company" is ambiguous to the extent that it does not specify which officials can commit the Company

to excusing employees from work. However, although the evidence clearly shows that Director of Industrial Relations Shover has always made the determination as to which employees shall and which shall not receive holiday pay, this is different from the decision to excuse an employee from work. A supervisor is a Company representative and an employee who is told by him that he has permission to leave early can rightfully assume that he has the Company's leave to do so, whether the supervisor has made the decision himself or is merely passing the word down from higher authority.

2.   Although Acting Supervisor Brown attached an implied condition when he excused the grievant one-half hour early to the effect that he must work the day following the holiday, the grievant's failure to do so was excusable under the exceptions listed in the last sentence of Article 11.5. * * *

4.   The Company has the right to refuse to authorize absences on either or part of either qualifying days for reasons other than those listed in Article 11.5. But once an absence is authorized then it must be construed as an excused absence under the Agreement. * * *

6.   Both parties agree that the grievant's request to be excused one-half hour early on the work day before the holiday was not for the purpose of stretching the holiday. His offer to make up the time by working during his lunch hour is simple evidence of good faith.

The Board of Arbitration is cognizant of the many hours which both parties have spent examining numerous clock cards, absenteeism reports, and office memos in search of exceptions to Company Exhibit 1. Our failure to comment in detail on the fruit of these labors is not due to a lack of appreciation for the work but rather to our conclusion that, regardless of what has been past practice, Article 11.5 clearly gives the Company the right to make exceptions to requirements for holiday pay and that where, as here, it excuses an employee on one of the required days, it must not deny him holiday pay.

Award

The grievance is sustained. Mr. Leroy A. DeJaynes must be paid holiday pay for December 24 and 25, 1968.

Dissenting Opinion

SPROWL, Company Arbitrator, Dissenting:—The decision of the majority is so patently contrary to the unequivocal language of the last sentence of Article 5 of the collective bargaining agreement and to the uniform application of that provision by the parties since its first incorporation into the contract in 1954 that I must record my vigorous dissent.

This provision of the contract required the grievant employee, DeJaynes, who was off because of illness the day after the Christmas 1968 holiday, to have worked the full work day prior to that holiday in order to qualify for holiday pay.

DeJaynes requested a pass to leave the plant one half hour early on the work day before this holiday, and was given such pass by his supervisor only after being warned that in leaving work early on that day he had not worked the full day as required in order to qualify for holiday pay; and consequently it was absolutely essential that he work the full day after the holiday, otherwise he would not receive any holiday pay.

DeJaynes accepted this risk and left the plant early, fully cognizant of the fact that if he did not work the full day after the Christmas holiday, he would lose his holiday pay.

Unfortunately, he was unable to report for work the day after the holiday because of illness.

The evidence is undisputed that the exception for "authorized" absences contained in the first sentence of Article 5 does not apply to and in practice has never been applied to employees on sick or accident leave or leaves of absence, such employees being treated of separately in the last sentence of Article 5. Be that as it may, however, in *view of the caveat* given DeJaynes at the time he asked for and received a pass to leave early the day before the holiday in question, the issuance of that pass can under no stretch of the imagination be construed to be an authorization of his absence, which would entitle him to holiday pay. Where an employee is warned that failure to work will disqualify him for holiday pay, holiday pay is consistently denied. See Goodyear Tire & Rubber Co., 44 LA 1212, and Morgan Bros. Laundry, 14 LA 201, 205.

Under the unambiguous language of the pertinent provisions of the contract and the uniform construction placed thereon by the parties in the fifteen years since its adoption in 1954, the Company was absolutely correct in denying holiday pay to DeJaynes.

Where, as here, such a clear-cut practice has been established over a period of years, there is no justification whatsoever for an arbitration panel to resort to rules of construction which are only available in the absence of such a prior practice.

It should also be noted that on five different occasions since 1954 the Union proposed in its negotiations with the Company that the holiday pay provision of the contract be changed to permit an employee in the circumstances in which DeJaynes found himself here, to receive holiday pay even though absent because of illness.

Not one of these proposals was incorporated into the agreement between the parties; yet the majority, by its decision, has accomplished for the Union what it was unable to achieve through negotiations.

Such a deliberate rewriting of a contract is beyond the powers of the arbitration panel and should not be condoned.

For the foregoing reasons, it is my opinion that the grievance should be denied.

Notes and Questions

1.   Arbitrator Kesselman seems to suggest that the only reason for the "surrounding day" requirement is to prevent employees from prolonging the holiday. Is it the *only* reason? Would an employee who turned up seven hours late on the day before the holiday or left seven hours early on the day after be entitled to holiday pay because he or she was not prolonging the holiday? Consider National Uniform Service, 104 LA 901 (Jerome A. Klein, 1995). The agreement required employees to "report for work" the day before a holiday. The arbitrator awarded holiday pay to employees who reported 30 and 42 minutes late the day before Thanksgiving because they were not trying to stretch the holiday. In the arbitral equivalent of dicta, however, he stated that an employee who reported nearly seven hours late would not be eligible for holiday pay because the contractual provision's meaning depends on "common sense" and "fundamental logic."

2.   *Outboard Marine*'s dissenting arbitrator Sprowl argued that the union failed in five negotiations to win holiday pay for employees on sick leave. If true, what relevance should that information have? What is the dissenting arbitrator's precise objection to the majority's decision? *Is* there a relationship between the "excuse" provision and the last sentence of Article 11.5?

3.   Suppose Article 11.5 in *Outboard Marine* said nothing about sick leave. Would an employee absent because of illness on the preceding or succeeding day be entitled to holiday pay? Would the absence be "authorized by the Company" if the collective agreement provided for paid sick leave? Before getting too generous with the employer's money, ask yourself what reason an absent employee is most likely to offer for missing the qualifying day. Of course there are other reasons, too. What would the result be if the employee missed work on the qualifying day because of: (a) a bereavement leave, as in Allis–Chalmers Corp., 60 LA 1296 (Harry Platt, 1973)? (b) a disciplinary suspension, as in Inmont Corp., 60 LA 1125 (Peter Kelliher, 1973)?

4.   What if the "surrounding day" occurs when the employee is not working because of (a) a layoff, as in Allis–Chalmers Corp., 72 LA 840 (Raymond Goetz, 1979)? (b) A strike, as in Kansas Bakery Employers' Labor Council, 54 LA 754 (Russell Bauder, 1970)? (c) A vacation? Is there some general principle that can address all these problems?

5.   One purpose of contractual holidays is to *offer* employees the chance to stay home for a day without losing pay. Another purpose, however, might be to *force* the employer to shut down so that no one need choose between leisure and extra pay. An employer's breach of a promise to shut down for a holiday raises a difficult remedial problem. In Kroger Co., 85 LA 1198 (Theodore St. Antoine, 1985), the contract required closings on December 25 and January 1. Nevertheless, Kroger opened for business on January 1, 1985. The union asked the arbitrator to order compensation of quadruple pay and a disgorgement of all profits earned that day. The arbitrator denied the request for quadruple pay:

> If a damage award to employees is not to be merely a penalty in disguise, there must be evidence of a measurable injury suffered by them, either individually or as a class. I do not mean that it would be

impossible to attach a dollar value to a January 1 with family and friends, perhaps watching a bowl game (I note that neither Michigan nor Michigan State appeared in a bowl game on January 1, 1985), but I do not find that such a showing was made here.

85 LA at 1203. He did order disgorgement of profits, though. Is disgorgement any less a penalty than a damage award? What should happen to the "disgorged" money? Rather than resolve that question himself, the arbitrator ordered that the funds "shall be disposed of by the Union in its capacity as the exclusive bargaining representative of the employees."

6.   Collective agreements frequently list the negotiated holidays by date or name, for example "July 4" or "Independence Day." What happens when the stated date or holiday falls on a Sunday and a federal or state proclamation defines Monday, July 5 as the date for the legal celebration of the holiday? The problem is contractual, not legal: the government proclamation does not entitle an employee to a holiday. Most arbitrators stick closely to the contract, holding that when the agreement designates a holiday, a substitute can be created only by mutual agreement. See, for example, Stein, Inc., 71 LA 124 (Jerome Klein, 1978).

7.   Note that all of the problems discussed in these notes could have been avoided by careful drafting. Why do parties not answer foreseeable questions during negotiations?

3.   VACATIONS[3]

Like holidays, paid vacations in the United States are almost exclusively a matter of bargaining or market pressure. Outside the construction industry, which typically provides only sporadic employment unsuitable for vacation arrangements, 99% of collective agreements provide for paid vacations. The length of an employee's vacation entitlement varies with length of service. The median length of required service is one year for one week of vacation, two years for two weeks, eight years for three weeks, 15 years for four weeks, 21 years for five weeks, and 28 years for six weeks. Of course not all employers provide that many weeks of vacation. Nevertheless, the trend toward longer vacations by senior employees was unmistakable at least through the middle 1990s. In 1971, only 22% of collective bargaining agreements provided for five weeks of vacation; by 1995, 60% did so. During the same period, the percentage of agreements providing for six weeks of vacation grew from 5% to 22%.[4] By European standards, this pattern is unbelievably stingy. In most of Western Europe, laws require a minimum of five weeks of vacation for *all* employees.

3. Bibliographic Suggestions: Roger I. Abrams and Dennis R. Nolan, *The Common Law of the Labor Agreement: Vacations*, 5 Industrial Relations Law Journal 603 (1983); Shyam Das, *Fringe Benefits*, The Common Law of the Workplace: The Views of Arbitrators (Theodore J. St. Antoine, ed., 1998), 306, 306–11; Sharon Henderson Ellis, *Vacations and Vacation Pay*, Chapter 31

of Labor and Employment Arbitration (Tim Bornstein, Ann Gosline, and Marc Greenbaum, eds., 2d ed. 1997); Arnold M. Zack and Richard I. Bloch, Labor Agreement in Negotiation and Arbitration 283–89 (2d Ed. 1995).

4. Basic Patterns, *supra* footnote 2, at 101–10.

Vacation clauses typically impose two requirements for vacation pay: a length of service requirement (usually one year to qualify for any vacation) and a work requirement of a certain number of hours worked in a certain period (usually half or more of a standard year's hours). Most also require that the applicant be an "available" employee at the time of the vacation sought.

Grievances over vacation rights take three main forms: disputes over the scheduling of vacations (who decides, and how?); disputes over eligibility for vacations or vacation pay; and disputes over the computation of vacation pay (is the three weeks' pay, for example, to mean three weeks at the straight time rate, or does it include the shift differential, the dangerous work premium, and the overtime the employee would have worked?).

REICHOLD CHEMICALS, INC.
66 LA 745 (Paul D. Jackson, 1976).*

BACKGROUND

The collective bargaining agreement between the parties terminated March 31, 1975. Negotiations for a new contract proving unsuccessful, the Union struck from June 10, 1975 until September 2, 1975. The strike was ended by a new agreement effective April 1, 1975. A settlement agreement concluding the strike was entered into September 3, 1975.

On September 4, 1975, the employer published on its bulletin board the following:

Note

There have been some inquiries as to exactly what the vacation policy is for 1975. Here is what has been decided:

For those with 15 years or more of service, you are allowed 120 hours vacation in the remainder of 1975.

For those with 9 years or more, you are allowed 90 hours.

For those with more than one year, you are allowed 60 hours.

Your supervisor will begin to schedule vacations as soon as he has all the information needed from you as to time preferences.

The effect of this notice was to reduce all vacations by one-fourth, on the basis that the strike lasted for one-quarter of the year. * * * [The union filed unfair labor practice charges, which the Board deferred to arbitration pursuant to its *Collyer Insulated Wire* doctrine.]

THE ISSUES

Shortly after the strike settlement the union raised three grievances of which only one is involved in this arbitration. In Item No. 3 of its letter of September 8, 1975 to the employer, the union referred to the notice on the bulletin board as an unprecedented prorating of vacations. * * *

Since the parties have agreed that the issues to be decided are to be selected by me, I will dispose of this question. First, with regard to the problem created by the proration of vacation benefits for the strike period, in order properly to dispose of this question, it is necessary to take into account the different periods of time involved, the time in which vacations became fully earned and also the time in which vacations must be taken, whether in 1975 or thereafter, all in reference to the strike period. * * *

FINDINGS AND CONCLUSIONS

Wages are paid for services rendered by the employee to his employer. Unless there is an overriding agreement, a statute or a principle of law, the withholding of services ordinarily justifies the withholding of wages.

Vacations are recognized as a form of deferred wages.

It is the primary function of the arbitrator to resolve disputes by endeavoring to ascertain the intent of the parties from the language of the collective bargaining agreement. The Union is right as the employer acknowledged at the hearing that the bulletin notice of September 4, 1975 was partly incorrect because it failed to take into account the situation of those employees who had already completed their necessary qualifying service for vacations prior to the commencement of the strike. The employer has stated that it will rectify this error and pay the vacation benefits to those employees thus qualified. This acknowledgment will be recognized by the award. The question remains however whether or not the employer is entitled, in the next vacation year, to deduct from the vacation benefits of each employee one-fourth thereof based upon the length of the strike which was a work period of three months or one-fourth of a calendar year. The further question remains as to proration of vacation benefits of employees who had not completed their qualifying year at the time of the strike.

Article XIV, Vacations, provides that employees "after the completion of one (1) year's service shall be granted two (2) weeks' vacation with pay, said vacation to be taken within six months after the anniversary of completion of one year's service." The article then goes on to provide for longer vacations for those with longer periods of service. The union seeks to equate the vacation article and its "service" language with Article IV, Seniority, which provides that "seniority shall be the length of service accumulated by a fulltime employee from the day of his original employment * * * "and further provides that "accumulation of service" can only be broken under certain conditions and in certain situations, none of which include a strike. Since seniority cannot be broken, (that is to say, the *"accumulation of service"*) by a strike, the *"completion of one year's service"* as provided in Article XIV also cannot be considered as having been broken by a strike and the vacation qualifying time should be accumulated and credited for the entire period of the strike according to the union. This would mean, following the argument to its logical conclusion, that for every year a strike continued an employee should receive a paid vacation.

Article XIV is intended to provide vacation benefits for employees who perform work for the company and who complete a minimum amount of work (service) within an anniversary year calculated from the date of first employment, which, coincidentally, is also the date from which calculations are made for the purpose of seniority. [Article XIV, Paragraph (2) provided that an employee would not receive credit toward vacation pay for time spent on a layoff.] It makes little sense to enforce Paragraph (2) of Article XIV authorizing the employer to prorate vacation benefits in the event of involuntary lay-off of the employee but not to allow proration of vacation for not working during a strike. Use of the word "service" in Article XIV, in my opinion means service rendered, that is to say, "*worked*." This is recognized indirectly in Paragraph (2) of Article XIV, which, in referring to proration of vacation pay, refers to proration "at one (1) day for each month *worked*."

Where the parties wish to refer specifically to the employee's employment relationship with the company (service) as distinguished from service rendered (working time) they demonstrate an awareness and ability to do so. Thus in Paragraph (2) of Article XIV which is concerned with the employer's right to prorate vacation pay in case of lay-off, death, or termination for any cause, the parties use the words "provided he had *completed* one year of employment."

In the absence of any specific indication in the written agreement that the parties wished to give vacation credit for strike time, adherence to the general [principle] that vacation pay is a form of wages payable when earned and earned when worked, is a reasonable conclusion. In making this determination, some consideration is given to the fact that in a previous situation following a strike, the parties specifically negotiated and agreed upon the granting of vacation credit for strike time. This is a circumstance that the union should have been aware of at the conclusion of the strike in 1975. More importantly, it is clear evidence of the fact that the parties recognized that the contract, which is identical now to the former one in this regard, did not specifically cover this problem or provide for it and that a special agreement was needed to justify payment for the strike time.

Award

The right of the employer to prorate employee vacation benefits in 1975 for absences due to striking is sustained and the grievances are denied with the caveat that employees who fulfilled their qualifying vacation requirements for the year 1975 prior to the commencement of the strike shall not have their vacation prorated in 1975, but the period covered by the strike may be prorated for the purposes of calculating vacations in the following anniversary year. No coercion or discrimination is found to have been intended since the employer's interpretation and application of the collective bargaining agreement and relevant law was correct. The parties shall share equally in the costs and expenses of this arbitration.

Notes and Questions

1. Why did the union think that employees were entitled to vacation credit for time spent on strike? Is the union's argument as absurd as Arbitrator Jackson makes it out to be? Do you think, for example, that the union's argument leads to the "logical conclusion, that for every year a strike continued an employee should receive a paid vacation?" If not, where would you draw the line?

2. Many of the most common vacation eligibility disputes parallel those over eligibility for holidays. What happens, for example, if an employee missed the requisite number of hours worked because of a sick leave or layoff rather than a strike? Should the employee receive the full vacation pay, no vacation pay, or *pro rata* vacation pay? One frequent key to this range of disputes is the assertion that vacation pay is simply a form of deferred compensation. Thus one earns vacation pay only when one works — and that would not include time spent on leave, layoff, or strike. See, *e.g.*, Frye Copysystems, Inc., 65 LA 1249 (Sol Yarowsky, 1975). Of course the parties can change that presumption in their contract or in their practices. See Fabick Machinery Co., 104 LA 555 (Mark Suardi, 1995).

3. *Disputes Over Vacation Scheduling*

(a) Agreements frequently provide that employees may select vacation times by seniority, usually with some limitations to protect the employer's ability to carry on its work. Suppose an employer denies the employee's requested vacation dates and unilaterally substitutes a different period. If the plant is to be shut down for lack of work in February, for example, an employer might order all employees to take their vacations in February and thus eliminate some staffing problems during the rest of the year. The problem is that not every employee will relish a February vacation. Arbitrators uniformly recognize that employers have wide discretion in managing the operation unless limited by the contract. If the employer's reason is insufficient, however, an arbitrator will sustain the grievance. The Abrams and Nolan article cited in footnote 3 discusses this range of issues, but one early case deserves brief quotation.

Harry Shulman, the distinguished Permanent Umpire at Ford Motor Company, held that employees could refuse to take their vacations during an indefinite layoff because a "vacation" during a layoff was not a vacation at all:

> A vacation is a period of rest between periods of work. A layoff is a period of anxiety and hardship between periods of work. The tremendous difference lies in the assurance of the vacationer that he will return to work at the end of his vacation and the equal assurance of the employee on layoff that he does not know when he will return to work. The basic difference, with its financial, emotional, and psychological

implications, is not obliterated by a form of words or by the receipt of income for a part of the indefinite period of layoff.

Ford Motor Co., 3 LA 829, 831 (1946). Are you persuaded by Shulman? Isn't the real difference between a vacation and a layoff that the former is paid?

(b) What remedy should the successful scheduling-dispute grievant receive? An extra week's vacation? Extra pay in lieu of vacation? Wouldn't either of those remedies over-compensate the grievant? Or should the arbitrator try to evaluate the worth of a vacation at the desired time (the first week in June, say) versus one at the ordered time (the second week in February, for example) and award the difference? A few arbitrators have tried to make such calculations but Arbitrator Ralph Seward admitted that he could not "assign a monetary value to grievants' mental discomfort" and settled for putting the company on notice that future violations might result in "either a further vacation on the proper dates or pay-in-lieu thereof." Bethlehem Steel Co., 31 LA 857, 858 (1958). Consider again Arbitrator St. Antoine's remarks about holiday pay in Kroger Co., 85 LA 1198, 1203 (1985), quoted in endnote 5 after *Outboard Marine*.

(c) How much discretion does an employer have when dealing with employee requests for vacations? For example, may it deny last-minute vacation requests by employees with excessive sick leave usage while granting such requests by employees with good attendance records? See Cuyahoga Falls Board of Education, 114 LA 1565 (Tobie Braverman, 2000): "An employee who uses substantial sick leave, triggering a chain of events involving difficult to find substitutes on a too frequent basis, should not expect the same degree of accommodation for last minute vacation leave requests as an employee who regularly reports for work and uses sick leave with its concomitant building operation disruptions less regularly." Do you see anything wrong with using vacation scheduling as an incentive to minimize sick leave usage?

4. This case—indeed, almost every case in this chapter—forced the arbitrator to decide how to go about interpreting the parties' agreement. Faced with contractual silence or ambiguous language, how should an arbitrator decide what the parties intended? Can they even be said to have "intended" anything when the contract gives no indication they even considered the issue? One simple answer would be to deny all grievances not founded on a clear contractual provision, but that would deprive many parties of their legitimate expectations and would demand too much of labor negotiators. (Because unions bear the burden of proof in contractual grievances, it would also give employers the benefit of every omission or ambiguity.) How then should a conscientious arbitrator resolve an interpretive dispute?

Like judges, arbitrators have several helpful canons of interpretation: give words their normal meanings absent any indication of a contrary intent; interpret questionable provisions as consistent with law rather than as inconsistent; construe documents as a whole, to harmonize provisions and give effect to all clauses; avoid forfeitures and harsh or absurd results; give specific language greater weight than general language; view provisions in light of their context, their negotiation background, and the parties' and industry's practices; resolve intractable ambiguities against the drafter; and so on, *ad infinitum*. The problem with such guidelines is that they are too general to solve many specific cases. Moreover, interpretive guideposts do not always point in the same direction. For good discussions of these issues, see Elkouri and Elkouri, How Arbitration Works 427–84 (Alan Miles Rubin, Editor-in-Chief, 6th ed. 2003) and Marvin F. Hill, Jr. and Anthony V. Sinicropi, Evidence in Arbitration 346–66 (2d ed. 1987).

4. LEAVES OF ABSENCE[5]

Unless limited by the agreement, management has the right to grant, withhold, or condition leaves of absence. Almost all agreements have some leave provisions, including funeral leave (86% of the contracts in one sample), personal leave (76%), union business leave (78%), and paid and unpaid sick leave (31% and 50%, respectively).[6] A well-drafted leave provision will specify the requirements for leave, the length of leave, and the effect of the leave on pay, vacations, holidays, insurance, and seniority. Unfortunately, few leave provisions are so thorough. Because of the diversity of topics and requirements, the range of potential problems is almost infinite.

(a) Medical or Sick Leave[7]

Sick-leave abuse is a constant worry for employers. Arbitrators recognize that employers may impose reasonable rules to prevent abuse, but what is "reasonable?" At the very least, employers may require medical investigations and documentation of frequent or extended absences due to claimed illnesses or injuries. As Arbitrator Ralph Neas concluded in Hormel Fine Frozen Foods, 75 LA 1129, 1141 (1980),

> Although there may not be an abuse of its discretion in such matters and absent any contractual restrictions, the Company has the right to require proof of illness in order to avoid fraud, invalid claims or other abuses of the system. Such rights include the privilege of requiring a doctor's certification, questioning the claimant and the attending physician, requiring submission of additional medical documentation, and to generally conduct a thorough investigation of any questionable claim when there is reasonable cause.

Resolving disputes over the existence or magnitude of a medical problem then becomes an evidentiary problem.

5. See generally, Andria S. Knapp, *Leaves of Absence*, Chapter 30 of Labor and Employment Arbitration (Tim Bornstein, Ann Gosline, and Marc Greenbaum, eds., 2d ed. 2002). See also Arnold M. Zack and Richard I. Bloch, Labor Agreement in Negotiation and Arbitration 289–301 (2d ed. 1995).

6. Basic Patterns, *supra* footnote 2, at 71–77.

7. Bibliographic Suggestions: Joan G. Dolan, *Arbitration of Health–Related Issues, With Special Reference to the ADA*, 47 Pro-

ceedings of the National Academy of Arbitrators 42 (1994); Harvey A. Nathan and Lisa Salkovitz Kohn, *Sickness, Accident, and Health Benefits*, Chapter 35 of Labor and Employment Arbitration (Tim Bornstein, Ann Gosline, and Marc Greenbaum, eds., 2d ed. 1998); and Arnold M. Zack and Richard I. Bloch, The Labor Agreement in Negotiation and Arbitration 272–301 (2d ed. 1983). The first two deal not only with sick leave, but also with other forms of contractual benefits triggered by accident or illness such as medical insurance.

Does Arbitrator Neas's formulation trouble you? Should your employer have the rights to demand documentation and to question your doctor every time you call in sick? Even if you are just absent a day because of a cold? Wouldn't forcing you to get a doctor's excuse for every absence be a misuse of scarce medical resources? If the employer could not demand proof of claimed illness, however, how can the employer assure that you are not just taking an unauthorized paid vacation at the employer's expense? Some employees have responded to employers' demands for medical documentation by entering the "market" for false or forged excuses. Doctors have been known to write excuses even without proof of illness, but more commonly a staff member will do so, perhaps for a small charge.

Abuse of sick leave is a perennial reason for discharge. Before concluding that the employee abused sick leave, however, the employer had better be sure of its evidence. Consider the situation presented in Universal Frozen Foods, 103 LA 238 (Katrina I. Boedecker, 1994). The grievant had taken sick leave because of an asserted back injury. The employer fired him after reviewing video tapes showing him walking normally, working on a car, and loading and unloading a pickup truck. It turned out, however, that the employee had planned to return to work after securing a doctor's release during an appointment that was scheduled shortly after the video tapes were taken but was reinjured in an automobile accident a day before his appointment. As a result, he was still unable to work at the time the employer fired him. The arbitrator therefore ordered his reinstatement.

Most employers do not question their professional and managerial employees' claims to sick leave. Why then do they doubt their clerical and manufacturing employees? Is it simple class bias? Or are there solid reasons why some types of employees are less likely than others to cheat on medical leave?

Occasionally arbitrators see the reverse problem—the employer forcing an unwilling employee into a medical leave. This is most common when the employer fears the employee may have psychological problems that could interfere with work or endanger other employees. In light of recent incidents of workplace violence, those concerns are more common and more reasonable than ever before. Mandatory sick leave pending a medical examination is generally legitimate, provided the employer has adequate reasons. See Reckitt & Colman, Inc., 108 LA 726 (John R. Thornell, 1997) (mandatory medical leave for a troubled employee was appropriate where the contract allowed the employer to relieve employees for lack of work or "other legitimate reasons"). If the employer acts without sufficient reason, however, it will be liable to the employee for the resulting economic harm. Boces, First Supervisory District, Erie County, New York, 82 LA 1269 (Irving H. Sabghir, 1984) (school district erred in placing a teacher on leave, because the district's doctor was not board certified in psychiatry and the teacher's doctor did not recommend psychiatric evaluation; the leave became proper only after a psychiatrist recommended against her return to work).

Workers usually accumulate sick leave each month. The collective bargaining agreement normally specifies how much leave they may accumulate. Without careful drafting, however, those provisions may give rise to other disputes. In Huntleigh Transportation Services, 101 LA 784 (Charles J. Marino, 1993), the contract limited accrual to "22 sick days." Most employees worked five traditional eight-hour shifts per week, so they could accumulate 176 hours of leave. One employee who worked four ten-hour shifts each week argued that she should be able to accumulate 220 hours. The arbitrator rejected her claim, holding that all benefits were based on a normal 40–hour work week; that meant that the parties' expectation was for a maximum of 176 hours.

A NOTE ON THE IMPACT OF FEDERAL STATUTES ON SICK LEAVE RULES

Before 1990, sick leave benefits were almost exclusively a matter of contract. Since then, Congress passed two statutes that bar employers from taking some actions and require employers to take others when faced with an injured or ill employee (or, in some cases, with an injured or ill member of an employee's family). Indeed, sick leave, family care leave, and parental leave are now governed as much by federal law as by contract.

The first important federal statute was the Americans with Disabilities Act (ADA) of 1990, 42 U.S.C. § 12101 *et seq*. The ADA does not deal expressly with sick leave, but it does prohibit discrimination against "qualified individuals with a disability." It also requires employers to provide reasonable accommodations to employees whose disability prevents them from performing their regular jobs. Because some disabilities can interfere with regular attendance, the ADA may supersede contractual sick-leave rules. The term "may" is important, because regular attendance may be an essential function of the job; if so, an employee who cannot meet that standard would not be "qualified" under the ADA and would therefore not be entitled to an accommodation.

The second law to affect sick-leave rules was the Family and Medical Leave Act (FMLA) of 1993, 29 U.S.C. § 2601 *et seq*. The FMLA guarantees covered employees up to 12 weeks of unpaid leave within any 12–month period if they cannot work because of a serious medical condition (or because of the need to care for a family member with a serious medical condition). The leave need not be consecutive and can even be used to cover sporadic absences. In short, the employer may not deny leave or otherwise punish an employee who satisfies FMLA requirements, no matter how restrictive the contractual sick-leave provision might be.

The details of these laws are beyond the scope of this book. For a concise but thorough discussion of the issues, see Robert B. Gordon and Christopher L. Ekman, *Attendance Control Issues Under the ADA and FMLA*, 13 The Labor Lawyer 393 (1997). And for several examples of how arbitrators have dealt with such questions, see Notes on Current Issues of External Law in Section V.B. of this book.

(b) Funeral or Bereavement Leave

Funeral and bereavement leave provisions are a fruitful source of grievances. Decisions often turn on small differences in wording. For example, if the leave clause refers to the "funeral" rather than to "bereavement," the employee might be entitled to leave *only* for the time necessary to attend the funeral, and not for time spent grieving, comforting other bereaved family members, or administering the deceased's estate. See, for example, Penn Emblem Co., 101 LA 884 (Lloyd L. Byars, 1993) (where the contract provided three days of leave "to attend the funeral," only employees who actually attended the funeral were entitled to leave; those who attended were to get three full days of leave, however, because the agreement did not specify "up to" three days). A company may even require verification from the funeral home that the employee attended the funeral. Amax Zinc Co., Inc., 67 LA 536 (Robert Penfield, 1976). On the other hand, arbitrators have broadly defined the types of personal relationships justifying the leave, *e.g.*, Foremost Dairies, Inc., 43 LA 616 (James Greenwald, 1964) (the contractual term "brother" includes a step-brother); Georgia–Pacific Corp., 63 LA 163 (Gerald Cohen, 1974) ("close relatives" include those close by "affinity" as well as "consanguinity").

(c) *Union Business Leave*

Employers are understandably suspicious of employees' requests for leaves of absence for union business. (Their suspicion increases when the request is for *paid* leave, as some contracts provide for time spent investigating and processing grievances.) They sometimes challenge the reasonableness of such leave requests. When they do, employees often and understandably refuse to specify just what they intend to do while on union business leave.

When the employer does learn the purpose, it may react with horror. Why, the employer might wonder, should I assist the employee to plan a strike against me, Consolidation Coal Co., 83 LA 992 (Marvin Feldman, 1984), negotiate a contract at a competitor's plant, Hurd Millwork Corp., 58 LA 253 (Clark Hazelwood, 1972), or work for political causes, Consolidation Coal Co., 84 LA 1042 (Marvin Feldman, 1985)? The most common arbitral answer is that "union activity" is a general term suitable for broad interpretation. (Prudent arbitrators are not likely to offer the more obvious answer: "Because you were foolish enough to agree to that clause.") As Arbitrator Feldman put it in the 1985 *Consolidation Coal* case,

> Union activities mean union activities. They do not mean some, those that are liked, those that involve non-political activity, but rather it means *all* union activity. To hold otherwise would be to change the terms of the contract * * * [emphasis in original].

84 LA at 1044. If the employer wants to limit the use of union leave, it should do so in negotiations. Even then, the employer should enforce the limitation consistently. See Motor Wheel Corp., 102 LA 922 (Gerald B. Chattman, 1994).

5. INSURANCE

As health care costs have risen dramatically over the last decades, more and more unions have fought to obtain, increase, or at least preserve health insurance benefits. For the same reason, employers have struggled to shift more of the burden of medical costs onto employees' shoulders, for example by limiting some coverages and increasing deductibles and co-payments. Most of these issues are hammered out in negotiations. In several recent and well-publicized disputes, employers have won only part of the insurance concessions they initially sought, but those union victories tend to be accompanied by much lower wage increases that one would have expected. In effect, unions are spending more of their bargaining chips for health care than for wages or other benefits. In the public sector, they often take their demands to interest arbitration, e.g., School District of Cumberland, 115 LA 916 (Gil Vernon, 2000), and Town of Union City, 117 LA 1544 (Ann Holman Woolf, 2002).

While plan details may be resolved in negotiations, their implementation often provokes grievances. Collective bargaining agreements seldom get down to the level of specificity needed to determine exactly what treatment an ill employee may obtain or which drugs the doctor may prescribe, yet group health plans routinely adopt rules on such matters. Suppose an employer who has negotiated a health insurance requirement with the union representing its employees chooses a new plan administrator. So long as the plan remains the same, the union shouldn't care who administers it, right? And yet those changes often result in grievances. A recent example is provided by School Board of Miami, 118 LA 1742 (Nicholas Duda, Jr., 2003). After negotiating the health insurance provision the employer selected a new carrier that was more expensive for employees. The arbitrator found that the employer violated the contract both by failing to negotiate with the union before the change and by imposing extra costs on the employees. He ordered the School Board to compensate employees for their losses.

Less frequently, life insurance provisions end up in arbitration. Arbitrator Russell C. Neas dealt with that issue in Muzak LLC Dallas, 116 LA 945 (2001). The parties to a first collective bargaining agreement discussed retention of the existing life insurance benefit but did not incorporate anything about it in the contract. Shortly after ratification of the contract, the company stopped paying for life insurance. At the arbitration the union argued that the parties had verbally agreed to continue the program while the company denied making such an agreement. Arbitrator Neas found it more likely than not that there was such an agreement because the employees had given the union a mandate to preserve the plan, the union would not likely let the plan expire by default, and the probability of the union negotiating retention is much greater than the probability of the company taking it back.

H. SUBCONTRACTING

1. INTRODUCTION[1]

"Subcontracting" has many meanings in the labor relations context. At its narrowest, the term refers to an employer's use of another company to perform the employer's usual work at its usual location. At its broadest, it refers to any decision to purchase products or services that the employer's own employees could make or do. "Subcontracting" is virtually synonymous with the older term, "contracting-out," and it encompasses the newer term, "outsourcing," or buying goods or services from outside suppliers. It is similar to, and raises similar problems as, transfer of work to another facility or to employees outside the bargaining unit; collective bargaining agreements and arbitrators therefore often treat the issues as subject to the same principles. See John Burroughs, *The Bases and Limits of Arbitral Decision-making in Plant Relocation and Transfer of Work Disputes*, 7 Industrial Relations Law Journal 362, 371–72 (1985).

For employers, the critical issues in subcontracting cases are efficiency and cost. Often another firm can provide better goods or services, or provide them more cheaply or more quickly. Unions and employees on the other hand, worry about job security (subcontracting might result in layoffs or a smaller bargaining unit), about contractual security (subcontracting may undermine the substantive provisions of the collective bargaining agreement), and about power (subcontracting might reduce the union's bargaining leverage).

At least some types of subcontracting are mandatory subjects of bargaining, according to the Supreme Court's decision in Fibreboard Paper Products Corp. v. NLRB, 379 U.S. 203, 85 S.Ct. 398, 13 L.Ed.2d 233 (1964). That case involved the most blatant form of subcontracting. In the Court's terms, the issue was "the replacement of employees in the existing bargaining unit with those of an independent contractor to do the same work under similar conditions of employment." The Court was careful to state that its decision did not "encompass other forms of

---

1. Bibliographic Suggestions: Roger I. Abrams and Dennis R. Nolan, *Subcontracting Disputes in Labor Arbitration: Productive Efficiency Versus Job Security*, 15 University of Toledo Law Review 7 (1983); Donald Crawford, *The Arbitration of Disputes Over Subcontracting*, 13 Proceedings of the National Academy of Arbitrators 51 (1960); G. Allan Dash, Jr., *The Arbitration of Subcontracting Disputes*, 16 Industrial and Labor Relations Review 208 (1962–63); Marcia Greenbaum, *The Arbitration of Subcontracting Disputes: An Addendum*, 16 Industrial and Labor Relations Review 221 (1962–63); James Gross, *Value Judgments in the Decisions of Labor Arbitrators*, 21 Industrial and Labor Relations Review 55 (1967–68); Edwin H. Jacobs, *Subcontracting Arbitration: How the Issues are Decided*, 21 Cleveland State Law Review 162 (1972); Marlisse McCammon & John L. Cotton, *Arbitration Decisions in Subcontracting Disputes*, 29 Industrial Relations 135 (1990); Russell Smith, *Subcontracting and Union–Management Legal and Contractual Relations*, 17 Western Reserve Law Review 1272 (1966); *Subcontracting in the 1990s*, 49 Proceedings of the National Academy of Arbitrators 201–35 (1996); and Steven M. Wolf, *Subcontracting*, Chapter 25 of Labor and Employment Arbitration (Tim Bornstein, Ann Gosline, and Marc Greenbaum, eds., 2d ed. 2000).

'contracting out' or 'subcontracting' which arise daily in our complex economy." Thus employers need not bargain about many types of subcontracting: neither about subcontracting that involves a major decision going to the core of entrepreneurial control (to use Justice Stewart's term from his *Fibreboard* concurrence), nor about the routine decisions of an employer to buy its light bulbs and note pads rather than make them.

Subcontracting disputes come to arbitration in one of two ways. Some involve an express contractual provision on subcontracting. Others involve a union's claim that the collective agreement impliedly limits the employer's power to subcontract. The former cases are usually the easier to resolve.

2. CONTRACTUAL PROVISIONS ON SUBCONTRACTING

Negotiators often include subcontracting rights or restrictions in the collective bargaining agreement. The most recent study found subcontracting mentioned in 55% of the sample contracts. Bureau of National Affairs, Basic Patterns in Union Contracts 80 (14th ed. 1995). Subcontracting provisions vary widely, although the extremes (unqualified rights to subcontract and unqualified prohibitions on the practice) are very rare. Between the extremes, and in differing degrees of severity, subcontracting clauses may require advance notice to the union; require discussion with the union before a subcontracting decision; permit only "reasonable" subcontracting; forbid subcontracting if qualified employees are on layoff or would be laid off because of the subcontracting; or permit subcontracting only in specified circumstances (*e.g.*, emergencies, or where employees are unavailable or unqualified, or where the employer lacks the necessary facilities or tools).

In the BNA survey, 49% of the subcontracting clauses required advance notice or discussion; 31% forbade subcontracting in layoff situations; and 39% permitted subcontracting only if the employees lacked the necessary skills or equipment. Twenty-four percent required that any subcontracting follow contractual standards, and 15% required it to follow past practice.

Even clear contractual provisions can lead to arbitrable disputes. In a comprehensive paper on the subject, Arbitrator Donald Crawford raised some of the major questions, which we paraphrase here:

(a) What is "normal or regular bargaining unit work?" Is work of the sort performed by outside contractors before the contract was signed included under the definition of "work normally performed by the unit employees?" Is work involving the construction of new facilities "production and maintenance work?"

(b) What is "reasonable effort?" What is "possible?"

(c) Is the employer prohibited from contracting out work when bargaining unit employees are already working overtime?

(d) Did the contracting out result in the reduction or lay-off of a unit employee?

See Crawford, *supra* footnote 1, at 52–53.

FAIRMONT GENERAL HOSPITAL, INC.
105 LA 247 (Irwin J. Dean, Jr., 1995).*

Background

The Employer operates a hospital in Fairmont, West Virginia. Certain of its non-professional staff, including employees in the Medical Records Department, are members of a bargaining unit which is represented by the Union. The parties agree that the instant dispute involves the proper interpretation of provisions of the collective bargaining agreement relating to subcontracting of work that could be completed by employees at the Hospital. * * *

The facts underlying this grievance are not materially in dispute. In about July, 1993, the Employer discovered that an approximately six (6) month backlog of work had arisen in its Medical Records department. The Medical Records transcriptionists transcribe daily dictation performed by physicians as they render patient care. Such reports include admissions summaries [and] discharge summaries as well as post-operative records. The Employer observes that the six (6) month backlog in transcription had generated repeated complaints from physicians and that it did not comply with standards of the Joint Commission on Hospital Accreditation which mandated that post-operative reports be transcribed within twenty-four (24) to forty-eight (48) hours and that discharge summaries be completed within fifteen (15) days of a patient's leaving the hospital. Because the transcribed information is part of a patient's medical history and often required where a patient is readmitted to hospital confinement, the backlog disrupted the orderly operations of the Medical Records Department. Where patients were readmitted, physicians would require immediate transcription of prior records, necessitating that the dictation tapes would have to be located and transcribed immediately.

The Employer recognized that it would face a review by the Joint Commission on Hospital Accreditation in late August, 1993. Because discovery of the significant transcription backlog might jeopardize its continued accreditation, the Employer sought estimates from a subcontractor in an effort to relieve its backlog. The subcontractor indicated that it could provide this service and that the Employer could expect a forty-eight (48) hour turn around on tapes submitted to it for transcription. Pursuant to the terms of the parties' agreement, the Employer's desire to subcontract the delayed transcription was discussed with the Union on August 2, 1993. At that meeting, the Employer estimated that it had approximately ninety (90) overdue transcription tapes comprising 1,377.5 minutes of dictation. In response to the Employer's indication that it intended to subcontract this work, the Union responded that it believed that bargaining unit personnel could, if worked on an overtime basis, complete the work within the three (3) week deadline prior to the arrival of the Joint Commission representatives.

The Union estimated that the backlog could be cleared within the requisite time if each of the nine (9) transcriptionists employed in the Medical Records Department worked an additional 2.36 shifts, or 18.9 hours. The Employer responded that although the transcriptionists had incurred 2,400 overtime hours during the past eighteen (18) months, a significant backlog still remained. The Employer submitted that it did not feel that the bargaining unit could complete the work within the time limitations even were the bargaining unit members assigned to overtime. The Union also raised concerns at the meeting that the outside subcontractor would not produce as error-free a work product as bargaining unit members could produce. The Employer acknowledged these Union concerns by indicating it would have the transcription done in multiple batches so that they could be reviewed for accuracy.

Although the employer initially estimated the backlog at 1,377.5 minutes of dictation, ultimately a total of 2,257 minutes was subcontracted. Maintaining that at their then existing productivity level bargaining unit employees could have completed the work if each employee had been assigned an additional ten (10) hours of overtime work per week, the Union filed this grievance contending that the decision to subcontract was improper. The Employer has denied this grievance, contending that the contract requires it only to meet and discuss subcontracting decisions with the Union and does not require Union consent or agreement before bargaining unit work may be contracted out. The parties were unable to resolve their dispute through the preliminary stages of the grievance procedure set forth in the collective bargaining agreement, and the matter has accordingly been referred to this Arbitrator for full, final and binding resolution. * * *

ISSUE

Did the Employer violate the provisions of the collective bargaining agreement in effect between the parties when it subcontracted transcription work customarily performed by employees of the Medical Records Department? If so, what shall the appropriate remedy be?

PERTINENT CONTRACT PROVISIONS

* * *

Article XXVII. Subcontracting—Work Preservation

It is the Hospital's intention to use its own bargaining unit employees when it is reasonable and practical to perform bargaining unit work within the Hospital. In accordance with the above, the Hospital, from time to time, may determine it desirable to contract out such work. To assure the interests of the Union and employees are considered in reaching such contracting-out decisions, the parties agree to the following:

Section A.   A Contracting–Out–Committee shall be established and shall consist of six (6) persons. One-half (½) of the Committee shall consist of two (2) employees and one (1) union officer from the affected department and the other half shall be designated by the Hospital.

Section B.   The Committee shall attempt to resolve problems in connection with the operations, application, and administration of this contracting-out provision.

Section C.   Before the Hospital decides to contract out work which comes within the scope of this Article, the committee will meet and discuss the effects and reasons for the subcontracting.

Section D.   It is the intent of the parties that the members of the Contracting–Out–Committee shall engage in a discussion of the problems involved in a good faith effort to arrive at mutual understandings so that disputes and complaints can be avoided. * * *

DISCUSSION

At issue in this proceeding is whether the Employer has violated the provisions of the collective bargaining agreement by subcontracting work which the Union argues should have been performed by the transcriptionists in the Medical Records Department. Both parties agree that the facts are not materially disputed and that the only question which the Arbitrator must decide is the scope of the collective bargaining agreement's restrictions on subcontracting. The Employer insists that the only restriction on its right to subcontract bargaining unit work is its compliance with the meet and discuss requirements of Article XXVII. Under that provision, so long as the Employer informs the Union in advance of the possibility of subcontracting and considers in good faith any alternative recommendations which the Union may offer to preserve the work for the bargaining unit, it has complied with the agreement.

The Union counters that a fair reading of Article XXVII limits the Employer's right to subcontract to those instances in which the parties are able to reach some mutual agreement that the subcontracting is necessary or desirable. Under the Union's construction of Article XXVII, the Employer must justify subcontracting by identifying specific factors such as the lack of sufficient expertise among bargaining unit personnel to complete a job within necessary time restrictions. In such instances, the parties have reached agreement to divide the work between the bargaining unit and subcontractors according to their respective abilities to perform each component of the work.

In this case, the Employer does not dispute that bargaining unit personnel were capable of performing the transcription work in question, but contends that its decision to subcontract was reasonable given the extent of the backlog and the short period of time in which it was required to resolve the backlog prior to the Joint Commission inspection. The Union submits that because this work is concededly within the capabilities of the bargaining unit, its agreement was required prior to subcontracting inasmuch as the subcontracting provisions expressly require the Employer to maximize the utilization of bargaining unit employees.

After carefully considering the evidence and able arguments advanced by each of the parties, the Arbitrator is unable to agree with the Union that its prior consent is required in all instances in which the Employer may desire to subcontract bargaining unit work. As the Employer correctly observes, the provision in question requires only that the Employer meet and discuss with the Union prior to subcontracting.

The constraints placed upon the Employer under the work preservation provisions contained in Article XXVII of the agreement are twofold: First, the Employer must utilize bargaining unit personnel to perform bargaining unit work whenever allocation of such work within the bargaining unit is reasonable and practical. Secondly, before any final decision to contract out bargaining unit work is made, the matter must be submitted to the bilateral Contracting–Out–Committee for discussion. There is no requirement stated under Article XXVII, or any other provision of the contract, which renders a subcontracting action contingent upon Union approval.

Article XXVII reserves to management final authority over the decision of whether or not to contract out bargaining unit work; Union consent to contract out such work is not a prerequisite to a valid subcontracting action. The prerequisite which is established by the agreement, that is, that the Contracting–Out–Committee meet and discuss the effects of, and reasons for the subcontracting, is a device for ensuring that management's decision to subcontract any particular item of bargaining unit work is a well-considered one. The meet-and-discuss requirement of Article XXVII serves, in part, to ensure that the Employer has explored reasonable, practical alternatives to enlisting subcontractors before it arrives at a final determination on whether or not work will be contracted out. The function of a meet-and-discuss prerequisite to subcontracting is well stated in Inland–Rome, Inc., 93 LA (BNA) 666 (Williams, 1989), a decision cited by the Employer:

> The only reason for having such language would have to be to require the Company to justify, give reasons, and/or analyze the desire or the decision of the Company to contract specified work. * * * [W]hile the language per se implies an agreement might result, it does not require the Union to approve, okay, or sign off on the proposed work. If, after discussion, of reasons, justifications, analysis, etc., the parties still do not agree, the Company would be free to let the contract subject to the Union right to file a grievance and go to arbitration. This puts some pressure on the Company to be sure that its position is correct. * * *

Although the Arbitrator cannot accept the Union's argument that an attempt to reach a mutual agreement requires that an agreement in fact be concluded, he is unable to accept the Employer's position that its obligations are limited to discussing proposed subcontracting with the Union. As the Union correctly observes, the collective bargaining agreement contains an obligation of exercising good faith effort toward the objective of preserving bargaining unit work to the extent practicable. The Employer would hardly meet this requirement were it to blithely ignore Union recommendations or engage in a consistent refusal to accept reasonable alternatives. Nor could the Employer claim compliance with the agreement if management failed to timely undertake reasonable, necessary measures to avoid a need for employing outside contractors. Union testimony suggested that the Employer has not maintained normal staffing levels. Even assuming the inaccuracy of such testimony, however, it is clear that the backlog of work ultimately addressed by the outside contractor accumulated over an extended period. The record does not reflect any effort by the Hospital to cure the backlog as it developed by utilizing bargaining unit personnel. The Employer by failing to maintain proper staffing levels or otherwise failing to timely address a mounting work load, has created an artificial need for subcontracting. However, because of its commitment to reserve work for the bargaining unit, acceptance of a blanket right to subcontract under such circumstances would effectively vitiate its commitment to utilize bargaining unit personnel where practical.

After carefully considering the evidence adduced at the arbitration hearing, the Arbitrator must conclude that the Employer has indeed violated its commitment to the bargaining unit when it elected to subcontract the transcription work and rejected the Union's suggestion that it be accomplished on an overtime basis. The Employer's principal objection to utilizing employees at overtime was its desire to complete transcription of the backlogged tapes prior to the Joint Commission inspection, as well as some marginal cost savings which it anticipated. As the evidence indicated, however, the extensive backlog which the Employer confronted at the end of July, 1993, had been a problem of some duration. The Employer indicated that there were repeated complaints by physicians of dilatory turnaround in dictation transcription. As a result, the Arbitrator must find that the Employer was aware of this problem for some time but neglected to address it until the eve of the Joint Commission inspection. Moreover, there is no evidence to suggest that the Employer did not have sufficient advance notice of the inspection to address the transcription backlog without resort to using subcontractors.

The evidence in this case indicates that to the extent the Employer faced a crisis in August, 1993, that crisis arose because it failed to take corrective action at an earlier time. Obviously, a six (6) month transcription backlog requires at least six (6) months to develop. The causes for the backlog may include inadequate staffing in the department or inadequate supervision which would prevent any backlog from occurring, assuming that staffing levels were sufficient. Of course, other factors might result in a backlog, such as an unusually heavily patient census. However, the record does not support any inference that unusual dictation requirements beyond those normally expected had contributed to the delay in tape transcription. What the evidence does suggest is that the Employer allowed the backlog to become problematic and to use that fact as a justification for subcontracting. Because the subcontracting provisions require retention of work within the bargaining unit to the extent feasible, the Employer's obligation of good faith under those provisions is hardly satisfied where it seeks to justify subcontracting because of a situation the Employer itself has allowed to develop.

Although the Employer submits that it acted in good faith in rejecting the Union's suggestion of addressing the backlog by the use of bargaining unit employees on overtime, the Arbitrator must agree with the Union that its suggestion was indeed reasonable. The Union's computations indicate that each transcriptionist in the Medical Records Department would have been required to work approximately ten (10) hours of overtime during the three (3) weeks prior to the Joint Commission inspection. Moreover, that estimate may be higher for the reason that the Employer could have utilized a part-time transcriptionist for a full forty (40) hours, thereby saving some of the required overtime. As both parties acknowledge, costs of retaining the work within the bargaining unit, as opposed to subcontracting, would have been marginal, certainly less than $500.00. The Arbitrator must conclude therefore that the Employer did not act in good faith to preserve the disputed work for the bargaining unit.

As the above discussion indicates, the grievance will be sustained. An appropriate award follows.

Award

The grievance is sustained.

The Employer is directed to comply with the subcontracting provisions of the parties' collective bargaining agreement as interpreted by this award. The Employer is also directed to make each affected employee whole for compensation they lost as the result of the Employer's subcontracting decision. The Arbitrator finds that the work lost to the transcriptionists is in the amount of two hundred eighty (280) hours which shall be appropriately apportioned among them and paid at the applicable straight or overtime rates.

Notes and Questions

1. Do you read Article XXVII the same way Arbitrator Dean does? He reads more into a simple "notify and discuss" clause than most arbitrators would. The reason employers bargain for such clauses and resist "mutual agreement" clauses is precisely so that the employer will be free to make the final decision. See, for example, the case discussed by Arbitrator Dean, Inland–Rome, Inc., 93 LA 666 (J. Earl Williams, 1989): "If, after discussion of reasons, justification, analysis, etc., the parties still do not agree, the

Company would be free to let the contract subject to the Union right to file a grievance and go to arbitration." Similarly, if the agreement only requires notification, the employer need not even meet with the union before subcontracting, Water Pipe Extension, Bureau of Engineering Laborers' Local 1092 v. City of Chicago, 318 Ill.App.3d 628, 251 Ill.Dec. 915, 741 N.E.2d 1093 (2000) (enforcing an arbitration award to that effect). From what part of that Article does Arbitrator Dean draw his conclusion that the employer may not subcontract work to solve a problem of its own creation?

2.   Does it matter whether doing the work in house would require overtime pay? Obviously it did not matter to Arbitrator Dean, perhaps because the contractor's charges were close to the Hospital's overtime rate. Suppose the contrast were starker, so that an outside contractor could perform the work at the Hospital's straight-time rate, while using the Hospital's own employees would require overtime at time-and-a-half. Note that Article XXVII requires the Hospital to use its own employees only "when it is reasonable and practical to perform bargaining unit work within the Hospital." Would an arbitrator find the Hospital's decision to contract out the work "unreasonable" if using the Hospital's employees cost 50% more?

3.   Does a contract that grants an employer certain rights to subcontract also contain implied restrictions on those rights? Consider the recent case of Rock–Tenn Co. v. Paper, Allied–Industrial, Chemical & Energy Workers International Union, 2003 WL 22398814 (N.D. Tex. 2003). During negotiations the company proposed to drop all its trucking operations but dropped the proposal in the face of the union's objections. The ultimate contract contained this subcontracting provision: "Nothing in this Agreement shall limit in anyway [sic] the Company's subcontracting work or shall require the Company to perform any particular work in this plant rather than elsewhere." The company unilaterally subcontracted all its "long-haul" (over 100 miles) trucking. Notwithstanding that sentence, an arbitrator found a violation of the agreement. Relying on the company's withdrawal of its proposal, the arbitrator held that it "did not act in good faith and evaded the spirit of [the] Agreement by these actions." The judge vacated the award, holding that it did not "draw its essence" from the agreement because it conflicted with the quoted term and because the arbitrator "exceeded his authority" by finding an implied limitation. Does that decision itself comply with the letter, let alone the spirit, of *Enterprise Wheel*, Section III.C.

4.   A typical exception to a work-preservation clause allows subcontracting if the work "cannot be performed by the bargaining unit." How strictly should an arbitrator interpret such a term? "Cannot" under any circumstances? "Cannot" without interfering with other work? "Cannot" without additional costs? See Browning–Ferris Industries of Ohio, Inc., 118 LA 602 (Charles Z. Adamson, 2003) (subcontracting certain work did not violate the agreement because employees were already working substantial overtime and could not have completed the work in the necessary time period), and Boeing Satellite Systems, 119 LA 241 (Lionel Richman, 2003) (finding a violation in subcontracting work while competent employees were laid off, despite contention that it would "make no sense to call in a laid-off employee for one day's work").

5.   Relevant contract provisions often seem inconsistent or unclear. In Besser Co., 117 LA 1413 (Sol M. Elkin, 2002), the agreement limited subcontracting but allowed the company to "introduce new or improved production methods, equipment or facilities, or change or eliminate existing equipment or methods." The company hired an outside firm to store and maintain its tool inventory. "Subcontracting" or "improved production methods?" (Subcontracting.) In Mrs. Baird's Bakery/Bimbo Bakeries USA, 117 LA 1042 (Diane Dunham Massey, 2002), the agreement described staffing rules for the employer's distribution business and contained a "zipper clause" stating that "no other agreements" (besides the collective bargaining agreement) shall affect the parties' relationship. The company stopped distributing its own products and began using independent contractors. Violation of the staffing rules or a matter outside the agreement? (Decision not covered by the agreement.)

6.   *Remedies for subcontracting violations.* What remedy should an arbitrator award after sustaining a subcontracting grievance? If the agreement imposed only a "meet and discuss" obligation, should the union receive any retrospective remedy? See Marvin Hill and Anthony Sinicropi, Remedies in Arbitration 344–54 (2d ed. 1991). Hill and Sinicropi report several cases in which the arbitrator awarded monetary damages even though the employer's only obligation was to discuss proposed subcontracting decisions. A more recent example is United States Steel, 119 LA 1057 (Shyam Das, 2004). The agreement obliged the company to "provide written notice" to a joint committee before entering into any subcontracting arrangement. It specified in detail what information the notice was to contain.

For several years the practice was for the company to offer overtime work to its employees and to hire outside contractors for any work rejected by its employees. Rather than notice in advance, the joint committee discussed such contracting after the fact—although often over the union's protests. Arbitrator Das found a violation of the notice requirement The union prudently did not seek a remedy for those employees who had worked overtime or refused to work overtime but instead asked for compensation for employees who otherwise would have performed the work. The arbitrator agreed, although he limited the potential beneficiaries to those in classifications that traditionally had performed similar work.

Other arbitrators have devised novel remedies. One awarded the affected employees an equivalent number of hours of overtime work. Still another ordered the parties to bargain about a decision to eliminate a position but awarded the grievant back pay and continued pay until settlement or impasse. If the agreement prohibits the challenged subcontracting, must the employer pay its employees the money they would have earned had they performed the work? Or would that be punitive for the employer and a windfall (pay for work not performed) for the employees? (Recall the debate over "monetary" and "make-up" remedies for overtime bypasses, endnote 2 in Section VII.F.2.)

3.   SUBCONTRACTING DISPUTES UNDER SILENT CONTRACTS

Resolving disputes over the meaning of subcontracting clauses is relatively easy. That probably explains why few reported subcontracting cases involve express provisions. The more difficult cases are those in which the contract is silent about subcontracting. Resolution of such disputes raises a theoretical problem that permeates labor arbitration, namely the familiar conflict between the "reserved rights" and "implied obligations" theories discussed in Section VII.C. The reserved rights theory asserts that management exclusively retains all powers not limited by an express contractual provision. The implied obligations theory, on the other hand, asserts that the nature of the collective bargaining relationship, the collective bargaining agreement, or general contractual provisions like recognition and seniority clauses, impose tacit limitations on the employer's powers.

The "pristine" version of the reserved rights theory holds that without an express contractual restriction, management's power to subcontract is unlimited. The purest arbitral statement of this approach is from Arbitrator Marion Beatty's decision in American Sugar Refining Co., 37 LA 334, 337–38 (1971):

> Arbitrators are not soothsayers and "wise men" employed to dispense equity and goodwill according to their own notions of what is best for the parties, nor are they kings like Solomon with unlimited wisdom or courts of unlimited jurisdiction. Arbitrators are employed to interpret the working agreement as the parties themselves wrote it.

> I am not unmindful that some arbitrators have read contracting-out restrictions into contracts containing no clear statements on the subject. In contract interpretation, we are trying to ascertain the mutual intention of the parties. We must be guided primarily by the language used. Admittedly, certain inferences may be read into it, but they should be only those inferences which clearly and logically follow from the language used and which reasonable men must have mutually intended. To go far afield in search of veiled inferences or ethereal or celestial factors is a mistake. I believe Labor contracts are much more earthly; they are not written in fancy language purposely containing hidden meanings.

> When an arbitrator finds that the parties have not dealt with the subject of contracting-out in their working agreement, but that the employer is nevertheless prohibited from contracting-out (a) unless he acted in good faith; (b) unless he acts in conformity with past practice; (c) unless he acts reasonably; (d) unless his act does not deprive a substantial number of employees of employment; (e) unless his acts were dictated by the requirements of the business; (f) if his act is barred by the recognition clause; (g) if his act is barred by the seniority provisions of the working agreement; or (h) if his act violates the spirit of the agreement, the arbitrator may be in outer space and reading the stars instead of the contract.

Subcontracting may undercut contractual wage and seniority provisions, however, and may even lessen the utility of the recognition agreement. Unions therefore argue that, singly or together, these clauses prohibit any subcontracting. Arbitrator Saul Wallen expressed the implied obligations theory well in one of the first published awards on the subject, a case involving the transfer of work to employees outside the bargaining unit:

> If one of the purposes of the contract as a whole, and of the seniority provisions in particular, is to assure the bargaining unit employees a measure of job security, then such security would be meaningless if the company's view were in this case to prevail. For it would mean that without regard to prior custom or practice as to the assignment of work, the Company could continuously narrow the area of available job opportunities in which the seniority clause functions by transferring duties performed by bargaining unit employees not covered by the agreement. Not only the seniority clause but the entire agreement could thus be vitiated.

New Britain Machine Co., 8 LA 720, 722–23 (1947).

Moreover, collective bargaining agreements contain the same implied covenants of good faith and fair dealing found in other contracts. Applied to subcontracting, these covenants mean that the employer must not "seek a substitute labor supply at lower wages or inferior standards." They do not, however, "reach subcontracting which is based on business considerations other than the cost of acquiring labor under the collective agreement." Archibald Cox, *The Legal Nature of Collective Bargaining Agreements*, 57 Michigan Law Review 1, 31–32 (1958).

In the early days of arbitration, the division over these theories led to confusing and contradictory arbitration awards. In 1949, for example, one arbitrator bluntly claimed that "arbitration decisions are unanimous to the effect that the company has the right to subcontract work unless the contract specifically restricts that right," International Harvester Co., 12 LA 707, 709 (Whitley McCoy, 1949). Just two years later, another arbitrator concluded that arbitrators are "virtually unanimous in holding that a Company may not unilaterally remove a job from the bargaining unit, even when there is no express limitation to that effect in the agreement or when there is a management rights clause," Bethlehem Steel Co., 16 LA 111, 113 (Charles Killingsworth, 1951).

Although there may still be a few arbitrators in each camp, most arbitrators now take a middle course. The most common view is that even a silent contract implies *some* restrictions on management's power to subcontract. Most arbitrators would agree that even under a silent contract an employer could not simply fire all bargaining unit employees and subcontract their work. Arbitrators divide over the source and nature of those implied restrictions as well as on their application. The main line of division is between those using a subjective test such as "good faith" and those using a relatively objective test such as "reasonableness." Whatever the test, each case is likely to turn on several factors such as the type and importance of the business justifications for subcontracting, the type of work involved, past practices and bargaining history, and the subcontracting's impact on employees and the union.

Here is one clear and oft-cited statement of the consensus:

> In the absence of contractual language relating to contracting out of work, the general arbitration rule is that management has the right to contract out work as long as the action if performed in good faith, it represents a reasonable business decision, it does not result in a subversion of the labor agreement, and it does not have the effect of seriously weakening the bargaining unit or important parts of it.

Shenango Valley Water Co., 53 LA 741, 744–45 (Thomas J. McDermott, 1969). And here is another:

> Subcontracting, when not limited by contractual language, is not a right to be exercised with unfettered abandon. Inherent in every Collective Bargaining Agreement is job security for the bargaining unit members. That principal was set forth over a half century ago by Arbitrator Saul Wallen in the off cited passage from New Britain Mach. Co.,8 LA(BNA) 720, 722 (1947):

>> Job security is an inherent element of the labor contract, a part of its very being. If wages is the heart of the labor agreement, job security may be considered its soul. * * *

> Thus, outsourcing which has as its central purpose nothing more than the transferring of work customarily performed by the bargaining unit to non-bargaining unit members, must be strongly presumed to be an attack on not only the bargaining unit, but on the very purpose of the collective bargaining process. To permit such attack would render the collective bargaining process an exercise in futility, with hard won Labor Agreements being circumvented by outsourcing.

Certainty is not a hallmark of arbitration awards on subcontracting, as one exasperated arbitrator noted:

> Because of the importance which they attach to the issue, both parties have cited certain decisions of other arbitrators in support of their position, and the umpire has supplemented these citations by his own research into the reported cases. Beyond revealing that other companies and unions have faced this same question of implied obligations—have presented similar agreements, and voiced similar fears—the cases show little uniformity of either theoretical agreement or ultimate decision. Within each group of decisions, moreover, there are conflicts of principle and approach. The umpire has returned from his exploration of the cases a sadder—if not a wiser—man, echoing the plaint of Omar Khayyam: "Myself when young did eagerly frequent Doctor and Saint and heard great argument about it and about: but evermore came out by that same door wherein I went."

Bethlehem Steel Co., 30 LA 678, 682 (Ralph Seward, 1958).

ALLIS–CHALMERS MFG. CO.

39 LA 1213 (Russell Smith, 1962).*

[This case involves two subcontracting grievances, one over certain janitorial work and the other over the manufacture of certain component parts. Employees were on layoff during all the challenged subcontracting, and employees had previously done the same or similar work. The contract said nothing about subcontracting, and the Company therefore challenged the arbitrability of the grievances.]

DISCUSSION

I. Jurisdiction

The initial question for decision is whether, as the Company contends, the claims made by the instant grievances fall outside the jurisdictional authority of the Referee. The Company relies upon Reference Paragraph 167 of the Agreement, which provided as follows:

> The jurisdictional authority of the Impartial Referee is defined as and limited to the determination of any grievance which is a controversy between the parties or between the Company and employees covered by this agreement concerning compliance with any provision of this agreement and is submitted to him consistent with the provisions of this agreement.

The Company notes that the first step of the grievance procedure contemplates that an employee may present "any grievance concerning his employment," but asserts that this provision is much broader than the "arbitration clause" above quoted in that the latter limits arbitrable grievances to those which allege a violation of some express provision or provisions of the Agreement. The Company reasons that, inasmuch as the claim of the Union does not rest on any specific provision of the Agreement relating to the matter of subcontracting (or, more accurately, contracting out) of work encompassed by the defined bargaining unit, but, instead, rests on alleged implications derived from a composite of provisions (the definition of the bargaining unit, specified wage rates, seniority, etc.), the Referee has no jurisdiction.

This contention, in the Referee's judgment, is without merit and must be rejected. Without elaborating the point, it seems to the Referee that the Company is reading into Reference Paragraph 167 a limitation which is not there. The paragraph does not state that a grievance must concern and involve a "provision" which explicitly touches the subject matter of the grievance. It simply says, in effect, that the grievance must involve a controversy concerning compliance with "any provision" of the Agreement. This language does not foreclose the consideration of a claim based on the theory that one or more cited provisions of the Agreement give rise to an implied limitation or restriction on managerial action. There can be no doubt that in the area of contractual obligations generally it is frequently necessary, in order to give effect to the intent of the parties, to determine whether the specific provisions of the agreement, fairly and properly construed, import obligations not specifically stated. This is true at least as much in the case of labor agreements as in the case of other kinds of contracts.

The Referee therefore concludes that the instant grievances present claims which are within his jurisdiction to decide. The basic issue is whether, from the provisions defining the bargaining unit, specifying the wage structure, providing seniority rights, and otherwise providing rights and benefits to employees, there arises an implied prohibition upon the contracting out of work of kinds normally and customarily done by employees in the bargaining unit. This is a contention which involves a controversy concerning compliance with a provision of the Agreement alleged to be implicit in the specified provisions.

II. *Implied Limitations*

Insofar as the Union's case is predicated, as it appears at least in part to be, on the broad proposition that the labor agreement, taken as a whole or in the light of the specific provisions cited, gives rise to an implied absolute and unqualified prohibition upon the contracting out of work normally and customarily performed by employees in the bargaining unit, the contention must be dismissed as untenable. The Referee considered this matter in Referee Case No. 8, 1959–1961 Agreement, Springfield Works, and there stated:

> The Referee has considered this general problem more than once. He is unable to accept as sound the broad proposition asserted by the Union that an absolute prohibition upon the contracting out of work done by bargaining unit employees can properly be implied from the "recognition," "wage," and "seniority" provisions of the contract. None of these provisions literally, historically, or in context is a guarantee to employees in the defined bargaining unit that the work which was there when the unit was first recognized will continue to be there. Rather, they assure that, insofar as persons are employed by the Company to perform work of the kinds which are included within the defined unit, there will be recognition by the Company of the Union as the bargaining representative of such persons, and that such persons will be entitled to the benefits of the wage, seniority, and other provisions of the labor agreement.

The Referee adheres to this position. * * *

Both parties in their briefs make extensive reference to the decisions of other arbitrators in the area of subcontracting. Such citation is understandable, since it is literally possible to cite prior decisions which range throughout the entire spectrum of possibilities. Some, at the one extreme, hold that, absent a specific contractual restriction, the employer retains complete freedom in the matter. Others, at the other extreme, hold that the employer is prohibited from contracting out any work normally performed by unit employees. Most decisions fall somewhere in between, holding that there is some kind of implicit limitation on the right to contract out work, but also freedom to do so under some circumstances. The Referee has examined (more than once) the reported cases, as have others. His distinct impression is that in most instances, at least in recent years, the result in the particular case was to uphold the employer's right to take the protested action, while the opinion indicated the view that there are limitations based on factors not presented by the facts of the particular case. * * * Sometimes a detailed catalog of such prohibited types or circumstances of subcontracting was set forth, by way of dicta; the more usual pattern has been to express the limitation in terms of such broad criteria as the necessity of "good faith," or "fair dealing," or the requisite of "sound business judgment," or the absence of evidence that the action "arbitrarily reduced the scope of the bargaining unit." In most instances, the arbitrator stressed the importance of looking closely at "the facts and circumstances" of the case, and these, of course, have been almost infinitely varied. * * *

The present Referee, while rejecting the Union's view that there exists an absolute (implied) prohibition on the contracting out of work of kinds regularly and normally performed by bargaining unit employees, likewise rejects the Company's view that it has complete freedom in this respect. In the Springfield case he indicated that "a standard of 'good faith' may be applicable, difficult of definition as this may be." Upon further reflection, he is prepared now to say that he thinks this standard is implicit in the union-management relationship represented by the parties' Agreement, in view of the quite legitimate interests and expectations which the employees and the Union have in protecting the fruits of their negotiations with the Company.

Past Practice

"Past practice" in subcontracting for services and for the manufacturing of components may properly be taken into account as a factor negating the existence of any broad, implied limitation on subcontracting, but not as eliminating the restriction altogether. Moreover, an unsuccessful Union attempt to negotiate into the contract specific restrictions on subcontracting, as was the case in the parties' negotiations of their 1959–1961 Agreement, is likewise a fact which may help to support the claim that the parties have recognized that the Company has substantial latitude in the matter of subcontracting. Yet it would be unrealistic to interpret futile bargaining efforts as meaning the parties were in agreement that the Agreement implies no restriction at all. Parties frequently try to solidify through bargaining a position which they could otherwise take, or to broaden rights which otherwise might arguably exist. Thus, the Referee does not find either in the evidence of past practice, here adduced or in the history of the negotiations of the 1959–1961 Agreement, a satisfactory basis for concluding that the Company has complete, untrammeled freedom in the matter of subcontracting. Nor, incidentally, does he attach any special significance to the decisions of the National Labor Relations Board holding that the matter of subcontracting is a "bargainable" issue under the National Labor Relations Act. The parties did bargain on this subject without reaching agreement on any specific provision for inclusion in their Agreement. The question here is whether the Agreement they reached may properly be said to imply some kind of limitation on the Company's freedom to subcontract. In the Referee's judgment, some limitation may properly be implied, narrow though it may be.

Real difficulty arises, however, in attempting to lay down a set of specific criteria to be used in determining whether, in a subcontracting situation, an employer has acted in bad faith. Many arbitrators have sought to do this, and the wide variation in the results of their deliberations of itself casts some doubt on the wisdom of such efforts and to suggest that detailed specification may best be left to the collective bargaining process. In general, it seems to the Referee that "good faith" is present when the managerial decision to contract out work is made on the basis of a rational consideration of factors related to the conduct of an efficient, economical operation, and with some regard for the interests and expectations of the employees affected by the decision, and that "bad faith" is present when the decision is arbitrary (i.e., lacks any rational basis) or fails to take into account at all the interests and expectations of employees affected. Without attempting anything like a complete "catalog," the following would appear, at least *prima facie*, to be instances of bad faith: (1) To negotiate a collective agreement with the Union representative covering classifications of work while withholding from the Union the fact that the employer contemplates, in the immediate future, a major change in operations which will eliminate such work; (2) entering into a "subcontracting" arrangement which is a subterfuge, in the sense that the "employees" of the ostensible "subcontractor" become in substance the employees of the employer; (3) the commingling of employees of a subcontractor, working under a different set of wages or other working conditions, regularly and continuously with employees of the employer performing the same kinds of work; (4) contracting out work for the specific purpose of undermining or weakening the Union or depriving employees of employment opportunities. On the other hand, the Referee does not consider that it is *per se* arbitrary, unreasonable, or an act of bad faith to contract out work primarily to reduce production costs. After all, a prime managerial obligation is to conduct an efficient and profitable enterprise, and doing so serves, in the long run, the best interests of employees as well as stockholders.

The observations made above do not resolve cases. The facts of the particular case must be examined, especially in relation to the considerations underlying the managerial decision to contract out the work in question. Of necessity, the Referee, having taken the position that the managerial discretion is subject to the implied limitation that it must be exercised in good faith, cannot escape the necessity and responsibility for making a judgment on this matter. As a matter of procedure, it seems evident that management should explain *why* it made the decision, and that it is then appropriate for the Union to attempt either to show that the considerations motivating the decision, as disclosed by management, indicate bad faith, or else that other considerations of a kind indicating bad faith in fact motivated the decision.

III. Particular Grievances

(1) The "Janitorial" Work

The only part of the work undertaken by Don's Window Cleaning Company on October 29 and 30, 1960, which is here protested is floor cleaning. Company testimony is to the effect that this work (in addition to other work) was "let" to the outside contractor, rather than assigned at least in part to bargaining unit employees, on an overtime basis, because of these considerations: (1) The necessity of insuring that the work would be completed over the week-end; (2) lack of certainty as to when the floor washing would take place; (3) lack of certainty as to how many people would be required to do such work; (4) the difficulty of getting unit personnel to come in "on emergencies" or on overtime; (5) the inability of some of the unit personnel to handle "scrubbing machines;" (6) the necessity of coordinating the floor cleaning with the moving and other operations involved; (7) the limitations, under State law, of the number of hours which women could be required to work consecutively; and (8) safety factors. Economic considerations, such as the overtime premium payments which would have been required, were not, apparently, involved in the determination.

The Union does not claim that these considerations were not the factors motivating the decision. Its claim is that the Company judgment concerning some of them (e.g., the difficulty of coordinating the work of Company employees with the work of employees of the outside contractor) was unsound. It seems to the Referee, however, that the factors which management took into account were within the range of considerations which could rationally be taken into account, and that there is no evidence that the total judgment reached was either arbitrary or unreasonable, or failed to take into account the natural desires of unit personnel to avail themselves of an overtime opportunity. On the whole, the conclusion must be that there is no evidence of bad faith.

(2) The Contracting Out of Work on Components

With respect to the so-called "operating mechanisms," Company testimony indicates that the primary reason for the subcontracting to Kramer Company was economic—i.e., the fact that the price for the component as bid by the contractor, taken together with other applicable cost factors, would be substantially lower than the costs previously experienced by the Company in manufacturing the mechanism. Another consideration was apparently the fact that, according to the Company, planned time schedules were not met in connection with its earlier manufacture of this component.

With respect to the so-called "stationary contacts," Company testimony is to the effect that the primary consideration motivating the decision to have Fansteel Metallurgical Company process the components, complete, was the shorter procurement cycle which would and did result, namely, 60 days as compared with 120 days under the prior practice. In addition, according to the Company, the unit cost was reduced from $3.37 to $2.02.

The Union does not contend that these considerations did not, in fact, motivate the decisions to contract out the work in question, although, in the case of the stationary contacts, there was Union testimony to the effect that the length of the procurement cycle had been due to delays in Fansteel's part of the work, not in the processing done in the Company's shops. With respect to the matter of procurement time, however, the fact is that it was reduced, in accordance with the Company's expectations, whatever the reason may have been.

As in the case of the janitorial work, the Referee concludes that the considerations which management took into account, although in these instances primarily or partially economic, indicate that its decisions were not arbitrary or unreasonable, and were not taken in bad faith. No ulterior purpose is indicated in terms either of the status of the Union or of employees in the bargaining unit, nor is there any showing, if this has relevance, that the effect of such subcontracting was to curtail bargaining unit jobs in any substantial way. The Referee repeats that, in his view, cost considerations as a basis for subcontracting, do not of themselves, necessarily indicate bad faith. Manufacturing operations commonly involve some contracting out or purchasing of components, or work thereon, and considerable flexibility in this regard is to be expected in the interest of an efficient and economically sound enterprise. It may fairly be presumed, indeed, that the Company on occasion takes contracts to supply components, or to perform work on components, for other manufacturing concerns. The existence of a substantial degree of managerial discretion, therefore, does not necessarily harm the employees of the Company. They may actually gain thereby, rather than lose, in their over-all employment opportunities.

AWARD

Union Grievances Nos. 1802–59–B (filed October 31, 1960) and 1183–262–A (filed December 7, 1961) are denied.

Notes and Questions

1.   (a) On what basis does Arbitrator Smith find the dispute arbitrable? In United Steelworkers of America v. Warrior and Gulf Navigation Co., 363 U.S. 574, 80 S.Ct. 1347, 4 L.Ed.2d 1409 (1960) (reprinted in Section III.B.), the Court held arbitrable a subcontracting grievance even though the agreement said nothing about subcontracting and the arbitration provision excluded "matters which are strictly a function of management." Even before *Warrior & Gulf*, arbitrators managed to find a basis for resolving such grievances. Several courts were more dubious. For an exhaustive discussion

of the precedents, see Celanese Corp. of America, 33 LA 925 (Samuel Dash, 1959). After *Warrior and Gulf*, courts and arbitrators alike found subcontracting grievances arbitrable, unless the agreement specifically excluded them.

(b) When the *Warrior and Gulf* case finally went before an arbitrator after the Supreme Court's decision, he found implied limitations on contracting out. He held that the employer had violated those limits on at least one occasion by subcontracting work while some employees were on layoff. Warrior & Gulf Navigation Co., 36 LA 695 (J. Fred Holly, 1961). Why should that fact affect the result?

2. What do you make of Arbitrator Smith's treatments of past practice and the union's unsuccessful attempt to negotiate a specific restriction on subcontracting? Does the union's bargaining failure prove that the contract did *not* bar subcontracting? See Simonds Industries, Inc., 104 LA 41 (Robert Rybolt, 1994) (using bargaining history and the employer's 17–year practice to conclude that the agreement did not bar subcontracting).

3. (a) Whether the critical test is objective or subjective, a multitude of factors will bear on its application. Many arbitrators have tried to find all the pertinent factors, producing lists of five, six, eleven, and twelve items. The greater the number of pertinent factors, of course, the greater the likelihood they will point in different directions. That leaves the decision maker free to reach virtually any result, simply by choosing to emphasize some factors rather than others. The variances led one arbitrator to conclude:

> After examining these studies and many of the decision discussed, it is fair to conclude that no one, whatever his initial inclinations or prejudices, will go away from them without finding something he likes. Like the town fair, there is something there for everyone.

KVP Sutherland Paper Co., 40 LA 737, 740 (Sanford Kadish, 1963). Another arbitrator, after boiling the considerations down to three (the type of work subcontracted, the reasons for and conditions of the subcontracting, and the impact on the bargaining unit and its members), warned:

> * * * there is no certainty in this area, no absolute truth. The most an arbitrator can do is to make a careful examination of the contract and the facts and try to render a decision which protects the Union's side of the bargain without depriving the Employer of its side.

Uniroyal, Inc., 76 LA 1049, 1053 (Dennis R. Nolan, 1981).

For a good discussion of the most commonly used criteria, see Marvin Hill and Anthony Sinicropi, Management Rights 451–63 (1986).

(b) What criteria did Arbitrator Smith use? Who wins and who loses if an arbitrator uses those criteria? What other criteria could he have used? In which direction would the alternative criteria point? What sort of subcontracting would violate the criteria Arbitrator Smith used?

(c) Some cases, of course, are relatively clear. In Miller and Co., 102 LA 197 (1993), Arbitrator James R. Cox approved the employer's subcontracting of its briquette production to a nonunion company. The agreement was silent on subcontracting, so the arbitrator used a standard similar to

Arbitrator Smith's: "Management's right to contract out is dependent upon whether the subcontracting is undertaken in good faith, is a reasonable business decision, and does not subvert the labor contract." Using that test, he found no violation where the briquette operation was losing a million and a half dollars a year and the subcontractor's costs were lower because of efficiency rather than lower wages. See also Gaylord Container Corp., 106 LA 461 (Barry J. Baroni, 1996) (no violation where the employer lacked qualified employees and specialized equipment needed to do the work safely and to comply with OSHA standards, the work was an incidental part of the total job, and arose because of an emergency). Most cases are far more complicated.

4.   How successful are subcontracting grievances? There has been no recent study, but several earlier studies (all cited in footnote 1), using somewhat different classification schemes, reached surprisingly consistent results, finding management winning about 65–84% of the cases. See Dash (70%, in a study of 64 cases from 1947–59); Greenbaum (78%, in a study of 50 cases from 1959–62); Smith, (84%, in a study of 77 cases from 1962–66); and Jacobs (65.5%, in a study of 51 cases from 1968–71).

5.   Do arbitrators share, perhaps unconsciously, certain values that determine the results in subcontracting cases? In a provocative study, James Gross re-examined the cases used in earlier studies and found "a dominant value theme—efficiency, as the *summum bonum*." Gross, *supra* footnote 1, at 70. Why should efficiency, of all possible values, be arbitrators' "highest good?" Gross speculates that arbitrators are selected by parties to whom efficiency is already an important value, and thus are likely (consciously or not) to apply the parties' value patterns. Moreover, the parties may *think* that efficiency is important to arbitrators and thus may persuade the arbitrator that efficiency is the key value.

Does that speculation persuade you? Unions have half the say in selecting arbitrators, yet invariably appear on the "inefficient" side of subcontracting disputes. Why would they then try to persuade the arbitrator that efficiency is the key value? Why would the jointly-selected arbitrator be more likely to prize efficiency than whatever other alternative values the union might assert? A more recent study used statistical analysis of subcontracting cases to conclude that case variables such as the particular facts and issues, not external factors, determined results. McCammon & Cotton, *supra* footnote 1.

6.   Are all efficiency arguments on the employers' side? If efficiency is likely to prove a losing issue for unions in subcontracting cases, what other values can a union assert in opposition to efficiency? How could anyone argue *against* efficiency? Or is that the wrong question to ask in these cases? If so, what is the *right* question?

7.   The contemporary debate over "outsourcing" simply adds an international dimension to traditional subcontracting disputes. See, e.g., Katherine V. W. Stone, *Employee Representation in the Boundaryless Workplace*, 77 Chicago–Kent Law Review 773 (2002). Does it matter, either for the affected employees or for arbitrators interpreting collective bargaining clauses, whether the disputed work is performed by another company in India,

another company across the street, or by employees of another company working in the employer's own plant?

I. UNION SECURITY[1]

1. INTRODUCTION

A union gains the right to represent employees when selected "by the majority of the employees in a unit appropriate for" collective bargaining. Labor Management Relations Act, § 9(a), 29 U.S.C.A. § 159(a). The group for which the union bargains is termed, appropriately, the bargaining unit. Section 9(a) provides that the selected representative becomes "the exclusive representative of all the employees in such unit for the purposes of collective bargaining in respect to rates of pay, wages, hours of employment, or other conditions of employment." "Exclusive representative" means just that: once a bargaining unit selects a representative, the employees (even those who opposed the union) may no longer represent themselves (or choose others to represent them) in bargaining over the listed subjects. This unique characteristic of American labor law is known as the "exclusivity principle."

As the exclusive representative, the union must fairly represent *all* employees, even those who choose not to join. (This refers to the "duty of fair representation" discussed in Section V.A., *supra*.) Representing employees is expensive. Among other things, representation involves negotiating a collective bargaining agreement, monitoring the employer's compliance with the agreement, processing grievances, arbitrating unresolved disputes, paying the bills for the local union organization, and advising employees on work-related matters. Local unions also must contribute to the support of regional and national union organizations. Many unions also engage in political activity, from registering voters and supporting or opposing legislation to helping candidates for office. The statutory duty to represent all employees fairly, even though only some may choose to pay dues, presents the union with a difficult dilemma.

The dilemma posed by the statute has two solutions. If unions could refuse to represent non-members (or could charge for services to non-members), members would bear only their own expenses. Alternatively, if unions could force all employees to join, or at least to pay dues, the added income would presumably cover the expenses of representing reluctant members or non-members. American unions favor the second

1. Bibliographic Suggestions: Thomas R. Haggard, Compulsory Unionism, The NLRB, and the Courts: A Legal Analysis of Union Security Agreements 191–209 (1977); Billie Ann Brotman, *A Comparison Between Arbitral and National Labor Relations Board Decisions Concerning Union Security Clauses*, 37 Labor Law Journal 849 (1986); Kenneth G. Dau–Schmidt, *Union Security Agreements Under the National Labor Relations Act: The Statute, the Constitution, and the Court's Opinion in* Beck, 27 Harvard Journal on Legislation 51 (1990); Peter Florey, *Fair Share Proceedings: A Case for Common Sense*, 44 Arbitration Journal 35 (March, 1989); Thomas R. Haggard, *Union Security in the Context of Labor Arbitration*, 47 Proceedings of the National Academy of Arbitrators 110 (1995); and Martin H. Malin, *The Legal Status of Union Security Fee Arbitration after* Chicago Teachers Union v. Hudson, 29 Boston College Law Review 857 (1988).

solution. They have long argued that, because by law the exclusive representative must represent all employees in the bargaining unit, all employees should either join the union or at least contribute to its expenses. Employees who do not contribute, unions argue, are "free riders" who get the benefits of unionization without paying the fare. To prevent free riders, unions try to negotiate contractual provisions requiring represented employees to join or pay, on penalty of losing their jobs. (The obvious counter to the free rider argument is that some employees do not think unionization benefits them. If the collective agreement nevertheless requires them to support the union, they become "forced riders," required to pay for services they do not want.) Depending on one's perspective, these provisions are either "union security" or "compulsory unionism" clauses.

The primary forms of union security agreements are these:

(a) **Closed Shop Agreements.** The closed shop agreement prohibits an employer from hiring anyone except union members in good standing. As explained later, the closed shop is now illegal.

(b) **Union Shop Agreements.** The union shop agreement allows the employer to hire without regard to union membership, but obliges new employees to join the union within a certain time, usually thirty days. (It is sometimes said that under the closed shop, the union determines who the employees will be, while under the union shop the employer determines who the union's members will be.) This is the strongest form of union security agreement permitted by law.

Unions lacking the bargaining strength to obtain a full union shop agreement may settle for less. The "modified union shop" agreement exempts certain employees, usually those of high seniority at the time of the agreement, from the requirement of union membership. "Maintenance of membership" agreements, as the term suggests, oblige all employees who are members of the union to remain so. Moreover, court decisions have limited the "membership" a union can demand to payment of uniform dues and fees. Unless an employee chooses to become a full member, the union may not force him or her to comply with union rules, fine them for violations such as crossing picket lines, etc. This limitation blurs the distinction between the union shop and the next category, the agency shop.

(c) **Agency Shop Agreements.** The agency shop agreement does not require employees to join the union, but rather to pay the amount of money union members would pay in dues and fees. Especially in the public sector, the preferred term for the agency shop is a "fair share" agreement, which requires employees to pay "their" share of the union's costs of representing employees. As discussed later in this section, court decisions have further reduced the amount of money unions may demand from non-members. Because not all of a union's expenses are properly chargeable to non-members, the "fair" share may be less—usually very slightly less—than the usual dues and fees.

(d) Checkoff Agreements. "Checkoff" refers to an employee's checking a box on a form to allow the employer to deduct union dues from the employee's paycheck and pass them on to the union. Employers almost always agree to a checkoff provision because it costs the employer little or nothing and yet is very important to the union's economic security. A checkoff arrangement saves the union the burden of collecting the dues itself, makes it more difficult for employees to avoid payment, and avoids the annoyance employees might feel if they had to write a check each month. Even if employees must pay a fee to the union, they need not do so by checkoff. Checkoff agreements are the weakest, but universally legal, form of union security provision.

Sixty-four percent of the contracts in the Bureau of National Affairs survey include union shop clauses; 10% modified union shop clauses; 4% maintenance of membership clauses; 10% contain agency shop clauses; and 95% include the checkoff. Basic Patterns in Union Contracts 97–100 (14th Ed. 1995).

2. THE LEGAL STATUS OF UNION SECURITY AGREEMENTS

The legal status of union security clauses is a complicated topic extending far beyond the scope of this book.[2] Because parties in union security arbitrations often refer to legal requirements, however, a brief discussion is helpful.

From the passage of the Wagner Act in 1935 until 1947, federal law did not restrict union security agreements. One of the many compromises in the Taft–Hartley Act of that year forbade closed shop agreements [§ 8(a)(3)], allowed states to prohibit union shop and agency shop agreements [§ 14(b)], and expressly authorized checkoffs [§ 302(c)(4)]. More than twenty states, mostly in the South and West, have used their authority under § 14(b) to outlaw some forms of union security agreements. (Proponents of such state restrictions termed them "right to work" laws, meaning that employees would have a right to retain their jobs even if they chose not to join the union. States that have adopted those laws are thus termed "right to work states.") In the remaining states, union shop agreements are common.

Over the last 50 years, litigation over union security agreements has run along two sometimes criss-crossing tracks. One track involves public employees who claim that union security clauses in public-sector collective bargaining agreements violate their First Amendment rights to association (or, more accurately, to non-association). The second track involves private sector employees, initially in occupations covered by the

2. For a magisterial, if somewhat dated, discussion of the entire field, see Thomas R. Haggard, Compulsory Unionism, The NLRB, and the Courts: A Legal Analysis of Union Security Agreements 191–209 (1977).

Railway Labor Act, who raise both statutory and constitutional claims.[3] Despite the divergent claims, the Supreme Court has tried to harmonize the constitutional and statutory authorities, interpreting the RLA and NLRA to provide the same protections to private-sector employees as the Constitution provides to their public-sector counterparts. In the course of this litigation, the Court has established several principles affecting arbitrations over union security clauses. All references are to the cases cited in footnote 3.

(a) Neither the union shop nor the agency shop violates the Constitution, whether negotiated in the private or public sectors (*Hanson, Street, Abood*).

(b) The only "membership" a union can require, however, is the payment of dues and fees, as opposed to broader forms of membership that might require participation in activities or might subject a person to union discipline. This limitation whittles the membership requirement down to its "financial core," and effectively makes the union shop no more than an agency shop by another name (*Radio Officers, General Motors*). Nevertheless, negotiating a clause that simply uses the statutory language rather than spelling out the limited meaning the courts have given it does not violate the law (*Miller*).

(c) Compulsory fees are a "significant impingement on First Amendment rights * * * justified by the governmental interest in industrial peace." The government therefore cannot force objecting non-members, financial core members, or fee-payers to support union activities other than those "necessarily or reasonably incurred for the purpose of performing the duties of an exclusive representative of the employees in dealing with the employer on labor-management issues" (*Ellis, Beck*). This effectively reduces the agency shop (and thus the union shop) to a representation-fee agreement, like those found in public-sector "fair share" clauses (*Street, Allen, Abood, Ellis*). While unions may require full members to contribute to all their lawful expenses (*Allis-Chalmers*), employees may resign

---

3. The major cases are these: Radio Officers' Union v. NLRB, 347 U.S. 17, 74 S.Ct. 323, 98 L.Ed. 455 (1954); Railway Employees' Department v. Hanson, 351 U.S. 225, 76 S.Ct. 714, 100 L.Ed. 1112 (1956); International Association of Machinists v. Street, 367 U.S. 740, 81 S.Ct. 1784, 6 L.Ed.2d 1141 (1961); Brotherhood of Railway and Steamship Clerks, Freight Handlers, Express and Station Employees v. Allen, 373 U.S. 113, 83 S.Ct. 1158, 10 L.Ed.2d 235 (1963); NLRB v. General Motors Corp., 373 U.S. 734, 83 S.Ct. 1453, 10 L.Ed.2d 670 (1963); NLRB v. Allis–Chalmers Mfg. Co., 388 U.S. 175, 87 S.Ct. 2001, 18 L.Ed.2d 1123 (1967); Abood v. Detroit Board of Education, 431 U.S. 209, 97 S.Ct. 1782, 52 L.Ed.2d 261 (1977); Ellis v. Brotherhood of Railway, Air-line and Steamship Clerks, Freight Handlers, Express and Station Employees, 466 U.S. 435, 104 S.Ct. 1883, 80 L.Ed.2d 428 (1984); Pattern Makers' League of North America v. NLRB, 473 U.S. 95, 105 S.Ct. 3064, 87 L.Ed.2d 68 (1985); Chicago Teachers Union, Local No. 1 v. Hudson, 475 U.S. 292, 106 S.Ct. 1066, 89 L.Ed.2d 232 (1986); Communications Workers of America v. Beck, 487 U.S. 735, 108 S.Ct. 2641, 101 L.Ed.2d 634 (1988); Lehnert v. Ferris Faculty Association, 500 U.S. 507, 111 S.Ct. 1950, 114 L.Ed.2d 572 (1991); Air Line Pilots Association v. Miller, 523 U.S. 866, 118 S.Ct. 1761, 140 L.Ed.2d 1070 (1998); and Marquez v. Screen Actors Guild, 525 U.S. 33, 119 S.Ct. 292, 142 L.Ed.2d 242 (1998).

full membership and become financial core members at any time (*Pattern Makers*).

(d) Expenditures chargeable to nonmembers include negotiating and administering the collective bargaining agreement, conventions, social activities, and publications, but exclude political or ideological activities (*Street, Allen*), union organizing, and certain types of litigation (*Ellis*). The Supreme Court's sharp division in *Lehnert*, which produced four opinions, illustrates the difficulty of categorizing expenditures.

(e) To prevent unions from exacting improper support, the Supreme Court has required them to provide fair procedures by which objecting employees can determine what percentage of the union's expenditures are for "nonchargeable" purposes and thereby proportionately reduce their compulsory payments. It is not enough for a union to decide which expenditures are chargeable and rebate the excess charges, because that would amount to a forced loan from the employee to the union (*Ellis, Hudson*). According to the Court, a public sector union must provide an adequate explanation for its allocations, must place in an escrow account the reasonably debatable portion of the objector's dues, and must provide the dissenting employee a reasonably prompt decision by an impartial decisionmaker (*Hudson*). The Supreme Court has not yet specifically required the same procedures for private-sector fee objectors. It may very well do so, however, considering its previous attempts to harmonize the First Amendment, the RLA, and the NLRA.

(f) Arbitration can be an expeditious means for such a neutral decision, but only if the objecting employee agrees to that process. If a union unilaterally adopts an arbitration procedure for challenging agency shop fees, objectors need not arbitrate before suing in federal court (*Miller*). Although *Hudson* required unions and employers to implement procedures for a prompt decision before a neutral decisionmaker, it does not oblige objectors to use those procedures. Arbitration is a matter of contract, so a party need not arbitrate a claim unless he or she agrees to do so.

One obvious result of these decisions is to strengthen the hand of the individual employee against the union in monetary matters. The right of employees to resign from full membership at any time could (if employees knew about and exercised their rights) severely limit the union's ability to force them to contribute to special projects, such as organizing campaigns, other striking unions, and strike funds. Limiting "chargeable" expenditures to collective bargaining and related matters restricts the union's ability to engage in political efforts—or would do so if many employees objected to those activities. While the amount of money actually lost due to objecting employees is small—very few employees object, and most of the agency fees are for chargeable purposes[4]—record-keeping and litigation can be troublesome and expensive.

---

4. In one major union, dissenting dues-payers numbered only 0.01% of the membership; non-chargeable expenses average about 20% of total expenditures. See the

More importantly, the employees' rights to adequate information and to a hearing before an impartial decisionmaker expose to scrutiny financial affairs that many unions would rather keep confidential. The Supreme Court's decisions have spawned a lively debate over the conflict between individual and collective rights.[5]

3. THE RELATIONSHIP BETWEEN UNION SECURITY LAW AND ARBITRATION

You read in Chapter V.B. how arbitrators divide over the applicability of external law in arbitration proceedings. One school argues that because every contract is subject to the law, arbitrators should resolve any legal issues involved in the dispute. To ignore legal questions, they assert, would result in arbitration awards permitting or even ostensibly requiring illegal conduct. The other school claims that arbitrators are creatures of the contract, and thus have only the authority the parties delegate to them; usually this means the power to resolve disputes over the "interpretation and application of this agreement." An arbitration decision based solely on external law would not "draw its essence" from the collective bargaining agreement, and thus would not merit judicial enforcement under the third of the *Trilogy* cases, United Steelworkers of America v. Enterprise Wheel & Car Corp., 363 U.S. 593, 80 S.Ct. 1358, 4 L.Ed.2d 1424 (1960). On the other hand, the *Enterprise Wheel* Court expressly stated that an arbitrator could look to the law "for help in determining the sense of the agreement."

Union security disputes exacerbate the external-law problem because constitutional and statutory laws govern every aspect: which employees are covered, what the union can demand from covered employees, which expenditures the union may charge objectors, and what procedures the union must provide for objectors. An arbitrator's failure to resolve the legal questions in such cases almost begs for subsequent litigation, and virtually ensures that the award will not have the virtue of "finality." In fact, though, union security arbitrations seldom present difficult external-law questions because labor and management usually concede the law's governing nature.

article by Kenneth G. Dau–Schmidt cited in note 1, especially at 53, nn. 13–14. In 1988, the International Union of Electronic, Electrical, Salaried, Machine and Furniture Workers (IUE) had only three requests for financial core status from its 180,000 members. 132 Labor Relations Reporter 461 (1989).

5. Among the better contributions to this debate are Milton L. Chappell, *From Abood to Tierney: You've Come a Long Way*, 15 Ohio Northern University Law Review 1 (1988); Dau–Schmidt, *supra* note 1; Roger Hartley, *Constitutional Values and Adjudication of Taft–Hartley Act Dues Objector Cases*, 41 Hastings Law Journal 1 (1989); Elena Matsis, *Procedural Rights of Fair Share Objectors After* Hudson *and* Beck, 6 The Labor Lawyer 251 (1990); Dennis C. Shea, *Unions, Union Membership, and Union Security*, 11 Seton Hall Legislative Journal 1 (1987); and Edwin Vieira, Jr., Communications Workers of America v. Beck: *A Victory for Nonunion Employees Already Under Attack*, 11 Government Union Review 1 (1990).

UNDS
112 LA 14 (Herbert L. Haber, 1999).*

The Company is an over-the-road regional trucker headquartered at its terminal in Edison, New Jersey and operating a small warehouse facility in Winchester, Virginia. Its Agreement with the Union covers all of its drivers, including those assigned to the Winchester terminal. That Agreement provides in pertinent part as follows:

ARTICLE 2. UNION RECOGNITION

[Section 3 obliged employees to "become and remain members in good standing" as a condition of employment, required those who were not members to pay the "agreed-upon agency fee," and directed the employer to collect the fee and remit it to the union each month. In Section 4 the employer agreed discharge employees who did not tender the required fees.]

[BACKGROUND]

In a letter dated July 9, 1997, the Union advised Thomas Baio, Company Vice–President, that several workers had "failed to tender the initiation fees, periodic dues or agency fees" required by the Agreement and demanded that the Company "suspend the work privileges of those Drivers." Attached to the letter were "Suspension Notices" that had been sent to each of the Drivers informing them that "your dues are in arrears in the amount of $xxxx.00 which places your standing in the Union and the industry in serious jeopardy." The notices also stated that "you are now, because of your dues delinquency, a member in bad standing and subject to suspension of your work privileges." All of the affected employees, Harry Flesher, Richard Ewing, Robert Bracklehurst, Constance Cross and Herman Vangrift, had been recruited for, and were assigned to, the Winchester terminal.

Cross and Bracklehurst responded to the Union notices of dues delinquency by letter, declining to join the Union and rejecting the request for fee payment claiming coverage under the provisions of Virginia's "Right-to-Work" laws. A letter from the Virginia Department of Labor and Industry, dated July 23, 1997, jointly addressed to them, was also received by the Company and Union. In that letter the Commonwealth notes the receipt of complaints from Company employees at the Company's Winchester facility alleging Union threats of job loss for their failure to join or pay dues and awareness of the Union's demand that the Company suspend drivers who have failed to join or pay dues. It then goes on to state:

> Threats and intimidation in connection with union membership constitute criminal violations under Sections 40.1–66 and–69 of the Code of Virginia (1950), as amended. It is also a criminal violation of Sections 40.1–60 and–62 of the Code for the employer to terminate

* Reprinted with permission from *Labor Arbitration Reporter–Labor Arbitration Reports*, 112 LA 14. Copyright 1999 by The Bureau of National Affairs, Inc. (800–372–1033) <http://www.bna.com>.

or take any other adverse action against employees because they decline to join the Union or pay fees. * * *

Please be assured that the Commonwealth will take all available steps to enforce its Right-to-Work laws, including its protection of employees from threats, intimidation, and adverse action of any kind. * * * This is to request that you immediately take steps to insure that no representative or agent of your Union violates these criminal statutes.

The Company did not suspend the named employees and the grievance followed.

[POSITIONS OF THE PARTIES]

At the hearing the Company stated that * * * it had not acted to suspend its Winchester Terminal employees, because of its belief that the Union's notices seeking dues payment to those employees were not in compliance with federal law and because of its concern that suspending the working privileges of the non-dues paying employees would constitute criminal violations of Virginia law.

The Company points out that the Agreement confirms the applicability of federal law and that the terms, manner, and procedures to be followed by the Union in attempting to collect agency fees and dues are well established under that law. It observes that the Supreme Court, in NLRB v. General Motors, 373 U.S. 734 [53 LRRM 2313] (1963), held that the "burdens of [Union] membership upon which employment may be conditioned, are expressly limited to the payment of initiation fees and monthly dues," and that such membership is "whittled down to its financial core" (742); that in Communication Workers v. Beck, 487 U.S. 735 [128 LRRM 2729] (1988), the Court went on to further explicate its earlier holding by noting that Section8(a)(3) of the National Labor Relations Act ("NLRA")29 U.S.C. Section 158(a)(3)

> authorizes the exaction of only those fees and dues necessary to 'performing the duties of an exclusive bargaining representative of the employees in dealing with the employer on labor-management issues,' "(762–63);

and that the National Labor Relations Board ("NLRB"), in its implementation of the law, requires that a union, in moving to collect fees and dues from nonmember employees under a negotiated union-security clause, must

> at a minimum give the employee reasonable notice of the delinquency including a statement of the precise amount and months for which dues are owed and of the method used to compute the amount, tell the employee when to make the required payments, and explain to the employee that failure to pay will result in discharge. California Saw & Knife Works, 320 NLRB 224 232 [151 LRRM 1121].

It further notes that the Board requires that the notice to the affected employee also inform the employee that

> he has the right to be or remain a nonmember and that nonmembers have the right (1) to object to paying for union activities not germane to the union's duties as bargaining agent and to obtain a reduction in fees for such activities; (2) to be given sufficient information to enable the employee to intelligently decide whether to object; and (3) to be apprised of any internal union procedures for filing objections. If the employee chooses to object, he must be apprised of the percentage of the reduction, the basis for the calculation, and the right to challenge these figures, Id. 233.

The Company points out that in California Saw, the Board, after first noting the Section 8(a)(3) provisions that an employer acting under a negotiated union-security clause will not be deemed to have committed an unfair labor practice if it discharges an employee at the union's request for failure to tender dues and fees provided it has reasonable grounds to believe the discharge is proper, went on to state that

> [i]n determining whether such grounds exist, the employer has a duty of inquiry 'where the employer is aware of * * * facts that would lead [it] to believe that the discharge may be for an improper purpose'. (246)

The Company asserts that the record of these proceedings confirms the validity of its initial belief that the Union's agency fee collection procedures violate the federal law. It observes that Union witnesses stated that the Union collects more than 100% of union dues from agency fees payers and acknowledged the absence of any Union established formal procedure by which employees can obtain an accounting of union expenditures or object to such expenditures not germane to bargaining unit activities, and it notes that the Union's "Suspension Notice" of claimed due delinquencies did not stipulate the "precise amount and month" of such claimed delinquencies nor provide notice of the employee's Beck rights as required by the NLRB (See California Saw 232–233). The Company avers that, by these failures, the Union's request for the termination of the affected employees violates federal law, and by extension the Agreement, and that, accordingly, the Union's grievance seeking enforcement of that improper request must be denied. It also argues that the affected employees cannot be charged for back dues or fees because the Union cannot exact or collect dues until such time as it provides an accounting and objection procedure as required by Beck.

With respect to the issue of the applicability of Virginia law in this dispute, the Company points out that it has been specifically advised by the Virginia Department of Labor and Industry that the Commonwealth would vigorously enforce its Rights-to-Work laws and that the Commonwealth has already made a preliminary determination of its jurisdiction over these employees and had informed the Union that the Union's failure to register with the Commonwealth is in violation of its law.

Moreover, the Company argues that, in the absence of Union compliance with the responsibilities imposed on it by Beck and California Saw, inquiry into Virginia Law applicability in this proceeding is premature and unnecessary to determine this grievance, and that a fresh review of its compliance would be required by any future implementation of the indicated notices and procedures by the Union. Finally, the Company * * * it observes that application of this "continuing contract"/job situs test in the instant matter, which would require consideration of the overall time the affected workers spend in Virginia versus others states, would necessitate testimony by these employees and the submission of relevant evidence. * * *

The Union, for its part, [contends] that the central issue in these proceedings is the applicability for the Virginia statute and it observes that the Supreme Court has addressed this question in Mobil Oil and has established "predominant job situs" as the controlling factor. * * * The Union asserts that an examination of the driver's mileage and DOT records will establish that the affected employees will confirm that they spend no more than 5% to 10% of their time in Commonwealth of Virginia.

The Union does not dispute the applicability of Federal Law in this matter. It maintains, however, that the Company's reliance on General Motors and Beck is misplaced. It argues that the Courts and the Board have uniformly held that the use of language requiring union membership in contractual union-security clauses is permissible so long as it is clear that such "membership" involves no more than the payment of regular dues (citations omitted), and that Beck's holding that the Union's fees are limited to its expenses for activities germane to collective bargaining, contract administration and grievance adjustment, as opposed to expenditures for political or ideological causes, are not applicable here because all of the Union's income and assets are devoted to "core" issues. * * *

DISCUSSION

It is undisputed that Federal Law governs in this matter and that any application of Virginia's Right-to-Work law would be based on a determination of work activity using the "predominant job situs" rule as the controlling factor. I also find it indisputable the reasonableness of the Company's concern that it would be vulnerable to unfair labor practice charges and criminal liability were it to accede to the Union's request that the named employees be discharged for failure to pay dues, given its more accurate interpretation of the Federal Law requirements for Union behavior in this area.

While the law relating to the collective bargaining agreement use of "membership" as applying to agency fee payments is currently unsettled—different Circuit Courts offering a variety of holdings in this connection—the notice and procedural requirements associated with agency fee payments are clearly established by the Board in California

Saw (later confirmed by the Seventh Circuit, enf'd Machinists v. NLRB, 133 F.3d 1012 [157 LRRM 2287] [1998]). The Board has declared that the Union is required to inform members of the bargaining unit covered by its negotiated union security clause that they have

> the right to be or remain a nonmember and that nonmembers have the right (1) to object to paying for union activities not germane to the union's duties as bargaining agent and to obtain a reduction in fees for such activities; (2) to be given sufficient information to enable the employee to intelligently decide whether to object; and (3) to be apprised of any internal union procedures for filing objections. If the employee chooses to object, he must be apprised of the percentage of the reduction, the basis for the calculation, and the right to challenge these figures. (Id. 33).

The Board also requires that any notice of claimed delinquency of dues or fee payments sent to an agency fee payer include "a statement of the precise amount and months for which dues are owed and of the method used to compute the calculation" (id.). In the case at bar, the Union's "Suspension Notice," its only communication in this regard to the affected employees, is not in compliance with these Board mandated requirements. Nor is its statement permitting it to assess agency fee payments which may exceed dues payable monthly by union members by 5% in compliance with these Federal regulations. Until the Union meets all of these requirements, its request for the discharge of agency fee payers for non-payment of dues violates both Federal Law and its Agreement. Given these circumstances, its grievance must be denied.

AWARD

In the light of the above finding, and because further evidentiary hearing would be required with respect to the question of the applicability of Virginia Law in this situation, I do not address that issue at this time. Should this matter of Agency Fee collection again be brought before me in my capacity as Impartial Chairman under the Agreement, I will expect the parties to be prepared to address both the question of the Union's substantive and procedural compliance with the Federal Law, and the applicability of the Virginia Right to Work Law to the matter.

Notes and Questions

1. Because both parties agreed that federal and state law controlled the case and presented their legal arguments to him, Arbitrator Haber had authority to apply external law. Often that is not the case. In Hartford Provision Co., 89 LA 590 (Howard R. Sacks, 1987), the employer wanted the arbitrator to consider the law while the union's position wavered. Said the arbitrator, "Accordingly, I do not think I would be violating the mandate of the parties if I were to take jurisdiction of that issue, and I have formulated the submission accordingly." He also found that it would be "sensible" for him to deal with the legal issues:

> If I were simply to follow the contract, and order the Employer to take steps to enforce the union security provision, the inevitable result would

be that the Employer would challenge my order in some other forum. Thus, enforcing the contract as written will produce not finality, but simply another proceeding in another forum. On the other hand, if I decide the statutory issue, there is a fair chance that the result will be final. The issue does not appear unusually difficult; I have had training and experience in interpreting statutes, including the NLRA; and the issue has been briefed by experienced labor lawyers.

2. Not all arbitrators are so eager to resolve statutory questions. In City of Effingham, Illinois, 108 LA 1131 (Harvey A. Nathan, 1997), the arbitrator refused to consider an opinion of the General Counsel of the Illinois Labor Relations Board that the union security clause violated Illinois law:

A labor arbitrator is not the guardian of the public interest. He does not sit as a public officer or as an agent of a regulatory body. The labor arbitrator is the guardian of the contract. He is limited to interpreting the contract and in resolving disputes in a manner which is true to the contract. If there is an issue of public policy or statutory interpretation outside the four corners of the contract, that is for a public body.

3. Arbitrator Haber's task was also made easier because of the union's clear failure to comply with the notification requirements announced by the Board in California Saw. By denying the grievance on that ground, he put off for another day the much more difficult questions of whether Virginia's right to work law barred compulsory collection of dues and whether, if it did not, the union's charges and procedures complied with federal law.

4. ARBITRATION OF UNION SECURITY DISPUTES

Union security disputes reaching arbitration fall into two main categories. The first category (of which Hartford Provision is a good example) includes claims that the employer breached the collective bargaining agreement by not enforcing a union or agency shop provision. The second, following in the wake of Hudson and other court decisions, involves determination of the amount of money unions may charge fee objectors.

(a) Enforcement of Union Security Agreements

J. W. WELLS LUMBER CO.
42 LA 678 (Robert Howlett, 1964).*

[Section 6 of the parties' agreement provided that "All present employees of the Company and all new employees, after the expiration of their period of probationary employment * * * who do not join the Union shall, as a condition of employment, pay to the Union each month a service charge as a contribution toward the administration of this Agreement, in an amount equal to that paid by other employees of the bargaining unit who are members of the Union * * *. There will be no

* Reprinted with permission from Labor Arbitration Reporter–Labor Arbitration Reports, 42 LA 678. Copyright 1964 by The Bureau of National Affairs, Inc. (800–372–1033) <http://www.bna.com>.

check-off of these dues by the Company." When some employees failed to pay, the union posted a notice warning them that continued failure "will result in your discharge." The union then asked the company to terminate the employees who still did not pay. The company refused, arguing that it was up to the union to persuade the employees to pay or to sue them for the money. Section 7 forbade the arbitration board "to add to, to ignore, or to modify" the agreement.]

The evidence and analysis of the contract disclose that the grievance has merit and should be sustained.

Payment of the service charge in an amount equal to the union's initiation fees and dues is a "condition of employment." "Condition" means that an employee is not entitled to employment *unless* the initiation fees and dues, or services charges, are paid. * * *

An employee who does not pay the service charge has not fulfilled this condition of employment; hence is not entitled to retain employee status. * * *

This condition is no different than other conditions of employment which, if not met, may lead to dismissal, even though a collective contract does not affirmatively state that non-compliance with the condition will result in dismissal. An employee who is not qualified to perform the work of this job may be terminated, and an arbitrator will affirm a management decision of dismissal even though the contract does not include a provision authorizing dismissal. And as a corollary, and perhaps more to the point here, arbitrators will reinstate employees discharged for insufficient reasons, even though the affirmative power of reinstatement is not mentioned, or the contract does not limit discharge to "just cause." * * *

Here, the Union has the right to receive a service charge from non-member employees; employees who fail to pay the service charge (or initiation fee and dues, if members) are not entitled to retain employee status.

The agreement neither requires that enforcement be found outside the collective contract nor prohibits the arbitrator from applying a remedy. To the contrary, the contract vests in the arbitrator the power to direct compliance with the contract.

Section 7 contains a complete grievance procedure. The purpose of the grievance procedure is stated in the first paragraph of the Section:

> It is the intent of this Article to provide an efficient and orderly means of satisfactorily adjusting complaints and grievances. A grievance is a claim that rights have been violated because of a violation or misinterpretation of the terms of this Agreement.

The thrust of the paragraph is adjustment of complaints and grievances. If a complaint or grievance has merit, adjustment requires affirmative action to correct the violation or misinterpretation of the contract. The contract recognizes that the Board of Arbitration is to render a binding decision, for it sets up an arbitration procedure which provides for a hearing and a "finding and decision (which shall be) final and binding upon the Company, the Union and the Employees." Section 7 decrees that the "function of the Board of Arbitration shall be of a judicial nature."

Any tribunal which has judicial power has authority to enter an order subject to enforcement. A method of enforcement is provided by both Michigan and Federal law. [The arbitrator then discussed the Michigan arbitration statute, § 301(a) of the LMRA, and the *Steelworkers Trilogy*.]

I recognize the limiting nature of Carr v. Kalamazoo Vegetable Parchment Co., 354 Mich. 327, 332 (1958):

> An arbitrator is not a chancellor. He possesses no equitable powers excepting as the submission may expressly grant such. He is in no position to mollify, qualify, or straddle, and he has no right to dictate specific types of relief outside the scope of the submitted issue or issues, once he has decided the latter.

The decision, however, does not limit an arbitrator's power to dictate relief *inside* the scope of the submitted issue. By indirection, it says that an arbitrator has power to dictate relief applicable to the submitted issue.

In summary:

1.   Under the provisions of Section 6, employees who do not pay the service charge as provided thereunder are not entitled to continue as employees of J. W. Wells Lumber Company and must be terminated.

2.   Management is required under the provisions of the contract to notify such employees of termination.

3.   As arbitrator I have the power under the contract to direct termination of employees who do not pay the service charge in Section 6.
* * *

I shall stay the execution of my award until June 1, 1964. If by that date, the delinquent employees named above have not paid all monthly service charges due prior to March 1, 1964 (through February, 1964), such employees shall, as of June 1, 1964, be terminated as employees of J. W. Wells Lumber Company pursuant to the rules established in the Award.

Notes and Questions

1.   Why does the arbitrator discuss the employer's power to discharge unqualified employees, and the arbitrator's power to reinstate improperly discharged employees? How does the arbitrator get from the terms of Section 6 to his order to the employer? Does he "add to" or "modify" the Agreement in violation of Section 7?

2.   *Remedies for violations of union security agreements.* Did Arbitrator Howlett exceed his remedial authority by ordering termination of employees

who failed to pay union dues? What alternative remedies might he have ordered?

(a) Normally the arbitrator will direct the employer to fire the objecting employees, although there is a strong tendency to give them one last chance to pay the required money just as Arbitrator Howlett did. See, *e.g.*, Westinghouse Electric Corp., 56 LA 588 (Sidney A. Wolff, 1971) (employer must fire the employee if he does not pay the money owed within another 30 days); Colwell General, Inc., 104 LA 1036 (Robert H. Brunner, 1995) ("we balk at outright firing of [the non-payers] even though bound by the contract to do so. Rather, it is directed that [they] be given another opportunity in light of this decision to join the Union by tender of initiation fee and dues, within ten days of receipt of this decision by the Company"); and Oklahoma Fixture Co., 114 LA 1733 (Ed W. Bankston, 2000) (giving fee objectors three months to pay accumulated dues of about $1,500 each). In Savoy Laundry and Linen Supply, Inc., 48 LA 760, 763 (Clyde W. Summers, George Froehlich, and George F. McDonough, 1967), the arbitration board admitted that the contract called for dismissal but nevertheless urged "the Union not to assert that right without mercy, but rather to give the present employees an opportunity to pay their dues and avoid dismissal."

(b) If the employer belatedly fires the offending employee, the union would still be out the dues and fees it would otherwise have received. Must the union sue the employee, or can it force the employer to make up the difference? In Great Western Carpet Cushion Co., Inc., 95 LA 1057, 1060 (Leo Weiss, 1990), the arbitrator gave the employees ten days to resolve their differences with the union and ordered the employer to fire those who failed to do so. He also ordered the employer to pay the union the dues and initiation fees the objecting employees would have paid to the union. On reconsideration, though, he dropped the initiation fee obligation, reasoning that this was a one-time assessment which the employees should pay even if they belatedly joined the union. Unlike missed dues payments, initiation fees did not increase because of the company's breach. Arbitrator Jerry Fullmer, in St. Elizabeth Health Center, 118 LA 37 (2002), found that the employer repeatedly deducted far less from employees' pay than the union was owed. Because it would be impossible, due to employee turnover and other factors, to make up the amount due by means of future wage deductions, he directed the employer to pay the union directly.

(c) Assuming the employees signed a checkoff agreement, should an arbitrator just order the employer to deduct the dues from the employees' pay, since it's really the *employees'* obligation? Can you think of any legal problems with such an order? (In *Great Western*, Arbitrator Weiss placed the burden on the employer because it had misled the employees into thinking they did not have to pay.)

(d) Whether the employer itself is liable to the union may turn on whether the employees had ever authorized the employer to deduct union fees. State wage-payment statutes usually prohibit unauthorized deductions from wages, so if the employees have not signed a checkoff agreement, the employer could not legally deduct money for the union. The only remedy in such a case would be an order to comply with the union security clause and discharge the non-payers. See Yukon Manufacturing, Inc., 105 LA 339

(Barry C. Brown, 1995). Once the employees sign a checkoff agreement, however, they may be held to its terms even if they later resign from full union membership, City of Effingham, Illinois, 108 LA 1131 (Harvey A. Nathan, 1997).

3.   You now know that a union may not demand more from represented employees than payment of certain dues and fees, but how many affected employees know that? Whose job is it to inform them? If a union fails to inform employees of the agency fee option and instead tells them they must "join" the union, may it still insist that the employer fire those who do not join? Until 1998, it was arguable that a union's failure to advise employees of their rights might violate its duty of fair representation. In the *Marquez* case cited at footnote 3, the Supreme Court held that it did not. In any event, as Arbitrator Weiss held in the *Great Western* case, a possible breach by the union of its duty of fair representation would not be a defense for an employer's breach of its contractual obligations under the union security agreement.

Shortly after taking office in 2001, President George W. Bush issued Executive Order 13,201, 66 Fed. Reg. 11,221 (2001). The Order directed federal government contractors to post notices informing their employees that those who are not members of the union "can object to the use of their payments for certain purposes and can only be required to pay their share of union costs relating to collective bargaining, contract administration, and grievance adjustment." The United Auto Workers quickly challenged the Executive Order in court, arguing that it was preempted by the National Labor Relations Act. In a 2–1 decision, the D.C. Circuit rejected the union's arguments. UAW–Labor Employment and Training Corp. v. Chao, 325 F.3d 360 (2003), cert. denied, ___ U.S. ___, 124 S.Ct. 2014, 158 L.Ed.2d 490 (2004).

4.   Some arbitrators are still reluctant to apply external law to contract disputes unless the parties explicitly authorize them to do so. That doesn't seem to be the case with union security arbitrations. The law so permeates the field that most arbitrators use it without a qualm. In UNDS, 112 LA 14 (Herbert L. Haber, 1999), for example, the union filed a grievance seeking to force the employer to discharge five employees for non-payment of fees. The arbitrator concluded that the union had not properly notified the employees of their obligation, had not given them sufficient information about the chargeability of union expenditures, and had charged them more in agency fees than the union charged its members in monthly dues. Because these practices violated the NLRA as interpreted by the Supreme Court, the arbitrator denied the grievance.

5.   *Conscientious objection to membership or dues payment.* Does an employee's conscientious objection to joining or supporting a union excuse the employer from enforcing a union security agreement? In Union Pacific Railroad Co., 22 LA 20, 21 (Edgar L. Warren, 1954), an employee subject to a union shop agreement refused to join or to pay an agency fee, explaining:

> There are thousands of Christians in this country including some in this company's employ who honor God and pray for what is right and many such persons believe membership in unions involves a violation of the laws of God. I would ask you to read from 2 Corinthians Vi 14–18—"Be

not unequally yoked together with unbelievers * * * what part hath he that believeth with an infidel or unbeliever." Place these inspired words alongside the scripture in I Cor. 14.37 "Let him acknowledge that the things I write are the commandments of the Lord" and you will see that to those who accept the Bible or the Scriptures as the Word of God and would obey it, the bond of unionism with men who do not even nominally believe in the Lord would constitute disobedience to the Lord's commandments.

The union rejected the employee's offer to contribute to the Red Cross an amount equal to dues and fees. The arbitrator declined to rule on the constitutionality of the union shop and directed the employer to fire the employee. (The grievant's case was not strengthened by evidence he had previously belonged to an association the union regarded as a "company union.")

Cases like this led Congress to amend the NLRA in 1980. Section 19 now permits some conscientious objectors to contribute money in lieu of union dues to one of three charities specified in the collective agreement. Section 19 only protects members of a religious group whose "established and traditional tenets or teachings" prohibit union membership. One court has held that this limitation violates the First Amendment's Establishment Clause. Wilson v. NLRB, 920 F.2d 1282 (6th Cir.1990), cert. denied, 505 U.S. 1218, 112 S.Ct. 3025, 120 L.Ed.2d 896 (1992).

6. *Checkoffs.* Checkoff arrangements are the weakest and superficially the simplest of union security agreements. Nevertheless, they pose many potential legal and contractual problems, involving such difficulties as determining which employees the provision covers, which union claims are "dues and fees" and which are something else, and whether the checkoff authorization is effective after a contract expires or an employee resigns from the union. See generally, Thomas R. Haggard, *Union Checkoff Arrangements Under the National Labor Relations Act,* 39 DePaul Law Review 567 (1990). Professor Haggard finds that the NLRB seldom defers to arbitration decisions on checkoff disputes, so he suggests that the Board simply do away with the middleperson and resolve all such conflicts itself.

7. *Hiring hall agreements.* A stronger type of union security agreement, not discussed above, is the employer's promise to obtain employees through a union-run hiring hall. Although hiring halls are by law prohibited from discriminating against non-members, in fact some of them do. In any event, the mere fact that the hiring hall provides access to work is a powerful incentive to join the union. Rarely do hiring hall matters reach arbitration. When they do, it is usually in the context of an allegation that an employer hired workers from some other source. See, e.g., Levernier Construction, Inc., 113 LA 152 (James J. Gallagher, 1999). The hiring-hall agreement allowed employers to hire from other sources if the union could not provide qualified employees within 48 hours. On occasion the hiring hall was unable to provide workers in a timely manner. Levernier needed cement masons for an emergency job that had to be completed over the next two days and therefore hired four non-union workers. The arbitrator found that the emergency nature of the work excused compliance with the normal hiring hall procedures but still found a violation because the employer

should at least have contacted the union to see if it could provide the needed workers the next day.

(b) Compulsory Fee Disputes

INTERNATIONAL BROTHERHOOD OF FIREMEN AND OILERS, LOCAL 100
95 LA 189 (Nicholas Duda, 1990).*

[Certain employees of the Akron School Board protested the amount of the so-called "fair share" fee the union claimed they had to pay, which amounted to 48.4% of the usual dues. After the Supreme Court's decision in Chicago Teachers Union, Local 1 v. Hudson, 475 U.S. 292, 106 S.Ct. 1066, 89 L.Ed.2d 232 (1986), the union adopted the American Arbitration Association's "Rules for Impartial Determination of Union Fees" to deal with such disputes. It notified non-members of the proposed fee for the 1989–90 school year. Seven employees challenged the proposal, but only three remain in this arbitration. Each had left the union because of dissatisfaction with some action or policy.]

The specific question is whether 48.4% of the expenditures of Local #100 are properly chargeable to fair share payers as their pro rata shares of the cost of collective bargaining, contract administration, or grievance adjustment? If not, what percentage of the expenses are properly chargeable to fair share payers? * * *

The Categories of Expenditures for Which Challengers Were Charged

The fee payers' challenges are before this Arbitrator for decision with the burden of proving chargeability on the Union. The Union claims that all expenditures it charged were for collective bargaining, contract administration and grievance adjustment. Those are valid reasons to charge under federal (e.g. Abood) and state law (O.R.C. 4117).

All calculations for the computations to determine the amount of fair share for the year 1989–1990 were based on expenditures for the 12 month period beginning October 1, 1988 and ending September 30, 1989, the prior year. The Arbitrator finds that reference period to be comparable, reasonable and not improper. The Local spent $71,413.08 in the reference period including $36,853.75 given to the International Union and the Regional AFL–CIO Labor Council. The Local Union spent $34,559.33 for other purposes. The Union did not attempt to charge the fee payers for any payments to the International Union or to the regional union organization.

At the arbitration hearing, the Arbitrator assured the Challengers as indicated above, that there was no legal prohibition per se against fair share fees. On hearing that, two of the Challengers indicated that they were not interested in challenging the chargeability of any of the Local's expenditures which amounted to $34,559.33 because of the acknowledged honesty and integrity of Mr. Willoughby. However, one Challenger and therefore the Arbitrator insisted the Union show details and proof about the expenditures and categories for which fair share payers were being charged. In addition to the data presented to the Arbitrator at the hearing, other information was later sent to the Arbitrator at his request from the Shaker Heights Business Representatives and from Certified Public Accountants for the Akron, Cuyahoga Falls and Tallmadge units.

The Arbitrator reviewed each of the expense categories and the proof in detail. Although the Local is of substantial size in respect to total employees and number of bargaining units, the staff and administrative work is performed by only one full time worker—Business Agent and Treasurer Willoughby—aided by one part time office worker paid only $5,000/year. Much work is performed by volunteers who receive no money or a flat monthly amount so nominal it might more properly be considered a token, probably not fully reimbursing for time and out-of-pocket expenses in connection with collective bargaining duties. Thus, the amounts the Union charge were quite modest, reflecting an economical operation of the Local.

In addition however, the Local was very conservative in setting the categories for which non-members would be charged. Over one half of the Local's expenditures were to its International. Certainly a case could have been made that some of the money sent to the International was chargeable under the applicable standards. However, the Local made no attempt to establish such a claim. That reluctance might stem from the reality that seeking another $30 from each of 10–15 employees, for a total of $300–$400 for the 1989–1990 school year would have required a much larger expenditure involving time and travel expenses, etc. by International officers who would have participated in a broader hearing.

The vast majority of expenditures charged were directly related to contract negotiation and grievance administration. For example, the $20,000.00 in wages for the Business Agent and part-time employee and the various expenses for meetings, transportation, etc. are clearly chargeable as direct collective bargaining expenses. Most of the other expense categories deal with items such as rent, services (utilities, phone, etc.), and payroll cost, all of which re chargeable as related to collective bargaining. The $1,349.60 for "Legal & Audit" is also chargeable as indirect collective bargaining expense.

There were only two items that were at all questionable. The first item was a "donation" of $359 for a table of six at a dinner sponsored by the Community Action Council whose membership is confined to AFL–CIO Unions and business organizations. Six members of the executive board attend that dinner each year, including 1988–1989, as representatives of Local 100. Activities of the Council are intended to benefit community employers and employees. However, the local has only considered Union members for attendance as representatives of the Union.

Inasmuch as this dinner was a "Union members only" function, the expenditure for tickets is not chargeable to non-members.

The other item questioned was an amount of $3,000 given to the Shaker Heights unit when it separated into its own administration * * * Local #100 tendered them $3,000 or approximately $20 per member which was considerably less than each person's proportionate "share" of the treasury.

Under the circumstances the Arbitrator does not consider this "expenditure" to be violative of the constitutional and statutory standards. The item was in the nature of a partial disbursement of savings to the Shaker Heights unit assuming the collective bargaining responsibility for 20% of the bargaining members and labor agreements. In light of the reduced work obligation and attendant costs to Local #100 resulting from relinquishment of the Shaker Heights collective bargaining responsibility, the $3,000 was a modest expenditure in relation to collective bargaining and therefore chargeable.

In view of the foregoing, the total expenditures ($34,559.33) claimed from fair share payers must be reduced by $359.39. Stated another way, the non-chargeable expenses should be increased by the same amount to become $37,213.14. That figure divided by the total expenditures— $71,413.08—results in 52.1 percentage of rebate, rather than the 51.6% determined by the Union.

Under the Union's rebate percentage, a full time person was "rebated" $5.68 per month from the dues amount of $11.00. The revision determined by the Arbitrator increases the rebate amount to $5.73 per month, a difference of only 5 cents per month. The same type of adjustment, using 52.1, should be made in the rebate due other types of employees.

The Challenger Complaints About Union Performance

Under the law, the Arbitrator has jurisdiction to determine the fair share fee for the 1989–1990 school year. He may do so despite a challenger's prior refusal to accept the Union's determination. (Actually such challenge is the basis for the Arbitrator's involvement.) However, the Arbitrator's authority is limited to that issue. He cannot consider the claim to overcharges in 1985 or earlier. Similarly, the Arbitrator has no jurisdiction to review complaints the Challengers have held against the Union for many years. As explained by the Arbitrator at the hearing, other forums are available to pursue such claims.

Award

Although the fair share fee provision is permitted under state and federal law, the specific rebate percentage determined by the Union for school year 1989–1990 must be changed from 51.6% to 52.11%. The Union is directed to make that change.

Notes and Questions

1. This relatively simple case gives you a peek at a complex problem, that of determining just which expenditures the union can charge to dues objectors. Do you agree with Arbitrator Duda's conclusions? Why or why not? For a thorough discussion of the possible categories of union expenditures, see Roger Hartley, *Constitutional Values and Adjudications of Taft–Hartley Dues Objector Cases, supra* footnote 5. Professor Hartley interprets the cases to permit charges for "nonexpressive activity," "expressive activities engaged in as contract negotiator or administrator," and "other expressive activity supporting the collective bargaining function," but not for "expressive activity not bearing a real and substantial relationship to collective bargaining generally" or for tangible benefits non-members cannot receive. Would accepting his proposed categories solve union security fee disputes?

2. Arbitrator Duda found that the union must rebate 52.11% of the usual dues to objecting employees; in other words, only 47.89% of the local's expenditures were properly chargeable to them. This is an unusually low percentage, primarily because the local did not present evidence on the nature of the regional and national bodies' expenditures. Transportation Communications International Union, 93 LA 732 (James Harkless, 1989) presents a striking contrast. Arbitrator Harkless sustained the union's determination that 99% of the local's expenditures were chargeable, and accepted a determination by the same Professor Hartley cited in the previous note that 82% of the national organization's expenditures were chargeable. (Like several other unions, this one hired an arbitrator to help it classify its expenditures after the recent Supreme Court cases.) Other cases produce similar figures, *e.g.,* United Automobile Workers, 94 LA 1272 (Alan Walt, 1990) (84%); California Federation of Teachers, 95 LA 25 (David A. Concepcion, 1990) (90%); and Association of Professional Flight Attendants, 107 LA 548 (David A. Concepcion, 1996) (98%).

3. As these high figures indicate, arbitrators have been quite sympathetic to union claims that challenged expenditures are "germane" to the union's representation obligations. UAW Locals 6000, 723, 571, 699, and 70, 94 LA 1272 (Alan Walt, 1990) is a good example. Arbitrator Walt rejected challenges to union expenditures for (a) support of a family education center used by bargaining unit members' families, because "family participation and support becomes crucial" if there is a strike; (b) assistance to retired members who are no longer members of the bargaining unit; (c) a Civil Rights Fund use to implement union policies regarding fair employment practices; (d) purchase of union jackets for officers and staff so that members could identify them in and out of the plant; and (e) expenses of attendance at the union's drug and alcohol training seminar. The Arbitrator found that 86% of the International's expenditures were chargeable, as were 93–99% of the various locals' expenditures.

4. Fee disputes present some unique procedural problems.

(a) The normal grievance involves a dispute between the employer and the union. Fee disputes, in contrast, usually involve differences between some employees and the union. Nevertheless, unless the union establishes a special *Hudson*-type procedure, the matter might squeeze somewhat uneasily into the usual arbitration procedure in which employees are not formal parties. Can the objectors count on the employer to represent their interests? Why or why not? If not, must the union allow the objectors to participate as parties? Will they be likely to do so? How much of a stake does the individual objector have in a fee dispute? (Typical union dues amount to one or two hours' pay per month.) If you had that small a stake, how much time and effort would you invest in a protest? (The grievants in Arbitrator Duda's case "won" an extra five cents per month.) Even if the individual objectors are willing to participate, how effective will they be? If they are unlikely to be effective on their own, who might speak on their behalf? Most of the major union security court cases have been brought by, or assisted by, the National Right to Work Legal Defense Foundation, an organization unions believe to be anti-union, not merely pro-dissenter.

(b) If the union does establish a *Hudson*-type procedure, should the objectors have to pay half the costs of the arbitration, the way the typical grievance arbitration parties do? Why or why not? If not, who *should* pay the bill? If the union pays the bills (including the arbitrator's fee), is that likely to prejudice the result? If the dispute is really between some employees and the union, should the employer have to pay any part of the costs? Many union security agreements have indemnity clauses, under which the union agrees to reimburse the employer for any costs of complying with the agreement. See, for example, Rutgers, The State University of New Jersey, 86 LA 649 (Jay Kramer, 1985) (requiring the union to indemnify the University for legal fees and costs incurred defending a suit by non-union faculty members who challenged the agency fee deduction).

(c) Even the fairest *Hudson*-type procedure may not protect the union from suit. The Supreme Court recently held (in the *Miller* case cited in footnote 3) that unions cannot force dissenting employees to exhaust a union-created arbitration procedure before bringing claims in federal court. That ruling leaves the choice of forum to the objector. Which forum would you recommend to an objector? Why?

(d) The union has the burden of establishing the percentage of its expenditures chargeable to objectors. Is this sufficient to guarantee an accurate result? If you represented a fee objector or a union in a fee dispute grievance, how would you prepare for the case? 2002/2003 Agency Fee Challengers and Washington Education Association, 2003 WL 23350926 (Carlton J. Snow, 2003), provides an illustration. The union presented substantial statistical data on classification of its expenditures at the local, state, and national levels, including an audit by a CPA that took about 400 hours of work. The fee challengers had a simpler approach:

> Fee challengers do not offer specific arguments that the assessed fees, as such, are improper. What the challengers maintain is that the Association is required to demonstrate the propriety of any assessed fee. It is the belief of the challengers that an objective evaluation of the evidence presented by the Association will show that the fees assessed by the Association are not legally justified. Without offering any specific challenge, they implicitly call into question the reliability of data used to compute the proposed fee.

Not surprisingly, the arbitrator ultimately accepted the union's evidence and estimates of the chargeable percentages.

5. As Arbitrator Duda's case indicates, the American Arbitration Association has promulgated a set of rules for union security fee dispute arbitrations, which parties are free to adopt. Under these rules, only a union may initiate the arbitration procedure. The AAA appoints the arbitrator but the union pays all expenses. Participants may have counsel.

A NOTE ON THE QUALITY OF ARBITRATORS'
UNION–SECURITY DECISIONS

How *well* do arbitrators deal with potential conflicts between the law and the union-security agreement? One study of arbitration cases reviewed by the NLRB under its *Spielberg* doctrine found that "arbitrators interpret and apply the contract's written word, without considering the National Labor Relations Act or conducting an in-depth analysis of Board decisions," and thus uphold contract provisions the Board would find invalid. Brotman, *supra* footnote 1. Brotman's sample is skewed, however, since it deals only with the tiny minority of arbitration cases in which a party later challenges the result before the Board. A much broader survey of union-security arbitration cases reached the opposite conclusion: "most arbitrators will concern themselves with problems of statutory interpretation, while a few limit their decisions strictly to a construction of the contract." Thomas R. Haggard, Compulsory Unionism, the NLRB, and the Courts, *supra* footnote 1.

Professor Haggard also concluded (at 208–09) that arbitrators did a good job in union security cases:

> Like the statutes that authorize them, union security agreements are often ambiguously worded and, many times, merely copy the exact words of the statute itself. As have the courts, labor arbitrators have thus been confronted with many difficult problems of interpretation. They must not only determine what the law allows, but also, within that maximum, determine exactly how far the parties intended to go, and then apply the contract to factual situations that are often excruciatingly complex.

> By and large, labor arbitrators have done an admirable job in the field. The decisions reflect a keen appreciation of the underlying interests of both the employer and the union. But more important is the apparent arbitral regard for the rights of the individual employee who stands to lose the most through an adverse decision.

In his 1995 update, however, Professor Haggard emphasized the problems faced by dissenting employees. The union opposes them and often the employer remains neutral or supports the union's position:

> As a result, many violations go unremedied. The employer acquiesces in the union's demands, and the adversely affected employee either is unaware of the violation or lacks the power to file a grievance individually. Even when employers resist union demands and grievances are filed, do the employers always litigate union security issues as vigorously as they would an issue directly affecting the pocketbook or the ability to manage?

The AAA-sanctioned fair share arbitrations are more troublesome. Since the participants are limited to the union and the objecting employees, the representation an employer might provide in a normal union-employer arbitration is lacking. Moreover, protesting employees often are neither represented by counsel nor possess the expertise to evaluate and challenge the union's complicated and extensive financial data. It is to the credit of arbitrators who have heard some of these cases that they have attempted to assist the employees in framing the issues and in evaluating the financial data. One can, however, seriously question whether this is either appropriate or adequate. The fact that the arbitrator is paid by the union raises serious "appearance of justice" questions.

The problem is even broader than that. After more than 50 years under the NLRA, employers, unions, and arbitrators have become parts of an essentially conservative, well-entrenched, labor-management relations "establishment." The parties are familiar with each other and with the spoken and unspoken "rules of the game." Exclusive representation, collective contracts, the coincidence of employee and union interests, and the supremacy of the group over the individual are the fundamental premises underlying this miniature, unionized industrial society. Dissident employees do not fit easily into this cozy picture. They are not part of the "club." They reject the fundamental premises. They resent the compulsion they have been subjected to by their employer and a union that they dislike. And they are justifiably suspicious of and cynical about any process, allegedly created to vindicate their rights, that is established and controlled by one or both of these parties.

* * * Although the "establishment" has provided procedures for the adjudication of these disputes, it has done so only because the law requires it. In sum, it is not an environment in which dissident employees are likely to feel welcome. In light of these considerations, the question is this: Are the traditional arbitration and AAA-sanctioned procedures truly capable of providing the kind of justice, and appearance of justice, required in this unusual situation? That the answer to that question might be "no" should be of concern to the arbitration community.

Union Security in the Context of Labor Arbitration, supra note 1, at 122–23.

Some of these concerns may have influenced the Supreme Court when it decided in *Miller* not to require dissenters to use a union-promulgated arbitration procedure. Do you agree with Professor Haggard's skepticism about the use of arbitration to resolve union security disputes? If so, what alternatives are there?

Chapter VIII

ARBITRATION IN THE PUBLIC SECTOR

A. STATE AND LOCAL GOVERNMENT[1]

1. INTRODUCTION

In many respects public-sector arbitration mirrors private-sector arbitration. In the typical discipline case involving a government employee, for example, the issues, evidence, and procedure may differ little from a similar case down the street in a manufacturing or retail business. In other respects, however, the differences are enormous.

Perhaps the greatest difference is that public sector arbitration is far more likely than private sector arbitration to involve *interest* disputes rather than grievances. Very rarely do parties in the private sector turn over their unresolved negotiating issues to an arbitrator. Most public-sector collective bargaining statutes, in contrast, *require* arbitration of negotiation impasses, primarily because most states prohibit public sector strikes and lockouts. Without the opportunity to strike or arbitrate, public-sector unionists say, collective bargaining would be reduced to "collective begging." Public-sector interest arbitration can take several forms having little counterpart in the private sector such as "med-arb" (a dispute resolution system in which a mediator who cannot bring the parties to agreement switches hats to decide the remaining issues as an arbitrator) and "final-offer" arbitration (in which the arbitrator must choose either the employer's or the union's last offer). The last option comes in two varieties, final offer by package and final offer by issue.

---

1. Bibliographic Suggestions: Arvid Anderson, *Public Sector Arbitration*, in Labor Arbitrator Development: A Handbook 93 (Christopher A. Barreca, Anne Harmon Miller, and Max Zimny, eds. 1983); Joseph R. Grodin, June M. Weisberger, and Martin H. Malin, Public Sector Employment: Cases and Materials 326–418 (2004); Joseph R. Grodin and Joyce M. Najita, *Judicial Response to Public–Sector Arbitration*, in Public Sector Bargaining 229 (Benjamin Aaron, Joyce M. Najita, and James L. Stern, eds., 2nd ed. 1988); Jerome Lefkowitz, *The Legal Framework of Labor Arbitration in the Public Sector*, in Labor Arbitration: A Practical Guide for Advocates 30 (Max Zimny, William F. Dolson, and Christopher A. Barreca, eds. 1990).

The second major distinction is that constitutions and statutes play a much greater role when the employer is a government agency. Constitutional restrictions on government action are part of the reason, but a greater explanation is that states regulate their own labor relations much more tightly than the federal government regulates private-sector labor relations. Most state statutes limit the scope of bargaining and codify management rights, for instance. Many statutes expressly subordinate the collective agreement to state laws and regulations. Frequently the contract itself will incorporate pertinent laws.

The last of the major differences is that public-sector arbitration decisions are subject to administrative and judicial review to a degree unknown in the private sector.

This chapter begins by exploring grievance arbitration in the public sector, including constitutional and statutory limitations on such arbitration. It then investigates interest arbitration in the public sector, again with some consideration of the applicable constitutional and statutory limitations. The chapter concludes with notes on interest arbitration in the private sector and in other countries.

2. GRIEVANCE ARBITRATION[2]

SCHOOL COMMITTEE OF DANVERS v. TYMAN

Supreme Judicial Court of Massachusetts, 1977.
372 Mass. 106, 360 N.E.2d 877.

WILKINS, JUSTICE: The defendants appeal from an order * * * granting a stay of arbitration concerning certain grievances asserted on behalf of the defendant Tyman, a nontenured teacher in the Danvers school system. * * * We conclude that arbitration should not have been stayed and that an order should be entered * * * directing the parties to proceed to arbitration.

The basic circumstances are not in dispute. The Danvers Teachers' Association (association) and the Danvers school committee (school committee) entered into a collective bargaining agreement for the period from September 1, 1973, to June 30, 1975. The agreement provided that a grievance, as defined therein, could be processed through four levels, the last of which called for final and binding arbitration. The agreement

---

2. Bibliographic Suggestions: George W. Bohlander, *Public Sector Grievance Arbitration: Structure and Administration*, 21 Journal of Collective Negotiations in the Public Sector 271 (1992); Charles Craver, *The Judicial Enforcement of Public Sector Grievance Arbitration*, 58 Texas Law Review 329 (1980); Clarence R. Deitsch and David A. Dilts, The Arbitration of Rights Disputes in the Public Sector (1990); Harry Graham, *Grievance Arbitration in State and Local Government in the 1990s and Beyond*, Labor Arbitration Under Fire 72 (James L. Stern and Joyce M. Najita, eds. 1997); James W. Mastriani and Robert E. Anderson, *Public Sector Scope of Bargaining and Arbitrability*, Chapter 47 of Labor and Employment Arbitration (Tim Bornstein, Ann Gosline, and Marc Greenbaum, eds. 2nd ed. 1997); and Debra J. Mesch, *Grievance Arbitration in the Public Sector: A Conceptual Framework and Empirical Analysis of Public and Private Sector Arbitration Cases*, 15 Review of Public Personnel Administration 22 (1995).

also set forth certain procedures to be followed in the evaluation of the work performance of a teacher. Those procedures included notice to a teacher of any material placed in his or her file which was derogatory to the teacher's conduct, service, character or personality; an opportunity to review that material; and a right to reply in writing. Each teacher was entitled to be advised promptly in detail of any complaints about him or her made to the school administration or to the school committee. The agreement contained a provision that "[t]he Committee retains its statutory right to rehire or not to rehire non-tenure teachers * * *."

The defendant Tyman was hired as a teacher of English for the school year commencing September 1971. In the early part of April, 1974, during the third year of her employment and, hence, during the last possible year of nontenured status, * * * the school committee voted not to rehire Tyman and on April 12, 1974, notified her in writing of its decision. A grievance was filed in May which alleged a failure to follow appropriate evaluation procedures, inadequate classroom observations and evaluations, and discrimination. The defendants did not seek explicitly to arbitrate the school committee's decision not to reappoint Tyman to a fourth year as a teacher in the school system. Arbitration was requested by the association in July, and, after a continuance a hearing was scheduled for September 10, 1974.

On September 9, 1974, the school committee filed a complaint in the Superior Court seeking, in effect, an order granting a stay of the arbitration proceeding. It is clear from the complaint that the school committee's argument was that arbitration of the grievance was barred because, under [State law], the school committee had an absolute power to pass on the question whether a non-tenured teacher's contract should be renewed. On that same day, the matter was argued by counsel and, on the basis of the complaint and the arguments of counsel, the judge entered an order granting a stay of arbitration because "the claim sought to be arbitrated does not state a controversy covered by the provision for arbitration." The defendants have appealed. On our own motion, we transferred the case here for decision.

The fundamental issue in this case arises from the tension between (1) the terms of the lawfully authorized collective bargaining agreement between the association and the school committee providing for final and binding arbitration * * *, and (2) the traditional authority of school committees in the matter of contract renewal resulting in tenure for teachers. The Legislature could have, but has not, resolved this dispute by stating explicitly, as it has in other instances * * *, whether and how far the agreement may override existing law. Our function in this case is to assess the Legislature's overall intention in light of (1) its apparent grant of full authority to school committees to agree to arbitration of "any dispute concerning the interpretation or application of * * * [a collective bargaining] agreement" * * *, and (2) the continuing, apparently unfettered, statutory authority of a school committee to determine that a non-tenured teacher "is not to be employed for the following school year." * * *

Views of various State courts have not been consistent concerning the extent to which, if at all, a school committee may assert an absolute authority to grant or deny tenure to probationary teachers in opposition to a claim of arbitrability of questions relating to nonrenewal of the teacher's contract. See Note, *Public Sector Grievance Procedures, Due Process, and the Duty of Fair Representation*, 89 Harv. L. Rev. 752, 757 n. 28 (1976). Because traditions and statutory provisions vary among States, the divergence of opinion is understandable.

In some States, the courts have held that a probationary employee may be discharged as a matter of discretion and that resort to contractual grievance procedures is impermissible. * * * In Illinois, a school board's duties in appointing teachers have been held to be nondelegable, and the failure to follow contractual evaluation procedures does not restrict a school board's statutory rights and powers to decide in its discretion not to renew a probationary teacher's contract. * * * Thus, in Illinois an arbitrator may not award an employment contact as a remedy for the violation of evaluation procedures contained in a collective bargaining agreement. * * *

In Michigan, on the other hand, the question whether a school board agreed to arbitrate the nonrenewal of a probationary teacher's contract has been left to determination by an arbitrator. *Kaleva–Norman–Dickson School Dist. No. 6 v. Kaleva–Norman–Dickson School Teachers' Ass'n*, 393 Mich. 583, 595, 89 LRRM 2078 (1975). In that opinion, no particular consideration was given to any argument that the school board had no authority to delegate to an arbitrator the question of the propriety of its failure to renew a nontenured teacher's contract. * * *

Arbitration should not have been stayed in this case. Judicial intervention is not warranted where no conflict has arisen between the consequences of the arbitration proceedings called for in the collective bargaining agreement and any nondelegable authority of the school committee.

We accept the school committee's argument that, against its will, it may not delegate to an arbitrator its authority to make decisions concerning tenure. The nondelegable authority of an incumbent school committee in the appointment and reappointment of academic personnel has a long tradition. * * * Although the Legislature has granted procedural safeguards to nontenured teachers who have been teaching for more than ninety days, where they are threatened with dismissal during a school year * * *, no such protection has been granted to such teachers when the subject of renewal or nonrenewal of their contracts is involved. Indeed, the legislature has expressly indicated that the procedural safeguards applicable to dismissal of nontenured teachers do not apply to the renewal of their contracts. * * * It is true that the tenure statute * * * has the effect of reducing the traditional, wide discretion of school committees by granting protection to teachers who have acquired tenure. It is also true that by failure to send a timely notice a teacher may acquire tenure without a conscious, affirmative act by a school committee. * * * But the fact remains that a school committee's authority to determine questions of contract renewal and tenure during the first three years of a teacher's term of employment has been left unchanged by legislation. We do not find in legislative authorization for school teachers to bargain collectively concerning "wages, hours, and other terms and conditions of employment" * * *, and to arbitrate grievances * * *, an intent to permit a school committee to bargain away its traditional authority to make tenure decisions if it so wishes. Whenever the Legislature has limited the powers of school committees, it has done so in express terms, and it is expected that a radical departure from prior policy would be clearly indicated, and not left to doubtful implication. * * *

Although a school committee may not surrender its authority to make tenure decisions, there is no reason why a school committee may not bind itself to follow certain procedures precedent to the making of any such decision. In this case, the school committee agreed to submit to arbitration on a wide range of subjects. Unless there is positive assurance that an arbitration clause is not susceptible to an interpretation that covers the asserted dispute, or unless no lawful relief conceivably can be awarded by the arbitrator, an order to arbitrate should not be denied. See *United Steelworkers of America v. Warrior & Gulf Navigation Co.*, 363 U.S. 574, 582–83 (1960); * * *. In this case, no occasion for a stay of the arbitration arises merely from the possibility of an arbitrator's award which might purport to intrude into the school committee's inviolate authority.

Any threat to the school committee's authority has not matured yet because it is far from clear that the arbitrator's award will encroach on the school committee's exclusive domain. The agreement to follow certain procedures preliminary to exercising its right to decide a tenure question, and to permit arbitration of a claim that it has failed to follow those procedures, does not impinge on a school committee's right to make the ultimate tenure decision. If a violation is found by the arbitrator, he may not grant tenure to the teacher, but he may fashion a remedy which falls short of intruding into the school committee's exclusive domain. Some violations of evaluation procedures may be trivial and not justify any relief. Not all violations of a teacher's rights, even constitutional rights, will justify reinstatement. *Mt. Healthy City School Dist. Bd. of Educ. v. Doyle*, 429 U.S. 274 (1977). The arbitrator might direct merely that the omitted procedures be followed and the teacher's record corrected as appears appropriate. However, in other cases, the failure to follow evaluation procedures may be shown to have so prejudiced a teacher's position that more substantial relief may be in order. It would be premature in this case to announce any limits on the scope of an arbitrator's award in such a case, provided it does not award tenure to the teacher. * * * We leave open the question of the validity of an award which imposes sanctions because of the failure of a school committee to follow evaluation procedures although no teacher was harmed by the omission.

If a school committee wishes to deny the application of evaluation procedures to nontenured teachers or to deny such a teacher the right to arbitrate any failure to follow such agreed procedures, the school committee can say so explicitly in the collective bargaining agreement. Once a school committee agrees to follow certain procedures and to permit binding arbitration concerning its alleged failure to adhere to those practices, we see no public policy considerations which prevent full implementation of the terms of the agreement subject, however, to the retention in favor of the school committee of its nondelegable rights. Indeed, adherence to the evaluation procedures may be expected to provide information to the school committee which will permit it to make a fairer and more informed judgment concerning a teacher. The fact that ultimately the school committee may make the tenure decision without regard to information produced pursuant to evaluation procedures in no way justifies a school committee's failure to follow the terms of its agreement both to make such evaluations and to permit arbitration of its alleged failure to do so.

The collective bargaining agreement provides that the meaning of the agreement is a "grievance" which can be submitted to arbitration. * * * The meaning of the agreement is for the arbitrator and not for the courts. The school committee may argue to the arbitrator that the grievances asserted here are not ones which may be the subject of arbitration because of the reservation by the committee of its statutory right "not to rehire non-tenure teachers." The decision of the arbitrator on such a question of interpretation will be final and not subject to review.

The order granting a stay of arbitration is vacated, and an order shall be entered * * * directing the parties to proceed to arbitration.

So ordered.

Notes and Questions

1.   The court states that a School Committee "against its will * * * may not delegate to an arbitrator its authority to make decisions concerning tenure." What does the court mean by "against its will"? And what does it mean by the word "delegate"? Suppose the School Committee agreed that it would not deny tenure arbitrarily or unreasonably, and that its agreement on that score could be enforced in court rather than through arbitration. Would that constitute a "delegation" to the court? If the union demanded the provision and the employer unsuccessfully resisted it, would the School Committee's delegation be "against its will?" Does it matter whether the "delegation" is to arbitration rather than to a court?

2.   A legislature first empowers a school board to decide tenure questions, then empowers the board to negotiate collective agreements about "terms and conditions of employment." Presumably the legislators know that collective agreements typically include arbitration clauses. Is there any reason to believe the legislature intended to deny the board power to submit tenure disputes to arbitration? Would it matter if the collective-bargaining

statute defined the scope of bargaining and management's reserved rights but said nothing about tenure decisions?

3. Public-sector grievance arbitration has often been attacked on state constitutional grounds. The usual form of the attack, alluded to in *School Committee of Danvers*, is to claim that the arbitration agreement is an impermissible "delegation of governmental power" to a private individual. Grodin and Najita, *supra* footnote 1, sum up the cases at 232–34 (footnotes omitted):

> While it is sometimes said that courts at common law disapproved the arbitration of public-sector grievances as an unlawful delegation of governmental power, close examination of the cases cited in support of that proposition reveal either that the court was not talking about arbitration at all, or that it confused grievance arbitration with interest arbitration, or that its objection to arbitration stemmed from the court's view that the underlying collective-bargaining agreement was itself beyond the authority of the public entity. In any event, once legislatures in many states came to give their blessing to collective bargaining in the public sector, courts began to accept grievance arbitration as an appropriate means to give effect to an otherwise valid contract even in the absence of express statutory authority. * * *

> Many of the modern statutes explicitly authorize, and in at least two cases actually mandate, provisions for binding grievance arbitration. Thus, except in states where collective bargaining agreements are not yet permitted, there appears to be no question as to the general validity of agreements to arbitrate public-sector labor grievances.

4. Constitutional questions affect public-sector arbitration in another way. Public employees have constitutional rights against their employer that private employees lack, *e.g.*, protections from some searches and seizures. Occasionally a public-sector grievant may try to raise these issues in arbitration. Does the arbitrator have authority to rule on such extra-contractual questions? If so, is the arbitrator's decision on them entitled to the same deference as the arbitrator's interpretation of the agreement? See McGrath v. State, 312 N.W.2d 438 (Minn.1981), for one example. Prison guards engaged in a "sick-out" to protest discipline imposed on one of their colleagues after an escape. The employer then disciplined the protestors for abuse of sick-leave privileges. The guards first sued, alleging violation of their due process, equal protection, and free speech rights under the U.S. Constitution. The trial court dismissed the claims because they had not yet exhausted their remedy (arbitration) under the collective agreement. The guards then arbitrated the dispute. After the arbitrator upheld the discipline the guards returned to court.

The Minnesota Supreme Court found their constitutional arguments to be without merit but then stated at 441:

> The fact that we decline to interfere with the arbitration process does not confer upon the arbitrator the right to decide constitutional issues. We have already indicated that arbitrators are without such authority in Minnesota. * * * We now expressly hold this to be the rule in Minnesota irrespective of the language of the arbitration agreement. In the normal case, where the constitutional violations alleged are of a general

nature the arbitrator is to proceed. The alleged constitutional violations may be raised at the time of judicial review of the arbitration determination.

Does this holding mean that the arbitrator cannot offer an opinion on the constitutional issues or simply that the arbitrator's opinion is worthless? Suppose the agreement incorporates all relevant constitutional and statutory provisions. Could the arbitrator *not* follow that part of the agreement? Justice Scott, concurring in *McGrath*, stated that an arbitrator should determine constitutional questions if the parties indicated a "clear intent" to arbitrate such disputes. The Minnesota Supreme Court later rejected his suggestion in County of Hennepin v. Law Enforcement Labor Services, Inc., Local No. 19, 527 N.W.2d 821, 825 (Minn.1995) ("We reaffirm our holdings in *City of Richfield* and *McGrath* and again hold that in the public sector an arbitrator has no authority to make constitutional determinations, irrespective of the language of the arbitration agreement").

5. May parties to a collective agreement waive or modify an individual employee's constitutional rights? The few courts to address this question have generally answered in the affirmative. See, for example, Barnica v. Kenai Peninsula Borough School District, 46 P.3d 974 (Alaska 2002) (favorably citing an earlier holding that a collective bargaining agreement could waive an employee's state constitutional right to a pretermination hearing so long as the remedy substituted was "fair, reasonable and efficacious") and Spencer v. New York City Transit Authority, 1999 WL 51814 (E.D.N.Y. 1999) ("It is firmly established in New York that unions may waive individual employees' constitutional rights, including due process requirements, through collective bargaining agreements"). Note how this issue parallels the question raised (but not answered) in Alexander v. Gardner–Denver Co., 415 U.S. 36, 94 S.Ct. 1011, 39 L.Ed.2d 147 (1974) and Wright v. Universal Maritime Service Corp., 525 U.S. 70, 119 S.Ct. 391, 142 L.Ed.2d 361 (1998) (both discussed in Section IV.B.3., *supra*): may a union waive an individual employee's statutory right to sue by agreeing to contract provisions requiring arbitration of such claims?

6. Statutory limitations are another matter entirely. As Grodin and Najita point out, *supra* footnote 1, collective bargaining statutes may expressly limit the scope of bargaining. As a result, the government agency may not delegate to an arbitrator power over some statutorily reserved management right. Similarly, other laws may define a specific decision-maker who may not delegate that authority to an arbitrator. In the field of education, for example, several state courts have held that a school board may not allow an arbitrator to exercise its power to decide tenure questions. (Even the *School Committee of Danvers* court strongly implied that the school board could not arbitrate the *merits* of a tenure dispute.) A few other courts have refused to allow arbitration of discharges of police officers and probation officers.

Absent some specific restriction, however, state courts apply the same presumption of arbitrability to public sector cases as federal courts do in private-sector cases. One relatively early New York case, Acting Superintendent of Schools of Liverpool Central School District v. United Liverpool Faculty Association, 42 N.Y.2d 509, 399 N.Y.S.2d 189, 369 N.E.2d 746

(1977), took a narrower view, holding that the test of arbitrability in public sector labor disputes was closer to the strict commercial arbitration rule than to the liberal *Steelworkers Trilogy* approach: "the agreement to arbitrate must be express, direct and unequivocal as to the issues or disputes to be submitted to arbitration; anything less will lead to a denial of arbitration." Later New York cases retreated from that view and enforced broad arbitration clauses. In any event, almost all courts recognize that a public employer may bind itself as to the manner in which it exercises its statutory prerogatives, *e.g.*, School Committee of Pittsfield v. United Educators of Pittsfield, 438 Mass. 753, 784 N.E.2d 11 (2003) (quoting an earlier opinion, the court wrote that "a school committee may bind itself to follow certain procedures with respect to decisions committed to its exclusive authority, and a failure to observe those procedures may be the basis for an arbitrable grievance").

7. Professor Charles Craver, *supra* footnote 2, concludes that most state courts accept the private-sector standard of judicial review, namely that courts are not to review the merits of an award "so long as it draws its essence from the collective bargaining agreement." United Steelworkers of America v. Enterprise Wheel & Car Corp., 363 U.S. 593, 80 S.Ct. 1358, 4 L.Ed.2d 1424 (1960). Grodin and Najita, *supra* footnote 1, agree. Perhaps so, but there remains a certain residue of distrust.

County of Allegheny v. Allegheny County Prison Employees Independent Union, 476 Pa. 27, 381 A.2d 849 (1977), is a good example. Private-sector arbitrators routinely enforce obligations drawn from past practices, and courts routinely enforce such decisions. In *County of Allegheny*, the arbitrator found that the employer erred by departing from binding past practices that (a) required employment of a guard to supervise the guards' lounge during meals and (b) allowed guards to select for their meals any food available from the jail kitchen (rather than having to accept the meals offered to prisoners). The collective bargaining agreement included a standard "integration" or "zipper" clause stating that the agreement represented "the full and complete agreement and commitment between the parties thereto." The arbitrator concluded that the zipper clause did not apply. That would have ended the matter in a private-sector case. A majority of the Pennsylvania Supreme Court, in contrast, differed with the arbitrator's interpretation: "we hold only that where a collective bargaining agreement not only makes no mention whatever of past practices but does include a broad integration clause, an award which incorporates into the agreement, as separately enforceable conditions of the employment relationship, past practices which antedate the effective date of that agreement cannot be said to 'draw its essence from the collective bargaining agreement.' " *Contra*, Ramsey County v. American Federation of State, County and Municipal Employees, Local 8, 309 N.W.2d 785 (Minn.1981) (upholding an award based on past practice, despite explicitly contrary contract language).

Grodin and Najita summarize the differences between the two sectors over judicial review, *supra* note 1, at 242–44:

> First, the courts appear less inclined to defer to an arbitration award where there exists a statute covering the subject matter, even if the statute is not deemed preemptive. * * * Such decisions reflect,

perhaps, the unwillingness of courts to accept the full implications of collective bargaining and arbitration in an area still permeated by legislation. * * *

Second, courts in the public sector appear less tolerant than those in the private sector of awards that rely on past practice to establish obligations not expressed in the agreement. * * * [C]ases such as these may reflect a judicial assumption that in the public sector it is to be expected that limitations on managerial authority will be express rather than implied.

Finally, even where the arbitrator's award is based upon express contract language, courts in some cases have displayed a greater propensity than in the private sector to overturn the arbitrator's interpretation. * * *

Should courts give less deference to public-sector arbitration awards than to private-sector awards? Why or why not?

CITY OF LAKE WORTH
101 LA 78 (Roger I. Abrams, 1993).*

On October 28, 1991, the Palm Beach County Police Benevolent Association (Lieutenants) filed a class grievance regarding the City of Lake Worth's failure to pay wage increases in accordance with the Agreement. On November 4, 1991, the Chief of Police denied the grievance because Florida state law, Section 447.309(2), "operates to make the collective bargaining agreement subject to the approval, through the medium of appropriations, of the City Commission." * * *

I. ISSUES * * *

Did the City violate the Agreement when it failed to pay wage increases due under Article 27 for fiscal year 91–92? If so, what shall the remedy be?

II. PROVISIONS OF THE AGREEMENT AND STATE LAW * * *
ARTICLE 4: MANAGEMENT RIGHTS

Section 3. If in the sole discretion of the Mayor or the Mayor's designee, it is determined that civil emergency conditions exist, including but not limited to riots, civil disorders, hurricane conditions, similar catastrophes, or exigencies, the provisions of this agreement may be suspended by the Mayor or the Mayor's designee during the time of the declared emergency, provided that rates and monetary fringe benefits shall not be suspended.

ARTICLE 31: GRIEVANCE PROCEDURE
* * * ARBITRATION REFERRAL

3. The arbitrator shall not have the power to add to, subtract from, modify, or alter the terms of the collective bargaining agreement in

* Reprinted with permission from *Labor Arbitration Reporter–Labor Arbitration Reports*, 101 LA 78. Copyright 1994 by The Bureau of National Affairs, Inc. (800–372–1033) <http://www.bna.com>.

arriving at a decision on the issue or issues presented and shall confine his decision solely to the interpretation and application of the agreement.

ARTICLE 33: SAVINGS CLAUSE

This Agreement constitutes the entire agreement between the PBA and the City * * *. This Agreement will not be interpreted so as to deprive any employee of any benefits or protections granted by the laws of the State of Florida, ordinances of the City of Lake Worth, or personnel rules and regulations of the Lake Worth Civil Service Board.

Florida State Statute Public Employees

447.309   Collective bargaining; approval or rejection.

(1) After an employee organization has been certified pursuant to the provisions of this part, the bargaining agent for the organization and the chief executive officer of the appropriate public employer or employers, jointly, shall bargain collectively in the determination of the wages, hours, and terms and conditions of employment of the public employees within the bargaining unit. * * * Any collective bargaining agreement reached by the negotiators shall be reduced to writing, and such agreement shall be signed by the chief executive officer and the bargaining agent. Any agreement signed by the chief executive officer and the bargaining agent shall not be binding on the public employer until such agreement has been ratified by the public employer and by public employees who are members of the bargaining unit, subject to the provisions of subsections (2) and (3). * * *

(2) Upon execution of the collective bargaining agreement, the chief executive shall, in his annual budget request or by other appropriate means, request the legislative body to appropriate such amounts as shall be sufficient to fund the provisions of the collective bargaining agreement. If less than the requested amount is appropriated, the collective bargaining agreement shall be administered by the chief executive officer on the basis of the amounts appropriated by the legislative body. The failure of the legislative body to appropriate funds sufficient to fund the collective bargaining agreement shall not constitute, or be evidence of, any unfair labor practice.

III.   BACKGROUND FACTS

The Police Benevolent Association of Palm Beach County represents a bargaining unit of six lieutenants who work for the Police Department of the City of Lake Worth. In 1989, the parties agreed to a three-year collective bargaining agreement, providing for a 5 percent across-the-board annual increase and a 3 percent merit increase. The Union had wanted a one-year contract, but the City insisted on a multi-year agreement to achieve labor stability. The City Manager recommended City Commission approval of the three-year contract for the Union police officers in order to set "the necessary labor perimeters." The City Manager explained that the three-year contract achieved the goal of "stabilizing the floundering" labor relationship.

During the spring of 1991, the Union learned that the City was preparing not to fund the third year of the negotiated wage increase for Union members and for the other unionized City employees. City Manager John Kelly sought to reopen the collective bargaining agreement with the Lieutenants. [Union leader] Garson refused to do so. He and other union leaders later met with Kelly. When Kelly said he would not recommend to the City that they fund the pay raises, Garson said it was "kind of a shock to me." * * *

Former City Commissioner Michael Coonerty testified that in May 1991 John Kelly notified the Commissioners of a budget problem. Kelly recommended that the Commission cut back some City services and that it not fund the contractual wage increases for unionized employees. Coonerty testified: "We knew we were in trouble." None of the Commissioners suggested not funding the contractual wage increases. It was the City Manager's idea. In an executive session, Kelly said: "There is a state law that specifically states that we do not have to fund a contract if there is not enough funds." The Commission acted based on Kelly's advice.

On cross-examination, Coonerty said he voted not to fund the increases "in the best interest of the City." He acknowledged he did consider the effect on collective bargaining: "I'm a politician after all!" He said this was the hardest decision he ever had to make, and "I knew it was going to hurt." He said that they had to look at the broader picture. They thought the choice was either to fund the contracts or lay off employees. He knew that the unions would never trust the City again and the union-management relationship would never be the same. He acknowledged that the City Commission could have raised taxes, but he felt that that was not in the best interest of the citizens of the City. If taxes went up, he said, it "can hurt my political career."[3] * * *

[Charles Z.] Powers [the City's Finance Director] explained that as early as December 1990 or January 1991 before the budget process began, the City Manager received advice from City Attorney Alan Fallik that one option available to the City was not to fund the Union Contract increases under state law. Mr. Power testified that the City Manager was required to propose a budget that included the Contract increases, but Kelly did not want his proposal accepted. The City Manager explained to the Commission: "I had to fund those things. You don't." The City Commission did not.

IV. CONTENTIONS OF THE PARTIES

[The Union argued that the City should be bound by three earlier arbitration awards, one of them by Arbitrator Abrams, holding that the City violated its agreements with other unions by not funding them; that external law did not apply, and if it did the statute would violate the federal and state constitutions; and that the City violated the agreement out of "the worst sort of political expediency."]

3. Mr. Coonerty is no longer on the Lake Worth City Commission.

[According to Arbitrator Abrams, the City "relies totally on Florida law which it argues supports its failure to pay the wage increase. Section 447.309(2) gives the City the 'option of underfunding' the agreement." The state constitutional right to bargain must be balanced against the City's obligations as guardian of public funds. The previous arbitration awards were erroneous. The City's brief stated that it was "most unfortunate that arbitrators see fit to deprive public employers of fundamental rights of government and to grant public employees the unconditional right to receive funding in direct violation of law." Arbitrator Abrams paraphrased the City's position about his earlier opinion: "This Arbitrator wrongly stated in his earlier decision that the City claims it had the right only to breach union contracts but must fulfill all other contracts with vendors. In fact, the City has the right not to fulfill any contract it wants."]

V. Discussion and Opinion

A. Introduction : The City Commission of the City of Lake Worth, Florida, made a decision during 1991 not to appropriate the funds needed to meet its contract obligations with its unions, including the small P.B.A. Lieutenants Union. The increases were mandated under the respective binding and enforceable collective bargaining agreements. * * * In its brief, the Union argues that the Arbitrator must follow the earlier arbitration opinions and that the City is "collaterally estopped" from rearguing the issues. * * *

Those opinions are of great assistance in resolving this dispute, but they are not controlling unless the parties' Agreement makes them so.

The resolution of the merits of this dispute does parallel this Arbitrator's analysis in the I.B.E.W. case. Much of the reasoning and some of the language used in that opinion is usefully applied here. The City makes many of the same arguments. It makes no pretense about its contractual obligations. It again claims that under state law it was not required to live up to its agreement.[7]

The Arbitrator wrote in the I.B.E.W. case that the City was claiming that it must fulfill every contract it has with every vendor, except one—the contract with unionized employees who sells their labor to the City. Apparently, the Arbitrator was wrong. The City now retorts in its brief with one of the most breathtaking arguments ever made to this Arbitrator. The City claims that under the Florida Constitution it has the right not to honor any and all contracts it has executed simply by not appropriating the required funds, including, presumably, those contracts that have been partially performed, such as the present Agreement. That would make doing business with a governmental entity a matter of roulette. Will it pay? Will it not? It depends on how it feels at the

7. In the I.B.E.W. case, the Arbitrator termed that "a remarkable claim," and the City criticizes the use of the adjective in its current brief. It remains a "remarkable claim," however, to suggest that every con-tract promise with financial implications—virtually every provision in the collective bargaining agreement—is voidable at will by the public employer without the need to demonstrate a compelling reason.

moment. That cannot possibly be the way the business of government is to be conducted in the State of Florida. The Florida Constitution does not allow a municipality to create a "shell game" when dealing with its vendors. * * *

B.   *Analysis of External Law*: The City says the Arbitrator must apply external law and the Union insists to the contrary. * * *

The Agreement here provides: "The arbitrator shall not have the power to add to, subtract from, modify, or alter the terms of the collective bargaining agreement in arriving at a decision on the issue or issues presented and *shall confine his decision solely to the interpretation and application of the agreement*" (emphasis added). The direction to the arbitrator is clear: Look "solely" at the terms of the Agreement.

There really can be no question that the Agreement required the City to pay wage increases and merit increases during its third year. The City admits as much. For good reason or bad reason or for no reason at all, the City Commission decided not to live up to those promises. There was evidence in the record from the Union expert's testimony in other proceedings that the increases could have been funded through a variety of sources without affecting services at all. The City says that is all beside the point. It could decide it did not want to pay what it promised it would pay. The City does not claim that the external law allows it to nullify contract clauses only for good reasons. Its argument is broader than that. *The City says it can decide not to fulfill its financial obligations for any reason at any time.*

The basis for the City's claim is Florida Statutes Section 447.309(2), quoted above, which addresses collective bargaining in the public sector. As applied to a municipality such as the City of Lake Worth, Section 447.309(2) would require the City Manager to request that the City Commission appropriate money to fund the provisions of the Agreement. (The evidence shows that the City Manager John Kelly did that, although he hoped the City Commission would not follow his request and worked to make sure it would not.) The statute then says "if less than the requested amount is appropriated, the collective bargaining agreement shall be administered by the [City Manager] on the basis of the amounts appropriated by the legislative body." Did the Florida Legislature intend to allow municipalities, such as Lake Worth, to jettison their contract promises? * * *

In its brief, the City attempts to explain away the most recent Florida Supreme Court decision involving legislative underfunding of a collective bargaining agreement. In *Chiles v. United Faculty of Florida*, 615 So.2d 671 (Fla.1993), Justice Gerald Kogan addressed "a matter of great public importance." The State Legislature had resolved a bargaining impasse by authorizing a 3% raise for various classes of public employees. Because of a projected budget shortfall, it then postponed and finally eliminated the planned pay raises. The unions representing the affected employees sued based on the constitutional protection of the right to bargain collectively contained in the Florida Constitution. The

Court distinguished the *P.B.A.* Case, decided less than three months earlier, based on the fact that here "an agreement was reached and funded, then unilaterally modified by the legislature, and finally unilaterally abrogated by the legislature." [In *State v. P.B.A.*, 613 So.2d 415 (Fla.1992), the Florida Supreme Court held that public employees do not have a right to demand that the State Legislature appropriate funds for a collective bargaining agreement negotiated by the Governor.] The Court rejected the State's argument that public employee bargaining agreements cannot ever constitute fully binding contracts: "The right to contract is one of the most sacrosanct rights guaranteed by our fundamental law." In dictum, the Court said that the Legislature does have the right "to reduce previously approved appropriations to pay public workers' salaries made pursuant to a collective bargaining agreement, but only where it can demonstrate a compelling state interest * * *. Before that authority can be exercised, however, the legislature must demonstrate that [there are] no other reasonable alternative means of preserving its contract with public workers, either in whole or in part." The Court suggested that if the employer could void a promise at will "we necessarily would be required to conclude that there was no contract here at all for lack of mutuality * * *." The Court ordered the Legislature to implement the pay raise.

The City argues that in the *Chiles* case appropriations were actually made for the raises in question, then postponed, while here the City Commission refused to make the appropriations required in the third year of the Agreement. That ignores the fact that the City Commission here had ratified the three-year agreement as a whole. The City and the Union then performed under that three-year Agreement (not a series of one-year agreements) for two full years before the City reneged on its promise. The City actually received a substantial part of its bargain, the extended stability in labor relations that the City Manager used as the rationale for the three-year contract demand.

As the most recent word from the Supreme Court, *Chiles* stands generally for the proposition that promises made by a legislative body are enforceable. As applied here, that means that once the City Commission ratified the three-year Agreement and enjoyed the benefits of that Agreement, it was bound to fulfill its obligations. As the Supreme Court said in Chiles: "The right to contract is one of the most sacrosanct rights guaranteed by our fundamental law." The City cannot take advantage of that right when it suits its purpose, and then vitiate that right without compelling reason when it decides it no longer wants to keep its word. * * *

None of the opinions addressing on Section 447.309(2) offer[s] a definitive reading of the legislative intent, in particular with regard to contract liability as determined in arbitration. The last sentence in the Section 447.309(2) paragraph does clarify the purpose of the provision, however. The statute says that the failure of the legislative body to appropriate sufficient funds "shall not constitute, or be evidence of, any unfair labor practice." The provision appears to have been designed to keep the State Public Employment Relations Commission out of the business of second guessing the legislative judgments of local municipalities. It does not free the City from its contract obligations that might be perfected in another forum, such as arbitration. * * *

As the Arbitrator stated in the I.B.E.W. case, reading Section 447.309(2) as the City suggests would make collective bargaining a cruel joke. The heart of negotiations is the wage promise. The City pressed the Union for a three-year contract. The Union wanted a one-year deal, but finally agreed to the City's demand. The length of the contract is also a crucial element in bargaining. The two provisions—wage increases and length of the contract—are interrelated. A three-year contract may provide the labor stability management seeks, but it creates risks for a union. It is "betting" that inflation will not render the negotiated wage increase a mirage. With a one-year agreement, the union can attempt to recalibrate the wage scale annually. When the Union here agreed to the City's demand for a three-year agreement, it had good reason to trust that the *quid pro quo* would follow, the payment of the negotiated wage increase over the three years.

If one party to the Agreement can ignore its promises for any reason or no reason at all, was there ever any real collective bargaining? We must remember that public employees enjoy the protection of a Florida Constitutional provision, Article I, Section 6, which expressly supports collective bargaining. Section 447.309(2) should not be read in a way that would render it subject to constitutional question. The Legislature should be presumed to have enacted a constitutional statute. There is no evidence in the record or in any available research that demonstrates that it was the State Legislature's intention to permit Constitutionally-protected collective bargaining to be destroyed by legislative bodies at the local level.[17]

C. Applicability of External Law: Although the external law on its face and as interpreted by the courts does not excuse the City's action, in order to resolve this dispute the Arbitrator need not look to external law. Nothing in the parties' Agreement requires the contract arbitrator to read, interpret and apply enacted legislation. The City argues that all state laws are part of the Agreement. Where does it say that in the Agreement? The City points to Article 4 that protects management rights. If the decision to underfund is an inherent management right, then the City does not need external law. It would have this right by contract. Obviously, this is not an inherent management function. Otherwise, the wage promise would be a sham. That could not have been what the parties intended. * * *

---

17. The City's argument concerning the effect of Section 447.309(2) is brought to the extreme towards the end of its brief when it argues that not only does this provision override the constitutional right of public employees to bargain collectively, but the City doubts that it could even waive the "right to underfund" if it wanted to. That means that the parties to a public sector labor relationship in Florida cannot reach a binding agreement. Even if the public employer expressly agrees not to nullify the terms of an agreement, it is incapable of keeping that promise. According to the City's argument, there can be no real public sector collective bargaining in Florida.

A careful reading of the Agreement demonstrates that the parties did not intend to incorporate external law. The parties expressly provided in Article 4, Section 3, that in case of civil emergency the Mayor may suspend the provisions of the Agreement "provided that rates and monetary fringe benefits shall not be suspended." This is the clearest evidence that the parties intended that employees would be paid in accordance with the terms of the Agreement throughout the term of the Agreement. Even in the case of a civil emergency, "rates shall not be suspended." * * *

D. *The Contract*: The Agreement requires the payment of wages at certain rates. Nothing in the Agreement excuses that payment. As a legislative body, the City Commission approved the collective bargaining agreement. That action contemplated three years of wage and merit increases. The City has not offered any reason that would justify underfunding because of a financial emergency situation, and the Arbitrator need not address such hypothetical circumstances. The Agreement is plain on its face. The wage increases should have been paid. * * *

The City argues that it is "most unfortunate that arbitrators see fit to deprive public employers of fundamental rights of government and to grant public employees the unconditional right to receive funding in direct violation of law." The arbitrators do not "deprive" parties of rights or "grant" parties rights. They read, interpret and apply contracts. It is "most unfortunate" that the City does not appreciate the binding nature of its obligations.

E. *Final and Binding Decision*: Although the citizens may be the ultimate judge of the actions of their elected officials, the parties have provided for a private, self-contained, and final-and-binding system for resolving disputes concerning alleged violations of their Agreement through arbitration. The Arbitrator's power is to enforce the Agreement, a binding pact between the City and the Union. The Arbitrator's power comes from the Contract and the power of his decisions depends upon fidelity to the terms of the Agreement.

One would have hoped now that the City has arbitrated and lost four virtually identical cases that it would turn its course of action towards rebuilding its relationship with its employees and their unions. Regretfully, it is likely to continue to fight this battle in court. It persists in the belief that its word is good for as long as it wants to keep it and no longer. * * *

[The statute must be read in a manner consistent with Florida's constitutional protection of the right of public employees to bargain collectively.] The term "to bargain collectively" has a well understood meaning. It means to give-and-take across the negotiation table, reach agreement (if you can), and then keep your promises. To read Section 407.309(2) to allow the public employer to escape from its promises in the absence of the most compelling circumstances would make a mockery of collective bargaining. As Lewis Carroll wrote in Alice in Wonderland: "Everything's got a moral, if you can only find it." Here the moral is: "When you make a deal, you live by it."

The Agreement controls, and it was violated here.

VI. Award

The City violated the Agreement when it failed to pay wage increases due under Article 27 for fiscal year 91–92. By way of remedy, the employees should be made whole with all legal interest paid.

Notes and Questions

1.   Does the arbitrator's approach differ because of the governmental status of the employer? *Should* it? Why or why not? Did you notice anything different about this opinion's tone, compared to that of the other arbitration opinions you have read? If so, in what ways is it different? Why might the arbitrator, a careful draftsman in full control of his craft, have chosen this tone rather than some other? How would *you* have written the award?

2.   Why does Arbitrator Abrams hold that the three previous awards, all on the same issue and all involving the same employer, are not determinative? And why does he hold that "external law does not apply"? How could the State's collective bargaining law *not* apply? If it does not apply, why does he deal with the legal issues at such length? If Florida, like some other states, expressly made the collective agreement subject to state laws, or if the agreement itself incorporated those laws, the arbitrator might not be able to avoid legal issues.

Some authorities differ with Arbitrator Abrams and conclude that external law automatically applies in public-sector grievance arbitration. See generally, Charles Craver, *The Judicial Enforcement of Public Sector Grievance Arbitration*, *supra* footnote 2. Whether or not the arbitrator expressly applies external law, courts reviewing public-sector awards will overturn an award that conflicts with an applicable statute, *e.g.*, Allegheny Valley School District v. Allegheny Valley Educational Association, 25 Pa.Cmwlth. 559, 360 A.2d 762 (1976) and Local 1219, International Association of Fire Fighters v. Connecticut Labor Relations Board, 171 Conn. 342, 370 A.2d 952 (1976) (refusing to enforce awards that conflict with statutory pay provisions). If the award ignores the law but reaches a result permitted by the law, however, there may be no reversible error.

3.   The City did not claim that a financial emergency forced it to "underfund" the contract's third year. Should an arbitrator's approach differ if the employer does make such a plea? Why or why not?

4.   This case indicates how complex public-sector cases can be, compared to their private sector counterparts.

(a) Because constitutions, statutes, and common law rules apply even to what in the private sector would be routine contract-breach or discipline cases, public sector parties rely much more heavily on lawyers. A good study of the phenomenon is Mitchell A. Sherr, *Legal Representation of Public Sector Employers and Unions in Grievance Arbitration*, 23 Journal of Collective Negotiations in the Public Sector 203 (1994).

(b) Public-sector cases often present an issue that rarely appears in the private sector: who is the "employer?" Governments divide powers in ways no private business could afford. Is the employer in a typical school case the superintendent who negotiates the agreement? The school board that makes budgetary policy? The county that levies the taxes funding the schools? The state that provides another part of the budget? All of them? One problem is determining who has power to negotiate and sign agreements. A bigger problem is deciding against whom any remedy should run.

5. Apart from obvious differences such as those mentioned in the previous note, public sector arbitration closely resembles its private sector counterpart. Many of the issues are the same, the same arbitrators and lawyers may work in both sectors, and the procedures are virtually identical. Shouldn't the results therefore be similar, too? So you might think. One careful empirical study (Mesch, cited in footnote 2 at the beginning of this subsection) reached surprising conclusions. After surveying almost 4,000 discipline arbitration cases in both sectors over seven years, the author found that "outcomes tend to favor the grievant in the public sector—the grievant wins more frequently, is terminated less often, and receives a shorter suspension." Why might that be? Her study did not provide an answer but Mesch does pose several hypotheses. Perhaps, she suggests, it is just a statistical anomaly because more serious public sector cases might go through civil service channels rather than to arbitration. Or it might be due to "environmental and institutional constraints found within each sector." Or "it may be that public sector arbitration is currently in embryonic stage of development." Can you think of other explanations?

6. Attempting to use the grievance arbitration process to settle what are really interest disputes is hardly rare in the private sector, but it is especially common in the public sector because strikes are often illegal or impractical. Consider Independent School District No. 319, 1995 WL 600955 (Mario F. Bognanno, 1995). For many years teachers gave mid-term progress reports to students who were in danger of failing. In 1993, the School District required them to give such reports to all students. The Agreement was silent on the subject; in other contexts, the parties might have addressed it in negotiations. The teachers' union instead filed a grievance asserting that the new rule violated the collective agreement because the employer adopted it without bargaining, because it increased their workload, and because it violated teachers' rights to evaluate students as they deem appropriate. Arbitrator Bognanno found that teachers had ample time to do the extra reports and that the requirement affected only the frequency, not the manner, of evaluation. The District did not have to bargain before implementing the new rule, he held, because the rule was not a "term or condition of employment" and because the management rights clause allowed the employer to operate the school system "as it deems fit."

3. INTEREST ARBITRATION[3]

Resolution of bargaining disputes in the private sector is relatively simple. If negotiations deadlock, the parties may seek the aid of a

---

3. Bibliographic Suggestions: Arvid Anderson, Loren Krause, and Parker A. De- naco, *Public Sector Interest Arbitration and Fact Finding: Standards and Procedures,*

mediator. If that fails, economic force usually determines the outcome. Dispute resolution in the public sector is far more complicated because most states prohibit public-sector strikes and lockouts. Of the thirty-six states with collective bargaining statutes, only thirteen allow any public-sector strikes, and most of those states severely limit the right. (Of course public-sector strikes are illegal in states without public-sector bargaining statutes.) Banning strikes could leave unionized employees with no bargaining leverage. Most states have therefore provided alternative forms of dispute resolution. If negotiations deadlock, the governing statute usually mandates one or more of a variety of procedures: mediation, fact-finding, "med-arb," arbitration, or intervention of a state labor-relations agency. About thirty states provide some form of interest arbitration.

The Olson chapter cited in footnote 3 discusses the range of dispute-resolution procedures, as does Strategies for Impasse Resolution (Harry Kershen and Clair Meirowitz, eds. 1992). This section deals only with the arbitration option. We use the term "interest arbitration" to signify arbitration of the parties' respective *interests* rather than of their *rights*—in other words, arbitration of the substance of the collective bargaining agreement rather than its interpretation or application.

(a) Constitutional Issues

Unsurprisingly, interest arbitration has presented state courts with even more difficult constitutional issues than grievance arbitration. After all, the interest arbitrator can, within the statutory limitations, set the wages, hours, and other benefits for the entire bargaining unit. Those determinations necessarily affect the public employer's budget, and in turn the levels of taxation. Thus the concern for an unconstitutional delegation of power is even greater in this type of arbitration.

Compared to "rights" or "grievance" arbitration, interest arbitration is remarkably open-ended. Rather than interpreting what the agreement *means*, the arbitrator decides what the terms of the agreement *will be*. This raises a range of issues virtually unique to the public sector. May the arbitrator constitutionally decide what a government must do? If so, how does interest arbitration fit into a democratic political system? What limits bind the arbitrator? What factors should influence the arbitrator's award? Precedent? Comparability? Ability to pay? Social goals? This section can only scratch the surface of these difficult questions. For further enlightenment, see the sources listed in footnote 3.

Chapter 48 of Labor and Employment Arbitration (Tim Bornstein, Ann Gosline, and Marc Greenbaum, eds., 2nd ed. 1999); Charles B. Craver, *The Judicial Enforcement of Public Sector Interest Arbitration*, 21 Boston College Law Review 557 (1980); David A. Dilts and William J. Walsh, Collective Bargaining and Impasse Resolution in the Public Sector (1988); Joseph R. Grodin, *Political Aspects of Public Sector Interest Arbitration*, 64 California Law Review 678 (1976); J. Joseph Loewenberg, *Interest Arbitration: Past, Present, and Future*, Labor Arbitration Under Fire 111 (James L. Stern and Joyce M. Najita, eds. 1997); Charles J. Morris, *The Role of Interest Arbitration in a Collective Bargaining System*, The Future of Labor Arbitration 197 (1976); and Craig A. Olson, *Dispute Resolution in the Public Sector*, in Public Sector Bargaining, *supra* note 1, at 160.

JUDICIAL RESPONSE TO PUBLIC–SECTOR ARBITRATION

Joseph R. Grodin and Joyce M. Najita.
Public Sector Bargaining, 229, 253–57 (Benjamin Aaron,
Joyce M. Najita, and James L. Stern, eds.)
Public Sector Bargaining, Industrial Relations
Research Association Series, 2nd ed. 1988.

VALIDITY OF INTEREST ARBITRATION

Statutes mandating interest arbitration for public employees have been challenged on a variety of state constitutional grounds, most of them involving either the relationship of state to local authority, the relationship of arbitration to the legislative process, or a combination of the two. The first category of challenge—that the statute intrudes impermissibly upon the autonomy of a "home rule" city or county—has been uniformly rejected by the courts and need not concern us here. The second category, involving the relationship of arbitration to the legislative process, may take a variety of forms: that the statute constitutes an unlawful delegation of legislative power to private parties, that the statute contains insufficient standards or safeguards to guide or check arbitral discretion, that it represents an unconstitutional delegation of the taxing power, or that the method by which arbitrators are chosen violates the "one man, one vote" principle. The third category of challenge stems from the provisions, known as "ripper clauses," found in 18 state constitutions and prohibiting the legislature from delegating to a "special or private body" any power to interfere with "municipal moneys or to perform municipal functions."

Prior to 1975, Pennsylvania was the only state in which interest arbitration was held constitutionally impermissible, and that was on the basis of a ripper clause that has subsequently been amended to permit arbitration. After that amendment, the state interest-arbitration statute was sustained. The supreme court of Wyoming upheld that state's interest-arbitration statute despite a ripper clause in the state's constitution, and the courts of Rhode Island, Maine, and Nebraska (which have no ripper clauses) rejected constitutional challenges based on other grounds. The supreme court of Maine was equally divided on the question of unlawful delegation, but since the lower court had sustained the statute, the effect of the division was to affirm. Thus, by the end of 1974 the score stood 5–0 in favor of constitutionality.

Since that time, interest arbitration's constitutional batting average has been rising. The highest courts in Connecticut, Maine, New Jersey, Minnesota, New York, Massachusetts, Washington, and Michigan have sustained the constitutionality of interest arbitration in those states; and courts in South Dakota, Colorado, Utah, and Maryland have reached the opposite conclusion. While each of the latter state constitutions contains ripper clauses, the decisions in Colorado and Utah went beyond those clauses to rely generally on unconstitutional delegation doctrine. In

California, the supreme court in a footnote in one case rather summarily dispensed with a constitutional attack raised by an amicus curiae to the constitutionality of a city-charter provision calling for binding interest arbitration; however, the vitality of that footnote is dampened somewhat by the reasoning of the same court in an opinion which holds that an arrangement by a general-law city for interest arbitration would constitute an impermissible delegation of wage-fixing authority under a state statute providing that "by resolution or ordinance the city council shall fix the compensation of all appointive officers."

The delegation issue is the most formidable of the constitutional issues, and its various ramifications are best reflected in the diverse opinions that comprise the Michigan supreme court's decision in *Dearborn Fire Fighters Union v. City of Dearborn* [394 Mich. 229, 231 N.W.2d 226 (1975)]. The Michigan statute mandates interest arbitration for police and fire department labor disputes; like most interest-arbitration statutes, it provides for a tripartite arbitration panel composed of one delegate named by each of the parties and a neutral member to be selected by those two. In the event they fail to agree upon selection, then the neutral is appointed by the chair of the Michigan Employment Relations Commission (MERC). The city of Dearborn, at impasse in negotiations with both police and fire department employees, declined to designate a delegate to the arbitration panels, and so the MERC chairman appointed the neutral for each panel, and the two-person panels proceeded to consider and issue awards. The city refused to comply with the awards, and litigation ensued.

The four justices sitting on the case each wrote a separate opinion. Justice Levin, joined by Chief Justice Kavanagh, summarized their argument for the unconstitutionality of the statute as follows:

> The arbitrator/chairman of the panel is entrusted with the authority to decide major questions of public policy concerning the conditions of public employment, the levels and standards of public services and the allocation of public revenues. Those questions are legislative and political, not judicial or quasi-judicial. The act is structured to insulate the arbitrator/chairman's decision from review in the political process. It is not intended that he be, nor is he in fact, accountable within the political process for his decision. This is not consonant with the constitutional exercise of political power in a representative democracy.

Although the statute contained both standards to guide the exercise of the delegated power and procedural safeguards such as provisions for hearing, statement of findings and conclusions, and judicial review—characteristics generally considered adequate to validate the delegation of legislative authority—Justices Levin and Kavanagh considered the statute defective because it allocated such authority to private persons who did not have continuing responsibility for its exercise, ad hoc and "expendable" arbitrators who were not accountable in any meaningful way. The fact that the neutral arbitrator in the *Dearborn* case happened to have been appointed by the MERC chairman did not make the arbitrator any more accountable in their view, since the statute called for the MERC chairman to appoint an "impartial" person rather than someone who would seek to render a decision "which will have the support of the electorate or of their elected representatives." The availability of judicial review of the award, while possibly assuring against the arbitrary exercise of discretionary power, could not in their opinion fulfill the constitutional need for "review and accountability through the political process":

> It is the unique method of appointment, requiring independent decision makers without accountability to a governmental appointing authority, and the unique dispersal of decision-making power among numerous *ad hoc* decision makers, only temporarily in office, precluding assessment of responsibility for the consequences of their decisions on the level of public resources and the cost of government, which renders invalid this particular delegation of legislative power.

The two remaining judges, whose combined opinions carried the day, agreed upon the conclusion in the particular case, but for quite different reasons. Justice Coleman adopted a pragmatic approach, reasoning that some system of interest arbitration was clearly called for if strikes were to be avoided and that the choice between ad hoc arbitrators and a permanent arbitration board involved a balancing process that should be left to the legislature. Justice Williams, in a lengthier and more analytical opinion, argued that whether a person to whom power is delegated should be characterized as "a private person, or better . . . a non-politically accountable person" should depend, not upon the label the persons wears, but upon the "underlying reality"; and this reality, in the justice's opinion, should be viewed from the perspective of four criteria:

> First, how close by appointment is the person or agency to the elective process and political accountability? * * *

> Second, how clearly restricted is the operation of the person or agency by standards written into the law and the possibility of judicial review?

> Third, how much is the person or agency held to public accountability by the length of tenure on and the public exposure of the job?

> Fourth, * * * the importance and breadth of power granted.

Applying these criteria, Justice Williams found:

1. While selection of the arbitration panels is outside the ordinary political processes, appointment of the neutral by the MERC chairman "guarantees high public visibility and accountability."

2. While operators operate independently, the statute's specific and ample standards plus provision for judicial review assure a "high degree of legal accountability."

3.   While tenure of arbitrators is brief, arbitrators are motivated both by professional dedication and concern for continuing acceptability; they operate in the focus of "intense public and media scrutiny"; and they are subject to legal standards, all evidencing a "considerable degree of personal accountability."

4.   While the job is important, the areas of discretion are "suitably delimited."

Justice Williams concluded that while selection of the arbitrator by the parties would pose serious constitutional doubt, so long as the MERC chairman appointed the arbitrator, the statute was constitutional.

The accountability issue was later treated in detail in the June 1980 decision of the Michigan supreme court in *City of Detroit v. Detroit Police Officers Association* [294 N.W.2d 68]. In that decision, the majority held that the 1976 amendments changing the method of appointing the neutral chairperson of the arbitration panel removed any doubts regarding the panel's accountability that existed after the *Dearborn* decision. Chairpersons are now appointed by the MERC from its permanent arbitration panel. The court reasoned that persons whose names appear on that panel will be concerned with the long-term impact of their decisions because they must be residents of Michigan and because they remain on the panel until removed by MERC. They serve in many disputes, so they are not "hit-and-run arbitrators," the court stated. As appointees of MERC the arbitrators acquire a kind of political accountability they would not have if appointed by the partisan members of the arbitration panel. The majority believes that the "tension" between independence and political accountability was balanced by the act's standards to guide the panel, by the public atmosphere in which the act operates, and by the act's provision for judicial review. In deciding whether the arbitration panel's award was supported by the evidence, the court tackled the extremely important matter of the weight to be given to each of the eight factors which the law requires the arbitration panel to consider. The court held that the legislature mandated the arbitration panel to weigh the factors and that such was a constitutional delegation of authority. Listing the factors may be necessary before courts will uphold the constitutionality of interest-arbitration statutes, but the weight to be given each factor must be determined on a case-by-case basis before a decision can be reached.

Notes and Questions

1.   The Michigan cases discussed in this excerpt ultimately approved interest arbitration because the arbitrator is in some sense "politically accountable." Isn't that exactly backwards? Isn't arbitral *independence*, rather than "accountability," essential to any arbitration system? Or is arbitral independence essential only for grievance arbitration? If so, what is it about interest arbitration that justifies the distinction? Is it possible for an arbitrator to make a completely objective decision if he or she is also required to consider political factors?

Do you understand why the issue of arbitrator "accountability" is so significant? A public-sector interest arbitrator ultimately allocates scarce public resources. An award of a wage increase to fire fighters, for example, might mean less money for public housing or road repair or might force the government to raise taxes. Are those proper functions for an unelected private citizen who may not even live in the jurisdiction? See Grodin, *Political Aspects of Public Sector Interest Arbitration, supra* footnote 3.

2.   Grodin and Najita mention some state courts that have found public sector interest arbitration unconstitutional. A surprising recent addition to that list (and the only one since 1981) is California. In County of Riverside v. Superior Court, 30 Cal.4th 278, 132 Cal.Rptr.2d 713, 66 P.3d 718 (2003), the California Supreme Court unanimously struck down that state's local government interest arbitration law. It held that the law violated constitutional provisions requiring that the "governing body shall provide for the * * * compensation * * * of employees" and prohibiting the legislature from delegating "to a private person or body power to * * * interfere with county or municipal corporation * * * money * * * or perform municipal functions." See generally, Note, *Binding Interest Arbitration in the Public Sector: A "New" Proposal for California and Beyond*, 55 Hastings Law Journal 245 (2003).

Do you share those concerns? Who *should* decide employment terms if the public employer and union cannot agree? Or is the real problem not interest arbitration but strikes or even public sector collective bargaining itself?

3.   Why do most states still prohibit public sector strikes and lockouts? Do you find those reasons persuasive? State and federal courts alike have upheld those prohibitions against constitutional attack. Rejected claims have cited constitutional provisions on freedom of speech and association, prohibitions on denials of liberty and property, and requirements of equal protection. Can you formulate the types of arguments a union could make on those grounds? Why do you suppose the courts have rejected those arguments? More than a dozen states permit some types of public sector strikes. Does this suggest that the reasons for strike prohibitions are faulty? Or might something else be at work?

4.   Do state courts have (or should they have) a greater role in determining arbitrability in public sector disputes than federal courts do under the *Steelworkers Trilogy*? Why or why not? See Grodin and Najita, *supra* footnote 1, at 257–59.

(b) Practical Application

CITY OF OAK CREEK
98 LA 325 (Arvid Anderson, 1991).*

The dispute involves some 51 members of a blue collar unit which includes highway, engineering, clerical, parks and recreation employees.

The City also bargains with police and fire units and with a recently certified unit of 16 sewer and water works employees. At the time of the interest arbitration hearing, the parties had reached tentative agreements on most of the issues. However, two major issues remained. The City is seeking a change in the subcontracting language in the current agreement. In exchange for this grant, the City is offering an additional .75% increase in hourly wages effective on 7/1/91. This is the equivalent of about 6 cents per hour.

The second major issue is the City's desire to limit the health insurance options available to unit members. Currently unit members can choose between WPS, WHO, Family Health Plan, Samaritan Health Plan, and Compcare. Under the City's final offer, the City would have the right to eliminate all of the HMO options except for Family Health Plan which it agreed to maintain as an option through 1992. It is the Union's position to maintain the status quo. The City also alleges that there is a dispute regarding the coverage of retirees under the medical plan. However, the Union's position is that the City has a right to do whatever it seeks to do with respect to retirees and does not regard this as an issue. The relevant current contract language and final offers are as follows:

ARTICLE 1—SECTION 3 RECOGNITION

Section 3 No employee shall be displaced, laid off, reduced or deprived of any of the benefits of this Agreement because of any future Agreement entered into between the City and another governmental agency or industrial firm.

Union's proposal: Maintain Status Quo

City's proposal:

b.   Article 3—Management–Employees Rights (2–3)

Add new paragraph "J"—Effective July 1, 1991, to subcontract or contract for goods or services as long as no bargaining unit employee is laid-off.

c.   On the same date the subcontracting language is effective (July 1, 1991), all wages rates shall be increased by .75% in addition to the across-the-board increase contained in Article 10.

ARTICLE 17—INSURANCE

Section 1: Hospital Insurance. Effective January 1, 1989, City agrees to provide and pay the full premium for hospital and surgical insurance, including major medical. The carrier shall be Wisconsin Physicians Service (WPS) Health Incentive Program, or such other Carrier that provides duplicate or better coverage and service as that in effect on July 1, 1988 under the Wisconsin Physicians Service (WPS) Health Incentive Program (HIP).

Section 2: Health Maintenance Organization. The Municipality shall offer membership in any Health Maintenance Organization which has been certified by the United States Department of Health, Education, and Welfare, or agreed upon by the Union. The Municipality shall pay for an employee electing this coverage an amount of this premium not to exceed City's contribution to the then existing medical insurance. The following health maintenance organizations are currently offered by the City: Wisconsin Health organization (WHO), Family Health Plan (FHP), Samaritan Health Plan and Compcare. The City Reserves the right to add HMOs which are federally certified.

Union's Proposal: Maintain Status Quo

City's Proposal:

The City may withdraw the HMOs (except that for 1990–1992, Family Health Plan would remain as an HMO alternative) as health care providers, as long as it gives the Union thirty (30) days notice at the end of the calendar year.

With respect to wages, the parties are in basic agreement. The first year of the contract from 7/1/90 to 6/30/91 a 2.00% increase effective on 7/1/90 and another 2.00% increase effective 1/1/91. Effective on 7/1/91 the City and the Union have agreed also on a 2.25% wage increase to be effective and another increase of 2.00% to be effective on 1/1/91. In addition, the City would propose an additional .75% per hour effective 7/1/91 provided the arbitrator adopts the City's proposed language regarding subcontracting.

POSITION OF THE PARTIES

The City asserts there is a compelling need to change the subcontracting language based on the bargaining history and changes in the City's operation. Of immediate concern is the City's need to comply with state mandated recycling. The City introduced three arbitration awards to demonstrate its contention that there is a need for a change. The first involved a grievance over the City's attempt to subcontract the work of mounting tires on rims and the balancing of tires. The arbitrator in that case concluded, that since the mounting and balancing of tires often resulted in overtime for bargaining employees, such overtime was a "benefit" under the contract language and the grievance was upheld; meaning that no employees could be deprived of a benefit as a result of the subcontracting.

In the second grievance, the City contracted out paving work in the summer of 1985. The arbitrator in that case viewed the phrase "benefits of this agreement" as something more than fringe benefits. Since the employees would have received overtime and out of classification pay, the arbitrator viewed those as benefits. However, the arbitrator also upheld the City's right to subcontract in certain instances based on past practice, but in general the Union's grievance was upheld.

The last grievance involved the contracting out of survey crew work in September of 1986. In that grievance the Union argued that employees had lost the benefits of overtime as a result of the subcontracting. However, in that decision the arbitrator concluded that there was no loss of benefits and the grievance was denied. Nevertheless the City concluded that, because of the uncertain definition afforded by arbitrators to the phrase "any benefits", that clearly a change was called for. The City pointing out that in two of the decisions overtime was included in "any benefit", but in the one case overtime was not considered to be "any benefit". The City argues that it has attempted to change the language by bargaining; but has been unsuccessful and therefore, seeks arbitration as a remedy.

The City has also alleged that while it has no intention to subcontract out snow plowing, which is a substantial source of overtime benefits, it is interested in discussing the problems associated with recycling. At present the City does not see how keeping recycling in house would be a cost benefit and believes that it would be more cost effective to subcontract such work. While the Union has suggested that it is willing to discuss the recycling issue, no agreement has been reached.

The City also introduced copies of the subcontracting language in the six area south shore municipalities, namely, Cudahy, Franklin, Greendale, Greenfield, St. Francis and South Milwaukee. The City asserts that none of those south shore municipalities have sub-contract language which is as restrictive as that of Oak Creek. The City also suggests that the language in the other six communities more closely resembles that proposed by the City, namely, that the municipality may subcontract as long as no employees are laid off.

With respect to wages, the City emphasizes that its offer is reasonable and in conformity with that offered by the other six municipalities and that that offer would be increased in the event the City's subcontracting proposal is accepted.

With respect to health insurance, the City introduced as an expert witness its health consultant, William J. Martin, to demonstrate the City's dilemma of being unable to obtain reasonable bids as an alternative to its present costs. The City could not obtain reasonable bids because it did not have 80% of its employees in HMOs and because it did not have a two-year record of the claims experience of the employees under the present plans. Furthermore, the mixing of retirees with current employees also discouraged competitive bidders. Thus, in the absence of claims experience for a minimum of two years and because of the current percentage of retirees of 30% in the City's plan, the City was unable to attract bidders. The City's current rate of participation in HMOs is approximately 28%, while Martin testified the industry standard is 80% participation in the standard plan.

The City also emphasized that the other units, police, fire and the sewer and water workers, had accepted the City's health modifications. As an extreme example of the skyrocketing health insurance costs, the City points out that its monthly premium per family coverage [under] one of the plans is now $520.00 per month or nearly $200.00 higher than the other plans. Thus, the City argues that it has submitted substantial evidence in support of its two requested changes.

It is the Union's position that the City has failed to meet its burden in seeking a change in the status quo. The Union submitted a number of arbitration citations to show (1) that the party seeking a proposed change must demonstrate a need for the change; (2) if there has been a demonstration of a need for a change, then the party proposing the change must demonstrate that it has provided quid pro quo for the proposed change; and (3) that arbitrators require that there must be clear and convincing evidence of the need for those changes. The Union points out that it did agree in bargaining to certain changes suggested by the City with respect to health insurance, but that for its right to discontinue the HMOs, the City has not offered any quid pro quo whatsoever.

With respect to subcontracting, the Union asserts the City has not demonstrated a sufficient need for the proposed change. The only work which the City claims it wishes to subcontract is recycling, which is an issue that the Union has been prepared to discuss, and that it is willing to discuss subcontracting issues on a case by case basis. The City also has not shown any economic necessity for the proposed changes in subcontracting language; that its proposal of .75% or 6 cents per hour is not adequate to compensate the Union members for possible substantial losses of overtime earnings.

As for health insurance, and the City's desire to eliminate most of the HMOs, the City has not shown that such elimination will result in substantial reductions in the cost of health insurance. Under the City's proposal, the City would retain the most costly plan, the WPS, and eliminate the least inexpensive [sic] WHO plan. Twenty percent of its membership would come under the more expensive plan than the ones they are presently in because the less expensive plans would be eliminated. On top of that an additional 11% of the membership could switch to the more expensive WPS plan. For a family, this plan could amount to over $200.00 per month to the City per family. Therefore, it is difficult to see the financial justification for the City's proposal. Furthermore, the City has not offered any quid pro quo for its health insurance proposal. The Union emphasizes also that it has already agreed to increase the prescription drug card deductible to a pre-certification requirement that could lead to out of pocket cost for Union members and a reduction in cash incentive for the WPS/HIP Plan.

The Union stresses that it was the City's insistence on employee participation in HMOs that put it in the position it is now in. A few years ago, the City wanted to increase [the] number of employees participating in the HMOs. As a result now 80% of its members have HMO coverage. Now the City is seeking to switch but does not give adequate reasons for such suggestions. The other external comparables show that the area employees have at least two HMO choices and one employer, South Milwaukee, offers six HMO plans. In sum, the Union asserts that the City has failed to demonstrate a sufficient need for its proposed changes.

Discussion

This case presents the dilemma facing arbitrators in total package final offers which link both economic and non-economic issues. This case is also complicated because it involves significant merits on both sides. However, the arbitrator must chose one of the final offers regardless of the deficiencies in making such choice. This arbitrator believes that it would be far preferable to separate the economic issues from the non-economic issues, but he recognizes that is a legislative issue.

First with respect to the issue of subcontracting, this arbitrator has concluded that the City has made a persuasive case for change. The City illustrated its case with three grievance arbitration opinions which gave differing results essentially interpreting the same subcontracting clause and the meaning of "any benefits". The City had also attempted to negotiate a change without success. In addition none of the comparable communities has a similar highly restrictive clause. Furthermore, the Union's own exhibits of clauses in nearby Franklin and Cudahy were not as restrictive as that now existing. In essence the cities of Franklin and Cudahy may subcontract as long as no layoffs occur. While the cited clauses are more restrictive in stating that subcontracting will not be used to undermine the Union, the central principle is that the City may subcontract as long as no layoffs occur. The City has asserted that it does not intend to subcontract snow plowing, but no such limitation is proposed.

In consideration of its subcontracting proposal, the City offers another .75% across the board wage increase. There is no way at present of showing that the amount is either adequate, inadequate or overly generous to compensate the employees who presumably will lose some overtime. There is simply no way telling at this point. However, the contract has less than nine months to run and the parties will have another opportunity to evaluate the subcontracting language and the experience thereunder.

With respect to the wage offer, the additional .75% increase is more than that offered to other Unions and to employees of comparable communities. Thus, the wage offer itself is very fair; but again that is without an accurate evaluation of the value of the subcontracting article.

With respect to the issue of health insurance, the City has also made a persuasive case. Again, however, the negotiations have been clouded by the cost of providing health insurance for retirees. The Union has made it clear that it is not bargaining for retirees and that the City is free to do whatever it wishes for them.

The strongest point in favor of the City is that the three other units, police, fire and sewer and water, have accepted the City's offer. While different conditions of work may effect the subcontracting issue as it relates to the police, fire and sewer and water units, the same cannot be said of health insurance. No reasonable distinction can be made as to why significantly different health plans should be made available to different units. The City currently pays the highest standard plan among the comparable communities. Again, the City pays the entire employee premium for the HMOs as well as providing four HMOs. In addition, the City has been hit with an intolerable $200 per month increase for one of the plans. While the City has agreed to maintain the more expensive plan for this contract, it can seek to change that in the next agreement.

The City has assured that employees will not be forced to see new doctors because employees can elect coverage under the standard plan and thus may continue their current doctor-patient relationship. In addition the City has assured that there will be no waiting period or pre-existing conditions clauses on the transfer to another carrier.

With respect to the City's right to withdraw from the HMOs (except for 1990–1992) the Family Health Plan would remain as a health care provider so long as it gives the Union Thirty (30) days' notice at the end of that calendar year. As for the Union's claim that there is no quid pro quo for the City's offer, this arbitrator concludes that the City's proposal is generous and does not require such separate consideration. Furthermore the three other units have accepted the plan with the same wage rate proposal, excluding .75% per hour effective 7/1/91.

Thus on balance for the reasons stated above, the arbitrator has selected the City's final offer and so

AWARDS

The City's final offer as set forth above.

Notes and Questions

1. *City of Oak Creek* illustrates the use of "final offer" arbitration. Several state statutes oblige the arbitrator to choose either the union's or the employer's final offer. No matter how ridiculous the arbitrator may find those positions, he or she may not impose a more reasonable result. Why would a legislature enact a final-offer system rather than conventional arbitration?

2. Wisconsin's law obliged Arbitrator Anderson to choose one party's final offer "package." That is, winner takes all, even if some aspects of the package are outrageous. Some other jurisdictions allow the arbitrator to choose among the final offers on each issue—for example, an arbitrator could select the union's wage proposal, the employer's health insurance proposal, the union's subcontracting proposal, and the employer's discipline proposal. Which of the two options, final offer by "package" or by "issue," is better, and why? One other possibility is to lump cost items as a package but deal with non-cost items separately. What are the advantages and disadvantages of that approach?

3. How does this case differ from the private sector cases you have previously read? How does the arbitrator's approach differ?

4. How did Arbitrator Anderson choose between the two proposals? What factors did he regard as decisive? Are there other factors he should have considered? These questions raise the problem of *standards* for interest arbitration. Regardless of whether the state law uses final-offer arbitration, if arbitration of interest disputes is to be something more than a gamble, there must be some restrictions on the arbitrator's discretion. (Even if the law imposes no standards, the courts will, when a party seeks review of an award.) Section 4 of this chapter provides some information on the "standards" issue.

5. However questionable any interest arbitration decision may seem, it will at least have the virtue of finality. In contrast, some other public-sector dispute resolution procedures are anything but final. In Olmstead Township, 109 LA 237 (Alan Miles Ruben, 1997), for instance, an established arbitrator served as a fact-finder pursuant to an Ohio statute. He went though an analysis of the issues in the same way that Arbitrator Anderson did, but each of his conclusions was phrased as a "recommendation" rather than as an "award." Why would a state opt for fact-finding rather than (or in addition to) arbitration? What benefits of fact-finding might counter-balance the disadvantage of the lack of finality?

4. STANDARDS IN INTEREST ARBITRATION

Most public sector interest arbitration statutes specify the factors an arbitrator must use when reaching a decision. (The Anderson, Krause, and Denaco chapter cited at footnote 3 contains at § 48.05 a thorough discussion of the most common standards used in public sector interest arbitration.) Here, for example, is the pertinent section of the Wisconsin Municipal Employment Relations Act that governed the *City of Oak Creek* case, W.S.A. § 111.70(4)7r (West 1997):

7. Factors Considered. In making any decision under the arbitration procedures authorized by this paragraph, the arbitrator shall give weight to the following factors:

   a. The lawful authority of the municipal employer.

   b. Stipulations of the parties.

   c. The interests and welfare of the public and the financial ability of the unit of government to meet the costs of the proposed settlement.

   d. Comparison of the wages, hours and conditions of employment of the municipal employes involved in the arbitration proceedings with the wages, hours and conditions of employment of other employes performing similar services.

   e. Comparison of the wages, hours and conditions of employment of the municipal employes involved in the arbitration proceedings with the wages, hours and conditions of employment of other employes generally in public employment in the same community and in comparable communities.

   f. Comparison of the wages, hours and conditions of employment of the municipal employes involved in the arbitration proceedings with the wages, hours and conditions of employment of other employes in private employment in the same community and in comparable communities.

g.   The average consumer prices for goods and services, commonly known as the cost-of-living.

h.   The overall compensation presently received by the municipal employes, including direct wage compensation, vacations, holidays and excused time, insurance and pensions, medical and hospitalization benefits, the continuity and stability of employment, and all other benefits received.

i.   Changes in any of the foregoing circumstances during the pendency of the arbitration proceedings.

j.   Such other factors, not confined to the foregoing, which are normally or traditionally taken into consideration in the determination of wages, hours and conditions of employment through voluntary collective bargaining, mediation, fact-finding, arbitration or otherwise between the parties, in the public service or in private employment.

To complicate matters further, the statute subjects those factors to a "factor given greatest weight" (state laws and directives limiting municipal expenditures) and a "factor given greater weight" ("economic conditions in the jurisdiction of the municipal employer").

Notes and Questions

1.   Does a listing of factors like Wisconsin's ease the arbitrator's burden or limit the arbitrator's discretion? How did the list affect Arbitrator Anderson's decision in *City of Oak Creek*? Did he consider all the required statutory criteria? If not, why not? Should the courts throw out his award if he did not?

2.   Imagine an interest arbitration of municipal wages in your town. How would an arbitrator apply these factors? Would they all point to the same result? If not, which will trump the others? Will six out of the ten listed give the victory to the employer? What if the union's four are clear and substantial while the employer's six are dubious and trivial?

3.   Consider just one factor, comparability. In subsections d., e., and f., the Wisconsin statute directs the arbitrator to compare the subject employees' wages, hours, and conditions of employment with those of employees performing similar services and with those of private-and public-sector employees in "the same community and in comparable communities." What sort of evidence will this require? How will the parties obtain and present it? In almost every case, the union will have some evidence that some employees in some communities earn more than the arbitrating employees, while the employer will be able to show that some employees in some communities earn less. Where does that leave the arbitrator? Should the arbitrator decide that some employees (or some communities) are "more comparable" than others? Must the arbitrator aim for the middle of the pack? What if (as is often the case) the wages of comparable public-sector employees differ widely

from those of comparable private-sector employees? One could easily raise as many questions about each of the other listed factors. How, for example, could an arbitrator apply subsection c., "the interests and welfare of the public and the financial ability of the unit of government to meet the costs of the proposed settlement"?

4. Would an arbitrator who wanted to reach a particular result have any difficulty justifying that result, whatever it might be, under the Wisconsin statute? Could the arbitrator simply fall back on subsection j.?

On the other hand, does a statutory list of multiple factors simply give a reviewing court more reasons for overturning an interest arbitration award? Hillsdale PBA Local 207 v. Borough of Hillsdale, 137 N.J. 71, 644 A.2d 564 (1994), for example, involved a final-offer arbitration statute for police and firefighters that directed arbitrators to consider eight factors, including among others the public welfare, comparisons with other public and private employers, financial effect on the community, the cost of living, and the continuity and stability of police and fire-department employment. The arbitrator quoted the relevant statute, found that the Borough was able to pay, and held that the union's proposal was more reasonable than the employer's. The parties did not offer evidence on all eight factors and the arbitrator did not address all of them. The New Jersey Supreme Court overturned the arbitrator's decision. Here is the court's explanation:

> Although compulsory arbitration is essentially adversarial, the public is a silent party to the process. Compulsory interest arbitration * * *. affects the public in many ways, most notably in the cost and adequacy of police and fire-protection services. Indeed, Section 16g expressly requires the arbitrator to consider the effect of an award on the general public. Hence, an award runs the risk of being found deficient if it does not expressly consider "the interests and welfare of the public." * * *

> As the statute states, an arbitrator need not rely on all factors, but only on those that the arbitrator deems relevant. An arbitrator should not deem a factor irrelevant, however, without first considering the relevant evidence. An arbitrator who requires additional evidence may request the parties to supplement their presentations. * * *

> Whether or not the parties adduce evidence on a particular factor, the arbitrator's opinion should explain why the arbitrator finds that factor irrelevant. Without such an explanation, the opinion and award may not be a "reasonable determination of the issues." Neither the parties, the public, nor a reviewing court can ascertain if the determination is reasonable or if the arbitrator has given "due weight" to the relevant factors.

What will that decision mean in practice? Does it just mean that arbitrators have to add a few sentences explaining why factors A, B, and C aren't relevant while factors D, E, and F are? Or would a court expect more? If you were arbitrating a public sector dispute in New Jersey, how would you proceed? Suppose neither party presented any evidence about "the interests and welfare of the public." Presumably you should "request the parties to supplement their presentations," to use the court's language. What would you ask them to provide?

In Town of Union City, Oklahoma, 117 LA 1544 (Anne Holman Woolf, 2002), one public employer tried to prove that its offer best satisfied the "interest and welfare of the public" standard by putting its offer and the union's up to a vote of the residents. Residents voted for the Town's offer. Does the vote end the matter? After pointing out that only 28% of the eligible voters participated and that the proposition "only briefly summarized" the nineteen disputed issues, Arbitrator Holman rejected the city's contention. The public-interest standard, she wrote, "is a complex and multifaceted concept which involves consideration of many significant components, including but not limited to the outcome of any particular election." In choosing the union's proposal, she gave greater weight to the 40% per year turnover rate for police officers.

5. Whatever factors the law may require an arbitrator to consider, other factors will also play a role. In County of Carlton, 104 LA 773 (Joseph L. Daly, 1995), for example, the union representing certain County employees sought an interest arbitration award of five floating holidays. Its main argument was comparability, because other County of Carlton employees already had that fringe benefit. The arbitrator agreed, reasoning that the bargaining unit would otherwise "have a 'sense of grievance' * * * when it compares its lot with the other employees in the area."

6. You should now be able to see why interest arbitration cases tend to be long, complex, expensive, and uncertain. Given those difficulties, why do you suppose states continue to mandate interest arbitration rather than deciding wages and other conditions by statute or allowing use of economic pressure?

A NOTE ON INTEREST ARBITRATION IN THE PRIVATE SECTOR

Except during wartime, interest arbitration in the United States is largely a public-sector phenomenon. Unions and employers both understandably dislike *compulsory* interest arbitration, but their opposition to *voluntary* interest arbitration is almost as strong. Why do you suppose that is so? Why would virtually all private sector agreements provide for grievance arbitration, and almost none for interest arbitration? If you represented a private-sector union or employer, why might you favor or disfavor interest arbitration?

There have been a few exceptions. Most of these have been of the last-resort variety: deadlocked parties in a situation where a strike would be suicidal might opt for arbitration, particularly if their positions are not far apart. Very rarely do parties provide for interest arbitration before reaching a deadlock.

Perhaps the most significant pre-deadlock exception was the "Experimental Negotiating Agreement," or ENA, used in the steel industry in the 1970s. After a disastrous series of strikes during contract negotiations, the parties realized that the American steel industry was losing business to foreign competitors whenever a collective bargaining agreement was about to expire. Businesses needing steel simply could not take the risk that the supply would be cut off by a labor dispute. When customers could not shift to foreign steel, they tended to stockpile steel in preparation for a possible strike; that made for a painful boom-and-bust cycle, and for production inefficiencies.

The result was the ENA, an interest-arbitration provision added to the 1973 agreement between the steel industry and the United Steelworkers. Foregoing the right to strike was enormously controversial within the union. A group of dissidents even sued in federal court, unsuccessfully, to block implementation of the ENA. Once it was in the contract, however, the parties were exceedingly reluctant to use it. There is good reason to believe the industry and union reached agreements in 1974 and 1977 partly because they feared what an interest arbitrator might do. Severe competitive pressures forced employers to let the ENA lapse in the 1980s. Since then, neither the steel industry nor—with one exception—any other major private industry in the United States has routinely relied on arbitration to resolve interest disputes.[4]

The one exception is professional baseball. A quarter-century ago, team owners and the union representing baseball players established a form of interest arbitration to resolve some salary disputes. [Roger Abrams concisely describes the origins of baseball's salary arbitration in Legal Bases: Baseball and the Law 115–33 (1998).] Unlike most economic disputes in unionized settings, baseball arbitration applies only to *individual* salary disputes, and usually only to players whose recent success has given them unusual leverage. It is unusual, too, in using a very limited form of final-offer arbitration. The only issue before the arbitrator is the player's salary for a given year, and the arbitrator must choose either the player's offer or the owner's offer. Though criticized from time to time by both sides (but not at the same time), the salary arbitration system has long outlived the ENA. See John L. Fizel, *Play Ball: Baseball Arbitration After 20 Years*, 49 Dispute Resolution Journal No. 2, 42 (June 1994).

Although no other industries generally use interest arbitration, occasionally certain parties will use it to resolve an intractable bargaining dispute. The problem of standards discussed in the previous section occurs with even greater force in those cases. Unless the parties' arbitration agreement specifies standards, the arbitrator will lack even the rudimentary guidance provided by state public-sector statutes.

The lack of controlling standards also makes judicial review problematic. How can a court decide whether an arbitrator exceeded his or her authority if no document defines that authority? As a result, courts are less likely to overturn a private sector interest award than a public sector one. Naturally, there are exceptions. In one relatively recent case, an arbitrator awarded a large retroactive wage increase for drivers at the New York Daily News. The arbitrator noted that the newspaper had not advanced a defense of inability to pay and had refused to provide financial data sought by the union. In further proceedings, the Daily News asserted that it lost nearly $18 million in 1998 and that it had no cash reserve with which to pay the award. The arbitrator noted the plea but made no findings about it. A federal judge

4. A few employers and unions in the airline industry, where work stoppages are particularly costly, have occasionally used interest arbitration. See the symposium on *Industry Specific Arbitration Issues: The Airline Industry*, 55 Proceedings of the National Academy of Arbitrators 132–62 (2002).

overturned the award, not because the arbitrator's decision was wrong, but because he failed to "conduct a thorough examination of the News's finances which the large awarded wage increase made absolutely necessary."[5]

5. COMPARATIVE NOTE

SETTLEMENT OF DISPUTES OVER INTERESTS

Alvin L. Goldman.
Comparative Labour Law and Industrial Relations in Industrialised
Market Economies 541–45. Roger Blainpain and Chris Engels,
Editors, 6th ed., Kluwer, 1999.

One distinguishing feature of interests dispute settlement through Adjudication is the assumption that the result will be a principled decision. A variable in the adjudicative process, therefore, is the nature and source of the guiding principles. Should they reflect only the goals of the disputing parties or should they reflect the broader concerns of social and economic policy? The answer in some countries is to attempt to provide public policy oriented guidelines. For example, in Israel an arbitral decision is supposed to be guided by 'fairness' and 'justice'.

Another variable in the Adjudication model is the structure and source of the impartial members of the tribunal. Frequently such people are professors or retired high ranking civil servants. Often they have had legal training. In some systems, such as Australia and some Canadian provinces, the adjudicators are fulltime government employees who are specifically assigned this responsibility. In Germany, where appointment is made by the parties, most commonly the impartial adjudicators are labour court judges.

When discussing Adjudication of interests disputes, one must begin with the foremost example of Australia and New Zealand where for most of the 20th Century Adjudication was a central mechanism for resolving interests disputes. New Zealand's system of comprehensive interests arbitration was abandoned in large measure in 1984 and totally abandoned in 1991. During the early 1990s a majority of Australian states and the federal parliament significantly reduced the role of Adjudication of interests disputes and by 1996 the remaining states had similar changes under consideration. Perhaps most significant, in early 1996 national elections were won by a political coalition committed to further reduction of the role of Adjudication in resolving employment interests disputes. Although compulsory interest arbitration may soon be a relic of 'down-under' history, it continues to warrant examination both because rejuvenation remains a possibility and because this unique structure endured longer than most other legal structures regulating labor-management interests disputes resolution in advanced economic systems.

---

5. Daily News L.P. v. Newspaper & Mail Deliverers' Union of New York and Vicini- ty, 1999 WL 1095613 (S.D.N.Y. 1999).

In Australia, because of its federated structure and the significant role that state governments play in much of the employment relations area, the available Adjudication machinery varies depending upon which set of laws control a particular employment relationship. Yerbury and Isaac divide the various arbitral tribunal structures into three classes: curial types, tripartite boards, and a mixture of the two. The curial type bodies are presided over by legally trained judges assisted by lay members called commissioners. These tribunals operate with greater formality than the tripartite boards which consist of equal representatives from each side and are presided over by a neutral. Whatever the tribunal, its awards are enforceable in the manner of legislative enactments.

Up to the early 1990s, interests disputes could be brought to an arbitral tribunal either on the initiative of a party or through the tribunal's own intervention. Once the arbitral process was initiated, the parties generally negotiated a settlement, with or without the aid of government conciliators. However, negotiated settlements often were submitted for award certification since only certified arbitration awards were judicially enforceable. Applications for such consent awards were rejected if the Commission found that they would be contrary to the public interest. Arbitration awards of the Industrial Relations Commission were binding on all employees and employers in the classification defined by the award regardless of whether their representative organization, if any, was a party to the dispute. At various times the Commission defined the public interest as requiring consideration of labour market flexibility, employment growth, comparative worth, monetary stability, price stability, and foreign competition.

Changes introduced in the early to mid–1990s vary by jurisdiction but included allowing collective agreements to be enforced without prior tribunal approval as an award, restricting the subject matter scope of tribunal authority, and confining awards to the enterprise. In the case of a couple of states, subject to commission oversight, the amended laws permit employers to enter directly into 'workplace agreements' with individual employees or with the workforce. That is, to establish agreements without negotiating with a union.

In Canada, several provincial governments as well as the federal government require parties reaching an impasse in the negotiation of an initial collective agreement to submit to binding third party resolution. In a couple of provinces the administrative agency that supervises labor-management relations serves as the Adjudication tribunal. Specially selected tripartite boards or single arbitrators serve this function in the other jurisdictions.

With respect to its own workers, the federal government in Canada requires the representative union to elect, prior to commencing negotiations, whether impasses will be resolved by conciliation subject to an ultimate right to strike, or by compulsory arbitration by a tribunal consisting of a labour and a management representative plus an impartial member drawn from permanent panels. About half of all provincial government workers in Canada are subject to arbitration mechanisms in the event of collective bargaining impasses.

Bargaining impasses in Greece may be resolved by Adjudication by an Administrative Arbitration Court consisting of judges together with employer and union representatives. The dispute initially is heard and decided by a First Level Administrative Arbitration Court whose decision is subject to review by a Second Level Administrative Arbitration Court.

Traditionally, interests arbitration has played a minor role in non government labour relations in the USA. At times it has been available by contractual arrangement in a few industries, including steel, and is used to resolve impasses concerning the individual compensation rates for athletes in some professional sports.

In contrast, interests arbitration is widely used in the employment relations of government workers in the USA. Impasses in collective bargaining for postal workers, for example, are required to be submitted to arbitration if fact finding and conciliation efforts fail. The mandated arbitration procedure requires each side to designate an arbiter with a third to be selected by those two arbitrators. The parties equally share the costs and have the right to adopt an alternative procedure by mutual consent.

A variety of interests arbitration formats have been adopted as mandatory settlement procedures for state and local government workers in the USA. A few state courts have rejected such legislation on the ground that it violates the constitutional prerogatives and responsibilities of executive and legislative officers. Among the states in which impasse arbitration has survived judicial scrutiny, several limit mandatory arbitration to certain groups of workers such as police and fire fighters. A few states use a tripartite format while others provide for an award by a single arbiter. In some instances the tribunal must choose between each side's final bargaining offer package while in other jurisdictions the tribunal must separately choose between each side's last offer with respect to each disputed issue. A format used in some states in the US requires the arbiter to select from among the parties' last offers or the fact finder's recommendation to the parties. (Fact finding and conciliation generally are earlier mandated stages of the procedure under these state laws.) And, other states allow the arbitrator to shape the award without restriction respecting the parties' bargaining positions. Often the legislature has enacted a list of criteria to be weighed by such tribunals as the basis for decision.

Several studies attempt to assess the impact of interests arbitration upon government employee labour relations in the USA. One observation is that while collective bargaining continues to be the dominant model for resolving such disputes, even when arbitration is available, some parties become dependent upon arbitration if available. An explanation for this dependence is the presence of special problems regarding the parties' respective power positions and political or personal pressures. In any event, the difference in results between negotiated settlements and arbitral awards does not appear to be very great. * * *

Many nations have policies that give preference to Adjudication machinery that is established by the disputing parties. For example, in the USA impasses concerning postal worker interests disputes are submitted to a statutory arbitration tribunal only if the parties have not agreed to their own arbitral mechanism. In Germany, the parties shape the mechanism for resolving works council disputes and make every effort to reach a settlement even when the mechanism for adjudicative resolution has been initiated.

In most national systems, Adjudication is seldom or never used to resolve interests disputes. Even when it is available, its greatest impact is not in its actual use but in the impetus it gives the parties to find their own solutions rather than become the victim of the third party's 'wisdom'. This is illustrated by the Swedish newspaper industry where, for over fifty years, by agreement the parties were required to submit deadlocked negotiations to arbitration. Nevertheless, they managed to reach mutual agreement on all but one occasion.

Acceptance of the Adjudication model for settling interests disputes largely results either from a desire to avoid an alternative of prolonged economic warfare or avoid work stoppages by those who provide important public services. The Adjudication model, even when applied through the generally informal processes of arbitration, is relatively time consuming because the arbiters need to be appointed, or at least notified, the issues must be framed, and the decision makers must be educated concerning the competing contentions and considerations. In addition, to the extent that there are neutral principles to be applied, at best they are vague and broad.

There is always the danger, too, that the 'impartial' party will harbor secret biases or will reach an impractical solution. On the other hand, because social or economic justice is not a precise science, no particular dispute resolution mechanism is innately superior to the rest. Therefore, the benefit of having a method available to definitively resolve the parties differences often outweighs the disadvantages and dangers of relying upon an impartial third party's imposed decision. Unresolved interests differences are costly when they create open economic warfare; they are costly, as well, when they fester in the form of uncertainties or repressed discontent.

Notes and Questions

1.   How do these foreign systems of dispute resolution differ from the American approach? What are the respective advantages and disadvantages?

2.   Professor Goldman notes that New Zealand abandoned and Australia severely limited their systems of compulsory arbitration of interest disputes. Why might a country with compulsory interest arbitration decide to abandon that approach? *Compare* Dennis R. Nolan, *R.I.P.: Compulsory Labour Arbitration in New Zealand, 1894–1984*, 12 Comparative Labor Law

Journal 411 (1991) (compulsory arbitration lost the support of both unions and management by the 1980s because it weakened unions, deterred serious collective bargaining, limited labor market flexibility, raised labor costs to uncompetitive levels, politicized industrial relations, and failed to prevent strikes) *with* Ellen J. Dannin, *Labor Law Reform in New Zealand*, 13 New York Law School Journal of International and Comparative Law 1 (1992) (employer associations' reform efforts were actually "an attack on the existence of unions as bodies with any sort of authority or power and an attempt to aggrandize the power of the corporations").

3. In both countries, labor party governments took the first steps away from compulsory arbitration. Conservative governments then extended (the Australian federal government and some of its states) or completed (New Zealand and other Australian states) the process. In 1999, New Zealand returned the Labour Party to power, but its election platform conspicuously avoided any suggestion of a return to compulsory arbitration. If, as Dannin argues, employers opposed compulsory arbitration as "an attack on the existence of unions" and to "aggrandize the power of the corporations," why would a Labour government accede to their wishes?

B. THE FEDERAL GOVERNMENT[1]

Collective bargaining in the federal government is relatively young. Perforce, labor arbitration is, too. President Kennedy first formalized federal sector collective bargaining in Executive Order 10988 in 1962. Under the executive order, arbitrators had broad jurisdiction but could only issue advisory awards that were subject to the approval of the agency head. In 1969, President Nixon revised federal sector arbitration in Executive Order 11491, for the first time permitting (but not requiring) binding grievance arbitration and authorizing the newly-established Federal Labor Relations Council to review exceptions to arbitration awards. Finally, as part of a broad legislative revision and codification of federal sector labor relations, Congress set the scope and procedure for arbitration of federal employees' grievances in the Civil Service Reform Act (CSRA) of 1978, 5 U.S.C.A. § 7101 *et seq.*

In many respects federal sector arbitration parallels private sector arbitration. Parties select their own arbitrators (usually through the Federal Mediation and Conciliation Service), present cases with the usual informality, limit arbitrators to interpretation and application of the collective agreement, and share the costs. In other respects, however,

1. Bibliographic Suggestions: On the origins of federal sector collective bargaining, see Albert A. Blum and I. B. Helburn, *Federal Labor–Management Relations: The Beginning*, 26 Journal of Collective Negotiations in the Public Sector 255 (1997). On federal sector grievance arbitration, see Grievance Arbitration in the Federal Service (Dennis K. Reischl and Ralph R. Smith, eds., 1987); Anthony Ingrassia, *Federal Sector Arbitration: A Management Viewpoint*, 43 Proceedings of the National Academy of Arbitrators 203 (1991); William V. Luneberg, *The Federal Personnel Complaint, Appeal, and Grievance Systems: A Structural Overview and Proposed Revisions*, 78 Kentucky Law Journal 1 (1989); Dennis R. Nolan, *Federal Sector Labor Arbitration: Differences, Problems, Cures*, 14 Pepperdine Law Review 805 (1987); and M. David Vaughn, *The Future of Arbitration in the Federal Sector and Postal Service*, Labor Arbitration Under Fire 88 (James L. Stern and Joyce M. Najita, eds. 1997).

there are extraordinary differences. Chief among the differences are these:

1. *Applicability of Laws and Regulations.* Every collective agreement in the federal sector is subject to all federal laws and to government-wide rules and regulations, CSRA § 7117(a). Section 7122(a) declares deficient an award that is "contrary to any law, rule, or regulation." Most federal-sector collective agreements include a provision expressly subordinating the agreement to applicable laws. As a result, arbitrators interpreting those agreements must consider statutory and regulatory issues that never affect the usual private sector arbitration.

2. *Limited Scope of Bargaining.* Many of the most fundamental subjects in private sector bargaining, including wages and salaries, holidays and vacations, and pension and health benefits, are set by law for federal government employees. Section § 7117(a) (which incorporates all federal laws) and § 7106 (which establishes broad and non-negotiable management rights) severely limit the subjects of collective bargaining in the federal sector. (A union may, however, negotiate over the procedures management will follow in exercising its statutory rights.) This restricted scope of bargaining places far more weight on arbitration, because often it will be the only way a union can demonstrate its worth and the only way employees can gain significant benefits.

3. *Limitations on Arbitral Procedures.* In the private sector, arbitrators have almost unlimited authority over arbitration procedures including selection of the applicable interpretive rules and the required quantum of proof. In the federal sector, arbitrators must apply the critical substantive rules and some procedural rules followed by related federal bodies.

Cornelius v. Nutt, 472 U.S. 648, 105 S.Ct. 2882, 86 L.Ed.2d 515 (1985), for example, involved a discharge case in which the employees had the choice between arbitration and a claim before the Merit Systems Protection Board (MSPB). They chose to arbitrate, and the arbitrator overturned the discharges because of the agency's procedural errors. Had the employees gone instead to the MSPB, that body would have found the errors harmless and would have sustained the discharges. The Supreme Court held that in such cases the arbitrator must follow the same harmful-error standard used by the MSPB, *as interpreted by the MSPB*. When deciding whether to mitigate serious disciplinary penalties, arbitrators must now apply the twelve factors listed by the MSPB in Douglas v. Veterans Administration, 5 M.S.P.R. 280, 313 (1981). Some lower courts have interpreted *Nutt* broadly as requiring arbitrators to follow the MSPB's *procedural* rules as well as its substantive rules. See, *e.g.*, Huey v. Department of Health and Human Services, 782 F.2d 1575 (Fed.Cir.1986).

Federal sector arbitrators must similarly follow statutory specifications on the necessary quantum of proof. For example, in cases of removals or demotions for unacceptable performance ("§ 4303 cases"), the arbitrator must uphold the agency's action if it is supported by "substantial evidence" rather than applying the usual "just cause" standard. In cases of "adverse actions" (removal or other major discipline for "such cause as will promote the efficiency of the service"), the arbitrator must sustain the decision if the agency presents a "preponderance of the evidence" rather than insisting on "clear and convincing" proof or proof "beyond a reasonable doubt."

4. *Review of Arbitration Awards.* Less than one percent of private sector arbitration awards are challenged in court, primarily because the Supreme Court's *Enterprise Wheel* decision so limited the grounds for review that a challenger almost never wins. CSRA § 7122(a), in contrast, expressly provides for review of arbitration awards by the Federal Labor Relations Authority (FLRA). In addition to the usual private-sector grounds for judicial review, the FLRA may modify or set aside an award if it "is contrary to any law, rule, or regulation." Because of the ease of challenging awards and the broader ground for reviewing them, parties file exceptions to a fifth or more of federal sector awards.

The differences between the sectors continue after appeal. Courts overturn very few of the rare appeals from private sector arbitration awards. The FLRA, though, modifies or reverses almost 20% of the appeals it receives. (See the Ingrassia article cited at footnote 1.) FLRA decisions reviewing arbitration awards are appealable to the federal courts, adding yet another layer of possible review.

This combination of factors—more complex issues presented in arbitration and a far greater likelihood of successful review—exposes federal sector arbitrators to potentially embarrassing second-guessing. Devine v. White, 711 F.2d 1082 (D.C.Cir.1983), illustrates the risk. A nonlawyer arbitrator set aside a disciplinary sanction without considering the statutory requirement (whether there had been a "harmful" error). The Court of Appeals returned the case to the arbitrator for reconsideration. The arbitrator reaffirmed his decision, but apparently not in words sufficiently clear for the Court. Per curiam, the Court complained that "it is difficult to fathom any coherent line of reasoning" in the opinion; "we are hard-pressed to identify either a glimmer of reasoned consideration, to which we might defer, or a hint that his observations bear any significant relation to the real world." The opinion, said the court, forced it "to choose between placing its stamp of approval on utter gibberish" or conducting a "de novo review on a hopelessly inadequate record." (The court chose the former option.)

The FLRA and the courts thus hold arbitrators to high legal standards. They must apply pertinent statutes, rules, regulations, and administrative interpretations, even if the parties never mention those authorities. It is hardly surprising that many arbitrators, especially nonlawyers, decline to accept federal sector cases.

5. *Limitations on, and Additions to, Arbitral Remedial Authority.* Paradoxically, federal sector arbitrators have both more and less remedial authority than their private-sector counterparts. On one hand, arbitrators may not restrict management's statutory rights even by way of remedying a management breach of the agreement. For example, an arbitrator who finds that an agency wrongly denied the grievant a promotion may not simply order the grievant promoted because § 7106(a)(2)(C) gives management the exclusive right to fill positions. The arbitrator may only order the agency to make another decision, avoiding the errors that tainted the first. Similarly, an arbitrator may award back pay only after making certain findings of fact required by the Back Pay Act, 5 U.S.C. § 5596(a). Private sector arbitrators have legal authority, though they seldom use it, to award interest on back pay awards, but federal sector arbitrators may not award interest against the federal government.

On the other hand, federal sector arbitrators may, on appropriate findings, award reasonable attorney fees to the grievant or the grievant's union. They may even ignore the usual rule of *functus officio* (which holds that an arbitrator's final award extinguishes his or her legal authority) in order to rule on such a request.

U.S. CUSTOMS SERVICE, LAREDO TEXAS AND CHAPTER 145, NATIONAL TREASURY EMPLOYEES UNION

Federal Labor Relations Authority.
17 FLRA 68 (1985).

This matter is before the Authority on exceptions to the award of Arbitrator A. Dale Allen, Jr. filed by the Agency under section 7122(a) of the Federal Service Labor–Management Relations Statute and part 2425 of the Authority's Rules and Regulations.

The dispute in this matter concerns the denial of the requests of two female customs inspectors to exchange shifts with two male customs inspectors. The exchange requests were denied on the basis that the shifts requested to be exchanged would have been left without a female customs inspector on duty to conduct personal searches of female suspects. Grievances were filed and submitted to arbitration claiming that in denying the exchanges the Activity had violated provisions of the parties' collective bargaining agreement.[2]

Before the Arbitrator, the Activity argued that there could be no violation of the collective bargaining agreement because the shift exchange provisions pertained only to qualified employees. In this regard the Activity explained that the very nature of the agency mission demands assignment by sex in some instances and that with respect to personal searches, an employee of a specific sex becomes the category of employee which must be ordered and assigned to conduct a personal search depending on the sex of the person waiting to be searched. Thus, the Activity contended that when, as in this case, the employee request-

---

2. The provisions pertinently provide that subject to approval, qualified employees shall be allowed to exchange shifts and overtime assignments.

ing the shift exchange is the only woman assigned to the shift, only other women are qualified employees for shift exchange purposes. The Arbitrator agreed with the Activity insofar as personal searches are concerned that sex is a valid basis and qualification for the assignment. However, the Arbitrator rejected the necessity for the assignment of a female inspector to the shifts sought to be exchanged. He indicated that the incidence of personal searches of females is low and that the Activity has other alternatives: use of females from other federal agencies, from local law enforcement agencies, from the deputizing of civilians, and from call-back overtime of a female inspector. Accordingly, as his award the Arbitrator sustained the grievances and directed that as long as present conditions prevail, the type of shift exchanges involved in this case are to be granted.

As one of its exceptions, the Agency contends that the award is contrary to management's right to assign work under section 7106(a)(2)(B) of the Statute. The Authority agrees.

The Authority has repeatedly recognized that the plain language of section 7106 provides that "nothing" in the Statute shall "affect the authority" of an agency to exercise the rights enumerated in that section. E.g., Professional Air Traffic Controllers Organization and Federal Aviation Administration, 5 FLRA 763, 767 (1981). Therefore, the Authority has consistently held that no arbitration award may interpret or enforce a provision of a collective bargaining agreement so as to improperly deny an agency the authority to exercise its rights under that section, id., or so as to result in the substitution of the arbitrator's judgment for that of the agency in the exercise of those rights, e.g., American Federation of Government Employees, AFL–CIO, Local 2782 and Department of Commerce, Bureau of the Census, Washington, D.C., 6 FLRA 314, 321 (1981). Section 7106(a)(2)(B) of the Statute, in particular, reserves to management officials the authority to assign work. Encompassed within that authority is the discretion to establish the particular qualifications needed to perform the work assignment to be done and to exercise judgment in determining whether a particular employee meets those qualifications. Laborers International Union of North America, AFL–CIO, Local 1276 and Veterans Administration, National Cemetery Office, San Francisco, California, 9 FLRA 703, 706 (1982). In terms of this case, as already noted, the Activity denied the disputed shift exchanges because it determined that the employees who were to exchange with the grievants were not qualified. Thus, the Arbitrator has negated the exercise by management of its right to establish qualifications and to determine whether particular employees meet those qualifications when the Arbitrator, as the award, sustained the grievances and directed that as long as present conditions prevail, the type of shift exchanges involved in this case are to be granted. In so directing, the Arbitrator has substituted his judgment for that of the Activity as to which employees are qualified for a particular work assignment and compels the Activity to treat male and female customs inspectors as functional equivalents when the Activity has determined otherwise in order that the work assignment of personal searches may be accomplished regardless of the sex of the suspect. Consequently, the Authority finds that the award interferes with management's right to assign work and is therefore contrary to section 7106(a)(2)(B). See Veterans Administration Hospital, Lebanon, Pennsylvania and American Federation of Government Employees, AFL–CIO, Local 1966, 11 FLRA No. 43 (1983).

Accordingly, the award is set aside.

NATIONAL FEDERATION OF FEDERAL EMPLOYEES, LOCAL 2030 AND U.S. DEPARTMENT OF THE INTERIOR, BUREAU OF LAND MANAGEMENT

56 FLRA 667 (2000).

[The Arbitrator sustained a grievance alleging that the Agency had failed to promote the grievant in a timely manner, ordered the Agency to retroactively promote the grievant with back pay, and directed that the parties split the arbitration costs. Both parties filed exceptions.]

II.   BACKGROUND AND ARBITRATOR'S AWARD

The grievant is a dispatcher at the Agency who directs firefighters to fires in the forest and grassland areas served by the Agency. Before beginning his employment with the Agency, the grievant was employed with the National Park Service (NPS) as a GS–0462–5 forestry technician fire dispatcher. On July 6, 1997, he began employment with the Agency as a GS–4555–5/6/7 range technician (fire dispatcher)—a permanent part time position. "The three-grade designation connoted that this was a career ladder position, whereby [the grievant] could move from grade 5 through grade 6, and ultimately to grade 7." Award at 4. Though the grievant was guaranteed at least six months' work a year, he worked eight to nine months and was off duty the remaining months. In 1997, he worked until November 12, returning to work on March 9, 1998. On September 30, 1998, he completed his first full year of performance with the Agency.

In the grievant's Performance Improvement and Position Review (PIPR) for the period July to October 1997, the grievant's supervisor rated his performance as effective and in one of the five job elements, rated him as exceptional. For fiscal year 1998, the grievant was rated as effective and in three of the five elements, he was rated exceptional. The grievant received a copy of the 1998 PIPR on November 16, 1998, sixteen days after it was due. Shortly thereafter, he received a step increase within the Grade 5.

Subsequently, the grievant contacted his supervisor to discuss his concerns about his promotion to GS–6. The supervisor informed the grievant that she had never intended to withhold his promotion; that she had assumed he was a GS–6; and that she was surprised to learn that he was a Grade 5. She informed the grievant that she would look into the matter and initiated a personnel action requesting that his promotion be expedited. She also learned that the grievant would not be entitled to back pay.

On December 6, 1998, the grievant was promoted to Grade 6, effective that day. On December 28, he filed a grievance contending that he should have been promoted to the GS–6, step 1 level, effective either April 28 or July 6. The grievance was not resolved and was submitted to arbitration.

The Arbitrator stated the issue as:

Is Grievant * * * entitled to back pay and other employee benefits either from the time he was employed by the [NPS] on April 28, 1997, or from the time he was transferred to the [Agency] on July 6, [1997] to the time he was promoted from a GS–5 to a GS–6, effective December 6, 1998?

* * *

The Arbitrator next addressed the merits of the grievance. According to the Arbitrator, under the career ladder program, the grievant had to satisfy the following major requirements to be eligible for promotion: (1) specialized experience; (2) time in grade; and (3) satisfactory performance. The Arbitrator found that the grievant had satisfied all three requirements by the time management should have promoted him to GS–6.

The Arbitrator further stated that the Agency, rather than the grievant or the Union, was responsible for pursuing the grievant's promotion. The Arbitrator found that the Agency "was primarily responsible for initiating the paper work necessary to promote [g]rievant ... under the career ladder program[,]" which "is impliedly demonstrated by the [Agreement] and the Regulations governing [the Agency's] operations." Id. at 12. The Arbitrator found that throughout the Agreement, references to promotion "uniformly require that management initiate the process whereby an employee is promoted to the next higher grade." Id. The Arbitrator referenced Article 15.6B, which provides that "[e]mployees eligible for promotion 'can and normally' will be promoted as soon as they meet all the regulatory requirements for promotion." Id. The Arbitrator stated that this provision and other references in the contract "are written in such a fashion as to indicate that it is management that is expected to make the first move when it comes to promotion within the career ladder program." Id. at 13.

The Arbitrator found that the grievant's supervisor failed to initiate the paper work necessary for the grievant to be promoted under the career ladder program to GS–6. The Arbitrator distinguished American Federation of Government Employees, San Francisco Region and Office of Program Operations, Field Operations, Social Security Administration, San Francisco Region, 7 FLRA 622 (1982) (SSA), which was cited by the Agency and involved ministerial action that was not taken by an agency to effect a promotion. The Arbitrator found that although the supervisor's failure to commence the procedure for promoting the grievant "may not be considered 'ministerial' in nature, it was most certainly non-discretionary." Id. at 14. According to the Arbitrator, the "moment that the [g]rievant had satisfied all the requirements for promotion . . . , it was [the supervisor's] duty to start the process." Id.

Relying on Social Security Administration and American Federation of Government Employees, Local 3342, 51 FLRA 1700 (1996) (Local 3342), and other Authority decisions, the Arbitrator determined that the employee was entitled to back pay. The Arbitrator found that management had failed to carry out its responsibilities under the career ladder program and that the grievant had not only satisfied all the requirements for promotion from GS–5 to GS–6, but was actually working at the full performance level of a GS–7. Accordingly, the Arbitrator directed the Agency to recognize the effective date of the grievant's promotion to GS–6 as April 28 and to restore back pay and other benefits to him.

III.   UNION'S EXCEPTIONS

* * * The "Union's exceptions apply 'only' * * * to the [arbitration] fees/costs which the Arbitrator assessed to the Union and the Agency." Exceptions at 1. The Union contends that the Arbitrator did not comply with Article 5.15 in assessing these costs and, therefore, his action manifestly disregards the Agreement and does not draw its essence from the Agreement. Id. at 2. Specifically, the Union asserts that "[s]ince there was no SPLIT * * * or question in the Arbitrator's decision as to whom he considered the winner * * * the Arbitrator is required by [Article 5.15] to order the losing party to pay the Arbitrator's fees and expenses." Id. at 5.

According to the Union, since there was no split or confusion as to whom the "clear and convincing winner" was, the Arbitrator showed a "clear manifest disregard of [Article 5.15A of] the agreement" and his award does not represent a plausible interpretation of this provision. Id. at 10. The Union states that the Arbitrator was made aware of Article 5.15 because the Agency pointed the provision out and argued it in its brief. The Union asserts that as the Arbitrator's determination of costs is not justified or tied to a specific article of the Agreement, there can be no plausible interpretation of the Agreement, and therefore the plain wording of the contract must stand. Accordingly, the Union argues that under Article 5.15, the Agency is the loser and should be held liable for the payment of all the Arbitrator's fees and expenses. * * *

[The Agency did not file an opposition to the union's exceptions.]

B.   Analysis and Conclusions

The Arbitrator's Determination Requiring the Costs and Expenses of the Arbitration to Be Split Between the Parties Draws its Essence from the Agreement.

In order for an award to be found deficient as failing to draw its essence from the collective bargaining agreement, it must be established that the award: (1) cannot in any rational way be derived from the agreement; (2) is so unfounded in reason and fact and so unconnected with the wording and purposes of the agreement as to manifest an infidelity to the obligation of the arbitrator; (3) does not represent a plausible interpretation of the agreement; or (4) evidences a manifest disregard of the agreement. * * *

The Union argues that the Arbitrator's action in requiring it to pay an equal share of the costs and expenses of the arbitration manifestly disregards the Agreement because the Agency was the losing party and Article 5.15 provides that the fees and expenses shall be borne by the losing party. While Article 5.15 indicates that the arbitrator's fees and expenses shall be paid by the losing party, it also explicitly states that "[i]f in the arbitrator's judgment, neither party is the clear losing party, then the arbitrator will indicate the percentage of the arbitration costs each will pay."

This provision permits the Arbitrator to exercise his judgment in determining how the costs should be divided when, in the Arbitrator's judgment, neither party is the clear losing party. As indicated by the attachment to the Union's exception, the determination of arbitration fees and expenses under Article 5.15 was presented to the Arbitrator by the Agency in its closing brief. In his decision, the Arbitrator determined who should pay the fees and expenses of the arbitration and listed such fees and expenses and the amount or percentage that each party was required to pay. The Arbitrator split the fees and expenses.

By such action, the Arbitrator interpreted the provision and, pursuant to the discretion expressly granted him by the Agreement, determined that neither party was the clear losing party. Thus, the Union has not established, given the discretion permitted under the provision, that the Arbitrator's award cannot in any rational way be derived from the Agreement or evidences a manifest disregard of the Agreement; or represents an implausible interpretation of the Agreement. * * * Accordingly, this exception provides no basis for finding the award deficient.

IV. AGENCY'S EXCEPTIONS

A. *Positions of the Parties*

1. Agency

* * * Second, the Agency contends that the award is based on a nonfact. The Agency asserts that the non-fact supporting the award of retroactive promotion and back pay was that the grievant "was not aware that he had not been promoted until December 28, 1998 when he filed [the] ... grievance." Id. at 22 (emphasis omitted). The Agency contends that allowing this non-fact to support the Arbitrator's conclusion "flies directly in the face of facts the Arbitrator specifically determined, namely that [the grievant] knew in early April 1998" based on an

e-mail from a personnel staffing specialist that he was eligible for promotion to GS–6 as of April 28, 1998. Id. This finding, in the Agency's view, is a " 'gross mistake of fact but for which a different result would have been reached." Id. at 24. The Agency argues that the award should be set aside or at least modified to limit any back pay to the 30–day time frame preceding the filing of the grievance.

Third, the Agency contends that the retroactive promotion and award of back pay is contrary to the Back Pay Act, 5 U.S.C. § 5596. The Agency contends that there was no "administrative or clerical error which occurred because the process approving a promotion had never begun." Id. The Agency claims that as the delay in the grievant's promotion "preceded any approval of [the] promotion by the properly authorized official[,]" the award of a retroactive promotion with back pay is contrary to the Back Pay Act. Id. * * *

2. Union's Opposition

The Union asserts that the Agency is re-arguing issues presented before the Arbitrator and has not established that the award does not draw its essence from the Agreement or is based on a non-fact. * * *

The Union further asserts that the award does not violate the Back Pay Act. The Union contends that the Arbitrator found that the Agency violated Article 15.6B of the Agreement, pertaining to promotions, and that the promotion in the career ladder program was "non-discretionary." Id. at 10. The Union asserts that the Arbitrator cited as support for his decision relevant Authority cases that involve the application of the Back Pay Act. Accordingly, the Union asserts that the award shows the connection between the Agreement and the unjustified or unwarranted personnel action that resulted in a withdrawal or reduction of an employee's pay, allowances, and differentials.

B. Analysis and Conclusions

* * *

2. The Award Is Not Based on a Nonfact

To establish that an award is based on a nonfact, the appealing party must demonstrate that a central fact underlying the award is clearly erroneous, but for which a different result would have been reached by the arbitrator. * * * However, the Authority will not find an award deficient on the basis of an arbitrator's determination of any factual matter that the parties disputed at arbitration. * * * Additionally, "[t]he mere fact that the appealing party disputes an arbitral finding does not provide a basis for finding that an award is based on a nonfact." American Federation of Government Employees, Local 1923 and U.S. Department of Health and Human Services, Health Care Finance Administration, Baltimore, Maryland, 51 FLRA 576, 579 (1995). These principles appropriately accord deference to an arbitrator's factual findings because the parties have bargained for the facts to be found by an arbitrator whom they have chosen. * * *

The question of whether the grievant could reasonably be expected to be aware of any incident occurring on April 28 or July 6 giving rise to the grievance was in dispute before the Arbitrator. The Arbitrator, based on the record evidence, resolved the question and determined that it was not reasonable for the grievant to be aware of such incident. Consequently, the Agency has not demonstrated that the award is based on a nonfact.

Additionally, as previously noted, the Arbitrator determined, based on the facts of this case, including his finding that the grievant could not reasonably be aware of any incident occurring on April 28 or July 6, that the grievance was timely filed under Article 5.6 of the parties' Agreement. The Agency's contention challenges the Arbitrator's procedural arbitrability determination. Such a contention does not provide a basis for finding the award deficient. See, for example, Veterans Administration Medical Center, Birmingham, Alabama and American Federation of Government Employees, Local 2207, 35 FLRA 553, 556–57 (1990) (exception contending that arbitrator's award was based on a nonfact failed to establish that the award was deficient because contention challenged the arbitrator's procedural arbitrability determination).

3. The Award of a Retroactive Promotion and Back Pay is Not Contrary to the Back Pay Act

The Agency contends that the award is contrary to the Back Pay Act. In reviewing arbitration awards for consistency with law, rule, or regulation, the Authority reviews the questions of law raised by the Arbitrator's award and the Agency exceptions de novo. * * * In applying the standard of de novo review, the Authority assesses whether the arbitrator's legal conclusions are consistent with the applicable standard of law, based on the underlying factual findings. * * * In making that assessment, the Authority defers to the arbitrator's underlying factual findings. See id. The Authority also defers to an arbitrator on questions of contract interpretation. * * *

An award of backpay is authorized under the Back Pay Act only when an arbitrator finds that: (1) the aggrieved employee was affected by an unjustified or unwarranted personnel action; and (2) the personnel action resulted in the withdrawal or the reduction of an employee's pay, allowances, or differentials. * * * A violation of a collective bargaining agreement constitutes an unjustified or unwarranted personnel action under the Act. * * *

In this case, the Arbitrator found that the grievant was employed in a career ladder position, that he satisfied the three major requirements for a career ladder promotion under the Agreement, and that he was therefore entitled to a retroactive promotion. The Agency disagrees and argues that the award of retroactive promotion is contrary to the Back Pay Act because the delay in approving the grievant's promotion preceded an approval by the properly authorized official.

We conclude that the award is not contrary to the Back Pay Act. In this regard, a career-ladder promotion is the direct result of an agency's decision to select an employee and place the employee in a career-ladder position in the agency. The agency's selection of an employee and the placement of that employee in a career-ladder position also constitutes the agency's decision to promote that employee noncompetitively at appropriate stages in the employee's career up to the full performance level of the position, once the requisite conditions have been met. * * * The Arbitrator found that provisions in the parties' Agreement, including Article 15.6B, require management to initiate the "nondiscretionary" process whereby an employee is promoted to the next higher grade once the employee has satisfied all the requirements for a career ladder promotion, and that the Agency failed to comply with these provisions. Award at 14. The Arbitrator further found that the grievant had not only satisfied all the requirements for promotion from GS–5 to GS–6, as indicated by his PIPR, but was actually working at the full performance level of GS–7.

Thus, the Arbitrator's findings establish that the grievant occupied a career ladder position and, in accordance with the terms of the Agreement, was entitled to a nondiscretionary career ladder promotion when the requisite conditions were met. * * * Further, the Arbitrator's finding that the Agency failed to comply with the Agreement by failing to initiate the nondiscretionary process to timely promote the grievant satisfies the requirement under the Back Pay Act for an unjustified or unwarranted personnel action but for which the grievant would have been promoted to GS–6 as of April, 1998. * * *

Accordingly, the award is not contrary to the Back Pay Act.

V. Decision

The Agency and the Union's exceptions are denied.

Notes and Questions

1. What do these decisions suggest about the type of arbitrator you would select for a federal sector case? About the type of hearing you would want the arbitrator to conduct? About the role of arbitration in the federal sector, as contrasted to the private sector? Consider that in the interest of readability, both excerpts eliminate many citations to FLRA decisions and other authorities.

2. What, precisely, was Arbitrator Allen's error in *U.S. Customs Service*? What should he have done instead? Suppose (a reasonable assumption in federal sector arbitration) that neither advocate told the arbitrator about the controlling statute. Should arbitrators conduct their own research? (You see the result if they do not.) If so, should they apply the law they find without notifying the parties of their discoveries? Or should they, weeks after closing the hearings, reopen them for debate on the arbitrators' research? Finally, just how long will all this take, and who will pay the bills?

3. What is the effect of "setting aside" an award? When the problem is merely that the arbitrator did not consider an issue or wrote ambiguously, the FLRA often directs the parties to remand the case to the arbitrator. If the arbitrator errs, however, the grievant may be stuck without a remedy. It

thus is extremely important for federal sector parties to choose their arbitrators carefully and to alert them to the many pitfalls in this area.

4. What do you make of the parties' exceptions to the arbitrator's decision in *Bureau of Land Management*? Do you think the Union really believed that the award "manifestly disregards the Agreement and does not draw its essence from the Agreement?" Or that the Agency really believed that the arbitrator's decision was based on a "nonfact" and that it violated the Back Pay Act? If your answer to either question is no, then what might be going on in that case? Consider that each party's litigation costs must have been many times greater than the amount of back pay at issue.

Chapter IX

PERSPECTIVES ON LABOR ARBITRATION

A. ARBITRAL ETHICS[1]

1. INTRODUCTION

Confidence in the arbitrator's integrity is essential to labor arbitration. Arbitral ethics thus was one of the first concerns of the National Academy of Arbitrators, the professional association of labor arbitrators. In fact, membership and ethics committees were the first created by the Academy after its formation in 1947. In 1951, the Academy worked with the American Arbitration Association and the Federal Mediation and Conciliation Service to draft the Code of Ethics and Procedural Standards for Labor–Management Arbitration. In addition to establishing standards of conduct for arbitrators, the Code also attempted to state rules governing the conduct and behavior of the parties' advocates. In 1974, the three groups substantially revised the Code—among other things, they dropped the effort to regulate advocates' conduct—and published the Code of Professional Responsibility for Arbitrators of Labor–Management Disputes. The current version is reprinted in Appendix D.

---

1. Bibliographic Suggestions: Paul R. Hays, Labor Arbitration: A Dissenting View (1966); Deseriee A. Kennedy, *Predisposed with Integrity: The Elusive Quest for Justice in Tripartite Arbitrations*, 8 Georgetown Journal of Legal Ethics 749 (1995); Jean T. McKelvey, *Ethics Then and Now: A Comparison of Ethical Practices*, 38 Proceedings of the National Academy of Arbitrators 283 (1986); Dennis R. Nolan and Roger I. Abrams, *Arbitral Immunity*, 11 Industrial Relations Law Journal 228 (1989); Francis Xavier Quinn, *Ethical Boundaries Between Arbitrators and the Parties*, 55 Proceedings of the National Academy of Arbitrators 165 (2002); Alan Scott Rau, *Integrity in Private Judging*, 38 South Texas Law Review 485 (1997); Arnold Zack, *Partners in the Code—The NAA and the Designating Agencies*, 41 Proceedings of the National Academy of Arbitrators 216 (1989) (with Responses by representatives of the American Arbitration Association and the Federal Mediation and Conciliation Service); Maureeen A. Weston, *Reexamining Arbitral Immunity in an Age of Mandatory and Professional Arbitration*, 88 Minnesota Law Review 449 (2004); Perry A. Zirkel and Peter D. Winebrake, *Legal Boundaries for Partiality and Misconduct of Labor Arbitrators*, 1992 Detroit College of Law Review 679.

The Code has no legal force and is anything but self-executing. It contains no general procedure for enforcement and imposes no penalties. There is, however, an enforcement mechanism covering some arbitrators. The Academy's Committee on Professional Responsibility and Grievances (CPRG) issues advisory opinions on ethics questions[2] and handles complaints alleging violation of the Code, but it has jurisdiction only over Academy members. Moreover, the most severe sanction is expulsion from the Academy, an action that has no effect on the arbitrator's ability to hear cases. The appointing agencies—the AAA and FMCS—require arbitrators on their lists to abide by the Code but do not themselves interpret it. Their sole weapon for enforcing arbitral ethics is removal of an arbitrator from their lists. The paper by Arnold Zack cited at footnote 1 and the agencies' responses to it discuss the strengths and weaknesses of the Code's processes.

A party harmed by an arbitrator's ethical lapse has two other possible remedies: it can either sue the arbitrator for damages or seek "vacatur" of a tainted award. The first option is a virtual nullity. State and federal courts have granted arbitrators a broad immunity comparable to a judge's. Section 14 of the Revised Uniform Arbitration Act expressly grants arbitrators immunity from civil liability "to the same extent as a judge of a court of this State acting in a judicial capacity," provides that they may not be required to testify or produce records in subsequent litigation, and authorizes an award of attorney's fees and expenses if the arbitrator successfully resists a party's suit or subpoena. (A convenient guide to materials on arbitral immunity can be found on the Academy's website at http://www.naarb.org/immunity/reference.html). One study (Nolan and Abrams, *supra* footnote 1) found that no arbitrator has ever been held liable for misfeasance, although some have lost cases based on their total nonfeasance. A related "testimonial privilege" protects arbitrators from having to testify in litigation over their decisions.

The second option is slightly more successful but often provides little comfort. A vacated award may simply mean more litigation or the continuation of an unresolved dispute. Moreover, the standards for judging an arbitrator's alleged misdeeds make vacatur on ethical grounds hard to obtain. The Federal Arbitration Act, for example, permits vacatur for an award "procured by corruption, fraud, or undue means," where there was "evident partiality or corruption in the arbitrators," or for arbitral misconduct prejudicing a party's rights, 9 U.S.C.A. § 10 (1988). Mere "appearance of bias," the applicable standard when a party seeks a judge's recusal, is not sufficient.[3]

---

2. The Committee issued 22 advisory opinions—five of which have been withdrawn—between 1953 and 1991. The most accessible publication of the Committee's opinions is in Binder 3 of BNA's Labor Relations Reporter, at page 221 in the section titled "Nondecisional Material."

3. See Perry A. Zirkel and Peter D. Winebrake, *Legal Boundaries for Partiality and Misconduct of Labor Arbitrators, supra* footnote 1, at 685–86.

Even without legal enforcement, the Code guides arbitral conduct before, during, and after the hearing. Reading the Code at this point will make the following material more intelligible.

2. PREHEARING CONDUCT[4]

DISCLOSURE AND RECUSEMENT—WHEN TO TELL AND WHEN TO LEAVE
Walter J. Gershenfeld.
44 Proceedings of the National Academy of Arbitrators 218 (1992).

The key section of the Code is 2.B, which requires arbitrators to disclose "any current or past managerial, representational, or consultative relationship with any company or union involved in a proceeding" for which the arbitrator is being considered or has been designated to serve. Section 2.B. also requires disclosure of "any pertinent pecuniary interest" or "any close personal relationship" between either party and the arbitrator. The arbitrator is enjoined to withdraw if "the arbitrator believes or perceives that there is a clear conflict of interest." * * *

There is a duty to tell the parties anything about yourself that you have reason to believe they should know in connection with a given case. There is an obligation to recuse yourself when a conflict of interest appears to be present. * * *

SUMMARY

Disclosure and recusement continue to be important Code requirements in a variety of circumstances if a fair and proper hearing is to take place. If any erring is to be done, it should be on the side of disclosure and recusement, whichever is applicable. One notable exception occurs when an arbitrator is asked to engage in recusement simply because one party does not like a ruling made in the course of the hearing. This type of request, whether sincere or tactical, should generally not be honored.

Some of the situations requiring disclosure raise questions about the application of the Code as written. One involves financial holdings by an arbitrator. *De facto*, it appears neither the parties nor arbitrators expect disclosure of small holdings in large private organizations in *ad hoc* cases. Government bonds, particularly of large entities such as federal or state governments or large cities, are apparently covered by the Code but

4. Bibliographic Suggestions: In addition to the Gershenfeld article excerpted in this subsection, see Comment, *What an Arbitrator Should Investigate and Disclose: Proposing a New Test for Evident Partiality Under the Federal Arbitration Act*, 53 Case Western Reserve University Law Review 815 (2003); Lee Epstein, *The "Agreed" Case: A Problem in Ethics*, 20 Arbitration Journal 41 (1965); Joseph Krislov, *Disclosure Problems of the Academic Arbitrator*, 52 Dispute Resolution Journal 54 (Fall, 1997); Note, *The Standard of Impartiality* as *Applied to Arbitrators by the Federal Courts and Codes of Ethics*, 3 Georgetown Journal of Legal Ethics 821 (1990); Francis Xavier Quinn, *Ethical Boundaries Between Arbitrators and the Parties*, 55 Proceedings of the National Academy of Arbitrators 165 (2002); Herbert L. Sherman, Jr., *Labor Arbitrator's Duty of Disclosure*, 31 University of Pittsburgh Law Review 377 (1970) and *Arbitrator's Duty of Disclosure—A Sequel*, 24 Proceedings of the National Academy of Arbitrators 203 (1971).

are often ignored as disclosure items in practice. The time has come for us to address necessary Code changes involving stock and bond holdings.

We have a healthy heritage from past arbitrators and advocates who know and respect each other, who conform to the Code by making no secret of their friendship, and who may believe that no one should challenge an arbitrator's impartiality simply because of friendship with an advocate. The world today tends to be more suspicious in many ways than in the past, and arbitrators are well advised to make friendship disclosures routine so that all people at a hearing, especially those from the shop floor, are not puzzled by what is happening in an arbitration that affects them.

Other situations that in the past were not unusual, such as training one set of parties in the arbitration process, now raise questions of prerecusement if an arbitrator accepts a training assignment with that party. Cases close to home in the public sector (particularly in small communities) are more often becoming a basis for recusement. New types of relationships among the parties are also emerging as arbitrators and advocates find themselves coming together in such milieus as commercial arbitration while still meeting in labor arbitration settings.

No one ever said that questions of ethics were easy or resolvable for all time by given pronouncements. Disclosure and recusement require regular review if we are to keep up with new circumstances and changes in the perception of existing situations.

Notes and Questions

1. Experienced arbitrators are likely to know some parties, advocates, or witnesses as professional colleagues, social acquaintances, former employers, or former students. In fact, some advocates regard an arbitrator's familiarity with the industry and participants as a plus. Professor Herbert Sherman, in the articles cited at footnote 4, reported the results of an extensive survey of arbitrators and labor and management advocates about the arbitrator's duty of disclosure. Some obvious situations drew a consensus of all three groups. Each group agreed (by percentages ranging from 74–93%) that an arbitrator should disclose substantial stock holdings in the company. On many issues, however, the groups diverged. For example, 61% of arbitrators and 55% of union advocates, but only 35% of management advocates, believed that an arbitrator should disclose a $500 consulting fee received 10 years ago from one of the parties for a matter not related to labor relations. Does that type of split suggest that the arbitrator can ethically choose either answer?

Even when a majority of all groups agreed, there was often a substantial minority. A majority of each group said that a professor-arbitrator need not disclose that one of the advocates was a former student, but a strong minority of each (from 26–35%) expected disclosure. What should an arbitrator do to comply with the Code? What would you expect (or want, if that is different) your professor to do when you appear before him or her in a few years?

2. Failure to disclose has become a favorite basis for parties challenging arbitration awards in employment arbitration situations. Comment, *What an Arbitrator Should Investigate and Disclose: Proposing a New Test for Evident Partiality Under the Federal Arbitration Act*, 53 Case Western Reserve Law Review 815 (2003). California's Judicial Council, on direction of the legislature, recently imposed extraordinarily strict (some would say draconian) disclosure rules on arbitrators. They contain 17 categories and 21 subcategories of disclosure. See generally, Jay Folberg, *Arbitration Ethics— Is California the Future?*, 18 Ohio St. J. on Disp. Resol. 343 (2003); Note, *A New Era of Disclosure: California Judicial Council Enacts Arbitrator Ethics Standards*, 2003 J. Disp. Resol. 271; Francis Xavier Quinn, *Ethical Boundaries Between Arbitrators and the Parties*, 55 Proceedings of the National Academy of Arbitrators 165 (2002). The rules exclude labor arbitration but there is nevertheless a widespread expectation that practices in labor arbitration will have to change in the direction of greater disclosure. For example, labor arbitrators and parties have long believed that everyone understood that arbitrators handled cases from scores if not hundreds of parties and that they often dealt with the same advocates in different cases. No one expected an arbitrator to disclose previous arbitration service with Union X or that Company Y's lawyer had appeared before her last year representing Company Z. In California, those sorts of contacts in non-labor cases must be disclosed, and designating agencies like the AAA expect similar disclosure.

Should labor arbitrators also make such disclosures? The assumption of general knowledge may have been accurate when and where labor arbitration was a relatively tight community. Now, however, arbitrators often work in a wide geographic region or even nationwide, and none of the participants may have met before. Moreover, unions understandably worry about duty of fair representation suits by grievants. The union advocate may have no problem with the arbitrator's previous experience but the grievant—whose job may be at stake and who likely has little understanding of the dispute resolution system—may view *any* prior connection between the arbitrator and the employer as evidence of bias.

3. One easy answer to such questions is to disclose *everything* ("I think I may once have attended the same Mets game as the company lawyer * * *."). One distinguished arbitrator (Quinn, *supra* note 4 at 172) wrote: "Even if you believe that the parties will find your disclosure unnecessary or even humorous, it is better to err on the side of disclosure.... No exceptions are made for de minimis situations." Is there anything wrong with that answer? Does disclosure have a downside? Can there be "too much" disclosure?

4. Lawyers, like members of many other professions, once regarded advertising as unethical. They did so, that is, until the Federal government told them that such prohibitions violated antitrust laws. Until very recently, Code § 1.C.3. also prohibited advertising. Several interpretive opinions of the Academy's CPRG strictly interpreted that prohibition. Opinion No. 14, for example, found a violation when an arbitrator merely sent his resume to labor and management representatives and Opinion No. 16 criticized a change-of-address announcement that included information about the arbitrator's qualifications. Opinion No. 19 dealt with an arbitrator who distrib-

uted ball-point pens with his new address rather than using a business card. The pens conveyed the same information as a business card, the Committee recognized, but

> they also constituted a useful writing tool which, to the extent it was thereafter used, would serve as a continuing reminder of the arbitrator's availability. These characteristics convert the pens into a form of advertising or solicitation prohibited by [the Code].

In 2002, the Federal Trade Commission became concerned that the Code's advertising ban violated Federal antitrust laws. After lengthy negotiations and internal debate, the Academy and its Code Partners, the FMCS and AAA, agreed to drop the prohibition. In June of 2003, the Academy adopted this substitute:

> 3. An arbitrator shall not engage in conduct that would appear to compromise the arbitrator's impartiality.

> a. Arbitrators may disseminate or transmit truthful information about themselves through brochures or letters, among other means, provided that such material and information is disclosed, disseminated or transmitted in good faith to representatives of both management and labor.

The object of the last phrase, which the FTC accepted, was to avoid any implication that the arbitrator, by contacting only one side, favored that party.

Problems

A. Your first case as an arbitrator involves a discharge. Before the hearing and outside the hearing of the other participants, the union's representative commented to you, "I've got a loser today. I don't expect to win this one." What should you do next? Read Code §§ 2.A., 2.D., and 2.I. before answering. You might also look at the Epstein article cited at note 4. For one attempt at an answer, see CPRG Opinion No. 6 (June 10, 1980).

B. Before your second arbitration case, an interest arbitration hearing on the union's demand for a wage increase from a city government, the two advocates approached you and stated that they had reached an agreement but that "political" problems with their constituents made it necessary for them to present the settlement as the decision of an arbitrator. They asked you to proceed with the hearing as normal but to embody their settlement in your award—at your usual fee, of course. What should you do now? Are there any pertinent differences in this case to cause you to act differently from the previous one?

Does it matter whether both parties or just one of them "informs" the arbitrator? See CPRG Opinion No. 6 (June 10, 1980). In the situation presented to the Committee, a union representative in a discharge case had made a comment similar to that in Problem A. The issues were whether the arbitrator should (a) withdraw from the case and (b) disclose the remark to the grievant. Section 2.A.2. of the Code expressly prohibits participation in any "collusive attempt by the parties to use arbitration for an improper purpose." Even when the attempt is unilateral rather than collusive, said the Committee, the arbitrator should not continue to serve "without the informed consent of the discharged employee" because it would not "uphold the dignity and integrity of the office" (§ 1.D.1.) and would be inconsistent with the "essential personal qualifications of honesty and integrity" referred to in § 1.A.

In the unilateral "informed" case, the Opinion states that the arbitrator should first determine whether the remark really was an attempt to influence the arbitrator and, if so, whether the arbitrator could disregard the remark and "do full justice to the parties." If the arbitrator believes it is possible to ignore the remark, he or she need not withdraw. Professor Benjamin Aaron, who voted for the Opinion, remains uncomfortable with it. He notes some unanswered questions:

> Can an arbitrator who has heard the manifestly improper comment by the union representative ever erase the incident from his subconscious? Suppose that rather than being influenced against the grievant as a consequence, he leans over backward to be fair: is he any less biased in his judgment? On the other hand, would he always be justified in disclosing to the grievant and to the employer an ill-advised remark that might poison the relationship between the parties for years to come? Could he not better serve the parties and the process by remaining silent but subsequently impressing upon the offending representative the seriousness of his misconduct? Or suppose the arbitrator feels that he must withdraw: should he, nevertheless, in the interest of protecting the integrity of the arbitration process, inform the grievant and the employer of the union representative's remark, or would this be an act of officious meddling?

Benjamin Aaron, *The Role of the Arbitrator in Ensuring a Fair Hearing*, 35 Proceedings of the National Academy of Arbitrators 30, 42 (1982). If you find those questions difficult to answer, you may be comforted by Professor Aaron's next sentence: "Inasmuch as I cannot resolve these questions to my own satisfaction, I can hardly presume to do more than leave them with you without further comment."

On the other hand, if *both* parties propose a solution to the arbitrator, as in Problem B, Code § 2.I. allows the arbitrator to issue the settlement as an award if he or she "believes that a suggested award is proper, fair, sound, and lawful." Before complying with such a request, however, the arbitrator must take care to understand the proposal, making any necessary inquiries.

3. HEARING CONDUCT[5]

The primary Code provision on the arbitrator's hearing conduct is § 5.A.1.: "An arbitrator must provide a fair and adequate hearing which assures that both parties have sufficient opportunity to present their respective evidence and argument." How could anyone disagree? The problem, of course, is in the application. Thus subsection 1.a. states that the arbitrator should "conform to the various types of hearing procedures desired by the parties." Even if the arbitrator doubts the procedure's fairness? Consider Problem B, above. Subsection 1.c. states that

5. Bibliographic Suggestion: Richard Mittenthal, *A Code Commentary—Conduct* *of the Hearing*, 41 Proceedings of the National Academy of Arbitrators 236 (1989).

the arbitrator "should not intrude into a party's presentation so as to prevent that party from putting forward its case fairly and adequately." Even if the arbitrator believes the union advocate is incompetent or biased against the grievant? What should an arbitrator do if one party insists on presenting 12 witnesses where one or two would do? The Mittenthal article cited at footnote 5 provides some guidance.

TEAMSTERS LOCAL 506 v. E. D. CLAPP CORP.
United States District Court, Northern District of New York, 1982.
551 F.Supp. 570 (1982), *affirmed mem.* 742 F.2d 1441 (2d Cir.1983).

This action was brought by petitioner, Local 506 [Union], seeking a vacatur of arbitration awards rendered on November 12, 1981. The Union contends that the awards were procured by corruption, fraud, or undue means within the meaning of 9 U.S.C. § 10(a), that there was evident partiality or corruptness on the part of the arbitrator within the meaning of 9 U.S.C. § 10(b), that the arbitrator was guilty of misconduct within the meaning of 9 U.S.C. § 10(c), and that the arbitrator exceeded his powers within the meaning of 9 U.S.C. § 10(d). Respondent E.D. Clapp Corporation [Company] denies these allegations and requests that the Petition to Vacate be denied in all respects.

[Pursuant to the collective bargaining agreement, the New York State Mediation Board appointed arbitrator John Beich.] Arbitrator Beich communicated frequently with Union President Paul Bush and Company President Spencer S. Berger from the date of his appointment on February 6, 1981 to the first of the alleged "hearings" on July 1, 1981. On this date, the parties gathered in Auburn, New York. Although this fact is undisputed, the events of that day are subject to varied interpretation. According to the Company, the parties agreed that Beich could decide the question of whether the subject disputes were arbitrable before proceeding to the merits. This view is supported by the affidavits of Company President Spencer S. Berger, Assistant to the President William C. Lavery, and Company counsel Stephen J. Vollmer. The Union argues, however, that no agreement was reached allowing the arbitrator to first decide the arbitrability question. This position is supported by the affidavits of Union counsel Peter P. Paravati, and Union President Paul Bush.

After this alleged "stipulation" was entered into, the Company contends that a hearing was held on the arbitrability issue. At this hearing, the Company claims that it presented its case on the arbitrability issue, and in so doing, also substantially presented its case on the merits. * * * To the contrary, the Union asserts that no formal hearing was held. Instead, the Union claims that at this July 1 meeting, Company President Berger refused to allow consideration of anything but the arbitrability issue despite the prior understanding that all issues were to be presented. Berger's conduct, according to the Union, created turmoil, disorder, and chaos, and that under no stretch of the imagination, could that July 1 meeting be considered a hearing. No witnesses were called and the dischargees were never heard from. * * *

Due to the high degree of acrimony between the parties, it was allegedly agreed that arbitrator Beich be allowed to conduct independent investigations of the disputes and engage in ex parte contacts with the parties and their representatives. According to the Company, this stipulation was signed by the Company as an accommodation to the arbitrator even though it was understood that the arbitrability issue would be reached first. * * * The Union asserts, however, that the stipulation was entered into for different reasons. It is claimed that arbitrator Beich requested the parties to sign the stipulation in order to "cover" for the arbitrator's past ex parte meetings with the parties. This stipulation, signed by Union President Paul Bush, was understood by Bush to only cover past conduct by the arbitrator. Moreover, Bush charges that the stipulation was altered after he signed it so that Beich could have ex parte contacts in the future. * * *

After the stipulation was entered into, it appears that the parties agreed to another meeting with the arbitrator. On September 1, 1981, the parties gathered again in Auburn, New York. Once again the events of that day are subject to dispute. According to the Union, Paul Bush objected to certain procedural matters, namely, the sequestration of witnesses. The Union claims that it continually objected to ex parte meetings between the Company and arbitrator Beich and attributes any and all delays to the Company. * * * Needless to say, the Company's version of this episode is quite different. According to the Company, when the sequestration of witnesses was requested by the Company, Paul Bush objected on the grounds that it would prevent him from preparing his cases and would be detrimental to the interest of the grievants. When Bush's objections were overruled, he verbally assaulted the arbitrator and was "personally insulting and provoking." This view is supported by the affidavits of Company President Spencer S. Berger, Assistant to the President William C. Lavery, and Company counsel Stephen J. Vollmer. In a supplemental affidavit, Paul Bush specifically denied the Company's account of his "tirade."

At some point in the proceedings on September 1, 1981, arbitrator Beich attempted to question Union witness Bruce Bergeron. According to the Union, Beich tried to coerce Bergeron into signing an agreement stipulating to certain facts before asking any questions. The Union further alleges that these facts by stipulation were prepared by the Company. * * * The Company asserts that all arbitrator Beich asked Bergeron was whether he had left the Company's plant on a given date. At this point, according to the Company, Bush "exploded" again and renewed his tirade against the arbitrator. * * *

The manner in which the September 1, 1981 proceedings concluded is also the subject of a controversy. According to the Union, and of primary importance to the instant Petition to Vacate, arbitrator Beich withdrew from his role as arbitrator and stormed out of the proceedings. As stated in the Union's Petition:

> 26.   At that point, Beich stood up and stated, "[expletive deleted] it, I quit, I'm prejudiced, I never wanted these cases, they are making a patsy out of me." (deletion in original).

> 27.   Bush responded that Beich was acting like a fool, that Bush had never heard of an arbitrator quitting like this, that if he did not sit down and stop this nonsense Bush would call Chairman Healy. Beich responded "I don't give a [expletive deleted] who you call, I quit." (deletion in original).

* * * The Company's version of the conclusion of the September 1, 1981 meeting bears no mention of Beich's resignation. In fact, the Company asserts that Beich in no way indicated that he was withdrawing or resigning from the case. According to the Company, the meeting concluded because Paul Bush would not allow it to proceed in an orderly fashion. * * *

Unfortunately, a stenographic record was not taken of either the July 1 or September 1 meetings. With regard to the latter meeting, the Court finds the discrepancies in the above stories to be incredible. Discounting the affidavits of counsel who were not present at the time, the Court is presented with four sworn affidavits, two of which tell diametrically opposed versions of the same incident from the other two. Clearly, the bounds of zealousness have been exceeded.

Following the adjournment of the September 1 meeting, a long series of correspondence flowed between the parties, arbitrator Beich, and Chairman Healy of the New York State Mediation Board. On September 3, 1981, Company President Spencer S. Berger wrote to arbitrator Beich concerning the meeting of two days prior. Berger acknowledged that the Company had agreed on July 30, 1981 to have Beich render his decision as to the arbitrability simultaneously with the merits determination. However, Berger wrote, in view of the Union's conduct at the meeting and its failure to live up to the conditions in the July 30 agreement, the Company was requesting an expedited ruling on the threshold question of arbitrability.

Apparently in response to a telephone conversation, Union President Paul Bush wrote to Chairman Healy concerning the "unilateral withdrawal" of arbitrator Beich. While the Union did not solicit the resignation, according to Bush, it nevertheless accepted it. The Union stated its position that it would accept a substitute arbitrator. This letter, dated September 23, 1981, seemingly crossed in the mail with a September 21 letter from Chairman Healy to Bush and Berger. The Chairman's letter makes no mention of any resignation by Beich, stating:

> After consultation with staff arbitrator, John Beich, Esq. relative to the pending arbitrations at E.D. Clapp, pleased be advised

that I have requested Mr. Beich to expedite his decisions about the threshold issues of arbitrability.

Upon receipt of his awards, we are prepared to take what other steps may be necessary to conclude these matters.

In response to Chairman Healy's letter, Paul Bush wrote to the Chairman on September 24. Mr. Bush expressed his dismay at the prospect of a decision on the issue of arbitrability alone, and reiterated his position that all issues must be decided simultaneously.

After Paul Bush's September 24 letter to Chairman Healy, the events take a strange twist. It appears, that at an American Arbitration Association seminar in Syracuse on October 1, Chairman Healy met with Union President Bush and counsel for the Union to discuss the pendency of the arbitration proceedings between the Union and the Company. No representative of the Company was present at this meeting. The next day, Chairman Healy wrote to Paul Bush and Spencer Berger and advised that the Mediation Board had held a special meeting to discuss the E.D. Clapp situation. Accordingly, in light of the "unusual nature of the circumstances under which Mr. Beich withdrew as arbitrator, the Board [became] fearful that whoever might be the 'loser' in his awards would seek judicial review" and decided to appoint a panel of arbitrators for new hearings. The Court is at a loss to explain the difference between Chairman Healy's position in this last letter and the September 21 letter relating to the need for expedited decisions on arbitrability. Inasmuch as the Chairman's September 21 letter referred to a consultation with arbitrator Beich after the September 1 hearing, the Court can only conclude that the Chairman was influenced by the meeting with the Union at the October 1 seminar.

On October 9, Company President Berger wrote to Chairman Healy expressing his dismay at the prospect of having new hearings and discarding all of the past work of arbitrator Beich. Berger asserts in his letter that the change in the Chairman's position could be traced to the October 1 seminar. The Company summarized its position that it expected procedural rulings from arbitrator Beich before the resolution of any substantive issues and that legal proceedings would be instituted to redress any perceived injustice. Berger wrote to arbitrator Beich on October 23 and reiterated his position that the arbitrability must be decided first. Moreover, Berger referred to past phone conversations in which Beich had reaffirmed the fact that he had not withdrawn from the case.

Finally, on November 12, 1981, the arbitrator rendered his decisions holding that all of the subject disputes were not arbitrable under the terms of the CBA. It is these decisions that the Union seeks to have vacated. * * *

In the present case, the Union seeks to have the arbitration awards vacated. Thus, the Court must look to the provision of the United States Arbitration Act, 9 U.S.C. § 10, that covers vacation of arbitration awards. Section 10 provides that the district court may vacate an arbitration award

> (a) Where the award was procured by corruption, fraud or undue means.

> (b) Where there was evident partiality or corruption in the arbitrators, or either of them.

> (c) Where the arbitrators were guilty of misconduct in refusing to postpone the hearing upon sufficient cause shown, or in refusing to hear evidence pertinent and material to the controversy; or of any other misbehavior by which the rights of any party have been prejudiced.

> (d) Where the arbitrators exceeded their powers, or so imperfectly executed them that a mutual, final, and definite award upon the subject matter submitted was not made.

However, it must be noted that the burden of proof in upsetting the awards rests squarely on the Union. Cook Indus., Inc. v. Itoh & Co. (America) Inc., 449 F.2d 106, 108 (2d Cir.1971), cert. denied, 405 U.S. 921, 92 S.Ct. 957, 30 L.Ed.2d 792 (1972); * * *

The Court is also aware that "[a]rbitration is essentially consensual and practical. The United States Arbitration Act is obviously designed to protect the integrity of the process with a minimum of insistence upon set formulae and rules." Commonwealth Coatings Corp. v. Continental Casualty Co., 393 U.S. 145, 154–55, 89 S.Ct. 337, 342, 21 L.Ed.2d 301 (1968) (Fortas, J., dissenting). Therefore, proof that arbitrator Beich violated the Arbitration Act must be clear and convincing and may not simply be speculation or hard feelings on the part of the Union.

The Union argues that the arbitrator was guilty of misbehavior to the prejudice of the Union by failing to disclose his ex parte communications with the Company. This argument is without merit. Both parties were guilty of having ex parte communications with the arbitrator as well as the Chairman of the New York State Mediation Board. The record is full of correspondence to the Chairman and the arbitrator indicating that the other party was not privy to the writing. Here, the acrimonious relationship between the parties led to a total breakdown of respect for the fairness of arbitration process.

As to the claim that the stipulation allowing ex parte contacts was altered after Paul Bush signed it, the Court refuses to speculate as whether the stipulation was in fact changed. Regardless, the Court finds that both the "original" and the "altered" stipulation cover the types of conduct practiced by both parties to this case.

The Union further argues that the arbitrator was guilty of partiality and corruption and of procuring the awards by corruption, fraud and undue means. These contentions may similarly be rejected. Upon a review of the entire record in this case and keeping in mind the heavy burden of proof on the party seeking a vacatur, it is clear that the Union has failed to meet this burden. Rather, the only thing that the record shows is that each party has presented its own version of the events leading up to the awards issued by arbitrator Beich on November 12, 1981. In the Court's view, these two views are entirely contradictory. Accordingly, it cannot be said that the Union has properly proved its case on this point. * * *

With regard to the Union's claim that the arbitrator was guilty of evident partiality, the Supreme Court has held that arbitrators should avoid the appearance of bias or partiality. Commonwealth Coatings Corp. v. Continental Casualty Co., 393 U.S. at 150, 89 S.Ct. at 340. However, an award will not be vacated on the grounds of evident partiality of the arbitrator unless the conduct of the arbitrator was so biased and prejudiced as to destroy fundamental fairness. Cook Indus., Inc. v. C. Itoh & Co. (America) Inc., 449 F.2d at 107–08; * * * In the instant case, there is no clear evidence of partiality on the part of the arbitrator. Again, the Court has been presented with conflicting stories and cannot determine whether arbitrator Beich was in fact partial to the detriment of the Union. In the absence of a record from the hearings, the Court declines to agree with the Union on this issue and finds that the arbitrator was not evidently partial within the meaning of Section 10 of the United States Arbitration Act. 9 U.S.C. § 10(b).

In addition, the Union claims that arbitrator Beich exceeded his powers by refusing to conduct a hearing and by issuing the awards after his resignation. As recounted earlier, there is certainly a conflict in the proof concerning the alleged resignation or withdrawal of the arbitrator on September 1, 1981. The Union claims that Beich explicitly withdrew. The Company claims that he did no such thing. With a clear conflict in the evidence, it cannot be said that the Union has met its burden of proof on this issue. Moreover, a common sense review of the record leads to the conclusion that Beich did not withdraw as arbitrator. First, if Beich had withdrawn, he would not have issued the arbitration awards on November 12. Second, Chairman Healy's letter of September 21 indicates that Beich made no mention of any withdrawal after consulting with the Chairman following the September 1 hearing. Thus, it seems unlikely that Beich did in fact withdraw.

The claim that Beich exceeded his powers by refusing to conduct a hearing raises a far more serious issue. If in fact, no hearings were held, then the awards would have to be vacated. In this regard, the Court must look to the two separate hearing dates, July 1 and September 1, to see if the Union was denied its right to be heard. On July 1, the record shows that the Company presented evidence to the arbitrator. For one reason or another, it appears that the Union did not present any evidence, or if any evidence was presented, that it did not constitute the Union's entire case. This did not amount to a violation of the Union's right to be heard because it was subsequently agreed that another hearing would be held. While it is heavily disputed that the parties agreed on July 1 to decide the issue of arbitrability first, the record discloses that the Company later agreed to allow consideration of the substantive issues simultaneously with the threshold issue of arbitrability. Still, the Company argues that this agreement was subject to the condition that no further hearings would be held.

On September 1, the parties assembled in Auburn, New York for the second hearing. As noted above, this hearing ended abruptly due to disturbances from one or both of the parties. Thus, the hearing ended without both sides being allowed to fully present all of their evidence via documents and/or testimony. In the Company's view, the termination of the September 1 hearing voided its prior agreement to allow for simultaneous consideration of the merits as well as arbitrability. Although the Company argues that its agreement was conditioned upon the fact that no further hearings would be held, it cannot unilaterally rescind its agreement after participating in the second hearing.

The law is clear that a federal court cannot overturn an arbitration award unless the party opposing the award shows that one of the statutory grounds enumerated in 9 U.S.C. § 10 exists. * * * Here, the Court finds that the arbitrator violated section 10(c) by refusing to hear evidence pertinent and material to the controversy. After the close of the hearing on September 1, 1981, the Union was not given an opportunity to complete its presentation of proof regarding the arbitrability and/or merits of the grievances then under consideration. In view of the agreement to allow simultaneous consideration of the merits along with arbitrability, principles of fundamental fairness required that the Union be given a full opportunity to present its case to the arbitrator for consideration. The Court expresses no opinion as to the correctness of the subject awards which found the grievances to be non-arbitrable. Nevertheless, assuming that the grievances were indeed non-arbitrable, the Union still should have been given a chance to present its case on both the arbitrability and merits issues. The parties agreed to have arbitrator Beich consider both questions together. Since the Union was not given the chance to present its case in full, the subject awards cannot stand. Accordingly, it is hereby

ORDERED, that petitioner's motion to vacate the arbitration awards rendered on November 12, 1981 be granted.

Notes and Questions

1. Just where did Arbitrator Beich go wrong? Do you think he could have avoided this mess? How? Did the arbitrator's errors constitute ethical violations? If so, of which section(s)?

2. The court did not judge the propriety of the arbitrator's alleged *ex parte* meetings with the parties. Would *ex parte* communications, without more, violate the Code? See §§ 4.1, 5.A.1., and 5.C. Would *ex parte* communications, without more, provide a basis for vacating the award? See Federal Arbitration Act § 10, in Appendix B. Incidentally, the court applied the FAA without debating the propriety of doing so. You saw in Chapter III that the Supreme Court in *Lincoln Mills* and the *Steelworkers Trilogy* used Section 301 of the Taft–Hartley Act, not the FAA, when dealing with labor arbitration. Was the district court in this case correct to use the FAA? Before you

answer, reread Section 301 and FAA Section 10 in Appendix B. Now do you see why the judge in this case turned to the FAA?

3. Obviously the animosity between the parties made the arbitrator's job difficult. How should an arbitrator deal with such difficult and angry people?

4. Most ethical issues at the hearing stage involve allegations that the arbitrator's procedural rulings—refusal of a continuance, accepting or rejecting challenged evidence, and so on—either displayed bias or deprived a party of a fair hearing. Since arbitrators have wide discretion in the conduct of the hearing and are not bound by rules of evidence (see § V.A., *supra*), the courts usually reject these claims. In some instances, however, the ruling may so impair a party's case that the courts will deny enforcement. See Zirkel and Winebrake, *supra* footnote 1, at 697–703.

5. Suppose the parties and arbitrator agree on a hearing date but one party then refuses to attend, or withdraws after an adverse procedural ruling. What may (should) the arbitrator do? Does § 5.C. of the Code answer the question? Contrast that provision with Greenway Coop. Serv. v. Frontier Commodities, Inc., 2000 WL 665387 (Minn. App. 2000, unpub.) (vacating a commercial arbitration award because the arbitrator began the arbitration before the second party arrived, despite a telephone call alerting her that the party was on the way).

A NOTE ON THE ETHICAL OBLIGATIONS OF PARTY–APPOINTED ARBITRATORS

Most discussions of arbitral ethics focus on jointly-appointed neutrals. Whether the arbitration agreement uses one, three, or five such neutrals, their ethical obligations remain the same. Many arbitration agreements provide for tripartite arbitration, however, and that format presents a distinct problem. In tripartite grievance arbitration, each party typically designates one or more of its own representatives to serve as "partisan" arbitrators. The "system boards of adjustment" established by airlines pursuant to the Railway Labor Act are perhaps the best examples. In tripartite interest arbitration, each party typically picks one arbitrator from an impartial source such as the American Arbitration Association, and those two pick a third. The impasse procedure established by law for the Postal Service is perhaps the most widely known example.

What are the ethical obligations of the party-appointed arbitrators in these situations? There has been little discussion of the issue in the literature. (Two notable exceptions, neither of which deals exclusively with labor arbitration, are the Kennedy and Rau articles cited in footnote 1.) The Code of Professional Responsibility for Arbitrators of Labor–Management Disputes expressly excludes from its scope "partisan representatives on tripartite boards" but applies otherwise to "any impartial person, irrespective of specific title, who serves in a covered arbitration dispute procedure." On the face of it, party-appointed arbitrators are neither fish nor fowl. They occupy, in the word of Professor Rau (*supra* note 1 at 498), "an uncomfortable and ambiguous position—not quite 'advocates,' perhaps, but not exactly 'judges' either."

The easiest case is that of clearly "partisan" arbitrators. As the Code exclusion indicates, no one expects them to be neutral in any meaningful sense. In fact, their main roles seem to be to make one last argument for their parties' cause within the tribunal's executive sessions and to help the neutral arbitrator avoid making unintended mistakes. It naturally follows that the Code and other ethical norms have little application to them. They need not disclose their relationships with the appointing party, remain objective, or avoid ex parte discussions. With only rare exceptions, both parties would be surprised if the arbitration board reached a unanimous vote.

Party-appointed "neutral" arbitrators in labor disputes have a more complicated role. They are subject to all the usual ethical rules, so they must disclose relationships with the parties and their representatives, remain objective, and avoid ex parte contacts. Unanimous votes are common in these cases. If the party-appointed arbitrators have any special role, it is merely to ensure that the arbitration board gives full attention to the arguments presented by their appointing parties.

In each situation, the key that turns the lock is the expectation of the parties. If they expect "their" arbitrator to be neutral and expect that the other's will be as well, the party-appointed arbitrators should act accordingly and follow all relevant ethical strictures. If they expect "their" arbitrator to be partisan and expect that the other's will be as well, the party-appointed arbitrators should remain true to their principals and needn't lose any sleep over Code violations.

This Note deals only with labor arbitration. The new code of ethics for commercial arbitrators takes a different approach, establishing a presumption of neutrality for party-appointed arbitrators. See Olga K. Byrne, *A New Code of Ethics for Commercial Arbitrators: The Neutrality of Party–Appointed Arbitrators on a Tripartite Panel*, 30 Fordham Urban Law Journal 1815 (2003).

4. POSTHEARING CONDUCT[6]

PHILADELPHIA NEWSPAPERS, INC. v. NEWSPAPER GUILD OF GREATER PHILADELPHIA, LOCAL 10

United States District Court for the Eastern District of Pennsylvania, 1987.
1987 WL 17744.

This case is before the Court on plaintiff's and defendant's cross motions for summary judgment. The subject of the action is the enforcement of a clarification of an arbitration award.

6. Bibliographic Suggestions: Erwin B. Ellman, *Arbitrator Ethics and the Second Look*—Functus Officio *in the National Labor Policy*, 13 Industrial Relations Law Journal 416 (1991–92); Charles M. Rehmus, *The Code and Postaward Arbitral Discretion*, 42 Proceedings of the National Academy of Arbitrators 127 (1990); Peter Seitz, *Problems of the Finality of Awards, or Functus Officio and All That*, 17 Proceedings of the National Academy of Arbitrators 174 (1964); and Charles A. Werner and David Holtzman, *Clarification of Arbitration Awards*, 3 The Labor Lawyer 183 (1987).

I. FACTUAL BACKGROUND

Plaintiff Philadelphia Newspapers, Inc. (P.N.I.) is a corporation which owns and publishes a daily newspaper known as the Philadelphia Daily News. Defendant Newspaper Guild of Greater Philadelphia, Local 10 (the Guild), an unincorporated association, is a labor organization which was the collective bargaining representative of employees at the Philadelphia Daily News during the time period relevant to this action. PNI and the Guild were parties to a collective bargaining agreement which provided for arbitration as a dispute resolution mechanism. Article 17(b) of the collective bargaining agreement stated,

> Subject to the provisions of Section (a) of this Article the Employer will not discharge any employee except for good and reasonable cause. * * * [T]he arbiter's decision shall be restricted solely to a finding of whether or not the discharge was for good and reasonable cause and if the decision is in favor of the Employer, the award shall be limited to sustaining the discharge, and if in favor of the employee or employees discharged, the award shall be limited to reinstatement with full pay for all time lost.

Robert T. Lawlor (Lawlor), a full-time editorial page cartoonist for the Philadelphia Daily News, produced a cartoon that was published on the editorial page on December 24, 1984. The cartoon included Lawlor's estranged wife's unpublished telephone number. On January 23, 1985 P.N.I. notified Lawlor of his discharge. The Guild grieved Lawlor's discharge under Article 17(b) of the Agreement. The Guild's grievance was not resolved and the dispute was submitted to arbitration.

The parties selected Louis Aronin as the arbitrator to hear the Guild's grievance over Lawlor's discharge. Arbitrator Aronin concluded hearings, and both parties had the opportunity to present witnesses for direct and cross-examination, to submit evidence, and to argue their respective positions. Pursuant to a written opinion and Award dated July 1, 1986, Arbitrator Aronin sustained the Guild's grievance and issued the following award:

> 1) Grievant Rob Lawlor was not discharged for just cause;
>
> 2) Grievant Rob Lawlor's discharge shall be converted to a two week disciplinary suspension without pay, effective January 23, 1985;
>
> 3) Grievant shall be reinstated with all rights and benefits to his former, or substantially equivalent, position, and shall be made whole for all losses suffered as a result of said discharge, less the two week suspension;
>
> 4) The undersigned will retain jurisdiction for 60 days from the date of this Award to resolve any problems which the parties are unable to resolve relating to the implementation of this Award.

By letter dated July 16, 1986, PNI confirmed to the Guild that Lawlor could return to employment and be assigned to the position of advertising artist. Lawlor accepted the advertising artist position and returned to work. The Guild, however, contended that offering Lawlor the position of advertising artist did not comply with the July 1 arbitration award. On July 24, 1986, the Guild requested that Arbitrator Aronin clarify his award to determine whether PNI's offering to Lawlor of the advertising artist's position complied with the arbitration award. PNI objected to the Guild's clarification request. On July 29, 1986, Arbitrator Aronin stated his intention to clarify the July 1 award unless good cause could be shown as to why he should not do so. The parties submitted briefs on the clarification request. On September 17, 1986, Arbitrator Aronin issued an "Order Clarifying Award" which stated, in part, that:

> [P]aragraph (3) of the Award dated July 1, 1986, is hereby clarified to require that Grievant Rob Lawlor shall be reinstated to his former position of Editorial Cartoonist, or if that job no longer exists because of reasons other than Grievant's discharge, then to a substantially equivalent position.

PNI has refused to reassign Lawlor as editorial page cartoonist for the Philadelphia Daily News. On October 22, 1986 PNI filed a complaint and petition to vacate the arbitrator's order clarifying the arbitration award and to preclude enforcement. PNI filed a motion for summary judgment and the Guild filed a cross motion for summary judgment.

II. Appropriate Legal Standard

A trial court may enter summary judgment if, after a review of all evidentiary material in the record, there is no genuine issue as to any material fact, and the moving party is entitled to judgment as a matter of law. * * * Because the parties have stipulated to the facts surrounding Arbitrator Aronin's exercise of authority, the Court can safely say that there are no genuine issues of material fact with reference to the arbitrator's actions. To determine if either party is entitled to judgment as a matter of law, the court must consider whether Arbitrator Aronin had the power to issue a clarification of this original award.

III. Discussion

PNI asserts that it has complied with Arbitrator Aronin's July 1, 1986 reinstatement directive and that the arbitrator lacked authority to clarify his award after it was rendered. It is a fundamental common law principle that an arbitrator becomes functus officio, and his authority is exhausted, when he renders a final award. La Vale Plaza, Inc. v. R.S. Noonan, Inc., 378 F.2d 569, 572 (3d Cir.1967). * * * The policy underlying this rule is to prevent a nonjudicial officer, potentially subject to outside communication and unilateral influence, from reexamining a final decision. * * *

The functus officio doctrine is explained by Updegraff in Arbitration and Labor Relations, 116 (BNA Books, 1970), and quoted with approval in How Arbitration Works, Elkouri and Elkouri; (4th ed. 1985 at p. 283). The authority and jurisdiction of arbitrators are entirely terminated by the completion and delivery of an award. They have thereafter no power to recall the same, to order a rehearing, to amend, or to "interpret" in such manner as may be regarded as authoritative. But they may correct clerical mistakes or obvious errors of arithmetical computation.

The common law doctrine of functus officio is also the basis for section VI(D)(1) of the Code of Professional Responsibility for Arbitrators of Labor–Management Disputes which states that "no clarification or interpretation of an award is permissible without the consent of both parties."

In the present case, Arbitrator Aronin originally ordered that PNI should reinstate Lawlor to his former or substantially equivalent position. PNI took prompt action to comply with this order. Since no further information or action was required for compliance with the arbitrator's order, this Court holds that the July 1, 1986 arbitration order was a final order. Arbitrator Aronin's further actions to clarify the award were taken without authority or jurisdiction to do so.

The functus officio doctrine does contain exceptions. An arbitrator can correct a mistake that is apparent on the face of an award, or he can adjudicate an issue previously submitted to him that was not adjudicated in the award. * * * Arbitrator Aronin did neither of these things. He readjudicated the issue of reinstatement, and he drastically changed his award. The original order gave PNI the option to place Lawlor in his former position or to place him in a substantially equivalent position. The clarification established a hierarchy requiring PNI to place Lawlor in his former position and allowing reinstatement to a substantially equivalent position only if Lawlor's former position no longer existed because of reasons other than Lawlor's discharge.

Arbitrator Aronin's retention of jurisdiction for 60 days to resolve any problems relating to implementation of his initial award does not prevent the initial award from being a final award that triggers application of the functus officio doctrine. Arbitrator Aronin lacked the authority to retain jurisdiction so that portion of his initial award is null and void.

An arbitrator's authority or jurisdiction is confined to the power conferred upon him by the parties through mutual consent. * * * The Supreme Court recently stated

> The willingness of parties to enter into agreements that provide for arbitration of specified disputes would be "drastically reduced," however, if a labor arbitrator had the "power to determine his own jurisdiction * * *." Were this the applicable rule, an arbitrator would not be constrained to resolve only those disputes that the parties have agreed in advance to settle by arbitration, but instead, would be empowered "to impose obligations outside the contract limited only by his understanding and conscience." This result undercuts the longstanding federal policy of promoting industrial harmony through the use of collective-bargaining agreements, and is

antithetical to the function of a collective-bargaining agreement as setting out the rights and duties of the parties. (citations omitted).

In light of the foregoing authority, it is clear that Arbitrator Aronin acted without authority both when he retained jurisdiction under the original award for implementation purposes and when he later clarified the award. None of the parties requested his retention of jurisdiction, and PNI clearly objected to it. Consequently, PNI's motion for summary judgment is partially granted with respect to those issues.

To entirely resolve PNI's motion for summary judgment, this Court would have to determine whether PNI complied with the arbitrator's July 1, 1986 reinstatement order. In other words, this court would have to decide if offering Lawlor a position as an Advertising Artist reinstated him in a "substantially equivalent position" within the meaning of the July 1, 1986 arbitration award. PNI asserts that both the advertising artist and the editorial cartoonist command the same rate of pay while seniority and other similar rights remain unimpaired. Consequently, PNI asserts that the positions are substantially equivalent. The Guild, on the other hand, contends that factors such as creative freedom, range of artistic skills utilized, and notariety [sic] within the profession and public should be considered in making the determination of whether the two positions are substantially equivalent. It is the Court's view that the parties have not demonstrated that this issue may be resolved on summary judgment. There appears to be genuine issues of material fact present regarding this issue that should be left to the factfinder to resolve so that it may determine if the two positions are substantially equivalent. This court, therefore cannot decide whether PNI has, in fact, complied with the July 1, 1986 arbitration award. The issue will be left to the fact finder.

ORDER

And now, this 28th day of September, 1987, it is hereby Ordered that plaintiff PNI's motion for summary judgment is Granted only to the extent that it seeks to have the arbitration clarification order vacated. The Guild's summary judgment motion is Granted only to the extent that it advocates enforcement of the July 1, 1986 arbitration award. No attorney's fees are awarded. The parties should prepare to go to trial on the issue of whether the positions of advertising artist and editorial cartoonist are substantially equivalent within the meaning of the July 1, 1986 arbitration award.

[Just before the trial on the merits, the union moved for reconsideration and for remand of the case to the arbitrator. On October 22, 1987, the court ruled on those requests. The supplementary opinion is found at 1987 WL 38.]

The Guild insists that the July 1, 1986 arbitration order must be remanded for clarification because it is ambiguous. There is nothing ambiguous within the terms of the order: "Grievant shall be reinstated with all rights and benefits to his former or substantially equivalent, position * * *." The confusion arose in this case only after PNI attempted to comply with the order by offering Lawlor a position as an Advertising Artist. Arbitrator Aronin then issued his clarification order basically concluding that PNI's actions were insufficient under his understanding of the July 1, 1986 award. These facts indicate that the original order was not ambiguous, but rather Arbitrator Aronin's clarification order created any ambiguity that may have existed. Since this Court has previously held that Arbitrator Aronin's clarification order is null and void because it was delivered without authority or jurisdiction, the July 1, 1986 order, clear on its face and lacking any ambiguity, controls. There is, therefore, no need for clarification of the order.

This case should be remanded to arbitration, however, to determine the collateral issue of whether PNI has complied with the July 1, 1986 award. The implementation of the July 1 award has created a new dispute between the parties. Keeping in mind the parties' commitment in their collective bargaining agreement to resolve labor disputes through arbitration, I think it is only fair that this collateral issue be resolved in arbitration. Matters of compliance constitute a separate and distinct grievance appropriate for arbitration. * * *

The parties disagree as to which arbitrator they should utilize in this case. PNI would like the case submitted to a new arbitrator selected under the arbitration clause of the collective bargaining agreement. The Guild would like the dispute remanded to Arbitrator Aronin, the original arbitrator in this case. Because this case does not involve a remand for clarification of an ambiguity, but rather it involves resolution of a new dispute between the parties. I will order that the case be submitted to a new arbitrator selected under the arbitration clause of the collective bargaining agreement. An appropriate Order follows.

ORDER

And now, this 21st day of October, 1987, upon consideration of defendant's motion to reconsider and motion to remand to arbitration, it is hereby Ordered:

1. The motion for reconsideration is Denied.

2. The motion for remand is Granted under the following circumstances. The parties shall expeditiously select a new arbitrator under the collective bargaining agreement to consider the following issues: (a) whether PNI has complied with the Arbitration Award by reinstating grievant Robert Lawlor to the position of Advertising Artist; and (b) If the July 1, 1986 award requires PNI to reinstate Mr. Lawlor to the position of Editorial Cartoonist, whether this action is prohibited by the first amendment to the United States Constitution.

3. Arbitration proceedings shall be concluded within sixty (60) days absent circumstances beyond the parties' control.

4. This Court shall retain jurisdiction pending resubmission of this dispute to an Arbitrator for entry of a final order.

Notes and Questions

1. *Clarification.* Why *shouldn't* the arbitrator have clarified his award on the union's request? Who knows better than he what he meant? Does the *functus officio* doctrine guarantee even more litigation before a final decision?

The Code's ban on reconsideration at the request of a single party is not the universal rule. Sections 9 and 13 of the Uniform Arbitration Act allow either party to seek (or a court to order) modification of an award to correct "an evident miscalculation of figures," "an evident mistake in the description of any person, thing or property," or an imperfection "in a matter of form, not affecting the merits of the controversy." Similarly, either party may seek modification "for the purpose of clarifying the award." (Presumably "clarifying" the award would not involve changing the award except on the limited grounds mentioned, but the line between a clarification and a change can be difficult to discern.) In 1998 and 1999, the Academy considered amending the Code to permit clarifications on the request of just one party. The main argument in favor of the change was that it would eliminate the need for a party seeking clarification to get a court to remand the matter to the arbitrator. The Academy dropped the proposal when some union advocates worried that employers might use unilateral requests for clarification in order to delay implementation of an award.

2. *Retention of jurisdiction.* The District Court even held that the arbitrator's retention of jurisdiction was improper. Why? Read the Supreme Court language quoted by the judge as justification for his statement that the arbitrator "lacked the authority to retain jurisdiction." Is that quotation persuasive? Or even on point?

Most other courts find no problem in an arbitrator's retention of jurisdiction. Doing so obviates disputes about whether an arbitrator can address a post-award request by a single party and finesses the principle of *functus officio* because the award, by its very terms, is not final. Is it significant that the 1974 Code revisions dropped a part of the 1951 Code that an award "should reserve no future duties to the arbitrator except by agreement of the parties?" See Rehmus, *supra* footnote 6.

What should an arbitrator do if retention of jurisdiction seems prudent because of predictable differences over the implementation of the award? For example, parties in a discharge case might present evidence on the merits of the case but not on the amount of back pay to be paid if the arbitrator sustains the grievance. Suppose an arbitrator sustains the grievance and orders reinstatement with back pay. Should he or she retain jurisdiction to settle disputes over the remedy, such as quantifying back pay, evaluating the employee's efforts to mitigate damages, or determining whether the position to which the employer assigned the returning employee was equivalent to the one held at the time of discharge? See John E. Dunsford, *The Case for Retention of Remedial Jurisdiction in Labor Arbitration Awards*, 31 Ga. L. Rev. 201 (1996) (arguing that "in virtually all cases of grievance arbitration where a remedy is called for, labor arbitrators ought to routinely retain jurisdiction of the award for the purpose of resolving any disputes * * * regarding the meaning, application, and implementation of that remedy").

3. *Remand to arbitration.*

(a) The District Court ultimately remands the case to arbitration, but to a different arbitrator. Why did the court not just resolve the question of the employer's compliance with the award itself? On what authority, and for what purpose, did the court order arbitration before a new arbitrator? If an appeals court reverses and remands a lower-court opinion, does it send the case to a different judge? On what authority, and for what purpose, did the court direct the new arbitrator to decide whether reinstatement of the grievant to his old job "is prohibited by the first amendment to the United States Constitution"?

(b) In rejecting the union's request for remand to the original arbitrator, the court implies that remand would have been appropriate if the award were really ambiguous. How does that position differ from Arbitrator Aronin's original retention of jurisdiction "to resolve any problems * * * relating to the implementation of this Award"?

(c) Suppose a court does remand an ambiguous award to the same arbitrator on the request of a single party. What should the arbitrator do in light of § 6.D.1. ("No clarification or interpretation * * * is permissible without the consent of *both* parties")? Does the court order supersede the Code?

4. The doctrine of *functus officio* is not as solid as *Philadelphia Newspapers* suggests. One writer (Ellman, *supra* footnote 6) argued that the doctrine should be eliminated from the Code because arbitrators ignore it and the courts typically remand ambiguous awards to the same arbitrator for clarification. In a typically forceful opinion, Judge Richard Posner suggested that "Since the case for the exceptions [to the *functus officio* rule] seems stronger than the case for the rule, perhaps the time has come to discard the rule." Glass Molders, Pottery, Plastics and Allied Workers International Union, Local 182B v. Excelsior Foundry Co., 56 F.3d 844, 847 (7th Cir.1995). True to his law and economics background, however, he recognized that if the doctrine were "as pointless as it seems to us to be," arbitration associations and parties would already have changed their rules to authorize arbitrators to reconsider their decisions:

> Sheer inertia, or for that matter the capaciousness of the exceptions for clarification and completion, may be responsible. But an alternative possibility that we must not ignore is that the people who are paying for arbitration believe it unwise to give arbitrators as broad a right to reconsider awards as might seem appropriate to us. Arbitration is a service sold in a competitive market. The rules adopted by the sellers are presumptively efficient.

Id. at 848.

5. *Functus officio* is hardly the only posthearing ethical issue.

(a) *Delays.* The most common posthearing problem is delay in issuing an award. See Code § 2.J., especially subsection 3. Slight delays are common but extreme cases can severely injure the parties. Total nonfeasance has led to the only successful damage actions brought against arbitrators, E.C. Ernst, Inc. v. Manhattan Construction Co., 551 F.2d 1026, rehearing granted in part 559 F.2d 268 (5th Cir.1977), cert. denied 434 U.S. 1067, 98 S.Ct. 1246, 55 L.Ed.2d 769 (1978); Graphic Arts International Union, Local 508 v.

Standard Register Co., 103 L.R.R.M. 2212 (S.D.Ohio 1978); and Baar v. Tigerman, 140 Cal.App.3d 979, 211 Cal.Rptr. 426 (1983). Unreasonable delay in submitting an award is also the most common reason for arbitrator discipline, both by the Academy and by listing agencies such as the AAA and FMCS.

(b) *Testimonial immunity.* Parties occasionally try to involve the arbitrator in subsequent litigation. Actions brought against the arbitrators fall to the claim of arbitral immunity, but what about requests or demands that the arbitrator testify? See § 6.E. of the Code, especially subsection 2. ("an arbitrator should not voluntarily participate in legal enforcement proceedings"). So strong is the immunity doctrine that federal courts have even awarded sanctions against parties who brought discovery motions against arbitrators, Nolan and Abrams, *supra* note 1, at 266, and the Revised Uniform Arbitration Act now incorporates the same principle.

(c) *Fee disputes.* Disputes over the arbitrator's fees and expenses may also raise ethical problems. Code § 2.K. is more specific than most Code provisions. Its thrust is that all charges should be reasonable, should correspond to actual work, and should be disclosed to the parties before appointment.

Occasionally parties think the arbitrator charged too much, but those disagreements seldom rise to the level of a possible ethical violation. One exception is New York Newspaper Printing Pressman's Union No. 2. v. New York Times Company, 1992 WL 122788 (S.D.N.Y.1992). The arbitrator stated a per diem fee of $600, held six days of hearings, and prepared an award within a month after receiving the parties' briefs. For a hearing of that length, the parties expected to be charged for the hearing plus five or six days of study time, or about $7,000. Just before mailing the award, however, the arbitrator telephoned each of the parties. According to the union's lawyer, the arbitrator said "that he considered the dispute to be an interest arbitration (as opposed to a contract arbitration) and therefore he had a right to negotiate a higher fee. He said that he believed $25,000 would be an appropriate fee * * *. [He] looked forward to hearing my response regarding his bill and that the award would be issued shortly." The Company's attorney reported a similar conversation, closing with the arbitrator's hope that the Times' payment would be prompt. The court clearly disapproved of the arbitrator's conduct but held that it provided no basis for overturning the award.

How would you advise your client to deal with the arbitrator's bill? One party to the *Pressman's Union* case later filed an ethics charge against the arbitrator. The Academy's CPRG allowed the arbitrator to resign from membership because of an illness that prevented him from arbitrating, and therefore did not have to decide the merits of the charge. If the arbitrator had refused to resign, how should the CPRG rule? Read Code § 2.K.

In a somewhat similar situation (the arbitrator charged 19.5 days of study time for a two-day hearing; the national average is about 2 days of study time for each day of hearing), the losing union refused to pay its share of the bill. The employer then filed a grievance against the union charging violation of the agreement to split the fee. In an extremely thorough opinion, Arbitrator Ira Jaffe strongly suggested that the arbitrator violated his ethical obligations to the parties. Accordingly, the union "was warranted in challenging its obligation to pay those billed fees" and its failure to pay thus did not violate the parties' agreement. Social Security Administration, 93 LA 1166 (1989). If a party filed an ethics complaint against the arbitrator, how should the CPRG rule? Reread Code § 2.K. Several provisions in that section might be relevant.

6. *Publication of awards*. You have probably noticed that most of the arbitration decisions in this book came from reports published by commercial firms like BNA and CCH. Did you happen to wonder how, if arbitration is private and non-governmental, the publishers obtained the awards and received permission to publish them?

Publication of awards serves many valuable purposes but it also could invade the privacy of the parties or other participants. The parties "own" the award, so an arbitrator may not publish it without their consent (§ 2.C.1.c.). Obtaining express consent is a hassle even if the parties have no real objection to publication. Simple inertia might therefore deprive practitioners of these valuable guides. As a result, and after lengthy debate, the National Academy of Arbitrators amended the Code to permit use of a negative option: "If the question of consent to the publication of the award is raised at the time the award is issued, the arbitrator may state in writing to each party that failure to answer the inquiry within 30 days will be considered an implied consent to publish." Section 2.C.1.c.

A (VERY BRIEF) NOTE ON THE ETHICAL OBLIGATIONS OF ADVOCATES

This note is very brief because there are virtually no rules governing the ethical obligations of advocates in labor arbitration, apart from lawyers' codes of professional responsibility. Nonlawyer advocates are subject neither to the lawyers' codes nor to the arbitrator's Code. Is that a problem? If so, who should address it, and how?

One recurring issue is presented by the union's representation of individual grievants. Unless there is a clear understanding to the contrary, a lawyer engaged by the union represents the union even if the grievance involves an individual. At times the union's interests may differ from those of the grievant. What should the lawyer do in such a situation? What should a nonlawyer union advocate do?

The difficulty stems in large part from the exclusivity principle that lies at the heart of American labor law. (See Section VII.I.1.) Once a majority of a given bargaining unit selects a bargaining representative, the representative's status is *exclusive*: it must represent all bargaining unit members, and no member may select another representative or represent himself or herself. Not infrequently, the interests of the collective may differ from those of the individual. For example, a junior employee may wish to challenge a seniority system that suits the needs of the majority but that bars her from choosing a different shift, or a union may want to concede some grievances in order to negotiate a wage increase. The courts have tried to accommodate these conflicting interests through the duty of fair representation, or DFR. (See Section V.A.)

The DFR obliges the union to represent all members fairly but allows it wide discretion to make decisions that may favor some and disfavor others. Where does that leave the advocate? See generally, Adrienne Saldana, *Conflicting Interests in Union Representation: Should Exclusivity Be Abolished?*, 6 Georgetown Journal of Legal Ethics 188 (1992), and Stephen Gillers, Regulation of Lawyers: Problems of Law and Ethics § II.B. (5th ed. 1998).

Lawyers' ethical rules may provide some guidance, or they may merely complicate the issue. In any event, the predicate to a lawyer's ethical obligation is usually a lawyer-client relationship. If the lawyer's client is the union, as courts normally hold, the lawyer may have few obligations toward the individual grievant, and the union's only duty is the nebulous one of "fairness."

B. CRITICISM OF LABOR ARBITRATION

1. INTRODUCTION

It would be amazing if an institution as widespread as labor arbitration did not draw some critics. Arbitrators themselves may be the institution's harshest critics; the annual Proceedings of the National Academy of Arbitrators are replete with minutely detailed examinations of almost every conceivable aspect of labor arbitration. Some outside critics focus on the same sorts of questions that occupy arbitrators, chiefly procedural matters affecting arbitration's efficiency. Subsection 2 presents some examples of that type of criticism. Other outside critics concentrate on more fundamental concerns. Judge Paul Hayes, for example, came to the conclusion that arbitrators' dependence upon the parties for their selection corrupted the entire process. Subsection 3 addresses Hayes's criticism and arbitrators' responses to it. Finally, some observers charge that the arbitration system or arbitrators themselves are biased. A few workers' advocates argue that arbitration, and the contractualism that spawns it, disserve workers by turning moral claims into technical questions of documentary interpretation. Other pro-labor commentators charge that arbitrators rule on the basis of values inimical to unions' interests. In contrast, management representatives routinely charge that arbitrators refuse to sustain discharges even when there is clearly just cause for discipline. Subsection 4 provides examples of each of these.

As you read the following selections, ask yourself why, if arbitration is so flawed, labor and management still include an arbitration provision in almost every collective bargaining agreement.

2. ARBITRATION'S EFFICIENCY[1]

Labor arbitration's boast—and its primary claim to legal preference—has always been that it is faster, cheaper, and simpler than

1. Bibliographic Suggestions: Reginald Alleyne, *Delawyerizing Labor Arbitration*, 50 Ohio State Law Journal 93 (1989); Anthony F. Bartlett, *Labor Arbitration: The*

litigation. In most respects, it is, but that has not prevented criticism. Some critics have minimized the differences between the two dispute resolution mechanisms. Others have worried that a once-efficient system has begun to imitate its alternative, thus losing its special appeal.

Here are some data to help you evaluate these criticisms. They come from the Fiscal Year 2003 statistics of the Federal Mediation and Conciliation Service. The FMCS closed a total of 2,746 labor arbitration files that year, up slightly from previous years.

Average Dollar Amounts

Per Diem Rate:	$ 763.87
Total Fee:	$3,047.54
Expenses:	$ 364.32
Total Charge:	$3,411.86

Average Days Billed

Hearing Days:	1.15
Travel Days:	0.48
Study Days:	2.35
Total Days Billed:	**3.98**

These cost statistics are relatively straightforward. Arbitrators' fees and expenses averaged about $3,400 per case. Most parties split the costs evenly, so each would pay about $1,700 per case. Of course parties also must pay their own expenses (lawyers, expert witnesses, lost time for participants, and so on) and any administrative agency costs (AAA charges, hearing room rental, transcript, or a small FMCS fee for providing a list of arbitrators). By any standard, these figures suggest that arbitration is much cheaper than litigation or strikes. The average arbitrator's rate is modest compared to most lawyers' charges. Arbitrators' per diems vary widely, however, from about $500 to $2,400. As in other fields, the experienced and widely acceptable arbitrators tend to charge the most.

What about the length of time it takes to resolve a grievance? The most recent study is that of Zirkel and Krahmal, *supra* note 1. While

Problem of Legalism, 62 Oregon Law Review 195 (1983); Richard N. Block and Jack Stieber, *The Impact of Attorneys and Arbitrators on Arbitration Awards*, 40 Industrial and Labor Relations Review 543 (1987); Marvin F. Hill, Jr. and Anthony V. Sinicropi, *Improving the Arbitration Process: A Primer for Advocates*, 27 Willamette Law Review 463 (1991); George Nicolau, *Can the Labor Arbitration Process Be Simplified? If So, in What Manner and at What Expense?*, 39 Proceedings of the National Academy of Arbitrators 69 (1987); Dennis R. Nolan and Roger I. Abrams, *Trends in Private Sector*

Grievance Arbitration, in Labor Arbitration Under Fire 42 (James L. Stern and Joyce M. Najita, eds., 1997); Jack Stieber, Richard N. Block, and Victor Nichol, *Elapsed Time in Grievance Arbitration*, 43 Proceedings of the National Academy of Arbitrators 128 (1991); Christine D. Ver Ploeg, *Labor Arbitration: The Participants' Perspective*, 43 Arbitration Journal 36 (March 1988); Perry A. Zirkel and Andriy Krahmal, *Creeping Legalism in Grievance Arbitration: Fact or Fiction?*, 16 Ohio State Journal on Dispute Resolution 243 (2001).

acknowledging some weaknesses in the data and noting some variation from year to year, the authors found a relatively steady increase in time from 1970 to 1997 (the last year for which the FMCS published those figures). They broke down the time into a pre-hearing phase (from the filing of a grievance through selection of an arbitrator to the start of the hearing) and a hearing-to-award phase. In 1970, for example, the average FMCS case took 196.6 days to go from grievance to hearing and 49 more days to reach an award, a total of 245.6 days. In 1997, the pre-hearing phase alone took 244.8 days (an increase of about 25%); the hearing-to-award phase rose to 67 days, an increase of almost 37%.

So clearly arbitration takes a lot longer than it used to. The data do not explain the reasons, but Zirkel and Krahmal attribute much of the rise to a more frequent use of lawyers, briefs and transcripts. (Note that those factors apply primarily at and after the hearing; they don't explain the 49-day increase in time to get to hearing.) Those factors and a few related ones are pejoratively termed by some observers as the "creeping legalism" of labor arbitration.

Interpreting the evidence is tricky. In order to judge whether arbitration is "too slow," one must first ask, "compared to what?" It is slower than formerly, but it is still considerably faster than the likely alternative, court litigation. Similarly, in order to judge whether the changes are "bad," and even assuming the authors have correctly identified the causes, one has to ask whether there is something wrong with using lawyers, briefs and transcripts. To put it differently, it is not sufficient simply to assume that the absence of court-like procedures in arbitration is good and their increasing presence is bad.

The materials in this section will not definitively answer those questions but it should provide some perspective on them. We begin with an early complaint about creeping legalism, follow up with a summary of one considered analysis of the issue, and conclude with several notes and questions to focus your attention.

CREEPING LEGALISM IN LABOR ARBITRATION: AN EDITORIAL

13 Arbitration Journal 129 (1958).

More than a dozen years have elapsed since, at the end of World War II, labor and management spokesmen at a government-sponsored conference unanimously urged inclusion of arbitration clauses in all collective bargaining contracts. Such provisions had been virtually compelled by government during the period of War Labor Board controls. Now that the emergency was over, and with the prospect of re-adjustment grievances before them, the parties wanted the advantages of arbitration they had become accustomed to, but without the element of compulsion.

The decade that followed saw a truly remarkable demonstration of what can be accomplished by voluntary means. Arbitration clauses, no longer required by law or regulation, were nevertheless written into most of the newly negotiated agreements. By 1949 the Bureau of Labor Statistics was able to report that 83 percent of collective bargaining contracts provided for grievance arbitration. Four years later, arbitration had reached the 90 percent level. It is certainly no exaggeration to say that labor-management arbitration today enjoys an unchallenged position in American industrial relations.

But in the course of this development—and perhaps because of the very speed with which it took place—certain practices and tendencies have appeared which, if not checked, may prevent companies and unions from getting the full benefit of their arbitration clauses. One of these problems is the growing superstructure of legal trappings which has been increasingly evident in arbitration cases. This trend was commented upon recently by Emanuel Stein, a well known arbitrator and head of New York University's Department of Economics. "A frustrating kind of legalism has crept into labor relations because the arbitrator has come to function like a judge and the parties have come to treat arbitration like litigation, with all the canons of construction familiar to the law of contracts," he told an audience of government labor experts.

We believe that Professor Stein is quite correct both in his observation of the facts and in placing responsibility on parties and arbitrators alike. The trend has, in fact, gone so far that unless it is reversed there is serious danger that arbitration will lose the very characteristics of speed, economy and informality that cause companies and unions to prefer this method of grievance settlement above all others.

An arbitration award within the last year may be cited as one example of legalism carried to what may indeed be called a frustrating extreme. In this case, management of a multi-plant company decided to cease operations for a week, designating the shut-down as a "vacation." When the employees applied for unemployment compensation, the authorities ruled that workers on vacation were not unemployed within the meaning of the state laws. The union thereupon filed a grievance, accusing the employer of misrepresenting a layoff as a vacation and demanding, as a remedy, that the company pay all workers the money they would have received in unemployment compensation if the closing of the plant had been reported differently. The matter then went to a tripartite board of arbitration.

During the hearings, both parties cited published awards. In addition, the impartial arbitrator did research among the volumes of reported cases. In the thousands of awards, there was only one case, according to the written opinion of the impartial arbitrator, that was similar to the one before him. And even this, he wrote, "was not quite on all fours * * * for, of course, the contract provisions differed." Nevertheless, the impartial member of the board went on to say, "it [the cited case] has stood in the books for five years, for all to read, as a warning that the designation of a shutdown as a vacation period with consequent effect upon rights to unemployment benefits, may involve a company in a breach of contract with consequent damages."

The grievance was upheld and the company was directed to pay employees the sum they would have collected from unemployment compensation funds of the state. We are not here quarreling with the finding or the remedy. Quite possibly, the arbitrator would have come to the same conclusion without the support he found in a five year old case. But the very notion that a published award is "in the books for all to read" is something borrowed from the field of litigation and utterly foreign to arbitration. The publication of arbitration awards undoubtedly serves a useful educational function, because they afford good insight into how industry in general copes with labor relations problems. But these awards are not subject to appeal, nor is there any way of knowing whether the relatively few awards that appear in print are truly representative of the total practice of arbitration. To speak of an award being "in the books," as if it were a court decision that has withstood appeals to higher bodies, is to place upon labor and management a burden they never undertook when they agreed to arbitrate differences arising under their own contract.

Admittedly, this is an extreme example. Arbitrators do not often tell parties in so many words that they should have known that they were violating their own contracts because another party, in another case reported years earlier, was similarly found in violation. But the incident described here is nevertheless significant, for it points up the results that may follow if the present drift toward unnecessary legalism is not halted.

The arbitrator in the case referred to above found, as we have said, only one published case resembling that before him. No such shortage faced another arbitrator hearing a discharge grievance at about the same time. Here is a record of the arbitrator's citations: To show why the burden of proof should be on management in discharge cases—five previous awards. To explain that regardless of burden of proof, the weight of evidence might shift from one side to another, depending on circumstances—two court cases. For a definition of the term "preponderance of evidence" he referred to three court cases and two NLRB proceedings. On the nature of "self defense"—seven court actions and three arbitration awards. Finally, the arbitrator addressed himself to the basic issue of whether the company's rule was reasonable that both employees engaging in fisticuffs could be discharged without regard to who was the aggressor. On this he found four court cases worth citing. Concluding that the issues in the case before him resembled those in one of the leading court cases rather than in the other, he rendered his decision accordingly. Altogether, by our calculations, there were twenty-six separate citations given before the decision was announced. The effect of this research on the arbitrator's bill for study time may be imagined. * * *

And so it goes, one arbitrator burdening his written opinion with numerous citations to support self-evident conclusions, while another, presumably after no less diligent research, regretfully reporting that "the arbitrator has been unable to locate any published case similar to the one before us." In fairness to the arbitrators it should be added that the malady is not altogether their fault. It must also be attributed in large measure to the parties who persist in citing cases despite the fact that they know that prior awards constitute no binding precedent. Under such circumstances, the arbitrator naturally wants the losing party to know that his citations have been considered. What better way is there to do this than to locate additional cases on his own? This practice having continued for a number of years, it is no longer possible to say whether parties cite cases because that is what they think the arbitrators want, or whether arbitrators cite cases to please the parties. Undoubtedly, there is truth in both suppositions, for cause and effect interact.

If arbitration is to serve the parties in the manner that was originally contemplated when labor and management began to adopt arbitration clauses on a voluntary basis, there must be a firm determination by parties and arbitrators to adhere more closely to first principles. On the part of company and union representatives, it will mean fewer attempts to lure the arbitrator with citation of plausible-sounding but really irrelevant awards. And the arbitrator must be content to let his opinion and award speak for itself; he should regard it as beneath the dignity of his office to punctuate his award with cited cases intended only to show that he has not departed too widely from the views of his brethren.

EVALUATING LEGALISM

The Arbitration Journal editorial shows an early concern with creeping legalism. The same concern is still voiced by some participants; see, for example, Ver Ploeg, *supra* footnote 1. In fact, if the Arbitration Journal published the same editorial today, few would think it archaic. The editorial focuses on citation of other cases, but how big a problem can that be? For some critics of arbitration, the participation of lawyers in labor arbitration and the techniques they bring with them (particularly transcripts and briefs that increase both time and costs) are pernicious. That attitude stems from the conviction, often unexamined, that simpler is better—that is, that an arbitration system without "legalism" is superior to a more formal system. A little thought will produce some counter arguments. Consider this brief excerpt from a much longer article that takes a more balanced view of the concept of "legalism."

LABOR ARBITRATION: THE PROBLEM
OF LEGALISM
Anthony F. Bartlett.
62 Oregon Law Review 195 (1983).

II. Legalism Within Labor Arbitration

* * *

The use of a written transcript of the proceedings is not widespread. When a transcript is used, however, it serves several useful functions.

First, it permits the arbitrator to concentrate fully on the matter at hand, because he is relieved of the necessity of taking notes. Second, it forces the parties to exercise more care in presentation of evidence and testimony, because they know that their statements are being recorded verbatim. Third, it is very useful in helping the arbitrator to analyze lengthy and complicated hearings, or hearings where the subject matter is highly technical. Fourth, it will prove useful if subsequent court review is necessary. Along with these advantages of a permanent record, there also are disadvantages. For instance, a written transcript will bring delay in the compilation of the award because it will have to be read by the arbitrator, and with delay comes additional expense. A transcript may also bring delay in to the hearing itself, as the parties may be lured into unnecessary rhetoric with its accompanying formality. Consequently, transcripts should be avoided unless a lengthy or very technical hearing is involved.

Posthearing briefs are often used in labor arbitration to keep the arbitrator fully conversant with the reasoning of the parties. The briefs, however, may bring an attendant delay and formality into the process, as the parties normally use them not only to summarize their arguments, but also to cite prior awards, articles, and cases that they feel support their respective positions. While posthearing briefs may be desirable in complex cases, in which an arbitrator has to analyze extensively each side's position, there is no need for them in a typical arbitration proceeding. Therefore, posthearing briefs should be used only in appropriate situations.

Representation by attorneys in labor arbitrations sometimes causes greater formality in the proceedings. Lawyers, by virtue of their training, tend to favor well-defined procedures and techniques for the resolution of disputes. The informal nature of an arbitration hearing can leave a person steeped in legal orthodoxy feeling most uncomfortable, if not downright insecure. Training and experience in labor relations, however, often overcome the inclination to think purely in terms of legal technique and instead promote thinking in terms of the practical nature of labor arbitration. Where a mature collective bargaining relationship exists, labor and management sometimes rely on a permanent arbitrator for the duration of their contract. An attorney appearing on several occasions before this type of arbitrator under the same contract will become familiar with much of the background of the collective agreement and will be in a position to form a good working relationship with both his adversary and the arbitrator. Consequently, there usually will be less inclination to rely on legal technicality, because while familiarity popularly may be thought to breed contempt—a doubtful proposition in labor relations—it undoubtedly breeds security.

Most labor arbitration, however, is of an ad hoc nature, so the security felt by the lawyer appearing before a permanent arbitrator will be somewhat greater than that of his counterpart appearing before a temporary arbitrator. Appearing before different arbitrators under contract provisions which differ from one agreement to another, the ad hoc representative may be forced to fall back on the tried and true legal techniques with which he is most at ease. This is borne out by the fact that ad hoc arbitration proceedings tend to be more formal than permanent arbitration proceedings. However, if lawyers contribute to legalism in labor arbitration—and the sheer quantity of criticism seems to indicate that they do—it is a fault shared equally, it seems, by nonlawyers. Lay representatives, in the view of some arbitration authorities, often take upon themselves what they fondly imagine to be the role of a lawyer in arbitration, while protesting that they are not doing so. Labor arbitration, despite the many positive aspects described by its proponents, must produce a winner and a loser. The arbitrator is commissioned to determine a dispute, not to play the role of mediator or conciliator. With this perspective in mind, it is easier to appreciate that the very informality of a typical arbitration proceedings may invite both attorneys and lay representatives alike to use whatever formalities they can muster to win the actual struggle at hand, without giving thought as to what they might be contributing to labor arbitration jurisprudence.

III.   LEGALISM: STATUS AND CONSEQUENCES

While informality is still considered an important feature of the labor arbitration process, it is clear that the increasingly sophisticated nature of the collective bargaining system and the requirements of external law are tending toward more legalism. The question that necessarily arises, then, is how crucial is informality in making arbitration acceptable to the parties? Arbitration, despite the protests against legalism, remains as popular as ever with employers and unions. This is perhaps because both are prepared to tolerate the overuse of legal techniques in their private forum in order to reap the other benefits of arbitration.

No matter how rigid arbitration procedures become, the process is still less formal than court proceedings, and it also is less expensive. In addition, the relaxed rules of evidence in the arbitral forum permit a wider consideration of extrinsic factors than would be possible in court. Consider, for example, the "therapeutic function" that arbitration serves in allowing parties to vent their frustrations by introducing evidence that is not directly material or relevant.

The advantages of arbitration tend to outweigh those of using the courts. Thus, complaints about legalism may be merely instances of minor frustration and irritation with some aspects of the process. These complaints, however, may indicate that the parties actually do attach real importance to informality in arbitration. The answer to questions concerning the importance of informality to management and labor are perhaps given, at least in part, by the continued resort to the labor arbitration process rather than the courts.

One hopeful sign regarding the desire to preserve the informality and availability of labor arbitration is the growth in the use of expedited procedures by both employers and unions. Expedited arbitration, unlike "regular" arbitration, normally includes only those procedural devices that are absolutely necessary to bring a disputed matter before an arbitrator for a quick and inexpensive resolution. While such procedures vary in different situations, most expedited arbitrations do not, for example, use posthearing briefs or written transcripts, and opinions do not accompany the awards. Since expedited arbitration usually is used in relatively simple cases and often when a large backlog of unresolved grievances exists, the growth of its use may be seen as indicating a large degree of frustration with regular arbitration. On a more optimistic note, however, it also shows that the labor arbitration community has an interest in keeping the regular system workable by reducing the strains upon it.

The innovations used in expedited arbitration easily could be extended throughout the arbitration system to certain aspects which tend to legalism. Briefs and transcripts provide a clear example: they are not merely indicators of an overly legalistic approach to arbitration, they also are a prime cause. Their use can be brought under control by the parties when drawing up their agreed arbitration procedures. Failing such foresight, their use may be restricted by the arbitrator, who ultimately is responsible for the procedures employed, unless there is a clear agreement of the parties or an express statutory requirement to the contrary.

Notes and Questions

1. At the beginning of this section we cited some figures from Zirkel and Krahmal, *supra* footnote 1, that suggested a steady increase in legalism. Now it is time for some qualifications. One necessary caveat is that the data are notoriously unreliable. The authors rely almost exclusively on figures from the FMCS that come from arbitrators' sporadic return of a post-award information form. The FMCS itself does not vouch for accuracy of its figures. A second is that the statistics do not in fact show clear trends. Take the crudest but potentially most revealing measure, the length of time it takes for a case to go from grievance to award. Yes, the total time went from 245.6 days in 1970 to 311.8 days in 1997—but in between, from 1983–87, it took from 345–402 days, so the 1997 figure could represent a substantial *decrease* over the previous decade. Or on the matter of costs, the number of days charged by arbitrators bounced within a narrow range from 3.64 to 3.98 between 1988–1998, with the last year right in the middle of that range. There are similar oddities in the figures for the use of transcripts and briefs.

In view of those figures, is it accurate to speak of "creeping legalism" or to fault arbitration for its lack of efficiency?

2. If the use of lawyers in arbitration makes the process slower and more expensive, why wouldn't the parties just represent themselves? Does it matter whether a party is represented by a lawyer or a lay person? See Block and Stieber, *supra* note 1. Their study of discharge cases concludes that if just one party has a lawyer, its odds of winning will rise, but that "awards in

cases in which both sides are represented by attorneys do not significantly differ from awards in cases in which neither is represented by an attorney." The authors suggest that the parties could reduce costs by agreeing not to use attorneys. For an early but full discussion of lawyers' impact on arbitration, see Sylvester Garrett, *The Role of Lawyers in Arbitration*, 14 Proceedings of the National Academy of Arbitrators 102 (1961), and the management and union responses following his paper.

But would "killing all the lawyers" eliminate legalism? Consider this description of non-lawyer union advocates, written by a union lawyer:

> Every staff rep or BA [Business Agent] has to function like a lawyer. The entire labor movement is like a giant bar association of nonlicensed attorneys. I have seen them in their windbreakers and ties, going into arbitrations, but they could be divorce lawyers, or DUI lawyers, or street lawyers, the kind who hustle cases in traffic court: no, I think they are more like divorce lawyers, on the 14th floor of the County Building, the kind that enraged husbands pull out guns and shoot. This is the bottom of the labor movement, eight rungs below [union presidents]. But this is the cutting edge of labor. This is where we pick up first-step grievances and DUIs. Actually this is where I pick up some cases myself.

Thomas Geoghegan, Which Side Are You On? 163 (2004).

3.   Are creeping "legalisms," to the extent they exist, really bad? For a strong defense of "legalism," see J. David Andrews, *A Management Attorney's View* (in a symposium titled *Legalism in Arbitration*), 38 Proceedings of the National Academy of Arbitrators 191 (1986). Some "legalisms" are simply practices regarded as routine or even essential in litigation, for example using an attorney, transcribing the hearing, and submitting briefs. Others are arbitral versions of the procedural protections now given criminal defendants. An arbitrator, for example, might reinstate a guilty employee because the employer violated the contractual procedural requirements or the notions of "industrial due process" or "industrial equal protection." What effects would you expect such decisions to have on labor relations? Are such concepts undesirable legalisms, or do they instead put meat on the bones of the "just cause" principle?

Suppose you were a party to an arbitration involving your own job or (if you expect to be on management's side of the class barricades, involving lots of money). Would you want your advocate to be a lawyer? To file a brief? To use a transcript when writing the brief? And if your answers are yes, wouldn't you be contributing to "legalism?" Would that make you feel guilty? Or just cautious?

4.   If you do find legalism a problem, what cures can you offer? The late Professor Reginald Alleyne, in *Delawyerizing Labor Arbitration*, 50 Ohio State Law Journal 93, 95, 107 (1989), blamed evidentiary disputes for much of the increased delay and cost of arbitration. With a certain hyperbole, he claims that

> Today, except for the absence of a high bench, oak-paneled walls, and an enrobed judge, a casual and short-term observer may fail to distinguish between a one-day labor arbitration contesting a one-day suspension from work and the trial of an antitrust case in federal district court.

He recommends adoption of these simplified evidentiary rules for labor arbitration hearings:

Rule One—*Presentation of Evidence*

(a) Both parties shall present to the arbitrator at the outset of the hearing an opening statement, outlining in summary form what each intends to prove.

(b) A party may call any witness it considers essential in proving its claim, in whatever order it desires, including a witness who would normally be called by the opposite party.

Rule Two—*Admissibility of Evidence*

(a) *Documentary Evidence*—Before testimony is presented, each party shall present to the arbitrator and to each other all documents it will rely upon during the presentation of its case. Each such document shall bear an exhibit number. Reference may be made to a document whenever a party chooses to do so during the hearing. No objection to a submitted document shall be allowed during the presentation of testimony. After both parties have presented their cases, including rebuttal, each may comment on the opposing party's documentary evidence. The comments should ordinarily be limited to matters of authenticity, relevance in light of the evidence as a whole, and other matters bearing on the impression the arbitrator should receive from the evidence.

(b) *Testimony*—All testimony shall be received without objection, except that either the arbitrator or a party may object to testimony that would (I) needlessly lengthen the time required to complete the hearing because of its lack of value to the arbitrator in resolving the issues presented by the grievance or (ii) violate the confidentiality of the husband-wife, priest-penitent, doctor-patient, or lawyer-client relationship, or the privilege against self-incrimination.

Rule Three—*Burden and Quantum of Proof*

(a) In all cases except grievances over the assignment of discipline, the party who filed the grievance shall proceed first and present its case. In grievances over discipline, the employer shall proceed first and present its case.

(b) The party first presenting its case shall have the burden of convincing the arbitrator that its position should be sustained.

Would you favor adoption of these rules for arbitrations? Why or why not? Would they cure the problem of creeping legalism, or at least minimize its effects?

5.   What can the *parties* do to simplify arbitration? Review the FMCS statistics at the start of this subsection and try to figure out how the parties might eliminate some of the time spent obtaining an award. Which of the obvious ways of reducing costs would you recommend to a client? Eliminate lawyers? Transcripts? Briefs? Hire a cheap arbitrator rather than an expensive one? Ask the arbitrator for a bare award, with no opinion? Insist on a bench decision? See generally, Hill and Sinicropi, *supra* footnote 1; Nicolau, *supra* footnote 1, and comments following his paper. In fact, there already is such an option, namely the expedited arbitration programs described by

Professor Bartlett. Both the FMCS and the AAA have separate rules governing expedited arbitrations. If there are so many ways to reduce delays and expenses, why do you suppose most parties have not adopted them?

6. What can *arbitrators* do to simplify arbitration? Arbitrator John Shearer, in *Reducing Costs of Arbitration Through Increasing the Parties' Options*, 40 Arbitration Journal 74 (June, 1985), offers some novel suggestions. First, he begins hearings by offering the parties a last chance to discuss settlement among themselves. Second, he offers them a choice between a full written award (including a statement of the facts); an abbreviated award discussing the evidence, reasoning, and findings; or a simple statement of the result. He claims that these simple practices have increased the settlement rate and decreased the cost of those cases that do go to hearing.

7. Notwithstanding the criticisms, virtually all collective agreements still include arbitration provisions, and often those provisions are more "legalistic" than earlier ones. What does that say about the depth of the parties' concerns? Parties must find some utility in the process, at least as compared to the alternatives. What might that utility be? Could it be that arbitration permits parties to ensure the enforcement of a different set of norms than would operate under the common law, as we suggested in the first chapter to this book? If so, what might those norms be, and how do they differ from the common law's? (A hint: labor law used to be called the law of "master and servant." Would arbitrators be likely to use that phrase? Why not?) To put the issue another way, is the decision to use arbitration a choice of *forum* (same norms, different judge) or a choice of *law* (different norms, different judge)?

3. ARBITRATION'S HONESTY

In the years after the Supreme Court's fulsome praise of labor arbitration in the *Steelworkers Trilogy* of 1960, arbitrators understandably basked in their glory. All the more surprising, then, when one of their own number charged them with institutional dishonesty. A former arbitrator, Judge Paul Hays of the U.S. Court of Appeals for the Second Circuit drew upon his personal experience, which made his indictment even more credible. Hays first delivered his attack as the Storrs lectures at Yale Law School in 1964. He published one of them the next year in the Yale Law Journal, then published the lot in 1966 as a book, Labor Arbitration: A Dissenting View.

Chapter 1 of his book critically reviewed the *Trilogy* decisions. He concluded that the few authorities cited by Justice Douglas did not support his unqualified endorsement of arbitration or of arbitrators. Nor, said Hays, are there any other authorities that would. Moreover, he found the Court lacking in an understanding of labor relations practice, and guilty of flawed logic.

Chapter 2 discussed the practice of labor arbitration. Hays's primary concern was the gap between the exemplary arbitrators—Yale Law School Dean Harry Shulman and Harvard Law School Professor Archibald Cox—who were the Court's models, and the normal arbitrators who decide most cases. He regarded the latter as sadly lacking in experience and training. Worse, he believed them driven by a desire for "acceptability" to render rigged awards and unjustified compromise awards, and to invent doctrines that allowed them to retain business by deciding more cases for unions. Hays also rejected arbitration's vaunted efficiency, claiming that arbitrators wrongly applied novel procedural rules that made arbitration less efficient than it should have been.

Chapter 3, from which the following excerpt comes, began by arguing that if arbitration depends on the law, the law should take an active role to correct arbitration's errors. That, however, would defeat the very purpose of labor arbitration. The chapter therefore ended by proposing a strict separation between arbitration and the law. The law, Judge Hays said, should provide a simple alternative to formal litigation and leave arbitration to its own devices.

LABOR ARBITRATION: A DISSENTING VIEW
Paul R. Hays.
Yale University Press, 1966.

It may be that, as the courts become more familiar with the real nature of the arbitration process, they will likewise recede from the more extreme positions respecting arbitration. A reading of Dean Shulman's lecture and a selective reading from some of Cox's work does not provide a sufficient basis for a judgment of the character of the arbitration process. Since labor arbitration plays such an important role in our system of justice, it is incumbent on the scholars to make much more extensive and careful studies of the process than have yet appeared. On the basis of these studies we must have disinterested evaluations of the process as a whole. Too much of the material that is now available consists of enthusiastic endorsement of arbitration by arbitrators who are making a living out of it, or by organizations whose object is to forward and advance the cause of arbitration.

In the meantime, until the courts can get a more realistic picture of the whole process, there are a number of points at which the courts can intervene, and some of the courts have been scrutinizing arbitration more closely at these points. The courts have been entrusted by Congress with the task of fashioning the law governing the collective bargaining agreement. As they continue with the process, the conflict between the courts and the arbitrators is bound to become keener. The desirability of uniformity will tend to force some kind of resolution of this conflict.

Pending these scholarly studies and evaluations, I am forced to the conclusion, based upon observation during twenty-three years of very active practice in the area of arbitration and as an arbitrator, and upon the hints I pick up in the literature here and there, that labor arbitration has fatal shortcomings as a system for the judicial administration of contract violations. I call labor arbitration "a system for the judicial administration of contract violations" since this is, I believe, all that is basically claimed for it. An arbitrator is a third party called in to determine a controversy over whether one of the parties to the collective bargaining agreement has violated that agreement. He is not a wise counselor and statesman whom the management or the union looks to for advice on how to run their affairs or how to increase production or lessen tensions. He is merely an ad hoc judge to whom is submitted the question of whether the collective bargaining agreement has been violated. The chances are very good that, in all but a tiny percentage of arbitrations, this is the first time he has had anything to do with the plant, and that he knows nothing of the background of the dispute or of the "common law" of the industry. In fact there is a considerable possibility that this is his first arbitration case. He has no expertise in these matters and is not expected to have any, since it is expected that he will listen to the evidence presented by the two parties and decide on the basis of that evidence whether the charge of contract violation is or is not sustained. For his task he requires exactly the same expertise which judges have and use every day. He must be expert in analyzing issues, in weighing evidence, and in contract interpretation.

There are only a handful of arbitrators who, like Shulman and Cox, have the knowledge, training, skill, and character to make them good judges and therefore good arbitrators. In literally thousands of cases every year, decisions are made by arbitrators who are wholly unfitted for their jobs—who do not have the requisite knowledge, training, skill, intelligence, and character.

A proportion of arbitration awards, no one knows how large a proportion, are decided not on the basis of the evidence or of the contract or other proper considerations, but in a way which in the arbitrator's opinion makes it likely that he will be hired for other arbitration cases. It makes no difference whether or not a large majority of cases is decided in this way. A system of adjudication in which the judge depends for his livelihood, or for a substantial part of his livelihood or even for substantial supplements to his regular income, on whether he pleases those who hire him to judge is per se a thoroughly undesirable system. In no proper system of justice should a judge be submitted to such pressures. On the contrary, a judge should be carefully screened from any pressure of this type. There are many discussions of arbitration which do not mention this aspect of the process. In my opinion no discussion of arbitration that does not consider the effect of the arbitrator's dependence on the good will of the parties is completely honest.

Another proportion of awards is rigged awards, rendered by arbitrators who are the creatures of those who hire them for the purpose of misleading others, usually the union membership, about the conduct of their representatives. While the number of such awards is probably not very large, the practice is so vicious that no system including such a practice can have any proper claim to being a system of justice.

It is my view that intervention by the courts, even if a broad intervention should be permitted, is not a sufficient answer to the shortcomings of labor arbitration. I believe that the courts should not lend themselves at all to the arbitration process. Labor arbitration is a private system of justice not based on law and not observant of law. There is no reason why it should be able to call on the legal system to enforce its decrees. Moreover, there is affirmative reason why the courts should not lend their enforcement powers to arbitration. We know that a large proportion of the awards of arbitrators are rendered by incompetents, that another proportion—we do not know how large but are permitted by the circumstances to suspect that it is quite large—is rendered on the basis of what award might be best for the arbitrator's future. We know there is another group of cases, though it is true that the courts are not called upon for enforcement of such cases, in which the arbitrator has rendered a rigged award.

Dean Shulman in his famous lecture suggested that "the law stay out" of arbitration. While his reasons for such a suggestion are quite different from mine, I wish to make the same suggestion, that law get out of labor arbitration and leave the procedure exclusively to the voluntary action of the parties. In this way those who believe that labor arbitration is a praiseworthy system of industrial justice will be able to have such a system working on its highest level, the level Shulman described and advocated. Those who believe, as I do, that labor arbitration is a usually undesirable and frequently intolerable procedure will not be offended by the requirement that our courts rubber stamp the questionable results which the arbitrators have reached.

No one envisaged labor arbitration as a complete and very extensive system of private justice when the arbitration statutes were adopted. Nobody thought of a system where people earned a living by conducting arbitrations. It is doubtful, for example, whether the United States Arbitration Act has any application to labor arbitration, but in any event it was not designed to cover labor arbitration as it has developed, and the sponsors of the Act did not have in mind any such system as has grown up.

Section 203(d) of the Labor Management Relations Act, 1947, so often quoted as indicating a national policy in favor of arbitration, says nothing of court enforcement, and may be read in fact to favor the courts keeping out of the procedure. Section 203(d) provides:

> Final adjustment by a method agreed upon by the parties is declared to be the desirable method for settlement of grievance disputes arising over the application of interpretation of an existing collective-bargaining agreement.

The Section then goes on to direct the Mediation and Conciliation Service to make its services available in grievance disputes "only as a last resort and in exceptional cases."

This provision thus expresses a strong policy in favor of purely voluntary adjustment by the parties. The interference of courts in the process may be thought of as just as contrary to the policy set forth as is the interference of the Mediation and Conciliation Service. The principle for which the section appears to stand is the principle of "hands off" by government agencies of whatever sort.

We may assume also that the intervention of courts has a much wider effect than that which results from the cases in which the courts actually play a role. The availability of resort to the courts must serve in countless situations to persuade reluctant parties to collective agreements to accept arbitration and to abide by awards. We are therefore not considering merely those comparatively few cases that now get into the court but also the thousands of cases that are now settled without resort to the courts.

If the use of the courts for the purpose of enforcing arbitration were withdrawn, it would of course leave the courts available for the enforcement of collective bargaining agreements through their regular procedures. Incidentally, to make arbitration purely voluntary would entail, as I see it, refusal to give effect to an arbitration clause as a defense to an action in the courts, as well as the refusal of affirmative action for the enforcement of a promise to arbitrate. For voluntary arbitration to be effective, the parties to the collective bargaining agreement must be genuinely willing to carry out the agreement to arbitrate without outside pressure from any official source.

There are certain procedural advantages in arbitration which some would want to see preserved. There is nothing about those procedural aspects that makes them indissolubly a part of a private system of judicial administration. They could all be readily adapted to a public system of justice and made available in our courts.

For those who believe, for example, that a special expertise in labor problems is desirable for those who pass upon violations of collective agreements, there is the suggestion that we set up in this country a system of labor courts after the model which has been so successful in countries like Germany, Sweden, and Denmark. Such courts could be operated with a simplified procedure like the procedure in small-claims courts, so that cases could readily be presented by personnel managers or union representatives without the necessity of being represented by counsel. On the other hand, the courts would be equipped to hear complex cases as well as simple cases and to give full scope to representation by counsel.

Specialized labor courts could be given jurisdiction to hear aspects of labor relations problems other than actions for breach of collective agreement. What these other aspects would be has been suggested in connection with prior proposals for labor courts. I have enough controversy on my hands as it is without venturing any further along this line.

As I have made clear I do not believe that any expertise other than the expertise of judges in general is required for the resolution of controversies over violations of collective bargaining agreements. I would be content therefore with a procedural reform which would make available for such cases a simple, speedy, and inexpensive remedy. If the suggestion that a procedure like that of the small-claims courts does not satisfy these requirements, then I suggest an alternative along the line of the New York Simplified Procedure for Court Determination of Disputes. That procedure could be specified in the collective bargaining agreement and the promise to submit to it would be specifically enforceable. The action is commenced without the service of a summons and without pleadings, by the filing of a statement setting forth the issues ("claims and defenses"). A submission to this simplified procedure constitutes a waiver of trial by jury. At the hearing, rules as to the admissibility of evidence are dispensed with. The court may hold a pretrial hearing and may direct pretrial discovery and the taking of depositions. Under the New York procedure no appeal is permitted. I would permit an appeal upon permission of the Court of Appeals.

This procedure has all the advantages of arbitration plus certain procedural advantages, like discovery, which are not available in arbitration. In addition it has the advantage of being presided over by a judge who is trained and skilled, who is a part of the judicial tradition, and who is protected by tenure. The judgments will be judgments in accordance with the law of collective bargaining agreements as that law is being fashioned by the courts. This law will be uniform throughout the nation, as Congress intended it to be uniform.

Perhaps I will be accused of stirring up trouble where none has existed. I plead in my own defense that I am deeply committed to the integrity of our court system and that I do not believe judges should stand idly by and let that court system be used as the handmaiden for a system of private adjudication which has so many fatal shortcomings as has labor arbitration.

ARBITRATORS AND JUDGES—DISPELLING THE HAYS HAZE*

Saul Wallen.
9 California Management Review 17 (1967).

Do the facts square with Judge Hays' theories? I submit they do not. His first point, it appears, is that there is nothing more to arbitrating than to judging; that it calls for no other kind of expertise; and that only those few qualified to be judges are qualified to be arbitrators.

First, I submit that labor arbitration is in fact a distinct specialty and that the generality of arbitrators who are experienced do have a knowledge of industrial relations, an understanding of the problems of the interrelationship of levels of authority in multilayered organizations such as companies and unions, some knowledge of the problems of trade union administration, some feeling for the problems of production and of the roadblocks and obstacles to smooth in-plant administration, a considerable knowledge of the processes of industry, and a wide acquaintanceship with the techniques of wage incentives, job evaluation, and other features of wage administration that are basically simple, but until mastered, are gibberish to the uninformed. Furthermore, they need this knowledge to analyze intelligently and decide many, though by no means all, of the cases that come before them.

This point may have escaped Judge Hays, but it has not escaped other distinguished scholars knowledgeable both in jurisprudence and in labor arbitration. I refer specifically to Professor Lon L. Fuller, Carter Professor of General Jurisprudence, Harvard Law School, who wrote:

> In the nature of things few judges can have had any very extensive experience in the field of industrial relations. Arbitrators, on the other hand, are compelled to acquire a knowledge of industrial processes, modes of compensation, complex incentive plans, job classifications, shift arrangements, and procedures for layoff and recall.

> Naturally not all arbitrators stand on a parity with respect to this knowledge. But there are open to the arbitrator, even the novice, quick methods of education not available to the courts * * *.

In this sense, the experienced arbitrator does have the kind of "expertise" to which the Supreme Court referred in the Trilogy. In many cases, he has served before with the same parties, has learned something of the particular plant and industry, and is already familiar with the pattern of their relationships and the peculiarities of their special terminology. In a significant number of relationships, he is their permanent umpire, serving for the contract's term and continually renewed as successive contracts are negotiated. But, even where the particular plant and the parties are new to him, his background enables him quickly to grasp and comprehend what often would be obscure to someone not previously exposed.

Of course he is not "the wise counselor and statesman to whom management and the union look for advice on how to run their affairs or how to increase production or lessen tensions." The language of the Supreme Court in the trilogy cases from which Judge Hays drew this quotation for his lecture was extravagant and implies a role few arbitrators play and fewer desire to preempt. But a good arbitrator is more than an "*ad hoc* judge * * * expert in analyzing issues, in weighing evidence, and in contract interpretation." He must do that in the specialized context of labor relations, in the special community of an industrial plant and a local union. To be meaningful and convincing to the parties, his decisions should impart an understanding and comprehension of that atmosphere and should convey to them the conviction that their controversy is being decided not with reference to abstractions remote from their ken but with reference to the realities which govern their day-to-day in-plant lives.

I do not mean to imply that this is an expertise judges could not quickly acquire if they made labor cases a field of concentration. But I believe it is also true that the "expertise which judges have and use every day * * * "that of "analyzing issues * * * weighing evidence, and

* * * contract interpretation" is only part of the expertise an arbitrator employs because the judge does not ordinarily employ them in the same specialized atmosphere as does the arbitrator.

TESTING ARBITRATORS

For these reasons, I find somewhat cavalier Judge Hays' dismissal of the average arbitrator as wholly unfitted for his job—as lacking the requisite knowledge, training, skill, intelligence, and character. His criticism does not square with the fact that, once established, arbitrators appear to have a high survivability rate and are chosen again and again by people who do not deem them unfitted for their jobs, who appear to show some regard for their skill and intelligence and even some admiration for their character. I cannot, of course, speak about all arbitrators. But I think it safe to say that the arbitrators who decide the majority of cases presented to arbitration in this country, the ones who, whether they practice full time, part time, or occasionally, are called back time and again to serve, have met a test no judge is ever called upon to meet—the test of the marketplace—the judgment of those in a position freely to contract for their services.

I turn next to Judge Hays' second sweeping generalization—"In fact, a proportion of arbitration awards, no one knows how large a proportion, is decided not on the basis of the evidence or of the contract or other proper considerations, but in a way calculated to encourage the arbitrator's being hired for other arbitration cases." This, I submit, is arrant nonsense. The surest way for an arbitrator not to be hired for other arbitration cases by at least one of the same parties is to render a decision without regard to the evidence or the contract. Surely, Judge Hays could not have had this type of case in mind.

Possibly, he meant that there are arbitrators who decide a dispute between Company A and Union B without regard to the evidence or the contract in order to encourage Union C and Company D to agree upon him for their cases. This presupposes a naivete on the part of the parties that does not in fact exist. As the reader undoubtedly knows, arbitrators are not chosen by caprice. "They are checked upon, cross-referenced, and indexed by trade associations, union research departments, law firms, individual industrial relations directors, and union business agents. There are even several firms that make a specialty of providing information about individual arbitrators and their performance as reported by companies that have used them before—a sort of private Federal Bureau of Investigation whose dossiers are available for a fee."

The statement that arbitration opinions which ignore the evidence or the contract are written so as to encourage either the same or other parties to hire the writer for other arbitration cases is, on analysis, incomprehensible.

I turn next to the third count in Judge Hays' indictment of arbitration. He charges that "A system of adjudication in which the judge depends for his livelihood, or for a substantial part of his livelihood or even for substantial supplements to his regular income, on pleasing those who hire him to judge is per se a thoroughly undesirable system.''

Apparently, Judge Hays views the majority of arbitrators as craven, cringing creatures who write their decisions in mortal fear of the displeasure of the losing party and who, therefore, let that fear temper their judgements in some way he does not explain. Or he may be implying that, because the arbitrator fears the displeasure of the loser, which displeasure may have the tangible effect of a loss of future income, he contrives to write his decisions in such a way that there will be no loser.

His statement misconceives the nature of the impact of arbitral decisions. It ignores the fact that, if an arbitrator makes a dishonest decision in order to please one party, he thereby automatically alienates another who holds a veto power over his future services. In arbitration, one man's pleasure is his opponent's pain, and the pressures on the arbitrator, to the extent they exist at all, are countervailing.

More than that, his charge does no credit to the parties in arbitration cases. It implies that losers in arbitration cases are automatically indignant; that they possess no sense of the worth of their case; that they are incapable of admitting that there may have been another side to the question at issue; and that they are automatically moved to economic retaliation against the decider. The facts are quite to the contrary. In the vast majority of arbitration cases, the losers takes his licking gracefully; from time to time he is even convinced by the decision; more often than not he knew he had a losing case when he entered or when he left the hearing room; and he is not at all impelled to work out his displeasure by blacklisting the arbitrator.

It must be conceded, however, that an arbitrator from time to time displeases some parties to a degree that they are impelled to apply economic sanctions against him. Does the fear that this may happen becloud his ability to make a fair decision? The answer is "No," for two reasons. The first is that a career arbitrator who gets past his first case quickly learns, if he did not already know, that he would do well to avoid becoming dependent solely on one set of parties and to so spread his activities that a loss of the business of one set of parties does not seriously curtail his income. If, on the other hand, he has chosen to put all his eggs in one basket, his work is under such close scrutiny that he can do no less than decide cases according to the merits if he expects to have his services continued beyond its current term or even beyond the current case.

The second reason is more fundamental. Judge Hays' charge denigrates arbitrators unfairly and exalts the judiciary unduly. It presupposes that arbitrators are without character, professional responsibility or pride in their calling, and that they are responsive only to the tug of money. At the same time, it assumes that judges, freed from money concerns by virtue of civil service status, are per se freed from pressures which may affect their decisions.

The first presupposition is a gratuitous attack on the character and accomplishments of the many hundreds of men who have served honorably and efficiently as arbitrators in many thousands of disputes over the years. It may surprise Judge Hays to learn that there are some men in this world who think that to meet the challenge to act honorably and decide fairly is more important than the possible loss of future income and that not all such men are judges. To impute to arbitrators as a class the sort of cravenness embodied in Judge Hays' third charge is unjust in the extreme.

The second assumption is equally groundless. The judiciary is made up of men—mortals like us all—who may have been insulated from the pressures of concern for money but who may be prey to other more subtle pressures that could conceivably affect their decisions—the elected judge concerned about reelection; the appointed judge sensitive to the possibility of pressure from his political mentor; the subtle biases of birth or class with their influence on unconscious behavior. The great Cardozo stated it aptly:

> The spirit of the age, as it is revealed to each of us, is too often only the spirit of the group in which the accidents of birth or education or occupation or fellowship have given us a place. No effort or revolution of mind will overthrow utterly and at all times the empires of these subconscious loyalties.

The essence of the judicial temperament does not lie in an absolute freedom from biases, predilections, or even temptations. Even the saints never achieved that state of grace. It lies in the possession and exercise of those traits of character and moral strength that enable a man to recognize and exorcize these human weaknesses.

What magic is there in the judicial robe that ensures that judges will not yield to the pressures which surround them that is not also present in the business suit donned by the arbitrator? Who is to say that the sum total of the pressures on judges is the less or the greater than on arbitrators? Judge Hays appears to feel confident that he can render these Olympian judgments on arbitrators as a class with scarcely a nod to arbitrators as individuals.

The plain and simple fact of the matter is that all but a tiny minority of the judiciary possess judicial temperament in the sense that I have used the term and discharge their responsibilities in a manner that is a credit to their noble calling. Judge Hays has not supported either with fact or with logic his charge that the vast majority of arbitrators have done less. * * *

SUGGESTED SOLUTIONS

In his Storrs lecture, Judge Hays posed optional solutions for the sad state of arbitration. In my opinion, they are as faulty as his diagnosis of the problem.

His first solution is "that the law get out of arbitration and leave the procedure exclusively to the parties." He would withdraw the courts from enforcement of awards, permitting those who think arbitration praiseworthy to indulge in it and relieving those, who, like him, think it is usually undesirable, from having to witness the spectacle of our courts rubber-stamping the questionable results which the arbitrators have reached.

This solution overlooks the basic fact that grievance handling in American industrial relations is based very largely on the unconditional or slightly limited no-strike, no-lockout clause. Does he propose that, with arbitration wholly voluntary, such clauses be repealed and that the strike or lockout weapon be freely employed as the enforcer of engagements to arbitrate or as the persuader in grievance settlements? Or, on the other hand, does he propose the continuance of such clauses and the installation of voluntarism only on arbitration as the means of finally disposing of grievances?

His alternative solution is equally impractical. He states:

For those who believe, for example, that a special expertise in labor problems is desirable for those who pass upon violations of collective bargaining agreements, there is the suggestion that we set up in this country a system of labor courts after the model which has been so successful in countries like Germany, Sweden, and Denmark.

This suggestion overlooks a number of crucial matters. One is that trade agreements in these countries are relatively short, simple documents covering only the broadest terms of employment and leaving either to legislative regulation or managerial discretion a whole host of other terms and conditions of employment. The volume and detail of the collective agreements found in American industrial relations is unique. As a consequence, those subjects susceptible of arbitration in the industrial courts of these countries are limited. By contrast, the variety and complexity of the issues that are arbitrated in the United States is many times greater and the tasks of the industrial courts would, thus, be many times compounded. * * *

But more than that, the industrial courts in the nations Judge Hays mentions hear grievances arising out of much smaller, much less diverse, and much more compact economies. The chances of successfully implanting such a system on the diversity we have here are problematical at best.

I do not wish to be misunderstood. I do not intend, in refuting Judge Hays' charges, to present arbitration as we know it today as a model of perfection or the men who practice it as paragons of virtue. Arbitration needs much constructive criticism, and occasionally it gets it. But it deserves better than Judge Hays' broadside.

Notes and Questions

1. Judge Hays cites little authority and no studies to support his charges. Readers therefore must take them on faith, or on his logic. Consider

his complaint that arbitrators' monetary dependence on the parties corrupts the process. Do you agree? Keep in mind that the parties jointly select and pay the arbitrator. Do those provisions ensure strict neutrality? If not, how could the arbitrator please one side without offending the other? Or is there some "corrupt" way to please both sides?

2. Hays describes arbitration as "a usually undesirable and frequently intolerable procedure." Undesirable and intolerable to whom? Arbitrators? Unions? Employers? Employees? Government? Judges? Society? See Ver Ploeg, *supra* footnote 1, for a recent study of participants' attitudes toward arbitration.

3. Who wins the debate, Hays or Wallen? Why?

4. One popular perception of arbitration, to which Hays alludes, is that arbitrators tend to "split the baby" to avoid annoying either side and thus losing future business. Glance back at the cases you read in Chapter VII, for example Section B. on Discipline and Discharge. Did any of those decisions reflect baby-splitting? Would baby-splitting be a good long-term career strategy for an arbitrator?

4. ARBITRATION'S IDEOLOGY

The last of the broad lines of criticism about arbitration emphasizes its implicit ideology. There are two branches. The first attack, which comes primarily from academic advocates of Critical Legal Studies (CLS), views arbitration as but one means by which capitalism de-fangs labor radicalism. By imposing collective bargaining as the core of American labor relations law, they argue, Congress forced workers to concern themselves with contractualism rather than justice, with procedures rather than substance. Arbitration simply serves as the mechanism for legitimizing employer dominance; it deludes workers into thinking they stand on equal terms with employers, while in reality arbitrators create and apply doctrines that give employers control over most important workplace decisions. In short, arbitration continues to operate within the very normative framework that collective bargaining was meant to displace.

The second attack is much simpler: it accuses arbitrators of sharing management's values on the broadest questions of labor relations. Viewed in this light, the problem is not arbitration itself, as the Critical Legal Studies attack argues, but arbitrators themselves.

(a) The Critical Legal Studies Attack[2]

Of the major CLS writings on labor relations, the one that concentrates most on arbitration is Katherine Stone's 1981 article, *The Post–*

2. The major CLS articles dealing with arbitration are Karl Klare, *Labor Law as Ideology*, 4 Industrial Relations Law Journal 450 (1981), and Katherine Van Wezel Stone, *The Post–War Paradigm in American Labor Law*, 90 Yale Law Journal 1509 (1981) and *The Legacy of Industrial Pluralism: The Tension Between Individual Employment Rights and the New Deal Collective Bargaining System*, 59 University of Chicago Law Review 575 (1992). The most important responses are Matthew W. Finkin, *Revisionism in Labor Law*, 43 Maryland Law Review 23 (1984) and James T. Carney, *In Defense of Industrial Pluralism*, 87 Dickinson Law Review 253 (1983). (Klare, Stone, and Finkin carried on their debate in later publications but said little more about arbitration.)

War Paradigm in American Labor Law, cited in footnote 2. The following excerpt summarizes the pertinent parts of that article.

THE STRUCTURE OF POST–WAR
LABOR RELATIONS

Katherine Van Wezel Stone.

11 New York University Review of Law and Social Change 125 (1982–83).

In my article which I will summarize in the next few minutes, I argue that there is a single, unified vision of collective bargaining that is embodied in all post-war labor law doctrine and all post-war writings about industrial relations. This vision is both a definition of what collective bargaining is, and a vision of the ideal relationship between unions and management in society as a whole. It has become so pervasive in all thinking and writing about labor relations that, like the ambient air, it is almost invisible.

What I will try to do today is to explain what that vision is and define its major elements so that we can look at it, evaluate it, understand its functions, and consider whether it is an accurate and useful description of the industrial world. First I will try to articulate that vision, then say something about how it has come to be embodied in and enforced by court decisions, and finally, provide some criticisms of it. I will argue that the vision fails to present a plausible description of the industrial world and that it entails a prescription for class relations which has harmed the development of union strength over the last twenty-five years in America.

I call the vision "industrial pluralism." It is the view that collective bargaining is industrial self-government. In this view, management and labor are seen as political parties—each one represents its constituencies at the bargaining table as political representatives represent theirs in a legislature. The negotiation process is described as a legislative process in which the two parties meet and legislate the rules by which the workplace will be governed. The rules that result—the collective bargaining agreement—are termed a statute or a constitution for the workplace.

The governmental metaphor is central to the industrial pluralist model. Private arbitration plays a key role in the model: that of the metaphoric judiciary. A collective bargaining agreement, like a statute, requires rule application and rule interpretation. A collective bargaining agreement gives rise to innumerable questions concerning the meaning of the rules when they are applied to the varied and often unanticipated situations that arise daily. In the industrial pluralist model, these questions are decided by the arbitrator, who is the judge: the neutral, impartial entity who can interpret and apply the rules because he was not part of the original rule-making process. With a separation between the judicial and the legislative function, the industrial pluralists claim that there is a separation of powers which makes the workplace a microcosmic democracy.

In this scheme arbitration is not a mere afterthought, but rather goes to the heart of the collective bargaining process. Under the National Labor Relations Act (NLRA), management and labor have a statutory duty to bargain and to produce a written agreement. The agreement that results specifies rules which limit management's discretion and provide certain benefits and protections that the workers or the union have been able to obtain. The question that repeatedly arises is, what happens when management breaks the agreement by failing to provide the benefits or afford the protections specified? If the union has no mechanism to enforce the agreement, then the duty to bargain under the NLRA is reduced to a meaningless charade, and the collective agreement itself is nothing but a sham. The central question under the NLRA, therefore, is, What power do unions have to enforce their collective bargaining agreements? Without that power, the rights conferred by the Act are chimeric at best. Under the industrial pluralist vision, the collective agreement is only enforceable at arbitration. The arbitrator, as judge, decides if there has been a breach and fashions a remedy.

The industrial pluralist vision has institutional implications for the role of industrial relations in the broader judicial and legal process. The principal implication is that other types of legal and judicial processes should be kept out of the workplace. The model describes the workplace as an autonomous, democratic institution. Any intervention by outside process, be it a court, an administrative agency, or legislative enactment, would only disrupt its self-regulating, democratic process. * * *

I want to set forth two criticisms of this vision. The first one concerns the implausibility of the vision as a description of labor relations. The view of management and labor as jointly establishing the rules for governing plant life presupposes the possibility of equal power of management and labor and equal input into industrial conditions. This presupposition, which I call the premise of joint sovereignty, is, I will argue, a false premise. * * *

The industrial pluralist viewpoint has also had detrimental effects on the labor movement as a whole because of its insistence on arbitration as the only method of deciding industrial disputes. Arbitration places all such disputes in a private, invisible forum. It does not afford the kind of due process protections one might hope to find in an administrative agency or a court. Arbitrators are not public officials, and are therefore neither bound to uphold public office, nor are they accountable to a public process. They are not bound by rules of procedure or evidence. Arbitration awards are seldom published and when they are published, they have little precedential value. As a result, various doctrines which offend notions of due process have become prevalent. For example, the "obey now—grieve later rule" says that if a worker is given an order that violates the collective agreement, the worker nonetheless must obey the order and file a grievance later. Failure to do so results in discipline for insubordination, even if the worker was correct about the contract violation. The rule is involved in almost all insubordination cases, which represent approximately twenty-five percent of all arbitrated discipline cases. It is a severe rule because the right which the worker claimed by the grievance is often the right not to follow an improper order. That right is entirely lost by having to grieve after the fact. Once the order is obeyed, the grievance is functionally moot.

Other arbitral doctrines also offend traditional notions of due process. One doctrine says that an employer's business justification can be sufficient to override or negate explicit terms in a collective bargaining agreement. Another holds that when there is a credibility question to be resolved, it should be resolved against the worker and in favor or the company because the grievant has a motive to lie. These doctrines and others of their ilk, although not held by all arbitrators nor present in all decisions, are deeply enmeshed in the arbitral decisional law. The prevalence of such management-serving arbitration doctrines must be attributed to the private and invisible nature of the arbitral forum where the public cannot easily monitor developing trends or mobilize pressure for change.

This brings me to a larger critique of industrial pluralism—that the privatized structure that has been set up by industrial pluralism to handle labor disputes has functioned to impede the development of classwide action among the labor movement as a whole. Because the settlements of labor disputes are rendered invisible, the disputes themselves come to be defined in the most minute, narrow and economistic fashion. It becomes difficult for any individual worker or union to identify trends and there is no point at which pressure could be applied to change them. This makes it very difficult to build classwide alliances around shared and pervasive problems. Because the theory dictates that the important decisions about labor relations are made in a privatized forum, and that the political process must keep out, the political process becomes unavailable as a forum in which struggle for change can take place. This means that the kind of forcefulness and militancy that can develop when people define their rights collectively and subject this definition to public debate has been systematically thwarted by the impact of the industrial pluralist vision.

———————

The late Professor David Feller of the University of California at Berkeley did as much as anyone to create what Stone calls "industrial pluralism." As counsel to the Steelworkers Union during the *Trilogy* cases, he persuaded the Supreme Court to view arbitration as a responsible and essential method of enforcing collective bargaining rights. Naturally he differed with Stone about arbitration's role; he believed that, far from depriving workers of their rights, arbitration protects them better than any available alternative. The following excerpt is from his response to Stone's paper, 11 New York University Review of Law and Social Change 136, 140–41 (1982–83).

Let me first confess to being an "industrial pluralist"; but I define the term somewhat differently than Ms. Stone. The problem with her paper and the longer article which appeared in the Yale Law Journal, which I have read with some care, is that it makes certain assumptions about "industrial pluralists" which are plainly incorrect.

First of all, she assumes that the premise of industrial pluralism is equal power at the bargaining table. That simply is not so. I am an industrial pluralist precisely because I recognize that there are enormous differences in the relative strengths of employers and unions at different locations. There are some places where unions are weak, because replacements are readily available if the union strikes, and therefore inequality of bargaining power exists. There are other locations where the reverse is true. * * *

Now let me briefly address the subject of arbitration. Ms. Stone argues that the institution of arbitration has given away the rights which workers would have in the courts. Again, however, what she says has very little to do with reality. If a worker believes she is denied a right secured under the collective bargaining agreement and she can show that the union breached its duty of fair representation in not taking her case to arbitration, or in presenting her case in arbitration, then under *Vaca v. Sipes*, she can obtain a judicial adjudication of her grievance.

I have read about four hundred cases involving breach of the duty of fair representation and the small number won by workers clearly shows that the assumption that workers would do better in the courts than in arbitration is erroneous. In many cases the courts find a breach of the duty of fair representation but then, having opened the courthouse door, they conclude that the employer's action was not a breach of the collective bargaining agreement.

This is particularly true in discharge cases. In the courts the plaintiff has the burden of proof, because she is suing for breach of contract. She has to prove that the employer violated the agreement by discharging her. But, in arbitration, the normal rule in a disciplinary case is that the employer has both the burden of coming forward with the evidence and the burden of proof. Indeed, many arbitrators say that discharge is industrial capital punishment and the employer must prove the employee's offense beyond a reasonable doubt. No court in the world has ever gone that far.

The late Arthur M. Ross summed it up humorously in an address years ago to the National Academy of Arbitrators on cases of discharge for sleeping on the job. He said, "[I]t is well established that the only reliable means of substantiating guilt beyond a reasonable doubt is to lift the grievant from the chair in which he has been snoring and bounce him off the floor until he opens his eyes, blinks in confusion, and angrily inquires, 'What's the big idea waking me up in the middle of a shift?' Otherwise the grievant may successfully claim that he was momentarily resting his eyes or that he was deep in meditation concerning the problems of the job."

I agree that in one sense the arbitration system and the grievance process have led to a lack of class consciousness among workers. The arbitration system does provide a channel for discontent and provides at least a modicum of justice. There is never perfect justice because you are never able to resolve all your problems through collective bargaining, not only because of the imbalances which exist in economic power, but also because not all problems can be anticipated. That's why at periodic intervals agreements are renegotiated not only with respect to wages and benefits but also with respect to the provisions governing the day-to-day relationship of the parties at the workplace. This too, I concede, has the effect of channelling [sic] discontent and may lead to less militancy than would immediate and spontaneous job action to redress grievances, although in the end the latter method clearly is less effective in providing substantive justice.

It is correct, therefore, to say that if you didn't have the grievance and arbitration system, there might be more class consciousness on the part of workers. But that seems to me to be just another way of saying that what we need is increasing misery of the working classes in order to get a revolution. In that thesis I do not concur.

Notes and Questions

1. Feller's credentials as a labor advocate are impeccable, but does he give too much credit to the fair representation doctrine's ability to protect employee rights? Might he be identifying workers' interests with the institution of labor unions? If so, is he wrong? Stone had the last word in their debate, 11 New York University Review of Law and Social Change 147, 148 (1982–83). She used it to renew her attack on the industrial pluralism that fosters arbitration, rather than on arbitration itself:

Both David Feller and Jack Getman agree with me that there is an imbalance of power [in the "day-to-day life under an existing contract"], but we disagree as to how it should be remedied. Apparently both of them believe that unions have more power under industrial pluralism than they would otherwise, and that is a good thing * * *. Indeed, I'm willing to concede that it may have been true at an earlier time. Industrial pluralism may have given unions a modicum of more power during the period of an expanding economy by expanding the realm of joint sovereignty, by chipping away at retained rights, and by obtaining nickel-and-dime increases in the wage bargains. Industrial pluralism may work well in a time when the economy is expanding because management has the ability to buy off workers with small concessions of money and power. During such times, management may not mind sharing a few marginal crumbs here and there. But once the economic picture changes and there is an economic downswing—as there is now and will be for some time—the incrementalist approach no longer works.

That is when the sphere of joint sovereignty shrinks and the illusion of equal power collapses.

* * * What becomes clear is that by having adopted the incrementalist approach earlier, a very high price has been paid. That price is that workers and the labor movement have, in some sense, ended up with the worst of both worlds. They are faced with the demobilizing effect of having third parties decide their disputes for them, and yet they have not received the potential benefits of that process. That is, they have neither been given the real due process rights which are promoted by third party dispute resolution, nor have they been given the opportunity to develop the kind of militancy that comes from defining rights in class-wide and public ways.

2.   How valid are Stone's criticisms of arbitration? (a) Is arbitration really as private as she claims? There are hundreds of volumes of published arbitration awards, but they represent only a small fraction of the total number. Either party can block publication of an award. (b) Who would benefit and who would lose by making contractual disputes more "public?" (c) Do the arbitration doctrines you've studied this semester "offend traditional notions of due process," as she claims? Are the doctrines she cites balanced by others that favor workers, as Feller suggests?

Here is an earthier, less academic criticism of labor arbitration from a labor union lawyer. Despite his different tone and language, isn't he on the same wavelength as Stone?

Here I must pause and say something about arbitration. Oh yes, arbitration. Nothing has been more psalmed, more solemnly, by more federal judges since the Trilogy, as if it were the greatest invention of man. I am so sick of judges writing psalms to arbitration. Have they ever seen one? No. All they know is, they can kick these cases out of court. * * *

What is arbitration? Arbitration is ... well, let me begin with the four steps of the grievance procedure, which are ... As I write this, I feel weak, the pen falls from my hand. This is so boring. Yet I am a labor lawyer, and I do arbitrations. * * *

I said arbitration is like a mini-lawsuit. Often, however, there is nothing mini about it. It can be just as long, just as expensive as a real lawsuit, sometimes worse. An arbitrator, unlike a judge, can charge by the hour, so for the union, which is broke, there are two meters running, the arbitrator's and its lawyer's. * * *

So, does this force expedite resolution? God no. Arbitration is like a lawsuit in drag. Mainly it drags on and on. * * *

No, most arbitrations are dull, transfer of bargaining unit work, etc. I sit in a Holiday Inn in Springfield, and as the case goes on, I remember Harvard, running along the Charles, drinking sherry in the junior common rooms, the sixties ... back when the standard was not twenty nanograms of cannabis, or even fifty, but anything you liked, and I would not lose my job. My mind wanders.... How did I end up doing arbitrations?

For some of the BAs [Business Agents] I feel sorry. After all, I went to law school, and I asked to be a lawyer. But these guys probably thought they would lead strikes or something.

The big issue in labor-management relations today is not who can survive a strike, but who can survive, without blinking, the arbitrator's bill. Most of the time, labor is no match for management. The company has more money, and it has a big, overstaffed personnel department. It can outspend, outbrief, and outman the union in any case, if it wants. It can do all the urinalysis it wants, and then, after two and a half years, it clobbers us in arbitration.

Thomas Geoghegan, Which Side Are You On? 164–66 (2004).

3. The focus of the CLS criticism is collective bargaining's *contractualism*. Arbitration is just one element. If contractualism harms workers' interests, what alternatives are there? Or is the criticism really about collective bargaining itself? If so, what are the alternatives? The thrust of Stone's writings is that unions should be more militant—that they should use economic force to gain their objectives, whatever they are, rather than peacefully seeking incremental improvements in contracts. Presumably that would mean striking over grievances rather than arbitrating them. If unions are too weak to make significant gains under contractualism, how could they be strong enough to strike successfully over routine grievances. Consider that unions represent barely 8% of the country's private sector workforce.

Recall at this point David Feller's statement that he is an industrial pluralist "precisely because I recognize that there are enormous differences in the relative strengths of employers and unions at different locations." In other words, he favors contractualism not because unions are as strong as employers but because contractualism is their most powerful weapon when they are *not* equally strong. Do you agree with Feller? With Stone? Neither?

(b) Charges of Arbitral Bias[3]

The second branch of ideological criticism simply argues that arbitrators are biased. In arbitration's early years, most of this criticism came from management advocates who charged that arbitrators either split awards or invented doctrines to prevent management from exercising its rights to determine methods of production and discipline employees. See, for example, Francis A. O'Connell, Jr., *The Labor Arbitrator: Judge or Legislator*, 18 Proceedings of the National Academy of Arbitrators 102 (1965), and William M. Saxton, *A Management Advocate's View* (in a symposium titled *The Discipline and Discharge Case: Two Devil's Advocates on What Arbitrators Are Doing Wrong*), 32 Proceedings of the

3. Bibliographic Suggestions: James B. Atleson, *Arbitration: The Presence of Values in a Rational Decisionmaking System*, 50 Proceedings of the National Academy of Arbitrators 225 (1997); James A. Gross, *Value Judgments in the Decisions of Labor Arbitrators*, 21 Industrial and Labor Relations Review 55 (1967), *The Influence of Values in the Arbitral Decisionmaking Process*, 50 Proceedings of the National Academy of Arbitrators 212 (1997), and *Incorporating Human Rights Principles into U.S. Labor Arbitration: A Proposal for Fundamental Change* (forthcoming in 8 Employee Rights & Employment Policy Journal); Richard D. Sibbernsen, *What Arbitrators Think About Technology Replacing Labor*, 64 Harvard Business Review 8 (March–April 1986).

National Academy of Arbitrators 63 (1980). More recently, union advocates and sympathetic academics charged that arbitrators have adopted
accepted values such as efficiency and hierarchy that favor employers.

THEIR OWN BRAND OF INDUSTRIAL JUSTICE: ARBITRATORS' EXCESSES IN DISCHARGE CASES*

John R. Phillips.
10 Employee Relations Law Journal 48 (1984).

INTRODUCTION

This article was prompted by four recent cases (all unreported), in
which the writer participated. In each case the collective bargaining
agreement incorporated the employer's work rules and gave the employer the right to discharge for just cause. [The author, a management labor
lawyer, then describes four cases in which arbitrators reinstated employees he thought deserved discharge.]

Are such utterly ridiculous awards unique? Can't an employer
secure relief from the courts? Shouldn't a company minimize the chance
of such injustices by negotiating restrictions on the arbitrator's authority? Tragically, the answers to these questions are no, rarely, and easier
said than done.

RECENT DISCHARGE AWARDS

The following is an illustrative list of a few indefensible awards in
the past few years, which became the law of the shops involved.

- *Tyrone Hydraulics, Inc.*, 75 Lab. Arb. 672 (1980) (Murphy, Arb.):
A white employee at a southern plant was discharged for giving his
"highly respected" black foreman a "very severe" kick after "coming to
the plant under the influence of liquor." The arbitrator reduced the
discharge to a thirty-day suspension because of the grievant's "state of
repentance, and his lack of intention or motive to in any way cause
disrespect to his foreman," even though several unit employees had told
the foreman "this action was demeaning to the foreman and that
discipline should be undertaken."

- *Powermatic/Houdaille, Inc.*, 71 Lab. Arb. 54 (1978) (Cocalis, Arb.):
The discharge of an employee who "placed his finger through or by the
fly of his pants" and told a young female employee, "Hey, big mama,
look what I have for you," was reduced to a suspension. The arbitrator
concluded that the behavior was not immoral: "[Had] the gesture been
made in the presence of only men, I doubt it would have been considered
immoral conduct."

- *Colt Industries*, 71 Lab. Arb. 181 (1978) (Larkin, Arb.): The
discharge of an employee who had "personality clashes" with his fore-

* Reprinted with permission of Aspen
Publishers, from John R. Phillips, *Their
Own Brand of Industrial Justice: Arbitrators' Excesses in Discharge Cases*, 10 Employee Relations Law Journal 48 (1984).

man was reduced to a suspension. Although the grievant and a nonemployee "friend" admittedly had dumped garbage on the foreman's lawn, started a fire at his premises, and made harassing phone calls to him, the grievant was not the "primary instigator" and had a "reasonably good work record for four years."

● *Chatham Supermarkets, Inc.*, 71 Lab. Arb. 1084 (1978) (Roumell, Arb.): A "volatile" packinghouse employee with prior discipline for insubordination and fighting was discharged after he threatened a female employee, "simultaneously pointing his five-inch boning knife directly at [her] face and shaking it at her." The arbitrator reduced the discharge to a suspension, reasoning that "a knife might be used to emphasize a point or to gesture during a discussion with other employees," and "the situation is comparable to a secretary who having a pencil in her hand may wave it during the discussion."

● *McDonnell Douglas Canada, Ltd.*, 74 Lab. Arb. 1103 (1980) (O'Shea, Arb.): The discharge of an employee who violated plant rules by possessing marijuana at work, and pleaded guilty to a criminal offense, was reduced to a four-month suspension. While the arbitrator found that possession is "a very serious offense" and "dr[ew] the inference that [the employee] would have used the drugs at work had he not been caught," he concluded the incident was "isolated" and there was no "ongoing drug problem with other employees in the plant."

● *Hughes Air Corp.*, 73 Lab. Arb. 148 (1979) (Barsamian, Arb.): A male flight attendant, at a motel on a paid layover between flights, grabbed a fifteen-year-old motel employee in the groin and suggested sexual activity. A month earlier, the grievant had propositioned another minor male at an airport. The grievant was discharged, and the arbitrator reinstated him with back pay. The arbitrator concluded that the company's reputation was not harmed because the motel operator, although preferring that the grievant not return to his motel, "did not consider or recommend the cancellation of the contract with the company to provide rooms for its flight attendants." The arbitrator also found this an "isolated incident" that did not justify "the industrial 'capital punishment' of discharge."

● *Ohio Valley Hospital Association*, 79 Lab. Arb. 929 (1982) (Abrams, Arb.): A nurse who committed an "appalling error," amounting to "gross incompetence and recklessness," by failing to tell her supervisor a patient had taken the wrong medicine and nearly died, was reinstated. According to the arbitrator, she "deserves the chance" to prove her competence.

● *General Electric Co.*, 71 Lab. Arb. 337 (1978) (Craver, Arb.): A discharged employee who "only struck [a fellow employee] with a gloved hand and wrestled him to the floor" around "highly dangerous machinery" was reinstated because of his "contrite manner" at the hearing.

● *Dayton Power & Light Co.*, 80 Lab. Arb. 19 (1982) (Heincz [*sic*], Arb.): An employee guilty of "disgraceful" sexual harassment was reinstated with a seven-month suspension because of "the present economic recession and dim prospect of reemployability."

Do arbitrators issue compromise awards, as these cases suggest, and maintain scorecards of their records to assure their continued employment? Many management representatives and commentators have responded in the affirmative. * * *

Awards such as those discussed above destroy confidence in the arbitration process and jeopardize industrial discipline. A recent Gallup Poll disclosed that "65 percent of Americans think the overall level of ethics in American Society has declined in the past decade." Arbitrators who reinstate employees guilty of violence, harassment, carelessness, or other misconduct promote disorder and anarchy in the work place. It is unfortunate that employers cannot replace such offenders with the many capable workers now on the nation's unemployment rolls. How can American businesses hope to rival domestic and foreign competition when hamstrung by such "industrial justice"? How do such awards contribute to the quality of America's work life? Too many arbitrators overlook the Supreme Court's assumption in *Warrior & Gulf* that they consider "the effect upon productivity of a particular result [and] its consequence to the morale of the shop." * * *

It is clear that: private-sector arbitration of labor disputes is here to stay; there is a strong presumption of arbitrability; arbitrators have broad decisional authority under the essence test; and reviewing courts will not embark on a plenary review of awards. Some scholars advocate new legislation prohibiting the discharge of *any* employee except for just cause, with the arbitration experience "provid[ing] guides for statutory protection." This is a foreboding notion, if arbitration awards are accepted as precedents.

Both management and labor are now being cautioned to be responsible in seeking monetary "givebacks" and relaxing outdated, inflexible jurisdictional rules. In the final analysis, this article is a plea to arbitrators to enforce contracts and work rules as they are written, to exhibit more common sense and concern themselves less with social reform, and, in the words of the Supreme Court, to demonstrate "some minimum level of integrity" in discharge cases.

THE ARBITRATOR'S ROLE IN DISCHARGE CASES: ANOTHER VIEWPOINT*

Robert Coulson.
10 Employee Relations Law Journal 61 (1984).

Phillips complains that arbitrators are too willing to reduce terminations to suspensions, undercutting management authority. And he is right! However, I have come across several awards that affirm harsh actions by management. For example:

* Reprinted with permission of Aspen Publishers, from Robert Coulson, *The Arbitrator's Role in Discharge Cases: Another Viewpoint*, 10 Employee Relations Law Journal 61 (1984).

● In *Union Oil Co. of Cal. and OCAW*, AAA 288 (Mar. 1982), a worker was fired for allowing twenty gallons of oil to spill out of a valve. The arbitrator upheld the discharge.

● In *Cessna Aircraft Co. and IAM*, AAA 290 (Oct. 1983), a "model employee" failed to note on her job application a prior back injury that occurred three years before she was hired. This was upheld as a reason to discharge her after she pulled a muscle while lifting a fifty-pound weight on the job. According to the arbitrator, she had "falsified material facts."

● In *Cooper Stevedoring Co. and IUOE*, AAA 292 (June 1983), a welder was fired for refusing to work on a Saturday when asked to do so late Friday afternoon. Again, the discharge was upheld.

● In *Mead Corp. and UPIU*, AAA 293 (Sept. 1983), an employee with nine years' seniority was terminated for attending the out-of-state funeral of a close friend, although telling the company that his wife's grandmother had died. The discharge was sustained.

● In *Brockway Glass and GPPAW*, AAA 295 (Dec. 1983), a worker was discharged for fighting with a supervisor even though the supervisor challenged him to fight, struck the first blow, and gave the grievant a severe beating. The arbitrator upheld the discharge.

● In *Sunbeam Corp. and ACTWU*, AAA (Jan. 1983), an employee was let go for claiming that he injured his knee at work when hospital records showed that he had been treated for an injury to the same knee two days earlier. His discharge was upheld by the arbitrator.

● In *Gwaltney of Smithfield and IBT*, AAA 296 (May 1983), four employees were discharged for leaving their work stations for their regular lunch break without permission. The company had canceled the break that day. The arbitrator concluded that the grievants were acting in defiance of the company, although they claimed that nobody had told them of the cancellation.

A union might complain that these kinds of awards poorly serve them. Certainly, the percentages seem to favor management. A majority of discharge cases confirm termination. Are these the same arbitrators cited by Mr. Phillips? Most likely they are the same worried professionals, making decisions based on the testimony of the witnesses and the presentations of the contesting advocates.

Ah, there's the rub: the advocates! Labor arbitrators are not impersonal robots responding solely to verbal signals. Unlike computers they are sensitive to the parties' presentations. Sometimes, messages are transmitted through words that appear in a transcript. But many signals are exchanged in other ways. They are reflected in subjective perceptions. For example, Phillips cites cases where an arbitrator reduced a penalty because the grievant "learned his lesson," was in a "state of repentance," or was "genuinely contrite" and "deserved a chance." These determinations can be made only by someone who personally observes the participants at the hearing.

Are there valid reasons for an arbitrator to reduce a discharge to a suspension? Phillips would say not. But what if the employer has signaled that a suspension would be acceptable? Can Phillips assure us that the employers were not content with these decisions? In my experience, not every grievance arbitration case is for winning.

Phillips uses his cases as a springboard to conclude that arbitrators are promoting "disorder and anarchy in the work place." He conjures up visions of workers attacking each other with five-inch boning knives, crashing expensive forklifts into each other, and dumping garbage on their foreman's lawn. Of course, we are appalled by such actions. But we should recall that the arbitrator actually heard the testimony and had an opportunity to test it against the work-place environment and prior incidents between the parties. An ad hoc arbitrator may not be familiar, at the outset, with the conditions in the particular work place, but by the time the hearing is concluded, the arbitrator will have a shrewd idea of what constitutes misconduct there and how much discipline is generally imposed.

The arbitrator must stay within the bounds of the contract, but as Phillips notes, with approval, the arbitrator must "administer the rule of law established by [the parties'] collective agreement." The contract is not simply a piece of paper signed by the parties. It is a living relationship, defined and redefined during its term by innumerable conversations, grievance conferences, and arbitration hearings. Harsh discipline may be equally as destructive to the employer-employee relationship as the overabundance of equity that so troubles lawyer Phillips.

Justice Douglas put it very well in *Enterprise Wheel & Car*, 363 U.S. 593 (1960).

> When an arbitrator is commissioned to interpret and apply the collective bargaining agreement, he is to bring his informed judgment to bear in order to reach a fair solution of a problem. This is especially true when it comes to formulating remedies. There the need is for flexibility in meeting a wide variety of situations.

Professional labor arbitrators are expected to exercise their best judgment. In *Enterprise Wheel*, the arbitrator did exactly what Phillips complains of: he converted the discharge of the grievants to a suspension. They had left their jobs in protest against the discharge of one employee. What could be more disruptive? In this landmark case, the Court upheld the arbitrator. Why should the situation be different today?

Notes and Questions

1. Are the decisions cited by Phillips as bad as he asserts? You might look at a few of the published awards to determine whether his descriptions are accurate and complete. In *Tyrone Hydraulics*, for example, the arbitrator found that the kick was only horseplay rather than a deliberate attack and that the employee unequivocally apologized; even so, the arbitrator imposed a 30–day suspension—a very stiff penalty, by industrial relations and arbi-

tral standards. In *Dayton Power*, the sexual harassment involved one incident by an employee with 28 years of satisfactory service; the victim did not even report the incident, believing that she could handle it herself. Even so, the arbitrator imposed a *seven-month* suspension. Phillips assumes that the only appropriate penalty in these cases was discharge. Do you agree? Should the principle of corrective (or "progressive") discipline apply in these as in other cases?

As you have already seen, the concept of "just cause" includes both substantive and procedural elements. Among the procedural elements are requirements of progressive discipline, equal treatment, and due process. Might employers' failure to meet these procedural requisites explain some of the decisions management representatives criticize? *Should* management's procedural errors invalidate otherwise justified discipline?

2. On the other hand, are the decisions cited by Coulson equally horrible in the other direction? If so, do the two extremes balance out? Do they suggest that arbitrators are *not* biased? Or might Coulson's cases, too, have explanations omitted from his brief summaries? In the *Gwaltney* case, for example, the employees didn't just "leave their workstations * * * without permission." They deliberately disobeyed a direct order, in defiance of the negotiated grievance procedure and a no-strike provision that authorized immediate discharge, and in violation of the universal rule of "obey first, grieve later."

3. Phillips was a management labor lawyer. Coulson was the President of the American Arbitration Association, a position giving him reason to defend arbitration from criticism. Do their jobs explain their inconsistent views? If not, what else might be at work?

ARBITRAL VALUE JUDGMENTS IN HEALTH AND SAFETY DISPUTES: MANAGEMENT RIGHTS OVER WORKERS' RIGHTS
James A. Gross and Patricia A. Greenfield.
34 Buffalo Law Review 645 (1986).

INTRODUCTION

The influence of personal beliefs and values on the judgments of judicial and quasi-judicial decision-makers, such as labor arbitrators, continues to be ignored almost totally in the literature of labor law and labor arbitration. The research that has been done on this subject, however, demonstrates that prevailing ideas about ethics, humanity, law, private property, economics and the nature of the employer-worker relationship not only condition the thinking of these decision-makers, but also provide them with the ultimate standards for judgment. These value judgments pre-position a decision-maker's approach to particular case situations, thereby exercising a powerful influence on the outcomes of those cases.

A study of arbitral decisions in cases involving subcontracting and out-of-unit transfers of work, for example, identified a dominant value theme: management rights are necessary for the continued existence of the free enterprise system, and the pursuit of efficiency is one of the most important and fundamental rights of management. The decisions studied demonstrated arbitral acceptance of efficiency as the greatest good and the resultant presumption that the right to subcontract is essential to the competitive survival of the firm.

That study focused on subcontracting because those decisions were very likely to contain value expressions and orientations given the clash between the goals of maximum efficiency and employee job security. This study focuses on health and safety disputes because the even more fundamental clash between management's rights to operate the enterprise and workers' rights to a safe and healthful workplace is most likely to evoke arbitral value judgments. * * *

For purposes of analysis, these safety and health cases were divided into four major categories: Refusals to work for reasons of safety or health; the formulation and implementation of safety rules; crew size determinations which raise safety issues; and disease and disability cases where safety is an important consideration. * * *

I. CONTROLLING ARBITRAL VALUE JUDGMENTS

A. *Refusal to Work Cases*

Almost forty years ago, distinguished arbitrator Harry Shulman set forth in *Ford Motor Company* the principle of "work first, grieve later." In that case, a union representative countermanded a management order temporarily assigning employees to work in higher job classifications because that order was allegedly in violation of a long-standing practice of temporary assignments to lower but not higher classifications. Shulman ruled that "normally" an employee must obey a legitimate work order even if the employee is convinced the order is improper. According to Shulman, the employees should have worked in the higher classification and then protested by filing a grievance since "the grievance procedure would have provided them adequate recompense for the wrong." Otherwise, Shulman said, individual action would be substituted for collective action and the grievance procedure would be replaced with extra-contractual methods so that no enterprise could operate:

> [A]n industrial plant is not a debating society. Its objective is production. When a controversy arises, production cannot wait for exhaustion of the grievance procedure. While that procedure is being pursued, production must go on. And someone must have the authority to direct the manner in which it is to go on until the controversy is settled. That authority is vested in supervision. It must be vested here because the responsibility for production is also vested here; and responsibility must be accompanied by authority. It is fairly vested there because the grievance procedure is capable of adequately recompensing employees for abuse of authority by supervision.

Shulman allowed for exceptions to his rule: when obedience to a management order would require commission of a criminal or otherwise unlawful act or create an "unusual health hazard or other serious sacrifice." Shulman's "work first, grieve later" rule, reflecting the underlying value judgment that management has the right to direct and control the workforce, has become an axiom of labor relations as has his "threat to health or safety" exception to the rule.

Arbitrators, however, do not literally except health and safety from the "work first, grieve later" rule. Arbitral application of the rule in cases where employees refuse to obey management orders because of perceived or actual threats to health and safety reflects an insubordination mode of analysis. Management's right to direct and control the workplace becomes the analytic starting point, and the challenge to that right, i.e., a refusal to work, is insubordination. This approach relegates the safety and health claim to an affirmative defense to the insubordination charge.

In this insubordination mode of analysis, the employer meets its burden of proof by establishing only the usual elements constituting insubordination—that a direct order was given to the employees by a legitimate management authority, that the employees were warned of the consequences of refusal, and that the employees refused to obey the order. As far as the employer is concerned, therefore, there is nothing that distinguishes a refusal to work for reasons of health or safety from any other type of refusal to work case. Certainly, the employer is not obliged to prove that the work assignment did not endanger an employee's healthy or safety. * * *

Consequently, the whole orientation to this type of refusal to work case takes a health and safety dispute and makes it a matter of insubordination with health and safety merely a mitigating factor. Although technically the employer carries the burden of proof in all discipline cases, the practical effect of this orientation in refusal to work for reasons of health and safety cases is to shift the burden of proof concerning the decisive issue to the discharged or otherwise disciplined employee. Arbitrators sustained some penalty against employees in two of every three of the 154 cases in which an employee refused to work for reasons of health or safety.

The effect of this mode of analysis on the outcome of these cases is even more severe for employees because arbitrators routinely place upon them the heaviest possible standards of proof. * * *

The insubordination mode of analysis used in the refusal to work cases, with its associated heavy burden of proof on employees, is the consequence of arbitrators' almost universal acceptance of the value judgment that management's freedom to operate the enterprise and direct the workforce is superior to all other rights including workers' right to a safe and healthful workplace. This value judgment is rooted in conceptions of the rights of private property, defined during an era dominated by a philosophy of free market economics, by courts that desired to encourage industrial undertakings by making the burdens on entrepreneurs as light as possible.

Arbitrators see refusals to work, even for reasons of health and safety, as dangerous threats to the management authority they consider essential to the operation of an enterprise for profit. For example, in upholding the discipline imposed on miners who refused to throw a breaker switch on a shuttlecar after one miner who touched the car received a mild electrical shock, an arbitrator warned that "utter chaos" would be the "logical end product of each crew member making the decision as to what is or is not unsafe" since "no production would ever take place and the mines would be shut down without employment." Another arbitrator foresaw "anarchy" at the workplace unless he enforced management's right to require obedience to its orders in the face of employees' refusal to work because of smoke and dust at their work areas. * * *

The management rights framework of analysis used by arbitrators in cases where employees have refused to work for reasons of safety and health has resulted in decisions that place property rights, and other factors such as profits, efficiency, cost-benefit analysis, technology, management authority, and economic progress, over human rights. In a case referred to previously (the employee who became ill, had nosebleeds, and vomited while working in the midst of offensive odors and fumes from packing house meat scraps), the arbitrator told the employee that the proper procedure was to get sick first and then grieve:

> It appears that the proper procedure should have been for the Union committee to have insisted that the employee go onto the job assigned and for the employee to have done so, then if he became ill as a result thereof to have asked for assignment to some other job * * *. [T]he failure of the employee to do so does not justify reinstatement with back pay.

* * * It should be noted that those employees who have followed the Shulman scheme, obeying first and protesting their allegedly unsafe and unhealthful working conditions later in the grievance procedure, have not lost their jobs but have been penalized in a substantial number of cases; arbitrators upheld the grievances of such employees in only twenty-five of ninety-nine reported cases.

[The authors repeat the analysis for the other three types of cases, formulation and implementation of safety rules by management, crew size reductions where the union raises safety objections, and disability cases where management argues that retaining an employee would present a safety hazard. They find that arbitrators tend to emphasize safety concerns in the safety rules and disability cases, but (like the refusal to work cases) not in the grievances challenging crew size reductions. They find a unifying theme in all categories.]

This apparent shift in emphasis to safety is not the result of reasoning from a different premise. The evidence shows that the basic management authority value orientation of arbitrators has not changed. The primacy of safety and health in these decisions is not inconsistent with its subordinate position in refusal to work cases because its ranking in the priorities of labor arbitrators depends upon one consistent, controlling factor: management rights. * * *

CONCLUSIONS

The analysis of these published decisions does more than confirm the existence of value premises in the decisions of labor arbitrators. It reveals that the management rights value judgment is dominant and that this value judgment clearly controls the appearance and use of another value judgment: the notion that a worker has a right to a safe and healthful workplace. More specifically, most arbitrators make safety and health concerns paramount only when those claims support management rights. The four major categories of decisions read together constitute a classic illustration of how the acceptance of a certain value judgment determines a decision-maker's whole orientation when deciding an issue.

One fundamental question raised by these findings is what value judgment should control at the workplace when workers' health and safety are concerned. The long-standing dominance in United States industrial history of the proposition that management rights must take precedence over all else should not obscure a more humane value judgment, one more in keeping with current law and policy concerning worker health and safety—a value judgment that would make the workers' right to a safe and healthful workplace paramount. As our review of safety rule and disease and disability cases has illustrated, arbitrators do, in fact, recognize workers' health and safety value judgments as important and valid, even "paramount," but only where these value judgments coincide with management rights. Where, as in the refusal to work and crew size cases, a worker health and safety value judgment comes into conflict with management rights concepts of profit, property, authority, efficiency, cost-benefit analysis, technology or "progress," worker health and safety is relegated, at most, to a range of secondary considerations. * * *

Serious questions remain of the ability of arbitration to deal adequately with these issues.

First, arbitrators in the main make the decision to ignore external laws concerning health and safety, a choice that deprives arbitrators of access, not only to alternative values and public policy guidelines, but also to important and relevant data (such as OSHA standards) concerning occupational safety and health. Safety and health disputes also routinely involve technical matters beyond the expertise of most arbitrators; a situation requiring, at least, the creation of special panels of arbitrators with demonstrated qualifications in this area. Finally, the traditional arbitral remedy power is often inadequate to deal not only with the broad scope of certain health and safety problems that range far beyond the situation of a single grievant, but also with the long-term effects of working with certain job-related materials and processes such as toxic chemicals, radiation and asbestos.

It is possible that these defects can be wholly or partially eliminated. But this study has demonstrated that as a consequence of the adoption and implementation of a management rights value judgment, arbitration has become part of an industrial relations system that has as its aim the maintenance of managerial control over all aspects of an enterprise. Arbitrators give health and safety priority only insofar as the assertion of the health and safety value judgment supports this managerial control, as in the safety rule and disease and disability cases. When the health and safety of the worker conflicts with the goals of managerial control, as in the refusal to work and crew size cases, management rights reign supreme.

Given the structure and nature of the arbitration process, the pervasiveness of the management rights value judgment, and the absence of any direct or systematic way to bring about change in arbitral values, there appears to be little chance that labor arbitrators will place the safety and health of men and women at the work place above all other considerations. As Justice Benjamin Cardozo noted, however, "if a rule continues to work injustice, it will eventually be reformulated. The principles themselves are continually retested; for if the rules derived from a principle do not work well, the principle itself must ultimately be re-examined." We hope that by identifying the management rights value judgment and its dominance in health and safety matter arbitrators will recognize that change is needed.

Notes and Questions

1. The study of subcontracting cases mentioned at the beginning of the Gross and Greenfield article is Professor Gross's own, *supra* footnote 3. In that study, Professor Gross found "efficiency" to be the controlling value judgment when arbitrators decide such cases:

> The argument has begun to move from legal confirmation to the validation of management rights through the free enterprise system— the notion that "management's right to manage" should be supported because it is the best thing to do. The argument moves a degree more. If management rights are essential to the free enterprise system, then the pursuit of "efficiency is one of the most important and fundamental rights of management." Constant innovation and increased efficiency advance the economic interests of all—the firm, the workers, the union and the consumer; there ought to be no obstructions. The argument has come to rest on the value judgment that free competition is worth more to society than it costs—a philosophy of progress wherein efficiency is endorsed as socially desirable.

Efficiency also seems to lie behind the management rights preference shown in the health and safety cases. Why should efficiency be the arbitrators' *summum bonum*?

2. Gross and Greenfield clearly detest what they term the "insubordination mode of analysis" in refusal-to-work cases. Why? Do you agree with them? If so, what alternative analysis do you suggest? Are there any hidden costs to alternative approaches?

3. Gross and Greenfield are clearly sympathetic to union claims in health and safety cases. Their conclusions about arbitral value judgments should be viewed in that light. You might find it interesting to look at the texts of some of the decisions they criticize and decide for yourself whether the arbitrators or their critics are correct. (You can find the citations in the published version of the Gross and Greenfield article.)

For example, the electrical-shock case they mention is Bethlehem Mines Corp., 73–2 ARB ¶ 8594 (Jay May, 1974). A car lost power after hitting a bump. An employee received a mild shock, more like static electricity than a high-voltage current. The supervisor ordered the employees to throw a circuit breaker, like the circuit breakers in most homes and offices, to see if power could be restored; if there really was a short, as the grievants feared, the breaker would simply have tripped again. There was no reason to believe that the circuit breaker itself posed any risk. In fact, employees had thrown circuit breakers previously after such power failures without harm. The contract allowed employees concerned about safety to call a union representative on the safety committee to examine the problem, but instead the grievants simply refused the order. The employer therefore disciplined them for insubordination. Federal and state mine safety officials later advised the parties that throwing the switch would not have violated any safety regulation.

The "smoke and dust" case the authors next mention is Bethlehem Mines Corp., 74–2 ARB ¶ 8367 (J. Thomas Rimer, 1974). The employees *assumed* without investigation that there was smoke in their work areas; their supervisor measured the smoke level and found it within legal limits. The arbitrator doubted the grievants' good faith—like the employees in the other *Bethlehem Mines* case, these grievants did not call for a safety committeeman as they could have—and found there was no hazardous condition. He therefore sustained the discipline imposed for insubordination.

In light of those additional facts, how do you view the authors' clear dislike of the *Bethlehem Mines* arbitrator's concerns about possible "chaos" and "anarchy" if each employee could decide what is or is not safe? Are the authors suggesting that every claim of a safety concern, however implausible, should immunize employees from discipline for insubordination? If that is their point, do you agree? Why or why not? If that is not their point, what is?

4. Compare an employer's study of arbitral views on the introduction of new technology. In the article cited at footnote 3, Richard Sibbernsen, a senior vice president at J.I. Case Company, found arbitrators cautiously receptive to managerial efforts to reduce staffing:

> Assuming that no restrictions exist in the language of the labor agreement, the key issue is simply whether the challenged manning reduction is a reasonable exercise of management discretion linked to legitimate operational needs * * *. [T]he critical arbitral question is usually whether the company has good and sufficient reasons to support its decisions. Although certain job eliminations have been deemed appropriate simply as a method of reducing costs, such action is difficult to justify in cases where the work has merely been rearranged and no substantial change in operations has occurred. In one case, the employer

had argued that the classification was eliminated because the duties were no longer being performed. On close inquiry, the arbitrator found that the same duties were in fact being performed by employees in other classifications.

Arbitrators have, however, held job eliminations to be proper where the principal duties or functions of the employees involved have ceased to exist because of the introduction of new equipment, technology, or work methods. In all such cases, management has been able to demonstrate that the jobs were eliminated because of radical changes in circumstances. The arbitral scrutiny focuses on whether the changes in the equipment or working conditions are material.

Repeatedly, automation and the modernization of operations are seen as "good cause" for the elimination of certain jobs. Some arbitrators have, however, denied grievances even in cases where no significant and demonstrable change in operations has occurred.

Of course, it is up to the union to show that any job combination, job elimination, or reduction in crew size is arbitrary, unreasonable, and causative of an undue, unsafe work load for remaining employees. Usually management refutes such allegations by presenting at hearings professional work method evaluations, industrial engineering studies, industry surveys, and supervisory or employee testimony that explain the work loads and the reasonableness of the challenged actions.

5. Just what is the real nature of this dispute? Is it simply that Sibbernsen likes arbitrators' value judgments while Gross and Greenfield do not? Should arbitrators not have *any* value judgments? Is that even conceivable? See Kenneth William Thornicroft, *Arbitrators, Social Values, and the Burden of Proof in Substance Abuse Cases,* 40 Labor Law Journal 582 (1989) (concluding, as if it were hot news, that "the burden of proof determined by arbitrators to apply in substance abuse cases is strongly influenced by societal norms and values").

Recall Justice Cardozo's comment quoted by Saul Wallen earlier in this chapter: "The spirit of the age, as it is revealed to each of us, is too often only the spirit of the group in which the accidents of birth or education or occupation or fellowship have given us a place." What values would "accidents of birth or education or occupation or fellowship" be likely to give to arbitrators? While most arbitrators are well-educated and nearly half are lawyers, a surprisingly high percentage of them have blue-collar origins, have worked in manual or menial jobs, or have been union members. Can the same be said of the likely alternative decision makers federal and state judges?

Or is the authors' point that arbitrators should have *different* value judgments from the rest of society? If so, what value judgments should trump the efficiency criterion spotted by Gross and Greenfield and by Sibbernsen? And why should an arbitrator's idiosyncratic value judgments carry more weight than those of other people? Or do Gross and Greenfield believe that arbitrators should only have value judgments that predispose them to favor unions' arguments?

Professor Gross has addressed some of these questions in his most recent work on the subject, *Incorporating Human Rights Principles into U.S. Labor Arbitration: A Proposal for Fundamental Change* (forthcoming in 8 Employee Rights & Employment Policy Journal). He argues that arbitrators should view "workers' rights" as "human rights" and should therefore apply a "human rights standard rather than a management rights standard" to health and safety cases. This might entail considering internationally-recognized lists of human rights such as the United Nations Universal Declaration of Human Rights, the International Covenant on Cultural and Political Rights, and the International Covenant on Economic, Social and Cultural Rights. Keeping in mind that most collective bargaining agreements limit arbitrators to interpreting and applying the parties' contract, how might you as a union advocate seek to use those international documents? What arguments would you expect to hear in response from the employer's advocate?

6. To the extent that values do influence arbitrators' decisions, are they the arbitrators' values or those of our industrial relations system as embodied in federal labor law? That may be a chicken-or-egg question. Arbitration was already gaining ground when Congress passed the National Labor Relations Act in 1935 and it was firmly established by the time of the Taft–Hartley Act in 1947. At least as interpreted by the Supreme Court in *Lincoln Mills* and the *Trilogy*, Congress intended collective bargaining and labor arbitration to settle labor disputes—in other words, to serve as non-disruptive means of alternative dispute resolution. Moreover, as we have mentioned a few times, arbitration occurs only when both parties choose it as their means of resolving grievances. Against that background, is it fair to point to *arbitrators'* values as if they worked their way unbidden into modern labor relations? For an extended exploration of this and related issues, see James B. Atleson, Values and Assumptions in American Labor Law (1983).

Part 2

INDIVIDUAL EMPLOYMENT ARBITRATION[1]

1. Bibliographic suggestions: Richard A. Bales, *The Laissez-Faire Arbitration Market and the Need for a Uniform Federal Standard Governing Employment and Consumer Arbitration*, 52 Kansas Law Review 583 (2004); Samuel Estreicher, *Saturns for Rickshaws: The Stakes in the Debate Over Predispute Employment Arbitration Agreements*, 16 Ohio State Journal on Dispute Resolution 559 (2001); Elizabeth Hill, *Due Process at Low Cost: An Empirical Study of Employment Arbitration Under the Auspices of the American Arbitration Association*, 18 Ohio State Journal on Dispute Resolution 777, 800 n.93, 818 (2003); Martin H. Malin, *Privatizing Justice—But By How Much? Questions Gilmer Did Not Answer*, 16 Ohio State Journal on Dispute Resolution 589 (2001); Lewis L. Maltby, Employment Arbitration and Workplace Justice, 38 University of San Francisco Law Review 105 (2003); Dennis R. Nolan, *Employment Arbitration After* Circuit City, 41 Brandeis Law Journal 853 (2003).

591

Chapter X

HISTORY AND BACKGROUND

A. INTRODUCTION

As discussed in Chapter I, common law courts were hostile to executory arbitration agreements. However, the Federal Arbitration Act (FAA), enacted in 1925 and re-codified in 1947, requires courts to enforce arbitration agreements related to commerce and maritime transactions. Section 2 of the FAA provides that arbitration agreements "shall be valid, irrevocable and enforceable, save upon such grounds as exist at law or in equity for the revocation of any contract." Section 3 permits a party to an arbitration agreement to obtain a stay of proceedings in federal court when an issue is referable to arbitration. Section 4 authorizes judicial enforcement of arbitration awards and permits a party to obtain an order compelling arbitration when another party has failed, neglected, or refused to comply with an arbitration agreement. Although the FAA thus changed the general common law rule of arbitration, the statute explicitly excluded "contracts of employment of ... workers engaged in foreign or interstate commerce."

Judicial hostility to arbitration remained. For example, in Wilko v. Swan, 346 U.S. 427, 74 S.Ct. 182, 98 L.Ed. 168 (1953), a buyer of securities sued the seller for fraud under Section 12(2) of the Securities Act of 1933. The Court refused to compel the buyer to arbitrate the claim despite the existence of an arbitration clause in the sales contract, holding instead that the arbitration clause was void as an invalid waiver of the substantive law created by the statute. Lower federal courts subsequently interpreted *Wilko* as creating a "public policy" defense to the enforcement of arbitration agreements under the FAA when statutory claims were at issue. See, e.g., American Safety Equip. Corp. v. J.P. Maguire & Co., 391 F.2d 821, 827–28 (2d Cir.1968).

However, as lower federal courts relying on *Wilko* were proclaiming the inferiority of arbitration for resolving statutory claims, the Supreme Court was beginning to signal its approval of arbitration as the preferred mechanism for resolving labor disputes arising under collective bargaining agreements. Beginning in the late 1940s, parties seeking to compel arbitration pursuant to arbitration clauses in collective bargaining agreements increasingly began looking to federal law, both to avoid the common law rule in most states that arbitration agreements were revocable and unenforceable, and in the hope that either the attitude of the federal judiciary or the provisions of the FAA would permit enforcement. In *Textile Workers Union v. Lincoln Mills*, 353 U.S. 448, 458, 77 S.Ct. 912, 1 L.Ed.2d 972 (1957), the Supreme Court held that federal courts have the authority to order specific performance of an arbitration agreement contained in a collective bargaining agreement. Instead of relying on the FAA, however, the Court relied on Section 301 of the Labor–Management Relations Act of 1947 ("LMRA") for this holding. See Chapter III.A.

In the 1960 *Steelworkers* Trilogy, the Court strongly endorsed the use of arbitration as a mechanism for resolving industrial disputes arising under collective bargaining agreements. See *supra* Chapters III.B and III.C. The Court again relied on Section 301 of the LMRA rather than the FAA. The Court did not overrule *Wilko*, but distinguished it on the basis that cases arising in the labor context were unique. In United Steelworkers of America v. Enterprise Wheel & Car Corp., 363 U.S. 593, 80 S.Ct. 1358, 4 L.Ed.2d 1424 (1960), the Court discouraged arbitrators from deciding issues of law by stating that an arbitrator's authority derives exclusively from the underlying collective bargaining agreement, and that if an arbitrator strayed from this authority by, for example, relying solely on external law, the resulting arbitral award could be vacated.

Four years later, Congress enacted Title VII, which prohibited employment discrimination on the basis of race, color, religion, sex, and national origin. This statute was followed by a slew of similar statutes that prohibited employment discrimination on the basis of age, pregnancy, and disability. State legislatures followed suit. State courts began to use contract and tort doctrines to soften the common law rule of employment-at-will. This explosion in employment rights was accompanied by a dramatic increase in litigated employment claims. See Clyde W. Summers, *Labor Law as the Century Turns: A Changing of the Guard*, 67 Nebraska Law Review 7 (1988) (noting that the principal source of worker protection was shifting from contractual rights negotiated through collective bargaining agreements to law-created individual employment rights).

The Supreme Court's distinction of *Wilko* and its reliance on Section 301 created a dichotomy in which collective bargaining issues were arbitrable but statutory issues were not. This dichotomy was challenged by the 1974 case of *Alexander v. Gardner–Denver Co.*, 415 U.S. 36, 94 S.Ct. 1011, 39 L.Ed.2d 147 (1974), which presented the issue of whether an employee's arbitration of a just-cause claim under a collective bargaining agreement foreclosed subsequent litigation of a statutory discrimination claim based on the same facts. In holding it did not, the Court denigrated arbitration as a forum for the resolution of statutory employment claims, citing the informality of arbitral procedures, the lack of labor arbitrators' expertise on issues of substantive law, and the absence of written opinions. *Gardner-Denver*, therefore, seemed to confirm the dichotomy between arbitrable collective bargaining issues and non-arbitrable statutory issues. Following this reasoning, several lower courts ruled that arbitration clauses contained in individual employment contracts, instead of in collective bargaining agreements, would not preclude subsequent suits under anti-discrimination laws. See, e.g., Utley v. Goldman Sachs & Co., 883 F.2d 184, 187 (1st Cir.1989).

The next major series of arbitration cases was the *Mitsubishi* Trilogy, decided between 1985 and 1989. In these cases, the Court enforced arbitration agreements covering antitrust, securities, and racketeering laws; and explicitly overruled *Wilko*. Rodriguez de Quijas v. Shearson/American Express, Inc., 490 U.S. 477, 479, 486, 109 S.Ct. 1917, 104 L.Ed.2d 526 (1989); Shearson/American Express, Inc. v. McMahon, 482 U.S. 220, 238, 242, 107 S.Ct. 2332, 96 L.Ed.2d 185 (1987); Mitsubishi Motors Corp. v. Soler Chrysler–Plymouth, Inc., 473 U.S. 614, 616, 640, 105 S.Ct. 3346, 87 L.Ed.2d 444 (1985). In doing so, the Court declared that "we are well past the time when judicial suspicion of the desirability of arbitration and of the competence of arbitral tribunals inhibited the development of arbitration as an alternative means of dispute resolution." *Mitsubishi*, 473 U.S. at 626–27, 105 S.Ct. at 3354, 87 L.Ed. at 451. The Court also interpreted the FAA as creating a presumption of arbitrability when the issue is whether arbitration is permitted under a particular statute: where a party to an arbitration agreement attempts to enforce the agreement as a defense against the other party's attempt to litigate a statutory claim, the statutory claim will be presumed arbitrable absent explicit evidence that Congress intended to preclude arbitration under the statute. *Id.* However, in a subsequent case, the Court held that this presumption does not apply when the issue is whether the parties have contractually agreed to arbitrate a particular claim. First Options of Chicago, Inc. v. Kaplan, 514 U.S. 938, 115 S.Ct. 1920, 131 L.Ed.2d 985 (1995).

Employers, concerned with the volume and cost of litigating individual employment rights, began to consider arbitration as an alternative to litigation. This was particularly true in the securities industry, where a standard-form arbitration clause originally intended primarily to cover broker-dealer disputes was increasingly invoked in disputes involving statutory employment rights such as discrimination claims. This trend began, slowly at first, to spread outside the securities industry, and arbitration provisions began to appear in employment agreements and employment handbooks. Attorneys representing employees challenged these arbitration provisions on the grounds that employment contracts fall within the FAA statutory exclusion and that compelled arbitration of statutory employment claims would be antithetical to the purposes of the underlying statutes. Arbitration agreements also were challenged on grounds that they were unconscionable, that they were adhesion contracts based on unequal bargaining power, and that specific procedures prescribed by the agreements were fundamentally unfair.

In the 1991 decision of *Gilmer v. Interstate/Johnson Lane Corporation*,[1] 500 U.S. 20, 111 S.Ct. 1647, 114 L.Ed.2d 26 (1991), the Supreme Court held for the first time that an employer could require a non-union employee to arbitrate rather than litigate a federal age discrimination claim pursuant to a predispute arbitration agreement that the employee had been required to sign as a condition of employment. The *Gilmer* Court stated that objections of unconscionability and procedural unfairness must be addressed on a case-by-case basis and that procedural differences between arbitration and litigation do not make arbitration fundamentally unfair. The Court declined to resolve the issue of whether the FAA applied to employment contracts, finding that the arbitration contract in that case was not an employment contract. This issue was resolved in a later case, *Circuit City Stores, Inc. v. Adams*, 532 U.S. 105, 121 S.Ct. 1302, 149 L.Ed.2d 234 (2001), in which the Court held that the FAA's exclusionary clause applies only to those workers directly engaged in foreign or interstate commerce such as railroad employees and truck drivers.

According to one commentator, *Gilmer* precipitated a "stampede" by employers to draft agreements with their employees requiring submission of employment disputes to binding arbitration.[2] Commentators in the popular press and in various trade journals quickly concluded that employment arbitration was becoming "the cornerstone of national labor policy," "an idea whose time has come," and that compulsory arbitration was "here to stay" as a method of resolving employment disputes.[3]

Many of the arbitration agreements imposed by employers immediately following *Gilmer* required employees to relinquish important employment rights. One employer, for example, required its employees, as a condition of employment, to sign an agreement providing that all employment claims would be arbitrated; that the employee's total remedy would be limited to the lesser of actual lost wages, six months' wages, or reinstatement; and that the arbitration would occur with no opportunity for the employee to conduct discovery.[4] Employer-sponsored "agreements" like this have sparked an intense debate—in recent judicial opinions, in the academic community, and in the popular press—about whether employment arbitration should be encouraged, or whether it should be banned as an unjustified encroachment on employees' rights. These unfair agreements also provoked an absolutist opposition to employment arbitration by plaintiffs' attorneys, and precipitated a large number of judicial decisions in which judges refused to enforce agreements containing provisions patently unfair to employees.

---

1. See *infra* Chapter X.B.

2. William M. Howard, *Arbitrating Employment Discrimination Claims: Do You Really Have To? Do You Really Want To?* 43 Drake Law Review 255, 255 (1994).

3. See, e.g., Ronald Turner, *Compulsory Arbitration of Employment Discrimination* *Claims with Special Reference to the 3 A's— Access, Adjudication and Acceptability*, 31 Wake Forest Law Review 231, 294 (1996).

4. Pony Express Courier Corp. v. Morris, 921 S.W.2d 817, 819 (Tex.App.—San Antonio 1996, n.w.h.).

Structurally, employment arbitration is similar to labor arbitration. Like labor arbitration, the arbitration hearing usually occurs in a conference room, lasts only a day or two, and is relatively informal compared to litigation. Both sides usually are represented by counsel, though the company often will agree not to use counsel at the hearing if the employee agrees to the same. The parties present their own witnesses and cross-examine opposing witnesses. Procedural and evidentiary rules are relaxed. Judicial review is extremely limited. Arbitrators are jointly selected by the parties, usually from lists supplied by an arbitration service such as the American Arbitration Association. (The AAA rules for employment arbitration are reproduced in Appendix C to this Book.) Almost all employment arbitrators are lawyers; some double as labor arbitrators. Like labor arbitration, employment arbitration is much faster than litigation; absent the necessity of a lawsuit to compel arbitration, employment arbitration usually is completed within a matter of months.

Although employment arbitration appears superficially very similar to labor arbitration, there are a few critical differences. One is the absence of a union. The arbitration agreement and the arbitration rules, instead of being the product of joint negotiation between the employer and a union, are promulgated unilaterally by the employer. Employees often are "offered" arbitration agreements on a "sign-it-or-be-fired (or not hired)" basis. Similarly, whereas a unionized grievant has the aid of a union representative or attorney throughout the grievance process and at the arbitration hearing, the plaintiff in an employment arbitration case must either find an attorney or go it alone.

Another major difference is the role of external law. In labor arbitration, an arbitrator who bases an award solely on external law exceeds the scope of the arbitrator's authority, and the award is unenforceable. In employment arbitration, the parties expressly contract for the arbitration of disputes concerning external law.

In 1995, representatives of the American Bar Association, the Society of Professionals in Dispute Resolution, the National Academy of Arbitrators, the Federal Mediation and Conciliation Service, the National Employment Lawyers' Association, the American Civil Liberties Union, and the International Ladies Garment Workers' Union drafted the Due Process Protocol for Mediation and Arbitration of Statutory Arbitration Disputes. See 9A Lab.Rel.Rep. (BNA) No. 142, at 534:401 (May 9, 1995). This Protocol, which is reproduced as Appendix E to this Book, set minimum procedural safeguards for inclusion in all employment arbitration agreements. For example, participants agreed that employment arbitrators ought to be qualified to decide statutory disputes, that employees should have a right to counsel in arbitration proceedings, and that arbitrators should be empowered to award the full panoply of damages permitted by law. However, participants could not reach consensus on whether employers should be permitted to require employees to sign predispute agreements to arbitrate statutory employment claims as a condition of employment. As will be seen, the Due Process Protocol has been extremely influential. See Margaret M. Harding, *The Limits of the Due Process Protocols*, 19 Ohio State Journal on Dispute Resolution 369 (2004).

This chapter begins with an examination of *Gilmer* and its antecedents. Chapter XI then analyzes some of the issues that lower courts have had to grapple with in applying *Gilmer*. These issues include the allocation of arbitration fees between employers and employees, the determination of whether arbitral procedures are sufficiently fair to warrant judicial enforcement of the underlying arbitration agreements, the use of external law, and the availability (and scope) of discovery and judicial review. Chapter XII examines several employment arbitration cases in detail. Chapter XII concludes this Part by considering the arguments both for and against compulsory arbitration as an employment dispute resolution process.

B.   THE LEGAL BACKGROUND

GILMER v. INTERSTATE/JOHNSON LANE CORPORATION

Supreme Court of the United States, 1991.
500 U.S. 20, 111 S.Ct. 1647, 114 L.Ed.2d 26.

JUSTICE WHITE delivered the opinion of the Court.

The question presented in this case is whether a claim under the Age Discrimination in Employment Act of 1967 (ADEA), can be subjected to compulsory arbitration pursuant to an arbitration agreement in a securities registration application. * * *

I.

Respondent Interstate/Johnson Lane Corporation (Interstate) hired petitioner Robert Gilmer as a Manager of Financial Services in May 1981. As required by his employment, Gilmer registered as a securities representative with several stock exchanges, including the New York Stock Exchange (NYSE). [The NYSE registration application provided that Gilmer "agree[d] to arbitrate any dispute, claim or controversy," including employment disputes, arising between him and Interstate.] * * *

Interstate terminated Gilmer's employment in 1987, at which time Gilmer was 62 years of age. [Gilmer sued Interstate in federal court for age discrimination. Interstate responded by filing a motion to compel arbitration. The District Court, relying on *Gardner-Denver*, denied the motion. The Fourth Circuit reversed.]

II.

The FAA [Federal Arbitration Act] was originally enacted in 1925, 43 Stat. 883, and then reenacted and codified in 1947 as Title 9 of the United States Code. Its purpose was to reverse the longstanding judicial hostility to arbitration agreements that had existed at English common law and had been adopted by American courts, and to place arbitration agreements upon the same footing as other contracts. Its primary substantive provision states that "[a] written provision in any maritime transaction or a contract evidencing a transaction involving commerce to settle by arbitration a controversy thereafter arising out of such contract or transaction * * * shall be valid, irrevocable, and enforceable, save upon such grounds as exist at law or in equity for the revocation of any contract." 9 U.S.C. § 2. The FAA also provides for stays of proceedings in federal district courts when an issue in the proceeding is referable to arbitration, § 3, and for orders compelling arbitration when one party has failed, neglected, or refused to comply with an arbitration agreement, § 4. These provisions manifest a "liberal federal policy favoring arbitration agreements." *Moses H. Cone Memorial Hospital v. Mercury Construction Corp.*, 460 U.S. 1, 24, 103 S.Ct. 927, 941, 74 L.Ed.2d 765 (1983).[2]

It is by now clear that statutory claims may be the subject of an arbitration agreement, enforceable pursuant to the FAA. Indeed, in recent years we have held enforceable arbitration agreements relating to claims arising under the Sherman Act, 15 U.S.C. §§ 1–7; § 10(b) of the Securities Exchange Act of 1934, 15 U.S.C. § 78j(b); the civil provisions of the Racketeer Influenced and Corrupt Organizations Act (RICO), 18 U.S.C. § 1961 *et seq.*; and § 12(2) of the Securities Act of 1933, 15 U.S.C. § 77l(2). In these cases we recognized that "[b]y agreeing to arbitrate a statutory claim, a party does not forgo the substantive rights afforded by the statute; it only submits to their resolution in an arbitral, rather than a judicial, forum." Mitsubishi [Motors Corp. v. Soler Chrysler–Plymouth, Inc., 473 U.S. 614, 628, 105 S.Ct. 3346, 3354 87 L.Ed.2d 444 (1985)].

Although all statutory claims may not be appropriate for arbitration, "[h]aving made the bargain to arbitrate, the party should be held to it unless Congress itself has evinced an intention to preclude a waiver of judicial remedies for the statutory rights at issue." *Ibid.* In this regard, we note that the burden is on Gilmer to show that Congress intended to

---

2. Section 1 of the FAA provides that "nothing herein contained shall apply to contracts of employment of seamen, railroad employees, or any other class of workers engaged in foreign or interstate commerce." 9 U.S.C. § 1. Several *amici curiae* in support of Gilmer argue that that section excludes from the coverage of the FAA all "contracts of employment." Gilmer, however, did not raise the issue in the courts below, it was not addressed there, and it was not among the questions presented in the petition for certiorari. In any event, it would be inappropriate to address the scope of the § 1 exclusion because the arbitration clause being enforced here is not contained in a contract of employment. * * * The record before us does not show, and the parties do not contend, that Gilmer's em-

ployment agreement with Interstate contained a written arbitration clause. Rather, the arbitration clause at issue is in Gilmer's securities registration application, which is a contract with the securities exchanges, not with Interstate. The lower courts addressing the issue uniformly have concluded that the exclusionary clause of § 1 of the FAA is inapplicable to arbitration clauses contained in such registration applications. * * * Unlike the dissent, see *post*, at 1659–1660, we choose to follow the plain language of the FAA and the weight of authority, and we therefore hold that § 1's exclusionary clause does not apply to Gilmer's arbitration agreement. Consequently, we leave for another day the issue raised by *amici curiae*.

preclude a waiver of a judicial forum for ADEA claims. If such an intention exists, it will be discoverable in the text of the ADEA, its legislative history, or an "inherent conflict" between arbitration and the ADEA's underlying purposes. Throughout such an inquiry, it should be kept in mind that "questions of arbitrability must be addressed with a healthy regard for the federal policy favoring arbitration." *Moses H. Cone, supra,* 460 U.S. at 24, 103 S.Ct. at 941.

III.

Gilmer concedes that nothing in the text of the ADEA or its legislative history explicitly precludes arbitration. He argues, however, that compulsory arbitration of ADEA claims pursuant to arbitration agreements would be inconsistent with the statutory framework and purposes of the ADEA. Like the Court of Appeals, we disagree.

A.

Congress enacted the ADEA in 1967 "to promote employment of older persons based on their ability rather than age; to prohibit arbitrary age discrimination in employment; [and] to help employers and workers find ways of meeting problems arising from the impact of age on employment." 29 U.S.C. § 621(b). To achieve those goals, the ADEA, among other things, makes it unlawful for an employer "to fail or refuse to hire or to discharge any individual or otherwise discriminate against any individual with respect to his compensation, terms, conditions, or privileges of employment, because of such individual's age." § 623(a)(1). This proscription is enforced both by private suits and by the EEOC. * * *

As Gilmer contends, the ADEA is designed not only to address individual grievances, but also to further important social policies. We do not perceive any inherent inconsistency between those policies, however, and enforcing agreements to arbitrate age discrimination claims. It is true that arbitration focuses on specific disputes between the parties involved. The same can be said, however, of judicial resolution of claims. Both of these dispute resolution mechanisms nevertheless also can further broader social purposes. The Sherman Act, the Securities Exchange Act of 1934, RICO, and the Securities Act of 1933 all are designed to advance important public policies, but, as noted above, claims under those statutes are appropriate for arbitration. "[S]o long as the prospective litigant effectively may vindicate [his or her] statutory cause of action in the arbitral forum, the statute will continue to serve both its remedial and deterrent function." *Mitsubishi, supra,* 473 U. S., at 637, 105 S.Ct. at 3359.

We also are unpersuaded by the argument that arbitration will undermine the role of the EEOC in enforcing the ADEA. An individual ADEA claimant subject to an arbitration agreement will still be free to file a charge with the EEOC, even though the claimant is not able to institute a private judicial action. Indeed, Gilmer filed a charge with the EEOC in this case. In any event, the EEOC's role in combating age discrimination is not dependent on the filing of a charge; the agency may receive information concerning alleged violations of the ADEA "from any source," and it has independent authority to investigate age discrimination. Moreover, nothing in the ADEA indicates that Congress intended that the EEOC be involved in all employment disputes. Such disputes can be settled, for example, without any EEOC involvement. * * * Finally, the mere involvement of an administrative agency in the enforcement of a statute is not sufficient to preclude arbitration. For example, the Securities Exchange Commission is heavily involved in the enforcement of the Securities Exchange Act of 1934 and the Securities Act of 1933, but we have held that claims under both of those statutes may be subject to compulsory arbitration.

Gilmer also argues that compulsory arbitration is improper because it deprives claimants of the judicial forum provided for by the ADEA. Congress, however, did not explicitly preclude arbitration or other nonjudicial resolution of claims, even in its recent amendments to the ADEA. "[I]f Congress intended the substantive protection afforded [by the ADEA] to include protection against waiver of the right to a judicial forum, that intention will be deducible from text or legislative history." *Mitsubishi*, 473 U.S. at 628, 105 S.Ct. at 3354. Moreover, Gilmer's argument ignores the ADEA's flexible approach to resolution of claims. The EEOC, for example, is directed to pursue "informal methods of conciliation, conference, and persuasion," 29 U.S.C. § 626(b), which suggests that out-of-court dispute resolution, such as arbitration, is consistent with the statutory scheme established by Congress. In addition, arbitration is consistent with Congress' grant of concurrent jurisdiction over ADEA claims to state and federal courts, see 29 U.S.C. § 626(c)(1) (allowing suits to be brought "in any court of competent jurisdiction"), because arbitration agreements, "like the provision for concurrent jurisdiction, serve to advance the objective of allowing [claimants] a broader right to select the forum for resolving disputes, whether it be judicial or otherwise." Rodriguez de Quijas [v. Shearson/American Express, Inc., 490 U.S. 477, 483, 109 S.Ct. 1917, 1921, 104 L.Ed.2d 526 (1989)].

B.

In arguing that arbitration is inconsistent with the ADEA, Gilmer also raises a host of challenges to the adequacy of arbitration procedures. Initially, we note that in our recent arbitration cases we have already rejected most of these arguments as insufficient to preclude arbitration of statutory claims. Such generalized attacks on arbitration "res[t] on suspicion of arbitration as a method of weakening the protections afforded in the substantive law to would-be complainants," and as such, they are "far out of step with our current strong endorsement of the federal statutes favoring this method of resolving disputes." *Rodriguez de Quijas, supra*, at 481, 109 S.Ct. at 1920. Consequently, we address these arguments only briefly.

Gilmer first speculates that arbitration panels will be biased. However, "[w]e decline to indulge the presumption that the parties and arbitral body conducting a proceeding will be unable or unwilling to retain competent, conscientious and impartial arbitrators." *Mitsubishi, supra,* 473 U.S. at 634, 105 S.Ct. at 3357–3358. In any event, we note that the NYSE arbitration rules, which are applicable to the dispute in this case, provide protections against biased panels. The rules require, for example, that the parties be informed of the employment histories of the arbitrators, and that they be allowed to make further inquiries into the arbitrators' backgrounds. In addition, each party is allowed one peremptory challenge and unlimited challenges for cause. Moreover, the arbitrators are required to disclose "any circumstances which might preclude [them] from rendering an objective and impartial determination." The FAA also protects against bias, by providing that courts may overturn arbitration decisions "[w]here there was evident partiality or corruption in the arbitrators." 9 U.S.C. § 10(b). There has been no showing in this case that those provisions are inadequate to guard against potential bias.

Gilmer also complains that the discovery allowed in arbitration is more limited than in the federal courts, which he contends will make it difficult to prove discrimination. It is unlikely, however, that age discrimination claims require more extensive discovery than other claims that we have found to be arbitrable, such as RICO and antitrust claims. Moreover, there has been no showing in this case that the NYSE discovery provisions, which allow for document production, information requests, depositions, and subpoenas * * *, will prove insufficient to allow ADEA claimants such as Gilmer a fair opportunity to present their claims. Although those procedures might not be as extensive as in the federal courts, by agreeing to arbitrate, a party "trades the procedures and opportunity for review of the courtroom for the simplicity, informality, and expedition of arbitration." *Mitsubishi, supra,* at 628, 105 S.Ct. at 3354. Indeed, an important counterweight to the reduced discovery in NYSE arbitration is that arbitrators are not bound by the rules of evidence.

A further alleged deficiency of arbitration is that arbitrators often will not issue written opinions, resulting, Gilmer contends, in a lack of public knowledge of employers' discriminatory policies, an inability to obtain effective appellate review, and a stifling of the development of the law. The NYSE rules, however, do require that all arbitration awards be in writing, and that the awards contain the names of the parties, a summary of the issues in controversy, and a description of the award issued. * * * In addition, the award decisions are made available to the public. * * * Furthermore, judicial decisions addressing ADEA claims will continue to be issued because it is unlikely that all or even most

ADEA claimants will be subject to arbitration agreements. Finally, Gilmer's concerns apply equally to settlements of ADEA claims, which, as noted above, are clearly allowed.[4]

It is also argued that arbitration procedures cannot adequately further the purposes of the ADEA because they do not provide for broad equitable relief and class actions. As the court below noted, however, arbitrators do have the power to fashion equitable relief. 895 F.2d, at 199–200. Indeed, the NYSE rules applicable here do not restrict the types of relief an arbitrator may award, but merely refer to "damages and/or other relief." * * * The NYSE rules also provide for collective proceedings. * * * But "even if the arbitration could not go forward as a class action or class relief could not be granted by the arbitrator, the fact that the [ADEA] provides for the possibility of bringing a collective action does not mean that individual attempts at conciliation were intended to be barred." *Nicholson v. CPC Int'l Inc.*, 877 F.2d 221, 241 (3d Cir.1989) (Becker, J., dissenting). Finally, it should be remembered that arbitration agreements will not preclude the EEOC from bringing actions seeking class-wide and equitable relief.

C.

An additional reason advanced by Gilmer for refusing to enforce arbitration agreements relating to ADEA claims is his contention that there often will be unequal bargaining power between employers and employees. Mere inequality in bargaining power, however, is not a sufficient reason to hold that arbitration agreements are never enforceable in the employment context. Relationships between securities dealers and investors, for example, may involve unequal bargaining power, but we nevertheless held in *Rodriguez de Quijas* and *McMahon* that agreements to arbitrate in that context are enforceable. As discussed above, the FAA's purpose was to place arbitration agreements on the same footing as other contracts. Thus, arbitration agreements are enforceable "save upon such grounds as exist at law or in equity for the revocation of any contract." 9 U.S.C. § 2. "Of course, courts should remain attuned to well-supported claims that the agreement to arbitrate resulted from the sort of fraud or overwhelming economic power that would provide grounds 'for the revocation of any contract.' "*Mitsubishi*, 473 U.S. at 627, 105 S.Ct. at 3354. There is no indication in this case, however, that Gilmer, an experienced businessman, was coerced or defrauded into agreeing to the arbitration clause in his registration application. As with the claimed procedural inadequacies discussed above, this claim of unequal bargaining power is best left for resolution in specific cases.

IV.

In addition to the arguments discussed above, Gilmer vigorously asserts that our decision in *Alexander v. Gardner–Denver Co.* and its

---

4. Gilmer also contends that judicial review of arbitration decisions is too limited. We have stated, however, that "although judicial scrutiny of arbitration awards necessarily is limited, such review is sufficient to ensure that arbitrators comply with the requirements of the statute" at issue. *Shearson/American Express Inc. v. McMahon*, 482 U.S. 220, 232, 107 S.Ct. 2332, 2340, 96 L.Ed.2d 185 (1987).

progeny * * * preclude arbitration of employment discrimination claims. Gilmer's reliance on these cases, however, is misplaced.

In *Gardner-Denver*, the issue was whether a discharged employee whose grievance had been arbitrated pursuant to an arbitration clause in a collective-bargaining agreement was precluded from subsequently bringing a Title VII action based upon the conduct that was the subject of the grievance. In holding that the employee was not foreclosed from bringing the Title VII claim, we stressed that an employee's contractual rights under a collective-bargaining agreement are distinct from the employee's statutory Title VII rights:

> In submitting his grievance to arbitration, an employee seeks to vindicate his contractual right under a collective-bargaining agreement. By contrast, in filing a lawsuit under Title VII, an employee asserts independent statutory rights accorded by Congress. The distinctly separate nature of these contractual and statutory rights is not vitiated merely because both were violated as a result of the same factual occurrence. 415 U.S. at 49–50, 94 S.Ct. at 1020.

We also noted that a labor arbitrator has authority only to resolve questions of contractual rights. The arbitrator's "task is to effectuate the intent of the parties" and he or she does not have the "general authority to invoke public laws that conflict with the bargain between the parties." By contrast, "in instituting an action under Title VII, the employee is not seeking review of the arbitrator's decision. Rather, he is asserting a statutory right independent of the arbitration process." We further expressed concern that in collective-bargaining arbitration "the interests of the individual employee may be subordinated to the collective interests of all employees in the bargaining unit."[5]

* * *

There are several important distinctions between the *Gardner-Denver* line of cases and the case before us. First, those cases did not involve the issue of the enforceability of an agreement to arbitrate statutory claims. Rather, they involved the quite different issue whether arbitration of contract-based claims precluded subsequent judicial resolution of statutory claims. Since the employees there had not agreed to arbitrate their statutory claims, and the labor arbitrators were not authorized to resolve such claims, the arbitration in those cases understandably was held not to preclude subsequent statutory actions. Second, because the arbitration in those cases occurred in the context of a collective-bargaining agreement, the claimants there were represented by their unions in the arbitration proceedings. An important concern therefore was the tension between collective representation and individ-

---

5. The Court in *Alexander v. Gardner–Denver Co.* also expressed the view that arbitration was inferior to the judicial process for resolving statutory claims. That "mistrust of the arbitral process," however, has been undermined by our recent arbitration decisions. *McMahon*, 482 U.S. at 231– 232, 107 S.Ct. at 2340. "[W]e are well past the time when judicial suspicion of the desirability of arbitration and of the competence of arbitral tribunals inhibited the development of arbitration as an alternative means of dispute resolution." Mitsubishi, 473 U.S. at 626–7, 105 S.Ct. At 3354.

ual statutory rights, a concern not applicable to the present case. Finally, those cases were not decided under the FAA, which, as discussed above, reflects a "liberal federal policy favoring arbitration agreements." *Mitsubishi*, 473 U.S. at 625, 105 S.Ct. at 3353. Therefore, those cases provide no basis for refusing to enforce Gilmer's agreement to arbitrate his ADEA claim.

V.

We conclude that Gilmer has not met his burden of showing that Congress, in enacting the ADEA, intended to preclude arbitration of claims under that Act. Accordingly, the judgment of the Court of Appeals is

Affirmed.

JUSTICE STEVENS, with whom JUSTICE MARSHALL joins, dissenting.

Section 1 of the Federal Arbitration Act (FAA) states:

> [N]othing herein contained shall apply to contracts of employment of seamen, railroad employees, or any other class of workers engaged in foreign or interstate commerce. 9 U.S.C. § 1.

The Court today, in holding that the FAA compels enforcement of arbitration clauses even when claims of age discrimination are at issue, skirts the antecedent question whether the coverage of the Act even extends to arbitration clauses contained in employment contracts, regardless of the subject matter of the claim at issue. In my opinion, arbitration clauses contained in employment agreements are specifically exempt from coverage of the FAA, and for that reason respondent Interstate/Johnson Lane Corporation cannot, pursuant to the FAA, compel petitioner to submit his claims arising under the Age Discrimination in Employment Act of 1967 (ADEA), 29 U.S.C. § 621 *et seq.*, to binding arbitration.

* * *

Notes and Questions

1. Strictly speaking, the holding in *Gilmer* applies only to statutory claims brought under the federal Age Discrimination in Employment Act. Since *Gilmer*, however, the lower federal courts have compelled arbitration of claims arising under virtually all federal employment statutes, state employment statutes, and state common law doctrines. See, e.g., EEOC v. Luce, Forward, Hamilton & Scripps, 345 F.3d 742 (9th Cir.2003) (Title VII of the Civil Rights Act of 1964); Singletary v. Enersys, Inc., 57 Fed.Appx. 161 (4th Cir.2003) (ADA and FMLA); Carter v. Countrywide Credit Industries, Inc., 362 F.3d 294 (5th Cir. 2004) (FLSA); Willis v. Dean Witter Reynolds, Inc., 948 F.2d 305, 308 (6th Cir.1991) (Kentucky statute prohibiting gender discrimination); Bender v. A.G. Edwards & Sons, Inc., 971 F.2d 698, 699 (11th Cir.1992) (common law claims of battery, intentional infliction of emotional distress, and negligent retention). Moreover, the FAA applies in state courts as well as federal courts. Moses H. Cone Memorial Hospital v.

Mercury Construction Corp., 460 U.S. 1, 24, 103 S.Ct. 927, 74 L.Ed.2d 765 (1983).

2. Does *Gilmer* effectively overrule *Gardner-Denver*, or are the cases distinguishable?

In Austin v. Owens–Brockway Glass Container, Inc., 78 F.3d 875, 881–82 (4th Cir.1996), an employee covered by a collective bargaining agreement containing both a nondiscrimination clause and an arbitration clause filed a lawsuit under the Americans with Disabilities Act. A divided panel of the Fourth Circuit held that the employee was bound by the arbitration clause and therefore precluded from litigating her claims. The court explained that "*Gilmer* thus rejects the principal concern in * * * *Gardner-Denver* * * *, that arbitration is an 'inappropriate forum' for the resolution of Title VII statutory rights."

Other circuits, however, have disagreed. In Pryner v. Tractor Supply Co., 109 F.3d 354, 365 (7th Cir.1997), Chief Judge Richard Posner of the Seventh Circuit stated:

> [W]e are timid about declaring decisions by the Supreme Court overruled when the Court has not said so. The conservative reading of Gilmer [sic] is that it just pruned some dicta from [*Gardner-Denver*]— and it certainly cannot be taken to hold that collective bargaining agreements can compel the arbitration of statutory rights. That issue was not before the Court or discussed by it.

See also Brisentine v. Stone & Webster Engineering Corp., 117 F.3d 519, 523 (11th Cir.1997) ("Distinguishing a prior precedent that is being overruled would make as much sense as pruning a plant that is being dug up and discarded. If the Supreme Court in *Gilmer* had intended to cast *Alexander* upon the judicial mulch heap, it would not have bothered to prune back that decision.").

When the Supreme Court granted certiorari on a subsequent Fourth Circuit case similar to *Austin*, most commentators assumed the Court would summarily reverse. Instead, the Court unanimously held that the arbitration clause at issue did not waive the right to a file discrimination suit because the clause was general and did "not contain a clear and unmistakable waiver of the covered employees' rights to a judicial forum for federal claims of employment discrimination." The Court expressly reserved the question of whether a clear and unmistakable collective waiver in a collective bargaining agreement would be effective. Wright v. Universal Maritime Serv. Corp., 525 U.S. 70, 119 S.Ct. 391, 142 L.Ed.2d 361 (1998). The Fourth Circuit quickly stepped through the door the Supreme Court had left open and, in Safrit v. Cone Mills Corp., 248 F.3d 306 (4th Cir.2001), interpreted a relatively routine labor arbitration clause as constituting a clear and unmistakable waiver of the employee's right to sue under Title VII for sex discrimination. Again, the Court dodged the issue. See 534 U.S. 995, 122 S.Ct. 464, 151 L.Ed.2d 381 (2001) (denying certiorari). But see Eastern Associated Coal Corp. v. Massey, 373 F.3d 530, 536–37 (4th Cir.2004) (holding that a collective bargaining agreement that required arbitration of claims arising under the federal Americans with Disabilities Act did not clearly and unmistakably require arbitration of claims arising under a parallel state statute).

(a) Is there a middle ground? One possibility is a "rebuttable presumption" standard—i.e., courts will presume that arbitration clauses found in collective bargaining agreements do not extend to statutory claims, but this presumption can be rebutted if explicit language in the collective bargaining agreement provides otherwise. What do you think of this approach? Should a union attorney seek to include such a waiver in a collective bargaining agreement, or resist an employer's effort to include one? Would a union attorney risk violating the duty of fair representation by proposing or agreeing to such a waiver?

(b) Assume the Supreme Court ultimately follows *Gardner-Denver* and holds that a union lacks the power to waive its members' rights to sue in federal court. Such a clause then would be a non-mandatory, and perhaps a prohibited, subject of bargaining. If so, the employer would be free to approach employees individually and demand individual waivers. Thus, the employer could impose unilaterally what the union could not grant, negotiate about, or strike to prevent. See Dennis R. Nolan, *Employment Arbitration After* Circuit City, 41 Brandeis Law Journal 853, 862–63 (2003); see also Air Line Pilots Ass'n, Int'l v. Northwest Airlines, Inc., 211 F.3d 1312 (D.C. Cir.2000) (per curiam en banc), cert. denied, 531 U.S. 1011, 121 S.Ct. 565, 148 L.Ed.2d 484 (2000), reinstating 199 F.3d 477 (D.C. Cir.1999) (in case arising under the Railway Labor Act, a union may not lawfully agree to binding arbitration of employees' discrimination claims, and such an arbitration clause therefore is not a mandatory subject of bargaining); see also Ann C. Hodges, *Arbitration of Statutory Claims in the Unionized Workplace: Is Bargaining with the Union Required?*, 16 Ohio State Journal on Dispute Resolution 513 (2001) (arguing that although employment arbitration is not a mandatory subject of bargaining under the National Labor Relations Act, employers nonetheless should not be permitted to impose statutory arbitration on employees individually); Ann C. Hodges, *Can Compulsory Arbitration Be Reconciled with Section 7 Rights?*, 38 Wake Forest Law Review 173 (2003) (arguing that arbitration agreements imposed on employees as a condition of employment violate Section 7 of the NLRA by requiring employees to waive their right to engage in the concerted activity of filing a judicial claim for enforcement of statutory or contractual rights); Theodore J. St. Antoine, Gilmer *in the Collective Bargaining Context*, 16 Ohio State Journal on Dispute Resolution 491 (2001) (arguing that unions should be free to make arbitration the exclusive forum for vindicating statutory rights).

(c) What happens if the remedy an employee seeks in litigation conflicts with the provisions of a collective bargaining agreement? In Brown v. Illinois Central Railroad Co., 254 F.3d 654 (7th Cir.), cert. denied, 534 U.S. 1041, 122 S.Ct. 616, 151 L.Ed.2d 539 (2001), the railroad disqualified an employee as a trainman because the employee's medical restrictions prevented him from being on call seven days a week. The employee sued, arguing that the ADA required the railroad to accommodate his disability by awarding him the job with a reduced work schedule. The Seventh Circuit dismissed the suit because the reduced work schedule conflicted with the seniority provision in the employee's collective bargaining agreement.

3. In June 1998, the Securities and Exchange Commission voted to permit the securities exchanges such as the NYSE to amend their U–4 forms (the registration forms, signed by employees, that contain the arbitration

provision) to exclude employment discrimination claims (though not other employment disputes) from the types of claims that must be arbitrated. Both the NYSE and the NASD have amended their U–4 forms accordingly. See 64 Federal Register 30081 (1999).

4.   What does the *Gilmer* Court mean when it says that "an important counterweight to the reduced discovery in NYSE arbitration is that arbitrators are not bound by the rules of evidence"?

5.   Section 3 of the FAA requires courts to stay judicial proceedings for "any issue referable to arbitration under an agreement in writing." Courts have consistently held that while the FAA "requires a writing, it does not require that the writing be signed by the parties." See, e.g., Tinder v. Pinkerton Security, 305 F.3d 728 (7th Cir.2002). Thus, it is usually sufficient for the party seeking to compel arbitration to show that the other party received a written copy of the arbitration agreement.

6.   The Seventh Amendment provides that "in Suits at common law, where the value in controversy shall exceed twenty dollars, the right of trial by jury shall be preserved...." This right may be waived, but courts generally require that the waiver be knowing and voluntary. See, e.g., Medical Air Technology Corp. v. Marwan Investment Inc., 303 F.3d 11, 18–19 (1st Cir.2002). Should courts use the Seventh Amendment to invalidate some or all employment arbitration agreements? See Jean R. Sternlight, *The Rise and Spread of Mandatory Arbitration as a Substitute for the Jury Trial*, 38 University of San Francisco Law Review 17 (2003) (yes); Stephen J. Ware, *Contractual Arbitration, Mandatory Arbitration, and State Constitutional Jury-Trial Rights*, 38 University of San Francisco Law Review 39 (2003) (no); Cooper v. MRM Investment Co., 367 F.3d 493, 502, 506 (6th Cir. 2004) (arbitration agreements need not expressly waive the right to jury trial because the loss of that right is a fairly obvious consequence of the agreement to arbitrate).

7.   How is the FAA's "liberal federal policy favoring arbitration" similar to, and different from, the policy favoring labor arbitration that the Supreme Court has read into § 301 of the LMRA? One obvious difference is the degree to which the laws have federalized arbitration.

As discussed above in Chapters III.A and IV.B, *Lincoln Mills* and its progeny resulted in the complete federalization of arbitration law under Section 301. This has not occurred under the FAA, however, because the statute expressly leaves room for state law. Section 2 of the FAA provides that arbitration agreements "shall be valid, irrevocable, and enforceable, *save upon such grounds that exist at law or in equity for the revocation of any contract*." Thus, notwithstanding the FAA's creation of a federal policy in favor of arbitration and a federal common law of arbitrability which preempts state law disfavoring arbitration, state contract law controls whether an arbitration agreement is valid. This will be discussed in more detail in Chapter XI.

8.   Might the Court's enthusiastic endorsement of compulsory arbitration be motivated in part by a self-interested desire to reduce the number of employment cases in already overloaded federal dockets? See Rebecca Hanner White, *Arbitration and the Administrative State*, 38 Wake Forest Law Review 1283, 1296 (2003) (courts, by enforcing predispute arbitration agree-

ments, can achieve more manageable caseloads and avoid becoming "super-personnel departments."). If so, is this an appropriate justification for a judicial doctrine?

9. The National Academy of Arbitrators (NAA) is the primary professional association of *labor* arbitrators. It has issued a Statement on Individual Contracts of Employment which provides: "At the hearing, the arbitrator should seek a comfortable balance between the traditional informality and efficiency of arbitration and court-like diligence in respecting and safeguarding the substantive statutory rights of the parties." Is this realistic?

10. In contrast to the Supreme Court's holding in *Gilmer* that binding arbitration clauses are enforceable in federal courts, the lower federal courts have uniformly refused to enforce private contractual provisions that require employees to participate in *nonbinding* ADR procedures prior to, but not in lieu of, filing a discrimination claim in court. For example, assume that an employer contractually requires its employees to submit discrimination claims to mediation (see Chapter XIII) or to a peer review panel (see Chapter XIV) prior to filing a discrimination claim. The lower federal courts will find such clauses unenforceable. See, e.g., Brennan v. King, 139 F.3d 258 (1st Cir.1998). Does it make any sense for courts to enforce private contractual provisions that require employees to forfeit their right to a judicial remedy for discrimination, but not provisions that require employees to pursue nonbinding ADR as a prerequisite to a discrimination suit? See Steven M. Warshawsky, Gilmer, *the Contractual Exhaustion Doctrine, and Federal Statutory Employment Discrimination Claims*, 19 The Labor Lawyer 285 (2004).

While courts have refused to make participation in nonbinding employment ADR a condition precedent to judicial enforcement, courts have consistently enforced agreements to engage in nonbinding ADR. Amy J. Schmitz, *Refreshing Contractual Analysis of ADR Agreements By Curing Bipolar Avoidance of Modern Common Law*, 9 Harvard Negotiation Law Review 1 (2004). Many courts have relied on the FAA, notwithstanding the fact that the FAA applies only to *arbitration* agreements. See, e.g., AMF Inc. v. Brunswick Corp., 621 F.Supp. 456 (E.D.N.Y. 1985). Other courts rely on contract principles or on their own inherent power to control their dockets. See Amy M. Pugh & Richard A. Bales, *The Inherent Power of the Federal Courts to Compel Participation in Nonbinding Forms of Alternative Dispute Resolution*, 42 Duquesne Law Review 1 (2003).

CIRCUIT CITY STORES, INC. v. ADAMS

Supreme Court of the United States, 2001.
532 U.S. 105, 121 S.Ct. 1302, 149 L.Ed.2d 234.

KENNEDY, J., delivered the opinion of the Court, in which REHNQUIST, C.J., and O'CONNOR, SCALIA, and THOMAS, JJ., joined. STEVENS, J., filed a dissenting opinion, in which GINSBURG and BREYER, JJ., joined, and in which SOUTER, J., joined as to Parts II and III. SOUTER, J., filed a dissenting opinion, in which STEVENS, GINSBURG , and BREYER, JJ., joined.

Justice KENNEDY delivered the opinion of the Court.

I.

[Saint Clair Adams applied for a job at Circuit City Stores, Inc., a national retailer of consumer electronics. Adams signed an employment application which contained an arbitration clause. Two years after she was hired, Adams filed an employment discrimination lawsuit against Circuit City in state court, asserting state law discrimination and tort claims. Circuit City sued in federal court under the FAA to enjoin the state-court action and to compel arbitration. The district court entered the requested order, and Adams appealed. The Ninth Circuit reversed, holding that the arbitration agreement between Adams and Circuit City was contained in a "contract of employment," and so was not subject to the FAA. Circuit City appealed, noting that the Ninth Circuit's conclusion that all employment contracts are excluded from the FAA conflicted with every other Court of Appeals to have addressed the question.]

II.

A.

* * *

[This case involves the FAA's] the exemption from coverage under § 1. The exemption clause provides the Act shall not apply "to contracts of employment of seamen, railroad employees, or any other class of workers engaged in foreign or interstate commerce." 9 U.S.C. § 1. Most Courts of Appeals conclude the exclusion provision is limited to transportation workers, defined, for instance, as those workers "actually engaged in the movement of goods in interstate commerce." [T]he Court of Appeals for the Ninth Circuit takes a different view and interprets the § 1 exception to exclude all contracts of employment from the reach of the FAA. This comprehensive exemption had been advocated by amici curiae in *Gilmer*, where we addressed the question whether a registered securities representative's employment discrimination claim under the Age Discrimination in Employment Act of 1967, could be submitted to arbitration pursuant to an agreement in his securities registration application. Concluding that the application was not a "contract of employment" at all, we found it unnecessary to reach the meaning of § 1. There is no such dispute in this case; while Circuit City argued in its petition for certiorari that the employment application signed by Adams was not a "contract of employment," we declined to grant certiorari on this point. So the issue reserved in *Gilmer* is presented here.

B.

Respondent, endorsing the reasoning of the Court of Appeals for the Ninth Circuit that the provision excludes all employment contracts, relies on the asserted breadth of the words "contracts of employment of . . . any other class of workers engaged in . . . commerce." Referring to our construction of § 2's coverage provision in *Allied-Bruce* [*Terminix v. Dobson*, 513 U.S. 265, 115 S.Ct. 834, 130 L.Ed.2d 753 (1995)]–concluding that the words "involving commerce" evidence the congressional intent to regulate to the full extent of its commerce power–respondent contends § 1's interpretation should have a like reach, thus exempting all employment contracts. The two provisions, it is argued, are coterminous; under this view the "involving commerce" provision brings within the FAA's scope all contracts within the Congress' commerce power, and the "engaged in ... commerce" language in § 1 in turn exempts from the FAA all employment contracts falling within that authority.

This reading of § 1, however, runs into an immediate and, in our view, insurmountable textual obstacle. Unlike the "involving commerce" language in § 2, the words "any other class of workers engaged in ... commerce" constitute a residual phrase, following, in the same sentence, explicit reference to "seamen" and "railroad employees." Construing the residual phrase to exclude all employment contracts fails to give independent effect to the statute's enumeration of the specific categories of workers which precedes it; there would be no need for Congress to use the phrases "seamen" and "railroad employees" if those same classes of workers were subsumed within the meaning of the "engaged in ... commerce" residual clause. The wording of § 1 calls for the application of the maxim *ejusdem generis*, the statutory canon that "[w]here general words follow specific words in a statutory enumeration, the general words are construed to embrace only objects similar in nature to those objects enumerated by the preceding specific words." Under this rule of construction the residual clause should be read to give effect to the terms "seamen" and "railroad employees," and should itself be controlled and defined by reference to the enumerated categories of workers which are recited just before it; the interpretation of the clause pressed by respondent fails to produce these results.

Canons of construction need not be conclusive and are often countered, of course, by some maxim pointing in a different direction. The application of the rule *ejusdem generis* in this case, however, is in full accord with other sound considerations bearing upon the proper interpretation of the clause. For even if the term "engaged in commerce" stood alone in § 1, we would not construe the provision to exclude all contracts of employment from the FAA. Congress uses different modifiers to the word "commerce" in the design and enactment of its statutes. The phrase "affecting commerce" indicates Congress' intent to regulate to the outer limits of its authority under the Commerce Clause. * * * [But] the general words "in commerce" and the specific phrase "engaged in commerce" are understood to have a more limited reach.

It is argued that we should assess the meaning of the phrase "engaged in commerce" in a different manner here, because the FAA was enacted when congressional authority to regulate under the commerce power was to a large extent confined by our decisions. When the FAA was enacted in 1925, respondent reasons, the phrase "engaged in commerce" was not a term of art indicating a limited assertion of congressional jurisdiction; to the contrary, it is said, the formulation came close to expressing the outer limits of Congress' power as then understood. Were this mode of interpretation to prevail, we would take into account the scope of the Commerce Clause, as then elaborated by the Court, at the date of the FAA's enactment in order to interpret what the statute means now.

A variable standard for interpreting common, jurisdictional phrases would contradict our earlier cases and bring instability to statutory interpretation. The Court has declined in past cases to afford significance, in construing the meaning of the statutory jurisdictional provisions "in commerce" and "engaged in commerce," to the circumstance that the statute predated shifts in the Court's Commerce Clause. * * * The plain meaning of the words "engaged in commerce" is narrower than the more open-ended formulations "affecting commerce" and "involving commerce." It would be unwieldy for Congress, for the Court, and for litigants to be required to deconstruct statutory Commerce Clause phrases depending upon the year of a particular statutory enactment.

* * *

In sum, the text of the FAA forecloses the construction of § 1 followed by the Court of Appeals in the case under review, a construction which would exclude all employment contracts from the FAA. * * * Section 1 exempts from the FAA only contracts of employment of transportation workers.

C.

As the conclusion we reach today is directed by the text of § 1, we need not assess the legislative history of the exclusion provision. We do note, however, that the legislative record on the § 1 exemption is quite sparse. Respondent points to no language in either committee report addressing the meaning of the provision, nor to any mention of the § 1 exclusion during debate on the FAA on the floor of the House or Senate. Instead, respondent places greatest reliance upon testimony before a Senate subcommittee hearing suggesting that the exception may have been added in response to the objections of the president of the International Seamen's Union of America. Legislative history is problematic even when the attempt is to draw inferences from the intent of duly appointed committees of the Congress. It becomes far more so when we consult sources still more steps removed from the full Congress and speculate upon the significance of the fact that a certain interest group sponsored or opposed particular legislation. We ought not attribute to Congress an official purpose based on the motives of a particular group that lobbied for or against a certain proposal—even assuming the precise intent of the group can be determined, a point doubtful both as a general rule and in the instant case. It is for the Congress, not the courts, to consult political forces and then decide how best to resolve conflicts in the course of writing the objective embodiments of law we know as statutes.

* * *

For the foregoing reasons, the judgment of the Court of Appeals for the Ninth Circuit is reversed, and the case is remanded for further proceedings consistent with this opinion.

It is so ordered.

Justice STEVENS, with whom Justice GINSBURG and Justice BREYER join, and with whom Justice SOUTER joins as to Parts II and III, dissenting.

* * *

I.

* * *

The history of the Act, which is extensive and well-documented, makes clear that the FAA was a response to the refusal of courts to enforce commercial arbitration agreements, which were commonly used in the maritime context. The original bill was drafted by the Committee on Commerce, Trade, and Commercial Law of the American Bar Association (ABA) upon consideration of "the further extension of the principle of *commercial* arbitration." Report of the Forty-third Annual Meeting of the ABA, 45 A.B.A. Rep. 75 (1920) (emphasis added). As drafted, the bill was understood by Members of Congress to "simply provid[e] for one thing, and that is to give an opportunity to enforce an agreement in *commercial* contracts and *admiralty* contracts." 65 Cong. Rec.1931 (1924) (remarks of Rep. Graham) (emphasis added). It is no surprise, then, that when the legislation was first introduced in 1922, it did not mention employment contracts, but did contain a rather precise definition of the term "maritime transactions" that underscored the commercial character of the proposed bill. Indeed, neither the history of the drafting of the original bill by the ABA, nor the records of the deliberations in Congress during the years preceding the ultimate enactment of the Act in 1925, contains any evidence that the proponents of the legislation intended it to apply to agreements affecting employment.

Nevertheless, the original bill was opposed by representatives of organized labor, most notably the president of the International Seamen's Union of America, because of their concern that the legislation might authorize federal judicial enforcement of arbitration clauses in employment contracts and collective-bargaining agreements. In response to those objections, the chairman of the ABA committee that drafted the legislation emphasized at a Senate Judiciary Subcommittee hearing that "[i]t is not intended that this shall be an act referring to labor disputes at all," but he also observed that "if your honorable committee should feel that there is any danger of that, they should add to the bill the following language, 'but nothing herein contained shall apply to seamen or any class of workers in interstate and foreign commerce.'" Similarly, another supporter of the bill, then Secretary of Commerce Herbert Hoover, suggested that "[i]f objection appears to the inclusion of workers' contracts in the law's scheme, it might be well amended by stating 'but nothing herein contained shall apply to contracts of employment of seamen, railroad employees, or any other class of workers engaged in interstate or foreign commerce.' " The legislation was reintroduced in the next session of Congress with Secretary Hoover's exclusionary language added to § 1, and the amendment eliminated organized labor's opposition to the proposed law.

That amendment is what the Court construes today. History amply supports the proposition that it was an uncontroversial provision that merely confirmed the fact that no one interested in the enactment of the FAA ever intended or expected that § 2 would apply to employment contracts. * * *

II.

A quarter century after the FAA was passed, many Courts of Appeals were presented with the question whether collective-bargaining agreements were "contracts of employment" for purposes of § 1's exclusion. The courts split over that question * * *. In *Textile Workers v. Lincoln Mills of Ala.*, 353 U.S. 448, 77 S.Ct. 923, 1 L.Ed.2d 972 (1957), [this] Court * * * held that § 301 [] provided the authority to compel arbitration. The fact that the Court relied on § 301 of the LMRA, a statutory provision that does not mention arbitration, rather than the FAA, a statute that expressly authorizes the enforcement of arbitration agreements, strongly implies that the Court had concluded that the FAA simply did not apply because § 1 exempts labor contracts.

III.

Times have changed. Judges in the 19th century disfavored private arbitration. The 1925 Act was intended to overcome that attitude, but a number of this Court's cases decided in the last several decades have pushed the pendulum far beyond a neutral attitude and endorsed a policy that strongly favors private arbitration. * * *

It is not necessarily wrong for the Court to put its own imprint on a statute. But when its refusal to look beyond the raw statutory text enables it to disregard countervailing considerations that were expressed by Members of the enacting Congress and that remain valid today, the Court misuses its authority. As the history of the legislation indicates, the potential disparity in bargaining power between individual employees and large employers was the source of organized labor's opposition to the Act, which it feared would require courts to enforce unfair employment contracts. * * * When the Court simply ignores the interest of the unrepresented employee, it skews its interpretation with its own policy preferences.

I respectfully dissent.

JUSTICE SOUTER, with whom JUSTICE STEVENS, JUSTICE GINSBURG, and JUSTICE BREYER join, dissenting.

* * *

[T]he majority today finds great significance in the fact that the generally phrased exemption for the employment contracts of workers "engaged in commerce" does not stand alone, but occurs at the end of a sequence of more specific exemptions: for "contracts of employment of seamen, railroad employees, or any other class of workers engaged in foreign or interstate commerce." * * * Like many interpretive canons, however, *ejusdem generis* is a fallback, and if there are good reasons not to apply it, it is put aside. There are good reasons here. As Adams argued, it is imputing something very odd to the working of the congressional brain to say that Congress took care to bar application of the Act to the class of employment contracts it most obviously had authority to legislate about in 1925, contracts of workers employed by carriers and handlers of commerce, while covering only employees "engaged" in less obvious ways, over whose coverage litigation might be anticipated with uncertain results * * *

Notes and Questions

1. Are you convinced by the Court's distinction of the phrases "involving commerce" and "engaged in ... commerce"? Is there anything "plain" about the meanings the Court attributes to these phrases? For insightful historical discussions of the FAA exclusion, see Matthew W. Finkin, *"Workers' Contracts" Under the United States Arbitration Act: An Essay in Historical Clarification*, 17 Berkeley Journal of Employment & Labor Law 282 (1996); Matthew W. Finkin, *Employment Contracts Under the FAA–Reconsidered*, 48 Labor Law Journal 329 (1997).

2. Does the Court's decision in this case conflict with its recent decisions favoring states rights? See Samuel Estreicher, *Saturns for Rickshaws: The Stakes in the Debate Over Predispute Employment Arbitration Agreements*, 16 Ohio State Journal on Dispute Resolution 559 (2001).

3. Following *Circuit City*, lower courts will have to determine which employees are and are not "transportation workers." See, e.g., Palcko v. Airborne Express, Inc., 372 F.3d 588, 593–94 (3d Cir.2004) (supervisor employed by package delivery service is within the exclusionary clause because her job is so closely related to the transportation of goods as to be in practical effect part of the shipping of the goods); (Harden v. Roadway Package Systems, Inc., 249 F.3d 1137 (9th Cir.2001) (delivery driver is within exclusionary clause); Perez v. Globe Airport Security Services, Inc., 253 F.3d 1280 (11th Cir.2001) (airport security guard is not within exclusionary clause).

4. The Supreme Court remanded *Circuit City* to the Ninth Circuit. The Ninth Circuit's subsequent decision is discussed in Chapter XI.B.2.

A NOTE ON *EEOC v. WAFFLE HOUSE*

EEOC v. Waffle House, 534 U.S. 279, 122 S.Ct. 754, 151 L.Ed.2d 755 (2002), involved an employee who was fired from his job as a Waffle House grill operator after he suffered a seizure at work. The employee, who had signed a predispute arbitration agreement, did not pursue arbitration, but instead filed a charge of discrimination with the Equal Employment Opportunity Commission (EEOC). The EEOC subsequently filed a complaint in federal district court against Waffle House for unlawful disability discrimination against the employee. Waffle House moved to stay the suit and compel arbitration. The district court denied the motion. The court of appeals reversed, ordering arbitration, but limiting the EEOC's potential remedies to injunctive relief.

The issue before the Court was whether an arbitration agreement between an employer and the employee barred the EEOC from pursuing victim-specific judicial relief, such as backpay, reinstatement, and damages, in an enforcement action. The Court, in a 6–3 decision authored by Justice Stevens, reversed the court of appeals, and held that the EEOC was free to seek victim-specific relief. The Court reasoned that Title VII, which created the EEOC, "makes the EEOC the master of its own case," and that the statute gave the agency–not the courts–the authority "to determine whether public resources should be committed to the recovery of victim-specific relief."

Justice Thomas, writing for the dissent, focused on § 706(g)(1) of Title VII. This section provides that, after a finding of liability, "the court may enjoin the respondent from engaging in such unlawful employment practice, and order *such affirmative action as may be appropriate,* which may include, but is not limited to, reinstatement or hiring of employees, with or without back pay ... *or any other equitable relief as the court deems appropriate*" (emphasis added). Justice Thomas reasoned that it was not "appropriate" to allow the EEOC to do on behalf of an employee that which the employee is precluded from doing for himself–i.e., to seek victim-specific relief in court on behalf of an employee who had agreed to arbitrate, rather than litigate, his claims.

Notes and Questions

1. The EEOC is the administrative agency created by Congress to administer Title VII, the Age Discrimination in Employment Act, and the Americans with Disabilities Act. The agency has only procedural rulemaking authority under Title VII, but has both substantive and procedural rulemaking authority under the other two statutes. See 29 U.S.C. § 628 (ADEA); 42 U.S.C. § 12116 (ADA); 110 Cong. Rec. 2575 (1964) (statement of Rep. Celler, who offered the amendment to Title VII eliminating the EEOC's substantive rulemaking powers). The EEOC does not have statutory authority to interpret the Federal Arbitration Act; nor does it have adjudicatory authority under any of the antidiscrimination statutes.

The EEOC has consistently opposed the enforcement of predispute arbitration agreements, but has been roundly ignored by the courts on this issue. See Chapter XII, *infra.*

2. The EEOC files suit in only a small percentage of the cases it considers. In fiscal year 2002, the EEOC received 84,442 charges of discrimination, and found reasonable cause in 6878 of the charges. However, the agency filed suit in only 364 cases, representing 0.43% of the total charges filed and 5.3% of the meritorious charges filed. See EEOC 2002 Annual Report, http://www.eeoc.gov/abouteeoc/annual_reports/annrep02.html (last accessed April 3, 2004); EEOC Litigation Statistics, FY 1992 Through FY 2002, http://www.eeoc.gov/stats/litigation.html (last accessed April 3, 2004).

In 1999, the EEOC launched a nationwide voluntary mediation program. The EEOC credits this program with helping it to reduce its backlog of charges and increase its conciliation rate. See http://www.eeoc.gov/mediate/index.html; see also Michael Z. Green, *Proposing A New Paradigm for EEOC Enforcement After 35 Years: Outsourcing Charge Processing By Mandatory Mediation*, 105 Dickinson Law Review 305 (2001) (arguing that mediation should be mandatory, that it should be outsourced to private mediators, and that the EEOC should reallocate its resources from charge processing to enforcement).

3. The Court left open the issue of whether the EEOC may pursue a claim that an employee already has brought to arbitration. How should lower courts resolve this issue? What if an employee signs a waiver or release instead of an arbitration agreement? See Senich v. American–Republican, Inc., 215 F.R.D. 40, 44–45 (D.Conn.2003) (permitting EEOC to seek victim-specific relief for employees who had signed a waiver and release as a condition of receiving benefits under an employer severance program).

4. Justices Souter, Stevens, Ginsburg, and Breyer dissented in *Circuit City Stores, Inc. v. Adams, supra*. However, each of these Justices joined the majority in *Waffle House*, and cited *Circuit City* for the proposition that the FAA applies to employment contracts. Can *Waffle House*, then, be seen as strengthening the institution of employment arbitration?

Chapter XI

JUDICIAL APPLICATION
OF *GILMER*

A. INTRODUCTION

Gilmer held that the FAA provides the legal authority for judicial enforcement of employment arbitration agreements. That statute, however, does not specify the scope of an arbitrator's authority or the arbitral procedures that must be used. Instead, the Supreme Court has stated consistently that these items are contractual, and therefore subject to the private agreement of the parties. See, e.g., Mitsubishi Motors Corp. v. Soler Chrysler–Plymouth, Inc., 473 U.S. 614, 625, 105 S.Ct. 3346, 87 L.Ed.2d 444 (1985) ("The 'liberal federal policy favoring arbitration agreements' manifested by [9 U.S.C. § 2] and the Act as a whole, is at bottom a policy guaranteeing the enforcement of private contractual arrangements: the Act simply 'creates a body of federal substantive law establishing and regulating the duty to honor an agreement to arbitrate.' " (quoting Moses H. Cone Memorial Hosp. v. Mercury Constr. Corp., 460 U.S. 1, 24, 25 n.32, 103 S.Ct. 927, 74 L.Ed.2d 765 (1983)) (citation omitted)). As a practical matter, this means that most employment arbitration agreements are drafted by employers. While many employers have drafted arbitration agreements that are scrupulously fair to employees, other employers have drafted lopsided arbitration agreements that, for example, limit damages, impose shortened statutes of limitation, impose filing fees and other prohibitive costs, restrict or eliminate discovery, and give the employer undue control over the selection of arbitrators.

Courts generally have agreed that the most egregious of these lopsided agreements should not be enforced. Courts are divided, however, on the proper source of authority for refusing enforcement. Some courts rely on the federal statutory law giving rise to the claim, reasoning that lopsided arbitration agreements are unenforceable because they are inconsistent with, for example, the federal antidiscrimination laws. Other courts rely on state-law breach-of-contract principles. A third group of courts, again looking to state law, finds that lopsided agreements are unenforceable because they are unconscionable. The first three cases in this Chapter will examine these sources of authority.

In addition to this source-of-authority division, the federal circuits also are divided on the point at which an arbitration agreement becomes sufficiently "lopsided" to merit non-enforcement. The remainder of this Chapter will consider in detail several of the issues that have arisen concerning how *Gilmer* should be applied to these issues.

B. CHALLENGING ARBITRAL PROCEDURES

1. FEDERAL LAW

COLE v. BURNS INTERNATIONAL SECURITY SERVICES

United States Court of Appeals, District of Columbia Circuit, 1997.
105 F.3d 1465.

HARRY T. EDWARDS, CHIEF JUDGE:

* * *

II. BACKGROUND

Clinton Cole used to work as a security guard at Union Station in Washington, D.C. for a company called LaSalle and Partners ("La-Salle"). In 1991, Burns Security took over LaSalle's contract to provide security at Union Station and required all LaSalle employees to sign a "Pre–Dispute Resolution Agreement" in order to obtain employment with Burns. * * *

In October 1993, Burns Security fired Cole. After filing charges with the Equal Employment Opportunity Commission, Cole filed the instant complaint in the United States District Court for the District of Columbia, alleging racial discrimination, harassment based on race, retaliation for his writing a letter of complaint regarding sexual harassment of a subordinate employee by another supervisor at Burns, and intentional infliction of emotional distress. Burns moved to compel arbitration of the dispute and to dismiss Cole's complaint pursuant to the terms of the contract. * * * [T]he trial court granted [the] motion and dismissed Cole's complaint.

* * *

2. *The Validity of the Agreement to Arbitrate in this Case*

The starting point of our analysis is the Supreme Court's decision in *Gilmer*. In that case, the Court held that an employee's agreement to arbitrate employment-related disputes may require him to arbitrate statutory claims under the ADEA because "[b]y agreeing to arbitrate a statutory claim, [an employee] does not forgo the substantive rights afforded by the statute; [he] only submits to their resolution in an arbitral, rather than a judicial, forum." The Court emphasized that "so long as the prospective litigant effectively may vindicate [his or her] statutory cause of action in the arbitral forum, the statute will continue to serve both its remedial and deterrent function." [Citations omitted.]

Obviously, *Gilmer* cannot be read as holding that an arbitration agreement is enforceable no matter what rights it waives or what burdens it imposes. Such a holding would be fundamentally at odds with our understanding of the rights accorded to persons protected by public statutes like the ADEA and Title VII. The beneficiaries of public statutes are entitled to the rights and protections provided by the law. Clearly, it would be unlawful for an employer to condition employment on an employee's agreement to give up the right to be free from racial or gender discrimination. *See Gardner–Denver*, 415 U.S. at 51, 94 S.Ct. at 1021 ("[T]here can be no prospective waiver of an employee's rights under Title VII). Any such condition of employment would violate Title VII, regardless of whether or not the agreement was viewed as a contract of adhesion. Thus, in a subsequent suit by the employee raising a viable claim of racial discrimination or sexual harassment, it would be no defense that the employee had signed a contract giving up her right to be free from discrimination.

Similarly, an employee cannot be required as a condition of employment to waive access to a neutral forum in which statutory employment discrimination claims may be heard. For example, an employee could not be required to sign an agreement waiving the right to bring Title VII claims in any forum. Although the employer could argue that such an agreement does not waive the substantive protections of the statute, surely such an agreement would nonetheless violate the law by leaving the employee's substantive rights at the mercy of the employer's good faith in adhering to the law. At a minimum, statutory rights include both a substantive protection and access to a neutral forum in which to enforce those protections.

3. *The Obligation to Pay Arbitrators' Fees*

* * * The arbitration agreement in this case presents an issue not raised by the agreement in *Gilmer:* can an employer condition employment on acceptance of an arbitration agreement that requires the employee to submit his or her statutory claims to arbitration and then requires the employee to pay all or part of the arbitrators' fees? This was not an issue in *Gilmer* (and other like cases), because, under NYSE Rules and NASD Rules, it is standard practice in the securities industry for employers to pay all of the arbitrators' fees. Employees may be required to pay a filing fee, expenses, or an administrative fee, but these expenses are routinely waived in the event of financial hardship.

Thus, in *Gilmer*, the Supreme Court endorsed a system of arbitration in which employees are not required to pay for the arbitrator assigned to hear their statutory claims. There is no reason to think that the Court would have approved arbitration in the absence of this arrangement. Indeed, we are unaware of any situation in American jurisprudence in which a beneficiary of a federal statute has been required to pay for the services of the judge assigned to hear her or his case. Under *Gilmer*, arbitration is supposed to be a reasonable substitute for a judicial forum. Therefore, it would undermine Congress's intent to prevent employees who are seeking to vindicate statutory rights from gaining access to a judicial forum and then require them to pay for the services of an arbitrator when they would never be required to pay for a judge in court.

In sum, we hold that Cole could not be required to agree to arbitrate his public law claims as a condition of employment if the arbitration agreement required him to pay all or part of the arbitrator's fees and expenses. In light of this holding, we find that the arbitration agreement in this case is valid and enforceable. We do so because we interpret the agreement as requiring Burns Security to pay all of the arbitrator's fees necessary for a full and fair resolution of Cole's statutory claims.

* * *

KAREN LECRAFT HENDERSON, CIRCUIT JUDGE, concurring in part and dissenting in part:

* * *

By conditioning arbitration on the employer's assumption of arbitrator costs, the majority engages in pure judicial fee shifting which finds no support in the FAA, *Gilmer* or the parties' agreement, not one of which addresses arbitration fee allocation. Yet, relying on this very silence, the majority now declares that the employer must bear the costs, regardless of the outcome or the merits of the parties' positions, because of the majority's own speculation on what the arbitration costs will be and who will be required to pay them—factual matters never presented to the district court or even argued by the parties on appeal. The issues of costs and their allocation were first posed by the panel sua sponte during oral argument. I question initially, therefore, whether we should address them at all. In any event, the majority has now resolved those issues on the basis of its own research, and its construction of the AAA Rules [see Appendix C], which were introduced only after argument at the panel's request. Because the district court dismissed the complaint on a bare record consisting of the pleadings and attached exhibits, I would at a minimum remand to afford that court the opportunity to develop an evidentiary record and to make findings of fact regarding the likely costs and their allocation. * * *

Notes and Questions

1. The issue of arbitration fees will be discussed in more detail in Section C of this Chapter.

2. At what point does an arbitration agreement become so lopsided that it is inconsistent with the remedial and deterrent functions of the underlying antidiscrimination statutes? Does Judge Edwards provide a meaningful standard? Must arbitral procedures mirror litigation procedures? If so, don't the parties lose the benefits of arbitration?

3. Perhaps over time, the courts will develop a standard, or at least a common understanding, to guide their decisions. Until then, however, the parties are left in the dark. Does an employer have an incentive to maintain a lopsided arbitration agreement even if it appears relatively certain that a court eventually will invalidate the agreement? What effect might such an agreement have on an employee who is contemplating a claim against the employer? On the employee's ability to retain an attorney for her claim?

2. STATE LAW: UNCONSCIONABILITY

CIRCUIT CITY STORES, INC. v. ADAMS
United States Court of Appeals, Ninth Circuit, 2002.
279 F.3d 889.

On Remand from the United States Supreme Court.

D.W. NELSON, CIRCUIT JUDGE:

The Supreme Court granted certiorari, reversed this court's prior decision, and remanded for proceedings in accordance with its opinion in *Circuit City Stores, Inc. v. Adams,* 532 U.S. 105, 121 S.Ct. 1302, 149 L.Ed.2d 234 (2001). Now that the Federal Arbitration Act ("FAA"), 9 U.S.C. § 1 *et seq.*, applies to the arbitration agreement in this case, we must decide whether the district court erred in exercising its authority under the Act to compel arbitration.

I. FACTUAL AND PROCEDURAL BACKGROUND

On October 23, 1995, Saint Clair Adams completed an application to work as a sales person at Circuit City. As part of the application, Adams signed the "Circuit City Dispute Resolution Agreement" ("DRA"). The DRA requires employees to submit all claims and disputes to binding arbitration.[1] Incorporated into the DRA are a set of "Dispute Resolution Rules and Procedures" ("dispute resolution rules" or "rules") that define the claims subject to arbitration, discovery rules, allocation of fees, and available remedies. Under these rules, the amount of damages is restricted: back pay is limited to one year, front pay to two years, and punitive damages to the greater of the amount of front and back pay awarded or $5000. In addition, the employee is required to split the costs of the arbitration, including the daily fees of the arbitrator, the cost of a reporter to transcribe the proceedings, and the expense of renting the room in which the arbitration is held, unless the employee prevails and the arbitrator decides to order Circuit City to pay the employee's share

---

1. The DRA specifies that job applicants agree to settle "all previously unasserted claims, disputes or controversies arising out of or relating to my application or candidacy for employment, employment and/or cessation of employment with Circuit City, *exclusively* by final and binding *arbitration* before a neutral Arbitrator. By way of example only, such claims include claims un- der federal, state, and local statutory or common law, such as Age Discrimination in Employment Act, Title VII of the Civil Rights Act of 1964, as amended, including the amendments to the Civil Rights Act of 1991, the Americans with Disabilities Act, the law of contract and law of tort." (emphasis in original).

of the costs. Notably, Circuit City is not required under the agreement to arbitrate any claims against the employee.

An employee cannot work at Circuit City without signing the DRA. If an applicant refuses to sign the DRA (or withdraws consent within three days), Circuit City will not even consider his application.

In November 1997, Adams filed a state court lawsuit against Circuit City and three co-workers alleging sexual harassment, retaliation, constructive discharge, and intentional infliction of emotional distress under the California Fair Employment and Housing Act ("FEHA"), Cal. Gov't Code § 12900 *et seq.,* and discrimination based on sexual orientation under Cal. Labor Code § 1102.1. Adams sought compensatory, punitive, and emotional distress damages for alleged repeated harassment during his entire term of employment.

Circuit City responded by filing a petition in federal district court for the Northern District of California to stay the state court proceedings and compel arbitration pursuant to the DRA. On April 29, 1998, the district court granted the petition. On appeal, we reversed on the ground that Section 1 of the FAA exempted Adams' employment contract from the FAA's coverage. *Circuit City Stores, Inc. v. Adams,* 194 F.3d 1070 (9th Cir.1999). The Supreme Court reversed our decision and remanded.

II. DISCUSSION

Circuit City has devised an arbitration agreement that functions as a thumb on Circuit City's side of the scale should an employment dispute ever arise between the company and one of its employees. We conclude that such an arrangement is unconscionable under California law.

A. *Applicable Law*

* * * Section 2 of the FAA provides that arbitration agreements "shall be valid, irrevocable, and enforceable, *save upon such grounds that exist at law or in equity for the revocation of any contract.*" 9 U.S.C. § 2 (emphasis added). In determining the validity of an agreement to arbitrate, federal courts "should apply ordinary state-law principles that govern the formation of contracts." *First Options of Chicago, Inc. v. Kaplan,* 514 U.S. 938, 944, 115 S.Ct. 1920, 131 L.Ed.2d 985 (1995). Thus, although "courts may not invalidate arbitration agreements under state laws applicable *only* to arbitration provisions," general contract defenses such as fraud, duress, or unconscionability, grounded in state contract law, may operate to invalidate arbitration agreements. *Doctor's Assocs., Inc. v. Casarotto,* 517 U.S. 681, 687, 116 S.Ct. 1652, 134 L.Ed.2d 902 (1996).

Adams argues that the DRA is an unconscionable contract of adhesion. Because Adams was employed in California, we look to California contract law to determine whether the agreement is valid. *See Ticknor v. Choice Hotels Int'l, Inc.,* 265 F.3d 931 (9th Cir.2001) (applying Montana law to decide whether arbitration clause was valid).

Under California law, a contract is unenforceable if it is both procedurally and substantively unconscionable. *Armendariz v. Found. Health Psychcare Svcs., Inc.*, 24 Cal.4th 83, 99 Cal.Rptr.2d 745, 6 P.3d 669, 690 (2000). When assessing procedural unconscionability, we consider the equilibrium of bargaining power between the parties and the extent to which the contract clearly discloses its terms. *Stirlen v. Supercuts, Inc.*, 51 Cal.App.4th 1519, 60 Cal.Rptr.2d 138, 145 (1997). A determination of substantive unconscionability, on the other hand, involves whether the terms of the contract are unduly harsh or oppressive. *Id.*

B.   *The DRA and Unconscionability*

The DRA is procedurally unconscionable because it is a contract of adhesion: a standard-form contract, drafted by the party with superior bargaining power, which relegates to the other party the option of either adhering to its terms without modification or rejecting the contract entirely. *Id.* at 145–46 (indicating that a contract of adhesion is procedurally unconscionable). Circuit City, which possesses considerably more bargaining power than nearly all of its employees or applicants, drafted the contract and uses it as its standard arbitration agreement for all of its new employees. The agreement is a prerequisite to employment, and job applicants are not permitted to modify the agreement's terms—they must take the contract or leave it. *See Armendariz*, 99 Cal.Rptr.2d 745, 6 P.3d at 690 (noting that few applicants are in a position to refuse a job because of an arbitration agreement).

The California Supreme Court's recent decision in *Armendariz* counsels in favor of finding that the Circuit City arbitration agreement is substantively unconscionable as well. In *Armendariz*, the California court reversed an order compelling arbitration of a FEHA discrimination claim because the arbitration agreement at issue required arbitration only of employees' claims and excluded damages that would otherwise be available under the FEHA. *Armendariz*, 99 Cal.Rptr.2d 745, 6 P.3d at 694. The agreement in *Armendariz* required employees, as a condition of employment, to submit all claims relating to termination of that employment—including any claim that the termination violated the employee's rights—to binding arbitration. *Id.* at 675. The employer, however, was free to bring suit in court or arbitrate any dispute with its employees. In analyzing this asymmetrical arrangement, the court concluded that in order for a mandatory arbitration agreement to be valid, some "modicum of bilaterality" is required. *Id.* at 692. Since the employer was not bound to arbitrate its claims and there was no apparent justification for the lack of mutual obligations, the court reasoned that arbitration appeared to be functioning "less as a forum for neutral dispute resolution and more as a means of maximizing employer advantage." *Id.*

The substantive one-sidedness of the *Armendariz* agreement was compounded by the fact that it did not allow full recovery of damages for which the employees would be eligible under the FEHA. *Id.* at 694. The exclusive remedy was back pay from the date of discharge until the date of the arbitration award, whereas plaintiffs in FEHA suits would be entitled to punitive damages, injunctive relief, front pay, emotional distress damages, and attorneys' fees.

We find the arbitration agreement at issue here virtually indistinguishable from the agreement the California Supreme Court found unconscionable in *Armendariz.* Like the agreement in *Armendariz,* the DRA unilaterally forces employees to arbitrate claims against the employer. The claims subject to arbitration under the DRA include "any and all employment-related legal disputes, controversies or claims *of an Associate* arising out of, or relating to, an Associate's application or candidacy for employment, employment or cessation of employment with Circuit City" (emphasis added). The provision does not require Circuit City to arbitrate its claims against employees. Circuit City has offered no justification for this asymmetry, nor is there any indication that "business realities" warrant the one-sided obligation. This unjustified one-sidedness deprives the DRA of the "modicum of bilaterality" that the California Supreme Court requires for contracts to be enforceable under California law.

And again as in *Armendariz,* the asymmetry is compounded by the fact that the agreement limits the relief available to employees. Under the DRA, the remedies are limited to injunctive relief, up to one year of back pay and up to two years of front pay, compensatory damages, and punitive damages in an amount up to the greater of the amount of back pay and front pay awarded or $5,000. By contrast, a plaintiff in a civil suit for sexual harassment under the FEHA is eligible for all forms of relief that are generally available to civil litigants—including appropriate punitive damages and damages for emotional distress. *See Commodore Home Sys., Inc. v. Superior Court of San Bernardino County,* 32 Cal.3d 211, 185 Cal.Rptr. 270, 649 P.2d 912, 914 (1982). The DRA also requires the employee to split the arbitrator's fees with Circuit City. This fee allocation scheme alone would render an arbitration agreement unenforceable.[5] *Cf. Cole v. Burns Intern. Security Svcs.,* 105 F.3d 1465 (D.C.Cir.1997) (holding that it is unlawful to require an employee, through a mandatory arbitration agreement, to share the costs of arbitration). But the DRA goes even further: it also imposes a strict one year statute of limitations on arbitrating claims that would deprive Adams of the benefit of the continuing violation doctrine available in FEHA suits. *See, e.g., Richards v. CH2M Hill, Inc.,* 26 Cal.4th 798, 111 Cal.Rptr.2d 87, 29 P.3d 175, 176 (2001). In short, and just like the agreement invalidated by the California Supreme Court in *Armendariz,* the DRA

---

5. A side note: whereas the arbitration agreements in *Cole* and *Green Tree Fin. Corp. v. Randolph,* 531 U.S. 79, 121 S.Ct. 513, 148 L.Ed.2d 373 (2000), were silent as to the allocation of fees, the DRA explicitly divides the costs of arbitration equally between employer and employee. While the DRA contains provisions which potentially limit the employee's liability for fees, the default rule is that employees will share equally in the cost of arbitration. As a result, we cannot interpret the agreement to prohibit sharing costs, as the court did in *Cole,* 105 F.3d at 1485, or find the issue of fees too speculative, as in *Green Tree,* 121 S.Ct. at 522.

forces Adams to arbitrate his statutory claims without affording him the benefit of the full range of statutory remedies.

In addition, our decision is entirely consistent with federal law concerning the enforceability of arbitration agreements. The Supreme Court, in *Gilmer v. Interstate/Johnson Lane Corp.,* 500 U.S. 20, 26, 111 S.Ct. 1647, 114 L.Ed.2d 26 (1991), held that "[b]y agreeing to arbitrate a statutory claim, [an employee] does not forgo the substantive rights afforded by the statute; [he] only submits to their resolution in an arbitral, rather than a judicial forum." While the Court in *Gilmer* affirmed that statutory rights can be resolved through arbitration, the decision also recognized that the arbitral forum must allow the employee to adequately pursue statutory rights. *Id.* at 28., 111 S.Ct. 1647

Courts have since interpreted *Gilmer* to require basic procedural and remedial protections so that claimants can effectively pursue their statutory rights. *See, e.g., Cole,* 105 F.3d at 1482 (listing five basic requirements that an arbitral forum must meet). We note that here, Circuit City's arbitration agreement fails to meet two of *Cole's* minimum requirements: it fails to provide for all of the types of relief that would otherwise be available in court, or to ensure that employees do not have to pay either unreasonable costs or any arbitrators' fees or expenses as a condition of access to the arbitration forum. *Id.*

Nor does our decision run afoul of the FAA by imposing a heightened burden on arbitration agreements. Because unconscionability is a defense to contracts generally and does not single out arbitration agreements for special scrutiny, it is also a valid reason not to enforce an arbitration agreement under the FAA. Indeed, the Supreme Court has specifically mentioned unconscionability as a "generally applicable contract defense[ ]" that may be raised consistent with § 2 of the FAA. *Doctor's Assocs.,* 517 U.S. at 687, 116 S.Ct. 1652. * * *

C. *Severability*

Under California law, courts have discretion to sever an unconscionable provision or refuse to enforce the contract in its entirety. *See* Cal. Civ.Code § 1670.5(a). In deciding whether to invalidate the contract,

> [c]ourts are to look to the various purposes of the contract. If the central purpose of the contract is tainted with illegality, then the contract as a whole cannot be enforced. If the illegality is collateral to the main purpose of the contract, and the illegal provision can be extirpated from the contract by means of severance or restriction, then such severance and restriction are appropriate.

Armendariz, 99 Cal.Rptr.2d 745, 6 P.3d at 696.

In this case, as in *Armendariz,* the objectionable provisions pervade the entire contract. In addition to the damages limitation and the fee-sharing scheme, the unilateral aspect of the DRA runs throughout the agreement and defines the scope of the matters that are covered. Removing these provisions would go beyond mere excision to rewriting the contract, which is not the proper role of this Court. *See id.* at 125, 99

Cal.Rptr.2d 745, 6 P.3d 669. Therefore, we find the entire arbitration agreement unenforceable.

III. Conclusion

Because we find that the DRA is an unconscionable contract of adhesion under California law, the order compelling arbitration is RE-VERSED.

Notes and Questions

1. The take-it-or-leave it nature of the arbitration "agreement" will be discussed in more detail in Section C of this Chapter; the issue of limitations on remedies will be discussed in more detail in Section D of this Chapter.

2. Section 2 of the FAA provides that arbitration agreements "shall be valid, irrevocable, and enforceable, save upon such grounds that exist at law or in equity for the revocation *of any contract*." Thus, the application of state law is constrained because courts must "apply ordinary state-law principles that govern the formation of contracts." First Options of Chicago, Inc. v. Kaplan, 514 U.S. 938, 944, 115 S.Ct. 1920, 131 L.Ed.2d 985 (1995). For example, in *Doctor's Associates, Inc. v. Casarotto*, 517 U.S. 681, 688, 116 S.Ct. 1652, 134 L.Ed.2d 902 (1996), the Supreme Court considered a Montana statute that required arbitration contracts to contain a "notice of arbitration" typed in underlined capital letters on the front page of the contract. A franchise agreement did not comply with this statute because the arbitration clause was on page nine, in ordinary type. The Supreme Court held that the Montana statute was preempted by the FAA because the Montana statute "condition[ed] the enforceability of arbitration agreements on compliance with a special notice requirement not applicable to contracts generally." The FAA "precludes States from singling out arbitration provisions for suspect status, requiring instead that such provisions be placed 'upon the same footing as other contracts.'" Thus, "courts may not invalidate arbitration agreements under state laws applicable *only* to arbitration provisions." For an extensive discussion of the subject, see Christopher R. Drahozal, *Federal Arbitration Act Preemption*, 79 Indiana Law Journal 393 (2004).

3. In Morrison v. Circuit City Stores, 317 F.3d 646 (6th Cir.2003), excerpted in Part D of this Chapter, the Sixth Circuit, en banc, examined the same arbitration agreement that the Ninth Circuit examined in *Adams* above. The Sixth Circuit held that under Ohio law, the arbitration agreement was neither procedurally nor substantively unconscionable. Thus, if courts use state contract law as a mechanism for invalidating lopsided arbitration agreements, the same arbitration agreement might be enforceable in one state but unenforceable in another. See also Carter v. Countrywide Credit Industries, Inc., 362 F.3d 294, 301 n.5 (5th Cir.2004) (enforcing under Texas law an arbitration agreement that was identical to an agreement the Ninth Circuit had refused to enforce, under California law, on unconscionability grounds). In *Textile Workers Union v. Lincoln Mills*, 353 U.S. 448, 77 S.Ct. 912, 1 L.Ed.2d 972 (1957), the Supreme Court federalized the law of labor arbitration because the Court feared that inconsistent state-court interpretations of collective bargaining agreements would discourage

collective bargaining and thereby foment labor unrest. Does this concern apply equally to employment arbitration? Why or why not?

4. Professor Robert S. Summers, describing the contract-law doctrine of good faith, stated:

In contract law, taken as a whole, good faith is an "excluder." It is a phrase without general meaning (or meanings) of its own and serves to exclude a wide range of heterogeneous forms of bad faith. In a particular context the phrase takes on a specific meaning, but usually this is only by way of contrast with the specific form of bad faith actually or hypothetically ruled out.

Robert S. Summers, *Good Faith in General Contract Law and the Sales Provisions of the Uniform Commercial Code*, 54 Virginia Law Review 195, 201 (1968). Can the same be said of unconscionability? What types of employment arbitration provisions should the unconscionability doctrine exclude?

5. The Ninth Circuit's decision not to sever the offending provisions had the effect of making the entire arbitration agreement unenforceable. Is this consistent with the pro-arbitration tenor of *Gilmer*? Is it consistent with the intent of the parties? Courts outside the Ninth Circuit are much more likely to sever the offending provisions and enforce the underlying agreement to arbitrate. See, e.g., Hadnot v. Bay, Ltd., 344 F.3d 474, 478 (5th Cir.2003) (severing provision that prohibited arbitrator from awarding punitive or exemplary damages); Gannon v. Circuit City Stores, Inc., 262 F.3d 677, 682 (8th Cir.2001) ("[I]f [courts] were to hold entire arbitration agreements unenforceable every time a particular term is held invalid, it would discourage parties from forming contracts under the FAA and severely chill parties from structuring their contracts in the most efficient manner for fear that minor terms eventually could be used to undermine the validity of the entire contract."). Since arbitration is contractual, what gives these courts the authority to judicially amend (as opposed to refusing to enforce) the contract? Doesn't a judicial approach that favors severance encourage employers to draft lopsided clauses? See Cooper v. MRM Investment Co., 367 F.3d 493, 502, 512 (6th Cir. 2004), quoting Brief of Amicus Curiae EEOC (an employer "will not be deterred from routinely inserting ... a deliberately illegal clause into the arbitration agreement it mandates for its employees if it knows that the worst penalty for such illegality is the severance of the clause after the employee has litigated the matter.").

3. STATE LAW: BREACH OF CONTRACT

HOOTERS OF AMERICA, INC. v. PHILLIPS
United States Court of Appeals for the Fourth Circuit, 1999.
173 F.3d 933.

Wilkinson, C.J.:

Annette R. Phillips alleges that she was sexually harassed while working at a Hooters restaurant. After quitting her job, Phillips threatened to sue Hooters in court. Alleging that Phillips agreed to arbitrate employment-related disputes, Hooters preemptively filed suit to compel arbitration under the Federal Arbitration Act, 9 U.S.C. § 4. Because Hooters set up a dispute resolution process utterly lacking in the rudiments of even-handedness, we hold that Hooters breached its agreement to arbitrate. Thus, we affirm the district court's refusal to compel arbitration.

I.

Appellee Annette R. Phillips worked as a bartender at a Hooters restaurant in Myrtle Beach, South Carolina. She was employed since 1989 by appellant, Hooters of Myrtle Beach (HOMB), a franchisee of appellant, Hooters of America (collectively Hooters).

Phillips alleges that in June 1996, Gerald Brooks, a Hooters official and the brother of HOMB's principal owner, sexually harassed her by grabbing and slapping her buttocks. After appealing to her manager for help and being told to "let it go," she quit her job. Phillips then contacted Hooters through an attorney claiming that the attack and the restaurant's failure to address it violated her Title VII rights. Hooters responded that she was required to submit her claims to arbitration according to a binding agreement to arbitrate between the parties.

This agreement arose in 1994 during the implementation of Hooters' alternative dispute resolution program. As part of that program, the company conditioned eligibility for raises, transfers, and promotions upon an employee signing an "Agreement to arbitrate employment-related disputes." The agreement provides that Hooters and the employee each agree to arbitrate all disputes arising out of employment, including "any claim of discrimination, sexual harassment, retaliation, or wrongful discharge, whether arising under federal or state law." The agreement further states that

> the employee and the company agree to resolve any claims pursuant to the company's rules and procedures for alternative resolution of employment-related disputes, as promulgated by the company from time to time ("the rules"). Company will make available or provide a copy of the rules upon written request of the employee.

The employees of HOMB were initially given a copy of this agreement at an all-staff meeting held on November 20, 1994. HOMB's general manager, Gene Fulcher, told the employees to review the agreement for five days and that they would then be asked to accept or reject the agreement. No employee, however, was given a copy of Hooters' arbitration rules and procedures. Phillips signed the agreement on November 25, 1994. When her personnel file was updated in April 1995, Phillips again signed the agreement.

After Phillips quit her job in June 1996, Hooters sent to her attorney a copy of the Hooters rules then in effect. Phillips refused to arbitrate the dispute.

Hooters filed suit in November 1996, to compel arbitration under 9 U.S.C. § 4. Phillips defended on the grounds that the agreement to arbitrate was unenforceable. Phillips also asserted individual and class counterclaims against Hooters for violations of Title VII and for a declaration that the arbitration agreements were unenforceable against the class. In response, Hooters requested that the district court stay the proceedings on the counterclaims until after arbitration, 9 U.S.C. § 3.

In March 1998, the district court denied Hooters' motions to compel arbitration and stay proceedings on the counterclaims. The court found that there was no meeting of the minds on all of the material terms of the agreement and even if there were, Hooters' promise to arbitrate was illusory. In addition, the court found that the arbitration agreement was unconscionable and void for reasons of public policy. Hooters filed this interlocutory appeal, 9 U.S.C. § 16.

[The court reviewed *Gilmer* and its progeny and concluded that employment disputes are, as a general matter, arbitrable.]

III.

Predispute agreements to arbitrate Title VII claims are thus valid and enforceable. The question remains whether a binding arbitration agreement between Phillips and Hooters exists and compels Phillips to submit her Title VII claims to arbitration * * * .

Hooters argues that Phillips gave her assent to a bilateral agreement to arbitrate. That contract provided for the resolution by arbitration of all employment-related disputes, including claims arising under Title VII. Hooters claims the agreement to arbitrate is valid because Phillips twice signed it voluntarily. Thus, it argues the courts are bound to enforce it and compel arbitration.

We disagree. The judicial inquiry, while highly circumscribed, is not focused solely on an examination for contractual formation defects such as lack of mutual assent and want of consideration * * * . Courts also can investigate the existence of "such grounds as exist at law or in equity for the revocation of any contract." 9 U.S.C. § 2. However, the grounds for revocation must relate specifically to the arbitration clause and not just to the contract as a whole. Prima Paint Corp. v. Flood & Conklin Mfg. Co., 388 U.S. 395, 402–04, 87 S.Ct. 1801, 18 L.Ed.2d 1270 (1967); see also Wick v. Atlantic Marine, Inc., 605 F.2d 166, 168 (5th Cir.1979). In this case, the challenge goes to the validity of the arbitration agreement itself. Hooters materially breached the arbitration agreement by promulgating rules so egregiously unfair as to constitute a complete default of its contractual obligation to draft arbitration rules and to do so in good faith.

Hooters and Phillips agreed to settle any disputes between them not in a judicial forum, but in another neutral forum—arbitration. Their agreement provided that Hooters was responsible for setting up such a forum by promulgating arbitration rules and procedures. To this end, Hooters instituted a set of rules in July 1996.

The Hooters rules when taken as a whole, however, are so one-sided that their only possible purpose is to undermine the neutrality of the proceeding. The rules require the employee to provide the company notice of her claim at the outset, including "the nature of the Claim" and "the specific act(s) or omissions(s) which are the basis of the Claim." Rule 6–2(1), (2). Hooters, on the other hand, is not required to file any responsive pleadings or to notice its defenses. Additionally, at the time of filing this notice, the employee must provide the company with a list of all fact witnesses with a brief summary of the facts known to each. Rule 6–2(5). The company, however, is not required to reciprocate.

The Hooters rules also provide a mechanism for selecting a panel of three arbitrators that is crafted to ensure a biased decision maker. Rule 8. The employee and Hooters each select an arbitrator, and the two arbitrators in turn select a third. Good enough, except that the employee's arbitrator and the third arbitrator must be selected from a list of arbitrators created exclusively by Hooters. This gives Hooters control over the entire panel and places no limits whatsoever on whom Hooters can put on the list. Under the rules, Hooters is free to devise lists of partial arbitrators who have existing relationships, financial or familial, with Hooters and its management. In fact, the rules do not even prohibit Hooters from placing its managers, themselves, on the list. Further, nothing in the rules restricts Hooters from punishing arbitrators who rule against the company by removing them from the list. Given the unrestricted control that one party (Hooters) has over the panel, the selection of an impartial decision maker would be a surprising result.

Nor is fairness to be found once the proceedings are begun. Although Hooters may expand the scope of arbitration to any matter, "whether related or not to the Employee's Claim," the employee cannot raise "any matter not included in the Notice of Claim." Rules 4–2, 8–9. Similarly, Hooters is permitted to move for summary dismissal of employee claims before a hearing is held, whereas the employee is not permitted to seek summary judgment. Rule 14–4. Hooters, but not the employee, may record the arbitration hearing "by audio or videotaping or by verbatim transcription." Rule 18–1. The rules also grant Hooters the right to bring suit in court to vacate or modify an arbitral award when it can show, by a preponderance of the evidence, that the panel exceeded its authority. Rule 21–4. No such right is granted to the employee.

In addition, the rules provide that upon 30 days notice Hooters, but not the employee, may cancel the agreement to arbitrate. Rule 23–1. Moreover, Hooters reserves the right to modify the rules, "in whole or in part," whenever it wishes and "without notice" to the employee. Rule 24–1. Nothing in the rules even prohibits Hooters from changing the rules in the middle of an arbitration proceeding.

If by odd chance the unfairness of these rules were not apparent on their face, leading arbitration experts have decried their one-sidedness. George Friedman, Senior Vice President of the American Arbitration

Association (AAA), testified that the system established by the Hooters rules so deviated from minimum due process standards that the Association would refuse to arbitrate under those rules. George Nicolau, former president of both the National Academy of Arbitrators and the International Society of Professionals in Dispute Resolution, attested that the Hooters rules "are inconsistent with the concept of fair and impartial arbitration." He also testified that he was "certain that reputable designating agencies, such as the AAA and Jams/Endispute, would refuse to administer a program so unfair and one-sided as this one." Additionally, Dennis Nolan, Professor of Labor Law at the University of South Carolina, declared that the Hooters rules "do not satisfy the minimum requirements of a fair arbitration system." He found that the "most serious flaw" was that the "mechanism [for selecting arbitrators] violates the most fundamental aspect of justice, namely an impartial decision maker." Finally, Lewis Maltby, member of the Board of Directors of the AAA, testified that "This is without a doubt the most unfair arbitration program I have ever encountered."

* * *

We hold that the promulgation of so many biased rules—especially the scheme whereby one party to the proceeding so controls the arbitral panel—breaches the contract entered into by the parties. The parties agreed to submit their claims to arbitration—a system whereby disputes are fairly resolved by an impartial third party. Hooters by contract took on the obligation of establishing such a system. By creating a sham system unworthy even of the name of arbitration, Hooters completely failed in performing its contractual duty.

Moreover, Hooters had a duty to perform its obligations in good faith * * *. By agreeing to settle disputes in arbitration, Phillips agreed to the prompt and economical resolution of her claims. She could legitimately expect that arbitration would not entail procedures so wholly one-sided as to present a stacked deck. Thus we conclude that the Hooters rules also violate the contractual obligation of good faith.

Given Hooters' breaches of the arbitration agreement and Phillips' desire not to be bound by it, we hold that rescission is the proper remedy. Generally, "rescission will not be granted for a minor or casual breach of a contract, but only for those breaches which defeat the object of the contracting parties." Rogers v. Salisbury Brick Corp., 299 S.C. 141, 382 S.E.2d 915, 917 (1989) * * *. As we have explained, Hooters' breach is by no means insubstantial; its performance under the contract was so egregious that the result was hardly recognizable as arbitration at all. We therefore permit Phillips to cancel the agreement and thus Hooters' suit to compel arbitration must fail.[2]

2. Phillips asserts that the Hooters rules also attempt to effect a waiver of substantive statutory rights by limiting the remedies that an arbitration panel may award. She further argues that employees cannot waive substantive statutory rights in predispute arbitration agreements, or at the very least, such waivers must be knowing and voluntary. Because we hold that no valid agreement to arbitrate exists in this case, we need not take up these questions.

By promulgating this system of warped rules, Hooters so skewed the process in its favor that Phillips has been denied arbitration in any meaningful sense of the word. To uphold the promulgation of this aberrational scheme under the heading of arbitration would undermine, not advance, the federal policy favoring alternative dispute resolution. This we refuse to do. The judgment of the district court is affirmed, and the case is remanded for further proceedings consistent with this opinion.

Notes and Questions

1. What provision of the arbitration agreement did Hooters breach? An express provision? An implied provision? If the latter, then given the contractual nature of arbitration agreements, on what authority did the court imply into the agreement a provision to which the parties did not agree? If an arbitrator had similarly implied a term into the agreement, would the arbitrator have exceeded the scope of her authority?

2. In *Hooters*, the arbitration agreement itself was silent concerning arbitral procedures; the arbitral rules were contained in a separate document to which Phillips and other employees were not given access until after a dispute had arisen. What would the court have done with the case if Hooters had informed Phillips up front of the lopsided rules to which she was putatively agreeing? Couldn't Hooters argue that it would be inappropriate for the court to imply a promise to create a fair agreement, since any such implied promise would be negated by the express terms of the agreement? Could a court hold that arbitration is *by definition* a fair process, and that lopsided agreements are not "arbitration" and therefore are not enforceable under the FAA?

3. Consider the following:

> Let us assume for a minute that for some reason all the rabbits and all the foxes decided to enter into a contract for mutual security, one provision of which were that any disputes arising out of the contract would be arbitrated by a panel of foxes. Somehow that shocks our consciences, and it doesn't help the rabbits very much either.

> Now, what happens if we have the same contract with the same arbitration provision, except that disputes will be arbitrated by a panel of wolves? Is there such a community of interest among foxes and wolves that the wolves cannot be impartial? Possibly. Now what happens if disputes will be resolved by a panel composed of one squirrel, one elephant, and one wolf? One might conclude that squirrels look like rabbits, wolves look like foxes, and elephants ought surely to be impartial.

> Animal law becomes procedurally very complex if for a moment we assume *arguendo* that we will absolutely prohibit an arbitration provision which provides for arbitration by a panel of foxes, and that we will also prohibit arbitration by a panel of wolves in recognition of their community of interest with foxes. What happens then if there is a sincere effort to obtain a fair panel of arbitrators, as for example the

squirrel, elephant, and wolf, and the decision in a forthcoming dispute is expected legitimately to go against the rabbits?

The rabbits, whom we may logically assume will have retained the services of some sharks to represent them, will go into court and plead "wolfery", that is to say, that the elephant also has a community of interest with the foxes and wolves, so that for all intents and purposes it is the same as if he were a wolf, which is the same as a fox. The rabbits will obviously demand a hearing and a full-blown jury trial on the question of whether an elephant looks more like a squirrel or more like a wolf, and as soon as the law gives the rabbits a hearing, the foxes, relying in good faith on arbitration, might as well kiss themselves goodbye, because not only will they be forced to go to arbitration, but they will also be forced to go through the whole thing again in court either in the first instance when the rabbits seek to enjoin arbitration, or after arbitration when they, the foxes, seek to enforce their award. The purpose of arbitration, namely just, speedy, economical conflict resolution is defeated if the foxes must demonstrate the fairness of the procedure in order to disprove the allegation of "wolfery".

However, if the courts attempt to avoid the problem of the frivolous plea of "wolfery", by writing strong syllabus points making arbitration provisions absolutely binding and enforceable in all cases, then all the fox lawyers come out of the woodwork and begin writing arbitration provisions, with wolves for arbitrators, into all contracts, regardless of the nature of the transaction. If the foxes are blessed with a strong bargaining position they will be able to take advantage of unwary rabbits on all occasions and defeat the prosecution of just claims against themselves.

Board of Education v. W. Harley Miller, Inc., 160 W.Va. 473, 478–79, 236 S.E.2d 439, 443 (1977). Which way does the parable cut? Is there an answer?

4. Should courts ever enforce predispute agreements in which employees waive or alter substantive rights? Does *Gilmer* offer firm guidance on this issue? What about an agreement that either shortens or extends the statute of limitations? See. e.g., Ingle v. Circuit City Stores, Inc., 328 F.3d 1165, 1175 (9th Cir.2003) (refusing to enforce an arbitration agreement which, among other things, imposed a one-year statute of limitations); EEOC v. River Oaks Imaging and Diagnostic, 67 Fair Empl. Prac. Cas. (BNA) 1243 (S.D.Tex.1995) (refusing to enforce arbitration clause that, among other things, gave employees *more* time to file arbitration claim than they had to file EEOC charge; extended filing period could lull employees into not filing timely charge with the EEOC). Would it matter whether statutes of limitations are considered "substantive" or "procedural"?

5. Should courts enforce arbitration agreements that contain forum selection clauses? Should courts consider such clauses on a case-by-case basis, or create a *per se* rule? See Domingo v. Ameriquest Mortgage Co., 70 Fed.Appx. 919 (9th Cir. 2003) (refusing to enforce arbitration agreement that, among other things, required an employee in Hawai'i to arbitrate a claim in California); Carter v. Countrywide Credit Industries, Inc., 362 F.3d 294 (5th Cir.2004) (enforcing arbitration agreement containing forum selection clause because employees all lived near the designated forum); Ciago v. Ameriquest Mortgage Co., 295 F.Supp.2d 324, 330 (S.D.N.Y.2003) (holding

that the validity and meaning of specific provisions within an arbitration agreement, including a forum selection clause that would require a New York employee to arbitrate in California, is a matter for the arbitrator to decide).

6. Should courts enforce arbitration agreements that forbid employees to bring claims as a class action? In Green Tree Financial Corp. v. Bazzle, 539 U.S. 444, 123 S.Ct. 2402, 156 L.Ed.2d 414 (2003), the Supreme Court considered a state court's decision ordering class arbitration under state law in the context of a consumer arbitration agreement that was silent about whether class arbitration was forbidden or allowed. After concluding that the agreement did not expressly forbid class arbitration, a plurality of the Court held that "[u]nder the terms of the parties' contracts, the question–whether the agreement forbids class arbitration–is for the arbitrator to decide." The Court found it significant that the contract's provision to submit to arbitration "*all* disputes, claims, or controversies arising from or relating to this contract or the relationships which result from this contract" reflected the parties' intent to commit a broad scope of questions to arbitration, including the class arbitration question, because that issue "relat[ed] to the contract." See also Carter v. Countrywide Credit Industries, Inc., 362 F.3d 294 (5th Cir.2004) (enforcing arbitration agreement that prohibited employees from bringing classwide arbitration); Ingle v. Circuit City Stores, Inc., 328 F.3d 1165, 1176 (9th Cir.2003) (refusing to enforce such an agreement); Jean R. Sternlight, *As Mandatory Binding Arbitration Meets the Class Action, Will the Class Action Survive*, 42 William and Mary Law Review 1 (2000) (arguing that courts should protect the right of employees to seek class relief); Matthew W. Finkin, *Employee Representation Outside the Labor Act: Thoughts on Arbitral Representation, Group Arbitration, and Workplace Committees*, 5 University of Pennsylvania Journal of Labor and Employment Law 75, 86 (2002) (arguing that contractual prohibitions on class actions run afoul of *Gilmer*'s admonition that arbitration is merely a substitute forum that does not involve the loss of substantive rights).

Section 7 of the National Labor Relations Act gives employees the right to engage in "concerted activities for the purpose of collective bargaining or other mutual aid or protection." Does this provision give employees the right to proceed collectively through a class action?

7. Did the attorneys for Hooters who drafted the one-sided arbitration rules at issue in that case serve the interests of their client? What would have been a more appropriate approach?

C. CONTRACT–FORMATION ISSUES

Recall that Section 2 of the FAA provides that arbitration agreements "shall be valid, irrevocable, and enforceable, save upon such grounds that exist at law or in equity for the revocation of any contract." Courts have construed the "any contract" language as indicating that state contract law applies to contract-formation issues. The most commonly-raised contract-formation issues are consideration, adhesion contracts, unconscionability, and notice. These issues often overlap. Consider how they apply to the case below.

TINDER v. PINKERTON SECURITY

United States Court of Appeals for the Seventh Circuit, 2002.
305 F.3d 728.

MANION, CIRCUIT JUDGE

Ilah Tinder began employment with Pinkerton on October 21, 1996, and was assigned to work as a security officer at a General Motors facility in Janesville, Wisconsin. The following day, Tinder received a copy of Pinkerton's employee handbook [which provided, among other things,] that Pinkerton reserved the right to change its policies [and] rules. When notifying its employees of policy or rule changes, Pinkerton typically inserts a "payroll stuffer" in the envelope with each employee's paycheck. Occasionally, notices of policy or rule changes are accompanied by acknowledgment forms that employees were required to sign and return to management.

In October 1997, Pinkerton issued to all of its employees as a payroll stuffer a color brochure entitled "Pinkerton's Arbitration Program." The brochure announced that Pinkerton was instituting a mandatory arbitration program effective January 1, 1998, broadly covering all legal claims including discrimination under the federal civil rights statutes. * * * The brochure emphasized that * * * both the employees and the company were bound by the policy * * * *. The brochure suggested that opting out of the program was not possible if the employee wished to remain on the job past the effective date of the policy:

Q. What if I do not want to be covered by this binding arbitration program?

A. Effective January 1, 1998, all employees, including the CEO, are covered by the program. By remaining employed at Pinkerton through the effective date, you are agreeing to be covered by the program and you waive your right to a court trial.

* * * The brochure was not accompanied by an acknowledgment form.

Tinder did not recall receiving or seeing the arbitration brochure. Pinkerton produced two affidavits stating that Tinder received the brochure, however. The first affidavit, from Director of Employee Relations Kathy Rasmussen, asserted that Pinkerton's central office distributed copies of the brochure to each of its district offices with instructions to insert it as a payroll stuffer in the envelope along with each employee's paycheck. According to Rasmussen, Pinkerton sent a memorandum to its district office managers along with the brochures emphasizing the importance of the program and the need to promptly distribute the brochures. Rasmussen went on to aver that Pinkerton's legal department later issued a second memorandum confirming that the brochure had been distributed to all district offices. In the second affidavit, Mark Cruciani, manager of Pinkerton's district office in Milwaukee, asserted that Tinder was paid through his office; that his office distributed the brochure to all of its employees along with their paychecks on the payday following the date Pinkerton instructed its district offices to circulate the brochure; and that Tinder received her salary by check, not by direct deposit into a bank account. * * *

In fall 1998, Tinder verbally complained to her supervisor, Bradley Bastain, that she believed she was the victim of gender discrimination on the job. Tinder complained that, unlike her male co-workers, she was required to work overtime, was not promptly paid for her work, and was not reimbursed for her purchase of boots for her uniform. Instead of taking action to remedy Tinder's complaints, Bastain admonished Tinder that he was tired of hearing her "continual complaints to upper management." In November 1998, Bastain informed Tinder that he was removing her from her assigned post, and warned her that her work hours would be reduced if she continued to complain about her work environment. Tinder alleged that after this, Bastain reduced her pay and refused to accommodate her request to take Sundays off so she could attend religious services. She interpreted these actions as retaliation for complaining about discrimination. Shortly after these events, Tinder quit.

Claiming constructive discharge and retaliation in violation of Title VII, Tinder filed charges with the United States Equal Employment Opportunity Commission, received a right-to-sue letter, and timely filed this lawsuit in March 2000. Pinkerton immediately moved to stay proceedings and compel arbitration, [and] the district court agreed.

Tinder argues that any agreement she made to submit her claims to arbitration was not supported by valid consideration. She also contends that the district court erred in compelling her to arbitrate because she had no notice of the policy's implementation; she neither signed any acknowledgment agreeing to be bound nor was she allowed to opt out; the policy was not implemented until after she began employment with the company; and the contract is illusory. We review *de novo* the district court's decision to compel arbitration based on its finding that an enforceable arbitration agreement existed between the parties.

The FAA mandates enforcement of valid, written arbitration agreements. * * * We evaluate agreements to arbitrate under the same standards as any other contract. Whether a binding arbitration agreement exists is determined under principles of state contract law. Because all relevant events occurred in Wisconsin, Wisconsin law determines the validity of the agreement.

* * * Wisconsin courts treat contracts concerning employment like any other contract. This includes agreements formed subsequent to an employment at-will that supplant or alter the nature of the employment relationship. In such a case, to be enforceable the agreement must be supported by consideration. In Wisconsin, consideration consists of either a detriment to the promisor or a benefit to the promisee. A promise for a promise, or the exchange of promises, is adequate consideration to support a bilateral contract. An employer's promise to arbitrate in

exchange for an employee's promise to do the same constitutes sufficient consideration to support the arbitration agreement.

Tinder points out, however, that Pinkerton unilaterally implemented its arbitration program without input from her or its employees. This, she argues, shows that she never promised to arbitrate her dispute. But Pinkerton's unilateral decision to implement the program does not demonstrate that Tinder did not agree to be bound. The agreement provided expressly that by remaining employed at Pinkerton after the effective date of the arbitration program Tinder, like all other employees, agreed to submit her claims to arbitration. Wisconsin recognizes that, because at-will employees are free to quit their jobs at any time, at-will employees give adequate consideration for employer promises that modify or supplant the at-will employment relationship by remaining on the job. Tinder remained on the job past the effective date of the program. Doing such evidenced her mutual promise to arbitrate her disputes with Pinkerton.

The party opposing arbitration must identify a triable issue of fact concerning the existence of the agreement in order to obtain a trial on the merits of the contract. The FAA does not expressly identify the evidentiary standard a party seeking to avoid compelled arbitration must meet. But courts that have addressed the question have analogized the standard to that required of a party opposing summary judgment under Rule 56(e) of the Federal Rules of Civil Procedure: the opposing party must demonstrate that a genuine issue of material fact warranting a trial exists. [Citations omitted.] Just as in summary judgment proceedings, a party cannot avoid compelled arbitration by generally denying the facts upon which the right to arbitration rests; the party must identify specific evidence in the record demonstrating a material factual dispute for trial.

In deciding whether the party opposing summary judgment (and by analogy compelled arbitration) has identified a genuine issue of material fact for trial, "the evidence of the non-movant is to be believed and all justifiable inferences are to be drawn in his favor." *Anderson v. Liberty Lobby, Inc.*, 477 U.S. 242, 255, 106 S.Ct. 2505, 91 L.Ed.2d 202 (1986). But Tinder's only evidence that she never received notice of the program was her own affidavit in which she avers that she "does not recall seeing or reviewing the Arbitration Program brochure that Defendant alleges was included with her payroll check in October, 1997," and this does not raise a genuine issue of material fact. Tinder asserted only that she does not remember receiving or seeing the brochure, whereas the uncontroverted affidavits of Kathy Rasmussen and Mark Cruciani indicate that the brochure was definitely sent and presumably received with her paycheck. Tinder's affidavit thus does not raise a genuine issue whether the brochure was distributed to her. [Citations omitted.] The district court therefore correctly compelled arbitration without a trial on whether a contract was formed.

Tinder also asserts that Pinkerton's promises were illusory because Pinkerton reserved the right to modify or terminate its policies at any time. But a valid arbitration agreement exists, and both parties are bound by it.

Because Tinder continued her at-will employment past the effective date of the arbitration policy, and because Pinkerton agreed to bind itself to the arbitration policy, we conclude that adequate consideration supported Tinder's agreement to arbitrate, and the agreement was enforceable under Wisconsin law. The district court therefore correctly compelled Tinder to submit her Title VII claims to arbitration. The judgment of the district court is

AFFIRMED.

Notes and Questions

1.   The _Tinder_ court held that under Wisconsin law, an employer is not required to give an employee "additional consideration" in return for the employee's promise to arbitrate, because the employer's reciprocal promise to arbitrate is sufficient. What if the arbitration agreement gives the employer the unilateral right to amend or cancel the agreement? See Floss v. Ryan's Family Steak Houses, Inc., 211 F.3d 306, 313 (6th Cir.2000); Cheek v. United Healthcare, 378 Md. 139, 835 A.2d 656 (Md.2003) (the employer's reservation of the right " 'to alter, amend, modify, or revoke" the [Arbitration] Policy at its sole and absolute discretion at any time with or without notice' creates no real promise, and therefore, insufficient consideration to support an enforceable agreement to arbitrate."). What if the agreement provides that all claims brought by employees must be arbitrated, but that the employer has the option of either arbitrating or litigating its claims? See Gibson v. Neighborhood Health Clinics, Inc., 121 F.3d 1126, 1130–32 (7th Cir.1997) (refusing to enforce agreement by which the employee, but not the employer, agreed to arbitrate all future claims).

2.   Pinkerton announced an arbitration program to employees and declared that by continuing to work after the implementation date, they were agreeing to the program. This raises the issue of whether the arbitration agreement was a contract of adhesion. See Circuit City Stores, Inc. v. Adams, 279 F.3d 889 (9th Cir.2002) (excerpted _supra_ XI.B.2). Are compulsory arbitration agreements adhesive? Can a generalization be made as to all such agreements, or must this issue be decided on a case-by-case basis? What factors should a court consider in making a determination of adhesion? What exactly does adhesion mean in the employment context? If it means "free from economic pressure," would _any_ contractual provision (e.g., rate-of-pay, or work hours) required by the employer be enforceable? Compare David S. Schwartz, _Enforcing Small Print to Protect Big Business: Employee and Consumer Rights Claims in an Age of Compelled Arbitration,_ 1997 Wisconsin Law Review 33, with Stephen J. Ware, _Consumer Arbitration as Exceptional Consumer Law (With a Contractualist Reply to Carrington & Haagen),_ 29 McGeorge Law Review 195 (1998). See also Cooper v. MRM Investment Co., 367 F.3d 493, 502, 505 (6th Cir. 2004) (to prove adhesion, employee must show that she would be unable to find suitable employment elsewhere if she refused to sign the employer's employment arbitration agreement).

3.   Tinder might have argued that Pinkerton's apparent retention of a unilateral right to modify the arbitration agreement was unconscionable. See, e.g., Circuit City Stores, Inc. v. Mantor, 335 F.3d 1101, 1107 (9th Cir.2003); Ingle v. Circuit City Stores, Inc., 328 F.3d 1165, 1179 (9th Cir.2003). In most states, a contract, to be unenforceable, must be both procedurally and substantively unconscionable. Procedural unconscionability describes the process of contract formation, and focuses on the relative bargaining power between the parties and on whether the drafting party attempted to hide some of the terms of the contract. Circuit City Stores, Inc. v. Adams, 279 F.3d 889, 892–93 (9th Cir.2002) (applying California law). The *Hooters* case is a good example of this, because Hooters required Phillips to sign the arbitration agreement without first giving her access to the arbitration rules which were incorporated by reference into the arbitration agreement. Many contract-formation challenges raise the issue of procedural unconscionability. See also Wilcox v. Valero Refining Co., 256 F.Supp.2d 687, 691 (S.D.Tex.2003) (holding that it was procedurally unconscionable under Texas law for an employer to implement a binding arbitration policy on an employee who already had initiated a lawsuit against the employer).

Substantive unconscionability refers to unduly harsh or oppressive contract terms. Many courts use a sliding scale of procedural and substantive unconscionability: the more substantively unconscionable the contract, the less evidence of procedural unconscionability is required before courts will void a contract as unenforceable, and vice-versa. While issues of procedural unconscionability often focus on contract formation, issues of substantive unconscionability may extend well beyond contract formation, as the *Hooters* case illustrates.

4.   Tinder argued that she could not have assented to Pinkerton's arbitration program because she could not recall having received notice of it.

(a) The Seventh Circuit recited the summary-judgment standard that required it to make all justifiable inferences in favor of Tinder. Did the court actually do this? Why didn't Tinder's affidavit create an issue of fact? Would the case have come out differently if Tinder had stated unequivocally in her affidavit that she had not received notice? What, if anything, should the court have made of the fact that Pinkerton had not required employees to sign and return an acknowledgment form?

(b) Other courts have taken a less jaundiced view of employees' notice claims. For example, in Buckley v. Nabors Drilling USA, Inc., 190 F.Supp.2d 958, 965 (S.D.Tex.2002), the employer mailed copies of its Dispute Resolution Policy (DRP) to employees with their paychecks. The court found that this was insufficient to prove an employee's consent to the DRP:

> Defendant argues that the mailing and assumed receipt of the DRP adequately establishes Buckley's acceptance of the terms of the DRP, including its binding arbitration provision. Portraying the DRP as a permissible contractual modification of the at-will employment relationship between itself and Buckley, Defendant believes that Buckley's continued employment [] after receiving the DRP constitutes acknowledgment and acceptance of the DRP under Louisiana law. The Court agrees with Defendant that an unsigned written arbitration agreement may be valid under the FAA. The Court further recognizes that the

mailing of a document may create a presumption that such document was received. However, even assuming that Buckley received the DRP, there is absolutely no evidence that Buckley actually read, or, more importantly, understood the contents of the DRP. Buckley never signed or returned the acknowledgment letter enclosed in the DRP mailing, which generally would tend to indicate that an agreement had been reached. Additionally, there is no indication that [Defendant] made any other attempts to notify Buckley of the DRP and its binding arbitration clause anytime thereafter. Without more proof that Buckley actually read and understood the terms of the DRP, this Court is loath to declare that Buckley entered into a binding arbitration agreement.

Similarly, in Campbell v. General Dynamics Governments Systems Corp, 321 F.Supp.2d 142 (D.Mass. 2004), the court held that an employer's mass e-mail message to employees advising them of the establishment of a new arbitration policy for legal claims and describing the policy only through links was insufficient notice. See also Prevot v. Phillips Petroleum Co., 133 F.Supp.2d 937, 939–41 (S.D.Tex. 2001) (applying Texas law) (invalidating arbitration agreements where the agreements were written in English and given to employees who understood only Spanish); American Heritage Life Insurance Co. v. Lang, 321 F.3d 533 (5th Cir.2003) (applying Mississippi law) (in a consumer arbitration case, an illiterate borrower who claimed a lender did not inform him that he was signing an arbitration agreement created an issue of fact on whether the borrower consented to arbitration).

(c) The conditions under which employers require employees to sign arbitration agreements can give rise to claims that the agreements should not be enforced. In Maye v. Smith Barney Inc., 897 F.Supp. 100 (S.D.N.Y. 1995), the plaintiffs claimed that they each were told to sign their names approximately seventy-five times on a variety of documents (including an arbitration agreement) in a period of two hours without anyone explaining the contents of the documents and without an adequate opportunity to read most of them. The plaintiffs also complained that when they were told to sign these documents the atmosphere was "intimidating, hurried, and tense." The United States District Court for the Southern District of New York nonetheless granted the employer's motion to compel arbitration. However, in Berger v. Cantor Fitzgerald Securities, 942 F.Supp. 963 (S.D.N.Y.1996), a different judge from the Southern District of New York refused to compel arbitration where the plaintiff advanced a similar argument. On facts similar to *Maye*, the Court denied the employer's motion to compel, and instead ordered the parties to engage in discovery concerning the circumstances surrounding the plaintiff's signing of the arbitration agreement. The Court distinguished *Maye* by noting that in *Maye*, the one-page arbitration agreement contained a detailed explanation of the arbitration procedures and expressly defined the employment disputes covered by the agreement, whereas in *Berger,* the U–4 form merely made reference to the NASD rules with which the plaintiff was not provided. Do you agree that the cases are distinguishable? See also Brennan v. Bally Total Fitness, 198 F.Supp.2d 377, 383 (S.D.N.Y.2002) (refusing to enforce arbitration agreement where employer gave employee no more than fifteen minutes to review a sixteen-page single-spaced agreement).

(d) The notice issue also arises when the arbitration agreement is unclear regarding its scope. For example, in Prudential Insurance Company of America v. Lai, 42 F.3d 1299 (9th Cir.1994), the Ninth Circuit held that it will not enforce an employment arbitration agreement that was not knowingly entered into by the aggrieved employee. (Subsequent decisions have attributed to *Lai* a "knowing and voluntary" requirement, based on legislative history cited by the *Lai* court in support of its holding.) In *Lai*, the court refused to enforce an arbitration agreement contained in a U–4 form (similar to the one the plaintiff in *Gilmer* had signed) because the employees who had signed the form lacked specific knowledge that they might have to arbitrate sexual discrimination claims; neither the Form U–4 nor the old NASD rule it incorporated "refer[ed] to employment disputes" or "describ[ed] any disputes the parties agreed to arbitrate." Similarly, in Nelson v. Cyprus Bagdad Copper Corp., 119 F.3d 756 (9th Cir.1997), the court refused to enforce arbitration provisions contained in an employee handbook, because the form signed by the employee acknowledging that he had "received and read" the handbook did not refer to, or provide that the employee agreed to, arbitration.

(e) Consider the following:

> [T]here is a good public policy reason to supervise contracts to substitute private dispute mechanisms for public ones. This proposition * * * is based on the assumption that choices between arbitration and litigation are likely systematically to be made by at least one of the parties on the basis of no information, inadequate information or misinformation, and that one party to the transaction is likely to know that * * * . This is a strong reason, therefore, to require the lowest cost avoider, presumably the party seeking to impose a mandatory arbitration agreement, to provide reliable information to the party being asked to give up the right to go to court.

Paul H. Haagen, *New Wineskins for New Wine: The Need to Encourage Fairness in Mandatory Arbitration*, 40 Arizona Law Review 1039, 1059–60 (1998). Do you agree?

D. ARBITRATION FEES

GREEN TREE FINANCIAL CORP.— ALABAMA v. RANDOLPH

Supreme Court of the United States, 2000.
531 U.S. 79, 121 S.Ct. 513 148 L.Ed.2d 373.

REHNQUIST, J.

[Purchaser of mobile home (Larketta Randolph) sued lender which had financed the purchase (Green Tree), asserting claims under the Truth in Lending Act and Equal Credit Opportunity Act. Green Tree moved to compel arbitration. The District Court granted Green Tree's motion to compel arbitration. Randolph appealed. The appellate court] determined that the arbitration agreement failed to provide the minimum guarantees that respondent could vindicate her statutory rights under the TILA. Critical to this determination was the court's observation that the arbitration agreement was silent with respect to payment of filing fees, arbitrators' costs, and other arbitration expenses. On that basis, the court held that the agreement to arbitrate posed a risk that respondent's ability to vindicate her statutory rights would be undone by "steep" arbitration costs, and therefore was unenforceable.

We now turn to the question whether Randolph's agreement to arbitrate is unenforceable because it says nothing about the costs of arbitration, and thus fails to provide her protection from potentially substantial costs of pursuing her federal statutory claims in the arbitral forum. [Randolph contends] that the arbitration agreement's silence with respect to costs and fees creates a "risk" that she will be required to bear prohibitive arbitration costs if she pursues her claims in an arbitral forum, and thereby forces her to forgo any claims she may have against [Green Tree]. Therefore, she argues, she is unable to vindicate her statutory rights in arbitration.

It may well be that the existence of large arbitration costs could preclude a litigant such as Randolph from effectively vindicating her federal statutory rights in the arbitral forum. But the record does not show that Randolph will bear such costs if she goes to arbitration. Indeed, it contains hardly any information on the matter. As the Court of Appeals recognized, "we lack ... information about how claimants fare under Green Tree's arbitration clause." The record reveals only the arbitration agreement's silence on the subject, and that fact alone is plainly insufficient to render it unenforceable. The "risk" that Randolph will be saddled with prohibitive costs is too speculative to justify the invalidation of an arbitration agreement.

To invalidate the agreement on that basis would undermine the "liberal federal policy favoring arbitration agreements." *Moses H. Cone Memorial Hospital,* 460 U.S., at 24, 103 S.Ct. 927. It would also conflict with our prior holdings that the party resisting arbitration bears the burden of proving that the claims at issue are unsuitable for arbitration. We have held that the party seeking to avoid arbitration bears the burden of establishing that Congress intended to preclude arbitration of the statutory claims at issue. See *Gilmer, supra; McMahon, supra.* Similarly, we believe that where, as here, a party seeks to invalidate an arbitration agreement on the ground that arbitration would be prohibitively expensive, that party bears the burden of showing the likelihood of incurring such costs. Randolph did not meet that burden. How detailed the showing of prohibitive expense must be before the party seeking arbitration must come forward with contrary evidence is a matter we need not discuss; for in this case neither during discovery nor when the case was presented on the merits was there any timely showing at all on the point. The Court of Appeals therefore erred in deciding that the arbitration agreement's silence with respect to costs and fees rendered it unenforceable.

MORRISON v. CIRCUIT CITY STORES

United States Court of Appeals for the Sixth Circuit, 2003, en banc.
317 F.3d 646.

MOORE, J.

Lillian Pebbles Morrison submitted an application for a managerial position at a Circuit City store in Cincinnati, Ohio. As part of the application process, Morrison was required to sign a document entitled "Dispute Resolution Agreement." This document contained an arbitration clause that required resolution of all disputes or controversies arising out of employment with Circuit City in an arbitral forum.

* * *

Pursuant to Rule 13 of the Dispute Resolution Agreement, Circuit City is required to advance all costs for the arbitration, but each party is required to pay one-half of the costs of arbitration following the issuance of an arbitration award, unless the arbitrator decides to use her discretionary power to require the losing party to pay all arbitration costs. Such costs include "the daily or hourly fees and expenses (including travel) of the Arbitrator who decides the case, filing or administrative fees charged by the Arbitration Service, the cost of a reporter [to] transcribe[ ] the proceeding, and expenses of renting a room in which the arbitration is held," as well as incidental costs such as "photocopying or the costs of producing witnesses or proof." Rule 13 further provides that all arbitration costs must be paid within ninety calendar days of the issuance of the arbitration award. In addition, that rule provides that, if an employee is able to pay her share of the arbitration costs within this ninety day period, her costs (not including attorney fees) are then limited to the greater of either five hundred dollars or three percent of her most recent annual compensation. An employee who is not able to arrange to pay this amount within ninety days of the award's issuance, however, must pay her entire share of the costs. Circuit City also reserves the right to deduct up to five percent of the employee's compensation per pay period to satisfy any outstanding obligation.

Rule 14 [] places limits on the amount of monetary damages that may be awarded, allowing for twelve months of back pay, "starting from the point at which the Associate knew or should have known of the events giving rise to the alleged violation," and allowing any back pay award to be "reduced by interim earnings, public or private benefits received, and amounts that could have been received with reasonable diligence." Additionally, Rule 14 states that an arbitrator may award only up to twenty-four months of front pay and limits any award of punitive damages to the greater of $5,000 or an amount equal to the sum of the front and back pay awards.

Morrison began her employment at Circuit City on or about December 1, 1995. Two years later, on December 12, 1997, she was terminated.

Morrison alleges that her termination was the result of race and sex discrimination. She filed this lawsuit on December 11, 1998 * * *

Morrison argue[s] on appeal that the cost-splitting provisions in the arbitration agreements have the effect of denying her an effective forum for the vindication of [her] statutory rights. The Supreme Court has made clear that statutory rights, such as those created by Title VII, may be subject to mandatory arbitration only if the arbitral forum permits the effective vindication of those rights. If, then, the splitting or sharing of the costs of the arbitral forum under a particular arbitration agreement effectively prevents the vindication of a plaintiff's statutory rights, those rights cannot be subject to mandatory arbitration under that agreement. [E]mployers should not be permitted to draft arbitration agreements that deter a substantial number of potential litigants from seeking any forum for the vindication of their rights. To allow this would fatally undermine the federal anti-discrimination statutes, as it would enable employers to evade the requirements of federal law altogether.

Although the Tenth, Eleventh, and D.C. Circuits have suggested that such cost-splitting provisions *per se* deny litigants an effective forum for the vindication of their statutory rights, most courts, including this one, that have addressed this question have held that this issue must be decided on a case-by-case basis. In *Green Tree Financial Corp.-Alabama v. Randolph,* 531 U.S. 79, 121 S.Ct. 513, 148 L.Ed.2d 373 (2000), the Supreme Court adopted a case-by-case approach to determining whether a cost-splitting provision in an arbitration agreement denies potential litigants the opportunity to vindicate their statutory rights.

We believe that the following propositions of law can be derived from *Green Tree.* First, in some cases, the potential of incurring large arbitration costs and fees will deter potential litigants from seeking to vindicate their rights in the arbitral forum. Under *Gilmer,* the arbitral forum must provide litigants with an effective substitute for the judicial forum; if the fees and costs of the arbitral forum deter potential litigants, then that forum is clearly not an effective, or even adequate, substitute for the judicial forum. Second, where that prospect deters potential litigants, the arbitration agreement, or, at minimum, the cost-splitting provision contained within it, is unenforceable under *Gilmer.* Third, the burden of demonstrating that incurring such costs is likely under a given set of circumstances rests, at least initially, with the party opposing arbitration.

However, *Green Tree* does not provide us with a standard for "[h]ow detailed the showing of prohibitive expenses must be" to support the conclusion that the provision, at minimum, is unenforceable. In that case, of course, the plaintiff had relied solely on the arbitration agreement's silence on the allocation of arbitration costs, and thus the risk of incurring such prohibitive costs was highly speculative, indeed. In the case[] before us, however, the arbitration agreement[] explicitly provide[s] for cost-splitting. Thus, we must determine the appropriate standard for determining whether a cost-splitting provision contained in an arbitration agreement is invalid.

The Fourth Circuit has posited such a standard. Under *Bradford v. Rockwell Semiconductor Systems, Inc.,* 238 F.3d 549, 556 (4th Cir.2001), the inquiry can be broken into three parts: (1) the potential litigant's ability to pay arbitration costs and fees; (2) the difference between the expected cost of arbitration to the litigant and the expected cost of a judicial forum; and (3) whether that difference "is so substantial as to deter the bringing of claims" in the arbitral forum. With respect to (1) and (2), *Bradford* emphasized that "an appropriate case-by-case inquiry must focus upon a claimant's expected or actual arbitration costs and his ability to pay those costs, measured against a baseline of the claimant's expected costs for litigation and his ability to pay those costs." *Id.* n. 5. In keeping with *Green Tree,* the party opposing arbitration–*i.e.,* the plaintiff–bears the burden of demonstrating these elements. *See Bradford,* 238 F.3d. at 557.

The *Bradford* test and similar approaches, however, suffer from at least two infirmities. First, requiring the plaintiff to come forward with concrete estimates of anticipated or expected arbitration costs asks too much at this initial stage in the proceedings. Before an arbitrator has been selected, for example, a plaintiff can only estimate the hourly rate that the arbitrator will charge. Under the *Bradford* case-by-case approach, such average figures may appear "too speculative" to support a finding that the costs are prohibitively expensive, even though the plaintiff has no other evidence of costs. Moreover, where arbitration agreements provide for the shifting of fees and costs by the arbitrator on the basis of the arbitrator's decision on the merits, potential litigants (and reviewing courts) may not be able to gauge the likelihood of success or cost-shifting, especially prior to discovery.

Second, the *Bradford* case-by-case approach is inadequate to protect the deterrent functions of the federal anti-discrimination statutes at issue. The issue is not only whether an individual claimant would be precluded from effectively vindicating his or her rights in an arbitral forum by the risk of incurring substantial costs, but also whether other similarly situated individuals would be deterred by those risks as well. A cost-splitting provision should be held unenforceable whenever it would have the "chilling effect" of deterring a substantial number of potential litigants from seeking to vindicate their statutory rights.

A number of courts have suggested that judicial review of arbitration awards will adequately safeguard the remedial and deterrent functions of federal anti-discrimination statutes. *Post hoc* judicial review of arbitration awards as a means of guaranteeing the adequacy of the arbitral forum for protecting federal statutory rights has a kind of superficial attractiveness. * * * Requiring plaintiffs to arbitrate their claims and then argue, either to the arbitrator or to the reviewing court, that the costs were prohibitive avoids the problem identified in *Green*

Tree, namely the "speculative" or "conjectural" nature of the costs of arbitration. * * *

This attractiveness is, however, only superficial; there are at least two problems with this approach. First, judicial review of arbitration awards is very narrow. Second, * * * [a]fter the plaintiff has arbitrated her claims, reviewing courts will not likely determine that this risk deterred the plaintiff; after all, the plaintiff has already arbitrated her claims. Deterrence occurs early in the process. If we do not know who will prevail on the ultimate cost-splitting question until the end, we know who has lost from the beginning: those whom the cost-splitting provision deterred from initiating their claims at all.

In sum, the *post hoc* judicial review approach places plaintiffs in a kind of "Catch–22." They cannot claim, in advance of arbitration, that the risk of incurring arbitration costs would deter them from arbitrating their claims because they do not know what the costs will be, but if they arbitrate and actually incur costs, they cannot then argue that the costs deterred them because they have already arbitrated their claims. Just as Yossarian could not escape flying combat missions by claiming that he was crazy because anyone wanting to be released from combat must be sane, under this approach potential litigants cannot escape arbitration by claiming that the costs are prohibitive until after arbitration, at which point the costs were not prohibitive, because the litigants actually arbitrated their disputes.

For these reasons, we reject the judicial-review approach * * *. [W]e adopt a case-by-case approach to this issue that we believe is more protective of statutory rights than that adopted by the Fourth Circuit in *Bradford.*

We hold that potential litigants must be given an opportunity, prior to arbitration on the merits, to demonstrate that the potential costs of arbitration are great enough to deter them and similarly situated individuals from seeking to vindicate their federal statutory rights in the arbitral forum. Our approach differs from the case-by-case approach advocated in *Bradford* by looking to the possible "chilling effect" of the cost-splitting provision on similarly situated potential litigants, as opposed to its effect merely on the actual plaintiff in any given case. This difference in approach is premised on *Gilmer,* which held that "[s]o long as the prospective litigant effectively may vindicate [his or her] statutory cause of action in the arbitral forum, the statute will continue to serve both its remedial and deterrent function." 500 U.S. at 28, 111 S.Ct. 1647 (quotation omitted). As *Gilmer* makes clear, federal anti-discrimination statutes play both a remedial and deterrent role. Although the former role is largely a matter of the rights of particular aggrieved individuals, the latter is a question of "broader social purposes." *Id.* The deterrent function of the laws in question is, in part, that employers who engage in discriminatory practices are aware that they may incur liability in more than one case. If, however, a cost-splitting provision would deter a substantial number of potential litigants, then that provision undermines the deterrent effect of the anti-discrimination statutes. Thus, in order to protect the statutory rights at issue, the reviewing court must look to more than just the interests and conduct of a particular plaintiff. [I]f the reviewing court finds that the cost-splitting provision would deter a substantial number of similarly situated potential litigants, it should refuse to enforce the cost-splitting provision in order to serve the underlying functions of the federal statute. In conducting this analysis, the reviewing court should define the class of such similarly situated potential litigants by job description and socioeconomic background. It should take the actual plaintiff's income and resources as representative of this larger class's ability to shoulder the costs of arbitration. * * *

In analyzing this issue, reviewing courts should consider the costs of litigation as the alternative to arbitration, as in *Bradford,* but they must weigh the potential costs of litigation in a realistic manner. In many, if not most, cases, employees (and former employees) bringing discrimination claims will be represented by attorneys on a contingency-fee basis. Thus, many litigants will face minimal costs in the judicial forum, as the attorney will cover most of the fees of litigation and advance the expenses incurred in discovery. * * *

This analysis will yield different results in different cases. It will find, in many cases, that high-level managerial employees and others with substantial means can afford the costs of arbitration, thus making cost-splitting provisions in such cases enforceable. In the case of other employees, however, this standard will render cost-splitting provisions unenforceable in many, if not most, cases.

On appeal, Circuit City argues that Morrison could have avoided having to pay half of the cost of the arbitration, under the terms of Rule 13, if she could have arranged to pay the greater of $500 or three percent of her annual salary (in this case, three percent of $54,060, or $1,622) within ninety days of the arbitrator's award. Circuit City argues that, given this provision, we must reach the conclusion that Morrison did not face prohibitive costs in the present case because, at most, she would have been required to pay $1,622 for the arbitral forum.

In the abstract, this sum may not appear prohibitive, but it must be considered from the vantage point of the potential litigant in a case such as this. Recently terminated, the potential litigant must continue to pay for housing, utilities, transportation, food, and the other necessities of life in contemporary society despite losing her primary, and most likely only, source of income. Unless she is exceedingly fortunate, the potential litigant will experience at least a brief period of unemployment. Turning to the arbitration agreement with her employer, the potential litigant finds that, as the default rule, she will be obligated to pay half the costs of any arbitration which she initiates.

Minimal research will reveal that the potential costs of arbitrating the dispute easily reach thousands, if not tens of thousands, of dollars, far exceeding the costs that a plaintiff would incur in court. Courts charge plaintiffs initial filing fees, but they do not charge extra for in-person hearings, discovery requests, routine motions, or written decisions, costs that are all common in the world of private arbitrators. Based on one recent study using costs and estimates provided by three major arbitration providers themselves, a plaintiff forced to arbitrate a typical $60,000 employment discrimination claim will incur costs, depending on which company is chosen to provide the arbitration, that range from three to nearly *fifty* times the basic costs of litigating in a judicial, rather than arbitral, forum.* * * Based on these considerations, along with the evidence that Morrison presented regarding her previous salary, we conclude that the default cost-splitting rule in the Circuit City arbitration agreement would deter a substantial percentage of potential litigants from bringing their claims in the arbitral forum. * * *

Based on this reasoning, we hold that Morrison has satisfied her burden in the present case in demonstrating that the cost-splitting arrangement in the Circuit City arbitration agreement would deter a substantial number of similarly situated persons from attempting to vindicate their statutory rights in the arbitral forum, and thus that the cost-splitting provision in the agreement was unenforceable with respect to her claims.

We also conclude that the limitations that the Circuit City arbitration agreement places on the damages a claimant may recover from arbitration are unenforceable. It is well-established that "a party does not forgo the substantive rights afforded by [a] statute [when she agrees to arbitrate a statutory claim but] only submits to their resolution in an arbitral, rather than a judicial, forum." *Gilmer,* 500 U.S. at 26, 111 S.Ct. 1647 (quotation omitted). In this case, however, the enforcement of the arbitration agreement would require Morrison to forego her substantive rights to the full panoply of remedies under Title VII and would thereby contravene Congress's intent to utilize certain damages as a tool for compensating victims of discrimination and for deterring employment discrimination more broadly. The critical question is not whether a claimant may obtain *some* amount of the entire range of remedies under Title VII, but whether the limitation on remedies at issue undermines the rights protected by the statute.

The limitation on remedies provision at issue in Morrison's case undermines both the remedial and deterrent principles of Title VII. The arbitration agreement's limitation on remedies clearly impedes Title VII's remedial goal of "making persons whole for injuries suffered through past discrimination." *Albemarle Paper Co. v. Moody,* 422 U.S. 405, 421, 95 S.Ct. 2362, 45 L.Ed.2d 280 (1975). The Supreme Court has consistently recognized that one of the objects of Title VII is "[c]ompensation for injuries caused by the prohibited discrimination." *See, e.g., McKennon v. Nashville Banner Publ'g Co.,* 513 U.S. 352, 358, 115 S.Ct. 879, 130 L.Ed.2d 852 (1995). In this case, the remedies potentially available to make Morrison whole were significantly limited under the arbitration agreement, which allows only injunctive relief, including reinstatement; one year of backpay and reimbursement for lost fringe benefits (which may be further reduced by interim earnings or public/private benefits received); two years of front pay if reinstatement is not possible; compensatory damages in accordance with applicable law; and punitive damages up to $5,000 or the sum of a claimant's backpay and front pay awards, whichever is greater.

In sum, the Circuit City arbitration agreement does more than limit Morrison's potential monetary remedy for discrimination by limiting any backpay and front pay awards. In addition, it also prevents the remedial principles of Title VII from being effectuated because it does not allow Morrison to be fully compensated for any harms caused by wrongful discrimination. Similarly, Circuit City's arbitration agreement undermines the deterrent purposes of Title VII by placing stringent limits on punitive damages available to Morrison and other claimants under the arbitration agreement.

Because the limitation on remedies found in the Circuit City arbitration agreement significantly undermines Title VII's remedial purpose of making victims of discrimination whole and its deterrent purposes of forcing employers to eliminate and prevent discriminatory practices in the workplace, we hold that the provision at issue in this case was not enforceable.

Notes and Questions

1. Prior to Cole v. Burns Int'l Security Services, 105 F.3d 1465 (D.C.Cir.1997) (discussed *supra* Chapter XI.B.1), the prevailing view of legal commentators seemed to be that sharing the cost of the arbitrator was an essential term of an enforceable arbitration agreement, on the theory that arbitrators might be perceived as biased if they were paid solely by employers. See, e.g., Shalu Tandon Buckley, *Practical Concerns Regarding the Arbitration of Statutory Employment Claims*, 11 Ohio State Journal on Dispute Resolution 149, 179–80 (1996); Reginald Alleyne, *Arbitrators' Fees: The Dagger in the Heart of Mandatory Arbitration for Statutory Discrimination Claims*, 6 University of Pennsylvania Journal of Labor & Employment Law 1 (2003). After *Cole* but before *Green Tree*, the judicial pendulum seemed to shift; many courts concluded that employee access to the dispute resolution forum is a more important concern, and that arbitration agreements that required employees to pay a significant part of the arbitrator's fees were unenforceable. See, e.g., Shankle v. B–G Maintenance Management of Colorado, Inc., 163 F.3d 1230 (10th Cir.1999) (refusing to enforce arbitration agreement that required employee to pay for one-half of the arbitration fees).

Since *Green Tree*, the pendulum seems to have shifted again, with most courts evaluating fee-splitting provisions on a case-by-case basis and requiring employees to prove that they cannot afford the costs of arbitration. See, e.g., Faber v. Menard, Inc., 367 F.3d 1048, 1053–54 (8th Cir.2004). In Blair v. Scott Specialty Gasses, 283 F.3d 595, 608 (3d Cir.2002), the Third Circuit held that an employee's affidavit demonstrating that she had negative income and negative assets did not relieve the district court of making a factual determination of her ability to afford the probable arbitration fees, but in Spinetti v. Service Corporation International, 324 F.3d 212 (3d Cir.2003), the Third Circuit affirmed the district court's determination of inability to pay. Cf. Cooper v. MRM Investment Co., 199 F.Supp.2d 771 (M.D.Tenn.2002) (finding that plaintiff could not afford arbitral fees where her income for the previous year was only $7253.74). Compare Roberson v. Clear Channel Broadcasting, Inc., 144 F.Supp.2d 1371 (S.D.Fla.2001) (even where employee demonstrates inability to afford arbitral fees, employer may still obtain order compelling arbitration by agreeing to pay those fees) with *Cooper*, 199 F.Supp.2d 771 (employer's agreement to pay fees does not entitle employer to order compelling arbitration if the fee provision might deter other employees from pursuing their claims).

2.   The D.C. Circuit seems to be backing away from the categorical approach it adopted in *Cole*. See Brown v. Wheat First Securities, Inc., 257 F.3d 821 (D.C. Cir.2001) (holding that *Cole* does not apply to state common law retaliatory discharge claims); LaPrade v. Kidder, Peabody & Co., 246 F.3d 702 (D.C. Cir.2001) (enforcing an award which taxed $8,376 in fees against successful plaintiff).

3.   Is the Sixth Circuit's determination in *Morrison* that courts should consider the effect of a fee-shifting provision on other employees consistent with *Green Tree*? Or does *Green Tree* limit a court's consideration to the particular employee who has challenged the fee-shifting provision?

4.   An empirical study of AAA employment arbitration found that AAA employment arbitrators exercised their discretion to reallocate arbitrator's fees to the employer in 70.25% of the cases, hearing fees in 71.3% of the cases, and some or all of the filing fees in 85.12% of the cases. Even when employees lost on the merits, the arbitrator nonetheless shifted some or all of the employee's share of these fees to the employer in approximately 65% of the cases. Elizabeth Hill, *Due Process at Low Cost: An Empirical Study of Employment Arbitration Under the Auspices of the American Arbitration Association*, 18 Ohio State Journal on Dispute Resolution 777, 812 (2003). Is this significant?

5.   The *Morrison* court, in addition to striking the fee-shifting provision, also struck Circuit City's attempt to cap the damages that an arbitrator could award. The Hooters agreement similarly restricted employees' potential remedies, both by placing a cap on certain types of remedies (punitive damages were limited to one year's gross compensation), and by forbidding the arbitrator from granting certain types of relief (the arbitrator could not enjoin any company policies or procedures). See Hooters of America, Inc. v. Phillips, 39 F.Supp.2d 582 (D.S.C.1998).

Courts confronted with such agreements generally have taken one of five routes. The first is to sever the claim for relief which the arbitrator is not permitted to resolve, require the parties to submit the remaining claims to arbitration, and stay the non-arbitrated claim for resolution by the court after an arbitration award has been made. See, e.g., DiCrisci v. Lyndon Guar. Bank of N.Y., 807 F.Supp. 947, 953–54 (W.D.N.Y.1992). The second route is to strike the arbitration clause altogether and allow the entire claim to be litigated. See, e.g., Paladino v. Avnet Computer Technologies, Inc., 134 F.3d 1054 (11th Cir.1998); Alexander v. Anthony Int'l, L.P., 341 F.3d 256, 267 (3d Cir.2003) (striking arbitration agreement which, among other things, limited employees' relief to reinstatement and "net pecuniary damages"). The third route is to strike the limitation-of-remedies clause and to give the arbitrator the authority to award damages to the full extent permitted by law. See, e.g., Hadnot v. Bay, Ltd., 344 F.3d 474, 478 n.14 (5th Cir.2003). The fourth route is to let the arbitrator decide whether to award the relief. See, e.g., Great Western Mortgage Corp. v. Peacock, 110 F.3d 222, 232 (3d Cir.1997); Gannon v. Circuit City Stores, Inc., 262 F.3d 677, 682 n.6 (8th Cir.2001). The final route is to enforce the agreement as written. Judge Richard Posner explains:

> [S]hort of authorizing trial by battle or ordeal or, more doubtfully, by a panel of three monkeys, parties can stipulate to whatever procedures they want to govern the arbitration of their disputes; parties are as free to specify idiosyncratic terms of arbitration as they are to specify any other terms in their contract. For that matter, parties to adjudication have considerable power to vary the normal procedures, and surely can stipulate that punitive damages will not be awarded.

Baravati v. Josephthal, Lyon & Ross, Inc., 28 F.3d 704, 709 (7th Cir.1994) (citations omitted).

Which of these approaches do you think is best? Which policies might be advanced by each approach? See David S. Schwartz, *Understanding Remedy–Stripping Arbitration Clauses: Validity, Arbitrability, and Preclusion Principles*, 38 University of San Francisco Law Review 49 (2003) (arguing that courts should strike "remedy-stripping" clauses in their entirety).

6. The Civil Rights Act of 1991 permits courts to award attorneys fees to prevailing parties. In Christiansburg Garment Co. v. EEOC, 434 U.S. 412, 98 S.Ct. 694, 54 L.Ed.2d 648 (1978), the Supreme Court held that a prevailing employer may only be awarded attorney fees where the employee's lawsuit was "frivolous"; allowing the routine award of attorney fees to prevailing employers would undermine Title VII by deterring employees from bringing claims. Under what circumstances should arbitrators award such fees? Should they do so regularly or selectively? Should a court refuse to enforce an arbitration agreement in which an employee waives the right to recover attorneys fees? Should a court refuse to enforce an arbitration award that denies attorneys fees to a prevailing claimant, or that awards attorneys fees to a losing claimant? See Perez v. Globe Airport Security Services, Inc., 253 F.3d 1280, 1287 (11th Cir.2001) (denying enforcement of arbitration agreement that contained clause requiring fee-splitting between the parties; clause impermissibly limited the employee's remedies contrary to the Title VII provision that provides fee-shifting to prevailing plaintiffs); George Watts & Son, Inc. v. Tiffany & Co., 248 F.3d 577 (7th Cir.2001) (an arbitrator's refusal to award attorney's fees to the prevailing party as authorized by state law cannot be vacated or modified for "manifest disregard" of the law).

Should courts enforce arbitration agreements with "loser pays" provisions in cases involving statutory disputes? Several courts have. See, e.g., Musnick v. King Motor Co., 325 F.3d 1255 (11th Cir.2003); Manuel v. Honda R & D Ams., Inc., 175 F.Supp.2d 987 (S.D. Ohio 2001).

7. Employers frequently insert into their arbitration agreements a clause similar to the following: "The employee has the right to be represent-

ed by an attorney at all times. However, if the employee elects not to bring a lawyer to the arbitration hearing, the Company also will agree not to bring a lawyer to the hearing." Might such a clause be misleading? Many companies arbitrating under such a clause use attorneys extensively in the preparation of their case and witnesses, even if the attorneys do not attend the hearing itself.

Orley Ashenfelter and David Bloom collected empirical evidence concerning the use and nonuse of attorneys in several different types of non-employment disputes. They found that the outcome of disputes is roughly the same if either both parties or neither party is represented by an attorney. Where only one party is represented by an attorney, however, that party's likelihood of prevailing increases substantially. The authors concluded that where the method of dispute resolution allows the parties a realistic option of representing themselves, the decision to retain lawyers presents a prisoner's dilemma: although it would be in both parties' best interest to represent themselves, both nonetheless will rationally hire lawyers to avoid the "sucker's payoff" a party receives when only one's opponent hires a lawyer. Orley Ashenfelter and David Bloom, Lawyers as Agent of the Devil in a Prisoner's Dilemma Game, 11–19 (National Bureau of Economic Research Working Paper No. 4447 (Sept. 1993)).

On the other hand, Richard Ross, Senior Associate General Counsel for Anheuser–Busch, has argued that it is in an employer's best interest to encourage and even pay for an employee's retention of an attorney in an arbitral proceeding. He explains:

> If the employee does not have a lawyer, the selection of an arbitrator is a little more difficult just because the employee is not familiar with the process. It can also be helpful in settling some disputes if the employee has someone to lean on for advice and counsel. An attorney can help the employee assess his or her claim realistically, and give the employee some assurance that any settlement is fair and reasonable.

Richard Ross, Interview by Peter Phillips, in CPR Institute for Dispute Resolution, How Companies Manage Employment Disputes: A Compendium of Leading Corporate Employment Programs 54 (2002).

E. DISCOVERY

In *Gilmer*, the plaintiff argued unsuccessfully that his arbitration agreement should not be enforced because discovery would be too limited. The *Gilmer* Court, after noting that the applicable arbitration rules permitted at least some discovery, observed that "by agreeing to arbitrate, a party 'trades the procedures and opportunity for review of the courtroom for the simplicity, informality, and expedition of arbitration.'" *Gilmer*, 500 U.S. at 31, 111 S.Ct. at 1655, 114 L.Ed.2d at 34, quoting *Mitsubishi,* 473 U.S. at 628, 105 S.Ct. at 3354, 87 L.Ed.2d at 451. Recall from Chapter VI.C that discovery in labor arbitration is similarly more limited than in civil litigation.

Gilmer does not provide lower courts with much guidance concerning how broad discovery must be to obtain judicial enforcement of an agreement to arbitrate. Consider the following cases:

CONTINENTAL AIRLINES, INC. v. MASON
United States Court of Appeals for the Ninth Circuit, 1996.
87 F.3d 1318 (table), 12 IER Cas. 160, 1996 WL 341758.

MEMORANDUM OPINION

Alecia B. Mason * * * appeals the district court's Order compelling arbitration of her claims against Continental Airlines of employment discrimination, wrongful termination, and infliction of emotional distress. * * * Mason['s] claim that the * * * arbitration procedure [contained in the company's employee handbook] was unconscionable because it did not provide for discovery or legal counsel is meritless. In order to be unconscionable, a contract clause must "shock the conscience." * * * There is nothing that shocks the conscience about an arbitration procedure that does not provide for discovery or legal representation. * * *

WILKS v. THE PEP BOYS
United States District Court for the Middle District of Tennessee, 2003.
241 F.Supp.2d 860.

TRAUGHER, District Judge.

[A group of employees sued their employer for alleged violations of the Fair Labor Standards Act. The employer moved to dismiss and compel arbitration. Each of the employees had signed an arbitration agreement. However, because the employer had modified its arbitration agreement on several occasions, each plaintiff had signed a different version of the arbitration agreement. Apparently, some of the arbitration agreements provided that arbitration would be conducted under rules promulgated by the American Arbitration Association (AAA), and other agreements provided that arbitration would be conducted under rules promulgated by the Judicial Arbitration and Mediation Services/Endispute (JAMS).]

The Agreement provides for the following discovery:

Each party shall have the right to take the deposition of one individual and any expert witness designated by another party. Each party also shall have the right to propound requests for production of documents to any party.... Additional discovery may be had only where the Arbitrator selected so orders, upon a showing of substantial need.

The plaintiffs contend that, in the context of this collective FLSA case, that provision is "lopsided" and, therefore, unconscionable. The plaintiffs maintain that the defendant will only need to depose each plaintiff (its one deposition), but that the plaintiffs will need to depose numerous managers and other supervisory personnel in order to prove their claims.

First, the plaintiffs' argument is made in the context of a collective FLSA action, as the plaintiffs wish this case to be, not as applicable to an individual arbitration on an individual claim made by an individual plaintiff. As to an individual claim, the most relevant party to be deposed by the plaintiff, in fact, will be the direct supervisor or manager of the plaintiff. So, in the context of an individual arbitration, this provision is not "lopsided."

However, again, the rules of AAA and JAMS provide relief for the plaintiffs from this discovery provision. Rule 7 of AAA's National Rules provides that: "The arbitrator shall have the authority to order such discovery . . . as the arbitrator considers necessary to a full and fair exploration of the issues in dispute, consistent with the expedited nature of arbitration." This standard, more liberal than the "substantial need" standard in the Agreement, would determine the scope of discovery because Rule 1 of the National Rules provides that if an "adverse material inconsistency exists between the arbitration agreement and these rules, the arbitrator shall apply these rules."

Likewise, JAMS procedure forecloses lopsided discovery in favor of the employer. Standard No. 4 of the Minimum Standards provides for the "exchange of core information prior to the arbitration," and the Comment to that Standard provides that, in addition to one deposition for each side, "[o]ther discovery should be available at the arbitrator's discretion." Rule 2 of the JAMS Rules & Procedures mandates that these Minimum Standards prevail over any inconsistent agreement between the parties.

* * *

The various versions of the Agreement, as it must be administered by AAA and JAMS, is [sic] valid and enforceable. Therefore, as to the plaintiffs and prospective plaintiffs who have executed the Mutual Agreement to Arbitrate Claims in versions that do not differ in material respects from the versions before the court, this litigation will be dismissed, and those plaintiffs will be compelled to arbitrate their FLSA claims.

WALKER v. RYAN'S FAMILY STEAK HOUSES, INC.

United States District Court for the Middle District of Tennessee, 2003.
289 F.Supp.2d 916.

TRAUGHER, District Judge.

[A group of employees sued their employer for alleged violations of the Fair Labor Standards Act. The employer moved to dismiss and compel arbitration.]

Since 1993, Ryan's has had in place an agreement with Employment Dispute Services, Inc. ("EDSI") under which EDSI [a for-profit arbitration provider] agrees to provide an arbitral forum for all Ryan's job applicants, employees, and the company itself, in exchange for annual payment from Ryan's. In turn, Ryan's requires all job applicants, prior to being considered for employment, to sign a document * * * under which applicants agree to submit any and all employment-related disputes to EDSI's arbitration process and forego their right to have claims heard in a judicial forum. If an applicant refuses to sign the Agreement, she will not be considered for employment with Ryan's. Ryan's is named in the Agreement as a third party beneficiary.

Although limited discovery provisions are common in arbitration as a means of streamlining the process, the limited discovery available in the EDSI forum burdens the employee-claimant far more heavily than the employer, suggesting structural bias in favor of the employer. Both parties may request production of documents and are required to exchange witness lists and documents to be offered into evidence prior to arbitration. (Docket No. 82, Ex. 1, 2000 Rules at 4–6.) However, parties are able to schedule only one deposition as of right, and additional depositions are strongly disfavored, even under the current Rules: "Either party may file a request with the adjudication panel for additional depositions, but such requests are not encouraged and shall be granted *in extraordinary fact situations only and for good cause shown." Id.* at 6 (emphasis added). Employment claims often require an employee to conduct many depositions (e.g., co-workers, supervisors, etc.) to make out her case, while employers are often able to defend such claims with only one deposition–that of the employee. Thus, employees usually have a need for more discovery than employers, and stringent limitations on depositions such as those promulgated by EDSI more heavily burden the employee than the employer. Additionally, this court has previously noted that the rules of the American Arbitration Association and the Judicial Arbitration and Mediation Services/Endispute are relatively liberal in affording additional discovery "where necessary to a full and fair exploration of the issues in dispute." *See Wilks v. Pep Boys*, 241 F.Supp.2d 860, 865 (M.D.Tenn.2003). This liberal attitude towards discovery stands in stark contrast to EDSI's strict requirement that additional discovery should issue only in "extraordinary fact situations" and "for good cause shown."

* * *

Although this court recognizes the liberal federal policy favoring arbitration, it finds that the circumstances of this case preclude submitting these claims to the EDSI arbitral forum. For the reasons stated herein, the defendant's motion to dismiss and petition to compel arbitration and stay proceedings will be denied.

WILLIAMS v. KATTEN, MUCHIN & ZAVIS
United States District Court, N.D. Illinois, Eastern Division, 1996.
1996 WL 717447.

MAROVICH, District Judge.

[Plaintiff Elaine Williams moved to vacate an arbitration award in her favor and to reinstate her employment discrimination claims in federal court. The arbitration award did not give Williams any front pay damages or compensatory damages for her alleged medical expenses and emotional harm. One of Williams' arguments supporting vacatur was that KMZ had refused to produce three of four of her proposed deponents. The arbitrator, after holding a pre-hearing discovery conference, had denied Williams' deposition requests.]

The AAA Rules, incorporated into the [arbitration] agreement, authorize an arbitrator to subpoena a witness and documents either independently or upon the request of a party, and empower the arbitrator to determine the appropriate scope of discovery. * * * While it may be true that Williams was not permitted to engage in discovery to the extent she had hoped, it is also true that "by agreeing to arbitrate, a party trades the procedures and opportunity for review of the courtroom for the simplicity, informality, and expedition of arbitration." *Gilmer*, 500 U.S. at 26 (citation omitted). * * *

Williams * * * claims that the arbitrator's discovery rulings in KMZ's favor prevented her from presenting facts critical to her claim and thereby denied her a fundamentally fair hearing. The Court is permitted to vacate an arbitrator's award where the arbitrators "refuse[d] to hear evidence pertinent and material to the controversy." 9 U.S.C. § 10(a)(3). However, the informal nature of arbitration proceedings effectuates the national policy favoring arbitration, and such proceedings require "expeditious and summary hearing, with only restricted inquiry into factual issues."

At the discovery hearing, the [a]rbitrator Simon ruled on the relevance of each discovery request, and explained, for example, why it would be inappropriate for Williams to depose the three individuals she had requested * * * [The arbitrator's] discovery rulings were not arbitrary and capricious as Williams would like this Court to believe; rather, the arbitrator offered the parties the opportunity to present to the panel "the most relevant evidence in support of [their] respective sides." Williams has failed to demonstrate that the arbitrator's discovery rulings in this case constitute the kind of fundamental error necessary to find that Williams was deprived of a fair hearing.

Notes and Questions

1. The arbitration rules promulgated by Hooters (see supra Chapter XI.B.3) would have entitled Phillips to take only one deposition of a Hooters representative, unless the arbitral panel granted broader discovery on a showing of substantial and demonstrable need. See Hooters of America, Inc. v. Phillips, 39 F.Supp.2d 582 (D.S.C.1998). Would you, as a judge, enforce an arbitration agreement containing such a clause? Should a judge make this ruling before or after arbitration has occurred? What if a sexual harassment plaintiff accuses more than one supervisor of harassing her?

2. In a typical employment case, who might the plaintiff want to depose? Who might the defendant want to depose? How should the arbitrator decide who will be deposed and who will not?

3. Do the parties have any less need for discovery in arbitration than in litigation?

4. Do restrictions on discovery fall hardest on employers or employees? Why? See Kinney v. United HealthCare Serv., Inc., 70 Cal.App.4th 1322, 83 Cal.Rptr.2d 348 (4 Dist.1999) ("Given that [the employer] is presumably in possession of the vast majority of evidence that would be relevant to employment-related claims against it, the limitations on discovery, although equally applicable to both parties, work to curtail the employee's ability to substantiate any claim against [the employer]."). See also Michael Z. Green, *Debunking the Myth of Employer Advantage from Using Mandatory Arbitration for Discrimination Claims*, 31 Rutgers Law Journal 399, 438–40 (2000) (arguing that employers often stand to lose as much as employees when discovery is restricted); Martin H. Malin, *Privatizing Justice–But By How Much? Questions* Gilmer *Did Not Answer*, 16 Ohio State Journal on Dispute Resolution 589 (2001) (arguing that discovery in employment arbitration should be left to the discretion of the arbitrator to determine on a case-by-case basis).

5. Is there an appropriate way to balance the parties' need for discovery against the desire for a quick and inexpensive resolution of the dispute? Should this balance be struck by arbitrators on a case-by-case basis, or would universal, judicially-created baseline rules be more appropriate? Would it be appropriate for arbitration agreements themselves to articulate the scope of discovery rights? What if the agreement explicitly forbids discovery? What if the agreement is silent regarding discovery? See Martin v. SCI Management L.P., 296 F.Supp.2d 462, 468 (S.D.N.Y.2003) (observing that a right to discovery should be read into such an agreement "insofar as discovery is necessary to enable the plaintiff to vindicate her statutory rights.").

6. Note that the first three discovery cases excerpted above are before the court on the defendant's motion to compel arbitration. The last case is before the court on the employee's motion to vacate an arbitration award. Should the procedural posture of the case affect the court's analysis of the discovery issue?

7. Judge Traugher, in the *Walker* case, compares the EDSI arbitration rules unfavorably with the arbitration rules of AAA and JAMS that he discussed in *Wilks*. Judge Traugher also noted that while AAA and JAMS are non-profit organizations, EDSI is a for-profit corporation, and that almost half of EDSI's 2002 gross income came from Ryan's Family Steak Houses. Are either or both of these facts troublesome? Do these facts justify a different outcome in the cases? Does Judge Traugher give more credence to an employee's need for discovery in *Walker* than he did in *Wilks*?

F. ARBITRATORS' USE OF EXTERNAL LAW

Recall from Chapter V.B that the role of external law in labor arbitration is a hotly contested issue. Individual employment arbitration agreements, however, often expressly give the arbitrator the authority to consider and resolve issues of external law. An agreement might, for example, contain language similar to the following:

The parties agree that any legal or equitable claims or disputes arising out of or in connection with the employment, the terms and conditions of employment, or the termination of employment will be settled by binding arbitration. This agreement applies, but is not limited, to the following types of claims or disputes: wrongful discharge under statutory and common law; employment discrimination based on federal, state, or local statute; . . . .

Some individual employment arbitration agreements go even further by providing that external law provides the *only* basis for the arbitrator's award of relief to the employee. This is most likely to be true when employment is at-will and the employer does not want to confer just-cause protection to its workers.

GENERAL DYNAMICS LAND SYSTEMS
111 LA 319 (Marvin J. Feldman, 1998).*

STATEMENT OF FACTS

The grievance in this matter arose under and by favor of a unilaterally promulgated Dispute Resolution Handbook, written and published by the company on August 1, 1997. The grievant in this matter was not represented by a union and there is no bargaining unit on the work premises. The grievant was a member of the class of employees covered by the Handbook.

The Handbook contained certain clauses relevant to the matter at hand. One such clause is found at Step 4 of that Handbook. It revealed the following:

STEP 4—Arbitration

If the decision of the Management Appeals Committee is not acceptable to the employee and the issue is based on a legally protected right, the employee may initiate the Arbitration Process. * * * Arbitration is the exclusive external remedy for employees to resolve their disputes based on legally protected rights. The arbitrator has the power to award the same remedies (e.g., money damages, reinstatement, punitive damages) as could otherwise be obtained in court. * * *

* * *

[Grievant was laid off from his position as a Fire Marshal without explanation. He appealed the layoff to a management committee, which recommended only that he be given an explanation. Grievant then filed an arbitration request form as follows:]

Violation of Law: Specify applicable local, state, or federal law, statute, regulations, or ordinance you claim the Company has violated: *unknown at this time : additional information forth coming.*

Details of Complaint: Attach separate statement or relevant supporting documents as applicable: *was laid-off wrongfully and disagrees with the [management committee's] decision.*

Award/Relief Sought: Total Dollar Amount/Description of other relief sought: *want my Fire Marshal job.*

* * *

OPINION AND DISCUSSION

*

[T]here is no statutory right of the Federal Government or any known statutory law of the State of Ohio that was violated. The grievant could not reveal any violation of any law involved, either. The right to perpetuate a grievance for merit consideration under the Dispute Resolution Handbook is narrow. It only allows merit consideration for an alleged violation by the company of a legally protected right. This matter does not fit into that definition.

AWARD

Grievance denied. A hearing on the merits is not warranted.

Notes and Questions

1. The arbitrator decided this case on the arbitral equivalent of a motion to dismiss. Should arbitrators be willing to consider such motions? What about summary judgment motions? What are the pros and cons of an arbitrator deciding a case on motions, without holding an arbitral hearing? Is a summary judgment motion feasible in arbitration, given that discovery is somewhat limited? Should (could?) arbitrators use a different legal standard for deciding summary judgment motions than courts do?

2. The grievant in this case apparently attempted, without success, to find a lawyer to represent him. Should the arbitrator have taken this into account? How might an employee's signing of an arbitration agreement affect her ability to attract a lawyer to her case?

3. Confusion often arises when arbitration clauses are vaguely worded and can be construed as limited either to nonemployment matters or to only certain types of employment claims. For example, in Prudential Insurance Company of America v. Lai, 42 F.3d 1299, 1305 (9th Cir.1994), the employee-plaintiffs signed forms containing agreements "to arbitrate any dispute, claim or controversy that * * * is required to be arbitrated under the rules, constitutions, or bylaws of the organizations with which I register." They subsequently registered with the National Association of Securities Dealers, which required that disputes "arising in connection with the business" of its members be arbitrated. When plaintiffs filed suit alleging that their supervisor had raped, harassed, and sexually abused them, the employer moved to dismiss the suit and to compel arbitration. The Ninth Circuit denied the motion, in part because the arbitration agreement appeared to be aimed at securities disputes, and did not even refer to employment disputes. Similarly, in Rudolph v. Alamo Rent A Car, Inc., 952 F.Supp. 311 (E.D.Va.1997), the

court refused to compel arbitration where an employment contract provided for arbitration only of contractual disputes but nowhere specifically provided for the arbitration of statutory disputes.

GLOBE FURNITURE RENTALS, INC.*
105 LA 888 (William C. Heekin, 1995).

[Grievant was a salesperson at the company's retail furniture store. The company discharged her, citing various performance deficiencies and a history of written warnings. Grievant brought claims for, among other things, racial and sexual harassment and intentional infliction of emotional distress.]

DISCUSSION AND FINDINGS

The matter to be resolved is felt best stated as follows: Did the instant termination violate the pertinent employment contract and/or applicable law?

The Grievant contends that she was improperly terminated in violation of both her employment contract and applicable law due to having been harassed, ridiculed, and abused by way of racial and sexual jokes which she alleges were pervasive at the workplace, to the extent that supervisors both participated and encouraged co-workers to behave similarly for the purpose of bringing about her discharge; culminating in the Employer seizing upon her glaucoma physical disability after several years of service. The Grievant suggests that the Employer's president was personally involved in the perpetration of this hostile work environment as indicated on the occasion towards the end of the final warning period when she overhead him state on a * * * store speaker telephone– "Haven't you gotten rid of that Black bitch yet?" In contrast, the Employer, while emphasizing that the Employees' Manual provides for the employment-at-will doctrine, contends that evidence firmly establishes the Grievant to have been terminated only for poor job performance and, thus, not race, sex, and/or alleged disability. Accordingly, what underlies much of this dispute is a basic question of fact: Did the Grievant establish, by a preponderance of the evidence, that the instant employment termination was to any extent premised upon her race, gender, and/or possible physical disability?

Initially, it is felt important to make several findings and observations. First and very importantly, it is undisputed that the Grievant bears the burden of proof to establish by a preponderance of the evidence that this discharge was pretextual or improperly motivated. Second and also very importantly, the record is held to overwhelmingly establish, mostly without rebuttal, that her work performance—for at least two years prior to the time in question—was, at the very least, substandard. Indeed this was the situation despite repeated counselings, additional

* Reprinted with permission from *Labor Arbitration Reporter–Labor Arbitration Reports*, 105 LA 886. Copyright 1995 by The Bureau of National Affairs, Inc. (800–372–1033) <http://www.bna.com>.

training, and the issuance of a final warning demanding improvement over a sixty day[] period. Third, almost all of the discrimination related allegations made by the Grievant involved herself as a witness, a witness who for obvious reasons cannot be understood as disinterested regarding the outcome of this arbitration. Fourth, much of the corroborating testimony regarding an alleged hostile work environment as to race and gender came from two former employees previously terminated by the Employer: Diana Pidcock and Theresa Tataru. Accordingly, these witnesses cannot be viewed as disinterested either. In essence, it is normal in the employment setting that involuntarily terminated employees bear at least some ill will towards their former employer. Moreover, the neutrality of Diana Pidcock is, in particular, suspect since there is reliable direct testimony in the record that she was discharged for having made anti-semitic statements directed towards the Employer's ownership. Finally here, it is fundamental, based upon human experience and common sense, that complaints raised by a dismissed employee subsequent to his/her termination are inherently questionable concerning the underlying actuality of the matter complained about.

With respect to an alleged hostile work environment based upon race, it appears that the Grievant was the only African American who worked at the Broad Street store, at least in the capacity of an inside sales person, during the several years period in question[, and that she was] * * * replaced by a Caucasian American. * * *

[T]he record falls far short of establishing underlying racial discrimination. Indeed the evidence offered mainly consists of general, undeveloped assertions made by the Grievant. The one specific instance cited was the aforementioned "Haven't you gotten rid of that Black bitch yet" statement, allegedly made over a Broad Street store speaker phone by the Employer's president—David Hoguet. Upon comparing this assertion of the Grievant with the fact that it apparently was not raised at the time; that it was specifically denied by Mr. Hoguet; that [other employees] testified that the particular telephone involved did not have a speaker phone feature—with only Theresa Tataru testifying to the contrary, * * *: on balance, the fact of the above statement having been made cannot be held as reliably proven in the record. Also, [other employees] denied making racial jokes of any kind in the presence of the Grievant * * *.

The record is * * * similar regarding the claim of an alleged hostile work environment based upon gender. Here, the testimony that sex related jokes were pervasive—offered by the Grievant, Tataru, and Pidcock—was specifically denied by the alleged principals involved * * *. Also, the other argued-for hostile work environment evidence in this regard—that of several bathing suit postcards from Florida having been displayed in the Broad Street store break room—is found to be reasonably, on its face, non-supportive. This follows upon viewing these postcards, postcards which reasonably cannot be seen as pornographic or in any way extreme. Indeed there is no reason to not accept the assertion of the Employer that postcards of this type, inclusive of the "wet T-shirt contest" postcard—however tasteless—are obtainable in virtually any Florida postcard shop. Very importantly, the record contains overwhelming testimony evidence that the Grievant never complained about these postcards, or the telling of sex related jokes, to management prior to being terminated. * * * [J]okes about sex likely were, on occasion, told at the store in the presence of the Grievant. However, [there is no evidence that Grievant was contemporaneously offended by the jokes or postcards]. Ultimately, the claim of a hostile work environment in this matter, as to race or gender, is found to fall far short of being supported by the totality of the evidence submitted. Thus, no violation of federal or state law regarding discrimination based on upon race or sex* * * is found to have occurred.

[T]he record is held to not support the Grievant's claim of intentional infliction of emotional distress as a matter of law or fact. * * *

Based upon all of the foregoing, it is held that there exists no basis upon which there can be a grant of the relief sought. No violation of law * * * is found to have occurred. Therefore, the grievance must be, and is, denied.

AWARD

The grievance is denied.

Notes and Questions

1. At the time the facts of the above grievance arose and the grievance was decided, the applicable law was as follows:

(a) Race discrimination

Grievant had the initial burden of producing evidence that she was a member of a protected class, that she was qualified for the position, that she had been fired, and that the position remained available. The burden of production of evidence then would shift to the employer to articulate a legitimate, nondiscriminatory reason for the firing. If the employer met this burden, the burden would revert to the grievant to prove, by a preponderance of the evidence, either that race discrimination more likely motivated the firing or that the employer's proffered reason for the firing was pretextual. The grievant retained the ultimate burden of persuading the factfinder that the employer intentionally discriminated against the grievant. St. Mary's Honor Center v. Hicks, 509 U.S. 502, 113 S.Ct. 2742, 125 L.Ed.2d 407 (1993); Texas Department of Community Affairs v. Burdine, 450 U.S. 248, 101 S.Ct. 1089, 67 L.Ed.2d 207 (1981).

(b) Sexual harassment

Grievant had to prove that the employer created a hostile working environment that was unwelcome, based on sex, severe and pervasive (both objectively and subjectively), and that the employer could be held liable under agency principles. Harris v. Forklift Systems, Inc., 510 U.S. 17, 114 S.Ct. 367, 126 L.Ed.2d 295 (1993); see also Burlington Industries, Inc. v. Ellerth, 524 U.S. 742, 118 S.Ct. 2257, 141 L.Ed.2d 633 (1998); Farragher v. City of Boca Raton, 524 U.S. 775, 118 S.Ct. 2275, 141 L.Ed.2d 662 (1998).

(c) Intentional Infliction of Emotional Distress

Grievant had to prove that (1) the employer either intended to cause emotional distress or knew or should have known that actions taken would result in serious emotional distress; (2) the employer's conduct was so extreme and outrageous as to go beyond all possible bounds of decency and was such that it could be considered utterly intolerable in a civilized community; (3) the employer's actions were the proximate cause of her psychic injury; and (4) the mental anguish she suffered was serious and of a nature that no reasonable person could be expected to endure it. Pyle v. Pyle, 11 Ohio App.3d 31, 34, 11 OBR 63, 66–67, 463 N.E.2d 98, 103 (1983).

2.   Do you agree with Arbitrator Heekin that the primary extant issues were issues of fact? Did Arbitrator Heekin correctly apply the law? Of what significance, if any, is his failure to cite any legal authority? If the grievant were to request judicial review of the arbitration award, should the court grant her request? On what ground? Should the standard of review be any different for the emotional distress claim than for the statutory claims?

3.   What do you make of Arbitrator Heekin's assumption that the credibility of a fired employee is automatically suspect on the basis of her mere status as a fired employee? Isn't one purpose of the arbitral hearing to resolve credibility issues? Why isn't the employer's credibility similarly suspect? Is Arbitrator Heekin essentially placing his thumb on the scale? Would a court start with this assumption?

G.   JUDICIAL REVIEW

Recall from Chapter III.C that judicial review of labor arbitration awards under § 301 of the Labor Management Relations Act is extremely limited. Employment arbitration, though governed by the Federal Arbitration Act, is likewise extremely limited. The FAA permits a reviewing court to vacate an arbitration award in limited circumstances, including "[w]here the award was procured by corruption, fraud or undue means"; "[w]here there [existed] evident partiality or corruption [by] the arbitrators"; where there existed specified misconduct by the arbitrators, or "[w]here the arbitrators exceeded their powers." 9 U.S.C. § 10 (1994). As the following case illustrates, courts also will vacate an arbitration award if the arbitrator acted in "manifest disregard of the law."

HALLIGAN v. PIPER JAFFRAY, INC.
United States Court of Appeals for the Second Circuit, 1998.
148 F.3d 197.

FEINBERG, J.:

I.   BACKGROUND

Halligan was hired by Piper in 1973 as a salesman of equity investments to financial institutions. As a condition of employment, Halligan was required by the industry self-regulatory organization, the

National Association of Securities Dealers (NASD), to sign a standard form (U–4) containing an agreement to arbitrate any future disputes. In 1988, Tad Piper succeeded his father as CEO of Piper. * * * Halligan contends that thereafter Halligan was forced from his job in December 1992 by Tad Piper and Halligan's supervisor, Bruce Huber, because of his age and despite his continuing high performance.

In October 1993, Halligan submitted his ADEA claim, along with other claims, to arbitration before a panel of NASD arbitrators. Before he could complete his own re-direct testimony, however, his health deteriorated and in early 1995 the arbitrators were advised that Halligan was unable to testify further. * * * After his death, Mrs. Halligan continued the arbitration.

During the arbitration hearings, Halligan presented the arbitrators with very strong evidence of age-based discrimination. Piper for its part has conceded throughout that Halligan was "basically qualified." Piper principally contended that Halligan had chosen to retire; it also argued that performance and health issues justified its conduct.

Before leaving Piper in December 1992, Halligan was making nearly $500,000 per year. He ranked fifth out of 25 institutional salesmen. He was ranked first from 1987 through 1991, and had consistently been among Piper's top salesmen. He testified as to repeated discriminatory statements by Tad Piper, Huber, and Halligan's younger partner [Marvin] Geisness. For example, Halligan testified that at a meeting on August 27, 1992, Tad Piper told him "you're too old. Our clients are young and they want young salesmen," and Huber told him "we want you out of here quickly." Tad Piper and Huber denied making such remarks. Halligan also testified that during a telephone conversation on September 10, 1992, Huber told him that "we want you out of Piper Jaffray by the end of the year," and that "if you don't leave, we will fire you." Halligan testified that he then asked if he could stay for the remainder of the year, and that Huber agreed. Huber testified that during the conversation, Halligan asked him what he should do. He testified that he advised Halligan to resign, and that Halligan agreed "then that's what it will be." Huber admitted that Halligan had never requested his advice before. There were no witnesses to this conversation.

Halligan's evidence also included his notes of this and other conversations, a witness who testified that he had seen Halligan recording notes, and several witnesses who heard Halligan say he was being "fired." In addition, Halligan called many witnesses who testified that Piper personnel had expressed their intention to oust Halligan on account of his age. John Dockendorff, a former client and later competitor, testified that in 1989 (the year after Tad Piper became CEO) Huber attempted to recruit him (in Dockendorff's words) to "learn as much as I could about [Halligan's] accounts," because Halligan "would get put out to pasture because he was getting old." All Piper personnel denied having made such statements, although their testimony was occasionally inconsistent or ambiguous. Halligan presented testimonials from current and former clients and colleagues who testified that Halligan was among the best in his field. Halligan refused to provide Piper with a letter of resignation. He also refused an offer of a retirement party and refused to write a letter to his clients saying he was retiring. On November 23, 1992, Halligan's lawyer sent a letter threatening suit if Halligan was terminated. In addition, Halligan testified that he approached Huber in November and asked him if he could keep his job. Huber replied that plans had already been made to close the New York office. Apparently, those plans consisted simply of termination notices to two support staff. Halligan's accounts were thereafter assigned to two younger men. Halligan testified that he unsuccessfully looked for a new job after leaving Piper.

Piper principally argued that it gave Halligan the options of retiring, agreeing to a new percentage split with Geisness or being assigned a new group of accounts, and that Halligan agreed to retire in the phone conversation on September 10, 1992. Piper also contended its conduct was justified by concerns over Halligan's performance and health. Halligan had surgery for oral cancer twice (in 1990 and 1991), but returned to work each time after approximately two weeks. Halligan conceded that the surgeries had caused slight speech impairment, but offered various witnesses who testified that Halligan was always able to perform his job. Piper discounted Halligan's objective evidence of performance, arguing that Halligan's accounts had more inherent potential and that the rankings failed to reflect the contributions that other employees had made to Halligan's success. In addition, Huber testified that he thought Halligan needed to develop accounts more effectively (although Huber was unable to identify specific accounts) and use the firm's research and other resources more efficiently. Piper submitted various memoranda related to these concerns, and offered testimony by various witnesses who, with the exception of one employee who had recently retired, were all Piper officers or major shareholders. Piper discounted the testimonials in favor of Halligan, arguing that it was not his clients and former colleagues whose expectations Halligan had to satisfy.

Huber was the only witness testifying that in the September 10th telephone conversation Halligan accepted the "option" of retirement, and Huber was contradicted as to key elements of his testimony by other Piper witnesses. For example, Huber testified that Geisness was not informed of the August 27 meeting before it took place, but both Tad Piper and Geisness testified to the contrary. Geisness testified that when he discussed this meeting with Huber, he asked Huber to keep the New York office open.

In March 1996, after extensive hearings, the arbitrators rendered a written award setting forth the claims and defenses of each party, and denying any relief to the Halligans. The award did not contain any explanation or rationale for the result.

In June 1996, Mrs. Halligan petitioned the district court to vacate the award under § 10(a) of the Federal Arbitration Act (FAA), 9 U.S.C. § 10(a). * * * The district judge refused. * * *

II. ANALYSIS

Mrs. Halligan argues in this court, among other things, that the arbitrators' award reflected manifest disregard of the law. Piper argues in response, among other things, that it is not the function of this court to reassess the evidence or make judgments about witness credibility and that the district court was able to adequately review the award—even in the absence of a written explanation—by inferring from the record grounds that support the arbitrators' award. * * *

B. Standard of Review of Award

The parties agree that review of arbitration awards is generally governed by the FAA. * * * In addition, relying on an observation by the Supreme Court in Wilko v. Swan, 346 U.S. 427, 436–37, 74 S.Ct. 182, 98 L.Ed. 168 (1953), overruled on other grounds in Rodriguez de Quijas v. Shearson/American Express, Inc., 490 U.S. 477, 109 S.Ct. 1917, 104 L.Ed.2d 526 (1989), this court has also recognized that an arbitration award may be vacated if it is in "manifest disregard of the law." * * * We have also pointed out, however, that the reach of the doctrine is "severely limited." * * * Indeed, we have cautioned that manifest disregard "clearly means more than error or misunderstanding with respect to the law." * * * We have further noted that to modify or vacate an award on this ground, a court must find both that (1) the arbitrators knew of a governing legal principle yet refused to apply it or ignored it altogether, and (2) the law ignored by the arbitrators was well defined, explicit, and clearly applicable to the case. DiRussa v. Dean Witter Reynolds Inc., 121 F.3d 818, 821 (2d Cir.1997), cert. denied, [522 U.S. 1154], 118 S.Ct. 695, 139 L.Ed.2d 639 (1998).

This case also arises in the context of other developments. In the aftermath of *Gilmer* * * * , mandatory binding arbitration of employment discrimination disputes as a condition of employment has caused increased controversy. Attention has focused on, among other things, whether additional procedural requirements are necessary to ensure that employees will be able, in the words of *Gilmer*, to "effectively * * * vindicate" their statutory rights in arbitration. 500 U.S. at 28, 111 S. Ct. 1647.

* * *

In addition, the federal courts have shown growing concern over the problem. For example, the D.C. Circuit has recently emphasized the necessity of adequate review in enforcing a mandatory, pre-dispute agreement to arbitrate Title VII discrimination claims. Cole v. Burns Int'l Sec. Serv., 105 F.3d 1465 (D.C.Cir.1997). Similarly, in Prudential Ins. Co. of Am. v. Lai, 42 F.3d 1299 (9th Cir.1994), the Ninth Circuit held that waivers of a judicial forum for statutory employment discrimination claims must be "knowing and voluntary" and refused to enforce an agreement to arbitrate that did not meet that standard. * * *

C. *Application of Standard of Review*

We turn now to review of the district court's decision in this case. Mrs. Halligan argued in the district court and repeats to us that the arbitration award reflected manifest disregard of the law. Mrs. Halligan makes a strong case for that proposition. Quite simply, Halligan presented overwhelming evidence that Piper's conduct after Tad Piper became CEO was motivated by age discrimination. Halligan testified to repeated discriminatory statements, and offered contemporaneous notes supporting his version of events, which were in turn backed by the testimony of a witness who saw him making notes. Halligan also presented the testimony of numerous other witnesses who testified that Piper personnel admitted that the company wanted Halligan out. Halligan presented powerful evidence of his performance, in the form of quantitative sales rankings and relevant witness testimony. Notwithstanding Piper's testimony as to Halligan's performance and health, Piper conceded before the arbitrators—and continues to do so—that Halligan's continuing performance was not so unsatisfactory as to justify discharge. Indeed, its principal argument has been that Halligan retired voluntarily. Halligan also made a very strong showing that he did not choose the "option" of quitting but was fired. The strength of Halligan's showing of discriminatory motive is most probative of whether Piper took discriminatory action, *i.e.*, fired him. In addition, the circumstantial evidence surrounding his departure, *e.g.*, his statements to various witnesses about his being "fired," his refusal to write to his clients announcing his "resignation," his retention of counsel, is consistent only with a finding that Halligan was pushed out of his job.

Moreover, this is not a case like *DiRussa* where we refused to find "manifest disregard" because DiRussa had not sufficiently brought the governing law to the attention of the arbitrators. There is no such problem here. The record indicates that counsel for both parties generally agreed on the applicable law (and still do on appeal), and explained it to the arbitrators. It is true that the district court stated that the record "does not indicate the Panel's awareness, prior to its determinations, of the standards for burdens of proof." If this observation meant that counsel did not explain the law sufficiently to the arbitrators, it is not correct. Perhaps the district court meant that the arbitrators did not state that they were ignoring the relevant standards for burdens of proof. That is true, but we doubt whether even under a strict construction of the meaning of manifest disregard, it is necessary for arbitrators to state that they are deliberately ignoring the law. *See* DeGaetano v. Smith Barney, Inc., 983 F. Supp. 459, 463 (S.D.N.Y.1997).

In view of the strong evidence that Halligan was fired because of his age and the agreement of the parties that the arbitrators were correctly advised of the applicable legal principles, we are inclined to hold that they ignored the law or the evidence or both. Moreover, the arbitrators did not explain their award. It is true that we have stated repeatedly that arbitrators have no obligation to do so. * * * But in *Gilmer*, when the Supreme Court ruled that an employee could be forced to assert an ADEA claim in an arbitral forum, the Court did so on the assumptions that the claimant would not forgo the substantive rights afforded by the statute, that the arbitration agreement simply changed the forum for enforcement of those rights and that a claimant could effectively vindicate his or her statutory rights in the arbitration. 500 U.S. at 26, 28, 111 S.Ct. 1647. This case puts those assumptions to the test. The Court also stated in *Gilmer* that "claimed procedural inadequacies" in arbitration "are best left for resolution in specific cases," 500 U.S. at 33, 111 S.Ct. 1647. At least in the circumstances here, we believe that when a reviewing court is inclined to hold that an arbitration panel manifestly disregarded the law, the failure of the arbitrators to explain the award can be taken into account. Having done so, we are left with the firm belief that the arbitrators here manifestly disregarded the law or the evidence or both.

Piper argues that the arbitration panel resolved the case in accordance with substantive ADEA law; for example, it credited Piper's witnesses rather than Halligan's. Had the arbitrators offered that explanation of the award, on this record it would have been extremely hard to accept—but they did not do even that. There is some authority permitting discretionary remand of a case to the arbitrators for a written explanation of their award. But in view of the entire record here, we see no persuasive reason for doing so.

We want to make clear that we are not holding that arbitrators should write opinions in every case or even in most cases. We merely observe that where a reviewing court is inclined to find that arbitrators manifestly disregarded the law or the evidence and that an explanation, if given, would have strained credulity, the absence of explanation may reinforce the reviewing court's confidence that the arbitrators engaged in manifest disregard.

For the reasons stated above, we reverse * * * [and] remand to the district court for further proceedings consistent with this opinion.

Notes and Questions

1. For a thorough discussion of how courts apply both the statutory (e.g., bias, misconduct, or corruption on the part of the arbitrator) and nonstatutory (e.g., manifest disregard) grounds for judicial review of arbitration awards, see Stephen L. Hayford, *A New Paradigm for Commercial Arbitration: Rethinking the Relationship Between Reasoned Awards and the Judicial Standards for Vacatur*, 66 George Washington Law Review 443 (1998). Elsewhere, Professor Hayford has argued that the nonstatutory grounds for review should either be justified on statutory grounds or rejected. Stephen L. Hayford, *Law in Disarray: Judicial Standards for Vacatur of Commercial Arbitration Awards*, 30 Georgia Law Review 731 (1996). Are the nonstatutory grounds, such as the manifest disregard stan-

dard, consistent with the statutory language of the FAA specifying the grounds upon which courts are permitted to review arbitral awards?

2.   Can a persuasive argument be made that the arbitrators in *Halligan* did *not* act in "manifest disregard" of "the law"? Was the court second-guessing the arbitration panel's fact-finding? Note also how the court expands "manifest disregard" to include "ignoring" the evidence. Isn't this just a back-door way of second-guessing the arbitrator's fact-finding?

3.   Should an arbitration decision's inconsistency with *arbitral* precedent satisfy the manifest disregard standard? Arbitration awards are not "law," and therefore are not legally binding. See Chapter VI.D for a discussion of the role of precedent in labor arbitration. Would it matter if the arbitral precedent involved the same employer? What if, for example, an employee challenged the employer's system for awarding promotions as creating a disparate impact on the basis of race, and pointed to a prior arbitration award that concluded that the employer's system had precisely that effect?

4.   Is it possible to have traditional (extraordinarily deferential) review of arbitration and still be consistent with *Gilmer*'s prescription that arbitration does not entail a loss of substantive rights? In *Cole*, excerpted in Chapter XI.B.1, Judge Edwards wrote:

> [T]he strict deference accorded to arbitration decisions in the collective bargaining arena may not be appropriate in statutory cases in which an employee has been forced to resort to arbitration as a condition of employment. * * * Two assumptions have been central to the Court's decisions in this area. First, the Court has insisted that, "[b]y agreeing to arbitrate a statutory claim, a party does not forego the substantive rights afforded by the statute; it only submits to their resolution in an arbitral, rather than a judicial, forum." Second, the Court has stated repeatedly that, "although judicial scrutiny of arbitration awards necessarily is limited, such review is sufficient to ensure that arbitrators comply with the requirements of the statute at issue." These twin assumptions regarding the arbitration of statutory claims are valid only if judicial review under the "manifest disregard of the law" standard is sufficiently rigorous to ensure that arbitrators have properly interpreted and applied statutory law.
>
> The value and finality of an employer's arbitration system will not be undermined by focused review of arbitral legal determinations. Most employment discrimination claims are entirely factual in nature and involve well-settled legal principles. * * * As a result, in the vast majority of cases, judicial review of legal determinations to ensure compliance with public law should have no adverse impact on the arbitration process. Nonetheless, there will be some cases in which novel or difficult legal issues are presented demanding judicial judgment. In such cases, the courts are empowered to review an arbitrator's award to ensure that its resolution of public law issues is correct. Indeed, at oral argument, Burns conceded the courts' authority to engage in such review. Because meaningful judicial review of public law issues is available, Cole's agreement to arbitrate is not unconscionable or otherwise unenforceable.

Cole, 105 F.3d at 1486–87 (citations omitted).

Is it fair to read *Cole* as only assuring judicial review for cases with "novel or difficult legal issues" and suggesting that in other cases, arbitrators will correctly find the applicable law and apply it to the facts? If that is true, then why is it that federal district court judges (in the eyes of the circuit courts) often err on issues such as the issuance of summary judgment? Is it likely that Judge Edwards would have supported judicial review of *Halligan* under the reasoning of *Cole*? Wouldn't the mere *process* of obtaining judicial review, even if the arbitration decision ultimately is undisturbed, undercut many of the reasons for choosing arbitration over litigation?

5. Should the procedures under which a claim is arbitrated be relevant to the standard of review? What about the arbitrator's qualifications (such as if the arbitrator is not a lawyer)? Should it be relevant that only one party to the arbitration was represented by an attorney? Should it matter whether the source of the underlying claim is statutory, common law, or contractual?

6. Some legal commentators have argued for expanded review of cases involving statutory claims. See, e.g., Julian J. Moore, Note, *Arbitral Review (or Lack Thereof): Examining the Procedural Fairness of Arbitrating Statutory Claims*, 100 Columbia Law Review 1572 (2000) (arguing for expanded judicial review). On the other hand, wouldn't expanded judicial review make arbitration a mere stepping-stone on the path to arbitration, and permit employers to delay employees' access to statutory remedies? See Dennis R. Nolan, *Employment Arbitration After* Circuit City, 41 Brandeis L.J. 854, 877–80, 887–89 (2003). Is there a middle ground? Consider the following possibilities:

- Wide deference to findings of fact, but increased review of conclusions of law.

- A deference standard modeled after the deference courts traditionally have given to administrative agencies. See NLRB v. Curtin Matheson Scientific, Inc., 494 U.S. 775, 110 S.Ct. 1542, 108 L.Ed.2d 801 (1990); Chevron U.S.A. v. Natural Resources Defense Council, Inc., 467 U.S. 837, 104 S.Ct. 2778, 81 L.Ed.2d 694 (1984); see also Calvin William Sharpe, *Integrity Review of Statutory Arbitration Awards*, 54 Hastings Law Journal 311 (2003) (proposing a standard in which courts give deference to "reasoned conclusions" even if the court would have reached a different result).

- A deference standard modeled after the *Collyer-Spielberg–Olin* standards (discussed *supra* in Chapter I.4.A) by which the NLRB will defer to arbitration. See Judith B. Sadler, *ADR and the NLRA: Will the Board Defer?*, 16 Ohio State Journal on Dispute Resolution 571 (2001).

- The deference standard used by courts in reviewing an award rendered by an arbitrator resolving a grievance under a collective bargaining agreement. See Chapter III.C *supra*.

7. *Cole* does not indicate whether the arbitrator will be required to issue a written opinion. Isn't the *Halligan* court, despite its protestations to the contrary, requiring arbitrators to issue a written opinion containing the

reasons for the award, as a virtual prerequisite to judicial enforcement? Under what circumstances would a party prefer (or not prefer) an arbitrator to issue a written opinion? How should an arbitrator decide whether to issue a written opinion? See Green v. Ameritech Corp., 200 F.3d 967 (6th Cir. 2000) (where the arbitration agreement provided that the arbitrator's award "shall be accompanied by an opinion which explains the arbitrator's decision with respect to each theory advanced by Plaintiff," arbitrator's "brief and conclusory" six-page opinion stating that plaintiff had not met his burden of proof on any of his theories was sufficient).

The AAA rules provide that the award "shall be in writing and * * * shall provide the written reasons for the award unless the parties agree otherwise." American Arbitration Association, National Rules for the Resolution of Employment Disputes (Jan. 1, 2004), § 34 (see Appendix C). Absent a written opinion, is meaningful judicial review possible? Should the parties be permitted to agree that the arbitrator will not issue an opinion? Should courts take the absence of a written opinion into consideration when determining whether the arbitrators manifestly disregarded the law?

8. Are transcripts of the arbitration hearing necessary to permit adequate judicial review? If arbitration must include written opinions, transcripts, and judicial review of the merits, is it still arbitration?

9. May the parties to an arbitration agreement contract for a different standard of review? In Hughes Training Inc. v. Cook, 254 F.3d 588 (5th Cir.2001), the arbitration agreement provided that "in actions seeking to vacate an [arbitration] award, the standard of review to be applied to the arbitrator's findings of fact and conclusions of law will be the same as that applied by an appellate court reviewing a decision of a trial court sitting without a jury." The employer appealed, among other things, the former employee's award of $200,000 for intentional inflic tion of emotional distress. The district court held that, as a matter of law, the conduct alleged by the former employee was not "extreme and outrageous," and therefore could not support a claim for emotional distress. The Fifth Circuit affirmed, holding that it "was not unfair for the arbitration agreement to include a standard of review that allowed the district court to assess the arbitrator's legal and factual conclusions," and that the district court "correctly adopted the standard of review incorporated into the parties' arbitration agreement." However, in Bowen v. Amoco Pipeline Co., 254 F.3d 925 (10th Cir. 2001), the Tenth Circuit held that parties cannot contractually expand the standards of judicial review created by the FAA. The court reasoned that limited review was required by the statute and that it "further[ed] the federal policy favoring arbitration by preserving the independence of the arbitration process." See also Margaret M. Maggio & Richard A. Bales, *Contracting Around the FAA: The Enforceability of Private Agreements to Expand Judicial Review of Arbitration Awards*, 18 Ohio State Journal on Dispute Resolution 571 (2002) (arguing that parties should be permitted to expand the scope of judicial review so long as the new scope is not an idiosyncratic standard); Amy J. Schmitz, *Ending a Mud Bowl: Defining Arbitration's Finality through Functional Analysis*, 37 Georgia Law

Review 123 (2002) (arguing that agreements that expand judicial review are not "arbitration agreements" enforceable under the FAA).

For a variation on the above theme, consider Little v. Auto Stiegler, 29 Cal.4th 1064, 63 P.3d 979, 130 Cal.Rptr.2d 892, (2003). The parties had signed an arbitration agreement providing that "[a]wards exceeding $50,000.00 shall include the arbitrator's written reasoned opinion and ... shall be subject to reversal and remand, modification, or reduction following review of the record and arguments of the parties by a second arbitrator who shall ... proceed according to the law and procedures available to appellate review by the California Court of Appeal of a civil judgment following court trial." The California Supreme Court refused to enforce the arbitration agreement, reasoning that, as a practical matter, this provision subjected employee, but not employer, victories to the possibility of reversal.

10.   Section 9 of the FAA provides that a party to arbitration may apply for judicial confirmation of an award "at any time within one year after the award is made." Does this provision impose a one-year statute of limitations on such actions? See Photopaint Technologies v. Smartlens, 335 F.3d 152 (2d Cir.2003) (yes); Val–U Construction Co. of S.D. v. Rosebud Sioux Tribe, 146 F.3d 573 (8th Cir.1998) (no); Teressa Elliott, *Conflicting Interpretations of the One–Year Requirement on Motions to Confirm Arbitration Awards*, ___ Creighton Law Review ___ (forthcoming Fall 2004).

Chapter XII

EMPLOYMENT ARBITRATION
IN PRACTICE

A. EMPLOYMENT ARBITRATION CASES

IN RE HOBBY LOBBY STORES, INC.
AND INDIVIDUAL GRIEVANT

115 LA 956 (John R. Phillips 2001).*

ISSUES

The arbitration arises out of the termination of G___'s employment from Hobby Lobby Stores, Inc. on November 3, 1999. The issues presented by the Claimant fall generally into two categories:

    1. Whether Claimant was terminated from his employment because of his national origin (Hispanic) in violation of Title VII of the Civil Rights Act of 1964, as amended.

    2. Whether Claimant was terminated in violation of the written terms of an employment agreement.

    3. If so, what is the appropriate remedy?

SUMMARY OF FACTS

Claimant was hired by Respondent at a store in Memphis, Tennessee, on May 16, 1996, and transferred to Waterloo, Iowa, at his request in November of 1997. On October 26, 1998, he was promoted to manager of Store #135 in Waterloo, Iowa, and, as such, was responsible for the overall operations and maintenance of the store, including store conditions.

His immediate supervisor was Sid Paul. No substantial adverse complaints about Claimant appear to have been received until some time in 1999 when complaints arose in two general categories—issues regard-

* Reprinted with permission from *Labor Arbitration Reporter–Labor Arbitration Reports*, 115 LA 956. Copyright 2001 by The Bureau of National Affairs, Inc. (800–372–1033) <http://www.bna.com>.

ing store condition and complaints from employees regarding his management style. On September 21, 1999, Regional Vice President Neill Spurgin and District Manager Dale Klein inspected Claimant's store. As a result of that visit, on September 24, 1999, claimant was given a list of deficient store items to fix within ten days. Although not explicit, it was reasonably understood that his job was in jeopardy if store conditions were not improved to Mr. Klein's satisfaction within that time period.

Shortly thereafter, on October 3, 1999, Stephanie Rowe submitted a harassment complaint to Respondent against Claimant, complaining of his management style. Respondent had previously received complaints regarding Claimant's management style from Cindy Way on April 16, 1999, Tamara Morelock (verbal complaint), and Dawn Huffman on or about April 10, 1999. Further, on October 25, 1999, Mr. Klein was told that Joleen Pietro, a co-manager, had bypassed the chain of command and had second-guessed her supervisor's (Sid Paul) decision that she travel to another store to assist on a temporary basis with the store's opening.

Ultimately, Claimant was discharged as a result of loss of confidence by Respondent and Claimant's inability to manage the store based on what has been characterized by Respondent as three "red flags": (1) the store visit on September 21, 1999, revealing that the store had reached a critical level and was in immediate need of attention; (2) the complaint of harassment received from Stephanie Rowe on October 3, 1999; and (3) the October 25, 1999 issue involving Joleen Pietro filing a complaint to Respondent's corporate office regarding Sid Paul, which was apparently interpreted as Claimant's failure to properly manage the store's co-management.

Respondent issued a handbook that provides for complaint procedure culminating in final and binding arbitration. The same handbook includes a progressive discipline procedure.

* * *

POSITION OF CLAIMANT

Claimant argues first that he was terminated because of his national origin (Hispanic), which would be unlawful under 42 U.S.C. § 2000e–2(a), which is Title VII of the Civil Rights Act of 1964, as amended. His claim in that respect is based in part on him being reminded that he had hired Fred Olive, a "black man" with a felony record and that Claimant was referred to in 1999 by Sid Paul as a "dark-haired Mexican." The other basis for Claimant's contention that the termination was based on national origin discrimination was that he was treated differently than other similarly situated managers in his district by Respondent. In support of that contention, testimony was elicited on cross-examination that non-Hispanic management employees Jackie Patton, Bob Davis, Kathy Pearson, and James Farris were given the opportunity to be demoted or take other positions rather than being terminated. Claimant's theory is based on disparate treatment rather than disparate impact theory.

Claimant also advances the claim that the termination was in violation of written terms of an employment agreement formed by Respondent requiring Claimant to sign an acknowledgment of an employee handbook and a binding arbitration provision. Claimant correctly notes that Iowa law provides for an exception to the at-will doctrine for discharges in violation of employee handbooks constituting a unilateral contract. *French v. Foods, Inc.* 495 N.W.2d 768 [8 IER Cases 506] (Iowa 1993). In support of Claimant's contention that a handbook constitutes a binding contract, Claimant notes that Respondent not only distributed the handbook but required him to sign the handbook and, further, to sign a memorandum contained in the handbook requiring employees to submit all claims relating to employment relations or termination to final and binding arbitration. Claimant references the progressive discipline provisions in the handbook and reasons that if the arbitration provisions in the handbook are binding, so are the progressive discipline provisions. Claimant further argues that, since no clear written notice was provided in accordance with the progressive discipline procedures, termination was violative of the progressive discipline provisions and, therefore, was a breach of the employment agreement created by the handbook.

POSITION OF RESPONDENT

Respondent argues that there is no evidence of national origin discrimination and cites to deposition testimony of Claimant that was reaffirmed on cross-examination during the hearing and that there was insufficient evidence that similarly situated individuals were treated more favorably. Specifically, Respondent points out that, upon cross-examination, Claimant was unable to provide any specific evidence of discriminatory intent against Hispanics and that reference to a "dark-haired Mexican" was, at most, a stray comment. Further, Respondent takes the position that Claimant's own evidence of similarly situated individuals being treated more favorably came from cross-examination of Respondent's witnesses and that the Claimant himself lacked knowledge of how they were treated or what their circumstances were. In reviewing the specifics of the five alleged comparables, Jackie Patton, Bob Davis, Ron Hall, Kathy Pearson, and James Farris, Respondent takes issue with their comparability and points out that, based on Dale Klein's testimony, to the extent the demotions or transfers were disciplinary, they lacked similarity to Claimant's issues of management style and store deficiencies.

Respondent maintains that excessive employee complaints led to loss of confidence in the Claimant's ability to manage his employees. Specifically, it notes that Claimant received more employee complaints than an average manager receives in ten years, resulting in a loss of confidence in his ability to satisfactorily manage his employees. Respondent specifically references the complaint of Stephanie Rowe filed on October 3,

1999, as well as the earlier complaints of Cindy Way, Tamara Morelock, and Dawn Huffman. Respondent also relies on the incident involving Joleen Pietro and Sid Paul on October 25, 1999, requiring Mr. Klein to intervene as a result of Ms. Pietro going outside of the chain of command, reflecting what was perceived by Mr. Paul and Mr. Klein to be a loss of control by Claimant over his employees.

Respondent essentially takes the position that even if there was a prima facie case of disparate treatment established, Respondent had legitimate non-discriminatory reasons for termination and that even if the reason offered for the termination were trivial or baseless, Respondent acted with a good-faith belief that the reason motivating it for termination were legitimate and non-discriminatory. Respondent correctly notes that the law is if the employer honestly believed in the non-discriminatory reasons it offered, even if the reasons are trivial or baseless, the reasons do not constitute a pretext for discrimination, *Jackson v. Brach Corp.*, 176 F.3d 971 [80 FED Case 853] (7th Cir.1999), or that even if they were unfair and incorrect, that does not necessarily evidence intentional discrimination for relief under the law. *Kariotis v. Navistar International Transportation Corp.*, 131 F.3d 672 [7 AD Cases 1313] (7th Cir.1997).

Respondent maintains that the Employee Handbook did not constitute an employment contract and that Respondent remained an at-will employee at any time and could be terminated without cause. Respondent points out that its employee handbook does not guarantee any employment protection; rather, it contains explicit and conspicuous disclaimers that negate any attempt to construe it as an employment contract.

With respect to the progressive discipline policy incorporated in the handbook, Respondent notes that the company is not obligated to follow the progressive discipline steps and that it retains the right to terminate an employee without any prior warning. Further, Respondent cites Claimant's testimony that he admitted that he was an at-will employee and had no employment agreement with Respondent. Thus, Respondent takes the position that lacking evidence of discrimination or the existence of a valid employment agreement, no remedy exists under which Claimant can challenge his termination.

Reasoning and Award

First, with the respect to the claim of unlawful national origin (Hispanic) discrimination under 42 U.S.C. § 2000E–2(a) of Title VII of the Civil Rights Act of 1964, as amended, Claimant's admissions in deposition and at the hearing that he was not claiming national origin discrimination are not dispositive. It appears that Claimant acknowledged that he has little or no direct evidence of discrimination, but does contend that he was treated differently than others similarly situated. His offered direct evidence was that management reminded him during their September 1999 review of his store that he had hired Fred Olive, a "black man" with a felony record and that he was referred to in 1999 by Sid Paul as a "dark-haired Mexican." Little inference can be drawn from the reference to Fred Olive and the evidence is that reference to Claimant by Sid Paul as a "dark-haired Mexican" was merely passing along the terminology used by a customer, not Sid Paul's own way of referring to the Claimant. Thus, at most the evidence constitutes stray comments and does not support the finding of unlawful discrimination based on national origin.

The other basis for claiming national origin discrimination was testimony elicited on cross-examination from Respondent's own witnesses that non-Hispanic management employees P___, D___, K___ and F___ were given the opportunity to be demoted or take other positions rather than being terminated. All were management employees working within the same district and at least some were given opportunities to be demoted or take other positions rather than being terminated for one reason or another. Claimant's own testimony with respect to the individuals was hearsay. However, testimony by Mr. Klein established that there were non-Hispanic management employees having performance problems or relationship problems who were given the opportunity to take demotions or other positions rather than being terminated. * * * The fact that several non-Hispanic management employees were given alternatives other than termination for one or the other bases upon which Claimant's termination was based certainly raises the question of whether Claimant was treated similarly. Offering alternatives to termination appears to be a practice of Respondent that was not accorded to the Claimant.

However, on the balance, there is an insufficient record upon which to find that these management individuals were similarly situated. One or possibly two had employee relations issues while two had store condition problems but no employee relations issues. None were shown to have had the extent of problems that Mr. Klein, the decision-maker, perceived Claimant had accumulated by November 1999. Certainly, none of the possible comparables had both store condition problems and employee relations problems. Further, there was a lack of evidence of the extent to which there had been a history of employee problems accumulating with respect to the other management employees who were given the opportunity to take demotions or other positions. It may well be that one or more of the management employees were similarly situated, but the record is simply insufficient to make such a finding. * * * Thus, Claimant's contention that he was treated differently than other similarly situated management employees must fail.

With respect to the claim that the termination was in violation of written terms of an employment agreement, the employee handbook must be viewed in its entirety and contains an explicit disclaimer that it is not a contract, "express or implied, guaranteeing employment for any duration". Clearly, that preserves at least an element of at-will status in the relationship. The element that it preserves is that the employment relationship is not for any specific duration of time, however. There were contractual aspects to the handbook as evidenced by the fact that the arbitration was required by a provision requiring employees to bring "all claims relating to employment relations or termination" under the arbitration procedure. Clearly, a contract existed that included final and binding arbitration. However, the law is clear that an employer can implement terms and conditions of employment, such as binding arbitration, without disrupting the at-will relationship. See *Patterson v. Tenant Healthcare, Inc.*, 113 F.3d 832 [73 FEP Cases 1822] (8th Cir.1997). Thus, the existence of a binding arbitration clause does not necessarily carry with it other limitations on at-will employment such as a just cause requirement for termination.

In this instance, the handbook did contain a progressive discipline policy which generally provided for verbal and written warning prior to termination. In fact, the form upon which the actual termination decision was recorded evidences that Respondent had a specific Employee Written Warning format for employee written warnings. In the portion of that form it indicates that the form is to be used for warnings as well as dismissals.

In this situation, Claimant was not given any kind of formal written warning and certainly the company's own Employee Written Warning form was never utilized prior to termination. However, even if contractual, the progressive discipline format contained in the employment handbook provided that disciplinary actions will "generally fall" within the categories of verbal, written and termination, but specifically stated that the company retained the right to terminate an employee without prior warning. Further, the policy concludes with the statement "while the above progressive discipline process is recommended as a general practice the Company is not obligated to follow same." Thus, while the circumstance under which the Claimant was terminated is certainly one in which most employers, particularly one such as Respondent, which "places extreme importance on treating its employees with dignity and respect," and which prides itself on being a Christina organization would accord progressive discipline, the Company was not contractually required to do so under the terms of its progressive discipline policy. Thus, even if the progressive discipline policy was contractually binding as a part of the handbook, it was not violated in this instance because it does not require prior written warning in every instance.

The disturbing part of this arbitration is that the Arbitrator finds that more than one of the bases upon which the termination rests were not legitimate. With respect to the store conditions, while it may be true that on September 21, 1999 the store conditions were deficient resulting in a list of items to be fixed within 10 days, the record taken as a whole of testimony, including that of management witnesses such as Dale Klein, leads one to conclude that the store employees, under Claimant's leadership, undertook extraordinary efforts to improve the store conditions and that almost every deficiency was improved by the end of the ten day period. Although the written summary of the reasons for termination signed by Mr. Klein and Mr. Paul incorrectly claimed that

20% of the deficiencies went unremedied at the next inspection, even Respondent's Post Hearing Brief (P.9) acknowledges that the Claimant made "adequate effort to remedy the conditions."

Next, the Arbitrator finds that, although perhaps not all, at least some of the complaints regarding the Claimant's management style were either unsupported or the criticisms of Claimant were not legitimate. For example, Tamara Morelock's alleged incident in which Claimant was to have said something derogatory over the walkie-talkie was totally unsupported by the testimony. That Sid Paul did little to investigate it yet passed it on to Dale Klein may be unconscionable, but was nevertheless a consideration by Dale Klein at the time of termination since he did not know that it lacked merit. The Arbitrator was particularly disturbed by the revelation at the hearing that Tamara Morelock, who remained employed by Respondent, was reported to have told other employees of Respondent that they need not honor the Arbitrator's subpoena served on them by Claimant and that in fact current employees known by Respondent and its counsel, in fact, failed to show up for the hearing. Testimony from such absent witnesses may well have been probative in this arbitration, but was not available because they failed to appear. That having been said, the Arbitrator refrains from drawing adverse inferences from their failure to appeal because the Respondent did offer to make subpoenaed witnesses who were current employees available for Claimant's counsel during a recess caucus.

Of particular concern among the reasons offered by the Respondent for the termination is the reliance placed on a letter written by Joleen Pietro on October 26, 1999. That was one of the final events immediately preceding termination. Essentially, she was criticized by Sid Paul because she jumped the chain of command and did not communicate properly. However, the testimony of Sid Paul and Joleen Pietro taken together leads to the inescapable conclusion that Ms. Pietro may have upset Mr. Paul, but that he had hung up on her and that she had written to corporate to complain about him. That Ms. Pietro complained about the situation can hardly be attributed to the claimant or to the store being "out of control" as Sid Paul testified and, in fact, was well within the spirit of the "all doors within the company are open" language of the Grievance Policy contained in the Employee Handbook. Moreover, no casual connection was ever established between the Claimant's management abilities and Ms. Pietro's complaint. Nevertheless, it was one of the issues presented to Dale Klein for his consideration in the summary of reasons on November 3, 1999 why the Claimant should be terminated. And Klein's reliance on such information, even if flawed was in good faith and neither discriminatory nor breach of an employment agreement.

AWARD

In summary, while the condition of the store had substantially improved and while at least some of the employee complaints regarding Claimant's management style lacked support, and while it was certainly unfair to attribute the Sid Paul/Joleen Pietro controversy to Claimant, there is no just cause or fairness standard, contractual or otherwise, under which to review the termination of Claimant's employment. It may well be that Claimant was treated unfairly, particularly under these circumstances and since the Company ignored the written elements of progressive discipline. However, in the absence of a just cause standard, and finding there to be insufficient evidence of discrimination and no breach of an employment agreement, the complaint is denied and the finding is entered in favor of Respondent.

This Award is in full settlement of all claims submitted to this Arbitration. All claims not expressly granted herein are, hereby, denied.

Notes and Questions

1. When Claimant was fired in 1999, the burdens of a Title VII race discrimination case were allocated as follows: First, the employee (or former or prospective employee) had the burden of producing evidence of a prima facie case, which required a showing (a) that the employee was a member of a class protected under Title VII, (b) that the employee was qualified for the position, (c) that the position was available, and (d) that the employee suffered an adverse employment action. Second, an employee making this showing would shift the burden to the employer of producing evidence of a legitimate, non-discriminatory reason for the adverse employment action. Third, an employer making this showing would shift the burden of persuasion back to the employee. There was a split of authority over what the employee was required to prove in this third stage. Some courts held that the employee must prove both that the employer's proffered reason for the adverse employment action was false *and* that discrimination was the true reason for the adverse employment action (the "pretext-plus" approach). See, e.g., Feliciano de La Cruz v. El Conquistador Resort, 218 F.3d 1, 6 (1st Cir.2000). Other courts held that the employee's showing that the employer's proffered reason was false would by itself permit, though not require, the factfinder to find discrimination (the "pretext-permissive" approach). See, e.g., Kline v. Tennessee Valley Authority, 128 F.3d 337, 347 (6th Cir.1997). The Eighth Circuit, the circuit in which Claimant's case arose, adopted both approaches, apparently without realizing the inconsistency. See Kim v. Nash Finch Co., 123 F.3d 1046, 1056–57 (8th Cir.1997); see also St. Mary's Honor Center v. Hicks, 509 U.S. 502, 512, 113 S.Ct. 2742, 2750, 125 L.Ed.2d 407 n.4 (1993) (similarly adopting both approaches without realizing the inconsistency). The Supreme Court ultimately adopted the pretext-permissive approach. Reeves v. Sanderson Plumbing Products, Inc., 530 U.S. 133, 120 S.Ct. 2097, 147 L.Ed.2d 105 (2000).

Did Arbitrator Phillips correctly apply the above burden-shifting framework to Claimant's race discrimination claim? Must an arbitrator use the same analytical framework that a court would? Why or why not? What would be the consequences of either answer?

2. On the issue of whether a good faith but incorrect reason can constitute discrimination, Arbitrator Phillips cited two Seventh Circuit cases despite the fact that this case arose in the Eighth Circuit. On the issue of whether a binding arbitration agreement within an employment handbook

makes the other provisions in that handbook contractually binding, he cited an Eighth Circuit case for an issue that is governed by state law. Though Arbitrator Phillips's conclusions of law on both points probably were correct, does his (mis)use of authority give you pause?

3.   Does Arbitrator Phillips give adequate weight to the possibility that *Sid Paul* might have been motivated by discriminatory animus?

4.   Arbitrator Phillips ultimately found that there was "an insufficient record" to support a finding that other management officials were similarly situated to Claimant. Arbitrator Phillips does not describe what discovery was requested or allowed prior to the arbitration hearing. Wouldn't the broad discovery permitted under the rules of civil procedure have cleared this up? Might not Claimant's lack of information have been exacerbated by the fact that several witnesses he attempted to call to testify at the arbitration hearing did not appear, apparently because a company representative had told them that they need not honor the Arbitrator's subpoena? What about the fact that the same person (Tamara Morelock) who discouraged the attendance of these witnesses also had previously complained about Claimant, a complaint that the Arbitrator explicitly found was "unsupported by the testimony"? Might *Morelock* have been motivated by discriminatory animus? Was it proper under these circumstances for the Arbitrator to "refrain[] from drawing adverse inferences" from the absence of these witnesses?

IN RE PHELPS DODGE MORENCI
AND INDIVIDUAL GRIEVANT
114 LA 819 (C. Chester Brisco, 2000).*

BACKGROUND

* * * The Grievant[, B____,] worked for the Company almost four years. Hired as a General Laborer on September 21, 1995, he successfully bid to AA Haul Truck Driver one month later. On February 13, 1999, he was transporting S____, also an AA Haul Truck Driver, from the active mining area to the mine gate to attend a problem-solving meeting. During the approximately 15–minute van ride, they conversed. B____ learned from S____ that an employee, Scott Adams, had been accused of sexual harassment and that was the purpose of the problem-solving meeting. The Grievant then made the comment according to S____, "that if he had been turned in for harassment, he would, I guess rape, or fuck the woman who turned him in." Asked if she was offended by this remark, S____ testified "At that time I really wasn't paying attention. I was preparing for the problem-solving . . . He was joking when he said it. I, I don't think he meant a personal threat to Phoenix [Sotello]. She just took it that way."

At the problem-solving meeting on February 13, 1999, S____ said nothing about the incident, although she had opportunity to do so.

Indeed, she did not report the incident to her coach or to anyone in management. However, S___ later described the incident to Sotello. How much later is not certain, and what was said is sharply disputed. Sotello thinks that S___ might have told her in "late March, maybe in April." She also thinks that S___ reported the incident to her within two or three days of its occurrence. These beliefs, obviously, cannot be reconciled. Sotello's testimony as to what S___ told her does not square with S___'s testimony about their conversation. Sotello testified that S___ revealed to her that:

> He [B___] asked her what was she going to the office for? And she told him that it was for a sexual harassment case. And that's when he said that if a woman ever turned him in for sexual harassment, he would, he would fuck her in the ass, with his fist, fuck her in the mouth, and rape her with his fist. And while she was telling me all of this, she was–I could see she was scared because she is so small, and she just, she looked at me, she says, "Phoenix, don't say anything to anybody. Don't tell anybody anything." And she, at the same time she kept looking at the bus, like she was afraid of something, because she kept looking to the bus, and looking back at me, and looking back to the buses. And I mean, she says, "Phoenix, please promise me, you're not going to say anything." And after that she went back to her bus, and I climbed in my van.

S___ testified that when she told Sotello of the incident "I was just having a conversation [with her], I had no idea that she was going to run to Human Resources." When asked if she was ever frightened of B___, S___ responded "No, that was another conversation Phoenix took out of context, and interpreted in her own words." S___ also testified that "What was said [by Sotello], and how—the way she repeated it, wasn't what I meant." S___ further testified that she did not recall telling Sotello not to tell anyone, but "I didn't tell her to go and tell."

Sotello, on her part, claimed that she "took it to the Company official right off the bat." She called for S___'s coach, Melvin Davis, and "he was there within a half an hour to 45 minutes." Sotello also said that the effect of what S___ had told her was so traumatic that "I got to the point where I wouldn't even come off my track to use the restroom in . . . that eight-hour shift . . . I developed urinary tract infection, whatever, but I was not going to climb off of my truck when someone was out there making those kind of threats. I wasn't going to go out there." She offered no further details of her trauma.

Investigation of the incident did not get underway until April. The investigation concluded in June, and in its course the company questioned 26 employees, none of whom were found to have any connection with B___'s conduct the prior February 13. B___ admitted he had said "if a woman filed a sexual harassment complaint against me, I would . . . go and rape her, because I figured I'd probably get fired, and so I would rape her in order to even the score." B___ denied using the graphic terms that Sotello reported he had used and claimed that he was joking.

According to Human Resources Manager Tom Green, S___ was evasive when questioned and she averred that B___ had not used the words Sotello reported he had used.

B___ testified that after the investigation he was under the impression from Tom Green that he would not be terminated, but he might receive some discipline. In July, B___ was called in and he was discharged on July 23, 1999, for his conduct on February 13, 1999. He filed for the problem solving complaint on the day of his discharge and this arbitration resulted.

ISSUES

1.   Did the Company have just cause to discharge B___ on July 23, 1999?

2.   If the answer to question number one is "No," what is the remedy?

* * *

POSITIONS OF THE PARTIES

The Company argues that it completed a proper investigation and concluded that the offensive remarks made by B___ were so gross, egregious, and such a direct violation of both the Guiding Principles and of Title VII of the Civil Rights Act of 1964, that the appropriate discipline was discharge. "Anything less than discharge would send a message that the Company has a level of tolerance for this type of proven violation ... B___'s actions show that he is incapable of maintaining a safe and non hostile environment for his co-workers and therefore unsuited to work in the high performing team environment here at Phelps Dodge Morenci, Inc."

The employee points out he and S___ were good friends, although he never had any contact with her outside of work. "The statement made by B___ to S___ was told to a co-worker, and that co-worker reported it to the Company four months later." The discipline, he concludes, "was not reasonably related to the seriousness of the incident." The Company, therefore, did not have just cause to discharge him.

OPINION

The Facts

The facts of B___'s misconduct that may be distilled from the conflicting evidence are difficult to ascertain. The parties stipulated to the fact that his comment to S___ occurred on February 13, 1999, during the van trip to the main gate. Exactly what words B___ used are disputed. The testimony of B___ and S___ is consistent. However, B___ has a motivation as the accused to at least shade the truth and S___, perhaps, is protecting B___. Nevertheless, they are the only percipient witnesses. S___ contradicts Sotello's version of what she told her. * * *

The evidence is difficult to fathom and arbitrators have no special divining rod by which to determine credibility. However, * * * [t]he Arbitrator concludes that the consistent testimony of B___ and of S___, absent any showing that they have colluded, plus the testimony of S___ that Sotello misrepresented her revelation, comprises a preponderance of the evidence. The Arbitrator finds that the utterances admitted by B___ are the true facts and that the testimony of Sotello as to those utterances is properly disregarded

We therefore examine the question of just cause for discharging B___ for having said to S___ on February 13, 1999, "if a woman filed a sexual harassment complaint against me, I would ... go and rape her, because I figured I'd probably get fired, and so I would rape her in order to even the score."

The Law

The Company has a legal duty as well a moral obligation to maintain a work place free from sexual harassment. The duty is well recognized in [the Company's harassment policy] which parallel[s] the proscriptions found in Title VII of the Civil Rights Act of 1964 (hereafter "Act"). The Act does not mention sexual harassment, but the concept derives from interpretation of the Act's prohibition against sex discrimination. See Bornstein, *Arbitration of Sexual Harassment*, in The Changing Face of Arbitration in theory and Practice, Proceedings of the 44th Annual Meetings of the national [sic] Academy of Arbitrators, ed. Gladys Gruenberg, pp. 109–142 (Washington: BNA Books 1992).

In *Meritor Savings Bank v. Vinson*, 477 U.S. 57, 67 [40 FEP Cases 1822] (1986), 106 S.Ct. 2399, the United States Supreme court endorsed the EEOC Guidelines issued in connection with enforcement of the Act. The Court adopted and approved the "hostile working environment" theory, and recognized that sexual harassment exists where "such conduct has the purpose or effect of unreasonably interfering with an individual's work performance or creating an intimidating, hostile, or offensive working environment."

The Company's case rests upon establishing that the single remark made by B___ to S___ created an "intimidating, hostile, or offensive working environment to another person, Sotello, who was not present and learned of the incident later—perhaps much later.

> Sexual harassment is "unwelcome verbal or physical conduct of a sexual nature." Because sexual attraction may often play a role in the day-to-day social exchange between employees, "the distinction between invited, uninvited-but-unwelcome, offensive-but-tolerated, and flatly rejected" sexual advances may well be difficult to discern. ... But this distinction is essential because sexual conduct becomes unlawful only when it is unwelcome. Bornstein, op. Cit., p. 134.

The EEOC guidelines make clear that prohibited sexual conduct must be unwelcome. The Company's [sexual harassment policy does] not specifically state that an element of prohibited sexual harassment is that it must be unwelcome, but the Policy refers to "unlawful discrimination" and to the Title VII of the Civil Rights Act and the Policy must be interpreted in the light of the law. Therefore, the Arbitrator concludes that the intent of the Policy is to confine its proscriptions to unlawful (unwelcome) conduct and it is appropriate to rely on the legal definition contained in the EEOC Guidelines as explained above.

Again, the evidence is that B____'s remark was not unwelcome as to Bowman. However, Tom Green focused on the issue of whether or not the remark was intended as a joke. Green testified, "I dismissed that it was a joke. I couldn't see in any fashion it could be a joke." The legal issue is not whether B____ intended the remark as a joke, but whether or not the remark, joke or not, was unwelcome to S____. She testified it was not.

Nevertheless, if harassing conduct sufficiently permeated the work environment, it may comprise unlawful harassment even though the offended person was not present at the time the remark was made. This also may be the result if the remark was directed specifically to a person not present. Sotello learned of B____'s comment only because S____ chose to confide in her. There is no evidence that B____'s comment permeated the work environment or that B____ directed his comment to Sotello.

In evaluating Sotello's claim that she was sexually harassed, the Arbitrator must apply the reasonable woman standard. That is, would a reasonable person in Sotello's position have considered the conduct of B____ severe or pervasive. In deciding whether or not the conduct was severe and pervasive enough to constitute a hostile working environment, the Arbitrator must consider the totality of the circumstances. These circumstances include:

> The frequency of the conduct
>
> The severity of the conduct
>
> Whether the conduct was physically threatening or humiliating or was a mere offensive utterance.
>
> Whether the conduct unreasonably interfered with complainant Sotello's work performance.

We note that B____ worked for the Company almost four years at the time of the incident and that he has no record of prior discipline. His conduct was a single utterance and there is no evidence that he engaged in similar conduct from February 13, 1999, until he was discharged 160 days later on July 23, 1999. The conduct was not physically threatening nor was it directed at a particular female in an effort to humiliate. B____'s conduct was certainly ignorant and in poor taste, but his language is properly characterized as mere offensive utterance.

Finally, the question is whether or not B____'s remark unreasonably interfered with Sotello's work performance. She claimed she was afraid to get out of her truck during her shift, even to go to the restroom. She did not elaborate as to when this occurred or how long she suffered from this mental state. Applying the standard of a reasonable woman, the Arbitrator finds that B___'s conduct was so remote as to time and circumstance that a reasonable woman would not have so reacted.

There are numerous arbitration decisions dealing with discipline for sexual harassment. These decisions distinguish between employees whose conduct comprised a pattern of repeated offenses where the discharge was sustained and those employees who engaged in a single instance of misconduct found insufficient to create a hostile working environment where the discharge was set aside [citations omitted].

The Arbitrator is mindful of the seriousness with which the Company holds the question of sexual harassment and of the extensive investigation it felt obliged to undertake. The investigation perhaps diverted its attention from the single incident upon which B___'s long delayed discharge is based. Certainly, if the hostile working environment existed as claimed by the Company it had a duty to act quickly. The passage of time, however, between the incident on February 13, 1999, and B___'s termination 160 days later, with no intervening incidents, supplies an additional reason for concluding that the Company has reacted too strongly to B___'s conduct, however boorish, ignorant and unnecessary. The company may maintain a strong and effective program against sexual harassment by applying discipline appropriate to the degree of misconduct. It is not necessary that every offensive utterance be cause for termination. Progressive discipline in the form of a final warning is appropriate in this case.

AWARD

1. The company did not have just cause to discharge B___ on July 23, 1999.

2. The remedy shall be that B___ is reinstated to his job as AA Haul Truck Driver effective July 23, 1999, with back pay and benefits, less interim earnings. This arbitration opinion shall comprise a final warning and counseling that a repetition of his behavior may be cause for discharge.

3. The Arbitrator retains jurisdiction solely for the purpose of the terms of this award.

Notes and Questions

1. Arbitrator Brisco framed the issue as whether the Company had "just cause" to discharge B___. Why did the arbitrator apply a just-cause standard to an individual arbitration case?

2. Note that this was not a Title VII harassment case brought by a victim of alleged harassment, but a wrongful discharge case brought by the alleged harassor. Does the different context change the way that Title VII law should be used in the case?

3. Do you agree that a single incident of misconduct can never support a sexual harassment claim? Compare Creamer v. Laidlaw Transit, Inc., 86 F.3d 167, 170 (10th Cir.1996) (holding that single incident of sexual harass-

ment was neither sufficiently pervasive nor severe to constitute a hostile work environment) with Hickman v. Laskodi, 45 Fed.Appx. 451 (6th Cir. 2002) (holding that a single serious threat of physical harm can suffice to state a sexual harassment claim); *Moring v. Arkansas Department of Corrections*, 243 F.3d 452, 456–57 (8th Cir.2001) (holding that evidence of an isolated harassing incident was sufficient to support the jury's finding of a sexually hostile work environment where the plaintiff's supervisor, clad in only boxer shorts, "touched her thigh and leaned in as if to kiss her").

4. Do you agree with the arbitrator's conclusion that B___'s remark was "not physically threatening"? With his conclusion that Sotello's fear was unreasonable under the circumstances? That a "reasonable woman" would not have reacted with fear upon learning of B___'s remark? Aren't these precisely the kind of issues for which juries are best suited? Consider the following:

> [A]rbitration [does not] seem suited to the adjudication of claims that rest not on a well-understood and well-accepted statutory standard but on the ascertainment of external community values. Take, for example, a claim of invasion of privacy or dignity [based on an employer's] electronic monitoring and surveillance. Such a case confronts the arbitrator not with the resolution of a factual dispute bearing on an agreed-on standard but to resolve what the standards are in the face of a strongly defended business practice. It seems one thing to call on an arbitrator to sort out claims of pretext or mixed motive in a discharge. It seems quite another to call on an arbitrator to decide if personal information routinely disseminated by the company for valid business purposes nevertheless exceeded "all bounds of civilized behavior" or if the routine administration of a personality test was "unreasonably offensive" to the larger community. To put those kinds of claims into the hands of an arbitrator, to be decided in a nonpublic hearing and to result in a nonpublic decision, is to preclude the kind of communal judgment the standards for deciding them necessarily implicate.

Matthew W. Finkin, *Modern Manorial Law*, 38 Industrial Relations 127, 133 (1999). Does Professor Finkin's preference for juries extend to sexual harassment cases, where the factfinder must decide when the alleged perpetrator's conduct has been "bad enough" to rise to the level of actionable harassment? Are there particular types of employment issues which judges and/or arbitrators are best suited to resolve?

5. Was it proper for the arbitrator to use the "reasonable woman" standard? The Ninth Circuit, the circuit in which this case arose, adopted the reasonable woman standard in 1991, Ellison v. Brady, 924 F.2d 872, 878–79 (9th Cir.1991), and still uses it today, Holly D. v. California Institute of Technology, 339 F.3d 1158, 1173 (9th Cir.2003). In Harris v. Forklift Systems, Inc., 510 U.S. 17, 114 S.Ct. 367, 126 L.Ed.2d 295 (1993), the Supreme Court appeared to use a "reasonable person" standard. Is there a meaningful difference between these standards?

6. Should it matter that Sotello was not the intended recipient of S___'s comment, but instead learned of the comment second-hand?

7.   The employer wins each of the two cases presented above. A review of published employment arbitration cases reveals that a striking proportion of them are employer victories, although, as Part B of this Chapter demonstrates, employee win rates are at least as good in arbitration as they are in litigation. What might be skewing the *published* cases? If an increasing number of cases are shifted from litigation to arbitration, what effect might this have on the development of discrimination law?

8.   Do either of the two cases presented above fit into the category of fact-intensive cases which Judge Edwards, in *Cole*, says should be largely unaffected by judicial review? If these cases were appealed, what approach should the reviewing court take?

9.   How do you think these cases would have been decided in labor arbitration? In litigation? Which forum would you prefer if you were counsel for an employee? For an employer? Why?

B.   NORMATIVE AND EMPIRICAL STUDIES OF EMPLOYMENT ARBITRATION

In 1997, the Equal Employment Opportunity Commission issued the EEOC Policy Statement on Employment Arbitration. This policy statement sharply criticized employment arbitration. However, as discussed in Chapter X, the EEOC has only procedural (not substantive) rulemaking authority under Title VII, and has no statutory authority to interpret the Federal Arbitration Act. Consequently, courts have largely ignored the EEOC Policy Statement. See Borg–Warner Protective Services Corp. v. EEOC, 81 F.Supp.2d 20 (D.D.C.2000).

The EEOC's impotence on the subject did not seem to diminish, at least immediately, the agency's opposition to employment arbitration. For example, in EEOC v. Waffle House, 534 U.S. 279, 122 S.Ct. 754, 151 L.Ed.2d 755 (2002), discussed in Chapter X, the EEOC brought suit in its own name on behalf of an aggrieved individual who had signed an arbitration agreement. Similarly, in Cooper v. MRM Investment Co., 367 F.3d 493, 496, 512 (6th Cir.2004), the EEOC filed an amicus curiae brief on behalf of an employee challenging the enforcement of an employment arbitration agreement.

More recently, however, the EEOC seems to have extended grudging acceptance to employment arbitration. In EEOC v. Luce, Forward, Hamilton & Scripps, 345 F.3d 742 (9th Cir.2003) (*en banc*), the EEOC sued a law firm seeking to invalidate its employment arbitration agreement. The federal district court agreed with the EEOC and enjoined enforcement of the agreement. The Ninth Circuit reversed, holding that the agreement was valid. The court remanded, however, giving the EEOC the opportunity to develop its "novel theory" that the firm illegally had "retaliated" against an employee by denying employment to him for refusing to sign the arbitration agreement. Ultimately, however, the EEOC settled the case, and agreed that with some minor revisions, the arbitration agreement would be in compliance with state and federal law. EEOC v. Luce, Forward, Hamilton & Scripps, No. LA CV 00–1322

(C.D. Cal.), settlement approved June 18, 2004. An EEOC spokesperson subsequently explained that although the EEOC policy statement opposing employment arbitration "is still technically in effect", there is "a lot of confusion" at the agency over the issue, and the agency is re-evaluating the continued vitality of the policy statement. See *EEOC Contravenes Policy, Allows Law Firm to Continue Mandatory Arbitration Plan*, 73 United States Law Week (BNA) (July 20, 2004) at 2043–44.

In any event, many legal commentators have joined the EEOC in criticizing employment arbitration. Employment arbitration has been criticized on the following grounds:

- It undermines the statutory right that employees have under the federal antidiscrimination laws to sue for enforcement, and undermines the fundamental right to trial by jury. See Jean R. Sternlight, *The Rise and Spread of Mandatory Arbitration as a Substitute for the Jury Trial*, 38 University of San Francisco Law Review 17 (2003). But doesn't this beg the question of whether employees can waive their statutory procedural rights?

- It fails to deter employers from violating antidiscrimination laws. Public enforcement of antidiscrimination laws through the courts is critical for deterring employer violations and exposing systemic patterns of discrimination. See David S. Schwartz, *Enforcing Small Print to Protect Big Business: Employee and Consumer Rights Claims in an Age of Compelled Arbitration,* 1997 Wisconsin Law Review 33 (the factors that make arbitration attractive, such as speed and low cost, all tend to reduce the employer's costs of defense and liability; employment arbitration permits an employer to "engage[] in a measure of 'self-regulation' by lowering the costs of violating the statute it would have faced under the regime of full judicial enforcement."); Clyde W. Summers, *Mandatory Arbitration: Privatizing Public Rights, Compelling the Unwilling to Arbitrate*, 6 University of Pennsylvania Journal of Labor and Employment Law 685, 704 (2004) (arbitration "limits consumers' and others' ability to know whether they are patronizing a lawbreaker"). But don't the possibility of damages, adverse publicity, and EEOC enforcement, still provide incentives for employers to comply with the law?

- Arbitration agreements are drafted by employers with little or no input from employees; it is unfair to permit employers to impose these "agreements" on employees on a "take-it-or-be-fired (or not hired)" basis. See Katherine Van Wezel Stone, *Mandatory Arbitration of Individual Employment Rights: The Yellow–Dog Contract of the 1990s*, 73 Denver University Law Review 1017 (1996). But don't employers impose other conditions of employment, such as work hours and salary, on a similar basis?

- Individual employees lack meaningful bargaining power. As a result, many arbitration agreements contain lopsided provisions that give every possible procedural advantage to the employer. See Richard A. Bales, *The Laissez–Faire Arbitration Market and the Need for a*

Uniform Federal Standard Governing Employment and Consumer Arbitration, 52 Kansas Law Review 583 (2004) (providing examples of lopsided provisions). But won't courts refuse to enforce egregiously lopsided arbitration "agreements"?

• The informal nature of arbitration results in a sort of second-class justice. See Katherine Van Wezel Stone, *Rustic Justice: Community and Coercion Under the Federal Arbitration Act*, 77 North Carolina Law Review 931 (1999). But does it? See *infra* Chapter XII.B.

• The absence of published arbitral opinions will stifle development of the law. See Samuel Estreicher, *Predispute Agreements to Arbitrate Statutory Employment Claims*, 72 New York University Law Review 1344 (1997) (concluding that mandatory publication of arbitral awards is "a close question"). But there is no empirical support for this argument; if anything, the number of published employment cases appears to have increased over the past fifteen years.

• Employers, but not individual employees, are repeat players in arbitration. This results in two systemic employer advantages. The first is that the employer is more familiar with the pool of potential arbitrators and therefore is in a better position than an employee to select an arbitrator favorable to its side. The second is that an arbitrator interested in generating future business will be predisposed to favor the employer. See Lisa B. Bingham, *On Repeat Players, Adhesive Contracts, and the Use of Statistics in Judicial Review of Employment Arbitration Awards*, 29 McGeorge Law Review 223 (1998); Lisa B. Bingham, *Employment Arbitration: The Repeat Player Effect*, 1 Employee Rights and Employment Policy Journal 189 (1997). But see Lisa B. Bingham & Shimon Sarraf, *Employment Arbitration Before and After the Due Process Protocol for Mediation and Arbitration Disputes Arising Out of Employment: Preliminary Evidence That Self–Regulation Makes A Difference*, in Alternative Dispute Resolution in the Employment Arena: Proceedings of New York University's 53d Annual Conference on Labor (Samuel Estreicher ed. 2001) (finding no statistically significant evidence that employers confronting the same arbitrator in a second case have a higher probability of success).

On the other hand, advocates for employment arbitration have pointed out that for all its flaws, arbitration provides access to a dispute resolution forum for employees to whom the courthouse doors are closed. Litigating a simple employment dispute from inception through trial can easily cost upwards of $100,000; few unemployed employees can afford to pay this out-of-pocket. While some employees are able to turn to contingency fee arrangements to secure legal representation, an attorney has little incentive to take an employment case unless the likelihood and quantity of recoverable damages appear large—i.e., when the employee has a high income (creating a large sum of lost wages) and/or the employer's conduct has been particularly egregious (creating the possibility of a punitive damages award). See Peter H. Huang, *A New Options Theory for Risk Multipliers of Attorney's Fees in Federal Civil Rights*

Litigation, 73 New York University Law Review 1943, 1945 (1998). Fee shifting statutes that permit prevailing plaintiffs to recover their attorneys' fees may marginally help employees find legal representation, but the fees are only awarded to plaintiffs who prevail, and are not adjusted to reflect the risk of loss. See City of Burlington v. Dague, 505 U.S. 557, 112 S.Ct. 2638, 120 L.Ed.2d 449 (rejecting contingency enhancements as inconsistent with the statutory requirement that fees be shifted only to prevailing parties). The EEOC is unable to fill the gap, because its meager resources permit it to file suit in only 0.43% of the cases it considers. EEOC 2002 Annual Report, http://www.eeoc.gov/abouteeoc/annual_reports/annrep02.html (last accessed April 3, 2004) (noting that 84,442 charges of discrimination were filed in fiscal year 2002); EEOC Litigation Statistics, FY 1992 Through FY 2002, http://www.eeoc.gov/stats/litigation.html (last accessed April 3, 2004) (noting that the EEOC filed 364 suits in fiscal year 2002).

A 1995 survey indicated that plaintiffs' attorneys accept only about 5% of the employment discrimination claims brought to them by prospective clients due largely to the attorneys' policy of accepting only those employment discrimination cases in which employees could demonstrate provable damages of, on average, at least $60,000. William M. Howard, *Arbitrating Claims of Employment Discrimination: What Really Does Happen? What Really Should Happen?*, 50 Dispute Resolution Journal 40, 45 (1995). Because "provable damages" correlate with salary, only high-income employees are able, in most cases, to attract an attorney to their case. See Elizabeth Hill, *Due Process at Low Cost: An Empirical Study of Employment Arbitration Under the Auspices of the American Arbitration Association*, 18 Ohio State Journal on Dispute Resolution 777, 783 (2003). The reported cases and limited empirical evidence available indicate that most employment claims are brought by high-income professional employees, and that low-income employees lack meaningful access to the courts for resolution of their employment disputes. See James N. Dertzouzos, Elaine Holland, and Patricia Ebener, RAND Inst. No. R–3602–ICJ, The Legal and Economic Consequences of Wrongful Termination 20–21 (1988); James W. Meeker and John Dombrink, *Access to the Civil Courts for Those of Low and Moderate Means*, 66 Southern California Law Review 2217, 2218 (1993); Bright v. Norshipco & Norfolk Shipbuilding & Drydock Corp., 951 F.Supp. 95, 98 (E.D.Va.1997) ("[W]e have simply priced the court system beyond the reach of most citizens, because the cost of litigation far exceeds the value of the decision itself.").

This has led many commentators to conclude that employment arbitration often works to the advantage of low-income employees. Professor Samuel Estreicher writes:

> In a world without employment arbitration as an available option, we would essentially have a "cadillac" system for the few and a "rickshaw" system for the many. The unspoken (yet undeniable) truth is that most claims filed by employees do not attract the attention of private lawyers because the stakes are too small and

outcomes too uncertain to warrant the investment of lawyer time and resources. These claims have only one place to go: filings with administrative agencies where they essentially languish, for the agencies themselves lack the staffing (and often even the inclination) to serve as lawyers for average claimants. The people who benefit under a litigation-based system are those whose salaries are high enough to warrant the costs and risks of a law suit undertaken by competent counsel; these are the folks who are likely to derive benefit from the considerable upside potential of unpredictable jury awards. Very few claimants, however, are able to obtain a position in this "litigation lottery."

Most plaintiff lawyers understandably value this system because it enables them to be highly selective about the cases they take on. Moreover, the sheer costs of defending a litigation and the risks of a jury trial create considerable settlement value irrespective of the substantive merits of the underlying claim. Thus, most cases where claimants obtain competent counsel will settle, and at sufficiently high values to give plaintiff lawyers ample economic rewards without actually having to try many law suits. Thus, the system works well for high-end claimants and most plaintiff lawyers, and not very well for average claimants.

A properly designed arbitration system, I submit, can do a better job of delivering accessible justice for average claimants than a litigation-based approach. It stands a better chance of providing Saturns for average claimants, in place of the rickshaws now available to the many so that a few can drive Cadillacs.

Samuel Estreicher, *Saturns for Rickshaws: The Stakes in the Debate Over Predispute Employment Arbitration Agreements*, 16 Ohio State Journal on Dispute Resolution 559, 563–64 (2001).

Consider these arguments as you read the following:

EMPLOYMENT ARBITRATION AND WORKPLACE JUSTICE
Lewis L. Maltby.
38 University of San Francisco Law Review 105 (2003).

II. EMPIRICAL DATA ON EMPLOYEE SUCCESS RATES

A. Results from Studies on Arbitration in the Employment Context

Ultimately, the facts speak for themselves—either employment arbitration has delivered justice to employees or it has not. Fortunately, a significant body of empirical evidence is now available to demonstrate whether justice has in fact been achieved through arbitration.

1. AAA Arbitration

The first significant work in this area was conducted by Professor Lisa Bingham of Indiana University. Professor Bingham found that, in 1992, employees in arbitrations conducted by the American Arbitration

Association ("AAA") prevailed in 73% of cases they filed against their employers. Two years later, Professor Bingham examined employee win rates in AAA arbitration again for the period extending from 1993 to 1995. In this time span, employees won 63% of the time.[8]

Lewis Maltby, President of the National Workrights Institute, examined AAA records for 2000 and found that employees won 66% of the time.[9] Theodore Eisenberg, a law professor at Cornell Law School, and Elizabeth Hill, a research fellow for the Center for Law and Labor, found an employee win rate of 43% in a sample of randomly selected AAA cases from 1999 to 2000.[10]

It is difficult to completely harmonize these results. At first blush, employee success rates might appear to be declining over time. * * * The only changes that occurred in AAA arbitration during the time period in which these studies were conducted were: 1) the development and adoption of the Due Process Protocol ("Protocol") [reproduced in Appendix C]; and 2) the creation of a new roster of employment arbitrators by AAA. Both of these developments, however, work to the advantage of employee plaintiffs and should have the effect of increasing their win rate. The most logical explanation for the different success rates is that the reported variations are simply the result of chance. * * *

The critical question is, "How often do employees prevail in arbitration?" None of these studies, taken individually, provides a clear answer to this question. Each study simply represents a different slice of the same data set and so each should be given equal weight. Therefore, aggregating the data provides the most meaningful interpretation of the data. The total number of employment arbitrations represented by all the studies was 557. Of these, employees won 346 cases, for a success rate of 62%.

* * *

B. Results from Studies on Litigation

Employees' success rates in arbitration mean little in isolation. They only become meaningful when compared to the success rates of similar cases resolved through litigation.

Eisenberg and Hill recently demonstrated that employee success rates, both in litigation and arbitration, vary dramatically with the legal theory involved in each employment dispute.[19] Specifically, employee success rates were determined to be much higher in either forum when

8. Lisa B. Bingham, *Employment Arbitration: The Repeat Player Effect*, 1 Employee Rights & Employment Policy Journal 189, 210 (1997).

9. Lewis L. Maltby, *The Myth of Second–Class Justice: Resolving Employment Disputes in Arbitration, in* How ADR Works 915, 921 (Norman Brand ed., 2002).

10. Theodore Eisenberg & Elizabeth Hill, *Employment Arbitration and Litigation: An Empirical Comparison*, 2003 Public Law & Legal Theory Res. Paper Series 1, 14, http://papers.ssrn.com/sol3/papers.cfm?abstract_id=389780 (last accessed [April 3, 2004]).

19. *See* Eisenberg & Hill, *supra* note 10, at 16.

the case involved a contract dispute, as compared to when the case involved a violation of a civil rights statute.

The fact that very few employment arbitrations involve civil rights disputes requires that we use litigation results from non-civil rights employment cases for comparison to arbitration results. Eisenberg and Hill analyzed the results of state court employment trials in 1996 from the Civil Trial Court Network, a project of the National Center for State Courts and the Bureau of Justice Statistics. The databases of the courts of general jurisdiction, as compared to the databases of the civil rights cases from federal courts, dealt with cases that more clearly resembled AAA cases.

The success rate of employee plaintiffs in these state court employment disputes was 57%. This is slightly lower than the 62% success rate achieved by employees in AAA arbitrations. It is difficult, however, to attribute any significance to this small difference. The fairest conclusion that can be drawn is that employees have as equal a chance of winning a state court trial as they do an AAA arbitration proceeding.

C. Effect of Summary Judgment

The conclusion that success rates in arbitration and litigation are equal, however, applies only when an employee plaintiff in civil court has a trial. However, many employees in civil court do not receive a trial. The majority of employment cases in federal court, some 60%, are resolved on summary judgment.[28] Employers win 98% of these summary judgment motions. In state court, the number of employment cases dismissed on summary judgment is much lower—only 15%. This does not occur in arbitration. Summary judgment in AAA arbitration is so rare as to be statistically insignificant. Virtually all employees who take their disputes to AAA arbitration receive a hearing on the merits.

This additional factor–the effect of summary judgment–requires a complete rethinking of the comparison of arbitration success rates to litigation success rates. The question is not, "How do employees who go to court and get a trial fare compared to employees who use arbitration?" The real question is, "How do all employees who take their disputes to court fare compared to all employees who take their disputes to arbitration?"

Looking at the data from this perspective reveals that 62% of all employees who turn to AAA arbitration achieve a decision in their favor. To create a comparable figure for litigation, we must factor in the rate of summary judgment for those cases that are analogous to those going to arbitration. Twenty two percent of AAA's employment caseload consists of federal civil rights cases. The remainder of the caseload is made up of contract claims and other legal disputes that more closely resemble state court claims. A weighted average analysis produces a rate of summary

28. Inter–University Consortium for Political and Social Research Database, case category 442 jobs (July 11, 1997) (on file with author).

judgment in litigation, regarding those cases comparable to AAA's cases, of 25%.

This has important implications for comparing AAA results to litigation results. Since 25% of litigated cases would have been dismissed on summary judgment, only 75% of these cases would have gone to trial. The 57% of cases employees were found to have won in court thus represents only 43% of the total cases brought by employees.

It is critical to remember that the source of all the arbitration data used in this analysis was the AAA. The AAA is well known for maintaining a roster that includes arbitrators of the highest quality, who scrupulously follow the Protocol. While other large providers of arbitration, such as JAMS/Endispute and the National Arbitration Forum, may match AAA's quality, it is almost inconceivable that all of the hundreds of providers in this unregulated field meet AAA's high standards. The above analysis shows that arbitration can provide victory rates that are as good or even better for employees than courts can provide. It does not prove that arbitration generally provides the high victory rates reported in this article.

D.   Size of Awards

Even if employees are more likely to win in arbitration proceedings than in court, this does not prove that arbitration is better for employees than litigation. Justice is not achieved merely because a deserving employee has won his or her case. Justice is served only if the amount the employee has received from a victory is fair, in terms of the harm the employee has suffered.

Initial figures on the amounts employees typically receive as the result of favorable arbitration decisions raised serious concerns. Professor Bingham found that the mean damages awarded by AAA arbitrators from January 1993 to December 1995 was $49,030.[33] By contrast, the mean damages awarded by district courts, for this same time period, was $530,611.[34] These findings seem to indicate that, while employees win more often in arbitration than in court, arbitration judgments undercompensate prevailing employees.

Insight gained from later research indicates that this analysis is too crude to be meaningful. The cases handled by AAA are mostly contract dispute cases and so are primarily economic in nature. Such cases offer very little opportunity for an arbitrator to award compensatory or punitive damages. The employment cases handled by federal district courts, in contrast, are predominantly statutory civil rights cases that frequently call for such damages.

33. Lisa B. Bingham, *Unequal Bargaining Power: An Account for the Repeat Player Effect in Employment Arbitration*, 50 Industrial Relations Research Association Proceedings 33, 38 (1998).

34. *Inter-University Database, supra* note 28.

More recently, Eisenberg and Hill compared the size of the awards in AAA arbitration proceedings to the size of awards in state court employment cases. The median AAA award was $63,120, while the median state court award was an almost identical $68,737.[38] The mean awards, however, were quite different. The mean AAA award was around $153,000,but the mean state court award was about $462,000. This indicates that most employees who prevailed in arbitration received awards comparable to what they would have received in court, but a few employees who took their claims to court received very large awards that they would not have received from arbitration.

These large jury awards, however, are seldom received in full by prevailing employees. It is commonplace for a trial court judge to reduce the size of a jury award against an employer. It is also routine practice for employers to appeal large trial court awards and use the cost and delay of appeal as a bargaining tool. Some experienced trial lawyers have estimated this "shrinkage" to be in excess of 50%. If these estimates are correct, the difference in mean awards would be reduced greatly, and might be eliminated altogether.

Notes and Questions

1. Despite Maltby's findings that most employees are substantially better off using AAA arbitration than they are using litigation, he nonetheless concludes that "[a]rbitration as a condition of employment is wrong and should be opposed." Do you agree?

2. How likely is it that parties to an employment dispute will agree to arbitration *after* a dispute has arisen? If you are an attorney representing a party in an employment case that already has been filed in court, under what circumstances would you recommend arbitration to your client? What factors would be important to you?

3. Why is it that employers are far more likely than employees to insist upon compulsory arbitration agreements? Why are employees far more likely than employers to challenge an agreement's enforceability in court? Must your answer to the two questions necessarily be the same?

4. The excerpt above indicates that arbitrators are less likely than jurors to render extremely large awards; arbitrators also appear far less likely than juries to award punitive damages. (For a counter-example, see Siegel v. Prudential Insurance Co., 67 Cal.App.4th 1270, 79 Cal.Rptr.2d 726 (2 Dist.1998) (refusing to vacate a million dollar award for punitive damages)). Assuming that perceptions are true, does arbitration permit employers to view employment disputes as just another predictable cost of doing business, as opposed to a threat that could put them out of business or seriously affect their bottom line? If so, is this likely to affect the degree of importance that employers attach to complying with employment laws?

5. Another difference between litigation and arbitration is the settlement rate. Only about 5% of court cases that are filed actually go to trial; the vast majority are settled. See Marc Galanter and Mia Cahill, *"Most Cases*

---

38. *See* Eisenberg & Hill, *supra* note 10, at 18.

Settle": Judicial Promotion and Regulation of Settlements, 46 Stanford Law Review 1339 (1994); Samuel R. Gross and Kent D. Syverud, *Don't Try: Civil Jury Verdicts in a System Geared to Settlement*, 44 UCLA Law Review 1, 2 (1996). Though some cases subject to arbitration agreements also settle, the settlement rate probably is significantly lower than for litigation.

6.　Elizabeth Hill, examining AAA arbitration, concluded that low-income employees proceeding *pro se* succeed in AAA arbitration at about the same rate as low-income employees with counsel. Elizabeth Hill, *Due Process at Low Cost: An Empirical Study of Employment Arbitration Under the Auspices of the American Arbitration Association*, 18 Ohio State Journal on Dispute Resolution 777, 800 n.93, 818 (2003). It is highly doubtful whether the same can be said for litigation, in which employees must first navigate the process of filing an EEOC charge, see Michael Selmi, *The Value of the EEOC: Reexamining the Agency's Role in Employment Discrimination Law*, 57 Ohio State Law Journal 1, 10–11, 25 (1996), and then must navigate the rules of civil procedure.

7.　Theodore Eisenberg and Elizabeth Hill, in a study discussed in the Maltby excerpt above, concluded that employment arbitration is much faster than employment litigation. Mean and median times in arbitration ranged from about seven to thirteen months; mean and median litigation times, in both state and federal courts, all exceeded twenty months. Theodore Eisenberg & Elizabeth Hill, *Employment Arbitration and Litigation: An Empirical Comparison*, 2003 Public Law & Legal Theory Research Paper Series 1, 14, http://papers.ssrn.com/sol3/papers.crm?abstract_id=389780 (last accessed [April 3, 2004]). Delay typically favors the employer. Richard A, Bales, Compulsory Arbitration: The Grand Experiment in Employment 154 (1997) ("An employer believing that an employee has a valid claim has ample motive to delay trial indefinitely, because doing so will both pressure the employee to accept a smaller settlement as her resources dwindle, and extend into the distant future the date that settlement or judgment must be paid out. Delay also may deter future suits by other employees by fostering the employer's reputation for vigorously defending and delaying all of its employment cases.").

A COMPARATIVE NOTE ON PROTECTING NON–UNION WORKERS

In the 1970s, when European economies were booming, the trend in European law was to afford workers strong job security protection. The more recent trend has been towards deregulation of the labor market and a restoration of the employer's unilateral power to discharge workers. See Bob Hepple, *European Rules on Dismissal Law?*, 18 Comparative Labor Law Journal 204 (1997). That being said, most European countries provide workers with far greater legal protection of job security than is available to American workers who are not covered by a collective bargaining agreement.

The methods used for resolving individual employment disputes (referred to in different countries as "grievances," "individual grievances," or "legal disputes") vary widely. Some countries resolve such disputes in their ordinary courts. Some countries channel employment disputes into specialized labor courts, administrative agencies, or industrial tribunals. A few countries, such as Sweden, rely heavily on arbitration. Many countries use several procedures for resolving employment disputes. For example, the labor-court country of Germany permits the parties to use arbitration; Britain uses a combination of labor courts, mediation, arbitration, and industrial tribunals. See generally Jean R. Sternlight, *In Search of the Best Procedure for Enforcing Employment Discrimination Laws: A Comparative Analysis*, 78 Tulane Law Review 1401 (2004); Roy J. Adams, Industrial Relations Under Liberal Democracy: North America in Comparative Perspective (1995); Alan Gladstone, *Settlement of Disputes Over Rights*, in Comparative Labour Law and Industrial Relations in Industrialized Market Economies 629 (Roger Blanpain and Chris Engels, eds., 7th ed. 2001); Alan Gladstone, Voluntary Arbitration of Interest Disputes: A Practical Guide (1984); Benjamin Aaron, *Settlement of Disputes Over Rights*, in Comparative Labour Law and Industrial Relations 260 (Roger Blanpain and Frances Millard, eds., 1982).

C. ETHICAL ISSUES IN EMPLOYMENT ARBITRATION

ETHICAL CONCERNS IN DRAFTING EMPLOYMENT ARBITRATION AGREEMENTS AFTER *CIRCUIT CITY* AND *GREEN TREE*

Martin H. Malin.
41 Brandeis Law Journal 779 (2003).

In representing a client, a lawyer's obligation is "zealously to protect and pursue a client's legitimate interests, within the bounds of the law."[105] * * * Professor David Luban has referred to the duty to zealously pursue the client's interests as the "principle of partisanship."[107] American lawyers have so internalized the principle of partisanship that their intuitive reaction when clients ask them to draft arbitration agreements to impose on their employees will be to draft as close to the line of enforceability as possible. * * * I suggest that lawyers should question their intuition.

There is a consensus that the principle of partisanship has its limits. The Supreme Court made this clear in Nix v. Whiteside,[117] [when the Court held that a criminal defense counsel was ethically obligated to advise the court if the client insisted on perjuring himself, just as the attorney would have been if the client announced an intent to tamper with witnesses or jurors]. Thus, lawyers have dual roles. They serve as representatives of their clients, but they also serve as officers of the court.

The justification of the adversary system that forms the basis for the Model Rules is the system's function in seeking truth. The system assumes that the most effective way to find the truth is to have both

105. Model Rules of Prof'l Conduct, pmbl. ¶ 9 (2002).

107. David Luban, Lawyers and Justice: An Ethical Study 11 (1988).

117. 475 U.S. 157 (1986).

parties zealously represented by advocates who will uncover and present their fullest and most favorable case, and, by cross examination, rebuttal and argument, will test to the maximum the case presented by the other side. Neither counsel is seeking the truth. Each counsel is presenting the case believed to have the greatest likelihood of winning, regardless of the truth. The combined partisan efforts of the opposing advocates are what is most likely to produce a complete and tested record that facilitates the tribunal's determination of where the truth lies. Thus, [w]hen attorneys present their clients' cases in the light most favorable to their clients, they serve the adversary system's truth seeking function.

* * *

[I]t is becoming increasingly difficult for employees to resist arbitration in the courts. When employees file suit, courts are increasingly likely to compel arbitration. The judicial embrace of arbitration at the front end has been accompanied by a judicial reluctance to disturb arbitration awards at the back end. * * * Thus, it appears that management lawyers, when drafting employment arbitration agreements for their clients, are creating the first and final forum in which their clients' employees will adjudicate their statutory claims. The Model Rules make clear that in carrying out this function, counsel's role is not limited to that of legal tactician.[160] Thus, in presenting the arbitration alternative to a client, a lawyer may counsel a client that the arbitral forum should be established with fair procedures that will ensure that employees using it will be able to vindicate their statutory rights. I contend, however, that not only is a lawyer permitted to so counsel the client, the ethical lawyer must do so.

Our nation's employment statutes provide the legal framework regulating the relationships between employers and employees. They are designed to remedy market failures and market excesses. Each statute contains its own enforcement provisions, including the public tribunals, typically courts or administrative agencies, before whom disputes over enforcement will be resolved. When representing a client before one of those tribunals, a lawyer is obligated to maintain the integrity of the tribunal. By so doing, the lawyer maintains the integrity of the overall legal framework, including the substantive provisions of the statute that the tribunal is empowered to enforce. It follows, a fortiori, that in creating a substitute tribunal, a lawyer remains obligated to ensure the integrity of the overall legal framework, including the substantive provisions of the statutes that the substitute tribunal will enforce. In other words, the lawyer is obligated when drafting the tribunal's structure and procedures to be true to the Supreme Court's vision that the arbitration

160. See Model Rules, supra note 105, at R. 2.1 ("In representing a client, a lawyer shall exercise independent professional judgment and render candid advice. In rendering advice, a lawyer may refer not only to law but to other considerations such as moral, economic, social and political factors, that may be relevant to the client's situation.").

agreement only substitutes a forum and does not impede the effective vindication of statutory rights.

* * *

[T]he lawyer's responsibility to maintain the integrity of the legal framework should inform the manner in which the lawyer presents the arbitration alternative to the client. In counseling a client, it is impossible for a lawyer to escape ethical, social and political considerations. The law's ambiguity precludes a lawyer from limiting her role to that of amoral tactician, neutrally and objectively informing the client of the probable legal consequences of a proposed course of action. The tone with which the lawyer presents the alternatives will affect the manner in which the client receives the lawyer's advice and the course of action likely to be taken.

For example, the lawyer can discuss employment statutes as infringements on employer autonomy that arm unscrupulous employees with vexatious weapons to extract unwarranted concessions from their employers. The lawyer can then portray arbitration as an opportunity to act strategically to force such vexatious claims into a forum that will be sympathetic to the employer's plight and hostile to insolent employees who dare to challenge the boss. Such a presentation will likely lead to an arbitration agreement that undermines the overall legal framework by stacking the deck in the employer's favor. I submit that such an approach falls outside the boundaries of the partisanship principle and breaches the lawyer's responsibilities to maintain the integrity of the justice system.

Alternatively, the lawyer can portray arbitration as a system that substitutes a less formal, less expensive and less time consuming process for litigation while maintaining the integrity of the underlying statutory regulatory framework. The lawyer can explain that moving to an arbitration system may actually lead to an increase in claims because the system will be more accessible to employees than the courts. Such an increase in claims, however, is likely to be offset by reduced litigation expenses and by arbitration's elimination of the employer's exposure to outlier jury awards. As a private forum, arbitration may also shield the employer from adverse publicity. The lawyer can further explain that the arbitration agreement may not waive employees' statutory rights but must merely substitute the arbitral forum for the courts as the venue where employees may effectively vindicate their statutory rights. Under such an approach, the client will decide whether arbitration is in its interests. If the client opts to impose arbitration on its employees, the system the lawyer will draft will be fair and even handed, lacking sharp practices that may stack the deck against employees.

In most cases, the client will follow the lawyer's lead and the path the lawyer chooses in presenting the arbitration alternative will dictate how the agreement is drafted. But, what if the lawyer presents the arbitration alternative appropriately and the client insists that the lawyer draft the agreement strategically to eliminate, to the maximum extent possible, what the client regards as meritless vexatious claims? The lawyer should attempt to dissuade the client from such strategic behavior. If the client continues to insist, the lawyer faces what the Model Rules call a "difficult ethical problem []."[164] The Model Rules leave it to each individual lawyer to strike the right balance in such circumstances between "responsibilities to clients, to the legal system and to the lawyer's own interest in remaining an upright person while earning a satisfactory living."

A lawyer who chooses to draft the arbitration agreement strategically must maintain her professional independence and should take steps to ensure that the client recognizes that independence as well. Otherwise, the client is likely to portray the arbitration system to its employees as something that has been blessed by the lawyer. If an employee questions specific details of the system, the client likely will respond that it is simply following the lawyer's orders. In so doing, the client will seek to clothe the arbitration system with a false legitimacy by playing on the lawyer's role as an officer of the court. To accomplish this, the lawyer should make clear to the client the ethical ramifications of drafting the arbitration agreement to stack the deck and also make clear that the moral responsibility for such action rests with the client and not the lawyer.

It may be argued that lawyers have no role preaching ethics to their clients. The lawyer's personal ethical code does not necessarily coincide with the client's. The lawyer may think it immoral for a client to layoff a large number of employees around Christmas time, particularly if those employees are not likely to find comparable employment elsewhere. The client, however, may regard the lay offs as justified, perhaps for reasons unknown to or unappreciated by the lawyer. Who made the lawyer king of morality? It is better, so the argument goes, for the lawyer to restrain himself to implementing the client's decision.

Regardless of the merits of the above argument, it has no application to the drafting of employment arbitration agreements. The lawyer who counsels a client that the agreement must be drafted fairly is not imposing her moral values on the client. Rather, she is upholding the legal framework as articulated by the Supreme Court. The Court has told us that employment arbitration must not affect substantive rights; it must merely substitute arbitration for litigation as the forum in which those rights may be vindicated.

Notes and Questions

1. Apart from the ethical concerns raised by Professor Malin, what other risks does an attorney incur by drafting a lopsided arbitration agreement? Consider the following comment of Richard Ross, Senior Associate General Counsel for Anheuser–Busch, discussing that company's dispute resolution program:

164. Model Rules, supra note 105, at pmbl. ¶ 8.

The enforceability of these programs will always be an issue. My philosophy on that is first, you cannot play games with these programs. If you try to use an employment ADR program to limit legal exposure or employee rights or remedies, you are going to get shot down. Second, no matter how fair and reasonable the program, there will always be some risk that a particular court will not enforce it.

Besides, the true key to a good employment ADR program is not legal enforceability. The key to a good program is whether it has sufficient credibility in the eyes of the employees that they willingly use it. If you can get your program to that level, you don't have to worry about enforceability.

Richard Ross, Interview by Peter Phillips, in CPR Institute for Dispute Resolution, How Companies Manage Employment Disputes: A Compendium of Leading Corporate Employment Programs 55 (2002).

2. Professor Malin's article discusses the ethical concerns of a lawyer who is drafting an arbitration agreement for an employer. To what extent do these ethical concerns apply to a lawyer who is representing the employer in an arbitration proceeding? Does this depend on whether the employee is represented by an attorney?

3. What types of ethical issues might arise for an *arbitrator* when the employer is represented by an attorney but the employee is not?

Most ethical codes governing arbitrators are enforced privately rather than by public law. An example is American Bar Association and American Arbitration Association, The Code of Ethics for Arbitrators in Commercial Disputes, Effective March 1, 2004, available at http://www.adr.org/index2.1.jsp?JSPssid=15729 (last accessed April 6, 2004). AAA demands that its arbitrators comply with the Code, and may remove arbitrators who fail to do so. In 2002, California promulgated, as part of the California Code of Civil Procedure, a mandatory ethical code for arbitrators, called The Ethics Standards for Neutral Arbitrators in Contractual Arbitration. See http://www.courtinfo.ca.gov/rules/appendix/appdiv6.pdf (last accessed April 6, 2004). These rules contain expansive disclosure requirements (discussed in more detail *supra* Chapter IX.A), increase parties' ability to disqualify arbitrators, and regulate many aspects of arbitrators' conduct. For general discussions of the California rules, see Jay Folberg, *Arbitration Ethics–Is California the Future?*, 18 Ohio State Journal on Dispute Resolution 343 (2003); Ruth V. Glick, *California Arbitration Reform: The Aftermath*, 38 University of San Francisco Law Review 119 (2003). The California rules currently are being challenged in the courts. See, e.g., Skinner v. Donaldson, Lufkin & Jenrette Securities Corp., No. C–03–2625VRW, 2003 WL 23174478 (N.D.Cal.2003) (California rules are preempted by the FAA); Jevne v. Superior Court, 6 Cal.Rptr.3d 542 (App.2 Dist. 2003) (California rules are not preempted by FAA, but are preempted by Securities Exchange Act of 1934); Mayo v. Dean Witter Reynolds, Inc., 258 F.Supp.2d 1097 (N.D.Cal.2003) (California rules are preempted by both FAA and Securities Exchange Act of 1934).

4. Do parties aggrieved by alleged misconduct on the part of the arbitrator have a cause of action against the arbitrator or the arbitral service provider? The universal answer of the courts has been "no." See, e.g.,

Brandon, Jones, Sandall, Zeide, Kohn, Chalal & Musso, P.A. v. MedPartners, Inc., 203 F.R.D. 677, 688 & n.8 (S.D.Fla.2001) (dissolving an injunction enjoining an arbitral organization from "conducting an improper arbitration"); Health Services Management Corp. v. Hughes, 975 F.2d 1253, 1260 n.6 (7th Cir.1992) (conferring immunity despite finding that arbitral organization "clearly violated" its own rule requiring disclosure of personal, financial, or professional relationships with either party); see also Dennis R. Nolan and Roger I. Abrams, *Arbitral Immunity*, 11 Industrial Relations Law Journal 228 (1989). These decisions are grounded in a common-law doctrine of arbitral immunity, and are predicated on the assumption that arbitrators are the functional equivalent of judges. *Are* arbitrators the functional equivalent of judges? See Maureen A. Weston, *Reexamining Arbitral Immunity in an Age of Mandatory and Professional Arbitration*, 88 Minnesota Law Review 449, 484 (2004) (arguing that arbitral immunity should be qualified, rather than absolute, because there are fewer procedural safeguards in private arbitration than in public courts). Recall from Chapter IX.A that another possible remedy for a party harmed by an arbitrator's ethical lapse is to seek vacatur of a tainted award.

*

Part 3

MEDIATION AND OTHER FORMS OF ALTERNATIVE DISPUTE RESOLUTION

Arbitration is not the only alternative form of dispute resolution available for resolving workplace disputes. Mediation is very commonly used, most commonly in the nonunion sector,[1] but also as a mechanism for resolving grievances in the union sector. Mediation is the process by which a neutral individual, usually chosen by the parties, helps the parties reach a mutually acceptable settlement. (Contrast this with arbitration, in which the arbitrator imposes a binding decision upon the parties.) The mediator encourages settlement by facilitating communication between the parties, helping the parties to focus on the real issues of the dispute, and creating settlement options.

In addition to mediation, there are several other alternative forms of dispute resolution. One of these is the use of peer review committees, in which the dispute is decided by a committee of the employee's peers and typically one or more management representatives. Another form of ADR is the use of "open door policies," which encourage employees to seek resolution of their disputes "up the chain of command" rather than through the courts. Similarly, some employers have ombudsmen who serve as a "go-between" between employees and management. A final type of ADR is early neutral evaluation, in which an independent third party makes an initial assessment of the merits of a dispute and encourages the parties to settle.

Some of these dispute resolution forms, particularly mediation and early neutral evaluation, are used on an ad hoc basis as a precursor or adjunct to litigation or binding arbitration. With less but increasing frequency, however, nonunion companies are becoming proactive and systematic with their dispute resolution policies in an attempt to resolve disputes less expensively and to preserve the employment relationship. These policies often combine several methods of alternative dispute

---

1. In the union sector, mediation has long been used to help settle the terms of new collective bargaining agreements. Moreover, Section 8(d)(3) of the NLRA requires that any party desiring to terminate or modify an existing collective bargaining agreement must notify the Federal Media-tion and Conciliation Service together with any state agency designed and empowered to mediate the dispute. Section 8(g) directs (rather than merely authorizes) the FMCS to intervene to effect a settlement in health care negotiations.

resolution and require that employees use the methods in a logical progression (for example, open door policy first, then mediation, then arbitration).

Although many of these comprehensive dispute resolution programs appear promising, they come with a major caveat. Because most of them are promulgated unilaterally by the employer and are not the product of negotiation through the collective bargaining process, there is real concern that the programs may not always be fair to employees.

This Part examines how each of these other forms of alternative dispute resolution can be used to resolve employment disputes. Chapter XIII focuses on mediation, since (aside from arbitration) mediation is by far the most common ADR technique used in the resolution of employment disputes in the nonunion workplace. This chapter addresses such issues as why parties choose mediation, what the proper role of a mediator is, a detailed description of the mediation process, how lawyers represent their clients in mediation, and the substantive law of mediation.

Chapter XIV explores several alternative forms of dispute resolution, such as peer review committees, open door policies, ombudsmen, and early neutral evaluation. The chapter concludes by examining how one company combined several dispute resolution methods into a comprehensive dispute resolution program.

Chapter XIII

MEDIATION[1]

A. WHY PARTIES CHOOSE MEDIATION

THE VANISHING TRIAL:
AN EXAMINATION OF TRIALS AND RELATED
MATTERS IN FEDERAL AND STATE COURTS

Marc Galanter.

459, 460–61, 485, 514–17 (Sept. 6, 2004 galley version).

To be published at 1 Journal of Empirical Legal Studies (Nov. 2004).

I. THE NUMBER OF CIVIL TRIALS

* * * Over the past generation or more, the legal world has been growing vigorously. On almost any measure—the number of lawyers, the amount spent on law, the amount of authoritative legal material, the size of the legal literature, the prominence of law in public consciousness—law has flourished and grown. It seems curious, then, to find a contrary pattern in one central legal phenomenon, indeed one that lies at the very heart of our image of our system—trials. The number of trials has not increased in proportion to these other measures. In some, perhaps most, forums, the absolute number of trials has undergone a sharp decline. * * *

[From 1962–2002 , federal] dispositions increased by factor of five—from 50,000 to 258,000 cases. But the number of civil trials in 2002 was

1. Bibliographic suggestions: American Arbitration Association, Dispute–Wise Management: Improving Economic and Non-Economic Outcomes in Managing Business Conflicts (2003); Lisa B. Bingham, *Mediation at Work: Transforming Workplace Conflict at the United States Postal Service*, in Human Capital Management Series (Oct. 2003); Peter J. Bishop, Winning in the Workplace (1995); John T. Dunlop and Arnold M. Zack, Mediation and Arbitration of Employment Disputes (1997); Kimberlee K. Kovach, Mediation: Principles and Practice (1994); Ann G. Leibowitz, ADR in Employment Cases (1996); Leonard L. Riskin and James E. Westbrook, Dispute Resolution and Lawyers (1987); E. Wendy Trachte–Huber and Stephen K. Huber, Mediation and Negotiation: Reaching Agreement in Law and Business (1998); Lon L. Fuller, *Mediation—Its Forms and Functions*, 44 Southern California Law Review 305 (1970); Jonathan R. Harkavy, *Privatizing Workplace Justice: The Advent of Mediation in Resolving Sexual Harassment Disputes*, 34 Wake Forest Law Review 135 (1999); L. Camille Hebert, *Establishing and Evaluating A Workplace Mediation Pilot Project: An Ohio Case Study*, 14 Ohio State Journal on Dispute Resolution 415 (1999).

more than 20 percent lower than the number in 1962—some 4,569 now to 5,802 then. So the portion of dispositions that were by trial was less than one sixth of what is was in 1962—1.8 percent now as opposed to 11.5 percent in 1962.

The drop in civil trials has not been constant over the 40–year period; it has been recent and steep. [I]n the early part of our period, there was an increase in trials, peaking in 1985, when there were 12,529. From then to now, the number of trials in federal court has dropped by more than 60% and the portion of cases disposed of by trial has fallen from 4.7 percent to 1.8 percent. * * *

IV.   CIVIL FILINGS

* * * Do these changing patterns of dispositions merely reflect changes in filings? Clearly the decline in trials is not simply a reflection of the cases coming to the federal courts, for the number of trials has declined while the number of filings has increased fivefold. Nor is the decline in trials simply a function of the changing makeup of a docket with fewer of the types of cases that are most likely to get tried and more of the types that rarely go to trial. * * * Instead, we see the drop in trial rates occurring in every category, suggesting that the difference lies in what happens in court rather than in a change in the makeup of the caseload. * * *

VIII.   OTHER FORUMS

One of the most prominent explanations of the decline of trials is the migration of cases to other forums. * * *

How much does ADR [and Internal Dispute Resolution] affect the trial docket of the courts? Once cases are filed in court, they may be deflected into mediation or arbitration with the encouragement of the court. * * * Alternatively, claimants may pursue matters in non-court forums without filing a case in court. They may do this either on their own volition or under the constraint of a mandatory arbitration clause. We know that a significant number of claims are kept out of the courts by such clauses, but we do not know how many. * * *

IX.   CAUSES AND CONSEQUENCES

For a long time, the vast majority of cases of almost every kind in both federal and state courts have terminated by settlement. * * * What we are seeing since the late 1980s is not only a continuation in the shrinkage of *percentage* of cases that go to trial, but a shrinkage of the *absolute number* of cases that go to trial. * * *

The first cluster of explanations are what might be called the diminished-supply argument, that is, that cases did not eventuate in trials because they did not get to court in the first place or, having come to court, they have departed for another forum. [But as noted above in Part I, the number of filings has consistently risen, not fallen.] * * *

A second major line of explanation is the diversion argument—that the claims and contests are there but they are in different forums. * * * [T]here seems to be some substance to this, but it should be kept in mind that the decline in trials is very general, across the board, and is not confined to sectors or localities where ADR has flourished.

A third explanation might be called the economic argument, that is, that going to trial has become more costly as litigation has become more technical, complex, and expensive. Rising costs of increasingly specialized lawyers, the need to deploy expensive experts, jury consultants, and all the associated expenses have priced some parties out of the market. For those who can afford to play, the increased transaction costs enlarge the overlap in settlement ranges. More and more of the players in the legal arena are corporate actors who view participation in the legal arena in terms of long-term strategy. Increasingly, they regard much legal involvement as just another business input, one that must be subjected to cost controls. One part of such control is alternative sourcing—diverting what might have been legal business into alternative forums.

PRIVATIZING WORKPLACE JUSTICE: THE ADVENT OF MEDIATION IN RESOLVING SEXUAL HARASSMENT DISPUTES

Jonathan R. Harkavy.
34 Wake Forest Law Review 135, 156–63 (1999).

A.   ADVANTAGES OF MEDIATION IN SEXUAL HARASSMENT DISPUTES

1.   Mediation provides a comfortable forum for all parties and thus is more likely to facilitate a workable resolution to a dispute than a more adversarial process involving rights adjudicated in a formal setting under a fixed set of rules. From the employee's standpoint, the safety of a mediated settlement conference permits her to assert her claims and confront her employer with less apprehension about being further victimized and with some (though not guaranteed) protection against retaliation. From the standpoint of the alleged harasser, the mediated settlement conference is also a safe forum for trying to explain (if not deny) the conduct at issue. Even from the standpoint of the employer, mediation offers an opportunity to meet a problem head-on and obtain feedback about it without fear of its position being misconstrued by either the victim or the harasser, both of whom may be productive, valued employees.

2.   Mediation provides a confidential forum for resolving disputes without revealing publicly the intimate and embarrassing details of conduct that might otherwise have to be disclosed in adjudication. Particularly from the standpoint of the victim, the confidentiality of mediation offers a considerable advantage over adjudicatory proceedings where intimacies and degradations would likely be revealed for public consumption and consequent personal embarrassment. * * * [M]ost accused harassers will assuredly prefer the confidentiality offered by

mediation, particularly if the alleged conduct might have an impact on their own marriages, other familial relationships, and employment opportunities.

3. The prospect of settlement at an early stage offers substantial advantages to all parties. The victim, who may be quite traumatized by the harassment, will be permitted to obtain appropriate treatment which she might not otherwise have been able to afford and will generally be able to get on with her life. * * * Likewise, the accused harasser can be brought to justice more quickly, punished more appropriately, and trained or sensitized more effectively through early intervention. Or, if the dispute is resolved without any attribution of responsibility, the accused harasser will be able to resume his employment with a minimum of interruption and embarrassment. From the standpoint of the employer, early settlement offers the obvious advantages of both cost savings and minimal diversion from the employer's ordinary business. * * *

4. Mediation provides an opportunity to redirect emotions in a productive manner. In contrast to the courtroom or the arbitral forum, where the adversarial process puts parties under stress by subjecting them to cross-examination in the context of rights and rules, mediation is designed to put the parties at ease in the context of exploring their interests and needs. That is not to say that emotions in a sexual harassment case are left outside the door of the conference room. Indeed, both the general session and the private caucuses may involve displays of emotion by all sides. Such displays are sometimes therapeutic and may ultimately be useful to mediators in ferreting out a victim's true concerns and interests. * * *

5. Adaptability of procedures and flexibility of outcomes are among mediation's primary advantages in sexual harassment cases. Aside from the obvious adjustability of procedures allowing mediation to be physically and emotionally comfortable, the range of remedies available to the parties is bounded only by their creativity. * * *

6. [T]here is considerable anecdotal evidence to suggest that both victims and their employers in sexual harassment cases can benefit financially from mediating these disputes. My own observation is that employers can avoid liability at the high end of the damage scale in mediated settlements, but are more likely to pay something in a greater number of cases. On the other hand, victims of sexual harassment can expect a more certain recovery through mediation, though they may have to forego the prospect of the maximum possible relief which is always available (though not often attainable) in court. * * *

7. The avoidance of troublesome precedent is a positive consequence of mediation's inherent privacy * * * * The fact that an employer may have paid one employee a certain amount of money to settle her claim may, in the mind of an employer's human resources manager, put a floor on future claims of the same kind, even though the surrounding circumstances might suggest a markedly different outcome. * * *

8. One of the principal values of mediation—the resolution of a dispute in a manner so that the parties can continue their business, professional, or personal relationships—makes mediation appear superior to adjudicatory forms of dispute resolution. Judicial litigation and private arbitration, with their emphasis on adversary procedures, tend to drive parties further apart, thus making continuance of the employer-employee relationship much more difficult. Mediation, by contrast, emphasizes a non-adversarial exploration of the parties' common interests and personal concerns, thereby making it far less likely that the employment relationship becomes irreparably fractured.

9. * * * The shift of focus in mediation away from the technical legal merits of a dispute lessens the impact that undecided legal issues may have on resolving a dispute. * * * By directing the parties' attention to their interests instead of to their legal positions, a mediator can sidestep the uncertainties in Title VII law to a far greater extent than is possible with other ADR techniques.

10. Perhaps the most significant advantage mediation has to offer in sexual harassment cases is personal empowerment and recognition. After all, in mediation it is a party herself, not some outside determinative force such as a jury, judge, or arbitrator, who decides whether or not to resolve her dispute and on what terms. Particularly for victims of sexual harassment, the prospect of controlling a situation instead of being controlled by it may be critical to recovering self-esteem, continuing employment, and stabilizing personal situations. * * *

B.   DISADVANTAGES OF MEDIATION IN SEXUAL HARASSMENT CASES

1. Mediation may impair the orderly development of a coherent sexual harassment jurisprudence. To the extent that it is successful in resolving large numbers of disputes, the cases left for adjudication may involve such unique factual situations that the resultant body of case law will be shaped—and possibly warped—by mediation's leftovers. * * *

2. The absence of public vindication is a distinct disadvantage of mediation. Particularly for victims of sexual harassment, personal vindication—being believed in a "he said/she said" situation—may be important to one's marriage, one's family, and one's self-esteem. A decision by an impartial adjudicator, whether a judge, jury, arbitrator, or evaluator, provides the kind of third-party vindication that mediation cannot * * *. Public vindication also may be important from the employers' standpoint. * * * Particularly after a dispute becomes common knowledge among other employees, the employer may need to pursue public vindication in order to maintain morale in the workplace.

3. Some parties, typically employers, but occasionally employees, believe that proposing or even agreeing to mediation is a sign of weakness or an admission of responsibility. Whatever disadvantage may be entailed by that perception, the increased use of mediation as an ADR device required by court rules will render that argument less substantial and virtually moot. * * *

4.   Disclosure of unrevealed information that may be used at trial is another perceived disadvantage of mediation. * * * Responsible mediators can minimize much of the worry about secret information and trial strategies through scrupulous adherence to their duty of confidentiality. * * *

5.   Mediated settlements may not fully serve the deterrence objective of Title VII. The lack of public disapproval, the prospect of cheaper and quicker settlements, and other advantageous aspects of privately negotiated and confidentially performed settlements may, in effect, provide an insufficient incentive to employers to control the conduct of supervisors. That is, some employers are more likely to obey the law fully if their feet are held to the fire of a public trial of a sexual harassment dispute. * * *

6.   The confidentiality of most mediated settlements of individual sexual harassment cases deprives the community of information about what the law actually is, who is violating the law, and what the costs of illegal conduct are. Some prominent members of the academic community see this aspect of mediation—and of settlement in general—as a substantial departure from sound public policy. * * *

7.   The absence of public scrutiny of how sexual harassment law is being developed and applied may be a significant disadvantage of privatizing workplace justice * * *. Moreover, justice achieved in private may be regarded by some as an abdication by our overworked court system to an essentially unregulated profession of mediators.

Notes and Questions

1.   Some commentators have suggested that a "litigation explosion" is one explanation for the recent surge in interest in ADR. See, e.g., Walter K. Olson, The Litigation Explosion 1–2, 7–8 (1991). However, the evidence for a dramatic increase in parties' propensity to litigate is equivocal. The litigation rates of many types of cases have been relatively level, while sharp increases in litigation rates have occurred in particular types of cases such as family law, criminal law, and certain types of product liability cases. See Carl Tobias, *Public Law Litigation and the Federal Rules of Civil Procedure*, 74 Cornell Law Review 270, 287–89 (1989) (reviewing debate over litigation explosion); see also Arthur R. Miller, *The Pretrial Rush to Judgment: Are the "Litigation Explosion," "Liability Crisis," and Efficiency Cliches Eroding Our Day in Court and Jury Trial Committments?*, 78 New York University Law Review 982 (2003) (arguing that the purported litigation explosion is a political excuse for the increased judicial use of summary judgment).

Wouldn't an appropriate response to the increase in federal court litigation be to add more federal judges? Although Congress has increased somewhat the number of federal judges over the last forty years, that increase has lagged far behind the rise in federal litigation. See William M. Richman and William L. Reynolds, *Elitism, Expediency, and the New Certiorari: Requiem for the Learned Hand Tradition*, 81 Cornell Law Review 273, 274–75 n.3 (1996). Interestingly, one of the primary sources of opposition to expanding the number of federal judges has been the federal judiciary itself.

Many judges apparently believe that increasing the number of judges would erode the bench's quality and undermine collegiality. *Id.* at 300–04, 323–25 (discussing judicial responses to proposals to expand the number of federal appeals court judges); see also Carl Tobias, *The New Certiorari and a National Study of the Appeals Courts*, 81 Cornell Law Review 1264 (1996) (replying to Richman and Reynolds). Under these circumstances, is it appropriate for a federal judge to suggest that the solution to the increase in federal litigation is to dispose of more cases through ADR?

2. Regardless of the cause, the empirical evidence demonstrates that very few employment cases go to trial. Roughly 60% of employment cases filed in federal court, and 15% of employment cases filed in state court, are decided on summary judgment. Lewis Maltby, *Employment Arbitration and Workplace Justice*, 38 University of San Francisco Law Review 105, 112–13 (2003). Only about 7% of federal cases, and 3% of state cases, are resolved by trial. Bureau of Justice Statistics, U.S. Department of Justice, NCJ–153177, Special Report: Civil Justice Survey of State Courts 1–2 (1995); Judith Resnik, *Trial As Error, Jurisdiction As Injury: Transforming the Meaning of Article III*, 113 Harvard Law Review 924, 925–28 (2000). The rest, presumably, are withdrawn or settled.

3. Is litigation obsolete? Are there instances in which it would be in the client's best interest to have a litigated resolution rather than a mediated settlement? Can you provide examples of such circumstances?

4. Are mediated settlements as likely as litigated determinations to enhance employer compliance with statutes such as Title VII? Why or why not?

5. Consider the following argument: "Settlement is for me the civil analogue of plea bargaining: Consent is often coerced; the bargain may be struck by someone without authority; the absence of a trial and judgment renders subsequent judicial involvement troublesome; and although dockets are trimmed, justice may not be done." Owen M. Fiss, *Against Settlement*, 93 Yale Law Journal 1073, 1075 (1984). Fiss argues that the following types of cases are particularly inappropriate for ADR: (1) where one party has disproportionate bargaining power or resources compared to the other party, (2) where securing settlement or consent is difficult, (3) where post-judgment supervision is necessary, and (4) where there is a need for authoritative interpretation of the law. He provides as an example a suit between a member of a racial minority and a municipal police department over alleged brutality. Would many or most employment disputes satisfy these criteria?

Andrew McThenia and Thomas Shaffer, in a response to Fiss' article, write that "settlement is neither an avoidance mechanism nor a truce. Settlement is a process of reconciliation in which the anger of broken relationships is to be confronted rather than avoided, and in which healing demands not a truce but confrontation." Andrew W. McThenia and Thomas L. Shaffer, *For Reconciliation*, 94 Yale Law Journal 1660 (1985). Do you agree?

In a continuation of the debate, Carrie Menkel–Meadow argues that settlement advances party autonomy and is a rational and legitimate response to overcrowded judicial dockets. She argues further that if the private interests in settling a case outweigh the public interest in litigating it, the private interests should be respected. Carrie Menkel–Meadow, *Whose Dispute Is It Anyway?: A Philosophical and Democratic Defense of Settlement (in Some Cases)*, 83 Georgetown Law Journal 2663 (1995).

Do you find any of these arguments persuasive? For further discussion of settlement in the context of unequal bargaining bargaining power between the parties, *see infra* Chapter XIII.F.

B. THE MEDIATOR'S ROLE

"WHAT'S GOING ON" IN MEDIATION: AN EMPIRICAL ANALYSIS OF THE INFLUENCE OF A MEDIATOR'S STYLE ON PARTY SATISFACTION AND MONETARY BENEFIT

E. Patrick McDermott and Ruth Obar.
9 Harvard Negotiation Law Review 75, 80–83, 85–86, 89–90, 105, 107 (2004).

The use of mediation to resolve a wide range of legal and other disputes continues to increase. As mediation enters the mainstream, business, community, and legal dispute resolution scholars have paid increasing attention to the dynamics of the mediation process. We use quantitative analysis from a large database of cases mediated at the Equal Employment Opportunity Commission (EEOC) to describe "what's going on" in the field of mediation.

Using a database of 645 employment law cases mediated under the EEOC's mediation program, we analyzed various self-reported mediator behavior. We first examined the types of mediator behavior (facilitative, evaluative or hybrid) used by mediators in this "facilitative" program. [The types of mediation are described below.] We then examined whether a particular mediation style resulted in a higher participant satisfaction rating across procedural due process and distributive variables, whether a particular style resulted in a higher settlement agreement, and whether representation affected the amount of money obtained in mediation. * * *

VI. THE LITERATURE—EVALUATION VERSUS FACILITATION

In order to determine how facilitative and evaluative techniques are being used in mediation, we first had to identify these techniques. We note at the outset that there is no consensus in the field regarding the exact characteristics of facilitative versus evaluative mediator conduct. We present an overview of the literature. We then classify mediator behavior for our analysis.

A. *Facilitative Mediation and Its Advocates*

Robert A. Baruch Bush and Joseph Folger advocate a form of facilitative mediation known as transformative mediation.[25] They see the

---

25. ROBERT A. BARUCH BUSH & JOSEPH FOLGER, THE PROMISE OF MEDIATION: RESPONDING TO CONFLICT THROUGH EMPOWERMENT AND RECOGNITION (1994), at 81–95 * * *.

mediator as a process person who does not contribute any information to the process other than agenda structuring. Transformative mediation takes a "social/communicative view of conflict." Thus, transformative mediation posits that the transformation of the negative interaction between parties in conflict into a positive relationship based on mutual empowerment and recognition is what matters most to the parties, even more than the particular terms of a settlement.

Mediator conduct in this style includes facilitating "recognition" by each party of the other party's vantage point. Such conduct includes paraphrasing and reframing to encourage complementary validation. Bush and Folger oppose any evaluative conduct, believing that evaluative mediation undermines such validation and also inhibits creativity in the mediation problem-solving process. Bush and other facilitative advocates such as Kovach and Love, believe that evaluation necessarily involves mediator coercion and pressure. * * *

Professors Kimberlee Kovach and Lela Love are prominent proponents of facilitative mediation.[33] They entered the debate by excoriating evaluative mediation, arguing that it is not mediation but rather some other type of dispute resolution process. * * * Kovach and Love appear to depart from Folger and Bush's description of facilitative mediation as agenda structuring that avoids any mediator coercion or pressure. Kovach and Love support the use of some evaluative behavior in mediation. They state that so long as the mediator does not take an actual position, as would a judge, arbitrator, or neutral expert, this conduct is reconcilable in a pure facilitative mediation model. For example, they claim that the following activities, while admittedly evaluative, are appropriate as "essential parts of a mediator's facilitative role ..." These activities include:

- reframing;
- structuring of the bargaining agenda;
- probing of assessments and positions;
- challenging proposals;
- urging parties to obtain additional resources or information;
- suggesting possible resolutions (for the purpose of stimulating parties to generate options); and
- reality testing or checking.

According to Kovach and Love, if these activities are motivated by and result in the stimulation of party evaluation and decision-making, they "comport more with a facilitative orientation." * * * Kovach and Love believe that as long as the mediator does not give an opinion on the merits/damages due to a party, all other mediator opinions, assertions,

---

33. Kimberlee K. Kovach & Lela P. Love, *Evaluative Mediation is an Oxymoron*, 14 ALTERNATIVES TO HIGH COST LITIG. 31, 31 (1996)[;] * * * Lela P. Love, *The Top* *Ten Reasons Why Mediators Should Not Evaluate*, 24 FLA. STATE U. L. REV. 937, 938–39 (1997).

challenges, and actions are acceptable in a facilitative mediation. The mediator must not " 'answer' the question posed by the dispute" or the mediator would be engaging in improper evaluative conduct. * * *

B. Evaluative Mediation

Leonard R. Riskin posits that "the mediator who evaluates assumes that the participants want and need her to provide some guidance as to the appropriate grounds for settlement–based on law, industry practice or technology—and that she is qualified to give such guidance by virtue of her training, experience, and objectivity."[59] Thus, an evaluative mediator helps the parties to understand the strengths and weaknesses of their positions and the likely outcome of litigation or whatever other process they will use if they fail to reach a resolution in mediation. According to Riskin, mediator techniques that are associated with evaluative mediation include:

- assessing the strengths and weaknesses of each side's case;
- predicting outcomes of court or other processes;
- proposing position-based compromise agreements;
- urging or pushing the parties to settle or to accept a particular settlement proposal or range;
- educating herself about the underlying interests;
- predicting the impact of not settling; and
- developing and offering proposals.

Riskin notes that much of this evaluative conduct occurs in private caucus.

In response to those who claim that evaluative mediation is not mediation, Riskin replies, "It is too late for commentators or mediation organizations to tell practitioners who are widely recognized as mediators that they are not, in the same sense that it is too late for the Pizza Association of Naples, Italy to tell Domino's that its product is not the genuine article."[65] * * *

VII. THE RESEARCH

This paper is based on data from our comprehensive study of the EEOC mediation program. Our first study was a comprehensive study of charging party and respondent opinions regarding various procedural and distributive elements of the EEOC mediation program. Our second study addressed mediator feedback on the dynamics of the mediation process, including participant (charging party, respondent, mediator) conduct that facilitates resolution of the dispute, reasons the dispute was not resolved, mediator tactics, behaviors that act as barriers to a resolution, the role of legal counsel and other representatives, and the turning

---

59. [Leonard R. Riskin, *Understanding Mediators' Orientations, Strategies, and Techniques: A Grid for the Perplexed*, 1 HARV. NEGOT. L. REV. 7 (1996).]

65. *Id.* at 24.

point(s) in a successful mediation. Mediator evaluations of the skills of the parties' legal and non-legal representatives were also highlighted in the report. * * *

IX. Conclusions and Implications

* * *

A. The Critical Role of Representation in Mediation

We set out to give some insight to the facilitative-evaluative debate. While we have done so, our key finding relates to the role of counsel in mediation. Mediation programs often downplay the role of counsel. Some programs ask that counsel remain in the background. Many mediators treat counsel as an obstacle to the dispute resolution process. Our results indicate that if the amount of money obtained in settlement is important, the charging party in employment mediation is at a decided disadvantage without counsel. This disadvantage is even more pronounced in an evaluative mediation. The practical implications of these findings include: (1) Participants, particularly charging parties in employment mediation, should be advised of the benefits of counsel and forewarned that they may obtain a lower monetary settlement without representation; (2) Counsel should think twice about allowing a client to participate in mediation without his presence; and (3) Mediation models that limit the role of representation are inherently suspect.

B. "Feel Good" versus "More Money"

This data provides great insight into how employment mediation works. Our data suggest that both sides of the facilitative-evaluative debate have sound arguments. Those in the facilitative camp are correct that their mediation style clearly produces higher disputant satisfaction ratings on both procedural due process and distributive measures. Although charging parties in an employment mediation often obtain significantly less money in settlement using facilitative mediation rather than evaluative mediation, charging parties are more likely to report that they obtained what they wanted. It is fair to say that facilitative conduct is more pleasing to the parties. One may argue that this is because there are intrinsic and non-monetary gains that are met in facilitative mediation but not evaluative mediation. However, others may argue that where a charging party is clearly obtaining much less money in facilitative mediation, such high disputant satisfaction ratings are a pyrrhic victory.

As important, while evaluative mediation offers the highest potential payout, this occurs only where there is legal representation. Absent legal representation, evaluative mediation appears to result in lower settlement amounts. Research is necessary to determine if evaluative conduct and/or comments are used to intimidate unrepresented charging parties into settling.

THE THEORY AND PRACTICE OF MEDIATION: REPLY TO PROFESSOR SUSSKIND

Joseph B. Stulberg.
6 Vermont Law Review 85, 86–88, 91–94, 96–97 (1981).

Lon Fuller, the distinguished professor and arbitrator, described the goal of the mediator in elegant fashion when he wrote: "[T]he central quality of mediation [is] its capacity to reorient the parties towards each other, not by imposing rules on them, but by helping them to achieve a new and shared perception of their relationship, a perception that will redirect their attitude and dispositions toward one another."[15] What functions of office does the mediator have that enable him to fulfill that objective? A brief listing would include the following functions.

A mediator is a catalyst. Succinctly stated, the mediator's presence affects how the parties interact. His presence should lend a constructive posture to the discussions rather than cause further misunderstanding and polarization, although there are no guarantees that the latter condition will not result. * * * Much as the chemical term catalyst connotes, the mediator's presence alone creates a special reaction between the parties. Any mediator, therefore, takes on a unique responsibility for the continued integrity of the discussions.

A mediator is also an educator. He must know the desires, aspirations, working procedures, political limitations, and business constraints of the parties. He must immerse himself in the dynamics of the controversy to enable him to explain (although not necessarily justify) the reasons for a party's specific proposal or its refusal to yield in its demands. He may have to explain, for example, the meaning of certain statutory provisions that bear on the dispute, the technology of machinery that is the focus of discussion, or simply the principles by which the negotiation process goes forward.

Third, the mediator must be a translator. The mediator's role is to convey each party's proposals in a language that is both faithful to the desired objectives of the party and formulated to insure the highest degree of receptivity by the listener. The proposal of an angry neighbor that the "young hoodlum" not play his stereo from 11:00 p.m. to 7:00 a.m. every day becomes, through the intervention and guidance of a mediator, a proposal to the youth that he be able to play his stereo on a daily basis from 7:00 a.m. to 11:00 p.m.

Fourth, the mediator may also expand the resources available to the parties. Persons are occasionally frustrated in their discussions because of a lack of information or support services. The mediator, by his personal presence and with the integrity of his office, can frequently gain access for the parties to needed personnel or data. * * *

15. Lon Fuller, *Mediation—Its Forms and Functions,* 44 Southern California Law   Review 305, 325 (1971).

Fifth, the mediator often becomes the bearer of bad news. Concessions do not always come readily; parties frequently reject a proposal in whole or in part. The mediator can cushion the expected negative reaction to such a rejection by preparing the parties for it in private conversations. Negotiations are not sanitized. They can be extremely emotional. Persons can react honestly and indignantly, frequently launching personal attacks on those representatives refusing to display flexibility. Those who are the focus of such an attack will, quite understandably, react defensively. The mediator's function is to create a context in which such an emotional, cathartic response can occur without causing an escalation of hostilities or further polarization.

Sixth, the mediator is an agent of reality. Persons frequently become committed to advocating one and only one solution to a problem. There are a variety of explanations for this common phenomenon, ranging from pride of authorship in a proposal to the mistaken belief that compromising means acting without principles. The mediator is in the best position to inform a party, as directly and as candidly as possible, that its objective is simply not obtainable through those specific negotiations. He does not argue that the proposal is undesirable and therefore not obtainable. Rather, as an impartial participant in the discussions, he may suggest that the positions the party advances will not be realized, either because they are beyond the resource capacity of the other parties to fulfill or that, for reasons of administrative efficiency or matters of principle, the other parties will not concede. If the proposing party persists in its belief that the other parties will relent, the question is reduced to a perception of power. The mediator's role at that time is to force the proposing party to reassess the degree of power that it perceives it possesses.

The last function of a mediator is to be a scapegoat. No one ever enters into an agreement without thinking he might have done better had he waited a little longer or demanded a little more. A party can conveniently suggest to its constituents when it presents the settlement terms that the decision was forced upon it. In the context of negotiation and mediation, that focus of blame—the scapegoat—can be the mediator.
* * *

[A] mediator must be neutral with regard to outcome. Parties negotiate because they lack the power to achieve their objectives unilaterally. They negotiate with those persons or representatives of groups whose cooperation they need to achieve their objective. If the mediator is neutral and remains so, then he and his office invite a bond of trust to develop between him and the parties. If the mediator's job is to assist the parties to reach a resolution, and his commitment to neutrality ensures confidentiality, then, in an important sense, the parties have nothing to lose and everything to gain by the mediator's intervention. In these two bases of assistance and neutrality there is no way the mediator could jeopardize or abridge the substantive interests of the respective parties.

How is this trust exemplified in practice? Suppose a party advocates certain proposals because of internal political divisions which might impede discussions. For tactical reasons, however, the party does not want to reveal these internal divisions to the other parties. A mediator to whom such information is entrusted can direct discussions so that such a dilemma can be overcome. The mediator's vigorous plea made in the presence of all parties to remove the proposal from further discussions, for example, might provide a safe, face-saving way for that party to drop its demand.

There is a variety of information that parties will entrust to a neutral mediator, including a statement of their priorities, acceptable trade-offs, and their desired timing for demonstrating movement and flexibility. All of these postures are aimed to achieve a resolution without fear that such information will be carelessly shared or that it will surface in public forums in a manner calculated to embarrass or exploit the parties into undesired movement. This type of trust is secured and reinforced only if the mediator is neutral, has no power to insist upon a particular outcome, and honors the confidences placed in him. If any of these characteristics is absent, then the parties must calculate what information they will share with the mediator, just as they do in communicating with any of the parties to the controversy.

Notes and Questions

1. Does Stulberg advocate evaluative or facilitative mediation? Which approach would you take if you were a mediator? Must a mediator be either/or, or can a mediator borrow from each? Is Stulberg's description of the mediator's role accurate? Realistic? Achievable?

2. Might different circumstances call for different types of mediation? For example, in a continuing relationship, facilitative mediation might be more appropriate because it produces greater understanding and ability to work together. Are these factors as important when the parties likely will never meet again, as when a discharged employee does not seek reinstatement? Which type of mediator would you choose if you represented a plaintiff (defendant) and believed you had a strong (weak) case?

3. Stulberg's ideal of the "neutral mediator" is not universally shared. Lawrence Susskind has argued that environmental mediators should be concerned about the substantive outcome of mediation agreements (for example, about the impact on unrepresented or under-represented groups), and not just on reaching agreement. Lawrence Susskind, *Environmental Mediation and the Accountability Problem*, 6 Vermont Law Review 1 (1981). Do you agree?

Could a similar argument be made in the employment context? Is any nonparty similarly at risk in the resolution of employment disputes? What about a fellow employee who didn't get the raise or promotion, or who is disadvantaged by the employer's affirmative action, or who is "bumped" from her job to make room for a successful plaintiff? If a consensual settlement between employer and employee is likely to create future problems for either party from parties not at the table, is it appropriate for the mediator to raise the issue? How might this affect the parties' confidence in the mediator and the mediation process? Would it turn the process into a tripartite negotiation, and transform the mediator into an advocate? Might it affect the parties' willingness to mediate future cases?

4. How might a mediator let the parties "vent" without letting the mediation become unduly adversarial?

5. In what ways is the role of the mediator similar to the role of an arbitrator? In what ways is it different? How are the attributes of an ideal mediator similar to those of an ideal arbitrator? How might they differ?

6. If you had a career objective of becoming a mediator, how would you go about pursuing that objective? See generally E. Wendy Trachte–Huber and Stephen K. Huber, Reaching Agreement in Law and Business 711–56 (1998) (discussing training, registration, certification, and licensure requirements).

C. DESCRIPTION OF THE PROCESS

ALTERNATIVE DISPUTE RESOLUTION: AN INTRODUCTION

Carolyn Chalmers and Laura Cooper.

1997.

Little can be said about the mediation process that will be true of all mediations. Mediation, by its very nature, is a malleable model of dispute resolution. Indeed, of all the ADR processes, mediation grants the parties and their advocates the greatest control over both the shape of the process and the substantive outcome. The nature of the neutral's participation varies greatly depending on the individual mediator. Mediation also assumes different features depending on the subject matter being mediated.

Consider the following employment discrimination dispute as an illustration of the mediation process. The employer's attorney, the manager of the division involved, and perhaps a human resource professional would typically represent the company. The plaintiff worker, her lawyer, and perhaps a friend, family member, or supporting witness would be present for the plaintiff. The mediator might begin with a group meeting with all the participants to ensure that no lingering conflict of interest issues exist and to discuss the process. Frequently, counsel will make opening remarks about the client's settlement position. After these remarks conclude, the mediator might elicit general information from the parties about the nature of the dispute. From here, the group might split into separate caucuses. In meeting with the plaintiff and her counsel, the mediator would elicit more of the plaintiff's story, attempt to identify her current interests, and identify her settlement demand. The mediator's subsequent meeting with the employer and its counsel would also involve listening, identifying interests, and obtaining a settlement proposal. These first two caucus meetings may absorb half of a day. The parties' storytelling and the mediator's listening are essential elements to developing rapport and building the foundation of trust necessary for the difficult decisions that lie ahead.

The mediator may focus the next round of caucus meetings on "reality testing" the parties' perceptions of the dispute. In these meetings, the mediator helps parties identify the weaknesses in their case and the strengths of the opposing party's case. Additional settlement proposals and counter-proposals are exchanged. As the process proceeds, the caucus meetings with the mediator get shorter and the pace of the shuttle diplomacy quickens. The parties focus increasingly on what compromises they are willing to accept to settle the dispute.

Toward the end of the process, difficult compromises are usually made. Settlements are generally both below what one party expected and above what the other had planned. As the choice between litigation and settlement emerges, parties may have strong emotional reactions. If the mediator negotiates this stage successfully, she may write down the provisions of the agreement for parties and counsel to review. This can lead to the identification of additional issues best resolved before the parties adjourn the mediation. At the close of the process, the mediator often reconvenes the group meeting to confirm the agreement, if one has been reached, and to thank the parties for their active participation.

THE MEDIATION PROCESS: PRACTICAL STRATEGIES FOR RESOLVING CONFLICT

Christopher W. Moore.
212–19; 221; 227–29 (2003).

The mediator's first activities in this phase of intervention should set a positive tone and meet the basic needs of safety. A mediator accomplishes this nonverbally through the physical arrangement of the parties in the room and verbally with his or her opening statement. The opening statement usually contains approximately eleven elements. These include:

1. Introduction of the mediator and, if appropriate, the parties

2. Commendation of the willingness of the parties to cooperate and seek a solution to their problems and to address relationship issues

3. Definition of mediation and the mediator's role

4. Statement of impartiality and neutrality (when appropriate)

5. Description of mediation procedures

6. Explanation of the concept of the caucus (private meetings)

7. Definition of the parameters of confidentiality (when appropriate)

8. Description of logistics, scheduling, and length of meetings

9. Suggestions for behavioral guidelines or ground rules

10. Answers to questions posed by the parties

11. Joint commitment to begin

* * *

DEFINITION OF MEDIATION AND THE MEDIATOR'S ROLE

[T]he mediator should define mediation and the mediator's role in dispute resolution. * * * Mediators * * * usually try to explain mediation and the mediator's role in the most informal language possible. Explanations vary considerably, but they usually cover (1) a brief description of what the parties will do during the current session; (2) what a mediator is; (3) what the mediator can do for the parties; and (4) the potential outcome of mediation. For example:

During the next meeting or two, you will be engaging in discussions and searching for a joint solution that will meet your needs and satisfy your interests. * * * My role as mediator will be to help you identify problems or issues that you want to talk about, help you clarify needs that must be met, assist you in developing a problem-solving process that will enable you to reach your goals, [and] keep you focused and on the right track * * *.

Next, the mediator should describe his or her authority relationship with the disputants:

As I told each of you previously, mediation is a voluntary process. You are here because you want to see if you can find solutions to issues that concern you * * *. My role is to assist you in doing this. I do not have the authority, nor will I attempt, to make decisions for you. * * * My role is to advise you on procedure, and on how you might best talk about these issues. If you reach an agreement, we (or I) will write it down in the form of a memorandum of understanding. This agreement can become legally binding if it involves issues covered by law, or it may be left as an informal agreement. * * * You do not lose any rights to go to court if you use mediation and are unable to reach an agreement. * * *

DESCRIPTION OF MEDIATION PROCEDURES

Next, the mediator should describe the procedures to be followed. * * * Here is a common description of negotiation procedures:

At this time, I would like to briefly describe the process that I propose you follow to begin the session. * * * Both of you have a significant amount of information about the situation that you are responding to. Although I have briefly spoken with each of you about these matters, I do not have the detailed understanding that each of you does. I suggest that we begin the discussion today with a brief description from each of you *about the situation and issues that brought you to mediation. This will educate all of us about the issues you want to discuss and the interests that are important to you and give us a common perception of the problem. Each of you will have a chance * * * to present your view of the situation. I request that you not interrupt the other while he or she is explaining a viewpoint, and that you hold your questions until the end of the presentation. * * **

During your presentations, I may ask some clarifying questions or probe your description so that I can gain a greater understanding of how you perceive the situation. My probing is not to put you on the spot but rather to broaden our mutual understanding of the problem. At the end of each of your presentations, there will be a time for the other person (or parties) to ask questions of clarification. This is not a time to debate the issues, but to clarify issues and perceptions about the problem(s) at hand.

At the end of the presentation and questions we will turn to the other (or next) person (or party) to repeat the process until a representative of each view has had an opportunity to speak. At this point, we will clearly identify both the issues that you would like to discuss in more depth and the interests that you would like to have satisfied. [Then we will] develop some potential solutions and assess whether one or more of these options will meet your needs. * * *

The mediator should clearly explain the stages of the problem-solving process and should take care not to present herself as an authority figure. It is the disputants' process, not the mediator's. The process description is a procedural suggestion, not an order.

EXPLANATION OF THE CAUCUS OR PRIVATE MEETINGS

Next, the mediator should explain the concept of the caucus with each party:

There may be a need, at some time in the course of our meetings, for each of you to take some time for yourself away from the joint meeting (and confer with other members of your group, if it is a group dispute) or to meet with me individually as a mediator. This type of break or meeting is not unusual. It allows you time to refocus and reflect on your short-and long-term goals, handle strong emotions, explore options or proposals, gather your facts to develop new settlement options, or reach a consensus within your group (if applicable). At times, I may call such a meeting,

but you may initiate one also. If I call a separate meeting, it is not to make a deal but to explore issues that might be more comfortable for you to discuss in private. What is discussed in these separate meetings will be considered by me to be confidential. I will not reveal what we have talked about with the other party (or parties) unless you instruct me to do so.
* * *

Suggestions for Behavioral Guidelines

At this time, the mediator should shift his or her focus to behavioral guidelines that will facilitate an orderly discussion. Guidelines that mediators may suggest include procedures to handle interruptions, agreements about the role of witnesses and relationships with the press, conditions for smoking, identification of those with whom disputants may discuss negotiations, delineation of what can or should be disclosed by the parties, and so on.

* * *

Opening Statements by Parties

Parties in dispute usually start with opening statements of their own. These statements are usually designed to outline their substantive interests, establish a bargaining procedure, and build rapport with the other side. * * *

Facilitation of Communication and Information Exchange

The most critical task for disputants at this stage of negotiation is to maximize accurate information exchange. They may be hindered in doing so by * * * excessive posturing, extreme demands designed to signal how intensely the parties feel about the issues or how much they want the other party or parties to move, jumbled or unstructured communication, inaccurate listening, intense emotional outbursts, or total dysfunction of one or more parties.

The mediator's main task, therefore, is to help the parties communicate about substantive issues in dispute and minimize the psychological damage resulting from emotional exchanges. To facilitate this communication, mediators use a variety of communication techniques, * * * includ[ing]:

Restatement. The mediator listens to what has been said and feeds back the content to the party in the party's own words.

Paraphrase. The mediator listens to what has been said and restates the content back to the party using different words that have the same meaning as the original statement. This is often called reframing.

Active Listening. The mediator decodes a spoken message and then feeds back to the speaker the emotions of the message. This is commonly used in conciliation.

Summarization. The mediator condenses the message of a speaker.

Expansion. The mediator receives a message, feeds it back to the listener in an expanded and elaborated form, and then checks to verify accurate perception.

Ordering. The mediator helps a speaker order ideas into some form of sequence (historical, size, importance, amount, and so on).

Grouping. The mediator helps a speaker identify common ideas or issues and combine them into logical units.

Structuring. The mediator assists a speaker in organizing and arranging his or her thoughts and speech into a coherent message.

Separating or fractionating. The mediator divides an idea or an issue into smaller component parts.

Generalization. The mediator identifies general points or principles in a speaker's presentation.

Probing questions. The mediator asks questions to encourage a speaker to elaborate on an idea.

Questions of clarification. The mediator asks questions to obtain clarification of particular points.

Mediators use these communication skills to help parties communicate more accurately with each other. Ideally, the parties use them too.

Notes and Questions

1. How should the following factors affect the structure of the mediation:

(a) The number of parties.

(b) The type of dispute (e.g., discrimination, claim for overtime compensation, wrongful discharge).

(c) The personalities of the parties.

(d) The personalities of the lawyers.

(e) The reluctance of one or more of the parties to mediate the dispute.

(f) The amount of time that the parties have allotted to the mediation session.

2. Moore recommends that the mediator give a lengthy, detailed opening statement. Is this wise? What approach would you take? Similarly, what is the purpose of the caucus? What should one party be doing while the other party is caucusing with the mediator?

3. How vigorously should the mediator "reality test" the parties' perceptions of the dispute? What should the mediator do upon becoming convinced that one of the parties has unrealistic expectations?

4. What should the mediator do if, during opening statements, (a) one of the parties becomes unduly hostile, or (b) one of the attorneys repeatedly interrupts the other party's opening statement?

5. Some mediators require the parties to submit a "position statement" to the mediator prior to the mediation. This statement typically is confidential and not shared with the opposing party. How might such a statement be useful to a mediator? Are there any drawbacks? As an attorney for one of the parties, how would you approach such a statement? Would you be more or less adversarial than in the mediation session itself? Than your posture in the litigation?

6. Under most circumstances, the parties split the mediator's fee. Under what circumstances would it be appropriate for one party to pay a disproportionate share or all of the fee? Would that create a conflict of interest on the part of the mediator? See Allison Balc, *Making It Work at Work: Mediation's Impact on Employee/Employer Relationships and Mediator Neutrality*, 2 Pepperdine Dispute Resolution Law Journal 241, 254–58 (2002). What does mediation offer the parties in an employment dispute that could not be accomplished simply by direct negotiations between counsel for the employer and employee? See Norman Brand, *What You Can Learn From Mediators to Make You a Better Negotiator*, in How ADR Works 263–65 (Norman Brand, ed., 2002) (describing strategies, such as active listening, that advocates can use to help settle cases).

7. Even parties to a successful mediation are potentially unhappy-plaintiffs because they got less than they hoped for, defendants because they gave more than they wanted. In fact, empirical research demonstrates that clients are significantly more satisfied with mediation than they are with adjudication or arbitration. James S. Kakalik, Terence Dunworth, Laural A. Hill, Daniel McCaffrey, Marian Oshiro, Nicholas M. Pace, and Mary E. Vaiana, *Just, Speedy, and Inexpensive? An Evaluation of Judicial Case Management Under the Civil Justice Reform Act*, Rand MR–800–ICJ [http://www.rand.org/publications/MR/MR800/] (1996) (finding high satisfaction levels among legal clients that had participated in mediation); Chris Guthrie and James Levin, *"Party Satisfaction" Perspective on a Comprehensive Mediation Statute*, 13 Ohio State Journal of Dispute Resolution 885, 907 n.7 (1998) (summarizing empirical research); see also Michael J. Yelnosky, *Title VII, Mediation, and Collective Action*, 1999 University of Illinois Law Review 583, 602–04 (discussing participant satisfaction with employment mediation).

D.   HOW LAWYERS REPRESENT CLIENTS IN MEDIATION

ALTERNATIVE DISPUTE RESOLUTION: AN INTRODUCTION

Carolyn Chalmers and Laura Cooper.

1997.

The lawyer's role in mediation involves advising the client about ADR options, effectively evaluating a case for its amenability to mediation, selecting the appropriate process for resolving the dispute, persuading the other side to participate, preparing the client for the process, selecting a suitable neutral, and advocating effectively on the client's behalf during the mediation process.

1) Advise the Client About ADR Options. While all attorneys are duty-bound to vigorously and zealously represent their clients, zealous representation means more than just vigorous advocacy; it means fully advising the client of all relevant considerations pertaining to the lawful means of solving the client's particular problem. A lawyer's duty to inform clients about ADR processes arises from several sources. Implicit in the ethical considerations articulated in the Model Rules of Professional Responsibility is the obligation to keep clients informed. In some states, court rules require counsel to inform clients about ADR options. Potential malpractice exposure also encourages attorneys to advise clients about ADR options that may avoid both risks and predictable costs. Because studies show that the attorney's attitude toward ADR is the most significant determinant of the party's attitude toward ADR, a competent explanation of ADR greatly increases the client's consideration of, and benefit from, an ADR process.

2) Assess Whether the Dispute Is Amenable to Mediation. Certain disputes are suitable for mediation while others are not. No litmus test exists to guide the lawyer when making this judgment. The attorney must understand the mediation process and then carefully analyze how mediation would affect the client's interests and the dynamics of the dispute. Some types of cases are considered intrinsically good mediation candidates. For example, complex disputes that involve dense facts and massive discovery are well suited to mediation because a neutral with subject-matter expertise can evaluate the case and assist the parties in identifying the disputed issues. Additionally, business disputes, where the parties have an ongoing business relationship, are thought to be particularly well suited to mediation. Because mediation is a confidential process, it is also appropriately considered where the client is particularly sensitive to disclosing certain business or personal information or where litigation addresses high visibility issues.

3) Determine the Appropriate Stage to Pursue Mediation. Attorneys should coordinate their litigation goals with their settlement goals so that mediation is explored at the earliest point consistent with preserv-

ing the client's option to litigate effectively. Although mediating early in the dispute may save the parties time and money by avoiding discovery expenses, the parties also must have in hand the information from which to bargain effectively and to evaluate settlement options. Thus, counsel will often perform the core, critical discovery, and then allow the mediation process to bridge the absence of full discovery. Counsel must, however, evaluate how the information disclosed during mediation will affect opportunities to take effective depositions and to prevail on anticipated motions in the event mediation does not succeed. Determining the point at which the client's chance to reach a successful mediated solution is maximized is an art that emerges in the context of specific case analysis.

4) Persuade the Opposing Party to Mediate. An attorney with a client interested in mediation may encounter an unwilling opposing counsel or party. Persistent persuasive communications with the opposing party is an initial technique to overcome this hurdle to mediation. One might forward to the unwilling counsel a copy of a current article that discusses the benefits of mediation and suggest that it be reviewed with the opposing party. Attorneys sometimes respond to reminders about their professional responsibility to inform clients about ADR. It may be helpful to emphasize the non-binding nature of mediation.

Another technique for getting the other side to mediate involves enlisting the support of the judicial branch. In many jurisdictions, courts have authority to order an ADR process, including mediation. Finally, some mediation service providers are committed to securing the participation of the reluctant opposing party or counsel. Counsel can request that a mediator assist in overcoming this initial obstacle to mediation.

5) Select the Appropriate Mediator. Within the confines of peremptory challenges and for-cause dismissals, lawyers are able to select the jury that will hear their case. Even the most skillful forum shopper, however, cannot ordinarily select the judge who will hear a case because judge assignment is a random process. The ability to select the mediator, however, is one of mediation's great advantages over litigation.

There is arguably no more important decision about the mediation process than the selection of the mediator. The success of mediation and the ultimate outcome of a conflict "depend heavily upon matching the right mediator to the right dispute."[95] Rosenberg and Folberg's empirical study highlights this point. The authors noted that the neutral's "personal skills, attitudes, and behavior were by far the most significant determinants of participant satisfaction * * *."[97]

The lawyer is responsible for recommending knowledgeable and experienced mediators to the client. In order to make an informed selection, counsel must understand the substantive law and facts in-

95. [Arthur A. Chaykin, *Selecting the Right Mediator*, Dispute Resolution Journal, Sept. 1994, at 58.]

97. [Joshua D. Rosenberg and H. Jay Folberg, *Alternative Dispute Resolution: An Empirical Analysis*, 46 Stanford Law Review 1487,1528 (1994).]

volved in the dispute. The attorney must effectively analyze what the real problem is that needs to be addressed as well as the obstacles that have prevented settlement to date. If the chief impediment to settlement is the parties' widely differing view of liability or damages, then the client should strongly consider a mediator experienced in the relevant subject matter. By contrast, if the chief impediment to settlement is the emotional intensity of the parties or counsel, a mediator with strong facilitative and counseling skills may be most helpful. These categories of disputes are not mutually exclusive, and counsel may require a mediator who possesses both subject-matter expertise and facilitative skills.

To be effective, a mediator must be viewed by both parties as neutral. A very practical but important concern is the mediator's reputation for having the time and energy to stay with a thorny problem or difficult parties in order to reach a solution. The mediator needs to have the personality and temperament necessary to be effective with the particular parties and attorneys involved.

Selecting the right mediator requires that the lawyer know the qualifications and styles of individual mediators. Lawyers can gather information about potential mediators by requesting resumes and references, searching electronic legal data bases for past experiences, discussing prospective mediators with legal colleagues, and conducting telephone interviews of prospective mediators. Telephone interviews commonly include discussions of relevant experience, identification of references, explanation of the mediator's approach, and administrative matters such as fee and schedule information.

6) Prepare for the Mediation. Mediation advocacy presents a particular challenge to the lawyer. As in litigation, the lawyer must be thoroughly familiar with the facts and law relevant to the case. At the same time, the mediation process demands that the lawyer be skilled at packaging salient points in a manner persuasive to both the mediator as well as the opposing party. *Indeed, the lawyer's and client's chief objective during the mediation is to impress upon the opposing party and counsel the validity and reasonableness of their position.* By contrast, in litigation, the lawyer's focus is on persuading the judge and jury. This difference has profound implications for the attorney's preparation.

The lawyer must also prepare the client for the mediation. At a minimum, this involves providing the client with an evaluation of the liability and damage issues of the case. More often, it also involves educating the client about the mediation process, evaluating the client's interests, anticipating settlement options and strategies, and preparing the client to be able to answer anticipated mediator questions. Only when the client is prepared both substantively and procedurally is the potential for settlement maximized.

If properly prepared, the client may be a valuable mediation participant.[100] Thus, the lawyer should also prepare his or her client to

---

100. Tom Arnold, *Twenty Common Errors in Mediation Advocacy*, 423 PLI/Pat 433 (1995). Arnold states that "CEO's settle a larger percentage of cases than any VP

persuade the opposing party. Although many lawyers are reluctant to allow their clients to participate directly in the mediation, the lawyer's fear of damaging admissions made by the client is somewhat alleviated by the confidential nature of mediation. Once prepared, the attorney and the client must decide on the respective roles they will perform in articulating the client's views. A party may find it more difficult to address sensitive issues than an attorney might. At the same time, however, even an inarticulate party is usually the best advocate on the issue of injury. Sometimes, an issue broached by a party may be viewed with less favor by the opposing party than one raised in the first instance by counsel. Client participation can sometimes defuse the gladiator dynamics that develops between two attorney advocates.

7) Advocate Effectively in the Mediation. The lawyer should avoid donning the litigator's mantle in the mediation context. Effective advocacy in mediation is ultimately addressed to the other party, not a judge or jury. In performing this important function, Tom Arnold, an experienced mediator and mediation practitioner, suggests that there are several tactics an attorney should not employ during a mediation. Lawyers should not make harsh attacks on the opposing party. Denigrating the other party leads to an atmosphere of distrust where neither party will generously yield. Advocates should also avoid issuing ultimatums or attempt to intimidate the other party and should resist the temptation to adopt a moralistic tone. Arrogant displays are counter-productive and create an atmosphere of distrust.

The informality and flexibility of mediation can camouflage the very real contribution that persuasive advocacy can make. Mediation advocacy includes the proper use of advocacy tools, exhibits, charts, copies of relevant cases or contracts with key phrases highlighted. Effective mediation advocacy is also accomplished by the willing give-and-take between parties that allows a settlement to be reached. Finally, if the parties reach an agreement, it is the lawyer's task to ensure that the agreement is memorialized into a written, enforceable contract that details both parties' legal rights and responsibilities.

Notes and Questions

1. Do you agree that some disputes are not suitable for mediation? Can a generalization be made about employment disputes?

2. Which party, the employer or employee, is most likely to be interested in mediating the following disputes:

and/or house counsel or other party agent * * * . Any lesser agent than the CEO, even with the explicit 'authority,' but who is to some degree concerned about review or criticism back at the office by a constituency which was not a participant in the give and take of mediation, is not the best 'client' to settle the case." Arnold goes on to note that "[a]n interesting mix of personality traits, charity towards others and their mistakes, conciliatory attitude, creativity, (and) flexibility * * * is the preferred client representative for a mediation." *Id*.

(a) A sexual harassment claim, where the employee's chances of winning at trial are moderate and there is a potential for a large damage award.

(b) A wage dispute, in which the employee's chances of winning at trial are high but damages are unlikely to exceed a few thousand dollars.

(c) A race discrimination claim with a large potential damage award, but where the employer has a reasonable chance of getting the case dismissed on a summary judgment motion.

(d) A class action discrimination claim.

(e) A dispute concerning an employee's shift assignment, where that employee is covered by a collective bargaining agreement containing grievance and arbitration provisions.

3.   For each of the above disputes, which of the following mediators would be the best choice from the employee's perspective? From the employer's perspective?

(a) A retired federal court judge who is extremely familiar with employment law and who has a reputation for telling parties in mediation exactly how the former judge thinks the case will be resolved if it is tried.

(b) A professional mediator who has no particular expertise in employment law, but who is well-known for an ability to get the parties talking amicably at the bargaining table.

4.   What would be the costs and benefits to both the employer and the employee of undertaking mediation at the following points in an employment dispute?

(a) Before a suit is filed.

(b) After suit is filed, but before any discovery has occurred.

(c) After some limited discovery has occurred (What specific forms of discovery would likely be of particular importance to the employee? To the employer?).

(d) After full discovery.

(e) After the employer has filed a motion for summary judgment.

Does the point at which mediation occurs affect the type of mediator that either party might prefer? Does the type of case affect the time at which mediation should occur?

5.   What criteria should be used to determine whether the client should speak directly (for example, in an opening statement) in a mediation? Is this different for employees and employers? What potential benefits and risks are there? How should a lawyer prepare a client for participation in mediation?

6.   Under what circumstances is an expeditious settlement of an employment case not in the *lawyer's* economic interests? Is there a potential conflict of interest between the lawyer's and the client's interests in ADR? Can a lawyer satisfactorily resolve such a conflict? How? Are there any practical reasons for a lawyer to "do the right thing"?

7. Should either or both of the parties bring a settlement offer with them to the mediation? What are the advantages and disadvantages of making such a settlement offer either immediately prior to the session, or even at the very beginning of the mediation session?

8. Does the nature of attorney advocacy in mediation differ from the nature of attorney advocacy in litigation? In arbitration? If so, how? See Jean R. Sternlight, *Lawyers' Representation of Clients in Mediation: Using Economics and Psychology to Structure Advocacy in a Nonadversarial Setting*, 14 Ohio State Journal on Dispute Resolution 269 (1999). Does the relationship between the lawyer and the client differ in mediation, arbitration, and litigation? If so, how?

E. THE LAW AFFECTING THE MEDIATION PROCESS

1. CONFIDENTIALITY

NIELSEN–ALLEN v. INDUSTRIAL MAINTENANCE CORP.

United States District Court of the Virgin Islands, 2004.
2004 WL 502567.

Order on Defendant Hovensa's Motion for
Sanctions Against Plaintiff's Counsel

RESNICK, MAGISTRATE J.

* * *

In its motion Hovensa claims that during court-ordered mediation in the discrimination case of *Virginia Moorehead v. Hovensa*, plaintiff's counsel disclosed to the mediator and her client, the settlement amount reached in this case, in violation of the confidentiality agreement. Plaintiff counters that Hovensa's motion, which recounts what transpired in the mediation, itself violates the applicable rules of confidentiality and should be stricken.

DISCUSSION

Hovensa asserts that plaintiff's counsel's disclosure, to the mediator, of the settlement amount reached in a different, unrelated case, constitutes bad faith and is sanctionable. Plaintiff argues that the disclosure was within the context of mediation; that the mediator's communications are confidential; and that Local Rule of Civil Procedure 3.2(4) & (5) prevent Hovensa from disclosing any matter discussed in mediation in a subsequent motion for sanctions. Plaintiff also argues that the confidentiality provision in the Moorehead settlement agreement does not apply to Moorehead's attorney.

Mediation is a process designed to facilitate settlement and is not a trial in itself. Indeed, the purpose of confidentiality in mediation is to promote "a candid and informal exchange regarding events in the past.... This frank exchange is achieved only if the participants know that what is said in the mediation will not be used to their detriment through later court proceedings and other adjudicatory processes." (Nat. Conf. of Comrs. On U. State Laws, U. Mediation Act (may [sic] 2001) § 2.

Thus, there is a strong preference for confidentiality within the mediation context. Title 28 U.S.C. § 652(d) allows each local court to adopt rules prescribing disclosure of mediation communications. Pursuant to such statute, this Court promulgated LRCi 3.2 which not only makes such communications inadmissible, but creates a mediation privilege, giving the holder the right "to refuse to disclose, and to prevent any person present at the proceeding from disclosing communications made during such proceeding." LRCi 3.2(4). The sole exception to this rule allows the mediator to notify the referring judge that a party acted in bad faith. LRCi 3.2(e)(2). Thus, the creation of the mediation privilege in this court indicates a strong desire to protect the sanctity of the mediation proceedings.

A majority of jurisdictions recognize and enforce such a privilege. In *Foxgate Homeowners' Association, Inc. v. Bramalea California, Inc.,* 25 P.3d 1117, (Cal.2001), the Court ruled that there were "no exceptions to the confidentiality of mediation communications.... Neither a mediator nor a party may reveal communications made during mediation." In *Sheldone v. Pennsylvania Turnpike Commission,* 104 F.Supp.2d 511, (W.D.Pa.2000), the Court explained that the mediation privilege established in local rules was "rooted in the imperative need for confidence and trust", and that disclosure of communications uttered in mediation would violate such trust. *Id.* at 513. The Court continued:

> If participants cannot rely on the confidential treatment of everything that transpires during [mediation] sessions then *counsel of necessity will feel constrained to conduct themselves in a cautious, tightlipped, noncommittal manner more suitable to poker players in a high-stakes game than to adversaries attempting to arrive at a just resolution of a civil dispute. This atmosphere* if allowed to exist *would surely destroy the effectiveness of a program which has led to settlements ... , thereby expediting cases at a time when ... judicial resources ... are sorely taxed.*

Id. citing Lake Utopia Paper Ltd. v. Connelly Containers, Inc., 608 F.2d 928, 930 (2d Cir.1979) cert. den. 444 U.S. 1076 (1980) (emphasis in original). The Court in *Calka v. Kucker Kraus & Bruh,* 167 F.3d 144 (2d Cir.1999) found that a confidentiality rule similar to the one in this case was violated where the attorney disclosed confidential statements in a sanctions motion. The privilege was also used to bar the use of statements as a basis for criminal charges in *U.S. v. Gullo,* 672 F.Supp. 99, 103 (W.D.N.Y.1987) and a contractor's admissions at a mediation proceeding were ruled inadmissible in a subsequent criminal prosecution in *Byrd v. State,* 367 S.E.2d 300, 302 (Ct.App.Ga.1988).

Applying the cloak of mediation to the facts of this matter appears inequitable to Hovensa who negotiated settlement of the *Nielsen-Allen* case and applied confidentiality thereto for the express purpose of avoiding having such settlement amount established as a benchmark in future similar employment cases. Such result highlights the need for exceptions to mediation confidentiality, which has been the subject of several scholarly discussions. *See e.g.,* Mori Irvine, *Serving Two Masters: The Obligation Under the Rules of Professional Conduct to Report Attorney Misconduct in a Confidential Mediation,* 26 Rutgers Law Journal, 155 (1994). The commentaries lament the fact that statutes which provide a blanket protection for mediation communications create a conflict with an attorney's duty to report unethical or criminal conduct which may occur during such proceedings. * * * To that end, certain courts have attempted to carve exceptions such as in cases of ongoing or future criminal activity; if a court determines that fairness to third parties warrants disclosure; or to "uphold the administration of justice." * * * However, [this court] does not agree that a court "may fashion an exception for bad faith in mediation because failure to authorize reporting of such conduct during mediation may lead to "an absurd result" or "fail to carry out the legislative policy of encouraging mediation." [*Foxgate,*] 25 P.3d *at* 1128. Accordingly, the Court finds that the mediation privilege set forth in LRCi 3.2 prohibits consideration of Hovensa's motion for sanctions.

Further, even if Hovensa's motion was to be considered, Hovensa acknowledges that no specific rule or statute was violated in this instance, and asks the Court to invoke its inherent powers to sanction the plaintiff. It is well settled that the Court's inherent powers to sanction conduct before it must be premised on a finding of bad faith. *Roadway Express Inc. v. Piper,* 447 U.S. 752, 767 (1980) * * *. Thus, Hovensa must establish that the targeted conduct in this case was undertaken "in bad faith, vexatiously, wantonly, or for oppressive reasons." *Chambers v. NASCO, Inc.,* 501 U.S. 32, 55 (1991). Because the mediation was court ordered in this case, the Court has authority over the parties' conduct.

The Court notes that plaintiff's counsel made the statements in the context of a mediation proceeding which is itself confidential. The mediator to whom the comment was made, and Ms. Moorhead, are also bound by the rule of confidentiality. The cases cited by the defendant involve much more substantial publication, and to parties outside of mediation. *See, e.g. Toon v. Wackenhut Corrections Corp.,* 250 F.3d 950, (5th Cir.2001) (Court found bad faith where attorney deliberately filed confidential materials without seal); [s]ee also Lawson v. Brown's Daycare Center, Inc.,* (unsealed disclosure to court in disciplinary complaint).

The Court recognizes that a rule which imposes a blanket restriction on disclosing all communications made in mediation may imply immunity from sanctions by shielding parties who disobey court orders or otherwise violate ethical rules in such context, and that LRCi 3.2 should be amended to provide for appropriate exceptions to the rule. However, in this case, the conduct targeted is nothing more than the attorney's statement to the mediator in the presence of Ms. Moorhead, that the current case should settle for the same dollar amount as a similar but unrelated, case. The mediator has no power to decide and is only a facilitator of settlement. Thus, such statement did not interfere with the trial process and was not published to any party outside of the litigation itself.

Upon consideration, the Court finds that the conduct in question does not support the finding of bad faith required for imposition of a sanction. Because the Court found that Hovensa's motion may not be considered and that even if it was to be considered, the subject conduct by plaintiff's attorney would not qualify as sanctionable conduct, the Court need not consider plaintiff's argument regarding whether the confidentiality agreement in the *Moorhead* matter applied to plaintiff's counsel.

Accordingly, it is hereby ORDERED AS FOLLOWS:

1. that HOVENSA's motion for sanctions is DENIED.

2. the attorney's portion of settlement proceeds deposited with the Court pursuant to the Order dated November 11, 2003 shall not be disbursed and shall remain on deposit pending further Order of the Court (i.e., to allow Hovensa to file any timely appeal of this Order).

UNIFORM MEDIATION ACT
http://www.law.upenn.edu/bll/ulc/mediat/2003finaldraft.htm
(last accessed May 24, 2004).

(Adopted by the National Conference of the Commissioners on Uniform State Laws and approved by the Delegates of the American Bar Association in 2001, and amended in 2003.)

SECTION 4. PRIVILEGE AGAINST DISCLOSURE; ADMISSIBILITY; DISCOVERY.

(a) Except as otherwise provided in Section 6, a mediation communication is privileged as provided in subsection (b) and is not subject to discovery or admissible in evidence in a proceeding unless waived or precluded as provided by Section 5.

(b) In a proceeding, the following privileges apply

(1) A mediation party may refuse to disclose, and may prevent any other person from disclosing, a mediation communication.

(2) A mediator may refuse to disclose a mediation communication, and may prevent any other person from disclosing, a mediation communication of the mediator.

(3) A nonparty participant may refuse to disclose, and may prevent any other person from disclosing, a mediation communication of the nonparty participant.

(c) Evidence or information that is otherwise admissible or subject to discovery does not become inadmissible or protected from discovery solely by reason of its disclosure or use in a mediation.

SECTION 5.   WAIVER AND PRECLUSION OF PRIVILEGE.

(a) A privilege under Section 4 may be waived in a record or orally during a proceeding if it is expressly waived by all parties to the mediation and:

   (1) in the case of the privilege of a mediator, it is expressly waived by the mediator; and

   (2) in the case of the privilege of a nonparty participant, it is expressly waived by the nonparty participant.

(b) A person that discloses or makes a representation about a mediation communication which prejudices another person in a proceeding is precluded from asserting a privilege under Section 4, but only to the extent necessary for the person prejudiced to respond to the representation or disclosure.

(c) A person that intentionally uses a mediation to plan, attempt to commit or commit a crime, or to conceal an ongoing crime or ongoing criminal activity is precluded from asserting a privilege under Section 4.

SECTION 6.   EXCEPTIONS TO PRIVILEGE.

(a) There is no privilege under Section 4 for a mediation communication that is:

   (1) in an agreement evidenced by a record signed by all parties to the agreement;

   (2) available to the public under [insert statutory reference to open records act] or made during a session of a mediation which is open, or is required by law to be open, to the public;

   (3) a threat or statement of a plan to inflict bodily injury or commit a crime of violence;

   (4) intentionally used to plan a crime, attempt to commit or commit a crime, or to conceal an ongoing crime or ongoing criminal activity;

   (5) sought or offered to prove or disprove a claim or complaint of professional misconduct or malpractice filed against a mediator;

   (6) except as otherwise provided in subsection (c), sought or offered to prove or disprove a claim or complaint of professional misconduct or malpractice filed against a mediation party, nonparty participant, or representative of a party based on conduct occurring during a mediation; or

(7) sought or offered to prove or disprove abuse, neglect, abandonment, or exploitation in a proceeding in which a child or adult protective services agency is a party, * * *.

(b) There is no privilege under Section 4 if a court, administrative agency, or arbitrator finds, after a hearing in camera, that the party seeking discovery or the proponent of the evidence has shown that the evidence is not otherwise available, that there is a need for the evidence that substantially outweighs the interest in protecting confidentiality, and that the mediation communication is sought or offered in:

(1) a court proceeding involving a felony [or misdemeanor]; or

(2) except as otherwise provided in subsection (c), a proceeding to prove a claim to rescind or reform or a defense to avoid liability on a contract arising out of the mediation.

(c) A mediator may not be compelled to provide evidence of a mediation communication referred to in subsection (a)(6) or (b)(2).

(d) If a mediation communication is not privileged under subsection (a) or (b), only the portion of the communication necessary for the application of the exception from nondisclosure may be admitted. Admission of evidence under subsection (a) or (b) does not render the evidence, or any other mediation communication, discoverable or admissible for any other purpose.

SECTION 7.   PROHIBITED MEDIATOR REPORTS.

(a) Except as required in subsection (b), a mediator may not make a report, assessment, evaluation, recommendation, finding, or other communication regarding a mediation to a court, administrative agency, or other authority that may make a ruling on the dispute that is the subject of the mediation.

(b) A mediator may disclose:

(1) whether the mediation occurred or has terminated, whether a settlement was reached, and attendance;

(2) a mediation communication as permitted under Section 6; or

(3) a mediation communication evidencing abuse, neglect, abandonment, or exploitation of an individual to a public agency responsible for protecting individuals against such mistreatment.

(c) A communication made in violation of subsection (a) may not be considered by a court, administrative agency, or arbitrator.

SECTION 8. CONFIDENTIALITY.

Unless subject to the [insert statutory references to open meetings act and open records act], mediation communications are confidential to the extent agreed by the parties or provided by other law or rule of this State.

Comment

The evidentiary privilege granted in Sections 4–6 assures party expectations regarding the confidentiality of mediation communications against disclosures in subsequent legal proceedings. However, it is also possible for mediation communications to be disclosed outside of proceedings, for example to family members, friends, business associates and the general public. Section 8 focuses on such disclosures.

Notes and Questions

1.   Do you agree with the outcome of the *Nielsen-Allen* case? Won't an employer be reluctant to settle future cases in mediation if the employer knows that the settlement value can be used as a benchmark in a subsequent case? How would the *Nielsen-Allen* case have been decided under the UMA? Would the UMA permit Hovensa to complain to the state bar association about opposing counsel's disclosure? Should it?

2.   Dennis Sharp and Peter Robinson separately have posited several hypotheticals to illustrate the complexity of mediation confidentiality. Dennis Sharp, *The Many Faces of Mediation Confidentiality*, 53 Dispute Resolution Journal 56 (1998); Peter Robinson, *Centuries of Contract Common Law Can't Be All Wrong: Why the UMA's Exception to Mediation Confidentiality in Enforcement Proceedings Should Be Embraced and Broadened*, 2003 Journal of Dispute Resolution 135, 143–48 (2003). For each of the hypotheticals below, when is disclosure permitted under the UMA? When is disclosure required? Does it make a difference whether the disclosing entity is a party or the mediator? Are there any limits on how the disclosure may subsequently be used?

(a) The plaintiff in an employment dispute, during the mediation session, credibly threatens to kill his former supervisor.

(b) The former employee reveals to the mediator that she has embezzled several thousand dollars from the employer. Can or must the mediator disclose this information to the employer? To law enforcement authorities?

(c) Subsequent to mediation, the parties agree to resolve the dispute by binding arbitration. At the arbitration hearing, the employer seeks to introduce admissions made by the plaintiff "for what they [the admissions] are worth."

(d) The case settled in mediation, but the plaintiff files suit seeking to have the settlement agreement set aside because the mediator failed to disclose that he formerly was an in-house attorney for the employer. What if the action is against the mediator for damages caused by the nondisclosure?

(e) The plaintiff in a sexual harassment suit sues her employer and her supervisor in his individual capacity. Following mediation, the supervisor settles, but the employer does not. Prior to trial, the plaintiff and employer agree that certain statements made during the mediation will be admissible in court.

(f) Several days after an unsuccessful mediation session, the mediator telephones the parties and unsuccessfully attempts to further assist them in settling the dispute. When the case goes to trial, can the mediator be compelled to testify about what was said during those conversations?

(g) After mediation, the parties disagreed about whether an agreement handwritten by the mediator and signed by both parties was an enforceable agreement or merely a summary of terms for future discussion.

(h) A party relied on misrepresentations by her union that she was only entitled to six months of pack pay, when she actually was entitled to eighteen months of back pay.

(i) A typographical error in the settlement agreement led to a $600,000 windfall for one party.

(j) A plaintiff with age discrimination claims unknowingly and involuntarily waived her rights in a mediated agreement, in violation of the Older Workers' Benefits Protection Act.

(k) A mediated agreement to settle a workers' compensation claim did not specify whether it also was intended to settle a discrimination claim.

3.   In light of the exceptions to confidentiality, what would you advise a client, prior to mediation, about the extent of confidentiality afforded to mediation communications? Are these exceptions likely to undermine significantly the ability of parties to communicate effectively with mediators? If you were a mediator, what, if anything, would you tell the parties about confidentiality at the beginning of a mediation session?

4.   Should confidentiality be extended to arbitration and other types of ADR? Should the scope of confidentiality be any different when settlement negotiations are not assisted by a third-party neutral?

5.   Should employers be able to keep their employment wrongs secret merely by settling them? See Eric D. Green, *A Heretical View of the Mediation Privilege*, 2 Ohio State Journal of Dispute Resolution 1 (1986).

2.   ENFORCEABILITY OF MEDIATED AGREEMENTS

JACOBS v. NEW YORK FINANCIAL CENTER HOTEL

United States District Court for the Southern District of New York, 1997.
1997 WL 375737.

Defendants move to dismiss the complaint pursuant to Fed.R.Civ.P. 12(b)(6) or for summary judgment pursuant to Fed.R.Civ.P. 56, claiming that plaintiff's employment discrimination suit should be dismissed because the parties entered into a settlement agreement which released the claims brought in the present suit. Plaintiff argues that the settlement agreement is unenforceable because his waiver of the Age Discrimination in Employment Act ("ADEA") claims was not knowing and voluntary as defined in the Older Workers Benefit Protection Act ("OWBPA"), 29 U.S.C. § 626(f) (amending the ADEA).

BACKGROUND

The settlement agreement is a handwritten document drafted during a single mediation session on Friday, April 5, 1996, which was initiated at plaintiff's request and lasted approximately five hours. Under the agreement, plaintiff was to receive $65,000 and a letter of recommendation in exchange for withdrawing and waiving the employment discrimination claims he had filed with the Equal Employment Opportunity Commission ("EEOC"). Plaintiff's counsel telephoned defendants' counsel three or four days after the mediation to tell her plaintiff was rejecting the agreement because he wanted more money. After attempts at renegotiation failed, plaintiff filed this suit on September 18, 1996.

DISCUSSION

Section 626(f) of the OWBPA states, in pertinent part,

(f) Waiver

(1) An individual may not waive any right or claim under this chapter [the ADEA] unless the waiver is knowing and voluntary....

(2) A waiver in settlement of a[n ADEA] charge filed with the Equal Opportunity Employment Commission. alleging age discrimination of a kind prohibited under section 623 or 633a of this title may not be considered knowing and voluntary unless at a minimum–* * *

(B) the individual is given a reasonable period of time within which to consider the settlement agreement.

(3) In any dispute that may arise over whether any of the requirements, conditions, and circumstances set forth in subparagraph (A) or (B) of paragraph (2), have been met, the party asserting the validity of a waiver shall have the burden of proving in a court of competent jurisdiction that a waiver was knowing and voluntary pursuant to paragraph (1) or (2).

In this case, Mr. Jacobs did not have a reasonable time in which to consider the settlement agreement as required by § 626(f)(2)(B).

Since that clause does not describe what constitutes a reasonable time, the OWBPA paragraphs that apply to waivers of claims that have not been filed with the EEOC, see § 626(f)(1), provide a starting point for that determination. Section 626(f)(1)(F)(i) requires that an employee who has not filed an ADEA claim be given "at least 21 days within which to consider the agreement"; under § 626(f)(1)(G) a waiver of a claim is not valid unless it allows for a seven-day revocation period after its execution.

Here, in contrast with either the seven-or 21–day periods, plaintiff had only a few hours to consider the settlement agreement. He also claims to have been under pressure because the mediator told him that defendants' offer was open only during the mediation session. The short, intense time was insufficient to allow full consideration of the terms of the agreement. Indeed, once plaintiff had an opportunity to think it over, he rejected the settlement agreement.

Defendants' arguments that plaintiff "had months prior to the mediation to consider his settlement needs" and that plaintiff's counsel should not have allowed his client to sign the agreement "if [the] client [did] not have sufficient time to consider a proposal" are unavailing. Since there is no evidence that plaintiff knew before the mediation session what defendants' offer would be, plaintiff's time to consider the settlement agreement did not begin until the terms were made known to him. *Cf. Bormann v. AT & T Communications, Inc.,* 875 F.2d 399, 403 (2d Cir.1989) (quoting *EEOC v. Am. Express Publ'g Corp.,* 681 F.Supp. 216, 219 (S.D.N.Y.1988)) (one factor to consider in determining whether waiver of Title VII claim is valid is "the amount of time the plaintiff had possession of or access to the agreement before signing it").

Plaintiff cites cases from other circuits which hold that a waiver of ADEA claims that does not comply with the OWBPA is either void, *see Oberg v. Allied Van Lines, Inc.,* 11 F.3d 679, 682–83 (7th Cir.1993), or voidable, *see Blistein v. St. John's College,* 74 F.3d 1459, 1465 (4th Cir.1996); *Wamsley v. Champlin Ref. and Chem., Inc.,* 11 F.3d 534, 538–39 (5th Cir.1993). The only court in the Second Circuit to address this issue held such an agreement voidable. *Hodge v. New York College of Podiatric Med.,* 940 F.Supp. 579, 584 (S.D.N.Y.1996). A voidable contract may be enforced if the party opposing enforcement ratifies it "by accepting the benefits conferred by the agreement." *Id.* Here, plaintiff did not receive any benefits under the settlement agreement: he neither accepted the money nor received a letter of recommendation. Thus, plaintiff did not ratify the agreement, and it is unenforceable under either approach.

CONCLUSION

Defendants' motion is denied.

So ordered.

Notes and Questions

1. The OWBPA applies only to waivers of federal age discrimination claims, not to other types of discrimination claims or to common law claims. In those types of cases, courts use the common law of contracts (offer/acceptance/consideration) as the default rule for determining the enforceability of a mediated agreement. See, e.g., Strategic Staff Management, Inc. v. Roseland, 260 Neb. 682, 686, 619 N.W.2d 230, 234 (2000).

2.   Enforceability issues often arise when the terms of the mediated agreement are ambiguous, or when one party attempts to add or subtract terms to or from the mediated agreement, or when it is unclear whether a mediated agreement was reached at all. See Jaynes v. Austin, 20 Fed.Appx. 421 (6th Cir. 2001) (enforcing mediation agreement and rejecting employer's post-mediation attempt to add additional terms to the agreement). In a subsequent action to enforce the purported agreement, the party seeking enforcement will want to testify to the terms of the purported agreement, and may want to subpoena the mediator's testimony. How does Section 6 of the Uniform Mediation Act deal with this? See also NLRB v. Joseph Macaluso, Inc., 618 F.2d 51 (9th Cir.1980) (approving NLRB's decision refusing to subpoena a mediator in an unfair labor practice proceeding).

3.   Once the parties have agreed on a dollar figure to settle the case and on whether the employee will be reinstated, they typically are relieved to have settled the case and emotionally exhausted from the day's events. Under these circumstances, it is tempting to leave the mediation session without drafting a written settlement agreement. However, reducing an agreement reached in mediation to writing, preferably before the mediation session is concluded, may be a necessary predicate to judicial enforcement; some jurisdictions will not enforce a settlement agreement—including an agreement reached in mediation—unless the agreement is in writing. See, e.g., Fla. R. Civ. P. 1.730(b); Tex. R. Civ. P. 11; see also Regents of the Univ. of Cal. v. Sumner, 42 Cal.App.4th 1209, 50 Cal.Rptr.2d 200, 202 (1996) (parties can reach an enforceable oral agreement by dictating terms of agreement into a tape recorder after the mediation has ended); Smith v. Columbia Gas Transmission Corp., 176 F.3d 475 (unpublished op.) (4th Cir.1999) (enforcing a written settlement agreement that accurately reflected a verbal agreement reached in mediation). Under what circumstances might a party prefer *not* to reduce a mediation agreement to writing?

4.   The 1997 version of the Minnesota Civil Mediation Act provided that a mediated settlement agreement is not binding unless it states it is binding. Minn. Stat. § 572.35(1). In Haghighi v. Russian–American Broadcasting Co., 577 N.W.2d 927, 930 (Minn.1998) (*Haghighi I*), the Minnesota Supreme Court refused to enforce a handwritten settlement agreement, signed on each page by the parties, because it did not state that it was binding. See also Haghighi v. Russian–American Broadcasting Co., 173 F.3d 1086 (8th Cir.1999) (applying *Haghighi I*). The statute, amended in 1999, now provides: "A mediated settlement agreement is not binding unless (1) it contains a provision stating that it is binding * * * or (2) the parties were otherwise advised of the conditions in clause (1)." Minn. Stat. Ann. § 572.35 (West 1999).

Are there any reasons to impose greater requirements for enforcement of a mediated settlement agreement than would be imposed for enforcement of a settlement agreement created in the absence of mediation?

5.   What are the social implications of resolving employment disputes through private ADR mechanisms? How will the proliferation of mediation affect the development of legal doctrines in employment law? Is there any important function performed by a public resolution of employment cases (in

open trials, reported cases, and publicized verdicts) that will be lost by private resolution? Or are the values served by ADR equally, if not more, compelling? Does it matter whether the dispute raises significant issues of statutory construction, or whether it is "just" a run-of-the-mill contract interpretation case?

Does the public nature of litigation impose a barrier to plaintiffs coming forward with employment claims? If so, would this barrier be lessened somewhat by the availability of private ADR mechanisms?

Are the answers to any of these questions different for mediation than for arbitration?

6. Court reporters are rarely present at mediation sessions. Under what circumstances might a party want one present?

F. MEDIATION ETHICS

1. ETHICS AND THE MEDIATOR

A NOTE ON MEDIATOR AND ARBITRATOR ETHICS
Norman Brand.
in How ADR Works 82–89 (Norman Brand, ed., 2002).

The standards of behavior for mediators promulgated by various entities generally cover six areas: voluntariness, impartiality, disclosure, competence, confidentiality, and compensation. Each of these areas requires some explanation and raises some questions for the neutral.

A. VOLUNTARINESS

There are two aspects to voluntariness. First, any party is free to withdraw from mediation at any time. Second, the parties must reach a voluntary, uncoerced agreement. The Model Standards of Conduct for Mediators [promulgated jointly by the American Arbitration Association, the American Bar Association, and the Society of Professionals in Dispute Resolution SPIRD] also state that "[p]arties shall be given the opportunity to consider all proposed options." These elements raise the following questions for the neutral. First, is it ethically appropriate to participate in mandatory programs where a court orders the parties to mediate? The California Dispute Resolution Council (CDRC) Standards differentiate between being mandated to the mediation process, which it deems acceptable, and a mediator mandating the extent to which a party must participate, which it deems not acceptable. There is a subsidiary question of what role, if any, a mediator should take in reporting what occurred in mediation to a court that mandated the mediation. Most mediators believe that they should only indicate whether a party attended with the people the court asked to attend. If a mediator provides anything beyond that in a "report to the court," she acquires coercive power. If a mediator can blame a party for unreasonable mediation behavior, he has such coercive power. Moreover, parties who are mandated to mediation may be more likely to posture before a mediator who will be reporting their behavior to the court in which they are litigating.

The final consideration is the requirement in the Model Standards that parties be given an opportunity to consider "all proposed options." It is likely that the drafters saw this as an analog to the lawyer's responsibility to transmit offers of compromise and settlement to the client. The difficulty, as most veteran mediators know, is that some "proposed options" amount to a gratuitous insult. Conveying that proposed option may very well end the mediation with one side walking out in anger. A useful alternative, employed by many veteran mediators, is to decline to carry the proposed option to the other side, but offer to reconvene a joint session so the party proposing the option can convey it–while counseling that party on the likely response to the inflammatory option. This way the mediator is not tainted by the insult and can work to save the mediation if anger erupts.

B.   Impartiality

There are three aspects to impartiality: (1) the mediator's own ability to remain impartial, (2) the appearance of impartiality, and (3) potential grounds for a reasonable person to call the mediator's impartiality into question. The first aspect is internal. There are certain issues about which each of us feels strongly that there is a "right and wrong." To the extent that this feeling will impair a mediator's ability to listen to one side or to report a position fairly to the other side, the mediator should not take the case. The "appearance of partiality" standard for mediator conduct is more troublesome. Where the standards are enforced through sanctions, a charge that a mediator engaged in conduct that gave the appearance of partiality is difficult to evaluate. As veteran mediators know, it is sometimes necessary to play devil's advocate, to convey the other side's convictions, and that could appear to an unhappy party, in retrospect, as partiality. Thus, the rule creates a tension between the mediator's legitimate efforts to move the parties to resolution and the fear of subsequent attacks on the process by a party with buyer's or seller's remorse. The third aspect of impartiality is considered in detail in the next section.

C.   Disclosure

What a mediator should disclose is less controversial than how it is characterized. The Model Standards use the phrase "conflict of interest" and define it as "a dealing or relationship that might create an impression of possible bias." While the definition makes sense, the same phrase is used in ethics for attorneys where it has a different meaning and a well-developed body of law. As a consequence, some have jumped to the erroneous conclusion that a mediator has a conflict of interest because she formerly was a partner of one of the attorneys in the mediation, or she formerly represented one of the parties in the mediation. Neither of these relationships constitutes a conflict of interest for a mediator, but they should be disclosed. In fact, the other side may want that mediator because of the former relationship, which could bring credibility and trust.

The CDRC Standards provide a more workable model for mediation disclosure. They do not posit that mediators have conflicts of interest as lawyers understand that term. Instead, the Standards require disclosure of "potential grounds upon which a mediator's impartiality might reasonably be challenged." These include personal and professional relationships, as well as previous cases with one or both parties or their attorneys. Both the mediator and the parties have a continuing obligation to disclose. If either party asks the mediator to withdraw after a disclosure, he must do so.

Because mediation is voluntary, it is not clear whether there are any appropriate sanctions for failure to disclose. If parties make a voluntary, uncoerced agreement, then the mediator's past relationships or cases are irrelevant. If one side learns a fact that makes it uncomfortable with the mediator, that side can simply withdraw from the mediation. Finally, it is difficult to posit a "repeat player" bias in mediators. Because mediators do not have any power to dictate the terms of an agreement, the only way they could influence a decision is by "beating up" on one side. This behavior is unlikely to be successful with a represented party and is likely to adversely affect the mediator's reputation and acceptability.

D. COMPETENCE

A continuing question in mediation is whether parties want process or substantive expertise in their mediators. Both sets of standards sidestep that question and simply require mediators to have the competence that will meet the reasonable expectation of the parties. This criterion becomes more important when a court mandates mediation and provides a list of mediators, because the court may be thought to provide some assurance of competence. [However], the courts rely chiefly on training as a competence threshold.

The real question for mediators is: "What are these parties looking for?" Many mediators have a conference call with the parties before the mediation in order to ascertain details such as whether there will be premediation briefs, whether the briefs will be shared with the other party, and who will attend. It is a good practice for the mediator to use this conference call to ascertain the parties' expectations about the mediation. If the parties erroneously believe that the mediator has some expertise or experience that she lacks, that needs to be disclosed during this call. Similarly, if the parties have unrealistic expectations about what the mediator can do to promote agreement, those expectations must be discussed. In sum, the mediator must be sure that there is a fit between his skill, style, and ability and what the parties expect.

E. CONFIDENTIALITY

Confidentiality is critical to mediation. The law of the jurisdiction controls postmediation confidentiality. The ground rules established at the mediation by the mediator and the parties control confidentiality during the mediation. Jurisdictions differ in the extent to which they will enforce the confidentiality of communications made in mediation against discovery and use in litigation. * * *

Confidentiality during the mediation is also important, to both the mediator and the parties, to increase the chance of settlement. Each party must feel comfortable about telling the mediator things it does not want the other side to know. It is critical for the mediator to establish the confidentiality rules with the parties at the first joint session. For instance, in order to permit the parties to speak freely in private caucus with her, the mediator may adopt a practice of checking with the party at the end of the caucus to ask whether she can convey certain specific information. Anything that is not mentioned is not conveyed. In this way, the mediator and the party can be assured that there will be no inadvertent sharing of information the party deems confidential. The critical issue for mediator ethics is to establish a specific method for preserving confidentiality during the mediation that is acceptable to the parties.

F. COMPENSATION

Both the Model and CDRC Standards require the mediator to disclose all fees, charges, and costs before the mediation, and both forbid contingent fees. While both require that fees be "reasonable," the real determinant of fees is the marketplace. The only ethical issue for mediators occurs in those jurisdictions where court-annexed programs require the mediator to provide a certain number of hours free or for a token payment before charging his normal fee. It is sometimes asserted that a mediator slowed the progress of the free mediation to convert it into a fee-generating mediation. While that may or may not be true, any system that requires the mediator to provide free (or almost free) services before she can charge creates a potential dilemma for the mediator. * * *

Mediators have a number of options for avoiding this potential for an ethical dilemma. First, they can decline to participate in the combination programs. If one separates her pro bono work from her compensated work, there is no potential ethical problem. Second, those mediators who participate in the programs should attempt to provide the parties with a realistic assessment, during the mediation, of whether the case is likely to be settled and an estimate of the hours needed. * * * By making a realistic prediction early in the case–based on observations about the dynamics of the case—the mediator can avoid being accused of manipulating the process to produce a fee.

Where mediation is not court-annexed, the market for employment mediators is similar to the market for labor arbitrators. While there are no written awards to study, there is a great deal of informal information sharing. * * * [Both the plaintiff and defense bars are well-organized, and thus have access to information about employment mediators similar to the information traditionally shared about labor arbitrators.] In the segment of employment mediation practice that is not court-annexed, the same market forces that effectively regulate labor arbitrator ethics regulate employment mediator ethics. The parties, who can freely choose any mediator, know their skills, styles, and competence. Any ethical failures, lack of skill, or perceived biases are quickly known and have immediate financial consequences. The parties regulate employment mediator ethics by choosing which mediator to employ.

Notes and Questions

1. Note 3 following the Stulberg excerpt, in Part B of this chapter, raises the issue of whether the mediator must be neutral with respect to the substantive outcome of mediated agreements. A related issue is whether the mediator must be neutral with regard to the parties' ability to bargain effectively in the mediation itself. Owen Fiss, in his article *Against Settlement*, 93 Yale Law Journal 1073 (1984), noted that the parties to a dispute rarely possess equal bargaining power. Is this likely to be particularly true in employment disputes? Why? Under what circumstances? See Cynthia Grant Bowman and Elizabeth M. Schneider, *Feminist Legal Theory, Feminist Lawmaking, and the Legal Profession*, 67 Fordham Law Review 249, 269 (1998) (women are often disadvantaged by informal processes such as mediation); Mori Irvine, Note, *Mediation: Is It Appropriate for Sexual Harassment Grievances?*, 9 Ohio State Journal on Dispute Resolution 27, 40 (1993) (mediation is inappropriate for the resolution of sexual harassment claims because there is an imbalance of power between the harasser / employer and the victim that cannot be reconciled in mediation); but see Vivian Berger, *Employment Mediation in the Twenty–First Century: Challenges in a Changing Environment*, 5 University of Pennsylvania Journal of Labor & Employment Law 487, 534 (2003) (noting that "[m]any critics of ADR indulge in the fantasy of 'litigation romanticism,' failing to consider the ways in which formal adversarial proceedings, in courts or agencies, handicap the weaker party–often to a much greater degree [than ADR].").

Should the mediator take any steps to equalize a significant disparity in bargaining power? See Emily M. Calhoun, *Workplace Mediation: The First–Phase, Private Caucus in Individual Discrimination Disputes*, 9 Harvard Negotiation Law Review 187 (2004) (arguing that a mediator should schedule a private caucus with the discrimination complainant prior to the mediation session to enable the mediator to understand the complainant's group-based identity); Carrie A. Bond, Note, *Shattering the Myth: Mediating Sexual Harassment Disputes in the Workplace*, 65 Fordham Law Review 2489, 2515–16 (1997) (arguing that mediation can be structured to account for power imbalances between the parties; a mediator might, for example, not require that the parties meet or negotiate face-to-face). Is the feminist critique of mediation itself sexist and demeaning to women, or does it express legitimate concerns about the perpetuation of inequality?

2. Consider also instances when the mediator is confronted by (a) a legally sophisticated party across from a legally unsophisticated party, (b) a fully informed party across from a woefully ignorant party, and (c) a party with an effective advocate across from a party with no advocate at all. Recall

McDermott and Obar's conclusion that non-represented parties are significantly disadvantaged in mediation. Can the mediator achieve bargaining equality while still remaining neutral? Would action to achieve bargaining equality raise a question of mediator ethics? Would a mediator's inaction in the face of an obvious disparity in bargaining power raise a question of mediator ethics?

3.   Brand notes that there is an inherent tension between court-ordered mediation and the mediation ideal of voluntariness. Some parties, however, may not want to participate in mediation, at least at the time and under the circumstances ordered by the court. Legislatures and courts have responded by adopting "good faith" requirements for mediation, but such a nebulous standard is difficult to enforce and itself gives apparent coercive authority to the mediator. See generally John Lande, *Using Dispute System Design Methods to Promote Good–Faith Participation in Court–Connected Mediation Programs*, 50 UCLA Law Review 69 (2002).

4.   May a mediator give advice or information to the parties? Some jurisdictions expressly permit it. See Connecticut Formal Ethics Opinion 35 (1982); see also Oregon Formal Ethics Opinion 488 (1983) (a lawyer-mediator may give all parties in a divorce mediation information on legal rules and explain whether party proposals are within reasonable legal tolerances). Other jurisdictions forbid it. See Wisconsin Formal Ethics Op. E–79–2 (1980). The rationales against permitting a mediator to offer advice or information are that it would compromise the mediator's neutrality and that, if the mediator is not a lawyer, it might constitute the unauthorized practice of law. Still other jurisdictions distinguish between advice and information, and permit mediators to give the latter but not the former. See Maryland Formal Ethics Opinion 80-55A (1980). However, the distinction between advice and information often is anything but a bright line. See 1 Nancy H. Rogers and Craig A. McEwen, Mediation: Law, Policy and Practice 10 11 to 10 13 (2d ed. 1994). See also Robert B. Moberly, *Mediator Gag Rules: Is It Ethical for Mediators to Evaluate or Advise?*, 38 South Texas Law Review 669 (1997) (suggesting that mediators should be free to either dispense or not dispense advice; the parties' ability to select their own mediator functions as a market that can "help sort out the mediator style most appropriate for particular cases and parties.").

5.   Should the parties unhesitatingly share confidential information with the mediator? Are there circumstances under which an attorney should advise the client to keep certain information private, even from the mediator? Might this compromise the mediation process? How?

6.   Is it ever appropriate for a mediator to pressure the parties to settle? See Vitakis–Valchine v. Valchine, 793 So.2d 1094, (Fla. Dist. Ct. App. 2001) (holding that trial court could refuse to enforce mediation agreement where mediator had told party that if no agreement were reached, the mediator would report to the trial judge that mediation had failed because of that party); Randle v. Mid Gulf, Inc., 1996 WL 447954 (Tex. App.–Houston [14th Dist.], writ denied) (holding that trial court could refuse to enforce mediation agreement where mediator would not permit party to leave the mediation without an agreement although the party was complaining of chest

pains, had a history of heart problems, and had not taken his heart medication that day).

7. Recall from Chapter IX.A that there is a strong legislative and judicial trend toward broadening arbitrators' disclosure requirements. Do you agree with Brand that disclosure is less important for a mediator?

8. Courts have consistently held that arbitrators and mediators enjoy qualified immunity from civil liability. See Jacqueline M. Nolan–Haley, *Informed Consent in Mediation: A Guiding Principle for Truly Educated Decisionmaking*, 74 Notre Dame Law Review 775, 802 (1999); Dennis Nolan and Roger Abrams, *Arbitral Immunity*, 11 Industrial Relations Law Journal 228 (1989). For extended discussion on mediator liability, see Michael Moffitt, *Suing Mediators*, 83 Boston University Law Review 147 (2003); Michael Moffitt, *Ten Ways to Get Sued: A Guide for Mediators*, 8 Harvard Negotiation Law Review 81 (2003).

9. Consider one litigator's approach to mediation:

> The worst, negative aspect of it is, if ... I act for the Big Bad Wolf against Little Red Riding Hood and I don't want this dispute resolved, I want to tie it up as long as I possibly can, and mandatory mediation is custom made. I can waste more time, I can string it along, I can make sure this thing never gets resolved because as you've already figured out, I know the language. I know how to make it look like I'm heading in that direction. I make it look like I can make all the right noises in the world, like this is the most wonderful thing to be involved in when I have no intention of ever resolving this. I have the intention of making this the most expensive, longest process but is it going to feel good. It's going to feel so nice, we're going to be here and we're going to talk the talk but we're not going to walk the walk. You can tie anybody up and keep them farther away from getting their dispute resolved through mandatory mediation process or a mediation process than anything else.

Julie Macfarlane, *Culture Change? A Tale of Two Cities and Mandatory Court–Connected Mediation*, 2002 Journal of Dispute Resolution 241, 267 (quoting a Toronto litigator). What might a mediator do when she perceives that a party or advocate has this attitude? As you read the following section, consider whether the Model Rules of Professional Responsibility provide a constraint on advocates.

2. ETHICS AND THE ADVOCATE

SOME ETHICAL ISSUES SURROUNDING MEDIATION

Robert P. Burns.
70 Fordham Law Review 691, 692–701 (2001).

I. TWO TRADITIONAL ISSUES IN NEGOTIATION ETHICS

A. *The Question of Truthfulness*

The most important ethical issues surrounding the mediations in which lawyers participate relate to: (1) the appropriate level of candor for the dialogue that occurs during the mediations and (2) the appropriate division of authority between lawyer and client before and during the mediations. These are the very same issues that surround negotiation ethics, though the addition of the mediator changes the context within which they arise.

At one extreme, mediation can simply be facilitated share bargaining. Here the underlying premise of a mediation is that there is a relatively fixed pie to divide and that the mediation is a "zero-sum game." One person's gain is the other person's loss and neither party gains in any way from the other party's "success." The process of the mediation, like share-bargaining negotiation, is employed both to determine whether there is a zone of cooperative success, a so-called bargaining range created by the overlap between the parties bottom lines, and then to settle as close to the other party's bottom line as possible. The ethical issues surrounding this style of negotiation are all intertwined with obligations of candor or truthfulness; and one can easily see why. Both parties to this kind of negotiation perceive themselves better off settling anywhere in the settlement range created by the overlap between bottom lines than not settling. But, both parties are conceived as solely self-interested and so each is better off settling at the point in the settlement range that represents precisely the "opponent's" bottom line. From a purely self-interested point of view, each party is best served by the opponent's misunderstanding the party's own bottom line, believing that it is identical to his own. So if a plaintiff will settle for $10,000 and a defendant will offer as much as $20,000 to avoid further litigation, it is in our purely self-interested plaintiff's interest that the defendant perceive that he will accept no less than $20,000. For it is still in the interest of the defendant that he settle for $20,000 rather than go to trial. The process of this sort of negotiation involves "information bargaining" to discover the opponent's bottom line, while convincingly sequencing offers and engaging in other behaviors, of which the negotiation literature offers a full panoply, to convince the opponent that the bottom line is other than where it actually is.

The obvious way to avoid this morally distasteful, if sometimes subtle, dance of deception, or at least misdirection, is simply to be utterly candid about the underlying facts of one's own situation as well as one's bottom line. Indeed, full candor would not involve simply answering questions posed by one's negotiating partner honestly. It would involve volunteering all information that each party would like to know. Such candor would suggest the apparently courteous expedient of splitting the difference between the bottom lines, something that would seem to provide "equal respect" to the participants. Of course, splitting the difference is dependent on a high level of candor from each side, candor that is inconsistent with our assumption of the mutual indifference of the parties and cannot practically be guaranteed by the usual means of incentives and penalties.

The ethical and legal rules that control this sort of negotiation try to balance the ideals of "telling the truth" and "preventing the negotiating partner from taking advantage. * * * The current lawyer codes strike the following balance * * * . There is generally no requirement that a lawyer inform a negotiating partner of any fact,[10] however clear it is that the negotiator would want to know that fact, would profit from knowing it, or suffers from major misunderstanding of that fact. In that sense, they are wholly coherent with the share bargaining style of negotiating described above. Current rules impose some limits on a purely strategic style by prohibiting "false statement[s] of material fact or law"[11] to opponents. Practically, that limits strategic misdirection solely to "agenda setting" that avoids whole areas that contain factual material of which the negotiator seeks to avoid discussion and "blocking" of specific inquiries. * * *

The complexity and ambiguity of the authoritative interpretations of the Rule shows the depth of the tensions among the competing moral considerations here. The Comment to Model Rule 4.1 provides some consolation to the hard bargainer: "A lawyer is required to be truthful when dealing with others on a client's behalf, but generally has no affirmative duty to inform an opposing party of relevant facts."[12] The exception to the exception, however, can create situations that call for extraordinarily, if not impossibly, refined judgments: "A misrepresentation can occur if the lawyer incorporates or affirms a statement of another person that the lawyer knows is false. Misrepresentations can also occur by failure to act."[13] The Comment to the Ethics 2000 Commission version of Comment 1 to Rule 4.1 drops the extremely unhelpful last phrase "failure to act," but substitutes language that may not be more helpful in resolving individual cases: "Misrepresentations can also occur by . . . partially true but misleading statements or omissions that are the equivalent of affirmative false statements."[14]

The Comment to the current version of the Model Rules goes on to incorporate language that has caused a fair degree of consternation:

> This Rule refers to statements of fact. Whether a particular statement should be regarded as one of fact can depend on the circumstances. Under generally accepted conventions in negotiation, certain types of statements ordinarily are not taken as statements of material fact. Estimates of price or value placed on the subject of a transaction and a party's intentions as to an acceptable settlement of a claim are in this category, and so is the existence of an undisclosed principal except where nondisclosure of the principal would constitute fraud.[15]

Other than the examples provided by the Comment, there seems to be one other major category of statements that would be outside the confines of "material fact," namely the willingness of a client to go to trial rather than reach a settlement.

---

10. MODEL RULES OF PROF'L CONDUCT R. 4.1 cmt. 1 (1999).

11. R. 4.1(a).

12. R. 4.1 cmt. 1.

13. *Id.*

14. [*Id.*]

15. R. 4.1 cmt. 2.

This extremely strategic attitude toward truth-telling, doling out bits of information often out of context, may get in the way of "problem solving" or "integrative" styles of negotiation and the "broad facilitative" style of mediation that parallel it. Problem solving is normally thought to require a higher level of candor between negotiating partners. This is because a key aspect of the problem-solving enterprise is to separate positions taken for the kinds of strategic reasons just described from the underlying interests or "needs" that animate the parties. Purely positional bargaining may blind both parties to the negotiation of possibilities for collaboration (ways that "enlarge the pie" for distribution). To give an extreme example, one of the classic strategic ploys is "br'er rabbit," where the negotiator insists that one outcome (that he secretly desires above all) is the most disfavored of all outcomes. If the opponent wants him to submit to that outcome, the opponent is going to have to pay a very high price indeed. From a problem-solving point of view, however, the use of such a ploy may well prevent the negotiating partner from proposing alternatives that provide even more of the secretly desired alternative. * * *

B. The Question of Client Authority

The other set of ethical issues that surround negotiation have to do with the fostering of client autonomy. Specifically, they involve the interpretation of Model Rule 1.2, which provides that "[a] lawyer shall abide by a client's decision concerning the objectives of representation . . . and shall consult with the client as to the means by which they are to be pursued."[17] The Rule provides explicitly that a lawyer "shall abide by a client's decision whether to accept an offer of settlement of a matter."[18] This provision includes as an obvious corollary a requirement that a lawyer convey to the client any offer concerning which the lawyer does not already have clear authority to accept or reject.

Two sorts of difficulties arise in the application of this rule. The first has to do with the choice in negotiating strategy itself. Is the decision to pursue a hard positional bargaining strategy or an integrative or problem-solving approach a choice of means or a choice of the goals of the representation? It seems that it could be either. If the client's goals in the representation are solely extrinsic to the process—maximizing recovery in a tort claim—it would seem that choice of negotiating style would be a means. If the client includes maintaining cordial relations with the opposing party as a goal of the representation, it would still seem that the choice of negotiating strategy is a means rather than an end, though here the choice of an integrative strategy might be the only competent one. One could, however, envision a client who saw it as a goal of the representation to communicate with the negotiating party in a candid and non-manipulative manner, even if that surrendered some tactical advantages. Such a client would consider integrative bargaining to be a

17. R.1.2(a). Rule 1.4 mandates "reasonable communication with the client" * * *.

18. R. 1.2(a).

matter of ethics, not of strategy. In a Kantian idiom, he might say not that honesty is the best policy, but that honesty is better than any policy. For such a client, negotiating in a certain manner could well become a goal of the representation on which, according to the casuistry suggested by Rule 1.2, the client holds ultimate authority.* * *

The second set of problems surrounding the application of the rule are practical. In lawyer-to-lawyer negotiation, the attorneys face a shifting set of proposals in an indeterminate relationship to each other. Often one's opponent is offering trade-offs between possibilities, each precise combination cannot easily be anticipated and the movement from one to the other may be fluid. Withdrawal from the negotiation to consult with the client every time a slight modification is tentatively proposed may be impractical and, from a purely strategic point of view, may reveal aspects of the client's position that ought to be withheld. I do not think there is any easy answer to this practical problem, though its force can be blunted by good initial client interviewing and a firm sense of the priorities among the client's goals.

The second difficulty in the application of the rule requiring client control of the goals of representation in negotiation is more a problem in the lawyer's moral psychology. In lawyer-to-lawyer negotiation the attorney largely controls the pattern of offers from the opponent and completely controls the flow of information to the client. The client is dependent on the lawyer's reporting of the opponent's factual assertions and the offers made. More importantly, the client is dependent upon his lawyer's judgment about what resolutions are feasible and when the opponent has reached his resistance point. When a lawyer says to his or her client, this point is "non-negotiable" or "they will not budge on this," it is likely that the client will follow his lead. Finally, the ethical rules all but prevent a lawyer from contacting a represented opposing party when he or she believes that offers (and, a fortiori, information) are not being conveyed to that party by his or her lawyer.[25]

The client is thus highly dependent upon the lawyer's honesty— primarily with himself—about what he is saying to his client and what he is doing in the negotiation. And there are strong motives to be less than candid with oneself. Often a lawyer will honestly believe that his client is not acting in her own best interests, that she is too willing to settle on unfavorable terms in a divorce, perhaps, simply to avoid even the threat of a trial that the lawyer believes is extremely remote. The temptation to resort to the paternalistic manipulation of information here can be great. Second, every fee structure will create some potential conflict of interest between client and lawyer. This is true whether the lawyer is charging a flat fee, an hourly fee, or a contingent fee. In each case, it is a matter of purely contingent fact that the lawyer's financial self-interest will be exactly congruent with his client's goals in the

25. The Model Rules do not absolutely prohibit client-to-client contact under these circumstances but there is a risk here that a lawyer will be accused of orchestrating an improper end-run around the lawyer representing the opposing party. *See, e.g.,* Trumbull County Bar Ass'n v. Makridis, 671 N.E.2d 31 (Ohio 1996).

representation. Only the lawyer's sense of professional obligation—his or her "purity of heart"–can assure that it is the client's goals that are being advanced.

Notes and Questions

1. Professor Burns refers to two models of negotiation: share-bargaining and problem-solving. Are these models commensurate with McDermott and Obar's distinction between the evaluative and facilitative styles of mediating?

2. Professor Burns refers to bargaining tactics that share-bargaining negotiators may use "to convince the opponent that the bottom line is other than where it actually is." Judge Wayne Brazil notes that these tactics may include:

> Advancing arguments known or suspected to be specious, concealing significant information, obscuring weaknesses, attempting to divert the attention of other parties away from the main analytical or evidentiary chance, misleading others about the existence or persuasive power of evidence not yet formally presented (e.g., projected testimony from percipient or expert witnesses), resisting well-made suggestions, intentionally injecting hostility or friction into the process, remaining rigidly attached to positions not sincerely held, delaying other parties' access to information, or needlessly protracting the proceedings—simply to gain time, or to wear down the other parties or to increase their cost burdens.

Wayne D. Brazil, *Continuing the Conversation About the Current Status and the Future of ADR: A View from the Courts*, 2000 Journal of Dispute Resolution 11, 29 (2000). Are any of these tactics prohibited by the Model Rules? Should they be? See Kimberlee K. Kovach, *New Wine Requires New Wineskins: Transforming Lawyer Ethics for Effective Representation in a Non–Adversarial Approach to Problem Solving: Mediation*, 28 Fordham Urban Law Journal 935, 952 (2001) (arguing that such tactics make mediation almost indistinguishable from litigation). Are there strategic risks (other than the opportunity cost of disregarding the problem-solving approach to mediation) to using these tactics? Might these tactics be appropriate in some contexts (e.g., negotiating a collective bargaining agreement) but not in others?

3. The problem-solving model of negotiating settlements also can be applied to negotiating labor agreements. This model of labor negotiating is called "interest-based bargaining." Harry C. Katz & Thomas A. Kochan, An Introduction to Collective Bargaining and Industrial Relations 191–93 (2d ed. 2000). Interest-based bargaining should not be confused with interest arbitration (discussed supra at Chapter VIII.A), in which labor negotiators give an arbitrator the authority to write the substantive terms of a collective bargaining agreement. When interest-based bargaining fails, the parties may turn to interest arbitration. This transition is often difficult because the two concepts are theoretically incompatible. Interest-based bargaining is based on cooperative self-determination, whereas interest arbitration is based on adversarial delegation.

4.   After Professor Burns's article went to press, two of the applicable Model Rules were amended. Rule 1.2(a) now reads: "[A] lawyer shall abide by a client's decisions concerning the objectives of the representation ... and, *as required by Rule 1.4,* shall consult with the client as to the means by which they are to be pursued" (emphasis added to denote change from prior Rule). Rule 1.4, which mandates reasonable communication with the client, now also requires that a lawyer "reasonably consult with the client about the means by which the client's objectives are to be accomplished." Does the new language provide a clear answer to whether the lawyer or the client holds ultimate authority with regards to means? See also Restatement (Third) of the Law Governing Lawyers § 21(2) (2000) (unequivocally giving the client such authority).

5.   What is a "material fact" as to which the opponent is entitled to truthfulness under M.R. 4.1(a)? Consider the following scenarios:

(a) A former employee suing her former employer for discrimination is claiming front pay as part of her damages. Unbeknownst to the employer, the employee, shortly before the mediation session, received an employment offer from another company at a larger salary than she had been making with her former employer. Is/should the former employee (be) required to disclose this fact? Would it affect your answer if you knew the former employee had accepted the offer? Rejected the offer? Whether the offer was still pending?

(b) A former employee reasonably believes that she has a valid employment claim against her former employer for at least $150,000. Under normal circumstances, she would not accept a penny less than $150,000 to settle her claim. However, she has a pressing need for immediate cash to make a necessary down payment for needed surgery for her child, and for this reason is willing to settle at mediation for $100,000. Is the former employer entitled to learn of and benefit from knowledge of the former employee's immediate need for cash?

(c) A former employee, a devout Bhuddist, believes he was discriminated against on the basis of his religion. He also believes that going to trial is inconsistent with his religious beliefs. Is the former employer entitled to know of the former employee's attitude toward trial?

G.   GRIEVANCE MEDIATION[1]

Grievance mediation represents one way of dealing with disputes arising under a collective bargaining agreement. Some collective bargain-

1. Bibliographic suggestions: Jeanne M. Brett and Stephen B. Goldberg, *Grievance Mediation in the Coal Industry: A Field Experiment,* 37 Industrial and Labor Relations Review 49 (Oct.1993); Peter Feuille, *Grievance Mediation,* in Employment Dispute Resolution in the Changing Workplace (Adrienne E. Eaton and Jeffery H. Keefe, eds.) (1999); Walter J. Gershenfeld, *Alternatives for Labor Arbitrators,* 53 Dispute Resolution Journal 53 (1998); Stephen B. Goldberg, *Grievance Mediation: A Successful Alternative to Labor Arbitration,* 5 Negotiation Journal 9 (1989); Mori Irvine, *Mediation: Is It Appropriate for Sexual Harassment Grievances?,* 9 Ohio State Journal on Dispute Resolution 27 (1993); Joshua M. Javits, *Crisis Negotiations: How Labor and Management Can Best Navigate Major Changes in the Midterm Contract Period,* 13 World Arbitration and Mediation Report 130, 134 (2002).

ing agreements include grievance mediation as a step in the grievance process. Though empirical evidence is sketchy, it appears that a relatively small number of collective bargaining agreements have taken this approach.[2]

As the Chalmers and Cooper excerpt in Section C discussed, mediation comes in all shapes and sizes. Not only do different mediators have different mediating styles, but the parties can define the goals, issues, and structure of the mediation session. The mediation process described in the excerpt below is somewhat different from earlier descriptions of mediation. In this process, the structure seems slightly more adversarial, and the mediator seems to have more responsibility to offer an independent evaluation of the merits of the case, than in most mediations.

LOW PROFILE/HIGH POTENTIAL: A LOOK AT GRIEVANCE MEDIATION

Richard N. Block, John Beck, and A. Robin Olson.
51 Dispute Resolution Journal 55 (1996).

In early 1991, the parties [at a large unionized manufacturing plant in the Midwest] established an unstructured grievance mediation procedure as an extra step prior to arbitration. The procedure was established primarily because the parties perceived some distinct advantages in terms of speed and cost in resolving disputes without the necessity of arbitration.

Under the procedure created, a grievance could be brought to mediation only if both sides agreed. There were no constraints on the actions of the mediator or the parties, as it was believed that the parties did not have sufficient experience with mediation to establish constraints. Thus, the mediator had no obligation to issue an advisory award if the parties did not settle, although nothing prevented the mediator from offering a view on the merits of the grievance. The mediator could issue a binding opinion if so requested by both parties.

During this period the parties submitted 22 grievances to mediation at four separate two-day sessions. As in the typical arbitration proceeding, each party invited whomever it wished to attend the session. Typically, the company representatives included one or two human resources officials, and the supervisor or supervisors involved in the grievance. Union representatives usually included the international representative, the local president, several members of the bargaining committee, the steward involved in the grievance, and the grievant.

In a typical session, one representative of each side would present its version of the factual situation along with arguments as to why it believed its position was meritorious under the agreement. The other party would then present its view of the situation. In order to encourage

---

2. BNA, Basic Patterns in Union Contracts 37 (14th Ed. 1995) (14 of 400 contracts in representative sample had mediation provisions).

the free flow of information, other attendees would be permitted to provide their views on the matter. There was no direct-or cross-examination, however.

Following the joint session, the mediator would then ask the parties to separate, and provide each party with a view of both the merits of the grievance and the interests involved. The mediator might suggest a settlement and indicate who would prevail in arbitration, if the case went to that step.

* * *

[The authors analyzed the outcomes of mediation and interviewed representatives of each of the parties.]

[G]rievance mediation did not result in outcomes that were more favorable to one party than the other.

* * *

The results of the interviews suggested that grievance mediation had benefits in six specified areas. First, there seemed to be consensus that grievance mediation is less costly and less time consuming than arbitration. Several grievances could be addressed in a single day, and the parties often had a response on the same day. The longest response time was seven days.

Second, the parties agreed that grievance mediation facilitated interest-based rather than rights-based bargaining. It permitted the parties to address the reasons why issues arose, and the interests underlying those issues. Once this was accomplished, it helped to facilitate a solution to the problem with which both parties could live.

Third, the parties agreed that grievance mediation eliminated the "scar tissue" and surprises of arbitration. The parties did not lose control of a situation by placing the decision in an arbitrator's hands. Grievance mediation also gave them access to the neutral and the ability to influence the mediator's recommendation in private, away from the other party. Each party, in private, could inform the mediator of what was truly important to them. This could then be incorporated into a recommendation.

Fourth, the parties believed that a key advantage was that the procedure was informal and unstructured. This permitted a flow of ideas that the mediator could adopt, if appropriate.

Fifth, the parties believed that another key advantage was that the mediator could facilitate communications by explaining to each the other party's point of view on an issue. By talking to each party individually, the mediator could develop a resolution and then encourage both parties to accept it, thereby giving each party a gracious way out of a difficult situation. Neither party believed it was embarrassed; the incentive to "lay in the weeds" and wait for a future mistake was reduced. The mediator can also provide a prediction on how an arbitrator might rule on the case if it went to arbitration. This further reinforced the tendency of the grievance mediation process to develop a resolution based on the merits of the grievance.

Sixth, the parties believed that grievance mediation had a large educational component. It could be used by the parties to educate each other about their concerns and problems, it could be a vehicle for both sides to understand the role of a third party in their relationship, and it could be used to educate the mediator on the points of view of the parties on particular issues.

[Despite these benefits, the employer was not as enthusiastic about the use of mediation as the union was.] It appears that employers find some benefit to the formality, structure and costs associated with arbitration. * * * [T]he employer seemed to find some benefit in forcing the union to make an economic calculus regarding taking cases to arbitration rather than permitting the union the option of going to mediation.

Notes and Questions

1. Many grievance mediation procedures, unlike the one described above, require the mediator to issue an advisory opinion if the grievance is not resolved by the mediation. What purpose does this serve? Why isn't such an opinion issued in more typical mediations? Under what circumstances would you, as an attorney representing a nonunion client in an employment case, prefer the mediator to issue an advisory opinion? When would you prefer that the mediator not issue an opinion? Would the knowledge that the mediator will issue an opinion affect the parties' (and their attorneys') conduct and/or the likelihood of settlement during the mediation session? How?

2. If mediation is faster and cheaper, why might an employer prefer to go directly to arbitration? See Peter Feuille, *Grievance Mediation,* in Employment Dispute Resolution and Worker Rights in the Changing Workplace 187, 200–03 (1999) ("employers may perceive mediation as a process designed primarily to persuade management to give something to the union that the union could not obtain in arbitration").

3. How is the mediation process described above more like arbitration than like a typical mediation? How is it more like mediation?

4. How valuable would you expect grievance mediation to be to a union? Put another way, if you were a union representative negotiating a collective bargaining agreement with an employer, would you make significant wage concessions to get the employer to agree to a grievance mediation procedure?

5. The flip side of grievance mediation is when the parties agree, in a collective bargaining agreement, to mediate claims *not* covered by the bargaining agreement, such as interpersonal claims, communication difficulties, or (sometimes) legal claims. See Ann C. Hodges, *Mediation and the Transformation of American Labor Unions*, 69 Missouri Law Review 365 (2004). What are the advantages and disadvantages to each party of including such a clause in a collective bargaining agreement?

5. Would it be accurate to characterize grievance mediation as an extension of the process of collective bargaining?

Chapter XIV

OTHER METHODS[1]

Mediation and arbitration are just two of the many forms of ADR. The flexibility that the parties have in designing an ADR approach often tends to create hybrid forms that defy easy categorization. Moreover, the various forms of ADR are not mutually exclusive; some companies have incorporated several forms of ADR into a comprehensive dispute resolution system. This Chapter highlights some of the most common other forms of ADR that are used in the workplace.

A. OPEN DOOR POLICIES

KORSLUND v. DYNCORP TRI– CITIES SERVICES, INC.

Court of Appeals of Washington, 2004.
121 Wash.App. 295, 88 P.3d 966.

KATO, C.J.

Steven M. Korslund, Virginia A. Miller, and John Acosta appeal the dismissal of their claims against DynCorp Tri–Cities Services, Inc., (DynCorp) and Fluor Daniel Hanford, Inc. (Fluor), arising from their allegations of safety violations, mismanagement, and fraud at the Hanford Nuclear Reservation. * * * The plaintiffs were longtime workers in the [Fire Systems Maintenance] group. Ms. Miller and Mr. Acosta were journeyman electricians and longtime work partners. Mr. Korslund was the fire systems administrator and the lead engineer in the FSM group. * * *

Beginning in early 1997, Mr. Korslund participated in two investigations that were critical of DynCorp's safety practices. In his weekly

1. Bibliographic suggestions: E. Patrick McDermott with Arthur Eliot Berkeley, Alternative Dispute Resolution in the Workplace (1996); Mary P. Rowe and Michael M. Baker, *Are You Hearing Enough Employee Concerns?*, 62 Harvard Business Review 127 (1984); A. Balfour, *Five Types of Nonunion Grievance Systems*, 61 Personnel 67 (1984).

reports to management beginning in March 1997, Mr. Korslund referred to safety violations and other work-related problems. He also reported * * * that some workers were abusing overtime. * * * Also during the first half of 1997, Ms. Miller and Mr. Acosta became concerned about [their supervisor's] inexperience in the field, about what they believed were instances of mismanagement and fraud in the FSM group, and about abuse of work hours by FSM's pipefitters.

[Korslund, Miller, and Acosta filed several written internal complaints. Subsequently, they claimed that they were ostracized, threatened, harassed, reprimanded, falsely accused of misconduct, and transferred, in retaliation for their complaints. Korslund and Miller took long-term medical leave; Acosta continued to work but complained of depression and anxiety. They sued their employer for, among other things, "breach of promises of specific treatment in specific situations." The trial court granted the employer's motion for summary judgment, and the plaintiffs appealed.]

* * *

We next consider whether the court properly dismissed the plaintiffs' claims for breach of promises of specific treatment in specific situations. In addition to the public policy tort, *Thompson* [*v. St. Regis Paper Co.*, 102 Wash.2d 219, 685 P.2d 1081 (1984)] also recognized that employee policy documents may create enforceable obligations:

> [I]f an employer, for whatever reason, creates an atmosphere of job security and fair treatment with promises *of specific treatment in specific situations* and an employee is induced thereby to remain on the job and not actively seek other employment, those promises are enforceable components of the employment relationship. We believe that by his or her unilateral objective manifestation of intent, the employer creates an expectation, and thus an obligation of treatment in accord with those written promises. *See* Restatement (Second) of Contracts § 2 (1981) (promise is a manifestation of intention *to act or refrain from acting in a specified way,* so made as to justify a promise in understanding a commitment has been made).

> It may be that employers will not always be bound by statements in employment manuals. They can specifically state in a conspicuous manner that nothing contained therein is intended to be part of the employment relationship and are simply general statements of company policy. Additionally, policy statements as written may not amount to promises of specific treatment and merely be general statements of company policy and, thus, not binding. Moreover, the employer may specifically reserve a right to modify those policies or write them in a manner that retains discretion to the employer.

Thompson, 102 Wash.2d at 230–31, 685 P.2d 1081. The elements of this contract-based claim are: (1) a promise of specific treatment in a specific situation; (2) justifiable reliance on the promise by the employee; and (3) a breach of the promise by the employer. *Bulman v. Safeway, Inc.,* 144 Wash.2d 335, 340–41, 27 P.3d 1172 (2001). * * *

Fluor's Employee Concerns Program (ECP) "provides a way to assure appropriate attention and response to any concerns related to: Safety; Health; Security; Quality; Environmental Protection; Business Ethics; Compliance with laws and regulations; Fraud, abuse, or mismanagement; or Physical Working Conditions." The document entitled "Resolving Employee Concerns" provides in pertinent part:

2.1   Managers

[Fluor]   is committed to open, honest, two-way communications with all employees. [Fluor]'s open door policy encourages employees to bring unresolved issues or concerns to the attention of management at any level necessary. Every member of management and supervision has the responsibility to facilitate concern resolution through support and application of this and the open door policy.

Management must ensure that employees who raise concerns or who testify or otherwise participate in congressional investigations are not harassed, intimidated, or subject to any discriminatory or retaliatory actions. Any employee who engages in or condones any of these actions against another employee will be subject to appropriate corrective measures.

2.2   Employees

Employees are free to discuss any matter of concern at any time with their supervisor, managers, or Employee Concern Points-of-Contact (POCs) without recrimination or reprisal. Normally, employees should seek to resolve concerns first by working with immediate managers or the appropriate service or oversight organization. However, if an employee believes that normal management processes have not or will not resolve a concern or if an employee does not know how to deal with a concern, any of the resources below are available:

- Workforce Development/Diversity (employment discrimination or sexual harassment)
- Human Resources (all personnel issues)
- Grievance procedure (contract-related issues for bargaining unit employees, only)
- The ECP

The plaintiffs contend this document specifically promises to take disciplinary action against any person who retaliates against employees for submitting concerns. The defendants point out that the company retains for itself the discretion to determine the appropriate corrective measures. "A supposed promise may be illusory if it is so indefinite it cannot be enforced or if its performance is optional or discretionary on the part of the promisor." *Stewart v. Chevron Chem. Co.,* 111 Wash.2d 609, 613, 762 P.2d 1143 (1988). While it is true that the company retains discretion to determine the appropriate sanction, its policy expressly states that *some* corrective measure will be taken. The policy does not use language suggesting discretion, such as "should," *see Stewart,* 111 Wash.2d at 613, 762 P.2d 1143, or "make every effort," *see Clark County Pub. Util. Dist. No. 1 v. Int'l Bhd. of Elec. Workers,* 111 Wash.App. 690, 695, 45 P.3d 1127 (2002), *rev'd on other grounds,* 150 Wash.2d 237, 76 P.3d 248 (2003). The document uses the word "will," which indicates disciplinary action is mandatory. *See McClintick v. Timber Prods. Mfrs., Inc.,* 105 Wash.App. 914, 922, 21 P.3d 328 (2001). There is at least a fact question whether Fluor intended a promise of specific action in specific situations.

On the question of justifiable reliance, the defendants direct the court's attention to evidence that Ms. Miller and Mr. Acosta were only vaguely aware of the "Resolving Employee Concerns" document. *See Hill v. J.C. Penney, Inc.,* 70 Wash.App. 225, 235, 852 P.2d 1111 ("Statements contained in a supervisor's manual providing for specific treatment are not enforceable if the employer did not distribute the manual to employees, the employee is not aware of the provisions, and the employee consequently does not rely on the provisions."), *review denied,* 122 Wash.2d 1023, 866 P.2d 39 (1993). All of the plaintiffs stated in declarations, however, that they were aware of the companies' policies from various sources, including the Hanford website, postings on bulletin boards, discussions with other workers, e-mail communications, and notices in the company newsletter. This evidence creates at least a factual question as to the plaintiffs' justifiable reliance on the "Resolving Employee Concerns" document.

The defendants also contend there was no justifiable reliance because there is no evidence the plaintiffs were induced "to remain on the job and not actively seek other employment." *Thompson,* 102 Wash.2d at 230, 685 P.2d 1081. But evidence of inducement is not an element of the claim. In context, the quoted language from *Thompson* makes it clear that justifiable reliance itself demonstrates the employee accepted the promise as a component of the employment relationship. For example, in *Bulman,* 144 Wash.2d at 354, 27 P.3d 1172, the court concluded that because the plaintiff had failed to establish that he was aware of the policies, he could not prove justifiable reliance and thus the policies were not an inducement to remain employed.

The plaintiffs' justifiable reliance here is bolstered by Fluor's requirement that employees face discharge if they fail to report legal or ethical violations. A document entitled "Legal and Ethical Conduct" provides in pertinent part:

2.8   Reporting Obligations

Employees who believe that [Fluor] standards of conduct, laws, or government regulations are not being met or observed are expected to report the circumstances to their supervisors or any level of management, or if circumstances dictate, to other internal resources such as the Employee Concerns Program, Human Resources, the legal department or others. Government resources include the DOE Employee Concerns Program, the Inspector General, the Government Accountability Office and others.

. . . .

2.11 Violations

Violation of these rules by any employee may result in the employee's discharge. Civil charges against the employee may also be filed.

This mandatory reporting requirement, coupled with the document prohibiting retaliation, demonstrates an overall policy of encouraging reporting of violations, first by requiring reports and second by promising that reporters will not be subject to harassment or disciplinary action. The plaintiffs allege they were relying on this overall policy, and they have established at least a factual question on justifiable reliance.

On the question of breach of the promise, the plaintiffs have presented circumstantial evidence that their supervisors either retaliated directly or encouraged others to do so when they raised workplace concerns. All of the plaintiffs were long-term employees in Hanford's FSM group, apparently without serious disciplinary incident. But shortly after they began submitting safety and other concerns, they were subjected to harassment by coworkers and disciplinary actions by their supervisors, including (in Mr. Korslund's case) being relieved of some responsibilities and accused of misconduct and (in Ms. Miller's and Mr. Acosta's cases) being transferred to another work area. This temporal proximity of events is circumstantial evidence of retaliation in violation of the ethic's [sic] booklet's promise. * * * There is at least a factual question on breach of the promises. * * * [Thus, the trial] court erred in dismissing the plaintiff's claims that the defendants breached promises contained in the [Employee Concerns Program] document.

Notes and Questions

1. How likely is it that employees will feel comfortable bypassing or challenging their supervisor up the chain of command? Doesn't the *Korslund* case illustrate why they might hesitate to do so? Does a company policy guaranteeing no retaliation effectively alleviate their concerns?

2. How are supervisors likely to react to a company policy that encourages employees to bypass them in the chain of command? How would you expect a member of upper management to react when an assembly-line employee complains that she was not properly credited with two hours of overtime worked the preceding week?

3. The Supreme Court has held that an employer accused of sexual harassment may assert an affirmative defense by showing that (1) the employer exercised reasonable care to prevent and correct promptly any sexually harassing behavior, and (2) the plaintiff-employee failed to take advantage of corrective and preventative measures made available to her by the employer. Burlington Industries v. Ellerth, 524 U.S. 742, 765, 118 S.Ct. 2257, 2270, 141 L.Ed.2d 633 (1998); Faragher v. City of Boca Raton, 524 U.S. 775, 807, 118 S.Ct. 2275, 2293, 141 L.Ed.2d 662 (1998). Consequently,

employers often implement open-door policies as part of their sexual harassment policies. See, e.g., Fisher v. Electronic Data Systems, 278 F.Supp.2d 980 (S.D. Iowa 2003) (granting summary judgment for employer; employee knew of employer's open-door policy but unreasonably failed to report harassing conduct for more than a year); Koerber v. Journey's End, Inc., 2004 WL 723850 (N.D. Ill. March 31, 2004) (entering judgment for employee after bench trial; employer's purported open-door policy was not in writing, not posted in the workplace, and not disseminated to or discussed with employees).

4. The statutory and tort law of many states protects employees who "blow the whistle" on their employer for violating the law or engaging in other conduct that is against public policy. See, e.g., Nees v. Hocks, 272 Or. 210, 536 P.2d 512 (Or. 1975) (awarding damages to employee fired because she served on jury duty). The scope of protection varies widely among the states: some protect only public employees, others all employees; some protect only reports to law enforcement agencies, others protect all public disclosures; some cover only reports of illegal conduct, others cover reports of any unethical conduct or conduct harmful to the public. See Steven L. Willborn, Stewart J. Schwab, and John F. Burton, Employment Law: Cases and Materials 176–80 (3d ed. 2002); see also Stewart J. Schwab, *Wrongful Discharge Law and the Search for Third Party Effects*, 74 Texas Law Review 1943, 1966–72 (1996).

Does a company's open-door policy create a contract cause of action for an employee discharged for internal whistleblowing? Must the open-door policy also contain an anti-retaliation clause? Can the employer argue that the open-door policy and/or anti-retaliation clause is *never* contractually binding? What can an employer do to help protect itself from employee suits claiming that a supervisor retaliated against the employee as a result of the employee's use of the open-door policy?

5. Assume that the *Korslund* plaintiffs were right and their department head was inappropriately crediting employees with overtime work that those employees had not performed. Isn't it in the employer's best interest to encourage other employees to report this problem so the problem can be fixed? Why didn't the employer protect the *Korslund* plaintiffs in this case? Is this an example of where a mid-level supervisor's interests diverge from the employer's interests? If so, is an open-door policy the best way to correct such a divergence? The next section considers another possible way.

B. OMBUDSMEN

An ombudsman is a person employed by a company to help resolve personnel disputes. Like a mediator, an ombudsman functions as a sort of "go-between" between the aggrieved employee and the company (and/or the employee's managers or supervisors). Also like a mediator, the ombudsman does not have independent authority to impose a resolution of the dispute, but attempts to find a "middle ground" on which everyone can agree. As the following cases illustrate, there is some tension between the ombudsman's ostensible role as a neutral and the ombudsman's status as an employee of the employer.

KIENTZY v. McDONNELL DOUGLAS CORP.

United States District Court, E.D. Missouri, 1991.
133 F.R.D. 570.

DAVID D. NOCE, United States Magistrate Judge.

This action is before the Court upon the motion of Therese Clemente for an order, under Federal Rule of Civil Procedure 26(c)(1), protecting from pretrial discovery, by both plaintiff and defendant, the communications she received in her position as a company ombudsman of defendant McDonnell Douglas Corporation ("MDC"). * * *

Plaintiff Mary Kientzy alleges in this action that MDC terminated her from employment as a security officer on account of her gender, in violation of Title VII of the Civil Rights Act of 1964, 42 U.S.C. § 2000e et seq., and the Missouri Human Rights Act, § 213.055 R.S.Mo. (1986). * * *

Plaintiff has noticed Therese Clemente for deposition * * *. The purpose of the ombudsman program and office is to mediate, in a strictly confidential environment, disputes between MDC employees and between employees and management.

Plaintiff Kientzy was terminated from employment in August, 1988, following the decision of a company disciplinary committee. After the disciplinary committee made its decision, plaintiff went to Ms. Clemente in her position as ombudsman; MDC nevertheless terminated her. Plaintiff argues that Ms. Clemente received information about plaintiff's situation from company employees, including a member of the disciplinary committee who has since died.

Plaintiff argues that the information received by Clemente is relevant to the trial of the action and is discoverable, on two grounds. First, she argues that the statements made to Clemente by defendant's personnel may evidence discriminatory animus in the decision to terminate her. Second, she argues that the ombudsman program is a company procedure for appealing her dismissal and that the ombudsman thus participated in the final decision to terminate her. For the reasons set forth below, the Court agrees with movant that the confidential communications made to her are protected from disclosure by Federal Rule of Evidence 501.

Rule 501 requires that this Court assay the ombudsman's claim of privilege by interpreting the principles of the common law "in light of reason and experience." Four cardinal factors have been discerned for this purpose:

> (1) the communication must be one made in the belief that it will not be disclosed; (2) confidentiality must be essential to the maintenance of the relationship between the parties; (3) the relationship should be one that society considers worthy of being fostered; and (4) the injury to the relationship incurred by disclosure

must be greater than the benefit gained in the correct disposal of litigation.

In re Doe, 711 F.2d 1187, 1193 (2d Cir. 1983); *Mattson v. Cuyuna Ore Co.*, 178 F. Supp. 653, 654 n. 2 (D.Minn.1959). Each of these four factors is present in this case.

First, ombudsman Clemente received the subject communications in the belief that they would be kept confidential. The [defendant's] ombudsman office is constituted as an independent and neutral entity. It has no authority to make company policy. Its head has the position of company vice-president, independent of the company's human resources and personnel offices. The office has direct access to the company president. Ombudsman Clemente is bound by the Code of Ethics of the Corporate Ombudsman Association, which provides for the confidentiality of communications. The office has adopted procedures to assure such confidentiality. The [Company] Ombudsman Office has given its strict pledge of confidentiality to all employees and to the company. All new employees are so advised and defendant has repeatedly restated to its employees that they may rely on the confidentiality of the ombudsman's office. Since it opened in 1985, the * * * ombudsman's office has received approximately 4800 communications. Defendant has sought, but has been refused, access to the ombudsman's files and records regarding plaintiff. The company has indicated it will not request them in the future.

Second, confidentiality of communications is essential to relationships between the ombudsman's office and defendant's employees and defendant's management. The function of the * * * ombudsman's office is to receive communications and to remedy workplace problems, in a strictly confidential atmosphere. Without this confidentiality, the office would be just one more non-confidential opportunity for employees to air disputes. The ombudsman's office provides an opportunity for complete disclosure, without the specter of retaliation, that does not exist in the other available, non-confidential grievance and complaint procedures.

Third, the relationship between the ombudsman office and defendant's employees and management is worthy of societal support. The Court takes judicial notice of the fact that MDC * * * [is] a very large federal government contractor[] in the aircraft, space, and other industries. It is important that [its] employees have an opportunity to make confidential statements and to receive confidential guidance, information, and aid to remedy workplace problems to, [sic] benefit themselves and possibly the nation. This is true in spite of the possibility that such actions may be perceived by an employee to be against company or fellow employees' interests.

Fourth, the harm caused by a disruption of the confidential relationship between the ombudsman's office and others in plaintiff's case would be greater than the benefit to plaintiff by disclosure. A successful ombudsman program resolves many problems informally and more quickly than other more formal procedures, including court actions. A court order that Clemente disclose the information communicated to her in confidence, or that her informants disclose what they told her in confidence about plaintiff, would destroy the reputation and principle of confidentiality that the * * * ombudsman program and office now enjoys and needs to perform its function. The utility of that program and office, in resolving disputes in this workplace and thus diminishing the need for more formal resolution procedures, is founded on the confidentiality of its communications to and from company officials and employees. * * * The societal benefit from this confidentiality is paramount to plaintiff's need for disclosure.

* * *

For the reasons set forth above,

IT IS HEREBY ORDERED that the motion of Theresa Clemente for a protective order is sustained.

CARMAN v. McDONNELL DOUGLAS CORP.
United States Court of Appeals, Eighth Circuit, 1997.
114 F.3d 790.

RICHARD S. ARNOLD, CHIEF JUDGE

In October 1992, McDonnell Douglas Aircraft Corporation laid off Frank Carman as part of a reduction in force of its management staff. Carman then sued McDonnell Douglas, claiming that his termination violated the Age Discrimination in Employment Act, the Missouri Human Rights Act, and the Employee Retirement Income Security Act of 1974. In the course of discovery, the District Court denied Carman's request for the production of certain documents, holding that they were protected by the "Ombudsman Privilege." The District Court later granted summary judgment to McDonnell Douglas, a decision which Carman now appeals. Because we hold that the District Court lacked sufficient justification for creating an ombudsman privilege and denying Carman's discovery request, we reverse and remand. * * *

III.

We now turn to the issue of the "ombudsman privilege." In the context of this case, the term "ombudsman" refers to an employee outside of the corporate chain of command whose job is to investigate and mediate workplace disputes. The corporate ombudsman is paid by the corporation and lacks the structural independence that characterizes government ombudsmen in some countries and states, where the office of ombudsman is a separate branch of government that handles disputes between citizens and government agencies. Nonetheless, the corporate ombudsman purports to be an independent and neutral party who promises strict confidentiality to all employees and is bound by the Code of Ethics of the Corporate Ombudsman Association, which requires the ombudsman to keep communications confidential. McDonnell Douglas argues for recognition of an evidentiary privilege that would protect corporate ombudsmen from having to disclose relevant employee communications to civil litigants.

Federal Rule of Evidence 501 states that federal courts should recognize evidentiary privileges according to "the principles of the common law" interpreted "in the light of reason and experience." The beginning of any analysis under Rule 501 is the principle that "the public has a right to every man's evidence." Hardwicke, L.C.J., quoted in 12 *Cobbett's Parliamentary History* 675, 693 (1742) (quoted with approval in *United States v. Bryan,* 339 U.S. 323, 331, 70 S.Ct. 724, 730, 94 L.Ed. 884 (1950)). Accordingly, evidentiary privileges "are not lightly created." *United States v. Nixon,* 418 U.S. 683, 710, 94 S.Ct. 3090, 3108, 41 L.Ed.2d 1039 (1974). A party that seeks the creation of a new evidentiary privilege must overcome the significant burden of establishing that "permitting a refusal to testify or excluding relevant evidence has a public good transcending the normally predominant principle of utilizing all rational means for ascertaining truth." *Trammel v. United States,* 445 U.S. 40, 50, 100 S.Ct. 906, 912, 63 L.Ed.2d 186 (1980) (quoting *Elkins v. United States,* 364 U.S. 206, 234, 80 S.Ct. 1437, 1454, 4 L.Ed.2d 1669 (1960) (Frankfurter, J., dissenting)).

The first important factor for assessing a proposed new evidentiary privilege is the importance of the relationship that the privilege will foster. The defendant argues that ombudsmen help resolve workplace disputes prior to the commencement of expensive and time-consuming litigation. We agree that fair and efficient alternative dispute resolution techniques benefit society and are worthy of encouragement. To the extent that corporate ombudsmen successfully resolve disputes in a fair and efficient manner, they are a welcome and helpful addition to a society that is weary of lawsuits.

Nonetheless, far more is required to justify the creation of a new evidentiary privilege. First, McDonnell Douglas has failed to present any evidence, and indeed has not even argued, that the ombudsman method is more successful at resolving workplace disputes than other forms of alternative dispute resolution, nor has it even pointed to any evidence establishing that its own ombudsman is especially successful at resolving workplace disputes prior to the commencement of litigation. In recognizing a privilege for the McDonnell Douglas ombudsman's office in 1991, the court in *Kientzy v. McDonnell Douglas Corp.,* 133 F.R.D. 570, 572 (E.D.Mo.1991), found that the office had received approximately 4,800 communications since 1985, but neither the court nor McDonnell Douglas in the present case provides us with any context to evaluate the significance of this statistic.

Second, McDonnell Douglas has failed to make a compelling argument that most of the advantages afforded by the ombudsman method would be lost without the privilege. Even without a privilege, corporate ombudsmen still have much to offer employees in the way of confidentiality, for they are still able to promise to keep employee communications confidential from management. Indeed, when an aggrieved employee or an employee-witness is deciding whether or not to confide in a company ombudsman, his greatest concern is not likely to be that the statement will someday be revealed in civil discovery. More likely, the employee will fear that the ombudsman is biased in favor of the company, and that the ombudsman will tell management everything that the employee says. The denial of an ombudsman privilege will not affect the ombudsman's ability to convince an employee that the ombudsman is neutral, and creation of an ombudsman privilege will not help alleviate the fear that she is not.

We are especially unconvinced that "no present or future [McDonnell Douglas] employee could feel comfortable in airing his or her disputes with the Ombudsman because of the specter of discovery." An employee either will or will not have a meritorious complaint. If he does not and is aware that he does not, he is no more likely to share the frivolousness of his complaint with a company ombudsman than he is with a court. If he has a meritorious complaint that he would prefer not to litigate, then he will generally feel that he has nothing to hide and will be undeterred by the prospect of civil discovery from sharing the nature of his complaint with the ombudsman. The dim prospect that the employee's complaint might someday surface in an unrelated case strikes us as an unlikely deterrent. Again, it is the perception that the ombudsman is the company's investigator, a fear that does not depend upon the prospect of civil discovery, that is most likely to keep such an employee from speaking openly.

McDonnell Douglas also argues that failure to recognize an ombudsman privilege will disrupt the relationship between management and the ombudsman's office. In cases where management has nothing to hide, this is unlikely. It is probably true that management will be less likely to share damaging information with an ombudsman if there is no privilege. Nonetheless, McDonnell Douglas has provided no reason to believe that management is especially eager to confess wrongdoing to ombudsmen when a privilege exists, or that ombudsmen are helpful at resolving disputes that involve violations of the law by management or supervisors. If the chilling of management-ombudsman communications occurs only in cases that would not have been resolved at the ombudsman stage anyway, then there is no reason to recognize an ombudsman privilege.

IV.

We disagree with the District Court's holding that employee communications to Therese Clemente were protected from discovery by an ombudsman privilege. The judgment is reversed, and the cause remanded for further proceedings consistent with this opinion. * * *

It is so ordered.

Notes and Questions

1. Because Missouri is in the Eighth Circuit, *Carman* effectively overruled *Kientzy*. Which opinion do you find more persuasive?

The *Carman* court refused to extend a privilege to ombudsmen in part because the employer in that case could not show the superiority of the ombudsman process to other forms of ADR. But doesn't the efficacy of an ombudsman depend on confidentiality, without which employees may not be candid with an ombudsman? For further discussion of the confidentiality issue, see Christina M. Kuta, Comment, *Universities, Corporations, and States Use Them–Now It's Time to Protect Them: An Analysis of the Public and Private Sector Ombudsman and the Continued Need for a Privileged Relationship*, 27 Southern Illinois University Law Journal 389, 404 (2003);William L. Kandel and Sheri L. Frumer, *The Corporate Ombudsman and Employment Law: Maintaining the Confidentiality of Communications*, 19 Employee Relations Law Journal 587 (1994). See also Solorzano v. Shell Chemical Co., 2000 WL 1145766 (E.D.La. Aug. 14, 2000) (finding no need to recognize federal common law privilege for ombudsmen because a narrowly-drawn protective order would suffice to accommodate the need for confidentiality); Coles v. Perry, 217 F.R.D. 1, 8 (D.C.D.C.2003) (applying Federal Rule of Evidence 408, which bars admission of conduct or statements made during compromise negotiations when offered to prove liability, in granting defendant's motion to exclude discussions between plaintiff and defendant's equal employment opportunity officer). For a review of the limited empirical literature regarding ombudsmen, see Lisa B. Bingham, *Employment Dispute Resolution: The Case for Mediation*, ___ Conflict Resolution Quarterly ___ (forthcoming Fall 2004).

2. Many employees in company personnel departments spend much of their time investigating allegations of employee misconduct. No doubt their investigations would be more effective if they could guarantee confidentiality to employees who gave them information. Could these investigations be privileged under Rule 501? Why or why not? Should courts allow these investigations to be privileged?

3. If an employee's statements to an ombudsman were privileged, would employees nonetheless likely be reticent to disclose information to the ombudsman? If so, under what circumstances?

4. Are ombudsmen supposed to be neutral in a dispute between an employee and a supervisor? Between an employee and the company? See Karl A. Slaikeu and Ralph H. Hasson, Controlling the Costs of Conflict 55 (1999) (answering both questions affirmatively). *Can* ombudsmen be neutral in the latter situation? Are ombudsmen really supposed to be independent, or are they merely functionaries of the employer? Are they really Personnel Department employees with a neutral veneer?

5. When an employee is sexually harassed by a co-worker, the employer is liable only for the actionable sexual harassment of which it knew or should have known. If an employee informs a company ombudsman that she has been sexually harassed, may the ombudsman's knowledge of the claim be imputed to the company? What if the employee requests that the ombudsman keep the entire matter confidential? If you were the ombudsman in this situation, what would you do?

6. How effective would you expect ombudsmen to be at resolving workplace disputes? Are there certain types of disputes that you would expect ombudsmen to be better at resolving than others? What powers

should ombudsmen have? If they disagree with a personnel decision by an employer, what, if anything, should they do?

7.   Given a choice between an open door policy or an ombudsman, which do you believe most employees would prefer? Why?

8.   The American Bar Association's sections on Administrative Law and Regulatory Practice and on Dispute Resolution have developed Standards for the Establishment and Operation of the Ombudsman Offices. The Standards emphasize independence, impartiality, and confidentiality. See 54 Admin. L. Rev. 535 and 543 (2002).

C. PEER REVIEW SYSTEMS

Peer review systems shift some personnel decisions from the company to the aggrieved employee's peers. The peer review "hearing" usually has the appearance of an adjudication: the grieving employee tells his or her side of the story and presents witnesses, the company tells its side of the story and presents witnesses, and the peer review panel, functioning as judge or jury or both, renders a decision. Employees often perceive peer review systems as a fair way of making personnel decisions. Employers often like peer review systems because it makes it less likely that employees will "blame" the employer for discharge decisions. Anecdotal evidence indicates that peer review panels are likely to deal more strictly with employees than personnel departments would.

Because there are few legal restrictions on peer review systems, the systems vary widely. The panel may be chosen randomly or from a specified pool of selected or trained employees. The panel may be restricted to employees in the aggrieved employee's work group or department, or may be chosen company-wide. The panel may or may not have authority to hear a wide range of employee grievances. The panel's decisions may be binding or merely advisory on the company.

One legal restriction on peer review systems is § 8(a)(2) of the National Labor Relations Act. This section forbids employers from dominating labor organizations. Although § 2(5) of the NLRA generally defines "labor organization" extremely broadly, the term is limited in the sense that it applies only to organizations that "deal[ ] with" the employer. To protect legitimate labor organizations from company unions, an employer may "deal with" a labor organization only if employees have designated the organization to be their exclusive bargaining representative. In Keeler Brass Automotive Group, 317 NLRB 1110 (1995), the National Labor Relations Board held that an employer-sponsored grievance committee violated the NLRA because it did not have full decisional authority over the grievances it heard; in practice, the committee would make a recommendation to management, management would respond with a counterproposal, and the committee and company would continue "back and forth explaining themselves until an acceptable result was achieved." Cf. Sparks Nugget, Inc., 230 NLRB 275 (1977), *enforcement granted in part and denied in part, sub nom. NLRB*

v. Silver Spur Casino, 623 F.2d 571 (9th Cir.1980) (grievance committee did not deal with employer, and consequently did not violate NLRA, because committee's decision on grievances was final).

BERNHOLC v. KITAIN
Supreme Court, Nassau County, New York, 2000.
186 Misc.2d 697, 720 N.Y.S.2d 737.

ANTHONY L. PARGA, J.

Motion by the defendants for an order, pursuant to 22 NYCRR § 216.1 and CPLR 3103(a), sealing the court record relating to this action and prohibiting the plaintiff from disclosing to any third party the information relating to the internal peer review proceedings and Quality Management activities conducted by defendants, is denied in its entirety and consequently the temporary restraining order is vacated.

The application at bar is apparently one of first impression. Reported cases granting a protective order concerning the subject documents have arisen in the context of medical malpractice actions and not in cases such as the one at bar, which is primarily an action sounding in defamation and breach of contract.

This action arises out of the defendants' imposition of monitoring procedures on the plaintiff, a physician, after an incident which occurred on March 8, 2000, in the defendant Hospital's operating room while the plaintiff was the attending anesthesiologist. The plaintiff did not appear for a hearing held on July 10, 2000, as part of the Hospital's peer review process. The plaintiff's refusal to comply with the conditions imposed on him was deemed by the defendants to be a resignation by the plaintiff of his position with the Hospital's Department of Anesthesiology. Shortly thereafter plaintiff commenced his lawsuit, seeking monetary damages from the eight causes of action he has alleged. The defendants then obtained *ex parte* a temporary restraining order (Roberto, J.) sealing the record in this action and prohibiting the plaintiff from disclosing to third parties information relating to the peer review process. With the seal in place, the defendants subsequently moved to dismiss the complaint and have purportedly annexed confidential materials from the hearing in support of their motion.

The defendants argue that the integrity of the peer review process would best be preserved if these records were not made accessible to the public since (a) state and federal statutes (*see,* Public Health Law 2805–m(2); Education Law § 6527; 42 U.S.C. § 11137[b]) mandate that the peer review process be kept confidential and not disclosed to the public, and (b) since the defendants need to rely on evidence adduced by the peer review process in order to defend themselves. They further contend that future investigations into issues relating to the physician's professional conduct would be compromised, as well as the confidentiality of records related to the individual patient.

The law has always favored the public's right of access to court proceedings and to inspect and copy judicial documents * * *. In response to concern that the practice of sealing records of settlements in tort actions would prevent consumers from learning about, for example, potential defects in products, New York promulgated Rule 216.1[a] of the Uniform Rules for the New York State Trial Courts (22 NYCRR) to require the courts to take into account the public's interest and exercise their discretion in overriding the parties' wishes to seal the records * * *. The rule provides that "[e]xcept where otherwise provided by statute or rule, a court shall not enter an order in any action or proceeding sealing the court records, whether in whole or in part, except upon a written finding of good cause, which shall specify the grounds thereof. In determining whether good cause has been shown, the court shall consider the interests of the public as well as the parties." (22 NYCRR 216.1[a]). "[G]ood cause" requires a legitimate or sound basis to justify the sealing of court documents (*Danco Laboratories, Ltd. v. Chemical Works of Gedeon Richter, Ltd., supra* at 8, 711 N.Y.S.2d 419; *Matter of Conservatorship of Ethel Brownstone,* 191 A.D.2d 167, 594 N.Y.S.2d 31).

In applying these principles to the motion at bar, the Court finds that the defendants failed to sufficiently establish good cause to seal this court record. The blanket protection sought by the defendants is not justified since plaintiff's eight causes of action (e.g., defamation, intentional infliction of emotional distress, breach of contract, breach of the medical staff's by-laws, etc.) extend beyond an examination of defendant's confidential professional review process. The purpose of Education Law § 6527 and Public Health Law § 2805–m is to promote the quality of hospital and medical care through self-review without fear of reprisal by guaranteeing confidentiality to those persons performing the review function * * *. These statutes were "not intended, however, to extend protection to persons whose conduct is subject to review" (van-Bergen v. Long Beach Med. Center, [277 A.D.2d 374], 374–375, 717 N.Y.S.2d 191; *see, Bryant v. Bui,* 265 A.D.2d 848, 849, 695 N.Y.S.2d 790). This includes defendant Kitain as well as the plaintiff, who chose not to appear at a peer review hearing, even though the cloak of confidentiality might inure to his benefit. This is not a medical malpractice action, and this plaintiff is not attempting "to circumvent the confidentiality provisions of Education Law § 6527(3) and article 28 of the Public Health Law" (*Logue v. Velez,* 677 N.Y.S.2d 6, 699 N.E.2d 365). The gravamen of plaintiff's complaint reveals a bitter dispute between an employer and a ten year physician/employee at one of the major medical centers in this country, and the public (if not the patient involved in the incident) has a right to know what purportedly transpired between these parties and led to the disintegration of the parties' employment relationship and the damages allegedly sustained by the plaintiff.

The denial of defendants' motion does not preclude a future application by either of the parties during the discovery phase of this litigation for a protective order concerning the defendants' peer review/quality assurance file surrounding the subject incident.

Notes and Questions

1. Peer review committees are commonly used by hospitals to help physicians identify and correct mistakes, and by higher education to make tenure decisions. See, e.g., Bredice v. Doctors Hospital, Inc., 50 F.R.D. 249 (D.D.C.1970), aff'd without opin., 479 F.2d 920 (D.C.Cir.1973) (recognizing the self-critical or self-evaluative privilege in the context of a hospital peer review conference on the care and treatment of patients); University of Pennsylvania v. EEOC, 493 U.S. 182, 110 S.Ct. 577, 107 L.Ed.2d 571 (1990) (holding that neither common law privilege nor First Amendment freedom of speech shield peer review materials from subpoena in discrimination suit). Are employment peer review committees analogous to hospital and university peer review committees? Why or why not?

2. An employee complains to the company's personnel department that her supervisor is sexually harassing her. The personnel department investigates the allegation, determines it to be accurate, and fires the supervisor. The supervisor appeals his firing through the company's peer review process. The peer review panel disagrees with the personnel department's findings and orders reinstatement. What should the company do?

3. Is there a risk that peer review panels will tend to perpetuate the stereotypes and discrimination that many employment statutes were designed to eliminate? What if, for example, the aggrieved employee in note 2 was the first female employee the company had ever hired to work in its small-engine maintenance department?

4. What are the benefits and drawbacks to peer review from an employee's perspective? From upper management's perspective? From the perspective of a front-line supervisor? From the perspective of an employee in the company's Personnel Department?

5. If you were designing a peer review system, what method would you use to determine who sits on the panel for a given grievance? Is it advisable for nonmanagement employees to hear a management employee's grievance, and vice versa? Would you allow grievants to cross-examine witnesses? For further discussion of procedural issues that often arise under peer review systems, see Cynthia F. Cohen, *Justice and Peer Review Systems: A Framework for Analysis*, 28 Journal of Collective Negotiations 83 (1999).

6. As discussed in the text preceding the *Bernholc* case, the purpose of Section 8(a)(2) of the NLRA is to prevent employers from imposing company unions on employees. Notwithstanding the balance struck by *Keeler Brass* and *Sparks Nugget*, a recent study shows that one of the prime motives for employers to institute peer-review systems is union avoidance. See Alexander J.S. Colvin, *Institutional Pressures, Human Resource Strategies, and the Rise of Nonunion Dispute Resolution Procedures*, 56 Industrial and Labor Relations Review 375 (2003).

7. Might another motivation for peer review systems be to deter litigation? If the peer review panel finds for the employee, the employer can quickly re-instate the employee to minimize damages. If the panel finds for

the employer, the employee likely will have a difficult time finding an attorney. Why might this be so?

8.   One company, Farmers Insurance Group, has created a variation on the theme of peer review committees. Employees are contractually entitled to have discharge decisions reviewed by a "termination review board." The termination review board is composed of (1) an agent of Farmers selected by the discharged employee, (2) the Farmers regional manager, and (3) a third party mutually selected by the other two parties. The recommendations of the board are not binding. In Saeta v. Superior Court, 117 Cal.App.4th 261, 11 Cal.Rptr.3d 610 (2 Dist. 2004), the third board member was a retired judge. The board found that the plaintiff's discharge was justified. The plaintiff then sued Farmers, and sought to depose the retired judge. The retired judge objected, but the plaintiff filed a motion to compel, which the trial court granted. The retired judge then filed a mandamus petition to block the deposition. The appellate court, however, found that because the review board proceeding was "neither an arbitration nor a mediation," the evidentiary privileges applicable to those procedures did not apply. The court therefore denied the retired judge's mandamus petition, and permitted the plaintiff to depose him.

D.   EARLY NEUTRAL EVALUATION

Early neutral evaluation (ENE) is the process by which a neutral evaluator, chosen jointly by the aggrieved employee and the company, renders a nonbinding advisory opinion concerning the merits of the case. It is usually preceded by an informal "hearing" at which the parties present their arguments and evidence (or summaries of evidence). The purpose is to narrow the issues and to help the parties understand the strengths and weaknesses of their (and their opponent's) case. ENE often is most useful when one or both parties have unrealistically assessed the merits or settlement value of their case.

A typical ENE session opens with the evaluator making a short opening statement which explains the purposes of the program and the procedure to be followed. After the evaluator's opening statement, the plaintiff presents a summary of his or her case. This summary may include the presentation of documents. It also includes an explanation of the legal theories of the case. After the plaintiff's presentation, the defense makes a similar presentation. During the presentations, the evaluator may ask questions, but typically the presentations may not be interrupted by the other side.

After the parties have completed their respective presentations, the evaluator identifies the issues on which the parties agree and may encourage the parties to stipulate to those issues. Next, the evaluator, with the assistance of the parties, identifies the specific areas of dispute.

After the parties and the evaluator have agreed to the issues, the evaluator moves to another room to prepare a case evaluation. This case evaluation is th evaluator's assessment of the strengths and weaknesses of each party's case, together with facts to support the evaluator's assessment. The assessment also sets forth the evaluator's opinion as to which party will prevail on the merits and why. The assessment may estimate the damages, if any, that the evaluator believes may be awarded.

After the evaluator has completed the written assessment is complete, the evaluator rejoins the parties. Without disclosing the case evaluation, the evaluator asks the parties if they are willing to discuss settlement. Frequently, the experience of having heard the other party's presentation of its case creates a strong motivation to settle. If both parties are willing to discuss settlement, then settlement discussions begin, with the evaluator functioning as a mediator. If either party willing to discuss settlement, however, the evaluator then presents the case evaluation to the parties.

Notes and Questions

1. It is unclear whether, and if so to what extent, ENE aids settlement and reduces the costs of dispute resolution. Compare David I. Levine, *Northern District of California Adopts Early Neutral Evaluation to Expedite Dispute Resolution*, 72 Judicature 235 (1989) (finding significant benefits from use of ENE) with James S. Kakalik, Terence Dunworth, Laural A. Hill, Daniel McCaffrey, Marian Oshiro, Nicholas M. Pace, and Mary E. Vaiana, *Just, Speedy, and Inexpensive? An Evaluation of Judicial Case Management Under the Civil Justice Reform Act*, Rand MR–800–ICJ [http://www.rand.org/publications/MR/MR800/] (1996) (finding that ENE had no discernable effect on time to disposition, litigation costs, or attorney views of fairness or satisfaction with case management).

2. ENE usually occurs shortly after a lawsuit has been filed, though it occasionally is used beforehand. Are employers or the employees in the best position, during the early phases of litigation, to present their best possible case in an ENE proceeding? Assuming that some discovery will occur before the ENE proceeding, what discovery is likely to be most important to employers? To employees?

3. How is the role of an ENE evaluator different from the role of a mediator? As an attorney representing a party in an employment lawsuit, would you look for different qualities in an ENE evaluator than you would in a mediator? What are the advantages and disadvantages of ENE as compared to mediation? Would it be advisable to use both ENE and mediation in the same case? To use the same person as both the ENE evaluator and the mediator?

Would your answers be the same if you were comparing ENE to arbitration?

4. What kinds of feedback from the ENE neutral are likely to be most useful to the parties? What kinds of feedback are most likely to foster settlement?

5. Why does the ENE evaluator only discuss the case assessment with the parties after the parties have rejected settlement discussions? Why might a party reject settlement discussions following an ENE session?

E. MULTISTEP APPROACHES

DRAFTING ADR PROGRAMS: MANAGEMENT–INTEGRATED CONFLICT MANAGEMENT SYSTEMS

James N. Adler.

in How ADR Works 794–95 (Norman Brand, ed., 2002).

In light of the expense, frequent delays, and often unpredictable decisions in court, I believe employers should consider developing an ADR system tailored to their own culture, employment environment, and needs. Surely, most employers can devise a fairer, faster, more user-friendly, less expensive and more effective way to resolve employee disputes than the present judicial system. Many employers, moreover, have accepted this challenge, developing a variety of ADR procedures that better serve the interests of both the employer and its employees. * * *

One of the most innovative and comprehensive programs has been implemented by Brown & Root, Inc. (now part of Halliburton Company), which developed an elaborate predispute grievance and arbitration system applicable to all of its employees nationwide. Although the final step in the Brown & Root procedure is binding, neutral arbitration, the company has trained many of its employees to be mediators and attempts through its program to encourage early resolution through direct negotiation and mediation. Most unusually, Brown & Root will pay 80 percent of any employee's attorneys' fees up to a maximum of $2,500. As a result, employees have been able to select and secure more effective legal counsel, and most cases have been settled expeditiously. After a number of years' experience with its program, Brown & Root has found employee satisfaction high and the company's costs of resolving employee claims substantially reduced.

A different approach was chosen by TRW Space & Electronics Group, which was concerned about the effect on employee morale if it required employees to agree to an arbitration forum, thus precluding any resort to the court system. TRW's solution was to implement a system of mandatory but nonbinding, arbitration. Under this program, all employee claims that cannot be settled must be arbitrated as a precondition to filing a lawsuit. If the employee accepts an arbitrator's decision, TRW has agreed in advance to accept it as well. If the employee rejects the arbitrator's decision, the employee is free to proceed in court.

Yet another approach was employed by Rockwell International Corp. Motivated largely by legal fees of over $1 million and the substantial time required of its executives to successfully defend a single wrongful termination lawsuit, Rockwell instituted a program of binding arbitration. Although agreement to the arbitration procedures was voluntary, only those employees agreeing to the program would remain eligible for certain stock options. Some employers that have not wanted to require all existing employees to forego judicial remedies in favor of arbitration have treated the arbitration procedures as a benefit that existing employees could select through an opt-in or opt-out mechanism. Some companies, for example, have instituted dispute settlement procedures leading to binding arbitration for resolution of all employee disputes, but have permitted existing employees to opt-out of these procedures if they did so within a certain period after the procedures were promulgated.

Most employers who have addressed these issues, however, have taken a more traditional approach and have required, through employee handbooks or otherwise, that all employees agree to binding, neutral arbitration or employee disputes as a condition of employment or of continued employment.

Notes and Questions

1. Halliburton's Dispute Resolution Program consists of four steps. First, an open-door policy encourages employees to go up the chain of command to resolve a dispute. The company guarantees that it will not retaliate against employees for doing so, and the company has an extensive training session on mediation to help front-line supervisors resolve disputes. Second, an employee may initiate a Conference, in which the employee and a company representative confer with an internal mediator to try to resolve the dispute. The third step is mediation, with a mediator selected by an outside organization such as AAA. Both mediation and the fourth step, binding arbitration, are available only for the resolution of legal disputes. Both Halliburton and the employee participate equally in the selection of the arbitrator. The employee pays a "$50 processing fee," and Halliburton pays for the remainder of the mediator's and/or arbitrator's fees. See Richard A. Bales, Compulsory Arbitration: The Grand Experiment in Employment 102–14 (1997).

2. Evaluate the strengths and weaknesses of the dispute resolution programs described above from the following perspectives: a rank-and-file employee, an on-the-line supervisor, a human resources director, a stockholder. Are employees better off with each program than they would be without them? Are there any respects in which they are disadvantaged by the program? Is this approach a realistic option for most companies? Why or why not?

3. Why would Halliburton offer to pay the legal expenses of employees who claim that Halliburton violated a legally protected right? Why does Halliburton limit outside mediation and arbitration to claims based on legally protected rights?

4. A Halliburton employee seeks advice from you, an attorney, on an employment dispute. The employee has not yet attempted to resolve the dispute through the company's Dispute Resolution Program. What do you advise, given the open-door policy? What questions should you ask before deciding what advice to give? What role, if any, should you play in attempting to resolve the dispute at this point? What would you do if the dispute concerns an allegation of employment discrimination, the time for filing a discrimination charge with the Equal Employment Opportunity Commission is about to expire, and the employee has not yet attempted to use the open-

door policy? What if the policy did not contain an anti-retaliation clause, and the employee fears retaliation?

5. Why would a company adopt an approach like that of TRW? What is the point of institutionalizing an ADR program if the employee can just sue anyway? Why is it that relatively few employers (Rockwell International excepted) give employees a choice about whether to sign a predispute arbitration agreement?

Appendix A

RESEARCHING LABOR ARBITRATION AND ALTERNATIVE DISPUTE RESOLUTION IN EMPLOYMENT

Suzanne Thorpe and Laura J. Cooper*

Introduction
Bibliographies
Major Texts
Arbitration Awards
Information About Dispute Resolution Professionals
Procedural and Ethical Rules
Other Resources on Workplace Dispute Resolution
> Books
> Periodicals
> Web Sites

Introduction

What kinds of information can we expect to find when doing research in alternative dispute resolution? To the extent that ordinary issues of law arise when considering methods of alternative dispute resolution, such as whether an agreement to arbitrate is judicially enforceable or whether communications in the course of mediation enjoy an evidentiary privilege, ordinary sources of legal research remain appropriate. This research guide generally does not describe those research tools.

Much of what goes on within mediation or arbitration is, however, beyond the immediate reach of traditional legal doctrines and processes

* Suzanne Thorpe is the Associate Director for Faculty, Research and Instructional Services at the University of Minnesota Law School Library. Laura J. Cooper is the J. Stewart & Mario Thomas McClendon Professor in Law and Alternative Dispute Resolution at the University of Minnesota Law School. An earlier version of this research guide was published at 91 Law Library Journal 367 (1999).

of enforcement. The legal system affords arbitrators and mediators a broad range of discretion untouched by legal controls. The question is often not a matter of what the neutral may legally do, but rather what the neutral might or should do.

Consider, for example, the concept of precedent and its role in legal research. Appellate court decisions establish a body of precedent binding on lower courts whose decisions are subject to judicial review by those appellate courts. In arguing a case to a lower court, it is therefore critical to locate the decisions of appropriate appellate courts that would be binding on that lower court. Within a system of labor arbitration, however, arbitrator awards generally are not subject to judicial review on the merits. The decisions of a court, or even of another arbitrator, will not have the force of precedent. An advocate in a labor arbitration forum, therefore, is not looking for decisions that would constitute precedent in the pending arbitration proceeding, but rather for decisions that might have persuasive authority because of their analytical power.

The ability to conduct research regarding disputes resolved in alternative forums is also limited by party privacy. While courts and their decisions are open to the public, mediation and arbitration nearly always occur in private. Privacy often is one of the reasons the parties have selected mediation or arbitration. Research sources, therefore, cannot possibly provide comprehensive access to the decisions of arbitrators or the outcomes of mediated settlements. For example, arbitration awards are only published if all of the parties to the arbitration have authorized publication. Some labor arbitrators request permission from the parties in all of the cases they decide; some never do.

As compared to the tools used in a traditional legal context, research tools in alternative dispute resolution are thus likely to be much less complete and their use is much less likely to be critical to the resolution of the dispute.

This guide lists sources that discuss arbitration and other means of employment dispute resolution in unionized and nonunionized settings. After identifying comprehensive bibliographies on these topics, the guide presents texts that dispute resolution practitioners consider to be essential reference tools. Sources that contain arbitration awards, sources that provide information about alternative dispute resolution professionals, and texts of procedure and ethics rules follow next. The last portion of the guide covers other texts, periodicals, and Web sites that offer additional commentary on arbitration, mediation, and other types of employment dispute resolution. Both hardcopy and electronic works are listed. In the interest of currency, with few exceptions, only monographs that have appeared since 1990 are included.

Bibliographies

"Annual Bibliography Issue," *Ohio State Journal on Dispute Resolution*.

Starting in 1992, the last issue of each volume of this journal is an extensive bibliography of articles and books related to dispute resolution published during the preceding year. Works are listed alphabetically by author. Each entry provides a brief description of the work followed by subject classification numbers. Works covering labor and employment dispute resolution are classified under "93–labor general," "94–labor-discrimination," "95–labor–management (union)," "96–labor-employment (non-union)." A table lists works alphabetically by author under each classification number.

Coleman, Charles J., Theodora T. Haynes, and Marie T. Gibson McGraw, *Labor and Employment Arbitration: An Annotated Bibliography, 1991–1996*. Ithaca, N.Y.: ILR Press, 1997.

This bibliography updates and expands on the 1994 work described in the next entry. It provides almost 600 short summaries of books and articles covering most aspects of American and Canadian labor arbitration and general employment dispute resolution. The bibliography is arranged into seventeen broad format (e.g., general studies, biographies) and topical categories that are further subdivided by more specific topics. Author and subject indexes also are included. This book updates labor arbitration materials published since *Labor Arbitration: An Annotated Bibliography*, noted immediately below, and includes employment arbitration publications since 1991.

Coleman, Charles J. and Theodora T. Haynes, eds., *Labor Arbitration: An Annotated Bibliography*. Ithaca, N.Y.: ILR Press, 1994.

This work provides commentary about more than 1,000 works that cover American and Canadian labor arbitration. Included are monographs published since 1950, articles published in nonlegal journals since 1970, and articles published in law journals since 1980. The work is arranged in two parts: books and monographs followed by periodicals and proceedings. Both parts are subdivided under the following headings: arbitration and dispute settlement; arbitrator characteristics; development of arbitration; grievances and grievance mediation; advocacy; arbitrability, management rights, past practice; discipline and discharge; compensation, work rules, remedies; arbitration and the law; interest arbitration; nonunion employees and wrongful discharge; and arbitration in specific industries.

Hinchcliff, Carole L., *Dispute Resolution: A Selected Bibliography, 1987–1988*. Washington, D.C.: American Bar Association, 1991.

This annotated bibliography lists articles and books published from 1987 to 1988 in alphabetical order by author. A classified list of subjects and subject index is included. The entry for each work indicates which of these subject(s) is relevant. This bibliography is continued through annual bibliographies in the *Ohio State Journal of Dispute Resolution*.

Major Texts

Alternative Dispute Resolution of Employment Disputes

Brand, Norman, ed., *How ADR Works*. Washington, D.C.: Bureau of National Affairs, 2002.

Despite its title suggesting an even broader focus, this is a comprehensive treatise on workplace dispute resolution, including arbitration and mediation, collective bargaining and statutory disputes, and the creation of innovative dispute resolution programs in the union and non-union setting. The book includes more than fifty chapters and more than a dozen appendices. It was created by the American Bar Association Section on Labor and Employment Law and offers chapters by both neutrals and attorney advocates. It includes chapters on counseling clients about ADR and offers several perspectives on how to prepare clients for arbitration and mediation, and how to present cases in those procedures. Several arbitrators and mediators write about how they conduct their proceedings and what they expect of the parties. Other sections provide guidance on drafting settlement agreements and sample agreements.

Arbitration Under Collective Bargaining Agreements

Bornstein, Tim, Ann Gosline, and Marc Greenbaum, eds., *Labor and Employment Arbitration*. 2d ed. New York, N.Y.: Matthew Bender, 1997–. 2 vols.

Numerous experts have contributed to this authoritative two-volume looseleaf work that provides comprehensive coverage of important procedural and substantive elements of labor arbitration. Volume I focuses on the arbitration process, arbitrability, contract interpretation, and specific contract issues subject to arbitration. Volume II covers additional arbitration issues, external statutory and case law affecting labor arbitration, nonunion employment arbitration, and arbitration in selected industries. A detailed index is also provided. This work is kept up to date through periodic supplementation.

National Academy of Arbitrators, *Proceedings of the . . . Annual Meeting*. Washington, D.C.: Bureau of National Affairs, 1948–.

This is an annual compilation of papers and reports presented at the organization's annual meeting. Its volumes are the richest source of research and commentary on labor arbitration. Each volume also has a distinctive title and includes bibliographic references and an index. A cumulative index is separately published in: Gladys W. Gruenberg, Joyce M. Najita, and Dennis R. Nolan, *The National Academy of Arbitrators: Fifty Years in the World of Work* (Washington, D.C.: Bureau of National Affairs, 1998), which also includes a history of the organization. Volumes subsequent to 1998 include a cumulative author index. The volume for the 55th Annual Meeting includes a topical index for 1998–2002.

Ruben, Alan Miles, ed., *Elkouri & Elkouri: How Arbitration Works*. 6th ed. Washington, D.C.: Bureau of National Affairs, 2003.

For more than four decades, this work has been the leading treatise on the practice of labor arbitration. It is authored by expert arbitration practitioners who offer in-depth analyses of the substance and process of arbitration. Topics covered include the history and role of arbitration, arbitration tribunals, arbitrability, techniques used, law and evidence used, and specific contract issues subject to arbitration, remedies available, public sector arbitration, and state and local government issues. Under discharge and discipline, a table of offenses cites arbitration awards according to the severity of penalty imposed. Each chapter provides references to relevant topic numbers from the BNA's *Labor Arbitration Reports Cumulative Digest Index* facilitating location of more recent cases related to each subject addressed in the treatise. Numerous references to arbitrations and court decisions are provided. The work also provides a table of arbitrators, table of arbitration awards, table of cases, table of statutes, and a subject index.

St. Antoine, Theodore J., ed., *The Common Law of the Workplace: The Views of Arbitrators*. Washington, D.C.: Bureau of National Affairs, 1998.

This work represents an effort by the National Academy of Arbitrators to create a reference source that conveniently restates the principles derived from fifty years of arbitration decisions. The principles are organized under the following headings: practice and procedure, contract interpretation, management and union rights, job assignments, seniority, discipline and discharge, wages and hours, safety and health, fringe benefits, and remedies. Following each stated principle are comments, illustrations, and citations to articles and books discussing the principle.

Schoonhoven, Ray J., ed., *Fairweather's Practice and Procedure in Labor Arbitration*. 4th ed. Washington, D.C.: Bureau of National Affairs, 1999.

This practice manual thoroughly explains the rationale and history of labor arbitration procedure. Topics covered include submitting a case, selecting an arbitrator, resolving arbitrability issues, obtaining evidence, utilizing witnesses, and conducting a hearing. The work also covers burdens of proof, standard of review, due process, remedies, and post-award proceedings. One chapter focuses on arbitration in the nonunionized workplace. Tables of awards and cases by party and an index are also provided.

Arbitration of Common Law and Statutory Disputes

Bales, Richard A., *Compulsory Arbitration: The Grand Experiment in Employment*. Ithaca, N.Y.: ILR Press, 1997.

This is one of the few works dealing exclusively with dispute resolution in the nonunionized workplace. It provides an overview of the practice of arbitration and the statutory and common law basis for mandatory arbitration in employment, followed by an examination of the Equal Employment Opportunity Commission's treatment of compulsory arbitration. It then discusses arbitration in the securities and construction industries and finishes with considerations for drafting enforceable arbitration agreements and policy considerations in arbitration. The work contains bibliographic references and an index.

Bornstein, Tim, Ann Gosline, and Marc Greenbaum, eds., *Labor and Employment Arbitration*. 2d ed. New York, N.Y.: Matthew Bender, 1997–. 2 vols.

Described in the previous section, chapter 45 of this book provides a brief overview of the major case law, statutory law, and organizations involved in nonunion employment arbitration.

Carbonneau, Thomas E., *Employment Arbitration*. Yonkers, N.Y.: Juris Publishing, 2000–.

This practical work begins with a brief overview of the history and process of arbitration in the nonunion workplace, followed by a review of congressional and judicial developments related to employment arbitration. The last part of the work focuses on integrating arbitration into the workplace through employment handbooks, model policies, and agreements. A case table and subject index are provided.

Mediation of Workplace Disputes

Few monographic works cover mediation of workplace disputes. Periodical and continuing legal education literature are currently the best sources of information on this topic.

Alternative Dispute Resolution: What the Business Lawyer Needs to Know 1999. New York, N.Y.: Practising Law Institute, 1999.

This continuing education publication covers many aspects of alternative dispute resolution. It is useful because it reprints several introductory articles on mediation produced by the American Arbitration Association and the American Bar Association. Included are model mediation standards and practical tips for preparing clients and conducting successful mediation sessions.

Berger, Vivian, "Employment Mediation in the Twenty–First Century: Challenges in a Changing Environment," *University of Pennsylvania Journal of Labor and Employment Law*, 5 (Spring 2003): 487–543.

This article reviews recent trends that have caused employment discrimination litigation to be less desirable and discusses why and when mediation is a better alternative to such litigation. The last part of the article covers best practices in workplace mediation.

Miller, Kathryn E., "How to Prepare for and Participate in an Employment Mediation," *The Journal of Alternative Dispute Resolution in Employment* 1 (Fall 1999): 45–52.

This article provides a practical guide for advocates in employment mediation on such issues as determining the best time for mediation, using administrative agency dispute resolution processes, selecting a neutral and preparing for mediation.

Miller, Kathryn E., "Making Mediation Work for You and Your Clients in Employment Cases," *Employee Rights Quarterly*: *ERQ* 3 (Fall 2002): 53–63.

This article, written for attorneys considering mediation, looks at mediation in relation to litigation. It describes types of mediation and discusses the process of mediation, ways to involve clients, possible monetary and non-monetary demands available, and fees.

Shaw, Margaret L., "Employment Disputes." In *Mediating Legal Disputes: Effective Strategies for Lawyers and Mediators*, 441. Boston: Little, Brown, 1996.

This chapter describes the reasons why mediation is well-suited to resolve employment disputes. It also discusses the particular challenges facing employment mediators and provides a procedural overview of employment mediation. Case studies illustrating mediation of wrongful termination and disability accommodation disputes are included.

Simon, Howard A. and Yaroslav Sochynsky, "In–House Mediation of Employment Disputes: ADR for the 1990s," *Employment Relations Law Journal* 21 (Summer 1995): 29–51.

After briefly describing various methods of employment dispute resolution, this article compares several existing in-house mediation programs and offers tips on designing similar programs.

Weinstein, Rebecca Jane, *Mediation in the Workplace: A Guide for Training, Practice, and Administration*. Westport, CT; London: Quorum Books, 2001.

This work offers a blend of theoretical and practical information on workplace mediation aimed at mediators, employees, and employers. After describing how conflict can be managed through mediation, the work details the process of mediation from start to finish. The author offers tips on the physical environment, questioning techniques, caucusing, confidentiality, documentation, and final agreements. These tips are reinforced by a series of workplace-based exercises and mock mediations. The final part of the work provides information to assist in designing an in-house mediation program, including sample policies and forms. Bibliographical references and an index are also provided.

Workplace Dispute Resolution Programs

CPR Institute for Dispute Resolution, *How Companies Manage Employment Disputes: A Compendium of Leading Corporate Employment Programs*. CPR Institute for Dispute Resolution (2002).

Corporate attorneys serving as members of the CPR Employment Disputes Committee created this valuable guide to the design of comprehensive workplace dispute resolution programs, including such features as informal dispute resolution, mediation and arbitration. The book includes a study of programs of twenty employers, useful introductory materials on ADR methods, sample policies and educational materials, and interviews with corporate executives about their experiences in implementing dispute resolution programs. The book provides an excellent resource for attorneys or companies desiring to learn the best practices in design of corporate dispute resolution programs.

Arbitration Awards

Although most arbitration awards are not published, several specialized reporting services provide full texts and summaries of selected awards. Most reports are available in both paper and electronic formats. Each service offers helpful indexes and tables for identifying awards by topic, party, and arbitrator.

Major Sources for Full Texts and Summaries

Labor Arbitration Reports. Washington, D.C.: Bureau of National Affairs, 1946–.

This looseleaf work is published weekly as a component of the *Labor Relations Reporter* and is the leading source for full texts and summaries of labor arbitration awards. Preceding the text of each award are headnotes that describe the issues involved in the arbitration. A classification number is assigned to each headnote denoting the subject matter of the award according to the publisher's detailed classification scheme. This numbering scheme is used to group together summaries of awards on the same topic in the publication's case digest. Each weekly report also contains summaries of the cases, an outline of classifications, and lists of arbitrators and cases in the report. Semi-annually, these looseleaf reports are replaced by a bound volume. A full search of cumulative digests may require consulting several separate digests in looseleaf format, as well as several paperback and hardbound digests. The looseleaf volumes of the *Labor Relations Reports* include a "Master Index" covering recent reports. This index offers a section on labor arbitration that contains a topic finder (overview of the classification scheme) and separate cumulative digests for each volume of *Labor Arbitration Reports*. The digest entries contain the summaries that appear in the headnotes described earlier. The Master Index volume contains a digest for both the current looseleaf reports and for recent bound volumes. It also provides tables listing arbitration awards by arbitrator, party, and contract term. Arbitrator biographies are included as well. The weekly reports and digests are periodically replaced by bound volumes, initially in paperback and later in hardbound.

Labor Arbitration Reports is also available in electronic form on LexisNexis (LRRLA) from 1980 to date and on Westlaw (LRR–LA) from 1979 to date. They can also be found in the publisher's *Labor and Employment Law Library* which is available both on CD ROM and on the Web at <http://laborandemploymentlaw.bna.com/>. The awards in the CD ROM version lag three to four weeks behind other hardcopy and electronic versions of the service. All of the electronic versions offer the advantage of key word searches of the full texts and summaries, including searches by arbitrator. Classification number searches are also possible, but the Westlaw and LexisNexis versions do not provide an outline of the classification scheme, so it may be necessary to consult the Master Index of the paper version of this work in order to identify useful classification numbers. The CD ROM and Web versions include the alphabetical topic finder and the classification outline found in the paper version. Selecting items from either the topic finder or the classification outline will yield related headnote summaries and, most often, the full texts of the decisions containing these headnotes. Unfortunately, none of the electronic versions offers as useful a compilation of cases as the hardcopy cumulative digests. Of the electronic versions, the one on the BNA's own Web site is the easiest to use.

Awards submitted to BNA but not selected by its editors for publication in *Labor Arbitration Reports* are not available on BNA's own web site, but are available on Westlaw in the database (LA–UNP). No indexing or summaries are available for these "unpublished" awards. On Westlaw, one may search both published and unpublished awards in the database (LA–COMB).

Labor Arbitration Awards. Chicago, Ill.:CCH, 1961–.

This looseleaf work appears monthly. Each issue provides the full texts of selected recent arbitration awards. Each award is preceded by a very short summary of the award and information on the source of the arbitrator's selection. The looseleaf contains alphabetically arranged topical indexes, one for recent awards and one for earlier awards. The indexes offer short phrases describing awards. Tables listing awards by party and arbitrator, arbitrator biographies, and advisory ethics opinions of the National Academy of Arbitrators are also provided in this volume. Periodically, the contents of the looseleaf volume are replaced by bound volumes. Each bound volume contains the awards, a topical index, and the party and arbitrator tables covering the awards included. The publication is also available on CD ROM and on the web at <http://hr.cch.com>. New materials appear initially in the looseleaf version and are later available on the web (approximately a week later) and CD ROM (approximately a month later).

Labor Arbitration Information System (LAIS). Fort Washington, Penn.: LRP, 1981–.

This monthly looseleaf service, formerly called *Labor Arbitration Index* (1970–1980), offers the most comprehensive index to labor arbitration awards available. While it does not index every award published, more than 2,500 awards are indexed annually, including those reported in *Labor Arbitration Reports*, *Labor Arbitration Awards*, and other publications. Awards are indexed under a topical classification scheme and, for each award there is a brief summary indicating the prevailing party. An alphabetical list of topical categories and a subject index for the classification scheme are offered. Awards also are listed by arbitrator, by employer, and by union. Each year, the monthly indexes and finding lists are replaced by bound volumes. This service provides full text of selected awards and summarizes awards published elsewhere. Each award is assigned at least one classification number identifying the subject matter of the award. This number can be used to locate other awards on the same topic in the index. The service includes a helpful user guide.

Labor Arbitration Information System is available in several electronic formats. It appears as a semi-annual *Arbitration Database on CD ROM* which includes summaries of arbitration awards and biographical data on arbitrators that have appeared since 1978 in the publisher's *Labor Arbitration Information System*. The same data is available through Arbsearch.com, a fee-based service on the Web at <http://www.arbsearch.com>. Westlaw provides access to *Labor Arbitration Information System* (LAIS), but this version is usually less current than the other electronic versions. The electronic versions offer the advantage of key word searches, including searches by arbitrator, union, subject, and employer. They provide subject and LAIS classification number searching of arbitration case summaries published by various publishers. The publisher provides a fee-based research service, *Instant Computer Arbitration Search (ICAS)* that conducts customized searches in the *Labor Arbitration Information System* database.

Other Sources for Full Texts and Summaries

ARBIT.

This private database, which contains full texts of selected awards issued since 1960, was originally created by a group of private attorneys. It is now available on Westlaw (ARBIT) although it is not updated regularly.

Arbitration Award Summaries. St. Paul, Minn.: Minnesota Bureau of Mediation Services, 1983–.

This monthly source provides summaries of public and private sector arbitration awards issued in Minnesota. Awards are indexed by arbitrator, subject, employer, and union.

Arbitration in the Schools. Horsham, Penn.: LRP Publications, 1970–.

This monthly report from the American Arbitration Association summarizes selected arbitration awards and fact-finding recommendations involving employees of educational institutions. It includes semi-annual and annual indexes with lists of arbitrators.

Arbitrators' Qualification Reports. Charlotte, N.C.: R. C. Simpson.

This fee-based service provides unpublished awards of arbitrators. To order, contact R. C. Simpson at 5950 Fairview Rd, Charlotte, N.C. 28210–3104; telephone: (704) 553–0716; fax: (704) 553–0734.

Government Employee Relations Report. Washington, D.C.: Bureau of National Affairs, 1963–.

The weekly "Current Reports" section of this work occasionally contains summaries of arbitrator rulings, usually with citations to sources providing the full text. The rulings are included in the "administrative rulings" portion of this section. The index to the "Current Reports" lists arbitration summaries under the heading "arbitration."

Labor Arbitration in Government. Horsham, Penn.: LRP Publications, 1972–.

This source from the American Arbitration Association provides monthly summaries of arbitration awards involving federal, state, and local government employees (excluding those in schools).

National Arbitration Center.< http://www.lawmemo.com/arb/award/default.htm >

This free Web site provides full texts of several hundred awards from 1988 to date, submitted by the arbitrators who are listed in the arbitrator directory on the site. Awards are searchable by keyword. A chronological list of awards is provided.

PersonNet.com. Eagan, Minn.: West Group. <http://www.personnet.com/>

A subset of this fee-based database, *Arbitrators' Decisions*, contains the full texts of arbitration awards on federal government human resource issues beginning in 1973. It also includes selected federal court decisions related to these awards from 1978 to date. The awards and cases in the *Arbitrators' Decisions* database can also be searched on Westlaw (PNET–ARB). It is also possible to search Westlaw separately for the awards (ARB-DEC) or federal court decisions (ARB–CS).

Summary of Labor Arbitration Awards. Horsham, Penn.: LRP Publications, 1959–.

This monthly service from the American Arbitration Association summarizes arbitration awards in the private sector. It provides semi-annual and annual indexes listing cases by arbitrator and topic. The full text of these awards is available upon request from the Association.

Citator

Shepard's Labor Arbitration Citations. Colorado Springs, Colo.: Shepards, 1989–.

This work contains references to state and federal cases on labor arbitration and to statutes and regulations pertaining to labor arbitration. It is useful for determining whether awards published in *Labor Arbitration Awards* or *Labor Arbitration Reports* have been cited in subsequent awards in these two publications. It also provides a table of cases and arbitration awards by name of party. Unfortunately, it does not provide information about court decisions that enforce or vacate arbitration awards.

Information About Dispute Resolution Professionals

Publications, Services, and Databases

The sources discussed below for finding alternative dispute resolution professionals should be used with some caution. Frequently, they only include individuals who volunteer biographical information or pay to be listed, so there are likely to be numerous omissions. In addition, the information, once provided, may not be kept current. When possible, it is advisable to compare listings information from several sources.

Arbitrators' Qualification Reports. Charlotte, N.C.: R. C. Simpson.

This service provides reports on arbitrators, listing the awards that they have made by subject, recommendations of parties who have used the arbitrator, and lists of published awards by the arbitrator. The service can provide some unpublished arbitration awards. To order, contact R. C. Simpson at 5950 Fairview Rd, Charlotte, N.C. 28210–3104; telephone: (704) 553–0716; fax: (704) 553–0734.

Arbitrators' Biographies. Chicago, Ill. CCH, 1961–.

This directory of arbitrators appears initially in the looseleaf volume of the *Labor Arbitration Awards* set discussed earlier. It provides alphabetical listings of arbitrators whose awards appear in the service. These listings include address and telephone information, affiliations, current and past positions, publications, issues arbitrated, and the industries involved. Each bound volume of the set contains a directory of the arbitrators whose awards appear in the volume.

Arbsearch.com. Horsham: Penn., LRP. <http://www.arbsearch.com>

This fee-based Web service offered by LRP, publisher of the *Labor Arbitration Information System*, allows subscribers to search for information on over 4,000 arbitrators, including biographies, summaries of awards arbitrated, and statistical analyses by prevailing party of the awards. It links to summaries of their awards with citations.

Directory of Arbitrators. Washington, D.C.: Bureau of National Affairs, 1937–.

This directory initially appears in looseleaf format in the labor arbitration section of the Master Index volume of the *Labor Relations Reporter* described earlier. It subsequently appears in the bound cumulative digest and index volumes of this publication. Biographies are arranged alphabetically by name and provide address and telephone information, education, experience, professional affiliations, and lists of cases, contracts arbitrated, and industries involved. The directory is also available on LexisNexis (ARBBIO) and on Westlaw (LRR–DIR).

Instant Computer Arbitration Search (ICAS). Fort Washington, Penn.: LRP.

This fee-based service conducts searches on its database, *Labor Arbitration Information System*, discussed earlier. Reports with information about individual arbitrators, including summaries of awards arbitrated, biographical data, and statistical analyses by prevailing party of the awards are provided. The awards included in the database are also found in the *Labor Arbitration Information System*. For further information, call (800) 341–7874, ext. 274.

Martindale-Hubbell Dispute Resolution Directory. Summit, N.J.: Martindale–Hubbell, 1994–.

This directory provides contact information and practice areas for dispute resolution professionals. Individuals are listed alphabetically under each U.S. geographic jurisdiction. Indexes by practice area and name are also provided. It is available on LexisNexis (DRD) and on the Web at <http://www.martindale.com/xp/Martindale/Dispute_Resolution

/Search_Dispute_Resolution_Directory/qual_search.xml>.

National Arbitration Center. Salem, Ore.: LawMemo.com <http://
  www.lawmemo.com/arb/award/default.htm>

This free Web site provides contact information and detailed biographies for arbitrators who pay to be listed. Arbitrators are listed by state and can be found through key word searching. Links are provided to awards submitted by the arbitrators.

PersonNet.com. Eagan, Minn.: West Group. <http://www.person-
  net.com/>

From the fee-based database, *Arbitrators' Decisions*, containing federal sector arbitration awards, this resource includes biographical data and statistics for arbitrators whose awards are contained in the database. The statistics list union wins, management wins and split decisions for those federal sector cases in the database. The biographies and statistics in the *Arbitrators' Decisions* database, described earlier, can also be searched on Westlaw (PNET–ARB). It is also possible to search Westlaw separately for the biographies (ARB–BIO) or statistics (ARB–STAT).

Other Sources

Alliance for Education in Dispute Resolution.

This consortium of universities and professional dispute resolution organizations provides training and educational programs on employment mediation and arbitration. It also conducts research on workplace alternative dispute resolution. Its web site at <http://www.ilr.cornell.edu/alliance/> includes a roster of employment arbitrators and mediators who have completed its training programs. For further information, contact the Alliance through the Cornell Institute on Conflict Resolution, 621 Catherwood Library Tower, Ithaca, New York 14853–5378; (607) 255–6974.

American Arbitration Association.

This organization is dedicated to dispute resolution through mediation, arbitration, democratic elections, and other voluntary methods. It maintains a "Roster of Neutrals," a list of arbitrators considered by this organization to be experts in arbitration. Names of neutrals may be obtained for a charge from the regional offices of the association, which can be found at its Web site at <http://www.adr.org/>. This association also provides biographical information on mediators at <http://www.mediatorindex.com/>. For further information, contact the Association at 140 W. 51st St., New York, N.Y. 10020; (212) 484–4000.

CPR Institute for Dispute Resolution.

This organization, created by corporations using ADR services, is dedicated to developing new procedures for dispute resolution and to providing educational programs to promote alternative dispute resolution. It maintains international and national rosters of 700 prominent attorneys, former judges, legally-trained executives, and academics available to mediate or arbitrate a business or public dispute. Information on these individuals can be obtained for a fee from the organization's Web site at <http://www.cpradr.org/panels.htm>. For further information, contact the Institute at 366 Madison Ave., New York, N.Y. 10017–3122; (212) 949–6490.

Federal Mediation and Conciliation Service. Office of Arbitration Services.

This independent government agency promotes sound and stable labor-management relations through mediation and arbitration services. It maintains a roster of approximately 1,250 active arbitrators and provides lists of arbitrators and their qualifications for a fee. Further information about this service is available through its Web site at <http://www.fmcs.gov>. For further information, contact the Service at 2100 K St., N.W., Washington, D.C. 20427; (202) 606–8100.

National Mediation Board.

The Board was established by the Railway Labor Act, governing railroad and airline labor relations. It provides mediation services for the resolution of "major disputes" involving rates of pay, rules, or working conditions and provides arbitration services for "minor disputes" (employee grievances arising under collective bargaining agreements). The Board maintains a roster of those certified to serve as arbitrators of railroad and airline grievances. For further information, contact the Board at 1301 K Street NW, Suite 250 East, Washington, D.C. 20005–7011; 202–692–5000, or at its Web site at <www.nmb.gov>.

Resources Available Only to Union Advocates.

A few larger national unions with centralized arbitration departments, including the United Steelworkers Union and the United Automobile Workers Union, maintain private lists rating arbitrators, only available to representatives of or advocates for those unions. The AFL–CIO Lawyers Coordinating Committee in approximately 2000 launched an online service accessible only by its members (attorneys who represent unions). Attorneys who have experience with particular arbitrators are asked whether they would use that arbitrator again. Once there are a minimum number of responses, the service reports the responses as a numerical rating separately for the categories of discharge cases, contract language cases and interest arbitration. The service also identifies lawyers who have used particular arbitrators so the lawyers may be contacted for further information. The AFL–CIO Lawyers Coordinating Committee is located at 815 Sixteenth Street, N.W., 6th Floor, Washington, D.C. 20006; (202) 637–5214.

Procedural and Ethical Rules

The following sources shape the process of alternative dispute resolution and the conduct of the professionals who are involved. Although hard copies are available, only electronic versions are listed since these contain the most up to date changes. BNA's *Labor and Employment Law Library* includes many of the sources discussed below.

American Arbitration Association. *Labor Arbitration Rules.* <http://www.adr.org/index2.1.jsp?JSPssid=15747>

These rules contain procedures for parties who use the labor arbitration services of the American Arbitration Association pursuant to an arbitration clause in a collective bargaining agreement. *Expedited Labor Arbitration Procedures* are included.

American Arbitration Association. *National Rules for the Resolution of Employment Disputes.* <http://www.adr.org/index2.1.jsp?JSPssid=15747>

These rules set forth procedures for arbitration or mediation of employment disputes by parties, not subject to a collective bargaining agreement, who agree to observe them.

Due Process Protocol for Mediation and Arbitration of Statutory Disputes Arising out of the Employment Relationship. <http://www.adr.org/index2.1.jsp?JSPssid=15769>

This protocol represents the work of a Task Force on Alternative Dispute Resolution, composed of delegates from organizations with experience in workplace alternative dispute resolution. It sets guidelines to ensure fairness and equity in resolving statutory workplace disputes.

Model Standards of Conduct for Mediators. <http://www.adr.org/index2.1.jsp?JSPssid=15718>

These standards were jointly developed by the American Arbitration Association, the American Bar Association, and the Society of Professionals in Dispute Resolution. They are intended to guide mediators and to instill confidence in parties and the general public about the process of mediation.

Code of Professional Responsibility for Arbitrators of Labor–Management Disputes of the Federal Mediation and Conciliation Service, National Academy of Arbitrators, American Arbitration Association. <http://www.fmcs.gov/internet/itemDetail.asp?categoryID=198 & itemID=16989> <http//www.naarb.org/code/html >

This code governs voluntary arbitration of disputes arising under collective bargaining agreements. It applies to members of the National Academy of Arbitrators and arbitrators on the rosters of the American Arbitration Association and the Federal Mediation and Conciliation Service.

Code of Professional Responsibility, Advisory Opinions

The Committee on Professional Responsibility of the National Academy of Arbitrators issues advisory opinions interpreting the Code of Professional Responsibility for Arbitrators of Labor Management Disputes. These numbered advisory opinions each state a factual circumstance and then discuss it and assess the ethical conduct for an arbitrator in that situation. As of 2004, some of the advisory opinions have been rescinded and others are being revised in light of recent amendments to the Code related to arbitrator advertising and solicitation. The current advisory opinions are posted in the web-based BNA *Labor and Employment Law Library* at <http://laborandemploymentlaw.bna.com/>. (On the home page of the BNA Labor and Employment Law Library, click "Complete Library," then under "Labor Arbitration" click "Labor Arbitration Rules, Procedures and Directories," and under that click "National Academy of Arbitrators Committee on Professional Responsibility and Grievances Advisory Opinions.") Following revision, they are also likely to be posted on the web site of the National Academy of Arbitrators at <http//www.naarb.org/>.

Other Resources on Workplace Dispute Resolution

Books

Bognanno, Mario F. and Charles J. Coleman, eds., *Labor Arbitration in America*. New York, N.Y.: Praeger, 1992.

This work reports on the results of a survey conducted from 1986 to 1987 of professional arbitrators in Canada and the United States. It profiles their backgrounds, qualifications, earnings, and work. A list of agencies that supplied names of arbitrators and an index are included.

Brand, Norman, ed., *Discipline and Discharge in Arbitration*. Washington, D.C.: Bureau of National Affairs, 1998. *2001 Supplement*. Anne L. Draznin, ed. Washington, D.C.: Bureau of National Affairs, 2001.

This is a comprehensive treatise on arbitration of employee discipline and discharge under collective bargaining agreements. The first chapter provides a practical guide to advocacy in discipline cases. Other chapters address theories of just cause, evidentiary and procedural questions, remedies, consideration of external law, and judicial review. Most of the book is devoted to analysis of arbitration decisions, organized according to the basis of the employee's conduct, including attendance, job performance, substance abuse, dishonesty, workplace and off-duty misconduct and union activities. Each section includes numerous citations to relevant published arbitration awards. The book includes a detailed index and table of court cases cited. The supplement covers decisions issued between 1996 and 2000. It includes the 1995 Due Process Protocol for Mediation and Arbitration of Statutory Disputes Arising Out of the Employment Relationship and provides tables of arbitration decisions, arbitrators and court cases that cover both the main volume and the supplement.

Carbonneau, Thomas E., *The Law and Practice of Arbitration*. Huntington, N.Y.: Juris Publishing, 2004.

Chapter 8 of this general work on arbitration focuses on workplace arbitration. It provides an in-depth analysis of the major cases related to labor and employment arbitration law. It also includes provisions for a model arbitration agreement.

Coulson, Robert, *Labor Arbitration: What You Need to Know*. Rev. 5th ed. Edited with additional material by Kristine L. Sova. Huntington, N.Y.: Juris Publishing, 2003.

This work is a handbook for persons engaged in labor arbitration. It highlights issues to consider before arbitrating, how to select an arbitrator, how an arbitration proceeds, and when arbitration is used in the public sector. Much of the work consists of useful appendices: the American Arbitration Association Labor Arbitration Rules, a glossary of useful terminology, summaries of leading N.L.R.B. and court decisions, standards for "just cause" in disciplinary and discharge cases, a bibliography of books on labor arbitration, and texts of major statutes. A directory of the offices of the American Arbitration Association is also included.

Denenberg, Tia Schneider and R.V. Denenberg, *Alcohol and Other Drugs: Issues in Arbitration*. Washington, D.C.: Bureau of National Affairs, 1991.

This work discusses legal and policy issues related to alcohol and drug use and abuse in the workplace. It addresses drug testing, evidentiary matters, and work rules. Relevant arbitration and court rulings are excerpted and a topically-arranged table of arbitration rulings and an index are provided.

Dolson, William F., Max Zimny, and Christopher A. Barreca, eds., *Labor Arbitration: Cases and Materials for Advocates*. Washington, D.C.: Bureau of National Affairs, 1997.

This work is a companion to the Zimny training text discussed later. It is designed for training labor arbitration advocates. It includes materials for simulated arbitrations and contains sample documents, forms, hearing transcripts, and awards. Topics covered include discipline and discharge, seniority, leaves, holidays, strikes, and management rights.

Dunlop, John Thomas and Arnold M. Zack, *Mediation and Arbitration of Employment Disputes*. San Francisco: Jossey–Bass Publishers, 1997.

This work traces the development of alternative dispute resolution through union contracts and statutory law and examines due process provisions in employer-promulgated dispute resolution systems. It also discusses and advocates use of the Due Process Protocol of Mediation and Arbitration of Statutory Disputes Arising Out of the Employment Relationship. The text of the Protocol is included along with a Massachusetts state policy implementing it.

Eaton, Adrienne E. and Jeffery H. Keefe, eds., *Employment Dispute Resolution and Worker Rights in the Changing Workplace*. Champaign, IL : Industrial Relations Research Association, 1999.

This scholarly work examines developments and research trends related to modern workplace dispute resolution. Initial chapters focus on arbitration practices in the nonunion sector and discuss the need for more research on the resolution of employment disputes. They are followed by chapters covering union grievance procedures and mediation practice. Later chapters examine the effects of new organizational structures such as teams on dispute resolution and then highlight dispute resolution in the public sector and building trades. Each chapter provides an extensive bibliography of useful readings. In their introduction, the editors identify gaps in current research and recommend new areas for further study.

Elkouri, Frank and Edna Asper Elkouri, *Resolving Drug Issues*. Washington, D.C.: Bureau of National Affairs, 1993.

This work provides arbitrators and advocates with helpful scientific and legal information on drug use, abuse, and testing in the employment context. Following an overview of the drugs commonly involved in grievances, commentary on the applicable constitutional, statutory, regulatory, and case law governing drug cases is provided. Appendices contain selected executive branch guidelines and orders and numerous arbitrations involving drug use are cited and analyzed throughout the text. A case table and an index are provided.

Estreicher, Samuel and David Sherwyn, eds., *Alternative Dispute Resolution in the Employment Arena: Proceedings of the New York University 53rd Annual Conference on Labor*. New York, N.Y.: Kluwer Law International, 2004.

The proceedings of this conference provide a comprehensive review of the current law and practice of alternative dispute resolution in the workplace. Part one focuses on arbitration and peer review of statutory employment claims and presents the ADR policies of several major U.S. companies. The second part describes several empirical studies of employment arbitration. This is followed by a review of major litigation involving arbitration of labor and employment arbitration. A final part provides perspectives on mediation.

Federal Administrative Dispute Resolution Deskbook. Chicago, Ill.: American Bar Association. Section of Administrative Law and Regulatory Practice, 2001.

This work discusses the forms of alternative dispute resolution used by various federal agencies. It provides commentaries on legislation, offers practical tips and discusses experiences in specific agencies. Several chapters focus on labor and employment dispute resolution including chapter 4 on labor arbitration services of the Federal Mediation and Conciliation Service; chapter 15 on alternative dispute resolution in the federal workplace; and chapter 16 on mediation of federal employment discrimination charges. Bibliographical references are provided.

Gleason, Sandra E., ed., *Workplace Dispute Resolution: Directions for the 21st Century*. East Lansing, Mich.: Michigan State University Press, 1997.

This work analyzes the history and future of various types of dispute resolution in unionized and nonunionized employment settings. It includes sociological and psychological perspectives from the United States, Europe, and Japan. Bibliographic references and an index are provided.

Gorman, Robert A. and Matthew W. Finkin, *Basic Text on Labor Law: Unionization and Collective Bargaining.* 2d ed. St. Paul, Minn.: West (2004).

This is a comprehensive treatise on the law of labor-management relations. It covers several topics related to arbitration including the legal status of collective bargaining agreements, substantive and procedural arbitrability, duties of a successor employer, judicial review of labor arbitration awards, injunctions, deferral, preemption and the duty of fair representation.

Green, Jon W. and John W. Robinson, IV, eds., *Employment Litigation Handbook.* Chicago, Ill.: Section of Litigation, American Bar Association, 1998.

This work, designed for employment law attorneys, emphasizes litigation issues, but two chapters cover mediation and arbitration of employment disputes. Chapters 14 and 15 offer short employer and employee perspectives on these forms of alternative dispute resolution. Topics covered include laws and procedural rules governing arbitration and mediation, circumstances leading to mandatory or voluntary arbitration and mediation, pitfalls of arbitration, and tips for avoiding mandatory arbitration. Bibliographic references are provided.

Grenig, Jay E., *Alternative Dispute Resolution with Forms.* St. Paul, Minn.: West Publishing Co., 1997.

This is a comprehensive treatise on all methods of alternative dispute resolution. It is updated by a pocket part. Chapter 15 addresses mediation, arbitration and fact-finding in labor and employment disputes. Appendix D includes forms for a wide variety of documents used in arbitration and mediation. The treatise is distributed with a computer disk including the forms. The treatise is also available on Westlaw (ADR).

Hadley, Ernest C., *A Guide to Federal Sector Labor Arbitration.* 2d ed. Arlington, Va.: Dewey Publications, 1999.

This is a comprehensive treatise on the grievance and arbitration process for federal employees. It broadly covers substance, procedure and remedies. Additional topics include whistleblower protections, the right to union representation and review of arbitration awards.

Hancock, William A., ed., *Corporate Counsel's Guide to Alternative Dispute Resolution in the Employment Context, Business Laws.* 2d ed. Chesterland, Ohio: Business Laws, 1996.

This work is intended as a handbook to assist corporate attorneys in developing alternative dispute resolution policies and programs. It discusses programs in place at several corporations and includes sample forms, policies, and procedures. Appendices provide information about various organizations and government agencies involved in alternative dispute resolution and their rules for settling disputes. A topical index is included.

Hardin, Patrick and John E. Higgins, Jr., eds., *The Developing Labor Law: The Board, the Courts, and the National Labor Relations Act.* 4th ed. Washington, D.C.: Bureau of National Affairs, 2002. 2 vols.

Although most of this work discusses legal developments surrounding the National Labor Relations Act, chapters 17 and 18 focus on the role of arbitration in labor relations. It is thoroughly indexed and provides extensive footnote references to cases. It is kept current through cumulative supplements.

Hauck, Vern E., *Arbitrating Race, Religion, and National Origin Discrimination Grievances.* Westport, Conn.: Quorum Books, 1997.

This work focuses on arbitration of discrimination grievances based on race, religion, and national origin in both unionized and nonunionized workplaces. Part one of the book discusses the history and practice of arbitration in these types of cases; part two analyzes court rulings and arbitration awards for selected issues in each category of discrimination. A bibliography and index are included.

Hauck, Vern E., *Arbitrating Sex Discrimination Grievances.* Westport, Conn.: Quorum Books, 1998.

This work focuses on arbitration of discrimination grievances related to employment status, employment conditions, sexual harassment, pregnancy, and childbearing. Part one reproduces the text of the author's earlier work covering arbitration of race, religion, and national origin discrimination grievances. Part two examines specific court decisions and arbitration awards for selected issues for each type of discrimination. Both a bibliography and an index are provided.

Hauck, Vern E., *Arbitrating Sexual Harassment Cases.* Washington, D.C.: Bureau of National Affairs, 1995.

This work provides full texts and abstracts of arbitration awards and court decisions from the mid–1940s to the early 1990s related to sexual harassment. Also included are tables of awards and cases arranged by harassment issue, citation, and party names and government policies related to sexual harassment. Brief analyses of the law are reprinted from other sources. Appendices contain arbitration and ethics rules, statutes, and a test recommended for determining "just cause" discipline. An index and table of cases are also provided.

Hill, Marvin F. and Anthony V. Sinicropi, *Evidence in Arbitration.* 2d ed. Washington, D.C.: Bureau of National Affairs, 1987.

Although labor arbitrators do not generally adhere to the strict evidentiary rules applicable in judicial tribunals, there are principles of evidence arbitrators generally follow. This treatise addresses admission of evidence, rules of contract interpretation, and the effect of collateral proceedings and prior arbitration awards. This books is extensively footnoted with citations to arbitration awards and includes an index.

Hill, Marvin F. and Anthony V. Sinicropi, *Management Rights: A Legal and Arbitral Analysis*. Washington, D.C.: Bureau of National Affairs, 1986.

This volume addresses the theories of management rights and past practice in arbitration and then offers a comprehensive survey of the application of these theories to a wide range of workplace issues from minor work rules to major business decisions. It includes bibliographical references and an index.

Hill, Marvin F. and Anthony V. Sinicropi, *Remedies in Arbitration*. 2d ed. Washington, D.C.: Bureau of National Affairs, 1991.

This work first examines the sources of authority for arbitral remedies. It then provides in-depth commentary on remedies for discharge and disciplinary cases and remedies for nondisciplinary cases.

Hill, Marvin F. and Anthony V. Sinicropi, *Winning Arbitration Advocacy*. Washington, D.C.: Bureau of National Affairs, 1997.

This work offers practical tips for successful arbitration advocacy from pre-hearing through post-hearing and identifies common mistakes made by advocates. It also provides information about interest arbitration and for particular types of grievance cases, including drug and alcohol, discrimination, and off-duty misconduct. An index and bibliographic references are included.

Koven, Adolph M. and Susan L. Smith, *Just Cause: The Seven Tests*. 2d ed. Revised by Donald F. Farwell. Washington, D.C.: Bureau of National Affairs, 1992.

This book comments on tests developed by arbitrator Carroll R. Daugherty to determine if just cause existed for discharge and disciplinary actions. These tests are notice, reasonable rules and orders, the existence and quality of the employer's investigation, proof of misconduct, equality of treatment, and type of penalty. The work includes a detailed index and bibliographic references to cases.

Kramer, Henry S., *Alternative Dispute Resolution in the Workplace*. New York, N.Y.: Law Journal Seminars Press, 1998.

This desk reference for legal counsel, human resources managers, employers, employees, unions, and public interest groups provides legal guidance in the construction and management of alternative dispute resolution systems. It discusses the advantages and disadvantages of each type of system and offers practical advice for successful dispute resolution. Eleven chapters cover the development of alternative dispute resolution and its use for resolving statutory disputes, "at will" employment disputes, and disputes under collective bargaining agreements. Court-annexed alternative dispute resolution, securities industry applications, privately developed systems, and human resources considerations are also covered. The work includes an index and appendices with sample alternative dispute resolution agreements, statutes, and rules of practice.

Leslie, Douglas L., ed., *Railway Labor Act*. Washington, D.C.: Bureau of National Affairs, 1995. *2001 Cumulative Supplement*.

This book and its supplement provide a comprehensive treatise on the Railway Labor Act, governing labor relations in the airline and railroad industries. It was written by members of the Railway and Airline Labor Law Committee of the American Bar Association, Section of Labor and Employment Law, and includes an index and table of cases. Chapter 5 provides an overview of the complex system for resolution of disputes arising under collective bargaining agreements in the airline and railroad industries. The book also includes the text of the Railway Labor Act, and a mediation manual and rules of the National Mediation Board.

Loughran, Charles S., *How to Prepare and Present a Labor Arbitration Case: Strategy and Tactics for Advocates*. Washington, D.C.: Bureau of National Affairs, 1996.

This one-volume work guides readers through all phases of labor arbitration and serves as a excellent "how to" manual for novice arbitration advocates. Topics covered include selecting an arbitrator, preparing witnesses, assembling evidence, presenting the case, and challenging arbitration awards. It also provides forms, model questions, arbitration and evidence rules, and a bibliography.

McDermott, E. Patrick and Arthur Eliot Berkeley, *Alternative Dispute Resolution in the Workplace: Concepts and Techniques for Human Resource Executives and Their Counsel*. Westport, Conn.: Quorum Books, 1996.

This work traces the development of alternative dispute resolution in employment, contrasts its benefits to litigation, and introduces a few corporate dispute resolution programs currently in existence. The appendix includes a detailed analysis of the Brown & Root Dispute Resolution Program. A bibliography and index are included.

Nolan, Dennis R., *Labor and Employment Arbitration in a Nutshell*. St Paul, Minn.: West Group, 1998.

This work provides a basic overview of the history and practice of arbitration in union and nonunion workplaces. Topics include arbitration procedure and practice, applicable external laws affecting arbitration, the interplay between arbitration and administrative or judicial tribunals, and issues subject to arbitration. Appendixes provide arbitration rules and forms and selected statutes. Tables of cases and statutes and an index are provided.

Resolving Employment Disputes: A Practical Guide. New York, N.Y.: American Arbitration Association, 1997–.

This brief work provides an introductory overview of various forms of alternative dispute resolution that can be utilized in the workplace. It includes sample ADR clauses and the Due Process Protocol. The guide is kept up to date on the Web at <http://adr.org>.

Stern, James L. and Joyce M. Najita, eds., *Labor Arbitration Under Fire*. Ithaca, N.Y.: ILR Press, 1997.

This work contains essays by scholars and practitioners that cover the development and impact of private and public sector labor arbitration since the 1960s. Union and nonunion arbitration are discussed from the perspectives of both employers and employees. Included are an index and table of cases.

Wilkinson, John H., ed., *Donovan Leisure Newton & Irvine ADR Practice Handbook*. New York, N.Y.: John Wiley & Sons, 1990.

This work, consisting of contributions by scholars and practitioners, provides both historical background and practical information on general alternative dispute resolution. It outlines the steps involved in arbitration and mediation and recommends tactics to use. Also included are chapters describing the relationship between alternative dispute resolution and litigation, ethical concerns, client counseling, and implementation of corporate dispute resolution programs. The work provides a case table and topical index and 1993 cumulative supplement.

Zack, Arnold M., *A Handbook for Grievance Arbitration: Procedural and Ethical Issues*. New York, N.Y.: American Arbitration Association and Lexington Books, 1992.

This work, aimed at arbitrators and advocates, presents procedures for conducting arbitrations and the ethical issues involved. It includes a bibliography and an index.

Zack, Arnold M., *Arbitrating Discipline and Discharge Cases*. Horsham, Penn.: LRP Publications, 2000.

This work is designed as a guide for parties confronting workplace discipline and discharge matters. It covers the nature of disciplinary rules and causes for discipline and discharge. After discussing pre-arbitration considerations and procedures, the work details the process of arbitration and explains the remedies available. In concluding, the author provides recommendations for decreasing costs and increasing efficiency in arbitration. An index is included.

Zack, Arnold M., and Richard I. Bloch, *Labor Agreement in Negotiation and Arbitration*. 2d ed. Washington, D.C.: Bureau of National Affairs, 1995.

This work provides an introduction to techniques for resolving disputes through careful labor contract negotiation and for arbitration when required by agreement. It covers preparing and presenting an arbitration case. The text includes sections on arbitral decisionmaking regarding typical contract provisions and hypothetical problems and discussion questions related to each type of provision. An index and bibliographic references are provided.

Zimny, Max, William F. Dolson, and Christopher A. Barreca, eds., *Labor Arbitration: A Practical Guide for Advocates*. Washington, D.C.: Bureau of National Affairs, 1990.

This work, providing commentary from both union and management experts, is intended primarily as a training tool for beginning arbitration advocates. The topics covered include historical and legal foundations for arbitration, practices and procedures, and the internal and external laws governing arbitration. An index and bibliographic references are provided.

Periodicals

Indexes

Only a few periodicals focus specifically on labor arbitration and other forms of dispute resolution in employment, but general legal periodicals often contain articles on these topics. To identify articles of interest, consult:

Index to Legal Periodicals & Books. Bronx, N.Y.: H. W. Wilson, 1926–.

For articles published since 1980, this index is available on CD–ROM, on the Web at <http://www.hwwilson.com/databases/legal.htm>, and on LexisNexis (ILP) and Westlaw (ILP).

Current Law Index. Los Altos, Calif.: Information Access, 1980–.

This index is also available as *LegalTrac* on CD–ROM and on the Web at <http://infotrac.galegroup.com>, and on LexisNexis (LGLIND) and Westlaw (LRI).

Alternative Dispute Resolution Journals

ADR & the Law: A Report of the American Arbitration Association, the Fordham International Law Journal and the Fordham Urban Law Journal. New York, N.Y.: American Arbitration Association, 1997–.

Formerly *Arbitration and the Law* (1981–1994), each volume of this annual publication contains a section on labor arbitration which includes case digests and short articles. It has an annual index and case table in each volume.

Cardozo Journal of Conflict Resolution. New York, N.Y.: Benjamin N. Cardozo School of Law. Yeshiva University, 1999–. <http://www.cardozojcr.com/issues.html>

This Web-based semi-annual journal, formerly *Cardozo Online Journal of Conflict Resolution* (1998–1999), contains student-edited articles on all aspects of dispute resolution.

The Dispute Resolution Journal of the American Arbitration Association. New York, N.Y.: American Arbitration Association, 1993–.

Formerly *The Arbitration Journal* (1937–1993), this quarterly journal covers the full spectrum of the dispute resolution field including labor relations. It contains short articles by practitioners and scholars. It is also available on LexisNexis (DRJNL) and Westlaw (DRJ) from 1993.

Dispute Resolution Magazine. Washington, D.C.: American Bar Association. Section of Dispute Resolution, 1994–.

This quarterly magazine contains practitioner-oriented articles on a wide range of dispute resolution topics. It also includes summaries of recent judicial and legislative developments and a calendar of upcoming conferences and meetings.

Harvard Negotiation Law Review. Cambridge, Mass.: Harvard Law School, 1996–.

This annual student-edited journal is aimed at lawyers and legal scholars. It provides interdisciplinary treatment of negotiation as it relates to law and legal institutions. It is also available on LexisNexis (HRVNLR) from 1997 and on Westlaw (HVNLR) from 1996.

Journal of Alternative Dispute Resolution in Employment. Riverwoods, Ill., CCH, 1999–2001.

This short-lived quarterly periodical was aimed at human resources and dispute resolution professionals. Each issue included discussions of recent case law, mediation, arbitration, technological changes, regulatory developments, and ethics issues arising in the employment arena.

Journal of American Arbitration. Huntington, N.Y.: Juris Publications., 2001–.

This semi-annual journal is jointly edited by law students at the Tulane Arbitration Institute and Penn State Dickinson School of Law. It covers developments in all aspects of U.S. arbitration law.

Journal of Dispute Resolution. Columbia, Mo.: Center for the Study of Dispute Resolution, School of Law, University of Missouri–Columbia, 1988–.

Formerly the *Missouri Journal of Dispute Resolution* (1984–1987), this semi-annual publication is published in conjunction with the Center for the Study of Dispute Resolution. It contains scholarly articles on all forms of alternative dispute resolution. It also is available on LexisNexis (JDISPR) from 1995 and Westlaw (JDR) from 1993.

Ohio State Journal on Dispute Resolution. Columbus, OH: Ohio State University College of Law, 1985–.

This quarterly journal is published in cooperation with the American Bar Association Section of Dispute Resolution. It contains scholarly and practitioner-oriented articles covering many aspects of dispute resolution. The fourth issue of each volume contains a selective bibliography of books and articles on dispute resolution.[1] This journal is available on LexisNexis (OHSJDR) from 1995 and on Westlaw (OHSJDR) from 1985.

Pepperdine Dispute Resolution Law Journal. Malibu: Calif., 2000–.

This student-edited journal is published three times a year. It provides scholarly articles on dispute resolution issues of importance to students, practitioners and academics. It is available on LexisNexis (PEPPDR) from 2000 and Westlaw (PEPDRLJ) from 2000.

---

1. See Bibliographies section *supra*.

Labor and Employment Journals

Berkeley Journal of Employment and Labor Law. Berkeley, Calif.: University of California Press, 1993–.

Formerly titled *Industrial Relations Law Journal* (1976–1992), this semi-annual scholarly journal provides comprehensive coverage of employment and labor law. Each volume includes an index and book reviews. It is also available on Westlaw (BERKJELL) from 1984.

Employee Relations Law Journal. New York, N.Y.: Executive Enterprises Publications Co., 1975–.

This quarterly practitioner-oriented journal covers equal opportunity, occupational health and safety, labor-management relations, and employee benefits and compensation problems. This journal is available on Westlaw (EMRELLJ) from 1986.

Employee Responsibilities and Rights Journal. New York, N.Y.: Plenum Press, 1988–.

This quarterly journal is published for the Council on Employee Responsibilities and Rights. It contains scholarly articles on employment issues written by lawyers, economists, sociologists, psychologists, and philosophers.

Employee Rights and Employment Policy Journal. Chicago, Ill. Chicago–Kent College of Law and the National Employee Rights Institute, 1997–.

This semi-annual scholarly journal addresses both legal and employment policy issues in the union and nonunion workplace.

Hofstra Labor Law Journal. Hempstead, N.Y.: Hofstra University, 1984–1997.

This quarterly scholarly journal is available on LexisNexis (HLABLJ) from 1993 and on Westlaw (HOFLLJ) from 1984.

Industrial and Labor Relations Review. Ithaca, N.Y.: New York State School of Industrial and Labor Relations, Cornell University, 1947–.

This journal covers all aspects of the employment relationship, with a focus on academic empirical studies. It is also available on Westlaw (ILBRELREV) from 1989.

Labor Law Journal. Chicago, Ill. CCH, 1949–.

This monthly practitioner-oriented journal offers short articles on labor issues. An annual index is provided.

The Labor Lawyer. Chicago, Ill. American Bar Association, 1985–.

This journal appears three times per year and is aimed at practitioners, judges, administrators, and the interested public. An annual index is provided. This journal is also available on Westlaw (LABLAW) from 1987.

New York University Annual Conference on Labor. *Proceedings*. New York, N.Y.: New York University, 1948–.

Formerly the *New York University Annual National Conference on Labor* (1977–1996) and the *New York University Annual Conference on Labor* (1948–1976), this annual publication contains the papers presented by scholars, practitioners, and human resources professionals at each conference. Consolidated indexes are available for 1948–1983 (v. 1–35) and 1984–1989 (v. 36–41).

Web Sites

Major Organizations

Alliance for Education in Dispute Resolution.[2] <http://www.ilr.cornell.edu/alliance/>

The Alliance's Web site includes information on its training programs and research projects, a "resource library" containing articles, bibliographies, guides, protocols, standards, and statutes.

American Arbitration Association.[3] <http://www.adr.org/>

The Association's Web site is replete with information about alternative dispute resolution. It has separate pages for labor and employment that include ethics and arbitration rules, disciplinary rulings, model procedures, sample forms, articles, practice guides, state and federal statutes, information on the association's regional offices, bibliographies, publication order forms, and links to other Internet sites. It also has a library page that provides access to library research and document services. Information about its roster of neutrals is also available.

American Bar Association. Section of Dispute Resolution. <http://www.abanet.org/dispute/home.html>

This section of the American Bar Association supports legal professionals engaged in myriad forms of dispute resolution. It offers continuing education programs and online discussion forums and publishes books, periodicals, and conference reports that are listed on its Web site. It also provides links to other organizations and resources related to dispute resolution. Additional information is available from the Section at 740 15th St., NW, Washington, D.C. 20005–1009; (202) 662–1680.

Association for Conflict Resolution.[4] <http://www.acrnet.org/>

This organization of arbitrators, mediators, hearing examiners, and dispute resolution fact-finders includes a Workplace Section that issues news alerts and a newsletter. The organization offers information and educational programs promoting dispute resolution. This site contains information about the organization, its programs, and its publications. It also provides links to discussion lists and other relevant Internet sites.

CPR Institute for Dispute Resolution.[5] < http://www.cpradr.org/>

2. See *supra* description of Alliance for Education in Dispute Resolution.

3. See *supra* description of the American Arbitration Association.

4. ACR was formed in 2001 by the merger of the Society of Professionals in Dispute Resolution, the Academy of Family Mediators and the Conflict Resolution Education Network.

5. See *supra* description of CPR Institute for Dispute Resolution.

The Institute's Web site includes a monthly newsletter, model rules and procedures, information for ordering its publications and products, and biographical information on dispute resolution neutrals. The Web site includes model policies for a comprehensive employment dispute resolution program, the CPR Program to Resolve Employment Disputes.

National Academy of Arbitrators. <http://www.naarb.org/>

The Academy works to improve understanding and use of labor arbitration through research and educational programs. Its Web site provides information about the organization and its members, its code of ethics and ethics opinions, and the text of the Due Process Protocol for Mediation and Arbitration of Statutory Disputes Arising Out of the Employment Relationship.

National Mediation Board. <http://www.nmb.gov/index.html>

This board's Web site includes descriptions of its mediation and arbitration services and alternative dispute resolution training programs. Contact information, forms, regulations, and brief statistical information on the mediation and arbitration cases before the Board are also provided.

Databases of Resources

CRInfo (Conflict Resolution Information Source). <http://www.crin-fo.org/>

This Web site is maintained by the Conflict Research Consortium at the University of Colorado. It provides references and links to over 20,000 print and electronic resources and organizations related to conflict resolution. It is possible to run searches by broad topics and by key words. Many of the listings include brief annotations.

WorksonWorks. <http://www.worksonwork.irc.umn.edu>

This database is maintained by the staff of the Georgianna E. Herman Reference Room at the Industrial Relations Center of the University of Minnesota. It provides references to over 70,000 books, journal articles, working papers, proceedings, and Web sites on industrial relations topics. It is searchable by key word, author, title, and subject.

Appendix B

STATUTORY EXCERPTS

Labor Management Relations Act (29 U.S.C. §§ 141–197).

Sections 1; 2(5); 7; 8(a); 8(b) 1, 2, 3; 8(d); 9(a); 10(a); 10(f); 10(h); 13; 14(b); 201(b); 203(d); and 301.

Norris–LaGuardia (Anti–Injunction) Act (29 U.S.C. §§ 101–115).

United States Arbitration Act (9 U.S.C. §§ 1–16).

Uniform Arbitration Act.

LABOR MANAGEMENT RELATIONS ACT
29 U.S.C. §§ 141–197.

Section 1. The denial by some employers of the right of employees to organize and the refusal by some employers to accept the procedure of collective bargaining lead to strikes and other forms of industrial strife or unrest, which have the intent or the necessary effect of burdening or obstructing commerce by (a) impairing the efficiency, safety, or operation of the instrumentalities of commerce; (b) occurring in the current of commerce; (c) materially affecting, restraining, or controlling the flow of raw materials or manufactured or processed goods from or into the channels of commerce, or the prices of such materials or goods in commerce; or (d) causing diminution of employment and wages in such volume as substantially to impair or disrupt the market for goods flowing from or into the channels of commerce.

The inequality of bargaining power between employees who do not possess full freedom of association or actual liberty of contract, and employers who are organized in the corporate or other forms of ownership association substantially burdens and affects the flow of commerce, and tends to aggravate recurrent business depressions, by depressing wage rates and the purchasing power of wage earners in industry and by preventing the stabilization of competitive wage rates and working conditions within and between industries.

Experience has proved that protection by law of the right of employees to organize and bargain collectively safeguards commerce from injury, impairment, or interruption, and promotes the flow of commerce by removing certain recognized sources of industrial strife and unrest, by encouraging practices fundamental to the friendly adjustment of industrial disputes arising out of differences as to wages, hours, or other working conditions, and by restoring equality of bargaining power between employers and employees.

Experience has further demonstrated that certain practices by some labor organizations, their officers, and members have the intent or the necessary effect of burdening or obstructing commerce by preventing the free flow of goods in such commerce through strikes and other forms of industrial unrest or through concerted activities which impair the interest of the public in the free flow of such commerce. The elimination of such practices is a necessary condition to the assurance of the rights herein guaranteed.

It is hereby declared to be the policy of the United States to eliminate the causes of certain substantial obstructions to the free flow of commerce and to mitigate and eliminate these obstructions when they have occurred by encouraging the practice and procedure of collective bargaining and by protecting the exercise by workers of full freedom of association, self-organization, and designation of representatives of their own choosing, for the purpose of negotiating the terms and conditions of their employment or other mutual aid or protection.

Section 2. (5) The term "labor organization" means any organization of any kind, or any agency or employee representation committee or plan, in which employees participate and which exists for the purpose, in whole or in part, of dealing with employers concerning grievances, labor disputes, wages, rates of pay, hours of employment, or conditions of work. * * *

Section 7. Employees shall have the right to self-organization, to form, join or assist labor organizations, to bargain collectively through representatives of their own choosing, and to engage in other concerted activities for the purpose of collective bargaining or other mutual aid or protection, and shall also have the right to refrain from any or all of such activities except to the extent that such right may be affected by an agreement requiring membership in a labor organization as a condition of employment as authorized in section 8(a)(3).

Section 8.

(a) It shall be an unfair labor practice for an employer—

    (1) to interfere with, restrain, or coerce employees in the exercise of the rights guaranteed in section 7 of this act;

    (2) to dominate or interfere with the formation or administration of any labor organization or contribute financial or other support to it: *Provided*, That subject to rules and regulations made and published by the Board pursuant to section 6 of this

act, an employer shall not be prohibited from permitting employees to confer with him during working hours without loss of time or pay;

(3) by discrimination in regard to hire or tenure of employment or any term or condition of employment to encourage or discourage membership in any labor organization; *Provided*, That nothing in this act, or any other statute of the United States, shall preclude an employer from making an agreement with a labor organization (not established, maintained, or assisted by any action defined in this subsection as an unfair labor practice) to require as a condition of employment membership therein on or after the thirtieth day following the beginning of such employment or the effective date of such agreement, whichever is the later, (i) if such labor organization is the representative of the employees as provided in section 9(a), in the appropriate collective-bargaining unit covered by such agreement when made; and (ii) unless following an election held as provided in section 9(e) within one year preceding the effective date of such agreement the Board shall have certified that at least a majority of the employees eligible to vote in such election have voted to rescind the authority of such labor organization to make such an agreement: *Provided further*, that no employer shall justify any discrimination against an employee for nonmembership in a labor organization (A) if he has reasonable grounds for believing that such membership was not available to the employee on the same terms and conditions generally applicable to other members or (B) if he has reasonable grounds for believing that membership was denied or terminated for reasons other than the failure of the employee to tender the periodic dues and the initiation fees uniformly required as a condition of acquiring or retaining membership;

(4) to discharge or otherwise discriminate against an employee because he has filed charges or given testimony under this act;

(5) to refuse to bargain collectively with the representatives of his employees, subject to the provisions of section 9(a).

(b) It shall be an unfair labor practice for a labor organization or its agents—

(1) to restrain or coerce (A) employees in the exercise of the rights guaranteed in section 7: *Provided*, That this paragraph shall not impair the right of a labor organization to prescribe its own rules with respect to the acquisition or retention of membership therein; or (B) an employer in the selection of his representatives for the purposes of collective bargaining or the adjustment of grievances;

(2) to cause or attempt to cause an employer to discriminate against an employee in violation of subsection (a)(3) of this section or to discriminate against an employee with respect to

whom membership in such organization has been denied or
terminated on some ground other than his failure to tender the
periodic dues and the initiation fees uniformly required as a
condition of acquiring or retaining membership;

(3) to refuse to bargain collectively with an employer, provided
it is the representative of his employees subject to the provisions of section 9(a); * * *

(d) For the purposes of this section, to bargain collectively is the
performance of the mutual obligation of the employer and the
representative of the employees to meet at reasonable times and
confer in good faith with respect to wages, hours, and other
terms and conditions of employment, or the negotiation of an
agreement, or any question arising thereunder, and the execution of a written contract incorporating any agreement reached
if requested by either party, but such obligation does not compel
either party to agree to a proposal or require the making of a
concession: *provided*, That where there is in effect a collective-
bargaining contract covering employees in an industry affecting
commerce, the duty to bargain collectively shall also mean that
no party to such contract shall terminate or modify such contract, unless the party desiring such termination or modification—

(1) serves a written notice upon the other party to the contract
of the proposed termination or modification sixty days prior to
the expiration date thereof, or in the event such contract
contains no expiration date, sixty days prior to the time it is
proposed to make such termination or modification;

(2) offers to meet and confer with the other party for the
purpose of negotiating a new contract or a contract containing
the proposed modifications;

(3) notifies the Federal Mediation and Conciliation Service
within thirty days after such notice of the existence of a dispute,
and simultaneously therewith notifies any State or Territorial
agency established to mediate and conciliate disputes within the
State or Territory where the dispute occurred, provided no
agreement has been reached by that time; and

(4) continues in full force and effect, without resorting to strike
or lock-out, all the terms and conditions of the existing contract
for a period of sixty days after such notice is given or until the
expiration date of such contract, whichever occurs later: * * *

Section 9. (a) Representatives designated or selected for the purposes of collective bargaining by the majority of the employees in a unit
appropriate for such purposes, shall be the exclusive representatives of
all the employees in such unit for the purposes of collective bargaining in
respect to rates of pay, wages, hours of employment, or other conditions
of employment: *Provided*, That any individual employee or a group of

employees shall have the right at any time to present grievances to their employer and to have such grievances adjusted, without the intervention of the bargaining representative, as long as the adjustment is not inconsistent with the terms of a collective-bargaining contract or agreement then in effect: *Provided further*, That the bargaining representative has been given opportunity to be present at such adjustment.

Section 10. (a) The Board is empowered, as hereinafter provided, to prevent any person from engaging in any unfair labor practice (listed in section 8) affecting commerce. This power shall not be affected by any other means of adjustment or prevention that has been or may be established by agreement, law, or otherwise: * * *

  (f) Any person aggrieved by a the final order of Board granting or denying in whole or in part the relief sought may obtain a review of such order in any United States court of appeals in the circuit wherein the unfair labor practice in question was alleged to have been engaged in or wherein such person resides or transacts business, or in the United States Court of Appeals for the District of Columbia, by filing in such a court a written petition praying that the order of the Board be modified or set aside. A copy of such petition shall be forthwith transmitted by the clerk of the court to the Board, and thereupon the aggrieved party shall file in the court the record in the proceeding, certified by the Board, as provided in section 2112 of title 28. Upon the filing of such petition, the court shall proceed in the same manner as in the case of an application by the Board under subsection (e) of this section, and shall have the same jurisdiction to grant to the Board such temporary relief or restraining order as it deems just and proper, and in like manner to make and enter a decree enforcing, modifying, and enforcing as so modified, or setting aside in whole or in part the order of the Board; the findings of the Board with respect to questions of fact if supported by substantial evidence on the record considered as a whole shall in like manner be conclusive. * * *

  (h) When granting appropriate temporary relief or a restraining order, or making and entering a decree enforcing, modifying, and enforcing as so modified or setting aside in whole or in part an order of the Board, as provided in this section, the jurisdiction of courts sitting in equity shall not be limited by chapter 6 of this title. * * *

Section 13. Nothing in this Act, except as specifically provided for herein, shall be construed so as either to interfere with or impede or diminish in any way the right to strike, or to affect the limitations or qualifications on that right.

Section 14. (b) Nothing in this Act shall be construed as authorizing the execution or application of agreements requiring membership in a labor organization as a condition of employment in any State or

Territory in which such execution or application is prohibited by State or Territorial law.

Section 201. That it is the policy of the United States that—

* * *

(b) the settlement of issues between employers and employees through collective bargaining may be advanced by making available full and adequate governmental facilities for conciliation, mediation, and voluntary arbitration to aid and encourage employers and the representatives of their employees to reach and maintain agreements concerning rates of pay, hours, and working conditions, and to make all reasonable efforts to settle their differences by mutual agreement reached through conferences and collective bargaining or by such methods as may be provided for in any applicable agreement for the settlement of disputes;

* * *

Section 203. (d) Final adjustment by a method agreed upon by the parties is hereby declared to be the desirable method for settlement of grievance disputes arising over the application or interpretation of an existing collective-bargaining agreement. The [Federal Mediation and Conciliation] Service is directed to make its conciliation and mediation services available in the settlement of such grievance disputes only as a last resort and in exceptional cases.

Section 301. (a) Suits for violation of contracts between an employer and a labor organization representing employees in an industry affecting commerce as defined in this Act, or between any such labor organizations, may be brought in any district court of the United States having jurisdiction of the parties, without regard to the citizenship of the parties.

(b) Any labor organization which represents employees in an industry affecting commerce as defined in this Act and any employer whose activities affect commerce as defined in this Act shall be bound by the acts of its agents. Any such labor organization may sue or be sued as an entity and in behalf of the employees whom it represents in the courts of the United States. Any money judgment against a labor organization in a district court of the United States shall be enforceable only against the organization as an entity and against its assets, and shall not be enforceable against any individual member or his assets.

NORRIS–LA GUARDIA (ANTI–INJUNCTION) ACT
29 U.S.C. §§ 101–115.

An Act

To amend the Judicial Code and to define and limit the jurisdiction of courts sitting in equity, and for other purposes.

Sec. 1. Issuance of Restraining Orders and Injunctions; Limitation; Public Policy.

No court of the United States, as herein defined, shall have jurisdiction to issue any restraining order or temporary or permanent injunction in a case involving or growing out of a labor dispute, except in a strict conformity with the provisions of this Act; nor shall any such restraining order or temporary or permanent injunction be issued contrary to the public policy declared in this Act.

Sec. 2. Public Policy in Labor Matters Declared.

In the interpretation of this Act and in determining the jurisdiction and authority of the courts of the United States, as such jurisdiction and authority are herein defined and limited, the public policy of the United States is hereby declared as follows:

Whereas under prevailing economic conditions, developed with the aid of governmental authority for owners of property to organize in the corporate and other forms of ownership association, the individual unorganized worker is commonly helpless to exercise actual liberty of contract and to protect his freedom of labor, and thereby to obtain acceptable terms and conditions of employment, wherefore, though he should be free to decline to associate with his fellows, it is necessary that he have full freedom of association, self-organization, and designation of representatives of his own choosing, to negotiate the terms and conditions of his employment, and that he shall be free from the interference, restraint, or coercion of employers of labor, or their agents, in the designation of such representatives or in self-organization or in other concerted activities for the purpose of collective bargaining or other mutual aid or protection; therefore, the following definitions of and limitations upon the jurisdiction and authority of the courts of the United States are enacted.

Sec. 3. Nonenforceability of Undertakings in Conflict With Public Policy; "Yellow Dog" Contracts.

Any undertaking or promise, such as is described in this section, or any other undertaking or promise in conflict with the public policy declared in section 2 of this Act is hereby declared to be contrary to the public policy of the United States, shall not be enforceable in any court of the United States and shall not afford any basis for the granting of legal or equitable relief by any such court, including specifically the following:

Every undertaking or promise hereafter made, whether written or oral, express or implied, constituting or contained in any contract or agreement of hiring or employment between any individual, firm, company, association, or corporation, and any employee or prospective employee of the same, whereby

(a) Either party to such contract or agreement undertakes or promises not to join, become, or remain a member of any labor organization or of any employer organization; or

(b) Either party to such contract or agreement undertakes or promises that he will withdraw from an employment relation in the event that he joins, becomes, or remains a member of any labor organization or of any employer organization.

Sec. 4. Enumeration of Specific Acts Not Subject to Restraining Orders or Injunctions.

No court of the United States shall have jurisdiction to issue any restraining order or temporary or permanent injunction in any case involving or growing out of any labor dispute to prohibit any person or persons participating or interested in such dispute (as these terms are herein defined) from doing, whether singly or in concert, any of the following acts:

(a) Ceasing or refusing to perform any work or to remain in any relation of employment;

(b) Becoming or remaining a member of any labor organization or of any employer organization, regardless of any such undertaking or promise as is described in section 3 of this Act;

(c) Paying or giving to, or withholding from, any person participating or interested in such labor dispute, any strike or unemployment benefits or insurance, or other moneys or things of value;

(d) By all lawful means aiding any person participating or interested in any labor dispute who is being proceeded against in, or is prosecuting, any action or suit in any court of the United States or of any State;

(e) Giving publicity to the existence of, or the facts involved in, any labor dispute, whether by advertising, speaking, patrolling, or by any other method not involving fraud or violence;

(f) Assembling peaceably to act or to organize to act in promotion of their interests in a labor dispute;

(g) Advising or notifying any person of an intention to do any of the acts heretofore specified;

(h) Agreeing with other persons to do or not to do any of the acts heretofore specified; and

(i) Advising, urging, or otherwise causing or inducing without fraud or violence the acts heretofore specified, regardless of any such undertaking or promise as is described in section 3 of this Act.

Sec. 5. Doing in Concert of Certain Acts as Constituting Unlawful Combination or Conspiracy Subjecting Person to Injunctive Remedies.

No court of the United States shall have jurisdiction to issue a restraining order or temporary or permanent injunction upon the ground that any of the persons participating or interested in a labor dispute constitute or are engaged in any unlawful combination or conspiracy because of the doing in concert of the acts enumerated in section 4 of this Act.

Sec. 6. Responsibility of Officers and Members of Associations or Their Organizations for Unlawful Acts of Individual Officers, Members, and Agents.

No officer or member of any association or organization, and no association or organization participating or interested in a labor dispute, shall be held responsible or liable in any court of the United States for the unlawful acts of individual officers, members, or agents, except upon clear proof of actual participation in, or actual authorization of, such acts, or of ratification of such acts after actual knowledge thereof.

Sec. 7. Issuance of Injunctions in Labor Disputes; Hearings; Findings of Court; Notice to Affected Persons; Temporary Restraining Order; Undertakings.

No court of the United States shall have jurisdiction to issue a temporary or permanent injunction in any case involving or growing out of a labor dispute, as herein defined, except after hearing the testimony of witnesses in open court (with opportunity for cross-examination) in support of the allegations of a complaint made under oath, and testimony in opposition thereof, if offered, and except after findings of fact by the court, to the effect

(a) That unlawful acts have been threatened and will be committed unless restrained or have been committed and will be continued unless restrained, but no injunction or temporary restraining order shall be issued on account of any threat or unlawful act excepting against the person or persons, association, or organization making the threat or committing the unlawful act or actually authorizing or ratifying the same after actual knowledge thereof;

(b) That substantial and irreparable injury to complainant's property will follow;

(c) That as to each item of relief granted greater injury will be inflicted upon complainant by the denial of relief than will be inflicted upon defendants by the granting relief;

(d) That complainant has no adequate remedy at law; and

(e) That the public officers charged with the duty to protect complainant's property are unable or unwilling to furnish adequate protection.

Such hearing shall be held after due and personal notice thereof has been given, in such manner as the court shall direct, to all known persons against whom relief is sought, and also to the chief of those public officials of the county and city within which the unlawful acts have been threatened or committed charged with the duty to protect complainant's property: *Provided, however,* That if a complainant shall also allege that, unless a temporary restraining order shall be issued without notice, a substantial and irreparable injury to complainant's property will be unavoidable, such a temporary restraining order may be issued upon testimony under oath, sufficient, if sustained, to justify the court in issuing a temporary injunction upon a hearing after notice. Such a temporary restraining order shall be effective for no longer than five days and shall become void at the expiration of said five days. No temporary restraining order or temporary injunction shall be issued except on condition that complainant shall first file an undertaking with adequate security in an amount to be fixed by the court sufficient to recompense those enjoined for any loss, expense, or damage caused by the improvident or erroneous issuance of such order or injunction, including all reasonable costs (together with a reasonable attorney's fee) and expense of defense against the order or against the granting of any injunctive relief sought in the same proceeding and subsequently denied by the court.

The undertaking mentioned in this section shall be understood to signify an agreement entered into by the complainant and the surety upon which a decree may be rendered in the same suit or proceeding against said complainant and surety, upon a hearing to assess damages of which hearing complainant and surety shall have reasonable notice, the said complainant and surety submitting themselves to the jurisdiction of the court for that purpose. But nothing herein contained shall deprive any party having a claim or cause of action under or upon such undertaking from electing to pursue his ordinary remedy by suit at law or in equity.

Sec. 8. Noncompliance With Obligations Involved in Labor Disputes or Failure to Settle by Negotiation or Arbitration as Preventing Injunctive Relief.

No restraining order or injunctive relief shall be granted to any complainant who has failed to comply with any obligation imposed by law which is involved in the labor dispute in question, or who has failed to make every reasonable effort to settle such dispute either by negotiation or with the aid of any available governmental machinery of mediation or voluntary arbitration.

Sec. 9. Granting of Restraining Order or Injunction as Dependent on Previous Findings of Fact; Limitation on Prohibitions Included in Restraining Orders and Injunctions.

No restraining order or temporary or permanent injunction shall be granted in a case involving or growing out of a labor dispute, except on the basis of findings of fact made and filed by the court in the record of the case prior to the issuance of such restraining order or injunction; and every restraining order or injunction granted in a case involving or growing out of a labor dispute shall include only a prohibition of such specific act or acts as may be expressly complained of in the bill of complaint or petition filed in such case and as shall be expressly included in said findings of fact made and filed by the court as provided in this Act.

Sec. 10. Review by Court of Appeals of Issuance or Denial of Temporary Injunctions; Record; Precedence.

Whenever any court of the United States shall issue or deny any temporary injunction in a case involving or growing out of a labor dispute, the court shall, upon the request of any party to the proceedings and on his filing the usual bond for costs, forthwith certify as in ordinary cases the record of the case to the court of appeals for its review. Upon the filing of such record in the court of appeals, the appeal shall be heard and the temporary injunctive order affirmed, modified, or set aside expeditiously.

Sec. 11. Contempts; Speedy and Public Trial; Jury.*

In all cases arising under this Act in which a person shall be charged with contempt in a court of the United States (as herein defined), the accused shall enjoy the right to a speedy and public trial by an impartial jury of the State and district wherein the contempt shall have been committed: *Provided*, That this right shall not apply to contempts committed in the presence of the court or so near thereto as to interfere directly with the administration of justice or to apply to the misbehavior, misconduct, or disobedience of any officer of the court in respect to the writs, orders, or process of the court.

Sec. 12. Contempts; Demand for Retirement of Judge Sitting in Proceeding.*

The defendant in any proceeding for contempt of court may file with the court a demand for the retirement of the judge sitting in the proceeding, if the contempt arises from an attack upon the character or conduct of such judge and if the attack occurred elsewhere than in the presence of the court or so near thereto as to interfere directly with the administration of justice. Upon the filing of any such demand the judge shall thereupon proceed no further, but another judge shall be designated in the same manner as is provided by law. The demand shall be filed prior to the hearing in the contempt proceeding.

Sec. 13. Definitions of Terms and Words Used in Chapter.

When used in this Act, and for the purposes of this Act—

(a) A case shall be held to involve or to grow out of a labor dispute when the case involves persons who are engaged in the same industry, trade, craft, or occupation; or have direct or indirect interests therein; or who are employees of the same employer; or who are members of the same or an affiliated organization of employers or employees; whether such dispute is (1) between one or more employers or associations of employers and one or more employees or associations of employees; (2) between one or more employers or associations of employers and one or more employers or associations of employers; or (3) between one or more employees or associations of employees and one or more

---

* S11 and 12 were repealed by Act of June 25, 1948 (62 Stat. 862), a codification of the provisions of Title 18 of the United States Code. The substance of Section 11 was reenacted in the same Act (62 Stat. 844, 18 U.S.C. § 3692 (1970)); the substance of Section 12 is now found in Rules 42(a) and (b) of the Federal Rules of Criminal Procedure.

employees or associations of employees; or when the case involves any conflicting or competing interests in a "labor dispute" (as hereinafter defined) or "persons participating or interested" therein (as hereinafter defined).

(b) A person or association shall be held to be a person participating or interested in a labor dispute if relief is sought against him or it, and if he or it is engaged in the same industry, trade, craft, or occupation in which such dispute occurs, or has a direct or indirect interest therein, or is a member, officer, or agent of any association composed in whole or in part of employers or employees engaged in such industry, trade, craft, or occupation.

(c) The term "labor dispute" includes any controversy concerning terms or conditions or employment, or concerning the association or representation of persons in negotiating, fixing, maintaining, changing, or seeking to arrange terms or conditions of employment, regardless of whether or not the disputants stand in the proximate relation of employer and employee.

(d) The term "court of the United States" means any court of the United States whose jurisdiction has been or may be conferred or defined or limited by Act of Congress, including the courts of the District of Columbia.

Sec. 14.   Separability of Provisions.

If any provision of this Act or the application thereof to any person or circumstance is held unconstitutional or otherwise invalid, the remaining provisions of this Act and the application of such provisions to other persons or circumstances shall not be affected thereby.

Sec. 15.   Repeal of Conflicting Acts.

All acts and parts of acts in conflict with the provisions of this Act are repealed.

FEDERAL ARBITRATION ACT
9 U.S.C. §§ 1–16.

§ 1.   "Maritime Transactions" and "Commerce" Defined; Exceptions to Operation of Title

"Maritime transactions," as herein defined, means charter parties, bills of lading of water carriers, agreements relating to wharfage, supplies furnished vessels or repairs of vessels, collisions, or any other matters in foreign commerce which, if the subject of controversy, would be embraced within admiralty jurisdiction; "commerce," as herein defined, means commerce among the several States or with foreign nations, or in any Territory of the United States or in the District of Columbia, or between any such Territory and another, or between any such Territory and any State or foreign nation, or between the District of Columbia and any State or Territory or foreign nation, but nothing herein contained shall apply to contracts of employment of seamen, railroad employees, or any other class of workers engaged in foreign or interstate commerce.

§ 2. Validity, Irrevocability, and Enforcement of Agreements to Arbitrate

A written provision in any maritime transaction or a contract evidencing a transaction involving commerce to settle by arbitration a controversy thereafter arising out of such contract or transaction, or the refusal to perform the whole or any part thereof, or an agreement in writing to submit to arbitration an existing controversy arising out of such a contract, transaction, or refusal, shall be valid, irrevocable, and enforceable, save upon such grounds as exist at law or in equity for the revocation of any contract.

§ 3. Stay of Proceedings Where Issue Therein Referable to Arbitration

If any suit or proceeding be brought in any of the courts of the United States upon any issue referable to arbitration under an agreement in writing for such arbitration, the court in which such suit is pending, upon being satisfied that the issue involved in such suit or proceeding is referable to arbitration under such an agreement, shall on application of one of the parties stay the trial of the action until such arbitration has been had in accordance with the terms of the agreement, providing the applicant for the stay is not in default in proceeding with such arbitration.

§ 4. Failure To Arbitrate Under Agreement; Petition to United States Court Having Jurisdiction for Order to Compel Arbitration; Notice and Service Thereof; Hearing and Determination

A party aggrieved by the alleged failure, neglect, or refusal of another to arbitrate under a written agreement for arbitration may petition any United States district court which, save for such agreement, would have jurisdiction under Title 28, in a civil action or in admiralty of the subject matter of a suit arising out of the controversy between the parties, for an order directing that such arbitration proceed in the manner provided for in such agreement. Five days' notice in writing of such application shall be served upon the party in default. Service thereof shall be made in the manner provided by the Federal Rules of Civil Procedure. The court shall hear the parties, and upon being satisfied that the making of the agreement for arbitration or the failure to comply therewith is not in issue, the court shall make an order directing the parties to proceed to arbitration in accordance with the terms of the agreement. The hearing and proceedings under such agreement, shall be within the district in which the petition for an order directing such arbitration is filed. If the making of the arbitration agreement or the failure, neglect, or refusal to perform the same be in issue, the court shall proceed summarily to the trial thereof. If no jury trial be demanded by the party alleged to be in default, or if the matter in disputes is within admiralty jurisdiction, the court shall hear and determine such issue. Where such an issue is raised, the party alleged to be in default may, except in cases of admiralty, on or before the return day of the notice of application, demand a jury trial of such issue, and upon such demand the court shall make an order referring the issue or issues to a jury in the manner provided by the Federal Rules of Civil Procedure, or may specially call a jury for that purpose. If the jury find that no agreement in writing for arbitration was made or that there is no default in proceeding thereunder, the proceeding shall be dismissed. If the jury find that an agreement for arbitration was made in writing and that there is a default in proceeding thereunder, the court shall make an order summarily directing the parties to proceed with the arbitration in accordance with the terms thereof.

§ 5. Appointment of Arbitrators or Umpire

If in the agreement provision be made for a method of naming or appointing an arbitrator or arbitrators or an umpire, such method shall be followed; but if no method be provided therein, or if a method be provided and any party thereto shall fail to avail himself of such method, or if for an other reason there shall be a lapse in the naming of an arbitrator or arbitrators or umpire, or in filling a vacancy, then upon the application of either party to the controversy the court shall designate and appoint an arbitrator or arbitrators or umpire, as the case may require, who shall act under the said agreement with the same force and effect as if he or they had been specifically named therein; and unless otherwise provided in the agreement the arbitration shall be by a single arbitrator.

§ 6. Application Heard as Motion

Any application to the court hereunder shall be made and heard in the manner provided by law for the making and hearing of motions, except as otherwise herein expressly provided.

§ 7. Witnesses Before Arbitrators;
Fees; Compelling Attendance

The arbitrators selected either as prescribed in this title or otherwise, or a majority of them, may summon in writing any person to attend before them or any of them as a witness and in a proper case to bring with him or them any book, record, document, or paper which may be deemed material as evidence in the case. The fees for such attendance shall be the same as the fees of witnesses before masters of the United States courts. Said summons shall issue in the name of the arbitrator or arbitrators, or a majority of them, and shall be signed by the arbitrators, or a majority of them, and shall be directed to the said person and shall be served in the same manner as subpoenas to appear and testify before the court; if any person or persons so summoned to testify shall refuse or neglect to obey said summons, upon petition the United States district court for the district in which such arbitrators, or a majority of them, are sitting may compel the attendance of such person or persons before said arbitrator or arbitrators, or punish said person or persons for contempt in the same manner provided on February 12, 1925, for securing the attendance of witnesses or their punishment for neglect or refusal to attend in the courts of the United States.

§ 8. Proceedings Begun by Libel in Admiralty and Seizure of Vessel or Property

If the basis of jurisdiction be a cause of action otherwise justiciable in admiralty, then, notwithstanding anything herein to the contrary the party claiming to be aggrieved may begin his proceeding hereunder by libel and seizure of the vessel or other property of the other party according to the usual course of admiralty proceedings, and the court shall then have jurisdiction to direct the parties to proceed with the arbitration and shall retain jurisdiction to enter its decree upon the award.

§ 9. Award of Arbitrators; Confirmation; Jurisdiction; Procedure

If the parties in their agreement have agreed that a judgment of the court shall be entered upon the award made pursuant to the arbitration, and shall specify the court, then at any time within one year after the award is made any party to the arbitration may apply to the court so specified for an order confirming the award, and thereupon the court must grant such an order unless the award is vacated, modified, or corrected as prescribed in sections 10 and 11 of this title. If no court is specified in the agreement of the parties, then such application may be made to the United States court in and for the district within which such award was made. Notice of the application shall be served upon the adverse party, and thereupon the court shall have jurisdiction of such party as though he had appeared generally in the proceeding. If the adverse party is a resident of the district within which the award was made, such service shall be made upon the adverse party or his attorney as prescribed by law for service of notice of motion in an action in the same court. If the adverse party shall be a nonresident, then the notice of the application shall be served by the marshal of any district within which the adverse party may be found in like manner as other process of the court.

§ 10. Same; Vacation; Grounds; Rehearing

(a) In any of the following cases the United States court in and for the district wherein the award was made may make an order vacating the award upon the application of any party to the arbitration—

(1) Where the award was procured by corruption, fraud, or undue means.

(2) Where there was evident partiality or corruption in the arbitrators, or either of them.

(3) Where the arbitrators were guilty of misconduct in refusing to postpone the hearing, upon sufficient cause shown, or in refus-

ing to hear evidence pertinent and material to the controversy; or of any other misbehavior by which the rights of any party have been prejudiced.

(4) Where the arbitrators exceeded their powers, or so imperfectly executed them that a mutual, final, and definite award upon the subject matter submitted was not made.

(5) Where an award is vacated and the time within which the agreement required the award to be made has not expired the court may, in its discretion, direct a rehearing by the arbitrators.

(b) The United States district court for the district wherein an award was made that was issued pursuant to section 580 of title 5 may make an order vacating the award upon the application of a person, other than a party to the arbitration, who is adversely affected or aggrieved by the award, if the use of arbitration or the award is clearly inconsistent with the factors set forth in section 572 of title 5.

§ 11. Same; Modification or Correction; Grounds; Order

In either of the following cases the United States court in and for the district wherein the award was made may make an order modifying or correcting the award upon the application of any party to the arbitration—

(a) Where there was an evident material miscalculation of figures or an evident material mistake in the description of any person, thing, or property referred to in the award.

(b) Where the arbitrators have awarded upon a matter not submitted to them, unless it is a matter not affecting the merits of the decision upon the matter submitted.

(c) Where the award is imperfect in matter of form not affecting the merits of the controversy.

The order may modify and correct the award, so as to effect the intent thereof and promote justice between the parties.

§ 12. Notice of Motions to Vacate or Modify; Service; Stay of Proceedings

Notice of a motion to vacate, modify, or correct an award must be served upon the adverse party or his attorney within three months after the award is filed or delivered. If the adverse party is a resident of the district within which the award was made, such service shall be made upon the adverse party or his attorney as prescribed by law for service of notice of motion in an action in the same court. If the adverse party shall be a nonresident then the notice of the application shall be served by the marshal of any district within which the adverse party may be found in like manner as other process of the court. For the purposes of the motion any judge who might make an order to stay the proceedings in an action brought in the same court may make an order, to be served with the notice of motion, staying the proceedings of the adverse party to enforce the award.

§ 13. Papers Filed With Order on Motions; Judgment; Docketing; Force and Effect; Enforcement

The party moving for an order confirming, modifying, or correcting an award shall, at the time such order is filed with the clerk for the entry of judgment thereon, also file the following papers with the clerk:

(a) The agreement; the selection or appointment, if any, of an additional arbitrator or umpire; and each written extension of the time, if any, within which to make the award.

(b) The award.

(c) Each notice, affidavit, or other paper used upon an application to confirm, modify, or correct the award, and a copy of each order of the court upon such an application.

The judgment shall be docketed as if it was rendered in an action.

The judgment so entered shall have the same force and effect, in all respects, as, and be subject to all the provisions of law relating to, a judgment in an action; and it may be enforced as if it had been rendered in an action in the court in which it is entered.

§ 14. Contracts Not Affected

This title shall not apply to contracts made prior to January 1, 1926.

§ 15. Inapplicability of the Act of State doctrine

Enforcement of arbitral agreements, confirmation of arbitral awards, and execution upon judgments based on orders confirming such awards shall not be refused on the basis of the Act of State doctrine.

§ 16. Appeals

(a) An appeal may be taken from—

(1) an order—

(A) refusing a stay of any action under section 3 of this title,

(B) denying a petition under section 4 of this title to order arbitration to proceed,

(C) denying an application under section 206 of this title to compel arbitration,

(D) confirming or denying confirmation of an award or partial award, or

(E) modifying, correcting, or vacating an award;

(2) an interlocutory order granting, continuing, or modifying an injunction against an arbitration that is subject to this title; or

(3) a final decision with respect to an arbitration that is subject to this title.

(b) Except as otherwise provided in section 1292(b) of title 28, an appeal may not be taken from an interlocutory order—

(1) granting a stay of any action under section 3 of this title;

(2) directing arbitration to proceed under section 4 of this title;

(3) compelling arbitration under section 206 of this title; or

(4) refusing to enjoin an arbitration that is subject to this title.

UNIFORM ARBITRATION ACT

(Adopted by the National Conference of the Commissioners on Uniform State Laws in 1955 and amended in 1956; approved by the Delegates of the American Bar Association on August 26, 1955 and August 30, 1956; and further amended in 2000.)

Section 1. Definitions. In this [Act]:

(1) "Arbitration organization" means an association, agency, board, commission, or other entity that is neutral and initiates, sponsors, or administers an arbitration proceeding or is involved in the appointment of an arbitrator.

(2) "Arbitrator" means an individual appointed to render an award, alone or with others, in a controversy that is subject to an agreement to arbitrate.

(3) "Court" means [a court of competent jurisdiction in this State].

(4) "Knowledge" means actual knowledge.

(5) "Person" means an individual, corporation, business trust, estate, trust, partnership, limited liability company, association, joint venture, government; governmental subdivision, agency, or instrumentality; public corporation; or any other legal or commercial entity.

(6) "Record" means information that is inscribed on a tangible medium or that is stored in an electronic or other medium and is retrievable in perceivable form.

Section 2. Notice.

(a) Except as otherwise provided in this [Act], a person gives notice to another person by taking action that is reasonably necessary to inform the other person in ordinary course, whether or not the other person acquires knowledge of the notice.

(b) A person has notice if the person has knowledge of the notice or has received notice.

(c) A person receives notice when it comes to the person's attention or the notice is delivered at the person's place of residence or place of business, or at another location held out by the person as a place of delivery of such communications.

Section 3. When [Act] Applies.

(a) This [Act] governs an agreement to arbitrate made on or after [the effective date of this [Act]].

(b) This [Act] governs an agreement to arbitrate made before [the effective date of this [Act]] if all the parties to the agreement or to the arbitration proceeding so agree in a record.

(c) On or after [a delayed date], this [Act] governs an agreement to arbitrate whenever made.

Section 4. Effect of Agreement to Arbitrate; Nonwaivable Provisions.

(a) Except as otherwise provided in subsections (b) and (c), a party to an agreement to arbitrate or to an arbitration proceeding may waive or, the parties may vary the effect of, the requirements of this [Act] to the extent permitted by law.

(b) Before a controversy arises that is subject to an agreement to arbitrate, a party to the agreement may not:

(1) waive or agree to vary the effect of the requirements of Section 5(a), 6(a), 8, 17(a), 17(b), 26, or 28;

(2) agree to unreasonably restrict the right under Section 9 to notice of the initiation of an arbitration proceeding;

(3) agree to unreasonably restrict the right under Section 12 to disclosure of any facts by a neutral arbitrator; or

(4) waive the right under Section 16 of a party to an agreement to arbitrate to be represented by a lawyer at any proceeding or hearing under this [Act], but an employer and a labor organization may waive the right to representation by a lawyer in a labor arbitration.

(c) A party to an agreement to arbitrate or arbitration proceeding may not waive, or the parties may not vary the effect of, the requirements of this section or Section 3(a) or (c), 7, 14, 18, 20(d) or (e), 22, 23, 24, 25(a) or (b), 29, 30, 31, or 32.

Section 5. [Application] for Judicial Relief.

(a) Except as otherwise provided in Section 28, an [application] for judicial relief under this [Act] must be made by [motion] to the court and heard in the manner provided by law or rule of court for making and hearing [motions].

(b) Unless a civil action involving the agreement to arbitrate is pending, notice of an initial [motion] to the court under this [Act] must be served in the manner provided by law for the service of a summons in a civil action. Otherwise, notice of the motion must be given in the manner provided by law or rule of court for serving [motions] in pending cases.

Section 6.   Validity of Agreement to Arbitrate.

(a) An agreement contained in a record to submit to arbitration any existing or subsequent controversy arising between the parties to the agreement is valid, enforceable, and irrevocable except upon a ground that exists at law or in equity for the revocation of a contract.

(b) The court shall decide whether an agreement to arbitrate exists or a controversy is subject to an agreement to arbitrate.

(c) An arbitrator shall decide whether a condition precedent to arbitrability has been fulfilled and whether a contract containing a valid agreement to arbitrate is enforceable.

(d) If a party to a judicial proceeding challenges the existence of, or claims that a controversy is not subject to, an agreement to arbitrate, the arbitration proceeding may continue pending final resolution of the issue by the court, unless the court otherwise orders.

Section 7.   [Motion] to Compel or Stay Arbitration.

(a) On [motion] of a person showing an agreement to arbitrate and alleging another person's refusal to arbitrate pursuant to the agreement:

> (1) if the refusing party does not appear or does not oppose the [motion], the court shall order the parties to arbitrate; and

> (2) if the refusing party opposes the [motion], the court shall proceed summarily to decide the issue and order the parties to arbitrate unless it finds that there is no enforceable agreement to arbitrate.

(b) On [motion] of a person alleging that an arbitration proceeding has been initiated or threatened but that there is no agreement to arbitrate, the court shall proceed summarily to decide the issue. If the court finds that there is an enforceable agreement to arbitrate, it shall order the parties to arbitrate.

(c) If the court finds that there is no enforceable agreement, it may not pursuant to subsection (a) or (b) order the parties to arbitrate.

(d) The court may not refuse to order arbitration because the claim subject to arbitration lacks merit or grounds for the claim have not been established.

(e) If a proceeding involving a claim referable to arbitration under an alleged agreement to arbitrate is pending in court, a [motion] under this section must be made in that court. Otherwise a [motion] under this section may be made in any court as provided in Section 27.

(f) If a party makes a [motion] to the court to order arbitration, the court on just terms shall stay any judicial proceeding that involves a claim alleged to be subject to the arbitration until the court renders a final decision under this section.

(g) If the court orders arbitration, the court on just terms shall stay any judicial proceeding that involves a claim subject to the arbitration. If a claim subject to the arbitration is severable, the court may limit the stay to that claim.

Section 8.   Provisional Remedies.

(a) Before an arbitrator is appointed and is authorized and able to act, the court, upon [motion] of a party to an arbitration proceeding and for good cause shown, may enter an order for provisional remedies to protect the effectiveness of the arbitration proceeding to the same extent and under the same conditions as if the controversy were the subject of a civil action.

(b) After an arbitrator is appointed and is authorized and able to act:

(1) the arbitrator may issue such orders for provisional remedies, including interim awards, as the arbitrator finds necessary to protect the effectiveness of the arbitration proceeding and to promote the fair and expeditious resolution of the controversy, to the same extent and under the same conditions as if the controversy were the subject of a civil action and

(2) a party to an arbitration proceeding may move the court for a provisional remedy only if the matter is urgent and the arbitrator is not able to act timely or the arbitrator cannot provide an adequate remedy.

(c) A party does not waive a right of arbitration by making a [motion] under subsection (a) or (b).

Section 9.   Initiation of Arbitration.

(a) A person initiates an arbitration proceeding by giving notice in a record to the other parties to the agreement to arbitrate in the agreed manner between the parties or, in the absence of agreement, by certified or registered mail, return receipt requested and obtained, or by service as authorized for the commencement of a civil action. The notice must describe the nature of the controversy and the remedy sought.

(b) Unless a person objects for lack or insufficiency of notice under Section 15(c) not later than the beginning of the arbitration hearing, the person by appearing at the hearing waives any objection to lack of or insufficiency of notice.

Section 10.   Consolidation of Separate Arbitration Proceedings.

(a) Except as otherwise provided in subsection (c), upon [motion] of a party to an agreement to arbitrate or to an arbitration proceeding, the court may order consolidation of separate arbitration proceedings as to all or some of the claims if:

(1) there are separate agreements to arbitrate or separate arbitration proceedings between the same persons or one of them is a party to a separate agreement to arbitrate or a separate arbitration proceeding with a third person;

(2) the claims subject to the agreements to arbitrate arise in substantial part from the same transaction or series of related transactions;

(3) the existence of a common issue of law or fact creates the possibility of conflicting decisions in the separate arbitration proceedings; and

(4) prejudice resulting from a failure to consolidate is not outweighed by the risk of undue delay or prejudice to the rights of or hardship to parties opposing consolidation.

(b) The court may order consolidation of separate arbitration proceedings as to some claims and allow other claims to be resolved in separate arbitration proceedings.

(c) The court may not order consolidation of the claims of a party to an agreement to arbitrate if the agreement prohibits consolidation.

Section 11. Appointment of Arbitrator; Service as a Neutral Arbitrator.

(a) If the parties to an agreement to arbitrate agree on a method for appointing an arbitrator, that method must be followed, unless the method fails. If the parties have not agreed on a method, the agreed method fails, or an arbitrator appointed fails or is unable to act and a successor has not been appointed, the court, on [motion] of a party to the arbitration proceeding, shall appoint the arbitrator. An arbitrator so appointed has all the powers of an arbitrator designated in the agreement to arbitrate or appointed pursuant to the agreed method.

(b) An individual who has a known, direct, and material interest in the outcome of the arbitration proceeding or a known, existing, and substantial relationship with a party may not serve as an arbitrator required by an agreement to be neutral.

Section 12. Disclosure by Arbitrator.

(a) Before accepting appointment, an individual who is requested to serve as an arbitrator, after making a reasonable inquiry, shall disclose to all parties to the agreement to arbitrate and arbitration proceeding and to any other arbitrators any known facts that a reasonable person would consider likely to affect the impartiality of the arbitrator in the arbitration proceeding, including:

(1) a financial or personal interest in the outcome of the arbitration proceeding; and

(2) an existing or past relationship with any of the parties to the agreement to arbitrate or the arbitration proceeding, their counsel or representatives, a witness, or another arbitrators.

(b) An arbitrator has a continuing obligation to disclose to all parties to the agreement to arbitrate and arbitration proceeding and to any other arbitrators any facts that the arbitrator learns after accepting appointment which a reasonable person would consider likely to affect the impartiality of the arbitrator.

(c) If an arbitrator discloses a fact required by subsection (a) or (b) to be disclosed and a party timely objects to the appointment or continued service of the arbitrator based upon the fact disclosed, the objection may be a ground under Section 23(a)(2) for vacating an award made by the arbitrator.

(d) If the arbitrator did not disclose a fact as required by subsection (a) or (b), upon timely objection by a party, the court under Section 23(a)(2) may vacate an award.

(e) An arbitrator appointed as a neutral arbitrator who does not disclose a known, direct, and material interest in the outcome of the arbitration proceeding or a known, existing, and substantial relationship with a party is presumed to act with evident partiality under Section 23(a)(2).

(f) If the parties to an arbitration proceeding agree to the procedures of an arbitration organization or any other procedures for challenges to arbitrators before an award is made, substantial compliance with those procedures is a condition precedent to a [motion] to vacate an award on that ground under Section 23(a)(2).

Section 13. Action by Majority. If there is more than one arbitrator, the powers of an arbitrator must be exercised by a majority of the arbitrators, but all of them shall conduct the hearing under Section 15(c).

Section 14. Immunity of Arbitrator; Competency to Testify; Attorney's Fees and Costs.

(a) An arbitrator or an arbitration organization acting in that capacity is immune from civil liability to the same extent as a judge of a court of this State acting in a judicial capacity.

(b) The immunity afforded by this section supplements any immunity under other law.

(c) The failure of an arbitrator to make a disclosure required by Section 12 does not cause any loss of immunity under this section.

(d) In a judicial, administrative, or similar proceeding, an arbitrator or representative of an arbitration organization is not competent to testify, and may not be required to produce records as to any statement, conduct, decision, or ruling occurring during the arbitration proceeding, to the same extent as a judge of a court of this State acting in a judicial capacity. This subsection does not apply:

(1) to the extent necessary to determine the claim of an arbitrator, arbitration organization, or representative of the arbitration organization against a party to the arbitration proceeding; or

(2) to a hearing on a [motion] to vacate an award under Section 23(a)(1) or (2) if the [movant] establishes prima facie that a ground for vacating the award exists.

(e) If a person commences a civil action against an arbitrator, arbitration organization, or representative of an arbitration organization arising from the services of the arbitrator, organization, or representative or if a person seeks to compel an arbitrator or a representative of an arbitration organization to testify or produce records in violation of subsection (d), and the court decides that the arbitrator, arbitration organization, or representative of an arbitration organization is immune from civil liability or that the arbitrator or representative of the organization is not competent to testify, the court shall award to the arbitrator, organization, or representative reasonable attorney's fees and other reasonable expenses of litigation.

Section 15. Arbitration Process.

(a) An arbitrator may conduct an arbitration in such manner as the arbitrator considers appropriate for a fair and expeditious disposition of the proceeding. The authority conferred upon the arbitrator includes the power to hold conferences with the parties to the arbitration proceeding before the hearing and, among other matters, determine the admissibility, relevance, materiality and weight of any evidence.

(b) An arbitrator may decide a request for summary disposition of a claim or particular issue:

(1) if all interested parties agree; or

(2) upon request of one party to the arbitration proceeding if that party gives notice to all other parties to the proceeding, and the other parties have a reasonable opportunity to respond.

(c) If an arbitrator orders a hearing, the arbitrator shall set a time and place and give notice of the hearing not less than five days before the hearing begins. Unless a party to the arbitration proceeding makes an objection to lack or insufficiency of notice not later than the beginning of the hearing, the party's appearance at the hearing waives the objection. Upon request of a party to the arbitration proceeding and for good cause shown, or upon the arbitrator's own initiative, the arbitrator may adjourn the hearing from time to time as necessary but may not postpone the hearing to a time later than that fixed by the agreement to arbitrate for making the award unless the parties to the arbitration proceeding consent to a later date. The arbitrator may hear and decide the controversy upon the evidence produced although a party who was duly notified of the arbitration proceeding did not appear. The court, on request, may direct the arbitrator to conduct the hearing promptly and render a timely decision.

(d) At a hearing under subsection (c), a party to the arbitration proceeding has a right to be heard, to present evidence material to the controversy, and to cross-examine witnesses appearing at the hearing.

(e) If an arbitrator ceases or is unable to act during the arbitration proceeding, a replacement arbitrator must be appointed in accordance with Section 11 to continue the proceeding and to resolve the controversy.

Section 16. Representation by lawyer. A party to an arbitration proceeding may be represented by a lawyer.

Section 17. Witnesses; Subpoenas; Depositions; Discovery.

(a) An arbitrator may issue a subpoena for the attendance of a witness and for the production of records and other evidence at any hearing and may administer oaths. A subpoena must be served in the manner for service of subpoenas in a civil action and, upon [motion] to the court by a party to the arbitration proceeding or the arbitrator, enforced in the manner for enforcement of subpoenas in a civil action.

(b) In order to make the proceedings fair, expeditious, and cost effective, upon request of a party to or a witness in an arbitration proceeding, an arbitrator may permit a deposition of any witness to be taken for use as evidence at the hearing, including a witness who cannot be subpoenaed for or is unable to attend a hearing. The arbitrator shall determine the conditions under which the deposition is taken.

(c) An arbitrator may permit such discovery as the arbitrator decides is appropriate in the circumstances, taking into account the needs of the parties to the arbitration proceeding and other affected persons and the desirability of making the proceeding fair, expeditious, and cost effective.

(d) If an arbitrator permits discovery under subsection (c), the arbitrator may order a party to the arbitration proceeding to comply with the arbitrator's discovery-related orders, issue subpoenas for the attendance of a witness and for the production of records and other evidence at a discovery proceeding, and take action against a noncomplying party to the extent a court could if the controversy were the subject of a civil action in this State.

(e) An arbitrator may issue a protective order to prevent the disclosure of privileged information, confidential information, trade secrets, and other information protected from disclosure to the extent a court could if the controversy were the subject of a civil action in this State.

(f) All laws compelling a person under subpoena to testify and all fees for attending a judicial proceeding, a deposition, or a discovery proceeding as a witness apply to an arbitration proceeding as if the controversy were the subject of a civil action in this State.

(g) The court may enforce a subpoena or discovery-related order for the attendance of a witness within this State and for the production of records and other evidence issued by an arbitrator in connection with an arbitration proceeding in another State upon conditions determined by the court so as to make the arbitration proceeding fair, expeditious, and cost effective. A subpoena or discovery-related order issued by an arbitrator in another State must be served in the manner provided by law for service of subpoenas in a civil action in this State and, upon [motion] to the court by a party to the arbitration proceeding or the arbitrator, enforced in the manner provided by law for enforcement of subpoenas in a civil action in this State.

Section 18. Judicial Enforcement of Preaward Ruling by Arbitrator. If an arbitrator makes a preaward ruling in favor of a party to the arbitration proceeding, the party may request the arbitrator to incorporate the ruling into an award under Section 19. A prevailing party may make a [motion] to the court for an expedited order to confirm the award under Section 22, in which case the court shall summarily decide the [motion]. The court shall issue an order to confirm the award unless the court vacates, modifies, or corrects the award under Section 23 or 24.

Section 19. Award.

(a) An arbitrator shall make a record of an award. The record must be signed or otherwise authenticated by any arbitrator who concurs with the award. The arbitrator or the arbitration organization shall give notice of the award, including a copy of the award, to each party to the arbitration proceeding.

(b) An award must be made within the time specified by the agreement to arbitrate or, if not specified therein, within the time ordered by the court. The court may extend or the parties to the arbitration proceeding may agree in a record to extend the time. The court or the parties may do so within or after the time specified or ordered. A party waives any objection that an award was not timely made unless the party gives notice of the objection to the arbitrator before receiving notice of the award.

Section 20. Change of Award by Arbitrator.

(a) On [motion] to an arbitrator by a party to an arbitration proceeding, the arbitrator may modify or correct an award:

(1) upon a ground stated in Section 24(a)(1) or (3);

(2) because the arbitrator has not made a final and definite award upon a claim submitted by the parties to the arbitration proceeding; or

(3) to clarify the award.

(b) A [motion] under subsection (a) must be made and notice given to all parties within 20 days after the movant receives notice of the award.

(c) A party to the arbitration proceeding must give notice of any objection to the [motion] within 10 days after receipt of the notice.

(d) If a [motion] to the court is pending under Section 22, 23, or 24, the court may submit the claim to the arbitrator to consider whether to modify or correct the award:

(1) upon a ground stated in Section 24(a)(1) or (3);

(2) because the arbitrator has not made a final and definite award upon a claim submitted by the parties to the arbitration proceeding; or

(3) to clarify the award.

(e) An award modified or corrected pursuant to this section is subject to Sections 19(a), 22, 23, and 24.

Section 21. Remedies; Fees and Expenses of Arbitration Proceeding.

(a) An arbitrator may award punitive damages or other exemplary relief if such an award is authorized by law in a civil action involving the same claim and the evidence produced at the hearing justifies the award under the legal standards otherwise applicable to the claim.

(b) An arbitrator may award reasonable attorney's fees and other reasonable expenses of arbitration if such an award is authorized by law in a civil action involving the same claim or by the agreement of the parties to the arbitration proceeding.

(c) As to all remedies other than those authorized by subsections (a) and (b), an arbitrator may order such remedies as the arbitrator considers just and appropriate under the circumstances of the arbitration proceeding. The fact that such a remedy could not or would not be granted by the court is not a ground for refusing to confirm an award under Section 22 or for vacating an award under Section 23.

(d) An arbitrator's expenses and fees, together with other expenses, must be paid as provided in the award.

(e) If an arbitrator awards punitive damages or other exemplary relief under subsection (a), the arbitrator shall specify in the award the basis in fact justifying and the basis in law authorizing the award and state separately the amount of the punitive damages or other exemplary relief.

Section 22. Confirmation of Award. After a party to an arbitration proceeding receives notice of an award, the party may make a [motion] to the court for an order confirming the award at which time the court shall issue a confirming order unless the award is modified or corrected pursuant to Section 20 or 24 or is vacated pursuant to Section 23.

Section 23. Vacating Award.

(a) Upon [motion] to the court by a party to an arbitration proceeding, the court shall vacate an award made in the arbitration proceeding if:

(1) the award was procured by corruption, fraud, or other undue means;

(2) there was:

(A) evident partiality by an arbitrator appointed as a neutral arbitrator;

(B) corruption by an arbitrator; or

(C) misconduct by an arbitrator prejudicing the rights of a party to the arbitration proceeding;

(3) an arbitrator refused to postpone the hearing upon showing of sufficient cause for postponement, refused to consider evidence material to the controversy, or otherwise conducted the hearing contrary to Section 15, so as to prejudice substantially the rights of a party to the arbitration proceeding;

(4) an arbitrator exceeded the arbitrator's powers;

(5) there was no agreement to arbitrate, unless the person participated in the arbitration proceeding without raising the objection under Section 15(c) not later than the beginning of the arbitration hearing; or

(6) the arbitration was conducted without proper notice of the initiation of an arbitration as required in Section 9 so as to prejudice substantially the rights of a party to the arbitration proceeding.

(b) A [motion] under this section must be filed within 90 days after the [movant] receives notice of the award pursuant to Section 19 or within 90 days after the [movant] receives notice of a modified or corrected award pursuant to Section 20, unless the [movant] alleges that the award was procured by corruption, fraud, or other undue means, in which case the [motion] must be made within 90 days after the ground is known or by the exercise of reasonable care would have been known by the [movant].

(c) If the court vacates an award on a ground other than that set forth in subsection (a)(5), it may order a rehearing. If the award is vacated on a ground stated in subsection (a)(1) or (2), the rehearing must be before a new arbitrator. If the award is vacated on a ground stated in subsection (a)(3), (4), or (6), the rehearing may be before the arbitrator who made the award or the arbitrator's successor. The arbitrator must render the decision in the rehearing within the same time as that provided in Section 19(b) for an award.

(d) If the court denies a [motion] to vacate an award, it shall confirm the award unless a [motion] to modify or correct the award is pending.

Section 24.   Modification or Correction of Award.

(a) Upon [motion] made within 90 days after the [movant] receives notice of the award pursuant to Section 19 or within 90 days after the [movant] receives notice of a modified or corrected award pursuant to Section 20, the court shall modify or correct the award if:

(1) there was an evident mathematical miscalculation or an evident mistake in the description of a person, thing, or property referred to in the award;

(2) the arbitrator has made an award on a claim not submitted to the arbitrator and the award may be corrected without affecting the merits of the decision upon the claims submitted; or

(3) the award is imperfect in a matter of form not affecting the merits of the decision on the claims submitted.

(b) If a [motion] made under subsection (a) is granted, the court shall modify or correct and confirm the award as modified or corrected. Otherwise, unless a motion to vacate is pending, the court shall confirm the award.

(c) A [motion] to modify or correct an award pursuant to this section may be joined with a [motion] to vacate the award.

Section 25.   Judgment on Award; Attorney's Fees and Litigation Expenses.

(a) Upon granting an order confirming, vacating without directing a rehearing, modifying, or correcting an award, the court shall enter a judgment in conformity therewith. The judgment may be recorded, docketed, and enforced as any other judgment in a civil action.

(b) A court may allow reasonable costs of the [motion] and subsequent judicial proceedings.

(c) On [application] of a prevailing party to a contested judicial proceeding under Section 22, 23, or 24, the court may add reasonable attorney's fees and other reasonable expenses of litigation incurred in a judicial proceeding after the award is made to a judgment confirming, vacating without directing a rehearing, modifying, or correcting an award.

Section 26.   Jurisdiction.

(a) A court of this State having jurisdiction over the controversy and the parties may enforce an agreement to arbitrate.

(b) An agreement to arbitrate providing for arbitration in this State confers exclusive jurisdiction on the court to enter judgment on an award under this [Act].

Section 27.   Venue. A [motion] pursuant to Section 5 must be made in the court of the [county] in which the agreement to arbitrate specifies the arbitration hearing is to be held or, if the hearing has been held, in the court of the [county] in which it was held. Otherwise, the [motion] may be made in the court of any [county] in which an adverse party resides or has a place of business or, if no adverse party has a residence or place of business in this State, in the court of any [county] in this State. All subsequent [motions] must be made in the court hearing the initial [motion] unless the court otherwise directs.

Section 28.   Appeals.

(a) An appeal may be taken from:

(1) an order denying a [motion] to compel arbitration;

(2) an order granting a [motion] to stay arbitration;

(3) an order confirming or denying confirmation of an award;

(4) an order modifying or correcting an award;

(5) an order vacating an award without directing a rehearing; or

(6) a final judgment entered pursuant to this [Act].

(b) An appeal under this section must be taken as from an order or a judgment in a civil action.

Section 29.   Uniformity of Application and Construction. In applying and construing this uniform act, consideration must be given to the need to promote uniformity of the law with respect to its subject matter among States that enact it.

Section 30.   Relationship to Electronic Signatures in Global and National Commerce Act. The provisions of this Act governing the legal effect, validity, and enforceability of electronic records or electronic signatures, and of contracts performed with the use of such records or signatures conform to the requirements of Section 102 of the Electronic Signatures in Global and National Commerce Act.

Section 31.   Effective Date. This [Act] takes effect on [effective date].

Section 32.   Repeal. Effective on [delayed date should be the same as that in Section 3(c)], the [Uniform Arbitration Act] is repealed.

Section 33.   Savings Clause. This [Act] does not affect an action or proceeding commenced or right accrued before this [Act] takes effect. Subject to Section 3 of this [Act], an arbitration agreement made before the effective date of this [Act] is governed by the [Uniform Arbitration Act].

Appendix C

AMERICAN ARBITRATION ASSOCIATION RULES

LABOR ARBITRATION RULES

Amended and effective May 1, 2004.

Introduction

Every year, labor and management enter into thousands of collective bargaining agreements. Virtually all of these agreements provide for arbitration of unresolved grievances. For decades, the American Arbitration Association (AAA) has been a leading administrator of labor-management disputes.

The American Arbitration Association is a public-service, not-for-profit organization offering a broad range of dispute resolution services to business executives, attorneys, individuals, trade associations, unions, management, consumers, families, communities, and all levels of government. Services are available through AAA headquarters in New York City and through offices located in major cities throughout the United States. Hearings may be held at locations convenient for the parties and are not limited to cities with AAA offices. In addition, the AAA serves as a center for education and training, issues specialized publications, and conducts research on all forms of out-of-court dispute settlement.

Arbitration is a tool of industrial relations. Like other tools, it has limitations as well as advantages. In the hands of an expert, it produces useful results. When abused or made to do things for which it was never intended, the outcome can be disappointing. For these reasons, all participants in the process-union officials, employers, personnel executives, attorneys, and the arbitrators themselves-have an equal stake in orderly, efficient, and constructive arbitration procedures. The AAA's Labor Arbitration Rules provide a time-tested method for efficient, fair, and economical resolution of labor-management disputes. By referring to them in a collective bargaining agreement, the parties can take advantage of these benefits.

The parties can provide for arbitration of future disputes by inserting the following clause into their contracts:

Any dispute, claim, or grievance arising from or relating to the interpretation or application of this agreement shall be submitted to arbitration administered by the American Arbitration Association under its Labor Arbitration Rules. The parties further agree to accept the arbitrator's award as final and binding on them.

For relatively uncomplicated grievances, parties who use the labor arbitration services of the American Arbitration Association may agree to use expedited procedures that provide a prompt and inexpensive method for resolving disputes. This option responds to a concern about rising costs and delays in processing grievance-arbitration cases. The AAA's Expedited Labor Arbitration Procedures, by eliminating or streamlining certain steps, are intended to resolve cases within a month of the appointment of the arbitrator.

Labor Arbitration Rules

1. Agreement of Parties

The parties shall be deemed to have made these rules a part of their arbitration agreement whenever, in a collective bargaining agreement or submission, they have provided for arbitration by the American Arbitration Association (hereinafter the AAA) or under its rules. These rules and any amendment thereof shall apply in the form obtaining when the arbitration is initiated. The parties, by written agreement, may vary the procedures set forth in these rules.

2. Name of Tribunal

Any tribunal constituted by the parties under these rules shall be called the Labor Arbitration Tribunal.

3. Administrator

When parties agree to arbitrate under these rules and an arbitration is instituted thereunder, they thereby authorize the AAA to administer the arbitration. The authority and obligations of the administrator are as provided in the agreement of the parties and in these rules.

4. Delegation of Duties

The duties of the AAA may be carried out through such representatives or committees as the AAA may direct.

5. Panel of Labor Arbitrators

The AAA shall establish and maintain a Panel of Labor Arbitrators and shall appoint arbitrators therefrom as hereinafter provided.

6. Office of Tribunal

The general office of the Labor Arbitration Tribunal is the headquarters of the AAA, which may, however, assign the administration of an arbitration to any of its regional offices.

7. Initiation under an Arbitration Clause in a Collective Bargaining Agreement

Arbitration under an arbitration clause in a collective bargaining agreement under these rules may be initiated by either party in the following manner:

(a) by giving written notice to the other party of its intention to arbitrate (demand), which notice shall contain a statement setting forth the nature of the dispute and the remedy sought, and

(b) by filing at any regional office of the AAA three copies of the notice, together with a copy of the collective bargaining agreement or such parts thereof as relate to the dispute, including the arbitration provisions. After the arbitrator is appointed, no new or different claim may be submitted except with the consent of the arbitrator and all other parties.

8. Answer

The party upon whom the demand for arbitration is made may file an answering statement with the AAA within ten (10) days after notice from the AAA, simultaneously sending a copy to the other party. If no answer is filed within the stated time, it will be treated as a denial of the claim. Failure to file an answer shall not operate to delay the arbitration.

9. Initiation under a Submission

Parties to any collective bargaining agreement may initiate an arbitration under these rules by filing at any regional office of the AAA two copies of a written agreement to arbitrate under these rules (submission), signed by the parties and setting forth the nature of the dispute and the remedy sought.

10. Fixing of Locale

The parties may mutually agree on the locale where the arbitration is to be held. If the locale is not designated in the collective bargaining agreement or submission, and if there is a dispute as to the appropriate locale, the AAA shall have the power to determine the locale and its decision shall be binding.

11. Qualifications of Arbitrator

Any neutral arbitrator appointed pursuant to Section 12, 13, or 14 or selected by mutual choice of the parties or their appointees, shall be subject to disqualification for the reasons specified in Section 17. If the parties specifically so agree in writing, the arbitrator shall not be subject to disqualification for those reasons. Unless the parties agree otherwise, an arbitrator selected unilaterally by one party is a party-appointed arbitrator and is not subject to disqualification pursuant to Section 17.

The term "arbitrator" in these rules refers to the arbitration panel, whether composed of one or more arbitrators and whether the arbitrators are neutral or party appointed.

12. Appointment from Panel

If the parties have not appointed an arbitrator and have not provided any other method of appointment, the arbitrator shall be appointed in the following manner: immediately after the filing of the demand or submission, the AAA shall submit simultaneously to each party an identical list of names of persons chosen from the Panel of Labor Arbitrators. Each party shall have ten (10) days from the mailing date in which to strike any name to which it objects, number the remaining names to indicate the order of preference, and return the list to the AAA.

If a party does not return the list within the time specified, all persons named therein shall be deemed acceptable.

From among the persons who have been approved on both lists, and in accordance with the designated order of mutual preference, the AAA shall invite the acceptance of an arbitrator to serve. If the parties fail to agree upon any of the persons named, if those named decline or are unable to act, or if for any other reason the appointment cannot be made from the submitted lists, the administrator shall have the power to make the appointment from among other members of the panel without the submission of any additional list.

13. Direct Appointment by Parties

If the agreement of the parties names an arbitrator or specifies a method of appointing an arbitrator, that designation or method shall be followed. The notice of appointment, with the name and address of the arbitrator, shall be filed with the AAA by the appointing party. Upon the request of any appointing party, the AAA shall submit a list of members of the panel from which the party may, if it so desires, make the appointment.

If the agreement specifies a period of time within which an arbitrator shall be appointed and any party fails to make an appointment within that period, the AAA may make the appointment.

If no period of time is specified in the agreement, the AAA shall notify the parties to make the appointment and if within ten (10) days thereafter such arbitrator has not been so appointed, the AAA shall make the appointment.

14. Appointment of Neutral Arbitrator by Party–Appointed Arbitrators

If the parties have appointed their arbitrators or if either or both of them have been appointed as provided in Section 13, and have authorized those arbitrators to appoint a neutral arbitrator within a specified time and no appointment is made within that time or any agreed extension thereof, the AAA may appoint a neutral arbitrator who shall act as chairperson.

If no period of time is specified for appointment of the neutral arbitrator and the parties do not make the appointment within ten (10) days from the date of the appointment of the last party-appointed arbitrator, the AAA shall appoint a neutral arbitrator who shall act as chairperson.

If the parties have agreed that the arbitrators shall appoint the neutral arbitrator from the panel, the AAA shall furnish to the party-appointed arbitrators, in the manner prescribed in Section 12, a list selected from the panel, and the appointment of the neutral arbitrator shall be made as prescribed in that section.

15. Number of Arbitrators

If the arbitration agreement does not specify the number of arbitrators, the dispute shall be heard and determined by one arbitrator, unless the parties otherwise agree.

16. Notice to Arbitrator of Appointment

Notice of the appointment of the neutral arbitrator shall be mailed to the arbitrator by the AAA and the signed acceptance of the arbitrator shall be filed with the AAA prior to the opening of the first hearing.

17. Disclosure and Challenge Procedure

No person shall serve as a neutral arbitrator in any arbitration under these rules in which that person has any financial or personal interest in the result of the arbitration. Any prospective or designated neutral arbitrator shall immediately disclose any circumstance likely to affect impartiality, including any bias or financial or personal interest in the result of the arbitration. Upon receipt of this information from the arbitrator or another source, the AAA shall communicate the information to the parties and, if it deems it appropriate to do so, to the arbitrator. Upon objection of a party to the continued service of a neutral arbitrator, the AAA, after consultation with the parties and the arbitrator, shall determine whether the arbitrator should be disqualified and shall inform the parties of its decision, which shall be conclusive.

18. Vacancies

If any arbitrator should resign, die, or otherwise be unable to perform the duties of the office, the AAA shall, on proof satisfactory to it, declare the office vacant. Vacancies shall be filled in the same manner as that governing the making of the original appointment, and the matter shall be reheard by the new arbitrator.

19. Date, Time, and Place of Hearing

The arbitrator shall fix the date, time, and place for each hearing. At least five (5) days prior thereto, the AAA shall mail notice of the date, time, and place of hearing to each party, unless the parties otherwise agree.

20. Representation

Any party may be represented by counsel or other authorized representative.

21. Stenographic Record and Interpreters

Any party wishing a stenographic record shall make arrangements directly with a stenographer and shall notify the other parties of such arrangements in advance of the hearing. The requesting party or parties shall pay the cost of the record. If the transcript is agreed by the parties to be or, in appropriate cases, determined by the arbitrator to be the official record of the proceeding, it must be made available to the arbitrator and to the other party for inspection, at a time and place determined by the arbitrator.

Any party wishing an interpreter shall make all arrangements directly with the interpreter and shall assume the costs of the service.

22. Attendance at Hearings

Persons having a direct interest in the arbitration are entitled to attend hearings. The arbitrator shall have the power to require the retirement of any witness or witnesses during the testimony of other witnesses. It shall be discretionary with the arbitrator to determine the propriety of the attendance of any other person.

23. Postponements

The arbitrator for good cause shown may postpone the hearing upon the request of a party or upon his or her own initiative and shall postpone when all of the parties agree thereto.

24. Oaths

Before proceeding with the first hearing, each arbitrator may take an oath of office and, if required by law, shall do so. The arbitrator may require witnesses to testify under oath administered by any duly qualified person and, if required by law or requested by either party, shall do so.

25. Majority Decision

Whenever there is more than one arbitrator, all decisions of the arbitrators shall be by majority vote. The award shall also be made by majority vote unless the concurrence of all is expressly required.

26. Order of Proceedings

A hearing shall be opened by the filing of the oath of the arbitrator, where required; by the recording of the date, time, and place of the hearing and the presence of the arbitrator, the parties, and counsel, if any; and by the receipt by the arbitrator of the demand and answer, if any, or the submission.

Exhibits may, when offered by either party, be received in evidence by the arbitrator. The names and addresses of all witnesses and exhibits in order received shall be made a part of the record.

The arbitrator may vary the normal procedure under which the initiating party first presents its claim, but in any case shall afford full and equal opportunity to all parties for the presentation of relevant proofs.

27. Arbitration in the Absence of a Party or Representative

Unless the law provides to the contrary, the arbitration may proceed in the absence of any party or representative who, after due notice, fails to be present or fails to obtain a postponement. An award shall not be made solely on the default of a party. The arbitrator shall require the other party to submit such evidence as may be required for the making of an award.

28. Evidence

The parties may offer such evidence as is relevant and material to the dispute, and shall produce such additional evidence as the arbitrator may deem necessary to an understanding and determination of the dispute. An arbitrator authorized by law to subpoena witnesses and documents may do so independently or upon the request of any party. The arbitrator shall be the judge of the relevance and materiality of the evidence offered and conformity to legal rules of evidence shall not be necessary. All evidence shall be taken in the presence of all of the arbitrators and all of the parties except where any of the parties is absent in default or has waived the right to be present.

29. Evidence by Affidavit and Filing of Documents

The arbitrator may receive and consider the evidence of witnesses by affidavit, giving it only such weight as seems proper after consideration of any objection made to its admission.

All documents that are not filed with the arbitrator at the hearing, but arranged at the hearing or subsequently by agreement of the parties to be submitted, shall be filed with the AAA for transmission to the arbitrator. All parties shall be afforded opportunity to examine such documents.

30. Inspection

Whenever the arbitrator deems it necessary, he or she may make an inspection in connection with the subject matter of the dispute after written notice to the parties, who may, if they so desire, be present at the inspection.

31. Closing of Hearings

The arbitrator shall inquire of all parties whether they have any further proof to offer or witness to be heard. Upon receiving negative replies or if satisfied that the record is complete, the arbitrator shall declare the hearings closed and a minute thereof shall be recorded. If briefs or other documents are to be filed, the hearings shall be declared closed as of the final date set by the arbitrator for filing with the AAA. If documents are to be filed as provided in Section 29 and the date for their receipt is later than the date set for the receipt of briefs, the later date shall be the date of closing the hearing. The time limit within which the arbitrator is required to make an award shall commence to run, in the absence of another agreement by the parties, upon the closing of the hearings.

32.   Reopening of Hearings

The hearings may for good cause shown be reopened by the arbitrator at will or on the motion of either party at any time before the award is made but, if the reopening of the hearings would prevent the making of the award within the specific time agreed upon by the parties in the contract out of which the controversy has arisen, the matter may not be reopened unless both parties agree to extend the time. When no specific date is fixed in the contract, the arbitrator may reopen the hearings and shall have thirty (30) days from the closing of the reopened hearings within which to make an award.

33.   Waiver of Oral Hearings

The parties may provide, by written agreement, for the waiver of oral hearings. If the parties are unable to agree as to the procedure, the AAA shall specify a fair and equitable procedure.

34.   Waiver of Rules

Any party who proceeds with the arbitration after knowledge that any provision or requirement of these rules has not been complied with and who fails to state an objection thereto in writing shall be deemed to have waived the right to object.

35.   Extensions of Time

The parties may modify any period of time by mutual agreement. The AAA or the arbitrator may for good cause extend any period of time established by these rules, except the time for making the award. The AAA shall notify the parties of any such extension of time and its reason therefor.

36.   Serving of Notice

Each party to a submission or other agreement that provides for arbitration under these rules shall be deemed to have consented and shall consent that any papers, notices, or process necessary or proper for the initiation or continuation of an arbitration under these rules; for any court action in connection therewith; or for the entry of judgment on an award made thereunder may be served upon the party by mail addressed to the party or its representative at the last known address or by personal service, in or outside the state where the arbitration is to be held.

The AAA and the parties may also use facsimile transmission, telex, telegram, or other written forms of electronic communication to give the notices required by these rules.

37. Time of Award

The award shall be rendered promptly by the arbitrator and, unless otherwise agreed by the parties or specified by law, no later than thirty (30) days from the date of closing the hearings, with five (5) additional days for mailing if briefs are to be filed.

If oral hearings have been waived, the award shall be rendered no later than thirty (30) days from the date of transmitting the final statements and proofs to the arbitrator.

38. Form of Award

The award shall be in writing and shall be signed either by the neutral arbitrator or by a concurring majority if there is more than one arbitrator. The parties shall advise the AAA whenever they do not require the arbitrator to accompany the award with an opinion.

39. Award upon Settlement

If the parties settle their dispute during the course of the arbitration, the arbitrator may, upon their request, set forth the terms of the agreed settlement in an award.

40. Delivery of Award to Parties

Parties shall accept as legal delivery of the award the placing of the award or a true copy thereof in the mail by the AAA, addressed to the party at its last known address or to its representative; personal service of the award; or the filing of the award in any other manner that is permitted by law.

41. Release of Documents for Judicial Proceedings

The AAA shall, upon the written request of a party, furnish to such party, at its expense, certified facsimiles of any papers in the AAA's possession that may be required in judicial proceedings relating to the arbitration.

42. Judicial Proceedings and Exclusion of Liability

(a) Neither the AAA nor any arbitrator in a proceeding under these rules is a necessary party in judicial proceedings relating to the arbitration.

(b) Neither the AAA nor any arbitrator shall be liable to any party for any act or omission in connection with any arbitration conducted under these rules.

43. Administrative Fees

As a not-for-profit organization, the AAA shall prescribe an administrative fee schedule to compensate it for the cost of providing administrative services. The schedule in effect at the time of filing shall be applicable.

44. Expenses

The expenses of witnesses for either side shall be paid by the party producing such witnesses.

Expenses of the arbitration, other than the cost of the stenographic record, including required traveling and other expenses of the arbitrator and of AAA representatives and the expenses of any witness or the cost of any proof produced at the direct request of the arbitrator, shall be borne equally by the parties, unless they agree otherwise, or unless the arbitrator, in the award, assesses such expenses or any part thereof against any specified party or parties.

45. Communication with Arbitrator

There shall be no communication between the parties and a neutral arbitrator other than at oral hearings, unless the parties and the arbitrator agree otherwise. Any other oral or written communication from the parties to the arbitrator shall be directed to the AAA for transmittal to the arbitrator.

46. Interpretation and Application of Rules

The arbitrator shall interpret and apply these rules insofar as they relate to the arbitrator's powers and duties. When there is more than one arbitrator and a difference arises among them concerning the meaning or application of any such rule, it shall be decided by a majority vote. If that is unobtainable, the arbitrator or either party may refer the question to the AAA for final decision. All other rules shall be interpreted and applied by the AAA.

Administrative Fees

Full Service Administrative Fee

The initial administrative fee is $175 for each party, due and payable at the time of filing. No refund of the initial fee is made when a matter is withdrawn or settled after the filing of the demand for arbitration or submission.

Arbitrator Compensation

Unless mutually agreed otherwise, the arbitrator's compensation shall be borne equally by the parties, in accordance with the fee structure disclosed in the arbitrator's biographical profile submitted to the parties.

Hearing Room Rental

Hearing rooms are available on a rental basis at AAA offices. Please check with your Case Management Center or local AAA office for specific availability and rates.

Postponement Fees

A fee of $150 is payable by a party causing a second postponement of any scheduled hearing that is subsequently rescheduled by the AAA.

List Only Service

Parties can contact the AAA and request one (1) list of no more than fifteen names. Within 48 hours of receipt of the joint request the AAA will submit a list with a return date of 10 days. If the parties mutually agree on the selection of an arbitrator, the AAA closes its file. The administrative fee for list only is $50 per party.

List with Appointment

Parties can contact the AAA and request one (1) list of no more than fifteen names. Within 48 hours of receipt of the joint request the AAA will submit a list with a return date of 10 days, for review and appointment of the arbitrator based on the parties' mutual selection. The AAA will notify the parties of the selection of the arbitrator. The administrative fee for list with appointment is $75 per party.

Expedited Labor Arbitration Procedures

In response to the concern of parties over rising costs and delays in grievance arbitration, the American Arbitration Association has established expedited procedures under which cases are scheduled promptly and awards rendered no later than seven (7) days after the hearings. In return for giving up certain features of traditional labor arbitration, such as transcripts, briefs, and extensive opinions, the parties using these simplified procedures can get quick decisions and realize certain cost savings.

Leading labor arbitrators have indicated a willingness to offer their services under these procedures, and the Association makes every effort to assign the best possible arbitrators with early available hearing dates. Since the establishment of these procedures, an ever increasing number of parties has taken advantage of them.

E1. Agreement of Parties

These procedures shall apply whenever the parties have agreed to arbitrate under them, the Streamlined Labor Arbitration Rules, or the Expedited Labor Arbitration Rules of the American Arbitration Association, in the form obtaining when the arbitration is initiated.

These procedures shall be applied as set forth below, in addition to any other portion of the Labor Arbitration Rules that is not in conflict with these expedited procedures.

E2. Appointment of Neutral Arbitrator

The AAA shall appoint a single neutral arbitrator from its Panel of Labor Arbitrators, who shall hear and determine the case promptly.

E3. Qualifications of Neutral Arbitrator

No person shall serve as a neutral arbitrator in any arbitration in which that person has any financial or personal interest in the result of the arbitration. Prior to accepting an appointment, the prospective arbitrator shall disclose any circumstance likely to prevent a prompt hearing or to create a presumption of bias. Upon receipt of such information, the AAA shall immediately replace that arbitrator or communicate the information to the parties.

E4. Vacancies

The AAA is authorized to substitute another arbitrator if a vacancy occurs or if an appointed arbitrator is unable to serve promptly.

E5. Date, Time, and Place of Hearing

The arbitrator shall fix the date, time, and place of the hearing, notice of which must be given at least 24 hours in advance. Such notice may be given orally or by facsimile.

E6. No Stenographic Record

There shall be no stenographic record of the proceedings.

E7. Proceedings

The hearing shall be conducted by the arbitrator in whatever manner will most expeditiously permit full presentation of the evidence and arguments of the parties. The arbitrator shall make an appropriate minute of the proceedings. Normally, the hearing shall be completed within one day. In unusual circumstances and for good cause shown, the arbitrator may schedule an additional hearing to be held within seven (7) days.

E8. Post-hearing Briefs

There shall be no post-hearing briefs.

E9. Time of Award

The award shall be rendered promptly by the arbitrator and, unless otherwise agreed by the parties, no later than seven (7) days from the date of the closing of the hearing.

E10. Form of Award

The award shall be in writing and shall be signed by the arbitrator. If the arbitrator determines that an opinion is necessary, it shall be in summary form.

Administrative Fees

Initial Administrative Fee

The initial administrative fee is $100 for each party, due and payable at the time of filing. No refund of the initial fee is made when a matter is withdrawn or settled after the filing of the demand for arbitration or submission.

Arbitrator Compensation

Unless mutually agreed otherwise, the arbitrator's compensation shall be borne equally by the parties, in accordance with the fee structure disclosed in the arbitrator's biographical profile submitted to the parties.

Hearing Room Rental

Hearing rooms are available on a rental basis at AAA offices. Please check with your Case Management Center or local AAA office for specific availability and rates.

Postponement Fees

A fee of $150 is payable by a party causing a second postponement of any scheduled hearing that is subsequently rescheduled by the AAA.

NATIONAL RULES FOR THE RESOLUTION OF EMPLOYMENT DISPUTES

Amended and Effective January 1, 2004.

INTRODUCTION

Federal and state laws reflecting societal intolerance for certain workplace conduct, as well as court decisions interpreting and applying those statutes, have redefined responsible corporate practice and employee relations. Increasingly, employers and employees face workplace disputes involving alleged wrongful termination, sexual harassment, or discrimination based on race, color, religion, sex, national origin, age and disability.

As courts and administrative agencies become less accessible to civil litigants, employers and their employees now see alternative dispute resolution ("ADR") as a way to promptly and effectively resolve workplace disputes. ADR procedures are becoming more common in contracts of employment, personnel manuals and employee handbooks. Increasingly, corporations and their employees look to the American Arbitration Association as a resource in developing prompt and effective employment procedures for employment-related disputes.

These rules have been developed for employers and employees who wish to use a private alternative to resolve their disputes, enabling them to have complaints heard by an impartial person with expertise in the employment field. These procedures benefit both the employer and the individual employee by making it possible to resolve disputes without extensive litigation.

ROLE OF THE AMERICAN ARBITRATION ASSOCIATION

The American Arbitration Association, founded in 1926, is a not-for-profit, public service organization dedicated to the resolution of disputes through mediation, arbitration, elections, and other voluntary dispute resolution procedures. Over 4,000,000 workers are now covered by employment ADR plans administered by the AAA.

In addition, the AAA provides education and training, specialized publications, and research on all forms of dispute settlement. With 36 offices worldwide and cooperative agreements with arbitral institutions in 41 other nations, the American Arbitration Association is the nation's largest private provider of ADR services.

For seventy-five years, the American Arbitration Association has set the standards for the development of fair and equitable dispute resolution procedures. The development of the *National Rules for the Resolution of Employment Disputes*, and the reconstitution of a select and diverse roster of expert neutrals to hear and resolve disputes, are the most recent initiatives of the Association to provide private, efficient and cost-effective procedures for out-of-court settlement of workplace disputes.

LEGAL BASIS OF EMPLOYMENT ADR

Since the beginning of this decade, Congress has twice reaffirmed the important role of ADR in the area of employment discrimination–in the Americans with Disabilities Act in 1990, and a year later in Section 118 of the Civil Rights Act in 1991. While technically not dealing with a contract of employment, the seminal court case dealing with the arbitration of disputes relating to the non-union workplace is *Gilmer v. Interstate/Johnson Lane, 500 U.S. 20, 111 S.Ct. 1647 (1991)*. The Supreme Court refused to invalidate Gilmer's agreement with the New York Stock Exchange that he would arbitrate disputes with his employer (Interstate/Johnson Lane) simply because he was obliged to sign it in order to work as a securities dealer whose trades were executed on the Exchange. Although the Gilmer Court found that the Age Discrimination in Employment Act did not preclude arbitration of age discrimination claims, it specifically declined to decide whether employment arbitration agreements were the type of "contracts of employment" which are not made enforceable by the Federal Arbitration Act.

Since *Gilmer*, lower federal courts have generally enforced employer-imposed ADR programs, as long as the programs are fair. Some courts have held that the employee must have received adequate notice of the program. However, the issue of binding arbitration programs that are a condition of employment is still giving rise to litigation.

THE FAIRNESS ISSUE: THE DUE PROCESS PROTOCOL

The Due Process Protocol for Mediation and Arbitration of Statutory Disputes Arising Out of the Employment Relationship was developed in 1995 by a special task force composed of individuals representing management, labor, employment, civil rights organizations, private administrative agencies, government, and the American Arbitration Association. The *Due Process Protocol*, which was endorsed by the Association in 1995, seeks to ensure fairness and equity in resolving workplace disputes. The *Due Process Protocol* encourages mediation and arbitration of statutory disputes, provided there are due process safeguards. It conveys the hope that ADR will reduce delays caused by the huge backlog of cases pending before administrative agencies and the courts. The *Due Process Protocol* "recognizes the dilemma inherent in the timing of an agreement to mediate and/or arbitrate statutory disputes" but does not take a position on whether an employer can require a pre-dispute, binding arbitration program as a condition of employment.

The *Due Process Protocol* has been endorsed by organizations representing a broad range of constituencies. They include the American Arbitration Association, the American Bar Association Labor and Employment Section, the American Civil Liberties Union, the Federal Mediation and Conciliation Service, the National Academy of Arbitrators, and the National Society of Professionals in Dispute Resolution. The National Employment Lawyers Association has endorsed the substantive provisions of the *Due Process Protocol*. It has been incorporated into the ADR procedures of the Massachusetts Commission Against Discrimination (MCAD) and into the *Report of the United States Secretary of Labor's Task Force in Excellence in State and Local Government*.

AAA's EMPLOYMENT ADR RULES

On June 1, 1996, the Association issued *National Rules for the Resolution of Employment Disputes*. The rules reflected the guidelines outlined in the *Due Process Protocol* and were based upon the AAA's *California Employment Dispute Resolution Rules*, which were developed by a committee of employment management and plaintiff attorneys, retired judges and arbitrators, in addition to Association executives. The revised rules were developed for employers and employees who wish to use a private alternative to resolve their disputes. The rules enabled parties to have complaints heard by an impartial person of their joint selection, with expertise in the employment field. Both employers and individual employees benefit by having experts resolve their disputes without the costs and delay of litigation. The rules included procedures which ensure due process in both the mediation and arbitration of employment disputes. After a year of use, the rules have been amended to address technical issues.

AAA's POLICY ON EMPLOYMENT ADR

The AAA's policy on employment ADR is guided by the state of existing law, as well as its obligation to act in an impartial manner. In following the law, and in the interest of providing an appropriate forum for the resolution of employment disputes, the Association administers dispute resolution programs which meet the due process standards as outlined in its *National Rules for the Resolution of Employment Disputes and the Due Process Protocol*. If the Association determines that a dispute resolution program on its face substantially and materially deviates from the minimum due process standards of the *National Rules for the Resolution of Employment Disputes and the Due Process Protocol*, the Association may decline to administer cases under that program. Other issues will be presented to the arbitrator for determination.

NOTIFICATION

If an employer intends to utilize the dispute resolution services of the Association in an employment ADR plan, it shall, at least 30 days prior to the planned effective date of the program: (1) notify the Association of its intention to do so; and (2) provide the Association with a copy of the employment dispute resolution plan. If an employer does not comply with this requirement, the Association reserves the right to decline its administrative services. Copies of all plans should be sent to the American Arbitration Association's Office of Program Development, 335 Madison Avenue, New York, NY 10017; FAX: 212–716–5913.

DESIGNING AN ADR PROGRAM

The guiding principle in designing a successful employment ADR system is that it must be fair in fact and perception. The American Arbitration Association has considerable experience in administering and assisting in the design of employment ADR plans, which gives it an informed perspective on how to effectively design ADR systems, as well as the problems to avoid. Its guidance to those designing employment ADR systems is summarized as follows:

- The American Arbitration Association encourages employers to consider the wide range of legally-available options to resolve workplace disputes outside the courtroom.

- A special emphasis is placed by the Association on encouraging the development of in-house dispute resolution procedures, such as open door policies, ombuds, peer review, and internal mediation.

- The Association recommends an external mediation component to resolve disputes not settled by the internal dispute resolution process.

- Programs which use arbitration as a final step may employ:
  - pre-dispute, voluntary final and binding arbitration;
  - pre-dispute, mandatory nonbinding arbitration;
  - pre-dispute, mandatory final and binding arbitration; or
  - post-dispute, voluntary final and binding arbitration.

- Although the AAA administers binding arbitration systems that have been required as a condition of initial or continued employment such programs must be consistent with the Association's *National Rules for the Resolution of Employment Disputes and the Due Process Protocol.*

Specific guidance on the responsible development and design of employment ADR systems is contained in the Association's publication, *Resolving Employment Disputes: A Practical Guide*, which is available from any AAA office.

ALTERNATIVE DISPUTE RESOLUTION OPTIONS

OPEN DOOR POLICY: Employees are encouraged to meet with their immediate manager or supervisor to discuss problems arising out of the workplace environment. In some systems, the employee is free to approach anyone in the chain of command.

OMBUDS: A neutral third party (either from within or outside the company) is designated to confidentially investigate and propose settlement of employment complaints brought by employees.

PEER REVIEW: A panel of employees (or employees and managers) works together to resolve employment complaints. Peer review panel members are trained in the handling of sensitive issues.

INTERNAL MEDIATION: A process for resolving disputes in which a neutral third person from within the company, trained in mediation techniques, helps the disputing parties negotiate a mutually acceptable settlement. Mediation is a nonbinding process in which the parties discuss their disputes with an impartial person who assists them in reaching a settlement. The mediator may suggest ways of resolving the dispute but may not impose a settlement on the parties.

FACT-FINDING: The investigation of a complaint by an impartial third person (or team) who examines the complaint and the facts and issues a non-binding report. Fact-finding is particularly helpful for allegations of sexual harassment, where a fact-finding team, composed of one male and one female neutral, investigates the allegations and presents its findings to the employer and the employee.

ARBITRATION: Arbitration is generally defined as the submission of disputes to one or more impartial persons for final and binding determination. It can be the final step in a workplace program that includes other dispute resolution methods. There are many possibilities for designing this final step. They include:

PRE-DISPUTE, VOLUNTARY FINAL AND BINDING ARBITRATION: The parties agree in advance, on a voluntary basis, to use arbitration to resolve disputes and they are bound by the outcome.

PRE-DISPUTE, MANDATORY NONBINDING ARBITRATION: The parties must use the arbitration process to resolve disputes, but they are not bound by the outcome.

PRE-DISPUTE, MANDATORY FINAL AND BINDING ARBITRATION: The parties must arbitrate unresolved disputes and they are bound by the outcome.

POST-DISPUTE, VOLUNTARY FINAL AND BINDING ARBITRATION: The parties have the option of deciding whether to use final and binding arbitration after a dispute arises.

TYPES OF DISPUTES COVERED

The dispute resolution procedures contained in this booklet can be inserted into an employee personnel manual, an employment application of an individual employment agreement, or can be used for a specific dispute. They do not apply to disputes arising out of collective bargaining agreements.

National Rules for the Resolution of Employment Disputes

1. Applicable Rules of Arbitration

The parties shall be deemed to have made these rules a part of their arbitration agreement whenever they have provided for arbitration by the American Arbitration Association (hereinafter "AAA") or under its *National Rules for the Resolution of Employment Disputes*. If a party establishes that an adverse material inconsistency exists between the arbitration agreement and these rules, the arbitrator shall apply these rules.

If, within 30 days after the Association's commencement of administration, a party seeks judicial intervention with respect to a pending arbitration, the Association will suspend administration for 60 days to permit the party to obtain a stay of arbitration from the court.

These rules, and any amendment of them, shall apply in the form obtaining at the time the demand for arbitration or submission is received by the AAA.

2. Notification

An employer intending to incorporate these rules or to refer to the dispute resolution services of the AAA in an employment ADR plan, shall, at least 30 days prior to the planned effective date of the program:

     i) notify the Association of its intention to do so and,

     ii) provide the Association with a copy of the employment dispute resolution plan.

Compliance with this requirement shall not preclude an arbitrator from entertaining challenges as provided in Section 1. If an employer does not comply with this requirement, the Association reserves the right to decline its administrative services.

3. AAA as Administrator of the Arbitration

When parties agree to arbitrate under these rules, or when they provide for arbitration by the AAA and an arbitration is initiated under these rules, they thereby authorize the AAA to administer the arbitration. The authority and duties of the AAA are prescribed in these rules, and may be carried out through such of the AAA's representatives as it may direct.

4. Initiation of Arbitration

Arbitration shall be initiated in the following manner.

a.   The parties may submit a joint request for arbitration.

b.   In the absence of a joint request for arbitration:

(i) The initiating party (hereinafter "Claimant[s]") shall:

(1) File a written notice (hereinafter "Demand") of its intention to arbitrate at any regional office of the AAA, within the time limit established by the applicable statute of limitations if the dispute involves statutory rights. If no statutory rights are involved, the time limit established by the applicable arbitration agreement shall be followed. Any dispute over such issues shall be referred to the arbitrator. The filing shall be made in duplicate, and each copy shall include the applicable arbitration agreement. The Demand shall set forth the names, addresses, and telephone numbers of the parties; a brief statement of the nature of the dispute; the amount in controversy, if any; the remedy sought; and requested hearing location.

(2) Simultaneously mail a copy of the Demand to the party (hereinafter "Respondent[s]").

(3) Include with its Demand the applicable filing fee, unless the parties agree to some other method of fee advancement.

(ii) The Respondent(s) shall file an Answer with the AAA within 10 days after the date of the letter from the AAA acknowledging receipt of the Demand. The Answer shall provide the Respondent's brief response to the claim and the issues presented. The Respondent(s) shall make its filing in duplicate with the AAA, and simultaneously shall mail a copy of the Answer to the Claimant.

(iii) The Respondent(s):

(1) May file a counterclaim with the AAA within 10 days after the letter from the AAA acknowledging receipt of the Demand. The filing shall be made in duplicate. The counterclaim shall set forth the nature of the claim, the amount in controversy, if any, and the remedy sought.

(2) Simultaneously shall mail a copy of any counterclaim to the Claimant.

(3) Shall include with its filing the applicable filing fee provided for by these rules.

(iv) The Claimant may file an Answer to the counterclaim with the AAA within 10 days after the date of the letter from the AAA acknowledging receipt of the counterclaim. The Answer shall provide Claimant's brief response to the counterclaim and the issues presented. The Claimant shall make its filing in duplicate with the AAA, and simultaneously shall mail a copy of the Answer to the Respondent(s).

c. The form of any filing in these rules shall not be subject to technical pleading requirements.

5. Changes of Claim

Before the appointment of the arbitrator, if either party desires to offer a new or different claim or counterclaim, such party must do so in writing by filing a written statement with the AAA and simultaneously mailing a copy to the other party(s), who shall have 10 days from the date of such mailing within which to file an answer with the AAA. After the appointment of the arbitrator, a party may offer a new or different claim or counterclaim only at the discretion of the arbitrator.

6. Administrative and Mediation Conferences

Before the appointment of the arbitrator, any party may request, or the AAA, in its discretion, may schedule an administrative conference with a representative of the AAA and the parties and/or their representatives. The purpose of the administrative conference is to organize and expedite the arbitration, explore its administrative aspects, establish the most efficient means of selecting an arbitrator, and to consider mediation as a dispute resolution option. There is no administrative fee for this service.

At any time after the filing of the Demand, with the consent of the parties, the AAA will arrange a mediation conference under its Mediation Rules to facilitate settlement. The mediator shall not be any arbitrator appointed to the case, except by mutual agreement of the parties. There is no administrative fee for initiating a mediation under AAA Mediation Rules for parties to a pending arbitration.

7. Discovery

The arbitrator shall have the authority to order such discovery, by way of deposition, interrogatory, document production, or otherwise, as the arbitrator considers necessary to a full and fair exploration of the issues in dispute, consistent with the expedited nature of arbitration.

8. Arbitration Management Conference

As soon as possible after the appointment of the arbitrator but not later than 60 days thereafter, the arbitrator shall conduct an Arbitration Management Conference with the parties and/or their representatives, in person or by telephone, to explore and resolve matters that will expedite the arbitration proceedings. The specific matters to be addressed include:

> (i) the issues to be arbitrated;

> (ii) the date, time, place and estimated duration of the hearing;

(iii) the resolution of outstanding discovery issues and establishment of discovery parameters;

(iv) the law, standards, rules of evidence and burdens of proof that are to apply to the proceeding;

(v) the exchange of stipulations and declarations regarding facts, exhibits, witnesses and other issues;

(vi) the names of witnesses (including expert witnesses), the scope of witness testimony, and witness exclusion;

(vii) the value of bifurcating the arbitration into a liability phase and damages phase;

(viii) the need for a stenographic record;

(ix) whether the parties will summarize their arguments orally or in writing;

(x) the form of the award;

(xi) any other issues relating to the subject or conduct of the arbitration;

(xii) the allocation of attorney's fees and costs.

The arbitrator shall issue oral or written orders reflecting his or her decisions on the above matters and may conduct additional conferences when the need arises.

There is no AAA administrative fee for an Arbitration Management Conference.

9. Location of the Arbitration

The parties may designate the location of the arbitration by mutual agreement. In the absence of such agreement before the appointment of the arbitrator, any party may request a specific hearing location by notifying the AAA in writing and simultaneously mailing a copy of the request to the other party(s). If the AAA receives no objection within 10 days of the date of the request, the hearing shall be held at the requested location. If a timely objection is filed with the AAA, the AAA shall have the power to determine the location and its decision shall be final and binding. After the appointment of the arbitrator, the arbitrator shall resolve all disputes regarding the location of the hearing.

10. Date and Time of Hearing

The arbitrator shall have the authority to set the date and time of the hearing in consultation with the parties.

11. Qualifications to Serve as Arbitrator and Rights of Parties to Disqualify Arbitrator

a. Standards of Experience and Neutrality

(i) Arbitrators serving under these rules shall be experienced in the field of employment law.

(ii) Arbitrators serving under these rules shall have no personal or financial interest in the results of the proceedings in which they are appointed and shall have no relation to the underlying dispute or to the parties or their counsel that may create an appearance of bias.

(iii) The roster of available arbitrators will be established on a non-discriminatory basis, diverse by gender, ethnicity, background and qualifications.

(iv) The Association may, upon request of a party or upon its own initiative, supplement the list of proposed arbitrators in disputes arising out of individually negotiated employment contracts with persons from the regular Commercial Roster, to allow the Association to respond to the particular needs of the dispute. In multi-arbitrator disputes, at least one of the arbitrators shall be experienced in the field of employment law.

b. Standards of Disclosure by Arbitrator

Prior to accepting appointment, the prospective arbitrator shall disclose all information that might be relevant to the standards of neutrality set forth in this Section, including but not limited to service as a neutral in any past or pending case involving any of the parties and/or their representatives or that may prevent a prompt hearing.

c. Disqualification for Failure to Meet Standards of Experience and Neutrality

An arbitrator may be disqualified in two ways:

(i) No later than 10 days after the appointment of the arbitrator, all parties jointly may challenge the qualifications of an arbitrator by communicating their objection to the AAA in writing. Upon receipt of a joint objection, the arbitrator shall be replaced.

(ii) Any party may challenge the qualifications of an arbitrator by communicating its objection to the AAA in writing. Upon receipt of the objection, the AAA either shall replace the arbitrator or communicate the objection to the other parties. If any party believes that the objection does not merit disqualification of the arbitrator, the party shall so communicate to the AAA and to the other parties within 10 days of the receipt of the objection from the AAA. Upon objection of a party to the service of an arbitrator, the AAA shall determine whether the arbitrator should be disqualified and shall inform the parties of its decision, which shall be conclusive.

12. Number and Appointment of Neutral Arbitrators

a. If the parties do not specify the number of arbitrators, the dispute shall be heard and determined by one arbitrator. If the parties cannot agree upon the number of arbitrators, the AAA shall have the authority to determine the number of arbitrators.

b. If the parties have not appointed an arbitrator and have not provided any method of appointment, the arbitrator shall be appointed in the following manner:

(i) Immediately after it receives the Demand, the AAA shall mail simultaneously to each party a letter containing an identical list of the names of all arbitrators who are members of the regional Employment Dispute Resolution Roster.

(ii) Each party shall have 10 days from the date of the letter in which to select the name of a mutually acceptable arbitrator to hear and determine their dispute. If the parties cannot agree upon a mutually acceptable arbitrator, they shall so notify the AAA. Within 10 days of the receipt of that notice, the AAA shall send the parties a shorter list of arbitrators who are members of the regional Employment Dispute Resolution Roster. Each party shall have 10 days from the date of the letter containing the revised list to strike any names objected to, number the remaining names in order of preference, and return the list to the AAA. If a party does not return the list within the time specified, all of the listed persons shall be deemed acceptable to that party.

(iii) The AAA shall invite the acceptance of the arbitrator whom both parties have selected as mutually acceptable or, in the case of resort to the ranking procedure, the arbitrator who has received the highest rating in the order of preference that the parties have specified.

(iv) If the parties fail to agree on any of the persons whom the AAA submits for consideration, or if mutually acceptable arbitrators are unable to act, or if for any other reason the appointment cannot be made from the list of persons whom the AAA submits for consideration, the AAA shall have the power to make the appointment from among other members of the Roster without the submission of additional lists.

13. Vacancies

If for any reason an arbitrator is unable to perform the duties of the office, the AAA may, on proof satisfactory to it, declare the office vacant. The vacancy shall be filled in accordance with applicable provisions of these Rules.

In the event of a vacancy in a panel of neutral arbitrators after the hearings have commenced, the remaining arbitrator or arbitrators may continue with the hearing and determination of the controversy, unless the parties agree otherwise.

14. Representation

Any party may be represented by counsel or other authorized representative. For parties without representation the AAA will, upon request, provide reference to institutions which might offer assistance. A party who intends to be represented shall notify the other party and the

AAA of the name and address of the representative at least 10 days prior to the date set for the hearing or conference at which that person is first to appear. If a representative files a Demand or an Answer, the obligation to give notice of representative status is deemed satisfied.

15. Stenographic Record

Any party desiring a stenographic record shall make arrangements directly with a stenographer and shall notify the other parties of these arrangements at least three days in advance of the hearing. The requesting party or parties shall pay the cost of the record. If the transcript is agreed by the parties, or determined by the arbitrator to be the official record of the proceeding, it must be provided to the arbitrator and made available to the other parties for inspection, at a date, time, and place determined by the arbitrator.

16. Interpreters

Any party wishing an interpreter shall make all arrangements directly with the interpreter and shall assume the costs of the service.

17. Attendance at Hearings

The arbitrator shall have the authority to exclude witnesses, other than a party, from the hearing during the testimony of any other witness. The arbitrator also shall have the authority to decide whether any person who is not a witness may attend the hearing.

18. Confidentiality

The arbitrator shall maintain the confidentiality of the arbitration and shall have the authority to make appropriate rulings to safeguard that confidentiality, unless the parties agree otherwise or the law provides to the contrary.

19. Postponements

The arbitrator: (1) may postpone any hearing upon the request of a party for good cause shown; (2) must postpone any hearing upon the mutual agreement of the parties; and (3) may postpone any hearing on his or her own initiative.

20. Oaths

Before proceeding with the first hearing, each arbitrator may take an oath of office and, if required by law, shall do so. The arbitrator may require witnesses to testify under oath administered by any duly qualified person and, if it is required by law or requested by any party, shall do so.

21. Majority Decision

All decisions and awards of the arbitrators must be by a majority, unless the unanimous decision of all arbitrators is expressly required by the arbitration agreement or by law.

22.   Order of Proceedings and Communication with Arbitrators

A hearing shall be opened by: (1) filing the oath of the arbitrator, where required; (2) recording the date, time, and place of the hearing; (3) recording the presence of the arbitrator, the parties, and their representatives, if any; and (4) receiving into the record the Demand and the Answer, if any. The arbitrator may, at the beginning of the hearing, ask for statements clarifying the issues involved.

The parties shall bear the same burdens of proof and burdens of producing evidence as would apply if their claims and counterclaims had been brought in court.

Witnesses for each party shall submit to direct and cross examination as approved by the arbitrator.

With the exception of the rules regarding the allocation of the burdens of proof and going forward with the evidence, the arbitrator has the authority to set the rules for the conduct of the proceedings and shall exercise that authority to afford a full and equal opportunity to all parties to present any evidence that the arbitrator deems material and relevant to the resolution of the dispute.

Documentary and other forms of physical evidence, when offered by either party, may be received in evidence by the arbitrator.

The names and addresses of all witnesses and a description of the exhibits in the order received shall be made a part of the record.

There shall be no ex parte communication with the arbitrator, unless the parties and the arbitrator agree to the contrary in advance of the communication.

23.   Arbitration in the Absence of a Party or Representative

Unless the law provides to the contrary, the arbitration may proceed in the absence of any party or representative who, after due notice, fails to be present or fails to obtain a postponement. An award shall not be based solely on the default of a party. The arbitrator shall require the party who is in attendance to present such evidence as the arbitrator may require for the making of the award.

24.   Evidence

The parties may offer such evidence as is relevant and material to the dispute and shall produce such evidence as the arbitrator deems necessary to an understanding and determination of the dispute. An arbitrator or other person authorized by law to subpoena witnesses or documents may do so upon the request of any party or independently.

The arbitrator shall be the judge of the relevance and materiality of the evidence offered, and conformity to legal rules of evidence shall not be necessary. The arbitrator may in his or her discretion direct the order of proof, bifurcate proceedings, exclude cumulative or irrelevant testimony or other evidence, and direct the parties to focus their presentations on issues the decision of which could dispose of all or part of the case. All evidence shall be taken in the presence of all of the arbitrators and all of the parties, except where any party is absent, in default, or has waived the right to be present.

25. Evidence by Affidavit or Declaration and Post–Hearing Filing of Documents or Other Evidence

The arbitrator may receive and consider the evidence of witnesses by affidavit, but shall give it only such weight as the arbitrator deems it entitled to after consideration of any objection made to its admission.

If the parties agree or the arbitrator directs that documents or other evidence may be submitted to the arbitrator after the hearing, the documents or other evidence shall be filed with the AAA for transmission to the arbitrator, unless the parties agree to a different method of distribution. All parties shall be afforded an opportunity to examine such documents or other evidence and to lodge appropriate objections, if any.

26. Inspection or Investigation

An arbitrator finding it necessary to make an inspection or investigation in connection with the arbitration shall direct the AAA to so advise the parties. The arbitrator shall set the date and time, and the AAA shall notify the parties. Any party who so desires may be present during the inspection or investigation. In the event that one or all parties are not present during the inspection or investigation, the arbitrator shall make an oral or written report to the parties and afford them an opportunity to comment.

27. Interim Measures

At the request of any party, the arbitrator may take whatever interim measures he or she deems necessary with respect to the dispute, including measures for the conservation of property.

Such interim measures may be taken in the form of an interim award and the arbitrator may require security for the costs of such measures.

28. Closing of Hearing

The arbitrator shall specifically inquire of all parties whether they have any further proofs to offer or witnesses to be heard. Upon receiving negative replies or if satisfied that the record is complete, the arbitrator shall declare the hearing closed.

If briefs are to be filed, the hearing shall be declared closed as of the final date set by the arbitrator for the receipt of briefs. If documents are to be filed as provided in Section 25 and the date set for their receipt is later than that set for the receipt of briefs, the later date shall be the date of closing the hearing. The time limit within which the arbitrator is required to make the award shall commence to run, in the absence of other agreements by the parties, upon closing of the hearing.

29. Reopening of Hearing

The hearing may be reopened by the arbitrator upon the arbitrator's initiative, or upon application of a party for cause shown, at any time before the award is made. If reopening the hearing would prevent the making of the award within the specific time agreed on by the parties in the contract(s) out of which the controversy has arisen, the matter may not be reopened unless the parties agree on an extension of time. When no specific date is fixed in the contract, the arbitrator may reopen the hearing and shall have 30 days from the closing of the reopened hearing within which to make an award.

30. Waiver of Oral Hearing

The parties may provide, by written agreement, for the waiver of oral hearings in any case. If the parties are unable to agree as to the procedure, the AAA shall specify a fair and equitable procedure.

31. Waiver of Objection/Lack of Compliance with These Rules

Any party who proceeds with the arbitration after knowledge that any provision or requirement of these rules has not been complied with, and who fails to state objections thereto in writing, shall be deemed to have waived the right to object.

32. Extensions of Time

The parties may modify any period of time by mutual agreement. The AAA or the arbitrator may for good cause extend any period of time established by these Rules, except the time for making the award. The AAA shall notify the parties of any extension.

33. Serving of Notice

Each party shall be deemed to have consented that any papers, notices, or process necessary or proper for the initiation or continuation of an arbitration under these Rules; for any court actions in connection therewith; or for the entry of judgment on an award made under these procedures may be served on a party by mail addressed to the party or its representative at the last known address or by personal service, in or outside the state where the arbitration is to be held.

The AAA and the parties may also use facsimile transmission, telex, telegram, or other written forms of electronic communication to give the notices required by these Rules.

34. The Award

a. The award shall be made promptly by the arbitrator and, unless otherwise agreed by the parties or specified by law, no later than 30 days from the date of closing of the hearing or, if oral hearings have been waived, from the date of the AAA's transmittal of the final statements and proofs to the arbitrator.

b.   An award issued under these rules shall be publicly available, on a cost basis. The names of the parties and witnesses will not be publicly available, unless a party expressly agrees to have its name made public in the award.

c.   The award shall be in writing and shall be signed by a majority of the arbitrators and shall provide the written reasons for the award unless the parties agree otherwise. It shall be executed in the manner required by law.

d.   The arbitrator may grant any remedy or relief that the arbitrator deems just and equitable, including any remedy or relief that would have been available to the parties had the matter been heard in court. The arbitrator shall, in the award, assess arbitration fees, expenses, and compensation as provided in Sections 38, 39, and 40 in favor of any party and, in the event any administrative fees or expenses are due the AAA, in favor of the AAA.

e.   The arbitrator shall have the authority to provide for the reimbursement of representative's fees, in whole or in part, as part of the remedy, in accordance with applicable law.

f.   If the parties settle their dispute during the course of the arbitration, the arbitrator may set forth the terms of the settlement in a consent award.

g.   The parties shall accept as legal delivery of the award the placing of the award or a true copy thereof in the mail, addressed to a party or its representative at the last known address, personal service of the award, or the filing of the award in any manner that may be required by law.

h.   The arbitrator's award shall be final and binding. Judicial review shall be limited, as provided by law.

35.   Modification of Award

Within 20 days after the transmittal of an award, any party, upon notice to the other parties, may request the arbitrator to correct any clerical, typographical, technical or computational errors in the award. The arbitrator is not empowered to redetermine the merits of any claim already decided.

The other parties shall be given 10 days to respond to the request. The arbitrator shall dispose of the request within 20 days after transmittal by the AAA to the arbitrator of the request and any response thereto.

If applicable law requires a different procedural time frame, that procedure shall be followed.

36.   Release of Documents for Judicial Proceedings

The AAA shall, upon the written request of a party, furnish to the party, at that party's expense, certified copies of any papers in the AAA's case file that may be required in judicial proceedings relating to the arbitration.

37. Judicial Proceedings and Exclusion of Liability

a.   No judicial proceeding by a party relating to the subject matter of the arbitration shall be deemed a waiver of the party's right to arbitrate.

b.   Neither the AAA nor any arbitrator in a proceeding under these rules is or shall be considered a necessary or proper party in judicial proceedings relating to the arbitration.

c.   Parties to these procedures shall be deemed to have consented that judgment upon the arbitration award may be entered in any federal or state court having jurisdiction.

d.   Neither the AAA nor any arbitrator shall be liable to any party for any act or omission in connection with any arbitration conducted under these procedures.

38. Administrative Fees*

As a not-for-profit organization, the AAA shall prescribe filing and other administrative fees to compensate it for the cost of providing administrative services. The AAA administrative fee schedule in effect at the time the demand for arbitration or submission agreement is received shall be applicable.

AAA fees shall be paid in accordance with the Administrative Fee Schedule (see below).

The AAA may, in the event of extreme hardship on any party, defer or reduce the administrative fees. (To ensure that you have the most current information, see our Web site at www.adr.org).

39. Expenses

Unless otherwise agreed by the parties, the expenses of witnesses for either side shall be borne by the party producing such witnesses. All expenses of the arbitration, including required travel and other expenses of the arbitrator, AAA representatives, and any witness and the costs relating to any proof produced at the direction of the arbitrator, shall be borne by the employer, unless the parties agree otherwise or unless the arbitrator directs otherwise in the award as provided for in the Administrative Fee Schedule.

---

* Pursuant to Section 1284.3 of the California Code of Civil Procedure, consumers with a gross monthly income of less than 300% of the federal poverty guidelines are entitled to a waiver of arbitration fees and costs, exclusive of arbitrator fees. This law applies to all consumer agreements subject to the California Arbitration Act, and to all consumer arbitrations conducted in California. Only those disputes arising out of employer promulgated plans are included in the consumer definition. If you believe that you meet these requirements, you must submit to the AAA a declaration under oath regarding your monthly income and the number of persons in your household. Please contact the AAA's Western Case Management Center at 1–877–528–0879 if you have any questions regarding the waiver of administrative fees. (Effective January 1, 2003).

40. Neutral Arbitrator's Compensation

Arbitrators shall charge a rate consistent with the arbitrator's stated rate of compensation. If there is disagreement concerning the terms of compensation, an appropriate rate shall be established with the arbitrator by the AAA and confirmed to the parties.

Any arrangement for the compensation of a neutral arbitrator shall be made through the AAA and not directly between the parties and the arbitrator. Payment of the arbitrator's fees and expenses shall be made by the AAA from the fees and moneys collected by the AAA for this purpose.

41. Deposits

The AAA may require deposits in advance of any hearings such sums of money as it deems necessary to cover the expenses of the arbitration, including the arbitrator's fee, if any, and shall render an accounting and return any unexpended balance at the conclusion of the case.

42. Interpretation and Application of Rules

The arbitrator shall interpret and apply these rules as they relate to the arbitrator's powers and duties. When there is more than one arbitrator and a difference arises among them concerning the meaning or application of these Rules, it shall be resolved by a majority vote. If that is not possible, either an arbitrator or a party may refer the question to the AAA for final decision. All other procedures shall be interpreted and applied by the AAA.

Administrative Fee Schedule for Disputes Arising Out of Employer–Promulgated Plans:

Administrative Fee

The AAA's administrative fees are based on filing and service charges. Arbitrator compensation is not included in this schedule. Unless the employee chooses to pay a portion of the arbitrator's compensation, such compensation shall be paid in total by the employer. Arbitrator compensation and administrative fees are not subject to reallocation by the arbitrator(s) except upon the arbitrator's determination that a claim or counterclaim was filed for purposes of harassment or is patently frivolous.

Filing Fees

In cases before a single arbitrator, a nonrefundable filing fee capped in the amount of $125, is payable in full by the employee when a claim is filed, unless the plan provides that the employee pay less. A nonrefundable fee in the amount of $625 is payable in full by the employer, unless the plan provides that the employer pay more.

In cases before three or more arbitrators, a nonrefundable filing fee capped in the amount of $125, is payable in full by the employee when a claim is filed, unless the plan provides that the employee pay less. A nonrefundable fee in the amount of $1,375 is payable in full by the employer, unless the plan provides that the employer pay more.

Hearing Fees

For each day of hearing held before a single arbitrator, an administrative fee of $300 is payable by the employer.

For each day of hearing held before a multi-arbitrator panel, an administrative fee of $500 is payable by the employer.

There is no AAA hearing fee for the initial Arbitration Management Conference.

Postponement/Cancellation Fees

A fee of $150 is payable by a party causing a postponement of any hearing scheduled before a single arbitrator.

A fee of $250 is payable by a party causing a postponement of any hearing scheduled before a multi-arbitrator panel.

Hearing Room Rental

The hearing fees described above do not cover the rental of hearing rooms, which are available on a rental basis. Check with the administrator for availability and rates. Hearing room rental fees will be borne by the employer.

Suspension for Nonpayment

If arbitrator compensation or administrative charges have not been paid in full, the administrator may so inform the parties in order that one of them may advance the required payment. If such payments are not made, the arbitrator may order the suspension or termination of the proceedings. If no arbitrator has yet been appointed, the administrator may suspend the proceedings.

For Disputes Arising Out of Individually–Negotiated Employment Agreements and Contracts:

The AAA's Commercial Fee Schedule, listed below, will apply to disputes arising out of individually-negotiated employment agreements and contracts, even if such agreements and contracts reference or incorporate an employer-promulgated plan. Any questions or disagreements about whether a matter arises out of an employer-promulgated plan or an individually-negotiated agreement or contract shall be determined by the AAA and its determination shall be final.

Administrative Fee

The administrative fees of the AAA are based on the amount of the claim or counterclaim. Arbitrator compensation is not included in this schedule. Unless the parties agree otherwise, arbitrator compensation and administrative fees are subject to allocation by the arbitrator in the award.

Fees

An initial filing fee is payable in full by the filing party when a claim, counterclaim or additional claim is filed. A case service fee will be incurred for all cases that proceed to their first hearing. This fee will be payable in advance at the time that the first hearing is scheduled. This fee will be refunded at the conclusion of the case if no hearings have occurred. However, if the Association is not notified at least 24 hours before the time of the scheduled hearing, the case service fee will remain due and will not be refunded.

These fees will be billed in accordance with the following schedule:

Amount of Claim	Initial Filing Fee	Case Service Fee
Above $0 to $10,000	$500	$200
Above $10,000 to $75,000	$750	$300
Above $75,000 to $150,000	$1,500	$750
Above $150,000 to $300,000	$2,750	$1,250
Above $300,000 to $500,000	$4,250	$1,750
Above $500,000 to $1,000,000	$6,000	$2,500
Above $1,000,000 to $7,000,000	$8,000	$3,250
Above $7,000,000 to $10,000,000	$10,000	$4,000
No Amount Stated**	$3,250	$1,250

** This fee is applicable only when a claim or counterclaim is not for a monetary amount. Where a monetary claim amount is not known, parties will be required to state a range of claims or be subject to the highest possible filing fee.

Fee Schedule for Claims in Excess of $10 Million

The following is the fee schedule for use in disputes involving claims in excess of $10 million. If you have any questions, please consult your local AAA office or case management center.

Claim Size	Fee	Case Service Fee
$10 million and above	Base fee of $12,500 plus .01% of the amount of claim above $10 million.	$6,000
	Filing fees capped at $65,000	

Fees are subject to increase if the amount of a claim or counterclaim is modified after the initial filing date. Fees are subject to decrease if the amount of a claim or counterclaim is modified before the first hearing.

The minimum fees for any case having three or more arbitrators are $2,750 for the filing fee, plus a $1,250 case service fee. Expedited Procedures are applied in any case where no disclosed claim or counterclaim exceeds $75,000, exclusive of interest and arbitration cost

Parties on cases held in abeyance for one year by agreement, will be assessed an annual abeyance fee of $300. If a party refuses to pay the assessed fee, the other party or parties may pay the entire fee on behalf of all parties, otherwise the matter will be closed.

Refund Schedule

The AAA offers a refund schedule on filing fees. For cases with claims up to $75,000, a minimum filing fee of $300 will not be refunded. For all cases, a minimum fee of $500 will not be refunded. Subject to the minimum fee requirements, refunds will be calculated as follows:

- 100% of the filing fee, above the minimum fee, will be refunded if the case is settled or withdrawn within five calendar days of filing.

- 50% of the filing fee, in any case with filing fees in excess of $500, will be refunded if the case is settled or withdrawn between six and 30 calendar days of filing. Where the filing fee is $500, the refund will be $200.

- 25% of the filing fee will be refunded if the case is settled or withdrawn between 31 and 60 calendar days of filing.

No refund will be made once an arbitrator has been appointed (this includes one arbitrator on a three-arbitrator panel). No refunds will be granted on awarded cases.

Note: The date of receipt of the demand for arbitration with the AAA will be used to calculate refunds of filing fees for both claims and counterclaims.

Hearing Room Rental

The fees described above do not cover the rental of hearing rooms, which are available on a rental basis. Check with the AAA for availability and rates.

Employment Mediation Rules

1. Agreement of Parties

Whenever, by provision in an employment dispute resolution program, or by separate submission, the parties have provided for mediation or conciliation of existing or future disputes under the auspices of the American Arbitration Association (hereinafter "AAA") or under these rules, they shall be deemed to have made these rules, as amended and in effect as of the date of the submission of the dispute, a part of their agreement.

2. Initiation of Mediation

Any party to an employment dispute may initiate mediation by filing with the AAA a submission to mediation or a written request for mediation pursuant to these rules, together with the applicable administrative fee.

3. Request for Mediation

A request for mediation shall contain a brief statement of the nature of the dispute and the names, addresses, and telephone numbers of all parties to the dispute and those who will represent them, if any, in the mediation. The initiating party shall simultaneously file two copies of the request with the AAA and one copy with every other party to the dispute.

4. Appointment of Mediator

Upon receipt of a request for mediation, the AAA will appoint a qualified mediator to serve. Normally, a single mediator will be appointed unless the parties agree otherwise or the AAA determines otherwise. If the agreement of the parties names a mediator or specifies a method of appointing a mediator, that designation or method shall be followed.

5. Qualifications of Mediator

No person shall serve as a mediator in any dispute in which that person has any financial or personal interest in the result of the mediation, except by the written consent of all parties. Prior to accepting an appointment, the prospective mediator shall disclose any circumstance likely to create a presumption of bias or prevent a prompt meeting with the parties. Upon receipt of such information, the AAA shall either replace the mediator or immediately communicate the information to the parties for their comments. In the event that the parties disagree as to whether the mediator shall serve, the AAA will appoint another mediator. The AAA is authorized to appoint another mediator if the appointed mediator is unable to serve promptly.

6. Vacancies

If any mediator shall become unwilling or unable to serve, the AAA will appoint another mediator, unless the parties agree otherwise.

7. Representation

Any party may be represented by a person of the party's choice. The names and addresses of such persons shall be communicated in writing to all parties and to the AAA.

8. Date, Time, and Place of Mediation

The mediator shall fix the date and the time of each mediation session. The mediation shall be held at the appropriate regional office of the AAA, or at any other convenient location agreeable to the mediator and the parties, as the mediator shall determine.

9. Identification of Matters in Dispute

At least ten (10) days prior to the first scheduled mediation session, each party shall provide the mediator with a brief memorandum setting forth its position with regard to the issues that need to be resolved. At the discretion of the mediator, such memoranda may be mutually exchanged by the parties.

At the first session, the parties will be expected to produce all information reasonably required for the mediator to understand the issues presented. The mediator may require any party to supplement such information.

10. Authority of Mediator

The mediator does not have the authority to impose a settlement on the parties but will attempt to help them reach a satisfactory resolution of their dispute. The mediator is authorized to conduct joint and separate meetings with the parties and to make oral and written recommendations for settlement. Whenever necessary, the mediator may also obtain expert advice concerning technical aspects of the dispute, provided that the parties agree and assume the expenses of obtaining such advice. Arrangements for obtaining such advice shall be made by the mediator or the parties, as the mediator shall determine.

The mediator is authorized to end the mediation whenever, in the judgment of the mediator, further efforts at mediation would not contribute to a resolution of the dispute between the parties.

11. Privacy

Mediation sessions are private. The parties and their representatives may attend mediation sessions. Other persons may attend only with the permission of the parties and with the consent of the mediator.

12. Confidentiality

Confidential information disclosed to a mediator by the parties or by witnesses in the course of the mediation shall not be divulged by the mediator. All records, reports, or other documents received by a mediator while serving in that capacity shall be confidential. The mediator shall not be compelled to divulge such records or to testify in regard to the mediation in any adversary proceeding or judicial forum.

The parties shall maintain the confidentiality of the mediation and shall not rely on, or introduce as evidence in any arbitral, judicial, or other proceeding

(a) views expressed or suggestions made by another party with respect to a possible settlement of the dispute;

(b) admissions made by another party in the course of the mediation proceedings;

(c) proposals made or

(d) views expressed by the mediator; or the fact that another party had or had not indicated willingness to accept a proposal for settlement made by the mediator.

13. No Stenographic Record

There shall be no stenographic record of the mediation process.

14. Termination of Mediation

The mediation shall be terminated

(a) by the execution of a settlement agreement by the parties;

(b) by a written declaration of the mediator to the effect that further efforts at mediation are no longer worthwhile; or

(c) by a written declaration of a party or parties to the effect that the mediation proceedings are terminated.

15. Exclusion of Liability

Neither the AAA nor any mediator is a necessary party in judicial proceedings relating to the mediation.

Neither the AAA nor any mediator shall be liable to any party for any act or omission in connection with any mediation conducted under these rules.

16. Interpretation and Application of Rules

The mediator shall interpret and apply these rules insofar as they relate to the mediator's duties and responsibilities. All other rules shall be interpreted and applied by the AAA.

17. Expenses

The expenses of witnesses for either side shall be paid by the party producing such witnesses. All other expenses of the mediation, including required traveling and other expenses of the mediator and representatives of the AAA, and the expenses of any witness and the cost of any proofs or expert advice produced at the direct request of the mediator, shall be borne equally by the parties unless they agree otherwise.

Mediation Fee Schedule

The mediation filing fee is $325 per party. In addition, the parties are responsible for compensating the mediator at his or her published rate, for conference and study time (hourly or per diem).

All expenses are generally borne equally by the parties. The parties may adjust this arrangement by agreement.

Before the commencement of the mediation, the AAA shall estimate anticipated total expenses. Each party shall pay its portion of that amount as per the agreed upon arrangement. When the mediation has terminated, the AAA shall render an accounting and return any unexpended balance to the parties.

Rules, forms, procedures and guides, as well as information about applying for a fee reduction or deferral, are subject to periodic change and updating. To ensure that you have the mist [sic] current information see our website at www.adr.org.

Appendix D

CODE OF PROFESSIONAL RESPONSIBILITY FOR ARBITRATORS OF LABOR MANAGEMENT DISPUTES

National Academy of Arbitrators
American Arbitration Association
Federal Mediation and Conciliation Service
As amended and in effect June 2003
Preamble

Background

The provisions of this Code deal with the voluntary arbitration of labor-management disputes and certain other arbitration and related procedures which have developed or become more common since it was first adopted.

Voluntary arbitration rests upon the mutual desire of management and labor in each collective bargaining relationship to develop procedures for dispute settlement which meet their own particular needs and obligations. No two voluntary systems, therefore, are likely to be identical in practice. Words used to describe arbitrators (Arbitrator, Umpire, Impartial Chair, Chair of Arbitration Board, etc.) may suggest typical approaches, but actual differences within any general type of arrangement may be as great as distinctions often made among the several types.

Arbitrators of labor-management disputes are sometimes asked to serve as impartial third parties under a variety of arbitration and related procedures dealing with the rights and interests of employees in connection with their employment and/or representation by a union. In some cases these procedures may not be the product of voluntary agreement between management and labor. They may be established by statute or ordinance, ad hoc agreement, individual employment contract, or through procedures unilaterally adopted by employers and unions. Some of the procedures may be designed to resolve disputes over new or revised contract terms, where the arbitrator may be referred to as a Fact Finder or a member of an Impasse Panel or Board of Inquiry, or the like. Others may be designed to resolve disputes over wrongful termination or other employment issues arising under the law, an implied or explicit individual employment contract, or an agreement to resolve a lawsuit. In some such cases the arbitrator may be referred to as an Appeal Examiner, Hearing Officer, Referee, or other like titles. Finally, some procedures may be established by employers to resolve employment disputes under personnel policies and handbooks or established by unions to resolve disputes with represented employees in agency shop or fair share cases.

The standards of professional responsibility set forth in this Code are intended to guide the impartial third party serving in all of these diverse procedures.

Scope of Code

This Code is a privately developed set of standards of professional behavior for arbitrators who are subject to its provisions. It applies to voluntary arbitration of labor-management disputes and the other arbitration and related procedures described in the Preamble, hereinafter referred to as "covered arbitration dispute procedures."

The word "arbitrator," as used hereinafter in the Code, is intended to apply to any impartial person, irrespective of specific title, who serves in a covered arbitration dispute procedure in which there is conferred authority to decide issues or to make formal recommendations.

The Code is not designed to apply to mediation or conciliation, as distinguished from arbitration, nor to other procedures in which the third party is not authorized in advance to make decisions or recommendations. It does not apply to partisan representatives on tripartite boards. It does not apply to commercial arbitration or to uses of arbitration other than a covered arbitration dispute procedure as defined above.

Format of Code

Bold Face type, sometimes including explanatory material, is used to set forth general principles. *Italics* are used for amplification of general principles. Ordinary type is used primarily for illustrative or explanatory comment.

Application of Code

Faithful adherence by an arbitrator to this Code is basic to professional responsibility.

The National Academy of Arbitrators will expect its members to be governed in their professional conduct by this Code and stands ready, through its Committee on Professional Responsibility and Grievances, to advise its members as to the Code's interpretation. The American

Arbitration Association and the Federal Mediation and Conciliation Service will apply the Code to the arbitrators on their rosters in cases handled under their respective appointment or referral procedures. Other arbitrators and administrative agencies may, of course, voluntarily adopt the Code and be governed by it.

In interpreting the Code and applying it to charges of professional misconduct, under existing or revised procedures of the National Academy of Arbitrators and of the administrative agencies, it should be recognized that while some of its standards express ethical principles basic to the arbitration profession, others rest less on ethics than on considerations of good practice. Experience has shown the difficulty of drawing rigid lines of distinction between ethics and good practice, and this Code does not attempt to do so. Rather, it leaves the gravity of alleged misconduct and the extent to which ethical standards have been violated to be assessed in the light of the facts and circumstances of each particular case.

1. ARBITRATOR'S QUALIFICATIONS AND RESPONSIBILITIES TO THE PROFESSION

A. General Qualifications

1. Essential personal qualifications of an arbitrator include honesty, integrity, impartiality and general competence in labor relations matters.

An arbitrator must demonstrate ability to exercise these personal qualities faithfully and with good judgment, both in procedural matters an in substantive decisions

   a. Selection by mutual agreement of the parties or direct designation by an administrative agency are the effective methods of appraisal of this combination of an individual's potential and performance, rather than the fact of placement on a roster of an administrative agency or membership in a professional association of arbitrators.

2. An arbitrator must be as ready to rule for one party as for the other on each issue, either in a single case or in a group of cases. Compromise by an arbitrator for the sake of attempting to achieve personal acceptability is unprofessional.

B. Qualifications for Special Cases

1. When an arbitrator decides that a case requires specialized knowledge beyond the arbitrator's competence, the arbitrator must decline appointment, withdraw, or request technical assistance.

   a. An arbitrator may be qualified generally but not for specialized assignments. Some types of incentive, work standard, job evaluation, welfare program, pension, or insurance cases may require specialized knowledge, experience or competence. Arbitration of contract terms also may require distinctive background and experience.

b. Effective appraisal by an administrative agency or by an arbitrator of the need for special qualifications requires that both parties make know the special nature of the case prior to appointment of the arbitrator.

C. Responsibilities To The Profession

1. An arbitrator must uphold the dignity and integrity of the office and endeavor to provide effective service to the parties.

a. To this end, an arbitrator should keep current with principles, practices and developments that are relevant to the arbitrator's field of practice.

2. An arbitrator shall not make false or deceptive representations in the advertising and/or solicitation of arbitration work.

3. An arbitrator shall not engage in conduct that would appear to compromise the arbitrator's impartiality.

a. Arbitrators may disseminate or transmit truthful information about themselves through brochures or letters, among other means, provided that such material and information is disclosed, disseminated or transmitted in good faith to representatives of both management and labor.

4. An experienced arbitrator should cooperate in the training of new arbitrators.

2. RESPONSIBILITIES TO THE PARTIES

A. Recognition of Diversity in Arbitration Arrangements

1. An arbitrator should conscientiously endeavor to understand and observe, to the extent consistent with professional responsibility, the significant principles governing each arbitration system in which the arbitrator serves.

a. Recognition of special features of a particular arbitration arrangement can be essential with respect to procedural matters and may influence other aspects of the arbitration process.

2. Such understanding does not relieve an arbitrator from a corollary responsibility to seek to discern and refuse to lend approval or consent to any collusive attempt by the parties to use arbitration for an improper purpose.

3. An arbitrator who is asked to arbitrate a dispute under a procedure established unilaterally by an employer or union, to resolve an employment dispute or agency shop or fair share dispute, has no obligation to accept such appointment. Before accepting such an appointment, an arbitrator should consider

**the possible need to disclose the existence of any ongoing rela-
tionships with the employer or union.**

a.   If the arbitrator is already serving as an umpire, permanent
arbitrator or panel member under a procedure where the employer
or union has the right unilaterally to remove the arbitrator from
such a position, those facts should be disclosed.

B.   Required Disclosures

**1.   Before accepting an appointment, an arbitrator must
disclose directly or through the administrative agency involved,
any current or past managerial, representational, or consultative relationship with any company or union involved in a
proceeding in which the arbitrator is being considered for appointment or has been tentatively designated to serve. Disclosure must also be made of any pertinent pecuniary interest.**

a.   The duty to disclose includes membership on a Board of
Directors, full-time or part-time service as a representative or advocate, consultation work for a fee, current stock or bond ownership
(other than mutual fund shares or appropriate trust arrangements)
or any other pertinent form of managerial, financial or immediate
family interest in the company or union involved.

**2.   When an arbitrator is serving concurrently as an advo-
cate for or representative of other companies or unions in labor
relations matters, or has done so in recent years, such activities
must be disclosed before accepting appointment as an arbitrator.**

**An arbitrator must disclose such activities to an administra-
tive agency if on that agency's active roster or seeking
placement on a roster. Such disclosure then satisfies this
requirement for cases handled under that agency's referral.**

a.   It is not necessary to disclose names of clients or other
specific details. It is necessary to indicate the general nature of the
labor relations advocacy or representational work involved, whether
for companies or unions or both, and a reasonable approximation of
the extent of such activity.

b.   *An arbitrator on an administrative agency's roster has a
continuing obligation to notify the agency of any significant changes
pertinent to this requirement.*

c.   When an administrative agency is not involved, an arbitrator must make such disclosure directly unless the arbitrator is
certain that both parties to the case are fully aware of such activities.

**3.   An arbitrator must not permit personal relationships to
affect decision-making.**

**Prior to acceptance of an appointment, an arbitrator must
disclose to the parties or to the administrative agency in-**

volved any close personal relationship or other circumstance, in addition to those specifically mentioned earlier to this section, which might reasonably raise a question as to the arbitrator's impartiality.

    a.   Arbitrators establish personal relationships with many company and union representatives, with fellow arbitrators, and with fellow members of various professional associations. There should be no attempt to be secretive about such friendships or acquaintances but disclosure is not necessary unless some feature of a particular relationship might reasonably appear to impair impartiality.

4.   If the circumstances requiring disclosure are not known to the arbitrator prior to acceptance of appointment, disclosure must be made when such circumstances become known to the arbitrator.

5.   The burden of disclosure rests on the arbitrator. After appropriate disclosure, the arbitrator may serve if both parties so desire. If the arbitrator believes or perceives that there is a clear conflict of interest, the arbitrator should withdraw, irrespective of the expressed desires of the parties.

C.   Privacy of Arbitration

1.   All significant aspects of an arbitration proceeding must be treated by the arbitrator as confidential unless this requirement is waived by both parties or disclosure is required or permitted by law.

    a.   Attendance at hearings by persons not representing the parties or invited by either or both of them should be permitted only when the parties agree or when an applicable law requires or permits. Occasionally, special circumstances may require that an arbitrator rule on such matters as attendance and degree of participation of counsel selected by a grievant.

    b.   *Discussion of a case at any time by an arbitrator with persons not involved directly should be limited to situations where advance approval or consent of both parties is obtained or where the identity of the parties and details of the case are sufficiently obscured to eliminate any realistic probability of identification.*

    A commonly recognized exception is discussion of a problem in a case with a fellow arbitrator. *Any such discussion does not relieve the arbitrator who is acting in the case from sole responsibility for the decision and the discussion must be considered as confidential.*

    Discussion of aspects of a case in a classroom without prior specific approval of the parties is not a violation provided the arbitrator is satisfied that there is no breach of essential confidentiality.

c. *It is a violation of professional responsibility for an arbitrator to make public an award without the consent of the parties.*

An arbitrator may ask the parties whether they consent to the publication of the award either at the hearing or at the time the award is issued.

(1) *If such question is asked at the hearing it should be asked in writing as follows:*

"Do you consent to the submission of the award in this matter for publication?

Yes ( )   No ( )

If you consent you have the right to notify the arbitrator within 30 days after the date of the award that you revoke your consent."

It is desirable but not required that the arbitrator remind the parties at the time of the issuance of the award of their right to withdraw their consent to publication.

(2) If the question of consent to the publication of the award is raised at the time the award is issued, the arbitrator may state in writing to each party that failure to answer the inquiry within 30 days will be considered an implied consent to publish.

d. It is not improper for an arbitrator to donate arbitration files to a library of a college, university or similar institution without prior consent of all parties involved. When the circumstances permit, there should be deleted from such donations any cases concerning which one or both of the parties have expressed a desire for privacy. As an additional safeguard, an arbitrator may also decide to withhold recent cases or indicate to the donee a time interval before such cases can be made generally available.

e. *Applicable laws, regulations, or practices of the parties may permit or even require exceptions to the above noted principles of privacy.*

D. Personal Relationships with the Parties

1. An arbitrator must make every reasonable effort to conform to arrangements required by an administrative agency or mutually desired by the parties regarding communications and personal relationships with the parties.

a. *Only an "arm's-length" relationship may be acceptable to the parties in some arbitration arrangements or may be required by the rules of an administrative agency. The arbitrator should then have no contact of consequence with representatives of either party while handling a case without the other party's presence or consent.*

b.   *In other situations, both parties may want communications and personal relationships to be less formal. It is then appropriate for the arbitrator to respond accordingly.*

E.   Jurisdiction

1.   An arbitrator must observe faithfully both the limitations and inclusions of the jurisdiction conferred by an agreement or other submission under which the arbitrator serves.

2.   A direct settlement by the parties of some or all issues in a case, at any stage of the proceedings, must be accepted by the arbitrator as removing further jurisdiction over such issues.

F.   Mediation by an Arbitrator

1.   When the parties wish at the outset to give an arbitrator authority both to mediate and to decide or submit recommendations regarding residual issues, if any, they should so advise the arbitrator prior to appointment. If the appointment is accepted, the arbitrator must perform a mediation role consistent with the circumstances of the case.

a.   Direct appointments, also, may require a dual role as mediator and arbitrator of residual issues. This is most likely to occur in some public sector cases.

2.   When a request to mediate is first made after appointment, the arbitrator may either accept or decline a mediation role.

a.   *Once arbitration has been invoked, either party normally has a right to insist that the process be continued to decision.*

b.   *If one party requests that the arbitrator mediate and the other party objects, the arbitrator should decline the request.*

c.   *An arbitrator is not precluded from suggesting mediation. To avoid the possibility of improper pressure, the arbitrator should not so suggest unless it can be discerned that both parties are likely to be receptive. In any event, the arbitrator's suggestion should not be pursued unless both parties readily agree.*

G.   Reliance by an Arbitrator on Other Arbitration Awards or on Independent Research

1.   An arbitrator must assume full personal responsibility for the decision in each case decided.

a.   *The extent, if any, to which an arbitrator properly may rely on precedent, on guidance of other awards, or on independent research is dependent primarily on the policies of the parties on these matters, as expressed in the contract, or other agreement, or at the hearing.*

b.   When the mutual desires of the parties are not known or when the parties express differing opinions or policies, the arbitrator may exercise discretion as to these matters, consistent with the acceptance of full personal responsibility for the award.

H.   Use of Assistants

1.   An arbitrator must not delegate any decision-making function to another person without consent of the parties.

a.   *Without prior consent of the parties, an arbitrator may use the services of an assistant for research, clerical duties, or preliminary drafting under the direction of the arbitrator, which does not involve the delegation of any decision-making function.*

b.   *If an arbitrator is unable, because of time limitations or other reasons, to handle all decision-making aspects of a case, it is not a violation of professional responsibility to suggest to the parties an allocation of responsibility between the arbitrator and an assistant or associate. The arbitrator must not exert pressure on the parties to accept such a suggestion.*

I.   Consent Awards

1.   Prior to issuance of an award, the parties may jointly request the arbitrator to include in the award certain agreements between them, concerning some or all of the issues. If the arbitrator believes that a suggested award is proper, fair, sound, and lawful, it is consistent with professional responsibility to adopt it.

a.   *Before complying with such a request, an arbitrator must be certain of understanding the suggested settlement adequately in order to be able to appraise its terms. If it appears that pertinent facts or circumstances may not have been disclosed, the arbitrator should take the initiative to assure that all significant aspects of the case are fully understood. To this end, the arbitrator may request additional specific information and may question witnesses at a hearing.*

J.   Avoidance of Delay

1.   It is a basic professional responsibility of an arbitrator to plan a work schedule so that present and future commitments will be fulfilled in a timely manner.

a.   *When planning is upset for reasons beyond the control of the arbitrator, every reasonable effort should nevertheless be exerted to fulfill all commitments. If this is not possible, prompt notice at the arbitrator's initiative should be given to all parties affected. Such notices should include reasonably accurate estimates of any additional time required. To the extent possible, priority should be given to cases in process so that other parties may make alternative arbitration arrangements.*

2.   An arbitrator must cooperate with the parties and with any administrative agency involved in avoiding delays.

a. An arbitrator on the active roster of an administrative agency must take the initiative in advising the agency of any scheduling difficulties that can be foreseen.

b. Requests for services, whether received directly or through an administrative agency, should be declined if the arbitrator is unable to schedule a hearing as soon as the parties wish. If the parties, nevertheless, jointly desire to obtain the services of the arbitrator and the arbitrator agrees, arrangements should be made by agreement that the arbitrator confidently expects to fulfill.

c. An arbitrator may properly seek to persuade the parties to alter or eliminate arbitration procedures or tactics that cause unnecessary delay.

3. Once the case record has been closed, an arbitrator must adhere to the time limits for an award, as stipulated in the labor agreement or as provided by regulation of an administrative agency or as otherwise agreed.

a. If an appropriate award cannot be rendered within the required time, it is incumbent on the arbitrator to seek an extension of time from the parties.

b. If the parties have agreed upon abnormally short time limits for an award after a case is closed, the arbitrator should be so advised by the parties or by the administrative agency involved, prior to acceptance of appointment.

K. Fees and Expenses

1. An arbitrator occupies a position of trust in respect to the parties and the administrative agencies. In charging for services and expenses, the arbitrator must be governed by the same high standards of honor and integrity that apply to all other phases of arbitration work.

An arbitrator must endeavor to keep total charges for services and expenses reasonable and consistent with the nature of the case or cases decided.

Prior to appointment, the parties should be aware of or be able readily to determine all significant aspects of an arbitrator's bases for charges for fees and expenses.

a. Services Not Primarily Chargeable on a Per Diem Basis

By agreement with the parties, the financial aspects of many "permanent" arbitration assignments, of some interest disputes, and of some "ad hoc" grievance assignments do not include a per diem fee for services as a primary part of the total understanding. In such situations, the arbitrator must adhere faithfully to all agreed-upon arrangements governing fees and expenses.

b. Per Diem Basis for Charges for Services

(1) *When an arbitrator's charges for services are determined primarily by a stipulated per diem fee, the arbitrator should establish in advance the bases for application of such per diem fee and for determination of reimbursable expenses.*

Practices established by an arbitrator should include the basis for charges, if any, for:

(a) hearing time, including the application of the stipulated basic per diem hearing fee to hearing days of varying lengths;

(b) study time;

(c) necessary travel time when not included in charges for hearing time;

(d) postponement or cancellation of hearings by the parties and the circumstances in which such charges will normally be assessed or waived;

(e) office overhead expenses (secretarial, telephone, postage, etc.);

(f) the work of paid assistants or associates.

(2) *Each arbitrator should be guided by the following general principles:*

(a) *Per diem charges for a hearing should not be in excess of actual time spent or allocated for the hearing.*

(b) *Per diem charges for study time should not be in excess of actual time spent.*

(c) *Any fixed ratio of study days to hearing days, not agreed to specifically by the parties, is inconsistent with the per diem method of charges for services.*

(d) *Charges for expenses must not be in excess of actual expenses normally reimbursable and incurred in connection with the case or cases involved.*

(e) *When time or expense are involved for two or more sets of parties on the same day or trip, such time or expense charges should be appropriately prorated.*

(f) *An arbitrator may stipulate in advance a minimum charge for a hearing without violation of (a) or (e) above.*

(3) *An arbitrator on the active roster of an administrative agency must file with the agency the individual bases for determination of fees and expenses if the agency so requires. Thereafter, it is the responsibility of each such arbitrator to advise the agency promptly of any change in any basis for charges.*

Such filing may be in the form of answers to a questionnaire devised by an agency or by any other method adopted by or approved by an agency.

Having supplied an administrative agency with the information noted above, an arbitrator's professional responsibility of disclosure under this Code with respect to fees and expenses has been satisfied for cases referred by that agency.

(4) If an administrative agency promulgates specific standards with respect to any of these matters which are in addition to or more restrictive than an individual arbitrator's standards, an arbitrator on its active roster must observe the agency standards for cases handled under the auspices of that agency, or decline to serve.

(5) When an arbitrator is contacted directly by the parties for a case or cases, the arbitrator has a professional responsibility to respond to questions by submitting the bases for charges for fees and expenses.

(6) When it is know to the arbitrator that one or both of the parties cannot afford normal charges, it is consistent with professional responsibility to charge lesser amounts to both parties or to one of the parties if the other party is made aware of the difference and agrees.

(7) If an arbitrator concludes that the total of charges derived from the normal basis of calculation is not compatible with the case decided, it is consistent with professional responsibility to charge lesser amounts to both parties.

2.   An arbitrator must maintain adequate records to support charges for services and expenses and must make an accounting to the parties or to an involved administrative agency on request.

3.   RESPONSIBILITIES TO ADMINISTRATIVE AGENCIES

A.   General Responsibilities

1.   An arbitrator must be candid, accurate, and fully responsive to an administrative agency concerning qualifications, availability, and all other pertinent matters.

2.   An arbitrator must observe policies and rules of an administrative agency in cases referred by that agency.

3.   An arbitrator must not seek to influence an administrative agency by any improper means, including gifts or other inducements to agency personnel.

a.   It is not improper for a person seeking placement on a roster to request references from individual having knowledge of the applicant's experience and qualifications.

b.   Arbitrators should recognize that the primary responsibility of an administrative agency is to serve the parties.

4. PREHEARING CONDUCT

1.   All prehearing matters must be handled in a manner that fosters complete impartiality by the arbitrator.

a.   The primary purpose of prehearing discussions involving the arbitrator is to obtain agreement on procedural matters so that the hearing can proceed without unnecessary obstacles. If differences of opinion should arise during such discussions and, particularly, if such differences appear to impinge on substantive matters, the circumstances will suggest whether the matter can be resolved informally or may require a prehearing conference or, more rarely, a formal preliminary hearing. When an administrative agency handles some or all aspects of the arrangements prior to a hearing, the arbitrator will become involved only if differences of some substance arise.

b.   *Copies of any prehearing correspondence between the arbitrator and either party must be made available to both parties.*

5. HEARING CONDUCT

A. General Principles

1.   An arbitrator must provide a fair and adequate hearing which assures that both parties have sufficient opportunity to present their respective evidence and argument.

a.   *Within the limits of this responsibility, an arbitrator should conform to the various types of hearing procedures desired by the parties.*

b.   An arbitrator may: encourage stipulations of fact; restate the substance of issues or arguments to promote or verify understanding; question the parties' representatives or witnesses, when necessary or advisable, to obtain additional pertinent information; and request that the parties submit additional evidence, either at the hearing or by subsequent filing.

c.   *An arbitrator should not intrude into a party's presentation so as to prevent that party from putting forward its case fairly and adequately.*

B. Transcripts or Recordings

1.   Mutual agreement of the parties as to use or non-use of a transcript must be respected by the arbitrator.

a.   *A transcript is the official record of a hearing only when both parties agree to a transcript or an applicable law or regulation so provides.*

b.   *An arbitrator may seek to persuade the parties to avoid use of a transcript, or to use a transcript if the nature of the case appears to require one. However, if an arbitrator intends to make appointment to a case contingent on mutual agreement to a transcript, that requirement must be made known to both parties prior to appointment.*

c.   If the parties do not agree to a transcript, an arbitrator may permit one party to take a transcript at its own cost. The arbitrator may also make appropriate arrangements under which the other party may have access to a copy, if a copy is provided to the arbitrator.

d.   Without prior approval, an arbitrator may seek to use a personal tape recorder to supplement note taking. The arbitrator should not insist on such a tape recording if either or both parties object.

C.   Ex Parte Hearings

1.   In determining whether to conduct an ex parte hearing, an arbitrator must consider relevant legal, contractual, and other pertinent circumstances.

2.   An arbitrator must be certain, before proceeding ex parte, that the party refusing or failing to attend the hearings has been given adequate notice of the time, place, and purposes of the hearing.

D.   Plant Visits

1.   An arbitrator should comply with a request of any party that the arbitrator visit a work area pertinent to the dispute prior to, during, or after a hearing. An arbitrator may also initiate such a request.

a.   *Procedures for such visits should be agreed to by the parties in consultation with the arbitrator.*

E.   Bench Decisions or Expedited Awards

1.   When an arbitrator understands, prior to acceptance of appointment, that a bench decision is expected at the conclusion of the hearing, the arbitrator must comply with the understanding unless both parties agree otherwise.

a.   *If notice of the parties' desire for a bench decision is not given prior to the arbitrator's acceptance of the case, issuance of such a bench decision is discretionary.*

b.   *When only one party makes the request and the other objects, the arbitrator should not render a bench decision except under most unusual circumstance.*

2.   When an arbitrator understands, prior to acceptance of appointment, that a concise written award is expected within a stated time period after the hearing, the arbitrator must comply with the understanding unless both parties agree otherwise.

6.   POST HEARING CONDUCT

A.   Post Hearing Briefs and Submissions

1.   An arbitrator must comply with mutual agreements in respect to the filing or nonfiling of post hearing briefs or submissions.

> a.   An arbitrator may either suggest the filing of post hearing briefs or other submissions or suggest that none be filed.

> b.   When the parties disagree as to the need for briefs, an arbitrator may permit filing but may determine a reasonable time limitation.

2.   An arbitrator must not consider a post hearing brief or submission that has not been provided to the other party.

B.   Disclosure of Terms of Award

1.   An arbitrator must not disclose a prospective award to either party prior to its simultaneous issuance to both parties or explore possible alternative awards unilaterally with one party, unless both parties so agree.

> a.   Partisan members of tripartite boards may know prospective terms of an award in advance of its issuance. Similar situations may exist in other less formal arrangements mutually agreed to by the parties. In any such situation, the arbitrator should determine and observe the mutually desired degree of confidentiality.

C.   Awards and Opinions

1.   The award should be definite, certain, and as concise as possible.

> a.   When an opinion is required, factors to be considered by an arbitrator include: desirability of brevity, consistent with the nature of the case and any expressed desires of the parties; need to use a style and form that is understandable to responsible representatives of the parties, to the grievant and supervisors, and to others in the collective bargaining relationship; necessity of meeting the significant issues; forthrightness to an extent not harmful to the relationship of the parties; and avoidance of gratuitous advice or discourse not essential to disposition of the issues.

D.   Clarification of Interpretation of Awards

1.   No clarification or interpretation of an award is permissible without the consent of both parties.

2.   Under agreements which permit or require clarification or interpretation of an award, an arbitrator must afford both parties an opportunity to be heard.

E.   Enforcement of Award

1.   The arbitrator's responsibility does not extend to the enforcement of an award.

2.   In view of the professional and confidential nature of the arbitration relationship, an arbitrator should not voluntarily participate in legal enforcement proceedings.

Appendix E

A DUE PROCESS PROTOCOL FOR MEDIATION AND ARBITRATION OF STATUTORY DISPUTES ARISING OUT OF THE EMPLOYMENT RELATIONSHIP

May 9, 1995.

The following protocol is offered by the undersigned individuals, members of the Task Force on Alternative Dispute Resolution in Employment, as a means of providing due process in the resolution by mediation and binding arbitration of employment disputes involving statutory rights. The signatories were designated by their respective organizations, but the protocol reflects their personal views and should not be construed as representing the policy of the designating organizations.

Genesis

This Task Force was created by individuals from diverse organizations involved in labor and employment law to examine questions of due process arising out of the use of mediation and arbitration for resolving employment disputes. In this protocol we confine ourselves to statutory disputes.

The members of the Task Force felt that mediation and arbitration of statutory disputes conducted under proper due process safeguards should be encouraged in order to provide expeditious, accessible, inexpensive and fair private enforcement of statutory employment disputes for the 100,000,000 members of the workforce who might not otherwise have ready, effective access to administrative or judicial relief. They also hope that such a system will serve to reduce the delays which now arise out of the huge backlog of cases pending before administrative agencies and courts and that it will help forestall an even greater number of such cases.

A. Pre or Post Dispute Arbitration

The Task Force recognizes the dilemma inherent in the timing of an agreement to mediate and/or arbitrate statutory disputes. It did not achieve consensus on this difficult issue. The views in this spectrum are set forth randomly, as follows:

- Employers should be able to create mediation and/or arbitration systems to resolve statutory claims, but any agreement to mediate and/or arbitrate disputes should be informed, voluntary, and not a condition of initial or continued employment.

- Employers should have the right to insist on an agreement to mediate and/or arbitrate statutory disputes as a condition of initial or continued employment.

- Postponing such an agreement until a dispute actually arises, when there will likely exist a stronger re-disposition to litigate, will result in very few agreements to mediate and/or arbitrate, thus negating the likelihood of effectively utilizing alternative dispute resolution and overcoming the problems of administrative and judicial delays which now plague the system.

- Employees should not be permitted to waive their right to judicial relief of statutory claims arising out of the employment relationship for any reason.

- Employers should be able to create mediation and/or arbitration systems to resolve statutory claims, but the decision to mediate and/or arbitrate individual cases should not be made until after the dispute arises.

- The Task Force takes no position on the timing of agreements to mediate and/or arbitrate statutory employment disputes, though it agrees that such agreements be knowingly made. The focus of this protocol is on standards of exemplary due process.

B. Right of Representation

1. Choice of Representative

Employees considering the use of or, in fact, utilizing mediation and/or arbitration procedures should have the right to be represented by a spokesperson of their own choosing. The mediation and arbitration procedure should so specify and should include reference to institutions which might offer assistance, such as bar associations, legal service associations, civil rights organizations, trade unions, etc.

2. Fees for Representation

The amount and method of payment for representation should be determined between the claimant and the representative. We recommend, however, a number of existing systems which provide employer reimbursement of at least a portion of the employee's attorney fees, especially for lower paid employees. The arbitrator should have the authority to provide for fee reimbursement, in whole or in part, as part of the remedy in accordance with applicable law or in the interests of justice.

3. Access to Information

One of the advantages of arbitration is that there is usually less time and money spent in pre-trial discovery. Adequate but limited pre-trial discovery is to be encouraged and employees should have access to all information reasonably relevant to mediation and/or arbitration of their claims. The employees' representative should also have reasonable pre-hearing and hearing access to all such information and documentation.

Necessary pre-hearing depositions consistent with the expedited nature of arbitration should be available. We also recommend that prior to selection of an arbitrator, each side should be provided with the names, addresses and phone numbers of the representatives of the parties in that arbitrator's six most recent cases to aid them in selection.

C. Mediator and Arbitrator Qualification

1. Roster Membership

Mediators and arbitrators selected for such cases should have skill in the conduct of hearings, knowledge of the statutory issues at stake in the dispute, and familiarity with the workplace and employment environment. The roster of available mediators and arbitrators should be established on a non-discriminatory basis, diverse by gender, ethnicity, background, experience, etc. to satisfy the parties that their interest and objectives will be respected and fully considered.

Our recommendation is for selection of impartial arbitrators and mediators. We recognize the right of employers and employees to jointly select as mediator and/or arbitrator one in whom both parties have requisite trust, even though not possessing the qualifications here recommended, as most promising to bring finality and to withstand judicial scrutiny. The existing cadre of labor and employment mediators and arbitrators, some lawyers, some not, although skilled in conducting hearings and familiar with the employment milieu is unlikely, without special training, to consistently possess knowledge of the statutory environment in which these disputes arise and of the characteristics of the non-union workplace.

There is a manifest need for mediators and arbitrators with expertise in statutory requirements in the employment field who may, without special training, lack experience in the employment area and in the conduct of arbitration hearings and mediation sessions. Reexamination of rostering eligibility by designating agencies, such as the American Arbitration Association, may permit the expedited inclusion in the pool of this most valuable source of expertise.

The roster of arbitrators and mediators should contain representatives with all such skills in order to meet the diverse needs of this caseload.

Regardless of their prior experience, mediators and arbitrators on the roster must be independent of bias toward either party. They should reject cases if they believe the procedure lacks requisite due process.

2. Training

The creation of a roster containing the foregoing qualifications dictates the development of a training program to educate existing and potential labor and employment mediators and arbitrators as to the statutes, including substantive, procedural and remedial issues to be confronted and to train experts in the statutes as to employer procedures governing the employment relationship as well as due process and fairness in the conduct and control of arbitration hearings and mediation sessions.

Training in the statutory issues should be provided by the government agencies, bar associations, academic institutions, etc., administered perhaps by the designating agency, such as the AAA, at various locations throughout the country. Such training should be updated periodically and be required of all mediators and arbitrators. Training in the conduct of mediation and arbitration could be provided by a mentoring program with experienced panelists.

Successful completion of such training would be reflected in the resume or panel cards of the arbitrators supplied to the parties for their selection process.

3. Panel Selection

Upon request of the parties, the designating agency should utilize a list procedure such as that of the AAA or select a panel composed of an odd number of mediators and arbitrators from its roster or pool. The panel cards for such individuals should be submitted to the parties for their perusal prior to alternate striking of the names on the list, resulting in the designation of the remaining mediator and/or arbitrator.

The selection process could empower the designating agency to appoint a mediator and/or arbitrator if the striking procedure is unacceptable or unsuccessful. As noted above, subject to the consent of the parties, the designating agency should provide the names of the parties and their representatives in recent cases decided by the listed arbitrators.

4. Conflicts of Interest

The mediator and arbitrator for a case has a duty to disclose any relationship which might reasonably constitute or be perceived as a conflict of interest. The designated mediator and/or arbitrator should be required to sign an oath provided by the designating agency, if any, affirming the absence of such present or preexisting ties.

5. Authority of the Arbitrator

The arbitrator should be bound by applicable agreements, statutes, regulations and rules of procedure of the designating agency, including the authority to determine the time and place of the hearing, permit reasonable discovery, issue subpoenas, decide arbitrability issues, preserve order and privacy in the hearings, rule on evidentiary matters, determine the close of the hearing and procedures for post-hearing submissions, and issue an award resolving the submitted dispute.

The arbitrator should be empowered to award whatever relief would be available in court under the law. The arbitrator should issue an opinion and award setting forth a summary of the issues, including the type(s) of dispute(s), the damages and/or other relief requested and awarded, a statement of any other issues resolved, and a statement regarding the disposition of any statutory claim(s).

6. Compensation of the Mediator and Arbitrator

Impartiality is best assured by the parties sharing the fees and expenses of the mediator and arbitrator. In cases where the economic condition of a party does not permit equal sharing, the parties should make mutually acceptable arrangements to achieve that goal if at all possible. In the absence of such agreement, the arbitrator should determine allocation of fees. The designating agency, by negotiating the parties share of costs and collecting such fees, might be able to reduce the bias potential of disparate contributions by forwarding payment to the mediator and/or arbitrator without disclosing the parties share therein.

D. Scope of Review

The arbitrator's award should be final and binding and the scope of review should be limited.

*

Appendix F

ON WRITING THE POST–HEARING BRIEF

DOUGLAS E. RAY, ON WRITING THE
POST–HEARING BRIEF
47 Arbitration Journal 58–60 (December 1992).

Recent statistics compiled by the American Arbitration Association indicate that post-hearing briefs are filed in almost 65 percent of labor arbitration cases. Despite the common use of briefs, however, not all advocates take full advantage of this form of argumentation. The purpose of this article is to provide a few simple guidelines that can make the post-hearing brief a more effective form of argument. Although the examples given are from the field of labor arbitration, the basic principles will apply to other forms of arbitration as well.

The best brief is one that makes it easy for the arbitrator to decide your way. Such a brief will provide the arbitrator everything he or she needs to write a clear opinion favoring your position. Although it is clearly the arbitrator's job to ferret out the facts and apply them to the contract, arbitrators, like advocates, are mere mortals. You do not wish to run the risk that the arbitrator will miss an important fact or misunderstand your position. This is especially true if you have asked for 30 or more days in which to submit briefs. The time required to submit briefs may delay ultimate resolution to a point where the arbitrator is no longer as familiar with the matter as immediately after the hearing. For this reason, special care should be taken to stress important facts.

The task of making things easy for the arbitrator begins even before reaching the body of the brief. A cover page, for example, can help the arbitrator easily find your brief among the many case documents and minimize the risk of misfiling. The cover should contain the names of the parties, the case number followed by a parenthetical describing the case (*e.g.*, *Wilson overtime claim*) and a label such as *Company's Post–Hearing Brief*. The name and address of the representative submitting the brief should appear on the cover as well as the last page. Similarly, if the brief is more than a few pages, a table of contents can be helpful. By looking at the table of contents, the arbitrator should be able to under-stand the argument based on clear statements of your position set out in section headings and subsection headings. Such headings should be simple declarative sentences.

The Issue

The issue to be decided should be set out in a separate section. Identify whether the parties have stipulated to this as the issue or whether it is your side's position as to the issue. Given the limited jurisdiction of an arbitrator, you do not want to risk confusion in this area.

Statement of Facts

A section on background or statement of facts is very important. To begin this section, first examine a well written arbitration decision. What does the arbitrator need to know to begin the opinion? Bear in mind that the hearing was 30 to 45 days ago and the arbitrator does not always have the case at the forefront of his or her mind. A brief that identifies the company and plant and explains what is produced, that identifies the union and the part of the workforce it represents and that identifies the grievant and the grievant's position is appreciated. The statement should then give a history of the case. What did the company do? When? When was the grievance filed? By whom? What did it allege? How did the Company respond? When was the arbitration hearing held? Where? Did the parties stipulate as to jurisdiction? Were there other stipulations?

By laying this foundation, you may get the arbitrator used to relying on your brief as a valuable guide to what happened. If it is accurate, the descriptions of events or testimony which follow may be seen as more reliable. At this point you will put in accurate facts or an accurate rendition of what the witnesses testified to at hearing. The more reliable your rendition, the more credibility your arguments will have. You need not recount every fact or bit of testimony. Tell your story clearly, insuring that facts that help you come out. Sometimes section headings within the Statement of Facts will make it seem more clear and orga-nized. The arbitrator has a duty to find the facts, but you want to make it as easy as possible for the arbitrator to see those facts you believe are important. Use citations to the transcript if one is available. If not, make clear which witness testified to each fact so the arbitrator can confirm your statement in notes from the hearing.

It is important to include a section setting forth the contract sections on which you rely. The arbitrator has a copy of the contract but your goal is to make it very easy for the arbitrator to understand your position and very easy to find your authority.

The Argument

The argument section should begin with a one or two paragraph introduction to the argument that sets out your entire argument in simple direct language. It is then followed by arguments identified by section headings stated in simple declarative sentences.

Arguments should be arrayed in logical order. Put your most persuasive argument first. In some cases, start by stressing that the other party has the burden of proof and provide citations to general authorities. This will provide the filter through which you will want the arbitrator to read the arguments which follow.

Each section has a point to make that is supported by fact, contract, rules and/or cases. Make sure that the arbitrator understands the point a section makes by beginning a complicated section with a brief summary of the section. This helps the arbitrator understand why you are providing the arguments which follow.

Sometimes the section heading can be crafted so as to perfectly summarize your position. If this is the case, you can begin the section by setting out a contract provision or a fact from hearing which you will use as a springboard for argument.

Setting out a contract provision, fact or general rule of interpretation will not necessarily help you prevail unless you provide the logical link to your argument by immediately showing how it applies. "The contract states * * *." "This is important because * * *." "In particular, the use of the word * * * indicates * * *." "Therefore, on these facts, the parties intended * * *."

Similarly, "It is a general rule of contract interpretation that * * *." (citation to treatise or authority); "This rule applies fully here because * * *. Therefore * * *."

Finally, "At hearing, W admitted that * * *. This is important because * * *. Therefore * * *."

In summary, you want to make each point very clearly. Do not rely on the arbitrator to make linkages. You want to place together the rule, fact or contract provision, the application and the conclusion to be drawn. You know your case far better than the arbitrator does and what is obvious to you may not be clear to the arbitrator unless you explain your thinking clearly.

Make Your Argument Before Distinguishing Theirs

Within a section you want to clearly make your side's argument before attempting to rebut arguments on related points made by the other side. Why? Your argument is the most important and should come first. Second, you want the arbitrator to understand your position and be persuaded by it before considering your opponent's position. You never want the arbitrator confused as to where you stand. Having made your argument as to the meaning of a section or the existence of a fact, it is far easier to then say "Although the Union/Company argues that * * * such position is unsupported by the facts/common rules of interpretation * * *."

Stress Contract and Fact–Based Arguments

Including arbitration cases in your brief can help persuade the arbitrator to rule your way by showing other logical interpretations of similar facts and contracts. Do not be confused as to the arbitrator's job, however. It is to find facts and apply them to *your* contract. Other cases are not binding. They may be persuasive, however. Because they are not binding you should introduce them in support of a fact and contract-based argument you have just made within the section.

As with most arguments, a discussion of cases should be introduced with a simple declarative sentence explaining why you will be talking about cases. "A number of arbitrators reviewing similar facts under similar contracts have reached the same result. For example, in *X Co.*, 99 LA xxx (Mantle 1954), the arbitrator held that * * *." Once having introduced the case, make it work for you by stressing similarities to your case. "As in our case, the contract in *X Co.* provided * * *." Where possible, try to establish that your case is even stronger. "In this case, not only did Grievant * * * and * * * as did the grievant in *X Co.* but the instant Grievant * * * as well. Therefore * * *." Put in a few other citations with parentheticals to show similar outcomes. This helps the arbitrator see that the case discussed is not an aberration. "*See also Y Co.*, 89–1 CCH ARB para 12,309 (Skowron 1989), holding that * * *."

Briefs which merely string together a list of citations are less helpful. Indeed, cases taken from footnotes in treatises may not always accurately reflect the rule for which they are cited. All cases cited should be read to insure they help your cause.

If you believe particular cases support your argument, consider attaching copies of the most important ones to your brief. This is particularly helpful if your arbitrator lacks access to a good labor library.

Use Repetition and Other Tactics

When discussing contract language, try to use the exact contract language when making declarative statements about it. For example, "The contract states that ' * * * fully utilized * * *.' In this case, the Company 'fully utilized' the workforce by * * *."

Often, too, you will want to follow up quotes from arbitration treatises or arbitration opinions with a direct application. "Here, too, there was an 'egregious violation' of the contract justifying * * *." Repeating the exact language should help lead the reader to accept the connection.

Use transitions between sections to demonstrate that you should win for several independent reasons and to put emphasis on powerful points. "Not only was the contract violated because * * * but * * * as well."

Avoid Weakness

Often an advocate undercuts the strength of a good argument by saying things like, "Even assuming that the action violated the contract, the remedy called for * * *." Another way of showing weakness is to use "assuming arguendo." It is far better to use transitions that do not appear to concede the point, such as "Not only does the grievance lack merit because * * *. but the remedy requested is beyond the arbitrator's authority as well because * * *." or "the remedy requested is beyond the arbitrator's authority as well because * * *." You do not want the arbitrator to think that you do not fully believe in the persuasiveness of the position you have just taken.

Making a Strong Conclusion

In your conclusion, you will want to briefly but powerfully restate your position. Then tell the arbitrator exactly the outcome you want. If there is a dispute over potential remedy, make sure the arbitrator knows your position. Sometimes you will have to put in a separate last argument section of the argument if the scope of the remedy involves a controversial point.

Before you write the conclusion, reread the brief. Have you made it easy for the arbitrator to answer the question "why are they telling me this?" If it is not clear, add an introductory sentence to the unclear section explaining that "To fully understand Article IV of the contract, it is necessary to consider other sections as well because * * *. Thus, Article V(a) which provides * * * is important because it demonstrates * * *."

Check for spelling, grammar, punctuation and credibility. Your reputation and your persuasiveness depend on it.

*

Index

References are to pages

DISCOVERY—Cont'd
Under National Labor Relations Act, 241–42

DUE PROCESS OF ARBITRATION
Generally, 216–39
Access to arbitration, 218–21, 691–92
Confrontation, 230–32
Constitution, application of in arbitration, 216–17
Contractual due process rights, 234–39
Search and seizure, 226–30
Self-incrimination, 216–17, 222–26
Separate representation, 221
Surprise, 232–34
Third-party intervention, 221–22

DUE PROCESS PROTOCOL FOR MEDIA-TION AND ARBITRATION OF STATUTO-RY DISPUTES ARISING OUT OF THE EMPLOYMENT RELATIONSHIP, Text, 891–95

DUTY OF FAIR REPRESENTATION
Generally, 144–70
Apportionment of damages, 162–69
Collective bargaining, 145–49
Enforcement, 157–58, 169–70
Exhausting internal procedures, 170
Grievance arbitration, 149–62
Jury trial, 169–70
National Labor Relations Act, 149–62
Negligence, 160–61
Origins of, 145–49
Punitive damages, 169–70
Race discrimination, 145–47
Railway Labor Act, 145–49
Statute of limitations, 169
Women, 161

EFFICIENCY OF ARBITRATION
See CRITICISM OF ARBITRATION

EMPIRICAL STUDIES
Of arbitration fees, 650
Of Employment arbitration, 692–97
Of Employment litigation, 713
Of Mediation, 714–17

EQUAL EMPLOYMENT OPPORTUNITY COMMISSION
Generally, 599–600, 614–16, 688–89

ETHICS
See also CODE OF PROFESSIONAL RESPONSIBILITY
Generally, 522–47, 698–703, 744–56
Advocates, 546–47, 750–56
Disclosure, 524–28
Hearing conduct, 528–36
In employment arbitration, 698–703
In mediation, 744–56
Party-appointed arbitrators, 536–37
Posthearing conduct, 537–46

ETHICS—Cont'd
Prehearing conduct, 524–28

EVIDENCE
Admission of, 199–216
Error, 78–79, 199
Hearsay, 206–16
Judicial review of evidentiary decisions, 78–79, 213
Relevance, 204
Subpoenas, 243

EXTERNAL LAW
See also DEFERRAL TO ARBITRA-TION
Generally, 170–98
Application of, 187–96
Current issues, 196–98
In employment arbitration, 657–63
Views on arbitral compliance with, 170–87

FAMILY MEDICAL LEAVE ACT, 196–98

FEDERAL ARBITRATION ACT
Generally, 6
As source of guidance in labor arbitration, 78, 83
Contracts of employment exception, 598, 608–14
In employment arbitration, 592–616, 663–72
Text, 820–26
Writing Requirement, 607

FEDERAL COMMON LAW
See also ARBITRABILITY
Generally, 33–45, 592
Section 301 of Labor Management Rela-tions Act, 33, 35–40

FEDERAL GOVERNMENT, ARBITRATION IN
See PUBLIC SECTOR, ARBITRATION IN

FEDERAL MEDIATION AND CONCILIA-TION SERVICE
Generally, 11

FEES
Arbitration, 641–52
Mediation, 727, 747–48

FOREIGN DISPUTE RESOLUTION METH-ODS
Generally, 26–27, 697–98

FRINGE BENEFITS
Generally, 406–23
Holiday pay, 406–13
Insurance, 423
Leaves of absence, 419–22
Vacations, 413–19

GRIEVANCE MEDIATION
Generally, 756–59

†

0–314–14765–9

90000

9 780314 147653